Collins

New
SCHOOL
DICTIONARY

Collins
An imprint of HarperCollinsPublishers

First Published 1999

Latest reprint 2001

© HarperCollins Publishers 1999

10 9 8 7 6

ISBN 0 00 765936-9

Collins® and Bank of English® are registered trademarks of
HarperCollins Publishers Limited

The HarperCollins website address is
www.**fire**and**water**.com

A catalogue record for this book
is available from the British Library.

Corpus Acknowledgments
We would like to thank those authors and publishers
who kindly gave permission for copyright material to be
used in the Bank of English. We would also like to thank
Times Newspapers Ltd for providing valuable data.

Typographical design by Kerry Aylin

Typeset by Stewart C Russell

Printed and bound in Germany by
Elsnerdruck, Berlin

Introduction

Collins New School Dictionary is an indispensable language and literacy resource for today's students.

In Britain, the National Literacy Strategy set ambitious targets for students to acquire dictionary skills at every stage of their education. This is because if you know how to use a dictionary effectively you can improve your performance in all subjects, not just English or Modern Languages.

Collins New School Dictionary has been created to meet the needs of students today. Through research among teachers and students, Collins discovered the features that would be most helpful, and incorporated these into this dictionary.

Collins New School Dictionary is easy to use. On the outer edge of each page is a marker highlighting the letter of the alphabet shown on the page. At the top of each page the first and last words featured on the page are clearly shown. The type is large and clear, and extra features are marked by helpful symbols. Each definition within an entry is separated by a sense number, so even longer entries are easy to read and understand.

The entries themselves are written in simple, straightforward language, without any confusing abbreviations. Many of them are full sentences, and all of them are easy to follow. There are helpful examples of the word in use in real English sentences. Spelling help is given for all forms of the entry word. Simple pronunciations are given for awkward words.

Collins New School Dictionary has even more ways to help. There are interesting word histories that increase knowledge of language. Similar words features at many entries offer alternative words for common words and help build vocabulary. Usage notes give spelling tips, advice on when to use a word, and reminders on which words should be used together. Grammar boxes give helpful information on how English works.

Special attention has been given to the vocabulary of a wide range of school examination subjects, so you can find definitions for key words in Geography, RE, Science, and many other subjects.

For easy access Collins has included the Key Words feature at the front of the dictionary. This lists, by topic, entries where you will find some extra help. So, for instance, you can check up on confusable words; words that come from Latin; terms used in Geography. These groupings can be the starting point for projects to increase your knowledge and understanding of English. There is also a photocopiable Dictionary Skills workpack to accompany this dictionary, containing dozens of classroom activities to develop dictionary skills.

Collins New School Dictionary is relevant, accessible, and student-friendly, and offers essential help on the route to success.

Editorial Staff

Editorial Director
Diana Treffry

Managing Editor
Sheila Ferguson

Senior Lexicographer
Elspeth Summers

Lexicographers
Andrew Holmes   Mary O'Neill
Ian Brookes   Lorna Gilmour

Computing Staff
Stewart C Russell   Jane Creevy

Editorial Assistance
Susan Dunsmore

Teacher Reader
Geoff Barton

Australian Editor
W A Krebs
Associate Professor in Literature and Communications
Bond University, Queensland

New Zealand Editor
Elizabeth Gordon
Associate Professor, Department of Linguistics
University of Canterbury

South African Editor
Geoffrey Hughes
Professor, Department of English
University of the Witwatersrand

How To Use The Dictionary

Collins New School Dictionary is easy to use and understand. Below are some entries showing the dictionary's main features, along with an explanation of what they are.

The entry word

How to say the word

fiend fiends
Said "feend" NOUN **1** a devil or evil spirit. **2** a very wicked or cruel person. **3** AN INFORMAL USE someone who is very keen on a particular thing EG *a fitness fiend.*
▥ from Old English *feond* meaning 'enemy'

Advice on when to use the word

An example of the word being used

Word history ▥ explains the word comes from

What the word means

Other words that come from the entry word

fish fishes fishing fished
NOUN **1** a cold-blooded creature living in water that has a spine, gills, fins, and a scaly skin. **2** Fish is the flesh of fish eaten as food.
▶ VERB **3** To fish is to try to catch fish for food or sport. **4** If you fish for information, you try to get it in an indirect way.
fishing NOUN, **fisherman** NOUN
☑ The plural of the noun *fish* can be either *fish* or *fishes*, but *fish* is more common.

Definition number

Usage note ☑ gives more information on how the word is used

Similar words list ▤ shows other words with the same meaning

flinch flinches flinching flinched
VERB If you flinch, you make a sudden small movement in fear or pain.
▤ cringe, recoil, wince

Other forms of the word

The word's part of speech

full stop full stops
NOUN the punctuation mark (.) used at the end of a sentence and after an abbreviation or initial.

> **What does the Full Stop do?**
> The **full stop** (.) marks the end of any sentence which is not a question or an exclamation.
> *The train is leaving.*
> A full stop is also used after an abbreviation or initial.
> *etc.   Dr. Jenkins   J.R. Hartley*
> A full stop is also used after an expression that stands by itself but is not a complete sentence.
> *Good morning.*

Grammar box gives more information on the way English works

Key Words

As well as all the usual information you expect to find in a dictionary – definitions, spelling help, pronunciations, and examples – *Collins New School Dictionary* contains extra features that will help you understand more about the English language, and feel more confident about your reading and writing. These extra features are word histories, usage notes, similar words lists, grammar boxes, and school subject vocabulary. To find out more about these features, look at the entries for the words listed on these pages.

🏛 Word Histories

If you want to find out where words come from you can look at the word histories in many entries. The word histories are marked by the symbol 🏛. Modern English words have come from many different sources. Below are some examples.

Words from Latin	**Words from Greek**	**Words from Old English**
apricot	acrobat	acre
chapel	dinosaur	bless
dismal	encyclopedia	daisy
hibernate	gorilla	earwig
migraine	hippopotamus	fiend
muscle	moustache	holiday
slave	parasite	walnut
vaccine	toxic	werewolf

Words from Arabic	**Words from Hindi**	**Words from French**
alcove	bangle	interfere
assassin	bungalow	menagerie
checkmate	gymkhana	oboe
cotton	juggernaut	parlour
genie	loot	plumber
giraffe	mandir	sabotage
hazard	shampoo	souvenir
racquet	thug	suede

Words named after people	**Other interesting words**
boycott	anorak
platonic	berserk
sandwich	bikini
saxophone	chocolate
shrapnel	denim
sideburn	jumbo
tarmac	paper
teddy bear	tulip

☑ Usage Notes

If you want to know more about how words should be used, you can look at the usage notes in many entries. The usage notes are marked by the symbol ☑. There are several kinds of usage note: tips on spelling; help with words that are often confused; advice on when you should use a word and when to avoid it; and reminders on which words go together. Below are some examples of entries where you can find this help.

Spelling Tips
accommodate
black
environment
hamster
licence
pronunciation
yank

Confusing Words
amoral & immoral
flaunt & flout
hoard & horde
loath & loathe
loose & lose
principal & principle
their & there

When to use a word
alternative
between
chairman
disinterested
elder
less
plus

Words which go together
acquainted
bored
demand
inside
outside
provided
try

▤ Similar Words

When you are writing, it is good to vary the words you use. This keeps your reader interested, and helps to increase your vocabulary. If you want to know another word to use instead of one you have used already, look to see if there is a similar word list at the entry for the word you want to replace. Similar words lists are marked by the symbol ▤. Then you can pick a similar word, or synonym, to put in your writing. Below are some examples of common words that have similar words lists in their entries.

Common Verbs	Common Nouns	Common Adjectives
appear	area	brave
beat	choice	depressed
catch	energy	excellent
finish	fight	happy
harm	grief	lively
imagine	job	modern
mix	noise	ordinary
recognize	opinion	rude
scare	thought	silly
warn	victory	weird

Grammar Boxes

Throughout the dictionary there are grammar boxes at the end of entries. These boxes contain rules and advice on English grammar, as well as helpful examples. Below are some entries where you can find out more about grammar.

Punctuation	Parts of Speech	Parts of a Sentence
apostrophe	adjective	clause
bracket	adverb	phrase
colon	conjunction	sentence
comma	interjection	
dash	noun	
exclamation mark	part of speech	**Gender**
full stop	preposition	feminine
hyphen	pronoun	gender
inverted comma	verb	masculine
punctuation		neuter
question mark		
semicolon		

Verbs	Nouns	Adjectives
active	noun	adjective
future	plural	comparative
passive	possessive	superlative
past tense		
present tense		
tense		
verb		

School Subject Vocabulary

As an extra feature of this dictionary we have included a wide range of words related to school subjects. Subjects like History, Geography, Science and Religious Studies have their own specialist vocabulary, and many of these words have been added to give extra help to students who are studying these subjects. Below are some of the subjects covered, and examples of entries relating to them.

History	Geography	Mathematics
armistice	acid rain	addition
civil war	climate	division
colony	deforestation	fraction
conquest	ecosystem	median
democracy	equator	multiplication
emperor	glaciation	parallelogram
ghetto	mineral	scale
holocaust	plateau	square
nationalism	rainforest	subtraction
republic	settlement	trapezium
treaty	stratum	volume

Modern Languages
article
case
comparative
imperative
infinitive
subjunctive
superlative
vocabulary

English
comedy
dialect
limerick
paragraph
register
simile
slang
tragedy

Poetry
alliteration
couplet
foot
irony
meter
rhyme
sonnet
stanza

Sociology
alienate
capitalism
discriminate
hierarchy
Marxism
polygamy
racism
welfare state

Psychology
attitude
ego
extrovert
introvert
neurosis
peer
self-esteem
stereotype

Religious Studies
apostle
bar mitzvah
dharma
hajj
khanda
puja
scripture
sin

Food Technology
carbohydrate
cholesterol
fat
gelatine
monounsaturated
nutrient
polyunsaturated
salmonella

Business Studies
asset
cash flow
fiscal
inflation
liquidation
privatization
spreadsheet
VAT

Media Studies
broadsheet
director
libel
producer
royalties
screenplay
tabloid
World Wide Web

Science
acid
amplitude
capillary
cell
current
DNA
enzyme
frequency

Science
kinetic energy
nucleus
ovary
protein
radiation
solution
velocity
xylem

Design and Technology
alloy
cantilever
forge
hacksaw
laminated
plastic
rivet
template

BANK *of* ENGLISH

This dictionary has been compiled by referring to the Bank of English, a unique database of the English language with examples of over 323 million words enabling Collins lexicographers to analyse how English is actually used today and how it is changing. This is the evidence on which the changes in this dictionary are based.

The Bank of English was set up as a joint initiative by HarperCollins Publishers and Birmingham University to be a resource for language research and lexicography. It contains a very wide range of material from books, newspapers, radio, TV, magazines, letters, and talks reflecting the whole spectrum of English today. Its size and range make it an unequalled resource and the purpose-built software for its analysis is unique to Collins Dictionaries.

This ensures that Collins Dictionaries accurately reflect English as it is used today in a way that is most helpful to the dictionary user as well as including a range of rarer and historical words and meanings.

a an
ADJECTIVE The indefinite article 'a', or 'an' if the next sound is a vowel, is used when you are talking about one of something EG *an apple... There was a car parked behind the hedge.*

The Indefinite Article

The word *a* is known as the **indefinite article**. You use it before a singular noun to refer to any example of that noun, or to avoid being specific about which example you mean.
  a school   a woman

The word *an* is used instead of *a* when a word begins with a vowel sound.
  an elephant   an umpire

The word *an* is also used instead of *a* when words sound as though they begin with a vowel.
  an hour   an honour

The word *a* is used instead of *an* when words that begin with a vowel sound as though they begin with a consonant.
  a union   a European

Also look at the grammar box at **the**.

---

aardvark aardvarks
NOUN an ant-eating African animal with a long snout.
🔲 from obsolete Afrikaans meaning 'earth pig'

aback
ADVERB If you are taken aback, you are very surprised.

abacus abacuses
NOUN a frame with beads that slide along rods, used for counting.
🔲 from Greek *abax* meaning 'board covered with sand for doing sums on'

abalone abalones
Said "ab-a-**lone**-ee" NOUN a shellfish which can be eaten.

abandon abandons abandoning abandoned
VERB **1** If you abandon someone or

something, you leave them or give them up for good. ▶ NOUN **2** If you do something with abandon, you do it in an uncontrolled way EG *He began to laugh with abandon.*
abandoned ADJECTIVE, **abandonment** NOUN
🔳 (sense 1) desert, forsake, leave

abate abates abating abated
VERB If something abates, it becomes less EG *His anger abated.*

abattoir abattoirs
Said "ab-a-**twah**" NOUN a place where animals are killed for meat.

abbey abbeys
NOUN a church with buildings attached to it in which monks or nuns live.

abbot abbots
NOUN the monk or priest in charge of all the monks in a monastery.

abbreviate abbreviates abbreviating abbreviated
VERB To abbreviate something is to make it shorter.

abbreviation abbreviations
NOUN a short form of a word or phrase. An example is 'W', which is short for 'West'.

abdicate abdicates abdicating abdicated
VERB If a king or queen abdicates, he or she gives up being a king or queen.
abdication NOUN

abdomen abdomens
NOUN the front part of your body below your chest, containing your stomach and intestines.
abdominal ADJECTIVE

abduct abducts abducting abducted
VERB To abduct someone is to take them away by force.
abduction NOUN

aberration aberrations
NOUN something that is not normal

or usual.

abet abets abetting abetted
VERB If you abet someone, you help
them to do something EG *You've
aided and abetted criminals to evade
justice.*

abhor abhors abhorring abhorred
VERB; A FORMAL WORD If you abhor
something, you hate it.
abhorrence NOUN, **abhorrent** ADJECTIVE

abide abides abiding abided
VERB 1 If you can't abide something,
you dislike it very much. 2 If you
abide by a decision or law, you act
in agreement with it.

ability abilities
NOUN the intelligence or skill
needed to do something EG *the
ability to get on with others.*
◼ capability, proficiency, skill

abject
ADJECTIVE very bad EG *abject failure.*
abjectly ADVERB

ablaze
ADJECTIVE on fire.

able abler ablest
ADJECTIVE 1 If you are able to do
something, you can do it.
2 Someone who is able is very
clever or talented.

ably
Said "ay-blee" ADVERB skilfully and
successfully EG *He is ably supported by
the cast.*

abnormal
ADJECTIVE not normal or usual.
abnormally ADVERB

abnormality abnormalities
NOUN something that is not normal
or usual.
◼ irregularity, oddity, peculiarity

aboard
PREPOSITION OR ADVERB on a ship or
plane.

abode abodes
NOUN; AN OLD-FASHIONED WORD Your
abode is your home.

abolish abolishes abolishing
abolished
VERB To abolish something is to do
away with it EG *the campaign to
abolish hunting.*
abolition NOUN
◼ do away with, eliminate, end

abominable
ADJECTIVE very unpleasant or
shocking.
abominably ADVERB

Aborigine Aborigines
Said "ab-or-rij-in-ee" NOUN someone
descended from the people who
lived in Australia before Europeans
arrived.
Aboriginal ADJECTIVE
▥ borrowed from *aborigines*, the
Latin word for the pre-Roman
inhabitants of Italy

abort aborts aborting aborted
VERB 1 If a plan or activity is
aborted, it is stopped before it is
finished. 2 If a pregnant woman
aborts, the pregnancy ends too
soon and the baby dies.

abortion abortions
NOUN If a woman has an abortion,
the pregnancy is ended deliberately
and the baby dies.

abortive
ADJECTIVE unsuccessful EG *an abortive
bank raid.*

abound abounds abounding
abounded
VERB If things abound, there are very
large numbers of them.

about
PREPOSITION OR ADVERB 1 of or
concerning. 2 approximately and
not exactly. ▶ ADVERB 3 in different
directions EG *There were some bottles
scattered about.* ▶ ADJECTIVE 4 present
or in a place EG *Is Jane about?* ▶ PHRASE
5 If you are **about to** do
something, you are just going to do
it.

above
PREPOSITION OR ADVERB 1 directly over
or higher than something EG *above
the clouds.* 2 greater than a level or
amount EG *The temperature didn't rise
above freezing point.*

above board
ADJECTIVE completely open and legal
EG *They assured me it was above board
and properly licensed.*
▣ an allusion to the difficulty of
cheating at cards with your hands
above the table

abrasion abrasions
NOUN an area where your skin has
been broken.

abrasive
ADJECTIVE 1 An abrasive substance is
rough and can be used to clean
hard surfaces. 2 Someone who is
abrasive is unpleasant and rude.

abroad
ADVERB in a foreign country.

abrupt
ADJECTIVE 1 sudden and quick EG *His
career came to an abrupt end.*
2 unfriendly and impolite.
abruptly ADVERB, **abruptness** NOUN

abscess abscesses
Said "ab-sess" NOUN a painful
swelling filled with pus.

abseiling
NOUN Abseiling is the sport of going
down a cliff or a tall building by
sliding down ropes.

absent
ADJECTIVE Something that is absent is
not present in a place or situation.
absence NOUN

absentee absentees
NOUN someone who is not present
when they should be.

absent-minded
ADJECTIVE forgetful.

absolute
ADJECTIVE 1 total and complete EG
absolute honesty. 2 having total
power EG *the absolute ruler.*
absolutely ADVERB

absolve absolves absolving absolved
VERB To absolve someone of
something is to state they are not
to blame for it.

absorb absorbs absorbing absorbed
VERB If something absorbs liquid or
gas, it soaks it up.
▣ soak up, take in

absorbent
ADJECTIVE Absorbent materials soak
up liquid easily.

absorption
NOUN 1 Absorption is the soaking up
of a liquid. 2 Absorption is great
interest in something EG *my father's
absorption in his business affairs.*

abstain abstains abstaining abstained
VERB 1 If you abstain from
something, you do not do it or
have it EG *The patients had to abstain
from alcohol.* 2 If you abstain in a
vote, you do not vote.
abstention NOUN
▣ (sense 1) forbear, keep from,
refrain

abstinence
NOUN Abstinence is deliberately not
doing something you enjoy.

abstract
ADJECTIVE 1 An abstract idea is based
on thoughts and ideas rather than
physical objects or events, for
example 'bravery'. 2 Abstract art is
a style of art which uses shapes
rather than images of people or
objects. 3 Abstract nouns refer to
qualities or ideas rather than to
physical objects, for example
'happiness' or 'a question'.
abstraction NOUN

absurd
ADJECTIVE ridiculous and stupid.
absurdly ADVERB, **absurdity** NOUN
▣ ludicrous, preposterous,
ridiculous

abundance
NOUN Something that exists in
abundance exists in large numbers
EG *an abundance of wildlife.*
abundant ADJECTIVE, **abundantly** ADVERB
▣ plenty, profusion

abuse abuses abusing abused
NOUN *Said "ab-yoose"* 1 Abuse is
cruel treatment of someone EG *child
abuse.* 2 Abuse is rude and unkind

A
B
C
D
E
F
G
H
I
J
K
L
M
N
O
P
Q
R
S
T
U
V
W
X
Y
Z

remarks directed towards someone. **3** The abuse of something is the wrong use of it EG *an abuse of power... alcohol abuse.* ▶ VERB *Said* "ab-yooze" **4** If you abuse someone, you speak insultingly to them. **5** To abuse someone also means to treat them cruelly. **6** If you abuse something, you use it wrongly or for a bad purpose.
▤ (sense 1) ill-treatment, injury, maltreatment
▤ (sense 5) ill-treat, maltreat

abusive
ADJECTIVE rude and unkind.
abusively ADVERB, **abusiveness** NOUN

abysmal
Said "ab-**biz**-ml" ADJECTIVE very bad indeed EG *an abysmal performance.*
abysmally ADVERB

abyss abysses
NOUN a very deep hole.
▥ from Greek *abussos* meaning 'bottomless'

acacia acacias
Said "a-**kay**-sha" NOUN a type of thorny shrub with small yellow or white flowers.

academic academics
ADJECTIVE **1** Academic work is work done in a school, college, or university. ▶ NOUN **2** someone who teaches or does research in a college or university.
academically ADVERB

academy academies
NOUN **1** a school or college, usually one that specializes in one particular subject EG *the Royal Academy of Dramatic Art.* **2** an organization of scientists, artists, writers, or musicians.
▥ from Greek *akadēmeia*, the name of the grove where Plato taught

accelerate accelerates accelerating accelerated
VERB To accelerate is to go faster.

acceleration
NOUN Acceleration is the rate at which the speed of something is increasing.

accelerator accelerators
NOUN the pedal in a vehicle which you press to make it go faster.

accent accents
NOUN **1** a way of pronouncing a language EG *She had an Australian accent.* **2** a mark placed above or below a letter in some languages, which affects the way the letter is pronounced. **3** An accent on something is an emphasis on it EG *The accent is on action and special effects.*

accentuate accentuates accentuating accentuated
VERB To accentuate a feature of something is to make it more noticeable.

accept accepts accepting accepted
VERB **1** If you accept something, you say yes to it or take it from someone. **2** If you accept a situation, you realize that it cannot be changed EG *He accepts criticism as part of his job.* **3** If you accept a statement or story, you believe it is true EG *The board accepted his explanation.* **4** If a group accepts you, they treat you as one of the group.
acceptance NOUN, **acceptable** ADJECTIVE, **acceptably** ADVERB

access accesses accessing accessed
NOUN **1** Access is the right or opportunity to use something or to enter a place. ▶ VERB **2** If you access information from a computer, you get it.

accessible
ADJECTIVE **1** easily reached or seen EG *The village was accessible by foot only.* **2** easily understood or used EG *guidebooks which present information in a clear and accessible style.*
accessibility NOUN

accession
NOUN A ruler's accession is the time when he or she becomes the ruler

of a country.

accessory accessories
NOUN **1** an extra part. **2** An accessory to a crime is someone who helps another person commit the crime.

accident accidents
NOUN **1** an unexpected event in which people are injured or killed. **2** Something that happens by accident happens by chance.

accidental
ADJECTIVE happening by chance.
accidentally ADVERB
■ inadvertent, unintentional, unplanned

acclaimed
ADJECTIVE If someone or something is acclaimed, they are praised enthusiastically.

accolade accolades
NOUN; A FORMAL WORD An accolade is great praise or an award given to someone.

accommodate accommodates accommodating accommodated
VERB **1** If you accommodate someone, you provide them with a place to sleep, live, or work. **2** If a place can accommodate a number of things or people, it has enough room for them.
☑ *Accommodate* has two *c*s and two *m*s.

accommodation
NOUN Accommodation is a place provided for someone to sleep, live, or work in.

accompaniment accompaniments
NOUN **1** The accompaniment to a song is the music played to go with it. **2** An accompaniment to something is another thing that comes with it EG *Melon is a good accompaniment to cold meats.*

accompany accompanies accompanying accompanied
VERB **1** If you accompany someone, you go with them. **2** If one thing accompanies another, the two things exist at the same time EG

severe pain accompanied by fever. **3** If you accompany a singer or musician, you play an instrument while they sing or play the main tune.

accomplice accomplices
NOUN An accomplice is a person who helps someone else to commit a crime.

accomplish accomplishes accomplishing accomplished
VERB If you accomplish something, you succeed in doing it.
☑ The *com* part of *accomplish* can sound like *kum* or *kom*.

accomplished
ADJECTIVE very talented at something EG *an accomplished cook.*

accomplishment accomplishments
NOUN Someone's accomplishments are the skills they have gained.

accord accords according accorded
VERB **1** If you accord someone or something a particular treatment, you treat them in that way EG *He was accorded a proper respect for his status.* ▶ NOUN **2** Accord is agreement. ▶ PHRASE **3** If you do something **of your own accord**, you do it willingly and not because you have been forced to do it.

accordance
PHRASE If you act **in accordance with** a rule or belief, you act in the way the rule or belief says you should.

according to
PREPOSITION **1** If something is true according to a particular person, that person says that it is true. **2** If something is done according to a principle or plan, that principle or plan is used as the basis for it.

accordion accordions
NOUN An accordion is a musical instrument like an expanding box. It is played by squeezing the two sides together while pressing the keys on it.

A
B
C
D
E
F
G
H
I
J
K
L
M
N
O
P
Q
R
S
T
U
V
W
X
Y
Z

accost accosts accosting accosted
VERB If someone accosts you, especially someone you do not know, they come up and speak to you EG *She says she is accosted when she goes shopping.*

account accounts accounting accounted
NOUN **1** a written or spoken report of something. **2** If you have a bank account, you can leave money in the bank and take it out when you need it. ▶ PLURAL NOUN **3** Accounts are records of money spent and received by a person or business. ▶ PHRASE **4** If you **take something into account**, you include it in your planning. **5 On account of** means because of. ▶ VERB **6** To account for something is to explain it EG *This might account for her strange behaviour.* **7** If something accounts for a particular amount of something, it is that amount EG *The brain accounts for three per cent of body weight.*

accountable
ADJECTIVE If you are accountable for something, you are responsible for it and have to explain your actions EG *The committee is accountable to Parliament.*
accountability NOUN

accountancy
NOUN Accountancy is the job of keeping or inspecting financial accounts.

accountant accountants
NOUN a person whose job is to keep or inspect financial accounts.

accounting
NOUN Accounting is the keeping and checking of financial accounts.

accrue accrues accruing accrued
VERB If money or interest accrues, it increases gradually.

accumulate accumulates accumulating accumulated
VERB If you accumulate things or they accumulate, they collect over a period of time.

accurate
ADJECTIVE completely correct or precise.
accurately ADVERB, **accuracy** NOUN
■ correct, exact, precise

accuse accuses accusing accused
VERB If you accuse someone of doing something wrong, you say they have done it.
accusation NOUN, **accuser** NOUN

accustom accustoms accustoming accustomed
VERB If you accustom yourself to something new or different, you get used to it.

ace aces
NOUN **1** In a pack of cards, an ace is a card with a single symbol on it. ▶ ADJECTIVE **2** AN INFORMAL USE good or skilful EG *an ace squash player.*

acerbic
Said "as-ser-bik" ADJECTIVE; A FORMAL WORD Acerbic remarks are harsh and bitter.

ache aches aching ached
VERB **1** If you ache, you feel a continuous dull pain in a part of your body. **2** If you are aching for something, you want it very much. ▶ NOUN **3** a continuous dull pain.

achieve achieves achieving achieved
VERB If you achieve something, you successfully do it or cause it to happen.
■ accomplish, attain, fulfil
☑ The *i* comes before the *e* in *achieve*.

achievement achievements
NOUN something which you succeed in doing, especially after a lot of effort.

acid acids
NOUN **1** a chemical liquid that turns litmus paper red. Strong acids can damage skin, cloth, and metal. ▶ ADJECTIVE **2** Acid tastes are sharp or sour.
acidic ADJECTIVE, **acidity** NOUN

acid rain

NOUN Acid rain is rain polluted by acid in the atmosphere which has come from factories.

acknowledge acknowledges
acknowledging acknowledged
VERB **1** If you acknowledge a fact or situation, you agree or admit it is true. **2** If you acknowledge someone, you show that you have seen and recognized them. **3** If you acknowledge a message, you tell the person who sent it that you have received it.
acknowledgment or **acknowledgement**
NOUN
☰ (sense 1) accept, admit, grant
☑ *Acknowledgment* and *acknowledgement* are both correct spellings.

acne
Said "ak-nee" NOUN Acne consists of lumpy spots that cover someone's face.

acorn acorns
NOUN the fruit of the oak tree, consisting of a pale oval nut in a cup-shaped base.

acoustic
Said "a-koo-stik" ADJECTIVE **1** relating to sound or hearing. **2** An acoustic guitar is not made louder with an electric amplifier.

acoustics
PLURAL NOUN The acoustics of a room are its structural features which are responsible for how clearly you can hear sounds made in it.

acquaintance acquaintances
NOUN someone you know slightly but not well.

acquainted
ADJECTIVE If you are acquainted with someone, you know them slightly but not well.
☑ You say that you are *acquainted with* someone.

acquire acquires acquiring
acquired
VERB If you acquire something, you obtain it.

acquisition acquisitions
NOUN something you have obtained.

acquit acquits acquitting
acquitted
VERB **1** If someone is acquitted of a crime, they have been tried in a court and found not guilty. **2** If you acquit yourself well on a particular occasion, you behave or perform well.
acquittal NOUN

acre acres
NOUN a unit for measuring areas of land. One acre is equal to 4840 square yards or about 4047 square metres.
⌂ from Old English *æcer* meaning 'field'

acrid
ADJECTIVE sharp and bitter EG *the acrid smell of burning plastic.*

acrimony
Said "ak-rim-on-ee" NOUN; A FORMAL WORD Acrimony is bitterness and anger.
acrimonious ADJECTIVE

acrobat acrobats
NOUN an entertainer who performs gymnastic tricks.
acrobatic ADJECTIVE, **acrobatics** PLURAL NOUN
⌂ from Greek *akrobates* meaning 'someone who walks on tiptoe'

acronym acronyms
NOUN a word made up of the initial letters of a phrase. An example of an acronym is 'BAFTA', which stands for 'British Academy of Film and Television Arts'.

across
PREPOSITION OR ADVERB **1** going from one side of something to the other. **2** on the other side of a road or river.

acrylic
Said "a-kril-lik" NOUN Acrylic is a type of man-made cloth.

act acts acting acted
VERB **1** If you act, you do something EG *It would be irresponsible not to act*

A
B
C
D
E
F
G
H
I
J
K
L
M
N
O
P
Q
R
S
T
U
V
W
X
Y
Z

swiftly. **2** If you act in a particular way, you behave in that way. **3** If a person or thing acts as something else, it has the function or does the job of that thing EG *She was able to act as an interpreter*. **4** If you act in a play or film, you play a part. ▶ NOUN **5** An act is a single thing someone does EG *It was an act of disloyalty to the King.* **6** An Act of Parliament is a law passed by the government. **7** In a play, ballet, or opera, an act is one of the main parts it is divided into.

≡ (sense 4) perform, play
≡ (sense 6) action, deed
≡ (sense 6) bill, decree, law

acting
NOUN Acting is the profession of performing in plays or films.

action actions
NOUN **1** something you do for a particular purpose EG *He had to take evasive action to avoid being hit*. **2** a physical movement. **3** In law, an action is a legal proceeding EG *a libel action*.

activate activates activating activated
VERB To activate something is to make it start working.
≡ set in motion, start

active
ADJECTIVE **1** Active people are full of energy and are always busy. **2** If someone is active in an organization, they are involved in it and work hard for it. **3** In grammar, a verb in the active voice is one where the subject does the action, rather than having it done to them.
actively ADVERB

The Active Voice

The **active** voice and the **passive** voice are two different ways of presenting information in a sentence. When a sentence is written in the **active** voice, the subject of the verb is doing the action. This is the most natural way of presenting information.

Anna is feeding the cat.
The cat chased a mouse.

Also look at the grammar box at **passive**.

activist activists
NOUN A political activist is a person who tries to bring about political and social change.

activity activities
NOUN **1** Activity is a situation in which a lot of things are happening at the same time. **2** something you do for pleasure EG *sport and leisure activities*.

actor actors
NOUN a man or woman whose profession is acting.

actress actresses
NOUN a woman whose profession is acting.

actual
ADJECTIVE real, rather than imaginary or guessed at EG *That is the official figure: the actual figure is much higher.*
actually ADVERB
☑ Don't use *actual* or *actually* when they don't add anything to the meaning of a sentence. Say *it's a fact* rather than *it's an actual fact*.

acumen
NOUN Acumen is the ability to make good decisions quickly EG *business acumen*.

acupuncture
NOUN Acupuncture is the treatment of illness or pain by sticking small needles into specific places in a person's body.
▥ from Latin *acus* meaning 'needle' added to 'puncture'

acute
ADJECTIVE **1** severe or intense EG *an acute shortage of accommodation*. **2** very intelligent EG *an acute mind*. **3** An acute angle is less than 90°. **4** In French and some other languages, an acute accent is a line sloping upwards from left to right placed over a vowel to indicate a change in pronunciation, as in the

word *café*.

ad ads

NOUN; AN INFORMAL WORD an advertisement.

AD

You use 'AD' in dates to indicate the number of years after the birth of Jesus Christ.

adage adages

Said "ad-dij" NOUN a saying that expresses some general truth about life.

adamant

ADJECTIVE If you are adamant, you are determined not to change your mind.

adamantly ADVERB

Adam's apple Adam's apples

NOUN The Adam's apple is the larynx, a lump that sticks out at the front of the neck.

🔲 from the story that a piece of the forbidden apple got stuck in Adam's throat

adapt adapts adapting adapted

VERB 1 If you adapt to a new situation, you change so you can deal with it successfully. 2 If you adapt something, you change it so it is suitable for a new purpose or situation.

adaptable ADJECTIVE, **adaptation** NOUN

adaptor adaptors; also spelt adapter

NOUN a type of electric plug which can be used to connect two or more plugs to one socket.

add adds adding added

VERB 1 If you add something to a number of things, you put it with the things. 2 If you add numbers together or add them up, you work out the total.

adder adders

NOUN a small poisonous snake.

addict addicts

NOUN someone who cannot stop taking harmful drugs.

addicted ADJECTIVE, **addiction** NOUN

addictive

ADJECTIVE If a drug is addictive, the people who take it cannot stop.

addition additions

NOUN 1 something that has been added to something else.
2 Addition is the process of adding numbers together.

🔲 (sense 1) extra, supplement

additional

ADJECTIVE extra or more EG *They made the decision to take on additional staff.*

additionally ADVERB

additive additives

NOUN something added to something else, usually in order to improve it.

address addresses addressing addressed

NOUN 1 the number of the house where you live, together with the name of the street and the town or village. 2 a speech given to a group of people. ▶ VERB 3 If a letter is addressed to you, it has your name and address written on it. 4 If you address a problem or task, you start to deal with it.

adept

ADJECTIVE very skilful at doing something EG *She is adept at motivating others.*

adequate

ADJECTIVE enough in amount or good enough for a purpose EG *an adequate diet.*

adequately ADVERB, **adequacy** NOUN

🔲 enough, satisfactory, sufficient

adhere adheres adhering adhered

VERB 1 If one thing adheres to another, it sticks firmly to it. 2 If you adhere to a rule or agreement, you do what it says. 3 If you adhere to an opinion or belief, you firmly hold that opinion or belief.

adherence NOUN

adherent adherents

NOUN An adherent of a belief is someone who holds that belief.

adhesive adhesives

A
B
C
D
E
F
G
H
I
J
K
L
M
N
O
P
Q
R
S
T
U
V
W
X
Y
Z

9

A
B
C
D
E
F
G
H
I
J
K
L
M
N
O
P
Q
R
S
T
U
V
W
X
Y
Z

NOUN **1** any substance used to stick two things together, for example glue. ▶ ADJECTIVE **2** Adhesive substances are sticky and able to stick to things.

adjacent
Said "ad-**jay**-sent" ADJECTIVE; A FORMAL WORD If two things are adjacent, they are next to each other EG *a hotel adjacent to the beach.*

adjective adjectives
NOUN a word that adds to the description given by a noun. For example, in 'They live in a large white Georgian house', 'large', 'white', and 'Georgian' are all adjectives.
adjectival ADJECTIVE

What is an Adjective?

An adjective is a word that tells you something about a noun. Adjectives are sometimes called "describing words".

Adjectives may indicate how many of a person or thing there are.
three men **some** fish

Adjectives may describe feelings or qualities.
a **happy** child a **strange** girl

Adjectives may describe size, age, temperature, or measurement.
a **large** envelope an **old** jacket

Adjectives may indicate colour.
red socks **dark** hair

Adjectives may indicate nationality or origin.
my **Indian** cousin a **northern** accent

Adjectives may indicate the material from which something is made.
a **wooden** box **denim** trousers

---

adjoining
ADJECTIVE If two rooms are next to each other and are connected, they are adjoining.

adjourn adjourns adjourning adjourned
VERB **1** If a meeting or trial is adjourned, it stops for a time EG *The case was adjourned until September.*
2 If people adjourn to another place, they go there together after a meeting EG *We adjourned to the lounge.*
adjournment NOUN

adjust adjusts adjusting adjusted
VERB **1** If you adjust something, you change its position or alter it in some other way. **2** If you adjust to a new situation, you get used to it.
adjustment NOUN, **adjustable** ADJECTIVE

ad-lib ad-libs ad-libbing ad-libbed
VERB **1** If you ad-lib, you say something that has not been prepared beforehand EG *I ad-lib on radio but use a script on TV.* ▶ NOUN **2** a comment that has not been prepared beforehand.
▣ short for Latin *ad libitum* meaning 'according to desire'

administer administers administering administered
VERB **1** To administer an organization is to be responsible for managing it. **2** To administer the law or administer justice is to put it into practice and apply it. **3** If medicine is administered to someone, it is given to them.

administration administrations
NOUN **1** Administration is the work of organizing and supervising an organization. **2** Administration is also the process of administering something EG *the administration of criminal justice.* **3** The administration is the group of people that manages an organization or a country.
administrative ADJECTIVE, **administrator** NOUN

admirable
ADJECTIVE very good and deserving to be admired.
admirably ADVERB

admiral admirals
NOUN the commander of a navy.
▣ from Arabic *amir* meaning 'commander'

admire admires admiring admired
VERB If you admire someone or something, you respect and approve of them.

admiration NOUN, **admirer** NOUN, **admiring** ADJECTIVE, **admiringly** ADVERB

admission admissions
NOUN **1** If you are allowed admission to a place, you are allowed to go in. **2** If you make an admission of something, you agree, often reluctantly, it is true EG *It was an admission of guilt.*

admit admits admitting admitted
VERB **1** If you admit something, you agree, often reluctantly, it is true. **2** To admit someone or something to a place or organization is to allow them to enter it. **3** If you are admitted to hospital, you are taken there to stay until you are better.

admittedly
ADVERB People use 'admittedly' to show that what they are saying contrasts with something they have already said or are about to say, and weakens their argument EG *My studies, admittedly only from books, taught me much.*

adolescent adolescents
NOUN a young person who is no longer a child but who is not yet an adult.
adolescence NOUN
📖 from Latin *adolescere* meaning 'to grow up'

adopt adopts adopting adopted
VERB **1** If you adopt a child that is not your own, you take him or her into your family as your son or daughter. **2** A FORMAL USE If you adopt a particular attitude, you start to have it.
adoption NOUN

adorable
ADJECTIVE sweet and attractive.

adore adores adoring adored
VERB If you adore someone, you feel deep love and admiration for them.
adoration NOUN

adorn adorns adorning adorned
VERB To adorn something is to decorate it EG *The cathedral is adorned with statues.*
adornment NOUN

adrenalin or **adrenaline**
Said "a-**dren**-al-in" NOUN Adrenalin is a substance which is produced by your body when you are angry, scared, or excited and which makes your heart beat faster.

adrift
ADJECTIVE OR ADVERB If a boat is adrift or goes adrift, it floats on the water without being controlled.

adulation
Said "ad-yoo-**lay**-shn" NOUN Adulation is great admiration and praise for someone.
adulatory ADJECTIVE

adult adults
NOUN a mature and fully developed person or animal.

adultery
NOUN Adultery is sexual intercourse between a married person and someone he or she is not married to.
adulterer NOUN, **adulterous** ADJECTIVE

adulthood
NOUN Someone's adulthood is the time during their life when they are an adult.

advance advances advancing advanced
VERB **1** To advance is to move forward. **2** To advance a cause or interest is to help it to be successful. **3** If you advance someone a sum of money, you lend it to them. ▶ NOUN **4** Advance in something is progress in it EG *scientific advance.* **5** a sum of money lent to someone. ▶ ADJECTIVE **6** happening before an event EG *The event received little advance publicity.*
▶ PHRASE **7** If you do something **in advance**, you do it before something else happens EG *We booked up the room well in advance.*
🔳 (sense 4) development, progress

advantage advantages
NOUN **1** a benefit or something that puts you in a better position.
▶ PHRASE **2** If you **take advantage of** someone, you treat them unfairly

A
B
C
D
E
F
G
H
I
J
K
L
M
N
O
P
Q
R
S
T
U
V
W
X
Y
Z

11

for your own benefit. **3** If you **take advantage of** something, you make use of it.

advantageous

ADJECTIVE likely to benefit you in some way EG *an advantageous marriage.*

advent

NOUN **1** The advent of something is its start or its coming into existence EG *The advent of the submarine changed naval warfare.* **2** Advent is the season just before Christmas in the Christian calendar.

adventure adventures

NOUN a series of events that are unusual and exciting.

adventurer adventurers

NOUN someone who enjoys doing dangerous and exciting things.

adventurous

ADJECTIVE willing to take risks and do new and exciting things.
adventurously ADVERB

adverb adverbs

NOUN a word that adds information about a verb or a following adjective or other adverb, for example, 'slowly', 'now', and 'here' which say how, when, or where something is done.
adverbial ADJECTIVE

What is an Adverb?

An adverb is a word that gives information about a verb. Many adverbs end with the letters -ly.

Adverbs of manner answer the question "how?".
  *She runs **quickly**.*
  *She sings **badly**.*

Adverbs of place answer the question "where?".
  *We travelled **northwards**.*
  *I live **here**.*

Adverbs of time answer the question "when?".
  *You must stop **immediately**.*
  *I arrived **yesterday**.*

Adverbs of degree answer the question

"to what extent?".
  *I **really** hope you will stay.*
  *I play golf **fairly** often.*

Adverbs of frequency answer the question "how often?".
  *We **sometimes** meet for lunch.*
  *You **never** answer my questions.*

Sometimes adverbs can refer to the whole sentence rather than just the verb.
  ***Fortunately**, she was not badly hurt.*

---

adversary adversaries

Said "ad-ver-sar-ee" NOUN someone who is your enemy or who opposes what you are doing.

adverse

ADJECTIVE unfavourable to you or opposite to what you want or need EG *adverse weather conditions.*
adversely ADVERB

adversity adversities

NOUN a time of danger or difficulty.

advert adverts

NOUN; AN INFORMAL WORD an advertisement.

advertise advertises advertising advertised

VERB **1** If you advertise something, you tell people about it in a newspaper or poster, or on TV. **2** To advertise is to make an announcement in a newspaper or poster, or on TV.
advertiser NOUN, **advertising** NOUN

advertisement advertisements

Said "ad-ver-tiss-ment" NOUN an announcement about something in a newspaper or poster, or on TV.
▤ ad, advert, commercial

advice

NOUN Advice is a suggestion from someone about what you should do.
▤ counsel, guidance, suggestion

advisable

ADJECTIVE sensible and likely to achieve the result you want EG *It is advisable to buy the visa before travelling.*
advisably ADVERB, **advisability** NOUN

advise advises advising advised
VERB **1** If you advise someone to do something, you tell them you think they should do it. **2** A FORMAL USE If you advise someone of something, you inform them of it.
adviser NOUN, **advisory** ADJECTIVE
■ (sense 1) counsel, recommend, suggest

advocate advocates advocating advocated
VERB **1** If you advocate a course of action or plan, you support it publicly. ▶ NOUN **2** An advocate of something is someone who supports it publicly. **3** A FORMAL USE a lawyer who represents clients in court.
advocacy NOUN

aerial aerials
Said "air-ee-al" ADJECTIVE **1** Aerial means happening in the air EG *aerial combat*. ▶ NOUN **2** a piece of wire for receiving television or radio signals.

aerial top dressing
NOUN In Australia and New Zealand, aerial top dressing is the spreading of fertilizer from an aeroplane onto land in remote country areas.

aerobics
NOUN Aerobics is a type of fast physical exercise, which increases the oxygen in your blood and strengthens your heart and lungs.
aerobic ADJECTIVE

aerodynamic
ADJECTIVE having a streamlined shape that moves easily through the air.

aeroplane aeroplanes
NOUN a vehicle with wings and engines that enable it to fly.

aerosol aerosols
NOUN a small metal container in which liquid is kept under pressure so that it can be forced out as a spray.
☑ *Aerosol* starts with *aer* and not with *air*.

aerospace
ADJECTIVE involved in making and designing aeroplanes and spacecraft.

aesthetic or **esthetic**
Said "eess-thet-ik" ADJECTIVE; A FORMAL WORD relating to the appreciation of beauty or art.
aesthetically ADVERB, **aesthetics** NOUN

afar
ADJECTIVE; A LITERARY WORD From afar means from a long way away.

affable
ADJECTIVE pleasant and easy to talk to.
affably ADVERB, **affability** NOUN

affair affairs
NOUN **1** an event or series of events EG *The funeral was a sad affair*. **2** To have an affair is to have a secret sexual or romantic relationship, especially when one of the people is married. ▶ PLURAL NOUN **3** Your affairs are your private and personal life EG *Why had he meddled in her affairs?*

affect affects affecting affected
VERB **1** If something affects you, it influences you in some way. **2** A FORMAL USE If you affect a particular way of behaving, you behave in that way EG *He affected an Italian accent*.

affectation affectations
NOUN An affectation is behaviour that is not genuine but is put on to impress people.

affection affections
NOUN **1** Affection is a feeling of love and fondness for someone. ▶ PLURAL NOUN **2** Your affections are feelings of love you have for someone.

affectionate
ADJECTIVE full of fondness for someone EG *an affectionate embrace*.
affectionately ADVERB

affiliate affiliates affiliating affiliated
VERB If a group affiliates itself to another, larger group, it forms a close association with it EG *organizations affiliated to the ANC*.
affiliation NOUN

A
B
C
D
E
F
G
H
I
J
K
L
M
N
O
P
Q
R
S
T
U
V
W
X
Y
Z

A
B
C
D
E
F
G
H
I
J
K
L
M
N
O
P
Q
R
S
T
U
V
W
X
Y
Z

affinity affinities
NOUN a close similarity or understanding between two things or people EG *There are affinities between the two poets.*

affirm affirms affirming affirmed
VERB If you affirm an idea or belief, you clearly indicate your support for it EG *We affirm our commitment to broadcast quality programmes.*
affirmation NOUN

affirmative
ADJECTIVE An affirmative word or gesture is one that means yes.

afflict afflicts afflicting afflicted
VERB If illness or pain afflicts someone, they suffer from it EG *She was afflicted by depression.*
affliction NOUN

affluent
ADJECTIVE having a lot of money and possessions.
affluence NOUN

afford affords affording afforded
VERB **1** If you can afford to do something, you have enough money or time to do it. **2** If you cannot afford something to happen, it would be harmful or embarrassing for you if it happened EG *We cannot afford to be complacent.*

affront affronts affronting affronted
VERB **1** If you are affronted by something, you are insulted and angered by it. ▶ NOUN **2** something that is an insult EG *Our prisons are an affront to civilized society.*
☑ Notice that *affront*, the noun, is followed by *to*.

afield
ADVERB Far afield means a long way away EG *competitors from as far afield as Russia and China.*

afloat
ADVERB OR ADJECTIVE **1** floating on water. **2** successful and making enough money EG *Companies are struggling hard to stay afloat.*

afoot

ADJECTIVE OR ADVERB happening or being planned, especially secretly EG *Plans are afoot to build a new museum.*

afraid
ADJECTIVE **1** If you are afraid, you are very frightened. **2** If you are afraid something might happen, you are worried it might happen.
☰ (sense 1) fearful, frightened, scared

afresh
ADVERB again and in a new way EG *The couple moved abroad to start life afresh.*

Africa
NOUN Africa is the second largest continent. It is almost surrounded by sea, with the Atlantic on its west side, the Mediterranean to the north and the Indian Ocean and the Red Sea to the east.

African Africans
ADJECTIVE **1** belonging or relating to Africa. ▶ NOUN **2** someone, especially a Black person, who comes from Africa.

African-American
African-Americans
NOUN an American whose ancestors came from Africa.

Afrikaans
Said "af-rik-**ahns**" NOUN Afrikaans is a language spoken in South Africa, similar to Dutch.

Afrikaner Afrikaners
NOUN a white South African with Dutch ancestors.

aft
ADVERB OR ADJECTIVE towards the back of a ship or boat.

after
PREPOSITION OR ADVERB **1** later than a particular time, date, or event. **2** behind and following someone or something EG *They ran after her.*
☰ (sense 1) afterwards, following, later

afterlife
NOUN The afterlife is a life some

people believe begins when you die.

aftermath

NOUN The aftermath of a disaster is the situation that comes after it.

afternoon afternoons

NOUN the part of the day between noon and about six o'clock.

aftershave

NOUN a pleasant-smelling liquid men put on their faces after shaving.

afterthought afterthoughts

NOUN something you do or say as an addition to something else you have already done or said.

afterwards

ADVERB after an event or time.

again

ADVERB 1 happening one more time EG *He looked forward to becoming a father again.* 2 returning to the same state or place as before EG *Her back began to hurt her again.*
■ (sense 1) anew, once more

against

PREPOSITION 1 touching and leaning on EG *He leaned against the wall.* 2 in opposition to EG *the Test match against England.* 3 in order to prevent EG *precautions against fire.* 4 in comparison with EG *The pound is now at its lowest rate against the dollar.*

age ages ageing or aging aged

NOUN 1 The age of something or someone is the number of years they have lived or existed. 2 Age is the quality of being old EG *a wine capable of improving with age.* 3 a particular period in history EG *the Iron Age.* ▶ PLURAL NOUN 4 AN INFORMAL USE Ages means a very long time EG *He's been talking for ages.* ▶ VERB 5 To age is to grow old or to appear older.

☑ *Ageing* and *aging* are both correct spellings.

aged

ADJECTIVE 1 *Rhymes with "raged"* having a particular age EG *people*

aged 16 to 24. 2 *Said "ay-dgid"* very old EG *an aged invalid.*

agency agencies

NOUN an organization or business which provides certain services EG *a detective agency.*

agenda agendas

NOUN a list of items to be discussed at a meeting.

agent agents

NOUN 1 someone who arranges work or business for other people, especially actors or singers. 2 someone who works for their country's secret service.

aggravate aggravates aggravating aggravated

VERB 1 To aggravate a bad situation is to make it worse. 2 AN INFORMAL USE If someone or something aggravates you, they make you annoyed.
aggravating ADJECTIVE, **aggravation** NOUN

☑ Some people think that using *aggravate* to mean 'annoy' is wrong.

aggregate aggregates

NOUN a total that is made up of several smaller amounts.

aggression

NOUN Aggression is violent and hostile behaviour.

aggressive

ADJECTIVE full of hostility and violence.
aggressively ADVERB, **aggressiveness** NOUN
■ belligerent, hostile

aggressor aggressors

NOUN a person or country that starts a fight or a war.

aggrieved

ADJECTIVE upset and angry about the way you have been treated.

aghast

Said "a-gast" ADJECTIVE shocked and horrified.

agile

ADJECTIVE able to move quickly and easily EG *He is as agile as a cat.*

A
B
C
D
E
F
G
H
I
J
K
L
M
N
O
P
Q
R
S
T
U
V
W
X
Y
Z

A
B
C
D
E
F
G
H
I
J
K
L
M
N
O
P
Q
R
S
T
U
V
W
X
Y
Z

agilely ADVERB, **agility** NOUN

agitate agitates agitating agitated

VERB **1** If you agitate for something, you campaign energetically to get it. **2** If something agitates you, it worries you.

agitation NOUN, **agitator** NOUN

agnostic agnostics

NOUN OR ADJECTIVE Someone who is an agnostic believes we cannot know definitely whether God exists or not.

agnosticism NOUN

▣ from Greek *agnōstos* meaning 'unknown'

ago

ADVERB in the past EG *She bought her flat three years ago.*

agog

ADJECTIVE excited and eager to know more about an event or situation EG *She was agog to hear his news.*

agonizing or **agonising**

ADJECTIVE extremely painful, either physically or mentally EG *an agonizing decision.*

agony

NOUN very great physical or mental pain.

▣ pain, suffering, torment

agoraphobia

Said "a-gor-a-foe-bee-a" NOUN Agoraphobia is the fear of open spaces.

agoraphobic ADJECTIVE

▣ from Greek *agora* meaning 'market place' + *phobia*

agrarian

Said "ag-rare-ee-an" ADJECTIVE; A FORMAL WORD relating to farming and agriculture EG *agrarian economies.*

agree agrees agreeing agreed

VERB **1** If you agree with someone, you have the same opinion as them. **2** If you agree to do something, you say you will do it. **3** If two stories or totals agree, they are the same. **4** Food that doesn't agree with you makes you ill.

▣ (sense 1) be of the same opinion, concur
▣ (sense 2) comply, consent

agreeable

ADJECTIVE **1** pleasant or enjoyable. **2** If you are agreeable to something, you are willing to allow it or to do it EG *She was agreeable to the project.*

agreeably ADVERB

agreement agreements

NOUN **1** a decision that has been reached by two or more people. **2** Two people who are in agreement have the same opinion about something.

agriculture

NOUN Agriculture is farming.

agricultural ADJECTIVE

aground

ADVERB If a boat runs aground, it becomes stuck in a shallow stretch of water.

ahead

ADVERB **1** in front EG *He looked ahead.* **2** more advanced than someone or something else EG *We are five years ahead of the competition.* **3** in the future EG *I haven't had time to think far ahead.*

aid aids aiding aided

NOUN **1** Aid is money, equipment, or services provided for people in need EG *food and medical aid.* **2** something that makes a task easier EG *teaching aids.* ▶ VERB **3** A FORMAL USE If you aid a person or an organization, you help or support them.

aide aides

NOUN an assistant to an important person, especially in the government or the army EG *the Prime Minister's closest aides.*

AIDS

NOUN AIDS is a disease which destroys the body's natural system of immunity to diseases. AIDS is an abbreviation for 'acquired immune deficiency syndrome'.

ailing
ADJECTIVE **1** sick or ill, and not getting better. **2** getting into difficulties, especially with money EG *an ailing company*.

ailment ailments
NOUN a minor illness.

aim aims aiming aimed
VERB **1** If you aim an object or weapon at someone or something, you point it at them. **2** If you aim to do something, you are planning or hoping to do it. ▶ NOUN **3** Your aim is what you intend to achieve. **4** If you take aim, you point an object or weapon at someone or something.
▤ (sense 1) point
▤ (sense 2) intend, mean, plan
▤ (sense 4) goal, intention, objective

aimless
ADJECTIVE having no clear purpose or plan.
aimlessly ADVERB, **aimlessness** NOUN

air airs airing aired
NOUN **1** Air is the mixture of oxygen and other gases which we breathe and which forms the earth's atmosphere. **2** An air someone or something has is the impression they give EG *an air of defiance*. **3** 'Air' is used to refer to travel in aircraft EG *I have to travel by air a great deal.*
▶ VERB **4** If you air your opinions, you talk about them to other people.

airborne
ADJECTIVE in the air and flying.

air-conditioning
NOUN a system of providing cool, clean air in buildings.
air-conditioned ADJECTIVE

aircraft
NOUN any vehicle which can fly.

airfield airfields
NOUN an open area of ground with runways where small aircraft take off and land.

air force air forces
NOUN the part of a country's armed services that fights using aircraft.

air gun air guns
NOUN a gun which uses air pressure to fire pellets.

air hostess air hostesses
NOUN a woman whose job is to look after passengers on an aircraft.

airless
ADJECTIVE having no wind or fresh air.

airlift airlifts
NOUN an operation to move people or goods by air, especially in an emergency.

airline airlines
NOUN a company which provides air travel.

airmail
NOUN the system of sending letters and parcels by air.

airman airmen
NOUN a man who serves in his country's air force.

airport airports
NOUN a place where people go to catch planes.

air raid air raids
NOUN an attack by enemy aircraft, in which bombs are dropped.

airship airships
NOUN a large, light aircraft, consisting of a rigid balloon filled with gas and powered by an engine, with a passenger compartment underneath.

airstrip airstrips
NOUN a stretch of land that has been cleared for aircraft to take off and land.

airtight
ADJECTIVE not letting air in or out.

airy airier airiest
ADJECTIVE full of fresh air and light.
airily ADVERB

aisle aisles
Rhymes with "mile" NOUN a long narrow gap that people can walk along between rows of seats or shelves.

A
B
C
D
E
F
G
H
I
J
K
L
M
N
O
P
Q
R
S
T
U
V
W
X
Y
Z

A

ajar

ADJECTIVE A door or window that is ajar is slightly open.

akin

ADJECTIVE; A FORMAL WORD similar EG *The taste is akin to veal.*

alabaster

NOUN Alabaster is a type of smooth stone used for making ornaments. 🏛 from Latin *alabaster* meaning 'vase for perfume'

alacrity

NOUN; A FORMAL WORD Alacrity is eager willingness EG *He seized this offer with alacrity.*

alarm alarms alarming alarmed

NOUN 1 Alarm is a feeling of fear and worry EG *The cat sprang back in alarm.* 2 an automatic device used to warn people of something EG *a car alarm.* ▶ VERB 3 If something alarms you, it makes you worried and anxious. **alarming** ADJECTIVE

alas

ADVERB unfortunately or regrettably EG *But, alas, it would not be true.*

Albanian Albanians

ADJECTIVE 1 belonging or relating to Albania. ▶ NOUN 2 someone who comes from Albania. 3 Albanian is the main language spoken in Albania.

albatross albatrosses

NOUN a large white sea bird.

albeit

Said "awl-bee-it" CONJUNCTION; A FORMAL WORD although EG *He was making progress, albeit slowly.*

albino albinos

NOUN a person or animal with very white skin, white hair, and pink eyes.

album albums

NOUN 1 a CD, cassette, or record with a number of songs on it. 2 a book in which you keep a collection of things such as photographs or stamps.

alchemy

Said "al-kem-ee" NOUN Alchemy was a medieval science that attempted to change ordinary metals into gold. **alchemist** NOUN

alcheringa

Said "al-cher-**ring**-ga" NOUN Alcheringa is the same as Dreamtime.

alcohol

NOUN Alcohol is any drink that can make people drunk; also the colourless flammable liquid found in these drinks, produced by fermenting sugar.

alcoholic alcoholics

ADJECTIVE 1 An alcoholic drink contains alcohol. ▶ NOUN 2 someone who is addicted to alcohol. **alcoholism** NOUN

alcopop alcopops

NOUN; AN INFORMAL WORD an alcoholic drink that tastes like a soft drink.

alcove alcoves

NOUN an area of a room which is set back slightly from the main part. 🏛 from Arabic *al-qubbah* meaning 'arch'

ale

NOUN Ale is a type of beer.

alert alerts alerting alerted

ADJECTIVE 1 paying full attention to what is happening EG *The criminal was spotted by an alert member of the public.* ▶ NOUN 2 a situation in which people prepare themselves for danger EG *The troops were on a war alert.* ▶ VERB 3 If you alert someone to a problem or danger, you warn them of it. **alertness** NOUN
🔲 (sense 1) attentive, vigilant, watchful

algae

Said "al-jee" PLURAL NOUN Algae are plants that grow in water or on damp surfaces.

algebra

NOUN Algebra is a branch of mathematics in which symbols and letters are used instead of numbers to express relationships between quantities.

algebraic ADJECTIVE
▣ from Arabic *al-jabr* meaning 'reunion'

Algerian Algerians
ADJECTIVE **1** belonging or relating to Algeria. ▶ NOUN **2** someone who comes from Algeria.

alias aliases
Said "ay-lee-ass" NOUN a false name EG *Leonard Nimoy, alias Mr Spock.*

alibi alibis
Said "al-li-bye" NOUN An alibi is evidence proving you were somewhere else when a crime was committed.

alien aliens
Said "ay-lee-an" ADJECTIVE **1** not normal to you EG *a totally alien culture.* ▶ NOUN **2** someone who is not a citizen of the country in which he or she lives. **3** In science fiction, an alien is a creature from outer space.

alienate alienates alienating alienated
VERB If you alienate someone, you do something that makes them become unsympathetic to you EG *The Council's approach alienated many local residents.*
alienation NOUN

alight alights alighting alighted
ADJECTIVE **1** Something that is alight is burning. ▶ VERB **2** If a bird or insect alights somewhere, it lands there. **3** A FORMAL USE When passengers alight from a vehicle, they get out of it at the end of a journey.

align aligns aligning aligned
Said "a-line" VERB **1** If you align yourself with a particular group, you support them. **2** If you align things, you place them in a straight line.
alignment NOUN

alike
ADJECTIVE **1** Things that are alike are similar in some way. ▶ ADVERB **2** If

people or things are treated alike, they are treated in a similar way.

alimony
Said "a-li-mon-ee" NOUN Alimony is money someone has to pay regularly to their wife or husband after they are divorced.

alive
ADJECTIVE **1** living. **2** lively and active.
▣ (sense 1) animate, living

alkali alkalis
Said "al-kal-eye" NOUN a chemical substance that turns litmus paper blue.
alkaline ADJECTIVE; **alkalinity** NOUN

all
ADJECTIVE, PRONOUN, OR ADVERB **1** used when referring to the whole of something EG *Why did he have to say all that?... She managed to finish it all.* ▶ ADVERB **2** 'All' is also used when saying the two sides in a game or contest have the same score EG *The final score was six points all.*

Allah
PROPER NOUN Allah is the Muslim name for God.

allay allays allaying allayed
VERB To allay someone's fears or doubts is to stop them feeling afraid or doubtful.

allege alleges alleging alleged
Said "a-lej" VERB If you allege that something is true, you say it is true but do not provide any proof EG *It is alleged that she died as a result of neglect.*
allegation NOUN, **alleged** ADJECTIVE

allegiance allegiances
Said "al-lee-jenss" NOUN Allegiance is loyal support for a person or organization.

allegory allegories
Said "al-li-gor-ee" NOUN a piece of writing or art in which the characters and events are symbols for something else. Allegories usually make some moral, religious, or political point. For

example, George Orwell's novel 'Animal Farm' is an allegory in that the animals who revolt in the farmyard are symbols of the political leaders in the Russian Revolution.

allergy allergies
Said "al-er-jee" NOUN a sensitivity someone has to something, so that they become ill when they eat it or touch it EG *an allergy to cows' milk*.

alleviate alleviates alleviating alleviated
VERB To alleviate pain or a problem is to make it less severe EG *measures to alleviate poverty*.
alleviation NOUN

alley alleys
NOUN a narrow passage between buildings.

alliance alliances
NOUN a group of people, organizations, or countries working together for similar aims.
■ association, league, union

alligator alligators
NOUN a large animal, similar to a crocodile.
▥ from Spanish *el lagarto* meaning 'lizard'

alliteration
NOUN; A LITERARY WORD Alliteration is the use of several words together which all begin with the same sound, for example 'the forest's ferny floor'.
alliterative ADJECTIVE

allocate allocates allocating allocated
VERB If you allocate something, you decide it should be given to a person or place, or used for a particular purpose EG *funds allocated for nursery education*.
allocation NOUN

allot allots allotting allotted
VERB If something is allotted to you, it is given to you as your share EG *Space was allotted for visitors' cars*.

allotment allotments

NOUN **1** a piece of land which people can rent to grow vegetables on. **2** a share of something.

allow allows allowing allowed
VERB **1** If you allow something, you say it is all right or let it happen. **2** If you allow a period of time or an amount of something, you set it aside for a particular purpose EG *Allow four hours for the paint to dry*.
allowable ADJECTIVE

allowance allowances
NOUN **1** money given regularly to someone for a particular purpose EG *a petrol allowance*. ▶ PHRASE **2** If you **make allowances** for something, you take it into account EG *The school made allowances for Muslim cultural customs*.

alloy alloys
NOUN a mixture of two or more metals.

all right or **alright**
ADJECTIVE **1** If something is all right, it is acceptable. **2** If someone is all right, they are safe and not harmed. **3** You say 'all right' to agree to something.

allude alludes alluding alluded
VERB If you allude to something, you refer to it in an indirect way.
☑ You *allude to* something. Do not confuse *allude* with *elude*.

allure
NOUN The allure of something is an exciting quality that makes it attractive EG *the allure of foreign travel*.
alluring ADJECTIVE

allusion allusions
NOUN an indirect reference to or comment about something EG *English literature is full of classical allusions*.

ally allies allying allied
NOUN **1** a person or country that helps and supports another. ▶ VERB **2** If you ally yourself with someone, you agree to help and support each other.
■ (sense 1) friend, helper, partner

◼ (sense 2) associate, join, unite

almanac almanacs
NOUN a book published every year giving information about a particular subject.

almighty
ADJECTIVE **1** very great or serious EG *I've just had an almighty row with the chairman.* ▶ PROPER NOUN **2** The Almighty is another name for God.

almond almonds
NOUN a pale brown oval nut.

almost
ADVERB very nearly EG *Over the past decade their wages have almost doubled.*
◼ just about, nearly, practically

alms
PLURAL NOUN; AN OLD-FASHIONED WORD
Alms are gifts of money, food, or clothing to poor people.

aloft
ADVERB up in the air or in a high position EG *He held aloft the trophy.*

alone
ADJECTIVE OR ADVERB not with other people or things EG *He just wanted to be alone.*
◼ by oneself, solitary, unaccompanied

along
PREPOSITION **1** moving, happening, or existing continuously from one end to the other of something, or at various points beside it EG *Put rivets along the top edge.* ▶ ADVERB **2** moving forward EG *We marched along.* **3** with someone EG *Why could she not take her along?* ▶ PHRASE **4** All along means from the beginning of a period of time right up to now EG *You've known that all along.*

alongside
PREPOSITION OR ADVERB **1** next to something EG *They had a house in the park alongside the river.* ▶ PREPOSITION **2** If you work alongside other people, you are working in the same place and cooperating with them EG *He was thrilled to work*

alongside Robert De Niro.
☑ Do not use *of* after *alongside*.

aloof
ADJECTIVE distant from someone or something.

aloud
ADVERB When you read or speak aloud, you speak loudly enough for other people to hear you.

alphabet alphabets
NOUN a set of letters in a fixed order that is used in writing a language.
alphabetical ADJECTIVE, **alphabetically** ADVERB

alpine
ADJECTIVE existing in or relating to high mountains EG *alpine flowers.*
▥ from *the Alps*, a mountain range in central Europe

already
ADVERB having happened before the present time or earlier than expected EG *She has already gone to bed.*

alright
another spelling of **all right**.
☑ Some people think that *all right* is the only correct spelling and that *alright* is wrong.

Alsatian Alsatians
Said "al-say-shn" NOUN a large wolflike dog.

also
ADVERB in addition to something that has just been mentioned.

altar altars
NOUN a holy table in a church or temple.

alter alters altering altered
VERB If something alters or if you alter it, it changes.
alteration NOUN

altercation altercations
NOUN; A FORMAL WORD a noisy disagreement.

alternate alternates alternating alternated
VERB **1** If one thing alternates with another, the two things regularly occur one after the other. ▶ ADJECTIVE

2 If something happens on alternate days, it happens on the first day but not the second, and happens again on the third day but not the fourth, and so on.
alternately ADVERB, **alternation** NOUN

alternating current alternating currents
NOUN An alternating current is a current that regularly changes its direction, so that the electrons flow first one way and then the other.

alternative alternatives
NOUN **1** something you can do or have instead of something else EG *alternatives to prison such as community service.* ▶ ADJECTIVE
2 Alternative plans or actions can happen or be done instead of what is already happening or being done.
alternatively ADVERB
☑ If there are more than two choices in a situation you should say *there are three choices* rather than *there are three alternatives* because the strict meaning of *alternative* is a choice between two things.

although
CONJUNCTION in spite of the fact that EG *He wasn't well-known in America, although he did make a film there.*

altitude altitudes
NOUN The altitude of something is its height above sea level EG *The mountain range reaches an altitude of 1330 metres.*

altogether
ADVERB **1** entirely EG *She wasn't altogether sorry to be leaving.* **2** in total; used of amounts EG *I get paid 1000 pounds a month altogether.*

aluminium
NOUN Aluminium is a silvery-white lightweight metal.

always
ADVERB all the time or for ever EG *She's always moaning.*

am
the first person singular, present tense of **be**.

a.m.
used to specify times between 12 midnight and 12 noon, eg *I get up at 6 a.m.* It is an abbreviation for the Latin phrase 'ante meridiem', which means 'before noon'.

amalgamate amalgamates amalgamating amalgamated
VERB If two organizations amalgamate, they join together to form one new organization.
amalgamation NOUN

amandla
NOUN In South Africa, amandla is a political slogan which calls for power for Black people.

amass amasses amassing amassed
VERB If you amass something such as money or information, you collect large quantities of it EG *He amassed a huge fortune.*

amateur amateurs
NOUN someone who does something as a hobby rather than as a job.

amateurish
ADJECTIVE not skilfully made or done.
amateurishly ADVERB

amaze amazes amazing amazed
VERB If something amazes you, it surprises you very much.
amazement NOUN
☰ astonish, astound, stun, surprise

amazing
ADJECTIVE very surprising or remarkable.
amazingly ADVERB

ambassador ambassadors
NOUN a person sent to a foreign country as the representative of his or her own government.

amber
NOUN **1** Amber is a hard, yellowish-brown substance used for making jewellery. ▶ NOUN OR ADJECTIVE
2 orange-brown.

ambidextrous
ADJECTIVE Someone who is ambidextrous is able to use both hands equally skilfully.

ambience

NOUN; A FORMAL WORD The ambience of a place is its atmosphere.

ambiguous

ADJECTIVE A word or phrase that is ambiguous has more than one meaning.
ambiguously ADVERB, **ambiguity** NOUN

ambition ambitions

NOUN **1** If you have an ambition to achieve something, you want very much to achieve it. **2** Ambition is a great desire for success, power, and wealth EG *He's talented and full of ambition.*

ambitious

ADJECTIVE **1** Someone who is ambitious has a strong desire for success, power, and wealth. **2** An ambitious plan is a large one and requires a lot of work EG *an ambitious rebuilding schedule.*

ambivalent

ADJECTIVE having or showing two conflicting attitudes or emotions.
ambivalence NOUN

amble ambles ambling ambled

VERB If you amble, you walk slowly and in a relaxed manner.

ambulance ambulances

NOUN a vehicle for taking sick and injured people to hospital.

ambush ambushes ambushing ambushed

VERB **1** To ambush someone is to attack them after hiding and lying in wait for them. ▶ NOUN **2** an attack on someone after hiding and lying in wait for them.

amen

INTERJECTION Amen is said by Christians at the end of a prayer. It means 'so be it'.

amenable

Said "am-mee-na-bl" ADJECTIVE willing to listen to suggestions, or to cooperate with someone EG *Both brothers were amenable to the arrangement.*
amenably ADVERB, **amenability** NOUN

amend amends amending amended

VERB **1** To amend something that has been written or said is to alter it slightly EG *Our constitution had to be amended.* ▶ PLURAL NOUN **2** If you make amends for something bad you have done, you say you are sorry and try to make up for it.
amendment NOUN

amenity amenities

Said "am-**mee**-nit-ee" NOUN Amenities are things that are available for the public to use, such as sports facilities or shopping centres.

America

NOUN America refers to the United States, or to the whole of North, South, and Central America.

American Americans

ADJECTIVE **1** belonging or relating to the United States, or to the whole of North, South, and Central America. ▶ NOUN **2** someone who comes from the United States.

amethyst amethysts

NOUN a type of purple semiprecious stone.
🏛 from Greek *amethustos* meaning 'not drunk'. It was thought to prevent intoxication

amiable

ADJECTIVE pleasant and friendly EG *The hotel staff were very amiable.*
amiably ADVERB, **amiability** NOUN

amicable

ADJECTIVE fairly friendly EG *an amicable divorce.*
amicably ADVERB

amid or **amidst**

PREPOSITION; A FORMAL WORD surrounded by EG *She enjoys cooking amid her friends.*
☑ The form *amidst* is a bit old-fashioned and *amid* is more often used.

amiss

ADJECTIVE If something is amiss, there is something wrong.

ammonia

NOUN Ammonia is a colourless, strong-smelling gas or liquid.

ammunition

NOUN Ammunition is anything that can be fired from a gun or other weapon, for example bullets and shells.

amnesia

NOUN Amnesia is loss of memory.

amnesty amnesties

NOUN an official pardon for political or other prisoners.

amoeba amoebas or amoebae

Said "am-mee-ba"; also spelt ameba

NOUN Amoebas are the smallest kind of living creature. They consist of one cell, which reproduces by dividing into two.

amok

Said "am-muk" PHRASE If a person or animal runs amok, they behave in a violent and uncontrolled way.

🏛 a Malay word

among or **amongst**

PREPOSITION 1 surrounded by EG The bike lay among piles of chains and pedals. 2 in the company of EG He was among friends. 3 between more than two EG The money will be divided among seven charities.

☑ If there are more than two things, you should use among. If there are only two things you should use between. The form amongst is a bit old-fashioned and among is more often used.

amoral

ADJECTIVE Someone who is amoral has no moral standards by which to live.

☑ Do not confuse amoral and immoral. You use amoral to talk about people with no moral standards, but immoral for people who are aware of moral standards but go against them.

amorous

ADJECTIVE passionately affectionate EG an amorous relationship.

amorously ADVERB, **amorousness** NOUN

amount amounts amounting amounted

NOUN 1 An amount of something is how much there is of it. ▶ VERB 2 If something amounts to a particular total, all the parts of it add up to that total EG Her vocabulary amounted to only 50 words.

▤ (sense 1) extent, number, quantity

amp amps

NOUN An amp is the same as an ampere.

ampere amperes

Said "am-pair" NOUN a unit which is used for measuring electric current.

amphetamine amphetamines

NOUN a drug that increases people's energy and makes them excited. It can have dangerous and unpleasant side effects.

amphibian amphibians

NOUN a creature that lives partly on land and partly in water, for example a frog or a newt.

amphibious

ADJECTIVE An amphibious animal, such as a frog, lives partly on land and partly in the water.

🏛 from Greek **amphibios** meaning 'having a double life'

amphitheatre amphitheatres

NOUN a large, semicircular open area with sloping sides covered with rows of seats.

ample

ADJECTIVE If there is an ample amount of something, there is more than enough of it.

amply ADVERB

amplifier amplifiers

NOUN a piece of equipment in a radio or stereo system which causes sounds or signals to become louder.

amplify amplifies amplifying amplified

VERB If you amplify a sound, you make it louder.

amplification NOUN

amplitude

NOUN In physics, the amplitude of a wave is how far its curve moves away from its normal position.

amputate amputates amputating amputated

VERB To amputate an arm or a leg is to cut it off as a surgical operation.
amputation NOUN

Amrit

NOUN **1** In the Sikh religion, Amrit is a special mixture of sugar and water used in rituals. **2** The Amrit or Amrit ceremony takes place when someone is accepted as a full member of the Sikh community, and drinks Amrit as part of the ceremony.

amuse amuses amusing amused

VERB **1** If something amuses you, you think it is funny. **2** If you amuse yourself, you find things to do which stop you from being bored.
amused ADJECTIVE, **amusing** ADJECTIVE

amusement amusements

NOUN **1** Amusement is the state of thinking something is funny.
2 Amusement is also the pleasure you get from being entertained or from doing something interesting.
3 Amusements are ways of passing the time pleasantly.

an

ADJECTIVE 'An' is used instead of 'a' in front of words that begin with a vowel sound.

☑ You use *an* in front of abbreviations that start with a vowel sound when they are read out loud: *an MA; an OBE.*

anachronism anachronisms

Said "an-**ak**-kron-izm" NOUN something that belongs or seems to belong to another time.
anachronistic ADJECTIVE
🔳 from Greek *anakhronismos* meaning 'mistake in time'

anaemia

Said "a-**nee**-mee-a" NOUN Anaemia is a medical condition resulting from too few red cells in a person's blood. People with anaemia look pale and feel very tired.
anaemic ADJECTIVE

anaesthetic anaesthetics

Said "an-niss-**thet**-ik" NOUN a substance that stops you feeling pain. A general anaesthetic stops you from feeling pain in the whole of your body by putting you to sleep, and a local anaesthetic makes just one part of your body go numb.

anaesthetist anaesthetists

NOUN a doctor who is specially trained to give anaesthetics.

anaesthetize anaesthetizes anaesthetizing anaesthetized; also spelt **anesthetize** or **anaesthetise**

VERB To anaesthetize someone is to give them an anaesthetic to make them unconscious.

anagram anagrams

NOUN a word or phrase formed by changing the order of the letters of another word or phrase. For example, 'triangle' is an anagram of 'integral'.

anal

Said "**ay**-nl" ADJECTIVE relating to the anus.

analgesic analgesics

Said "an-al-**jee**-sik" NOUN a substance that relieves pain.

analogy analogies

Said "an-**al**-o-jee" NOUN a comparison showing that two things are similar in some ways.
analogous ADJECTIVE

analyse analyses analysing analysed

VERB To analyse something is to investigate it carefully in order to understand it or find out what it consists of.

analysis analyses

NOUN Analysis is the process of investigating something in order to understand it or find out what it consists of EG *a full analysis of the problem.*

analyst analysts
NOUN a person whose job is to analyse things to find out about them.

analytic or **analytical**
ADJECTIVE using logical reasoning EG *Planning in detail requires an acute analytical mind.*
analytically ADVERB

anarchy
Said "an-nar-kee" NOUN Anarchy is a situation where nobody obeys laws or rules.
🏛 from Greek *anarkhos* meaning 'without a ruler'

anatomy anatomies
NOUN 1 Anatomy is the study of the structure of the human body or of the bodies of animals. 2 An animal's anatomy is the structure of its body.
anatomical ADJECTIVE, **anatomically** ADVERB

ANC
NOUN The ANC is one of the main political parties in South Africa. ANC is an abbreviation for 'African National Congress'.

ancestor ancestors
NOUN Your ancestors are the members of your family who lived many years ago and from whom you are descended.
ancestral ADJECTIVE
▇ forebear, forefather

ancestry ancestries
NOUN Your ancestry consists of the people from whom you are descended EG *a French citizen of Greek ancestry.*

anchor anchors anchoring anchored
NOUN 1 a heavy, hooked object at the end of a chain, dropped from a boat into the water to keep the boat in one place. ▶ VERB 2 To anchor a boat or another object is to stop it from moving by dropping an anchor or attaching it to something solid.

anchorage anchorages
NOUN a place where a boat can safely anchor.

anchovy anchovies
NOUN a type of small edible fish with a very strong salty taste.

ancient
Said "ayn-shent" ADJECTIVE 1 existing or happening in the distant past EG *ancient Greece.* 2 very old or having a very long history EG *an ancient monastery.*

ancillary
Said "an-sil-lar-ee" ADJECTIVE The ancillary workers in an institution are the people such as cooks and cleaners, whose work supports the main work of the institution.
🏛 from Latin *ancilla* meaning 'maidservant'

and
CONJUNCTION You use 'and' to link two or more words or phrases together.

androgynous
Said "an-droj-in-uss" ADJECTIVE; A FORMAL WORD having both male and female characteristics.

anecdote anecdotes
NOUN a short, entertaining story about a person or event.
anecdotal ADJECTIVE

anemone anemones
Said "an-em-on-ee" NOUN a plant with red, purple, or white flowers.

anew
ADVERB If you do something anew, you do it again EG *They left their life in Britain to start anew in France.*

angel angels
NOUN Angels are spiritual beings some people believe live in heaven and act as messengers for God.
angelic ADJECTIVE

anger angers angering angered
NOUN 1 Anger is the strong feeling you get when you feel someone has behaved in an unfair or cruel way. ▶ VERB 2 If something angers you, it makes you feel angry.

■ (sense 1) fury, rage, wrath
■ (sense 2) enrage, infuriate, madden

angina
Said "an-**jy**-na" NOUN Angina is a brief but very severe heart pain, caused by lack of blood supply to the heart. It is also known as 'angina pectoris'.

angle angles
NOUN **1** The distance between two lines at the point where they join together. Angles are measured in degrees. **2** the direction from which you look at something EG *He had painted the vase from all angles.* **3** An angle on something is a particular way of considering it EG *the same story from a German angle.*

angler anglers
NOUN someone who fishes with a fishing rod as a hobby.
angling NOUN
🔟 from Old English *angul* meaning 'fish-hook'

Anglican Anglicans
NOUN OR ADJECTIVE a member of one of the churches belonging to the Anglican Communion, a group of Protestant churches which includes the Church of England.

Anglo-Saxon Anglo-Saxons
NOUN **1** The Anglo-Saxons were a race of people who settled in England from the fifth century AD and were the dominant people until the Norman invasion in 1066. They were composed of three West Germanic tribes, the Angles, Saxons, and Jutes. **2** Anglo-Saxon is another name for **Old English.**

Angolan Angolans
Said "ang-**goh**-ln" ADJECTIVE
1 belonging or relating to Angola.
▸ NOUN **2** someone who comes from Angola.

angry angrier angriest
ADJECTIVE very cross or annoyed.
angrily ADVERB
■ enraged, furious, infuriated, mad

anguish
NOUN Anguish is extreme suffering.
anguished ADJECTIVE

angular
ADJECTIVE Angular things have straight lines and sharp points EG *He has an angular face and pointed chin.*

animal animals
NOUN any living being except a plant, or any mammal except a human being.
🔟 from Latin *anima* meaning 'life' or 'soul'

animate animates animating animated
VERB To animate something is to make it lively and interesting.

animated
ADJECTIVE lively and interesting EG *an animated conversation.*

animation
NOUN **1** Animation is a method of film-making in which a series of drawings are photographed. When the film is projected, the characters in the drawings appear to move. **2** Someone who has animation shows liveliness in the way they speak and act EG *The crowd showed no sign of animation.*
animator NOUN

animosity animosities
NOUN Animosity is a feeling of strong dislike and anger towards someone.

ankle ankles
NOUN the joint which connects your foot to your leg.

annex annexes annexing annexed; also spelt annexe
NOUN **1** an extra building which is joined to a larger main building. **2** an extra part added to a document. ▸ VERB **3** If one country annexes another, it seizes the other country and takes control of it.
annexation NOUN

annihilate annihilates annihilating annihilated
Said "an-**nye**-ill-ate" VERB If

A
B
C
D
E
F
G
H
I
J
K
L
M
N
O
P
Q
R
S
T
U
V
W
X
Y
Z

something is annihilated, it is completely destroyed.

annihilation NOUN

anniversary anniversaries

NOUN a date which is remembered because something special happened on that date in a previous year.

announce announces announcing announced

VERB If you announce something, you tell people about it publicly or officially EG *The team was announced on Friday morning.*

announcement NOUN

■ broadcast, make known, proclaim

announcer announcers

NOUN someone who introduces programmes on radio and television.

annoy annoys annoying annoyed

VERB If someone or something annoys you, they irritate you and make you fairly angry.

annoyance NOUN, **annoyed** ADJECTIVE

■ bother, exasperate, irritate, vex

annual annuals

ADJECTIVE **1** happening or done once a year EG *their annual conference.*
2 happening or calculated over a period of one year EG *the United States' annual budget for national defence.* ▶ NOUN **3** a book or magazine published once a year. **4** a plant that grows, flowers, and dies within one year.

annually ADVERB

annuity annuities

NOUN a fixed sum of money paid to someone every year from an investment or insurance policy.

annul annuls annulling annulled

VERB If a marriage or contract is annulled, it is declared invalid, so that legally it is considered never to have existed.

annulment NOUN

anoint anoints anointing anointed

VERB To anoint someone is to put oil on them as part of a ceremony.

anointment NOUN

anomaly anomalies

Said "an-**nom**-al-ee" NOUN

Something is an anomaly if it is unusual or different from normal.

anomalous ADJECTIVE

anon.

an abbreviation for **anonymous**.

anonymous

ADJECTIVE If something is anonymous, nobody knows who is responsible for it EG *The police received an anonymous phone call.*

anonymously ADVERB, **anonymity** NOUN

anorak anoraks

NOUN a warm waterproof jacket, usually with a hood.

▥ an Eskimo word

anorexia

NOUN Anorexia is a psychological illness in which the person refuses to eat because they are frightened of becoming fat.

▥ from Greek *an-* + *orexis* meaning 'no appetite'

another

ADJECTIVE OR PRONOUN Another thing or person is an additional thing or person.

answer answers answering answered

VERB **1** If you answer someone, you reply to them using words or actions or in writing. ▶ NOUN **2** the reply you give when you answer someone. **3** a solution to a problem.

■ (sense 1) reply, respond, retort
■ (sense 2) reply, response, retort

answerable

ADJECTIVE If you are answerable to someone for something, you are responsible for it EG *He must be made answerable for these terrible crimes.*

answering machine answering machines

NOUN a machine which records telephone calls while you are out.

ant ants

NOUN Ants are small insects that live

in large groups.

antagonism
NOUN Antagonism is hatred or hostility.

antagonist antagonists
NOUN an enemy or opponent.

antagonistic
ADJECTIVE Someone who is antagonistic towards you shows hate or hostility.
antagonistically ADVERB

antagonize antagonizes antagonizing antagonized; also spelt **antagonise**
VERB If someone is antagonized, they are made to feel anger and hostility.

Antarctic
NOUN The Antarctic is the region south of the Antarctic Circle.

Antarctic Circle
NOUN The Antarctic Circle is an imaginary circle around the southern part of the world.

ante-
PREFIX Ante- means before EG *antenatal*.

antecedent antecedents
Said "an-tis-see-dent" NOUN **1** An antecedent of a thing or event is something which happened or existed before it and is related to it in some way EG *the prehistoric antecedents of the horse.* **2** Your antecedents are your ancestors, the relatives from whom you are descended.

antelope antelopes
NOUN an animal which looks like a deer.

antenatal
ADJECTIVE concerned with the care of pregnant women and their unborn children EG *an antenatal clinic.*

antenna antennae or antennas
NOUN **1** The antennae of insects and certain other animals are the two long, thin parts attached to their heads which they use to feel with. The plural is 'antennae'. **2** In

Australian, New Zealand, and American English, an antenna is a radio or television aerial. The plural is 'antennas'.

anthem anthems
NOUN a hymn written for a special occasion.

anthology anthologies
NOUN a collection of writings by various authors published in one book.

anthropology
NOUN Anthropology is the study of human beings and their society and culture.
anthropological ADJECTIVE, **anthropologist** NOUN

anti-
PREFIX opposed to or opposite to something EG *antiwar marches.*

antibiotic antibiotics
NOUN Antibiotics are drugs or chemicals used in medicine to kill bacteria and cure infections.

antibody antibodies
NOUN Antibodies are substances produced in the blood which can kill the harmful bacteria that cause disease.

anticipate anticipates anticipating anticipated
VERB If you anticipate an event, you are expecting it and are prepared for it EG *She had anticipated his visit.*
anticipation NOUN

anticlimax anticlimaxes
NOUN If something is an anticlimax, it disappoints you because it is not as exciting as expected, or because it occurs after something that was very exciting.

anticlockwise
ADJECTIVE OR ADVERB moving in the opposite direction to the hands of a clock.

antics
PLURAL NOUN Antics are funny or silly ways of behaving.

antidote antidotes
NOUN a chemical substance that acts

against the effect of a poison.

antihistamine antihistamines
NOUN a drug used to treat an allergy.

antipathy
NOUN Antipathy is a strong feeling of dislike or hostility towards something or someone.

antiperspirant antiperspirants
NOUN a substance which stops you sweating when you put it on your skin.

antipodes
Said "an-tip-pod-eez" PLURAL NOUN The antipodes are any two points on the earth's surface that are situated directly opposite each other. In Britain, Australia and New Zealand are sometimes called the Antipodes as they are opposite Britain on the globe.
antipodean ADJECTIVE
▣ from Greek *antipous* meaning 'with the feet opposite'

antiquarian
ADJECTIVE relating to or involving old and rare objects EG *antiquarian books*.

antiquated
ADJECTIVE very old-fashioned EG *an antiquated method of teaching*.

antique antiques
Said "an-teek" NOUN **1** an object from the past that is collected because of its value or beauty.
▶ ADJECTIVE **2** from or concerning the past EG *antique furniture*.

antiquity antiquities
NOUN **1** Antiquity is the distant past, especially the time of the ancient Egyptians, Greeks, and Romans.
2 Antiquities are interesting works of art and buildings from the distant past.

anti-Semitism
NOUN Anti-Semitism is hatred of Jewish people.
anti-Semitic ADJECTIVE, **anti-Semite** NOUN

antiseptic
ADJECTIVE Something that is antiseptic kills germs.

antisocial

ADJECTIVE **1** An antisocial person is unwilling to meet and be friendly with other people. **2** Antisocial behaviour is annoying or upsetting to other people EG *Smoking in public is antisocial*.

antithesis antitheses
Said "an-tith-iss-iss" NOUN; A FORMAL WORD The antithesis of something is its exact opposite EG *Work is the antithesis of leisure*.

antivenene antivenenes
NOUN a substance which reduces the effect of a venom, especially a snake venom.

antler antlers
NOUN A male deer's antlers are the branched horns on its head.

antonym antonyms
NOUN a word which means the opposite of another word. For example, 'hot' is the antonym of 'cold'.

anus anuses
NOUN the hole between the buttocks.

anvil anvils
NOUN a heavy iron block on which hot metal is beaten into shape.

anxiety anxieties
NOUN Anxiety is nervousness or worry.

anxious
ADJECTIVE **1** If you are anxious, you are nervous or worried. **2** If you are anxious to do something or anxious that something should happen, you very much want to do it or want it to happen EG *She was anxious to have children*.
anxiously ADVERB

any
ADJECTIVE OR PRONOUN **1** one, some, or several EG *Do you have any paperclips I could borrow?* **2** even the smallest amount or even one EG *He was unable to tolerate any dairy products*. **3** whatever or whichever, no matter what or which EG *Any type of cooking oil will do*.

anybody

PRONOUN any person.

anyhow
ADVERB **1** in any case. **2** in a careless way EG *They were all shoved in anyhow*.

anyone
PRONOUN any person.

anything
PRONOUN any object, event, situation, or action.

anyway
ADVERB in any case.

anywhere
ADVERB in, at, or to any place.

Anzac Anzacs
NOUN **1** In World War I, an Anzac was a soldier with the Australia and New Zealand Army Corps. **2** an Australian or New Zealand soldier.

aorta
Said "ay-**or**-ta" NOUN the main artery in the body, which carries blood away from the heart.

apart
ADVERB OR ADJECTIVE **1** When something is apart from something else, there is a space or a distance between them EG *The couple separated and lived apart for four years… The gliders landed about seventy metres apart.* ▶ ADVERB **2** If you take something apart, you separate it into pieces.

apartheid
Said "ap-**par**-tide" NOUN In South Africa apartheid was the government policy and laws which kept people of different races apart. It was abolished in 1994.
🔟 an Afrikaans word

apartment apartments
NOUN a set of rooms for living in, usually on one floor of a building.

apathetic
ADJECTIVE not interested in anything.
▤ indifferent, uninterested

apathy
Said "**ap**-path-ee" NOUN Apathy is a state of mind in which you do not care about anything.

ape apes aping aped
NOUN **1** Apes are animals with a very short tail or no tail. They are closely related to man. Apes include chimpanzees, gorillas, and gibbons. ▶ VERB **2** If you ape someone's speech or behaviour, you imitate it.

aphid aphids
NOUN a small insect that feeds by sucking the juices from plants.

aphrodisiac aphrodisiacs
NOUN a food, drink, or drug which makes people want to have sex.

apiece
ADVERB If people have a particular number of things apiece, they have that number each.

aplomb
Said "uh-**plom**" NOUN If you do something with aplomb, you do it with great confidence.

apocalypse
Said "uh-**pok**-ka-lips" NOUN The Apocalypse is the end of the world.
apocalyptic ADJECTIVE
🔟 from Greek *apokaluptein* meaning 'to reveal'; the way the world will end is considered to be revealed in the last book of the Bible, called 'Apocalypse' or 'Revelation'

apocryphal
ADJECTIVE A story that is apocryphal is generally believed not to have really happened.

apolitical
Said "ay-**poll**-**it**-i-kl" ADJECTIVE not interested in politics.

apologetic
ADJECTIVE showing or saying you are sorry.
apologetically ADVERB

apologize apologizes apologizing apologized; also spelt **apologise**
VERB When you apologize to someone, you say you are sorry for something you have said or done.

apology apologies
NOUN something you say or write to

A
B
C
D
E
F
G
H
I
J
K
L
M
N
O
P
Q
R
S
T
U
V
W
X
Y
Z

tell someone you are sorry.

apostle apostles
NOUN The Apostles are the twelve followers who were chosen by Christ.

apostrophe apostrophes
Said "ap-poss-troff-ee" NOUN a punctuation mark used to show that one or more letters have been missed out of a word, for example "he's" for "he is". Apostrophes are also used with -s at the end of a noun to show that what follows belongs to or relates to the noun, for example *my brother's books*. If the noun already has an -s at the end, for example because it is plural, you just add the apostrophe, eg *my brothers' books*, referring to more than one brother.

What does the Apostrophe do?

The **apostrophe** (') is used to show possession. It is usually added to the end of a word and followed by an s.
Matthew's book   children's programmes

If a plural word already ends in -s, the apostrophe follows that letter.
my parents' generation   seven years' bad luck

You should not use an apostrophe to form plurals or possessive pronouns.
a pound of tomatoes [not *tomato's*]
I happen to be a fan of hers [not *her's*]

You can, however, add an apostrophe to form the plural of a number, letter, or symbol.
P's and Q's   7's   £'s

The apostrophe is also used to show that a letter or letters have been omitted.
rock'n'roll   Who's next?

---

appal appals appalling appalled
VERB If something appals you, it shocks you because it is very bad.

appalling
ADJECTIVE so bad as to be shocking EG *She escaped with appalling injuries.*

apparatus
NOUN The apparatus for a particular

task is the equipment used for it.

apparent
ADJECTIVE **1** seeming real rather than actually being real EG *an apparent hit and run accident.* **2** obvious EG *It was apparent that he had lost interest.*
apparently ADVERB
■ (sense 1) ostensible, seeming

apparition apparitions
NOUN something you think you see but that is not really there EG *a ghostly apparition on the windscreen.*

appeal appeals appealing appealed
VERB **1** If you appeal for something, you make an urgent request for it EG *The police appealed for witnesses to come forward.* **2** If you appeal to someone in authority against a decision, you formally ask them to change it. **3** If something appeals to you, you find it attractive or interesting. ▶ NOUN **4** a formal or serious request EG *an appeal for peace.* **5** The appeal of something is the quality it has which people find attractive or interesting EG *the rugged appeal of the Rockies.*
appealing ADJECTIVE

appear appears appearing appeared
VERB **1** When something which you could not see appears, it moves (or you move) so that you can see it. **2** When something new appears, it begins to exist. **3** When an actor or actress appears in a film or show, they take part in it. **4** If something appears to be a certain way, it seems or looks that way EG *He appeared to be searching for something.*
■ (sense 1) come into view, emerge, show up

appearance appearances
NOUN **1** The appearance of someone in a place is their arrival there, especially when it is unexpected. **2** The appearance of something new is the time when it begins to exist EG *the appearance of computer technology.* **3** Someone's or

something's appearance is the way they look to other people EG *His gaunt appearance had sparked fears for his health.*

appease appeases appeasing appeased

VERB If you try to appease someone, you try to calm them down when they are angry, for example by giving them what they want.
appeasement NOUN

appendage appendages
NOUN a less important part attached to a main part.

appendicitis
Said "app-end-i-site-uss" NOUN a painful illness in which a person's appendix becomes infected.

appendix appendices or appendixes
NOUN 1 Your appendix is a small closed tube forming part of your digestive system. 2 An appendix to a book is extra information placed after the end of the main text.
☑ The plural of the part of the body is *appendixes*. The plural of the extra section in a book is *appendices*.

appetite appetites
NOUN 1 Your appetite is your desire to eat. 2 If you have an appetite for something, you have a strong desire for it and enjoyment of it EG *She had lost her appetite for air travel.*

appetizing or **appetising**
ADJECTIVE Food that is appetizing looks and smells good, and makes you want to eat it.

applaud applauds applauding applauded
VERB 1 When a group of people applaud, they clap their hands in approval or praise. 2 When an action or attitude is applauded, people praise it.

applause
NOUN Applause is clapping by a group of people.

apple apples

NOUN a round fruit with smooth skin and firm white flesh.

appliance appliances
NOUN any machine in your home you use to do a job like cleaning or cooking EG *kitchen appliances.*

applicable
ADJECTIVE Something that is applicable to a situation is relevant to it EG *The rules are applicable to everyone.*

applicant applicants
NOUN someone who is applying for something EG *We had problems recruiting applicants for the post.*

application applications
NOUN 1 a formal request for something, usually in writing.
2 The application of a rule, system, or skill is the use of it in a particular situation.

apply applies applying applied
VERB 1 If you apply for something, you formally ask for it, usually by writing a letter. 2 If you apply a rule or skill, you use it in a situation EG *He applied his mind to the problem.* 3 If something applies to a person or a situation, it is relevant to that person or situation EG *The legislation applies only to people living in England and Wales.* 4 If you apply something to a surface, you put it on EG *She applied lipstick to her mouth.*

appoint appoints appointing appointed
VERB 1 If you appoint someone to a job or position, you formally choose them for it. 2 If you appoint a time or place for something to happen, you decide when or where it will happen.
appointed ADJECTIVE

appointment appointments
NOUN 1 an arrangement you have with someone to meet them. 2 The appointment of a person to do a particular job is the choosing of that person to do it. 3 a job or a position of responsibility EG *He applied for an appointment in Russia.*

A B C D E F G H I J K L M N O P Q R S T U V W X Y Z

A
B
C
D
E
F
G
H
I
J
K
L
M
N
O
P
Q
R
S
T
U
V
W
X
Y
Z

▤ (sense 1) date, engagement, meeting

apposite
Said "**app**-o-zit" ADJECTIVE well suited for a particular purpose EG *He went before Cameron could think of anything apposite to say.*

appraise appraises appraising appraised
VERB If you appraise something, you think about it carefully and form an opinion about it.
appraisal NOUN

appreciable
Said "a-**pree**-shuh-bl" ADJECTIVE large enough or important enough to be noticed EG *an appreciable difference.*
appreciably ADVERB

appreciate appreciates appreciating appreciated
VERB **1** If you appreciate something, you like it because you recognize its good qualities EG *He appreciates fine wines.* **2** If you appreciate a situation or problem, you understand it and know what it involves. **3** If you appreciate something someone has done for you, you are grateful to them for it EG *I really appreciate you coming to visit me.* **4** If something appreciates over a period of time, its value increases EG *The property appreciated by 50% in two years.*
appreciation NOUN
▤ (sense 1) prize, rate highly, value

appreciative
ADJECTIVE **1** understanding and enthusiastic EG *They were a very appreciative audience.* **2** thankful and grateful EG *I am particularly appreciative of the help.*
appreciatively ADVERB

apprehend apprehends apprehending apprehended
VERB; A FORMAL WORD **1** When the police apprehend someone, they arrest them and take them into custody. **2** If you apprehend something, you understand it fully EG *They were unable to apprehend his hidden meaning.*

apprehensive
ADJECTIVE afraid something bad may happen EG *I was very apprehensive about the birth.*
apprehensively ADVERB, **apprehension** NOUN

apprentice apprentices
NOUN a person who works for a period of time with a skilled craftsman in order to learn a skill or trade.
apprenticeship NOUN
▦ from Old French *aprendre* meaning 'to learn'

approach approaches approaching approached
VERB **1** To approach something is to come near or nearer to it. **2** When a future event approaches, it gradually gets nearer EG *As winter approached, tents were set up to accommodate refugees.* **3** If you approach someone about something, you ask them about it. **4** If you approach a situation or problem in a particular way, you think about it or deal with it in that way. ▶ NOUN **5** The approach of something is the process of it coming closer EG *the approach of spring.* **6** An approach to a situation or problem is a way of thinking about it or dealing with it. **7** a road or path that leads to a place.
approaching ADJECTIVE

appropriate appropriates appropriating appropriated
ADJECTIVE **1** suitable or acceptable for a particular situation EG *He didn't think jeans were appropriate for a vice-president.* ▶ VERB **2** A FORMAL USE If you appropriate something which does not belong to you, you take it without permission.
appropriately ADVERB, **appropriation** NOUN

approval
NOUN **1** Approval is agreement given to a plan or request EG *The plan will require approval from the local*

authority. **2** Approval is also admiration EG *She looked at James with approval.*

■ (sense 1) agreement, consent, permission

approve approves approving approved

VERB **1** If you approve of something or someone, you think that thing or person is acceptable or good. **2** If someone in a position of authority approves a plan or idea, they formally agree to it.

approved ADJECTIVE, **approving** ADJECTIVE

■ (sense 1) commend, favour, like
■ (sense 2) agree to, authorize, pass, permit

approximate

ADJECTIVE almost exact EG *What was the approximate distance between the cars?*

approximately ADVERB
■ close, near

apricot apricots

NOUN a small, soft, yellowish-orange fruit.

🏛 from Latin *praecox* meaning 'early ripening'

April

NOUN April is the fourth month of the year. It has 30 days.

🏛 from Latin *Aprīlis*

apron aprons

NOUN a piece of clothing worn over the front of normal clothing to protect it.

apt

ADJECTIVE **1** suitable or relevant EG *a very apt description.* **2** having a particular tendency EG *They are apt to jump to the wrong conclusions.*

aptitude

NOUN Someone's aptitude for something is their ability to learn it quickly and to do it well EG *I have a natural aptitude for painting.*

aquarium aquaria or aquariums

NOUN a glass tank filled with water in which fish are kept.

Aquarius

NOUN Aquarius is the eleventh sign of the zodiac, represented by a person carrying water. People born between January 20th and February 18th are born under this sign.

aquatic

ADJECTIVE **1** An aquatic animal or plant lives or grows in water. **2** involving water EG *aquatic sports.*

aqueduct aqueducts

NOUN a long bridge with many arches carrying a water supply over a valley.

Arab Arabs

NOUN a member of a group of people who used to live in Arabia but who now live throughout the Middle East and North Africa.

Arabic

NOUN Arabic is a language spoken by many people in the Middle East and North Africa.

arable

ADJECTIVE Arable land is used for growing crops.

arbitrary

ADJECTIVE An arbitrary decision or action is one that is not based on a plan or system.

arbitrarily ADVERB

arbitrate arbitrates arbitrating arbitrated

VERB When someone arbitrates between two people or groups who are in disagreement, they consider the facts and decide who is right.

arbitration NOUN, **arbitrator** NOUN

arc arcs

NOUN **1** a smoothly curving line. **2** In geometry, an arc is a section of the circumference of a circle.

arcade arcades

NOUN a covered passageway where there are shops or market stalls.

arcane

ADJECTIVE mysterious and difficult to understand.

arch arches arching arched

NOUN **1** a structure that has a curved

top supported on either side by a pillar or wall. **2** the curved part of bone at the top of the foot. ▶ VERB **3** When something arches, it forms a curved line or shape. ▶ ADJECTIVE **4** most important EG *my arch enemy.*

archaeology or **archeology**
Said "ar-kee-ol-loj-ee" NOUN Archaeology is the study of the past by digging up and examining the remains of buildings, tools, and other things.
archaeological ADJECTIVE, **archaeologist** NOUN
📖 from Greek *arkhaios* meaning 'ancient'

archaic
Said "ar-kay-ik" ADJECTIVE very old or old-fashioned.

archangel archangels
Said "ark-ain-jel" NOUN an angel of the highest rank.

archbishop archbishops
NOUN a bishop of the highest rank in a Christian Church.

archdeacon archdeacons
NOUN an Anglican clergyman ranking just below a bishop.

archeology
another spelling of **archaeology**.

archer archers
NOUN someone who shoots with a bow and arrow.

archery
NOUN Archery is a sport in which people shoot at a target with a bow and arrow.

archipelago archipelagos
Said "ar-kip-pel-lag-oh" NOUN a group of small islands.
📖 from Italian *arcipelago* meaning 'chief sea'; originally referring to the Aegean Sea

architect architects
Said "ar-kit-tekt" NOUN a person who designs buildings.

architecture
NOUN Architecture is the art or practice of designing buildings.
architectural ADJECTIVE

archive archives
Said "ar-kive" NOUN Archives are collections of documents and records about the history of a family or some other group of people.

arctic
NOUN **1** The Arctic is the region north of the Arctic Circle. ▶ ADJECTIVE **2** Arctic means very cold indeed EG *arctic conditions.*
📖 from Greek *arktos* meaning 'bear'; originally it referred to the northern constellation of the Great Bear

Arctic Circle
NOUN The Arctic Circle is an imaginary circle around the northern part of the world.

ardent
ADJECTIVE full of enthusiasm and passion.
ardently ADVERB

ardour
NOUN Ardour is a strong and passionate feeling of love or enthusiasm.

arduous
Said "ard-yoo-uss" ADJECTIVE tiring and needing a lot of effort EG *the arduous task of rebuilding the country.*

are
the plural form of the present tense of **be**.

area areas
NOUN **1** a particular part of a place, country, or the world EG *a built-up area of the city.* **2** The area of a piece of ground or a surface is the amount of space it covers, measured in square metres or square feet.
▣ (sense 1) district, region, zone

arena arenas
NOUN **1** a place where sports and other public events take place. **2** A particular arena is the centre of attention or activity in a particular situation EG *the political arena.*
📖 from Latin *harena* meaning 'sand', hence the sandy centre of

an amphitheatre where gladiators fought

Argentinian Argentinians
Said "ar-jen-**tin**-ee-an" ADJECTIVE
1 belonging or relating to Argentina. ▶ NOUN **2** someone who comes from Argentina.

arguable
ADJECTIVE An arguable idea or point is not necessarily true or correct and should be questioned.
arguably ADVERB

argue argues arguing argued
VERB **1** If you argue with someone about something, you disagree with them about it, sometimes in an angry way. **2** If you argue that something is the case, you give reasons why you think it is so EG *She argued that her client had been wrongly accused.*

argument arguments
NOUN **1** a disagreement between two people which causes a quarrel. **2** a point or a set of reasons you use to try to convince people about something.

argumentative
ADJECTIVE An argumentative person is always disagreeing with other people.

aria arias
Said "**ah**-ree-a" NOUN a song sung by one of the leading singers in an opera.
⌂ an Italian word meaning 'tune'

arid
ADJECTIVE Arid land is very dry because it has very little rain.

Aries
Said "**air**-reez" NOUN Aries is the first sign of the zodiac, represented by a ram. People born between March 21st and April 19th are born under this sign.

arise arises arising arose arisen
VERB **1** When something such as an opportunity or problem arises, it begins to exist. **2** A FORMAL USE To arise also means to stand up from a

sitting, kneeling, or lying position.

aristocracy aristocracies
NOUN a class of people who have a high social rank and special titles.

aristocrat aristocrats
NOUN someone whose family has a high social rank, and who has a title.
aristocratic ADJECTIVE

arithmetic
NOUN Arithmetic is the part of mathematics which is to do with the addition, subtraction, multiplication, and division of numbers.
arithmetical ADJECTIVE, **arithmetically** ADVERB
⌂ from Greek *arithmos* meaning 'number'

ark
NOUN In the Bible, the ark was the boat built by Noah for his family and the animals during the Flood.

arm arms arming armed
NOUN **1** Your arms are the part of your body between your shoulder and your wrist. **2** The arms of a chair are the parts on which you rest your arms. **3** An arm of an organization is a section of it EG *the political arm of the armed forces.*
▶ PLURAL NOUN **4** Arms are weapons used in a war. ▶ VERB **5** To arm someone is to provide them with weapons.

armada armadas
Said "ar-**mah**-da" NOUN a large fleet of warships.

armadillo armadillos
NOUN a mammal from South America which is covered with strong bony plates like armour.
⌂ a Spanish word meaning 'little armed man'

Armageddon
NOUN In Christianity, Armageddon is the final battle between good and evil at the end of the world.
⌂ from Hebrew *har megiddon*, the mountain district of Megiddo, the site of many battles

A
B
C
D
E
F
G
H
I
J
K
L
M
N
O
P
Q
R
S
T
U
V
W
X
Y
Z

A

armament armaments

NOUN Armaments are the weapons and military equipment that belong to a country.

armchair armchairs

NOUN a comfortable chair with a support on each side for your arms.

armed

ADJECTIVE A person who is armed is carrying a weapon or weapons.

armistice armistices

Said "ar-miss-tiss" NOUN an agreement in a war to stop fighting in order to discuss peace.

armour

NOUN In the past, armour was metal clothing worn for protection in battle.

armoured

ADJECTIVE covered with thick steel for protection from gunfire and other missiles EG *an armoured car.*

armoury armouries

NOUN a place where weapons are stored.

armpit armpits

NOUN the area under your arm where your arm joins your shoulder.

army armies

NOUN a large group of soldiers organized into divisions for fighting on land.

aroma aromas

NOUN a strong, pleasant smell.
aromatic ADJECTIVE
🏛 a Greek word meaning 'spice'

around

PREPOSITION **1** placed at various points in a place or area EG *There are many seats around the building.* **2** from place to place inside an area EG *We walked around the showroom.* **3** at approximately the time or place mentioned EG *The attacks began around noon.* ▶ ADVERB **4** here and there EG *His papers were scattered around.*

arouse arouses arousing aroused

VERB If something arouses a feeling in you, it causes you to begin to have this feeling EG *His death still arouses very painful feelings.*
arousal NOUN

arrange arranges arranging arranged

VERB **1** If you arrange to do something, you make plans for it. **2** If you arrange something for someone, you make it possible for them to have it or do it EG *The bank has arranged a loan for her.* **3** If you arrange objects, you set them out in a particular position EG *He started to arrange the books in piles.*
arrangement NOUN

array arrays

NOUN An array of different things is a large number of them displayed together.

arrears

PLURAL NOUN **1** Arrears are amounts of money you owe EG *mortgage arrears.* ▶ PHRASE **2** If you are paid **in arrears,** you are paid at the end of the period for which the payment is due.

arrest arrests arresting arrested

VERB **1** If the police arrest someone, they take them into custody to decide whether to charge them with an offence. ▶ NOUN **2** An arrest is the act of taking a person into custody.

arrival arrivals

NOUN **1** the act or time of arriving EG *The arrival of the train was delayed.* **2** something or someone that has arrived EG *The tourist authority reported record arrivals over Christmas.*

arrive arrives arriving arrived

VERB **1** When you arrive at a place, you reach it at the end of your journey. **2** When a letter or a piece of news arrives, it is brought to you EG *A letter arrived at her lawyer's office.* **3** When you arrive at an idea or decision you reach it. **4** When a moment, event, or new thing arrives, it begins to happen EG *The Easter holidays arrived.*

B C D E F G H I J K L M N O P Q R S T U V W X Y Z

arrogant
ADJECTIVE Someone who is arrogant behaves as if they are better than other people.
arrogantly ADVERB, **arrogance** NOUN

arrow arrows
NOUN a long, thin weapon with a sharp point at one end, shot from a bow.

arsenal arsenals
NOUN a place where weapons and ammunition are stored or produced.
📖 from Italian *arsenale* meaning 'dockyard', originally in Venice

arsenic
NOUN Arsenic is a very strong poison which can kill people.

arson
NOUN Arson is the crime of deliberately setting fire to something, especially a building.

art arts
NOUN **1** Art is the creation of objects such as paintings and sculptures, which are thought to be beautiful or which express a particular idea; also used to refer to the objects themselves. **2** An activity is called an art when it requires special skill or ability EG *the art of diplomacy*.
▶ PLURAL NOUN **3** The arts are literature, music, painting, and sculpture, considered together.

artefact artefacts
Said "**ar**-tif-fact" NOUN any object made by people.

artery arteries
NOUN **1** Your arteries are the tubes that carry blood from your heart to the rest of your body. **2** a main road or major section of any system of communication or transport.

artful
ADJECTIVE clever and skilful, often in a cunning way.
artfully ADVERB

arthritis
NOUN Arthritis is a condition in which the joints in someone's body become swollen and painful.
arthritic ADJECTIVE

artichoke artichokes
NOUN **1** A globe artichoke is a round green vegetable that has a cluster of fleshy leaves, the bottom part of which you can eat. **2** A Jerusalem artichoke is a small yellowish-white vegetable that grows underground and looks like a potato.
📖 from Arabic *al-kharshuf*

article articles
NOUN **1** a piece of writing in a newspaper or magazine. **2** a particular item EG *an article of clothing*. **3** In English grammar, 'a' and 'the' are sometimes called articles: 'a' (or 'an') is the indefinite article; 'the' is the definite article.

articulate articulates articulating articulated
ADJECTIVE **1** If you are articulate, you are able to express yourself well in words. ▶ VERB **2** When you articulate your ideas or feelings, you express in words what you think or feel EG *She could not articulate her grief.* **3** When you articulate a sound or word, you speak it clearly.
articulation NOUN

artificial
ADJECTIVE **1** created by people rather than occurring naturally EG *artificial colouring*. **2** pretending to have attitudes and feelings which other people realize are not real EG *an artificial smile*.
artificially ADVERB

artillery
NOUN **1** Artillery consists of large, powerful guns such as cannons. **2** The artillery is the branch of an army which uses large, powerful guns.

artist artists
NOUN **1** a person who draws or paints or produces other works of art. **2** a person who is very skilled at a particular activity.

artiste artistes

Said "ar-**teest**" NOUN a professional entertainer, for example a singer or a dancer.

artistic
ADJECTIVE 1 able to create good paintings, sculpture, or other works of art. 2 concerning or involving art or artists.
artistically ADVERB

artistry
NOUN Artistry is the creative skill of an artist, writer, actor, or musician EG *a supreme demonstration of his artistry as a cellist.*

arty artier artiest
ADJECTIVE; AN INFORMAL WORD interested in painting, sculpture, and other works of art.

as
CONJUNCTION 1 at the same time that EG *She waved at fans as she arrived for the concert.* 2 in the way that EG *They had talked as only the best of friends can.* 3 because EG *As I won't be back tonight, don't bother to cook a meal.* 4 when you are comparing things that are similar EG *It was as big as four football pitches.* ▶ PREPOSITION 5 You use 'as' when you are saying what role someone or something has EG *She worked as a waitress.* 6 You use **as if** or **as though** when you are giving a possible explanation for something EG *He looked at me as if I were mad.*

asbestos
NOUN Asbestos is a grey heat-resistant material used in the past to make fireproof articles.

ascend ascends ascending ascended
Said "ass-**end**" VERB; A FORMAL WORD To ascend is to move or lead upwards EG *We finally ascended to the brow of a steep hill.*

ascendancy
NOUN; A FORMAL WORD If one group has ascendancy over another, it has more power or influence than the other.

ascendant
ADJECTIVE 1 rising or moving upwards. ▶ PHRASE 2 Someone or something **in the ascendant** is increasing in power or popularity.

ascent ascents
NOUN an upward journey, for example up a mountain.

ascertain ascertains ascertaining ascertained
Said "ass-er-**tain**" VERB; A FORMAL WORD If you ascertain that something is the case, you find out it is the case EG *He had ascertained that she had given up smoking.*

ascribe ascribes ascribing ascribed
VERB 1 If you ascribe an event or state of affairs to a particular cause, you think that it is the cause of it EG *His stomach pains were ascribed to his intake of pork.* 2 If you ascribe a quality to someone, you think they have it.

ash ashes
NOUN 1 Ash is the grey or black powdery remains of anything that has been burnt. 2 a tree with grey bark and hard tough wood used for timber.

ashamed
ADJECTIVE 1 feeling embarrassed or guilty. 2 If you are ashamed of someone, you feel embarrassed to be connected with them.

ashen
ADJECTIVE grey or pale EG *Her face was ashen with fatigue.*

ashore
ADVERB on land or onto the land.

ashtray ashtrays
NOUN a small dish for ash from cigarettes and cigars.

Asia
NOUN Asia is the largest continent. It has Europe on its western side, with the Arctic to the north, the Pacific to the east, and the Indian Ocean to the south. Asia includes several island groups, including

Japan, Indonesia, and the Philippines.

Asian Asians
ADJECTIVE **1** belonging or relating to Asia. ▶ NOUN **2** someone who comes from India, Pakistan, Bangladesh, or from some other part of Asia.

aside asides
ADVERB **1** If you move something aside, you move it to one side. ▶ NOUN **2** a comment made away from the main conversation or dialogue that all those talking are not meant to hear.

ask asks asking asked
VERB **1** If you ask someone a question, you put a question to them for them to answer. **2** If you ask someone to do something, you tell them you want them to do it. **3** If you ask for something, you say you would like to have it. **4** If you ask someone's permission or forgiveness, you try to obtain it. **5** If you ask someone somewhere, you invite them there EG *Not everybody had been asked to the wedding.*

askew
ADJECTIVE not straight.

asleep
ADJECTIVE sleeping.

asparagus
NOUN Asparagus is a vegetable that has long shoots which are cooked and eaten.

aspect aspects
NOUN **1** An aspect of something is one of its features EG *Exam results illustrate only one aspect of a school's success.* **2** The aspect of a building is the direction it faces EG *The southern aspect of the cottage faces over fields.*

asphalt
NOUN Asphalt is a black substance used to make road surfaces and playgrounds.

aspiration aspirations
NOUN Someone's aspirations are their desires and ambitions.

aspire aspires aspiring aspired
VERB If you aspire to something, you have an ambition to achieve it EG *He aspired to work in music journalism.*
aspiring ADJECTIVE

aspirin aspirins
NOUN **1** Aspirin is a white drug used to relieve pain, fever, and colds. **2** a tablet of this drug.

ass asses
NOUN a donkey.

assailant assailants
NOUN someone who attacks another person.

assassin assassins
NOUN someone who has murdered a political or religious leader.
▦ from Arabic *hashshashin* meaning 'people who eat hashish'; the name comes from a medieval Muslim sect who ate hashish and went about murdering Crusaders

assassinate assassinates assassinating assassinated
VERB To assassinate a political or religious leader is to murder him or her.
assassination NOUN

assault assaults assaulting assaulted
NOUN **1** a violent attack on someone. ▶ VERB **2** To assault someone is to attack them violently.

assegai assegais
Said "ass-i-guy"; also spelt **assagai**
NOUN In South African English, an assegai is a sharp, light spear.

assemble assembles assembling assembled
VERB **1** To assemble is to gather together. **2** If you assemble something, you fit the parts of it together.

assembly assemblies
NOUN **1** a group of people who have gathered together for a meeting. **2** The assembly of an object is the fitting together of its parts EG *DIY assembly of units.*

A
B
C
D
E
F
G
H
I
J
K
L
M
N
O
P
Q
R
S
T
U
V
W
X
Y
Z

A B C D E F G H I J K L M N O P Q R S T U V W X Y Z

assent assents assenting assented
Said "as-**sent**" NOUN **1** If you give your assent to something, you agree to it. ▸ VERB **2** If you assent to something, you agree to it.

assert asserts asserting asserted
VERB **1** If you assert a fact or belief, you state it firmly and forcefully.
2 If you assert yourself, you speak and behave in a confident and direct way, so that people pay attention to you.

assertive
ADJECTIVE If you are assertive, you speak and behave in a confident and direct way, so that people pay attention to you.
assertively ADVERB, **assertiveness** NOUN

assess assesses assessing assessed
VERB If you assess something, you consider it carefully and make a judgment about it.
assessment NOUN
▤ appraise, judge, size up

assessor assessors
NOUN someone whose job is to assess the value of something.

asset assets
NOUN **1** a person or thing considered useful EG *He will be a great asset to the club.* ▸ PLURAL NOUN **2** The assets of a person or company are all the things they own that could be sold to raise money.

assign assigns assigning assigned
VERB **1** To assign something to someone is to give it to them officially or to make them responsible for it. **2** If someone is assigned to do something, they are officially told to do it.
▤ (sense 1) appoint, choose, select
▤ (sense 2) allocate, allot, give

assignation assignations
Said "ass-ig-**nay**-shn" NOUN; A LITERARY WORD a secret meeting with someone, especially a lover.

assignment assignments
NOUN a job someone is given to do.

assimilate assimilates assimilating assimilated
VERB **1** If you assimilate ideas or experiences, you learn and understand them. **2** When people are assimilated into a group, they become part of it.
assimilation NOUN

assist assists assisting assisted
VERB To assist someone is to help them do something.
assistance NOUN

assistant assistants
NOUN someone whose job is to help another person in their work.

associate associates associating associated
VERB **1** If you associate one thing with another, you connect the two things in your mind. **2** If you associate with a group of people, you spend a lot of time with them. ▸ NOUN **3** Your associates are the people you work with or spend a lot of time with.
▤ (sense 1) connect, link, relate
▤ (sense 2) consort, mix, socialize

association associations
NOUN **1** an organization for people who have similar interests, jobs, or aims. **2** Your association with a person or group is the connection or involvement you have with them. **3** An association between two things is a link you make in your mind between them EG *The place contained associations for her.*

assonance
NOUN Assonance is the use of similar vowel or consonant sounds in words near to each other or in the same word, for example 'a long storm'.

assorted
ADJECTIVE Assorted things are different in size and colour EG *assorted swimsuits.*

assortment assortments
NOUN a group of similar things that are different sizes and colours EG *an amazing assortment of old toys.*

assume assumes assuming
assumed
VERB **1** If you assume that something
is true, you accept it is true even
though you have not thought
about it EG *I assumed that he would
turn up.* **2** To assume responsibility
for something is to put yourself in
charge of it.
▣ (sense 1) believe, presume,
suppose, take for granted
▣ (sense 2) accept, shoulder, take
on

assumption assumptions
NOUN **1** a belief that something is
true, without thinking about it.
2 Assumption of power or
responsibility is the taking of it.

assurance assurances
NOUN **1** something said which is
intended to make people less
worried EG *She was emphatic in her
assurances that she wanted to stay.*
2 Assurance is a feeling of
confidence EG *He handled the car with
ease and assurance.* **3** Life assurance
is a type of insurance that pays
money to your dependants when
you die.

assure assures assuring assured
VERB If you assure someone that
something is true, you tell them it
is true.

asterisk asterisks
NOUN An asterisk is the symbol (*)
used in printing and writing.
▦ from Greek *asterikos* meaning
'small star'

astern
ADVERB OR ADJECTIVE; A NAUTICAL WORD
backwards or at the back.

asteroid asteroids
NOUN one of the large number of
very small planets that move
around the sun between the orbits
of Jupiter and Mars.

asthma
Said "ass-ma" NOUN a disease of the
chest which causes wheezing and
difficulty in breathing.
asthmatic ADJECTIVE

astonish astonishes astonishing
astonished
VERB If something astonishes you, it
surprises you very much.
astonished ADJECTIVE, **astonishing**
ADJECTIVE, **astonishingly** ADVERB,
astonishment NOUN

astound astounds astounding
astounded
VERB If something astounds you, it
shocks and amazes you.
astounded ADJECTIVE, **astounding**
ADJECTIVE

astray
PHRASE **1** To **lead someone astray** is
to influence them to do something
wrong. **2** If something **goes astray**,
it gets lost EG *The money had gone
astray.*

astride
PREPOSITION with one leg on either
side of something EG *He is pictured
astride his new motorbike.*

astringent astringents
Said "ass-**trin**-jent" NOUN a liquid
that makes skin less greasy and
stops bleeding.

astrology
NOUN Astrology is the study of the
sun, moon, and stars in order to
predict the future.
astrological ADJECTIVE, **astrologer** NOUN

astronaut astronauts
NOUN a person who operates a
spacecraft.
▦ from Greek *astron* meaning
'star' and *nautēs* meaning 'sailor'

astronomical
ADJECTIVE **1** involved with or relating
to astronomy. **2** extremely large in
amount EG *astronomical legal costs.*
astronomically ADVERB

astronomy
NOUN Astronomy is the scientific
study of stars and planets.
astronomer NOUN

astute
ADJECTIVE clever and quick at
understanding situations and
behaviour EG *an astute diplomat.*

asunder
ADVERB; A LITERARY WORD If something is torn asunder, it is violently torn apart.

asylum asylums
Said "ass-eye-lum" NOUN **1** AN OLD-FASHIONED USE a hospital for mental patients. **2** Political asylum is protection given by a government to someone who has fled from their own country for political reasons.

asymmetrical or asymmetric
Said "ay-sim-**met**-ri-kl" ADJECTIVE unbalanced or with one half not exactly the same as the other half.
asymmetry NOUN

at
PREPOSITION **1** used to say where someone or something is EG *Bert met us at the airport.* **2** used to mention the direction something is going in EG *He threw his plate at the wall.* **3** used to say when something happens EG *The game starts at 3 o'clock.* **4** used to mention the rate or price of something EG *The shares were priced at fifty pence.*

atheist atheists
Said "ayth-ee-ist" NOUN someone who believes there is no God.
atheistic ADJECTIVE, **atheism** NOUN

athlete athletes
NOUN someone who is good at sport and takes part in sporting events.

athletic
ADJECTIVE **1** strong, healthy, and good at sports. **2** involving athletes or athletics EG *I lost two years of my athletic career because of injury.*

athletics
NOUN Sporting events such as running, jumping, and throwing are called athletics.

Atlantic
NOUN The Atlantic is the ocean separating North and South America from Europe and Africa.
▦ from the *Atlas* mountains in Libya; the Atlantic lies to the west of these mountains

atlas atlases
NOUN a book of maps.
▦ from the giant *Atlas* in Greek mythology, who supported the sky on his shoulders

atmosphere atmospheres
NOUN **1** the air and other gases that surround a planet; also the air in a particular place EG *a musty atmosphere.* **2** the general mood of a place EG *a relaxed atmosphere.*
atmospheric ADJECTIVE

atom atoms
NOUN the smallest part of an element that can take part in a chemical reaction.

atomic
ADJECTIVE relating to atoms or to the power released by splitting atoms EG *atomic energy.*

atomic bomb atomic bombs
NOUN an extremely powerful bomb which explodes because of the energy that comes from splitting atoms.

atone atones atoning atoned
VERB; A FORMAL WORD If you atone for something wrong you have done, you say you are sorry and try to make up for it.

atrocious
ADJECTIVE extremely bad.

atrocity atrocities
NOUN an extremely cruel and shocking act.

attach attaches attaching attached
VERB If you attach something to something else, you join or fasten the two things together.

attaché attachés
Said "at-**tash**-ay" NOUN a member of staff in an embassy EG *the Russian Cultural Attaché.*

attached
ADJECTIVE If you are attached to someone, you are very fond of them.

attachment attachments
NOUN **1** Attachment to someone is a

feeling of love and affection for them. **2** Attachment to a cause or ideal is a strong belief in it and support for it. **3** a piece of equipment attached to a tool or machine to do a particular job.

attack attacks attacking attacked
VERB **1** To attack someone is to use violence against them so as to hurt or kill them. **2** If you attack someone or their ideas, you criticize them strongly EG *He attacked the government's economic policies.* **3** If a disease or chemical attacks something, it damages or destroys it EG *fungal diseases that attack crops.* **4** In a game such as football or hockey, to attack is to get the ball into a position from which a goal can be scored. ▶ NOUN **5** An attack is violent physical action against someone. **6** An attack on someone or on their ideas is strong criticism of them. **7** An attack of an illness is a short time in which you suffer badly with it.
attacker NOUN
▤ (sense 1) assault, set upon
▤ (sense 2) censure, criticize
▤ (sense 5) assault, onslaught

attain attains attaining attained
VERB; A FORMAL WORD If you attain something, you manage to achieve it EG *He eventually attained the rank of major.*
attainable ADJECTIVE, **attainment** NOUN

attempt attempts attempting attempted
VERB **1** If you attempt to do something, you try to do it or achieve it, but may not succeed EG *They attempted to escape.* ▶ NOUN **2** an act of trying to do something EG *He made no attempt to go for the ball.*

attend attends attending attended
VERB **1** If you attend an event, you are present at it. **2** To attend school, church, or hospital is to go there regularly. **3** If you attend to something, you deal with it EG *We*

have business to *attend* to first.
attendance NOUN

attendant attendants
NOUN someone whose job is to serve people in a place such as a garage or cloakroom.

attention
NOUN Attention is the thought or care you give to something EG *The woman needed medical attention.*

attentive
ADJECTIVE paying close attention to something EG *an attentive audience.*
attentively ADVERB, **attentiveness** NOUN

attest attests attesting attested
VERB; A FORMAL WORD To attest something is to show or declare it is true.
attestation NOUN

attic attics
NOUN a room at the top of a house immediately below the roof.

attire
NOUN; A FORMAL WORD Attire is clothing EG *We will be wearing traditional wedding attire.*

attitude attitudes
NOUN Your attitude to someone or something is the way you think about them and behave towards them.

attorney attorneys
Said "at-**turn**-ee" NOUN; AN AMERICAN WORD An attorney is the same as a lawyer.

attract attracts attracting attracted
VERB **1** If something attracts people, it interests them and makes them want to go to it EG *The trials have attracted many leading riders.* **2** If someone attracts you, you like and admire them EG *He was attracted to her outgoing personality.* **3** If something attracts support or publicity, it gets it.

attraction attractions
NOUN **1** Attraction is a feeling of liking someone or something very much. **2** something people visit for

A
B
C
D
E
F
G
H
I
J
K
L
M
N
O
P
Q
R
S
T
U
V
W
X
Y
Z

interest or pleasure EG *The temple is a major tourist attraction.* **3** a quality that attracts someone or something EG *the attraction of moving to seaside resorts.*

attractive

ADJECTIVE **1** interesting and possibly advantageous EG *an attractive proposition.* **2** pleasant to look at or be with EG *an attractive woman... an attractive personality.*
attractively ADVERB, **attractiveness** NOUN
≣ (sense 1) appealing, tempting
≣ (sense 2) charming, lovely, pleasant

attribute attributes attributing attributed

VERB **1** If you attribute something to a person or thing, you believe it was caused or created by that person or thing EG *Water pollution was attributed to the use of fertilizers... a painting attributed to Raphael.*
▶ NOUN **2** a quality or feature someone or something has.
attribution NOUN, **attributable** ADJECTIVE

attrition

NOUN Attrition is the constant wearing down of an enemy.

attuned

ADJECTIVE accustomed or well adjusted to something EG *His eyes quickly became attuned to the dark.*

aubergine aubergines

Said "oh-ber-jeen" NOUN a dark purple, pear-shaped vegetable. It is also called an **eggplant**.
▥ from Arabic *al-badindjan* meaning 'aubergine'

auburn

ADJECTIVE Auburn hair is reddish brown.

auction auctions auctioning auctioned

NOUN **1** a public sale in which goods are sold to the person who offers the highest price. ▶ VERB **2** To auction something is to sell it in an auction.

auctioneer auctioneers

NOUN the person in charge of an auction.

audacious

ADJECTIVE very daring EG *an audacious escape from jail.*
audaciously ADVERB, **audacity** NOUN

audible

ADJECTIVE loud enough to be heard EG *She spoke in a barely audible whisper.*
audibly ADVERB, **audibility** NOUN

audience audiences

NOUN **1** the group of people who are watching or listening to a performance. **2** a private or formal meeting with an important person EG *an audience with the Queen.*

audio

ADJECTIVE used in recording and reproducing sound EG *audio equipment.*

audit audits auditing audited

VERB **1** To audit a set of financial accounts is to examine them officially to check they are correct.
▶ NOUN **2** an official examination of an organization's accounts.
auditor NOUN

audition auditions

NOUN a short performance given by an actor or musician, so that a director can decide whether they are suitable for a part in a play or film or for a place in an orchestra.

auditorium auditoriums or auditoria

NOUN the part of a theatre where the audience sits.

augment augments augmenting augmented

VERB; A FORMAL WORD To augment something is to add something to it.

August

NOUN August is the eighth month of the year. It has 31 days.
▥ from the name of the Roman emperor *Augustus*

aunt aunts

NOUN Your aunt is the sister of your mother or father, or the wife of your uncle.

au pair au pairs
Said "oh **pair**" NOUN a young foreign girl who lives with a family to help with the children and housework and sometimes to learn the language.
▥ a French expression meaning 'on equal terms'

aura auras
NOUN an atmosphere that surrounds a person or thing EG *She has a great aura of calmness.*

aural
Rhymes with "**floral**" ADJECTIVE relating to or done through the sense of hearing EG *an aural comprehension test.*

auspices
Said "**aw**-spiss-eez" PLURAL NOUN; A FORMAL WORD If you do something under the auspices of a person or organization, you do it with their support EG *military intervention under the auspices of the United Nations.*

auspicious
ADJECTIVE; A FORMAL WORD favourable and seeming to promise success EG *It was an auspicious start to the month.*

austere
ADJECTIVE plain and simple, and without luxury EG *an austere grey office block.*
austerity NOUN

Australasia
Said "ost-ral-**lay**-sha" NOUN Australasia consists of Australia, New Zealand, and neighbouring islands in the Pacific.
Australasian ADJECTIVE

Australia
NOUN Australia is the smallest continent and the largest island in the world, situated between the Indian Ocean and the Pacific.

Australian Australians
ADJECTIVE **1** belonging or relating to Australia. ▸ NOUN **2** someone who comes from Australia.

Austrian Austrians
ADJECTIVE **1** belonging or relating to Austria. ▸ NOUN **2** someone who comes from Austria.

authentic
ADJECTIVE real and genuine.
authenticity NOUN

author authors
NOUN The author of a book is the person who wrote it.
☑ Use *author* to talk about both men and women writers, as *authoress* is now felt to be insulting.

authoritarian
ADJECTIVE believing in strict obedience EG *thirty years of authoritarian government.*
authoritarianism NOUN

authoritative
ADJECTIVE **1** having authority EG *his deep, authoritative voice.* **2** accepted as being reliable and accurate EG *an authoritative biography of the President.*
authoritatively ADVERB

authority authorities
NOUN **1** Authority is the power to control people EG *the authority of the state.* **2** In Britain, an authority is a local government department EG *local health authorities.* **3** Someone who is an authority on something knows a lot about it EG *the world's leading authority on fashion.* ▸ PLURAL NOUN **4** The authorities are the people who have the power to make decisions.

authorize authorizes authorizing authorized; also spelt authorise
VERB To authorize something is to give official permission for it to happen.
authorization NOUN

autobiography autobiographies
NOUN Someone's autobiography is an account of their life which they have written themselves.
autobiographical ADJECTIVE

autograph autographs
NOUN the signature of a famous person.

automated

47

A
B
C
D
E
F
G
H
I
J
K
L
M
N
O
P
Q
R
S
T
U
V
W
X
Y
Z

ADJECTIVE If a factory or way of making things is automated, it works using machinery rather than people.
automation NOUN

automatic
ADJECTIVE **1** An automatic machine is programmed to perform tasks without needing a person to operate it EG *The plane was flying on automatic pilot.* **2** Automatic actions or reactions take place without involving conscious thought. **3** A process or punishment that is automatic always happens as a direct result of something EG *The penalty for murder is an automatic life sentence.*
automatically ADVERB

automobile automobiles
NOUN; AN AMERICAN OR FORMAL WORD a car.

autonomous
Said "aw-ton-nom-uss" ADJECTIVE An autonomous country governs itself rather than being controlled by anyone else.
autonomy NOUN

autopsy autopsies
NOUN a medical examination of a dead body to discover the cause of death.

autumn autumns
NOUN Autumn is the season between summer and winter.
autumnal ADJECTIVE

auxiliary auxiliaries
NOUN **1** a person employed to help other members of staff EG *nursing auxiliaries.* ▶ ADJECTIVE **2** Auxiliary equipment is used when necessary in addition to the main equipment EG *Auxiliary fuel tanks were stored in the bomb bay.*

auxiliary verb auxiliary verbs
NOUN In grammar, an auxiliary verb is a verb which forms tenses of other verbs or questions. For example in 'He has gone', 'has' is the auxiliary verb and in 'Do you understand?', 'do' is the auxiliary verb.

avail
PHRASE If something you do is **of no avail** or **to no avail**, it is not successful or helpful.

available
ADJECTIVE **1** Something that is available can be obtained EG *Artichokes are available in supermarkets.* **2** Someone who is available is ready for work or free for people to talk to EG *She will no longer be available at weekends.*
availability NOUN
■ (sense 2) accessible

avalanche avalanches
Said "av-a-lahnsh" NOUN a huge mass of snow and ice that falls down a mountain side.

avant-garde
Said "av-vong-gard" ADJECTIVE extremely modern or experimental, especially in art, literature, or music.

avarice
NOUN; A FORMAL WORD Avarice is greed for money and possessions.
avaricious ADJECTIVE

avenge avenges avenging avenged
VERB If you avenge something harmful someone has done to you or your family, you punish or harm the other person in return EG *He was prepared to avenge the death of his friend.*
avenger NOUN

avenue avenues
NOUN a street, especially one with trees along it.

average averages averaging averaged
NOUN **1** a result obtained by adding several amounts together and then dividing the total by the number of different amounts EG *Six pupils were examined in a total of 39 subjects, an average of 6.5 subjects per pupil.* ▶ ADJECTIVE **2** Average means standard or normal EG *the average American teenager.* ▶ VERB **3** To

average a number is to produce that number as an average over a period of time EG *Monthly sales averaged more than 110,000.* ▸ PHRASE **4** You say **on average** when mentioning what usually happens in a situation EG *Men are, on average, taller than women.*

■ (sense 2) normal, ordinary, typical, usual

averse

ADJECTIVE unwilling to do something EG *He was averse to taking painkillers.*

aversion aversions

NOUN If you have an aversion to someone or something, you dislike them very much.

avert averts averting averted

VERB **1** If you avert an unpleasant event, you prevent it from happening. **2** If you avert your eyes from something, you turn your eyes away from it.

aviary aviaries

NOUN a large cage or group of cages in which birds are kept.

aviation

NOUN Aviation is the science of flying aircraft.

aviator aviators

NOUN; AN OLD-FASHIONED WORD a pilot of an aircraft.

avid

ADJECTIVE eager and enthusiastic for something.

avidly ADVERB

avocado avocados

NOUN a pear-shaped fruit, with dark green skin, soft greenish yellow flesh, and a large stone.

▥ from a South American Indian word *ahuacatl* meaning 'testicle', from its shape

avoid avoids avoiding avoided

VERB **1** If you avoid doing something, you make a deliberate effort not to do it. **2** If you avoid someone, you keep away from them.

avoidable ADJECTIVE, **avoidance** NOUN

■ (sense 1) dodge, refrain from, shirk

■ (sense 2) dodge, evade, keep away from

avowed

ADJECTIVE **1** A FORMAL WORD If you are an avowed supporter or opponent of something, you have declared that you support it or oppose it. **2** An avowed belief or aim is one you hold very strongly.

avuncular

ADJECTIVE friendly and helpful in manner towards younger people, rather like an uncle.

await awaits awaiting awaited

VERB **1** If you await something, you expect it. **2** If something awaits you, it will happen to you in the future.

awake awakes awaking awoke awoken

ADJECTIVE **1** Someone who is awake is not sleeping. ▸ VERB **2** When you awake, you wake up. **3** If you are awoken by something, it wakes you up.

awaken awakens awakening awakened

VERB If something awakens an emotion or interest in you, you start to feel this emotion or interest.

award awards awarding awarded

NOUN **1** a prize or certificate for doing something well. **2** a sum of money an organization gives to students for training or study. ▸ VERB **3** If you award someone something, you give it to them formally or officially.

aware

ADJECTIVE If you are aware of something, you know about it or realize it is there.

awareness NOUN

■ conscious of, knowing about, mindful of

awash

ADJECTIVE OR ADVERB covered with water EG *After the downpour the road was awash.*

A
B
C
D
E
F
G
H
I
J
K
L
M
N
O
P
Q
R
S
T
U
V
W
X
Y
Z

A

away

ADVERB **1** moving from a place EG *I saw them walk away*. **2** at a distance from a place EG *Our nearest vet is 12 kilometres away*. **3** in its proper place EG *He put his chequebook away*. **4** not at home, school, or work EG *She had been away from home for years.*

awe

NOUN; A FORMAL WORD Awe is a feeling of great respect mixed with amazement and sometimes slight fear.

awesome

ADJECTIVE **1** Something that is awesome is very impressive and frightening. **2** AN INFORMAL USE Awesome also means excellent or outstanding.

awful

ADJECTIVE **1** very unpleasant or very bad. **2** AN INFORMAL USE very great EG *It took an awful lot of courage.*
awfully ADVERB
◼ (sense 1) appalling, dreadful, terrible

awkward

ADJECTIVE **1** clumsy and uncomfortable EG *an awkward gesture*. **2** embarrassed or nervous EG *He was a shy, awkward young man*. **3** difficult to deal with EG *My lawyer is in an awkward situation.*
▦ from Old Norse *ofugr* meaning

'turned the wrong way'

awning awnings

NOUN a large roof of canvas or plastic attached to a building or vehicle.

awry

Said "a-rye" ADJECTIVE wrong or not as planned EG *Why had their plans gone so badly awry?*

axe axes axing axed

NOUN **1** a tool with a handle and a sharp blade, used for chopping wood. ▶ VERB **2** To axe something is to end it.

axiom axioms

NOUN a statement or saying that is generally accepted to be true.

axis axes

Said "ak-siss" NOUN **1** an imaginary line through the centre of something, around which it moves. **2** one of the two sides of a graph.

axle axles

NOUN the long bar that connects a pair of wheels on a vehicle.

ayatollah ayatollahs

NOUN an Islamic religious leader in Iran.
▦ from Arabic *ayatullah* meaning 'manifestation of God'

azure

Said "az-yoor" ADJECTIVE; A LITERARY WORD bright blue.

babble babbles babbling babbled
VERB When someone babbles, they talk in a confused or excited way.

baboon baboons
NOUN an African monkey with a pointed face, large teeth, and a long tail.
📖 from Old French *baboue* meaning 'grimace'

baby babies
NOUN a child in the first year or two of its life.
babyhood NOUN, **babyish** ADJECTIVE
◼ babe, infant

baby-sit baby-sits baby-sitting baby-sat
VERB To baby-sit for someone means to look after their children while that person is out.
baby-sitter NOUN, **baby-sitting** NOUN

bach baches baching bached
Said "batch" NOUN **1** In New Zealand, a small holiday cottage.
▶ VERB **2** AN INFORMAL USE In Australian and New Zealand English, to bach is to live and keep a house on your own, especially when you are not used to it.

bachelor bachelors
NOUN a man who has never been married.

back backs backing backed
ADVERB **1** When people or things move back, they move in the opposite direction from the one they are facing. **2** When people or things go back to a place or situation, they return to it EG *She went back to sleep.* **3** If you get something back, it is returned to you. **4** If you do something back to someone, you do to them what they have done to you EG *I smiled back at them.* **5** Back also means in the past EG *It happened back in the early eighties.* ▶ NOUN **6** the rear part of your body. **7** the part of something that is behind the front.

▶ ADJECTIVE **8** The back parts of something are the ones near the rear EG *an animal's back legs.* ▶ VERB **9** If a building backs onto something, its back faces in that direction. **10** When a car backs, it moves backwards. **11** To back a person or organization means to support or finance that person or organization.
back down VERB If you back down on a demand or claim, you withdraw and give up.
back out VERB If you back out of a promise or commitment, you decide not to do what you had promised to do.
back up VERB **1** If you back up a claim or story, you produce evidence to show that it is true. **2** If you back someone up, you help and support them.

backbone backbones
NOUN **1** the column of linked bones along the middle of a person's or animal's back. **2** Backbone is also strength of character.

backdate backdates backdating backdated
VERB If an arrangement is backdated, it is valid from a date earlier than the one on which it is completed or signed.

backdrop backdrops
NOUN the background to a situation or event EG *The visit occurred against the backdrop of the political crisis.*

backer backers
NOUN the backers of a project are the people who give it financial help.

backfire backfires backfiring backfired
VERB **1** If a plan backfires, it fails. **2** When a car backfires, there is a small but noisy explosion in its exhaust pipe.

background backgrounds
NOUN **1** the circumstances which

A
B
C
D
E
F
G
H
I
J
K
L
M
N
O
P
Q
R
S
T
U
V
W
X
Y
Z

help to explain an event or caused it to happen. **2** the kind of home you come from and your education and experience EG *a rich background.* **3** If sounds are in the background, they are there but no one really pays any attention to them EG *She could hear voices in the background.*

backing

NOUN Backing is support or help EG *The project got government backing.*

backlash

NOUN a hostile reaction to a new development or a new policy.

backlog backlogs

NOUN a number of things which have not yet been done, but which need to be done.

backpack backpacks

NOUN a large bag that hikers or campers carry on their backs.

backside backsides

NOUN; AN INFORMAL WORD the part of your body that you sit on.

backward

ADJECTIVE **1** Backward means directed behind you EG *without a backward glance.* **2** A backward country or society is one that does not have modern industries or technology. **3** A backward child is one who is unable to learn as quickly as other children of the same age.
backwardness NOUN

backwards

ADVERB **1** Backwards means behind you EG *Lucille looked backwards.* **2** If you do something backwards, you do it the opposite of the usual way EG *He instructed them to count backwards.*

bacon

NOUN Bacon is meat from the back or sides of a pig, which has been salted or smoked.

bacteria

PLURAL NOUN Bacteria are very tiny organisms which can cause disease.
bacterial ADJECTIVE
☑ The word *bacteria* is plural. The

singular form is *bacterium.*

bad worse worst

ADJECTIVE **1** Anything harmful or upsetting can be described as bad EG *I have some bad news... Is the pain bad?* **2** insufficient or of poor quality EG *bad roads.* **3** evil or immoral in character or behaviour EG *a bad person.* **4** lacking skill in something EG *I was bad at sports.* **5** Bad language consists of swearwords. **6** If you have a bad temper, you become angry easily.
badly ADVERB, **badness** NOUN
▤ (sense 3) evil, sinful, wicked, wrong

bade

a form of the past tense of **bid.**

badge badges

NOUN a piece of plastic or metal with a design or message on it that you can pin to your clothes.

badger badgers badgering badgered

NOUN **1** a wild animal that has a white head with two black stripes on it. ▶ VERB **2** If you badger someone, you keep asking them questions or pestering them to do something.

badminton

NOUN Badminton is a game in which two or four players use rackets to hit a shuttlecock over a high net.

Bafana bafana

PLURAL NOUN In South Africa, Bafana bafana is a name for the South African national soccer team.

baffle baffles baffling baffled

VERB If something baffles you, you cannot understand or explain it EG *The symptoms baffled the doctors.*
baffled ADJECTIVE, **baffling** ADJECTIVE

bag bags

NOUN **1** a container for carrying things in. ▶ PLURAL NOUN **2** AN INFORMAL USE Bags of something is a lot of it EG *bags of fun.*
▥ from Old Norse *baggi* meaning 'bundle'

baggage

NOUN Your baggage is the suitcases and bags that you take on a journey.

baggy baggier baggiest

ADJECTIVE Baggy clothing hangs loosely.

bagpipes

PLURAL NOUN a musical instrument played by squeezing air out of a leather bag through pipes, on which a tune is played.

bail bails bailing bailed

NOUN 1 Bail is a sum of money paid to a court to allow an accused person to go free until the time of the trial EG *He was released on bail.* ▶ VERB 2 If you bail water from a boat, you scoop it out.

bailiff bailiffs

NOUN 1 a law officer who makes sure that the decisions of a court are obeyed. 2 a person employed to look after land or property for the owner.

bait baits baiting baited

NOUN 1 a small amount of food placed on a hook or in a trap, to attract a fish or wild animal so that it gets caught. ▶ VERB 2 If you bait a hook or trap, you put some food on it to catch a fish or wild animal.

baize

NOUN Baize is a smooth woollen material, usually green, used for covering snooker tables.

bake bakes baking baked

VERB 1 To bake food means to cook it in an oven without using liquid or fat. 2 To bake earth or clay means to heat it until it becomes hard.

baker bakers

NOUN a person who makes and sells bread and cakes.

bakery bakeries

NOUN a building where bread and cakes are baked and sold.

bakkie bakkies

Said "buck-ee" NOUN In South African English, a bakkie is a small truck.

balaclava balaclavas

NOUN a close-fitting woollen hood that covers every part of your head except your face.

balance balances balancing balanced

VERB 1 When someone or something balances, they remain steady and do not fall over. ▶ NOUN 2 Balance is the state of being upright and steady. 3 Balance is also a situation in which all the parts involved have a stable relationship with each other EG *the chemical balance of the brain.* 4 The balance in someone's bank account is the amount of money in it.

balcony balconies

NOUN 1 a platform on the outside of a building with a wall or railing round it. 2 an area of upstairs seats in a theatre or cinema.

bald balder baldest

ADJECTIVE 1 A bald person has little or no hair on their head. 2 A bald statement or question is made in the simplest way without any attempt to be polite.

baldly ADVERB, **baldness** NOUN

🔲 from Middle English *ballede* meaning 'having a white patch'

bale bales baling baled

NOUN 1 a large bundle of something, such as paper or hay, tied tightly. ▶ VERB 2 If you bale water from a boat, you remove it using a container; also spelt **bail**.

balk balks balking balked; also spelt **baulk**

VERB If you balk at something, you object to it and may refuse to do it EG *He balked at the cost.*

ball balls

NOUN 1 a round object used in games such as cricket and soccer. 2 The ball of your foot or thumb is the rounded part where your toes join your foot or your thumb joins your hand. 3 a large formal social

A
B
C
D
E
F
G
H
I
J
K
L
M
N
O
P
Q
R
S
T
U
V
W
X
Y
Z

event at which people dance.
■ (sense 1) globe, orb, sphere

ballad ballads
NOUN **1** a long song or poem which tells a story. **2** a slow, romantic pop song.
▥ from Old French *ballade* meaning 'song for dancing to'

ballast
NOUN Ballast is any heavy material placed in a ship to make it more stable.

ballerina ballerinas
NOUN a woman ballet dancer.

ballet
Said "bal-lay" NOUN Ballet is a type of artistic dancing based on precise steps.

balloon balloons
NOUN **1** a small bag made of thin rubber that you blow into until it becomes larger and rounder. **2** a large, strong bag filled with gas or hot air, which travels through the air carrying passengers in a compartment underneath.
▥ from Italian *ballone* meaning 'large round object'

ballot ballots balloting balloted
NOUN **1** a secret vote in which people select a candidate in an election, or express their opinion about something. ▶ VERB **2** When a group of people are balloted, they are asked questions to find out what they think about a particular problem or question.
▥ from Italian *ballotta* meaning 'little round object'; in medieval Venice votes were cast by dropping black or white pebbles or balls into a box

ballpoint ballpoints
NOUN a pen with a small metal ball at the end which transfers the ink onto the paper.

ballroom ballrooms
NOUN a very large room used for dancing or formal balls.

balm

Said "bahm" NOUN; AN OLD-FASHIONED WORD Balm is a sweet-smelling soothing ointment.

balmy balmier balmiest
ADJECTIVE mild and pleasant EG *balmy summer evenings*.

balsa
NOUN Balsa is very lightweight wood.

balustrade balustrades
NOUN a railing or wall on a balcony or staircase.

bamboo
NOUN Bamboo is a tall tropical grass with hard, hollow stems used for making furniture.

ban bans banning banned
VERB **1** If something is banned, or if you are banned from doing it or using it, you are not allowed to do it or use it. ▶ NOUN **2** If there is a ban on something, it is not allowed.
■ (sense 1) forbid, outlaw, prohibit
■ (sense 2) disqualification, embargo, prohibition

banal
Said "ba-nahl" ADJECTIVE very ordinary and uninteresting EG *He made some banal remark*.
banality NOUN
▥ Old French *banal* referred to military service which all tenants had to do; hence the word came to mean 'common to everyone' or 'ordinary'

banana bananas
NOUN a long curved fruit with a yellow skin.
▥ from a West African language, via Portuguese

band bands
NOUN **1** a group of musicians who play jazz or pop music together, or a group who play brass instruments together. **2** a group of people who share a common purpose EG *a band of rebels*. **3** a narrow strip of something used to hold things together or worn as a decoration EG *an elastic band... a headband*.

bandage bandages bandaging

bandaged
NOUN **1** a strip of cloth wrapped round a wound to protect it. ▶ VERB **2** If you bandage a wound, you tie a bandage round it.

bandicoot bandicoots
NOUN a small Australian marsupial with a long pointed muzzle and a long tail.

bandit bandits
NOUN; AN OLD-FASHIONED WORD a member of an armed gang who rob travellers.
📖 from Italian **bandito** meaning 'man who has been banished or outlawed'

bandstand bandstands
NOUN a platform, usually with a roof, where a band can play outdoors.

bandwagon
PHRASE To **jump on the bandwagon** means to become involved in something because it is fashionable or likely to be successful.

bandy bandies bandying bandied
VERB If a name is bandied about, many people mention it.
📖 from Old French **bander** meaning 'to hit a tennis ball back and forth'

bane
NOUN; A LITERARY WORD Someone or something that is the bane of a person or organization causes a lot of trouble for them EG *the bane of my life*.
📖 from Old English **bana** meaning 'murderer'

bang bangs banging banged
VERB **1** If you bang something, you hit it or put it somewhere violently, so that it makes a loud noise EG *He banged down the receiver.* **2** If you bang a part of your body against something, you accidentally bump it. ▶ NOUN **3** a sudden, short, loud noise. **4** a hard or painful bump against something.

Bangladeshi Bangladeshis
Said "bang-glad-**desh**-ee" ADJECTIVE

1 belonging or relating to Bangladesh. ▶ NOUN **2** someone who comes from Bangladesh.

bangle bangles
NOUN an ornamental band worn round someone's wrist or ankle.
📖 from Hindi **bangri** meaning 'bracelet'

banish banishes banishing banished
VERB **1** To banish someone means to send them into exile. **2** To banish something means to get rid of it EG *It will be a long time before cancer is banished.*
banishment NOUN
▤ (sense 1) exile, expel, outlaw

banister banisters; also spelt **bannister**
NOUN a rail supported by posts along the side of a staircase.

banjo banjos or banjoes
NOUN a musical instrument, like a small guitar with a round body.

bank banks banking banked
NOUN **1** a business that looks after people's money. **2** a bank of something is a store of it kept ready for use EG *a blood bank.* **3** the raised ground along the edge of a river or lake. **4** the sloping side of an area of raised ground. ▶ VERB **5** When you bank money, you pay it into a bank. **6** If you bank on something happening, you expect it and rely on it.
banker NOUN, **banking** NOUN

bank holiday bank holidays
NOUN a public holiday, when banks are officially closed.

banknote banknotes
NOUN a piece of paper money.

bankrupt bankrupts bankrupting bankrupted
ADJECTIVE **1** People or organizations that go bankrupt do not have enough money to pay their debts. ▶ NOUN **2** someone who has been declared bankrupt. ▶ VERB **3** To bankrupt someone means to make them bankrupt EG *Restoring the house*

A B C D E F G H I J K L M N O P Q R S T U V W X Y Z

nearly bankrupted them.
bankruptcy NOUN

banksia banksias
NOUN an evergreen Australian tree or shrub with yellow flowers.

banner banners
NOUN a long strip of cloth with a message or slogan on it.

bannister
another spelling of **banister**.

banquet banquets
NOUN a grand formal dinner, often followed by speeches.

banter
NOUN Banter is friendly joking and teasing.

baobab baobabs
Said "bay-oo-bab" NOUN a small fruit tree with a very thick trunk which grows in Africa and northern Australia.

baptism
NOUN Baptism is the ceremony in which someone is baptized.

Baptist Baptists
NOUN OR ADJECTIVE a member of a Protestant church who believe that people should be baptized when they are adults rather than when they are babies.

baptize baptizes baptizing
baptized; also spelt **baptise**
VERB When someone is baptized water is sprinkled on them, or they are immersed in water, as a sign that they have become a Christian.
🔠 from Greek *baptein* meaning 'to dip in water'

bar bars barring barred
NOUN **1** a counter or room where alcoholic drinks are served. **2** a long, straight piece of metal. **3** a piece of something made in a rectangular shape EG *a bar of soap.* **4** The bars in a piece of music are the many short parts of equal length that the piece is divided into. ▶ VERB **5** If you bar a door, you place something across it to stop it being opened. **6** If you bar

someone's way, you stop them going somewhere by standing in front of them.

barb barbs
NOUN a sharp curved point on the end of an arrow or fish-hook.

barbarian barbarians
NOUN a member of a wild or uncivilized people.
🔠 from Greek *barbaros* meaning 'foreigner', originally 'person saying *bar-bar*'

barbaric
ADJECTIVE cruel or brutal EG *Ban the barbaric sport of fox hunting.*
barbarity NOUN

barbecue barbecues barbecuing
barbecued
NOUN **1** a grill with a charcoal fire on which you cook food, usually outdoors; also an outdoor party where you eat food cooked on a barbecue. ▶ VERB **2** When food is barbecued, it is cooked over a charcoal grill.
🔠 from a Caribbean word meaning 'framework'

barbed
ADJECTIVE A barbed remark is one that seems straightforward but is really unkind or spiteful.

barbed wire
NOUN Barbed wire is strong wire with sharp points sticking out of it, used to make fences.

barber barbers
NOUN a man who cuts men's hair.

barbiturate barbiturates
NOUN a drug that people take to make them calm or to put them to sleep.

bar code bar codes
NOUN a small pattern of numbers and lines on something you buy in a shop, which can be electronically scanned at a checkout to give the price.

bard bards
NOUN; A LITERARY WORD A bard is a poet. Some people call Shakespeare the

Bard.

bare bares baring bared

ADJECTIVE **1** If a part of your body is bare, it is not covered by any clothing. **2** If something is bare, it has nothing on top of it or inside it EG *bare floorboards... a small bare office*. **3** When trees are bare, they have no leaves on them. **4** The bare minimum or bare essentials means the very least that is needed EG *They were fed the bare minimum.* ▶ VERB **5** If you bare something, you uncover or show it.

▪ (sense 1) naked, nude, uncovered

▪ (sense 2) plain, stark

barefoot

ADJECTIVE OR ADVERB not wearing anything on your feet.

barely

ADVERB only just EG *The girl was barely sixteen.*

☑ Do not use *barely* with negative words like *not*: *she was barely sixteen* rather than *she was not barely sixteen*.

bargain bargains bargaining bargained

NOUN **1** an agreement in which two people or groups discuss and agree what each will do, pay, or receive in a matter which involves them both. **2** something which is sold at a low price and which is good value. ▶ VERB **3** When people bargain with each other, they discuss and agree terms about what each will do, pay, or receive in a matter which involves them both.

barge barges barging barged

NOUN **1** a boat with a flat bottom used for carrying heavy loads, especially on canals. ▶ VERB **2** AN INFORMAL USE If you barge into a place, you push into it in a rough or rude way.

baritone baritones

NOUN a man with a fairly deep singing voice.

bark barks barking barked

VERB **1** When a dog barks, it makes a short, loud noise, once or several times. ▶ NOUN **2** the short, loud noise that a dog makes. **3** the tough material that covers the outside of a tree.

barley

NOUN Barley is a cereal that is grown for food and is also used for making beer and whisky.

bar mitzvah

NOUN A Jewish boy's bar mitzvah is a ceremony that takes place on his 13th birthday, after which he is regarded as an adult.

▥ a Hebrew phrase meaning 'son of the law'

barmy barmier barmiest

ADJECTIVE; AN INFORMAL WORD mad or very foolish.

barn barns

NOUN a large farm building used for storing crops or animal food.

barnacle barnacles

NOUN a small shellfish that fixes itself to rocks and to the bottom of boats.

barometer barometers

NOUN an instrument that measures air pressure and shows when the weather is changing.

baron barons

NOUN a member of the lowest rank of the nobility.

baronial ADJECTIVE

baroness baronesses

NOUN a woman who has the rank of baron, or who is the wife of a baron.

baronet baronets

NOUN a man with an honorary knighthood which has been passed to him from his father.

barracks

NOUN a building where soldiers live.

▥ from Spanish *barraca* meaning 'hut'

barracuda barracudas

NOUN a large, fierce tropical fish with sharp teeth.

A
B
C
D
E
F
G
H
I
J
K
L
M
N
O
P
Q
R
S
T
U
V
W
X
Y
Z

barrage barrages

NOUN **1** A barrage of questions or complaints is a lot of them all coming at the same time. **2** Continuous artillery fire over a wide area, to prevent the enemy from moving.

≡ (sense 1) deluge, stream, torrent
≡ (sense 2) bombardment, fusillade, volley

barrel barrels

NOUN **1** a wooden container with rounded sides and flat ends. **2** The barrel of a gun is the long tube through which the bullet is fired.

barren

ADJECTIVE **1** Barren land has soil of such poor quality that plants cannot grow on it. **2** A barren woman or female animal is not able to have babies.

≡ (sense 1) desert, empty, unproductive
≡ (sense 2) infertile, sterile

barricade barricades barricading barricaded

NOUN **1** a temporary barrier put up to stop people getting past. ▶ VERB **2** If you barricade yourself inside a room or building, you put something heavy against the door to stop people getting in.

barrier barriers

NOUN a fence or wall that prevents people or animals getting from one area to another.

≡ barricade, fence, wall

barrister barristers

NOUN a lawyer who is qualified to represent people in the higher courts.

barrow barrows

NOUN **1** the same as a wheelbarrow. **2** a large cart from which fruit or other goods are sold in the street.

barter barters bartering bartered

VERB **1** If you barter goods, you exchange them for other goods, rather than selling them for money. ▶ NOUN **2** Barter is the activity of exchanging goods.

base bases basing based

NOUN **1** the lowest part of something, which often supports the rest. **2** A place which part of an army, navy, or air force works from. **3** In chemistry, a base is any compound that reacts with an acid to form a salt. ▶ VERB **4** To base something on something else means to use the second thing as a foundation or starting point of the first EG *The opera is based on a work by Pushkin.* **5** If you are based somewhere, you live there or work from there.

≡ (sense 1) bottom, foot, stand, support

baseball

NOUN Baseball is a team game played with a bat and a ball, similar to rounders.

basement basements

NOUN a floor of a building built completely or partly below the ground.

bases

NOUN **1** Said "bay-seez" the plural of **basis**. **2** Said "bay-siz" the plural of **base**.

bash bashes bashing bashed

VERB; AN INFORMAL WORD If you bash someone or bash into them, you hit them hard.

bashful

ADJECTIVE shy and easily embarrassed.

basic basics

ADJECTIVE **1** The basic aspects of something are the most necessary ones EG *the basic necessities of life.* **2** Something that is basic has only the necessary features without any extras or luxuries EG *The accommodation is pretty basic.* ▶ PLURAL NOUN **3** The basics of something are the things you need to know or understand EG *the basics of map-reading.*

basically ADVERB

≡ (sense 1) essential, necessary, vital

basilica basilicas

NOUN an oblong church with a rounded end called an apse.
🏛 from Greek *basilike* meaning 'royal hall'

basin basins
NOUN **1** a round wide container which is open at the top. **2** The basin of a river is a bowl of land from which water runs into the river.

basis bases
NOUN **1** The basis of something is the essential main principle from which it can be developed EG *The same colour theme is used as the basis for several patterns.* **2** The basis for a belief is the facts that support it EG *There is no basis for this assumption.*
▤ (sense 1) base, foundation
▤ (sense 2) foundation, ground, support

bask basks basking basked
VERB If you bask in the sun, you sit or lie in it, enjoying its warmth.

basket baskets
NOUN a container made of thin strips of cane woven together.

basketball
NOUN Basketball is a game in which two teams try to score goals by throwing a large ball through one of two circular nets suspended high up at each end of the court.

bass basses
Rhymes with "lace" NOUN **1** a man with a very deep singing voice. **2** a musical instrument that provides the rhythm and lowest part in the harmonies.

bass basses
Rhymes with "gas" NOUN a type of edible sea fish.

basset hound basset hounds
NOUN a smooth-haired dog with a long body and ears, and short legs.

bassoon bassoons
NOUN a large woodwind instrument.

bastard bastards
NOUN **1** AN OFFENSIVE USE People sometimes call someone a bastard when they dislike them or are very angry with them. **2** AN OLD-FASHIONED USE A bastard is someone whose parents were not married when he or she was born.

baste bastes basting basted
VERB When you baste meat that is roasting, you pour hot fat over it so that it does not become dry while cooking.

bastion bastions
NOUN; A LITERARY WORD something that protects a system or way of life EG *The country is the last bastion of communism.*

bat bats batting batted
NOUN **1** a specially shaped piece of wood with a handle, used for hitting the ball in a game such as cricket or table tennis. **2** a small flying animal, active at night, that looks like a mouse with wings.
▶ VERB **3** In certain sports, when someone is batting, it is their turn to try to hit the ball and score runs.

batch batches
NOUN a group of things of the same kind produced or dealt with together.

bated
PHRASE **With bated breath** means very anxiously.

bath baths
NOUN a long container which you fill with water and sit in to wash yourself.

bathe bathes bathing bathed
VERB **1** When you bathe, you swim or play in open water. **2** When you bathe a wound, you wash it gently. **3** A LITERARY USE If a place is bathed in light, a lot of light reaches it EG *The room was bathed in spring sunshine.*
bather NOUN, **bathing** NOUN

bathroom bathrooms
NOUN a room with a bath or shower, a washbasin, and often a toilet in it.

baths
NOUN The baths is a public swimming pool.

A
B
C
D
E
F
G
H
I
J
K
L
M
N
O
P
Q
R
S
T
U
V
W
X
Y
Z

baton batons

NOUN **1** a light, thin stick that a conductor uses to direct an orchestra or choir. **2** In athletics, the baton is a short stick passed from one runner to another in a relay race.

batsman batsmen

NOUN In cricket, the batsman is the person who is batting.

battalion battalions

NOUN an army unit consisting of three or more companies.

batten battens battening battened

NOUN a strip of wood that is fixed to something to strengthen it or hold it firm.

batten down VERB If you batten something down, you make it secure by fixing battens across it.

batter batters battering battered

VERB **1** To batter someone or something means to hit them many times EG *The waves kept battering the life raft.* ▶ NOUN **2** Batter is a mixture of flour, eggs, and milk, used to make pancakes, or to coat food before frying it.
battering NOUN

battery batteries

NOUN **1** a device for storing and producing electricity, for example in a torch or a car. **2** a large group of things or people. ▶ ADJECTIVE **3** A battery hen is one of a large number of hens kept in small cages for the mass production of eggs.

battle battles

NOUN **1** a fight between armed forces or a struggle between two people or groups with conflicting aims EG *the battle between town and country.* **2** A battle for something difficult is a determined attempt to obtain or achieve it EG *the battle for equality.*

battlefield battlefields

NOUN a place where a battle is or has been fought.

battlements

PLURAL NOUN The battlements of a castle consist of a wall built round the top, with gaps through which guns or arrows could be fired.

battleship battleships

NOUN a large, heavily armoured warship.

batty battier battiest

ADJECTIVE; AN INFORMAL WORD crazy or eccentric.

bauble baubles

NOUN a pretty but cheap ornament or piece of jewellery.

bawdy bawdier bawdiest

ADJECTIVE a bawdy joke or song contains humorous references to sex.
🏛 from Middle English *baude* meaning 'brothel keeper'

bawl bawls bawling bawled

VERB **1** AN INFORMAL WORD To bawl at someone means to shout at them loudly and harshly. **2** When a child is bawling, it is crying very loudly and angrily.

bay bays baying bayed

NOUN **1** a part of a coastline where the land curves inwards. **2** a space or area used for a particular purpose EG *a loading bay.* **3** Bay is a kind of tree similar to the laurel, with leaves used for flavouring in cooking. ▶ PHRASE **4** If you **keep something at bay**, you prevent it from reaching you EG *Eating oranges keeps colds at bay.* ▶ VERB **5** When a hound or wolf bays, it makes a deep howling noise.
🖼 (sense 1) cove, gulf, inlet

bayonet bayonets

NOUN a sharp blade that can be fixed to the end of a rifle and used for stabbing.
🏛 named after *Bayonne* in France, where it originated

bazaar bazaars

NOUN **1** an area with many small shops and stalls, especially in Eastern countries. **2** a sale to raise money for charity.
🏛 from Persian *bazar* meaning 'market'

BC

BC means 'before Christ' EG *in 49 BC.*

be am is are; being; was were; been

AUXILIARY VERB **1** 'Be' is used with a present participle to form the continuous tense EG *Crimes of violence are increasing.* **2** 'Be' is also used to say that something will happen EG *We are going to America next month.* **3** 'Be' is used to form the passive voice EG *The walls were being repaired.* ▶ VERB **4** 'Be' is used to give more information about the subject of a sentence EG *Her name is Melanie.*

The Verb Be

The verb **to be** has a lot of unusual forms, and does not follow the usual rules.

The main form is *be*. This is used with an auxiliary verb to make compound tenses, and after the preposition *to.*

*She will **be** five years old in April.*

The verb forms *am*, *are*, and *is* are used to talk about the present time. *Am* is used for the first person singular; *are* is used for the second person and for all plural forms; *is* is used for the third person singular.

*I **am** exhausted.*
*You **are** very welcome.*
*Robbie **is** always cheerful.*
*They **are** a pair of rascals.*

The present participle is *being*. This form is used with an auxiliary verb to make compound tenses.

*Matthew **was being** very helpful.*

The verb forms *was* and *were* talk about past time. *Was* is used for the first and third person singular; *were* is used for the second person and for all plural forms.

*I **was** exhausted.*
*You **were** very welcome.*
*Robbie **was** always cheerful.*
*They **were** a pair of rascals.*

The past participle is *been*. This form is used with an auxiliary verb to make compound tenses.

*I **shall have been** here five years in April.*
*Robbie **has been** polite at all times.*

---

beach beaches

NOUN an area of sand or pebbles beside the sea.
■ seashore, seaside, shore

beacon beacons

NOUN In the past, a beacon was a light or fire on a hill, which acted as a signal or warning.

bead beads

NOUN **1** Beads are small pieces of coloured glass or wood with a hole through the middle, strung together to make necklaces.
2 Beads of liquid are drops of it.

beady

ADJECTIVE Beady eyes are small and bright like beads.

beagle beagles

NOUN a short-haired dog with long ears and short legs.

beak beaks

NOUN A bird's beak is the hard part of its mouth that sticks out.

beaker beakers

NOUN **1** a cup for drinking out of, usually made of plastic and without a handle. **2** a glass container with a lip which is used in laboratories.

beam beams beaming beamed

NOUN **1** a broad smile. **2** A beam of light is a band of light that shines from something such as a torch. **3** a long, thick bar of wood or metal, especially one that supports a roof. ▶ VERB **4** If you beam, you smile because you are happy.

bean beans

NOUN Beans are the seeds or pods of a climbing plant, which are eaten as a vegetable; also used of some other seeds, for example the seeds from which coffee is made.

bear bears bearing bore borne

NOUN **1** a large, strong wild animal with thick fur and sharp claws.
▶ VERB **2** A FORMAL USE To bear something means to carry it or support its weight EG *The ice wasn't*

thick enough to bear their weight. **3** If something bears a mark or typical feature, it has it EG *The room bore all the signs of a violent struggle.* **4** If you bear something difficult, you accept it and are able to deal with it EG *He bore his last illness with courage.* **5** If you can't bear someone or something, you dislike them very much. **6** A FORMAL USE When a plant or tree bears flowers, fruit, or leaves, it produces them.
bearable ADJECTIVE

beard beards
NOUN the hair that grows on the lower part of a man's face.
bearded ADJECTIVE

bearer bearers
NOUN The bearer of something is the person who carries or presents it EG *the bearer of bad news.*

bearing
NOUN **1** If something has a bearing on a situation, it is relevant to it. **2** the way in which a person moves or stands.

beast beasts
NOUN **1** AN OLD-FASHIONED USE a large wild animal. **2** AN INFORMAL USE If you call someone a beast, you mean that they are cruel or spiteful.

beastly beastlier beastliest
ADJECTIVE; AN OLD-FASHIONED INFORMAL WORD cruel or spiteful.

beat beats beating beat beaten
VERB **1** To beat someone or something means to hit them hard and repeatedly EG *He threatened to beat her.* **2** If you beat someone in a race or game, you defeat them or do better than them. **3** When a bird or insect beats its wings, it moves them up and down. **4** When your heart is beating, it is pumping blood with a regular rhythm. **5** If you beat eggs, cream, or butter, you mix them vigorously using a fork or a whisk. ▸ NOUN **6** The beat of your heart is its regular pumping action. **7** The beat of a piece of music is its main rhythm. **8** A

police officer's beat is the area which he or she patrols.
▤ (sense 1) batter, hit, strike
▤ (sense 2) conquer, defeat, vanquish

beat up VERB To beat someone up means to hit or kick them repeatedly.
beater NOUN, **beating** NOUN

beaut beauts
AN INFORMAL WORD ▸ NOUN **1** In Australian and New Zealand English, a beaut is an outstanding person or thing. ▸ ADJECTIVE **2** In Australian and New Zealand English, beaut means good or excellent EG *a beaut house.*

beautiful
ADJECTIVE very attractive or pleasing EG *a beautiful girl... beautiful music.*
beautifully ADVERB
▤ attractive, gorgeous, lovely

beauty beauties
NOUN **1** Beauty is the quality of being beautiful. **2** A RATHER OLD-FASHIONED USE a very attractive woman. **3** The beauty of an idea or plan is what makes it attractive or worthwhile EG *The beauty of the fund is its simplicity.*

beaver beavers
NOUN an animal with a big, flat tail and webbed hind feet. Beavers build dams.

because
CONJUNCTION **1** 'Because' is used with a clause that gives the reason for something EG *I went home because I was tired.* ▸ PHRASE **2** Because of is used with a noun that gives the reason for something EG *He quit playing because of a knee injury.*

beck
If you are at someone's **beck and call**, you are always available to do what they ask.

beckon beckons beckoning beckoned
VERB **1** If you beckon to someone, you signal with your hand that you want them to come to you. **2** If you

say that something beckons, you mean that you find it very attractive EG *A career in journalism beckons*.

become becomes becoming became become
VERB To become something means to start feeling or being that thing EG *I became very angry... He became an actor.*

bed beds
NOUN **1** a piece of furniture that you lie on when you sleep. **2** A bed in a garden is an area of ground in which plants are grown. **3** The bed of a sea or river is the ground at the bottom of it.

bedclothes
PLURAL NOUN the sheets and covers that you put over you when you get into bed.

bedding
NOUN Bedding is sheets, blankets, and other covers that are used on beds.

bedlam
NOUN You can refer to a noisy and disorderly place or situation as bedlam EG *The delay caused bedlam at the station.*
🔲 from *Bedlam*, a shortened form of the Hospital of St. Mary of Bethlehem in London, which was an institution for the insane or mentally ill

bedpan bedpans
NOUN a container used as a toilet by people who are too ill to get out of bed.

bedraggled
ADJECTIVE A bedraggled person or animal is in a messy or untidy state.

bedridden
ADJECTIVE Someone who is bedridden is too ill or disabled to get out of bed.

bedrock
NOUN **1** Bedrock is the solid rock under the soil. **2** The bedrock of something is the foundation and principles on which it is based EG *His life was built on the bedrock of integrity.*

bedroom bedrooms
NOUN a room used for sleeping in.

bedspread bedspreads
NOUN a cover put over a bed, on top of the sheets and blankets.

bedstead bedsteads
NOUN the metal or wooden frame of an old-fashioned bed.

bee bees
NOUN a winged insect that makes honey and lives in large groups.

beech beeches
NOUN a tree with a smooth grey trunk and shiny leaves.

beef
NOUN Beef is the meat of a cow, bull, or ox.
🔲 from Old French *boef* meaning 'ox' or 'bull'

beefy beefier beefiest
ADJECTIVE; AN INFORMAL WORD A beefy person is strong and muscular.

beehive beehives
NOUN a container in which bees live and make their honey.

beeline
PHRASE; AN INFORMAL USE If you **make a beeline** for a place, you go there as quickly and directly as possible.

been
the past participle of **be**.

beer beers
NOUN an alcoholic drink made from malt and flavoured with hops.

beet beets
NOUN a plant with an edible root and leaves, such as sugar beet or beetroot.

beetle beetles
NOUN a flying insect with hard wings which cover its body when it is not flying.

beetroot beetroots
NOUN the round, dark red root of a type of beet, eaten as a vegetable.

befall befalls befalling befell

A
B
C
D
E
F
G
H
I
J
K
L
M
N
O
P
Q
R
S
T
U
V
W
X
Y
Z

A
B
C
D
E
F
G
H
I
J
K
L
M
N
O
P
Q
R
S
T
U
V
W
X
Y
Z

befallen

VERB; AN OLD-FASHIONED WORD If something befalls you, it happens to you EG *A similar fate befell my cousin.*

before

ADVERB, PREPOSITION, OR CONJUNCTION **1** 'Before' is used to refer to a previous time EG *Apply the ointment before going to bed.* ▶ ADVERB **2** If you have done something before, you have done it on a previous occasion EG *Never before had he seen such poverty.* ▶ PREPOSITION **3** A FORMAL USE Before also means in front of EG *They stopped before a large white villa.*
◨ (sense 1) earlier than, prior to
◨ (sense 2) previously

beforehand

ADVERB before EG *It had been agreed beforehand that they would spend the night there.*

befriend befriends befriending befriended

VERB If you befriend someone, you act in a kind and helpful way and so become friends with them.

beg begs begging begged

VERB **1** When people beg, they ask for food or money, because they are very poor. **2** If you beg someone to do something, you ask them very anxiously to do it.
◨ (sense 2) beseech, implore, plead

beggar beggars

NOUN someone who lives by asking people for money or food.

begin begins beginning began begun

VERB If you begin to do something, you start doing it. When something begins, it starts.
◨ commence, start

beginner beginners

NOUN someone who has just started learning to do something and cannot do it very well yet.
◨ learner, novice

beginning beginnings

NOUN The beginning of something is the first part of it or the time when it starts EG *They had now reached the beginning of the city.*

begonia begonias

Said "be-go-nya" NOUN a plant with brightly coloured flowers.

begrudge begrudges begrudging begrudged

VERB If you begrudge someone something, you are angry or envious because they have it EG *No one could begrudge him the glory.*

beguiling

Rhymes with "smiling" ADJECTIVE charming, but often in a deceptive way.

behalf

PHRASE To do something on behalf of someone or something means to do it for their benefit or as their representative.

behave behaves behaving behaved

VERB **1** If you behave in a particular way, you act in that way EG *They were behaving like animals.* **2** To behave yourself means to act correctly or properly.

behaviour

NOUN Your behaviour is the way in which you behave.

behead beheads beheading beheaded

VERB To behead someone means to cut their head off.

beheld

the past tense of **behold**.

behind

PREPOSITION **1** at the back of EG *He was seated behind the desk.* **2** responsible for or causing EG *He was the driving force behind the move.* **3** supporting someone EG *The whole country was behind him.* ▶ ADVERB **4** If you stay behind, you remain after other people have gone. **5** If you leave something behind, you do not take it with you.

behold

INTERJECTION; A LITERARY WORD You say 'behold' when you want someone

to look at something.
beholder NOUN

beige
Said "bayj" NOUN OR ADJECTIVE pale creamy-brown.

being beings
1 Being is the present participle of be. ▶ NOUN **2** Being is the state or fact of existing EG *The party came into being in 1923.* **3** a living creature, either real or imaginary EG *alien beings from a distant galaxy.*

belated
ADJECTIVE; A FORMAL WORD A belated action happens later than it should have done EG *a belated birthday present.*
belatedly ADVERB

belch belches belching belched
VERB **1** If you belch, you make a sudden noise in your throat because air has risen up from your stomach. **2** If something belches smoke or fire, it sends it out in large amounts EG *Smoke belched from the steelworks.* ▶ NOUN **3** the noise you make when you belch.

beleaguered
ADJECTIVE **1** struggling against difficulties or criticism EG *the beleaguered meat industry.* **2** besieged by an enemy EG *the beleaguered garrison.*

belfry belfries
NOUN the part of a church tower where the bells are.
▦ from Old French *berfrei* meaning 'tower'; because towers often contained bells this word was later changed to *belfrey*

Belgian Belgians
ADJECTIVE **1** belonging or relating to Belgium. ▶ NOUN **2** someone who comes from Belgium.

belief beliefs
NOUN **1** a feeling of certainty that something exists or is true. **2** one of the principles of a religion or moral system.
▤ (sense 2) creed, doctrine, faith

believe believes believing believed
VERB **1** If you believe that something is true, you accept that it is true. **2** If you believe someone, you accept that they are telling the truth. **3** If you believe in things such as God and miracles, you accept that they exist or happen. **4** If you believe in something such as a plan or system, you are in favour of it EG *They really believe in education.*
believable ADJECTIVE, **believer** NOUN

belittle belittles belittling belittled
VERB If you belittle someone or something, you make them seem unimportant EG *He belittled my opinions.*
▤ deprecate, disparage, scoff at

bell bells
NOUN **1** a cup-shaped metal object with a piece inside called a clapper that hits the sides, producing a ringing sound. **2** an electrical device that rings or buzzes in order to attract attention.

bellbird bellbirds
NOUN an Australian or New Zealand bird that makes a sound like a bell.

belligerent
ADJECTIVE aggressive and keen to start a fight or an argument.
belligerence NOUN

bellow bellows bellowing bellowed
VERB **1** When an animal such as a bull bellows, it makes a loud, deep roaring noise. **2** If someone bellows, they shout in a loud, deep voice. ▶ PLURAL NOUN **3** Bellows are a piece of equipment used for blowing air into a fire to make it burn more fiercely.

belly bellies
NOUN **1** Your belly is your stomach or the front of your body below your chest. **2** An animal's belly is the underneath part of its body.

belong belongs belonging

A B C D E F G H I J K L M N O P Q R S T U V W X Y Z

belonged

VERB **1** If something belongs to you, it is yours and you own it. **2** To belong to a group means to be a member of it. **3** If something belongs in a particular place, that is where it should be EG *It did not belong in the music room.*

belongings

PLURAL NOUN Your belongings are the things that you own.

beloved

Said "bil-**luv**-id" ADJECTIVE A beloved person or thing is one that you feel great affection for.

▤ adored, dear, loved, precious

below

PREPOSITION OR ADVERB **1** If something is below a line or the surface of something else, it is lower down EG *six inches below soil level.* **2** Below also means at or to a lower point, level, or rate EG *The temperature fell below the legal minimum.*

belt **belts** **belting** **belted**

NOUN **1** a strip of leather or cloth that you fasten round your waist to hold your trousers or skirt up. **2** In a machine, a belt is a circular strip of rubber that drives moving parts or carries objects along. **3** a specific area of a country EG *Poland's industrial belt.* ▸ VERB **4** AN INFORMAL USE To belt someone means to hit them very hard.

bemused

ADJECTIVE If you are bemused, you are puzzled or confused.

bench **benches**

NOUN **1** a long seat that two or more people can sit on. **2** a long, narrow worktable.

▤ (sense 1) form, pew, seat

bend **bends** **bending** **bent**

VERB **1** When you bend something, you use force to make it curved or angular. **2** When you bend, you move your head and shoulders forwards and downwards. ▸ NOUN **3** a curved part of something.

bent ADJECTIVE

▤ (sense 1) arch, bow, curve
▤ (sense 3) arch, bow, curve

beneath

PREPOSITION, ADJECTIVE AND ADVERB **1** an old-fashioned word for **underneath.** ▸ PREPOSITION **2** If someone thinks something is beneath them, they think that it is too unimportant for them to bother with it.

benefactor **benefactors**

NOUN a person who helps to support a person or institution by giving money.

▤ patron, sponsor, supporter

beneficial

ADJECTIVE Something that is beneficial is good for people EG *the beneficial effects of exercise.*

beneficially ADVERB

▤ advantageous, favourable, helpful

beneficiary **beneficiaries**

NOUN A beneficiary of something is someone who receives money or other benefits from it.

benefit **benefits** **benefiting** **benefited**

NOUN **1** The benefits of something are the advantages that it brings to people EG *the benefits of relaxation.* **2** Benefit is money given by the government to people who are unemployed or ill. ▸ VERB **3** If you benefit from something, it helps you.

▤ (sense 1) advantage, good, help
▤ (sense 3) gain, profit

benevolent

ADJECTIVE kind and helpful.

benevolence NOUN, **benevolently** ADVERB

benign

Said "be-**nine**" ADJECTIVE **1** Someone who is benign is kind and gentle. **2** A benign tumour is one that will not cause death or serious illness.

benignly ADVERB

bent

1 Bent is the past participle and past tense of **bend.** ▸ PHRASE **2** If you are **bent on** doing something, you are determined to do it.

bequeath bequeaths bequeathing bequeathed

VERB; A FORMAL WORD If someone bequeaths money or property to you, they give it to you in their will, so that it is yours after they have died.

bequest bequests

NOUN; A FORMAL WORD money or property that has been left to someone in a will.

berate berates berating berated

VERB; A FORMAL WORD If you berate someone, you scold them angrily EG *He berated them for getting caught.*

bereaved

ADJECTIVE; A FORMAL WORD You say that someone is bereaved when a close relative of theirs has recently died.
bereavement NOUN

bereft

ADJECTIVE; A LITERARY WORD If you are bereft of something, you no longer have it EG *The government seems bereft of ideas.*

beret berets

Said "**ber-ray**" NOUN a circular flat hat with no brim.

berm berms

NOUN **1** a narrow path at the edge of a slope, road, or canal. **2** In New Zealand English, a strip of grass between the road and the footpath in areas where people live.

berry berries

NOUN Berries are small, round fruits that grow on bushes or trees.

berserk

PHRASE If someone goes berserk, they lose control of themselves and become very violent.

📖 from Icelandic *berserkr*, a kind of Viking who wore a shirt (*serkr*) made from the skin of a bear (*björn*). They worked themselves into a frenzy before battle

berth berths

NOUN **1** a space in a harbour where a ship stays when it is being loaded or unloaded. **2** In a boat or caravan, a berth is a bed.

beseech beseeches beseeching beseeched or besought

VERB; A LITERARY WORD If you beseech someone to do something, you ask them very earnestly to do it EG *Her eyes beseeched him to show mercy.*
beseeching ADJECTIVE

beset

ADJECTIVE; A FORMAL WORD If you are beset by difficulties or doubts, you have a lot of them.

beside

PREPOSITION If one thing is beside something else, they are next to each other.
■ adjacent to, alongside, next to

besiege besieges besieging besieged

VERB **1** When soldiers besiege a place, they surround it and wait for the people inside to surrender. **2** If you are besieged by people, many people want something from you and continually bother you.

besought

a past tense and past participle of **beseech**.

best

1 the superlative of **good** and **well**.
▶ ADVERB **2** The thing that you like best is the thing that you prefer to everything else.
■ (sense 1) finest, supreme, top

best man

NOUN The best man at a wedding is the man who acts as the bridegroom's attendant.

bestow bestows bestowing bestowed

VERB; A FORMAL WORD If you bestow something on someone, you give it to them.

bet bets betting bet

VERB **1** If you bet on the result of an event, you will win money if something happens and lose money if it does not. ▶ NOUN **2** the act of betting on something, or the

A
B
C
D
E
F
G
H
I
J
K
L
M
N
O
P
Q
R
S
T
U
V
W
X
Y
Z

A
B
C
D
E
F
G
H
I
J
K
L
M
N
O
P
Q
R
S
T
U
V
W
X
Y
Z

amount of money that you agree to risk. ▸ AN INFORMAL PHRASE **3** You say I **bet** to indicate that you are sure that something is or will be so EG *I bet the answer is no.*
betting NOUN

betray betrays betraying betrayed
VERB **1** If you betray someone who trusts you, you do something which harms them, such as helping their enemies. **2** If you betray your feelings or thoughts, you show them without intending to.
betrayal NOUN, **betrayer** NOUN
▤ (sense 1) be disloyal to, double-cross
▤ (sense 2) give away, reveal

betrothal betrothals
NOUN; AN OLD-FASHIONED WORD an engagement to be married.
betrothed ADJECTIVE OR NOUN

better
1 the comparative of **good** and **well**. ▸ ADVERB **2** If you like one thing better than another, you like it more than the other thing. ▸ ADJECTIVE **3** If you are better after an illness, you are no longer ill.
▤ (sense 1) finer, greater, superior

between
PREPOSITION OR ADVERB **1** If something is between two other things, it is situated or happens in the space or time that separates them EG *flights between Europe and Asia.* **2** A relationship or difference between two people or things involves only those two.
☑ If there are two things you should use *between*. If there are more than two things you should use *among*.

beverage beverages
NOUN; A FORMAL WORD a drink.

bevy bevies
NOUN a group of people EG *a bevy of lawyers.*

beware
VERB If you tell someone to beware of something, you are warning

them that it might be dangerous or harmful.

bewilder bewilders bewildering bewildered
VERB If something bewilders you, it is too confusing or difficult for you to understand.
bewildered ADJECTIVE, **bewildering** ADJECTIVE, **bewilderment** NOUN

bewitch bewitches bewitching bewitched
VERB **1** To bewitch someone means to cast a spell on them. **2** If something bewitches you, you are so delighted by it that you cannot pay attention to anything else.
bewitched ADJECTIVE, **bewitching** ADJECTIVE

beyond
PREPOSITION **1** If something is beyond a certain place, it is on the other side of it EG *Beyond the hills was the Sahara.* **2** If something continues beyond a particular point, it continues further than that point EG *an education beyond the age of 16.* **3** If someone or something is beyond understanding or help, they cannot be understood or helped.

bias
NOUN Someone who shows bias favours one person or thing unfairly.
▤ favouritism, partiality, prejudice

biased or **biassed**
ADJECTIVE favouring one person or thing unfairly EG *biased attitudes.*
▤ one-sided, prejudiced

bib bibs
NOUN a piece of cloth or plastic which is worn under the chin of very young children when they are eating, to keep their clothes clean.

Bible Bibles
NOUN The Bible is the sacred book of the Christian religion.
biblical ADJECTIVE
▥ from Greek *biblia* meaning 'the books'

bicentenary bicentenaries

NOUN The bicentenary of an event is its two-hundredth anniversary.

biceps
NOUN Your biceps are the large muscles on your upper arms.

bicker bickers bickering bickered
VERB When people bicker, they argue or quarrel about unimportant things.

bicycle bicycles
NOUN a two-wheeled vehicle which you ride by pushing two pedals with your feet.

bid bids bidding bade bidden bid
NOUN 1 an attempt to obtain or do something EG *He made a bid for freedom*. 2 an offer to buy something for a certain sum of money. ▸ VERB 3 If you bid for something, you offer to pay a certain sum of money for it. 4 AN OLD-FASHIONED USE If you bid someone a greeting or a farewell, you say it to them.
☑ When *bid* means 'offer to pay a certain sum of money' (sense 3), the past tense and past participle is *bid*. When *bid* means 'say a greeting or farewell' (sense 4), the past tense is *bade* and the past participle is *bidden*.

biddy-biddy biddy-biddies
NOUN a prickly low-growing plant found in New Zealand.

bide bides biding bided
PHRASE If you **bide your time**, you wait for a good opportunity before doing something.

bidet bidets
Said "**bee-day**" NOUN a low basin in a bathroom which is used for washing your bottom in.
🏛 a French word meaning 'small horse'

big bigger biggest
ADJECTIVE large or important.
biggish ADJECTIVE, **bigness** NOUN
🖿 enormous, huge, large

bigamy
NOUN Bigamy is the crime of

marrying someone when you are already married to someone else.
bigamist NOUN

bigot bigots
NOUN someone who has strong and unreasonable opinions which they refuse to change.
bigoted ADJECTIVE, **bigotry** NOUN

bike bikes
NOUN; AN INFORMAL WORD a bicycle or motorcycle.

bikini bikinis
NOUN a small two-piece swimming costume worn by women.
🏛 after *Bikini* atoll, from a comparison between the devastating effect of the atom-bomb test and the effect caused by women wearing bikinis

bilateral
ADJECTIVE A bilateral agreement is one made between two groups or countries.

bile
NOUN Bile is a bitter yellow liquid produced by the liver which helps the digestion of fat.

bilge
NOUN the lowest part of a ship, where dirty water collects.

bilingual
ADJECTIVE involving or using two languages EG *bilingual street signs*.

bill bills
NOUN 1 a written statement of how much is owed for goods or services. 2 a formal statement of a proposed new law that is discussed and then voted on in Parliament. 3 a notice or a poster. 4 A bird's bill is its beak.
🖿 (sense 1) charges, invoice

billabong billabongs
NOUN In Australia, a billabong is a lagoon or pool formed from part of a river.

billboard billboards
NOUN a large board on which advertisements are displayed.

billet billets billeting billeted

A B C D E F G H I J K L M N O P Q R S T U V W X Y Z

VERB When soldiers are billeted in a building, arrangements are made for them to stay there.

billiards
NOUN Billiards is a game in which a long cue is used to move balls on a table.

billion billions
NOUN a thousand million. Formerly, a billion was a million million.
☑ As the meaning of *billion* has changed from one million million to one thousand million, a writer may mean either of these things when using it, depending on when the book or article was written.

billow billows billowing billowed
VERB 1 When things made of cloth billow, they swell out and flap slowly in the wind. 2 When smoke or cloud billows, it spreads upwards and outwards. ▶ NOUN 3 a large wave.

billy or **billycan billies** or **billycans**
NOUN In Australian and New Zealand English, a metal pot for boiling water over a camp fire.

bin bins
NOUN a container, especially one that you put rubbish in.

binary
Said "by-nar-ee" ADJECTIVE The binary system expresses numbers using only two digits, 0 and 1.

bind binds binding bound
VERB 1 If you bind something, you tie rope or string round it so that it is held firmly. 2 If something binds you to a course of action, it makes you act in that way EG *He was bound by that decision.*

bindi-eye bindi-eyes
NOUN a small Australian plant with prickly fruits.

binding bindings
ADJECTIVE 1 If a promise or agreement is binding, it must be obeyed. ▶ NOUN 2 The binding of a book is its cover.

binge binges
NOUN; AN INFORMAL WORD a wild bout of drinking or eating too much.

bingo
NOUN Bingo is a game in which players aim to match the numbers that someone calls out with the numbers on the card that they have been given.

binoculars
PLURAL NOUN Binoculars are an instrument with lenses for both eyes, which you look through in order to see objects far away.

biochemistry
NOUN Biochemistry is the study of the chemistry of living things.
biochemical ADJECTIVE, **biochemist** NOUN

biodegradable
ADJECTIVE If something is biodegradable, it can be broken down into its natural elements by the action of bacteria EG *biodegradable cleaning products.*

biography biographies
NOUN the history of someone's life, written by someone else.
biographer NOUN, **biographical** ADJECTIVE

biology
NOUN Biology is the study of living things.
biological ADJECTIVE, **biologically** ADVERB, **biologist** NOUN

bionic
ADJECTIVE having a part of the body that works electronically.

biopsy biopsies
NOUN an examination under a microscope of tissue from a living body to find out the cause of a disease.

birch birches
NOUN a tall deciduous tree with thin branches and thin bark.

bird birds
NOUN an animal with two legs, two wings, and feathers.

birth births
NOUN 1 The birth of a baby is when it comes out of its mother's womb at the beginning of its life. 2 The birth of something is its beginning

EG *the birth of modern art.*

birthday birthdays
NOUN Your birthday is the
anniversary of the date on which
you were born.

birthmark birthmarks
NOUN a mark on someone's skin that
has been there since they were
born.

biscuit biscuits
NOUN a small flat cake made of
baked dough.
🔲 from Old French *bes* + *cuit*
meaning 'twice-cooked'

bisect bisects bisecting bisected
VERB To bisect a line or area means
to divide it in half.

bisexual
ADJECTIVE sexually attracted to both
men and women.

bishop bishops
NOUN 1 a high-ranking clergyman in
some Christian Churches. 2 In
chess, a bishop is a piece that is
moved diagonally across the board.

bison
NOUN a large hairy animal related to
cattle.

bistro bistros
Said "bee-stroh" NOUN a small
informal restaurant.

bit bits
1 Bit is the past tense of **bite**.
▶ NOUN 2 A bit of something is a
small amount of it EG *a bit of coal.*
▶ AN INFORMAL PHRASE 3 A bit means
slightly or to a small extent EG
That's a bit tricky.
🟥 (sense 2) fragment, part, piece

bitch bitches
NOUN 1 a female dog. 2 AN OFFENSIVE
USE If someone refers to a woman as
a bitch, it means that they think
she behaves in a spiteful way.
bitchy ADJECTIVE

bite bites biting bit bitten
VERB 1 If you bite something, you
use your teeth to cut into it or
through it. 2 When an animal or
insect bites you, it cuts into your
skin with its teeth or mouth. ▶ NOUN
3 a small amount that you bite off
something with your teeth. 4 the
injury you get when an animal or
insect bites you.

bitter bitterest
ADJECTIVE 1 If someone is bitter, they
feel angry and resentful. 2 A bitter
disappointment or experience
makes people feel angry or
unhappy for a long time
afterwards. 3 In a bitter argument
or war, people argue or fight
fiercely and angrily EG *a bitter power
struggle.* 4 A bitter wind is an
extremely cold wind. 5 Something
that tastes bitter has a sharp,
unpleasant taste.
bitterly ADVERB, **bitterness** NOUN
🟥 (sense 1) acrimonious, resentful,
sour
🟥 (sense 5) acid, sharp, sour

bivouac bivouacs
Said "biv-oo-ak" NOUN a temporary
camp in the open air.

bizarre
Said "biz-zahr" ADJECTIVE very
strange or eccentric.

blab blabs blabbing blabbed
VERB; AN INFORMAL WORD When
someone blabs, they give away
secrets by talking carelessly.

black blacker blackest; blacks
NOUN OR ADJECTIVE 1 Black is the
darkest possible colour, like tar or
soot. 2 Someone who is Black is a
member of a dark-skinned race.
▶ ADJECTIVE 3 Black coffee or tea has
no milk or cream added to it.
4 Black humour involves jokes
about death or suffering.
blackness NOUN
🟥 (sense 1) dark, jet, pitch-black
✅ When you are writing about a
person or people, *Black* should start
with a capital letter.

blackberry blackberries
NOUN Blackberries are small black
fruits that grow on prickly bushes
called brambles.

blackbird blackbirds

A
NOUN a common European bird, the male of which has black feathers and a yellow beak.

blackboard blackboards
NOUN a dark-coloured board in a classroom, which teachers write on using chalk.

black box black boxes
NOUN an electronic device in an aircraft which collects and stores information during flights.

blackcurrant blackcurrants
NOUN Blackcurrants are very small dark purple fruits that grow in bunches on bushes.

blacken blackens blackening blackened
VERB To blacken something means to make it black EG *the smoke from the chimney blackened the roof.*

blackhead blackheads
NOUN a very small black spot on the skin caused by a pore being blocked with dirt.

blacklist blacklists blacklisting blacklisted
NOUN **1** a list of people or organizations who are thought to be untrustworthy or disloyal. ▶ VERB **2** When someone is blacklisted, they are put on a blacklist.

blackmail blackmails blackmailing blackmailed
VERB **1** If someone blackmails another person, they threaten to reveal an unpleasant secret about them unless that person gives them money or does something for them. ▶ NOUN **2** Blackmail is the action of blackmailing people.
blackmailer NOUN

black market
NOUN If something is bought or sold on the black market, it is bought or sold illegally.

blackout blackouts
NOUN If you have a blackout, you lose consciousness for a short time.

blacksmith blacksmiths
NOUN a person whose job is making

things out of iron, such as horseshoes.

bladder bladders
NOUN the part of your body where urine is held until it leaves your body.

blade blades
NOUN **1** The blade of a weapon or cutting tool is the sharp part of it. **2** The blades of a propeller are the thin, flat parts that turn round. **3** A blade of grass is a single piece of it.

blame blames blaming blamed
VERB **1** If someone blames you for something bad that has happened, they believe you caused it. ▶ NOUN **2** The blame for something bad that happens is the responsibility for letting it happen.
■ (sense 1) accuse, hold responsible

blameless
ADJECTIVE Someone who is blameless has not done anything wrong.

blanch blanches blanching blanched
VERB If you blanch, you suddenly become very pale.

bland blander blandest
ADJECTIVE dull and unexciting EG *a bland diet... bland pop music.*
blandly ADVERB

blank blanker blankest
ADJECTIVE **1** Something that is blank has nothing on it EG *a blank sheet of paper.* **2** If you look blank, your face shows no feeling or interest. ▶ NOUN **3** If your mind is a blank, you cannot think of anything or remember anything.

blanket blankets
NOUN **1** a large rectangle of thick cloth that is put on a bed to keep people warm. **2** A blanket of something such as snow is a thick covering of it.

blare blares blaring blared
VERB To blare means to make a loud, unpleasant noise EG *The radio blared pop music.*

blaspheme blasphemes

blaspheming blasphemed
VERB When people blaspheme, they are disrespectful about God or religion.

📖 from Greek *blapsis* meaning 'evil' and *phēmein* meaning 'to speak'

blasphemy blasphemies
NOUN Blasphemy is speech or behaviour that shows disrespect for God or religion.
blasphemous ADJECTIVE

blast blasts blasting blasted
VERB 1 When people blast a hole in something they make a hole with an explosion. ▶ NOUN 2 a big explosion, especially one caused by a bomb. 3 a sudden strong rush of wind or air.

blatant
ADJECTIVE If you describe something you think is bad as blatant, you mean that rather than hide it, those responsible actually seem to be making it obvious EG *a blatant disregard for the law.*

blaze blazes blazing blazed
NOUN 1 a large, hot fire. 2 A blaze of light or colour is a great or strong amount of it EG *a blaze of red.* 3 A blaze of publicity or attention is a lot of it. ▶ VERB 4 If something blazes it burns or shines brightly.

blazer blazers
NOUN a kind of jacket, often in the colours of a school or sports team.

bleach bleaches bleaching bleached
VERB 1 To bleach material or hair means to make it white, usually by using a chemical. ▶ NOUN 2 Bleach is a chemical that is used to make material white or to clean thoroughly and kill germs.

bleak bleaker bleakest
ADJECTIVE 1 If a situation is bleak, it is bad and seems unlikely to improve. 2 If a place is bleak, it is cold, bare, and exposed to the wind.

bleat bleats bleating bleated
VERB 1 When sheep or goats bleat, they make a high-pitched cry. ▶ NOUN 2 the high-pitched cry that a sheep or goat makes.

bleed bleeds bleeding bled
VERB When you bleed, you lose blood as a result of an injury.

bleep bleeps
NOUN a short high-pitched sound made by an electrical device such as an alarm.

blemish blemishes
NOUN a mark that spoils the appearance of something.

blend blends blending blended
VERB 1 When you blend substances, you mix them together to form a single substance. 2 When colours or sounds blend, they combine in a pleasing way. ▶ NOUN 3 A blend of things is a mixture of them, especially one that is pleasing. 4 a word formed by joining together the beginning and the end of two other words; for example, 'brunch' is a blend of 'breakfast' and 'lunch'.

blender blenders
NOUN a machine used for mixing liquids and foods at high speed.

bless blesses blessing blessed or blest
VERB When a priest blesses people or things, he or she asks for God's protection for them.

📖 from Old English *blædsian* meaning 'to sprinkle with sacrificial blood'

blessed
ADJECTIVE *Said "blest"* If someone is blessed with a particular quality or skill, they have it EG *He was blessed with a sense of humour.*
blessedly ADVERB

blessing blessings
NOUN 1 something good that you are thankful for EG *Good health is the greatest blessing.* ▶ PHRASE 2 If something is done **with someone's blessing**, they approve of it and support it.

blew

A
B
C
D
E
F
G
H
I
J
K
L
M
N
O
P
Q
R
S
T
U
V
W
X
Y
Z

A
B
C
D
E
F
G
H
I
J
K
L
M
N
O
P
Q
R
S
T
U
V
W
X
Y
Z

the past tense of **blow**.

blight blights blighting blighted
NOUN **1** something that damages or
spoils other things EG *the blight of the
recession.* ▶ VERB **2** When something
is blighted, it is seriously harmed EG
His life had been blighted by sickness.

blind blinds blinding blinded
ADJECTIVE **1** Someone who is blind
cannot see. **2** If someone is blind to
a particular fact, they do not
understand it. ▶ VERB **3** If something
blinds you, you become unable to
see, either for a short time or
permanently. ▶ NOUN **4** a roll of
cloth or paper that you pull down
over a window to keep out the
light.
blindly ADVERB, **blindness** NOUN

**blindfold blindfolds blindfolding
blindfolded**
NOUN **1** a strip of cloth tied over
someone's eyes so that they cannot
see. ▶ VERB **2** To blindfold someone
means to cover their eyes with a
strip of cloth.

blinding
ADJECTIVE A blinding light is so
bright that it hurts your eyes EG
There was a blinding flash.

blindingly
ADVERB; AN INFORMAL USE If something
is blindingly obvious, it is very
obvious indeed.

blink blinks blinking blinked
VERB When you blink, you close
your eyes quickly for a moment.

blinkers
PLURAL NOUN Blinkers are two pieces
of leather placed at the side of a
horse's eyes so that it can only see
straight ahead.

bliss
NOUN Bliss is a state of complete
happiness.
blissful ADJECTIVE, **blissfully** ADVERB

blister blisters blistering blistered
NOUN **1** a small bubble on your skin
containing watery liquid, caused by
a burn or rubbing. ▶ VERB **2** If

someone's skin blisters, blisters
appear on it as result of burning or
rubbing.

blithe
ADJECTIVE casual and done without
serious thought EG *a blithe disregard
for their safety.*
blithely ADVERB

blitz blitzes blitzing blitzed
NOUN **1** a bombing attack by enemy
aircraft on a city. ▶ VERB **2** When a
city is blitzed, it is bombed by
aircraft and is damaged or
destroyed.
📖 from German *Blitzkrieg*
meaning 'lightning war'

blizzard blizzards
NOUN a heavy snowstorm with
strong winds.

bloated
ADJECTIVE Something that is bloated
is much larger than normal, often
because there is a lot of liquid or
gas inside it.

blob blobs
NOUN a small amount of a thick or
sticky substance is.

bloc blocs
NOUN A group of countries or
political parties with similar aims
acting together is often called a
bloc EG *the world's largest trading bloc.*

block blocks blocking blocked
NOUN **1** A block of flats or offices is a
large building containing flats or
offices. **2** In a town, a block is an
area of land with streets on all its
sides EG *He lives a few blocks down.*
3 A block of something is a large
rectangular piece of it. ▶ VERB **4** To
block a road or channel means to
put something across it so that
nothing can get through. **5** If
something blocks your view, it is in
the way and prevents you from
seeing what you want to see. **6** If
someone blocks something, they
prevent it from happening EG *The
council blocked his plans.*
▤ (sense 3) bar, chunk, piece
▤ (senses 4, 5 & 6) obstruct

blockade blockades blockading blockaded
NOUN **1** an action that prevents goods from reaching a place. ▶ VERB **2** When a place is blockaded, supplies are prevented from reaching it.

blockage blockages
NOUN When there is a blockage in a pipe or tunnel, something is clogging it.
■ impediment, obstruction, stoppage

bloke blokes
NOUN; AN INFORMAL WORD a man.

blonde blondes
ADJECTIVE **1** Blonde hair is pale yellow in colour. The spelling 'blond' is used when referring to men. ▶ NOUN **2** A blonde, or blond, is a person with light-coloured hair.

blood
NOUN **1** Blood is the red liquid that is pumped by the heart round the bodies of human beings and other mammals. ▶ PHRASE **2** If something cruel is done **in cold blood**, it is done deliberately and in an unemotional way.

bloodhound bloodhounds
NOUN a large dog with an excellent sense of smell.

bloodless
ADJECTIVE **1** If someone's face or skin is bloodless, it is very pale. **2** In a bloodless coup or revolution, nobody is killed.

blood pressure
NOUN Your blood pressure is a measure of the force with which your blood is being pumped round your body.

bloodshed
NOUN When there is bloodshed, people are killed or wounded.

bloodshot
ADJECTIVE If a person's eyes are bloodshot, the white parts have become red.

bloodstained
ADJECTIVE covered with blood.

bloodstream
NOUN the flow of blood through your body.

bloodthirsty
ADJECTIVE Someone who is bloodthirsty enjoys using or watching violence.

blood transfusion blood transfusions
NOUN a process in which blood is injected into the body of someone who has lost a lot of blood.

blood vessel blood vessels
NOUN Blood vessels are the narrow tubes in your body through which your blood flows.

bloody bloodier bloodiest
ADJECTIVE OR ADVERB **1** Bloody is a common swearword, used to express anger or annoyance. ▶ ADJECTIVE **2** A bloody event is one in which a lot of people are killed EG *a bloody revolution*. **3** Bloody also means covered with blood EG *a bloody gash on his head*.

bloom blooms blooming bloomed
NOUN **1** a flower on a plant. ▶ VERB **2** When a plant blooms, it produces flowers. **3** When something like a feeling blooms, it grows EG *Romance can bloom where you least expect it*.

blossom blossoms blossoming blossomed
NOUN **1** Blossom is the growth of flowers that appears on a tree before the fruit. ▶ VERB **2** When a tree blossoms, it produces blossom.

blot blots blotting blotted
NOUN **1** a drop of ink that has been spilled on a surface. **2** A blot on someone's reputation is a mistake or piece of bad behaviour that spoils their reputation.
blot out VERB To blot something out means to be in front of it and prevent it from being seen EG *The smoke blotted out the sky*.

blotch blotches

A
B
C
D
E
F
G
H
I
J
K
L
M
N
O
P
Q
R
S
T
U
V
W
X
Y
Z

NOUN a discoloured area or stain.
blotchy ADJECTIVE

blouse blouses
NOUN a light shirt, worn by a girl or a woman.

blow blows blowing blew blown
VERB **1** When the wind blows, the air moves. **2** If something blows or is blown somewhere, the wind moves it there. **3** If you blow a whistle or horn, you make a sound by blowing into it. ▶ NOUN **4** If you receive a blow, someone or something hits you. **5** something that makes you very disappointed or unhappy EG *Marc's death was a terrible blow.*

blow up VERB **1** To blow something up means to destroy it with an explosion. **2** To blow up a balloon or a tyre means to fill it with air.

blubber
NOUN The blubber of animals such as whales and seals is the layer of fat that protects them from the cold.

bludge bludges bludging bludged
VERB; AN INFORMAL WORD **1** In Australian and New Zealand English, to bludge is to scrounge or cadge. **2** In Australian and New Zealand English, to bludge is also to avoid work or responsibilities.

bludgeon bludgeons bludgeoning bludgeoned
VERB To bludgeon someone means to hit them several times with a heavy object.

blue bluer bluest
ADJECTIVE OR NOUN **1** Blue is the colour of the sky on a clear, sunny day. ▶ PHRASE **2** If something happens **out of the blue**, it happens suddenly and unexpectedly. ▶ ADJECTIVE **3** Blue films and jokes are about sex.
bluish or **blueish** ADJECTIVE

bluebell bluebells
NOUN a woodland plant with blue, bell-shaped flowers.

bluebottle bluebottles

NOUN **1** a large fly with a shiny dark-blue body. **2** In Australia and New Zealand, a bluebottle is also a small stinging jellyfish.

blue-collar
ADJECTIVE Blue-collar workers do physical work as opposed to office work.

blueprint blueprints
NOUN a plan of how something is expected to work EG *the blueprint for successful living.*

bluff bluffs bluffing bluffed
NOUN **1** an attempt to make someone wrongly believe that you are in a strong position. ▶ VERB **2** If you are bluffing, you are trying to make someone believe that you are in a position of strength.

blunder blunders blundering blundered
VERB **1** If you blunder, you make a silly mistake. ▶ NOUN **2** a silly mistake.

blunt blunter bluntest
ADJECTIVE **1** A blunt object has a rounded point or edge, rather than a sharp one. **2** If you are blunt, you say exactly what you think, without trying to be polite.
■ (sense 2) forthright, outspoken, straightforward

blur blurs blurring blurred
NOUN **1** a shape or area which you cannot see clearly because it has no distinct outline or because it is moving very fast. ▶ VERB **2** To blur the differences between things means to make them no longer clear EG *The dreams blurred confusingly with her memories.*
blurred ADJECTIVE

blurt out blurts out blurting out blurted out
VERB If you blurt something out, you say it suddenly, after trying to keep it a secret.

blush blushes blushing blushed
VERB **1** If you blush, your face becomes red, because you are embarrassed or ashamed. ▶ NOUN

2 the red colour on someone's face when they are embarrassed or ashamed.

bluster blusters blustering blustered

VERB **1** When someone blusters, they behave aggressively because they are angry or frightened. ▶ NOUN **2** Bluster is aggressive behaviour by someone who is angry or frightened.

blustery

ADJECTIVE Blustery weather is rough and windy.

boa boas

NOUN **1** A boa, or a boa constrictor, is a large snake that kills its prey by coiling round it and crushing it. **2** a woman's long thin scarf of feathers or fur.

boar boars

NOUN a male wild pig, or a male domestic pig used for breeding.

board boards boarding boarded

NOUN **1** a long, flat piece of wood. **2** the group of people who control a company or organization. **3** Board is the meals provided when you stay somewhere EG *The price includes full board.* ▶ VERB **4** If you board a ship or aircraft, you get on it or in it. ▶ PHRASE **5** If you are on board a ship or aircraft, you are on it or in it.

boarder boarders

NOUN a pupil who lives at school during term.

boarding school boarding schools

NOUN a school where the pupils live during the term.

boardroom boardrooms

NOUN a room where the board of a company meets.

boast boasts boasting boasted

VERB **1** If you boast about your possessions or achievements, you talk about them proudly. ▶ NOUN **2** something that you say which shows that you are proud of what you own or have done.

boastful ADJECTIVE

■ (sense 1) blow your own trumpet, brag, crow

boat boats

NOUN a small vehicle for travelling across water.

bob bobs bobbing bobbed

VERB **1** When something bobs, it moves up and down. ▶ NOUN **2** a woman's hair style in which her hair is cut level with her chin.

bobbin bobbins

NOUN a small round object on which thread or wool is wound.

bobby bobbies

NOUN; AN OLD-FASHIONED INFORMAL WORD a policeman.

bode bodes boding boded

PHRASE; A LITERARY USE If something bodes ill, or bodes well, it makes you think that something bad, or good, will happen.

bodice bodices

NOUN the upper part of a dress.

bodily

ADJECTIVE **1** relating to the body EG *bodily contact.* ▶ ADVERB **2** involving the whole of someone's body EG *He was carried bodily up the steps.*

body bodies

NOUN **1** Your body is either all your physical parts, or just the main part not including your head, arms, and legs. **2** a person's dead body. **3** the main part of a car or aircraft, not including the engine. **4** A body of people is also an organized group.

■ (sense 1) build, figure, form, physique

bodyguard bodyguards

NOUN a person employed to protect someone.

bodywork

NOUN the outer part of a motor vehicle.

boer boers

Said "boh-er" NOUN In South Africa, a boer is a white farmer, especially one who is descended from the Dutch people who went to live in

A B C D E F G H I J K L M N O P Q R S T U V W X Y Z

A
B
C
D
E
F
G
H
I
J
K
L
M
N
O
P
Q
R
S
T
U
V
W
X
Y
Z

South Africa.

boerewors
Said "boo-rih-vorse" NOUN In South Africa, boerewors is a type of meat sausage.

bog bogs
NOUN an area of land which is always wet and spongy.
📖 from Gaelic *bogach* meaning 'swamp'

boggle boggles boggling boggled
VERB If your mind boggles at something, you find it difficult to imagine or understand.

bogus
ADJECTIVE not genuine EG *a bogus doctor*.

bohemian
Said "boh-hee-mee-an" ADJECTIVE Someone who is bohemian does not behave in the same way as most other people in society, and is usually involved in the arts.

boil boils boiling boiled
VERB 1 When a hot liquid boils, bubbles appear in it and it starts to give off steam. 2 When you boil a kettle, you heat it until the water in it boils. 3 When you boil food, you cook it in boiling water. ▶ NOUN 4 a red swelling on your skin.

boiler boilers
NOUN a piece of equipment which burns fuel to provide hot water.

boiling
ADJECTIVE; AN INFORMAL WORD very hot.

boisterous
ADJECTIVE Someone who is boisterous is noisy and lively.
📖 loud, noisy, rowdy, unruly

bold bolder boldest
ADJECTIVE 1 confident and not shy or embarrassed EG *He was not bold enough to ask them*. 2 not afraid of risk or danger. 3 clear and noticeable EG *bold colours*.
boldly ADVERB, **boldness** NOUN

bollard bollards
NOUN a short, thick post used to

keep vehicles out of a road.

bolster bolsters bolstering bolstered
VERB To bolster something means to support it or make it stronger EG *She relied on others to bolster her self-esteem*.

bolt bolts bolting bolted
NOUN 1 a metal bar that you slide across a door or window in order to fasten it. 2 a metal object which screws into a nut and is used to fasten things together. ▶ VERB 3 If you bolt a door or window, you fasten it using a bolt. If you bolt things together, you fasten them together using a bolt. 4 To bolt means to escape or run away. 5 To bolt food means to eat it very quickly.

bomb bombs bombing bombed
NOUN 1 a container filled with material that explodes when it hits something or is set off by a timer. ▶ VERB 2 When a place is bombed, it is attacked with bombs.
📖 from Greek *bombos* meaning 'a booming sound'

bombard bombards bombarding bombarded
VERB 1 To bombard a place means to attack it with heavy gunfire or bombs. 2 If you are bombarded with something you are made to face a great deal of it EG *I was bombarded with criticism*.
bombardment NOUN

bomber bombers
NOUN an aircraft that drops bombs.

bombshell bombshells
NOUN a sudden piece of shocking or upsetting news.

bona fide
Said "boh-na fie-dee" ADJECTIVE genuine EG *We are happy to donate to bona fide charities*.
📖 a Latin expression meaning 'in good faith'

bond bonds bonding bonded
NOUN 1 a close relationship between people. 2 A LITERARY USE Bonds are

chains or ropes used to tie a
prisoner up. **3** a certificate which
records that you have lent money
to a business and that it will repay
you the loan with interest. **4** Bonds
are also feelings or obligations that
force you to behave in a particular
way EG *the social bonds of community*.
▶ VERB **5** When two things bond or
are bonded, they become closely
linked or attached.
■ (sense 1) connection, link, tie

bondage
NOUN Bondage is the condition of
being someone's slave.

bone bones
NOUN Bones are the hard parts that
form the framework of a person's
or animal's body.
boneless ADJECTIVE

bonfire bonfires
NOUN a large fire made outdoors,
often to burn rubbish.
圙 from 'bone' + 'fire'; bones were
used as fuel in the Middle Ages

bonnet bonnets
NOUN **1** the metal cover over a car's
engine. **2** a baby's or woman's hat
tied under the chin.

bonny bonnier bonniest
ADJECTIVE; A SCOTTISH AND NORTHERN
ENGLISH WORD nice to look at.

bonus bonuses
NOUN **1** an amount of money added
to your usual pay. **2** Something
that is a bonus is a good thing that
you get in addition to something
else EG *The view from the hotel was an
added bonus.*

bony bonier boniest
ADJECTIVE Bony people or animals are
thin, with very little flesh covering
their bones.

boo boos booing booed
NOUN **1** a shout of disapproval. ▶ VERB
2 When people boo, they shout
'boo' to show their disapproval.

boobook boobooks
NOUN a small brown Australian owl
with a spotted back and wings.

book books booking booked
NOUN **1** a number of pages held
together inside a cover. ▶ VERB
2 When you book something such
as a room, you arrange to have it or
use it at a particular time.

bookcase bookcases
NOUN a piece of furniture with
shelves for books.

bookie bookies
NOUN; AN INFORMAL WORD a bookmaker.

booking bookings
NOUN an arrangement to book
something such as a hotel room.

book-keeping
NOUN Book-keeping is the keeping
of a record of the money spent and
received by a business.

booklet booklets
NOUN a small book with a paper
cover.

bookmaker bookmakers
NOUN a person who makes a living
by taking people's bets and paying
them when they win.

bookmark bookmarks
NOUN a piece of card which you put
between the pages of a book to
mark your place.

boom booms booming boomed
NOUN **1** a rapid increase in
something EG *the baby boom.* **2** a
loud deep echoing sound. ▶ VERB
3 When something booms, it
increases rapidly EG *Sales are
booming.* **4** To boom means to make
a loud deep echoing sound.

boomerang boomerangs
NOUN a curved wooden missile that
can be thrown so that it returns to
the thrower, originally used as a
weapon by Australian Aborigines.

boon boons
NOUN Something that is a boon
makes life better or easier EG *Credit
cards have been a boon to shoppers.*

boost boosts boosting boosted
VERB **1** To boost something means to
cause it to improve or increase EG
The campaign had boosted sales.

79

▶ NOUN **2** an improvement or increase eg *a boost to the economy*.
booster NOUN

boot boots booting booted
NOUN **1** Boots are strong shoes that come up over your ankle and sometimes your calf. **2** the covered space in a car, usually at the back, for carrying things in. ▶ VERB **3** AN INFORMAL USE If you boot something, you kick it. ▶ PHRASE **4** To boot means also or in addition eg *The story was compelling and well-written to boot*.

booth booths
NOUN **1** a small partly enclosed area eg *a telephone booth*. **2** a stall where you can buy goods.

booty
NOUN Booty is valuable things taken from a place, especially by soldiers after a battle.

booze boozes boozing boozed
AN INFORMAL WORD ▶ NOUN **1** Booze is alcoholic drink. ▶ VERB **2** When people booze, they drink alcohol.
boozer NOUN, **boozy** ADJECTIVE
🔲 from Old Dutch *busen* meaning 'to drink to excess'

border borders bordering bordered
NOUN **1** the dividing line between two countries. **2** a strip or band round the edge of something eg *plain tiles with a bright border*. **3** a long flower bed in a garden. ▶ VERB **4** To border something means to form a boundary along the side of it eg *Tall poplar trees bordered the fields*.

borderline
ADJECTIVE only just acceptable as a member of a class or group eg *a borderline case*.

bore bores boring bored
VERB **1** If something bores you, you find it dull and uninteresting. **2** If you bore a hole in something, you make it using a tool such as a drill. ▶ NOUN **3** someone or something that bores you.

bored

ADJECTIVE If you are bored, you are impatient because you find something uninteresting or because you have nothing to do.
boredom NOUN
✔ You can say that you are *bored with* or *bored by* someone or something, but you should not say *bored of*.

boring
ADJECTIVE dull and uninteresting.
▤ dull, tedious, uninteresting

born
VERB **1** When a baby is born, it comes out of its mother's womb at the beginning of its life. ▶ ADJECTIVE **2** You use 'born' to mean that someone has a particular quality from birth eg *He was a born pessimist*.

borne
the past participle of **bear**.

borough boroughs
Said "bur-uh" NOUN a town, or a district within a large town, that has its own council.

borrow borrows borrowing borrowed
VERB If you borrow something that belongs to someone else, they let you have it for a period of time.
borrower NOUN
✔ You *borrow* something *from* a person, not *off* them. Do not confuse *borrow* and *lend*. If you *borrow* something, you get it from another person for a while; if you *lend* something, someone gets it from you for a while.

Bosnian Bosnians
ADJECTIVE **1** belonging to or relating to Bosnia. ▶ NOUN **2** someone who comes from Bosnia.

bosom bosoms
NOUN **1** A woman's bosom is her breasts. ▶ ADJECTIVE **2** A bosom friend is a very close friend.

boss bosses bossing bossed
NOUN **1** Someone's boss is the person in charge of the place where they work. ▶ VERB **2** If someone bosses you around, they keep

telling you what to do.

bossy bossier bossiest
ADJECTIVE A bossy person enjoys telling other people what to do.
bossiness NOUN
■ dictatorial, domineering, overbearing

botany
NOUN Botany is the scientific study of plants.
botanic or **botanical** ADJECTIVE, **botanist** NOUN

botch botches botching botched
VERB; AN INFORMAL WORD If you botch something, you do it badly or clumsily.
■ bungle, mess up

both
ADJECTIVE OR PRONOUN 'Both' is used when saying something about two things or people.
☑ You can use *of* after *both*, but it is not essential. *Both the boys* means the same as *both of the boys*.

bother bothers bothering bothered
VERB **1** If you do not bother to do something, you do not do it because it takes too much effort or it seems unnecessary. **2** If something bothers you, you are worried or concerned about it. If you do not bother about it, you are not concerned about it EG *She is not bothered about money.* **3** If you bother someone, you interrupt them when they are busy. ▶ NOUN **4** Bother is trouble, fuss, or difficulty.
bothersome ADJECTIVE

bottle bottles bottling bottled
NOUN **1** a glass or plastic container for keeping liquids in. ▶ VERB **2** To bottle something means to store it in bottles.

bottleneck bottlenecks
NOUN a narrow section of road where traffic has to slow down or stop.

bottle store bottle stores
NOUN In Australian, New Zealand,

and South African English, a bottle store is a shop that sells sealed alcoholic drinks which can be drunk elsewhere.

bottom bottoms
NOUN **1** The bottom of something is its lowest part. **2** Your bottom is your buttocks. ▶ ADJECTIVE **3** The bottom thing in a series of things is the lowest one.
bottomless ADJECTIVE

bough boughs
Rhymes with "now" NOUN a large branch of a tree.

bought
the past tense and past participle of **buy**.
☑ Do not confuse *bought* and *brought*. *Bought* comes from *buy* and *brought* comes from *bring*.

boulder boulders
NOUN a large rounded rock.

boulevard boulevards
Said "boo-le-vard" NOUN a wide street in a city, usually with trees along each side.

bounce bounces bouncing bounced
VERB **1** When an object bounces, it springs back from something after hitting it. **2** To bounce also means to move up and down EG *Her long black hair bounced as she walked.* **3** If a cheque bounces, the bank refuses to accept it because there is not enough money in the account.
■ (sense 1) rebound, recoil, ricochet

bouncy
ADJECTIVE **1** Someone who is bouncy is lively and enthusiastic. **2** Something that is bouncy is capable of bouncing or being bounced on EG *a bouncy ball... a bouncy castle.*

bound bounds bounding bounded
ADJECTIVE **1** If you say that something is bound to happen, you mean that it is certain to happen. **2** If a person or a vehicle is bound for a place, they are going there. **3** If someone is bound by an agreement or

A B C D E F G H I J K L M N O P Q R S T U V W X Y Z

regulation, they must obey it.
▶ NOUN **4** a large leap. ▶ PLURAL NOUN
5 Bounds are limits which restrict
or control something EG *Their
enthusiasm knew no bounds.* ▶ PHRASE
6 If a place is **out of bounds**, you
are forbidden to go there. ▶ VERB
7 When animals or people bound,
they move quickly with large leaps
EG *He bounded up the stairway.*
8 Bound is also the past tense and
past participle of **bind**.

boundary boundaries
NOUN something that indicates the
farthest limit of anything EG *the city
boundary... the boundaries of taste.*

boundless
ADJECTIVE without end or limit EG *her
boundless energy.*

bountiful
ADJECTIVE; A LITERARY WORD freely
available in large amounts EG *a
bountiful harvest.*

bounty
NOUN **1** A LITERARY WORD Bounty is a
generous supply EG *autumn's bounty
of fruits.* **2** Someone's bounty is
their generosity in giving a lot of
something.

bouquet bouquets
Said "boo-kay" NOUN an attractively
arranged bunch of flowers.

bourgeois
Said "boor-jhwah" ADJECTIVE typical
of fairly rich middle-class people.

bourgeoisie
Said "boor-jhwah-zee" NOUN the
fairly rich middle-class people in a
society.

bout bouts
NOUN **1** If you have a bout of
something such as an illness, you
have it for a short time EG *a bout of
flu.* **2** If you have a bout of doing
something, you do it
enthusiastically for a short time.
3 a boxing or wrestling match.

boutique boutiques
Said "boo-teek" NOUN a small shop
that sells fashionable clothes.

bovine
ADJECTIVE; A TECHNICAL USE relating to
cattle.

bow bows bowing bowed
Rhymes with "now" VERB **1** When
you bow, you bend your body or
lower your head as a sign of respect
or greeting. **2** If you bow to
something, you give in to it EG *He
bowed to public pressure.* ▶ NOUN **3** the
movement you make when you
bow. **4** the front part of a ship.

bow bows
Rhymes with "low" NOUN **1** a knot
with two loops and two loose ends.
2 a long thin piece of wood with
horsehair stretched along it, which
you use to play a violin. **3** a long
flexible piece of wood used for
shooting arrows.

bowel bowels
Rhymes with "towel" NOUN Your
bowels are the tubes leading from
your stomach, through which
waste passes before it leaves your
body.
📖 from Latin *botellus* meaning
'little sausage'

bowerbird bowerbirds
NOUN a bird found in Australia, the
male of which builds a shelter
during courtship.

bowl bowls bowling bowled
Rhymes with "mole" NOUN **1** a round
container with a wide uncovered
top, used for holding liquid or for
serving food. **2** the hollow,
rounded part of something EG *a
toilet bowl.* **3** a large heavy ball used
in the game of bowls or tenpin
bowling. ▶ VERB **4** In cricket, to bowl
means to throw the ball towards
the batsman.
bowler NOUN

bowling
NOUN Bowling is a game in which
you roll a heavy ball down a
narrow track towards a group of
wooden objects called pins and try
to knock them down.

bowls

NOUN Bowls is a game in which the players try to roll large wooden balls as near as possible to a small ball.

bow tie bow ties
Rhymes with "low" NOUN a man's tie in the form of a bow, often worn at formal occasions.

box boxes boxing boxed
NOUN **1** a container with a firm base and sides and usually a lid. **2** On a form, a box is a rectangular space which you have to fill in. **3** In a theatre, a box is a small separate area where a few people can watch the performance together. ▶ VERB **4** To box means to fight someone according to the rules of boxing.

boxer boxers
NOUN **1** a person who boxes. **2** a type of medium-sized, smooth-haired dog with a flat face.

boxing
NOUN Boxing is a sport in which two people fight using their fists, wearing padded gloves.

box office box offices
NOUN the place where tickets are sold in a theatre or cinema.

boy boys
NOUN a male child.
boyhood NOUN, **boyish** ADJECTIVE
≡ lad, youngster, youth

boycott boycotts boycotting boycotted
VERB **1** If you boycott an organization or event, you refuse to have anything to do with it. ▶ NOUN **2** the boycotting of an organization or event EG *a boycott of the elections.*
▥ from the name of Captain C.C. Boycott (1832-1897), an Irish land agent, who offended the tenants, so that they refused to pay their rents
≡ (sense 1) ban, black, embargo

boyfriend boyfriends
NOUN Someone's boyfriend is the man or boy with whom they are having a romantic relationship.

bra bras
NOUN a piece of underwear worn by a woman to support her breasts.

braaivlies or **braai** braaivlieses or **braais**
Said "bry-flayss" NOUN In South African English, a braaivlies is a picnic where meat is cooked on an open fire.

brace braces bracing braced
VERB **1** When you brace yourself, you stiffen your body to steady yourself EG *The ship lurched and he braced himself.* **2** If you brace yourself for something unpleasant, you prepare yourself to deal with it EG *The police are braced for violent reprisals.* ▶ NOUN **3** an object fastened to something to straighten or support it EG *a neck brace.* ▶ PLURAL NOUN **4** Braces are a pair of straps worn over the shoulders and fastened to the trousers to hold them up.

bracelet bracelets
NOUN a chain or band worn around someone's wrist as an ornament.

bracing
ADJECTIVE Something that is bracing makes you feel fit and full of energy EG *the bracing sea air.*

bracken
NOUN Bracken is a plant like a large fern that grows on hills and in woods.

bracket brackets
NOUN **1** Brackets are a pair of written marks, ( ), [ ], or { }, placed round a word or sentence that is not part of the main text, or to show that the items inside the brackets belong together. **2** a range between two limits, for example of ages or prices EG *the four-figure price bracket.* **3** a piece of metal or wood fastened to a wall to support something such as a shelf.

What do Brackets do?

Brackets () enclose material that has been added to the text, but could be omitted

A
B
C
D
E
F
G
H
I
J
K
L
M
N
O
P
Q
R
S
T
U
V
W
X
Y
Z

A B C D E F G H I J K L M N O P Q R S T U V W X Y Z

and still leave a meaningful sentence. In formal writing this sort of material is usually marked off with commas or dashes, and brackets are used for giving references or translations of foreign phrases.

Buddhism is discussed in Chapter 7 (see pages 152-197).

The boat was called "La Ardilla Roja" (The Red Squirrel).

Square brackets [ ] are used to enclose remarks and explanations which are inserted by an author to make a quotation clearer.

The minister said, "I think that five million [pounds] should do it."

brag brags bragging bragged
VERB When someone brags, they boast about their achievements EG *Both leaders bragged they could win by a landslide.*

Brahma
Said "brah-ma" PROPER NOUN Brahma is a Hindu god and is one of the Trimurti.
▣ from a Sanskrit word meaning 'praise'

Brahman
Said "brah-men" NOUN In the Hindu religion Brahman is the ultimate and impersonal divine reality of the universe.

brahmin brahmins
Said "brah-min" NOUN a member of the highest or priestly caste in Hindu society.

braid braids braiding braided
NOUN **1** Braid is a strip of decorated cloth used to decorate clothes or curtains. **2** a length of hair which has been plaited and tied. ▶ VERB **3** To braid hair or thread means to plait it.

Braille
NOUN Braille is a system of printing for blind people in which letters are represented by raised dots that can be felt with the fingers.

brain brains
NOUN **1** Your brain is the mass of nerve tissue inside your head that controls your body and enables

you to think and feel; also used to refer to your mind and the way that you think EG *I admired his legal brain.* ▶ PLURAL NOUN **2** If you say that someone has brains, you mean that they are very intelligent.

brainchild
NOUN; AN INFORMAL WORD Someone's brainchild is something that they have invented or created.

brainwash brainwashes brainwashing brainwashed
VERB If people are brainwashed into believing something, they accept it unthinkingly because they are told it repeatedly.
brainwashing NOUN

brainwave brainwaves
NOUN; AN INFORMAL WORD a clever idea you think of suddenly.

brainy brainier brainiest
ADJECTIVE; AN INFORMAL WORD clever.

braise braises braising braised
VERB To braise food means to fry it for a short time, then cook it slowly in a little liquid.

brake brakes braking braked
NOUN **1** a device for making a vehicle stop or slow down. ▶ VERB **2** When a driver brakes, he or she makes a vehicle stop or slow down by using its brakes.

bramble brambles
NOUN a wild, thorny bush that produces blackberries.

bran
NOUN Bran is the ground husks that are left over after flour has been made from wheat grains.

branch branches branching branched
NOUN **1** The branches of a tree are the parts that grow out from its trunk. **2** A branch of an organization is one of a number of its offices or shops. **3** A branch of a subject is one of its areas of study or activity EG *specialists in certain branches of medicine.* ▶ VERB **4** A road that branches off from another

road splits off from it to lead in a different direction.

brand brands branding branded

NOUN **1** A brand of something is a particular kind or make of it EG *a popular brand of chocolate.* ▶ VERB **2** When an animal is branded, a mark is burned on its skin to show who owns it.

brandish brandishes brandishing branded

VERB; A LITERARY WORD If you brandish something, you wave it vigorously EG *He brandished his sword over his head.*

brand-new

ADJECTIVE completely new.

brandy

NOUN a strong alcoholic drink, usually made from wine.
▥ from Dutch *brandewijn* meaning 'burnt wine'

brash brasher brashest

ADJECTIVE If someone is brash, they are overconfident or rather rude.

brass

NOUN OR ADJECTIVE **1** Brass is a yellow-coloured metal made from copper and zinc. **2** In an orchestra, the brass section consists of brass wind instruments such as trumpets and trombones.

brassière brassières

NOUN; A FORMAL WORD a bra.

brat brats

NOUN; AN INFORMAL WORD A badly behaved child may be referred to as a brat.

bravado

Said "bra-**vah**-doh" NOUN Bravado is a display of courage intended to impress other people.

brave braver bravest; braves braving braved

ADJECTIVE **1** A brave person is willing to do dangerous things and does not show any fear. ▶ VERB **2** If you brave an unpleasant or dangerous situation, you face up to it in order to do something EG *His fans braved*

the rain to hear him sing.
bravely ADVERB, **bravery** NOUN
▤ (sense 1) courageous, daring, fearless, plucky

bravo

INTERJECTION People shout 'Bravo!' to express appreciation when something has been done well.

brawl brawls brawling brawled

NOUN **1** a rough fight. ▶ VERB **2** When people brawl, they take part in a rough fight.

brawn

NOUN Brawn is physical strength.
brawny ADJECTIVE

bray brays braying brayed

VERB **1** When a donkey brays, it makes a loud, harsh sound. ▶ NOUN **2** the sound a donkey makes.

brazen

ADJECTIVE When someone's behaviour is brazen, they do not care if other people think they are behaving wrongly.
brazenly ADVERB

brazier braziers

NOUN a metal container in which coal or charcoal is burned to keep people warm out of doors.

Brazilian Brazilians

ADJECTIVE **1** belonging or relating to Brazil. ▶ NOUN **2** someone who comes from Brazil.

breach breaches breaching breached

VERB **1** A FORMAL WORD If you breach an agreement or law, you break it. **2** To breach a barrier means to make a gap in it EG *The river breached its banks.* ▶ NOUN **3** A breach of an agreement or law is an action that breaks it EG *a breach of contract.* **4** a gap or break.
▤ (sense 3) contravention, infringement, violation

bread

NOUN Bread is a food made from flour and water, usually raised with yeast, and baked.

breadth

A B C D E F G H I J K L M N O P Q R S T U V W X Y Z

NOUN The breadth of something is the distance between its two sides.

breadwinner breadwinners
NOUN the person who earns the money in a family.

break breaks breaking broke broken
VERB **1** When an object breaks, it is damaged and separates into pieces. **2** If you break a rule or promise you fail to keep it. **3** When a boy's voice breaks, it becomes permanently deeper. **4** When a wave breaks, it falls and becomes foam. ▸ NOUN **5** a short period during which you rest or do something different.
■ (sense 1) crack, fracture, separate, snap
■ (sense 2) breach, contravene, disobey, violate

break down VERB **1** When a machine or a vehicle breaks down, it stops working. **2** When a discussion or relationship breaks down, it ends because of problems or disagreements.

break up VERB If something breaks up, it ends EG *The marriage broke up after a year.*
breakable ADJECTIVE

breakage breakages
NOUN the act of breaking something or a thing that has been broken.

breakaway
ADJECTIVE A breakaway group is one that has separated from a larger group.

breakdown breakdowns
NOUN **1** The breakdown of something such as a system is its failure EG *a breakdown in communications.* **2** the same as a nervous breakdown. **3** If a driver has a breakdown, their car stops working.

breaker breakers
NOUN Breakers are big sea waves.

breakfast breakfasts
NOUN the first meal of the day.

break-in break-ins
NOUN the illegal entering of a

building, especially by a burglar.

breakneck
ADJECTIVE; AN INFORMAL WORD Someone or something that is travelling at breakneck speed is travelling dangerously fast.

breakthrough breakthroughs
NOUN a sudden important development EG *a medical breakthrough.*

breakwater breakwaters
NOUN a wall extending into the sea which protects a coast from the force of the waves.

bream breams
Said "brim" NOUN an edible sea fish.

breast breasts
NOUN A woman's breasts are the two soft, fleshy parts on her chest, which produce milk after she has had a baby.

breath breaths
NOUN **1** Your breath is the air you take into your lungs and let out again when you breathe. ▸ PHRASE **2** If you are **out of breath**, you are breathing with difficulty after doing something energetic. **3** If you say something **under your breath**, you say it in a very quiet voice.

breathe breathes breathing breathed
VERB When you breathe, you take air into your lungs and let it out again.

breathless
ADJECTIVE If you are breathless, you are breathing fast or with difficulty.
breathlessly ADVERB, **breathlessness** NOUN

breathtaking
ADJECTIVE If you say that something is breathtaking, you mean that it is very beautiful or exciting.

bred
the past tense and past participle of breed.

breeches
Said "brit-chiz" PLURAL NOUN Breeches are trousers reaching to just below

the knee, nowadays worn especially for riding.

breed breeds breeding bred
NOUN **1** A breed of a species of domestic animal is a particular type of it. ▶ VERB **2** Someone who breeds animals or plants keeps them in order to produce more animals or plants with particular qualities. **3** When animals breed, they mate and produce offspring.
☰ (sense 3) multiply, procreate, reproduce

breeze breezes
NOUN a gentle wind.

brevity
NOUN; A FORMAL WORD Brevity means shortness EG *the brevity of his report*.

brew brews brewing brewed
VERB **1** If you brew tea or coffee, you make it in a pot by pouring hot water over it. **2** To brew beer means to make it, by boiling and fermenting malt. **3** If an unpleasant situation is brewing, it is about to happen EG *Another scandal is brewing*.
brewer NOUN

brewery breweries
NOUN a place where beer is made, or a company that makes it.

briar briars
NOUN a wild rose that grows on a dense prickly bush.

bribe bribes bribing bribed
NOUN **1** a gift or money given to an official to persuade them to make a favourable decision. ▶ VERB **2** To bribe someone means to give them a bribe.
bribery NOUN

bric-a-brac
NOUN Bric-a-brac consists of small ornaments or pieces of furniture of no great value.
▥ from a French phrase *à bric et à brac* meaning 'at random'

brick bricks
NOUN Bricks are rectangular blocks of baked clay used in building.

bricklayer bricklayers

NOUN a person whose job is to build with bricks.

bride brides
NOUN a woman who is getting married or who has just got married.
bridal ADJECTIVE

bridegroom bridegrooms
NOUN a man who is getting married or who has just got married.

bridesmaid bridesmaids
NOUN a woman who helps and accompanies a bride on her wedding day.

bridge bridges
NOUN **1** a structure built over a river, road, or railway so that vehicles and people can cross. **2** the platform from which a ship is steered and controlled. **3** the hard ridge at the top of your nose. **4** Bridge is a card game for four players based on whist.

bridle bridles
NOUN a set of straps round a horse's head and mouth, which the rider uses to control the horse.

brief briefer briefest; briefs briefing briefed
ADJECTIVE **1** Something that is brief lasts only a short time. ▶ VERB **2** When you brief someone on a task, you give them all the necessary instructions and information about it.
briefly ADVERB
☰ (sense 1) fleeting, momentary, quick, short

briefcase briefcases
NOUN a small flat case for carrying papers.

briefing briefings
NOUN a meeting at which information and instructions are given.

brier
another spelling of **briar**.

brigade brigades
NOUN an army unit consisting of three battalions.

A
B
C
D
E
F
G
H
I
J
K
L
M
N
O
P
Q
R
S
T
U
V
W
X
Y
Z

🔲 from Italian *brigare* meaning 'to fight'

brigadier brigadiers
Said "brig-ad-ear" NOUN an army officer of the rank immediately above colonel.

brigalow brigalows
NOUN a type of Australian acacia tree that grows in the bush.

bright brighter brightest
ADJECTIVE **1** strong and startling EG *a bright light.* **2** clever EG *my brightest student.* **3** cheerful EG *a bright smile.*
brightly ADVERB, **brightness** NOUN
■ (sense 1) brilliant, dazzling, shining, vivid

brighten brightens brightening brightened
VERB **1** If something brightens, it becomes brighter EG *The weather had brightened.* **2** If someone brightens, they suddenly look happier.
brighten up VERB To brighten something up means to make it more attractive and cheerful.

brilliant
ADJECTIVE **1** A brilliant light or colour is extremely bright. **2** A brilliant person is extremely clever. **3** A brilliant career is extremely successful.
brilliantly ADVERB, **brilliance** NOUN

brim brims
NOUN **1** The wide part of a hat is the part that sticks outwards at the bottom. ▶ PHRASE **2** If a container is filled **to the brim**, it is filled right to the top.

brine
NOUN Brine is salt water.

bring brings bringing brought
VERB **1** If you bring something or someone with you when you go to a place, you take them with you EG *You can bring a friend to the party.* **2** To bring something to a particular state means to cause it to be like that EG *Bring the vegetables to the boil.*
bring about VERB To bring something about means to cause it to happen

EG *We must try to bring about a better world.*
bring up VERB **1** To bring up children means to look after them while they grow up. **2** If you bring up a subject, you introduce it into the conversation EG *She brought up the subject at dinner.*

brink
NOUN If you are on the brink of something, you are just about to do it or experience it.

brisk brisker briskest
ADJECTIVE **1** A brisk action is done quickly and energetically EG *A brisk walk restores your energy.* **2** If someone's manner is brisk, it shows that they want to get things done quickly and efficiently.
briskly ADVERB, **briskness** NOUN

bristle bristles bristling bristled
NOUN **1** Bristles are strong animal hairs used to make brushes. ▶ VERB **2** If the hairs on an animal's body bristle, they rise up, because it is frightened.
bristly ADJECTIVE

British
ADJECTIVE belonging or relating to the United Kingdom of Great Britain and Northern Ireland.

Briton Britons
NOUN someone who comes from the United Kingdom of Great Britain and Northern Ireland.

brittle
ADJECTIVE An object that is brittle is hard but breaks easily.

broach broaches broaching broached
VERB When you broach a subject, you introduce it into a discussion.

broad broader broadest
ADJECTIVE **1** wide EG *a broad smile.* **2** having many different aspects or concerning many different people EG *A broad range of issues was discussed.* **3** general rather than detailed EG *the broad concerns of the movement.* **4** If someone has a broad accent, the way that they speak

makes it very clear where they come from EG *She spoke in a broad Irish accent.*

broad bean broad beans
NOUN Broad beans are light-green beans with thick flat edible seeds.

broadcast broadcasts broadcasting broadcast
NOUN **1** a programme or announcement on radio or television. ▶ VERB **2** To broadcast something means to send it out by radio waves, so that it can be seen on television or heard on radio.
broadcaster NOUN, **broadcasting** NOUN

broaden broadens broadening broadened
VERB **1** When something broadens, it becomes wider EG *His smile broadened.* **2** To broaden something means to cause it to involve more things or concern more people EG *We must broaden the scope of this job.*

broadly
ADVERB true to a large extent or in most cases EG *There are broadly two schools of thought on this.*

broad-minded
ADJECTIVE Someone who is broad-minded does not disapprove of behaviour or attitudes that many other people disapprove of.
■ liberal, open-minded, tolerant

broadsheet broadsheets
NOUN a newspaper with large pages and long news stories.

brocade
NOUN Brocade is a heavy, expensive material, often made of silk, with a raised pattern.
▥ from Spanish *brocado* meaning 'embossed fabric'

broccoli
NOUN Broccoli is a green vegetable, similar to cauliflower.

brochure brochures
Said "**broh**-sher" NOUN a booklet which gives information about a product or service.

brogue brogues

Said "**broag**" NOUN **1** a strong accent, especially an Irish one. **2** Brogues are thick leather shoes.
▥ from Irish Gaelic *brog* meaning 'boot' or 'shoe'

broke
1 the past tense of **break.** ▶ ADJECTIVE **2** AN INFORMAL USE If you are broke, you have no money.

broken
the past participle of **break.**

broker brokers
NOUN a person whose job is to buy and sell shares for other people.

brolga brolgas
NOUN a large grey Australian crane with a red-and-green head.

brolly brollies
NOUN; AN INFORMAL WORD an umbrella.

bronchitis
NOUN Bronchitis is an illness in which the two tubes which connect your windpipe to your lungs become infected, making you cough.

brontosaurus brontosauruses
NOUN a type of very large, plant-eating dinosaur.

bronze
NOUN Bronze is a yellowish-brown metal which is a mixture of copper and tin; also the yellowish-brown colour of this metal.

brooch brooches
Rhymes with "**coach**" NOUN a piece of jewellery with a pin at the back for attaching to clothes.

brood broods brooding brooded
NOUN **1** a family of baby birds. ▶ VERB **2** If you brood about something, you keep thinking about it in a serious or unhappy way.

brook brooks
NOUN a stream.

broom brooms
NOUN **1** a long-handled brush. **2** Broom is a shrub with yellow flowers.

broth

A
B
C
D
E
F
G
H
I
J
K
L
M
N
O
P
Q
R
S
T
U
V
W
X
Y
Z

brothel brothels
NOUN a house where men pay to have sex with prostitutes.

brother brothers
NOUN Your brother is a boy or man who has the same parents as you.
brotherly ADJECTIVE

brotherhood brotherhoods
NOUN **1** Brotherhood is the affection and loyalty that brothers or close male friends feel for each other. **2** a group of men with common interests or beliefs.

brother-in-law brothers-in-law
NOUN Someone's brother-in-law is the brother of their husband or wife, or their sister's husband.

brought
the past tense and past participle of **bring**.
☑ Do not confuse *brought* and *bought*. *Brought* comes from *bring* and *bought* comes from *buy*.

brow brows
NOUN **1** Your brow is your forehead. **2** Your brows are your eyebrows. **3** The brow of a hill is the top of it.

brown browner brownest
ADJECTIVE OR NOUN Brown is the colour of earth or wood.

brownie brownies
NOUN a junior member of the Guides.

browse browses browsing browsed
VERB **1** If you browse through a book, you look through it in a casual way. **2** If you browse in a shop, you look at the things in it for interest rather than because you want to buy something.

browser browsers
NOUN a piece of computer software that lets you look at websites on the World Wide Web.

bruise bruises bruising bruised
NOUN **1** a purple mark that appears on your skin after something has

NOUN Broth is soup, usually with vegetables in it.

hit it. ▶ VERB **2** If something bruises you, it hits you so that a bruise appears on your skin.

brumby brumbies
NOUN In Australia and New Zealand, a wild horse.

brunette brunettes
NOUN a girl or woman with dark brown hair.

brunt
PHRASE If you **bear the brunt** of something unpleasant, you are the person who suffers most EG *Women bear the brunt of crime.*

brush brushes brushing brushed
NOUN **1** an object with bristles which you use for cleaning things, painting, or tidying your hair.
▶ VERB **2** If you brush something, you clean it or tidy it with a brush. **3** To brush against something means to touch it while passing it EG *Her lips brushed his cheek.*

brusque
Said "broosk" ADJECTIVE Someone who is brusque deals with people quickly and without considering their feelings.
brusquely ADVERB

brussels sprout brussels sprouts
NOUN Brussels sprouts are vegetables that look like tiny cabbages.

brutal
ADJECTIVE Brutal behaviour is cruel and violent EG *the victim of a brutal murder.*
brutally ADVERB, **brutality** NOUN

brute brutes
NOUN **1** a rough and insensitive man. ▶ ADJECTIVE **2** Brute force is strength alone, without any skill EG *You have to open the lock gates using brute force.*
brutish ADJECTIVE

bubble bubbles bubbling bubbled
NOUN **1** a ball of air in a liquid. **2** a hollow, delicate ball of soapy liquid. ▶ VERB **3** When a liquid bubbles, bubbles form in it. **4** If

you are bubbling with something like excitement, you are full of it.
bubbly ADJECTIVE

buck bucks bucking bucked
NOUN **1** the male of various animals, including the deer and the rabbit. ▶ VERB **2** If a horse bucks, it jumps into the air with its feet off the ground.

bucket buckets
NOUN a deep round container with an open top and a handle.

buckle buckles buckling buckled
NOUN **1** a fastening on the end of a belt or strap. ▶ VERB **2** If you buckle a belt or strap, you fasten it. **3** If something buckles, it becomes bent because of severe heat or pressure.

bud buds budding budded
NOUN **1** a small, tight swelling on a tree or plant, which develops into a flower or a cluster of leaves. ▶ VERB **2** When a tree or plant buds, new buds appear on it.

Buddha
PROPER NOUN The Buddha is the title of Gautama Siddhartha, a religious teacher living in the 6th century BC in India and founder of Buddhism. Buddha means 'the enlightened one'.

Buddhism
NOUN Buddhism is a religion, founded by the Buddha, which teaches that the way to end suffering is by overcoming your desires.
Buddhist NOUN OR ADJECTIVE

budding
ADJECTIVE just beginning to develop EG *a budding artist.*

budge budges budging budged
VERB If something will not budge, you cannot move it.

budgerigar budgerigars
NOUN a small brightly coloured pet bird.

budget budgets budgeting budgeted
NOUN **1** a plan showing how much money will be available and how it will be spent. ▶ VERB **2** If you budget for something, you plan your money carefully, so as to be able to afford it.
budgetary ADJECTIVE

budgie budgies
NOUN; AN INFORMAL WORD a budgerigar.

buff buffs
ADJECTIVE **1** a pale brown colour. ▶ NOUN **2** AN INFORMAL USE someone who knows a lot about a subject EG *a film buff.*

buffalo buffaloes
NOUN a wild animal like a large cow with long curved horns.

buffer buffers
NOUN **1** Buffers on a train or at the end of a railway line are metal discs on springs that reduce shock when they are hit. **2** something that prevents something else from being harmed EG *keep savings as a buffer against unexpected cash needs.*

buffet buffets
Said "boof-ay" NOUN **1** a café at a station. **2** a meal at which people serve themselves.

buffet buffets buffeting buffeted
Said "buff-it" VERB If the wind or sea buffets a place or person, it strikes them violently and repeatedly.

bug bugs bugging bugged
NOUN **1** an insect, especially one that causes damage. **2** a small error in a computer program which means that the program will not work properly. **3** AN INFORMAL USE a virus or minor infection EG *a stomach bug.* ▶ VERB **4** If a place is bugged, tiny microphones are hidden there to pick up what people are saying.

bugle bugles
NOUN a brass instrument that looks like a small trumpet.
bugler NOUN

build builds building built
VERB **1** To build something such as a

A
B
C
D
E
F
G
H
I
J
K
L
M
N
O
P
Q
R
S
T
U
V
W
X
Y
Z

house means to make it from its parts. **2** To build something such as an organization means to develop it gradually. ▶ NOUN **3** Your build is the shape and size of your body.
builder NOUN
☰ (sense 1) assemble, construct, erect

building buildings
NOUN a structure with walls and a roof.

building society building societies
NOUN a business in which some people invest their money, while others borrow from it to buy a house.

bulb bulbs
NOUN **1** the glass part of an electric lamp. **2** an onion-shaped root that grows into a flower or plant.

Bulgarian Bulgarians
ADJECTIVE **1** belonging or relating to Bulgaria. ▶ NOUN **2** someone who comes from Bulgaria. **3** the main language spoken in Bulgaria.

bulge bulges bulging bulged
VERB **1** If something bulges, it swells out from a surface. ▶ NOUN **2** a lump on a normally flat surface.

bulk bulks
NOUN **1** a large mass of something EG *The book is more impressive for its bulk than its content.* **2** The bulk of something is most of it EG *the bulk of the world's great poetry.* ▶ PHRASE **3** To buy something **in bulk** means to buy it in large quantities.

bulky bulkier bulkiest
ADJECTIVE large and heavy EG *a bulky package.*
☰ cumbersome, large, unwieldy

bull bulls
NOUN the male of some species of animals, including the cow family, elephants and whales.

bulldog bulldogs
NOUN a squat dog with a broad head and muscular body.

bulldozer bulldozers
NOUN a powerful tractor with a broad blade in front, which is used for moving earth or knocking things down.

bullet bullets
NOUN a small piece of metal fired from a gun.

bulletin bulletins
NOUN **1** a short news report on radio or television. **2** a leaflet or small newspaper regularly produced by a group or organization.
▥ from Italian *bulletino* meaning 'small Papal edict'

bullion
NOUN Bullion is gold or silver in the form of bars.

bullock bullocks
NOUN a young castrated bull.

bullroarer bullroarers
NOUN a wooden slat attached to a string that is whirled round to make a roaring noise. Bullroarers are used especially by Australian Aborigines in religious ceremonies.

bully bullies bullying bullied
NOUN **1** someone who uses their strength or power to hurt or frighten other people. ▶ VERB **2** If someone bullies you into doing something, they make you do it by using force or threats.
▥ a 16th century word meaning 'fine fellow' or 'hired ruffian'

bump bumps bumping bumped
VERB **1** If you bump into something, you knock into it with a jolt. ▶ NOUN **2** a soft or dull noise made by something knocking into something else. **3** a raised, uneven part of a surface.
bumpy ADJECTIVE
☰ (sense 3) bulge, lump, protuberance

bumper bumpers
NOUN **1** Bumpers are bars on the front and back of a vehicle which protect it if there is a collision. ▶ ADJECTIVE **2** A bumper crop or harvest is larger than usual.

bun buns
NOUN a small, round cake.

bunch bunches bunching bunched
NOUN **1** a group of people or things.
2 A bunch of flowers is a number of them held or tied together. **3** A bunch of bananas or grapes is a group of them growing on the same stem. ▸ VERB **4** When people bunch together or bunch up, they stay very close to each other.

bundle bundles bundling bundled
NOUN **1** a number of things tied together or wrapped up in a cloth.
▸ VERB **2** If you bundle someone or something somewhere, you push them there quickly and roughly.

bung bungs bunging bunged
NOUN **1** a stopper used to close a hole in something such as a barrel.
▸ VERB **2** AN INFORMAL USE If you bung something somewhere, you put it there quickly and carelessly.

bungalow bungalows
NOUN a one-storey house.
▦ from Hindi *bangla* meaning 'house'

bungle bungles bungling bungled
VERB To bungle something means to fail to do it properly.

bunion bunions
NOUN a painful lump on the first joint of a person's big toe.

bunk bunks
NOUN a bed fixed to a wall in a ship or caravan.

bunker bunkers
NOUN **1** On a golf course, a bunker is a large hole filled with sand. **2** A coal bunker is a storage place for coal. **3** an underground shelter with strong walls to protect it from bombing.

bunting
NOUN Bunting is strips of small coloured flags displayed on streets and buildings on special occasions.

bunyip bunyips
NOUN a legendary monster said to live in swamps and lakes in Australia.

buoy buoys
Said "boy" NOUN a floating object anchored to the bottom of the sea, marking a channel or warning of danger.

buoyant
ADJECTIVE **1** able to float. **2** lively and cheerful EG *She was in a buoyant mood.*
buoyancy NOUN

burble burbles burbling burbled
VERB To burble means to makes a soft bubbling sound EG *The water burbled over the gravel.*

burden burdens
NOUN **1** a heavy load. **2** If something is a burden to you, it causes you a lot of worry or hard work.
burdensome ADJECTIVE
▤ (sense 1) load, weight
▤ (sense 2) millstone, trouble, worry

bureau bureaux
Said "byoo-roh" NOUN **1** an office that provides a service EG *an employment bureau.* **2** a writing desk with shelves and drawers.

bureaucracy
NOUN Bureaucracy is the complex system of rules and procedures which operates in government departments.
bureaucratic ADJECTIVE

bureaucrat bureaucrats
NOUN a person who works in a government department, especially one who follows rules and procedures strictly.

burgeoning
ADJECTIVE growing or developing rapidly EG *a burgeoning political crisis.*

burglar burglars
NOUN a thief who breaks into a building.
burglary NOUN

burgle burgles burgling burgled
VERB If your house is burgled, someone breaks into it and steals things.

A
B
C
D
E
F
G
H
I
J
K
L
M
N
O
P
Q
R
S
T
U
V
W
X
Y
Z

burial burials
NOUN a ceremony held when a dead person is buried.

burly burlier burliest
ADJECTIVE A burly man has a broad body and strong muscles.
■ brawny, well-built

burn burns burning burned or burnt
VERB 1 If something is burning, it is on fire. 2 To burn something means to destroy it with fire. 3 If you burn yourself or are burned, you are injured by fire or by something hot. ▶ NOUN 4 an injury caused by fire or by something hot.
■ (sense 1) be on fire, blaze
■ (sense 2) incinerate, set on fire
☑ You can write either *burned* or *burnt* as the past form of *burn*.

burp burps burping burped
VERB 1 If you burp, you make a noise because air from your stomach has been forced up through your throat. ▶ NOUN 2 the noise that you make when you burp.

burrow burrows burrowing burrowed
NOUN 1 a tunnel or hole in the ground dug by a small animal. ▶ VERB 2 When an animal burrows, it digs a burrow.

bursary bursaries
NOUN a sum of money given to someone to help fund their education.

burst bursts bursting burst
VERB 1 When something bursts, it splits open because of pressure from inside it. 2 If you burst into a room, you enter it suddenly. 3 To burst means to happen or come suddenly and with force EG *The aircraft burst into flames.* 4 AN INFORMAL USE If you are bursting with something, you find it difficult to keep it to yourself EG *We were bursting with joy.* ▶ NOUN 5 A burst of something is a short period of it EG *He had a sudden burst of energy.*
■ (sense 5) outbreak, rush, spate

bury buries burying buried
VERB 1 When a dead person is buried, their body is put into a grave and covered with earth. 2 To bury something means to put it in a hole in the ground and cover it up. 3 If something is buried under something, it is covered by it EG *My bag was buried under a pile of old newspapers.*

bus buses
NOUN a large motor vehicle that carries passengers.
▥ from Latin *omnibus* meaning 'for all'; buses were originally called omnibuses

bush bushes
NOUN 1 a thick plant with many stems branching out from ground level. 2 In Australia and South Africa, an uncultivated area outside of city areas is called the bush. 3 In New Zealand, the bush is land covered with rain forest.

bushman bushmen
NOUN 1 In Australia and New Zealand, someone who lives or travels in the bush. 2 In New Zealand, a bushman is also someone whose job it is to clear the bush for farming.

Bushman Bushmen
NOUN A Bushman is a member of a group of people in southern Africa who live by hunting and gathering food.

bushranger bushrangers
NOUN In Australia and New Zealand in the past, an outlaw living in the bush.

bushy bushier bushiest
ADJECTIVE Bushy hair or fur grows very thickly EG *bushy eyebrows.*

business businesses
NOUN 1 Business is work relating to the buying and selling of goods and services. 2 an organization which produces or sells goods or provides a service. 3 You can refer to any event, situation, or activity as a business EG *This whole business*

has upset me.

businessman NOUN, **businesswoman** NOUN

■ (sense 2) company, establishment, firm, organization

businesslike
ADJECTIVE dealing with things in an efficient way.

busker buskers
NOUN someone who plays music or sings for money in public places.

bust busts busting bust or busted
NOUN 1 a statue of someone's head and shoulders *a bust of Beethoven.*
2 A woman's bust is her chest and her breasts. ▶ VERB 3 AN INFORMAL USE If you bust something, you break it.
▶ ADJECTIVE 4 AN INFORMAL USE If a business goes bust, it becomes bankrupt and closes down.

bustle bustles bustling bustled
VERB 1 When people bustle, they move in a busy, hurried way.
▶ NOUN 2 Bustle is busy, noisy activity.

busy busier busiest; busies busying busied
ADJECTIVE 1 If you are busy, you are in the middle of doing something.
2 A busy place is full of people doing things or moving about EG *a busy seaside resort.* ▶ VERB 3 If you busy yourself with something, you occupy yourself by doing it.
busily ADVERB

■ (sense 1) employed, engaged, occupied

but
CONJUNCTION 1 used to introduce an idea that is opposite to what has gone before EG *I don't miss teaching but I miss the pupils.* 2 used when apologizing EG *I'm sorry, but I can't come tonight.* 3 except EG *We can't do anything but wait.*

butcher butchers
NOUN a shopkeeper who sells meat.

butler butlers
NOUN the chief male servant in a rich household.

▥ from Old French *bouteillier*

meaning 'person who deals with bottles'

butt butts butting butted
NOUN 1 The butt of a weapon is the thick end of its handle. 2 If you are the butt of teasing, you are the target of it. ▶ VERB 3 If you butt something, you ram it with your head.

butt in VERB If you butt in, you join in a private conversation or activity without being asked to.

butter butters buttering buttered
NOUN 1 Butter is a soft fatty food made from cream, which is spread on bread and used in cooking.
▶ VERB 2 To butter bread means to spread butter on it.

buttercup buttercups
NOUN a wild plant with bright yellow flowers.

butterfly butterflies
NOUN a type of insect with large colourful wings.

buttocks
PLURAL NOUN Your buttocks are the part of your body that you sit on.

button buttons buttoning buttoned
NOUN 1 Buttons are small, hard objects sewn on to clothing, and used to fasten two surfaces together. 2 a small object on a piece of equipment that you press to make it work. ▶ VERB 3 If you button a piece of clothing, you fasten it using its buttons.

buttonhole buttonholes
NOUN 1 a hole that you push a button through to fasten a piece of clothing. 2 a flower worn in your lapel.

buxom
ADJECTIVE A buxom woman is large, healthy, and attractive.

buy buys buying bought
VERB If you buy something, you obtain it by paying money for it.
buyer NOUN

buzz buzzes buzzing buzzed

A
B
C
D
E
F
G
H
I
J
K
L
M
N
O
P
Q
R
S
T
U
V
W
X
Y
Z

VERB **1** If something buzzes, it makes a humming sound, like a bee. ▶ NOUN **2** the sound something makes when it buzzes.

buzzard buzzards
NOUN a large brown and white bird of prey.

buzzer buzzers
NOUN a device that makes a buzzing sound, to attract attention.

by
PREPOSITION **1** used to indicate who or what has done something EG *The statement was issued by his solicitor.* **2** used to indicate how something is done EG *He frightened her by hiding behind the door.* **3** located next to EG *I sat by her bed.* **4** before a particular time EG *It should be ready by next spring.* ▶ PREPOSITION OR ADVERB **5** going past EG *We drove by his house.*

by-election by-elections
NOUN an election held to choose a new member of parliament after the previous member has resigned or died.

bygone
ADJECTIVE; A LITERARY WORD happening or existing a long time ago EG *the ceremonies of a bygone era.*

bypass bypasses
NOUN a main road which takes traffic round a town rather than through it.

bystander bystanders
NOUN someone who sees something happen but does not take part in it.

byte bytes
NOUN a unit of storage in a computer.

cab cabs
NOUN **1** a taxi. **2** In a lorry, bus, or train, the cab is where the driver sits.
🏛 from French *cabriolet* meaning 'light two-wheeled carriage'. Cabs were originally horse-drawn

cabaret cabarets
Said "kab-bar-ray" NOUN a show consisting of dancing, singing, or comedy acts.
🏛 from French *cabaret* meaning 'tavern'

cabbage cabbages
NOUN a large green leafy vegetable.
🏛 from Norman French *cabache* meaning 'head'

cabbage tree cabbage trees
NOUN a palm-like tree found in New Zealand with a tall bare trunk and big bunches of spiky leaves; also a similar tree found in eastern Australia.

cabin cabins
NOUN **1** a room in a ship where a passenger sleeps. **2** a small house, usually in the country and often made of wood. **3** the area where the passengers or the crew sit in a plane.

cabinet cabinets
NOUN **1** a small cupboard. **2** The cabinet in a government is a group of ministers who advise the leader and decide policies.

cable cables
NOUN **1** a strong, thick rope or chain. **2** a bundle of wires with a rubber covering, which carries electricity. **3** a message sent abroad by using electricity.

cable car cable cars
NOUN a vehicle pulled by a moving cable, for taking people up and down mountains.

cable television
NOUN a television service people can receive from underground wires which carry the signals.

cache caches
Said "kash" NOUN a store of things hidden away EG *a cache of guns.*

cachet
Said "kash-shay" NOUN; A FORMAL WORD Cachet is the status and respect something has EG *the cachet of shopping at Harrods.*

cackle cackles cackling cackled
VERB **1** If you cackle, you laugh harshly. ▶ NOUN **2** a harsh laugh.

cacophony
Said "kak-koff-fon-nee" NOUN; A FORMAL WORD a loud, unpleasant noise EG *a cacophony of barking dogs.*
🏛 from Greek *kakos* + *phōnē* meaning 'bad sound'

cactus cacti or cactuses
NOUN a thick, fleshy plant that grows in deserts and is usually covered in spikes.

cad cads
NOUN; AN OLD-FASHIONED WORD a man who treats people unfairly.

caddie caddies; also spelt caddy
NOUN **1** a person who carries golf clubs for a golf player. **2** A tea caddy is a box for keeping tea in.

cadence cadences
NOUN The cadence of someone's voice is the way it goes up and down as they speak.

cadet cadets
NOUN a young person being trained in the armed forces or police.

cadge cadges cadging cadged
VERB If you cadge something off someone, you get it from them and don't give them anything in return EG *I cadged a lift ashore.*

caesarean caesareans
Said "siz-air-ee-an"; also spelt caesarian and cesarean
NOUN A caesarean or caesarean section is an operation in which a baby is lifted out of a woman's

A B C D E F G H I J K L M N O P Q R S T U V W X Y Z

womb through a cut in her abdomen.

café cafés
Said "kaf-fay". NOUN **1** a place where you can buy light meals and drinks. **2** In South African English, a café is a corner shop or grocer's shop.

cafeteria cafeterias
Said "kaf-fit-ee-ree-ya". NOUN a restaurant where you serve yourself.

caffeine or **caffein**
Said "kaf-feen". NOUN Caffeine is a chemical in coffee and tea which makes you more active.

cage cages
NOUN a box made of wire or bars in which birds or animals are kept.
caged ADJECTIVE

cagey cagier cagiest
Said "kay-jee". ADJECTIVE; AN INFORMAL WORD cautious and not open EG *They're very cagey when they talk to me.*

cagoule cagoules
Said "ka-gool". NOUN a lightweight waterproof jacket with a hood.

cahoots
PHRASE; AN INFORMAL USE If you are **in cahoots** with someone, you are working closely with them on a secret plan.

cairn cairns
NOUN a pile of stones built as a memorial or a landmark.
▥ from Gaelic *carn* meaning 'heap of stones' or 'hill'

cajole cajoles cajoling cajoled
VERB If you cajole someone into doing something, you persuade them to do it by saying nice things to them.

cake cakes caking caked
NOUN **1** a sweet food made by baking flour, eggs, fat, and sugar. **2** A block of a hard substance such as soap. ▶ VERB **3** If something cakes or is caked, it forms or becomes covered with a solid layer EG *caked with mud.*
▥ from Old Norse *kaka* meaning

'oatcake'

calamity calamities
NOUN an event that causes disaster or distress.
calamitous ADJECTIVE

calcium
Said "kal-see-um". NOUN a soft white substance found in bones and teeth.

calculate calculates calculating calculated
VERB **1** If you calculate something, you work it out, usually by doing some arithmetic. **2** If something is calculated, it is deliberately planned to have a particular effect EG *Everything they said to each other was calculated to wound.*
calculation NOUN
▥ from Latin *calculus* meaning 'stone' or 'pebble'. The Romans used pebbles to count with

calculating
ADJECTIVE carefully planning situations to get what you want EG *Toby was always a calculating type.*

calculator calculators
NOUN a small electronic machine used for doing mathematical calculations.

calculus
NOUN Calculus is a branch of mathematics concerned with amounts that can change and rates of change.

calendar calendars
NOUN **1** a chart showing the date of each day in a particular year. **2** a system of dividing time into fixed periods of days, months, and years EG *the Jewish calendar.*
▥ from Latin *kalendae* the day of the month on which interest on debts was due

calf calves
NOUN **1** a young cow, bull, elephant, whale, or seal. **2** the thick part at the back of your leg below your knee.

calibre calibres
Said "kal-lib-ber". NOUN **1** the ability

or intelligence someone has EG *a player of her calibre.* **2** The calibre of a gun is the width of the inside of the barrel of the gun.

📖 from Arabic *qalib* meaning 'cobbler's last'

call calls calling called

VERB **1** If someone or something is called a particular name, that is their name EG *a man called Jeffrey.* **2** If you call people or situations something, you use words to describe your opinion of them EG *They called me crazy.* **3** If you call someone, you telephone them. **4** If you call or call out something, you say it loudly EG *He called out his daughter's name.* **5** If you call on someone, you pay them a short visit EG *Don't hesitate to call on me.* ▶ NOUN **6** If you get a call from someone, they telephone you or pay you a visit. **7** a cry or shout EG *a call for help.* **8** a demand for something EG *The call for art teachers was small.*

▤ (sense 1) christen, label, name

call off VERB If you call something off, you cancel it.

call up VERB If someone is called up, they are ordered to join the army, navy, or air force.

call box call boxes

NOUN a telephone box.

calling

NOUN **1** a profession or career. **2** If you have a calling to a particular job, you have a strong feeling that you should do it.

callous

ADJECTIVE cruel and not concerned with other people's feelings.

callously ADVERB, **callousness** NOUN

▤ hardhearted, heartless, unfeeling

calm calmer calmest; calms calming calmed

ADJECTIVE **1** Someone who is calm is quiet and does not show any worry or excitement. **2** If the weather or the sea is calm, it is still because there is no strong wind. ▶ NOUN **3** Calm is a state of quietness and peacefulness EG *He liked the calm of the evening.* ▶ VERB **4** To calm someone means to make them less upset or excited.

calmly ADVERB, **calmness** NOUN

▤ (sense 1) composed, cool, self-possessed

▤ (sense 3) peacefulness, quiet

▤ (sense 4) quieten, soothe

calorie calories

NOUN a unit of measurement for the energy food gives you EG *All alcohol is high in calories.*

calves

the plural of **calf**.

calypso calypsos

Said "kal-**lip**-soh" NOUN a type of song from the West Indies, accompanied by a rhythmic beat, about something happening at the time.

camaraderie

Said "kam-mer-**rah**-der-ree" NOUN Camaraderie is a feeling of trust and friendship between a group of people.

camber cambers

NOUN a slight downwards slope from the centre of a road to each side of it.

camel camels

NOUN a large mammal with either one or two humps on its back. Camels live in hot desert areas and are sometimes used for carrying things.

📖 from Hebrew *gamal*

cameo cameos

NOUN **1** a small but important part in a play or film played by a well-known actor or actress. **2** a brooch with a raised stone design on a flat stone of another colour.

camera cameras

NOUN a piece of equipment used for taking photographs or for filming.

📖 from Latin *camera* meaning 'vault'

camomile

A
B
C
D
E
F
G
H
I
J
K
L
M
N
O
P
Q
R
S
T
U
V
W
X
Y
Z

NOUN Camomile is a plant with a strong smell and daisy-like flowers which are used to make herbal tea.
📖 from Greek *khamaimēlon* meaning 'apple on the ground'

camouflage camouflages camouflaging camouflaged
Said "**kam**-mof-flahj" NOUN
1 Camouflage is a way of avoiding being seen by having the same colour or appearance as the surroundings. ▸ VERB **2** To camouflage something is to hide it by giving it the same colour or appearance as its surroundings.

camp camps camping camped
NOUN **1** a place where people live in tents or stay in tents on holiday. **2** a collection of buildings for a particular group of people such as soldiers or prisoners. **3** a group of people who support a particular idea or belief EG *the pro-government camp.* ▸ VERB **4** If you camp, you stay in a tent.
camper NOUN, **camping** NOUN

campaign campaigns campaigning campaigned
Said "kam-**pane**" NOUN **1** a set of actions aiming to achieve a particular result EG *a campaign to educate people.* ▸ VERB **2** To campaign means to carry out a campaign EG *He has campaigned against smoking.*
campaigner NOUN

camp-drafting
NOUN In Australia, camp-drafting is a competition in which men on horseback select cattle or sheep from a herd or flock.

campus campuses
NOUN the area of land and the buildings that make up a university or college.

can could
VERB **1** If you can do something, it is possible for you to do it or you are allowed to do it EG *You can go to the cinema.* **2** If you can do something, you have the ability to do it EG *I can speak Italian.*

can cans canning canned
NOUN **1** a metal container, often a sealed one with food or drink inside. ▸ VERB **2** To can food or drink is to seal it in cans.

Canadian Canadians
ADJECTIVE **1** belonging or relating to Canada. ▸ NOUN **2** someone who comes from Canada.

canal canals
NOUN a long, narrow man-made stretch of water.

canary canaries
NOUN a small yellow bird.

can-can can-cans
NOUN a lively dance in which women kick their legs high in the air to fast music.

cancel cancels cancelling cancelled
VERB **1** If you cancel something that has been arranged, you stop it from happening. **2** If you cancel a cheque or an agreement, you make sure that it is no longer valid.
cancellation NOUN

cancer cancers
NOUN **1** a serious disease in which abnormal cells in a part of the body increase rapidly, causing growths. **2** Cancer is also the fourth sign of the zodiac, represented by a crab. People born between June 21st and July 22nd are born under this sign.
cancerous ADJECTIVE
📖 from Latin *cancer* meaning 'crab'

candelabra or **candelabrum** candelabras
NOUN an ornamental holder for a number of candles.

candid
ADJECTIVE honest and frank.
candidly ADVERB, **candour** NOUN

candidate candidates
NOUN **1** a person who is being considered for a job. **2** a person taking an examination.
candidacy NOUN
📖 from Latin *candidatus* meaning 'white-robed'. In Rome, a candidate

wore a white toga

candied

ADJECTIVE covered or cooked in sugar EG *candied fruit.*

candle candles

NOUN a stick of hard wax with a wick through the middle. The lighted wick gives a flame that provides light.

candlestick candlesticks

NOUN a holder for a candle.

candy candies

NOUN; USED ESPECIALLY IN AMERICAN ENGLISH Candies are sweets.

🏛 from Arabic *qand* meaning 'cane sugar'

cane canes caning caned

NOUN **1** Cane is the long, hollow stems of a plant such as bamboo. **2** Cane is also strips of cane used for weaving things such as baskets. **3** a long narrow stick, often one used to beat people as a punishment. ▸ VERB **4** To cane someone means to beat them with a cane as a punishment.

canine

Said "**kay-nine**" ADJECTIVE relating to dogs.

canister canisters

NOUN a container with a lid, used for storing foods such as sugar or tea.

cannabis

NOUN Cannabis is a drug made from the hemp plant, which some people smoke.

canned

ADJECTIVE **1** Canned food is kept in cans. **2** Canned music or laughter on a television or radio show is recorded beforehand.

cannibal cannibals

NOUN a person who eats other human beings; also used of animals that eat animals of their own type.

cannibalism NOUN

cannon cannons or cannon

NOUN a large gun, usually on wheels, used in battles to fire heavy metal balls.

cannot

VERB Cannot is the same as can not EG *She cannot come home yet.*

canny

ADJECTIVE clever and cautious EG *canny business people.*

cannily ADVERB

canoe canoes

Said "**ka-noo**" NOUN a small, narrow boat that you row using a paddle.

canoeing NOUN

canon canons

NOUN **1** a member of the clergy in a cathedral. **2** a basic rule or principle EG *the canons of political economy.*

canopy canopies

NOUN a cover for something, used for shelter or decoration EG *a frilly canopy over the bed.*

🏛 from Greek *kōnōpeion* meaning 'bed with a mosquito net'

cantankerous

ADJECTIVE Cantankerous people are quarrelsome and bad-tempered.

canteen canteens

NOUN **1** the part of a workplace where the workers can go to eat. **2** A canteen of cutlery is a set of cutlery in a box.

canter canters cantering cantered

VERB When a horse canters, it moves at a speed between a gallop and a trot.

cantilever cantilevers

NOUN a long beam or bar fixed at only one end and supporting a bridge or other structure at the other end.

canton cantons

NOUN a political and administrative region of a country, especially in Switzerland.

canvas canvases

NOUN **1** Canvas is strong, heavy cloth used for making things such as sails and tents. **2** a piece of canvas on which an artist does a painting.

canvass canvasses canvassing canvassed

A B C D E F G H I J K L M N O P Q R S T U V W X Y Z

VERB **1** If you canvass people or a place, you go round trying to persuade people to vote for a particular candidate or party in an election. **2** If you canvass opinion, you find out what people think about a particular subject by asking them.

canyon canyons
NOUN a narrow river valley with steep sides.

cap caps capping capped
NOUN **1** a soft, flat hat, often with a peak at the front. **2** the top of a bottle. **3** Caps are small explosives used in toy guns. ▶ VERB **4** To cap something is to cover it with something. **5** If you cap a story or a joke that someone has just told, you tell a better one.

capable
ADJECTIVE **1** able to do something EG *a man capable of extreme violence.* **2** skilful or talented EG *She was a very capable woman.*
capably ADVERB, **capability** NOUN

capacity capacities
*Said "kap-**pas**-sit-tee"* NOUN **1** the maximum amount that something can hold or produce EG *a seating capacity of eleven thousand.* **2** A person's power or ability to do something EG *his capacity for consuming hamburgers.* **3** Someone's position or role EG *in his capacity as councillor.*

cape capes
NOUN **1** a short cloak with no sleeves. **2** a large piece of land sticking out into the sea EG *the Cape of Good Hope.*

caper capers
NOUN **1** Capers are the flower buds of a spiky Mediterranean shrub, which are pickled and used to flavour food. **2** a light-hearted practical joke EG *Jack would have nothing to do with such capers.*

capillary capillaries
*Said "kap-**pill**-lar-ree"* NOUN Capillaries are very thin blood vessels.

capital capitals
NOUN **1** The capital of a country is the city where the government meets. **2** Capital is the amount of money or property owned or used by a business. **3** Capital is also a sum of money that you save or invest in order to gain interest. **4** A capital or capital letter is a larger letter used at the beginning of a sentence or at a name.

capitalism
NOUN Capitalism is an economic and political system where businesses and industries are not owned and run by the government, but by individuals who can make a profit from them.
capitalist ADJECTIVE OR NOUN

capitalize capitalizes capitalizing capitalized; also spelt **capitalise**
VERB If you capitalize on a situation, you use it to get an advantage.

capital punishment
NOUN Capital punishment is legally killing someone as a punishment for a crime they have committed.

capitulate capitulates capitulating capitulated
VERB To capitulate is to give in and stop fighting or resisting EG *The Finns capitulated in March 1940.*
capitulation NOUN

cappuccino cappuccinos
*Said "kap-poot-**sheen**-oh"* NOUN coffee made with frothy milk.

capricious
*Said "kap-**prish**-uss"* ADJECTIVE often changing unexpectedly EG *the capricious English weather.*

Capricorn
NOUN Capricorn is the tenth sign of the zodiac, represented by a goat. People born between December 22nd and January 19th are born under this sign.
▣ from Latin *caper* meaning 'goat' and *cornu* meaning 'horn'

capsize capsizes capsizing

capsized
VERB If a boat capsizes, it turns upside down.

capsule capsules
NOUN **1** a small container with medicine inside which you swallow. **2** the part of a spacecraft in which astronauts travel.
🔟 from Latin *capsula* meaning 'little box'

captain captains captaining captained
NOUN **1** the officer in charge of a ship or aeroplane. **2** an army officer of the rank immediately above lieutenant. **3** a navy officer of the rank immediately above commander. **4** the leader of a sports team EG *captain of the cricket team.* ▸ VERB **5** If you captain a group of people, you are their leader.

caption captions
NOUN a title printed underneath a picture or photograph.

captivate captivates captivating captivated
VERB To captivate someone is to fascinate or attract them so that they cannot take their attention away EG *I was captivated by her.*
captivating ADJECTIVE

captive captives
NOUN **1** a person who has been captured and kept prisoner.
▸ ADJECTIVE **2** imprisoned or enclosed EG *a captive bird.*
captivity NOUN

captor captors
NOUN someone who has captured a person or animal.

capture captures capturing captured
VERB **1** To capture someone is to take them prisoner. **2** To capture a quality or mood means to succeed in representing or describing it EG *capturing the mood of the riots.* ▸ NOUN **3** The capture of someone or something is the capturing of them EG *the fifth anniversary of his capture.*

car cars

NOUN **1** a four-wheeled road vehicle with room for a small number of people. **2** a railway carriage used for a particular purpose EG *the buffet car.*

carafe carafes
Said "kar-**raf**" NOUN a glass bottle for serving water or wine.
🔟 from Arabic *gharrafah* meaning 'vessel for liquid'

caramel caramels
NOUN **1** a chewy sweet made from sugar, butter, and milk. **2** Caramel is burnt sugar used for colouring or flavouring food.

carat carats
NOUN **1** a unit for measuring the weight of diamonds and other precious stones. **2** a unit for measuring the purity of gold.

caravan caravans
NOUN **1** a vehicle pulled by a car in which people live or spend their holidays. **2** a group of people and animals travelling together, usually across a desert.
🔟 from Persian *karwan*

carbohydrate carbohydrates
NOUN Carbohydrate is a substance that gives you energy. It is found in foods like sugar and bread.

carbon
NOUN Carbon is a chemical element that is pure in diamonds and also found in coal. All living things contain carbon.

carburettor carburettors
Said "**kahr**-bur-ret-ter" NOUN the part of the engine in a vehicle in which air and petrol are mixed together.

carcass carcasses; also spelt carcase
NOUN the body of a dead animal.

card cards
NOUN **1** a piece of stiff paper or plastic with information or a message on it EG *a birthday card.*
2 Cards can mean playing cards EG *a poor set of cards with which to play.*
3 When you play cards, you play

A
B
C
D
E
F
G
H
I
J
K
L
M
N
O
P
Q
R
S
T
U
V
W
X
Y
Z

any game using playing cards.
4 Card is strong, stiff paper.
🏛 from Greek *khartēs* meaning 'papyrus leaf'

cardboard
NOUN Cardboard is thick, stiff paper.

cardiac
ADJECTIVE; A MEDICAL WORD relating to the heart EG *cardiac disease*.

cardigan cardigans
NOUN a knitted jacket that fastens up the front.

cardinal cardinals
NOUN **1** a high-ranking member of the Roman Catholic clergy who chooses and advises the Pope.
▶ ADJECTIVE **2** extremely important EG *a cardinal principle of law*.
🏛 from Latin *cardo* meaning 'hinge'. When something is important, other things hinge on it

care cares caring cared
VERB **1** If you care about something, you are concerned about it and interested in it. **2** If you care about someone, you feel affection towards them. **3** If you care for someone, you look after them.
▶ NOUN **4** Care is concern or worry. **5** Care of someone or something is treatment for them or looking after them EG *the care of the elderly*. **6** If you do something with care, you do it with close attention.

career careers careering careered
NOUN **1** the series of jobs that someone has in life, usually in the same occupation EG *a career in insurance*. ▶ VERB **2** To career somewhere is to move very quickly, often out of control EG *His car careered off the road*.

carefree
ADJECTIVE having no worries or responsibilities.

careful
ADJECTIVE **1** acting sensibly and with care EG *Be careful what you say to him*. **2** complete and well done EG *It needs very careful planning*.
carefully ADVERB

▣ (sense 1) cautious, prudent

careless
ADJECTIVE **1** done badly without enough attention EG *careless driving*. **2** relaxed and unconcerned EG *careless laughter*.
carelessly ADVERB, **carelessness** NOUN
▣ (sense 1) slapdash, sloppy

caress caresses caressing caressed
VERB **1** If you caress someone, you stroke them gently and affectionately. ▶ NOUN **2** a gentle, affectionate stroke.
▣ (sense 1) fondle, stroke

caretaker caretakers
NOUN **1** a person who looks after a large building such as a school.
▶ ADJECTIVE **2** having an important position for a short time until a new person is appointed EG *O'Leary was named caretaker manager*.

cargo cargoes
NOUN the goods carried on a ship or plane.

Caribbean
NOUN The Caribbean consists of the Caribbean Sea east of Central America and the islands in it.

caricature caricatures caricaturing caricatured
NOUN **1** a drawing or description of someone that exaggerates striking parts of their appearance or personality. ▶ VERB **2** To caricature someone is to give a caricature of them.

carjack carjacks carjacking carjacked
VERB If a car is carjacked, its driver is attacked and robbed, or the car is stolen.

carnage
Said "**kahr**-nij" NOUN Carnage is the violent killing of large numbers of people.

carnal
ADJECTIVE; A FORMAL WORD sexual and sensual rather than spiritual EG *carnal pleasure*.

carnation carnations
NOUN a plant with a long stem and white, pink, or red flowers.

carnival carnivals
NOUN a public festival with music, processions, and dancing.

carnivore carnivores
NOUN an animal that eats meat.
carnivorous ADJECTIVE

carol carols
NOUN a religious song sung at Christmas time.

carousel carousels
Said "kar-ros-sel" NOUN a merry-go-round.

carp carps carping carped
NOUN 1 a large edible freshwater fish. ▶ VERB 2 To carp means to complain about unimportant things.

carpel carpels
NOUN the seed-bearing female part of a flower.

carpenter carpenters
NOUN a person who makes and repairs wooden structures.
carpentry NOUN
🏛 from Latin *carpentarius* meaning 'wagon-maker'

carpet carpets carpeting carpeted
NOUN 1 a thick covering for a floor, usually made of a material like wool. ▶ VERB 2 To carpet a floor means to cover it with a carpet.

carriage carriages
NOUN 1 one of the separate sections of a passenger train. 2 an old-fashioned vehicle for carrying passengers, usually pulled by horses. 3 a machine part that moves and supports another part EG *a typewriter carriage.* 4 Someone's carriage is the way they hold their head and body when they move.

carriageway carriageways
NOUN one of the sides of a road which traffic travels along in one direction only.

carrier carriers

NOUN 1 a vehicle that is used for carrying things EG *a troop carrier.* 2 A carrier of a germ or disease is a person or animal that can pass it on to others.

carrier bag carrier bags
NOUN a bag made of plastic or paper, which is used for carrying shopping.

carrion
NOUN Carrion is the decaying flesh of dead animals.

carrot carrots
NOUN a long, thin orange root vegetable.

carry carries carrying carried
VERB 1 To carry something is to hold it and take it somewhere. 2 When a vehicle carries people, they travel in it. 3 A person or animal that carries a germ can pass it on to other people or animals EG *I still carry the disease.* 4 If a sound carries, it can be heard far away EG *Jake's voice carried over the cheering.* 5 In a meeting, if a proposal is carried, it is accepted by a majority of the people there.
= (sense 2) bear, convey, take
carry away VERB If you are carried away, you are so excited by something that you do not behave sensibly.
carry on VERB To carry on doing something means to continue doing it.
carry out VERB To carry something out means to do it and complete it EG *The conversion was carried out by a local builder.*

cart carts
NOUN a vehicle with wheels, used to carry goods and often pulled by horses or cattle.

cartilage
NOUN Cartilage is a strong, flexible substance found around the joints and in the nose and ears.

carton cartons
NOUN a cardboard or plastic container.

A
B
C
D
E
F
G
H
I
J
K
L
M
N
O
P
Q
R
S
T
U
V
W
X
Y
Z

cartoon cartoons

NOUN **1** a drawing or a series of drawings which are funny or make a point. **2** a film in which the characters and scenes are drawn.
cartoonist NOUN
▣ from Italian *cartone* meaning 'sketch on stiff paper'

cartridge cartridges

NOUN **1** a tube containing a bullet and an explosive substance, used in guns. **2** a thin plastic tube containing ink that you put in a pen.

cartwheel cartwheels

NOUN an acrobatic movement in which you throw yourself sideways onto one hand and move round in a circle with arms and legs stretched until you land on your feet again.

carve carves carving carved

VERB **1** To carve an object means to cut it out of a substance such as stone or wood. **2** To carve meat means to cut slices from it.

carving carvings

NOUN a carved object.

cascade cascades cascading cascaded

NOUN **1** a waterfall or group of waterfalls. ▶ VERB **2** To cascade means to flow downwards quickly EG *Gallons of water cascaded from the attic.*

case cases

NOUN **1** a particular situation, event, or example EG *a clear case of mistaken identity.* **2** a container for something, or a suitcase EG *a camera case.* **3** Doctors sometimes refer to a patient as a case. **4** Police detectives refer to a crime they are investigating as a case. **5** In an argument, the case for an idea is the reasons used to support it. **6** In law, a case is a trial or other inquiry. **7** In grammar, the case of a noun or pronoun is the form of it which shows its relationship with other words in a sentence EG *the*

accusative case. ▶ PHRASE **8** You say **in case** to explain something that you do because a particular thing might happen EG *I didn't want to shout in case I startled you.* **9** You say **in that case** to show that you are assuming something said before is true EG *In that case we won't do it.*
▤ (sense 1) instance, circumstance(s), situation

casement casements

NOUN a window that opens on hinges at one side.

cash cashes cashing cashed

NOUN **1** Cash is money in notes and coins rather than cheques. ▶ VERB **2** If you cash a cheque, you take it to a bank and exchange it for money.
▣ from Italian *cassa* meaning 'money-box'

cashew cashews

Said "kash-oo" NOUN a curved, edible nut.

cash flow

NOUN Cash flow is the money that a business makes and spends.

cashier cashiers

NOUN the person that customers pay in a shop or get money from in a bank.

cashmere

NOUN Cashmere is very soft, fine wool from goats.

cash register cash registers

NOUN a machine in a shop which records sales, and where the money is kept.

casing casings

NOUN a protective covering for something.

casino casinos

Said "kass-ee-noh" NOUN a place where people go to play gambling games.

cask casks

NOUN a wooden barrel.
▣ from Spanish *casco* meaning 'helmet'

casket caskets

NOUN a small box for jewellery or other valuables.

🔲 from Old French *cassette* meaning 'little box'

casserole casseroles
NOUN a dish made by cooking a mixture of meat and vegetables slowly in an oven; also used to refer to the pot a casserole is cooked in.

🔲 from Old French *casse* meaning 'ladle' or 'dripping pan'

cassette cassettes
NOUN a small flat container with magnetic tape inside, which is used for recording and playing back sounds.

cassette recorder cassette recorders
NOUN a machine used for recording and playing cassettes.

cassock cassocks
NOUN a long robe that is worn by some members of the clergy.

cassowary cassowaries
NOUN a large bird found in Australia with black feathers and a brightly coloured neck. Cassowaries cannot fly.

cast casts casting cast
NOUN 1 all the people who act in a play or film. 2 an object made by pouring liquid into a mould and leaving it to harden EG *the casts of classical sculptures*. 3 a stiff plaster covering put on broken bones to keep them still so that they heal properly. ▶ VERB 4 To cast actors is to choose them for roles in a play or film. 5 When people cast their votes in an election, they vote. 6 To cast something is to throw it. 7 If you cast your eyes somewhere, you look there EG *I cast my eyes down briefly*. 8 To cast an object is to make it by pouring liquid into a mould and leaving it to harden EG *An image of him has been cast in bronze*.

cast off VERB If you cast off, you untie the rope fastening a boat to a harbour or shore.

castanets
PLURAL NOUN Castanets are a Spanish musical instrument consisting of two small round pieces of wood that are clicked together with the fingers.

🔲 from Spanish *castañetas* meaning 'little chestnuts'

castaway castaways
NOUN a person who has been shipwrecked.

caste castes
NOUN 1 one of the four classes into which Hindu society is divided. 2 Caste is a system of social classes decided according to family, wealth, and position.

🔲 from Portuguese *casto* meaning 'pure'

caster sugar or **castor sugar**
NOUN Caster sugar is very fine white sugar used in cooking.

castigate castigates castigating castigated
VERB; A FORMAL WORD To castigate someone is to criticize them severely.

cast iron
NOUN 1 Cast iron is iron which is made into objects by casting. ▶ ADJECTIVE 2 A cast-iron excuse or guarantee is absolutely certain and firm.

castle castles
NOUN 1 a large building with walls or ditches round it to protect it from attack. 2 In chess, a castle is the same as a rook.

cast-off cast-offs
NOUN a piece of outgrown or discarded clothing that has been passed on to someone else.

castor castors; also spelt caster
NOUN a small wheel fitted to furniture so that it can be moved easily.

castor oil
NOUN Castor oil is a thick oil that comes from the seeds of the castor

A
B
C
D
E
F
G
H
I
J
K
L
M
N
O
P
Q
R
S
T
U
V
W
X
Y
Z

A
B
C
D
E
F
G
H
I
J
K
L
M
N
O
P
Q
R
S
T
U
V
W
X
Y
Z

oil plant. It is used as a laxative.

castrate castrates castrating castrated

VERB To castrate a male animal is to remove its testicles so that it can no longer produce sperm.
castration NOUN

casual

ADJECTIVE **1** happening by chance without planning EG *a casual remark.* **2** careless or without interest EG *a casual glance over his shoulder.* **3** Casual clothes are suitable for informal occasions. **4** Casual work is not regular or permanent.
casually ADVERB, **casualness** NOUN
■ (sense 2) careless, nonchalant, offhand

casualty casualties

NOUN a person killed or injured in an accident or war EG *Many of the casualties were office workers.*

casuarina casuarinas

Said "kass-you-a-**rine**-a" NOUN an Australian tree with jointed green branches.

cat cats

NOUN **1** a small furry animal with whiskers, a tail and sharp claws, often kept as a pet. **2** any of the family of mammals that includes lions and tigers.
⌂ from Latin *cattus*

catacomb catacombs

Said "**kat**-a-koom" NOUN Catacombs are underground passages where dead bodies are buried.
⌂ from Latin *catacumbas*, an underground cemetery near Rome

catalogue catalogues cataloguing catalogued

NOUN **1** a book containing pictures and descriptions of goods that you can buy in a shop or through the post. **2** a list of things such as the objects in a museum or the books in a library. ▶ VERB **3** To catalogue a collection of things means to list them in a catalogue.

catalyst catalysts

Said "**kat**-a-list" NOUN **1** something

that causes a change to happen EG *the catalyst which provoked civil war.* **2** a substance that speeds up a chemical reaction without changing itself.

catamaran catamarans

NOUN a sailing boat with two hulls connected to each other.
⌂ from Tamil *kattumaram* meaning 'tied logs'

catapult catapults catapulting catapulted

NOUN **1** a Y-shaped object with a piece of elastic tied between the two top ends used for shooting small stones. ▶ VERB **2** To catapult something is to throw it violently through the air. **3** If someone is catapulted into a situation, they find themselves unexpectedly in that situation EG *Tony has been catapulted into the limelight.*

cataract cataracts

NOUN **1** an area of the lens of someone's eye that has become white instead of clear, so that they cannot see properly. **2** a large waterfall.

catarrh

Said "kat-**tahr**" NOUN Catarrh is a condition in which you get a lot of mucus in your nose and throat.

catastrophe catastrophes

Said "kat-**tass**-trif-fee" NOUN a terrible disaster.
catastrophic ADJECTIVE

catch catches catching caught

VERB **1** If you catch a ball moving in the air, you grasp hold of it when it comes near you. **2** To catch an animal means to trap it EG *I caught ten fish.* **3** When the police catch criminals, they find them and arrest them. **4** If you catch someone doing something they should not be doing, you discover them doing it EG *He caught me playing the church organ.* **5** If you catch a bus or train, you get on it and travel somewhere. **6** If you catch a cold or a disease, you

become infected with it. **7** If something catches on an object, it sticks to it or gets trapped EG *The white fibres caught on the mesh.* ▶ NOUN **8** a hook that fastens or locks a door or window. **9** a problem or hidden complication in something.
☰ (sense 2) capture, snare, trap
☰ (sense 3) apprehend, arrest, capture
☰ (sense 6) contract, develop, go down with

catch on VERB **1** If you catch on to something, you understand it. **2** If something catches on, it becomes popular EG *This drink has never really caught on in New Zealand.*

catch out VERB To catch someone out is to trick them or trap them.

catch up VERB **1** To catch up with someone in front of you is to reach the place where they are by moving slightly faster than them. **2** To catch up with someone is also to reach the same level or standard as them.

catching
ADJECTIVE tending to spread very quickly EG *Measles is catching.*

catchy catchier catchiest
ADJECTIVE attractive and easily remembered EG *a catchy little tune.*

catechism catechisms
Said "kat-ik-kizm" NOUN a set of questions and answers about the main beliefs of a religion.

categorical
ADJECTIVE absolutely certain and direct EG *a categorical denial.*
categorically ADVERB

categorize categorizes
categorizing categorized; also
spelt **categorise**
VERB To categorize things is to arrange them in different categories.

category categories
NOUN a set of things with a particular characteristic in common EG *Occupations can be divided into four categories.*

cater caters catering catered
VERB To cater for people is to provide them with what they need, especially food.

caterer caterers
NOUN a person or business that provides food for parties and groups.

caterpillar caterpillars
NOUN the larva of a butterfly or moth. It looks like a small coloured worm and feeds on plants.
☰ from Old French *catepelose* meaning 'hairy cat'

catharsis catharses
Said "kath-**ar**-siss" NOUN; A FORMAL WORD Catharsis is the release of strong emotions and feelings by expressing them through drama or literature.
☰ from Greek *kathairein* meaning 'to purge' or 'to purify'

cathedral cathedrals
NOUN an important church with a bishop in charge of it.

Catholic Catholics
NOUN OR ADJECTIVE **1** a Roman Catholic. ▶ ADJECTIVE **2** If a person has catholic interests, they have a wide range of interests.
Catholicism NOUN
☰ from Greek *katholikos* meaning 'universal'
☑ When *Catholic* begins with a capital letter, it refers to the religion. When it begins with a small letter, it means 'covering a wide range'.

cattle
PLURAL NOUN Cattle are cows and bulls kept by farmers.

catty cattier cattiest
ADJECTIVE unpleasant and spiteful.
cattiness NOUN

catwalk catwalks
NOUN a narrow pathway that people walk along, for example over a stage.

Caucasian Caucasians
Said "kaw-**kayz**-yn" NOUN a person

A
B
C
D
E
F
G
H
I
J
K
L
M
N
O
P
Q
R
S
T
U
V
W
X
Y
Z

belonging to the race of people with fair or light-brown skin.

🏛 from *Caucasia*, a region in the former USSR

caught

the past tense and past participle of catch.

cauldron cauldrons

NOUN a large, round metal cooking pot, especially one that sits over a fire.

cauliflower cauliflowers

NOUN a large, round, white vegetable surrounded by green leaves.

cause causes causing caused

NOUN **1** The cause of something is the thing that makes it happen EG *the most common cause of back pain.* **2** an aim or principle which a group of people are working for EG *dedication to the cause of peace.* **3** If you have cause for something, you have a reason for it EG *They gave us no cause to believe that.* ▶ VERB **4** To cause something is to make it happen EG *This can cause delays.*

causal ADJECTIVE

causeway causeways

NOUN a raised path or road across water or marshland.

🏛 from Latin *calciatus* meaning 'paved with limestone'

caustic

ADJECTIVE **1** A caustic chemical can destroy substances EG *caustic liquids such as acids.* **2** bitter or sarcastic EG *your caustic sense of humour.*

caution cautions cautioning cautioned

NOUN **1** Caution is great care which you take to avoid danger EG *You will need to proceed with caution.* **2** a warning EG *Sutton was let off with a caution.* ▶ VERB **3** If someone cautions you, they warn you, usually not to do something again EG *A man has been cautioned by police.*

cautionary ADJECTIVE

cautious

ADJECTIVE acting very carefully to avoid danger EG *a cautious approach.*

cautiously ADVERB

cavalcade cavalcades

NOUN a procession of people on horses or in cars or in carriages.

cavalier

Said "kav-val-**eer**" ADJECTIVE arrogant and behaving without sensitivity EG *a cavalier attitude to women.*

cavalry

NOUN The cavalry is the part of an army that uses armoured vehicles or horses.

cave caves caving caved

NOUN **1** a large hole in rock, that is underground or in the side of a cliff. ▶ VERB **2** If a roof caves in, it collapses inwards.

caveman cavemen

NOUN Cavemen were people who lived in caves in prehistoric times.

cavern caverns

NOUN a large cave.

cavernous

ADJECTIVE large, deep, and hollow EG *a cavernous warehouse.*

caviar or **caviare**

Said "kav-vee-**ar**" NOUN Caviar is the tiny salted eggs of a fish called the sturgeon.

cavity cavities

NOUN a small hole in something solid EG *There were dark cavities in his back teeth.*

cavort cavorts cavorting cavorted

VERB When people cavort, they jump around excitedly.

caw caws cawing cawed

VERB When a crow or rook caws, it makes a harsh sound.

cc

an abbreviation for 'cubic centimetres'.

CD

an abbreviation for 'compact disc'.

CD-ROM

CD-ROM is a method of storing video, sound, or text on a compact disc which can be played on a computer using a laser. CD-ROM is an abbreviation for 'Compact Disc Read-Only Memory'.

cease ceases ceasing ceased
VERB **1** If something ceases, it stops happening. **2** If you cease to do something, or cease doing it, you stop doing it.

cease-fire cease-fires
NOUN an agreement between groups that are fighting each other to stop for a period and discuss peace.

ceaseless
ADJECTIVE going on without stopping EG *the ceaseless movement of the streets.*
ceaselessly ADVERB

cedar cedars
NOUN a large evergreen tree with wide branches and needle-shaped leaves.

cede cedes ceding ceded
Said "seed" VERB To cede something is to give it up to someone else EG *Haiti was ceded to France in 1697.*

ceiling ceilings
NOUN the top inside surface of a room.

celebrate celebrates celebrating celebrated
VERB **1** If you celebrate or celebrate something, you do something special and enjoyable because of it EG *a party to celebrate the end of the exams.* **2** When a priest celebrates Mass, he performs the ceremonies of the Mass.
celebration NOUN, **celebratory** ADJECTIVE

celebrated
ADJECTIVE famous EG *the celebrated Italian mountaineer.*

celebrity celebrities
NOUN a famous person.

celery
NOUN Celery is a vegetable with long pale green stalks.

celestial
Said "sil-lest-yal" ADJECTIVE; A FORMAL WORD concerning the sky or heaven EG *The telescope is pointed at a celestial object.*

celibate
Said "sel-lib-bit" ADJECTIVE Someone who is celibate does not marry or have sex.
celibacy NOUN

cell cells
NOUN **1** In biology, a cell is the smallest part of an animal or plant that can exist by itself. Each cell contains a nucleus. **2** a small room where a prisoner is kept in a prison or police station. **3** a small group of people set up to work together as part of a larger organization.

cellar cellars
NOUN a room underneath a building, often used to store wine.

cello cellos
Said "chel-loh" NOUN a large musical stringed instrument which you play sitting down, holding the instrument upright with your knees.
cellist NOUN

Cellophane
NOUN; A TRADEMARK Cellophane is thin, transparent plastic material used to wrap food or other things to protect them.

cellular
ADJECTIVE Cellular means relating to the cells of animals or plants.

celluloid
Said "sel-yul-loyd" NOUN Celluloid is a type of plastic which was once used to make photographic film.

Celsius
Said "sel-see-yuss" NOUN Celsius is a scale for measuring temperature in which water freezes at 0 degrees (0°C) and boils at 100 degrees (100°C). Celsius is the same as 'Centigrade'.

Celtic
Said "kel-tik" ADJECTIVE A Celtic language is one of a group of languages that includes Gaelic and Welsh.

cement cements cementing cemented

A B C D E F G H I J K L M N O P Q R S T U V W X Y Z

NOUN **1** Cement is a fine powder made from limestone and clay, which is mixed with sand and water to make concrete. ▶ VERB **2** To cement things is to stick them together with cement or cover them with cement. **3** Something that cements a relationship makes it stronger EG *to cement relations between them.*

cemetery cemeteries
NOUN an area of land where dead people are buried.

cenotaph cenotaphs
Said "sen-not-ahf" NOUN a monument built in memory of dead people, especially soldiers buried elsewhere.
🏛 from Greek *kenos* + *taphos* meaning 'empty tomb'

censor censors censoring censored
NOUN **1** a person officially appointed to examine books or films and to ban parts that are considered unsuitable. ▶ VERB **2** If someone censors a book or film, they cut or ban parts of it that are considered unsuitable for the public.
censorship NOUN

censure censures censuring censured
Said "sen-sher" NOUN **1** Censure is strong disapproval of something. ▶ VERB **2** To censure someone is to criticize them severely.

census censuses
NOUN an official survey of the population of a country.

cent cents
NOUN a unit of currency in the USA and in some other countries. In the USA, a cent is worth one hundredth of a dollar.

centaur centaurs
Said "sen-tawr" NOUN a creature in Greek mythology with the top half of a man and the lower body and legs of a horse.

centenary centenaries
Said "sen-teen-er-ee" NOUN the 100th anniversary of something.

centi-
PREFIX 'Centi-' is used to form words that have 'hundred' as part of their meaning EG *centimetre.*

Centigrade
Centigrade is another name for Celsius.
☑ Scientists say and write *Celsius* rather than *Centigrade.*

centilitre centilitres
NOUN a unit of liquid volume equal to one hundredth of a litre.

centimetre centimetres
NOUN a unit of length equal to ten millimetres or one hundredth of a metre.

centipede centipedes
NOUN a long, thin insect with many pairs of legs.

central
ADJECTIVE **1** in or near the centre of an object or area EG *central ceiling lights.* **2** main or most important EG *the central idea of this work.*
centrally ADVERB, **centrality** NOUN

Central America
NOUN Central America is another name for the Isthmus of Panama, the area of land joining North America to South America.

central heating
NOUN Central heating is a system of heating a building in which water or air is heated in a tank and travels through pipes and radiators round the building.

centralize centralizes centralizing centralized; also spelt centralise
VERB To centralize a system is to bring the organization of it under the control of one central group.
centralization NOUN

centre centres centring centred
NOUN **1** the middle of an object or area. **2** a building where people go for activities, meetings, or help EG *a health centre.* **3** Someone or something that is the centre of attention attracts a lot of attention.

▶ VERB **4** To centre something is to move it so that it is balanced or at the centre of something else. **5** If something centres on or around a particular thing, that thing is the main subject of attention EG *The discussion centred on his request.*
■ (sense 1) heart, middle

centrifugal
Said "sen-trif-**yoo**-gl" ADJECTIVE In physics, centrifugal force is the force that makes rotating objects move outwards.
🏛 from Latin *centrum* + *fugere* meaning 'to flee from the centre'

centripetal
Said "sen-**trip**-pee-tl" ADJECTIVE In physics, centripetal force is the force that makes rotating objects move inwards.
🏛 from Latin *centrum* + *petere* meaning 'to seek the centre'

centurion centurions
NOUN a Roman officer in charge of a hundred soldiers.

century centuries
NOUN **1** a period of one hundred years. **2** In cricket, a century is one hundred runs scored by a batsman.

ceramic ceramics
Said "sir-**ram**-mik" NOUN **1** Ceramic is a hard material made by baking clay to a very high temperature. **2** Ceramics is the art of making objects out of clay.

cereal cereals
NOUN **1** a food made from grain, often eaten with milk for breakfast. **2** a plant that produces edible grain, such as wheat or oats.
🏛 from Latin *cerealis* meaning 'concerning the growing of grain'

cerebral
Said "**ser**-reb-ral" ADJECTIVE; A FORMAL WORD relating to the brain EG *a cerebral haemorrhage.*

cerebral palsy
NOUN Cerebral palsy is an illness caused by damage to a baby's brain, which makes its muscles and limbs very weak.

ceremonial
ADJECTIVE relating to a ceremony EG *ceremonial dress.*
ceremonially ADVERB

ceremony ceremonies
NOUN **1** a set of formal actions performed at a special occasion or important public event EG *his recent coronation ceremony.* **2** Ceremony is very formal and polite behaviour EG *He hung up without ceremony.*

certain
ADJECTIVE **1** definite and with no doubt at all EG *He is certain to be in Italy.* **2** You use 'certain' to refer to a specific person or thing EG *certain aspects of the job.* **3** You use 'certain' to suggest that a quality is noticeable but not obvious EG *There's a certain resemblance to Joe.*

certainly
ADVERB **1** without doubt EG *My boss was certainly interested.* **2** of course EG *'Will you be there?' — 'Certainly'.*

certainty certainties
NOUN **1** Certainty is the state of being certain. **2** something that is known without doubt EG *There are no certainties and no guarantees.*

certificate certificates
NOUN a document stating particular facts, for example of someone's birth or death EG *a marriage certificate.*

certify certifies certifying certified
VERB **1** To certify something means to declare formally that it is true EG *certifying the cause of death.* **2** To certify someone means to declare officially that they are insane.

cervix cervixes or cervices
NOUN; A TECHNICAL WORD the entrance to the womb at the top of the vagina.
cervical ADJECTIVE

cessation
NOUN; A FORMAL WORD The cessation of something is the stopping of it EG *a swift cessation of hostilities.*

cf.

cf. means 'compare'. It is written after something in a text to mention something else which the the reader should compare with what has just been written.

CFC CFCs
NOUN CFCs are manufactured chemicals that are used in aerosol sprays. They damage the ozone layer. CFC is an abbreviation for 'chlorofluorocarbon'.

chaff
NOUN Chaff is the outer parts of grain separated from the seeds by beating.

chaffinch chaffinches
NOUN a small European bird with black and white wings.

chagrin
Said "**shag-rin**" NOUN; A FORMAL WORD Chagrin is a feeling of annoyance or disappointment.

chain chains chaining chained
NOUN **1** a number of metal rings connected together in a line EG *a bicycle chain*. **2** a number of things in a series or connected to each other EG *a chain of shops*. ▶ VERB **3** If you chain one thing to another, you fasten them together with a chain EG *They had chained themselves to railings*.

chain saw chain saws
NOUN a large saw with teeth fixed in a chain that is driven round by a motor.

chain-smoke chain-smokes chain-smoking chain-smoked
VERB To chain-smoke is to smoke cigarettes continually.

chair chairs chairing chaired
NOUN **1** a seat with a back and four legs for one person. **2** the person in charge of a meeting who decides when each person may speak. ▶ VERB **3** The person who chairs a meeting is in charge of it.

chair lift chair lifts
NOUN a line of chairs that hang from a moving cable and carry people up and down a mountain.

chairman chairmen
NOUN **1** the person in charge of a meeting who decides when each person may speak. **2** the head of a company or committee.
chairperson NOUN, **chairwoman** NOUN, **chairmanship** NOUN
☑ Some people don't like to use *chairman* when talking about a woman. You can use *chair* or *chairperson* to talk about a man or a woman.

chalet chalets
Said "**shall-lay**" NOUN a wooden house with a sloping roof, especially in a mountain area or a holiday camp.

chalice chalices
Said "**chal-liss**" NOUN a gold or silver cup used in Christian churches to hold the Communion wine.

chalk chalks chalking chalked
NOUN **1** Chalk is a soft white rock. Small sticks of chalk are used for writing or drawing on a blackboard. ▶ VERB **2** To chalk up a result is to achieve it EG *He chalked up his first win*.
chalky ADJECTIVE

challenge challenges challenging challenged
NOUN **1** something that is new and exciting but requires a lot of effort EG *It's a new challenge at the right time in my career*. **2** a suggestion from someone to compete with them. **3** A challenge to something is a questioning of whether it is correct or true EG *a challenge to authority*. ▶ VERB **4** If someone challenges you, they suggest that you compete with them in some way. **5** If you challenge something, you question whether it is correct or true.
challenger NOUN, **challenging** ADJECTIVE
▣ (sense 5) dispute, question

chamber chambers
NOUN **1** a large room, especially one used for formal meetings EG *the Council Chamber*. **2** a group of

A
B
C
D
E
F
G
H
I
J
K
L
M
N
O
P
Q
R
S
T
U
V
W
X
Y
Z

people chosen to decide laws or administrative matters. **3** a hollow place or compartment inside something, especially inside an animal's body or inside a gun EG *the chambers of the heart*.

chambermaid chambermaids
NOUN a woman who cleans and tidies rooms in a hotel.

chameleon chameleons
Said "kam-**mee**-lee-on" NOUN a lizard which is able to change the colour of its skin to match the colour of its surroundings.
📖 from Greek *khamai* + *leōn* meaning 'ground lion'

chamois leather chamois leathers
Said "**sham**-mee" NOUN a soft leather cloth used for polishing.

champagne champagnes
Said "sham-**pain**" NOUN Champagne is a sparkling white wine made in France.

champion champions championing championed
NOUN **1** a person who wins a competition. **2** someone who supports or defends a cause or principle EG *a champion of women's causes*. ▶ VERB **3** Someone who champions a cause or principle supports or defends it.
📖 from Latin *campus* meaning 'battlefield'

championship championships
NOUN a competition to find the champion of a sport.

chance chances chancing chanced
NOUN **1** The chance of something happening is how possible or likely it is EG *There's a chance of rain later*. **2** an opportunity to do something EG *Your chance to be a soap star!* **3** a possibility that something dangerous or unpleasant may happen EG *Don't take chances, he's armed*. **4** Chance is also the way things happen unexpectedly without being planned EG *I only found out by chance*. ▶ VERB **5** If you chance something, you try it

although you are taking a risk.
🟦 (sense 4) accident, coincidence, luck

chancellor chancellors
NOUN **1** the head of government in some European countries. **2** In Britain, the Chancellor is the Chancellor of the Exchequer. **3** the honorary head of a university.

Chancellor of the Exchequer
NOUN In Britain, the minister responsible for finance and taxes.

chandelier chandeliers
Said "shan-del-**leer**" NOUN an ornamental light fitting which hangs from the ceiling.

change changes changing changed
NOUN **1** a difference or alteration in something EG *Steven soon noticed a change in Penny's attitude*. **2** a replacement of something by something else EG *a change of clothes*. **3** Change is money you get back when you have paid more than the actual price of something. ▶ VERB **4** When something changes or when you change it, it becomes different EG *It changed my life*. **5** If you change something, you exchange it for something else. **6** When you change, you put on different clothes. **7** To change money means to exchange it for smaller coins of the same total value, or to exchange it for foreign currency.

changeable
ADJECTIVE likely to change all the time.
🟦 erratic, inconstant, variable

changeover changeovers
NOUN a change from one system or activity to another EG *the changeover between day and night*.

channel channels channelling channelled
NOUN **1** a wavelength used to receive programmes broadcast by a television or radio station; also the station itself EG *I was watching the*

other channel. **2** a passage along which water flows or along which something is carried. **3** The Channel or the English Channel is the stretch of sea between England and France. **4** a method of achieving something EG *We have tried to do things through the right channels.* ▶ VERB **5** To channel something such as money or energy means to direct it in a particular way EG *Their efforts are being channelled into worthy causes.*

chant chants chanting chanted
NOUN **1** a group of words repeated over and over again EG *a rousing chant.* **2** a religious song sung on only a few notes. ▶ VERB **3** If people chant a group of words, they repeat them over and over again EG *Crowds chanted his name.*

Chanukah
another spelling of **Hanukkah**.

chaos
Said "**kay**-oss" NOUN Chaos is a state of complete disorder and confusion.
chaotic ADJECTIVE

chap chaps chapping chapped
NOUN **1** AN INFORMAL USE a man. ▶ VERB **2** If your skin chaps, it becomes dry and cracked, usually as a result of cold or wind.

chapel chapels
NOUN **1** a section of a church or cathedral with its own altar. **2** a type of small church.
🏛 from Latin *capella* meaning 'small cloak'; originally used of the place where St Martin's cloak was kept as a relic

chaperone chaperones
Said "**shap**-per-rone"; also spelt **chaperon**
NOUN an older woman who accompanies a young unmarried woman on social occasions, or any person who accompanies a group of younger people.

chaplain chaplains
NOUN a member of the Christian clergy who regularly works in a hospital, school, or prison.
chaplaincy NOUN

chapter chapters
NOUN **1** one of the parts into which a book is divided. **2** a particular period in someone's life or in history.

char chars charring charred
VERB If something chars, it gets partly burned and goes black.
charred ADJECTIVE

character characters
NOUN **1** all the qualities which combine to form the personality or atmosphere of a person or place. **2** A person or place that has character has an interesting, attractive, or admirable quality EG *an inn of great character and simplicity.* **3** The characters in a film, play, or book are the people in it. **4** a person EG *an odd character.* **5** a letter, number, or other written symbol.
▤ (sense 1) nature, personality, quality

characteristic characteristics
NOUN **1** a quality that is typical of a particular person or thing EG *Silence is the characteristic of the place.*
▶ ADJECTIVE **2** Characteristic means typical of a particular person or thing EG *Two things are very characteristic of his driving.*
characteristically ADVERB

characterize characterizes characterizing characterized; also spelt **characterise**
VERB A quality that characterizes something is typical of it EG *a condition characterized by muscle stiffness.*

characterless
ADJECTIVE dull and uninteresting EG *a tiny characterless flat.*

charade charades
Said "shar-**rahd**" NOUN a ridiculous and unnecessary activity or pretence.
🏛 from Provençal *charrado*

meaning 'chat'

charcoal

NOUN Charcoal is a black form of carbon made by burning wood without air, used as a fuel and also for drawing.

charge charges charging charged

VERB **1** If someone charges you money, they ask you to pay it for something you have bought or received EG *The company charged 150 pounds on each loan.* **2** To charge someone means to accuse them formally of having committed a crime. **3** To charge a battery means to pass an electrical current through it to make it store electricity. **4** To charge somewhere means to rush forward, often to attack someone EG *The rhino charged at her.* ▶ NOUN **5** the price that you have to pay for something. **6** a formal accusation that a person is guilty of a crime and has to go to court. **7** To have charge or be in charge of someone or something means to be responsible for them and be in control of them. **8** an explosive put in a gun or other weapon. **9** An electrical charge is the amount of electricity that something carries.

charger chargers

NOUN a device for charging or recharging batteries.

chariot chariots

NOUN a two-wheeled open vehicle pulled by horses.

charisma

Said "kar-**riz**-ma" NOUN Charisma is a special ability to attract or influence people by your personality.
charismatic ADJECTIVE

charity charities

NOUN **1** an organization that raises money to help people who are ill, poor, or disabled. **2** Charity is money or other help given to poor, disabled, or ill people EG *to help raise money for charity.* **3** Charity is also a kind, sympathetic attitude towards people.
charitable ADJECTIVE

charlatan charlatans

Said "**shar**-lat-tn" NOUN someone who pretends to have skill or knowledge that they do not really have.

charm charms charming charmed

NOUN **1** Charm is an attractive and pleasing quality that some people and things have EG *a man of great personal charm.* **2** a small ornament worn on a bracelet. **3** a magical spell or an object that is supposed to bring good luck. ▶ VERB **4** If you charm someone, you use your charm to please them.

charmer charmers

NOUN someone who uses their charm to influence people.

charming

ADJECTIVE very pleasant and attractive EG *a rather charming man.*
charmingly ADVERB

chart charts charting charted

NOUN **1** a diagram or table showing information EG *He noted the score on his chart.* **2** a map of the sea or stars. ▶ VERB **3** If you chart something, you observe and record it carefully.

charter charters chartering chartered

NOUN **1** a document stating the rights or aims of a group or organization, often written by the government EG *the new charter for commuters.* ▶ VERB **2** To charter transport such as a plane or boat is to hire it for private use.
chartered ADJECTIVE

chase chases chasing chased

VERB **1** If you chase someone or something, you run or go after them in order to catch them or drive them away. ▶ NOUN **2** the activity of chasing or hunting someone or something EG *a high-speed car chase.*
▦ (sense 1) hunt, pursue

chasm chasms

A
B
C
D
E
F
G
H
I
J
K
L
M
N
O
P
Q
R
S
T
U
V
W
X
Y
Z

Said "kazm" NOUN **1** a deep crack in the earth's surface. **2** a very large difference between two ideas or groups of people EG *the chasm between rich and poor in America.*

chassis
Said "shas-ee" NOUN the frame on which a vehicle is built.
☑ The plural of *chassis* is also *chassis.*

chaste
Said "chayst" ADJECTIVE; AN OLD-FASHIONED USE not having sex with anyone outside marriage.
chastity NOUN

chastise chastises chastising chastised
VERB; A FORMAL WORD If someone chastises you, they criticize you or punish you for something you have done.

chat chats chatting chatted
NOUN **1** a friendly talk with someone, usually about things that are not very important. ▶ VERB **2** When people chat, they talk to each other in a friendly way.
☰ (senses 1 & 2) gossip, natter, talk
chat up VERB; AN INFORMAL USE If you chat up someone, you talk to them in a friendly way, because you are attracted to them.

chateau chateaux
Said "shat-toe" NOUN a large country house or castle in France.

chatter chatters chattering chattered
VERB **1** When people chatter, they talk very fast. **2** If your teeth are chattering, they are knocking together and making a clicking noise because you are cold. ▶ NOUN **3** Chatter is a lot of fast unimportant talk.

chatty chattier chattiest
ADJECTIVE talkative and friendly.

chauffeur chauffeurs
Said "show-fur" NOUN a person whose job is to drive another person's car.

chauvinist chauvinists
NOUN **1** a person who thinks their country is always right. **2** A male chauvinist is a man who believes that women are superior to women.
chauvinistic ADJECTIVE, **chauvinism** NOUN

cheap cheaper cheapest
ADJECTIVE **1** Something that is cheap costs very little money, and is sometimes of poor quality. **2** A cheap joke or cheap remark is unfair and unkind.
cheaply ADVERB
☰ (sense 1) inexpensive, reasonable

cheat cheats cheating cheated
VERB **1** If someone cheats, they do wrong or unfair things to win or get something that they want. **2** If you are cheated of or out of something, you do not get what you are entitled to. ▶ NOUN **3** a person who cheats.
☰ (sense 1) con, deceive, swindle

check checks checking checked
VERB **1** To check something is to examine it in order to make sure that everything is all right. **2** To check the growth or spread of something is to make it stop EG *a policy to check fast population growth.* ▶ NOUN **3** an inspection to make sure that everything is all right. **4** Checks are different coloured squares which form a pattern. ▶ PHRASE **5** If you keep something in check, you keep it under control EG *She kept her emotions in check.* ▶ ADJECTIVE **6** Check or checked means marked with a pattern of squares EG *check design.*
check out VERB If you check something out, you inspect it and find out whether everything about it is right.

checkmate
NOUN In chess, checkmate is a situation where one player cannot stop their king being captured and so loses the game.
🏛 from Arabic *shah mat* meaning 'the King is dead'

checkout checkouts
NOUN a counter in a supermarket where the customers pay for their goods.

checkpoint checkpoints
NOUN a place where traffic has to stop in order to be checked.

checkup checkups
NOUN an examination by a doctor to see if you are healthy.

cheek cheeks
NOUN **1** Your cheeks are the sides of your face below your eyes. **2** Cheek is speech or behaviour that is rude or disrespectful EG *an expression of sheer cheek*.
(sense 2) impertinence, impudence, insolence

cheeky cheekier cheekiest
ADJECTIVE rather rude and disrespectful.

cheer cheers cheering cheered
VERB **1** When people cheer, they shout with approval or in order to show support for a person or team.
▶ NOUN **2** a shout of approval or support.
cheer up VERB When you cheer up, you feel more cheerful.

cheerful
ADJECTIVE **1** happy and in good spirits EG *I had never seen her so cheerful.* **2** bright and pleasant-looking EG *a cheerful and charming place.*
cheerfully ADVERB, **cheerfulness** NOUN

cheerio
INTERJECTION Cheerio is a friendly way of saying goodbye.

cheery cheerier cheeriest
ADJECTIVE happy and cheerful EG *He gave me a cheery nod.*

cheese cheeses
NOUN a hard or creamy food made from milk.

cheesecake cheesecakes
NOUN a dessert made of biscuit covered with cream cheese.

cheetah cheetahs
NOUN a wild animal like a large cat with black spots.

from Sanskrit *citra* + *kaya* meaning 'speckled body'

chef chefs
NOUN a head cook in a restaurant or hotel.

chemical chemicals
NOUN **1** Chemicals are substances manufactured by chemistry.
▶ ADJECTIVE **2** involved in chemistry or using chemicals EG *chemical weapons.*
chemically ADVERB

chemist chemists
NOUN **1** a person who is qualified to make up drugs and medicines prescribed by a doctor. **2** a shop where medicines and cosmetics are sold. **3** a scientist who does research in chemistry.

chemistry
NOUN Chemistry is the scientific study of substances and the ways in which they change when they are combined with other substances.

chemotherapy
Said "keem-oh-**ther**-a-pee" NOUN Chemotherapy is a way of treating diseases such as cancer by using chemicals.

cheque cheques
NOUN a printed form on which you write an amount of money that you have to pay. You sign the cheque and your bank pays the money from your account.

chequered
Said "**chek**-kerd" ADJECTIVE **1** covered with a pattern of squares. **2** A chequered career is a varied career that has both good and bad parts.

cherish cherishes cherishing cherished
VERB **1** If you cherish something, you care deeply about it and want to keep it or look after it lovingly. **2** If you cherish a memory or hope, you have it in your mind and care deeply about it EG *I cherish the good memories I have of him.*

A B C D E F G H I J K L M N O P Q R S T U V W X Y Z

cherry cherries

NOUN **1** a small, juicy fruit with a red or black skin and a hard stone in the centre. **2** a tree that produces cherries.

cherub cherubs or cherubim

NOUN an angel, shown in pictures as a plump, naked child with wings. **cherubic** ADJECTIVE

chess

NOUN Chess is a board game for two people in which each player has 16 pieces and tries to move his or her pieces so that the other player's king cannot escape.

chest chests

NOUN **1** the front part of your body between your shoulders and your waist. **2** a large wooden box with a hinged lid.

chestnut chestnuts

NOUN **1** Chestnuts are reddish-brown nuts that grow inside a prickly green outer covering. **2** a tree that produces these nuts. ▶ ADJECTIVE **3** Something that is chestnut is reddish-brown.

chest of drawers chests of drawers

NOUN a piece of furniture with drawers in it, used for storing clothes.

chew chews chewing chewed

VERB When you chew something, you use your teeth to break it up in your mouth before swallowing it. **chewy** ADJECTIVE

chewing gum

NOUN Chewing gum is a kind of sweet that you chew for a long time, but which you do not swallow.

chic

Said "**sheek**" ADJECTIVE elegant and fashionable EG a chic restaurant.

chick chicks

NOUN a young bird.

chicken chickens chickening chickened

NOUN **1** a bird kept on a farm for its eggs and meat; also the meat of this bird EG roast chicken. ▶ VERB **2** AN INFORMAL USE If you chicken out of something, you do not do it because you are afraid.

chickenpox

NOUN Chickenpox is an illness which produces a fever and blister-like spots on the skin.

chicory

NOUN Chicory is a plant with bitter leaves that are used in salads.

chide chides chiding chided

VERB; AN OLD-FASHIONED WORD To chide someone is to tell them off.

chief chiefs

NOUN **1** the leader of a group or organization. ▶ ADJECTIVE **2** most important EG the chief source of oil. **chiefly** ADVERB

chieftain chieftains

NOUN the leader of a tribe or clan.

chiffon

Said "**shif-fon**" NOUN Chiffon is a very thin lightweight cloth made of silk or nylon.

chihuahua chihuahuas

Said "**chi-wah-wah**" NOUN a breed of very small dog with short hair and pointed ears.

chilblain chilblains

NOUN a sore, itchy swelling on a finger or toe.

child children

NOUN **1** a young person who is not yet an adult. **2** Someone's child is their son or daughter.
■ (sense 1) baby, kid, youngster

childhood childhoods

NOUN Someone's childhood is the time when they are a child.

childish

ADJECTIVE immature and foolish EG I don't have time for childish arguments. **childishly** ADVERB, **childishness** NOUN
■ immature, infantile, juvenile
✔ If you call someone childish, you think they are immature or foolish. If you call them childlike, you think they are innocent like a young

child.

childless
ADJECTIVE having no children.

childlike
ADJECTIVE like a child in appearance or behaviour EG *childlike enthusiasm*.

childminder childminders
NOUN a person who is qualified and paid to look after other people's children while they are at work.

Chilean Chileans
ADJECTIVE 1 belonging or relating to Chile. ▶ NOUN 2 someone who comes from Chile.

chill chills chilling chilled
VERB 1 To chill something is to make it cold EG *Chill the cheesecake*. 2 If something chills you, it makes you feel worried or frightened EG *The thought chilled her*. ▶ NOUN 3 a feverish cold. 4 a feeling of cold EG *the chill of the night air*.

chilli chillies
NOUN the red or green seed pod of a type of pepper which has a very hot, spicy taste.

chilly chillier chilliest
ADJECTIVE 1 rather cold EG *the chilly November breeze*. 2 unfriendly and without enthusiasm EG *a chilly reception*.

chilly-bin chilly-bins
NOUN; AN INFORMAL WORD In New Zealand English, a container for keeping food and drink cool that can be carried.

chime chimes chiming chimed
VERB When a bell chimes, it makes a clear ringing sound.

chimney chimneys
NOUN a vertical pipe or other hollow structure above a fireplace or furnace through which smoke from a fire escapes.
🏛 from Greek *kaminos* meaning 'fireplace' or 'oven'

chimpanzee chimpanzees
NOUN a small ape with dark fur that lives in forests in Africa.

chin chins
NOUN the part of your face below your mouth.

china chinas
NOUN 1 China is items like cups, saucers, and plates made from very fine clay. 2 AN INFORMAL WORD In South African English, a china is a friend.

Chinese
ADJECTIVE 1 belonging or relating to China. ▶ NOUN 2 someone who comes from China. 3 Chinese refers to any of a group of related languages and dialects spoken by Chinese people.

chink chinks
NOUN 1 a small, narrow opening EG *a chink in the roof*. 2 a short, light, ringing sound, like one made by glasses touching each other.

chintz
NOUN Chintz is a type of brightly patterned cotton fabric.
🏛 from Hindi *chint* meaning 'brightly coloured'

chip chips chipping chipped
NOUN 1 Chips are thin strips of fried potato. 2 In electronics, a chip is a tiny piece of silicon inside a computer which is used to form electronic circuits. 3 a small piece broken off an object, or the mark made when a piece breaks off. 4 In some gambling games, chips are counters used to represent money. ▶ VERB 5 If you chip an object, you break a small piece off it.

chipboard
NOUN Chipboard is a material made from wood scraps pressed together into hard sheets.

chipmunk chipmunks
NOUN a small rodent with a striped back.

chiropodist chiropodists
Said "kir-**rop**-pod-dist" NOUN a person whose job is treating people's feet.
chiropody NOUN

chirp chirps chirping chirped

A B C D E F G H I J K L M N O P Q R S T U V W X Y Z

A B C D E F G H I J K L M N O P Q R S T U V W X Y Z

VERB When a bird chirps, it makes a short, high-pitched sound.

chisel chisels chiselling chiselled
NOUN **1** a tool with a long metal blade and a sharp edge at the end which is used for cutting and shaping wood, stone, or metal.
▶ VERB **2** To chisel wood, stone, or metal is to cut or shape it using a chisel.

chivalry
Said "**shiv**-val-ree" NOUN Chivalry is polite and helpful behaviour, especially by men towards women.
chivalrous ADJECTIVE
▥ from Latin *caballarius* meaning 'horseman'

chive chives
NOUN Chives are grasslike hollow leaves that have a mild onion flavour.

chlorine
Said "**klaw**-reen" NOUN Chlorine is a poisonous greenish-yellow gas with a strong, unpleasant smell. It is used as a disinfectant for water, and to make bleach.

chloroform
Said "**klor**-rof-form" NOUN Chloroform is a colourless liquid with a strong, sweet smell used in cleaning products.

chlorophyll
Said "**klor**-rof-fil" NOUN Chlorophyll is a green substance in plants which enables them to use the energy from sunlight in order to grow.

chock-a-block or **chock-full**
ADJECTIVE completely full.

chocolate chocolates
NOUN **1** Chocolate is a sweet food made from cacao seeds. **2** a sweet made of chocolate. ▶ ADJECTIVE **3** dark brown.
▥ from Aztec *xococ* + *atl* meaning 'bitter water'

choice choices
NOUN **1** a range of different things that are available to choose from EG

a wider choice of treatments.
2 something that you choose EG You've made a good choice. **3** Choice is the power or right to choose EG I had no choice.
▤ (sense 1) range, selection, variety

choir choirs
Said "**kwire**" NOUN a group of singers, for example in a church.

choke chokes choking choked
VERB **1** If you choke, you stop being able to breathe properly, usually because something is blocking your windpipe EG *the diner who choked on a fish bone.* **2** If things choke a place, they fill it so much that it is blocked or clogged up EG *The canal was choked with old tyres.*

choko chokos
NOUN a fruit that is shaped like a pear and used as a vegetable in Australia and New Zealand.

cholera
Said "**kol**-ler-ra" NOUN Cholera is a serious disease causing severe diarrhoea and vomiting. It is caused by infected food or water.

cholesterol
Said "kol-**less**-ter-rol" NOUN Cholesterol is a substance found in all animal fats, tissues, and blood.

chook chooks
NOUN; AN INFORMAL WORD In Australian and New Zealand English, a chicken.

choose chooses choosing chose chosen
VERB To choose something is to decide to have it or do it EG *He chose to live in Kenya.*
▤ opt for, pick, select

choosy choosier choosiest
ADJECTIVE fussy and difficult to satisfy EG *You can't be too choosy about jobs.*

chop chops chopping chopped
VERB **1** To chop something is to cut it with quick, heavy strokes using an axe or a knife. ▶ NOUN **2** a small piece of lamb or pork containing a

bone, usually cut from the ribs.

chopper choppers
NOUN; AN INFORMAL WORD a helicopter.

choppy choppier choppiest
ADJECTIVE Choppy water has a lot of waves because it is windy.

chopstick chopsticks
NOUN Chopsticks are a pair of thin sticks used by people in the Far East for eating food.

choral
ADJECTIVE relating to singing by a choir EG *choral music*.

chord chords
NOUN a group of three or more musical notes played together.

chore chores
NOUN an uninteresting job that has to be done EG *the chore of cleaning*.

choreography
Said "kor-ree-og-raf-fee" NOUN Choreography is the art of composing dance steps and movements.
choreographer NOUN

chortle chortles chortling chortled
VERB To chortle is to laugh with amusement.

chorus choruses chorusing chorused
NOUN 1 a large group of singers; also a piece of music for a large group of singers. 2 a part of a song which is repeated after each verse. ▶ VERB 3 If people chorus something, they all say or sing it at the same time.
▨ from Greek *khoros*, the group of actors who gave the commentary in Classical plays

Christ
PROPER NOUN Christ is the name for Jesus. Christians believe that Jesus is the son of God.

christen christens christening christened
VERB When a baby is christened, it is named by a clergyman in a religious ceremony as a sign that it is a member of the Christian

church.

Christian Christians
NOUN 1 a person who believes in Jesus Christ and his teachings.
▶ ADJECTIVE 2 relating to Christ and his teachings EG *the Christian faith*. 3 good, kind, and considerate.
Christianity NOUN

Christian name Christian names
NOUN the name given to someone when they were born or christened.

Christmas Christmases
NOUN the Christian festival celebrating the birth of Christ, falling on December 25th.

chrome
Said "krome" NOUN Chrome is metal plated with chromium, a hard grey metal.

chromosome chromosomes
NOUN In biology, a chromosome is a part of a cell which contains genes that determine the characteristics of an animal or plant.

chronic
Said "kron-nik" ADJECTIVE lasting a very long time or never stopping EG *a chronic illness*.
chronically ADVERB

chronicle chronicles chronicling chronicled
NOUN 1 a record of a series of events described in the order in which they happened. ▶ VERB 2 To chronicle a series of events is to record or describe them in the order in which they happened.

chronological
Said "kron-nol-loj-i-kl" ADJECTIVE arranged in the order in which things happened EG *Tell me the whole story in chronological order*.
chronologically ADVERB

chronology
Said "kron-nol-loj-jee" NOUN The chronology of events is the order in which they happened.
▨ from Greek *khronos* meaning 'time' and *legein* meaning 'to say'

chrysalis chrysalises

Said "**kriss**-sal-liss" NOUN a butterfly or moth when it is developing from being a caterpillar to being a fully grown adult.

chrysanthemum chrysanthemums
Said "kriss-**an**-thim-mum" NOUN a plant with large, brightly coloured flowers.

chubby chubbier chubbiest
ADJECTIVE plump and round EG *his chubby cheeks.*

chuck chucks chucking chucked
VERB; AN INFORMAL WORD To chuck something is to throw it casually.

chuckle chuckles chuckling chuckled
VERB When you chuckle, you laugh quietly.

chug chugs chugging chugged
VERB When a machine or engine chugs, it makes a continuous dull thudding sound.

chum chums
NOUN; AN INFORMAL WORD a friend.

chunk chunks
NOUN a thick piece of something.
■ hunk, lump, piece

chunky chunkier chunkiest
ADJECTIVE Someone who is chunky is broad and heavy but usually short.

church churches
NOUN **1** a building where Christians go for religious services and worship. **2** In the Christian religion, a church is one of the groups with their own particular beliefs, customs, and clergy EG *the Catholic Church.*
▥ from Greek *kuriakon* meaning 'master's house'

Church of England
NOUN The Church of England is the Anglican church in England, where it is the state church, with the King or Queen as its head.

churchyard churchyards
NOUN an area of land around a church, often used as a graveyard.

churn churns
NOUN a container used for making milk or cream into butter.

chute chutes
Said "**shoot**" NOUN a steep slope or channel used to slide things down EG *a rubbish chute.*

chutney
NOUN Chutney is a strong-tasting thick sauce made from fruit, vinegar, and spices.

cider
NOUN Cider is an alcoholic drink made from apples.

cigar cigars
NOUN a roll of dried tobacco leaves which people smoke.
▥ from Mayan *sicar* meaning 'to smoke'

cigarette cigarettes
NOUN a thin roll of tobacco covered in thin paper which people smoke.

cinder cinders
NOUN Cinders are small pieces of burnt material left after something such as wood or coal has burned.

cinema cinemas
NOUN **1** a place where people go to watch films. **2** Cinema is the business of making films.

cinnamon
NOUN Cinnamon is a sweet spice which comes from the bark of an Asian tree.

cipher ciphers
Said "**sy**-fer"; also spelt **cypher**
NOUN a secret code or system of writing used to send secret messages.

circa
Said "**sir**-ka" PREPOSITION; A FORMAL WORD about or approximately; used especially before dates EG *portrait of a lady, circa 1840.*

circle circles circling circled
NOUN **1** a completely regular round shape. Every point on its edge is the same distance from the centre. **2** a group of people with the same interest or profession EG *a character well-known in yachting circles.* **3** an area of seats on an upper floor of a

theatre. ▶ VERB **4** To circle is to move round and round as though going round the edge of a circle EG *A police helicopter circled above.*

circuit circuits
Said "sir-kit" NOUN **1** any closed line or path, often circular, for example a racing track; also the distance round this path EG *three circuits of the 26-lap race remaining.* **2** An electrical circuit is a complete route around which an electric current can flow.

circular circulars
ADJECTIVE **1** in the shape of a circle. **2** A circular argument or theory is not valid because it uses a statement to prove a conclusion and the conclusion to prove the statement. ▶ NOUN **3** a letter or advert sent to a lot of people at the same time.
circularity NOUN

circulate circulates circulating circulated
VERB **1** When something circulates or when you circulate it, it moves easily around an area EG *an open position where the air can circulate freely.* **2** When you circulate something among people, you pass it round or tell it to all the people EG *We circulate a regular newsletter.*

circulation circulations
NOUN **1** The circulation of something is the act of circulating it or the action of it circulating EG *traffic circulation.* **2** The circulation of a newspaper or magazine is the number of copies that are sold of each issue. **3** Your circulation is the movement of blood through your body.

circumcise circumcises circumcising circumcised
VERB If a boy or man is circumcised, the foreskin at the end of his penis is removed. This is carried out mainly as part of a Muslim or Jewish religious ceremony.
circumcision NOUN

circumference circumferences
NOUN The circumference of a circle is its outer line or edge; also the length of this line.

circumstance circumstances
NOUN **1** The circumstances of a situation or event are the conditions that affect what happens EG *He did well in the circumstances.* **2** Someone's circumstances are their position and conditions in life EG *Her circumstances had changed.*

circus circuses
NOUN a show given by a travelling group of entertainers such as clowns, acrobats, and specially trained animals.

cistern cisterns
NOUN a tank in which water is stored, for example one in the roof of a house or above a toilet.

citadel citadels
NOUN a fortress in or near a city.

cite cites citing cited
VERB **1** A FORMAL WORD If you cite something, you quote it or refer to it EG *He cited a letter written by Newall.* **2** If someone is cited in a legal action, they are officially called to appear in court.

citizen citizens
NOUN The citizens of a country or city are the people who live in it or belong to it EG *American citizens.*
citizenship NOUN

citrus fruit citrus fruits
NOUN Citrus fruits are juicy, sharp-tasting fruits such as oranges, lemons, and grapefruit.

city cities
NOUN a large town where many people live and work.

civic
ADJECTIVE relating to a city or citizens EG *the Civic Centre.*

civil
ADJECTIVE **1** relating to the citizens of a country EG *civil rights.* **2** relating to people or things that are not connected with the armed forces EG

the history of civil aviation. **3** polite.
civilly ADVERB, **civility** NOUN

civil engineering
NOUN Civil engineering is the design and construction of roads, bridges, and public buildings.

civilian civilians
NOUN a person who is not in the armed forces.

civilization civilizations; also spelt civilisation
NOUN **1** a society which has a highly developed organization and culture EG *the tale of a lost civilization.* **2** Civilization is an advanced state of social organization and culture.

civilized
ADJECTIVE **1** A civilized society is one with a developed social organization and way of life. **2** A civilized person is polite and reasonable.

civil servant civil servants
NOUN a person who works in the civil service.

civil service
NOUN The civil service is the government departments responsible for the administration of a country.

civil war civil wars
NOUN a war between groups of people who live in the same country.

cl
an abbreviation for 'centilitres'.

clad
ADJECTIVE; A LITERARY WORD Someone who is clad in particular clothes is wearing them.

claim claims claiming claimed
VERB **1** If you claim that something is the case, you say that it is the case EG *He claims to have lived in the same house all his life.* **2** If you claim something, you ask for it because it belongs to you or you have a right to it EG *Cartier claimed the land for the King of France.* ▶ NOUN **3** a statement that something is the case, or that

you have a right to something EG *She will make a claim for damages.*
■ (sense 1) allege, assert, maintain

claimant claimants
NOUN someone who is making a claim, especially for money.

clairvoyant clairvoyants
ADJECTIVE **1** able to know about things that will happen in the future. ▶ NOUN **2** a person who is, or claims to be, clairvoyant.
▥ from French *clair* + *voyant* meaning 'clear-seeing'

clam clams
NOUN a kind of shellfish.

clamber clambers clambering clambered
VERB If you clamber somewhere, you climb there with difficulty.

clammy clammier clammiest
ADJECTIVE unpleasantly damp and sticky EG *clammy hands.*

clamour clamours clamouring clamoured
VERB **1** If people clamour for something, they demand it noisily or angrily EG *We clamoured for an explanation.* ▶ NOUN **2** Clamour is noisy or angry shouts or demands by a lot of people.

clamp clamps clamping clamped
NOUN **1** an object with movable parts that are used to hold two things firmly together. ▶ VERB **2** To clamp things together is to fasten them or hold them firmly with a clamp.
clamp down on VERB To clamp down on something is to become stricter in controlling it EG *The Queen has clamped down on all expenditure.*

clan clans
NOUN a group of families related to each other by being descended from the same ancestor.

clandestine
ADJECTIVE secret and hidden EG *a clandestine meeting with friends.*

clang clangs clanging clanged
VERB When something metal clangs

or when you clang it, it makes a loud, deep sound.

clank clanks clanking clanked
VERB If something metal clanks, it makes a loud noise.

clap claps clapping clapped
VERB 1 When you clap, you hit your hands together loudly to show your appreciation. 2 If you clap someone on the back or shoulder, you hit them in a friendly way. 3 If you clap something somewhere, you put it there quickly and firmly EG *I clapped a hand over her mouth.*
▶ NOUN 4 a sound made by clapping your hands. 5 A clap of thunder is a sudden loud noise of thunder.

claret clarets
NOUN a type of red wine, especially one from the Bordeaux region of France.

clarify clarifies clarifying clarified
VERB To clarify something is to make it clear and easier to understand EG *Discussion will clarify your thoughts.*
clarification NOUN

clarinet clarinets
NOUN a woodwind instrument with a straight tube and a single reed in its mouthpiece.

clarity
NOUN The clarity of something is its clearness.

clash clashes clashing clashed
VERB 1 If people clash with each other, they fight or argue. 2 Ideas or styles that clash are so different that they do not go together. 3 If two events clash, they happen at the same time so you cannot go to both. 4 When metal objects clash, they hit each other with a loud noise. ▶ NOUN 5 a fight or argument. 6 A clash of ideas, styles, or events is a situation in which they do not go together. 7 a loud noise made by metal objects when they hit each other.

clasp clasps clasping clasped
VERB 1 To clasp something means to hold it tightly or fasten it EG *He*

clasped his hands. ▶ NOUN 2 a fastening such as a hook or catch.

class classes classing classed
NOUN 1 A class of people or things is a group of them of a particular type or quality EG *the old class of politicians.* 2 a group of pupils or students taught together, or a lesson that they have together. 3 Someone who has class is elegant in appearance or behaviour. ▶ VERB 4 To class something means to arrange it in a particular group or to consider it as belonging to a particular group EG *They are officially classed as visitors.*
■ (sense 1) category, group, kind, type

classic classics
ADJECTIVE 1 typical and therefore a good model or example of something EG *a classic case of misuse.* 2 of very high quality EG *one of the classic films of all time.* 3 simple in style and form EG *the classic dinner suit.* ▶ NOUN 4 something of the highest quality EG *one of the great classics of rock music.* 5 Classics is the study of Latin and Greek, and the literature of ancient Greece and Rome.

classical
ADJECTIVE 1 traditional in style, form, and content EG *classical ballet.* 2 Classical music is serious music considered to be of lasting value. 3 characteristic of the style of ancient Greece and Rome EG *Classical friezes decorate the walls.*
classically ADVERB

classified
ADJECTIVE officially declared secret by the government EG *access to classified information.*

classify classifies classifying classified
VERB To classify things is to arrange them into groups with similar characteristics EG *We can classify the differences into three groups.*
classification NOUN

A B C D E F G H I J K L M N O P Q R S T U V W X Y Z

classy classier classiest
ADJECTIVE; AN INFORMAL WORD stylish and elegant.

clatter clatters clattering clattered
VERB 1 When things clatter, they hit each other with a loud rattling noise. ▶ NOUN 2 a loud rattling noise made by hard things hitting each other.

clause clauses
NOUN 1 a section of a legal document. 2 In grammar, a clause is a group of words with a subject and a verb, which may be a complete sentence or one of the parts of a sentence.

What is a Clause?
A **clause** is a group of words which form part of a sentence and express an idea or describe a situation. A clause often gives information about the main idea or situation.
Matthew ate a cake **which was covered in chocolate**.
Anna crossed the street **after looking carefully in both directions**.
Main Clauses and Subordinate Clauses
Clauses can be either **main clauses** or **subordinate clauses**.
A **main clause** is the core of a sentence. It would make sense if it stood on its own. Every sentence contains a main clause.
Matthew ate a cake which was covered in chocolate.
After looking carefully in both directions, **Anna crossed the road**.
A **subordinate clause** is a less important part of a sentence. It would not make sense on its own, but gives information about the main clause.
After looking carefully, Anna crossed the road.
Anna had to cross the road, **which was often very busy**.
Relative Clauses
Relative clauses give additional information about a person or thing mentioned in the main clause.
Relative clauses are introduced by a relative pronoun — who, whom, whose, which or that.
Robbie has a cat **who likes fish**.
Anna has one sister, **whose name is Rosie**.

claustrophobia
Said "klos-trof-foe-bee-ya" NOUN Claustrophobia is a fear of being in enclosed spaces.
claustrophobic ADJECTIVE

claw claws clawing clawed
NOUN 1 An animal's claws are hard, curved nails at the end of its feet. 2 The claws of a crab or lobster are the two jointed parts, used for grasping things. ▶ VERB 3 If an animal claws something, it digs its claws into it.

clay
NOUN Clay is a type of earth that is soft and sticky when wet and hard when baked dry. It is used to make pottery and bricks.

clean cleaner cleanest; cleans cleaning cleaned
ADJECTIVE 1 free from dirt or other unwanted substances or marks. 2 If humour is clean it is not rude and does not involve bad language. 3 A clean movement is skilful and accurate. 4 Clean also means free from fault or error EG a clean driving licence. ▶ VERB 5 To clean something is to remove dirt from it.
cleanly ADVERB, **cleaner** NOUN

cleanliness
Said "klen-lin-ness" NOUN Cleanliness is the practice of keeping yourself and your surroundings clean.

cleanse cleanses cleansing cleansed
Said "klenz" VERB To cleanse something is to make it completely free from dirt.

clear clearer clearest; clears clearing cleared
ADJECTIVE 1 easy to understand, see, or hear EG He made it clear he did not want to talk. 2 easy to see through EG a clear liquid. 3 free from

obstructions or unwanted things EG *clear of snow*. ▸ VERB **4** To clear an area is to remove unwanted things from it. **5** If you clear a fence or other obstacle, you jump over it without touching it. **6** When fog or mist clears, it disappears. **7** If someone is cleared of a crime, they are proved to be not guilty.
clearly ADVERB

▤ (sense 1) evident, obvious, plain
clear up VERB **1** If you clear up, you tidy a place and put things away. **2** When a problem or misunderstanding is cleared up, it is solved or settled.

clearance
NOUN **1** Clearance is the removal of old buildings in an area. **2** If someone is given clearance to do something, they get official permission to do it.

clearing clearings
NOUN an area of bare ground in a forest.

cleavage cleavages
NOUN the space between a woman's breasts.

cleaver cleavers
NOUN a knife with a large square blade, used especially by butchers.

cleft clefts
NOUN a narrow opening in a rock.

clementine clementines
NOUN a type of small citrus fruit that is a cross between an orange and a tangerine.

clench clenches clenching clenched
VERB **1** When you clench your fist, you curl your fingers up tightly. **2** When you clench your teeth, you squeeze them together tightly.

clergy
PLURAL NOUN The clergy are the ministers of the Christian Church.

clergyman clergymen
NOUN a male member of the clergy.

clerical
ADJECTIVE **1** relating to work done in an office EG *clerical jobs with the City Council*. **2** relating to the clergy.

clerk clerks
Said "klahrk" NOUN a person who keeps records or accounts in an office, bank, or law court.

clever cleverer cleverest
ADJECTIVE **1** intelligent and quick to understand things. **2** very effective or skilful EG *a clever plan*.
cleverly ADVERB, **cleverness** NOUN

▤ (sense 1) bright, intelligent, smart

clianthus
Said "klee-an-thuss" NOUN A clianthus is a plant found in Australia and New Zealand which has clusters of scarlet flowers.

cliché clichés
Said "klee-shay" NOUN an idea or phrase which is no longer effective because it has been used so much.

click clicks clicking clicked
VERB **1** When something clicks or when you click it, it makes a short snapping sound. ▸ NOUN **2** a sound of something clicking EG *I heard the click of a bolt*.

client clients
NOUN someone who pays a professional person or company to receive a service.

clientele
Said "klee-on-tell" PLURAL NOUN The clientele of a place are its customers.

cliff cliffs
NOUN a steep high rock face by the sea.

climate climates
NOUN **1** The climate of a place is the typical weather conditions there EG *The climate was dry in the summer*. **2** the general attitude and opinion of people at a particular time EG *the American political climate*.
climatic ADJECTIVE

climax climaxes
NOUN The climax of a process, story, or piece of music is the most exciting moment in it, usually near

A
B
C
D
E
F
G
H
I
J
K
L
M
N
O
P
Q
R
S
T
U
V
W
X
Y
Z

the end.

📖 from Greek *klimax* meaning 'ladder'

climb climbs climbing climbed
VERB **1** To climb is to move upwards. **2** If you climb somewhere, you move there with difficulty EG *She climbed out of the driving seat.* ▶ NOUN **3** a movement upwards EG *this long climb up the slope... the rapid climb in murders.*
climber NOUN

clinch clinches clinching clinched
VERB If you clinch an agreement or an argument, you settle it in a definite way EG *Peter clinched a deal.*

cling clings clinging clung
VERB To cling to something is to hold onto it or stay closely attached to it EG *still clinging to old-fashioned values.*

clingfilm
NOUN; A TRADEMARK a clear thin plastic used for wrapping food.

clinic clinics
NOUN a building where people go for medical treatment.

clinical
ADJECTIVE **1** relating to the medical treatment of patients EG *clinical tests.* **2** Clinical behaviour or thought is logical and unemotional EG *the cold, clinical attitudes of his colleagues.*
clinically ADVERB

clip clips clipping clipped
NOUN **1** a small metal or plastic object used for holding things together. **2** a short piece of a film shown by itself. ▶ VERB **3** If you clip things together, you fasten them with clips. **4** If you clip something, you cut bits from it to shape it EG *clipped hedges.*

clippers
PLURAL NOUN Clippers are tools used for cutting.

clipping clippings
NOUN an article cut from a newspaper or magazine.

clique cliques

Rhymes with **"seek"** NOUN a small group of people who stick together and do not mix with other people.

clitoris clitorises
Said **"klit-tor-riss"** NOUN a small highly sensitive piece of flesh near the opening of a woman's vagina.

cloak cloaks cloaking cloaked
NOUN **1** a wide, loose coat without sleeves. ▶ VERB **2** To cloak something is to cover or hide it EG *a land permanently cloaked in mist.*

cloakroom cloakrooms
NOUN a room for coats or a room with toilets and washbasins in a public building.

clock clocks
NOUN **1** a device that measures and shows the time. ▶ PHRASE **2** If you work **round the clock**, you work all day and night.

clockwise
ADJECTIVE OR ADVERB in the same direction as the hands on a clock.

clockwork
NOUN **1** Toys that work by clockwork move when they are wound up with a key. ▶ PHRASE **2** If something happens **like clockwork**, it happens with no problems or delays.

clog clogs clogging clogged
VERB **1** To clog something is to block it EG *pavements clogged up with people.* ▶ NOUN **2** Clogs are heavy wooden shoes.

cloister cloisters
NOUN a covered area in a monastery or a cathedral for walking around a square.

clone clones cloning cloned
NOUN **1** In biology, a clone is an animal or plant that has been produced artificially from the cells of another animal or plant and is therefore identical to it. ▶ VERB **2** To clone an animal or plant is to produce it as a clone.

close closes closing closed; closer closest

VERB 1 To close something is to shut it. **2** To close a road or entrance is to block it so that no-one can go in or out. **3** If a shop closes at a certain time, then it does not do business after that time. ▶ **ADJECTIVE OR ADVERB 4** near to something EG *a restaurant close to their home.* ▶ **ADJECTIVE 5** People who are close to each other are very friendly and know each other well. **6** You say the weather is close when it is uncomfortably warm and there is not enough air.
closely ADVERB, **closeness** NOUN, **closed** ADJECTIVE
■ (sense 4) near, nearby
close down VERB If a business closes down, all work stops there permanently.

closed shop closed shops
NOUN a factory or other business whose employees have to be members of a trade union.

closet closets closeting closeted
NOUN **1** a cupboard. ▶ VERB **2** If you are closeted somewhere, you shut yourself away alone or in private with another person. ▶ ADJECTIVE **3** Closet beliefs or habits are kept private and secret EG *a closet romantic.*

close-up close-ups
NOUN a detailed close view of something, especially a photograph taken close to the subject.

closure closures
Said "**klohz-yur**" NOUN **1** The closure of a business is the permanent shutting of it. **2** The closure of a road is the blocking of it so it cannot be used.

clot clots clotting clotted
NOUN **1** a lump, especially one that forms when blood thickens. ▶ VERB **2** When a substance such as blood clots, it thickens and forms a lump.

cloth cloths
NOUN **1** Cloth is fabric made by a process such as weaving. **2** a piece of material used for wiping or

protecting things.

clothe clothes clothing clothed
PLURAL NOUN **1** Clothes are the things people wear on their bodies. ▶ VERB **2** To clothe someone is to give them clothes to wear.

clothing
NOUN Clothing is the clothes people wear.

cloud clouds clouding clouded
NOUN **1** a mass of water vapour that forms in the air and is seen as a white or grey patch in the sky. **2** A cloud of smoke or dust is a mass of it floating in the air. ▶ VERB **3** If something clouds or is clouded, it becomes cloudy or difficult to see through EG *The sky clouded over.* **4** Something that clouds an issue makes it more confusing.
▥ from Old English *clud* meaning 'hill'

cloudy cloudier cloudiest
ADJECTIVE **1** full of clouds EG *the cloudy sky.* **2** difficult to see through EG *a glass of cloudy liquid.*
■ (sense 1) dull, overcast

clout
NOUN; AN INFORMAL WORD Someone who has clout has influence.

clove cloves
NOUN **1** Cloves are small, strong-smelling dried flower buds from a tropical tree, used as a spice in cooking. **2** A clove of garlic is one of the separate sections of the bulb.

clover
NOUN Clover is a small plant with leaves made up of three similar parts.

clown clowns clowning clowned
NOUN **1** a circus performer who wears funny clothes and make-up and does silly things to make people laugh. ▶ VERB **2** If you clown, you do silly things to make people laugh.

cloying
ADJECTIVE unpleasantly sickly, sweet,

A B C D E F G H I J K L M N O P Q R S T U V W X Y Z

A
B
C
D
E
F
G
H
I
J
K
L
M
N
O
P
Q
R
S
T
U
V
W
X
Y
Z

or sentimental EG *something less cloying than whipped cream.*

club clubs clubbing clubbed
NOUN **1** an organization of people with a particular interest, who meet regularly; also the place where they meet. **2** a thick, heavy stick used as a weapon. **3** a stick with a shaped head that a golf player uses to hit the ball. **4** Clubs is one of the four suits in a pack of playing cards. It is marked by a black symbol in the shape of a clover leaf. ▶ VERB **5** To club someone is to hit them hard with a heavy object.
≡ (sense 1) association, group, society
club together VERB If people club together, they all join together to give money to buy something.

cluck clucks clucking clucked
VERB When a hen clucks, it makes a short, repeated, high-pitched sound.

clue clues
NOUN something that helps to solve a problem or mystery.

clump clumps clumping clumped
NOUN **1** a small group of things close together. ▶ VERB **2** If you clump about, you walk with heavy footsteps.

clumsy clumsier clumsiest
ADJECTIVE **1** moving awkwardly and carelessly. **2** said or done without thought or tact EG *his clumsy attempts to catch her out.*
clumsily ADVERB, **clumsiness** NOUN
≡ (sense 1) awkward, gauche, ungainly

cluster clusters clustering clustered
NOUN **1** A cluster of things is a group of them together EG *a cluster of huts at the foot of the mountains.* ▶ VERB **2** If people cluster together, they stay together in a close group.

clutch clutches clutching clutched
VERB **1** If you clutch something, you hold it tightly or seize it. ▶ PLURAL

NOUN **2** If you are in someone's clutches, they have power or control over you.

clutter clutters cluttering cluttered
NOUN **1** Clutter is an untidy mess. ▶ VERB **2** Things that clutter a place fill it and make it untidy.

cm
an abbreviation for 'centimetres'.

co-
PREFIX Co- means together EG *Paula is now co-writing a book with Pierre.*

coach coaches coaching coached
NOUN **1** a long motor vehicle used for taking passengers on long journeys. **2** a section of a train that carries passengers. **3** a four-wheeled vehicle with a roof pulled by horses, which people used to travel in. **4** a person who coaches a sport or a subject. ▶ VERB **5** If someone coaches you, they teach you and help you to get better at a sport or a subject.
≡ (sense 4) instructor, trainer
≡ (sense 5) instruct, train

coal coals
NOUN **1** Coal is a hard black rock obtained from under the earth and burned as a fuel. **2** Coals are burning pieces of coal.

coalition coalitions
NOUN a temporary alliance, especially between different political parties forming a government.

coarse coarser coarsest
ADJECTIVE **1** Something that is coarse is rough in texture, often consisting of large particles EG *a coarse blanket.* **2** Someone who is coarse talks or behaves in a rude or rather offensive way.
coarsely ADVERB, **coarseness** NOUN

coast coasts coasting coasted
NOUN **1** the edge of the land where it meets the sea. ▶ VERB **2** A vehicle that is coasting is moving without engine power.
coastal ADJECTIVE

coastguard coastguards
NOUN an official who watches the sea near a coast to get help for sailors when they need it, and to prevent smuggling.

coastline coastlines
NOUN the outline of a coast, especially its appearance as seen from the sea or air.

coat coats coating coated
NOUN **1** a piece of clothing with sleeves which you wear outside over your other clothes. **2** An animal's coat is the fur or hair on its body. **3** A coat of paint or varnish is a layer of it. ▶ VERB **4** To coat something means to cover it with a thin layer of a something EG *walnuts coated with chocolate.*
coating NOUN

coax coaxes coaxing coaxed
VERB If you coax someone to do something, you gently persuade them to do it.
▤ cajole, persuade, talk into, wheedle

cobalt
NOUN Cobalt is a hard silvery-white metal which is used for producing a blue dye.

cobble cobbles
NOUN Cobbles or cobblestones are stones with a rounded surface that were used in the past for making roads.

cobbler cobblers
NOUN a person who makes or mends shoes.

cobra cobras
Said "koh-bra" NOUN a type of large poisonous snake from Africa and Asia.

cobweb cobwebs
NOUN the very thin net that a spider spins for catching insects.

cocaine
NOUN Cocaine is an addictive drug.
▥ from Spanish *coca* meaning 'preparation of cocoa leaves'

cock cocks

NOUN an adult male chicken; also used of any male bird.

cockatoo cockatoos
NOUN a type of parrot with a crest, found in Australia and New Guinea.

cockerel cockerels
NOUN a young cock.

Cockney Cockneys
NOUN a person born in the East End of London.

cockpit cockpits
NOUN The place in a small plane where the pilot sits.

cockroach cockroaches
NOUN a large dark-coloured insect often found in dirty rooms.

cocktail cocktails
NOUN an alcoholic drink made from several ingredients.

cocky cockier cockiest; cockies
AN INFORMAL WORD ▶ ADJECTIVE **1** cheeky or too self-confident. ▶ NOUN **2** In Australian English, a cockatoo. **3** In Australian and New Zealand English, a farmer, especially one whose farm is small.
cockiness NOUN

cocoa
NOUN Cocoa is a brown powder made from the seeds of a tropical tree and used for making chocolate; also a hot drink made from this powder.

coconut coconuts
NOUN a very large nut with white flesh, milky juice, and a hard hairy shell.

cocoon cocoons
NOUN a silky covering over the larvae of moths and some other insects.
▥ from Provençal *coucoun* meaning 'eggshell'

cod
NOUN a large edible fish.
☑ The plural of *cod* is also *cod*.

code codes
NOUN **1** a system of replacing the letters or words in a message with other letters or words, so that

A
B
C
D
E
F
G
H
I
J
K
L
M
N
O
P
Q
R
S
T
U
V
W
X
Y
Z

A
B
C
D
E
F
G
H
I
J
K
L
M
N
O
P
Q
R
S
T
U
V
W
X
Y
Z

nobody can understand the message unless they know the system. **2** a group of numbers and letters which is used to identify something EG *the telephone code for Melbourne*.

coded ADJECTIVE

coffee

NOUN Coffee is a substance made by roasting and grinding the beans of a tropical shrub; also a hot drink made from this substance.

📖 from Arabic *qahwah* meaning 'wine' or 'coffee'

coffin coffins

NOUN a box in which a dead body is buried or cremated.

cog cogs

NOUN a wheel with teeth which turns another wheel or part of a machine.

cognac

Said "**kon**-yak" NOUN Cognac is a kind of brandy.

coherent

ADJECTIVE **1** If something such as a theory is coherent, its parts fit together well and do not contradict each other. **2** If someone is coherent, what they are saying makes sense and is not jumbled or confused.

coherence NOUN

cohesive

ADJECTIVE If something is cohesive, its parts fit together well EG *The team must work as a cohesive unit*.

cohesion NOUN

coil coils coiling coiled

NOUN **1** a length of rope or wire wound into a series of loops; also one of the loops. ▶ VERB **2** If something coils, it turns into a series of loops.

coin coins coining coined

NOUN **1** a small metal disc which is used as money. ▶ VERB **2** If you coin a word or a phrase, you invent it.

coinage

NOUN The coinage of a country is

the coins that are used there.

coincide coincides coinciding coincided

VERB **1** If two events coincide, they happen at about the same time. **2** When two people's ideas or opinions coincide, they agree EG *What she said coincided exactly with his own thinking*.

coincidence coincidences

NOUN **1** what happens when two similar things occur at the same time by chance EG *I had moved to London, and by coincidence, Helen had too*. **2** the fact that two things are surprisingly the same.

coincidental ADJECTIVE, **coincidentally** ADVERB

coke

NOUN Coke is a grey fuel produced from coal.

colander colanders

Said "**kol**-an-der" NOUN a bowl-shaped container with holes in it, used for washing or draining food.

cold colder coldest; colds

ADJECTIVE **1** Something that is cold has a very low temperature. **2** If it is cold, the air temperature is very low. **3** Someone who is cold does not show much affection. ▶ NOUN **4** You can refer to cold weather as the cold EG *She was complaining about the cold*. **5** a minor illness in which you sneeze and may have a sore throat.

coldly ADVERB, **coldness** NOUN

cold-blooded

ADJECTIVE **1** Someone who is cold-blooded does not show any pity EG *two cold-blooded killers*. **2** A cold-blooded animal has a body temperature that changes according to the surrounding temperature.

cold war

NOUN Cold war is a state of extreme unfriendliness between countries not actually at war.

coleslaw

NOUN Coleslaw is a salad of chopped cabbage and other vegetables in mayonnaise.

🔲 from Dutch *koolsla* meaning 'cabbage salad'

colic
NOUN Colic is pain in a baby's stomach.

collaborate collaborates collaborating collaborated
VERB When people collaborate, they work together to produce something EG *The two bands have collaborated in the past.*
collaboration NOUN, **collaborator** NOUN

collage collages
Said "kol-lahj" NOUN a picture made by sticking pieces of paper or cloth onto a surface.

collapse collapses collapsing collapsed
VERB **1** If something such as a building collapses, it falls down suddenly. If a person collapses, they fall down suddenly because they are ill. **2** If something such as a system or a business collapses, it suddenly stops working EG *50,000 small firms collapsed last year.* ▸ NOUN **3** The collapse of something is what happens when it stops working EG *the collapse of his marriage.*

collapsible
ADJECTIVE A collapsible object can be folded flat when it is not in use EG *a collapsible ironing board.*

collar collars
NOUN **1** The collar of a shirt or coat is the part round the neck which is usually folded over. **2** a leather band round the neck of a dog or cat.

collateral
NOUN Collateral is money or property which is used as a guarantee that someone will repay a loan, and which the lender can take if the loan is not repaid.

colleague colleagues
NOUN A person's colleagues are the people he or she works with.

collect collects collecting collected
VERB **1** To collect things is to gather them together for a special purpose or as a hobby EG *collecting money for charity.* **2** If you collect someone or something from a place, you call there and take them away EG *We had to collect her from school.* **3** When things collect in a place, they gather there over a period of time EG *Food collects in holes in the teeth.*
collector NOUN

collected
ADJECTIVE calm and self-controlled.

collection collections
NOUN **1** a group of things acquired over a period of time EG *a collection of paintings.* **2** Collection is the collecting of something EG *tax collection.* **3** the organized collecting of money, for example for charity, or the sum of money collected.
📧 (sense 1) accumulation, compilation, set

collective collectives
ADJECTIVE **1** involving every member of a group of people EG *The wine growers took a collective decision.* ▸ NOUN **2** a group of people who share the responsibility both for running something and for doing the work.
collectively ADVERB

collective noun collective nouns
NOUN a noun that refers to a single unit made up of a number of things, for example 'flock' and 'swarm'.

college colleges
NOUN **1** a place where students study after they have left school. **2** a name given to some secondary schools. **3** one of the institutions into which some universities are divided. **4** In New Zealand English, a college can also refer to a teacher training college.

collide collides colliding collided
VERB If a moving object collides with something, it hits it.

collie collies
NOUN a dog that is used for rounding up sheep.

colliery collieries
NOUN a coal mine.

collision collisions
NOUN A collision occurs when a moving object hits something.
■ crash, impact, smash

colloquial
Said "kol-**loh**-kwee-al" ADJECTIVE Colloquial words and phrases are informal and used especially in conversation.
colloquially ADVERB, **colloquialism** NOUN

cologne
Said "kol-**lone**" NOUN Cologne is a kind of weak perfume.

colon colons
NOUN **1** the punctuation mark (:). **2** part of your intestine.

What does the Colon do?

The **colon** (:) and the **semicolon** (;) are often confused and used incorrectly.

The **colon** is used to introduce a list.
I bought fruit: pears, apples, grapes and plums.

The colon can be used to introduce a quotation.
He received a message which read: "You can't fool all of the people all of the time."

The colon can be used to introduce an explanation of a statement.
They did not enjoy the meal: the food was cold.

Also look at the grammar box at **semicolon**.

---

colonel colonels
Said "**kur**-nl" NOUN an army officer with a fairly high rank.

colonial
ADJECTIVE **1** relating to a colony. **2** In Australia, colonial is used to relate to the period of Australian history before the Federation in 1901.

colony colonies
NOUN **1** a country controlled by a more powerful country. **2** a group

of people who settle in a country controlled by their homeland.

colossal
ADJECTIVE very large indeed.

colour colours colouring coloured
NOUN **1** the appearance something has as a result of reflecting light. **2** Someone's colour is the normal colour of their skin. **3** Colour is also a quality that makes something interesting or exciting EG *bringing more culture and colour to the city.* ▶ VERB **4** If something colours your opinion, it affects the way you think about something.
coloured ADJECTIVE, **colourful** ADJECTIVE, **colourfully** ADVERB, **colourless** ADJECTIVE, **colouring** NOUN
■ (sense 1) hue, shade, tint

colour blind
ADJECTIVE Someone who is colour blind cannot distinguish between colours.

colt colts
NOUN a young male horse.

column columns
NOUN **1** a tall solid upright cylinder, especially one supporting a part of a building. **2** a group of people moving in a long line.

columnist columnists
NOUN a journalist who writes a regular article in a newspaper or magazine.

coma comas
NOUN Someone who is in a coma is in a state of deep unconsciousness.

comb combs combing combed
NOUN **1** a flat object with pointed teeth used for tidying your hair. ▶ VERB **2** When you comb your hair, you tidy it with a comb. **3** If you comb a place, you search it thoroughly to try to find someone or something.

combat combats combating combated
NOUN **1** Combat is fighting EG *his first experience of combat.* ▶ VERB **2** To combat something means to try to

stop it happening or developing EG *a way to combat crime*.

combination combinations
NOUN **1** a mixture of things EG *a combination of charm and skill*. **2** a series of letters or numbers used to open a special lock.

combine combines combining combined
VERB **1** To combine things is to cause them to exist together EG *to combine a career with being a mother*. **2** To combine things also means to join them together to make a single thing EG *Combine all the ingredients*. **3** If something combines two qualities or features, it has them both EG *a film that combines great charm and scintillating performances*.

combustion
NOUN Combustion is the act of burning something or the process of burning.

come comes coming came come
VERB **1** To come to a place is to move there or arrive there. **2** To come to a place also means to reach as far as that place EG *The sea water came up to his waist*. **3** 'Come' is used to say that someone or something reaches a particular state EG *They came to power in 1997... We had come to a decision*. **4** When a particular time or event comes, it happens EG *The peak of his career came early in 1990*. **5** If you come from a place, you were born there or it is your home. ▸ PHRASE **6** A time or event **to come** is a future time or event EG *The public will thank them in years to come*.

come about VERB The way something comes about is the way it happens EG *The discussion came about because of the proposed changes*.

come across VERB If you come across something, you find it by chance.

come off VERB If something comes off, it succeeds EG *His rescue plan had come off*.

come on VERB If something is coming on, it is making progress EG *Let's go*

and see how the grapes are coming on.

come up VERB If something comes up in a conversation or meeting, it is mentioned or discussed.

come up with VERB If you come up with a plan or idea, you suggest it.

comeback comebacks
NOUN To make a comeback means to be popular or successful again.

comedian comedians
NOUN an entertainer whose job is to make people laugh.

comedienne comediennes
Said "kom-mee-dee-en" NOUN a female comedian.

comedy comedies
NOUN a light-hearted play or film with a happy ending.
📖 from Greek *kōmos* meaning 'village festival' and *aeidein* meaning 'to sing'

comet comets
NOUN an object that travels around the sun leaving a bright trail behind it.

comfort comforts comforting comforted
NOUN **1** Comfort is the state of being physically relaxed EG *He settled back in comfort*. **2** Comfort is also a feeling of relief from worries or unhappiness EG *The thought is a great comfort to me*. ▸ PLURAL NOUN **3** Comforts are things which make your life easier and more pleasant EG *all the comforts of home*. ▸ VERB **4** To comfort someone is to make them less worried or unhappy.

comfortable
ADJECTIVE **1** If you are comfortable, you are physically relaxed. **2** Something that is comfortable makes you feel relaxed EG *a comfortable bed*. **3** If you feel comfortable in a particular situation, you are not afraid or embarrassed.
comfortably ADVERB

comic comics
ADJECTIVE **1** funny EG *a comic monologue*. ▸ NOUN **2** someone who

A
B
C
D
E
F
G
H
I
J
K
L
M
N
O
P
Q
R
S
T
U
V
W
X
Y
Z

tells jokes. **3** a magazine that contains stories told in pictures.

comical
ADJECTIVE funny EG *a comical sight*.

comma commas
NOUN the punctuation mark (,).

What does the Comma do?

The **comma** (,) indicates a short pause between different elements within a sentence. This happens, for example, when a sentence consists of two main clauses joined by a conjunction.
Anna likes swimming, but Matthew prefers fishing.

A comma may also separate an introductory phrase or a subordinate clause from the main clause in a sentence.
After a month of sunshine, it rained on Thursday.

However, a short introductory phrase does not need to be followed by a comma.
After lunch the classes continued.

When words such as *therefore, however,* and *moreover* are put into a sentence to show how a train of thought is progressing, they should be marked off by commas.
We are confident, however, that the operation will be successful.

The comma also separates items in a list or series.
I made this soup with carrots, leeks, and potatoes.

Commas separate the name of a person or people being addressed from the rest of the sentence.
Thank you, ladies and gentlemen, for your attention.

The comma also separates words in quotation marks from the rest of the sentence, if there is no question or exclamation mark at the end of the quotation.
"This is a terrific picture," she said.

---

command commands
commanding commanded
VERB **1** To command someone to do something is to order them to do it. **2** If you command something such as respect, you receive it

because of your personal qualities. **3** An officer who commands part of an army or navy is in charge of it.
▶ NOUN **4** an order to do something. **5** Your command of something is your knowledge of it and your ability to use this knowledge EG *a good command of English*.
▤ (sense 1) direct, order

What is a Command?

Commands are used to give orders, instructions, or warnings.

Commands are made by putting the verb at the start of the sentence. The verb is used in its **imperative form** which is the basic form without any endings added.
Come over here.

Commands do not need a subject, as people who are being told to do something already know who they are. So commands may consist of a single verb.
Stop!

The negative form of a command is introduced by *do not* or *don't*.
Don't put that on the table.

Commands often end with an exclamation mark rather than a full stop, especially if they express urgency.
Run for your life!

---

commandant commandants
Said "kom-man-dant" NOUN an army officer in charge of a place or group of people.

commander commanders
NOUN an officer in charge of a military operation or organization.

commandment commandments
NOUN The commandments are ten rules of behaviour that, according to the Old Testament, people should obey.

commando commandos
NOUN Commandos are soldiers who have been specially trained to carry out raids.

commemorate commemorates
commemorating commemorated
VERB **1** An object that

commemorates a person or an event is intended to remind people of that person or event. **2** If you commemorate an event, you do something special to show that you remember it.

commemorative ADJECTIVE, **commemoration** NOUN

commence commences commencing commenced
VERB; A FORMAL WORD To commence is to begin.
commencement NOUN

commend commends commending commended
VERB To commend someone or something is to praise them EG *He has been commended for his work.*
commendation NOUN, **commendable** ADJECTIVE

comment comments commenting commented
VERB **1** If you comment on something, you make a remark about it. ▶ NOUN **2** a remark about something EG *She received many comments about her appearance.*
▦ (sense 1) observe, remark

commentary commentaries
NOUN a description of an event which is broadcast on radio or television while the event is happening.

commentator commentators
NOUN someone who gives a radio or television commentary.

commerce
NOUN Commerce is the buying and selling of goods.

commercial commercials
ADJECTIVE **1** relating to commerce. **2** Commercial activities involve producing goods on a large scale in order to make money EG *the commercial fishing world.* ▶ NOUN **3** an advertisement on television or radio.
commercially ADVERB

commission commissions commissioning commissioned
VERB **1** If someone commissions a

piece of work, they formally ask someone to do it EG *a study commissioned by the government.*
▶ NOUN **2** a piece of work that has been commissioned. **3** Commission is money paid to a salesman each time a sale is made. **4** an official body appointed to investigate or control something.

commit commits committing committed
VERB **1** To commit a crime or sin is to do it. **2** If you commit yourself, you state an opinion or state that you will do something. **3** If someone is committed to hospital or prison, they are officially sent there.
committal NOUN
▦ (sense 1) do, perform, perpetrate

commitment commitments
NOUN **1** Commitment is a strong belief in an idea or system. **2** something that regularly takes up some of your time EG *business commitments.*

committed
ADJECTIVE A committed person has strong beliefs EG *a committed feminist.*

committee committees
NOUN a group of people who make decisions on behalf of a larger group.

commodity commodities
NOUN; A FORMAL WORD Commodities are things that are sold.

common commoner commonest; commons
ADJECTIVE **1** Something that is common exists in large numbers or happens often EG *a common complaint.* **2** If something is common to two or more people, they all have it or use it EG *I realized we had a common interest.* **3** 'Common' is used to indicate that something is of the ordinary kind and not special. **4** If you describe someone as common, you mean they do not have good taste or good manners. ▶ NOUN **5** an area

A B C D E F G H I J K L M N O P Q R S T U V W X Y Z

of grassy land where everyone can go. ▶ PHRASE **6** If two things or people have something **in common**, they both have it.
commonly ADVERB
▪ (sense 1) customary, frequent
▪ (sense 4) coarse, vulgar

commoner commoners
NOUN someone who is not a member of the nobility.

commonplace
ADJECTIVE Something that is commonplace happens often EG *Foreign holidays have become commonplace.*

common sense
NOUN Your common sense is your natural ability to behave sensibly and make good judgments.

Commonwealth
NOUN **1** The Commonwealth is an association of countries around the world that are or used to be ruled by Britain. **2** a country made up of a number of states EG *the Commonwealth of Australia.*

commotion
NOUN A commotion is a lot of noise and excitement.

communal
ADJECTIVE shared by a group of people EG *a communal canteen.*

commune communes
Said "**kom-yoon**" NOUN a group of people who live together and share everything.

communicate communicates communicating communicated
VERB **1** When people communicate with each other, they exchange information, usually by talking or writing to each other. **2** If you communicate an idea or a feeling to someone, you make them aware of it.
▪ (sense 2) convey, make known

communication communications
NOUN **1** Communication is the process by which people or animals exchange information. ▶ PLURAL NOUN

2 Communications are the systems by which people communicate or broadcast information, especially using electricity or radio waves.
▶ NOUN **3** A FORMAL USE a letter or telephone call.

communicative
ADJECTIVE Someone who is communicative is willing to talk to people.

communion
NOUN **1** Communion is the sharing of thoughts and feelings. **2** In Christianity, Communion is a religious service in which people share bread and wine in remembrance of the death and resurrection of Jesus Christ.

communism
NOUN Communism is the doctrine that the state should control the means of production and that there should be no private property.
communist ADJECTIVE OR NOUN

community communities
NOUN all the people living in a particular area; also used to refer to particular groups within a society EG *the heart of the local community... the Asian community.*

commute commutes commuting commuted
VERB People who commute travel a long distance to work every day.
commuter NOUN

compact
ADJECTIVE taking up very little space EG *a compact microwave.*

compact disc compact discs
NOUN a music or video recording in the form of a plastic disc which is played using a laser on a special machine, and gives good quality sound or pictures.

companion companions
NOUN someone you travel or spend time with.
companionship NOUN
▣ from Latin *com-* meaning 'together' and *panis* meaning

'bread'. A companion was originally someone you shared a meal with

company companies
NOUN **1** a business that sells goods or provides a service EG *the record company*. **2** a group of actors, opera singers, or dancers EG *the Royal Shakespeare Company*. **3** If you have company, you have a friend or visitor with you EG *I enjoyed her company*.

comparable
Said "**kom-pra-bl**" ADJECTIVE If two things are comparable, they are similar in size or quality EG *The skill is comparable to playing the violin.*
comparably ADVERB
■ equal, equivalent, on a par

comparative comparatives
ADJECTIVE **1** You add comparative to indicate that something is true only when compared with what is normal EG *eight years of comparative calm.* ▶ NOUN **2** In grammar, the comparative is the form of an adjective which indicates that the person or thing described has more of a particular quality than someone or something else. For example, 'quicker', 'better', and 'easier' are all comparatives.
comparatively ADVERB

What is a Comparative?

Many adjectives have three different forms. These are known as the **positive**, the **comparative**, and the **superlative**. The comparative and superlative are used when you make comparisons.

The **positive** form of an adjective is given as the entry in the dictionary. It is used when there is no comparison between different objects.
   *Matthew is **tall**.*

The **comparative** form is usually made by adding the ending *-er* to the positive form of the adjective. It shows that something possesses a quality to a greater extent than the thing it is being compared with.
   *Matthew is **taller** than Anna.*

You can also make comparisons by using the words *more* or *less* with the positive (not the comparative) form of the adjective.
   *Matthew is **more energetic** than Robbie.*

Irregular Comparative Forms

When the comparative and superlative of an adjective are not formed in the regular way, the irregular forms of the adjective are shown in the dictionary after the main entry.

Many adjectives — especially ones that have more than one syllable and do not end in *-y* — do not have separate spelling forms for the comparative and superlative. For these adjectives comparisons must be made using *more, less, most,* and *least.*

   beautiful ➤ more beautiful ➤ most beautiful
   boring ➤ less boring ➤ least boring

Look also at the grammar box at **superlative**.

compare compares comparing compared
VERB **1** When you compare things, you consider them together and see in what ways they are different or similar. **2** If you compare one thing to another, you say it is like the other thing EG *His voice is often compared to Michael Stipe's.*

comparison comparisons
NOUN When you make a comparison, you consider two things together and see in what ways they are different or similar.

compartment compartments
NOUN **1** a section of a railway carriage. **2** one of the separate parts of an object EG *a special compartment inside your vehicle.*

compass compasses
NOUN **1** an instrument with a magnetic needle for finding directions. ▶ PLURAL NOUN **2** Compasses are a hinged instrument for drawing circles.
☑ The proper name for the drawing instrument is *a pair of compasses.*

compassion
NOUN Compassion is pity and sympathy for someone who is

A B C D E F G H I J K L M N O P Q R S T U V W X Y Z

141

A
B
C
D
E
F
G
H
I
J
K
L
M
N
O
P
Q
R
S
T
U
V
W
X
Y
Z

suffering.

compassionate ADJECTIVE

compatible

ADJECTIVE If people or things are compatible, they can live or work together successfully.

compatibility NOUN

compatriot compatriots

NOUN Your compatriots are people from your own country.

compel compels compelling compelled

VERB To compel someone to do something is to force them to do it.

compelling

ADJECTIVE **1** If a story or event is compelling, it is extremely interesting EG *a compelling novel.* **2** A compelling argument or reason makes you believe that something is true or should be done EG *compelling new evidence.*

compensate compensates compensating compensated

VERB **1** To compensate someone is to give them money to replace something lost or damaged. **2** If one thing compensates for another, it cancels out its bad effects EG *The trip more than compensated for the hardship.*

compensatory ADJECTIVE, **compensation** NOUN

≡ (sense 1) recompense, refund
≡ (sense 2) make up for

compere comperes compering compered

Said "**kom**-pare" NOUN **1** the person who introduces the guests or performers in a show. ▶ VERB **2** To compere a show is to introduce the guests or performers.

compete competes competing competed

VERB **1** When people or firms compete, each tries to prove that they or their products are the best. **2** If you compete in a contest or game, you take part in it.

competent

ADJECTIVE Someone who is

competent at something can do it satisfactorily EG *a very competent engineer.*

competently ADVERB, **competence** NOUN

competition competitions

NOUN **1** When there is competition between people or groups, they are all trying to get something that not everyone can have EG *There's a lot of competition for places.* **2** an event in which people take part to find who is best at something. **3** When there is competition between firms, each firm is trying to get people to buy its own goods.

competitive

ADJECTIVE **1** A competitive situation is one in which people or firms are competing with each other EG *a crowded and competitive market.* **2** A competitive person is eager to be more successful than others. **3** Goods sold at competitive prices are cheaper than other goods of the same kind.

competitively ADVERB

competitor competitors

NOUN a person or firm that is competing to become the most successful.

compilation compilations

NOUN A compilation is a book, record, or programme consisting of several items that were originally produced separately EG *this compilation of his solo work.*

compile compiles compiling compiled

VERB When someone compiles a book or report, they make it by putting together several items.

complacent

ADJECTIVE If someone is complacent, they are unconcerned about a serious situation and do nothing about it.

complacency NOUN

complain complains complaining complained

VERB **1** If you complain, you say that you are not satisfied with something. **2** If you complain of pain or illness, you say that you have it.

■ (sense 1) find fault, grumble, moan

complaint complaints
NOUN If you make a complaint, you complain about something.

complement complements complementing complemented
VERB **1** If one thing complements another, the two things go well together EG *The tiled floor complements the pine furniture.* ▶ NOUN **2** If one thing is a complement to another, it goes well with it. In grammar, a complement is a word or phrase that gives information about the subject or object of a sentence. For example, in the sentence 'Rover is a dog', 'is a dog' is a complement.
complementary ADJECTIVE

complete completes completing completed
ADJECTIVE **1** to the greatest degree possible EG *a complete mess.* **2** If something is complete, none of it is missing EG *a complete set of tools.* **3** When a task is complete, it is finished EG *The planning stage is now complete.* ▶ VERB **4** If you complete something, you finish it. **5** If you complete a form, you fill it in.
completely ADVERB, **completion** NOUN
■ (sense 1) absolute, thorough, total
■ (sense 2) entire, full, whole

complex complexes
ADJECTIVE **1** Something that is complex has many different parts EG *a very complex problem.* ▶ NOUN **2** A complex is a group of buildings, roads, or other things connected with each other in some way EG *a hotel and restaurant complex.* **3** If someone has a complex, they have an emotional problem because of a past experience EG *an inferiority complex.*
complexity NOUN
■ (sense 1) complicated, intricate,

involved

complexion complexions
NOUN the quality of the skin on your face EG *a healthy glowing complexion.*

complicate complicates complicating complicated
VERB To complicate something is to make it more difficult to understand or deal with.

complicated
ADJECTIVE Something that is complicated has so many parts or aspects that it is difficult to understand or deal with.

complication complications
NOUN something that makes a situation more difficult to deal with EG *One possible complication was that it was late in the year.*

compliment compliments complimenting complimented
NOUN **1** If you pay someone a compliment, you tell them you admire something about them. ▶ VERB **2** If you compliment someone, you pay them a compliment.
▥ from Spanish *cumplir* meaning 'to do what is fitting'

complimentary
ADJECTIVE **1** If you are complimentary about something, you express admiration for it. **2** A complimentary seat, ticket, or publication is given to you free.

comply complies complying complied
VERB If you comply with an order or rule, you obey it.
compliance NOUN

component components
NOUN The components of something are the parts it is made of.

compose composes composing composed
VERB **1** If something is composed of particular things or people, it is made up of them. **2** To compose a piece of music, letter, or speech

A
B
C
D
E
F
G
H
I
J
K
L
M
N
O
P
Q
R
S
T
U
V
W
X
Y
Z

means to write it. **3** If you compose yourself, you become calm after being excited or upset.

composed
ADJECTIVE calm and in control of your feelings.

composer composers
NOUN someone who writes music.

composition compositions
NOUN **1** The composition of something is the things it consists of EG *the composition of the ozone layer.* **2** The composition of a poem or piece of music is the writing of it. **3** a piece of music or writing.

compost
NOUN Compost is a mixture of decaying plants and manure added to soil to help plants grow.

composure
NOUN Someone's composure is their ability to stay calm EG *Jarvis was able to recover his composure.*

compound compounds compounding compounded
NOUN **1** an enclosed area of land with buildings used for a particular purpose EG *the prison compound.* **2** In chemistry, a compound is a substance consisting of two or more different substances or chemical elements. ▶ VERB **3** To compound something is to put together different parts to make a whole. **4** To compound a problem is to make it worse by adding to it EG *Water shortages were compounded by taps left running.*

comprehend comprehends comprehending comprehended
VERB; A FORMAL WORD To comprehend something is to understand or appreciate it EG *He did not fully comprehend what was puzzling me.*
comprehension NOUN

comprehensible
ADJECTIVE able to be understood.

comprehensive comprehensives
ADJECTIVE **1** Something that is comprehensive includes everything

necessary or relevant EG *a comprehensive guide.* ▶ NOUN **2** a school where children of all abilities are taught together.
comprehensively ADVERB

compress compresses compressing compressed
VERB To compress something is to squeeze it or shorten it so that it takes up less space EG *compressed air.*
compression NOUN

comprise comprises comprising comprised
VERB; A FORMAL WORD What something comprises is what it consists of EG *The district then comprised 66 villages.*
☑ You do not need *of* after comprise. For example, you say *the library comprises 500,000 books.*

compromise compromises compromising compromised
NOUN **1** an agreement in which people accept less than they originally wanted EG *In the end they reached a compromise.* ▶ VERB **2** When people compromise, they agree to accept less than they originally wanted.
compromising ADJECTIVE

compulsion compulsions
NOUN a very strong desire to do something.

compulsive
ADJECTIVE **1** You use 'compulsive' to describe someone who cannot stop doing something EG *a compulsive letter writer.* **2** If you find something such as a book or television programme compulsive, you cannot stop reading or watching it.

compulsory
ADJECTIVE If something is compulsory, you have to do it EG *School attendance is compulsory.*
■ mandatory, obligatory

computer computers
NOUN an electronic machine that can quickly make calculations or store and find information.

computer-aided design
NOUN Computer-aided design is the

use of computers and computer graphics to help design things.

computerize computerizes computerizing computerized; also spelt **computerise**
VERB When a system or process is computerized, the work is done by computers.

computing
NOUN Computing is the use of computers and the writing of programs for them.

comrade comrades
NOUN A soldier's comrades are his fellow soldiers, especially in battle.
comradeship NOUN

con cons conning conned
AN INFORMAL WORD ▶ VERB **1** If someone cons you, they trick you into doing or believing something. ▶ NOUN **2** a trick in which someone deceives you into doing or believing something.

concave
ADJECTIVE A concave surface curves inwards, rather than being level or bulging outwards.

conceal conceals concealing concealed
VERB To conceal something is to hide it EG *He had concealed his gun.*
concealment NOUN

concede concedes conceding conceded
Said "kon-**seed**" VERB **1** If you concede something, you admit that it is true EG *I conceded that he was entitled to his views.* **2** When someone concedes defeat, they accept that they have lost something such as a contest or an election.

conceit
NOUN Conceit is someone's excessive pride in their appearance or abilities.
■ pride, self-importance

conceited
ADJECTIVE Someone who is conceited is too proud of their appearance or

abilities.
■ bigheaded, full of oneself, self-important

conceivable
ADJECTIVE If something is conceivable, you can believe that it could exist or be true EG *It's conceivable that you also met her.*
conceivably ADVERB

conceive conceives conceiving conceived
VERB **1** If you can conceive of something, you can imagine it or believe it EG *Could you conceive of doing such a thing yourself?* **2** If you conceive something such as a plan, you think of it and work out how it could be done. **3** When a woman conceives, she becomes pregnant.

concentrate concentrates concentrating concentrated
VERB **1** If you concentrate on something, you give it all your attention. **2** When something is concentrated in one place, it is all there rather than in several places EG *They are mostly concentrated in the urban areas.*
concentration NOUN

concentrated
ADJECTIVE A concentrated liquid has been made stronger by having water removed from it EG *concentrated apple juice.*

concentration camp concentration camps
NOUN a prison camp, especially one set up by the Nazis during World War Two.

concept concepts
NOUN an abstract or general idea EG *the concept of tolerance.*
conceptual ADJECTIVE, **conceptually** ADVERB

conception conceptions
NOUN **1** Your conception of something is the idea you have of it. **2** Conception is the process by which a woman becomes pregnant.

concern concerns concerning concerned

145

concern

NOUN **1** Concern is a feeling of worry about something or someone EG *public concern about violence*. **2** If something is your concern, it is your responsibility. **3** a business EG *a large manufacturing concern*. ▶ VERB **4** If something concerns you or if you are concerned about it, it worries you. **5** You say that something concerns you if it affects or involves you EG *It concerns you and me.* ▶ PHRASE **6** If something is of concern to you, it is important to you.

concerned ADJECTIVE

■ (sense 5) be relevant to, involve, regard

concerning

PREPOSITION You use 'concerning' to show what something is about EG *documents concerning arm sales to Iraq.*

concert concerts

NOUN a public performance by musicians.

concerted

ADJECTIVE A concerted action is done by several people together EG *concerted action to cut interest rates.*

concerto concertos or concerti

Said "kon-cher-toe" NOUN a piece of music for a solo instrument and an orchestra.

concession concessions

NOUN If you make a concession, you agree to let someone have or do something EG *Her one concession was to let me come into the building.*

conch conches

NOUN a shellfish with a large, brightly coloured shell; also the shell itself.

concise

ADJECTIVE giving all the necessary information using as few words as necessary EG *a concise guide.*

■ brief, short, succinct

conclude concludes concluding concluded

VERB **1** If you conclude something, you decide that it is so because of the other things that you know EG *An inquiry concluded that this was untrue.* **2** When you conclude something, you finish it EG *At that point I intend to conclude the interview.*

concluding ADJECTIVE, **conclusion** NOUN

conclusive

ADJECTIVE Facts that are conclusive show that something is certainly true.

conclusively ADVERB

concoct concocts concocting concocted

VERB **1** If you concoct an excuse or explanation, you invent one. **2** If you concoct something, you make it by mixing several things together.

concoction NOUN

concourse concourses

NOUN a wide hall in a building where people walk about or gather together.

concrete

NOUN **1** Concrete is a solid building material made by mixing cement, sand, and water. ▶ ADJECTIVE **2** definite, rather than general or vague EG *I don't really have any concrete plans.* **3** real and physical, rather than abstract EG *concrete evidence.*

concubine concubines

Said "kong-kyoo-bine" NOUN; AN OLD-FASHIONED WORD A man's concubine is his mistress.

concur concurs concurring concurred

VERB; A FORMAL WORD To concur is to agree EG *She concurred with me.*

concurrent

ADJECTIVE If things are concurrent, they happen at the same time.

concurrently ADVERB

concussed

ADJECTIVE confused or unconscious because of a blow to the head.

concussion NOUN

condemn condemns condemning condemned

VERB **1** If you condemn something,

you say it is bad and unacceptable EG *Teachers condemned the new plans.* **2** If someone is condemned to a punishment, they are given it EG *She was condemned to death.* **3** If you are condemned to something unpleasant, you must suffer it EG *Many women are condemned to poverty.* **4** When a building is condemned, it is going to be pulled down because it is unsafe.

condemnation NOUN
■ (sense 1) censure, criticize, disapprove
■ (sense 2) sentence
■ (sense 3) doom

condensation
NOUN Condensation is a coating of tiny drops formed on a surface by steam or vapour.

condense condenses condensing condensed
VERB **1** If you condense a piece of writing or a speech, you shorten it. **2** When a gas or vapour condenses, it changes into a liquid.

condescending
ADJECTIVE If you are condescending, you behave in a way that shows you think you are superior to other people.
■ patronizing, superior

condition conditions conditioning conditioned
NOUN **1** the state someone or something is in. ▶ PLURAL NOUN **2** The conditions in which something is done are the location and other factors likely to affect it EG *The very difficult conditions continued to affect our performance.* **3** a requirement that must be met for something else to be possible EG *He had been banned from drinking alcohol as a condition of bail.* **4** You can refer to an illness or other medical problem as a condition EG *a heart condition.* ▶ PHRASE **5** If you are **out of condition**, you are unfit. ▶ VERB **6** If someone is conditioned to behave or think in a certain way, they do it as a result of their upbringing or

training.
■ (sense 3) prerequisite, requirement, stipulation

conditional
ADJECTIVE If one thing is conditional on another, it can only happen if the other thing happens EG *You feel his love is conditional on you pleasing him.*

condolence condolences
NOUN Condolence is sympathy expressed for a bereaved person.

condom condoms
NOUN a rubber sheath worn by a man on his penis or by a woman inside her vagina as a contraceptive.

condone condones condoning condoned
VERB If you condone someone's bad behaviour, you accept it and do not try to stop it EG *We cannot condone violence.*

conducive
Said "kon-**joo**-siv" ADJECTIVE If something is conducive to something else, it makes it likely to happen EG *a situation that is conducive to relaxation.*

conduct conducts conducting conducted
VERB **1** To conduct an activity or task is to carry it out EG *He seemed to be conducting a conversation.* **2** A FORMAL USE The way you conduct yourself is the way you behave. **3** When someone conducts an orchestra or choir, they stand in front of it and direct it. **4** If something conducts heat or electricity, heat or electricity can pass through it. ▶ NOUN **5** If you take part in the conduct of an activity or task, you help to carry it out. **6** Your conduct is your behaviour.

conductor conductors
NOUN **1** someone who conducts an orchestra or choir. **2** someone who moves round a bus or train selling tickets. **3** a substance that conducts heat or electricity.

cone cones

NOUN **1** a regular three-dimensional shape with a circular base and a point at the top. **2** A fir cone or pine cone is the fruit of a fir or pine tree.

confectionery
NOUN Confectionery is sweets.

confederation confederations
NOUN an organization formed for business or political purposes.

confer confers conferring conferred
VERB When people confer, they discuss something in order to make a decision.

conference conferences
NOUN a meeting at which formal discussions take place.

confess confesses confessing confessed
VERB If you confess to something, you admit it EG *Your son has confessed to his crimes.*
■ admit, own up

confession confessions
NOUN **1** If you make a confession, you admit you have done something wrong. **2** Confession is the act of confessing something, especially a religious act in which people confess their sins to a priest.
■ (sense 1) acknowledgment, admission

confessional confessionals
NOUN a small room in some churches where people confess their sins to a priest.

confetti
NOUN Confetti is small pieces of coloured paper thrown over the bride and groom at a wedding.
▥ from Italian *confetto* meaning 'a sweet'

confidant confidants
Said "**kon**-fid-dant" NOUN; A FORMAL WORD a person you discuss your private problems with.
☑ When the person you discuss your private problems with is a girl or a woman, the word is spelt *confidante*.

confide confides confiding confided
VERB If you confide in or to someone, you tell them a secret EG *Marian confided in me that she was very worried.*

confidence confidences
NOUN **1** If you have confidence in someone, you feel you can trust them. **2** Someone who has confidence is sure of their own abilities or qualities. **3** a secret you tell someone.

confident
ADJECTIVE **1** If you are confident about something, you are sure it will happen the way you want it to. **2** People who are confident are sure of their own abilities or qualities.
confidently ADVERB
■ (sense 1) certain, positive, sure
■ (sense 2) assured, self-assured

confidential
ADJECTIVE Confidential information is meant to be kept secret.
confidentially ADVERB, **confidentiality** NOUN

confine confines confining confined
VERB **1** If something is confined to one place, person, or thing, it exists only in that place or affects only that person or thing. **2** If you confine yourself to doing or saying something, it is the only thing you do or say EG *They confined themselves to discussing the weather.* **3** If you are confined to a place, you cannot leave it EG *She was confined to bed for two days.* ▶ PLURAL NOUN **4** The confines of a place are its boundaries EG *outside the confines of the prison.*
confinement NOUN

confined
ADJECTIVE A confined space is small and enclosed by walls.

confirm confirms confirming confirmed
VERB **1** To confirm something is to

say or show that it is true EG *Police confirmed that they had received a call.* **2** If you confirm an arrangement or appointment, you say it is definite. **3** When someone is confirmed, they are formally accepted as a member of a Christian church.
confirmation NOUN
▣ (sense 1) prove, verify

confirmed
ADJECTIVE You use 'confirmed' to describe someone who has a belief or way of life that is unlikely to change EG *a confirmed bachelor.*

confiscate confiscates confiscating confiscated
VERB To confiscate something is to take it away from someone as a punishment.

conflict conflicts conflicting conflicted
NOUN **1** Conflict is disagreement and argument EG *conflict between workers and management.* **2** a war or battle. **3** When there is a conflict of ideas or interests, people have different ideas or interests which cannot all be satisfied. ▶ VERB **4** When ideas or interests conflict, they are different and cannot all be satisfied.
▣ (sense 1) disagreement, dissension
▣ (sense 2) battle, clash
▣ (sense 4) be incompatible, clash, disagree

conform conforms conforming conformed
VERB **1** If you conform, you behave the way people expect you to. **2** If something conforms to a law or to someone's wishes, it is what is required or wanted.
conformist NOUN OR ADJECTIVE

confront confronts confronting confronted
VERB **1** If you are confronted with a problem or task, you have to deal with it. **2** If you confront someone, you meet them face to face like an enemy. **3** If you confront someone with evidence or a fact, you present it to them in order to accuse them of something.

confrontation confrontations
NOUN a serious dispute or fight EG *a confrontation between police and fans.*

confuse confuses confusing confused
VERB **1** If you confuse two things, you mix them up and think one of them is the other EG *You are confusing facts with opinion.* **2** To confuse someone means to make them uncertain about what is happening or what to do. **3** To confuse a situation means to make it more complicated.
confused ADJECTIVE, **confusing** ADJECTIVE, **confusion** NOUN
▣ (sense 2) baffle, bewilder

congeal congeals congealing congealed
Said "kon-**jeel**" VERB When a liquid congeals, it becomes very thick and sticky.

congenial
Said "kon-**jeen**-yal" ADJECTIVE If something is congenial, it is pleasant and suits you EG *We wanted to talk in congenial surroundings.*

congenital
ADJECTIVE; A MEDICAL WORD If someone has a congenital disease or handicap, they have had it from birth but did not inherit it.

congested
ADJECTIVE **1** When a road is congested, it is so full of traffic that normal movement is impossible. **2** If your nose is congested, it is blocked and you cannot breathe properly.
congestion NOUN

conglomerate conglomerates
NOUN a large business organization consisting of several companies.

congratulate congratulates congratulating congratulated
VERB If you congratulate someone, you express pleasure at something good that has happened to them, or praise them for something they

A
B
C
D
E
F
G
H
I
J
K
L
M
N
O
P
Q
R
S
T
U
V
W
X
Y
Z

A
B
C
D
E
F
G
H
I
J
K
L
M
N
O
P
Q
R
S
T
U
V
W
X
Y
Z

have achieved.

congratulation NOUN, **congratulatory** ADJECTIVE

congregate congregates congregating congregated
VERB When people congregate, they gather together somewhere.

congregation congregations
NOUN the congregation are the people attending a service in a church.

congress congresses
NOUN a large meeting held to discuss ideas or policies EG *a medical congress*.

conical
ADJECTIVE shaped like a cone.

conifer conifers
NOUN any type of evergreen tree that produces cones.
coniferous ADJECTIVE

conjecture
NOUN Conjecture is guesswork about something EG *There was no evidence, only conjecture*.

conjugate conjugates conjugating conjugated
Said "kon-joo-gate" VERB When you conjugate a verb, you list the different forms of it you use with the pronouns 'I' 'you' (singular) 'he' 'she' 'it' 'you' (plural) and 'they'.

conjunction conjunctions
NOUN 1 In grammar, a conjunction is a word that links two other words or two clauses, for example 'and', 'but', 'while', and 'that'.
▶ PHRASE 2 If two or more things are done **in conjunction**, they are done together.

What is a Conjunction?

A conjunction is a word that joins two words or two parts of a sentence together. Conjunctions are sometimes called "joining words".

Co-ordinating conjunctions join items of equal importance.

*I ordered fish **and** chips.*

Contrasting conjunctions are a type of

co-ordinating conjunction which are used to join opposites or contrasting items.

*He was not walking **but** running.*

Correlative conjunctions are pairs of conjunctions, such as *either ... or*, or *both ... and*, each of which introduces a separate item in the sentence.

*She speaks **both** French **and** German.*
*You can drink **either** tea **or** coffee.*

Subordinating conjunctions join additional items to the main part of the sentence.

*He was happy **because** he had finished his work.*
*I will come **if** I have time.*

conjurer conjurers
NOUN someone who entertains people by doing magic tricks.

conker conkers
NOUN Conkers are hard brown nuts from a horse chestnut tree.

connect connects connecting connected
VERB 1 To connect two things is to join them together. 2 If you connect something with something else, you think of them as being linked EG *High blood pressure is closely connected to heart disease.*

connection connections; also spelt connexion
NOUN 1 a link or relationship between things. 2 the point where two wires or pipes are joined together EG *a loose connection*.
▶ PLURAL NOUN 3 Someone's connections are the people they know EG *He had powerful connections in the army.*

connoisseur connoisseurs
Said "kon-nis-sir" NOUN someone who knows a lot about the arts, or about food or drink EG *a great connoisseur of champagne.*
▨ from Old French *connoistre* meaning 'to know'

connotation connotations
NOUN The connotations of a word or name are what it makes you think of EG *a grey man for whom grey has no*

connotation of dullness.

conquer conquers conquering conquered
VERB **1** To conquer people is to take control of their country by force. **2** If you conquer something difficult or dangerous, you succeed in controlling it EG *Conquer your fear!*
conqueror NOUN

conquest conquests
NOUN **1** Conquest is the conquering of a country or group of people. **2** Conquests are lands captured by conquest.

conscience consciences
NOUN the part of your mind that tells you what is right and wrong.

conscientious
Said "kon-shee-en-shus" ADJECTIVE Someone who is conscientious is very careful to do their work properly.
conscientiously ADVERB
■ careful, meticulous, thorough

conscious
ADJECTIVE **1** If you are conscious of something, you are aware of it EG *She was not conscious of the time.* **2** A conscious action or effort is done deliberately EG *I made a conscious decision not to hide.* **3** Someone who is conscious is awake, rather than asleep or unconscious EG *Still conscious, she was taken to hospital.*
consciously ADVERB, **consciousness** NOUN

consecrated
ADJECTIVE A consecrated building or place is one that has been officially declared to be holy.

consecutive
ADJECTIVE Consecutive events or periods of time happen one after the other EG *eight consecutive games.*

consensus
NOUN Consensus is general agreement among a group of people EG *The consensus was that it could be done.*
✔ There are three ss in *consensus*, do not confuse the spelling with *census.* You should not say

consensus of opinion, as *consensus* already has *of opinion* in its meaning.

consent consents consenting consented
NOUN **1** Consent is permission to do something EG *Thomas reluctantly gave his consent to my writing this book.* **2** Consent is also agreement between two or more people EG *By common consent it was the best game of these championships.* ▶ VERB **3** If you consent to something, you agree to it or allow it.

consequence consequences
NOUN **1** The consequences of something are its results or effects EG *the dire consequences of major war.* **2** A FORMAL USE If something is of consequence, it is important.

consequent
ADJECTIVE Consequent describes something as being the result of something else EG *an earthquake in 1980 and its consequent damage.*
consequently ADVERB

conservation
NOUN Conservation is the preservation of the environment.
conservationist NOUN OR ADJECTIVE

conservative conservatives
NOUN **1** In Britain, a member or supporter of the Conservative Party, a political party that believes that the government should interfere as little as possible in the running of the economy. ▶ ADJECTIVE **2** In Britain, Conservative views and policies are those of the Conservative Party. **3** Someone who is conservative is not willing to accept changes or new ideas. **4** A conservative estimate or guess is a cautious or moderate one.
conservatively ADVERB, **conservatism** NOUN

conservatory conservatories
NOUN a room with glass walls and a glass roof in which plants are kept.

conserve conserves conserving conserved

A
B
C
D
E
F
G
H
I
J
K
L
M
N
O
P
Q
R
S
T
U
V
W
X
Y
Z

A
B
C
D
E
F
G
H
I
J
K
L
M
N
O
P
Q
R
S
T
U
V
W
X
Y
Z

VERB If you conserve a supply of something, you make it last EG *the only way to conserve energy*.

consider considers considering considered

VERB **1** If you consider something to be the case, you think or judge it to be so EG *The manager does not consider him an ideal team member*. **2** To consider something is to think about it carefully EG *If an offer were made, we would consider it*. **3** If you consider someone's needs or feelings, you take account of them. ◨ (sense 2) contemplate, think about

considerable

ADJECTIVE A considerable amount of something is a lot of it EG *a considerable sum of money*.
considerably ADVERB

considerate

ADJECTIVE Someone who is considerate pays attention to other people's needs and feelings.

consideration considerations

NOUN **1** Consideration is careful thought about something EG *a decision demanding careful consideration*. **2** If you show consideration for someone, you take account of their needs and feelings. **3** something that has to be taken into account EG *Money was also a consideration*.
◨ (sense 1) deliberation, thought

considered

ADJECTIVE A considered opinion or judgment is arrived at by careful thought.

considering

CONJUNCTION OR PREPOSITION You say considering to indicate that you are taking something into account EG *I know that must sound callous, considering that I was married to the man for seventeen years*.

consign consigns consigning consigned

VERB; A FORMAL WORD To consign something to a particular place is

to send or put it there.

consignment consignments

NOUN A consignment of goods is a load of them being delivered somewhere.

consist consists consisting consisted

VERB What something consists of is its different parts or members EG *The brain consists of millions of nerve cells*.

consistency consistencies

NOUN **1** Consistency is the quality of being consistent. **2** The consistency of a substance is how thick or smooth it is EG *the consistency of single cream*.

consistent

ADJECTIVE **1** If you are consistent, you keep doing something the same way EG *one of our most consistent performers*. **2** If something such as a statement or argument is consistent, there are no contradictions in it.
consistently ADVERB

console consoles consoling consoled

VERB *Said* "con-**sole**" **1** To console someone who is unhappy is to make them more cheerful. ▶ NOUN *Said* "con-**sole**" **2** a panel with switches or knobs for operating a machine.
consolation NOUN

consolidate consolidates consolidating consolidated

VERB To consolidate something you have gained or achieved is to make it more secure.
consolidation NOUN

consonant consonants

NOUN a sound such as 'p' or 'm' which you make by stopping the air flowing freely through your mouth.
▦ from Latin *consonare* meaning 'to sound at the same time'

consort consorts consorting consorted

VERB *Said* "con-**sort**" **1** A FORMAL WORD

If you consort with someone, you spend a lot of time with them.
▶ NOUN *Said "con-sort"* **2** the wife or husband of the king or queen.

consortium **consortia** or **consortiums**
NOUN a group of businesses working together.

conspicuous
ADJECTIVE If something is conspicuous, people can see or notice it very easily.
conspicuously ADVERB

conspiracy **conspiracies**
NOUN When there is a conspiracy, a group of people plan something illegal, often for a political purpose.

conspirator **conspirators**
NOUN someone involved in a conspiracy.

conspire **conspires conspiring conspired**
VERB **1** When people conspire, they plan together to do something illegal, often for a political purpose. **2** A LITERARY USE When events conspire towards a particular result, they seem to work together to cause it EG *Circumstances conspired to doom the business.*

constable **constables**
NOUN a police officer of the lowest rank.
⌑ from Latin *comes stabuli* meaning 'officer of the stable'

constabulary **constabularies**
NOUN a police force.

constant
ADJECTIVE **1** Something that is constant happens all the time or is always there EG *a city under constant attack.* **2** If an amount or level is constant, it stays the same. **3** People who are constant stay loyal to a person or idea.
constantly ADVERB, **constancy** NOUN
▤ (sense 2) fixed, steady, unchanging

constellation **constellations**
NOUN a group of stars.

consternation
NOUN Consternation is anxiety or dismay EG *There was some consternation when it began raining.*

constipated
ADJECTIVE Someone who is constipated is unable to pass solid waste.
constipation NOUN

constituency **constituencies**
NOUN a town or area represented by an MP.

constituent **constituents**
NOUN **1** An MP's constituents are the voters who live in his or her constituency. **2** The constituents of something are its parts EG *the major constituents of bone.*

constitute **constitutes constituting constituted**
VERB If a group of things constitute something, they are what it consists of EG *Jewellery constitutes 80 per cent of the stock.*

constitution **constitutions**
NOUN **1** The constitution of a country is the system of laws which formally states people's rights and duties. **2** Your constitution is your health EG *a very strong constitution.*
constitutional ADJECTIVE, **constitutionally** ADVERB

constrained
ADJECTIVE If a person feels constrained to do something, they feel that they should do that, even if they do not want to.

constraint **constraints**
NOUN something that limits someone's freedom of action EG *constraints on trade union power.*

constrict **constricts constricting constricted**
VERB To constrict something is to squeeze it tightly.
constriction NOUN

construct **constructs constructing constructed**
VERB To construct something is to build or make it.

A B C D E F G H I J K L M N O P Q R S T U V W X Y Z

153

construction constructions
NOUN **1** The construction of something is the building or making of it EG *the construction of the harbour.* **2** something built or made EG *a shoddy modern construction built of concrete.*

constructive
ADJECTIVE Constructive criticisms and comments are helpful.
constructively ADVERB

consul consuls
NOUN an official who lives in a foreign city and who looks after people there who are citizens of his or her own country.
consular ADJECTIVE

consulate consulates
NOUN the place where a consul works.

consult consults consulting consulted
VERB **1** If you consult someone, you ask for their opinion or advice. **2** When people consult each other, they exchange ideas and opinions. **3** If you consult a book or map, you look at it for information.

consultancy consultancies
NOUN an organization whose members give expert advice on a subject.

consultant consultants
NOUN **1** an experienced doctor who specializes in one type of medicine. **2** someone who gives expert advice EG *a management consultant.*

consultation consultations
NOUN **1** a meeting held to discuss something. **2** Consultation is discussion or the seeking of advice EG *There has to be much better consultation with the public.*
consultative ADJECTIVE

consume consumes consuming consumed
VERB **1** A FORMAL WORD If you consume something, you eat or drink it. **2** To consume fuel or energy is to use it up.

consumer consumers
NOUN someone who buys things or uses services EG *two new magazines for teenage consumers.*

consumerism
NOUN Consumerism is the belief that a country will have a strong economy if its people buy a lot of goods and spend a lot of money.

consuming
ADJECTIVE A consuming passion or interest is more important to you than anything else.

consummate consummates consummating consummated
Said "**kons**-yum-mate" VERB **1** To consummate something is to make it complete. **2** A FORMAL WORD If two people consummate a marriage or relationship, they make it complete by having sex. ▶ ADJECTIVE **3** *Said* "kon-**sum**-mit" You use 'consummate' to describe someone who is very good at something EG *a consummate politician.*
consummation NOUN

consumption
NOUN The consumption of fuel or food is the using of it, or the amount used.

contact contacts contacting contacted
NOUN **1** If you are in contact with someone, you regularly talk to them or write to them. **2** When things are in contact, they are touching each other. **3** someone you know in a place or organization from whom you can get help or information. ▶ VERB **4** If you contact someone, you telephone them or write to them.
■ (sense 4) get *or* be in touch with, reach

contact lens contact lenses
NOUN Contact lenses are small plastic lenses that you put in your eyes instead of wearing glasses, to help you see better.

contagious
ADJECTIVE A contagious disease can

be caught by touching people or things infected with it.

contain contains containing contained
VERB **1** If a substance contains something, that thing is a part of it EG *Alcohol contains sugar.* **2** The things a box or room contains are the things inside it. **3** A FORMAL USE To contain something also means to stop it increasing or spreading EG *efforts to contain the disease.*
containment NOUN

container containers
NOUN **1** something such as a box or a bottle that you keep things in. **2** a large sealed metal box for transporting things.
◼ (sense 1) holder, receptacle

contaminate contaminates contaminating contaminated
VERB If something is contaminated by dirt, chemicals, or radiation, it is made impure and harmful EG *foods contaminated with lead.*
contamination NOUN

contemplate contemplates contemplating contemplated
VERB **1** To contemplate is to think carefully about something for a long time. **2** If you contemplate doing something, you consider doing it EG *I never contemplated marrying Charles.* **3** If you contemplate something, you look at it for a long time EG *He contemplated his drawings.*
contemplation NOUN, **contemplative** ADJECTIVE

contemporary contemporaries
ADJECTIVE **1** produced or happening now EG *contemporary literature.* **2** produced or happening at the time you are talking about EG *contemporary descriptions of Lizzie Borden.* ▶ NOUN **3** Someone's contemporaries are other people living or active at the same time as them EG *Shakespeare and his contemporaries.*

contempt

NOUN If you treat someone or something with contempt, you show no respect for them at all.

contemptible
ADJECTIVE not worthy of any respect EG *this contemptible piece of nonsense.*

contemptuous
ADJECTIVE showing contempt.
contemptuously ADVERB

contend contends contending contended
VERB **1** To contend with a difficulty is to deal with it EG *They had to contend with injuries.* **2** A FORMAL USE If you contend that something is true, you say firmly that it is true. **3** When people contend for something, they compete for it.
contender NOUN

content contents contenting contented
PLURAL NOUN *Said* "con-tents" **1** The contents of something are the things inside it. ▶ NOUN *Said* "con-tent" **2** The content of an article or speech is what is expressed in it. **3** Content is the proportion of something that a substance contains EG *White bread is inferior in vitamin content.* ▶ ADJECTIVE *Said* "con-tent" **4** happy and satisfied with your life. **5** willing to do or have something EG *He would be content to telephone her.* ▶ VERB *Said* "con-tent" **6** If you content yourself with doing something, you do it and do not try to do anything else EG *He contented himself with an early morning lecture.*

contented
ADJECTIVE happy and satisfied with your life.
contentedly ADVERB, **contentment** NOUN

contention contentions
NOUN; A FORMAL WORD Someone's contention is the idea or opinion they are expressing EG *It is our contention that the 1980s mark a turning point in planning.*

contest contests contesting contested

contestant NOUN *Said* "con-test" **1** a competition or game EG *a boxing contest.* **2** a struggle for power EG *a presidential contest.* ▶ VERB *Said* "con-test" **3** If you contest a statement or decision, you object to it formally.

≣ (sense 1) competition, game, match

contestant contestants
NOUN someone taking part in a competition.

≣ competitor, player

context contexts
NOUN **1** The context of something consists of matters related to it which help to explain it EG *English history is treated in a European context.* **2** The context of a word or sentence consists of the words or sentences before and after it.

continent continents
NOUN **1** a very large area of land, such as Africa or Asia. **2** The Continent is the mainland of Europe.
continental ADJECTIVE

contingency contingencies
Said "kon-**tin**-jen-see" NOUN something that might happen in the future EG *I need to examine all possible contingencies.*

contingent contingents
NOUN **1** a group of people representing a country or organization EG *a strong South African contingent.* **2** a group of police or soldiers.

continual
ADJECTIVE **1** happening all the time without stopping EG *continual headaches.* **2** happening again and again EG *the continual snide remarks.*
continually ADVERB

≣ constant, incessant

continuation continuations
NOUN **1** The continuation of something is the continuing of it EG *the continuation of the human race.* **2** Something that is a continuation of an event follows it and seems like a part of it EG *a meeting which was a continuation of a conference.*

continue continues continuing continued
VERB **1** If you continue to do something, you keep doing it. **2** If something continues, it does not stop. **3** You also say something continues when it starts again after stopping EG *She continued after a pause.*

≣ (senses 2, 3 & 4) carry on, go on, proceed

continuous
ADJECTIVE **1** Continuous means happening or existing without stopping. **2** A continuous line or surface has no gaps or holes in it.
continuously ADVERB, **continuity** NOUN

contorted
ADJECTIVE twisted into an unnatural, unattractive shape.

contour contours
NOUN **1** The contours of something are its general shape. **2** On a map, a contour is a line joining points of equal height.

contra-
PREFIX Contra- means against or opposite to EG *contraflow.*

contraception
NOUN Contraception is methods of preventing pregnancy.

contraceptive contraceptives
NOUN a device or pill for preventing pregnancy.

contract contracts contracting contracted
NOUN **1** a written legal agreement about the sale of something or work done for money. ▶ VERB **2** When something contracts, it gets smaller or shorter. **3** A FORMAL USE If you contract an illness, you get it EG *Her husband contracted a virus.*
contractual ADJECTIVE, **contraction** NOUN

contractor contractors
NOUN a person or company who does work for other people or

companies EG *a building contractor.*

contradict **contradicts**
contradicting **contradicted**
VERB If you contradict someone, you
say that what they have just said is
not true, and that something else
is.
contradiction NOUN, **contradictory**
ADJECTIVE

contraption **contraptions**
NOUN a strange-looking machine or
piece of equipment.

contrary
ADJECTIVE **1** Contrary ideas or
opinions are opposed to each other
and cannot be held by the same
person EG *There isn't any contrary
evidence?* ▶ PHRASE **2** You say **on the
contrary** when you are
contradicting what someone has
just said.

contrast **contrasts** **contrasting**
contrasted
NOUN **1** a great difference between
things EG *the real contrast between the
two poems.* **2** If one thing is a
contrast to another, it is very
different from it EG *I couldn't imagine
a greater contrast to Maxwell.* ▶ VERB
3 If you contrast things, you
describe or emphasize the
differences between them. **4** If one
thing contrasts with another, it is
very different from it EG *The
interview contrasted completely with
the one she gave after Tokyo.*

contravene **contravenes**
contravening **contravened**
VERB; A FORMAL WORD If you
contravene a law or rule, you do
something that it forbids.

contribute **contributes**
contributing **contributed**
VERB **1** If you contribute to
something, you do things to help it
succeed EG *The elderly have much to
contribute to the community.* **2** If you
contribute money, you give it to
help to pay for something. **3** If
something contributes to an event
or situation, it is one of its causes EG

*The dry summer has contributed to
perfect conditions.*
contribution NOUN, **contributor** NOUN,
contributory ADJECTIVE
◼ (sense 2) donate, give

contrive **contrives** **contriving**
contrived
VERB; A FORMAL WORD If you contrive to
do something difficult, you succeed
in doing it EG *Anthony contrived to
escape with a few companions.*

contrived
ADJECTIVE Something that is
contrived is unnatural EG *a contrived
compliment.*

control **controls** **controlling**
controlled
NOUN **1** Control of a country or
organization is the power to make
the important decisions about how
it is run. **2** Your control over
something is your ability to make it
work the way you want it to. **3** The
controls on a machine are knobs or
other devices used to work it. ▶ VERB
4 To control a country or
organization means to have the
power to make decisions about
how it is run. **5** To control
something such as a machine or
system means to make it work the
way you want it to. **6** If you control
yourself, you make yourself behave
calmly when you are angry or
upset. ▶ PHRASE **7** If something is **out
of control**, nobody has any power
over it.
controller NOUN
◼ (sense 6) hold back, restrain

controversial
ADJECTIVE Something that is
controversial causes a lot of
discussion and argument, because
many people disapprove of it.

controversy **controversies**
Said "**kon**-triv-ver-see" *or*
"kon-**trov**-ver-see" NOUN discussion
and argument because many
people disapprove of something.
▥ from Latin *controversus*
meaning 'turned in an opposite

direction'

☑ Notice that there are two ways to say *controversy*. The first way is older, and the second is more becoming more common.

conundrum conundrums
NOUN; A FORMAL WORD a puzzling problem.

convalesce convalesces convalescing convalesced
VERB When people convalesce, they rest and regain their health after an illness or operation.

convection
NOUN Convection is the process by which heat travels through gases and liquids.

convene convenes convening convened
VERB 1 A FORMAL WORD To convene a meeting is to arrange for it to take place. 2 When people convene, they come together for a meeting.

convenience conveniences
NOUN 1 The convenience of something is the fact that it is easy to use or that it makes something easy to do. 2 something useful.

convenient
ADJECTIVE If something is convenient, it is easy to use or it makes something easy to do.
conveniently ADVERB
☐ handy, useful

convent convents
NOUN a building where nuns live, or a school run by nuns.

convention conventions
NOUN 1 an accepted way of behaving or doing something. 2 a large meeting of an organization or political group EG *the Democratic Convention.*

conventional
ADJECTIVE 1 You say that people are conventional when there is nothing unusual about their way of life. 2 Conventional methods are the ones that are usually used.
conventionally ADVERB

converge converges converging converged
VERB To converge is to meet or join at a particular place.

conversation conversations
NOUN If you have a conversation with someone, you spend time talking to them.
conversational ADJECTIVE,
conversationalist NOUN

converse converses conversing conversed
VERB *Said* "con-**verse**" 1 A FORMAL USE When people converse, they talk to each other. ▶ NOUN *Said* "**con**-verse" 2 The converse of something is its opposite EG *Don't you think that the converse might also be possible?*
conversely ADVERB

convert converts converting converted
VERB *Said* "con-**vert**" 1 To convert one thing into another is to change it so that it becomes the other thing. 2 If someone converts you, they persuade you to change your religious or political beliefs. ▶ NOUN *Said* "**con**-vert" 3 someone who has changed their religious or political beliefs.
conversion NOUN, **convertible** ADJECTIVE

convex
ADJECTIVE A convex surface bulges outwards, rather than being level or curving inwards.

convey conveys conveying conveyed
VERB 1 To convey information or ideas is to cause them to be known or understood. 2 A FORMAL USE To convey someone or something to a place is to transport them there.

conveyor belt conveyor belts
NOUN a moving strip used in factories for moving objects along.

convict convicts convicting convicted
VERB 1 To convict someone of a crime is to find them guilty. ▶ NOUN 2 someone serving a prison sentence.

conviction convictions
NOUN **1** a strong belief or opinion.
2 The conviction of someone is
what happens when they are found
guilty in a court of law.

convince convinces convincing
convinced
VERB To convince someone of
something is to persuade them that
it is true.
◼ persuade, sway

convincing
ADJECTIVE 'Convincing' is used to
describe things or people that can
make you believe something is true
EG *a convincing argument*.
convincingly ADVERB
◼ credible, persuasive, plausible

convoluted
Said "kon-vol-**yoo**-tid" ADJECTIVE
Something that is convoluted has
many twists and bends EG *the
convoluted patterns of these designs*.

convoy convoys
NOUN a group of vehicles or ships
travelling together.

convulsion convulsions
NOUN If someone has convulsions,
their muscles move violently and
uncontrollably.

coo coos cooing cooed
VERB When pigeons and doves coo,
they make a soft flutelike sound.

cook cooks cooking cooked
VERB **1** To cook food is to prepare it
for eating by heating it. ▶ NOUN
2 someone who prepares and cooks
food, often as their job.

cooker cookers
NOUN a device for cooking food.

cookery
NOUN Cookery is the activity of
preparing and cooking food.

cool cooler coolest; cools cooling
cooled
ADJECTIVE **1** Something cool has a
low temperature but is not cold.
2 If you are cool in a difficult
situation, you stay calm and
unemotional. ▶ VERB **3** When

something cools or when you cool
it, it becomes less warm.
coolly ADVERB, **coolness** NOUN

coolabah coolabahs; also spelt
coolibar
NOUN an Australian eucalypt that
grows along rivers.

coop coops
NOUN a cage for chickens or rabbits.

cooperate cooperates
cooperating cooperated
Said "koh-op-er-rate" VERB **1** When
people cooperate, they work or act
together. **2** To cooperate also
means to do what someone asks.
cooperation NOUN

cooperative cooperatives
Said "koh-op-er-ut-tiv" NOUN **1** a
business or organization run by the
people who work for it, and who
share its benefits or profits.
▶ ADJECTIVE **2** A cooperative activity is
done by people working together.
3 Someone who is cooperative does
what you ask them to.

coordinate coordinates
coordinating coordinated
Said "koh-or-din-ate" VERB **1** To
coordinate an activity is to
organize the people or things
involved in it EG *to coordinate the
campaign*. ▶ PLURAL NOUN
2 Coordinates are a pair of
numbers or letters which tell you
how far along and up or down a
point is on a grid.
coordination NOUN, **coordinator** NOUN

cop cops
NOUN; AN INFORMAL WORD a policeman.

cope copes coping coped
VERB If you cope with a problem or
task, you deal with it successfully.

copious
ADJECTIVE; A FORMAL WORD existing or
produced in large quantities EG *I
wrote copious notes for the solicitor*.

copper coppers
NOUN **1** Copper is a soft
reddish-brown metal. **2** Coppers
are brown metal coins of low value.

A B C D E F G H I J K L M N O P Q R S T U V W X Y Z

A B C D E F G H I J K L M N O P Q R S T U V W X Y Z

3 AN INFORMAL USE a policeman.

copse copses
NOUN a small group of trees growing close together.

copulate copulates copulating copulated
VERB; A FORMAL WORD To copulate is to have sex.
copulation NOUN

copy copies copying copied
NOUN **1** something made to look like something else. **2** A copy of a book, newspaper, or record is one of many identical ones produced at the same time. ▸ VERB **3** If you copy what someone does, you do the same thing. **4** If you copy something, you make a copy of it.
copier NOUN
▣ (sense 1) duplicate, replica, reproduction
▣ (sense 4) duplicate, reproduce

copyright copyrights
NOUN If someone has the copyright on a piece of writing or music, it cannot be copied or performed without their permission.

coral corals
NOUN Coral is a hard substance that forms in the sea from the skeletons of tiny animals called corals.

cord cords
NOUN **1** Cord is strong, thick string. **2** Electrical wire covered in rubber or plastic is also called cord.

cordial cordials
ADJECTIVE **1** warm and friendly EG *the cordial greeting.* ▸ NOUN **2** a sweet drink made from fruit juice.

cordon cordons cordoning cordoned
NOUN **1** a line or ring of police or soldiers preventing people entering or leaving a place. ▸ VERB **2** If police or soldiers cordon off an area, they stop people entering or leaving by forming themselves into a line or ring.

corduroy
NOUN Corduroy is a thick cloth with

parallel raised lines on the outside.

core cores
NOUN **1** the hard central part of a fruit such as an apple. **2** the most central part of an object or place EG *the earth's core.* **3** the most important part of something EG *the core of Asia's problems.*

cork corks
NOUN **1** Cork is the very light, spongelike bark of a Mediterranean tree. **2** a piece of cork pushed into the end of a bottle to close it.

corkscrew corkscrews
NOUN a device for pulling corks out of bottles.

cormorant cormorants
NOUN a dark-coloured bird with a long neck.

corn corns
NOUN **1** Corn refers to crops such as wheat and barley and to their seeds. **2** a small painful area of hard skin on your foot.

cornea corneas
*Said "*kor-nee-a*"* NOUN the transparent skin that covers the outside of your eyeball.
▥ from Latin *cornea tela* meaning 'horny web'

corner corners cornering cornered
NOUN **1** a place where two sides or edges of something meet EG *a small corner of one shelf... a street corner.* ▸ VERB **2** To corner a person or animal is to get them into a place they cannot escape from.

cornet cornets
NOUN a small brass instrument used in brass and military bands.

cornflour
NOUN Cornflour is a fine white flour made from maize and used in cooking to thicken sauces.

cornflower cornflowers
NOUN a small plant with bright flowers, usually blue.

cornice cornices
NOUN a decorative strip of plaster,

wood, or stone along the top edge of a wall.

corny corrier corriest
ADJECTIVE very obvious or sentimental and not at all original EG *corny old love songs*.

coronary coronaries
NOUN If someone has a coronary, blood cannot reach their heart because of a blood clot.

coronation coronations
NOUN the ceremony at which a king or queen is crowned.

coroner coroners
NOUN an official who investigates the deaths of people who have died in a violent or unusual way.

coronet coronets
NOUN a small crown.

corporal corporals
NOUN an officer of low rank in the army or air force.

corporal punishment
NOUN Corporal punishment is the punishing of people by beating them.

corporate
ADJECTIVE; A FORMAL WORD belonging to or done by all members of a group together EG *a corporate decision*.

corporation corporations
NOUN **1** a large business. **2** a group of people responsible for running a city.

corps
Rhymes with "more" NOUN **1** a part of an army with special duties EG *the engineering Corps*. **2** a small group of people who do a special job EG *the world press corps*.
✓ The plural of *corps* is also *corps*.

corpse corpses
NOUN a dead body.

corpuscle corpuscles
Said "kor-pus-sl" NOUN a red or white blood cell.

correa correas
NOUN an Australian shrub with large green and white flowers.

correct corrects correcting corrected
ADJECTIVE **1** If something is correct, there are no mistakes in it. **2** The correct thing in a particular situation is the right one EG *Each has the correct number of coins*. **3** Correct behaviour is considered to be socially acceptable. ▶ VERB **4** If you correct something which is wrong, you make it right.
correctly ADVERB, **correction** NOUN, **corrective** ADJECTIVE OR NOUN
▣ (sense 4) emend, rectify

correlate correlates correlating correlated
VERB If two things correlate or are correlated, they are closely connected or strongly influence each other EG *Obesity correlates with increased risk of stroke and diabetes*.
correlation NOUN

correspond corresponds corresponding corresponded
VERB **1** If one thing corresponds to another, it has a similar purpose, function, or status. **2** If numbers or amounts correspond, they are the same. **3** When people correspond, they write to each other. ▶

correspondence
NOUN **1** Correspondence is the writing of letters; also the letters written. **2** If there is a correspondence between two things, they are closely related or very similar.

correspondent correspondents
NOUN a newspaper, television, or radio reporter.

corresponding
ADJECTIVE **1** You use 'corresponding' to describe a change that results from a change in something else EG *the rise in interest rates and corresponding fall in house values*. **2** You also use 'corresponding' to describe something which has a similar purpose or status to something else EG *Alfard is the corresponding Western name for the*

A
B
C
D
E
F
G
H
I
J
K
L
M
N
O
P
Q
R
S
T
U
V
W
X
Y
Z

star.
correspondingly ADVERB

corridor corridors
NOUN a passage in a building or train.

corroboree corroborees
NOUN an Australian Aboriginal gathering or dance that is festive or warlike.

corrode corrodes corroding corroded
VERB When metal corrodes, it is gradually destroyed by a chemical or rust.
corrosion NOUN, **corrosive** ADJECTIVE

corrugated
ADJECTIVE Corrugated metal or cardboard has parallel folds to make it stronger.
▣ from Latin *corrugare* meaning 'to wrinkle up'

corrupt corrupts corrupting corrupted
ADJECTIVE 1 Corrupt people act dishonestly or illegally in return for money or power EG *corrupt ministers*.
▶ VERB 2 To corrupt someone means to make them dishonest or immoral.
corruptible ADJECTIVE
▤ (sense 2) crooked, dishonest
▤ (sense 2) deprave

corruption
NOUN Corruption is dishonesty and illegal behaviour by people in positions of power.
▤ depravity, immorality, vice

corset corsets
NOUN Corsets are stiff underwear worn by some women round their hips and waist to make them look slimmer.

cosmetic cosmetics
NOUN 1 Cosmetics are substances such as lipstick and face powder which improve a person's appearance. ▶ ADJECTIVE 2 Cosmetic changes improve the appearance of something without changing its basic character.

cosmic
ADJECTIVE belonging or relating to the universe.

cosmopolitan
ADJECTIVE A cosmopolitan place is full of people from many countries.
▣ from Greek *kosmos* meaning 'universe' and *politēs* meaning 'citizen'

cosmos
NOUN The cosmos is the universe.

cosset cossets cosseting cosseted
VERB If you cosset someone, you spoil them and protect them too much.

cost costs costing cost
NOUN 1 The cost of something is the amount of money needed to buy it, do it, or make it. 2 The cost of achieving something is the loss or injury in achieving it EG *the total cost in human misery*. ▶ VERB 3 You use 'cost' to talk about the amount of money you have to pay for things EG *The air fares were going to cost a lot*. 4 If a mistake costs you something, you lose that thing because of the mistake EG *a reckless gamble that could cost him his job*.

costly costlier costliest
ADJECTIVE expensive EG *the most costly piece of furniture*.

costume costumes
NOUN 1 a set of clothes worn by an actor. 2 Costume is the clothing worn in a particular place or during a particular period EG *eighteenth-century costume*.

cosy cosier cosiest; cosies
ADJECTIVE 1 warm and comfortable EG *her cosy new flat*. 2 Cosy activities are pleasant and friendly EG *a cosy chat*. ▶ NOUN 3 a soft cover put over a teapot to keep the tea warm.
cosily ADVERB, **cosiness** NOUN

cot cots
NOUN a small bed for a baby, with bars or panels round it to stop the baby falling out.
▣ from Hindi *khat* meaning 'bedstead'

cottage cottages
NOUN a small house in the country.

cottage cheese
NOUN Cottage cheese is a type of soft white lumpy cheese.

cotton cottons
NOUN **1** Cotton is cloth made from the soft fibres of the cotton plant. **2** Cotton is also thread used for sewing.
📖 from Arabic *qutn*

cotton wool
NOUN Cotton wool is soft fluffy cotton, often used for dressing wounds.

couch couches couching couched
NOUN **1** a long, soft piece of furniture which more than one person can sit on. ▶ VERB **2** If a statement is couched in a particular type of language, it is expressed in that language EG *a comment couched in impertinent terms*.

cough coughs coughing coughed
Said "koff" VERB **1** When you cough, you force air out of your throat with a sudden harsh noise. ▶ NOUN **2** an illness that makes you cough a lot; also the noise you make when you cough.

could
VERB **1** You use 'could' to say that you were able or allowed to do something EG *He could hear voices... She could come and go as she wanted*. **2** You also use 'could' to say that something might happen or might be the case EG *It could rain*. **3** You use 'could' when you are asking for something politely EG *Could you tell me the name of that film?*

coulomb coulombs
Said "koo-lom" NOUN a unit used to measure electric charge.

council councils
NOUN **1** a group of people elected to look after the affairs of a town, district, or county. **2** Some other groups have Council as part of their name EG *the World Gold Council*.

councillor councillors
NOUN an elected member of a local council.

counsel counsels counselling counselled
NOUN **1** A FORMAL USE To give someone counsel is to give them advice. ▶ VERB **2** To counsel people is to give them advice about their problems.
counselling NOUN, **counsellor** NOUN

count counts counting counted
VERB **1** To count is to say all the numbers in order up to a particular number. **2** If you count all the things in a group, you add them up to see how many there are. **3** What counts in a situation is whatever is most important. **4** To count as something means to be regarded as that thing EG *I'm not sure whether this counts as harassment*. **5** If you can count on someone or something, you can rely on them. ▶ NOUN **6** a number reached by counting. **7** A FORMAL USE If something is wrong on a particular count, it is wrong in that respect. **8** a European nobleman.
■ (sense 2) add (up), calculate, reckon

countdown countdowns
NOUN the counting aloud of numbers in reverse order before something happens, especially before a spacecraft is launched.

countenance countenances
NOUN; A FORMAL WORD Someone's countenance is their face.

counter counters countering countered
NOUN **1** a long, flat surface over which goods are sold in a shop. **2** a small, flat, round object used in board games. ▶ VERB **3** If you counter something that is being done, you take action to make it less effective EG *I countered that argument with a reference to our sales report*.

counteract counteracts counteracting counteracted
VERB To counteract something is to

reduce its effect by producing an opposite effect.

counterfeit counterfeits counterfeiting counterfeited
*Said "***kown**-ter-fit" ADJECTIVE
1 Something counterfeit is not genuine but has been made to look genuine to deceive people EG *counterfeit money.* ▸ VERB **2** To counterfeit something is to make a counterfeit version of it.

counterpart counterparts
NOUN The counterpart of a person or thing is another person or thing with a similar function in a different place EG *Unlike his British counterpart, the French mayor is an important personality.*

countess countesses
NOUN The wife of a count or earl, or a woman with the same rank as a count or earl.

counting
PREPOSITION You say 'counting' when including something in a calculation EG *nearly 4000 of us, not counting women and children.*

countless
ADJECTIVE too many to count EG *There had been countless demonstrations.*
≡ incalculable, innumerable

country countries
NOUN **1** one of the political areas the world is divided into. **2** The country is land away from towns and cities. **3** 'Country' is used to refer to an area with particular features or associations EG *the heart of wine country.*
≡ (sense 1) nation, state

countryman countrymen
NOUN Your countrymen are people from your own country.

countryside
NOUN The countryside is land away from towns and cities.

county counties
NOUN a region with its own local government.
🏛 from Old French *conté* meaning

'land belonging to a count'

coup coups
*Rhymes with "***you**" NOUN When there is a coup, a group of people seize power in a country.
🏛 from French *coup* meaning 'a blow'

couple couples coupling coupled
NOUN **1** two people who are married or having a sexual or romantic relationship. **2** A couple of things or people means two of them EG *a couple of weeks ago.* ▸ VERB **3** If one thing is coupled with another, the two things are done or dealt with together EG *Its stores combine high quality coupled with low prices.*

couplet couplets
NOUN two lines of poetry together, especially two that rhyme.

coupon coupons
NOUN **1** a piece of printed paper which, when you hand it in, entitles you to pay less than usual for something. **2** a form you fill in to ask for information or to enter a competition.

courage
NOUN Courage is the quality shown by people who do things knowing they are dangerous or difficult.
courageous ADJECTIVE, **courageously** ADVERB

courgette courgettes
*Said "***koor-jet**" NOUN a type of small marrow with dark green skin. Courgettes are also called **zucchini**.
🏛 from French *courgette* meaning 'little marrow'

courier couriers
*Said "***koo-ree-er**" NOUN **1** someone employed by a travel company to look after people on holiday. **2** someone employed to deliver special letters quickly.

course courses
NOUN **1** a series of lessons or lectures. **2** a series of medical treatments EG *a course of injections.* **3** one of the parts of a meal. **4** A course or a course of action is one

of the things you can do in a situation. **5** a piece of land where a sport such as golf is played. **6** the route a ship or aircraft takes. **7** If something happens in the course of a period of time, it happens during that period eg *Ten people died in the course of the day*. ▶ PHRASE **8** If you say **of course**, you are showing that something is totally expected or that you are sure about something eg *Of course she wouldn't do that*.

court courts courting courted
NOUN **1** a place where legal matters are decided by a judge and jury or a magistrate. The judge and jury or magistrate can also be referred to as the court. **2** a place where a game such as tennis or badminton is played. **3** the place where a king or queen lives and carries out ceremonial duties. ▶ VERB **4** AN OLD-FASHIONED USE If a man and woman are courting, they are spending a lot of time together because they intend to get married.

courteous
*Said "***kur-tee-yuss***"* ADJECTIVE Courteous behaviour is polite and considerate.
🔲 from Old French *corteis* meaning 'courtly-mannered'

courtesy
NOUN Courtesy is polite, considerate behaviour.

courtier courtiers
NOUN Courtiers were noblemen and noblewomen at the court of a king or queen.

court-martial court-martials court-martialling court-martialled
NOUN **1** a military trial. ▶ VERB **2** If a member of the armed forces is court-martialled, he or she is tried by a court martial.

courtship
NOUN; A FORMAL WORD Courtship is the activity of courting or the period of time during which a man and a woman are courting.

courtyard courtyards
NOUN a flat area of ground surrounded by buildings or walls.

cousin cousins
NOUN Your cousin is the child of your uncle or aunt.

cove coves
NOUN a small bay.

covenant covenants
*Said "***kuv-vi-nant***"* NOUN a formal written agreement or promise.

cover covers covering covered
VERB **1** If you cover something, you put something else over it to protect it or hide it. **2** If something covers something else, it forms a layer over it eg *Tears covered his face*. **3** If you cover a particular distance, you travel that distance eg *He covered 52 kilometres in 210 laps*. ▶ NOUN **4** something put over an object to protect it or keep it warm. **5** The cover of a book or magazine is its outside. **6** Insurance cover is a guarantee that money will be paid if something is lost or harmed. **7** In the open, cover consists of trees, rocks, or other places where you can shelter or hide.
cover up VERB If you cover up something you do not want people to know about, you hide it from them eg *Those who cover up weakness with strength*.
cover-up NOUN

coverage
NOUN The coverage of something in the news is the reporting of it.

covert
*Said "***kuv-vert***"* ADJECTIVE; A FORMAL WORD Covert activities are secret, rather than open.
covertly ADVERB

covet covets coveting coveted
*Said "***kuv-vit***"* VERB; A FORMAL WORD If you covet something, you want it very much.

cow cows
NOUN a large animal kept on farms for its milk.

A
B
C
D
E
F
G
H
I
J
K
L
M
N
O
P
Q
R
S
T
U
V
W
X
Y
Z

coward cowards
NOUN someone who is easily frightened and who avoids dangerous or difficult situations.
cowardly ADJECTIVE, **cowardice** NOUN

cowboy cowboys
NOUN a man employed to look after cattle in America.

cower cowers cowering cowered
VERB When someone cowers, they crouch or move backwards because they are afraid.
◼ cringe, shrink

cox coxes
NOUN a person who steers a boat.

coy coyer coyest
ADJECTIVE If someone is coy, they pretend to be shy and modest.
coyly ADVERB

coyote coyotes
Said "koy-**ote**-ee" NOUN a North American animal like a small wolf.

crab crabs
NOUN a sea creature with four pairs of legs, two pincers, and a flat, round body covered by a shell.

crack cracks cracking cracked
VERB 1 If something cracks, it becomes damaged, with lines appearing on its surface. 2 If you crack a joke, you tell it. 3 If you crack a problem or code, you solve it. ▶ NOUN 4 one of the lines appearing on something when it cracks. 5 a narrow gap. ▶ ADJECTIVE 6 A crack soldier or sportsman is highly trained and skilful.
◼ (sense 5) break, fracture, gap

cracker crackers
NOUN 1 a thin, crisp biscuit that is often eaten with cheese. 2 a paper-covered tube that pulls apart with a bang and usually has a toy and paper hat inside.

crackle crackles crackling crackled
VERB 1 If something crackles, it makes a rapid series of short, harsh noises. ▶ NOUN 2 a short, harsh noise.

cradle ▶ cradles cradling cradled

NOUN 1 a box-shaped bed for a baby.
▶ VERB 2 If you cradle something in your arms or hands, you hold it there carefully.

craft crafts
NOUN 1 an activity such as weaving, carving, or pottery. 2 a skilful occupation EG the writer's craft. 3 a boat, plane, or spacecraft.
☑ When craft means 'a boat, plane, or spacecraft' (sense 3), the plural is craft.

craftsman craftsmen
NOUN a man who makes things skilfully with his hands.
craftsmanship NOUN, **craftswoman** NOUN

crafty craftier craftiest
ADJECTIVE Someone who is crafty gets what they want by tricking people in a clever way.

crag crags
NOUN a steep rugged rock or peak.

craggy craggier craggiest
ADJECTIVE A craggy mountain or cliff is steep and rocky.

cram crams cramming crammed
VERB If you cram people or things into a place, you put more in than there is room for.
◼ pack, squeeze, stuff

cramp cramps
NOUN Cramp or cramps is a pain caused by a muscle contracting.

cramped
ADJECTIVE If a room or building is cramped, it is not big enough for the people or things in it.

cranberry cranberries
NOUN Cranberries are sour-tasting red berries, often made into a sauce.

crane cranes craning craned
NOUN 1 a machine that moves heavy things by lifting them in the air. 2 a large bird with a long neck and long legs. ▶ VERB 3 If you crane your neck, you extend your head in a particular direction to see or hear something better.

crank cranks cranking cranked
NOUN 1 AN INFORMAL USE someone with

strange ideas who behaves in an odd way. **2** a device you turn to make something move EG *The adjustment is made by turning the crank.* ▶ VERB **3** If you crank something, you make it move by turning a handle.
cranky ADJECTIVE

cranny crannies
NOUN a very narrow opening in a wall or rock EG *nooks and crannies.*

crash crashes crashing crashed
NOUN **1** an accident in which a moving vehicle hits something violently. **2** a sudden loud noise EG *the crash of the waves on the rocks.* **3** the sudden failure of a business or financial institution. ▶ VERB **4** When a vehicle crashes, it hits something and is badly damaged.

crash helmet crash helmets
NOUN a helmet worn by motor cyclists for protection when they are riding.

crate crates
NOUN a large box used for transporting or storing things.

crater craters
NOUN a wide hole in the ground caused by something hitting it or by an explosion.

cravat cravats
NOUN a piece of cloth a man can wear round his neck tucked into his shirt collar.
▥ from Serbo-Croat *Hrvat* meaning 'Croat'. Croat soldiers wore cravats during the Thirty Years' War

crave craves craving craved
VERB If you crave something, you want it very much EG *I crave her approval.*
craving NOUN

crawl crawls crawling crawled
VERB **1** When you crawl, you move forward on your hands and knees. **2** When a vehicle crawls, it moves very slowly. **3** AN INFORMAL USE If a place is crawling with people or things, it is full of them EG *The place is crawling with drunks.*
crawler NOUN

crayfish crayfishes or crayfish
NOUN a small shellfish like a lobster.
▥ from Old French *crevice* meaning 'crab'

crayon crayons
NOUN a coloured pencil or a stick of coloured wax.

craze crazes
NOUN something that is very popular for a short time.

crazy crazier craziest
ADJECTIVE; AN INFORMAL WORD **1** very strange or foolish EG *The guy is crazy... a crazy idea.* **2** If you are crazy about something, you are very keen on it EG *I was crazy about dancing.*
crazily ADVERB, **craziness** NOUN

creak creaks creaking creaked
VERB **1** If something creaks, it makes a harsh sound when it moves or when you stand on it. ▶ NOUN **2** a harsh squeaking noise.
creaky ADJECTIVE

cream creams
NOUN **1** Cream is a thick, yellowish-white liquid taken from the top of milk. **2** Cream is also a substance people can rub on their skin to make it soft. ▶ ADJECTIVE **3** yellowish-white.
creamy ADJECTIVE

crease creases creasing creased
NOUN **1** an irregular line that appears on cloth or paper when it is crumpled. **2** a straight line on something that has been pressed or folded neatly. ▶ VERB **3** To crease something is to make lines appear on it.
creased ADJECTIVE

create creates creating created
VERB **1** To create something is to cause it to happen or exist EG *This is absolutely vital but creates a problem.* **2** When someone creates a new product or process, they invent it.
creator NOUN, **creation** NOUN

creative

ADJECTIVE **1** Creative people are able to invent and develop original ideas. **2** Creative activities involve the inventing and developing of original ideas EG *creative writing*.
creatively ADVERB, **creativity** NOUN

creature creatures

NOUN any living thing that moves about.

crèche crèches

Said "**kresh**" NOUN a place where small children are looked after while their parents are working.
📖 from Old French *crèche* meaning 'crib' or 'manger'

credence

NOUN; A FORMAL WORD If something gives credence to a theory or story, it makes it easier to believe.

credentials

PLURAL NOUN Your credentials are your past achievements or other things in your background that make you qualified for something.

credible

ADJECTIVE If someone or something is credible, you can believe or trust them.
credibility NOUN

credit credits crediting credited

NOUN **1** If you are allowed credit, you can take something and pay for it later EG *to buy goods on credit*. **2** If you get the credit for something, people praise you for it. **3** If you say someone is a credit to their family or school, you mean that their family or school should be proud of them. ▶ PLURAL NOUN **4** The list of people who helped make a film, record, or television programme is called the credits. ▶ PHRASE **5** If someone or their bank account is **in credit**, their account has money in it. ▶ VERB **6** If you are credited with an achievement, people believe that you were responsible for it.

creditable

ADJECTIVE satisfactory or fairly good

168

EG *a creditable performance*.

credit card credit cards

NOUN a plastic card that allows someone to buy goods on credit.

creditor creditors

NOUN Your creditors are the people you owe money to.

creed creeds

NOUN **1** a religion. **2** any set of beliefs EG *the feminist creed*.

creek creeks

NOUN a narrow inlet where the sea comes a long way into the land.
📖 from Old Norse *kriki* meaning 'nook'

creep creeps creeping crept

VERB To creep is to move quietly and slowly.

creepy creepier creepiest

ADJECTIVE; AN INFORMAL WORD strange and frightening EG *a creepy feeling*.

cremate cremates cremating cremated

VERB When someone is cremated, their dead body is burned during a funeral service.
cremation NOUN

crematorium crematoriums or crematoria

NOUN a building in which the bodies of dead people are burned.

crepe

Said "**krayp**" NOUN **1** Crepe is a thin ridged material made from cotton, silk, or wool. **2** Crepe is also a type of rubber with a rough surface.

crescendo crescendos

Said "**krish-en-doe**" NOUN When there is a crescendo in a piece of music, the music gets louder.

crescent crescents

NOUN a curved shape that is wider in its middle than at the ends, which are pointed.

cress

NOUN Cress is a plant with small, strong-tasting leaves. It is used in salads.

crest crests

NOUN **1** The crest of a hill or wave is its highest part. **2** a tuft of feathers on top of a bird's head. **3** a small picture or design that is the emblem of a noble family, a town, or an organization.
crested ADJECTIVE

crevice crevices
NOUN a narrow crack or gap in rock.

crew crews
NOUN **1** The crew of a ship, aeroplane, or spacecraft are the people who operate it. **2** people with special technical skills who work together EG *the camera crew*.

crib cribs cribbing cribbed
VERB **1** AN INFORMAL USE If you crib, you copy what someone else has written and pretend it is your own work. ▶ NOUN **2** AN OLD-FASHIONED USE a baby's cot.

crib-wall crib-walls
NOUN In New Zealand English, a wooden wall built against a bank of earth to support it.

crick cricks
NOUN a pain in your neck or back caused by muscles becoming stiff.

cricket crickets
NOUN **1** Cricket is an outdoor game played by two teams who take turns at scoring runs by hitting a ball with a bat. **2** a small jumping insect that produces sounds by rubbing its wings together.
cricketer NOUN

crime crimes
NOUN an action for which you can be punished by law EG *a serious crime*.
■ misdemeanour, offence

criminal criminals
NOUN **1** someone who has committed a crime. ▶ ADJECTIVE **2** involving or related to crime EG *criminal activities*.
criminally ADVERB
■ (sense 1) crook, lawbreaker, offender

crimson

NOUN OR ADJECTIVE dark purplish-red.

cringe cringes cringing cringed
VERB If you cringe, you back away from someone or something because you are afraid or embarrassed.
🏛 from Old English *cringan* meaning 'to yield in battle'

crinkle crinkles crinkling crinkled
VERB **1** If something crinkles, it becomes slightly creased or folded. ▶ NOUN **2** Crinkles are small creases or folds.

cripple cripples crippling crippled
NOUN **1** someone who cannot move their body properly because it is weak or affected by disease. ▶ VERB **2** To cripple someone is to injure them severely so that they can never move properly again.
crippled ADJECTIVE, **crippling** ADJECTIVE

crisis crises
Said "kry-seez in the plural" NOUN a serious or dangerous situation.

crisp crisper crispest; crisps
ADJECTIVE **1** Something that is crisp is pleasantly fresh and firm EG *crisp lettuce leaves*. **2** If the air or the weather is crisp, it is pleasantly fresh, cold, and dry EG *crisp wintry days*. ▶ NOUN **3** Crisps are thin slices of potato fried until they are hard and crunchy.

crispy crispier crispiest
ADJECTIVE Crispy food is pleasantly hard and crunchy EG *a crispy salad*.

criterion criteria
Said "kry-teer-ee-on" NOUN a standard by which you judge or decide something.
✔ *Criteria* is the plural of *criterion*, and needs to be used with a plural verb.

critic critics
NOUN **1** someone who writes reviews of books, films, plays, or musical performances. **2** A critic of a person or system is someone who criticizes them publicly EG *the government's critics*.

A
B
C
D
E
F
G
H
I
J
K
L
M
N
O
P
Q
R
S
T
U
V
W
X
Y
Z

critical

ADJECTIVE **1** A critical time is one which is very important in determining what happens in the future EG *critical months in the history of the world.* **2** A critical situation is a very serious one EG *Rock music is in a critical state.* **3** If an ill or injured person is critical, they are in danger of dying. **4** If you are critical of something or someone, you express severe judgments or opinions about them. **5** If you are critical, you examine and judge something carefully EG *a critical look at the way he led his life.*
critically ADVERB

criticism criticisms

NOUN **1** When there is criticism of someone or something, people express disapproval of them. **2** If you make a criticism, you point out a fault you think someone or something has.

criticize criticizes criticizing criticized; also spelt **criticise**

VERB If you criticize someone or something, you say what you think is wrong with them.
■ disparage, find fault with

croak croaks croaking croaked

VERB **1** When animals and birds croak, they make harsh, low sounds. ▶ NOUN **2** a harsh, low sound.
🏛 from Old Norse *kraka* meaning 'crow'

Croatian Croatians

ADJECTIVE **1** belonging to or relating to Croatia. ▶ NOUN **2** someone who comes from Croatia. **3** Croatian is the form of Serbo-Croat spoken in Croatia.

crochet

Said "**kroh-shay**" NOUN Crochet is a way of making clothes and other things out of thread using a needle with a small hook at the end.

crockery

NOUN Crockery is plates, cups, and saucers.

crocodile crocodiles

NOUN a large scaly meat-eating reptile which lives in tropical rivers.
🏛 from Greek *krokodeilos* meaning 'lizard'

crocus crocuses

NOUN Crocuses are yellow, purple, or white flowers that grow in early spring.

croft crofts

NOUN a small piece of land, especially in Scotland, which is farmed by one family.
crofter NOUN

croissant croissants

Said "**krwus-son**" NOUN a light, crescent-shaped roll eaten at breakfast.
🏛 from French *croissant* meaning 'crescent'

crony cronies

NOUN; AN OLD-FASHIONED WORD Your cronies are the friends you spend a lot of time with.

crook crooks

NOUN **1** AN INFORMAL USE a criminal. **2** The crook of your arm or leg is the soft inside part where you bend your elbow or knee.

crooked

Said "**kroo-kid**" ADJECTIVE **1** bent or twisted. **2** Someone who is crooked is dishonest.

croon croons crooning crooned

VERB To croon is to sing or hum quietly and gently EG *He crooned a love song.*
🏛 from Old Dutch *kronen* meaning 'to groan'

crop crops cropping cropped

NOUN **1** Crops are plants such as wheat and potatoes that are grown for food. **2** the plants collected at harvest time EG *You should have two crops in the year.* ▶ VERB **3** To crop someone's hair is to cut it very short.

croquet

Said "**kroh-kay**" NOUN Croquet is a

game in which the players use long-handled mallets to hit balls through metal arches pushed into a lawn.

cross crosses crossing crossed; crosser crossest

VERB **1** If you cross something such as a room or a road, you go to the other side of it. **2** Lines or roads that cross meet and go across each other. **3** If a thought crosses your mind, you think of it. **4** If you cross your arms, legs, or fingers, you put one on top of the other. ▶ NOUN **5** a vertical bar or line crossed by a shorter horizontal bar or line; also used to describe any object shaped like this. **6** The Cross is the cross-shaped structure on which Jesus Christ was crucified. A cross is also any symbol representing Christ's Cross. **7** a written mark shaped like an X EG *I drew a small bicycle and put a cross by it.* **8** Something that is a cross between two things is neither one thing nor the other, but a mixture of both. ▶ ADJECTIVE **9** Someone who is cross is rather angry.
crossly ADVERB

crossbow crossbows
NOUN a weapon consisting of a small bow fixed at the end of a piece of wood.

cross-country
NOUN **1** Cross-country is the sport of running across open countryside, rather than on roads or on a track. ▶ ADVERB OR ADJECTIVE **2** across country.

cross-eyed
ADJECTIVE A cross-eyed person has eyes that seem to look towards each other.

crossfire
NOUN Crossfire is gunfire crossing the same place from opposite directions.

crossing crossings
NOUN **1** a place where you can cross a road safely. **2** a journey by ship to a place on the other side of the sea.

cross-legged
ADJECTIVE If you are sitting cross-legged, you are sitting on the floor with your knees pointing outwards and your feet tucked under them.

cross section cross sections
NOUN A cross section of a group of people is a representative sample of them.

crossword crosswords
NOUN a puzzle in which you work out the answers to clues and write them in the white squares of a pattern of black and white squares.

crotch crotches
NOUN the part of your body between the tops of your legs.

crouch crouches crouching crouched
VERB If you are crouching, you are leaning forward with your legs bent under you.

crow crows crowing crowed
NOUN **1** a large black bird which makes a loud, harsh noise. ▶ VERB **2** When a cock crows, it utters a loud squawking sound.

crowbar crowbars
NOUN a heavy iron bar used as a lever or for forcing things open.

crowd crowds crowding crowded
NOUN **1** a large group of people gathered together. ▶ VERB **2** When people crowd somewhere, they gather there close together or in large numbers.
■ (sense 1) mass, mob, multitude, throng

crowded
ADJECTIVE A crowded place is full of people.

crown crowns crowning crowned
NOUN **1** a circular ornament worn on a royal person's head. **2** The crown of something such as your head is the top part of it. ▶ VERB **3** When a king or queen is crowned, a crown is put on their head during their coronation ceremony. **4** When

A B C D E F G H I J K L M N O P Q R S T U V W X Y Z

something crowns an event, it is the final part of it EG *The news crowned a dreadful week.*

crucial
Said "kroo-shl" ADJECTIVE If something is crucial, it is very important in determining how something else will be in the future.
🔲 from Latin *crux* meaning 'a cross'
▪ critical, decisive, vital

crucifix crucifixes
NOUN a cross with a figure representing Jesus Christ being crucified on it.

crucify crucifies crucifying crucified
VERB To crucify someone is to tie or nail them to a cross and leave them there to die.
crucifixion NOUN

crude cruder crudest
ADJECTIVE 1 rough and simple EG *a crude weapon... a crude method of entry.* 2 A crude person speaks or behaves in a rude and offensive way EG *You can be quite crude at times.*
crudely ADVERB, **crudity** NOUN
▪ (sense 1) makeshift, primitive
▪ (sense 2) coarse, vulgar

cruel crueller cruellest
ADJECTIVE Cruel people deliberately cause pain or distress to other people or to animals.
cruelly ADVERB, **cruelty** NOUN
▪ brutal, callous, unkind

cruise cruises cruising cruised
NOUN 1 a holiday in which you travel on a ship and visit places.
▶ VERB 2 When a vehicle cruises, it moves at a constant moderate speed.

cruiser cruisers
NOUN 1 a motor boat with a cabin you can sleep in. 2 a large, fast warship.

crumb crumbs
NOUN Crumbs are very small pieces of bread or cake.

crumble crumbles crumbling crumbled
VERB When something crumbles, it breaks into small pieces.

crumbly
ADJECTIVE Something crumbly easily breaks into small pieces.

crumpet crumpets
NOUN a round, flat, breadlike cake which you eat toasted.

crumple crumples crumpling crumpled
VERB To crumple paper or cloth is to squash it so that it is full of creases and folds.

crunch crunches crunching crunched
VERB If you crunch something, you crush it noisily, for example between your teeth or under your feet.

crunchy crunchier crunchiest
ADJECTIVE Crunchy food is hard or crisp and makes a noise when you eat it.

crusade crusades
NOUN a long and determined attempt to achieve something EG *the crusade for human rights.*
crusader NOUN

crush crushes crushing crushed
VERB 1 To crush something is to destroy its shape by squeezing it. 2 To crush a substance is to turn it into liquid or powder by squeezing or grinding it. 3 To crush an army or political organization is to defeat it completely. ▶ NOUN 4 a dense crowd of people.

crust crusts
NOUN 1 the hard outside part of a loaf. 2 a hard layer on top of something EG *The snow had a fine crust on it.*

crusty crustier crustiest
ADJECTIVE 1 Something that is crusty has a hard outside layer. 2 Crusty people are impatient and irritable.

crutch crutches
NOUN a support like a long stick

A B C D E F G H I J K L M N O P Q R S T U V W X Y Z

which you lean on to help you walk when you have an injured foot or leg.

crux
NOUN the most important or difficult part of a problem or argument.

cry cries crying cried
VERB **1** When you cry, tears appear in your eyes. **2** To cry something is to shout it or say it loudly EG *'See you soon!' they cried*. ▸ NOUN **3** If you have a cry, you cry for a period of time. **4** a shout or other loud sound made with your voice. **5** a loud sound made by some birds EG *the cry of a seagull*.
■ (sense 1) sob, weep

crypt crypts
NOUN an underground room beneath a church, usually used as a burial place.
🏛 from Greek *kruptein* meaning 'to hide'

cryptic
ADJECTIVE A cryptic remark or message has a hidden meaning.

crystal crystals
NOUN **1** a piece of a mineral that has formed naturally into a regular shape. **2** Crystal is a type of transparent rock, used in jewellery. **3** Crystal is also a kind of very high quality glass.
crystalline ADJECTIVE

crystallize crystallizes crystallizing crystallized; also spelt **crystallise**
VERB **1** If a substance crystallizes, it turns into crystals. **2** If an idea crystallizes, it becomes clear in your mind.

cub cubs
NOUN **1** Some young wild animals are called cubs EG *a lion cub*. **2** The Cubs is an organization for young boys before they join the Scouts.

Cuban Cubans
Said "**kyoo**-ban" ADJECTIVE
1 belonging or relating to Cuba.
▸ NOUN **2** someone who comes from Cuba.

cube cubes cubing cubed
NOUN **1** a three-dimensional shape with six equally-sized square surfaces. **2** If you multiply a number by itself twice, you get its cube. ▸ VERB **3** To cube a number is to multiply it by itself twice.

cubic
ADJECTIVE used in measurements of volume EG *cubic centimetres*.

cubicle cubicles
NOUN a small enclosed area in a place such as a sports centre, where you can dress and undress.

cuckoo cuckoos
NOUN a grey bird with a two-note call that lays its eggs in other birds' nests.

cucumber cucumbers
NOUN a long, thin, green-skinned vegetable eaten raw.

cuddle cuddles cuddling cuddled
VERB **1** If you cuddle someone, you hold them affectionately in your arms. ▸ NOUN **2** If you give someone a cuddle, you hold them affectionately in your arms.

cuddly cuddlier cuddliest
ADJECTIVE Cuddly people, animals, or toys are soft or pleasing in some way so that you want to cuddle them.

cue cues
NOUN **1** something said or done by a performer that is a signal for another performer to begin EG *Chris never misses a cue*. **2** a long stick used to hit the balls in snooker and billiards.

cuff cuffs
NOUN the end part of a sleeve.

cufflink cufflinks
NOUN Cufflinks are small objects for holding shirt cuffs together.

cuisine
Said "**kwiz-een**" NOUN The cuisine of a region is the style of cooking that is typical of it.
🏛 from French *cuisine* meaning 'kitchen'

A B C D E F G H I J K L M N O P Q R S T U V W X Y Z

173

cul-de-sac cul-de-sacs
Said "kul-des-sak" NOUN a road that does not lead to any other roads because one end is blocked off.

culinary
ADJECTIVE; A FORMAL WORD connected with the kitchen or cooking.
🏛 from Latin *culina* meaning 'kitchen'

cull culls culling culled
VERB 1 If you cull things, you gather them from different places or sources EG *information culled from movies*. ▶ NOUN 2 When there is a cull, weaker animals are killed to reduce the numbers in a group.

culminate culminates culminating culminated
VERB To culminate in something is to finally develop into it EG *a campaign that culminated in a stunning success*.
culmination NOUN

culprit culprits
NOUN someone who has done something harmful or wrong.
🏛 from Anglo-French *culpable* meaning 'guilty' and *prit* meaning 'ready' (i.e. ready for trial)

cult cults
NOUN 1 A cult is a religious group with special rituals, usually connected with the worship of a particular person. 2 'Cult' is used to refer to any situation in which someone or something is very popular with a large group of people EG *the American sports car cult*.

cultivate cultivates cultivating cultivated
VERB 1 To cultivate land is to grow crops on it. 2 If you cultivate a feeling or attitude, you try to develop it in yourself or other people.
cultivation NOUN

culture cultures
NOUN 1 Culture refers to the arts and to people's appreciation of them EG *He was a man of culture*. 2 The culture of a particular society is its ideas, customs, and art EG *Japanese culture*. 3 In science, a culture is a group of bacteria or cells grown in a laboratory.
cultured ADJECTIVE, **cultural** ADJECTIVE

cumulative
ADJECTIVE Something that is cumulative keeps being added to.

cunjevoi cunjevois
Said "kun-jiv-voi" NOUN a very small Australian sea creature that lives on rocks.

cunning
ADJECTIVE 1 Someone who is cunning uses clever and deceitful methods to get what they want. ▶ NOUN 2 Cunning is the ability to get what you want using clever and deceitful methods.
cunningly ADVERB
🏛 from Old Norse *kunna* meaning 'to know'
🟰 (sense 1) crafty, sly, wily

cup cups cupping cupped
NOUN 1 a small, round container with a handle, which you drink out of. 2 a large metal container with two handles, given as a prize. ▶ VERB 3 If you cup your hands, you put them together to make a shape like a cup.

cupboard cupboards
NOUN a piece of furniture with doors and shelves.

curable
ADJECTIVE If a disease or illness is curable, it can be cured.

curate curates
NOUN a clergyman who helps a vicar or a priest.

curator curators
NOUN the person in a museum or art gallery in charge of its contents.

curb curbs curbing curbed
VERB 1 To curb something is to keep it within limits EG *policies designed to curb inflation*. ▶ NOUN 2 If a curb is placed on something, it is kept within limits EG *the curb on spending*.

curdle curdles curdling curdled

VERB When milk curdles, it turns sour.

curds

PLURAL NOUN Curds are the thick white substance formed when milk turns sour.

cure cures curing cured

VERB **1** To cure an illness is to end it. **2** To cure a sick or injured person is to make them well. **3** If something cures you of a habit or attitude, it stops you having it. **4** To cure food, tobacco, or animal skin is to treat it in order to preserve it. ▶ NOUN **5** A cure for an illness is something that cures it.

■ (sense 2) heal, make better

curfew curfews

NOUN If there is a curfew, people must stay indoors between particular times at night.

curiosity curiosities

NOUN **1** Curiosity is the desire to know about something or about many things. **2** something unusual and interesting.

curious

ADJECTIVE **1** Someone who is curious wants to know more about something. **2** Something that is curious is unusual and hard to explain.

curiously ADVERB

■ (sense 1) inquiring, inquisitive, nosy

curl curls curling curled

NOUN **1** Curls are lengths of hair shaped in tight curves and circles. **2** a curved or spiral shape EG *the curls of morning fog*. ▶ VERB **3** If something curls, it moves in a curve or spiral.

curly ADJECTIVE

curler curlers

NOUN Curlers are plastic or metal tubes that women roll their hair round to make it curly.

curlew curlews

Said "**kur**-lyoo" NOUN a large brown bird with a long curved beak and a loud cry.

currant currants

NOUN **1** Currants are small dried grapes often put in cakes and puddings. **2** Currants are also blackcurrants or redcurrants.

▥ sense 1 is from Middle English *rayson of Corannte* meaning 'Corinth raisin'

currawong currawongs

NOUN an Australian bird like a crow.

currency currencies

NOUN **1** A country's currency is its coins and banknotes, or its monetary system generally EG *foreign currency... a strong economy and a weak currency*. **2** If something such as an idea has currency, it is used a lot at a particular time.

current currents

NOUN **1** a strong continuous movement of the water in a river or in the sea. **2** An air current is a flowing movement in the air. **3** An electric current is a flow of electricity through a wire or circuit. ▶ ADJECTIVE **4** Something that is current is happening, being done, or being used now.

currently ADVERB

current affairs

PLURAL NOUN Current affairs are political and social events discussed in newspapers and on television and radio.

curriculum curriculums or curricula

Said "kur-**rik**-yoo-lum" NOUN the different courses taught at a school or university.

curriculum vitae curricula vitae

Said "**vee**-tie" NOUN Someone's curriculum vitae is a written account of their personal details, education, and work experience which they send when they apply for a job.

curried

ADJECTIVE Curried food has been flavoured with hot spices EG *curried lamb*.

curry curries currying curried

NOUN **1** Curry is an Indian dish

A
B
C
D
E
F
G
H
I
J
K
L
M
N
O
P
Q
R
S
T
U
V
W
X
Y
Z

made with hot spices. ▸ PHRASE **2** To **curry favour** with someone means to try to please them by flattering them or doing things to help them. 🔲 sense 1 is from Tamil *kari* meaning 'sauce'; sense 2 is from Old French *correer* meaning 'to make ready'

curse curses cursing cursed
VERB **1** To curse is to swear because you are angry. **2** If you curse someone or something, you say angry things about them using rude words. ▸ NOUN **3** what you say when you curse. **4** something supernatural that is supposed to cause unpleasant things to happen to someone. **5** a thing or person that causes a lot of distress EG *the curse of recession.*
cursed ADJECTIVE

cursor cursors
NOUN an arrow or box on a computer monitor which indicates where the next letter or symbol is.

cursory
ADJECTIVE When you give something a cursory glance or examination, you look at it briefly without paying attention to detail.

curt curter curtest
ADJECTIVE If someone is curt, they speak in a brief and rather rude way.
curtly ADVERB

curtail curtails curtailing curtailed
VERB; A FORMAL WORD To curtail something is to reduce or restrict it EG *Injury curtailed his career.*

curtain curtains
NOUN **1** a hanging piece of material which can be pulled across a window for privacy or to keep out the light. **2** a large piece of material which hangs in front of the stage in a theatre until a performance begins. 🔲 from Latin *cortina* meaning 'enclosed space'

curtsy curtsies curtsying curtsied; also spelt **curtsey**

VERB **1** When a woman curtsies, she lowers her body briefly, bending her knees, to show respect. ▸ NOUN **2** the movement a woman makes when she curtsies EG *She gave a mock curtsy.*

curve curves curving curved
NOUN **1** a smooth, gradually bending line. ▸ VERB **2** When something curves, it moves in a curve or has the shape of a curve EG *The track curved away below him... His mouth curved slightly.*
curved ADJECTIVE

cushion cushions cushioning cushioned
NOUN **1** a soft object put on a seat to make it more comfortable. ▸ VERB **2** To cushion something is to reduce its effect EG *We might have helped to cushion the shock for her.*

custard
NOUN Custard is a sweet yellow sauce made from milk and eggs or milk and a powder.

custodian custodians
NOUN the person in charge of a collection in an art gallery or a museum.

custody
NOUN **1** To have custody of a child means to have the legal right to keep it and look after it EG *She won custody of her younger son.* ▸ PHRASE **2** Someone who is **in custody** is being kept in prison until they can be tried in a court.
custodial ADJECTIVE

custom customs
NOUN **1** a traditional activity EG *an ancient Chinese custom.* **2** something usually done at a particular time or in particular circumstances by a person or by the people in a society EG *It was also my custom to do Christmas shows.* **3** Customs is the place at a border, airport, or harbour where you have to declare any goods you are bringing into a country. **4** A FORMAL USE If a shop or business has your custom, you buy

things or go there regularly EG *Banks are desperate to get your custom.*
■ (sense 1) convention, tradition
■ (sense 2) habit, practice

customary
ADJECTIVE usual EG *his customary modesty... her customary greeting.*
customarily ADVERB

custom-built or **custom-made**
ADJECTIVE Something that is custom-built or custom-made is made to someone's special requirements.

customer customers
NOUN **1** A shop's or firm's customers are the people who buy its goods. **2** AN INFORMAL USE You can use 'customer' to refer to someone when describing what they are like to deal with EG *a tough customer.*
■ (sense 1) buyer, client, consumer

cut cuts cutting cut
VERB **1** If you cut something, you use a knife, scissors, or some other sharp tool to mark it or remove parts of it. **2** If you cut yourself, you injure yourself on a sharp object. **3** If you cut the amount of something, you reduce it EG *Some costs could be cut.* **4** When writing is cut, parts of it are not printed or broadcast. **5** To cut from one scene or shot to another in a film is to go instantly to the other scene or shot. ► NOUN **6** a mark made with a knife or other sharp tool. **7** an injury caused by a sharp object. **8** a reduction EG *another cut in interest rates.* **9** a part in something written that is not printed or broadcast. **10** a large piece of meat ready for cooking. ► ADJECTIVE **11** Well cut clothes have been well designed and made EG *this beautifully cut coat.*
cut back VERB To cut back or cut back on spending means to reduce it.
cutback NOUN
cut down VERB If you cut down on an activity, you do it less often EG *cutting down on smoking.*
cut off VERB **1** To cut someone or something off means to separate

them from things they are normally connected with EG *The President had cut himself off from the people.* **2** If a supply of something is cut off, you no longer get it EG *The water had been cut off.* **3** If your telephone or telephone call is cut off, it is disconnected.
cut out VERB **1** If you cut out something you are doing, you stop doing it EG *Cut out drinking.* **2** If an engine cuts out, it suddenly stops working.

cute cuter cutest
ADJECTIVE pretty or attractive.

cuticle cuticles
NOUN Cuticles are the pieces of skin that cover the base of your fingernails and toenails.

cutlass cutlasses
NOUN a curved sword that was used by sailors.

cutlery
NOUN Cutlery is knives, forks, and spoons.
▦ from Latin *culter* meaning 'knife'

cutlet cutlets
NOUN a small piece of meat which you fry or grill.

cutting cuttings
NOUN **1** something cut from a newspaper or magazine. **2** a part cut from a plant and used to grow a new plant. ► ADJECTIVE **3** A cutting remark is unkind and likely to hurt someone.

CV
an abbreviation for **curriculum vitae.**

cyanide
Said "sigh-an-nide" NOUN Cyanide is an extremely poisonous chemical.

cyberpet cyberpets
NOUN an electronic toy that imitates the activities of a pet, and needs to be fed and entertained.

cyberspace
NOUN all of the data stored in a large computer, seen as a three-dimensional model.

A B C D E F G H I J K L M N O P Q R S T U V W X Y Z

cycle cycles cycling cycled
VERB **1** When you cycle, you ride a bicycle. ▶ NOUN **2** a bicycle or a motorcycle. **3** a series of events which is repeated again and again in the same order EG *the cycle of births and deaths*. **4** a single complete series of movements or events in an electrical, electronic, mechanical, or organic process. **5** a series of songs or poems intended to be performed or read together.
from Greek *kuklos* meaning 'ring' or 'wheel'

cyclical or **cyclic**
ADJECTIVE happening over and over again in cycles EG *a clear cyclical pattern*.

cyclist cyclists
NOUN someone who rides a bicycle.

cyclone cyclones
NOUN a violent tropical storm.

cygnet cygnets
Said "sig-net" NOUN a young swan.
from Latin *cygnus* meaning 'swan'

cylinder cylinders
NOUN **1** a regular three-dimensional shape with two equally-sized flat circular ends joined by a curved surface. **2** the part in a motor engine in which the piston moves backwards and forwards.
cylindrical ADJECTIVE

cymbal cymbals
NOUN a circular brass plate used as a percussion instrument. Cymbals are clashed together or hit with a stick.

cynic cynics

Said "sin-nik" NOUN a cynical person.
from Greek *kunikos* meaning 'dog-like'

cynical
ADJECTIVE believing that people always behave selfishly or dishonestly.
cynically ADVERB, **cynicism** NOUN

cypher
another spelling of **cipher**.

cypress cypresses
NOUN a type of evergreen tree with small dark green leaves and round cones.

cyst cysts
Said "sist" NOUN a growth containing liquid that can form under your skin or inside your body.

czar
another spelling of **tsar**.

czarina
another spelling of **tsarina**.

Czech Czechs
Said "chek" ADJECTIVE **1** belonging or relating to the Czech Republic. ▶ NOUN **2** someone who comes from the Czech Republic. **3** Czech is the language spoken in the Czech Republic.

Czechoslovak Czechoslovaks
Said "chek-oh-slow-vak" ADJECTIVE **1** belonging to or relating to the country that used to be Czechoslovakia. ▶ NOUN **2** someone who came from the country that used to be Czechoslovakia.

A B C D E F G H I J K L M N O P Q R S T U V W X Y Z

dab dabs dabbing dabbed
VERB **1** If you dab something, you touch it with quick light strokes EG *He dabbed some disinfectant on to the gash.* ▸ NOUN **2** a small amount of something that is put on a surface EG *a dab of perfume.*

dabble dabbles dabbling dabbled
VERB If you dabble in something, you work or play at it without being seriously involved in it EG *All his life he dabbled in poetry.*

dachshund dachshunds
Said "daks-hoond" NOUN a small dog with a long body and very short legs.
🏛 a German word meaning 'badger-dog'

dad or **daddy** dads or daddies
NOUN; AN INFORMAL WORD Your dad or your daddy is your father.

daddy-long-legs
NOUN a harmless flying insect with very long legs.

daffodil daffodils
NOUN a plant with a yellow trumpet-shaped flower.

daft dafter daftest
ADJECTIVE stupid and not sensible.
🏛 from Old English *gedæfte* meaning 'gentle'

dagga
NOUN; AN INFORMAL WORD In South African English, dagga is cannabis.

dagger daggers
NOUN a weapon like a short knife.

dahlia dahlias
Said "dale-ya" NOUN a type of brightly coloured garden flower.

daily
ADJECTIVE **1** occurring every day EG *our daily visit to the gym.* **2** of or relating to a single day or to one day at a time EG *the average daily wage.*

dainty daintier daintiest
ADJECTIVE very delicate and pretty.
daintily ADVERB

dairy dairies
NOUN **1** a shop or company that supplies milk and milk products. **2** In New Zealand, a small shop selling groceries, often outside of usual opening hours. ▸ ADJECTIVE **3** Dairy products are foods made from milk, such as butter, cheese, cream, and yogurt. **4** A dairy farm is one which keeps cattle to produce milk.

dais
Said "day-is" NOUN a raised platform, normally at one end of a hall and used by a speaker.

daisy daisies
NOUN a small wild flower with a yellow centre and small white petals.
🏛 from Old English *dæges eage* meaning 'day's eye', because the daisy opens in the daytime and closes at night

dale dales
NOUN a valley.

dalmatian dalmatians
NOUN a large dog with short smooth white hair and black or brown spots.

dam dams
NOUN a barrier built across a river to hold back water.

damage damages damaging damaged
VERB **1** To damage something means to harm or spoil it. ▸ NOUN **2** Damage to something is injury or harm done to it. **3** Damages is the money awarded by a court to compensate someone for loss or harm.
damaging ADJECTIVE

dame dames
NOUN the title given to a woman who has been awarded the OBE or one of the other British orders of chivalry.

damn damns damning damned

Said "dam" VERB 1 To damn something or someone means to curse or condemn them. ▶ INTERJECTION **2** 'Damn' is a swearword.
damned ADJECTIVE

damnation
Said "dam-**nay**-shun" NOUN Damnation is eternal punishment in Hell after death.

damp damper dampest
ADJECTIVE **1** slightly wet. ▶ NOUN **2** Damp is slight wetness, especially in the air or in the walls of a building.
dampness NOUN
🏛 from Old German *damp* meaning 'steam'

dampen dampens dampening dampened
VERB **1** If you dampen something, you make it slightly wet. **2** To dampen something also means to reduce its liveliness or strength EG *The whole episode has rather dampened my enthusiasm.*

damper
AN INFORMAL PHRASE To **put a damper** on something means to stop it being enjoyable.

damson damsons
NOUN a small blue-black plum; also the tree that the fruit grows on.
🏛 from Latin *prunum Damascenum* meaning 'Damascus plum'

dance dances dancing danced
VERB **1** To dance means to move your feet and body rhythmically in time to music. ▶ NOUN **2** a series of rhythmic movements or steps in time to music. **3** a social event where people dance with each other.
dancer NOUN, **dancing** NOUN

dandelion dandelions
NOUN a wild plant with yellow flowers which form a ball of fluffy seeds.

dandruff
NOUN Dandruff is small, loose scales of dead skin in someone's hair.

dandy dandies
NOUN; AN OLD-FASHIONED USE a man who always dresses in very smart clothes.

Dane Danes
NOUN someone who comes from Denmark.

danger dangers
NOUN **1** Danger is the possibility that someone may be harmed or killed. **2** something or someone that can hurt or harm you.
🟰 (sense 1) hazard, peril, risk

dangerous
ADJECTIVE able to or likely to cause hurt or harm.
dangerously ADVERB
🟰 hazardous, perilous, unsafe

dangle dangles dangling dangled
VERB When something dangles or when you dangle it, it swings or hangs loosely.

Danish
ADJECTIVE **1** belonging or relating to Denmark. ▶ NOUN **2** Danish is the main language spoken in Denmark.

dank danker dankest
ADJECTIVE A dank place is unpleasantly damp and chilly.

dapper
ADJECTIVE slim and neatly dressed.
🏛 from Old Dutch *dapper* meaning 'active' or 'nimble'

dappled
ADJECTIVE marked with patches of a different or darker shade.

dare dares daring dared
VERB **1** To dare someone means to challenge them to do something in order to prove their courage. **2** To dare to do something means to have the courage to do it. ▶ NOUN **3** a challenge to do something dangerous.
☑ When *dare* is used in a question or with a negative, it does not add an s: *dare she come?*; *he dare not come.*

daredevil daredevils
NOUN a person who enjoys doing

A B C D E F G H I J K L M N O P Q R S T U V W X Y Z

dangerous things.

dark darker darkest
ADJECTIVE **1** If it is dark, there is not enough light to see properly. **2** Dark colours or surfaces reflect little light and so look deep-coloured or dull. **3** 'Dark' is also used to describe thoughts or ideas which are sinister or unpleasant. ▸ NOUN **4** The dark is the lack of light in a place.
darkly ADVERB, **darkness** NOUN
▤ (sense 1) dim, murky

darken darkens darkening darkened
VERB If something darkens, or if you darken it, it becomes darker than it was.

darkroom darkrooms
NOUN a room from which daylight is shut out so that photographic film can be developed.

darling darlings
NOUN Someone who is lovable or a favourite may be called a darling. ▸ ADJECTIVE **2** much admired or loved EG *his darling daughter*.

darn darns darning darned
VERB **1** To darn a hole in a garment means to mend it with crossing stitches. ▸ NOUN **2** a part of a garment that has been darned.

dart darts darting darted
NOUN **1** a small pointed arrow. **2** Darts is a game in which the players throw darts at a round board divided into numbered sections. ▸ VERB **3** To dart about means to move quickly and suddenly from one place to another.

dash dashes dashing dashed
VERB **1** To dash somewhere means to rush there. **2** If something is dashed against something else, it strikes it or is thrown violently against it. **3** If hopes or ambitions are dashed, they are ruined or frustrated. ▸ NOUN **4** a sudden movement or rush. **5** a small quantity of something. **6** the

punctuation mark (—) which shows a change of subject, or which may be used instead of brackets.

What does the Dash do?

The **dash** (—) marks an abrupt change in the flow of a sentence, either showing a sudden change of subject, or marking off extra information. The dash can also show that a speech has been cut off suddenly.
I'm not sure — what was the question again?
"Go ahead and —" He broke off as Robbie seized his arm.

---

dashboard dashboards
NOUN the instrument panel in a motor vehicle.

dashing
ADJECTIVE A dashing man is stylish and confident EG *He was a dashing figure in his younger days.*

dasyure dasyures
Said "dass-ee-your" NOUN a small marsupial that lives in Australia and eats meat.

data
NOUN Data is information, usually in the form of facts or statistics.
▥ from Latin *data* meaning 'things given'
☑ *Data* is really a plural word, but it is usually used as a singular.

database databases
NOUN a collection of information stored in a computer.

date dates dating dated
NOUN **1** a particular day or year that can be named. **2** If you have a date, you have an appointment to meet someone; also used to refer to the person you are meeting. **3** a small dark-brown sticky fruit with a stone inside, which grows on palm trees. ▸ VERB **4** If you are dating someone, you have a romantic relationship with them. **5** If you date something, you find out the time when it began or was made. **6** If something dates from a

particular time, that is when it happened or was made. ▶ PHRASE **7** If something is **out of date**, it is old-fashioned or no longer valid.

datum
the singular form of **data**.

daub daubs daubing daubed
VERB If you daub something such as mud or paint on a surface, you smear it there.

daughter daughters
NOUN Someone's daughter is their female child.

daughter-in-law daughters-in-law
NOUN Someone's daughter-in-law is the wife of their son.

daunt daunts daunting daunted
VERB If something daunts you, you feel worried about whether you can succeed in doing it EG *He was not the type of man to be daunted by adversity.*
daunting ADJECTIVE

dawn dawns dawning dawned
NOUN **1** the time in the morning when light first appears in the sky. **2** the beginning of something EG *the dawn of the radio age.* ▶ VERB **3** If day is dawning, morning light is beginning to appear. **4** If an idea or fact dawns on you, you realize it.

day days
NOUN **1** one of the seven 24-hour periods of time in a week, measured from one midnight to the next. **2** Day is the period of light between sunrise and sunset. **3** You can refer to a particular day or days meaning a particular period in history EG *in Gladstone's day.*

daybreak
NOUN Daybreak is the time in the morning when light first appears in the sky.

daydream daydreams daydreaming daydreamed
NOUN **1** a series of pleasant thoughts about things that you would like to happen. ▶ VERB **2** When you daydream, you drift off into a daydream.

daylight
NOUN **1** Daylight is the period during the day when it is light. **2** Daylight is also the light from the sun.

day-to-day
ADJECTIVE happening every day as part of ordinary routine life.

day trip day trips
NOUN a journey for pleasure to a place and back again on the same day.

daze
PHRASE If you are **in a daze**, you are confused and bewildered.

dazed
ADJECTIVE If you are dazed, you are stunned and unable to think clearly.

dazzle dazzles dazzling dazzled
VERB **1** If someone or something dazzles you, you are very impressed by their brilliance. **2** If a bright light dazzles you, it blinds you for a moment.
dazzling ADJECTIVE

de-
PREFIX When de- is added to a noun or verb, it changes the meaning to its opposite EG *de-ice.*

deacon deacons
NOUN **1** In the Church of England or Roman Catholic Church, a deacon is a member of the clergy below the rank of priest. **2** In some other churches, a deacon is a church official appointed to help the minister.
deaconess NOUN

dead
ADJECTIVE **1** no longer living or supporting life. **2** no longer used or no longer functioning EG *a dead language.* **3** If part of your body goes dead, it loses sensation and feels numb. ▶ NOUN **4** the middle part of night or winter, when it is most quiet and at its darkest or coldest.

dead end dead ends
NOUN a street that is closed off at

one end.

deadline deadlines
NOUN a time or date before which something must be completed.

deadlock deadlocks
NOUN a situation in which neither side in a dispute is willing to give in.
◼ impasse, stalemate

deadly deadlier deadliest
ADJECTIVE **1** likely or able to cause death. ▶ ADVERB OR ADJECTIVE **2** 'Deadly' is used to emphasize how serious or unpleasant a situation is EG *He is deadly serious about his comeback.*

deadpan
ADJECTIVE OR ADVERB showing no emotion or expression.

deaf deafer deafest
ADJECTIVE **1** partially or totally unable to hear. **2** refusing to listen or pay attention to something EG *He was deaf to all pleas for financial help.*
deafness NOUN

deafening
ADJECTIVE If a noise is deafening, it is so loud that you cannot hear anything else.

deal deals dealing dealt
NOUN **1** an agreement or arrangement, especially in business. ▶ VERB **2** If you deal with something, you do what is necessary to sort it out EG *He must learn to deal with stress.* **3** If you deal in a particular type of goods, you buy and sell those goods. **4** If you deal someone or something a blow, you hurt or harm them EG *Competition from abroad dealt a heavy blow to the industry.*

dealer dealers
NOUN a person or firm whose business involves buying or selling things.

dealings
PLURAL NOUN Your dealings with people are the relations you have with them or the business you do

with them.

dean deans
NOUN **1** In a university or college, a dean is a person responsible for administration or for the welfare of students. **2** In the Church of England, a dean is a clergyman who is responsible for administration.
🏛 from Latin *decanus* meaning 'someone in charge of ten people'

dear dears; dearer dearest
NOUN **1** 'Dear' is used as a sign of affection EG *What's the matter, dear?* ▶ ADJECTIVE **2** much loved EG *my dear son.* **3** Something that is dear is very expensive. **4** You use 'dear' at the beginning of a letter before the name of the person you are writing to.
dearly ADVERB
◼ (sense 2) beloved, cherished
◼ (sense 3) costly, expensive

dearth
Said "**derth**" NOUN a shortage of something.

death deaths
NOUN Death is the end of the life of a person or animal.

debacle debacles
Said "**day-bah-kl**" NOUN; A FORMAL WORD a sudden disastrous failure.

debase debases debasing debased
VERB To debase something means to reduce its value or quality.

debatable
ADJECTIVE not absolutely certain EG *The justness of these wars is debatable.*
◼ doubtful, questionable

debate debates debating debated
NOUN **1** Debate is argument or discussion EG *There is much debate as to what causes depression.* **2** a formal discussion in which opposing views are expressed. ▶ VERB **3** When people debate something, they discuss it in a fairly formal manner. **4** If you are debating whether or not to do something, you are

A B C D E F G H I J K L M N O P Q R S T U V W X Y Z

considering it EG *He was debating whether or not he should tell her.*

debilitating

ADJECTIVE; A FORMAL WORD If something is debilitating, it makes you very weak EG *a debilitating illness.*

debit debits debiting debited

VERB **1** to take money from a person's bank account. ▶ NOUN **2** a record of the money that has been taken out of a person's bank account.

debrief debriefs debriefing debriefed

VERB When someone is debriefed, they are asked to give a report on a task they have just completed.
debriefing NOUN

debris

Said "**day-bree**" NOUN Debris is fragments or rubble left after something has been destroyed.
📖 from Old French *débrisier* meaning 'to shatter'

debt debts

Said "**det**" NOUN **1** a sum of money that is owed to one person by another. **2** Debt is the state of owing money.

debtor debtors

NOUN a person who owes money.

debut debuts

Said "**day-byoo**" NOUN a performer's first public appearance.

debutante debutantes

Said "**deb-yoo-tant**" NOUN; AN OLD-FASHIONED WORD a girl from the upper classes who has started going to social events.

decade decades

NOUN a period of ten years.
📖 from Greek *deka* meaning 'ten'

decadence

NOUN Decadence is a decline in standards of morality and behaviour.
decadent ADJECTIVE

decaffeinated

Said "**dee-kaf-in-ate-ed**" ADJECTIVE Decaffeinated coffee or tea has had

most of the caffeine removed.

decanter decanters

NOUN a glass bottle with a stopper, from which wine and other drinks are served.

decapitate decapitates decapitating decapitated

VERB To decapitate someone means to cut off their head.

decathlon decathlons

Said "**de-cath-lon**" NOUN a sports contest in which athletes compete in ten different events.
📖 from Greek *deka* meaning 'ten' and *athlon* meaning 'contest'

decay decays decaying decayed

VERB **1** When things decay, they rot or go bad. ▶ NOUN **2** Decay is the process of decaying.

deceased

A FORMAL WORD ▶ ADJECTIVE **1** A deceased person is someone who has recently died. ▶ NOUN **2** The deceased is someone who has recently died.

deceit

NOUN Deceit is behaviour that is intended to mislead people into believing something that is not true.
deceitful ADJECTIVE

deceive deceives deceiving deceived

VERB If you deceive someone, you make them believe something that is not true.

decelerate decelerates decelerating decelerated

VERB If something decelerates, it slows down.
deceleration NOUN

December

NOUN December is the twelfth and last month of the year. It has 31 days.
📖 from Latin *December* meaning 'the tenth month'

decency

NOUN **1** Decency is behaviour that is respectable and follows accepted moral standards. **2** Decency is also behaviour which shows kindness and respect towards people EG *No one had the decency to tell me to my face.*

decent

ADJECTIVE **1** of an acceptable standard or quality EG *He gets a decent pension.* **2** Decent people are honest and respectable EG *a decent man.*
decently ADVERB
▤ (sense 2) respectable

decentralize decentralizes decentralizing decentralized; also spelt decentralise

VERB To decentralize an organization means to reorganize it so that power is transferred from one main administrative centre to smaller local units.
decentralization NOUN

deception deceptions

NOUN **1** something that is intended to trick or deceive someone. **2** Deception is the act of deceiving someone.

deceptive

ADJECTIVE likely to make people believe something that is not true.
deceptively ADVERB
▤ false, misleading

decibel decibels

NOUN a unit of the intensity of sound.

decide decides deciding decided

VERB If you decide to do something, you choose to do it.
▤ make up one's mind, reach *or* come to a decision

deciduous

ADJECTIVE Deciduous trees lose their leaves in the autumn every year.

decimal decimals

ADJECTIVE **1** The decimal system expresses numbers using all the digits from 0 to 9. ▶ NOUN **2** a fraction in which a dot called a decimal point is followed by numbers representing tenths, hundredths, and thousandths. For example, 0.5 represents $\frac{5}{10}$ (or ½);

0.05 represents $\frac{5}{100}$ (or $\frac{1}{20}$).
▥ from Latin *decima* meaning 'a tenth'

decimate decimates decimating decimated

VERB To decimate a group of people or animals means to kill or destroy a large number of them.

decipher deciphers deciphering deciphered

VERB If you decipher a piece of writing or a message, you work out its meaning.

decision decisions

NOUN a choice or judgment that is made about something EG *The editor's decision is final.*
▤ judgment, resolution

decisive

Said "dis-**sigh**-siv" ADJECTIVE
1 having great influence on the result of something EG *It was the decisive moment of the race.* **2** A decisive person is able to make decisions firmly and quickly.
decisively ADVERB, **decisiveness** NOUN

deck decks

NOUN **1** a floor or platform built into a ship, or one of the two floors on a bus. **2** a pack of cards.

deck chair deck chairs

NOUN a light folding chair, made from canvas and wood and used outdoors.

declaration declarations

NOUN a firm, forceful statement, often an official announcement EG *a declaration of war.*
▤ assertion, statement

declare declares declaring declared

VERB **1** If you declare something, you say it firmly and forcefully EG *He declared early he was going to be famous.* **2** To declare something means to announce it officially or formally EG *Catholicism was declared the state religion.* **3** If you declare goods or earnings, you state what you have bought or earned, in order to pay tax or duty.

A B C D E F G H I J K L M N O P Q R S T U V W X Y Z

A
B
C
D
E
F
G
H
I
J
K
L
M
N
O
P
Q
R
S
T
U
V
W
X
Y
Z

≡ (sense 1) announce, proclaim, state

decline declines declining declined
VERB **1** If something declines, it becomes smaller or weaker. **2** If you decline something, you politely refuse to accept it or do it. ▸ NOUN **3** a gradual weakening or decrease EG *a decline in the birth rate.*

decode decodes decoding decoded
VERB If you decode a coded message, you convert it into ordinary language.

decompose decomposes decomposing decomposed
VERB If something decomposes, it decays through chemical or bacterial action.

decor
Said "day-kor" NOUN The decor of a room or house is the style in which it is decorated and furnished.

decorate decorates decorating decorated
VERB **1** If you decorate something, you make it more attractive by adding some ornament or colour to it. **2** If you decorate a room or building, you paint or wallpaper it.
≡ (sense 1) adorn, ornament

decoration decorations
NOUN **1** Decorations are features added to something to make it more attractive. **2** The decoration in a building or room is the style of the furniture and wallpaper.

decorative
ADJECTIVE intended to look attractive.

decorator decorators
NOUN a person whose job is painting and wallpapering rooms and buildings.

decorum
Said "dik-ore-um" NOUN; A FORMAL WORD Decorum is polite and correct behaviour.

decoy decoys
NOUN a person or object that is used

to lead someone or something into danger.

decrease decreases decreasing decreased
VERB **1** If something decreases or if you decrease it, it becomes less in quantity or size. ▸ NOUN **2** a lessening in the amount of something; also the amount by which something becomes less.
decreasing ADJECTIVE

decree decrees decreeing decreed
VERB **1** If someone decrees something, they state formally that it will happen. ▸ NOUN **2** an official decision or order, usually by governments or rulers.

dedicate dedicates dedicating dedicated
VERB If you dedicate yourself to something, you devote your time and energy to it.
dedication NOUN
≡ commit, devote

deduce deduces deducing deduced
VERB If you deduce something, you work it out from other facts that you know are true.
≡ conclude, reason

deduct deducts deducting deducted
VERB To deduct an amount from a total amount means to subtract it from the total.

deduction deductions
NOUN **1** an amount which is taken away from a total. **2** a conclusion that you have reached because of other things that you know are true.

deed deeds
NOUN **1** something that is done. **2** a legal document, especially concerning the ownership of land or buildings.

deem deems deeming deemed
VERB; A FORMAL USE If you deem something to be true, you judge or consider it to be true EG *His ideas*

were deemed unacceptable.

deep deeper deepest

ADJECTIVE **1** situated or extending a long way down from the top surface of something, or a long way inwards EG *a deep hole*. **2** great or intense EG *deep suspicion*. **3** low in pitch EG *a deep voice*. **4** strong and fairly dark in colour EG *The wine was deep ruby in colour.*

deeply ADVERB

deepen deepens deepening deepened

VERB If something deepens or is deepened, it becomes deeper or more intense.

deer

NOUN a large, hoofed mammal that lives wild in parts of Britain.
📖 from Old English *deor* meaning 'beast'

deface defaces defacing defaced

VERB If you deface a wall or notice, you spoil it by writing or drawing on it EG *She spitefully defaced her sister's poster.*

default defaults defaulting defaulted

VERB **1** If someone defaults on something they have legally agreed to do, they fail to do it EG *He defaulted on repayment of the loan.*
▶ PHRASE **2** If something happens **by default**, it happens because something else which might have prevented it has failed to happen.

defeat defeats defeating defeated

VERB **1** If you defeat someone or something, you win a victory over them, or cause them to fail. ▶ NOUN **2** Defeat is the state of being beaten or of failing EG *He was gracious in defeat.* **3** an occasion on which someone is beaten or fails to achieve something EG *It was a crushing defeat for the government.*

defecate defecates defecating defecated

VERB To defecate means to get rid of waste matter from the bowels

through the anus.

defect defects defecting defected

NOUN **1** a fault or flaw in something.
▶ VERB **2** If someone defects, they leave their own country or organization and join an opposing one.

defection NOUN

defective

ADJECTIVE imperfect or faulty EG *defective eyesight.*

defence defences

NOUN **1** Defence is action that is taken to protect someone or something from attack. **2** any arguments used in support of something that has been criticized or questioned. **3** the case presented, in a court of law, by a lawyer for the person on trial; also the person on trial and his or her lawyers. **4** A country's defences are its military resources, such as its armed forces and weapons.

defend defends defending defended

VERB **1** To defend someone or something means to protect them from harm or danger. **2** If you defend a person or their ideas and beliefs, you argue in support of them. **3** To defend someone in court means to represent them and argue their case for them. **4** In a game such as football or hockey, to defend means to try to prevent goals being scored by your opponents.

defender NOUN

defendant defendants

NOUN a person who has been accused of a crime in a court of law.

defensible

ADJECTIVE able to be defended against criticism or attack.

defensive

ADJECTIVE **1** intended or designed for protection EG *defensive weapons.*
2 Someone who is defensive feels unsure and threatened by other

A B C D E F G H I J K L M N O P Q R S T U V W X Y Z

people's opinions and attitudes EG *Don't get defensive, I was only joking.*
defensively ADVERB, **defensiveness** NOUN

defer defers deferring deferred
VERB **1** If you defer something, you delay or postpone it until a future time. **2** If you defer to someone, you agree with them or do what they want because you respect them.

deference
Said "def-er-ense" NOUN Deference is polite and respectful behaviour.
deferential ADJECTIVE

defiance
NOUN Defiance is behaviour which shows that you are not willing to obey someone or behave in the expected way EG *a gesture of defiance.*
defiant ADJECTIVE, **defiantly** ADVERB

deficiency deficiencies
NOUN a lack of something EG *vitamin deficiency.*
deficient ADJECTIVE

deficit deficits
Said "def-iss-it" NOUN the amount by which money received by an organization is less than money spent.

define defines defining defined
VERB If you define something, you say what it is or what it means EG *Culture can be defined in hundreds of ways.*

definite
ADJECTIVE **1** firm and unlikely to be changed EG *The answer is a definite 'yes'.* **2** certain or true rather than guessed or imagined EG *definite proof.*
definitely ADVERB

definition definitions
NOUN a statement explaining the meaning of a word or idea.

definitive
ADJECTIVE **1** final and unable to be questioned or altered EG *a definitive answer.* **2** most complete, or the best of its kind EG *a definitive history of science fiction.*
definitively ADVERB

deflate deflates deflating deflated
VERB **1** If you deflate something such as a tyre or balloon, you let out all the air or gas in it. **2** If you deflate someone, you make them seem less important.

deflect deflects deflecting deflected
VERB To deflect something means to turn it aside or make it change direction.
deflection NOUN

deforestation
NOUN Deforestation is the cutting down of all the trees in an area.

deformed
ADJECTIVE disfigured or abnormally shaped.

defraud defrauds defrauding defrauded
VERB If someone defrauds you, they cheat you out of something that should be yours.

defrost defrosts defrosting defrosted
VERB **1** If you defrost a freezer or refrigerator, you remove the ice from it. **2** If you defrost frozen food, you let it thaw out.

deft defter deftest
ADJECTIVE Someone who is deft is quick and skilful in their movements.
deftly ADVERB

defunct
ADJECTIVE no longer existing or functioning.

defuse defuses defusing defused
VERB **1** To defuse a dangerous or tense situation means to make it less dangerous or tense. **2** To defuse a bomb means to remove its fuse or detonator so that it cannot explode.

defy defies defying defied
VERB **1** If you defy a person or a law, you openly refuse to obey. **2** A FORMAL USE If you defy someone to do something that you think is impossible, you challenge them to

do it.

■ (sense 1) disregard, flout, resist

degenerate degenerates
degenerating degenerated
VERB **1** If something degenerates, it
becomes worse EG *The election
campaign degenerated into farce.*
▶ ADJECTIVE **2** having low standards
of morality. ▶ NOUN **3** someone
whose standards of morality are so
low that people find their
behaviour shocking or disgusting.
degeneration NOUN

degradation
NOUN Degradation is a state of
poverty and misery.

degrade degrades degrading
degraded
VERB If something degrades people,
it humiliates them and makes them
feel that they are not respected.
degrading ADJECTIVE
■ debase, demean

degree degrees
NOUN **1** an amount of a feeling or
quality EG *a degree of pain.* **2** a unit of
measurement of temperature; often
written as ° after a number EG *20°C.*
3 a unit of measurement of angles
in mathematics, and of latitude
and longitude EG *The yacht was 20°
off course.* **4** a course of study at a
university or college; also the
qualification awarded after passing
the course.

dehydrated
ADJECTIVE If someone is dehydrated,
they are weak or ill because they
have lost too much water from
their body.

deign deigns deigning deigned
Said "**dane**" VERB; A FORMAL WORD If
you deign to do something, you do
it even though you think you are
too important to do such a thing.

deity deities
NOUN a god or goddess.

deja vu
Said "**day-ja voo**" NOUN Deja vu is
the feeling that you have already
experienced in the past exactly the

same sequence of events as is
happening now.
🏛 from French *déjà vu* meaning
literally 'already seen'

dejected
ADJECTIVE miserable and unhappy.
dejection NOUN

delay delays delaying delayed
VERB **1** If you delay doing
something, you put it off until a
later time. **2** If something delays
you, it hinders you or slows you
down. ▶ NOUN **3** Delay is time
during which something is
delayed.
■ (sense 1) postpone, put off

delectable
ADJECTIVE very pleasing or delightful.

delegate delegates delegating
delegated
NOUN **1** a person appointed to vote
or to make decisions on behalf of a
group of people. ▶ VERB **2** If you
delegate duties, you give them to
someone who can then act on your
behalf.

delegation delegations
NOUN **1** a group of people chosen to
represent a larger group of people.
2 Delegation is the giving of duties,
responsibilities, or power to
someone who can then act on your
behalf.

delete deletes deleting deleted
VERB To delete something written
means to cross it out or remove it.
deletion NOUN

deliberate deliberates
deliberating deliberated
ADJECTIVE **1** done on purpose or
planned in advance EG *It was a
deliberate insult.* **2** careful and not
hurried in speech and action EG *She
was very deliberate in her movements.*
▶ VERB **3** If you deliberate about
something, you think about it
seriously and carefully.
deliberately ADVERB
■ (sense 1) intentional, planned

deliberation deliberations
NOUN Deliberation is careful

A
B
C
D
E
F
G
H
I
J
K
L
M
N
O
P
Q
R
S
T
U
V
W
X
Y
Z

A
B
C
D
E
F
G
H
I
J
K
L
M
N
O
P
Q
R
S
T
U
V
W
X
Y
Z

consideration of a subject.

delicacy delicacies

NOUN **1** Delicacy is grace and attractiveness. **2** Something said or done with delicacy is said or done tactfully so that nobody is offended. **3** Delicacies are rare or expensive foods that are considered especially nice to eat.

delicate

ADJECTIVE **1** fine, graceful, or subtle in character EG *a delicate fragrance*. **2** fragile and needing to be handled carefully EG *delicate antique lace*. **3** precise or sensitive, and able to notice very small changes EG *a delicate instrument*.

delicately ADVERB

delicatessen delicatessens

NOUN a shop selling unusual or imported foods.

📖 from German *Delikatessen* meaning 'delicacies'

delicious

ADJECTIVE very pleasing, especially to taste.

deliciously ADVERB

📘 delectable, scrumptious

delight delights delighting delighted

NOUN **1** Delight is great pleasure or joy. ▶ VERB **2** If something delights you or if you are delighted by it, it gives you a lot of pleasure.

delighted ADJECTIVE

delightful

ADJECTIVE very pleasant and attractive.

delinquent delinquents

NOUN a young person who commits minor crimes.

delinquency NOUN

delirious

ADJECTIVE **1** unable to speak or act in a rational way because of illness or fever. **2** wildly excited and happy.

deliriously ADVERB

deliver delivers delivering delivered

VERB **1** If you deliver something to

someone, you take it to them and give it to them. **2** To deliver a lecture or speech means to give it.

delivery deliveries

NOUN **1** Delivery or a delivery is the bringing of letters or goods to a person or firm. **2** Someone's delivery is the way in which they give a speech.

dell dells

NOUN; A LITERARY WORD a small wooded valley.

delta deltas

NOUN a low, flat area at the mouth of a river where the river has split into several branches to enter the sea.

delude deludes deluding deluded

VERB To delude people means to deceive them into believing something that is not true.

deluge deluges deluging deluged

NOUN **1** a sudden, heavy downpour of rain. ▶ VERB **2** To be deluged with things means to be overwhelmed by a great number of them.

delusion delusions

NOUN a mistaken or misleading belief or idea.

de luxe

Said "de **luks**" ADJECTIVE rich, luxurious, or of superior quality.

📖 from French *de luxe* meaning literally 'of luxury'

delve delves delving delved

VERB If you delve into something, you seek out more information about it.

demand demands demanding demanded

VERB **1** If you demand something, you ask for it forcefully and urgently. **2** If a job or situation demands a particular quality, it needs it EG *This situation demands hard work*. ▶ NOUN **3** a forceful request for something. **4** If there is a demand for something, a lot of people want to buy it or have it.

☑ The verb *demand* is either

followed by of or from: *at least one important decision was demanded of me; he had demanded an explanation from Daphne.*

demean demeans demeaning demeaned
VERB If you demean yourself, you do something which makes people have less respect for you.
demeaning ADJECTIVE

demeanour
NOUN Your demeanour is the way you behave and the impression that this creates.

demented
ADJECTIVE Someone who is demented behaves in a wild or violent way.

dementia
Said "dee-men-sha" NOUN; A MEDICAL WORD Dementia is a serious illness of the mind.

demi-
PREFIX Demi- means half.

demise
Said "dee-myz" NOUN; A FORMAL WORD Someone's demise is their death.

demo demos
NOUN; AN INFORMAL WORD a demonstration.

democracy democracies
NOUN Democracy is a system of government in which the people choose their leaders by voting for them in elections.

democrat democrats
NOUN a person who believes in democracy, personal freedom, and equality.

democratic
ADJECTIVE having representatives elected by the people.
democratically ADVERB
🖾 from Greek *dēmos* meaning 'the people' and *kratos* meaning 'power'

demography
NOUN Demography is the study of the changes in the size and structure of populations.
demographic ADJECTIVE

demolish demolishes demolishing

demolished
VERB To demolish a building means to pull it down or break it up.
demolition NOUN

demon demons
NOUN **1** an evil spirit or devil.
▶ ADJECTIVE **2** skilful, keen, and energetic EG *a demon squash player.*
demonic ADJECTIVE

demonstrate demonstrates demonstrating demonstrated
VERB **1** To demonstrate a fact or theory means to prove or show it to be true. **2** If you demonstrate something to somebody, you show and explain it by using or doing the thing itself EG *She demonstrated how to apply the make-up.* **3** If people demonstrate, they take part in a march or rally to show their opposition or support for something.

demonstration demonstrations
NOUN **1** a talk or explanation to show how to do or use something. **2** Demonstration is proof that something exists or is true. **3** a public march or rally in support of or opposition to something.
demonstrator NOUN

demote demotes demoting demoted
VERB A person who is demoted is put in a lower rank or position, often as a punishment.
demotion NOUN

demure
ADJECTIVE Someone who is demure is quiet, shy, and behaves very modestly.
demurely ADVERB

den dens
NOUN **1** the home of some wild animals such as lions or foxes. **2** a secret place where people meet.

denial denials
NOUN **1** A denial of something is a statement that it is untrue EG *He published a firm denial of the report.* **2** The denial of a request or something to which you have a

A B C D E F G H I J K L M N O P Q R S T U V W X Y Z

right is the refusal of it EG *the denial of human rights.*

denigrate denigrates denigrating denigrated
VERB; A FORMAL WORD To denigrate someone or something means to criticize them in order to damage their reputation.

denim denims
NOUN **1** Denim is strong cotton cloth, used for making clothes.
▶ PLURAL NOUN **2** Denims are jeans made from denim.
📖 from French *serge de Nîmes*, meaning 'serge (a type of cloth) from Nîmes'

denomination denominations
NOUN **1** a particular group which has slightly different religious beliefs from other groups within the same faith. **2** a unit in a system of weights, values, or measures EG *a high denomination note.*

denominator denominators
NOUN In maths, the denominator is the bottom part of a fraction.

denote denotes denoting denoted
VERB If one thing denotes another, it is a sign of it or it represents it EG *Formerly, a tan denoted wealth.*

denounce denounces denouncing denounced
VERB **1** If you denounce someone or something, you express very strong disapproval of them EG *He publicly denounced government nuclear policy.* **2** If you denounce someone, you give information against them EG *He was denounced as a dangerous agitator.*

dense denser densest
ADJECTIVE **1** thickly crowded or packed together EG *the dense crowd.* **2** difficult to see through EG *dense black smoke.*
densely ADVERB

density densities
NOUN the degree to which something is filled or occupied EG *a very high population density.*

dent dents denting dented
VERB **1** To dent something means to damage it by hitting it and making a hollow in its surface. ▶ NOUN **2** a hollow in the surface of something.

dental
ADJECTIVE relating to the teeth.

dentist dentists
NOUN a person who is qualified to treat people's teeth.

dentistry
NOUN Dentistry is the branch of medicine concerned with disorders of the teeth.

dentures
PLURAL NOUN Dentures are false teeth.

denunciation denunciations
NOUN A denunciation of someone or something is severe public criticism of them.

deny denies denying denied
VERB **1** If you deny something that has been said, you state that it is untrue. **2** If you deny that something is the case, you refuse to believe it EG *He denied the existence of God.* **3** If you deny someone something, you refuse to give it to them EG *They were denied permission to attend.*
▤ (sense 1) contradict, gainsay

deodorant deodorants
NOUN a substance or spray used to hide the smell of perspiration.

depart departs departing departed
VERB When you depart, you leave.
departure NOUN

department departments
NOUN one of the sections into which an organization is divided EG *the marketing department.*
departmental ADJECTIVE

depend depends depending depended
VERB **1** If you depend on someone or something, you trust them and rely on them. **2** If one thing depends on another, it is influenced by it EG *Success depends on the quality of the*

workforce.
■ (sense 1) count on, rely on, trust

dependable
ADJECTIVE reliable and trustworthy.

dependant dependants
NOUN someone who relies on
another person for financial
support.

dependence
NOUN Dependence is a constant
need that someone has for
something or someone in order to
survive or operate properly EG *He
was flattered by her dependence on him.*

dependency dependencies
NOUN a country or area controlled
by another country.

dependent
ADJECTIVE reliant on someone or
something.

depict depicts depicting depicted
VERB To depict someone or
something means to represent
them in painting or sculpture.

**deplete depletes depleting
depleted**
VERB To deplete something means to
reduce greatly the amount of it
available.
depletion NOUN

deplorable
ADJECTIVE shocking or regrettable EG
deplorable conditions.

**deplore deplores deploring
deplored**
VERB If you deplore something, you
condemn it because you feel it is
wrong.

**deploy deploys deploying
deployed**
VERB To deploy troops or resources
means to organize or position
them so that they can be used
effectively.
deployment NOUN

**deport deports deporting
deported**
VERB If a government deports
someone, it sends them out of the
country because they have

committed a crime or because they
do not have the right to be there.
deportation NOUN

**depose deposes deposing
deposed**
VERB If someone is deposed, they are
removed from a position of power.

**deposit deposits depositing
deposited**
VERB 1 If you deposit something,
you put it down or leave it
somewhere. 2 If you deposit money
or valuables, you put them
somewhere for safekeeping. ▶ NOUN
3 a sum of money given in part
payment for goods or services.

depot depots
Said "dep-oh" NOUN a place where
large supplies of materials or
equipment may be stored.

depraved
ADJECTIVE morally bad.

**depress depresses depressing
depressed**
VERB 1 If something depresses you, it
makes you feel sad and gloomy.
2 If wages or prices are depressed,
their value falls.
depressive ADJECTIVE

depressant depressants
NOUN a drug which reduces nervous
activity and so has a calming effect.

depressed
ADJECTIVE 1 unhappy and gloomy.
2 A place that is depressed has little
economic activity and therefore
low incomes and high
unemployment EG *depressed
industrial areas.*
■ (sense 1) dejected, despondent,
low-spirited

depression depressions
NOUN 1 a state of mind in which
someone feels unhappy and has no
energy or enthusiasm. 2 a time of
industrial and economic decline.

**deprive deprives depriving
deprived**
VERB If you deprive someone of
something, you take it away or

prevent them from having it.
deprived ADJECTIVE, **deprivation** NOUN

depth depths
NOUN **1** The depth of something is the measurement or distance between its top and bottom, or between its front and back. **2** The depth of something such as emotion is its intensity EG *the depth of her hostility.*

deputation deputations
NOUN a small group of people sent to speak or act on behalf of others.

deputy deputies
NOUN Someone's deputy is a person appointed to act in their place.

deranged
ADJECTIVE mad, or behaving in a wild and uncontrolled way.

derby derbies
Said "**dar-bee**" NOUN A local derby is a sporting event between two teams from the same area.

derelict
ADJECTIVE abandoned and falling into ruins.

deride derides deriding derided
VERB To deride someone or something means to mock or jeer at them with contempt.

derision
NOUN Derision is an attitude of contempt or scorn towards something or someone.

derivation derivations
NOUN The derivation of something is its origin or source.

derivative derivatives
NOUN **1** something which has developed from an earlier source. ▶ ADJECTIVE **2** not original, but based on or copied from something else EG *The record was not deliberately derivative.*

derive derives deriving derived
VERB **1** A FORMAL USE If you derive something from someone or something, you get it from them EG *He derived so much joy from music.* **2** If something derives from something

else, it develops from it.

derogatory
ADJECTIVE critical and scornful EG *He made derogatory remarks about them.*

descant descants
NOUN The descant to a tune is another tune played at the same time and at a higher pitch.

descend descends descending descended
VERB **1** To descend means to move downwards. **2** If you descend on people or on a place, you arrive unexpectedly.

descendant descendants
NOUN A person's descendants are the people in later generations who are related to them.

descended
ADJECTIVE If you are descended from someone who lived in the past, your family originally derived from them.

descent descents
NOUN **1** a movement or slope from a higher to a lower position or level. **2** Your descent is your family's origins.

describe describes describing described
VERB To describe someone or something means to give an account or a picture of them in words.

description descriptions
NOUN an account or picture of something in words.
descriptive ADJECTIVE

desert deserts deserting deserted
NOUN **1** a region of land with very little plant life, usually because of low rainfall. ▶ VERB **2** To desert a person means to leave or abandon them EG *His clients had deserted him.*
desertion NOUN
☑ The noun sense of *desert* (sense 1) is pronounced *dez*-ert. The verb sense (sense 2) is pronounced dez-*zert*.

A B C D E F G H I J K L M N O P Q R S T U V W X Y Z

deserter deserters
NOUN someone who leaves the armed forces without permission.

deserve deserves deserving deserved
VERB If you deserve something, you are entitled to it or earn it because of your qualities, achievements, or actions EG *He deserved a rest.*
■ be worthy of, justify, merit

deserving
ADJECTIVE worthy of being helped, rewarded, or praised EG *a deserving charity.*

design designs designing designed
VERB **1** To design something means to plan it, especially by preparing a detailed sketch or drawings from which it can be built or made.
▶ NOUN **2** a drawing or plan from which something can be built or made. **3** The design of something is its shape and style.
designer NOUN

designate designates designating designated
Said "dez-ig-nate" VERB **1** To designate someone or something means to formally label or name them EG *The room was designated a no smoking area.* **2** If you designate someone to do something, you appoint them to do it EG *He designated his son as his successor.*

designation designations
NOUN a name or title.

designing
ADJECTIVE crafty and cunning.

desirable
ADJECTIVE **1** worth having or doing EG *a desirable job.* **2** sexually attractive.
desirability NOUN

desire desires desiring desired
VERB **1** If you desire something, you want it very much. ▶ NOUN **2** a strong feeling of wanting something. **3** Desire for someone is a strong sexual attraction to them.
■ (sense 1) long for, want, wish for
■ (sense 2) longing, want, wish

desist desists desisting desisted
VERB; A FORMAL WORD To desist from doing something means to stop doing it.

desk desks
NOUN **1** a piece of furniture designed for working at or writing on. **2** a counter or table in a public building behind which a receptionist sits.

desktop
ADJECTIVE of a convenient size to be used on a desk or table EG *a desktop computer.*

desolate
ADJECTIVE **1** deserted and bleak EG *a desolate mountainous region.* **2** lonely, very sad, and without hope EG *He was desolate without her.*
desolation NOUN

despair despairs despairing despaired
NOUN **1** Despair is a total loss of hope. ▶ VERB **2** If you despair, you lose hope EG *He despaired of finishing it.*
despairing ADJECTIVE
■ (sense 1) desperation, hopelessness

despatch
another spelling of **dispatch**.

desperate
ADJECTIVE **1** If you are desperate, you are so worried or frightened that you will try anything to improve your situation EG *a desperate attempt to save their marriage.* **2** A desperate person is violent and dangerous. **3** A desperate situation is extremely dangerous or serious.
desperately ADVERB, **desperation** NOUN

despicable
ADJECTIVE deserving contempt.

despise despises despising despised
VERB If you despise someone or something, you dislike them very much.

despite
PREPOSITION in spite of EG *He fell asleep*

A
B
C
D
E
F
G
H
I
J
K
L
M
N
O
P
Q
R
S
T
U
V
W
X
Y
Z

despite all the coffee he'd drunk.'
■ in spite of, regardless of

despondent
ADJECTIVE dejected and unhappy.
despondency NOUN

dessert desserts
Said "diz-ert" NOUN a sweet food
served after the main course of a
meal.
▥ from French *desservir* meaning
'to clear the table after a meal'

destination destinations
NOUN a place to which someone or
something is going or is being sent.

destined
ADJECTIVE meant or intended to
happen EG *I was destined for fame and
fortune.*

destiny destinies
NOUN **1** Your destiny is all the things
that happen to you in your life,
especially when they are
considered to be outside human
control. **2** Destiny is the force
which some people believe
controls everyone's life.

destitute
ADJECTIVE without money or
possessions, and therefore in great
need.
destitution NOUN

**destroy destroys destroying
destroyed**
VERB **1** To destroy something means
to damage it so much that it is
completely ruined. **2** To destroy
something means to put an end to
it EG *The holiday destroyed their
friendship.*
■ (sense 1) demolish, ruin, wreck

destruction
NOUN Destruction is the act of
destroying something or the state
of being destroyed.
■ devastation, ruin

destructive
ADJECTIVE causing or able to cause
great harm, damage, or injury.
destructiveness NOUN

desultory

Said "dez-ul-tree" ADJECTIVE
unplanned, disorganized, and
without enthusiasm EG *A desultory,
embarrassed chatter began again.*

**detach detaches detaching
detached**
VERB To detach something means to
remove or unfasten it EG *The hood
can be detached.*
detachable ADJECTIVE

detached
ADJECTIVE **1** separate or standing
apart EG *a detached house.* **2** having
no real interest or emotional
involvement in something EG *He
observed me with a detached curiosity.*

detachment detachments
NOUN **1** Detachment is the feeling of
not being personally involved with
something EG *A stranger can view your
problems with detachment.* **2** a small
group of soldiers sent to do a
special job.

detail details
NOUN **1** an individual fact or feature
of something EG *We discussed every
detail of the performance.* **2** Detail is
all the small features that make up
the whole of something EG *Look at
the detail.*
detailed ADJECTIVE

detain detains detaining detained
VERB **1** To detain someone means to
force them to stay EG *She was being
detained for interrogation.* **2** If you
detain someone, you delay them EG
I mustn't detain you.

**detect detects detecting
detected**
VERB **1** If you detect something, you
notice it EG *I detected a glimmer of
interest in his eyes.* **2** To detect
something means to find it EG
Cancer can be detected by X-rays.
detectable ADJECTIVE

detection
NOUN **1** Detection is the act of
noticing, discovering, or sensing
something. **2** Detection is also the
work of investigating crime.

detective detectives

NOUN a person, usually a police officer, whose job is to investigate crimes.

detector detectors
NOUN an instrument which is used to detect the presence of something EG *a metal detector*.

detention
NOUN The detention of someone is their arrest or imprisonment.

deter deters deterring deterred
VERB To deter someone means to discourage or prevent them from doing something by creating a feeling of fear or doubt EG *99 per cent of burglars are deterred by the sight of an alarm box*.

detergent detergents
NOUN a chemical substance used for washing or cleaning things.

deteriorate deteriorates deteriorating deteriorated
VERB If something deteriorates, it gets worse EG *My father's health has deteriorated lately*.
deterioration NOUN

determination
NOUN Determination is great firmness, after you have made up your mind to do something EG *They shared a determination to win the war*.

determine determines determining determined
VERB **1** If something determines a situation or result, it causes it or controls it EG *The track surface determines his tactics in a race*. **2** To determine something means to decide or settle it firmly EG *The date has still to be determined*. **3** To determine something means to find out or calculate the facts about it EG *He bit the coin to determine whether it was genuine*.
■ (sense 2) decide, settle
■ (sense 3) ascertain, find out, verify

determined
ADJECTIVE firmly decided EG *She was determined not to repeat her error*.
determinedly ADVERB

■ intent on, resolute

deterrent deterrents
NOUN something that prevents you from doing something by making you afraid of what will happen if you do it EG *Capital punishment was no deterrent to domestic murders*.
deterrence NOUN

detest detests detesting detested
VERB If you detest someone or something, you strongly dislike them.

detonate detonates detonating detonated
VERB To detonate a bomb or mine means to cause it to explode.
detonator NOUN

detour detours
NOUN an alternative, less direct route.

detract detracts detracting detracted
VERB To detract from something means to make it seem less good or valuable.

detriment
NOUN Detriment is disadvantage or harm EG *a detriment to their health*.
detrimental ADJECTIVE

deuce deuces
Said "joos" NOUN In tennis, deuce is the score of forty all.

devalue devalues devaluing devalued
VERB To devalue something means to lower its status, importance, or worth.
devaluation NOUN

devastate devastates devastating devastated
VERB To devastate an area or place means to damage it severely or destroy it.
devastation NOUN

devastated
ADJECTIVE very shocked or upset EG *The family are devastated by the news*.

develop develops developing developed

A
B
C
D
E
F
G
H
I
J
K
L
M
N
O
P
Q
R
S
T
U
V
W
X
Y
Z

VERB **1** When something develops or is developed, it grows or becomes more advanced EG *The sneezing developed into a full blown cold.* **2** To develop an area of land means to build on it. **3** To develop an illness or a fault means to become affected by it.

developer developers
NOUN a person or company that builds on land.

development developments
NOUN **1** Development is gradual growth or progress. **2** The development of land or water is the process of making it more useful or profitable by the expansion of industry or housing EG *the development of the old docks.* **3** a new stage in a series of events EG *developments in technology.*
developmental ADJECTIVE

deviant deviants
ADJECTIVE **1** Deviant behaviour is unacceptable or different from what people consider as normal.
▶ NOUN **2** someone whose behaviour or beliefs are different from what people consider to be acceptable.

deviate deviates deviating deviated
VERB To deviate means to differ or depart from what is usual or acceptable.
deviation NOUN

device devices
NOUN **1** a machine or tool that is used for a particular purpose EG *a device to warn you when the batteries need changing.* **2** a plan or scheme EG *a device to pressurise him into selling.*

devil devils
NOUN **1** In Christianity and Judaism, the Devil is the spirit of evil and enemy of God. **2** an evil spirit.
▨ from Greek *diabolos* meaning 'slanderer', 'enemy', or 'devil'

devious
ADJECTIVE insincere and dishonest.
deviousness NOUN

devise devises devising devised

VERB To devise something means to work it out EG *Besides diets, he devised punishing exercise routines.*

devoid
ADJECTIVE lacking in a particular thing or quality EG *His glance was devoid of expression.*

devolution
NOUN Devolution is the transfer of power from a central government or organization to local government departments or smaller organizations.

devote devotes devoting devoted
VERB If you devote yourself to something, you give all your time, energy, or money to it EG *She has devoted herself to women's causes.*

devoted
ADJECTIVE very loving and loyal.

devotee devotees
NOUN a fanatical or enthusiastic follower of it.

devotion
NOUN Devotion to someone or something is great love or affection for them.
devotional ADJECTIVE

devour devours devouring devoured
VERB If you devour something, you eat it hungrily or greedily.

devout
ADJECTIVE deeply and sincerely religious EG *a devout Buddhist.*
devoutly ADVERB

dew
NOUN Dew is drops of moisture that form on the ground and other cool surfaces at night.

dexterity
NOUN Dexterity is skill or agility in using your hands or mind EG *He had learned to use the crutches with dexterity.*
dexterous ADJECTIVE

dharma
Said "dar-ma" NOUN In the Buddhist religion, dharma is ideal truth as

set out in the teaching of the
Buddha.
🔲 a Sanskrit word

diabetes
Said "dy-a-bee-tiss" NOUN Diabetes is
a disease in which someone has too
much sugar in their blood, because
they do not produce enough
insulin to absorb it.
diabetic NOUN OR ADJECTIVE

diabolical
ADJECTIVE **1** AN INFORMAL USE dreadful
and very annoying EG *The pain was
diabolical*. **2** extremely wicked and
cruel.

diagnose diagnoses diagnosing diagnosed
VERB To diagnose an illness or
problem means to identify exactly
what is wrong.

diagnosis diagnoses
NOUN the identification of what is
wrong with someone who is ill.
diagnostic ADJECTIVE

diagonal
ADJECTIVE in a slanting direction.
diagonally ADVERB
🔲 from Greek *diagōnios* meaning
'from angle to angle'

diagram diagrams
NOUN a drawing that shows or
explains something.

dial dials dialling dialled
NOUN **1** the face of a clock or meter,
with divisions marked on it so that
a time or measurement can be
recorded and read. **2** a part of a
device, such as a radio, used to
control or tune it. ▶ VERB **3** To dial a
telephone number means to press
the number keys to select the
required number.

dialect dialects
NOUN a form of a language spoken
in a particular geographical area.

dialogue dialogues
NOUN **1** In a novel, play, or film,
dialogue is conversation.
2 Dialogue is communication or
discussion between people or

groups of people EG *The union sought
dialogue with the council*.

dialysis
NOUN Dialysis is a treatment used
for some kidney diseases, in which
blood is filtered by a special
machine to remove waste products.
🔲 from Greek *dialuein* meaning
'to rip apart'

diameter diameters
NOUN The diameter of a circle is the
length of a straight line drawn
across it through its centre.

diamond diamonds
NOUN **1** a precious stone made of
pure carbon. **2** a shape with four
straight sides of equal length
forming two opposite angles less
than 90° and two opposite angles
greater than 90°. **3** Diamonds is
one of the four suits in a pack of
playing cards. It is marked by a red
diamond-shaped symbol. ▶ ADJECTIVE
4 A diamond anniversary is the
60th anniversary of an event.

diaphragm diaphragms
Said "dy-a-fram" NOUN In mammals,
the diaphragm is the muscular wall
that separates the lungs from the
stomach.

diarrhoea
Said "dy-a-ree-a" NOUN Diarrhoea is
a condition in which the faeces are
more liquid and frequent than
usual.

diary diaries
NOUN a book which has a separate
space or page for each day of the
year on which to keep a record of
appointments.
diarist NOUN

dice dices dicing diced
NOUN **1** a small cube which has each
side marked with dots representing
the numbers one to six. ▶ VERB **2** To
dice food means to cut it into small
cubes.
diced ADJECTIVE

dictate dictates dictating dictated
VERB **1** If you dictate something, you

A B C **D** E F G H I J K L M N O P Q R S T U V W X Y Z

say or read it aloud for someone else to write down. **2** To dictate something means to command or state what must happen EG *What we wear is largely dictated by our daily routine.*
dictation NOUN

dictator dictators
NOUN a ruler who has complete power in a country, especially one who has taken power by force.
dictatorial ADJECTIVE

diction
NOUN Someone's diction is the clarity with which they speak or sing.

dictionary dictionaries
NOUN a book in which words are listed alphabetically and explained, or equivalent words are given in another language.
▥ from Latin *dictio* meaning 'phrase' or 'word'

didgeridoo didgeridoos
NOUN an Australian musical wind instrument made in the shape of a long wooden tube.

die dies dying died
VERB **1** When people, animals, or plants die, they stop living.
2 When things die or die out, they cease to exist EG *That custom has died out now.* **3** When something dies, dies away, or dies down, it gradually fades away EG *The footsteps died away.* **4** AN INFORMAL USE If you are dying to do something, you are longing to do it. ▶ NOUN **5** a dice.
▤ (sense 1) expire, pass away, perish

diesel
Said "**dee**-zel" NOUN **1** a heavy fuel used in trains, buses, and lorries.
2 a vehicle with a diesel engine.

diet diets
NOUN **1** Someone's diet is the usual food that they eat EG *a vegetarian diet.* **2** a special restricted selection of foods that someone eats to improve their health or regulate their weight.

dietary ADJECTIVE
▥ from Greek *diaita* meaning 'mode of living'

dietician dieticians; also spelt dietitian
NOUN a person trained to advise people about healthy eating.

differ differs differing differed
VERB **1** If two or more things differ, they are unlike each other. **2** If people differ, they have opposing views or disagree about something.

difference differences
NOUN **1** The difference between things is the way in which they are unlike each other. **2** The difference between two numbers is the amount by which one is less than another. **3** A difference in someone or something is a significant change in them EG *You wouldn't believe the difference in her.*
▤ (sense 1) disparity, dissimilarity, distinction

different
ADJECTIVE **1** unlike something else.
2 unusual and out of the ordinary.
3 distinct and separate, although of the same kind EG *The lunch supports a different charity each year.*
differently ADVERB
▤ (sense 1) dissimilar, unlike
☑ You should say that one thing is *different from* another thing. Some people think that *different to* is incorrect. *Different than* is American.

differentiate differentiates differentiating differentiated
VERB **1** To differentiate between things means to recognize or show how one is unlike the other.
2 Something that differentiates one thing from another makes it distinct and unlike the other.
differentiation NOUN

difficult
ADJECTIVE **1** not easy to do, understand, or solve. **2** hard to deal with, especially because of being unreasonable or unpredictable EG *a*

difficult child.

■ (sense 1) demanding, hard, laborious

difficulty difficulties
NOUN **1** a problem EG *The central difficulty is his drinking.* **2** Difficulty is the fact or quality of being difficult.

diffident
ADJECTIVE timid and lacking in self-confidence.
diffidently ADVERB, **diffidence** NOUN

diffract diffracts diffracting diffracted
VERB When rays of light or sound waves diffract, they break up after hitting an obstacle.
diffraction NOUN

diffuse diffuses diffusing diffused
VERB **1** *Said* "dif-**yooz**" If something diffuses, it spreads out or scatters in all directions. ▶ ADJECTIVE **2** *Said* "dif-**yoos**" spread out over a wide area.
diffusion NOUN

dig digs digging dug
VERB **1** If you dig, you break up soil or sand, especially with a spade or garden fork. **2** To dig something into an object means to push, thrust, or poke it in. ▶ NOUN **3** a prod or jab, especially in the ribs. **4** AN INFORMAL USE A dig at someone is a spiteful or unpleasant remark intended to hurt or embarrass them. ▶ PLURAL NOUN **5** Digs are lodgings in someone else's house.

digest digests digesting digested
VERB **1** To digest food means to break it down in the gut so that it can be easily absorbed and used by the body. **2** If you digest information or a fact, you understand it and take it in.
digestible ADJECTIVE

digestion digestions
NOUN **1** Digestion is the process of digesting food. **2** Your digestion is your ability to digest food EG *Camomile tea aids poor digestion.*
digestive ADJECTIVE

digger diggers
NOUN In Australian English, digger is a friendly name to call a man.

digit digits
Said "**dij**-it" NOUN **1** A FORMAL USE Your digits are your fingers or toes. **2** a written symbol for any of the numbers from 0 to 9.

digital
ADJECTIVE displaying information, especially time, by numbers, rather than by a pointer moving round a dial EG *a digital watch.*
digitally ADVERB

dignified
ADJECTIVE full of dignity.

dignitary dignitaries
NOUN a person who holds a high official position.

dignity
NOUN Dignity is behaviour which is serious, calm, and controlled EG *She conducted herself with dignity.*

digression digressions
NOUN A digression in speech or writing is leaving the main subject for a while.

dilapidated
ADJECTIVE falling to pieces and generally in a bad condition EG *a dilapidated castle.*

dilate dilates dilating dilated
VERB To dilate means to become wider and larger EG *The pupil of the eye dilates in the dark.*
dilated ADJECTIVE, **dilation** NOUN

dilemma dilemmas
NOUN a situation in which a choice has to be made between alternatives that are equally difficult or unpleasant.
▥ from Greek *di-* meaning 'two' and *lemma* meaning 'assumption'
☑ A *dilemma* involves a difficult choice between two things. If there are more than two choices you should say *problem* or *difficulty*.

diligent
ADJECTIVE hard-working, and showing care and perseverance.

A B C D E F G H I J K L M N O P Q R S T U V W X Y Z

diligently ADVERB, **diligence** NOUN
■ conscientious, hard-working, industrious

dill
NOUN Dill is a herb with yellow flowers and a strong sweet smell.

dilly bag dilly bags
NOUN In Australian English, a dilly bag is a small bag used to carry food.

dilute dilutes diluting diluted
VERB To dilute a liquid means to add water or another liquid to it to make it less concentrated.
dilution NOUN

dim dimmer dimmest; dims dimming dimmed
ADJECTIVE **1** badly lit and lacking in brightness. **2** very vague and unclear in your mind EG *dim recollections*. **3** AN INFORMAL USE stupid or mentally dull EG *He is rather dim.*
▶ VERB **4** If lights dim or are dimmed, they become less bright.
dimly ADVERB, **dimness** NOUN

dimension dimensions
NOUN **1** A dimension of a situation is an aspect or factor that influences the way you understand it EG *This process had a domestic and a foreign dimension.* **2** You can talk about the size or extent of something as its dimensions EG *It was an explosion of major dimensions.* **3** The dimensions of something are also its measurements, for example its length, breadth, height, or diameter.

diminish diminishes diminishing diminished
VERB If something diminishes or if you diminish it, it becomes reduced in size or importance.

diminutive
ADJECTIVE very small.

dimple dimples
NOUN a small hollow in someone's cheek or chin.

din dins
NOUN a loud and unpleasant noise.

dinar dinars
Said "dee-nar" NOUN a unit of currency in several countries in Southern Europe, North Africa and the Middle East.

dine dines dining dined
VERB; A FORMAL USE To dine means to eat dinner in the evening EG *We dined together in the hotel.*

diner diners
NOUN **1** a person who is having dinner in a restaurant. **2** a small restaurant or railway restaurant car.

dinghy dinghies
Said "ding-ee" NOUN a small boat which is rowed, sailed, or powered by outboard motor.

dingo dingoes
NOUN an Australian wild dog.

dingy dingier dingiest
Said "din-jee" ADJECTIVE dusty, dark, and rather depressing EG *a dingy bedsit.*

dinkum
ADJECTIVE; AN INFORMAL WORD In Australian and New Zealand English, dinkum means genuine or right EG *a fair dinkum offer.*

dinner dinners
NOUN **1** the main meal of the day, eaten either in the evening or at lunchtime. **2** a formal social occasion in the evening, at which a meal is served.

dinosaur dinosaurs
Said "dy-no-sor" NOUN a large reptile which lived in prehistoric times.
▥ from Greek *deinos* + *sauros* meaning 'fearful lizard'

dint
PHRASE **By dint of** means by means of EG *He succeeds by dint of hard work.*

diocese dioceses
NOUN a district controlled by a bishop.
diocesan ADJECTIVE

dip dips dipping dipped
VERB **1** If you dip something into a liquid, you lower it or plunge it quickly into the liquid. **2** If

something dips, it slopes downwards or goes below a certain level EG *The sun dipped below the horizon*. **3** To dip also means to make a quick, slight downward movement EG *She dipped her fingers into the cool water*. ▶ NOUN **4** a rich creamy mixture which you scoop up with biscuits or raw vegetables and eat EG *an avocado dip*. **5** AN INFORMAL USE a swim.

diploma diplomas
NOUN a certificate awarded to a student who has successfully completed a course of study. 🏛 from Greek *diploma* meaning 'folded paper' or 'letter of recommendation'

diplomacy
NOUN **1** Diplomacy is the managing of relationships between countries. **2** Diplomacy is also skill in dealing with people without offending or upsetting them.
diplomatic ADJECTIVE, **diplomatically** ADVERB

diplomat diplomats
NOUN an official who negotiates and deals with another country on behalf of his or her own country.

dire direr direst
ADJECTIVE disastrous, urgent, or terrible EG *people in dire need*.

direct directs directing directed
ADJECTIVE **1** moving or aimed in a straight line or by the shortest route EG *the direct route*. **2** straightforward, and without delay or evasion EG *his direct manner*. **3** without anyone or anything intervening EG *Schools can take direct control of their own funding*. **4** exact EG *the direct opposite*. ▶ VERB **5** To direct something means to guide and control it. **6** To direct people or things means to send them, tell them, or show them the way. **7** To direct a film, a play, or a television programme means to organize the way it is made and performed.
▤ (sense 2) frank, open, straightforward

direct current
NOUN Direct current is a term used in physics to refer to an electric current that always flows in the same direction.

direction directions
NOUN **1** the general line that someone or something is moving or pointing in. **2** Direction is the controlling and guiding of something EG *He was chopping vegetables under the chef's direction*.
▶ PLURAL NOUN **3** Directions are instructions that tell you how to do something or how to get somewhere.

directive directives
NOUN an instruction that must be obeyed EG *a directive banning cigarette advertising*.

directly
ADVERB in a straight line or immediately EG *He looked directly at Rose*.

director directors
NOUN **1** a member of the board of a company or institution. **2** the person responsible for the making and performance of a programme, play, or film.
directorial ADJECTIVE

directorate directorates
NOUN a board of directors of a company or organization.

directory directories
NOUN a book which gives lists of facts, such as names and addresses, and is usually arranged in alphabetical order.

direct speech
NOUN the reporting of what someone has said by quoting the exact words.

dirge dirges
NOUN a slow, sad piece of music, sometimes played or sung at funerals.

dirt
NOUN **1** Dirt is any unclean

A
B
C
D
E
F
G
H
I
J
K
L
M
N
O
P
Q
R
S
T
U
V
W
X
Y
Z

substance, such as dust, mud, or stains. **2** Dirt is also earth or soil.

🏛 from Old Norse *drit* meaning 'excrement'

▣ (sense 1) filth, grime, muck

dirty dirtier dirtiest

ADJECTIVE **1** marked or covered with dirt. **2** unfair or dishonest EG *a dirty fight*. **3** about sex in a way that many people find offensive EG *dirty jokes*.

▣ (sense 1) filthy, grubby, mucky, unclean

dis-

PREFIX Dis- is added to the beginning of words to form a word that means the opposite EG *discontented*.

disability disabilities

NOUN a physical or mental condition or illness that restricts someone's way of life.

disable disables disabling disabled

VERB If something disables someone, it injures or harms them physically or mentally and severely affects their life.

disablement NOUN

disabled

ADJECTIVE lacking one or more physical powers, such as the ability to walk or to coordinate one's movements.

disadvantage disadvantages

NOUN an unfavourable or harmful circumstance.

disadvantaged ADJECTIVE

▣ drawback, handicap

disaffected

ADJECTIVE If someone is disaffected with an idea or organization, they no longer believe in it or support it EG *disaffected voters*.

disagree disagrees disagreeing disagreed

VERB **1** If you disagree with someone, you have a different view or opinion from theirs. **2** If you disagree with an action or proposal, you disapprove of it and believe it is wrong EG *He detested her*

and disagreed with her policies. **3** If food or drink disagrees with you, it makes you feel unwell.

disagreement NOUN

▣ (sense 1) differ, dispute, dissent

disagreeable

ADJECTIVE unpleasant or unhelpful and unfriendly EG *a disagreeable odour*.

disappear disappears disappearing disappeared

VERB **1** If something or someone disappears, they go out of sight or become lost. **2** To disappear also means to stop existing or happening EG *The pain has disappeared*.

disappearance NOUN

▣ fade away, vanish

disappoint disappoints disappointing disappointed

VERB If someone or something disappoints you, it fails to live up to what you expected of it.

disappointed ADJECTIVE, **disappointment** NOUN

disapprove disapproves disapproving disapproved

VERB To disapprove of something or someone means to believe they are wrong or bad EG *Everyone disapproved of their marrying so young*.

disapproval NOUN, **disapproving** ADJECTIVE

disarm disarms disarming disarmed

VERB **1** To disarm means to get rid of weapons. **2** If someone disarms you, they overcome your anger or doubt by charming or soothing you EG *Mahoney was almost disarmed by the frankness*.

disarming ADJECTIVE

disarmament

NOUN Disarmament is the reducing or getting rid of military forces and weapons.

disarray

NOUN Disarray is a state of disorder and confusion EG *Our army was in disarray and practically weaponless*.

disaster disasters
NOUN **1** an event or accident that causes great distress or destruction. **2** a complete failure.
disastrous ADJECTIVE, **disastrously** ADVERB
■ (sense 1) calamity, catastrophe

disband disbands disbanding disbanded
VERB When a group of people disbands, it officially ceases to exist.

disc discs; also spelt disk
NOUN **1** a flat round object EG *a tax disc… a compact disc.* **2** one of the thin circular pieces of cartilage which separate the bones in your spine. **3** a storage device used in computers.

discard discards discarding discarded
VERB To discard something means to get rid of it, because you no longer want it or find it useful.
■ dump, get rid of, throw away

discern discerns discerning discerned
Said "dis-ern" VERB; A FORMAL WORD To discern something means to notice or understand it clearly EG *The film had no plot that I could discern.*

discernible
ADJECTIVE able to be seen or recognized EG *no discernible talent.*

discerning
ADJECTIVE having good taste and judgment.
discernment NOUN

discharge discharges discharging discharged
VERB **1** If something discharges or is discharged, it is given or sent out EG *Oil discharged into the world's oceans.* **2** To discharge someone from hospital means to allow them to leave. **3** If someone is discharged from a job, they are dismissed from it. ▶ NOUN **4** a substance that is released from the inside of something EG *a thick nasal discharge.* **5** a dismissal or release from a job or an institution.

disciple disciples
Said "dis-sigh-pl" NOUN a follower of someone or something.

discipline disciplines disciplining disciplined
NOUN **1** Discipline is making people obey rules and punishing them when they break them. **2** Discipline is the ability to behave and work in a controlled way. ▶ VERB **3** If you discipline yourself, you train yourself to behave and work in an ordered way. **4** To discipline someone means to punish them.
disciplinary ADJECTIVE, **disciplined** ADJECTIVE

disc jockey disc jockeys
NOUN someone who introduces and plays pop records on the radio or at a night club.

disclose discloses disclosing disclosed
VERB To disclose something means to make it known or allow it to be seen.
disclosure NOUN

disco discos
NOUN a party or a club where people go to dance to pop records.

discomfort discomforts
NOUN **1** Discomfort is distress or slight pain. **2** Discomfort is also a feeling of worry or embarrassment. **3** Discomforts are things that make you uncomfortable.

disconcert disconcerts disconcerting disconcerted
VERB If something disconcerts you, it makes you feel uneasy or embarrassed.
disconcerting ADJECTIVE

disconnect disconnects disconnecting disconnected
VERB **1** To disconnect something means to detach it from something else. **2** If someone disconnects your fuel supply or telephone, they cut you off.

discontent
NOUN Discontent is a feeling of dissatisfaction with conditions or

A
B
C
D
E
F
G
H
I
J
K
L
M
N
O
P
Q
R
S
T
U
V
W
X
Y
Z

A
B
C
D
E
F
G
H
I
J
K
L
M
N
O
P
Q
R
S
T
U
V
W
X
Y
Z

with life in general EG *He was aware of the discontent this policy had caused.*
discontented ADJECTIVE

discontinue discontinues discontinuing discontinued
VERB To discontinue something means to stop doing it.

discord
NOUN Discord is unpleasantness or quarrelling between people.

discount discounts discounting discounted
NOUN 1 a reduction in the price of something. ▶ VERB 2 If you discount something, you reject it or ignore it EG *I haven't discounted her connection with the kidnapping case.*

discourage discourages discouraging discouraged
VERB To discourage someone means to take away their enthusiasm to do something.
discouraging ADJECTIVE, **discouragement** NOUN
■ demoralize, dishearten, put off

discourse discourses
A FORMAL WORD ▶ NOUN 1 a formal talk or piece of writing intended to teach or explain something.
2 Discourse is serious conversation between people on a particular subject.

discover discovers discovering discovered
VERB When you discover something, you find it or find out about it.
discovery NOUN, **discoverer** NOUN

discredit discredits discrediting discredited
VERB 1 To discredit someone means to damage their reputation. 2 To discredit an idea means to cause it to be doubted or not believed.

discreet
ADJECTIVE If you are discreet, you avoid causing embarrassment when dealing with secret or private matters.
discreetly ADVERB

discrepancy discrepancies

NOUN a difference between two things which ought to be the same EG *discrepancies in his police interviews.*

discrete
ADJECTIVE; A FORMAL WORD separate and distinct EG *two discrete sets of nerves.*

discretion
NOUN 1 Discretion is the quality of behaving with care and tact so as to avoid embarrassment or distress to other people EG *You can count on my discretion.* 2 Discretion is also freedom and authority to make decisions and take action according to your own judgment EG *Class teachers have very limited discretion in decision-making.*
discretionary ADJECTIVE

discriminate discriminates discriminating discriminated
VERB 1 To discriminate between things means to recognize and understand the differences between them. 2 To discriminate against a person or group means to treat them unfairly, usually because of their race, colour, or sex. 3 To discriminate in favour of a person or group means to treat them more favourably than others.
discrimination NOUN, **discriminatory** ADJECTIVE

discus discuses
NOUN a disc-shaped object with a heavy middle, thrown by athletes.

discuss discusses discussing discussed
VERB When people discuss something, they talk about it in detail.

discussion discussions
NOUN a conversation or piece of writing in which a subject is considered in detail.
■ conversation, discourse, talk

disdain
NOUN Disdain is a feeling of superiority over or contempt for someone or something EG *The candidates shared an equal disdain for the press.*

disdainful ADJECTIVE

disease diseases
NOUN an unhealthy condition in people, animals, or plants.
diseased ADJECTIVE

disembark disembarks disembarking disembarked
VERB To disembark means to land or unload from a ship, aircraft, or bus.

disembodied
ADJECTIVE **1** separate from or existing without a body EG *a disembodied skull*. **2** seeming not to be attached or to come from anyone EG *disembodied voices*.

disenchanted
ADJECTIVE disappointed with something, and no longer believing that it is good or worthwhile EG *She is very disenchanted with the marriage*.
disenchantment NOUN

disfigure disfigures disfiguring disfigured
VERB To disfigure something means to spoil its appearance EG *Graffiti or posters disfigured every wall*.

disgrace disgraces disgracing disgraced
NOUN **1** Disgrace is a state in which people disapprove of someone. **2** If something is a disgrace, it is unacceptable EG *The overcrowded prisons were a disgrace*. **3** If someone is a disgrace to a group of people, their behaviour makes the group feel ashamed EG *You're a disgrace to the school*. ▶ VERB **4** If you disgrace yourself or disgrace someone else, you cause yourself or them to be strongly disapproved of by other people.
■ (sense 1) dishonour, shame
■ (sense 4) discredit, dishonour, shame

disgraceful
ADJECTIVE If something is disgraceful, people disapprove of it strongly and think that those who are responsible for it should be ashamed.

disgracefully ADVERB
■ scandalous, shameful, shocking

disgruntled
ADJECTIVE discontented or in a bad mood.

disguise disguises disguising disguised
VERB **1** To disguise something means to change it so that people do not recognize it. **2** To disguise a feeling means to hide it EG *I tried to disguise my relief*. ▶ NOUN **3** something you wear or something you do to alter your appearance so that you cannot be recognized by other people.

disgust disgusts disgusting disgusted
NOUN **1** Disgust is a strong feeling of dislike or disapproval. ▶ VERB **2** To disgust someone means to make them feel a strong sense of dislike or disapproval.
disgusted ADJECTIVE
■ (sense 1) loathing, repugnance, revulsion
■ (sense 2) revolt, sicken

dish dishes
NOUN **1** a shallow container for cooking or serving food. **2** food of a particular kind or food cooked in a particular way EG *two fish dishes to choose from*.

disheartened
ADJECTIVE If you are disheartened, you feel disappointed.

dishevelled
Said "dish-ev-ld" ADJECTIVE If someone looks dishevelled, their clothes or hair look untidy.

dishonest
ADJECTIVE not truthful or able to be trusted.
dishonestly ADVERB

dishonesty
NOUN Dishonesty is behaviour which is meant to deceive people, either by not telling the truth or by cheating.

disillusioned

A B C D E F G H I J K L M N O P Q R S T U V W X Y Z

disinfectant disinfectants
NOUN a chemical substance that kills germs.

disintegrate disintegrates disintegrating disintegrated
VERB 1 If something disintegrates, it becomes weakened and is not effective EG *My confidence disintegrated.* 2 If an object disintegrates, it breaks into many pieces and so is destroyed.
disintegration NOUN

disinterest
NOUN 1 Disinterest is a lack of interest. 2 Disinterest is also a lack of personal involvement in a situation.

disinterested
ADJECTIVE If someone is disinterested, they are not going to gain or lose from the situation they are involved in, and so can act in a way that is fair to both sides EG *a disinterested judge.*
☑ Some people use *disinterested* to mean 'not interested', but the word they should use is *uninterested.*

disjointed
ADJECTIVE If thought or speech is disjointed, it jumps from subject to subject and so is difficult to follow.

disk
another spelling of **disc.**

dislike dislikes disliking disliked
VERB 1 If you dislike something or someone, you think they are unpleasant and do not like them. ▶ NOUN 2 Dislike is a feeling that you have when you do not like someone or something.
☰ (sense 2) aversion, distaste

dislocate dislocates dislocating dislocated
VERB To dislocate your bone or joint means to put it out of place.

dislodge dislodges dislodging

dislodged
VERB To dislodge something means to move it or force it out of place.

dismal
Said "diz-mal" ADJECTIVE rather gloomy and depressing EG *dismal weather.*
dismally ADVERB
🏛 from Latin *dies mali* meaning 'evil days'

dismantle dismantles dismantling dismantled
VERB To dismantle something means to take it apart.

dismay dismays dismaying dismayed
NOUN 1 Dismay is a feeling of fear and worry. ▶ VERB 2 If someone or something dismays you, it fills you with alarm and worry.

dismember dismembers dismembering dismembered
VERB; A FORMAL WORD To dismember a person or animal means to cut or tear their body into pieces.

dismiss dismisses dismissing dismissed
VERB 1 If you dismiss something, you decide to ignore it because it is not important enough for you to think about. 2 To dismiss an employee means to ask that person to leave their job. 3 If someone in authority dismisses you, they tell you to leave.
dismissal NOUN

dismissive
ADJECTIVE If you are dismissive of something or someone, you show that you think they are of little importance or value EG *a dismissive gesture.*

disorder disorders
NOUN 1 Disorder is a state of untidiness. 2 Disorder is also a lack of organization EG *The men fled in disorder.* 3 a disease EG *a stomach disorder.*
☰ (sense 2) chaos, confusion

disorganized or **disorganised**
ADJECTIVE If something is

ADJECTIVE If you are disillusioned with something, you are disappointed because it is not as good as you had expected.

208

disorganized, it is confused and badly prepared or badly arranged.
disorganization NOUN

disown disowns disowning disowned
VERB To disown someone or something means to refuse to admit any connection with them.

disparaging
ADJECTIVE critical and scornful EG *disparaging remarks*.

disparate
ADJECTIVE; A FORMAL WORD Things that are disparate are utterly different from one another.
disparity NOUN

dispatch dispatches dispatching dispatched; also spelt **despatch**
VERB 1 To dispatch someone or something to a particular place means to send them there for a special reason EG *The president dispatched him on a fact-finding visit.*
▶ NOUN 2 an official written message, often sent to an army or government headquarters.

dispel dispels dispelling dispelled
VERB To dispel fears or beliefs means to drive them away or to destroy them EG *The myths are being dispelled.*

dispensary dispensaries
NOUN a place where medicines are prepared and given out.

dispense dispenses dispensing dispensed
VERB 1 A FORMAL USE To dispense something means to give it out EG *They dispense advice.* 2 To dispense medicines means to prepare them and give them out. 3 To dispense with something means to do without it or do away with it EG *We'll dispense with formalities.*

dispenser dispensers
NOUN a machine or container from which you can get things EG *a cash dispenser.*

disperse disperses dispersing dispersed
VERB 1 When something disperses, it scatters over a wide area. 2 When people disperse or when someone disperses them, they move apart and go in different directions.
dispersion NOUN

dispirited
ADJECTIVE depressed and having no enthusiasm for anything.

dispiriting
ADJECTIVE Something dispiriting makes you depressed and unenthusiastic EG *a dispiriting defeat.*

displace displaces displacing displaced
VERB 1 If one thing displaces another, it forces the thing out of its usual place and occupies that place itself. 2 If people are displaced, they are forced to leave their home or country.

displacement
NOUN Displacement is the removal of something from its usual or correct place or position.

display displays displaying displayed
VERB 1 If you display something, you show it or make it visible to people. 2 If you display something such as an emotion, you behave in a way that shows you feel it. ▶ NOUN 3 an arrangement of things designed to attract people's attention.

displease displeases displeasing displeased
VERB If someone or something displeases you, they make you annoyed, dissatisfied, or offended.
displeasure NOUN

disposable
ADJECTIVE designed to be thrown away after use EG *disposable nappies.*

disposal
NOUN Disposal is the act of getting rid of something that is no longer wanted or needed.

dispose disposes disposing disposed
VERB 1 To dispose of something

A
B
C
D
E
F
G
H
I
J
K
L
M
N
O
P
Q
R
S
T
U
V
W
X
Y
Z

means to get rid of it. **2** If you are not disposed to do something, you are not willing to do it.

disprove disproves disproving disproved
VERB If someone disproves an idea, belief, or theory, they show that it is not true.

dispute disputes disputing disputed
NOUN **1** an argument. ▶ VERB **2** To dispute a fact or theory means to question the truth of it.

disqualify disqualifies disqualifying disqualified
VERB If someone is disqualified from a competition or activity, they are officially stopped from taking part in it EG *He was disqualified from driving for 18 months*.
disqualification NOUN

disquiet
NOUN Disquiet is worry or anxiety.
disquieting ADJECTIVE

disregard disregards disregarding disregarded
VERB **1** To disregard something means to pay little or no attention to it. ▶ NOUN **2** Disregard is a lack of attention or respect for something EG *He exhibited a flagrant disregard of the law*.

disrepair
PHRASE If something is **in disrepair** or **in a state of disrepair**, it is broken or in poor condition.

disrespect
NOUN Disrespect is contempt or lack of respect EG *his disrespect for authority*.
disrespectful ADJECTIVE

disrupt disrupts disrupting disrupted
VERB To disrupt something such as an event or system means to break it up or throw it into confusion EG *Strikes disrupted air traffic in Italy*.
disruption NOUN, **disruptive** ADJECTIVE

dissatisfied
ADJECTIVE not pleased or not

contented.
dissatisfaction NOUN

dissect dissects dissecting dissected
VERB To dissect a plant or a dead body means to cut it up so that it can be scientifically examined.
dissection NOUN

dissent dissents dissenting dissented
NOUN **1** Dissent is strong difference of opinion EG *political dissent*. ▶ VERB **2** When people dissent, they express a difference of opinion about something.
dissenting ADJECTIVE

dissertation dissertations
NOUN a long essay, especially for a university degree.

disservice
NOUN To do someone a disservice means to do something that harms them.

dissident dissidents
NOUN someone who disagrees with and criticizes the strict and unjust government of their country.

dissimilar
ADJECTIVE If things are dissimilar, they are unlike each other.

dissipate dissipates dissipating dissipated
VERB **1** A FORMAL WORD When something dissipates or is dissipated, it completely disappears EG *The cloud seemed to dissipate there*. **2** If someone dissipates time, money, or effort, they waste it.

dissipated
ADJECTIVE Someone who is dissipated shows signs of indulging too much in alcohol or other physical pleasures.

dissolve dissolves dissolving dissolved
VERB **1** If you dissolve something or if it dissolves in a liquid, it becomes mixed with and absorbed in the liquid. **2** To dissolve an organization or institution means

to officially end it.

dissuade dissuades dissuading dissuaded

Said "dis-**wade**" VERB To dissuade someone from doing something or from believing something means to persuade them not to do it or not to believe it.

distance distances distancing distanced

NOUN **1** The distance between two points is how far it is between them. **2** Distance is the fact of being far away in space or time. ▶ VERB **3** If you distance yourself from someone or something or are distanced from them, you become less involved with them.

distant

ADJECTIVE **1** far away in space or time. **2** A distant relative is one who is not closely related to you. **3** Someone who is distant is cold and unfriendly.

distantly ADVERB

■ (sense 3) aloof, reserved, standoffish

distaste

NOUN Distaste is a dislike of something which you find offensive.

distasteful

ADJECTIVE If you find something distasteful, you think it is unpleasant or offensive.

distil distils distilling distilled

VERB When a liquid is distilled, it is heated until it evaporates and then cooled to enable purified liquid to be collected.

distillation NOUN

distillery distilleries

NOUN a place where whisky or other strong alcoholic drink is made, using a process of distillation.

distinct

ADJECTIVE **1** If one thing is distinct from another, it is recognizably different from it EG *A word may have two quite distinct meanings.* **2** If something is distinct, you can

hear, smell, or see it clearly and plainly EG *There was a distinct buzzing noise.* **3** If something such as a fact, idea, or intention is distinct, it is clear and definite EG *She had a distinct feeling someone was watching them.*

distinctly ADVERB

distinction distinctions

NOUN **1** a difference between two things EG *a distinction between the body and the soul.* **2** Distinction is a quality of excellence and superiority EG *a man of distinction.* **3** a special honour or claim EG *It had the distinction of being the largest square in Europe.*

distinctive

ADJECTIVE Something that is distinctive has a special quality which makes it recognizable EG *a distinctive voice.*

distinctively ADVERB

distinguish distinguishes distinguishing distinguished

VERB **1** To distinguish between things means to recognize the difference between them EG *I've learned to distinguish business and friendship.* **2** To distinguish something means to make it out by seeing, hearing, or tasting it EG *I heard shouting but was unable to distinguish the words.* **3** If you distinguish yourself, you do something that makes people think highly of you.

distinguishable ADJECTIVE, **distinguishing** ADJECTIVE

distort distorts distorting distorted

VERB **1** If you distort a statement or an argument, you represent it in an untrue or misleading way. **2** If something is distorted, it is changed so that it seems strange or unclear EG *His voice was distorted.* **3** If an object is distorted, it is twisted or pulled out of shape.

distorted ADJECTIVE, **distortion** NOUN

distract distracts distracting

distracted
VERB If something distracts you, your attention is taken away from what you are doing.
distracted ADJECTIVE, **distractedly** ADVERB, **distracting** ADJECTIVE
■ divert, sidetrack

distraction distractions
NOUN **1** something that takes people's attention away from something. **2** an activity that is intended to amuse or relax someone.

distraught
ADJECTIVE so upset and worried that you cannot think clearly EG *He was distraught over the death of his mother.*

distress distresses distressing distressed
NOUN **1** Distress is great suffering caused by pain or sorrow. **2** Distress is also the state of needing help because of difficulties or danger.
▶ VERB **3** To distress someone means to make them feel alarmed or unhappy EG *Her death had profoundly distressed me.*
■ (sense 3) trouble, upset

distressing
ADJECTIVE very worrying or upsetting.

distribute distributes distributing distributed
VERB **1** To distribute something such as leaflets means to hand them out or deliver them EG *They publish and distribute brochures.* **2** If things are distributed, they are spread throughout an area or space EG *Distribute the cheese evenly on top of the quiche.* **3** To distribute something means to divide it and share it out among a number of people.
■ (sense 3) dispense, share out

distribution distributions
NOUN **1** Distribution is the delivering of something to various people or organizations EG *the distribution of vicious leaflets.* **2** Distribution is the sharing out of something EG *distribution of power.*

distributor distributors
NOUN a company that supplies goods to other businesses who then sell them to the public.

district districts
NOUN an area of a town or country EG *a residential district.*

district nurse district nurses
NOUN a nurse who visits and treats people in their own homes.

distrust distrusts distrusting distrusted
VERB **1** If you distrust someone, you are suspicious of them because you are not sure whether they are honest. ▶ NOUN **2** Distrust is suspicion.
distrustful ADJECTIVE

disturb disturbs disturbing disturbed
VERB **1** If you disturb someone, you break their peace or privacy. **2** If something disturbs you, it makes you feel upset or worried. **3** If something is disturbed, it is moved out of position or meddled with.
disturbing ADJECTIVE
■ (sense 2) trouble, upset, worry

disturbance disturbances
NOUN **1** Disturbance is the state of being disturbed. **2** a violent or unruly incident in public.

disuse
NOUN Something that has fallen into disuse is neglected or no longer used.
disused ADJECTIVE

ditch ditches
NOUN a channel at the side of a road or field, usually to drain away excess water.

dither dithers dithering dithered
VERB To dither means to be unsure and hesitant.

ditto
Ditto means 'the same'. In written lists, ditto is represented by a mark (,,) to avoid repetition.
▨ from Italian *detto* meaning 'said'

ditty ditties

NOUN; AN OLD-FASHIONED WORD a short simple song or poem.

dive dives diving dived

VERB **1** To dive means to jump into water with your arms held straight above your head. **2** If you go diving, you go down under the surface of the sea or a lake using special breathing equipment. **3** If an aircraft or bird dives, it flies in a steep downward path, or drops sharply.

diver NOUN, **diving** NOUN

diverge diverges diverging diverged

VERB **1** If opinions or facts diverge, they differ EG *Theory and practice sometimes diverged.* **2** If two things such as roads or paths which have been going in the same direction diverge, they separate and go off in different directions.

divergence NOUN, **divergent** ADJECTIVE

diverse

ADJECTIVE **1** If a group of things is diverse, it is made up of different kinds of things EG *a diverse range of goods and services.* **2** People, ideas, or objects that are diverse are very different from each other.

diversity NOUN

diversify diversifies diversifying diversified

VERB To diversify means to increase the variety of something EG *Has the company diversified into new areas?*

diversification NOUN

diversion diversions

NOUN **1** a special route arranged for traffic when the usual route is closed. **2** something that takes your attention away from what you should be concentrating on EG *A break for tea created a welcome diversion.* **3** a pleasant or amusing activity.

divert diverts diverting diverted

VERB To divert something means to change the course or direction it is following.

diverting ADJECTIVE

divide divides dividing divided

VERB **1** When something divides or is divided, it is split up and separated into two or more parts. **2** If something divides two areas, it forms a barrier between them. **3** If people divide over something or if something divides them, it causes strong disagreement between them. **4** In mathematics, when you divide, you calculate how many times one number contains another. ▶ NOUN **5** a separation EG *the class divide.*

dividend dividends

NOUN a portion of a company's profits that is paid to shareholders.

divine divines divining divined

ADJECTIVE **1** having the qualities of a god or goddess. ▶ VERB **2** To divine something means to discover it by guessing.

divinely ADVERB

divinity divinities

NOUN **1** Divinity is the study of religion. **2** Divinity is the state of being a god. **3** a god or goddess.

division divisions

NOUN **1** Division is the separation of something into two or more distinct parts. **2** Division is also the process of dividing one number by another. **3** a difference of opinion that causes separation between ideas or groups of people EG *There were divisions in the Party on economic policy.* **4** any one of the parts into which something is split EG *the Research Division.*

divisional ADJECTIVE

divisive

ADJECTIVE causing hostility between people so that they split into different groups EG *Inflation is economically and socially divisive.*

divisor divisors

NOUN a number by which another number is divided.

divorce divorces divorcing divorced

NOUN **1** Divorce is the formal and

A B C D E F G H I J K L M N O P Q R S T U V W X Y Z

legal ending of a marriage. ▶ VERB
2 When a married couple divorce,
their marriage is legally ended.
divorced ADJECTIVE, **divorcee** NOUN

divulge divulges divulging divulged
VERB To divulge information means
to reveal it.

DIY
NOUN DIY is the activity of making
or repairing things yourself. DIY is
an abbreviation for 'do-it-yourself'.

dizzy dizzier dizziest
ADJECTIVE having or causing a
whirling sensation.
dizziness NOUN

DNA
NOUN DNA is deoxyribonucleic acid,
which is found in the cells of all
living things. It is responsible for
passing on characteristics from
parents to their children.

do does doing did done; dos
VERB 1 Do is an auxiliary verb,
which is used to form questions,
negatives, and to give emphasis to
the main verb of a sentence. 2 If
someone does a task or activity,
they perform it and finish it EG *He
just didn't want to do any work.* 3 If
you ask what people do, you want
to know what their job is EG *What
will you do when you leave school?* 4 If
you do well at something, you are
successful. If you do badly, you are
unsuccessful. 5 If something will
do, it is adequate but not the most
suitable option EG *Home-made stock
is best, but cubes will do.* ▶ NOUN 6 AN
INFORMAL USE a party or other social
event.
■ (sense 2) carry out, execute,
perform

do up VERB 1 To do something up
means to fasten it. 2 To do up
something old means to repair and
decorate it.

docile
ADJECTIVE quiet, calm, and easily
controlled.

dock docks docking docked

NOUN 1 an enclosed area in a
harbour where ships go to be
loaded, unloaded, or repaired. 2 In
a court of law, the dock is the place
where the accused person stands or
sits. ▶ VERB 3 When a ship docks, it
is brought into dock at the end of
its voyage. 4 To dock someone's
wages means to deduct an amount
from the sum they would normally
receive. 5 To dock an animal's tail
means to cut part of it off.
docker NOUN

doctor doctors doctoring doctored
NOUN 1 a person who is qualified in
medicine and treats people who are
ill. 2 A doctor of an academic
subject is someone who has been
awarded the highest academic
degree EG *She is a doctor of philosophy.*
▶ VERB 3 To doctor something
means to alter it in order to deceive
people EG *Stamps can be doctored.*

doctorate doctorates
NOUN the highest university degree.
doctoral ADJECTIVE

doctrine doctrines
NOUN a set of beliefs or principles
held by a group.
doctrinal ADJECTIVE

document documents documenting documented
NOUN 1 a piece of paper which
provides an official record of
something. ▶ VERB 2 If you
document something, you make a
detailed record of it.
documentation NOUN

documentary documentaries
NOUN 1 a radio or television
programme, or a film, which gives
information on real events.
▶ ADJECTIVE 2 Documentary evidence
is made up of written or official
records.

dodge dodges dodging dodged
VERB 1 If you dodge or dodge
something, you move suddenly to
avoid being seen, hit, or caught.
2 If you dodge something such as

214

an issue or accusation, you avoid dealing with it.

dodgy

ADJECTIVE; AN INFORMAL WORD dangerous, risky, or unreliable EG *He has a dodgy heart.*

dodo dodos

NOUN a large, flightless bird which is now extinct.

doe does

NOUN a female deer, rabbit, or hare.

does

the third person singular of the present tense of **do**.

dog dogs dogging dogged

NOUN **1** a four-legged, meat-eating animal, kept as a pet, or to guard property or go hunting. ▶ VERB **2** If you dog someone, you follow them very closely and never leave them.

dog collar dog collars

NOUN; AN INFORMAL WORD a white collar with no front opening worn by Christian clergy.

dog-eared

ADJECTIVE A book that is dog-eared has been used so much that the corners of the pages are turned down or worn.

dogged

Said "dog-ged" ADJECTIVE showing determination to continue with something, even if it is very difficult EG *dogged persistence.*
doggedly ADVERB

dogma dogmas

NOUN a belief or system of beliefs held by a religious or political group.

dogmatic

ADJECTIVE Someone who is dogmatic about something is convinced that they are right about it.
dogmatism NOUN

doldrums

AN INFORMAL PHRASE If you are **in the doldrums**, you are depressed or bored.

dole doles doling doled

VERB If you dole something out, you give a certain amount of it to each individual in a group.

doll dolls

NOUN a child's toy which looks like a baby or person.

dollar dollars

NOUN the main unit of currency in Australia, New Zealand, the USA, Canada, and some other countries. A dollar is worth 100 cents.

dollop dollops

NOUN an amount of food, served casually in a lump.

dolphin dolphins

NOUN a mammal which lives in the sea and looks like a large fish with a long snout.

domain domains

NOUN **1** a particular area of activity or interest EG *the domain of science.*
2 an area over which someone has control or influence EG *This reservation was the largest of the Apache domains.*

dome domes

NOUN a round roof.
domed ADJECTIVE

domestic

ADJECTIVE **1** happening or existing within one particular country EG *domestic and foreign politics.*
2 involving or concerned with the home and family EG *routine domestic tasks.*

domesticated

ADJECTIVE If a wild animal or plant has been domesticated, it has been controlled or cultivated.

domesticity

NOUN; A FORMAL WORD Domesticity is life at home with your family.

dominance

NOUN **1** Dominance is power or control. **2** If something has dominance over other similar things, it is more powerful or important than they are EG *the dominance of the United States in the film business.*
dominant ADJECTIVE

A
B
C
D
E
F
G
H
I
J
K
L
M
N
O
P
Q
R
S
T
U
V
W
X
Y
Z

A B C D E F G H I J K L M N O P Q R S T U V W X Y Z

dominate dominates dominating dominated

VERB **1** If something or someone dominates a situation or event, they are the most powerful or important thing in it and have control over it EG *The civil service dominated public affairs.* **2** If a person or country dominates other people or places, they have power or control over them. **3** If something dominates an area, it towers over it EG *The valley was dominated by high surrounding cliffs.*

dominating ADJECTIVE, **domination** NOUN

domineering

ADJECTIVE Someone who is domineering tries to control other people EG *a domineering mother.*

dominion

NOUN Dominion is control or authority that a person or a country has over other people.

domino dominoes

NOUN Dominoes are small rectangular blocks marked with two groups of spots on one side, used for playing the game called dominoes.

don dons donning donned

NOUN **1** a lecturer at Oxford or Cambridge university. ▶ VERB **2** A LITERARY USE If you don clothing, you put it on.

donate donates donating donated

VERB To donate something to a charity or organization means to give it as a gift.

donation NOUN

done

the past participle of **do**.

donkey donkeys

NOUN an animal like a horse, but smaller and with longer ears.

donor donors

NOUN **1** someone who gives some of their blood while they are alive or an organ after their death to be used to help someone who is ill EG *a kidney donor.* **2** someone who gives

something such as money to a charity or other organization.

doodle doodles doodling doodled

NOUN **1** a drawing done when you are thinking about something else or when you are bored. ▶ VERB **2** To doodle means to draw doodles.

doom

NOUN Doom is a terrible fate or event in the future which you can do nothing to prevent.

doomed

ADJECTIVE If someone or something is doomed to an unpleasant or unhappy experience, they are certain to suffer it EG *doomed to failure.*

doomsday

NOUN Doomsday is the end of the world.

door doors

NOUN a swinging or sliding panel for opening or closing the entrance to something; also the entrance itself.

doorway doorways

NOUN an opening in a wall for a door.

dope dopes doping doped

NOUN **1** Dope is an illegal drug. ▶ VERB **2** If someone dopes you, they put a drug into your food or drink. 📖 from Dutch *doop* meaning 'sauce'

dormant

ADJECTIVE Something that is dormant is not active, growing, or being used EG *The buds will remain dormant until spring.*

dormitory dormitories

NOUN a large bedroom where several people sleep.

dormouse dormice

NOUN an animal, like a large mouse, with a furry tail.

dosage dosages

NOUN the amount of a medicine or a drug that should be taken.

dose doses

NOUN a measured amount of a

medicine or drug.

dossier dossiers
Said "doss-ee-ay" NOUN a collection of papers with information on a particular subject or person.

dot dots dotting dotted
NOUN **1** a very small, round mark.
▶ VERB **2** If things dot an area, they are scattered all over it EG *Fishing villages dot the coastline.* ▶ PHRASE **3** If you arrive somewhere **on the dot**, you arrive there at exactly the right time.

dote dotes doting doted
VERB If you dote on someone, you love them very much.
doting ADJECTIVE

double doubles doubling doubled
ADJECTIVE **1** twice the usual size EG *a double whisky.* **2** consisting of two parts EG *a double album.* ▶ VERB **3** If something doubles, it becomes twice as large. **4** To double as something means to have a second job or use as well as the main one EG *Their home doubles as an office.*
▶ NOUN **5** Your double is someone who looks exactly like you.
6 Doubles is a game of tennis or badminton which two people play against two other people.
doubly ADVERB

double bass double basses
NOUN a musical instrument like a large violin, which you play standing up.

double-cross double-crosses double-crossing double-crossed
VERB If someone double-crosses you, they cheat you by pretending to do what you both planned, when in fact they do the opposite.

double-decker double-deckers
ADJECTIVE **1** having two tiers or layers. ▶ NOUN **2** a bus with two floors.

double glazing
NOUN Double glazing is a second layer of glass fitted to windows to keep the building quieter or warmer.

doubt doubts doubting doubted
NOUN **1** Doubt is a feeling of uncertainty about whether something is true or possible. ▶ VERB **2** If you doubt something, you think that it is probably not true or possible.
▣ (sense 1) misgiving, qualm, uncertainty

doubtful
ADJECTIVE unlikely or uncertain.

dough
Rhymes with "go" NOUN **1** Dough is a mixture of flour and water and sometimes other ingredients, used to make bread, pastry, or biscuits. **2** AN INFORMAL USE Dough is money.

doughnut doughnuts
NOUN a ring of sweet dough cooked in hot fat.

dour
Rhymes with "poor" ADJECTIVE severe and unfriendly EG *a dour portrait of his personality.*

douse douses dousing doused; also spelt **dowse**
VERB If you douse a fire, you stop it burning by throwing water over it.

dove doves
NOUN a bird like a small pigeon.

dovetail dovetails dovetailing dovetailed
VERB If two things dovetail together, they fit together closely or neatly.

dowager dowagers
NOUN a woman who has inherited a title from her dead husband EG *the Empress Dowager.*

dowdy dowdier dowdiest
ADJECTIVE wearing dull and unfashionable clothes.

down downs downing downed
PREPOSITION OR ADVERB **1** Down means towards the ground, towards a lower level, or in a lower place. **2** If you go down a road or river, you go along it. ▶ ADVERB **3** If you put something down, you place it on a surface. **4** If an amount of something goes down, it decreases.

▶ ADJECTIVE **5** If you feel down, you feel depressed. ▶ VERB **6** If you down a drink, you drink it quickly. ▶ NOUN **7** Down is the small, soft feathers on young birds.

downcast
ADJECTIVE **1** feeling sad and dejected. **2** If your eyes are downcast, they are looking towards the ground.

downfall
NOUN **1** The downfall of a successful or powerful person or institution is their failure. **2** Something that is someone's downfall is the thing that causes their failure EG *His pride may be his downfall.*

downgrade downgrades downgrading downgraded
VERB If you downgrade something, you give it less importance or make it less valuable.

downhill
ADVERB **1** moving down a slope. **2** becoming worse EG *The press has gone downhill in the last 10 years.*

downpour downpours
NOUN a heavy fall of rain.

downright
ADJECTIVE OR ADVERB You use 'downright' to emphasize that something is extremely unpleasant or bad EG *Staff are often discourteous and sometimes downright rude.*

downstairs
ADVERB **1** going down a staircase towards the ground floor. ▶ ADJECTIVE OR ADVERB **2** on a lower floor or on the ground floor.

downstream
ADJECTIVE OR ADVERB Something that is downstream or moving downstream is nearer or moving nearer to the mouth of a river from a point further up.

down-to-earth
ADJECTIVE sensible and practical EG *a down-to-earth approach.*

downtrodden
ADJECTIVE People who are downtrodden are treated badly by those with power and do not have the ability to fight back.

downturn downturns
NOUN a decline in the economy or in the success of a company or industry.

downwards or downward
ADVERB OR ADJECTIVE **1** If you move or look downwards, you move or look towards the ground or towards a lower level EG *His eyes travelled downwards... She slipped on the downward slope.* **2** If an amount or rate moves downwards, it decreases.

downwind
ADVERB If something moves downwind, it moves in the same direction as the wind EG *Sparks drifted downwind.*

dowry dowries
NOUN A woman's dowry is money or property which her father gives to the man she marries.

doze dozes dozing dozed
VERB **1** When you doze, you sleep lightly for a short period. ▶ NOUN **2** a short, light sleep.

dozen dozens
NOUN A dozen things are twelve of them.

drab drabber drabbest
ADJECTIVE dull and unattractive. **drabness** NOUN
🔳 dreary, dull

draft drafts drafting drafted
NOUN **1** an early rough version of it of a document or speech. ▶ VERB **2** When you draft a document or speech, you write the first rough version of it. **3** To draft people somewhere means to move them there so that they can do a specific job EG *Various different presenters were drafted in.* **4** In Australian and New Zealand English, to draft cattle or sheep is to select some from a herd or flock.

drag drags dragging dragged
VERB **1** If you drag a heavy object somewhere, you pull it slowly and

with difficulty. **2** If you drag someone somewhere, you make them go although they may be unwilling. **3** If things drag behind you, they trail along the ground as you move along. **4** If an event or a period of time drags, it is boring and seems to last a long time.
▶ NOUN **5** Drag is the resistance to the motion of a body passing through air or a fluid.
■ (sense 1) draw, haul, pull

dragon dragons
NOUN In stories and legends, a dragon is a fierce animal like a large lizard with wings and claws that breathes fire.
📖 from Greek *drakōn* meaning 'serpent'

dragonfly dragonflies
NOUN a colourful insect which is often found near water.

dragoon dragoons dragooning dragooned
NOUN **1** Dragoons are soldiers. Originally, they were mounted infantry soldiers. ▶ VERB **2** If you dragoon someone into something, you force them to do it.

drain drains draining drained
VERB **1** If you drain something or if it drains, liquid gradually flows out of it or off it. **2** If you drain a glass, you drink all its contents. **3** If something drains strength or resources, it gradually uses them up EG *The prolonged boardroom battle drained him of energy and money.*
▶ NOUN **4** a pipe or channel that carries water or sewage away from a place. **5** a metal grid in a road, through which rainwater flows.

drainage
NOUN **1** Drainage is the system of pipes, drains, or ditches used to drain water or other liquid away from a place. **2** Drainage is also the process of draining water away, or the way in which a place drains EG *To grow these well, all you need is good drainage.*

drake drakes
NOUN a male duck.

drama dramas
NOUN **1** a serious play for the theatre, television, or radio. **2** Drama is plays and the theatre in general EG *Japanese drama.* **3** You can refer to the exciting events or aspects of a situation as drama EG *the drama of real life.*

dramatic
ADJECTIVE A dramatic change or event happens suddenly and is very noticeable EG *a dramatic departure from tradition.*
dramatically ADVERB

dramatist dramatists
NOUN a person who writes plays.

drape drapes draping draped
VERB If you drape a piece of cloth, you arrange it so that it hangs down or covers something in loose folds.

drastic
ADJECTIVE A drastic course of action is very severe and is usually taken urgently EG *It's time for drastic action.*
drastically ADVERB
■ extreme, radical

draught draughts
Said "draft" NOUN **1** a current of cold air. **2** an amount of liquid that you swallow. **3** Draughts is a game for two people played on a chessboard with round pieces.
▶ ADJECTIVE **4** Draught beer is served straight from barrels rather than in bottles.

draughtsman draughtsmen
NOUN a person who prepares detailed drawings or plans.

draughty draughtier draughtiest
ADJECTIVE A place that is draughty has currents of cold air blowing through it.

draw draws drawing drew drawn
VERB **1** When you draw, you use a pen or crayon to make a picture or diagram. **2** To draw near means to move closer. To draw away or draw

A
B
C
D
E
F
G
H
I
J
K
L
M
N
O
P
Q
R
S
T
U
V
W
X
Y
Z

back means to move away. **3** If you draw something in a particular direction, you pull it there smoothly and gently EG *He drew his feet under the chair*. **4** If you draw a deep breath, you breathe in deeply. **5** If you draw the curtains, you pull them so that they cover or uncover the window. **6** If something such as water or energy is drawn from a source, it is taken from it. **7** If you draw a conclusion, you arrive at it from the facts you know. **8** If you draw a distinction or a comparison between two things, you point out that it exists. ▸ NOUN **9** the result of a game or competition in which nobody wins.
draw up VERB To draw up a plan, document, or list means to prepare it and write it out.

drawback drawbacks
NOUN a problem that makes something less acceptable or desirable EG *Shortcuts usually have a drawback.*

drawbridge drawbridges
NOUN a bridge that can be pulled up or lowered.

drawer drawers
NOUN a sliding box-shaped part of a piece of furniture used for storing things.

drawing drawings
NOUN **1** a picture made with a pencil, pen, or crayon. **2** Drawing is the skill or work of making drawings.

drawing room drawing rooms
NOUN; AN OLD-FASHIONED WORD a room in a house where people relax or entertain guests.

drawl drawls drawling drawled
VERB If someone drawls, they speak slowly with long vowel sounds.

drawn
Drawn is the past participle of draw.

dread dreads dreading dreaded
VERB **1** If you dread something, you feel very worried and frightened

about it EG *He was dreading the journey*. ▸ NOUN **2** Dread is a feeling of great fear or anxiety.
dreaded ADJECTIVE

dreadful
ADJECTIVE very bad or unpleasant.
dreadfully ADVERB
▤ atrocious, awful, terrible

dream dreams dreaming dreamed or **dreamt**
NOUN **1** a series of events that you experience in your mind while asleep. **2** a situation or event which you often think about because you would very much like it to happen EG *his dream of winning the lottery*. ▸ VERB **3** When you dream, you see events in your mind while you are asleep. **4** When you dream about something happening, you often think about it because you would very much like it to happen. **5** If someone dreams up a plan or idea, they invent it. **6** If you say you would not dream of doing something, you are emphasizing that you would not do it EG *I wouldn't dream of giving the plot away*. ▸ ADJECTIVE **7** too good to be true EG *a dream holiday*.
dreamer NOUN

Dreamtime
NOUN In Australian Aboriginal legends, Dreamtime is the time when the world was being made and the first people were created.

dreamy dreamier dreamiest
ADJECTIVE Someone with a dreamy expression looks as if they are thinking about something very pleasant.

dreary drearier dreariest
ADJECTIVE dull or boring.

dregs
PLURAL NOUN The dregs of a liquid are the last drops left at the bottom of a container, and any sediment left with it.

drenched
ADJECTIVE soaking wet.

dress dresses dressing dressed

NOUN **1** a piece of clothing for women or girls made up of a skirt and top attached. **2** Dress is any clothing worn by men or women. ▶ VERB **3** When you dress, you put clothes on. **4** If you dress for a special occasion, you put on formal clothes. **5** To dress a wound means to clean it up and treat it.

dresser dressers
NOUN a piece of kitchen or dining room furniture with cupboards or drawers in the lower part and open shelves in the top part.

dress rehearsal dress rehearsals
NOUN the last rehearsal of a show or play, using costumes, scenery, and lighting.

dribble dribbles dribbling dribbled
VERB **1** When liquid dribbles down a surface, it trickles down it in drops or a thin stream. **2** If a person or animal dribbles, saliva trickles from their mouth. **3** In sport, to dribble a ball means to move it along by repeatedly tapping it with your foot or a stick. ▶ NOUN **4** a small quantity of liquid flowing in a thin stream or drops.

drift drifts drifting drifted
VERB **1** When something drifts, it is carried along by the wind or by water. **2** When people drift, they move aimlessly from one place or activity to another. **3** If you drift off to sleep, you gradually fall asleep. ▶ NOUN **4** A snow drift is a pile of snow heaped up by the wind. **5** The drift of an argument or a speech is its main point.
drifter NOUN

drill drills drilling drilled
NOUN **1** a tools for making holes EG an electric drill. **2** Drill is a routine exercise or routine training EG lifeboat drill. ▶ VERB **3** To drill into something means to make a hole in it using a drill. **4** If you drill people, you teach them to do something by repetition.

drink drinks drinking drank drunk
VERB **1** When you drink, you take liquid into your mouth and swallow it. **2** To drink also means to drink alcohol EG He drinks little and eats carefully. ▶ NOUN **3** an amount of liquid suitable for drinking. **4** an alcoholic drink.
drinker NOUN
▤ (sense 1) imbibe, sip, swallow
▤ (sense 2) booze, tipple

drip drips dripping dripped
VERB **1** When liquid drips, it falls in small drops. **2** When an object drips, drops of liquid fall from it. ▶ NOUN **3** a drop of liquid falling from something. **4** a device for allowing liquid food to enter the bloodstream of a person who cannot eat properly because they are ill.

drive drives driving drove driven
VERB **1** To drive a vehicle means to operate it and control its movements. **2** If something or someone drives you to do something, they force you to do it EG The illness of his daughter drove him to religion. **3** If you drive a post or nail into something, you force it in by hitting it with a hammer. **4** If something drives a machine, it supplies the power that makes it work. ▶ NOUN **5** a journey in a vehicle. **6** a private road that leads from a public road to a person's house. **7** Drive is energy and determination.
driver NOUN, **driving** NOUN

drivel
NOUN Drivel is nonsense EG He is still writing mindless drivel.
▥ from Old English *dreflian* meaning 'to dribble'

drizzle
NOUN Drizzle is light rain.

dromedary dromedaries
NOUN a camel which has one hump.

drone drones droning droned
VERB **1** If something drones, it makes a low, continuous humming noise.

A B C D E F G H I J K L M N O P Q R S T U V W X Y Z

A
B
C
D
E
F
G
H
I
J
K
L
M
N
O
P
Q
R
S
T
U
V
W
X
Y
Z

2 If someone drones on, they keep talking or reading aloud in a boring way. ▸ NOUN **3** a continuous low dull sound.

drool drools drooling drooled
VERB If someone drools, saliva dribbles from their mouth without them being able to stop it.

droop droops drooping drooped
VERB If something droops, it hangs or sags downwards with no strength or firmness.

drop drops dropping dropped
VERB **1** If you drop something, you let it fall. **2** If something drops, it falls straight down. **3** If a level or amount drops, it becomes less. **4** If your voice drops, or if you drop your voice, you speak more quietly. **5** If you drop something that you are doing or dealing with, you stop doing it or dealing with it EG *She dropped the subject and never mentioned it again.* **6** If you drop a hint, you give someone a hint in a casual way. **7** If you drop something or someone somewhere, you deposit or leave them there. ▸ NOUN **8** A drop of liquid is a very small quantity of it that forms or falls in a round shape. **9** a decrease EG *a huge drop in income.* **10** the distance between the top and bottom of something tall, such as a cliff or building EG *It is a sheer drop to the foot of the cliff.*

droplet droplets
NOUN a small drop.

droppings
PLURAL NOUN Droppings are the faeces of birds and small animals.

drought droughts
Rhymes with "shout" NOUN a long period during which there is no rain.

drove droves droving droved
1 Drove is the past tense of **drive**. ▸ VERB **2** To drove cattle or sheep is to drive them over a long distance.

drown drowns drowning drowned
VERB **1** When someone drowns or is drowned, they die because they have gone under water and cannot breathe. **2** If a noise drowns a sound, it is louder than the sound and makes it impossible to hear it.

drowsy drowsier drowsiest
ADJECTIVE feeling sleepy.

drudgery
NOUN Drudgery is hard uninteresting work.

drug drugs drugging drugged
NOUN **1** a chemical given to people to treat disease. **2** Drugs are chemical substances that some people smoke, swallow, smell, or inject because of their stimulating effects. ▸ VERB **3** To drug a person or animal means to give them a drug to make them unconscious. **4** To drug food or drink means to add a drug to it in order to make someone unconscious.
drugged ADJECTIVE

druid druids
Said "droo-id" NOUN a priest of an ancient religion in Northern Europe.

drum drums drumming drummed
NOUN **1** a musical instrument consisting of a skin stretched tightly over a round frame. **2** an object or container shaped like a drum EG *an oil drum.* **3** AN INFORMAL USE In Australian English, the drum is information or advice EG *The manager gave me the drum.* ▸ VERB **4** If something is drumming on a surface, it is hitting it regularly, making a continuous beating sound. **5** If you drum something into someone, you keep saying it to them until they understand it or remember it.

drumstick drumsticks
NOUN **1** a stick used for beating a drum. **2** A chicken drumstick is the lower part of the leg of a chicken, which is cooked and eaten.

drunk drunks
1 Drunk is the past participle of

A B C D E F G H I J K L M N O P Q R S T U V W X Y Z

drink. ▶ ADJECTIVE **2** If someone is drunk, they have drunk so much alcohol that they cannot speak clearly or behave sensibly. ▶ NOUN **3** a person who is drunk, or who often gets drunk.

drunken ADJECTIVE, **drunkenly** ADVERB, **drunkenness** NOUN

■ (sense 2) inebriated, intoxicated

dry drier or **dryer driest; dries drying dried**

ADJECTIVE **1** Something that is dry contains or uses no water or liquid. **2** Dry bread or toast is eaten without a topping. **3** Dry sherry or wine does not taste sweet. **4** Dry also means plain and sometimes boring EG *the dry facts.* **5** Dry humour is subtle and sarcastic. ▶ VERB **6** When you dry something, or when it dries, liquid is removed from it.

■ (sense 1) arid, dehydrated, parched

dry up VERB **1** If something dries up, it becomes completely dry. **2** AN INFORMAL USE If you dry up, you forget what you were going to say, or find that you have nothing left to say.

dryness NOUN, **drily** ADVERB

dry-clean dry-cleans dry-cleaning dry-cleaned

VERB When clothes are dry-cleaned, they are cleaned with a liquid chemical rather than with water.

dryer dryers; also spelt **drier**

NOUN a device for removing moisture from something by heating or by hot air EG *a hair dryer.*

dual

ADJECTIVE having two parts, functions, or aspects EG *a dual-purpose trimmer.*

dub dubs dubbing dubbed

VERB **1** If something is dubbed a particular name, it is given that name EG *Smiling has been dubbed 'nature's secret weapon'.* **2** If a film is dubbed, the voices on the soundtrack are not those of the actors, but those of other actors speaking in a different language.

dubious

Said "dyoo-bee-uss" ADJECTIVE **1** not entirely honest, safe, or reliable EG *dubious sales techniques.* **2** doubtful EG *I felt dubious about the entire proposition.*

dubiously ADVERB

■ (sense 1) questionable, suspect

duchess duchesses

NOUN a woman who has the same rank as a duke, or who is a duke's wife or widow.

duchy duchies

Said "dut-shee" NOUN the land owned and ruled by a duke or duchess.

duck ducks ducking ducked

NOUN **1** a bird that lives in water and has webbed feet and a large flat bill. ▶ VERB **2** If you duck, you move your head quickly downwards in order to avoid being hit by something. **3** If you duck a duty or responsibility, you avoid it. **4** To duck someone means to push them briefly under water.

duckling ducklings

NOUN a young duck.

duct ducts

NOUN **1** a pipe or channel through which liquid or gas is sent. **2** a bodily passage through which liquid such as tears can pass.

dud duds

NOUN something which does not function properly.

due dues

ADJECTIVE **1** expected to happen or arrive EG *The baby is due at Christmas.* **2** If you give something due consideration, you give it the consideration it needs. ▶ PHRASE **3 Due to** means because of EG *Headaches can be due to stress.* ▶ ADVERB **4 Due** means exactly in a particular direction EG *About a mile due west lay the ocean.* ▶ PLURAL NOUN **5 Dues** are sums of money that you pay regularly to an organization

A
B
C
D
E
F
G
H
I
J
K
L
M
N
O
P
Q
R
S
T
U
V
W
X
Y
Z

you belong to.

duel duels
NOUN **1** a fight arranged between two people using deadly weapons, to settle a quarrel. **2** Any contest or conflict between two people can be referred to as a duel.

duet duets
NOUN a piece of music sung or played by two people.

dug
Dug is the past tense and past participle of **dig**.

dugong dugongs
NOUN an animal like a whale that lives in warm seas.

dugout dugouts
NOUN **1** a canoe made by hollowing out a log. **2** A MILITARY WORD a shelter dug in the ground for protection.

duke dukes
NOUN a nobleman with a rank just below that of a prince.
🏛 from Latin *dux* meaning 'leader'

dull duller dullest; dulls dulling dulled
ADJECTIVE **1** not at all interesting in any way. **2** slow to learn or understand. **3** not bright, sharp, or clear. **4** A dull day or dull sky is very cloudy. **5** Dull feelings are weak and not intense EG *He should have been angry but felt only dull resentment.* ▶ VERB **6** If something dulls or is dulled, it becomes less bright, sharp, or clear.
dully ADVERB, **dullness** NOUN
◼ (sense 4) cloudy, overcast

duly
ADVERB **1** A FORMAL USE If something is duly done, it is done in the correct way EG *I wish to record my support for the duly elected council.* **2** If something duly happens, it is something that you expected to happen EG *Two chicks duly emerged from their eggs.*

dumb dumber dumbest
ADJECTIVE **1** unable to speak. **2** AN INFORMAL USE slow to understand or

stupid.

dumbfounded
ADJECTIVE speechless with amazement EG *She was too dumbfounded to answer.*

dummy dummies
NOUN **1** a rubber teat which a baby sucks or bites on. **2** an imitation or model of something which is used for display. ▶ ADJECTIVE **3** imitation or substitute.

dump dumps dumping dumped
VERB **1** When unwanted waste is dumped, it is left somewhere. **2** If you dump something, you throw it down or put it down somewhere in a careless way. ▶ NOUN **3** a place where rubbish is left. **4** a storage place, especially used by the military for storing supplies. **5** AN INFORMAL USE You refer to a place as a dump when it is unattractive and unpleasant to live in.

dumpling dumplings
NOUN a small lump of dough that is cooked and eaten with meat and vegetables.

dunce dunces
NOUN a person who cannot learn what someone is trying to teach them.

dune dunes
NOUN A dune or sand dune is a hill of sand near the sea or in the desert.

dung
NOUN Dung is the faeces from large animals, sometimes called manure.

dungarees
PLURAL NOUN Dungarees are trousers which have a bib covering the chest and straps over the shoulders.

dungeon dungeons
Said "dun-jen" NOUN an underground prison.

dunk dunks dunking dunked
VERB To dunk something means to dip it briefly into a liquid EG *He dunked a single tea bag into two cups.*

duo duos
NOUN **1** a pair of musical performers;

also a piece of music written for two players. **2** Any two people doing something together can be referred to as a duo.

dupe dupes duping duped
VERB **1** If someone dupes you, they trick you. ▶ NOUN **2** someone who has been tricked.
📖 from Old French *de huppe* meaning 'of the hoopoe', a bird thought to be stupid

duplicate duplicates duplicating duplicated
VERB **1** To duplicate something means to make an exact copy of it. ▶ NOUN **2** something that is identical to something else. ▶ ADJECTIVE **3** identical to or an exact copy of EG *a duplicate key*.
duplication NOUN

durable
ADJECTIVE strong and lasting for a long time.
durability NOUN

duration
NOUN The duration of something is the length of time during which it happens or exists.

duress
Said "dyoo-**ress**" NOUN If you do something under duress, you are forced to do it, and you do it very unwillingly.

during
PREPOSITION happening throughout a particular time or at a particular point in time EG *The mussels will open naturally during cooking*.

dusk
NOUN Dusk is the time just before nightfall when it is not completely dark.
📖 from Old English *dox* meaning 'dark' or 'swarthy'

dust dusts dusting dusted
NOUN **1** Dust is dry fine powdery material such as particles of earth, dirt, or pollen. ▶ VERB **2** When you dust furniture or other objects, you remove dust from them using a duster. **3** If you dust a surface with

powder, you cover it lightly with the powder.

dustbin dustbins
NOUN a large container for rubbish.

duster dusters
NOUN a cloth used for removing dust from furniture and other objects.

dustman dustmen
NOUN someone whose job is to collect the rubbish from people's houses.

dusty dustier dustiest
ADJECTIVE covered with dust.

Dutch
ADJECTIVE **1** belonging or relating to Holland. ▶ NOUN **2** Dutch is the main language spoken in Holland.

dutiful
ADJECTIVE doing everything you are expected to do.
dutifully ADVERB

duty duties
NOUN **1** Duties are things you ought to do or feel you should do, because it is your responsibility to do them EG *We have a duty as adults to listen to children*. ▶ PLURAL NOUN **2** Your duties are the tasks which you do as part of your job. ▶ NOUN **3** Duty is tax paid to the government on some goods, especially imports.
📲 (sense 1) obligation, responsibility

duty-free
ADJECTIVE Duty-free goods are sold at airports or on planes or ships at a cheaper price than usual because they are not taxed EG *duty-free vodka*.

duvet duvets
Said "**doo**-vay" NOUN a cotton quilt filled with feathers or other material, used on a bed in place of sheets and blankets.

dwarf dwarfs dwarfing dwarfed
VERB **1** If one thing dwarfs another, it is so much bigger that it makes it look very small. ▶ ADJECTIVE **2** smaller than average. ▶ NOUN **3** a person who is much smaller than average

A
B
C
D
E
F
G
H
I
J
K
L
M
N
O
P
Q
R
S
T
U
V
W
X
Y
Z

size.

dwell dwells dwelling dwelled or dwelt

VERB **1** A LITERARY USE To dwell somewhere means to live there. **2** If you dwell on something or dwell upon it, you think or write about it a lot.

dwelling dwellings

NOUN; A FORMAL WORD Someone's dwelling is the house or other place where they live.

dwindle dwindles dwindling dwindled

VERB If something dwindles, it becomes smaller or weaker.

dye dyes dyeing dyed

VERB **1** To dye something means to change its colour by applying coloured liquid to it. ▶ NOUN **2** a colouring substance which is used to change the colour of something such as cloth or hair.

dyke dykes; also spelt **dike**

NOUN a thick wall that prevents water flooding onto land from a river or from the sea.

dynamic dynamics

ADJECTIVE **1** A dynamic person is full of energy, ambition, and new ideas. **2** relating to energy or forces which produce motion. ▶ NOUN **3** In physics, dynamics is the study of the forces that change or produce the motion of bodies or particles. ▶ PLURAL NOUN **4** The dynamics of a society or a situation are the forces that cause it to change.

dynamite

NOUN Dynamite is a kind of explosive.

dynamo dynamos

NOUN a device that converts mechanical energy into electricity.

dynasty dynasties

NOUN a series of rulers of a country all belonging to the same family.

dysentery

Said "diss-en-tree" NOUN an infection of the bowel which causes fever, stomach pain, and severe diarrhoea.

dyslexia

Said "dis-lek-see-a" NOUN Dyslexia is difficulty with reading caused by a slight disorder of the brain.
dyslexic ADJECTIVE AND NOUN

each

ADJECTIVE OR PRONOUN **1** every one taken separately EG *Each time she went out, she would buy a plant.*
▶ PHRASE **2** If people do something to **each other**, each person does it to the other or others EG *She and Chris smiled at each other.*
☑ Wherever you use *each other* you could also use *one another*.

eager

ADJECTIVE wanting very much to do or have something.
eagerly ADVERB, **eagerness** NOUN

eagle eagles

NOUN a large bird of prey.

ear ears

NOUN **1** Your ears are the parts of your body on either side of your head with which you hear sounds. **2** An ear of corn or wheat is the top part of the stalk which contains seeds.

eardrum eardrums

NOUN Your eardrums are thin pieces of tightly stretched skin inside your ears which vibrate so that you can hear sounds.

earl earls

NOUN a British nobleman.
🏛 from Old English *eorl* meaning 'chieftain'

early earlier earliest

ADJECTIVE OR ADVERB **1** before the arranged or expected time EG *He wasn't late for our meeting, I was early.* **2** near the beginning of a day, evening, or other period of time EG *the early 1970s.*
🔲 (sense 1) premature, untimely

earmark earmarks earmarking earmarked

VERB If you earmark something for a special purpose, you keep it for that purpose.
🏛 from identification marks on the ears of domestic or farm animals

earn earns earning earned

VERB **1** If you earn money, you get it in return for work that you do. **2** If you earn something such as praise, you receive it because you deserve it.
earner NOUN

earnest

ADJECTIVE **1** sincere in what you say or do EG *I answered with an earnest smile.* ▶ PHRASE **2** If something begins **in earnest**, it happens to a greater or more serious extent than before EG *The battle began in earnest.*
earnestly ADVERB

earnings

PLURAL NOUN Your earnings are money that you earn.

earphones

PLURAL NOUN Earphones are small speakers which you wear on your ears to listen to a radio or cassette player.

earring earrings

NOUN Earrings are pieces of jewellery that you wear on your ear lobes.

earshot

PHRASE If you are **within earshot** of something, you can hear it.

earth earths

NOUN **1** The earth is the planet on which we live. **2** Earth is the dry land on the surface of the earth, especially the soil in which things grow. **3** a hole in the ground where a fox lives. **4** The earth in a piece of electrical equipment is the wire through which electricity can pass into the ground and so make the equipment safe for use.

earthenware

NOUN Earthenware is pottery made of baked clay.

earthly

ADJECTIVE concerned with life on earth rather than heaven or life after death.

earthquake earthquakes

NOUN a shaking of the ground caused by movement of the earth's crust.

earthworm earthworms
NOUN a worm that lives under the ground.

earthy earthier earthiest
ADJECTIVE **1** looking or smelling like earth. **2** Someone who is earthy is open and direct, often in a crude way EG *earthy language*.

earwig earwigs
NOUN a small, thin, brown insect which has a pair of pincers at the end of its body.
🏛 from Old English *earwicga* meaning 'ear insect'; it was believed to creep into people's ears

ease eases easing eased
NOUN **1** Ease is lack of difficulty, worry, or hardship EG *He had sailed through life with relative ease.* ▶ VERB **2** When something eases, or when you ease it, it becomes less severe or less intense EG *to ease the pain.* **3** If you ease something somewhere, you move it there slowly and carefully EG *He eased himself into his chair.*
▦ (sense 1) easiness, effortlessness
▦ (sense 2) alleviate, relieve

easel easels
NOUN an upright frame which supports a picture that someone is painting.
🏛 from Dutch *ezel* meaning 'ass' or 'donkey'

easily
ADVERB **1** without difficulty. **2** without a doubt EG *The song is easily one of their finest.*

east
NOUN **1** East is the direction in which you look to see the sun rise. **2** The east of a place is the part which is towards the east when you are in the centre EG *the east of Africa.* **3** The East is the countries in the south and east of Asia.
▶ ADJECTIVE OR ADVERB **4** East means in or towards the east EG *The entrance*

faces east. ▶ ADJECTIVE **5** An east wind blows from the east.

Easter
NOUN Easter is a Christian religious festival celebrating the resurrection of Christ.
🏛 from Old English *Eostre*, a pre-Christian Germanic goddess whose festival was at the spring equinox

easterly
ADJECTIVE **1** Easterly means to or towards the east. **2** An easterly wind blows from the east.

eastern
ADJECTIVE in or from the east EG *a remote eastern corner of the country.*

eastward or **eastwards**
ADVERB **1** Eastward or eastwards means towards the east EG *the eastward expansion of the city.*
▶ ADJECTIVE **2** The eastward part of something is the east part.

easy easier easiest
ADJECTIVE **1** able to be done without difficulty EG *It's easy to fall.* **2** comfortable and without any worries EG *an easy life.*
☑ Although *easy* is an adjective, it can be used as an adverb in fixed phrases like *take it easy.*

eat eats eating ate eaten
VERB **1** To eat means to chew and swallow food. **2** When you eat, you have a meal EG *We like to eat early.*
eat away VERB If something is eaten away, it is slowly destroyed EG *The sea had eaten away at the headland.*

eaves
PLURAL NOUN The eaves of a roof are the lower edges which jut out over the walls.

eavesdrop eavesdrops eavesdropping eavesdropped
VERB If you eavesdrop, you listen secretly to what other people are saying.
🏛 from Old English *yfesdrype* meaning 'water dripping down from the eaves'; people were supposed to stand outside in the

rain to hear what was being said inside the house

ebb ebbs ebbing ebbed
VERB **1** When the sea or the tide ebbs, it flows back. **2** If a person's feeling or strength ebbs, it gets weaker EG *The strength ebbed from his body*.

ebony
NOUN **1** Ebony is a hard, dark-coloured wood, used for making furniture. ▶ NOUN OR ADJECTIVE **2** very deep black.

ebullient
ADJECTIVE; A FORMAL WORD lively and full of enthusiasm.
ebullience NOUN

EC
NOUN The EC is an old name for the European Union. EC is an abbreviation for 'European Community'.

eccentric eccentrics
Said "ik-**sen**-trik" ADJECTIVE **1** having habits or opinions which other people think are odd or peculiar. ▶ NOUN **2** someone who is eccentric.
eccentricity NOUN, **eccentrically** ADVERB
▤ (sense 1) odd, peculiar, strange
▤ (sense 2) crank, oddball, weirdo

ecclesiastical
Said "ik-**leez**-ee-**ass**-ti-kl" ADJECTIVE of or relating to the Christian church.
▥ from Greek *ekklēsia* meaning 'assembly' or 'church'

echelon echelons
Said "**esh**-el-on" NOUN a level of power or responsibility in an organization.

echidna echidnas or echidnae
Said "ik-**kid**-na" NOUN a small, spiny mammal that lays eggs and has a long snout and claws, found in Australia.

echo echoes echoing echoed
NOUN **1** a sound which is caused by sound waves reflecting off a surface. **2** a repetition, imitation, or reminder of something EG *Echoes of the past are everywhere*. ▶ VERB **3** If a

sound echoes, it is reflected off a surface so that you can hear it again after the original sound has stopped.

eclipse eclipses
NOUN An eclipse occurs when one planet passes in front of another and hides it from view for a short time.

ecology
NOUN Ecology is the relationship between living things and their environment; also used of the study of this relationship.
ecological ADJECTIVE, **ecologically** ADVERB, **ecologist** NOUN

economic
ADJECTIVE **1** concerning the management of the money, industry, and trade of a country. **2** concerning making a profit EG *economic to produce*.

economical
ADJECTIVE **1** Something that is economical is cheap to use or operate. **2** Someone who is economical spends money carefully and sensibly.
economically ADVERB

economics
NOUN Economics is the study of the production and distribution of goods, services, and wealth in a society and the organization of its money, industry, and trade.

economist economists
NOUN a person who studies or writes about economics.

economy economies
NOUN **1** The economy of a country is the system it uses to organize and manage its money, industry, and trade; also used of the wealth that a country gets from business and industry. **2** Economy is the careful use of things to save money, time, or energy EG *Max dished up deftly, with an economy of movement*.
▥ from Greek *oikonomia* meaning 'domestic management'

ecosystem ecosystems

A B C D E F G H I J K L M N O P Q R S T U V W X Y Z

NOUN; A TECHNICAL WORD the relationship between plants and animals and their environment.

ecstasy ecstasies
NOUN **1** Ecstasy is a feeling of extreme happiness. **2** AN INFORMAL USE a strong illegal drug that can cause hallucinations.
ecstatic ADJECTIVE, **ecstatically** ADVERB

eczema
Said "ek-sim-ma" NOUN Eczema is a skin disease that causes the surface of the skin to become rough and itchy.
📖 from Greek *ekzein* meaning 'to boil over'

eddy eddies
NOUN a circular movement in water or air.

edge edges edging edged
NOUN **1** The edge of something is a border or line where it ends or meets something else. **2** The edge of a blade is its thin, sharp side. **3** If you have the edge over someone, you have an advantage over them. ▶ VERB **4** If you edge something, you make a border for it EG *The veil was edged with matching lace.* **5** If you edge somewhere, you move there very gradually EG *The ferry edged its way out into the river.*
■ (sense 1) border, brink, margin

edgy edgier edgiest
ADJECTIVE anxious and irritable.

edible
ADJECTIVE safe and pleasant to eat.

edifice edifices
Said "ed-if-iss" NOUN; A FORMAL WORD a large and impressive building.

edit edits editing edited
VERB **1** If you edit a piece of writing, you correct it so that it is fit for publishing. **2** To edit a film or television programme means to select different parts of it and arrange them in a particular order. **3** Someone who edits a newspaper or magazine is in charge of it.

edition editions

NOUN **1** An edition of a book or magazine is a particular version of it printed at one time. **2** An edition of a television or radio programme is a single programme that is one of a series.

editor editors
NOUN **1** a person who is responsible for the content of a newspaper or magazine. **2** a person who checks books and makes corrections to them before they are published. **3** a person who selects different parts of a television programme or a film and arranges them in a particular order.
editorship NOUN

editorial editorials
ADJECTIVE **1** involved in preparing a newspaper, book, or magazine for publication. **2** involving the contents and the opinions of a newspaper or magazine EG *an editorial comment.* ▶ NOUN **3** an article in a newspaper or magazine which gives the opinions of the editor or publisher on a particular topic.
editorially ADVERB

educate educates educating educated
VERB To educate someone means to teach them so that they gain knowledge about something.

educated
ADJECTIVE having a high standard of learning and culture.

education
NOUN **1** Education is the process of gaining knowledge and understanding through learning. **2** Education also refers to the system of teaching people at school or university.
educational ADJECTIVE, **educationally** ADVERB

eel eels
NOUN a long, thin, snakelike fish.

eerie eerier eeriest
ADJECTIVE strange and frightening EG *an eerie silence.*
eerily ADVERB

effect effects

NOUN **1** a direct result of someone or something on another person or thing EG *the effect of divorce on children.* **2** An effect that someone or something has is the overall impression or result that they have EG *The effect of the decor was cosy and antique.* ▶ PHRASE **3** If something **takes effect** at a particular time, it starts to happen or starts to produce results at that time EG *The law will take effect next year.*

effective

ADJECTIVE **1** working well and producing the intended results. **2** coming into operation or beginning officially EG *The agreement has become effective immediately.*
effectively ADVERB

effeminate

ADJECTIVE A man who is effeminate behaves, looks, or sounds like a woman.

efficient

ADJECTIVE capable of doing something well without wasting time or energy.
efficiently ADVERB, **efficiency** NOUN
■ capable, competent, proficient

effigy effigies

Said "ef-fij-ee" NOUN a statue or model of a person.

effluent effluents

Said "ef-loo-ent" NOUN Effluent is liquid waste that comes out of factories or sewage works.

effort efforts

NOUN **1** Effort is the physical or mental energy needed to do something. **2** an attempt or struggle to do something EG *I went to keep-fit classes in an effort to fight the flab.*
■ (sense 1) exertion, trouble, work

effortless

ADJECTIVE done easily.
effortlessly ADVERB

eg or e.g.

eg means 'for example', and is abbreviated from the Latin expression 'exempli gratia'.

egalitarian

ADJECTIVE favouring equality for all people EG *an egalitarian country.*

egg eggs

NOUN **1** an oval or rounded object laid by female birds, reptiles, fishes, and insects. A baby creature develops inside the egg until it is ready to be born. **2** a hen's egg used as food. **3** In a female animal, an egg is a cell produced in its body which can develop into a baby if it is fertilized.

eggplant eggplants

NOUN a dark purple pear-shaped vegetable. It is also called **aubergine**.

ego egos

Said "ee-goh" NOUN Your ego is your opinion of what you are worth EG *It'll do her good and boost her ego.*
📖 from Latin *ego* meaning 'I'

egocentric

ADJECTIVE only thinking of yourself and your own interests.

egoism or egotism

NOUN Egoism is behaviour and attitudes which show that you believe that you are more important than other people.
egoist or **egotist** NOUN, **egoistic**, **egotistic** or **egotistical** ADJECTIVE

Egyptian Egyptians

Said "ij-jip-shn" ADJECTIVE
1 belonging or relating to Egypt.
▶ NOUN **2** An Egyptian is someone who comes from Egypt.

eight eights

the number 8.
eighth

eighteen

the number 18.
eighteenth

eighty eighties

the number 80.
eightieth

either

ADJECTIVE, PRONOUN, OR CONJUNCTION
1 one or the other of two possible

alternatives EG *You can spell it either way... Either of these schemes would cost billions of pounds... Either take it or leave it.* ▶ ADJECTIVE **2** both one and the other EG *on either side of the head.*
☑ When *either* is followed by a plural noun, the following verb can be plural too: *either of these books are useful.*

ejaculate ejaculates ejaculating ejaculated

VERB **1** When a man ejaculates, he discharges semen from his penis. **2** If you ejaculate, you suddenly say something.
ejaculation NOUN
🏛 from Latin *jacere* meaning 'to throw'

eject ejects ejecting ejected

VERB If you eject something or someone, you forcefully push or send them out EG *He was ejected from the club.*
ejection NOUN
▤ expel, throw out

elaborate elaborates elaborating elaborated

ADJECTIVE **1** having many different parts EG *an elaborate system of drains.* **2** carefully planned, detailed, and exact EG *elaborate plans.* **3** highly decorated and complicated EG *elaborate designs.* ▶ VERB **4** If you elaborate on something, you add more information or detail about it.
elaborately ADVERB, **elaboration** NOUN
▤ (sense 3) complicated, fancy, ornate

eland elands

NOUN a large African antelope with twisted horns.

elapse elapses elapsing elapsed

VERB When time elapses, it passes by EG *Eleven years elapsed before you got this job.*

elastic

ADJECTIVE **1** able to stretch easily. ▶ NOUN **2** Elastic is rubber material which stretches and returns to its original shape.

elasticity NOUN

🏛 from Greek *elastikos* meaning 'pushing'

elation

NOUN Elation is a feeling of great happiness.
elated ADJECTIVE

elbow elbows elbowing elbowed

NOUN **1** Your elbow is the joint between the upper part of your arm and your forearm. ▶ VERB **2** If you elbow someone aside, you push them away with your elbow.

elder eldest; elders

ADJECTIVE **1** Your elder brother or sister is older than you. ▶ NOUN **2** a senior member of a group who has influence or authority. **3** a bush or small tree with dark purple berries.
☑ The adjectives *elder* and *eldest* can only be used when talking about the age of people within families. You can use *older* and *oldest* to talk about the age of other people or things.

elderly

ADJECTIVE **1** Elderly is a polite way to describe an old person. ▶ NOUN **2** The elderly are old people EG *Priority is given to services for the elderly.*

elect elects electing elected

VERB **1** If you elect someone, you choose them to fill a position, by voting EG *He's just been elected president.* **2** A FORMAL USE If you elect to do something, you choose to do it EG *I have elected to stay.* ▶ ADJECTIVE **3** A FORMAL USE voted into a position, but not yet carrying out the duties of the position EG *the vice-president elect.*

election elections

NOUN the selection of one or more people for an official position by voting.
electoral ADJECTIVE

electorate electorates

NOUN all the people who have the right to vote in an election.

electric

ADJECTIVE **1** powered or produced by electricity. **2** very tense or exciting EG *The atmosphere is electric.*
☑ The word *electric* is an adjective and should not be used as a noun.

electrical
ADJECTIVE using or producing electricity EG *electrical goods*.
electrically ADVERB

electrician electricians
NOUN a person whose job is to install and repair electrical equipment.

electricity
NOUN Electricity is a form of energy used for heating and lighting, and to provide power for machines.
🏛 from Greek *elektron* meaning 'amber'; in early experiments, scientists rubbed amber in order to get an electrical charge

electrified
ADJECTIVE connected to a supply of electricity.

electrifying
ADJECTIVE Something that is electrifying makes you feel very excited.

electrocute electrocutes electrocuting electrocuted
VERB If someone is electrocuted, they are killed by touching something that is connected to electricity.
electrocution NOUN

electrode electrodes
NOUN a small piece of metal which allows an electric current to pass between a source of power and a piece of equipment.

electron electrons
NOUN In physics, an electron is a tiny particle of matter, smaller than an atom.

electronic
ADJECTIVE having transistors or silicon chips which control an electric current.
electronically ADVERB

electronics
NOUN Electronics is the technology of electronic devices such as televisions, and computers; also the study of how these devices work.

elegant
ADJECTIVE attractive and graceful or stylish EG *an elegant and beautiful city*.
elegantly ADVERB, **elegance** NOUN

elegy elegies
Said "el-lij-ee" NOUN a sad poem or song about someone who has died.
🏛 from Greek *elegos* meaning 'lament sung to the flute'

element elements
NOUN **1** a part of something which combines with others to make a whole. **2** In chemistry, an element is a substance that is made up of only one type of atom. **3** A particular element within a large group of people is a section of it which is similar EG *criminal elements*. **4** An element of a quality is a certain amount of it EG *Their attack has largely lost the element of surprise.* **5** The elements of a subject are the basic and most important points. **6** The elements are the weather conditions EG *Our open boat is exposed to the elements.*

elemental
ADJECTIVE; A FORMAL WORD simple and basic, but powerful EG *elemental emotions*.

elementary
ADJECTIVE simple, basic, and straightforward EG *an elementary course in woodwork*.

elephant elephants
NOUN a very large four-legged mammal with a long trunk, large ears, and ivory tusks.

elevate elevates elevating elevated
VERB **1** To elevate someone to a higher status or position means to give them greater status or importance EG *He was elevated to the rank of major in the army.* **2** To elevate something means to raise it up.

A B C D E F G H I J K L M N O P Q R S T U V W X Y Z

A
B
C
D
E
F
G
H
I
J
K
L
M
N
O
P
Q
R
S
T
U
V
W
X
Y
Z

elevation elevations

NOUN **1** The elevation of someone or something is the raising of them to a higher level or position. **2** The elevation of a place is its height above sea level or above the ground.

eleven elevens

1 Eleven is the number 11. ▶ NOUN **2** a team of cricket or soccer players.

eleventh

elf elves

NOUN In folklore, an elf is a small mischievous fairy.

elicit elicits eliciting elicited

Said "il-**iss**-it" VERB **1** A FORMAL USE If you elicit information, you find it out by asking careful questions. **2** If you elicit a response or reaction, you make it happen EG He elicited sympathy from the audience.

eligible

Said "**el**-lij-i-bl" ADJECTIVE suitable or having the right qualifications for something EG You will be eligible for a grant in the future.

eligibility NOUN

eliminate eliminates eliminating eliminated

VERB **1** If you eliminate something or someone, you get rid of them EG They eliminated him from their inquiries. **2** If a team or a person is eliminated from a competition, they can no longer take part.

elimination NOUN

elite elites

Said "ill-**eet**" NOUN a group of the most powerful, rich, or talented people in a society.

Elizabethan

ADJECTIVE Someone or something that is Elizabethan lived or was made during the reign of Elizabeth I.

elk elks

NOUN a large kind of deer.

ellipse ellipses

NOUN a regular oval shape, like a circle seen from an angle.

elm elms

NOUN a tall tree with broad leaves.

elocution

NOUN Elocution is the art or study of speaking clearly or well in public.

elongated

ADJECTIVE long and thin.

elope elopes eloping eloped

VERB If someone elopes, they run away secretly with their lover to get married.

eloquent

ADJECTIVE able to speak or write skilfully and with ease EG an eloquent politician.

eloquently ADVERB, **eloquence** NOUN

else

ADVERB **1** other than this or more than this EG Can you think of anything else? ▶ PHRASE **2** You say or else to introduce a possibility or an alternative EG You have to go with the flow or else be left behind in the rush.

elsewhere

ADVERB in or to another place EG He would rather be elsewhere.

elude eludes eluding eluded

Said "ill-**ood**" VERB **1** If a fact or idea eludes you, you cannot understand it or remember it. **2** If you elude someone or something, you avoid them or escape from them EG He eluded the authorities.

elusive

ADJECTIVE difficult to find, achieve, describe, or remember EG the elusive million dollar prize.

elves

the plural of **elf**.

emaciated

Said "im-**may**-see-ate-ed" ADJECTIVE extremely thin and weak, because of illness or lack of food.

e-mail or **email**

NOUN the sending of messages from one computer to another.

emancipation

NOUN The emancipation of a person

means the act of freeing them from harmful or unpleasant restrictions.

embargo **embargoes**
NOUN an order made by a government to stop trade with another country.

embark **embarks embarking embarked**
VERB **1** If you embark, you go onto a ship at the start of a journey. **2** If you embark on something, you start it EG *He embarked on a huge spending spree.*

embarrass **embarrasses embarrassing embarrassed**
VERB If you embarrass someone, you make them feel ashamed or awkward EG *I won't embarrass you by asking for details.*
embarrassed ADJECTIVE, **embarrassing** ADJECTIVE, **embarrassment** NOUN

embassy **embassies**
NOUN the building in which an ambassador and his or her staff work; also used of the ambassador and his or her staff.

embedded
ADJECTIVE Something that is embedded is fixed firmly and deeply EG *glass decorated with embedded threads.*

ember **embers**
NOUN Embers are glowing pieces of coal or wood from a dying fire.

embittered
ADJECTIVE If you are embittered, you are angry and resentful about things that have happened to you.

emblazoned
Said "im-**blaze**-nd" ADJECTIVE If something is emblazoned with designs, it is decorated with them EG *vases emblazoned with bold and colourful images.*
▣ originally a heraldic term from Old French *blason* meaning 'shield'

emblem **emblems**
NOUN an object or a design representing an organization or an idea EG *a flower emblem of Japan.*

embody **embodies embodying embodied**
VERB **1** To embody a quality or idea means to contain it or express it EG *A young dancer embodies the spirit of fun.* **2** If a number of things are embodied in one thing, they are contained in it EG *the principles embodied in his report.*
embodiment NOUN

embossed
ADJECTIVE decorated with designs that stand up slightly from the surface EG *embossed wallpaper.*

embrace **embraces embracing embraced**
VERB **1** If you embrace someone, you hug them to show affection or as a greeting. **2** If you embrace a belief or cause you accept it and believe in it. ▶ NOUN **3** a hug.

embroider **embroiders embroidering embroidered**
VERB If you embroider fabric, you sew a decorative design onto it.

embroidery
NOUN Embroidery is decorative designs sewn onto fabric; also the art or skill of embroidery.

embroiled
ADJECTIVE If someone is embroiled in an argument or conflict they are deeply involved in it and cannot get out of it EG *The two companies are now embroiled in the courts.*

embryo **embryos**
Said "em-**bree**-oh" NOUN an animal or human being in the very early stages of development in the womb.
embryonic ADJECTIVE
▣ from Greek *embruon* meaning 'new-born animal'

emerald **emeralds**
NOUN **1** a bright green precious stone. ▶ NOUN OR ADJECTIVE **2** bright green.

emerge **emerges emerging emerged**
VERB **1** If someone emerges from a place, they come out of it so that

A
B
C
D
E
F
G
H
I
J
K
L
M
N
O
P
Q
R
S
T
U
V
W
X
Y
Z

they can be seen. **2** If something emerges, it becomes known or begins to be recognized as existing EG *It later emerged that he faced bankruptcy proceedings.*
emergence NOUN, **emergent** ADJECTIVE

emergency emergencies
NOUN an unexpected and serious event which needs immediate action to deal with it.
▣ crisis, extremity

emigrant emigrants
NOUN a person who leaves their native country and goes to live permanently in another one.

emigrate emigrates emigrating emigrated
VERB If you emigrate, you leave your native country and go to live permanently in another one.
emigration NOUN

eminence
NOUN **1** Eminence is the quality of being well-known and respected for what you do EG *lawyers of eminence.* **2** 'Your Eminence' is a title of respect used to address a Roman Catholic cardinal.

eminent
ADJECTIVE well-known and respected for what you do EG *an eminent scientist.*

eminently
ADVERB; A FORMAL WORD very EG *eminently reasonable.*

emir emirs
Said "em-eer" NOUN a Muslim ruler or nobleman.
▥ from Arabic *amir* meaning 'commander'

emission emissions
NOUN; A FORMAL WORD The emission of something such as gas or radiation is the release of it into the atmosphere.

emit emits emitting emitted
VERB To emit something means to give it out or release it EG *She emitted a long, low whistle.*
▣ exude, give off, give out

emotion emotions
NOUN a strong feeling, such as love or fear.

emotional
ADJECTIVE **1** causing strong feelings EG *an emotional appeal for help.* **2** to do with feelings rather than your physical condition EG *emotional support.* **3** showing your feelings openly EG *The child is in a very emotional state.*
emotionally ADVERB

emotive
ADJECTIVE concerning emotions, or stirring up strong emotions EG *emotive language.*

empathize empathizes empathizing empathized; also spelt **empathise**
VERB If you empathize with someone, you understand how they are feeling.
empathy NOUN

emperor emperors
NOUN a male ruler of an empire.
▥ from Latin *imperator* meaning 'commander-in-chief'

emphasis emphases
NOUN Emphasis is special importance or extra stress given to something.

emphasize emphasizes emphasizing emphasized; also spelt **emphasise**
VERB If you emphasize something, you make it known that it is very important EG *It was emphasized that the matter was of international concern.*

emphatic
ADJECTIVE expressed strongly and with force to show how important something is EG *I answered both questions with an emphatic 'Yes'.*
emphatically ADVERB

empire empires
NOUN **1** a group of countries controlled by one country. **2** a powerful group of companies controlled by one person.
▥ from Latin *imperium* meaning 'rule'

employ employs employing employed

VERB **1** If you employ someone, you pay them to work for you. **2** If you employ something for a particular purpose, you make use of it EG *the techniques employed in turning grapes into wine.*

■ (sense 1) engage, hire, take on

employee employees

NOUN a person who is paid to work for another person or for an organization.

employer employers

NOUN Someone's employer is the person or organization that they work for.

employment

NOUN Employment is the state of having a paid job, or the activity of recruiting people for a job.

empower empowers empowering empowered

VERB If you are empowered to do something, you have the authority or power to do it.

empress empresses

NOUN a woman who rules an empire, or the wife of an emperor.

empty emptier emptiest; empties emptying emptied

ADJECTIVE **1** having nothing or nobody inside. **2** without purpose, value, or meaning EG *empty promises.*
▸ VERB **3** If you empty something, or empty its contents, you remove the contents.

emptiness NOUN

■ (sense 1) bare, blank, vacant
■ (sense 3) clear, evacuate

emu emus

Said "ee-myoo" NOUN a large Australian bird which can run fast but cannot fly.

▥ from Portuguese *ema* meaning 'ostrich'

emulate emulates emulating emulated

VERB If you emulate someone or something, you imitate them because you admire them.

emulation NOUN

emulsion emulsions

NOUN a water-based paint.

enable enables enabling enabled

VERB To enable something to happen means to make it possible.

enact enacts enacting enacted

VERB **1** If a government enacts a law or bill, it officially passes it so that it becomes law. **2** If you enact a story or play, you act it out.

enactment NOUN

enamel enamels enamelling enamelled

NOUN **1** a substance like glass, used to decorate or protect metal or china. **2** The enamel on your teeth is the hard, white substance that forms the outer part. ▸ VERB **3** If you enamel something, you decorate or cover it with enamel.

enamelled ADJECTIVE

enamoured

Said "in-am-erd" ADJECTIVE If you are enamoured of someone or something, you like them very much.

encapsulate encapsulates encapsulating encapsulated

VERB If something encapsulates facts or ideas, it contains or represents them in a small space.

encased

ADJECTIVE Something that is encased is surrounded or covered with a substance EG *encased in plaster.*

enchanted

ADJECTIVE If you are enchanted by something or someone, you are fascinated or charmed by them.

enchanting

ADJECTIVE attractive, delightful, or charming EG *an enchanting baby.*

encircle encircles encircling encircled

VERB To encircle something or someone means to completely surround them.

enclave enclaves

NOUN a place that is surrounded by

A B C D E F G H I J K L M N O P Q R S T U V W X Y Z

A
B
C
D
E
F
G
H
I
J
K
L
M
N
O
P
Q
R
S
T
U
V
W
X
Y
Z

areas that are different from it in some important way, for example because the people there are from a different culture EG *a Muslim enclave in Bosnia.*

▣ from Old French *enclaver* meaning 'to enclose'

enclose **encloses** **enclosing** **enclosed**
VERB To enclose an object or area means to surround it with something solid.
enclosed ADJECTIVE

enclosure **enclosures**
NOUN an area of land surrounded by a wall or fence and used for a particular purpose.

encompass **encompasses** **encompassing** **encompassed**
VERB To encompass a number of things means to include all of those things EG *The book encompassed all aspects of maths.*

encore **encores**
Said "ong-kor" NOUN a short extra performance given by an entertainer because the audience asks for it.
▣ from French *encore* meaning 'again'

encounter **encounters** **encountering** **encountered**
VERB 1 If you encounter someone or something, you meet them or are faced with them EG *She was the most gifted child he ever encountered.* ▶ NOUN 2 a meeting, especially when it is difficult or unexpected.

encourage **encourages** **encouraging** **encouraged**
VERB 1 If you encourage someone, you give them courage and confidence to do something. 2 If someone or something encourages a particular activity, they support it EG *The government will encourage the creation of nursery places.*
encouraging ADJECTIVE, **encouragement** NOUN
▤ (sense 1) hearten, inspire

encroach **encroaches** **encroaching**

encroached
VERB If something encroaches on a place or on your time or rights, it gradually takes up or takes away more and more of it.
encroachment NOUN

encrusted
ADJECTIVE covered with a crust or layer of something EG *a necklace encrusted with gold.*

encyclopedia **encyclopedias**
Said "en-sigh-klop-ee-dee-a"; also spelt **encyclopaedia**
NOUN a book or set of books giving information about many different subjects.
▣ from Greek *enkuklios paideia* meaning 'general education'

encyclopedic or **encyclopaedic**
ADJECTIVE knowing or giving information about many different things.

end **ends** **ending** **ended**
NOUN 1 The end of a period of time or an event is the last part. 2 The end of something is the farthest point of it EG *the room at the end of the passage.* 3 the purpose for which something is done EG *the use of taxpayers' money for overt political ends.* ▶ VERB 4 If something ends or if you end it, it comes to a finish.

endanger **endangers** **endangering** **endangered**
VERB To endanger something means to cause it to be in a dangerous and harmful situation EG *a driver who endangers the safety of others.*
▤ jeopardize, put at risk

endear **endears** **endearing** **endeared**
VERB If someone's behaviour endears them to you, it makes you fond of them.
endearing ADJECTIVE, **endearingly** ADVERB

endeavour **endeavours** **endeavouring** **endeavoured**
Said "in-dev-er" VERB 1 A FORMAL WORD If you endeavour to do something, you try very hard to do it. ▶ NOUN 2 an effort to do or achieve

something.

endless

ADJECTIVE having or seeming to have no end.
endlessly ADVERB

endorse endorses endorsing endorsed

VERB **1** If you endorse someone or something, you give approval and support to them. **2** If you endorse a document, you write your signature or a comment on it, to show that you approve of it.
endorsement NOUN

endowed

ADJECTIVE If someone is endowed with a quality or ability, they have it or are given it EG *He was endowed with great willpower.*

endurance

NOUN Endurance is the ability to put up with a difficult situation for a period of time.

endure endures enduring endured

VERB **1** If you endure a difficult situation, you put up with it calmly and patiently. **2** If something endures, it lasts or continues to exist EG *The old alliance still endures.*
enduring ADJECTIVE

enema enemas

NOUN a liquid that is put into a person's rectum in order to empty their bowels.

enemy enemies

NOUN a person or group that is hostile or opposed to another person or group.
■ adversary, foe

energetic

ADJECTIVE having or showing energy or enthusiasm.
energetically ADVERB
■ active, lively, vigorous

energy energies

NOUN **1** Energy is the physical strength to do active things. **2** Energy is the power which drives machinery.

■ (sense 1) drive, stamina, vigour

enforce enforces enforcing enforced

VERB If you enforce a law or a rule, you make sure that it is obeyed.
enforceable ADJECTIVE, **enforcement** NOUN

engage engages engaging engaged

VERB **1** If you engage in an activity, you take part in it EG *Officials have declined to engage in a debate.* **2** To engage someone or their attention means to make or keep someone interested in something EG *He engaged the driver in conversation.*

engaged

ADJECTIVE **1** When two people are engaged, they have agreed to marry each other. **2** If someone or something is engaged, they are occupied or busy EG *Mr Anderson was otherwise engaged... The emergency number was always engaged.*

engagement engagements

NOUN **1** an appointment that you have with someone. **2** an agreement that two people have made with each other to get married.

engine engines

NOUN **1** a machine designed to convert heat or other kinds of energy into mechanical movement. **2** a railway locomotive.
▥ from Latin *ingenium* meaning 'ingenious device'

engineer engineers engineering engineered

NOUN **1** a person trained in designing and building machinery and electrical devices, or roads and bridges. **2** a person who repairs mechanical or electrical devices.
▶ VERB **3** If you engineer an event or situation, you arrange it cleverly, usually for your own advantage.

engineering

NOUN Engineering is the profession of designing and constructing machinery and electrical devices,

A B C D E F G H I J K L M N O P Q R S T U V W X Y Z

or roads and bridges.

English
ADJECTIVE **1** belonging or relating to England. ▶ NOUN **2** English is the main language spoken in the United Kingdom, the USA, Canada, Australia, New Zealand, and many other countries.

Englishman Englishmen
NOUN a man who comes from England.
Englishwoman NOUN

engrave engraves engraving engraved
VERB To engrave means to cut letters or designs into a hard surface with a tool.

engraving engravings
NOUN a picture or design that has been cut into a hard surface.
engraver NOUN

engrossed
ADJECTIVE If you are engrossed in something, it holds all your attention EG *He was engrossed in a video game.*

engulf engulfs engulfing engulfed
VERB To engulf something means to completely cover or surround it EG *Black smoke engulfed him.*

enhance enhances enhancing enhanced
VERB To enhance something means to make it more valuable or attractive EG *an outfit that really enhances his good looks.*
enhancement NOUN

enigma enigmas
NOUN anything which is puzzling or difficult to understand.

enigmatic
ADJECTIVE mysterious, puzzling, or difficult to understand EG *an enigmatic stranger.*
enigmatically ADVERB

enjoy enjoys enjoying enjoyed
VERB **1** If you enjoy something, you find pleasure and satisfaction in it. **2** If you enjoy something, you are lucky to have it or experience it EG

The mother has enjoyed a long life.

enjoyable
ADJECTIVE giving pleasure or satisfaction.

enjoyment
NOUN Enjoyment is the feeling of pleasure or satisfaction you get from something you enjoy.

enlarge enlarges enlarging enlarged
VERB **1** When you enlarge something, it gets bigger. **2** If you enlarge on a subject, you give more details about it.

enlargement enlargements
NOUN **1** An enlargement of something is the action of making it bigger. **2** something, especially a photograph, which has been made bigger.

enlighten enlightens enlightening enlightened
VERB To enlighten someone means to give them more knowledge or understanding of something.
enlightening ADJECTIVE, **enlightenment** NOUN

enlightened
ADJECTIVE well-informed and willing to consider different opinions EG *an enlightened government.*

enlist enlists enlisting enlisted
VERB **1** If someone enlists, they join the army, navy, or air force. **2** If you enlist someone's help, you persuade them to help you in something you are doing.

enliven enlivens enlivening enlivened
VERB To enliven something means to make it more lively or more cheerful.

en masse
Said "on **mass***"* ADVERB If a group of people do something en masse, they do it together and at the same time.

enormity enormities
NOUN **1** The enormity of a problem or difficulty is its great size and

seriousness. **2** something that is thought to be a terrible crime or offence.

enormous
ADJECTIVE very large in size or amount.
enormously ADVERB

enough
ADJECTIVE OR ADVERB **1** as much or as many as required EG *He did not have enough money for a coffee.* ▶ NOUN **2** Enough is the quantity necessary for something EG *There's not enough to go round.* ▶ ADVERB **3** very or fairly EG *She could manage well enough without me.*

enquire enquires enquiring enquired; also spelt **inquire**
VERB If you enquire about something or someone, you ask about them.

enquiry enquiries; also spelt **inquiry**
NOUN **1** a question that you ask in order to find something out. **2** an investigation into something that has happened and that needs explaining.

enrage enrages enraging enraged
VERB If something enrages you, it makes you very angry.
enraged ADJECTIVE

enrich enriches enriching enriched
VERB To enrich something means to improve the quality or value of it EG *new woods to enrich our countryside.*
enriched ADJECTIVE, **enrichment** NOUN

enrol enrols enrolling enrolled
VERB If you enrol for something such as a course or a college, you register to join or become a member of it.
enrolment NOUN

en route
Said "on **root**" ADVERB If something happens en route to a place, it happens on the way there.

ensconced
ADJECTIVE If you are ensconced in a particular place, you are settled there firmly and comfortably.

ensemble ensembles
Said "on-**som**-bl" NOUN **1** a group of things or people considered as a whole rather than separately. **2** a small group of musicians who play or sing together.

enshrine enshrines enshrining enshrined
VERB If something such as an idea or a right is enshrined in a society, constitution, or a law, it is protected by it EG *Freedom of speech is enshrined in the American Constitution.*

ensign ensigns
NOUN a flag flown by a ship to show what country that ship belongs to.

ensue ensues ensuing ensued
Said "en-**syoo**" VERB If something ensues, it happens after another event, usually as a result of it EG *He entered the house and an argument ensued.*
ensuing ADJECTIVE

ensure ensures ensuring ensured
VERB To ensure that something happens means to make certain that it happens EG *We make every effort to ensure the information given is correct.*

entangled
ADJECTIVE If you are entangled in problems or difficulties, you are involved in them.

enter enters entering entered
VERB **1** To enter a place means to go into it. **2** If you enter an organization or institution, you join and become a member of it EG *He entered Parliament in 1979.* **3** If you enter a competition or examination, you take part in it. **4** If you enter something in a diary or a list, you write it down.

enterprise enterprises
NOUN **1** a business or company. **2** a project or task, especially one that involves risk or difficulty.
▥ from French *entreprendre* meaning 'to undertake'

A B C D E F G H I J K L M N O P Q R S T U V W X Y Z

enterprising

ADJECTIVE ready to start new projects and tasks and full of boldness and initiative EG *an enterprising company*.

entertain entertains entertaining entertained

VERB **1** If you entertain people, you keep them amused or interested. **2** If you entertain guests, you receive them into your house and give them food and hospitality.

entertainer entertainers

NOUN someone whose job is to amuse and please audiences, for example a comedian or singer.

entertainment entertainments

NOUN Entertainment is anything that people watch for pleasure, such as shows and films.

enthral enthrals enthralling enthralled

Said "in-thrawl" VERB If you enthral someone, you hold their attention and interest completely.

enthralling ADJECTIVE

enthuse enthuses enthusing enthused

Said "inth-yooz" VERB If you enthuse about something, you talk about it with enthusiasm and excitement.

enthusiasm enthusiasms

NOUN Enthusiasm is interest, eagerness, or delight in something that you enjoy.

▣ from Greek *enthousiasmos* meaning 'possessed or inspired by the gods'

▤ keenness, passion, zeal

enthusiastic

ADJECTIVE showing great excitement, eagerness, or approval for something EG *She was enthusiastic about poetry*.

enthusiastically ADVERB

entice entices enticing enticed

VERB If you entice someone to do something, you tempt them to do it EG *We tried to entice the mouse out of the hole*.

enticing

ADJECTIVE extremely attractive and tempting.

entire

ADJECTIVE all of something EG *the entire month of July*.

entirely

ADVERB wholly and completely EG *He and I were entirely different*.

entirety

Said "en-tire-it-tee" PHRASE If something happens to something in its entirety, it happens to all of it EG *This message will now be repeated in its entirety*.

entitle entitles entitling entitled

VERB If something entitles you to have or do something, it gives you the right to have or do it.

entitlement NOUN

entity entities

Said "en-tit-ee" NOUN any complete thing that is not divided and not part of anything else.

entourage entourages

Said "on-too-rahj" NOUN a group of people who follow or travel with a famous or important person.

entrails

PLURAL NOUN Entrails are the inner parts, especially the intestines, of people or animals.

entrance entrances

Said "en-trunss" NOUN **1** The entrance of a building or area is its doorway or gate. **2** A person's entrance is their arrival in a place, or the way in which they arrive EG *Each creation is designed for you to make a dramatic entrance*. **3** Entrance is the right to enter a place EG *He had gained entrance to the Hall by pretending to be a heating engineer*.

entrance entrances entrancing entranced

Said "en-trahnss" VERB If something entrances you, it gives you a feeling of wonder and delight.

entrancing ADJECTIVE

entrant entrants

NOUN a person who officially enters a competition or an organization.

entrenched
ADJECTIVE If a belief, custom, or power is entrenched, it is firmly established.

entrepreneur entrepreneurs
*Said "on-tre-pren-**ur**"* NOUN a person who sets up business deals, especially ones in which risks are involved, in order to make a profit.
entrepreneurial ADJECTIVE

entrust entrusts entrusting entrusted
VERB If you entrust something to someone, you give them the care and protection of it EG *Miss Fry was entrusted with the children's education.*

entry entries
NOUN 1 Entry is the act of entering a place. 2 a place through which you enter somewhere. 3 anything which is entered or recorded EG *Send your entry to the address below.*
■ (sense 2) entrance, way in

envelop envelops enveloping enveloped
VERB To envelop something means to cover or surround it completely EG *A dense fog enveloped the area.*

envelope envelopes
NOUN a flat covering of paper with a flap that can be folded over to seal it, which is used to hold a letter.

enviable
ADJECTIVE If you describe something as enviable, you mean that you wish you had it yourself.

envious
ADJECTIVE full of envy.
enviously ADVERB

environment environments
NOUN 1 Your environment is the circumstances and conditions in which you live or work EG *a good environment to grow up in.* 2 The environment is the natural world around us EG *the waste which is dumped in the environment.*
environmental ADJECTIVE,

environmentally ADVERB
☑ There is an *n* before the *m* in *environment.*

environmentalist environmentalists
NOUN a person who is concerned with the problems of the natural environment, such as pollution.

envisage envisages envisaging envisaged
VERB If you envisage a situation or state of affairs, you can picture it in your mind as being true or likely to happen.

envoy envoys
NOUN a messenger, sent especially from one government to another.

envy envies envying envied
NOUN 1 Envy is a feeling of resentment you have when you wish you could have what someone else has. ▶ VERB 2 If you envy someone, you wish that you had what they have.

enzyme enzymes
NOUN a chemical substance, usually a protein, produced by cells in the body.

ephemeral
Said "if-em-er-al" ADJECTIVE lasting only a short time.

epic epics
NOUN 1 a long story of heroic events and actions. ▶ ADJECTIVE 2 very impressive or ambitious EG *epic adventures.*

epidemic epidemics
NOUN 1 an occurrence of a disease in one area, spreading quickly and affecting many people. 2 a rapid development or spread of something EG *the country's crime epidemic.*

epigram epigrams
NOUN a short saying which expresses an idea in a clever and amusing way.

epigraph
NOUN 1 a quotation at the beginning of a book. 2 an inscription on a

A
B
C
D
E
F
G
H
I
J
K
L
M
N
O
P
Q
R
S
T
U
V
W
X
Y
Z

monument or building.

epilepsy

NOUN Epilepsy is a condition of the brain which causes fits and periods of unconsciousness.

epileptic NOUN OR ADJECTIVE

episode episodes

NOUN **1** an event or period EG *After this episode, she found it impossible to trust him.* **2** one of several parts of a novel or drama appearing for example on television EG *I never miss an episode of Neighbours.*

epistle epistles

Said "ip-**piss**-sl" NOUN; A FORMAL WORD a letter.

epitaph epitaphs

Said "**ep**-it-ahf" NOUN some words on a tomb about the person who has died.

epithet epithets

NOUN a word or short phrase used to describe some characteristic of a person.

epitome

Said "ip-**pit**-om-ee" NOUN; A FORMAL WORD The epitome of something is the most typical example of its sort EG *She was the epitome of the successful woman.*

☑ Do not use *epitome* to mean 'the peak of something'. It means 'the most typical example of something'.

epoch epochs

Said "**ee**-pok" NOUN a long period of time.

eponymous

Said "ip-**on**-im-uss" ADJECTIVE; A FORMAL WORD The eponymous hero or heroine of a play or book is the person whose name forms its title EG *the eponymous hero of 'Eric the Viking'.*

🏛 from Greek *eponumos* meaning 'given as a name'

equal equals equalling equalled

ADJECTIVE **1** having the same size, amount, value, or standard. **2** If you are equal to a task, you have

the necessary ability to deal with it. ▶ NOUN **3** Your equals are people who have the same ability, status, or rights as you. ▶ VERB **4** If one thing equals another, it is as good or remarkable as the other EG *He equalled the course record of 63.*

equally ADVERB, **equality** NOUN

equate equates equating equated

VERB If you equate a particular thing with something else, you believe that it is similar or equal EG *You can't equate lives with money.*

equation equations

NOUN a mathematical formula stating that two amounts or values are the same.

equator

Said "ik-**way**-tor" NOUN an imaginary line drawn round the middle of the earth, lying halfway between the North and South poles.

equatorial ADJECTIVE

equestrian

Said "ik-**west**-ree-an" ADJECTIVE relating to or involving horses.

equilateral

ADJECTIVE An equilateral triangle has sides that are all the same length.

equilibrium equilibria

NOUN a state of balance or stability in a situation.

equine

ADJECTIVE relating to horses.

🏛 from Latin *equus* meaning 'horse'

equinox equinoxes

NOUN one of the two days in the year when the day and night are of equal length, occurring in September and March.

🏛 from Latin *aequinoctium* meaning 'equal night'

equip equips equipping equipped

VERB If a person or thing is equipped with something, they have it or are provided with it EG *The test boat was equipped with a folding propeller.*

= provide, supply

equipment
NOUN Equipment is all the things that are needed or used for a particular job or activity.
= apparatus, gear, tools

equitable
ADJECTIVE fair and reasonable.

equity
NOUN Equity is the quality of being fair and reasonable EG *It is important to distribute income with some sense of equity.*

equivalent equivalents
ADJECTIVE **1** equal in use, size, value, or effect. ▸ NOUN **2** something that has the same use, value, or effect as something else EG *One glass of wine is the equivalent of half a pint of beer.*
equivalence NOUN
= (sense 2) equal, match

era eras
Said "**ear**-a" NOUN a period of time distinguished by a particular feature EG *a new era of prosperity.*
from Latin ***aera*** meaning 'copper counters used for counting', hence for counting time

eradicate eradicates eradicating eradicated
VERB To eradicate something means to get rid of it or destroy it completely.
eradication NOUN

erase erases erasing erased
VERB To erase something means to remove it.

erect erects erecting erected
VERB **1** To erect something means to put it up or construct it EG *The building was erected in 1900.*
▸ ADJECTIVE **2** in a straight and upright position EG *She held herself erect and looked directly at him.*
= (sense 2) straight, upright, vertical

erection erections
NOUN **1** The erection of something is the process of erecting it.
2 anything which has been erected.
3 When a man has an erection, his penis is stiff, swollen, and in an upright position.

ermine
NOUN Ermine is expensive white fur.

erode erodes eroding eroded
VERB If something erodes or is eroded, it is gradually worn or eaten away and destroyed.

erosion
NOUN Erosion is the gradual wearing away and destruction of something EG *soil erosion.*

erotic
ADJECTIVE involving or arousing sexual desire.
erotically ADVERB, **eroticism** NOUN
from Greek ***erotikos*** meaning 'of love'

err errs erring erred
VERB If you err, you make a mistake.

errand errands
NOUN a short trip you make in order to do a job for someone.

erratic
ADJECTIVE not following a regular pattern or a fixed course EG *Police officers noticed his erratic driving.*
erratically ADVERB

erroneous
Said "ir-**rone**-ee-uss" ADJECTIVE Ideas or methods that are erroneous are incorrect or only partly correct.
erroneously ADVERB

error errors
NOUN a mistake or something which you have done wrong.

erudite
Said "**eh**-roo-dite" ADJECTIVE having great academic knowledge.

erupt erupts erupting erupted
VERB **1** When a volcano erupts, it violently throws out a lot of hot lava and ash. **2** When a situation erupts, it starts up suddenly and violently EG *A family row erupted.*
eruption NOUN

escalate escalates escalating escalated
VERB If a situation escalates, it

becomes greater in size, seriousness, or intensity.

escalator escalators
NOUN a mechanical moving staircase.

escapade escapades
NOUN an adventurous or daring incident that causes trouble.

escape escapes escaping escaped
VERB **1** To escape means to get free from someone or something. **2** If you escape something unpleasant or difficult, you manage to avoid it EG *He escaped the death penalty.* **3** If something escapes you, you cannot remember it EG *It was an actor whose name escapes me for the moment.*
▶ NOUN **4** an act of escaping from a particular place or situation EG *his escape from North Korea.* **5** a situation or activity which distracts you from something unpleasant EG *Television provides an escape.*

escapee escapees
Said "is-kay-**pee**" NOUN someone who has escaped, especially an escaped prisoner.

escapism
NOUN Escapism is avoiding the real and unpleasant things in life by thinking about pleasant or fantastic things EG *Most horror movies are simple escapism.*
escapist ADJECTIVE

eschew eschews eschewing eschewed
Said "is-**chew**" VERB; A FORMAL WORD If you eschew something, you deliberately avoid or keep away from it.

escort escorts escorting escorted
NOUN **1** a person or vehicle that travels with another in order to protect or guide them. **2** a person who accompanies another person of the opposite sex to a social event. ▶ VERB **3** If you escort someone, you go with them somewhere, especially in order to protect or guide them.

Eskimo Eskimos
NOUN a member of a group of

people who live in Northern Canada, Greenland, Alaska, and Eastern Siberia.

especially
ADVERB You say especially to show that something applies more to one thing, person, or situation than to any other EG *Regular eye tests are important, especially for the elderly.*

espionage
Said "**ess**-pee-on-ahj" NOUN Espionage is the act of spying to get secret information, especially to find out military or political secrets.
▣ from French *espionner* meaning 'to spy'

espouse espouses espousing espoused
VERB; A FORMAL WORD If you espouse a particular policy, cause, or plan, you give your support to it EG *They espoused the rights of man.*

espresso
NOUN Espresso is strong coffee made by forcing steam through ground coffee.
▣ from Italian *caffè espresso* meaning 'pressed coffee'
☑ The second letter of *espresso* is *s* and not *x*.

essay essays
NOUN a short piece of writing on a particular subject, for example one done as an exercise by a student.

essence essences
NOUN **1** The essence of something is its most basic and most important part, which gives it its identity EG *the very essence of being a woman.*
2 Essence is a concentrated liquid used for flavouring food EG *vanilla essence.*

essential essentials
ADJECTIVE **1** vitally important and absolutely necessary EG *Good ventilation is essential in the greenhouse.* **2** very basic, important, and typical EG *the essential aspects of international banking.* ▶ NOUN
3 something that is very important

or necessary EG *the bare essentials of furnishing.*

essentially ADVERB

establish **establishes** **establishing** **established**

VERB **1** To establish something means to set it up in a permanent way. **2** If you establish yourself or become established as something, you achieve a strong reputation for a particular activity EG *He had just established himself as a film star.* **3** If you establish a fact or establish the truth of something, you discover it and can prove it EG *Our first priority is to establish the cause of her death.*

established ADJECTIVE

■ (sense 1) create, found, set up

establishment **establishments**

NOUN **1** The establishment of an organization or system is the act of setting it up. **2** a shop, business, or some other sort of organization or institution. **3** The Establishment is the group of people in a country who have power and influence EG *lawyers, businessmen and other pillars of the Establishment.*

estate **estates**

NOUN **1** a large area of privately owned land in the country, together with all the property on it. **2** an area of land, usually in or near a city, which has been developed for housing or industry. **3** A LEGAL USE A person's estate consists of all the possessions they leave behind when they die.

estate agent **estate agents**

NOUN a person who works for a company that sells houses and land.

esteem

NOUN Esteem is admiration and respect that you feel for another person.

esteemed ADJECTIVE

estimate **estimates** **estimating** **estimated**

VERB **1** If you estimate an amount or quantity, you calculate it approximately. **2** If you estimate something, you make a guess about it based on the evidence you have available EG *Often it's possible to estimate a person's age just by knowing their name.* ▶ NOUN **3** an approximate calculation of an amount or quantity. **4** a guess you make about something based on the evidence you have available. **5** a formal statement from a company who may do some work for you, telling you how much it is likely to cost.

estimation **estimations**

NOUN **1** an approximate calculation of something that can be measured. **2** the opinion or impression you form about a person or situation.

estranged

ADJECTIVE **1** If someone is estranged from their husband or wife, they no longer live with them. **2** If someone is estranged from their family or friends, they have quarrelled with them and no longer keep in touch with them.

estrogen

NOUN a female sex hormone which regulates the reproductive cycle.

estuary **estuaries**

Said "est-yoo-ree" NOUN the wide part of a river near where it joins the sea and where fresh water mixes with salt water.

etc.

a written abbreviation for et cetera.

et cetera

*Said "it **set**-ra"* 'Et cetera' is used at the end of a list to indicate that other items of the same type you have mentioned could have been mentioned if there had been time or space.

☑ As *etc.* means 'and the rest', you should not write *and etc.*

etch **etches** **etching** **etched**

VERB **1** If you etch a design or pattern on a surface, you cut it into the surface by using acid or a sharp tool. **2** If something is etched on

A B C D **E** F G H I J K L M N O P Q R S T U V W X Y Z

your mind or memory, it has made such a strong impression on you that you feel you will never forget it.

etched ADJECTIVE

etching etchings
NOUN a picture printed from a metal plate that has had a design cut into it.

eternal
ADJECTIVE lasting forever, or seeming to last forever EG *eternal life*.
eternally ADVERB
■ endless, everlasting, perpetual

eternity eternities
NOUN **1** Eternity is time without end, or a state of existing outside time, especially the state some people believe they will pass into when they die. **2** a period of time which seems to go on for ever EG *We arrived there after an eternity*.

ether
Said "eeth-er" NOUN Ether is a colourless liquid that burns easily. Used in industry as a solvent and in medicine as an anaesthetic.

ethereal
Said "ith-ee-ree-al" ADJECTIVE light and delicate EG *misty ethereal landscapes*.
ethereally ADVERB

ethical
ADJECTIVE in agreement with accepted principles of behaviour that are thought to be right EG *teenagers who become vegetarian for ethical reasons*.
ethically ADVERB

ethics
PLURAL NOUN Ethics are moral beliefs about right and wrong EG *The medical profession has a code of ethics*.

Ethiopian Ethiopians
Said "eeth-ee-oh-pee-an" ADJECTIVE **1** belonging to or relating to Ethiopia. ▶ NOUN **2** someone who comes from Ethiopia.

ethnic
ADJECTIVE **1** involving different racial

groups of people EG *ethnic minorities*. **2** relating to a particular racial or cultural group, especially when very different from modern western culture EG *ethnic food*.
ethnically ADVERB

ethos
Said "eeth-oss" NOUN a set of ideas and attitudes that is associated with a particular group of people EG *the ethos of journalism*.

etiquette
Said "et-ik-ket" NOUN Etiquette is a set of rules for behaviour in a particular social situation.

etymology
Said "et-tim-ol-loj-ee" NOUN Etymology is the study of the origin and changes of form in words.

EU
NOUN EU is an abbreviation for 'European Union'.

eucalyptus or **eucalypt**
eucalyptuses or eucalypts
NOUN an evergreen tree, grown mostly in Australia; also the wood and oil from this tree.

Eucharist Eucharists
Said "yoo-kar-rist" NOUN a religious ceremony in which Christians remember and celebrate Christ's last meal with his disciples.
🏛 from Greek *eucharistia* meaning 'thanksgiving'

eunuch eunuchs
Said "yoo-nuk" NOUN a man who has been castrated.

euphemism euphemisms
NOUN a polite word or expression that you can use instead of one that might offend or upset people EG *action movies, a euphemism for violence*.
euphemistic ADJECTIVE, **euphemistically** ADVERB

euphoria
NOUN Euphoria is a feeling of great happiness.
euphoric ADJECTIVE

Europe

NOUN Europe is the second smallest continent. It has Asia on its eastern side, with the Arctic to the north, the Atlantic to the west, and the Mediterranean and Africa to the south.

European Europeans

ADJECTIVE **1** belonging or relating to Europe. ▶ NOUN **2** someone who comes from Europe.

European Union

NOUN The group of countries who have joined together under the Treaty of Rome for economic and trade purposes are officially known as the European Union.

euthanasia

Said "yooth-a-**nay**-zee-a" NOUN Euthanasia is the act of painlessly killing a dying person in order to stop their suffering.
🔲 from Greek *eu-* meaning 'easy' and *thanatos* meaning 'death'

evacuate evacuates evacuating evacuated

VERB If someone is evacuated, they are removed from a place of danger to a place of safety EG *A crowd of shoppers had to be evacuated from a store after a bomb scare.*
evacuation NOUN, **evacuee** NOUN

evade evades evading evaded

VERB **1** If you evade something or someone, you keep moving in order to keep out of their way EG *For two months he evaded police.* **2** If you evade a problem or question, you avoid dealing with it.

evaluate evaluates evaluating evaluated

VERB If you evaluate something, you assess its quality, value, or significance.
evaluation NOUN

evangelical

Said "ee-van-**jel**-ik-kl" ADJECTIVE Evangelical beliefs are Christian beliefs that stress the importance of the gospels and a personal belief in Christ.

evangelist evangelists

Said "iv-**van**-jel-ist" NOUN a person who travels from place to place preaching Christianity.
evangelize VERB, **evangelism** NOUN
🔲 from Greek *evangelion* meaning 'good news'

evaporate evaporates evaporating evaporated

VERB **1** When a liquid evaporates, it gradually becomes less and less because it has changed from a liquid into a gas. **2** If a substance has been evaporated, all the liquid has been taken out so that it is dry or concentrated.
evaporation NOUN

evasion evasions

NOUN Evasion is deliberately avoiding doing something EG *evasion of arrest.*

evasive

ADJECTIVE deliberately trying to avoid talking about or doing something EG *He was evasive about his past.*

eve eves

NOUN the evening or day before an event or occasion EG *on the eve of the battle.*

even evens evening evened

ADJECTIVE **1** flat and level EG *an even layer of chocolate.* **2** regular and without variation EG *an even temperature.* **3** In maths, numbers that are even can be divided exactly by two EG *4 is an even number.* **4** Scores that are even are exactly the same. ▶ ADVERB **5** 'Even' is used to suggest that something is unexpected or surprising EG *I haven't even got a bank account.* **6** 'Even' is also used to say that something is greater in degree than something else EG *This was an opportunity to obtain even more money.* ▶ PHRASE **7 Even if** or **even though** is used to introduce something that is surprising in relation to the main part of the sentence EG *She was too kind to say anything, even though she was jealous.*

A
B
C
D
E
F
G
H
I
J
K
L
M
N
O
P
Q
R
S
T
U
V
W
X
Y
Z

A
B
C
D
E
F
G
H
I
J
K
L
M
N
O
P
Q
R
S
T
U
V
W
X
Y
Z

evenly ADVERB
▤ (sense 1) flat, level, straight
▤ (sense 4) equal, level

evening evenings
NOUN the part of the day between late afternoon and the time you go to bed.

event events
NOUN **1** something that happens, especially when it is unusual or important. **2** one of the competitions that are part of an organized occasion, especially in sports. ▶ PHRASE **3** If you say **in any event**, you mean whatever happens EG *In any event we must get on with our own lives.*
▤ (sense 1) happening, incident, occurrence

eventful
ADJECTIVE full of interesting and important events.

eventual
ADJECTIVE happening or being achieved in the end EG *He remained confident of eventual victory.*

eventuality eventualities
NOUN a possible future event or result EG *equipment to cope with most eventualities.*

eventually
ADVERB in the end EG *Eventually I got to Berlin.*

ever
ADVERB **1** at any time EG *Have you ever seen anything like it?* **2** all the time EG *The President will come under ever more pressure to resign.* **3** 'Ever' is used to give emphasis to what you are saying EG *I'm as happy here as ever I was in England.* ▶ PHRASE **4** AN INFORMAL USE **Ever so** means very EG *Thank you ever so much.*

evergreen evergreens
NOUN a tree or bush which has green leaves all the year round.

everlasting
ADJECTIVE never coming to an end.

every
ADJECTIVE **1** 'Every' is used to refer to all the members of a particular group, separately and one by one EG *We eat out every night.* **2** 'Every' is used to mean the greatest or the best possible degree of something EG *He has every reason to avoid the subject.* **3** 'Every' is also used to indicate that something happens at regular intervals EG *renewable every five years.* ▶ PHRASE **4** **Every other** means each alternate EG *I see Lisa at least every other week.*

everybody
PRONOUN **1** all the people in a group EG *He obviously thinks everybody in the place knows him.* **2** all the people in the world EG *Everybody has a hobby.*
☑ *Everybody* and *everyone* mean the same.

everyday
ADJECTIVE usual or ordinary EG *the everyday drudgery of work.*

everyone
PRONOUN **1** all the people in a group. **2** all the people in the world.
☑ *Everyone* and *everybody* mean the same.

everything
PRONOUN **1** all or the whole of something. **2** the most important thing EG *When I was 20, friends were everything to me.*

everywhere
ADVERB in or to all places.

evict evicts evicting evicted
VERB To evict someone means to officially force them to leave a place they are occupying.
eviction NOUN

evidence
NOUN **1** Evidence is anything you see, read, or are told which gives you reason to believe something. **2** Evidence is the information used in court to attempt to prove or disprove something.

evident
ADJECTIVE easily noticed or understood EG *His love of nature is evident in his paintings.*
evidently ADVERB

evil evils

NOUN **1** Evil is a force or power that is believed to cause wicked or bad things to happen. **2** a very unpleasant or harmful situation or activity EG *the evils of war.* ▶ ADJECTIVE **3** Someone or something that is evil is morally wrong or bad EG *evil influences.*

evoke evokes evoking evoked

VERB To evoke an emotion, memory, or reaction means to cause it EG *Enthusiasm was evoked by the appearance of the Prince.*

evolution

Said "ee-vol-oo-shn" NOUN **1** Evolution is a process of gradual change taking place over many generations during which living things slowly change as they adapt to different environments. **2** Evolution is also any process of gradual change and development over a period of time EG *the evolution of the European Union.*
evolutionary ADJECTIVE

evolve evolves evolving evolved

VERB **1** If something evolves or if you evolve it, it develops gradually over a period of time EG *I was given a brief to evolve a system of training.* **2** When living things evolve, they gradually change and develop into different forms over a period of time.

ewe ewes

Said "yoo" NOUN a female sheep.

ex-

PREFIX former EG *her ex-husband.*

exacerbate exacerbates exacerbating exacerbated

Said "ig-zass-er-bate" VERB To exacerbate something means to make it worse.

exact exacts exacting exacted

ADJECTIVE **1** correct and complete in every detail EG *an exact replica of the Santa Maria.* **2** accurate and precise, as opposed to approximate EG *Mystery surrounds the exact circumstances of his death.* ▶ VERB **3** A

FORMAL WORD If somebody or something exacts something from you, they demand or obtain it from you, especially through force EG *The navy was on its way to exact a terrible revenge.*

exactly

ADVERB **1** with complete accuracy and precision EG *That's exactly what happened.* **2** You can use 'exactly' to emphasize the truth of a statement, or a similarity or close relationship between one thing and another EG *It's exactly the same colour.*

exaggerate exaggerates exaggerating exaggerated

VERB **1** If you exaggerate, you make the thing you are describing seem better, worse, bigger, or more important than it really is. **2** To exaggerate something means to make it more noticeable than usual EG *His Irish accent was exaggerated for the benefit of the joke he was telling.*
exaggeration NOUN

exalted

ADJECTIVE; A FORMAL WORD Someone who is exalted is very important.

exam exams

NOUN an official test set to find out your knowledge or skill in a subject.

examination examinations

NOUN **1** an exam. **2** If you make an examination of something, you inspect it very carefully EG *I carried out a careful examination of the hull.* **3** A medical examination is a check by a doctor to find out the state of your health.

examine examines examining examined

VERB **1** If you examine something, you inspect it very carefully. **2** To examine someone means to find out their knowledge or skill in a particular subject by testing them. **3** If a doctor examines you, he or she checks your body to find out the state of your health.

examiner examiners

NOUN a person who sets or marks an

exam.

example examples

NOUN **1** something which represents or is typical of a group or set EG *some examples of early Spanish music.* **2** If you say someone or something is an example to people, you mean that people can imitate and learn from them. ▶ PHRASE **3** You use **for example** to give an example of something you are talking about. ◼ (sense 1) sample, specimen

exasperate exasperates exasperating exasperated

VERB If someone or something exasperates you, they irritate you and make you angry.
exasperating ADJECTIVE, **exasperation** NOUN

excavate excavates excavating excavated

VERB To excavate means to remove earth from the ground by digging.
excavation NOUN

exceed exceeds exceeding exceeded

VERB To exceed something such as a limit means to go beyond it or to become greater than it EG *the first aircraft to exceed the speed of sound.*

exceedingly

ADVERB extremely or very much.

excel excels excelling excelled

VERB If someone excels in something, they are very good at doing it.

Excellency Excellencies

NOUN a title used to address an official of very high rank, such as an ambassador or a governor.

excellent

ADJECTIVE very good indeed.
excellence NOUN
◼ first-rate, outstanding, superb

except

PREPOSITION Except or except for means other than or apart from EG *All my family were musicians except my father.*

exception exceptions

252

NOUN somebody or something that is not included in a general statement or rule EG *English, like every language, has exceptions to its rules.*

exceptional

ADJECTIVE **1** unusually talented or clever. **2** unusual and likely to happen very rarely.
exceptionally ADVERB

excerpt excerpts

NOUN a short piece of writing or music which is taken from a larger piece.

excess excesses

NOUN **1** Excess is behaviour which goes beyond normally acceptable limits EG *a life of excess.* **2** a larger amount of something than is needed, usual, or healthy EG *an excess of energy.* ▶ ADJECTIVE **3** more than is needed, allowed, or healthy EG *excess weight.* ▶ PHRASE **4** In excess of a particular amount means more than that amount EG *a fortune in excess of 150 million pounds.* **5** If you do something to excess, you do it too much EG *She drank to excess.*

excessive

ADJECTIVE too great in amount or degree EG *using excessive force.*
excessively ADVERB

exchange exchanges exchanging exchanged

VERB **1** To exchange things means to give or receive one thing in return for another EG *They exchange small presents on Christmas Eve.* ▶ NOUN **2** the act of giving or receiving something in return for something else EG *an exchange of letters... exchanges of gunfire.* **3** a place where people trade and do business EG *the stock exchange.*

exchequer

Said "iks-**chek**-er" NOUN The exchequer is the department in the government in Britain and other countries which is responsible for money belonging to the state.

excise

NOUN Excise is a tax put on goods produced for sale in the country that produces them.

excitable
ADJECTIVE easily excited.

excite excites exciting excited
VERB **1** If somebody or something excites you, they make you feel very happy and nervous or very interested and enthusiastic. **2** If something excites a particular feeling, it causes somebody to have that feeling EG *This excited my suspicion.*
excited ADJECTIVE, **excitedly** ADVERB, **exciting** ADJECTIVE, **excitement** NOUN
■ (sense 1) arouse, thrill

exclaim exclaims exclaiming exclaimed
VERB When you exclaim, you cry out suddenly or loudly because you are excited or shocked.

exclamation exclamations
NOUN a word or phrase spoken suddenly to express a strong feeling.

exclamation mark exclamation marks
NOUN a punctuation mark (!) used in writing to express a strong feeling.

What does the Exclamation Mark do?

The **exclamation mark** (!) is used after emphatic expressions and exclamations.
I can't believe it!

The exclamation mark can lose its effect if used too much. After a sentence expressing mild excitement or humour, it is better to use a full stop.
It is a beautiful day.

---

exclude excludes excluding excluded
VERB **1** If you exclude something, you deliberately do not include it or do not consider it. **2** If you exclude somebody from a place or an activity, you prevent them from entering the place or taking part in the activity.
exclusion NOUN

exclusive exclusives
ADJECTIVE **1** available to or for the use of a small group of rich or privileged people EG *an exclusive club.* **2** belonging to a particular person or group only EG *exclusive rights to coverage of the Olympic Games.* ▶ NOUN **3** a story or interview which appears in only one newspaper or on only one television programme.
exclusively ADVERB

excrement
Said "eks-krim-ment" NOUN Excrement is the solid waste matter that is passed out of a person's or animal's body through their bowels.

excrete excretes excreting excreted
VERB When you excrete waste matter from your body, you get rid of it, for example by going to the lavatory or by sweating.
excretion NOUN, **excretory** ADJECTIVE

excruciating
Said "iks-kroo-shee-ate-ing" ADJECTIVE unbearably painful.
excruciatingly ADVERB
▥ from Latin *excruciare* meaning 'to torture'

excursion excursions
NOUN a short journey or outing.

excuse excuses excusing excused
NOUN **1** a reason which you give to explain why something has been done, has not been done, or will not be done. ▶ VERB **2** If you excuse yourself or something that you have done, you give reasons defending your actions. **3** If you excuse somebody for something wrong they have done, you forgive them for it. **4** If you excuse somebody from a duty or responsibility, you free them from it EG *He was excused from standing trial because of ill health.* ▶ PHRASE **5** You say **excuse me** to try to catch somebody's attention or to apologize for an interruption or for rude behaviour.

A B C D E F G H I J K L M N O P Q R S T U V W X Y Z

execute executes executing executed

VERB **1** To execute somebody means to kill them as a punishment for a crime. **2** If you execute something such as a plan or an action, you carry it out or perform it EG *The crime had been planned and executed in Montreal.*

execution NOUN

executioner executioners

NOUN a person whose job is to execute criminals.

executive executives

NOUN **1** a person who is employed by a company at a senior level. **2** The executive of an organization is a committee which has the authority to make decisions and ensure that they are carried out. ▶ ADJECTIVE **3** concerned with making important decisions and ensuring that they are carried out EG *the commission's executive director.*

executor executors

Said "ig-zek-yoo-tor" NOUN a person you appoint to carry out the instructions in your will.

exemplary

ADJECTIVE **1** being a good example and worthy of imitation EG *an exemplary performance.* **2** serving as a warning EG *an exemplary tale.*

exemplify exemplifies exemplifying exemplified

VERB **1** To exemplify something means to be a typical example of it EG *This aircraft exemplifies the advantages of European technological cooperation.* **2** If you exemplify something, you give an example of it.

exempt exempts exempting exempted

ADJECTIVE **1** excused from a rule or duty EG *people exempt from prescription charges.* ▶ VERB **2** To exempt someone from a rule, duty, or obligation means to excuse them from it.

exemption NOUN

exercise exercises exercising exercised

NOUN **1** Exercise is any activity which you do to get fit or remain healthy. **2** Exercises are also activities which you do to practise and train for a particular skill EG *piano exercises... a mathematical exercise.* ▶ VERB **3** When you exercise, you do activities which help you to get fit and remain healthy. **4** If you exercise your rights or responsibilities, you use them.

exert exerts exerting exerted

VERB **1** To exert pressure means to apply it. **2** If you exert yourself, you make a physical or mental effort to do something.

exertion exertions

NOUN Exertion is vigorous physical effort or exercise.

exhale exhales exhaling exhaled

VERB When you exhale, you breathe out.

exhaust exhausts exhausting exhausted

VERB **1** To exhaust somebody means to make them very tired EG *Several lengths of the pool left her exhausted.* **2** If you exhaust a supply of something such as money or food, you use it up completely. **3** If you exhaust a subject, you talk about it so much that there is nothing else to say about it. ▶ NOUN **4** a pipe which carries the gas or steam out of the engine of a vehicle.

exhaustion NOUN

■ (sense 1) fatigue, tire out, wear out

exhaustive

ADJECTIVE thorough and complete EG *an exhaustive series of tests.*

exhaustively ADVERB

exhibit exhibits exhibiting exhibited

VERB **1** To exhibit things means to show them in a public place for people to see. **2** If you exhibit your feelings or abilities, you display them so that other people can see them. ▶ NOUN **3** anything which is put on show for the public to see.

exhibition exhibitions
NOUN a public display of works of art, products, or skills.

exhibitor exhibitors
NOUN a person whose work is being shown in an exhibition.

exhilarating
ADJECTIVE Something that is exhilarating makes you feel very happy and excited.

exile exiles exiling exiled
NOUN **1** If somebody lives in exile, they live in a foreign country because they cannot live in their own country, usually for political reasons. **2** a person who lives in exile. ▶ VERB **3** If somebody is exiled, they are sent away from their own country and not allowed to return.

exist exists existing existed
VERB If something exists, it is present in the world as a real or living thing.

existence
NOUN **1** Existence is the state of being or existing. **2** a way of living or being EG an idyllic existence.

exit exits exiting exited
NOUN **1** a way out of a place. **2** If you make an exit, you leave a place. ▶ VERB **3** To exit means to go out.

exodus
NOUN An exodus is the departure of a large number of people from a place.

exotic
ADJECTIVE **1** attractive or interesting through being unusual EG exotic fabrics. **2** coming from a foreign country EG exotic plants.
▣ from Greek exotikos meaning 'foreign'

expand expands expanding expanded
VERB **1** If something expands or you expand it, it becomes larger in number or size. **2** If you expand on something, you give more details

about it EG The minister's speech expanded on the aims which he outlined last month.
expansion NOUN

expanse expanses
NOUN a very large or widespread area EG a vast expanse of pine forests.

expansive
ADJECTIVE **1** Something that is expansive is very wide or extends over a very large area EG the expansive countryside. **2** Someone who is expansive is friendly, open, or talkative.

expatriate expatriates
Said "eks-**pat**-ree-it" NOUN someone who is living in a country which is not their own.

expect expects expecting expected
VERB **1** If you expect something to happen, you believe that it will happen EG The trial is expected to end today. **2** If you are expecting somebody or something, you believe that they are going to arrive or to happen EG The Queen was expecting the chambermaid. **3** If you expect something, you believe that it is your right to get it or have it EG He seemed to expect a reply.
▤ (sense 1) anticipate, look forward to

expectancy
NOUN Expectancy is the feeling that something is about to happen, especially something exciting.

expectant
ADJECTIVE **1** If you are expectant, you believe that something is about to happen, especially something exciting. **2** An expectant mother or father is someone whose baby is going to be born soon.
expectantly ADVERB

expectation expectations
NOUN Expectation or an expectation is a strong belief or hope that something will happen.

expedient expedients
Said "iks-**pee**-dee-ent" NOUN **1** an

A B C D E F G H I J K L M N O P Q R S T U V W X Y Z

A
B
C
D
E
F
G
H
I
J
K
L
M
N
O
P
Q
R
S
T
U
V
W
X
Y
Z

action or plan that achieves a particular purpose but that may not be morally acceptable EG *Many firms have improved their profitability by the simple expedient of cutting staff.* ▶ ADJECTIVE **2** Something that is expedient is useful or convenient in a particular situation.
expediency NOUN

expedition expeditions
NOUN **1** an organized journey made for a special purpose, such as to explore; also the party of people who make such a journey. **2** a short journey or outing EG *shopping expeditions.*
expeditionary ADJECTIVE

expel expels expelling expelled
VERB **1** If someone is expelled from a school or club, they are officially told to leave because they have behaved badly. **2** If a gas or liquid is expelled from a place, it is forced out of it.

expend expends expending expended
VERB To expend energy, time, or money means to use it up or spend it.

expendable
ADJECTIVE no longer useful or necessary, and therefore able to be got rid of.

expenditure
NOUN Expenditure is the total amount of money spent on something.

expense expenses
NOUN **1** Expense is the money that something costs EG *the expense of installing a burglar alarm.* ▶ PLURAL NOUN **2** Expenses are the money somebody spends while doing something connected with their work, which is paid back to them by their employer.
◼ (sense 1) cost, expenditure, outlay

expensive
ADJECTIVE costing a lot of money.
expensively ADVERB

experience experiences experiencing experienced
NOUN **1** Experience consists of all the things that you have done or that have happened to you. **2** something that you do or something that happens to you, especially something new or unusual. ▶ VERB **3** If you experience a situation or feeling, it happens to you or you are affected by it.
◼ (sense 3) go through, undergo

experiment experiments experimenting experimented
NOUN **1** the testing of something, either to find out its effect or to prove something. ▶ VERB **2** If you experiment with something, you do a scientific test on it to prove or discover something.
experimentation NOUN, **experimental** ADJECTIVE, **experimentally** ADVERB

expert experts
NOUN **1** a person who is very skilled at doing something or very knowledgeable about a particular subject. ▶ ADJECTIVE **2** having or requiring special skill or knowledge EG *expert advice.*
expertly ADVERB
◼ (sense 1) authority, master, specialist

expertise
Said "eks-per-**teez**" NOUN Expertise is special skill or knowledge.

expire expires expiring expired
VERB When something expires, it reaches the end of the period of time for which it is valid EG *My contract expires in the summer.*
expiry NOUN

explain explains explaining explained
VERB If you explain something, you give details about it or reasons for it so that it can be understood.
explanation NOUN, **explanatory** ADJECTIVE
◼ clarify, elucidate, make clear

explicit
ADJECTIVE shown or expressed clearly

and openly EG *an explicit death threat.*
explicitly ADVERB

explode **explodes exploding exploded**
VERB **1** If something such as a bomb explodes, it bursts loudly and with great force, often causing damage. **2** If somebody explodes, they express strong feelings suddenly or violently EG *I half expected him to explode in anger.* **3** When something increases suddenly and rapidly, it can be said to explode EG *Sales of men's toiletries have exploded.*
from Latin *explodere* meaning 'to clap someone offstage', from *ex* meaning 'out of' + *plodere* meaning 'to clap'

exploit **exploits exploiting exploited**
VERB **1** If somebody exploits a person or a situation, they take advantage of them for their own ends EG *Critics claim he exploited black musicians.* **2** If you exploit something, you make the best use of it, often for profit EG *exploiting the power of computers.* ▶ NOUN **3** something daring or interesting that somebody has done EG *His courage and exploits were legendary.*
exploitation NOUN

explore **explores exploring explored**
VERB **1** If you explore a place, you travel in it to find out what it is like. **2** If you explore an idea, you think about it carefully.
exploration NOUN, **exploratory** ADJECTIVE, **explorer** NOUN

explosion **explosions**
NOUN a sudden violent burst of energy, for example one caused by a bomb.

explosive **explosives**
ADJECTIVE **1** capable of exploding or likely to explode. **2** happening suddenly and making a loud noise. **3** An explosive situation is one which is likely to have serious or dangerous effects. ▶ NOUN **4** a

substance or device that can explode.

exponent **exponents**
NOUN **1** An exponent of an idea or plan is someone who puts it forward. **2** A FORMAL USE An exponent of a skill or activity is someone who is good at it.

export **exports exporting exported**
VERB **1** To export goods means to send them to another country and sell them there. ▶ NOUN **2** Exports are goods which are sent to another country and sold.
exporter NOUN

expose **exposes exposing exposed**
VERB **1** To expose something means to uncover it and make it visible. **2** To expose a person to something dangerous means to put them in a situation in which it might harm them EG *exposed to tobacco smoke.* **3** To expose a person or situation means to reveal the truth about them.

exposition **expositions**
NOUN a detailed explanation of a particular subject.

exposure **exposures**
NOUN **1** Exposure is the exposing of something. **2** Exposure is the harmful effect on the body caused by very cold weather.

express **expresses expressing expressed**
VERB **1** When you express an idea or feeling, you show what you think or feel by saying or doing something. **2** If you express a quantity in a particular form, you write it down in that form EG *The result of the equation is usually expressed as a percentage.* ▶ ADJECTIVE **3** very fast EG *express delivery service.* ▶ NOUN **4** a fast train or coach which stops at only a few places.

expression **expressions**
NOUN **1** Your expression is the look on your face which shows what

you are thinking or feeling. **2** The expression of ideas or feelings is the showing of them through words, actions, or art. **3** a word or phrase used in communicating EG *the expression 'nosey parker'*.

expressive
ADJECTIVE **1** showing feelings clearly. **2** full of expression.

expressway expressways
NOUN a road designed for fast-moving traffic.

expulsion expulsions
NOUN The expulsion of someone from a place or institution is the act of officially banning them from that place or institution EG *the high number of school expulsions*.

exquisite
ADJECTIVE extremely beautiful and pleasing.

extend extends extending extended
VERB **1** If something extends for a distance, it continues and stretches into the distance. **2** If something extends from a surface or an object, it sticks out from it. **3** If you extend something, you make it larger or longer EG *The table had been extended to seat fifty*.

extension extensions
NOUN **1** a room or building which is added to an existing building. **2** an extra period of time for which something continues to exist or be valid EG *an extension to his visa*. **3** an additional telephone connected to the same line as another telephone.

extensive
ADJECTIVE **1** covering a large area. **2** very great in effect EG *extensive repairs*.
extensively ADVERB

extent extents
NOUN The extent of something is its length, area, or size.

exterior exteriors
NOUN **1** The exterior of something is its outside. **2** Your exterior is your outward appearance.

exterminate exterminates exterminating exterminated
VERB When animals or people are exterminated, they are deliberately killed.
extermination NOUN

external externals
ADJECTIVE existing or happening on the outside or outer part of something.
externally ADVERB

extinct
ADJECTIVE **1** An extinct species of animal or plant is no longer in existence. **2** An extinct volcano is no longer likely to erupt.
extinction NOUN

extinguish extinguishes extinguishing extinguished
VERB To extinguish a light or fire means to put it out.

extortionate
ADJECTIVE more expensive than you consider to be fair.

extra extras
ADJECTIVE **1** more than is usual, necessary, or expected. ▶ NOUN **2** anything which is additional. **3** a person who is hired to play a very small and unimportant part in a film.
■ (sense 1) added, additional, further

extract extracts extracting extracted
VERB **1** To extract something from a place means to take it out or get it out, often by force. **2** If you extract information from someone, you get it from them with difficulty. ▶ NOUN **3** a small section taken from a book or piece of music.

extraction
NOUN **1** Your extraction is the country or people that your family originally comes from EG *a Malaysian citizen of Australian extraction*. **2** Extraction is the process of taking or getting something out of a place.

extraordinary

ADJECTIVE unusual or surprising.
extraordinarily ADVERB
■ exceptional, remarkable, unusual

extravagant

ADJECTIVE **1** spending or costing more money than is reasonable or affordable. **2** going beyond reasonable limits.
extravagantly ADVERB, **extravagance** NOUN

extravaganza extravaganzas

NOUN a spectacular and expensive public show.

extreme extremes

ADJECTIVE **1** very great in degree or intensity EG *extreme caution*. **2** going beyond what is usual or reasonable EG *extreme weather conditions*. **3** at the furthest point or edge of something EG *the extreme northern corner of Spain.*
▶ NOUN **4** the highest or furthest degree of something.
extremely ADVERB

extremist extremists

NOUN a person who uses unreasonable or violent methods to bring about political change.
extremism NOUN

extremity extremities

NOUN The extremities of something are its furthest ends or edges.

extricate extricates extricating extricated

VERB To extricate someone from a place or a situation means to free them from it.

extrovert extroverts

NOUN a person who is more interested in other people and the world around them than their own thoughts and feelings.
🔲 from Latin *extra* meaning 'outwards' + *vertere* meaning 'to turn'

exuberant

ADJECTIVE full of energy and cheerfulness.
exuberantly ADVERB, **exuberance** NOUN

exude exudes exuding exuded

VERB If someone exudes a quality or feeling, they seem to have it to a great degree.

eye eyes eyeing or eying eyed

NOUN **1** the organ of sight. **2** the small hole at the end of a needle through which you pass the thread. ▶ VERB **3** To eye something means to look at it carefully or suspiciously.

eyeball eyeballs

NOUN the whole of the ball-shaped part of the eye.

eyebrow eyebrows

NOUN Your eyebrows are the lines of hair which grow on the ridges of bone above your eyes.

eyelash eyelashes

NOUN Your eyelashes are hairs that grow on the edges of your eyelids.

eyelid eyelids

NOUN Your eyelids are the folds of skin which cover your eyes when they are closed.

eyesight

NOUN Your eyesight is your ability to see.

eyesore eyesores

NOUN Something that is an eyesore is extremely ugly.

eyewitness eyewitnesses

NOUN a person who has seen an event and can describe what happened.

eyrie eyries

Said "ear-ee" NOUN the nest of an eagle or other bird of prey.

A B C D E F G H I J K L M N O P Q R S T U V W X Y Z

Ff Ff

fable fables

NOUN a story intended to teach a moral lesson.

📖 from Latin *fabula* meaning 'story'

fabled

ADJECTIVE well-known because many stories have been told about it EG *the fabled city of Troy*.

fabric fabrics

NOUN 1 Fabric is cloth EG *tough fabric for tents*. 2 The fabric of a building is its walls, roof, and other parts. 3 The fabric of a society or system is its structure, laws, and customs EG *the democratic fabric of American society*.

fabricate fabricates fabricating fabricated

VERB 1 If you fabricate a story or an explanation, you invent it in order to deceive people. 2 To fabricate something is to make or manufacture it.

fabrication NOUN

fabulous

ADJECTIVE 1 wonderful or very impressive EG *a fabulous picnic*. 2 not real, but happening in stories and legends EG *fabulous creatures*.

facade facades

Said "fas-**sahd**" NOUN 1 the front outside wall of a building. 2 a false outward appearance EG *the facade of honesty*.

face faces facing faced

NOUN 1 the front part of your head from your chin to your forehead. 2 the expression someone has or is making EG *a grim face*. 3 a surface or side of something, especially the most important side EG *the north face of Everest*. 4 the main aspect or general appearance of something EG *We have changed the face of language study*. ▶ VERB 5 To face something or someone is to be opposite them or to look at them or towards them EG

a room that faces on to the street. 6 If you face something difficult or unpleasant, you have to deal with it EG *She faced a terrible dilemma*.

▶ PHRASE 7 **On the face of it** means judging by the appearance of something or your initial reaction to it EG *On the face of it the palace looks gigantic*.

📘 (sense 1) countenance, visage

faceless

ADJECTIVE without character or individuality EG *anonymous shops and faceless coffee-bars*.

face-lift face-lifts

NOUN 1 an operation to tighten the skin on someone's face to make them look younger. 2 If you give something a face-lift, you clean it or improve its appearance.

facet facets

Said "**fas**-it" NOUN 1 a single part or aspect of something EG *the many facets of his talent*. 2 one of the flat, cut surfaces of a precious stone.

📖 from French *facette* meaning 'little face'

facetious

Said "fas-**see**-shuss" ADJECTIVE witty or amusing but in a rather silly or inappropriate way EG *He didn't appreciate my facetious suggestion*.

📖 from Latin *facetiae* meaning 'witty remarks'

facial

Said "**fay**-shal" ADJECTIVE appearing on or being part of the face EG *facial expressions*.

facilitate facilitates facilitating facilitated

VERB To facilitate something is to make it easier for it to happen EG *a process that will facilitate individual development*.

facility facilities

NOUN 1 a service or piece of equipment which makes it possible to do something EG *excellent shopping*

260

facilities. **2** A facility for something is an ability to do it easily or well EG *a facility for novel-writing.*

fact facts

NOUN **1** a piece of knowledge or information that is true or something that has actually happened. ▶ PHRASES **2 In fact, as a matter of fact**, and **in point of fact** mean 'actually' or 'really', and are used for emphasis or when making an additional comment EG *Very few people, in fact, have this type of skin.*

factual ADJECTIVE, **factually** ADVERB

faction factions

NOUN a small group of people belonging to a larger group, but differing from it in some aims or ideas EG *a conservative faction in the Church.*

fact of life facts of life

NOUN **1** The facts of life are details about sexual intercourse and how babies are conceived and born. **2** If you say that something is a fact of life, you mean that it is something that people expect to happen, even though they might find it shocking or unpleasant EG *War is a fact of life.*

factor factors

NOUN **1** something that helps to cause a result EG *House dust mites are a major factor in asthma.* **2** The factors of a number are the whole numbers that will divide exactly into it. For example, 2 and 5 are factors of 10. **3** If something increases by a particular factor, it is multiplied that number of times EG *The amount of energy used has increased by a factor of eight.*

■ (sense 1) cause, element, part

factory factories

NOUN a building or group of buildings where goods are made in large quantities.

faculty faculties

NOUN **1** Your faculties are your physical and mental abilities EG *My mental faculties are as sharp as ever.*

2 In some universities, a Faculty is a group of related departments EG *the Science Faculty.*

fad fads

NOUN an temporary fashion or craze EG *the latest exercise fad.*

fade fades fading faded

VERB If something fades, the intensity of its colour, brightness, or sound is gradually reduced.

faeces or feces

Said "fee-seez" PLURAL NOUN Faeces are the solid waste substances discharged from a person's or animal's body.

🏛 from Latin *faeces* meaning 'dregs'

fag fags

NOUN; AN INFORMAL WORD a cigarette.

Fahrenheit

Said "**far-ren-hite**" NOUN Fahrenheit is a scale of temperature in which the freezing point of water is 32° and the boiling point is 212°.

fail fails failing failed

VERB **1** If someone fails to achieve something, they are not successful. **2** If you fail an exam, your marks are too low and you do not pass. **3** If you fail to do something that you should have done, you do not do it EG *They failed to phone her.* **4** If something fails, it becomes less effective or stops working properly EG *The power failed... His grandmother's eyesight began to fail.* ▶ NOUN **5** In an exam, a fail is a piece of work that is not good enough to pass. ▶ PHRASE **6 Without fail** means definitely or regularly EG *Every Sunday her mum would ring without fail.*

■ (sense 1) be unsuccessful, flop

failing failings

NOUN **1** a fault in something or someone. ▶ PREPOSITION **2** used to introduce an alternative EG *Failing that, get a market stall.*

failure failures

NOUN **1** Failure is a lack of success EG *Not all conservation programmes ended*

in failure. **2** an unsuccessful person, thing, or action EG *The venture was a complete failure.* **3** Your failure to do something is not doing something that you were expected to do EG *a statement explaining his failure to turn up as a speaker.*
▤ (sense 2) flop, loser, washout

faint fainter faintest; faints fainting fainted

ADJECTIVE **1** A sound, colour, or feeling that is faint is not very strong or intense. **2** If you feel faint, you feel weak, dizzy, and unsteady. ▶ VERB **3** If you faint, you lose consciousness for a short time.
faintly ADVERB
▤ (sense 3) black out, pass out, swoon

fair fairer fairest; fairs

ADJECTIVE **1** reasonable and just EG *fair and prompt trials for political prisoners.* **2** quite large EG *a fair size envelope.* **3** moderately good or likely to be correct EG *He had a fair idea of what to expect.* **4** having light coloured hair or pale skin. **5** with pleasant and dry weather EG *Ireland's fair weather months.* ▶ NOUN **6** a form of entertainment that takes place outside, with stalls, sideshows, and machines to ride on. **7** an exhibition of goods produced by a particular industry EG *International Wine and Food Fair.*
fairly ADVERB, **fairness** NOUN
▤ (sense 1) impartial, just, unbiased

fairway fairways

NOUN the area of trimmed grass between a tee and a green on a golf course.

fairy fairies

NOUN In stories, fairies are small, supernatural creatures with magical powers.

fairy tale fairy tales

NOUN a story of magical events.

faith faiths

NOUN **1** Faith is a feeling of confidence, trust or optimism about something. **2** a particular religion.

faithful

ADJECTIVE **1** loyal to someone or something and remaining firm in support of them. **2** accurate and truthful EG *a faithful copy of an original.*
faithfully ADVERB, **faithfulness** NOUN
▤ (sense 1) loyal, steadfast, trusty

fake fakes faking faked

NOUN **1** an imitation of something made to trick people into thinking that it is genuine. ▶ ADJECTIVE **2** imitation and not genuine EG *fake fur.* ▶ VERB **3** If you fake a feeling, you pretend that you are experiencing it.
▤ (sense 1) copy, imitation, sham
▤ (sense 2) artificial, false, phoney
▤ (sense 3) feign, pretend, simulate

falcon falcons

NOUN a bird of prey that can be trained to hunt other birds or small animals.
▥ from Latin *falco* meaning 'hawk'

fall falls falling fell fallen

VERB **1** If someone or something falls or falls over, they drop towards the ground. **2** If something falls somewhere, it lands there EG *The spotlight fell on her.* **3** If something falls in amount or strength, it becomes less EG *Steel production fell about 25%.* **4** If a person or group in a position of power falls, they lose their position and someone else takes control. **5** Someone who falls in battle is killed. **6** If, for example, you fall asleep, fall ill, or fall in love, you change quite quickly to that new state. **7** If you fall for someone, you become strongly attracted to them and fall in love. **8** If you fall for a trick or lie, you are deceived by it. **9** Something that falls on a particular date occurs on that date. ▶ NOUN **10** If you have a fall, you accidentally fall over. **11** A fall of snow, soot, or other substance is a quantity of it that has fallen to the ground. **12** A fall in something is a reduction in its amount or strength. **13** In America, autumn is called the fall.

fall down VERB An argument or idea that falls down on a particular point is weak on that point and as a result will be unsuccessful.

fall out VERB If people fall out, they disagree and quarrel.

fall through VERB If an arrangement or plan falls through, it fails or is abandoned.

fallacy fallacies
Said "**fal-lass-ee**" NOUN something false that is generally believed to be true.
🔲 from Latin *fallacia* meaning 'deception'

fallopian tube fallopian tubes
Said "fal-**loh**-pee-an" NOUN The fallopian tubes in a woman's body are the pair of tubes along which the eggs pass from the ovaries to the uterus.

fallout
NOUN Fallout is radioactive particles that fall to the earth after a nuclear explosion.

fallow
ADJECTIVE Land that is fallow is not being used for crop growing so that it has the chance to rest and improve.

false
ADJECTIVE **1** untrue or incorrect EG *I think that's a false argument.* **2** not real or genuine but intended to seem real EG *false hair.* **3** unfaithful or deceitful.
falsely ADVERB, **falsity** NOUN

falsehood falsehoods
NOUN **1** Falsehood is the quality or fact of being untrue EG *the difference between truth and falsehood.* **2** a lie.

falsify falsifies falsifying falsified
VERB If you falsify something, you change it in order to deceive people.
falsification NOUN

falter falters faltering faltered
VERB If someone or something falters, they hesitate or become

unsure or unsteady EG *Her voice faltered.*

fame
NOUN Fame is the state of being very well-known.
🔲 prominence, renown, repute

famed
ADJECTIVE very well-known EG *an area famed for its beauty.*

familiar
ADJECTIVE **1** well-known or easy to recognize EG *familiar faces.*
2 knowing or understanding something well EG *Most children are familiar with stories.*
familiarity NOUN, **familiarize** VERB
🔲 (sense 1) recognizable, well-known

family families
NOUN **1** a group consisting of parents and their children; also all the people who are related to each other, including aunts and uncles, cousins, and grandparents. **2** a group of related species of animals or plants.
familial ADJECTIVE

family planning
NOUN Family planning is the practice of controlling the number of children you have, usually by using contraception.

famine famines
NOUN a serious shortage of food which may cause many deaths.

famished
ADJECTIVE; AN INFORMAL WORD very hungry.

famous
ADJECTIVE very well-known.
🔲 prominent, renowned, well-known

famously
ADVERB; AN OLD-FASHIONED WORD If people get on famously, they enjoy each other's company very much.

fan fans fanning fanned
NOUN **1** If you are a fan of someone or something, you like them very much and are very enthusiastic

A
B
C
D
E
F
G
H
I
J
K
L
M
N
O
P
Q
R
S
T
U
V
W
X
Y
Z

A B C D E F G H I J K L M N O P Q R S T U V W X Y Z

about them. **2** a hand-held or mechanical object which creates a draught of cool air when it moves. ▶ VERB **3** To fan someone or something is to create a draught in their direction EG *The gentle wind fanned her from all sides.*
≡ (sense 1) admirer, enthusiast, supporter

fan out VERB If things or people fan out, they move outwards in different directions.

fanatic fanatics
NOUN a person who is very extreme in their support for a cause or in their enthusiasm for a particular activity.
fanaticism NOUN
🏛 from Latin *fanaticus* meaning 'possessed by a god'

fanatical
ADJECTIVE If you are fanatical about something, you are very extreme in your enthusiasm or support for it.
fanatically ADVERB
≡ obsessive, overenthusiastic

fancy fancies fancying fancied; fancier fanciest
VERB **1** If you fancy something, you want to have it or do it EG *She fancied living in Canada.* ▶ ADJECTIVE **2** special and elaborate EG *dressed up in some fancy clothes.*
fanciful ADJECTIVE
≡ (sense 2) elaborate, ornate

fancy dress
NOUN Fancy dress is clothing worn for a party at which people dress up to look like a particular character or animal.

fanfare fanfares
NOUN a short, loud, musical introduction to a special event, usually played on trumpets.

fang fangs
NOUN Fangs are long, pointed teeth.

fantail fantails
NOUN **1** a pigeon with a large tail that can be opened out like a fan. **2** In Australia and New Zealand, a fantail is also a small, insect-eating

bird with a fan-shaped tail.

fantasize fantasizes fantasizing fantasized; also spelt **fantasise**
VERB If you fantasize, you imagine pleasant but unlikely events or situations.

fantastic
ADJECTIVE **1** wonderful and very pleasing EG *a fantastic view of the sea.* **2** extremely large in degree or amount EG *fantastic debts.* **3** strange and difficult to believe EG *fantastic animals found nowhere else on earth.*
fantastically ADVERB
≡ (sense 1) marvellous, wonderful

fantasy fantasies
NOUN **1** an imagined story or situation. **2** Fantasy is the activity of imagining things or the things that you imagine EG *She can't distinguish between fantasy and reality.*
🏛 from Greek *phantasia* meaning 'imagination'

far farther farthest; further furthest
ADVERB **1** If something is far away from other things, it is a long distance away. **2** Far also means very much or to a great extent or degree EG *far more important.* ▶ ADJECTIVE **3** Far means very distant EG *in the far south of Africa.* **4** Far also describes the more distant of two things rather than the nearer one EG *the far corner of the goal.* ▶ PHRASE **5** By far and far and away are used to say that something is the best EG *Walking is by far the best way to get around.* **6** So far means up to the present moment EG *So far, it's been good news.* **7** As far as, so far as, and in so far as mean to the degree or extent that something is true EG *As far as I know he is progressing well.*
≡ (sense 2) considerably, much
≡ (sense 3) distant, remote
✓ When you are talking about a physical distance you can use *farther* and *farthest* or *further* and *furthest*. If you are talking about extra effort or time, use *further* and *furthest*: *a further delay is likely.*

farce farces

NOUN **1** a humorous play in which ridiculous and unlikely situations occur. **2** a disorganized and ridiculous situation.

farcical ADJECTIVE

fare fares faring fared

NOUN **1** the amount charged for a journey on a bus, train, or plane. ▸ VERB **2** How someone fares in a particular situation is how they get on EG *The team have not fared well in this tournament.*

📖 from Old English *faran* meaning 'to go'

Far East

NOUN The Far East consists of the countries of East Asia, including China, Japan, and Malaysia.

Far Eastern ADJECTIVE

farewell

INTERJECTION **1** Farewell means goodbye. ▸ ADJECTIVE **2** A farewell act is performed by or for someone who is leaving a particular job or career EG *a farewell speech.*

far-fetched

ADJECTIVE unlikely to be true.

farm farms farming farmed

NOUN **1** an area of land together with buildings, used for growing crops and raising animals. ▸ VERB **2** Someone who farms uses land to grow crops and raise animals.

farmer NOUN, **farming** NOUN

📖 from Old French *ferme* meaning 'rented land'

farmhouse farmhouses

NOUN the main house on a farm.

farmyard farmyards

NOUN an area surrounded by farm buildings.

fascinate fascinates fascinating fascinated

VERB If something fascinates you, it interests you so much that you think about it and nothing else.

fascinating ADJECTIVE

🟦 absorb, enthral, intrigue

fascism

Said "**fash-izm**" NOUN Fascism is an extreme right-wing political ideology or system of government with a powerful dictator and state control of most activities. Nationalism is encouraged and political opposition is not allowed.

fascist NOUN OR ADJECTIVE

fashion fashions fashioning fashioned

NOUN **1** A fashion is a style of dress or way of behaving that is popular at a particular time. **2** The fashion in which someone does something is the way in which they do it. ▸ VERB **3** If you fashion something, you make or shape it.

🟦 (sense 1) style, trend, vogue

fashionable

ADJECTIVE Something that is fashionable is very popular with a lot of people at the same time.

fashionably ADVERB

🟦 in, in vogue, popular, trendy

fast faster fastest; fasts fasting fasted

ADJECTIVE OR ADVERB **1** moving, doing something, or happening quickly or with great speed. **2** If a clock is fast, it shows a time that is later than the real time. ▸ ADVERB **3** Something that is held fast is firmly fixed. ▸ PHRASE **4** If you are fast asleep, you are in a deep sleep. ▸ VERB **5** If you fast, you eat no food at all for a period of time, usually for religious reasons. ▸ NOUN **6** a period of time during which someone does not eat food.

🟦 (sense 1) quick, rapid, speedy, swift

fasten fastens fastening fastened

VERB **1** To fasten something is to close it or attach it firmly to something else. **2** If you fasten your hands or teeth around or onto something, you hold it tightly with them.

fastener NOUN, **fastening** NOUN

🟦 (sense 1) fix, secure

fast food

A B C D E F G H I J K L M N O P Q R S T U V W X Y Z

A B C D E F G H I J K L M N O P Q R S T U V W X Y Z

NOUN Fast food is hot food that is prepared and served quickly after you have ordered it.

fastidious
ADJECTIVE extremely choosy and concerned about neatness and cleanliness.

fat fatter fattest; fats
ADJECTIVE **1** Someone who is fat has too much weight on their body. **2** large or great EG *a fat pile of letters.* ▶ NOUN **3** Fat is the greasy, cream-coloured substance that animals and humans have under their skin, which is used to store energy and to help keep them warm. **4** Fat is also the greasy solid or liquid substance obtained from animals and plants and used in cooking.
fatness NOUN, **fatty** ADJECTIVE
▦ (sense 1) overweight, plump, podgy, tubby

fatal
ADJECTIVE **1** causing death EG *fatal injuries.* **2** very important or significant and likely to have an undesirable effect EG *The mistake was fatal to my plans.*
fatally ADVERB
▦ (sense 1) deadly, lethal, mortal

fatality fatalities
NOUN a death caused by accident or violence.

fate fates
NOUN **1** Fate is a power that is believed to control events. **2** Someone's fate is what happens to them EG *She was resigned to her fate.*
▦ (sense 1) destiny, providence

fateful
ADJECTIVE having an important, often disastrous, effect EG *fateful political decisions.*

father fathers fathering fathered
NOUN **1** A person's father is their male parent. **2** The father of something is the man who invented or started it EG *the father of Italian painting.* **3** 'Father' is used to address a priest in some Christian churches. **4** Father is another name for God. ▶ VERB **5** A LITERARY USE When a man fathers a child, he makes a woman pregnant.
fatherly ADJECTIVE, **fatherhood** NOUN

father-in-law fathers-in-law
NOUN A person's father-in-law is the father of their husband or wife.

fathom fathoms fathoming fathomed
NOUN **1** a unit for measuring the depth of water. It is equal to 6 feet or about 1.83 metres. ▶ VERB **2** If you fathom something, you understand it after careful thought EG *Daisy tries to fathom what it means.*

fatigue fatigues fatiguing fatigued
Said "fat-eeg" NOUN **1** Fatigue is extreme tiredness. ▶ VERB **2** If you are fatigued by something, it makes you extremely tired.

fault faults faulting faulted
NOUN **1** If something bad is your fault, you are to blame for it. **2** a weakness or imperfection in someone or something. **3** a large crack in rock caused by movement of the earth's crust. ▶ PHRASE **4** If you are **at fault**, you are mistaken or are to blame for something EG *If you were at fault, you accept it.* ▶ VERB **5** If you cannot fault someone, you cannot criticize them for what they are doing because they are doing it so well.
faultless ADJECTIVE, **faulty** ADJECTIVE
▦ (sense 2) defect, failing, flaw

favour favours favouring favoured
NOUN **1** If you regard someone or something with favour, you like or support them. **2** If you do someone a favour, you do something helpful for them. ▶ PHRASE **3** Something that is **in someone's favour** is a help or advantage to them EG *The arguments seemed to be in our favour.* **4** If you are **in favour of** something, you agree with it and think it should

happen. ▸ VERB **5** If you favour something or someone, you prefer that person or thing.
favourable ADJECTIVE, **favourably** ADVERB

favourite favourites
ADJECTIVE **1** Your favourite person or thing is the one you like best.
▸ NOUN **2** Someone's favourite is the person or thing they like best. **3** the animal or person expected to win in a race or contest.

favouritism
NOUN Favouritism is behaviour in which you are unfairly more helpful or more generous to one person than to other people.

fawn fawns fawning fawned
NOUN OR ADJECTIVE **1** pale yellowish-brown. ▸ NOUN **2** a very young deer. ▸ VERB **3** To fawn on someone is to seek their approval by flattering them.

fax faxes
NOUN an exact copy of a document sent electronically along a telephone line.

fear fears fearing feared
NOUN **1** Fear is an unpleasant feeling of danger. **2** a thought that something undesirable or unpleasant might happen EG *You have a fear of failure.* ▸ VERB **3** If you fear someone or something, you are frightened of them. **4** If you fear something unpleasant, you are worried that it is likely to happen EG *Artists feared that their pictures would be forgotten.*
fearless ADJECTIVE, **fearlessly** ADVERB
■ (sense 1) dread, fright, terror

fearful
ADJECTIVE **1** afraid and full of fear. **2** extremely unpleasant or worrying EG *The world's in such a fearful mess.*
fearfully ADVERB

fearsome
ADJECTIVE terrible or frightening EG *a powerful, fearsome weapon.*

feasible
ADJECTIVE possible and likely to

happen EG *The proposal is just not feasible.*
feasibility NOUN

feast feasts
NOUN a large and special meal for many people.

feat feats
NOUN an impressive and difficult achievement EG *It was an astonishing feat for Leeds to score six away from home.*

feather feathers
NOUN one of the light fluffy things covering a bird's body.
feathery ADJECTIVE

feature features featuring featured
NOUN **1** an interesting or important part or characteristic of something. **2** Someone's features are the various parts of their face. **3** a special article or programme dealing with a particular subject. **4** the main film in a cinema programme. ▸ VERB **5** To feature something is to include it or emphasize it as an important part or subject.
featureless ADJECTIVE

February
NOUN February is the second month of the year. It has 28 days, except in a leap year, when it has 29 days.
▥ from *Februa*, a Roman festival of purification

fed
the past tense and past participle of feed.

federal
ADJECTIVE relating to a system of government in which a group of states is controlled by a central government, but each state has its own local powers EG *The United States of America is a federal country.*

federation federations
NOUN a group of organizations or states that have joined together for a common purpose.

fed up

A
B
C
D
E
F
G
H
I
J
K
L
M
N
O
P
Q
R
S
T
U
V
W
X
Y
Z

ADJECTIVE; AN INFORMAL EXPRESSION
unhappy or bored.

fee fees
NOUN a charge or payment for a job, service, or activity.

feeble feebler feeblest
ADJECTIVE weak or lacking in power or influence EG *feeble and stupid arguments*.

feed feeds feeding fed
VERB **1** To feed a person or animal is to give them food. **2** When an animal or baby feeds, it eats. **3** To feed something is to supply what is needed for it to operate or exist EG *The information was fed into a computer database.* ▶ NOUN **4** Feed is food for animals or babies.

feedback
NOUN **1** Feedback is comments and information about the quality or success of something. **2** Feedback is also a condition in which some of the power, sound, or information produced by electronic equipment goes back into it.

feel feels feeling felt
VERB **1** If you feel an emotion or sensation, you experience it EG *I felt a bit ashamed.* **2** If you feel that something is the case, you believe it to be so EG *She feels that she is in control of her life.* **3** If you feel something, you touch it. **4** If something feels warm or cold, for example, you experience its warmth or coldness through the sense of touch EG *Real marble feels cold to the touch.* **5** To feel the effect of something is to be affected by it EG *The shock waves of this fire will be felt by people from all over the world.* ▶ NOUN **6** The feel of something is how it feels to you when you touch it EG *skin with a velvety smooth feel.* ▶ PHRASE **7** If you **feel like** doing something, you want to do it.
☰ (sense 1) be aware of, experience
☰ (sense 2) believe, consider, think

feeler feelers
NOUN An insect's feelers are the two

thin antennae on its head with which it senses things around it.

feeling feelings
NOUN **1** an emotion or reaction EG *feelings of envy.* **2** a physical sensation EG *a feeling of pain.* **3** Feeling is the ability to experience the sense of touch in your body EG *He had no feeling in his hands.* **4** Your feelings about something are your general attitudes or thoughts about it EG *He has strong feelings about our national sport.*

feet
the plural of **foot**.

feign feigns feigning feigned
Rhymes with "rain" VERB If you feign an emotion or state, you pretend to experience it EG *I feigned a headache.*

feline
Said "fee-line" ADJECTIVE belonging or relating to the cat family.
▥ from Latin *feles* meaning 'cat'

fell fells felling felled
1 the past tense of **fall**. ▶ VERB **2** To fell a tree is to cut it down.

fellow fellows
NOUN **1** A RATHER OLD-FASHIONED INFORMAL USE a man EG *I knew a fellow by that name.* **2** a senior member of a learned society or a university college. **3** Your fellows are the people who share work or an activity with you. ▶ ADJECTIVE **4** You use 'fellow' to describe people who have something in common with you EG *his fellow editors.*
▥ from Old Norse *felagi* meaning 'partner' or 'associate'

fellowship fellowships
NOUN **1** Fellowship is a feeling of friendliness that a group of people have when they are doing things together. **2** a group of people that join together because they have interests in common EG *the Dickens Fellowship.* **3** an academic post at a university which involves research work.

felt

1 the past tense and past participle of **feel**. ▶ NOUN **2** Felt is a thick cloth made by pressing short threads together.

female females
NOUN **1** a person or animal that belongs to the sex that can have babies or young. ▶ ADJECTIVE **2** concerning or relating to females.

feminine
ADJECTIVE **1** relating to women or considered to be typical of women. **2** belonging to a particular class of nouns in some languages, such as French, German, and Latin.
femininity NOUN

What is the Feminine?

Feminine nouns denote female people and animals.

The girl put on her coat. ➤ *girl* is **feminine**

It is customary to refer to countries and vehicles as if they were feminine.

The ship came into view, her sails swelling in the breeze.

Common nouns may be either masculine or feminine. Other words in the sentence may tell us if they are male or female.

The doctor parked his car.
The doctor parked her car.

Also look at the grammar boxes at **gender**, **masculine** and **neuter**.

---

feminism
NOUN Feminism is the belief that women should have the same rights and opportunities as men.
feminist NOUN OR ADJECTIVE

fen fens
NOUN The fens are an area of low, flat, very wet land in the east of England.

fence fences fencing fenced
NOUN **1** a wooden or wire barrier between two areas of land. **2** a barrier or hedge for the horses to jump over in horse racing or show jumping. ▶ VERB **3** To fence an area of land is to surround it with a fence. **4** When two people fence, they use special swords to fight

each other as a sport.

fend fends fending fended
PHRASE **1** If you have to **fend for yourself**, you have to look after yourself. ▶ VERB **2** If you fend off an attack or unwelcome questions or attention, you defend and protect yourself.

ferment ferments fermenting fermented
VERB When wine, beer, or fruit ferments, a chemical change takes place in it, often producing alcohol.
fermentation NOUN

fern ferns
NOUN a plant with long feathery leaves and no flowers.

ferocious
ADJECTIVE violent and fierce EG *ferocious dogs... ferocious storms*.
ferociously ADVERB, **ferocity** NOUN
▥ from Latin *ferox* meaning 'like a wild animal'

ferret ferrets
NOUN a small, fierce animal related to the weasel and kept for hunting rats and rabbits.
▥ from Old French *furet* meaning 'little thief'

ferry ferries ferrying ferried
NOUN **1** a boat that carries people and vehicles across short stretches of water. ▶ VERB **2** To ferry people or goods somewhere is to transport them there, usually on a short, regular journey.

fertile
ADJECTIVE **1** capable of producing strong, healthy plants EG *fertile soil*. **2** creative EG *fertile minds*. **3** able to have babies or young.
fertility NOUN

fertilize fertilizes fertilizing fertilized; also spelt **fertilise**
VERB **1** When an egg, plant, or female is fertilized, the process of reproduction begins by sperm joining with the egg, or by pollen coming into contact with the reproductive part of a plant. **2** To

A B C D E F G H I J K L M N O P Q R S T U V W X Y Z

fertilize land is to put manure or chemicals onto it to feed the plants.

fertilizer fertilizers; also spelt fertiliser
NOUN Fertilizer is a substance put onto soil to improve plant growth.

fervent
ADJECTIVE showing strong, sincere, and enthusiastic feeling EG *a fervent nationalist*.
fervently ADVERB

fervour
NOUN Fervour is a very strong feeling for or belief in something EG *a wave of religious fervour*.
📖 from Latin *fervor* meaning 'heat'

fester festers festering festered
VERB If a wound festers it becomes infected and produces pus.
📖 from Latin *fistula* meaning 'ulcer'

festival festivals
NOUN 1 an organized series of events and performances EG *the Cannes Film Festival*. 2 a day or period of religious celebration.

festive
ADJECTIVE full of happiness and celebration EG *a festive time of singing and dancing*.

festivity festivities
NOUN Festivity is celebration and happiness EG *the wedding festivities*.

festooned
ADJECTIVE If something is festooned with objects, the objects are hanging across it in large numbers.

fetch fetches fetching fetched
VERB 1 If you fetch something, you go to where it is and bring it back. 2 If something fetches a particular sum of money, it is sold for that amount EG *Portraits fetch the highest prices*.

fetching
ADJECTIVE attractive in appearance EG *a fetching purple frock*.

fete fetes feting feted
Rhymes with "date" NOUN 1 an outdoor event with competitions, displays, and goods for sale. ▶ VERB 2 Someone who is feted receives a public welcome or entertainment as an honour.

feud feuds feuding feuded
Said "fyood" NOUN 1 a long-term and very bitter quarrel, especially between families. ▶ VERB 2 When people feud, they take part in a feud.

feudalism
NOUN Feudalism is a social and political system that was common in the Middle Ages in Europe. Under this system, ordinary people were given land and protection by a lord, and in return they worked and fought for him.
feudal ADJECTIVE

fever fevers
NOUN 1 Fever is a condition occurring during illness, in which the patient has a very high body temperature. 2 A fever is extreme excitement or agitation EG *a fever of impatience*.

feverish
ADJECTIVE 1 in a state of extreme excitement or agitation EG *increasingly feverish activity*. 2 suffering from a high body temperature.
feverishly ADVERB

few fewer fewest
ADJECTIVE OR NOUN 1 used to refer to a small number of things EG *I saw him a few moments ago… one of only a few*. ▶ PHRASES 2 Quite a few or a good few means quite a large number of things.
☑ You use *fewer* to talk about things that can be counted: *fewer than five visits*. When you are talking about amounts that can't be counted you should use *less*.

fiancé fiancés
Said "fee-on-say" NOUN A woman's fiancé is the man to whom she is engaged.

fiancée fiancées
NOUN A man's fiancée is the woman

to whom he is engaged.

fiasco fiascos
Said "fee-**ass**-koh" NOUN an event or attempt that fails completely, especially in a ridiculous or disorganized way EG *The game ended in a complete fiasco.*

fib fibs fibbing fibbed
NOUN **1** a small, unimportant lie.
▶ VERB **2** If you fib, you tell a small lie.

fibre fibres
NOUN **1** a thin thread of a substance used to make cloth. **2** Fibre is also a part of plants that can be eaten but not digested; it helps food pass quickly through the body.
fibrous ADJECTIVE

fickle
ADJECTIVE A fickle person keeps changing their mind about who or what they like or want.
▦ from Old English *ficol* meaning 'treacherous' or 'deceitful'

fiction fictions
NOUN **1** Fiction is stories about people and events that have been invented by the author.
2 something that is not true.
fictional ADJECTIVE, **fictitious** ADJECTIVE

fiddle fiddles fiddling fiddled
VERB **1** If you fiddle with something, you keep moving it or touching it restlessly. **2** AN INFORMAL USE If someone fiddles something such as an account, they alter it dishonestly to get money for themselves. ▶ NOUN **3** AN INFORMAL USE a dishonest action or scheme to get money. **4** a violin.
fiddler NOUN

fiddly fiddlier fiddliest
ADJECTIVE small and difficult to do or use EG *fiddly nuts and bolts.*

fidelity
NOUN Fidelity is remaining firm in your beliefs, friendships, or loyalty to another person.

fidget fidgets fidgeting fidgeted
VERB **1** If you fidget, you keep changing your position because of nervousness or boredom. ▶ NOUN **2** someone who fidgets.
fidgety ADJECTIVE

field fields fielding fielded
NOUN **1** an area of land where crops are grown or animals are kept. **2** an area of land where sports are played EG *a hockey field.* **3** A coal field, oil field, or gold field is an area where coal, oil, or gold is found. **4** a particular subject or area of interest EG *He was doing well in his own field of advertising.* ▶ ADJECTIVE **5** A field trip or a field study involves research or activity in the natural environment rather than theoretical or laboratory work. **6** In an athletics competition, the field events are the events such as the high jump and the javelin which do not take place on a running track. ▶ VERB **7** In cricket, when you field the ball, you stop it after the batsman has hit it. **8** To field questions is to answer or deal with them skilfully.

fielder fielders
NOUN In cricket, the fielders are the team members who stand at various parts of the pitch and try to get the batsmen out or to prevent runs from being scored.

field marshal field marshals
NOUN an army officer of the highest rank.

fieldwork
NOUN Fieldwork is the study of something in the environment where it naturally lives or occurs, rather than in a class or laboratory.

fiend fiends
Said "feend" NOUN **1** a devil or evil spirit. **2** a very wicked or cruel person. **3** AN INFORMAL USE someone who is very keen on a particular thing EG *a fitness fiend.*
▦ from Old English *feond* meaning 'enemy'

fierce fiercer fiercest
ADJECTIVE **1** very aggressive or angry.

2 extremely strong or intense EG *a sudden fierce pain... a fierce storm.*

fiercely ADVERB

▣ (sense 1) ferocious, savage, wild

fiery fierier fieriest

ADJECTIVE **1** involving fire or seeming like fire EG *a huge fiery sun.*

2 showing great anger, energy, or passion EG *a fiery debate.*

fifteen

the number 15.

fifteenth

fifth fifths

1 The fifth item in a series is the one counted as number five. ▶ NOUN **2** one of five equal parts.

fifty fifties

the number 50.

fiftieth

fifty-fifty

ADVERB **1** divided equally into two portions. ▶ ADJECTIVE **2** just as likely not to happen as to happen EG *You've got a fifty-fifty chance of being right.*

fig figs

NOUN a soft, sweet fruit full of tiny seeds. It grows in hot countries and is often eaten dried.

fight fights fighting fought

VERB **1** When people fight, they take part in a battle, a war, a boxing match, or in some other attempt to hurt or kill someone. **2** To fight for something is to try in a very determined way to achieve it EG *I must fight for respect.* ▶ NOUN **3** a situation in which people hit or try to hurt each other. **4** a determined attempt to prevent or achieve something EG *the fight for independence.*

fighter NOUN

▣ (sense 1) battle, come to blows, struggle

▣ (sense 3) battle, conflict, struggle

figurative

ADJECTIVE If you use a word or expression in a figurative sense, you use it with a more abstract or imaginative meaning than its ordinary one.

figuratively ADVERB

figure figures figuring figured

NOUN **1** a written number or the amount a number stands for. **2** a geometrical shape. **3** a diagram or table in a written text. **4** the shape of a person whom you cannot see clearly EG *A human figure leaped at him.* **5** Your figure is the shape of your body EG *his slim and supple figure.* **6** a person EG *He was a major figure in the trial.* ▶ VERB **7** To figure in something is to appear or be included in it EG *the many people who have figured in his life.* **8** AN INFORMAL USE If you figure that something is the case, you guess or conclude this EG *We figure the fire broke out around four in the morning.*

figurehead figureheads

NOUN the leader of a movement or organization who has no real power.

figure of speech figures of speech

NOUN A figure of speech is an expression such as a simile or idiom in which the words are not used in their literal sense.

file files filing filed

NOUN **1** a box or folder in which a group of papers or records is kept; also used of the information kept in the file. **2** In computing, a file is a stored set of related data with its own name. **3** a line of people one behind the other. **4** a long steel tool with a rough surface, used for smoothing and shaping hard materials. ▶ VERB **5** When someone files a document, they put it in its correct place with similar documents. **6** When a group of people file somewhere, they walk one behind the other in a line. **7** If you file something, you smooth or shape it with a file.

fill fills filling filled

VERB **1** If you fill something or if it fills up, it becomes full. **2** If something fills a need, it satisfies the need EG *Ella had in some small way filled the gap left by Molly's absence.* **3** To fill a job vacancy is to appoint someone to do that job. ▶ NOUN **4** If you have had your fill of something, you do not want any more.

fill in VERB **1** If you fill in a form, you write information in the appropriate spaces. **2** If you fill someone in, you give them information to bring them up to date.

fillet fillets filleting filleted
NOUN **1** a strip of tender, boneless beef, veal, or pork. **2** a piece of fish with the bones removed. ▶ VERB **3** To fillet meat or fish is to prepare it by cutting out the bones.

filling fillings
NOUN **1** the soft food mixture inside a sandwich, cake, or pie. **2** a small amount of metal or plastic put into a hole in a tooth by a dentist.

filly fillies
NOUN a female horse or pony under the age of four.

film films filming filmed
NOUN **1** a series of moving pictures projected onto a screen and shown at the cinema or on television. **2** a thin flexible strip of plastic used in a camera to record images when exposed to light. **3** a very thin layer of powder or liquid on a surface. **4** Plastic film is a very thin sheet of plastic used for wrapping things. ▶ VERB **5** If you film someone, you use a cine camera or a video camera to record their movements on film. 🔲 from Old English *filmen* meaning 'membrane'

filter filters filtering filtered
NOUN **1** a device that allows some substances, lights, or sounds to pass through it, but not others EG *a filter against the harmful rays of the sun.* ▶ VERB **2** To filter a substance is to pass it through a filter. **3** If something filters somewhere, it

gets there slowly or faintly EG *Traffic filtered into the city.*
filtration NOUN

filth
NOUN **1** Filth is disgusting dirt and muck. **2** People often use the word filth to refer to very bad language or to sexual material that is thought to be crude and offensive.
filthy ADJECTIVE
🔲 from Old English *fylth* meaning 'pus' or 'corruption'
▤ (sense 1) dirt, muck, squalor

fin fins
NOUN a thin, flat structure on the body of a fish, used to help guide it through the water.

final finals
ADJECTIVE **1** last in a series or happening at the end of something. **2** A decision that is final cannot be changed or questioned. ▶ NOUN **3** the last game or contest in a series which decides the overall winner. ▶ PLURAL NOUN **4** Finals are the last and most important examinations of a university or college course.
▤ (sense 1) concluding, last

finale finales
Said "fin-**nah**-lee" NOUN the last section of a piece of music or show.

finalist finalists
NOUN a person taking part in the final of a competition.

finalize finalizes finalizing finalized; also spelt **finalise**
VERB If you finalize something, you complete all the arrangements for it.

finally
ADVERB If something finally happens, it happens after a long delay.
▤ (sense 1) at last, eventually
▤ (sense 2) in conclusion, lastly

finance finances financing financed
VERB **1** To finance a project or a large purchase is to provide the money for it. ▶ NOUN **2** Finance for

something is the money or loans used to pay for it. **3** Finance is also the management of money, loans, and investments.

financial
ADJECTIVE relating to or involving money.
financially ADVERB

financier financiers
NOUN a person who deals with the finance for large businesses.

finch finches
NOUN a small bird with a short strong beak.

find finds finding found
VERB **1** If you find someone or something, you discover them, either as a result of searching or by coming across them unexpectedly. **2** If you find that something is the case, you become aware of it or realize it EG *I found my fists were clenched.* **3** Something that is found in a particular place typically lives or exists there. **4** When a court or jury finds a person guilty or not guilty, they decide that the person is guilty or innocent EG *He was found guilty and sentenced to life imprisonment.* ▶ NOUN **5** If you describe something or someone as a find, you mean that you have recently discovered them and they are valuable or useful.
finder NOUN
■ (sense 1) come across, discover
find out VERB **1** If you find out something, you learn or discover something that you did not know. **2** If you find someone out, you discover that they have been doing something they should not have been doing.

findings
PLURAL NOUN Someone's findings are the conclusions they reach as a result of investigation.

fine finer finest; fines fining fined
ADJECTIVE **1** very good or very beautiful EG *a fine school... fine clothes.* **2** satisfactory or suitable EG

Pasta dishes are fine if not served with a rich sauce. **3** very narrow or thin EG *fine paper.* **4** A fine net or sieve has very small holes. Fine powder or dust consists of very small particles. **5** A fine detail, adjustment, or distinction is very delicate, exact, or subtle. **6** When the weather is fine, it is not raining and is bright or sunny. ▶ NOUN **7** a sum of money paid as a punishment. ▶ VERB **8** Someone who is fined has to pay a sum of money as a punishment.

finery
NOUN Finery is very beautiful clothing and jewellery.

finesse
Said "fin-ness" NOUN If you do something with finesse, you do it with skill and subtlety.

finger fingers fingering fingered
NOUN **1** Your fingers are the four long jointed parts of your hands, sometimes including the thumbs. ▶ VERB **2** If you finger something you feel it with your fingers.

fingernail fingernails
NOUN Your fingernails are the hard coverings at the ends of your fingers.

fingerprint fingerprints
NOUN a mark made showing the pattern on the skin at the tip of a person's finger.

finish finishes finishing finished
VERB **1** When you finish something, you reach the end of it and complete it. **2** When something finishes, it ends or stops. ▶ NOUN **3** The finish of something is the end or last part of it. **4** The finish that something has is the texture or appearance of its surface EG *a healthy, glossy finish.*
■ (sense 1) complete, conclude, end
■ (sense 3) close, conclusion, end

finite
Said "fie-nite" ADJECTIVE having a particular size or limit which cannot be increased EG *There's only*

finite money to spend.

Finn Finns
NOUN someone who comes from Finland.

Finnish
ADJECTIVE **1** belonging or relating to Finland. ▶ NOUN **2** Finnish is the main language spoken in Finland.

fir firs
NOUN a tall pointed evergreen tree that has thin needle-like leaves and produces cones.

fire fires firing fired
NOUN **1** Fire is the flames produced when something burns. **2** a pile or mass of burning material. **3** a piece of equipment that is used as a heater EG *a gas fire.* ▶ VERB **4** If you fire a weapon or fire a bullet, you operate the weapon so that the bullet or missile is released. **5** If you fire questions at someone, you ask them a lot of questions very quickly. **6** AN INFORMAL USE If an employer fires someone, he or she dismisses that person from their job. ▶ PHRASE **7** If someone **opens fire**, they start shooting.

firearm firearms
NOUN a gun.

fire brigade fire brigades
NOUN the organization which has the job of putting out fires.

fire engine fire engines
NOUN a large vehicle that carries equipment for putting out fires.

fire escape fire escapes
NOUN an emergency exit or staircase for use if there is a fire.

fire extinguisher fire extinguishers
NOUN a metal cylinder containing water or foam for spraying onto a fire.

firefighter firefighters
NOUN a person whose job is to put out fires and rescue trapped people.

firefly fireflies
NOUN an insect that glows in the dark.

fireplace fireplaces
NOUN the opening beneath a chimney where a fire can be lit.

fireproof
ADJECTIVE resistant to fire.

fire station fire stations
NOUN a building where fire engines are kept and where firefighters wait to be called out.

firework fireworks
NOUN a small container of gunpowder and other chemicals which explodes and produces coloured sparks or smoke when lit.

firing squad firing squads
NOUN a group of soldiers ordered to shoot a person condemned to death.

firm firmer firmest; firms
ADJECTIVE **1** Something that is firm does not move easily when pressed or pushed, or when weight is put on it. **2** A firm grasp or push is one with controlled force or pressure. **3** A firm decision is definite. **4** Someone who is firm behaves with authority that shows they will not change their mind. ▶ NOUN **5** a business selling or producing something.
firmly ADVERB, **firmness** NOUN

first
ADJECTIVE OR ADVERB **1** happening, coming, or done before everything or everyone else. ▶ ADJECTIVE **2** more important than anything else EG *Her cheese won first prize.* ▶ NOUN **3** something that has never happened or been done before.
firstly ADVERB
▣ (sense 2) chief, foremost, principal

first aid
NOUN First aid is medical treatment given to an injured person.

first class
ADJECTIVE **1** Something that is first class is of the highest quality or standard. **2** First-class accommodation on a train, aircraft, or ship is the best and most

A B C D E F G H I J K L M N O P Q R S T U V W X Y Z

A B C D E F G H I J K L M N O P Q R S T U V W X Y Z

expensive type of accommodation.
3 First-class postage is quick but more expensive.

first-hand
ADJECTIVE First-hand knowledge or experience is gained directly rather than from books or other people.

First Lady First Ladies
NOUN The First Lady of a country is the wife of a president.

first-rate
ADJECTIVE excellent.

fiscal
ADJECTIVE involving government or public money, especially taxes.
📖 from Latin *fiscus* meaning 'money-bag' or 'treasury'

fish fishes fishing fished
NOUN **1** a cold-blooded creature living in water that has a spine, gills, fins, and a scaly skin. **2** Fish is the flesh of fish eaten as food.
▶ VERB **3** To fish is to try to catch fish for food or sport. **4** If you fish for information, you try to get it in an indirect way.
fishing NOUN, **fisherman** NOUN
☑ The plural of the noun *fish* can be either *fish* or *fishes*, but *fish* is more common.

fishery fisheries
NOUN an area of the sea where fish are caught commercially.

fishmonger fishmongers
NOUN a shopkeeper who sells fish; also the shop itself.

fishy fishier fishiest
ADJECTIVE **1** smelling of fish. **2** AN INFORMAL USE suspicious or doubtful EG *He spotted something fishy going on.*

fission
Rhymes with "**mission**" NOUN
1 Fission is the splitting of something into parts. **2** Fission is also nuclear fission.

fissure fissures
NOUN a deep crack in rock.

fist fists
NOUN a hand with the fingers curled tightly towards the palm.

fit fits fitting fitted; fitter fittest
VERB **1** Something that fits is the right shape or size for a particular person or position. **2** If you fit something somewhere, you put it there carefully or securely EG *Very carefully he fitted the files inside the compartment.* **3** If something fits a particular situation, person, or thing, it is suitable or appropriate EG *a sentence that fitted the crime.*
▶ NOUN **4** The fit of something is how it fits EG *This bolt must be a good fit.* **5** If someone has a fit, their muscles suddenly start contracting violently and they may lose consciousness. **6** A fit of laughter, coughing, anger, or panic is a sudden uncontrolled outburst.
▶ ADJECTIVE **7** good enough or suitable EG *Housing fit for frail elderly people.* **8** Someone who is fit is healthy and has strong muscles as a result of regular exercise.
fitness NOUN
▤ (sense 3) match, suit
▤ (sense 5) convulsion, seizure, spasm

fitful
ADJECTIVE happening at irregular intervals and not continuous EG *a fitful breeze.*
fitfully ADVERB

fitter fitters
NOUN a person who assembles or installs machinery.

fitting fittings
ADJECTIVE **1** right or suitable EG *a fitting reward for his efforts.* ▶ NOUN **2** a small part that is fixed to a piece of equipment or furniture. **3** If you have a fitting, you try on a garment that is being made to see whether it fits properly.

five
the number 5.

fix fixes fixing fixed
VERB **1** If you fix something somewhere, you attach it or put it there securely. **2** If you fix something broken, you mend it.

3 If you fix your attention on something, you concentrate on it. **4** If you fix something, you make arrangements for it EG *The opening party is fixed for the 24th September.* **5** AN INFORMAL USE To fix something is to arrange the outcome unfairly or dishonestly. ▶ NOUN **6** AN INFORMAL USE something that has been unfairly or dishonestly arranged. **7** AN INFORMAL USE If you are in a fix, you are in a difficult situation. **8** an injection of a drug such as heroin.
fixed ADJECTIVE, **fixedly** ADVERB
■ (sense 2) mend, repair

fixation fixations
NOUN an extreme and obsessive interest in something.

fixture fixtures
NOUN **1** a piece of furniture or equipment that is fixed into position in a house. **2** a sports event due to take place on a particular date.

fizz fizzes fizzing fizzed
VERB Something that fizzes makes a hissing sound.

fizzle fizzles fizzling fizzled
VERB Something that fizzles makes a weak hissing or spitting sound.

fizzy fizzier fizziest
ADJECTIVE Fizzy drinks have carbon dioxide in them to make them bubbly.

fjord fjords
Said "fee-ord"; also spelt **fiord**
NOUN a long narrow inlet of the sea between very high cliffs, especially in Norway.
■ a Norwegian word

flab
NOUN Flab is large amounts of surplus fat on someone's body.

flabbergasted
ADJECTIVE extremely surprised.

flabby flabbier flabbiest
ADJECTIVE Someone who is flabby is rather fat and unfit, with loose flesh on their body.

flag flags flagging flagged

NOUN **1** a rectangular or square cloth which has a particular colour and design, and is used as the symbol of a nation or as a signal. ▶ VERB **2** If you or your spirits flag, you start to lose energy or enthusiasm.

flagrant
Said "**flay**-grant" ADJECTIVE very shocking and bad in an obvious way EG *a flagrant defiance of the rules.*

flagship flagships
NOUN **1** a ship carrying the commander of the fleet. **2** the most modern or impressive product or asset of an organization.

flail flails flailing flailed
VERB If someone's arms or legs flail about, they move in a wild, uncontrolled way.

flair
NOUN Flair is a natural ability to do something well or stylishly.

flak
NOUN **1** Flak is anti-aircraft fire. **2** If you get flak for doing something, you get a lot of severe criticism.
■ from the first letters of the parts of German *Fliegerabwehrkanone* meaning 'anti-aircraft gun'

flake flakes flaking flaked
NOUN **1** a small thin piece of something. ▶ VERB **2** When something such as paint flakes, small thin pieces of it come off.
flaky ADJECTIVE, **flaked** ADJECTIVE

flamboyant
ADJECTIVE behaving in a very showy and confident.
flamboyance NOUN

flame flames
NOUN **1** a flickering tongue or blaze of fire. **2** A flame of passion, desire, or anger is a sudden strong feeling.
■ from Latin *flamma* meaning 'blazing fire'

flamenco
NOUN Flamenco is a type of very lively, fast Spanish dancing, accompanied by guitar music.

flamingo flamingos or flamingoes

A B C D E F G H I J K L M N O P Q R S T U V W X Y Z

NOUN a long-legged wading bird with pink feathers and a long neck.

flammable

ADJECTIVE likely to catch fire and burn easily.

☑ Although *flammable* and *inflammable* both mean 'likely to catch fire', *flammable* is used more often as people sometimes think that *inflammable* means 'not likely to catch fire'.

flan flans

NOUN an open sweet or savoury tart with a pastry or cake base.

flank flanks flanking flanked

NOUN **1** the side of an animal between the ribs and the hip. ▶ VERB **2** Someone or something that is flanked by a particular thing or person has them at their side EG *He was flanked by four bodyguards.*

flannel flannels

NOUN **1** Flannel is a lightweight woollen fabric. **2** a small square of towelling, used for washing yourself. In Australian English it is called a **washer**.

flap flaps flapping flapped

VERB **1** Something that flaps moves up and down or from side to side with a snapping sound. ▶ NOUN **2** a loose piece of something such as paper or skin that is attached at one edge.

flare flares flaring flared

NOUN **1** a device that produces a brightly coloured flame, used especially as an emergency signal. ▶ VERB **2** If a fire flares, it suddenly burns much more vigorously. **3** If violence or a conflict flares or flares up, it suddenly starts or becomes more serious.

flash flashes flashing flashed

NOUN **1** a sudden short burst of light. **2** If a light flashes, it shines for a very short period, often repeatedly. **3** Something that flashes past moves or happens so fast that you almost miss it. **4** If you flash something, you show it

briefly EG *Michael Jackson flashed his face at the crowd.* ▶ PHRASE **5** Something that happens **in a flash** happens suddenly and lasts a very short time.

flashback flashbacks

NOUN a scene in a film, play, or book that returns to events in the past.

flashlight flashlights

NOUN a large, powerful torch.

flashy flashier flashiest

ADJECTIVE expensive and fashionable in appearance, in a vulgar way EG *flashy clothes.*

flask flasks

NOUN a bottle used for carrying alcoholic or hot drinks around with you.

flat flats; flats flatting flatted; flatter flattest

NOUN **1** a self-contained set of rooms, usually on one level, for living in. **2** In music, a flat is a note or key a semitone lower than that described by the same letter. It is represented by the symbol (♭). ▶ VERB **3** In Australian and New Zealand English, to flat is to live in a flat EG *flatting in London.* ▶ ADJECTIVE **4** Something that is flat is level and smooth. **5** A flat object is not very tall or deep EG *a low flat building.* **6** A flat tyre or ball has not got enough air in it. **7** A flat battery has lost its electrical charge. **8** A flat refusal or denial is complete and firm. **9** Something that is flat is without emotion or interest. **10** A flat rate or price is fixed and the same for everyone EG *The company charges a flat fee for its advice.* **11** A musical instrument or note that is flat is slightly too low in pitch. ▶ ADVERB **12** Something that is done in a particular time flat, takes exactly that time EG *They would find them in two minutes flat.*

flatly ADVERB, **flatness** NOUN

■ (sense 3) even, level

flathead flatheads

NOUN a common Australian edible

fish.

flatten flattens flattening flattened
VERB If you flatten something or if it flattens, it becomes flat or flatter.

flatter flatters flattering flattered
VERB 1 If you flatter someone, you praise them in an exaggerated way, either to please them or to persuade them to do something. 2 If you are flattered by something, it makes you feel pleased and important EG *He was very flattered because she liked him.* 3 If you flatter yourself that something is the case, you believe, perhaps mistakenly, something good about yourself or your abilities. 4 Something that flatters you makes you appear more attractive.
flattering ADJECTIVE
▤ (sense 1) butter up, praise

flattery
NOUN Flattery is flattering words or behaviour.

flatting
PHRASE In New Zealand English, to **go flatting** is to leave home and live with others in a shared house or flat.

flatulence
NOUN Flatulence is the uncomfortable state of having too much gas in your stomach or intestine.
▥ from Latin *flatus* meaning 'gust of wind'

flaunt flaunts flaunting flaunted
VERB If you flaunt your possessions or talents, you display them too obviously or proudly.
☑ Be careful not to confuse *flaunt* with *flout*, which means 'disobey'.

flautist flautists
NOUN someone who plays the flute.

flavour flavours flavouring flavoured
NOUN 1 The flavour of food is its taste. 2 The flavour of something is its distinctive characteristic or quality. ▶ VERB 3 If you flavour food

with a spice or herb, you add it to the food to give it a particular taste.
flavouring NOUN

flaw flaws
NOUN 1 a fault or mark in a piece of fabric or glass, or in a decorative pattern. 2 a weak point or undesirable quality in a theory, plan, or person's character.
flawed ADJECTIVE, **flawless** ADJECTIVE
▤ (sense 1) blemish, spot
▤ (sense 2) fault, weakness

flax
NOUN Flax is a plant used for making rope and cloth.

flay flays flaying flayed
VERB 1 To flay a dead animal is to cut off its skin. 2 To flay someone is to criticize them severely.

flea fleas
NOUN a small wingless jumping insect which feeds on blood.

fleck flecks
NOUN a small coloured mark or particle.
flecked ADJECTIVE

fled
the past tense and past participle of **flee**.

fledgling fledglings
NOUN 1 a young bird that is learning to fly. ▶ ADJECTIVE 2 Fledgling means new, or young and inexperienced EG *the fledgling American President.*

flee flees fleeing fled
VERB To flee from someone or something is to run away from them.

fleece fleeces fleecing fleeced
NOUN 1 A sheep's fleece is its coat of wool. ▶ VERB 2 To fleece someone is to overcharge or swindle them.

fleet fleets
NOUN a group of ships or vehicles owned by the same organization or travelling together.

fleeting
ADJECTIVE lasting for a very short time.

Flemish

NOUN Flemish is a language spoken in many parts of Belgium.

flesh
NOUN 1 Flesh is the soft part of the body. 2 The flesh of a fruit or vegetable is the soft inner part that you eat.
fleshy ADJECTIVE

flew
the past tense of fly.

flex flexes flexing flexed
NOUN 1 ia length of wire covered in plastic, which carries electricity to an appliance. ▶ VERB 2 If you flex your muscles, you bend and stretch them.

flexible
ADJECTIVE 1 able to be bent easily without breaking. 2 able to adapt to changing circumstances.
flexibility NOUN

flick flicks flicking flicked
VERB 1 If you flick something, you move it sharply with your finger. 2 If something flicks somewhere, it moves with a short sudden movement EG His foot flicked forward. ▶ NOUN 3 a sudden quick movement or sharp touch with the finger EG a sideways flick of the head.

flicker flickers flickering flickered
VERB 1 If a light or a flame flickers, it shines and moves unsteadily. ▶ NOUN 2 ia short unsteady light or movement of light EG the flicker of candlelight. 3 A flicker of a feeling is a very brief experience of it EG a flicker of interest.

flight flights
NOUN 1 a journey made by aeroplane. 2 Flight is the action of flying or the ability to fly. 3 Flight is also the act of running away. 4 A flight of stairs or steps is a set running in a single direction.

flight attendant flight attendants
NOUN a person who looks after passengers on an aircraft.

flimsy flimsier flimsiest
ADJECTIVE 1 made of something very thin or weak and not providing much protection. 2 not very convincing EG flimsy evidence.

flinch flinches flinching flinched
VERB If you flinch, you make a sudden small movement in fear or pain.
■ cringe, recoil, wince

fling flings flinging flung
VERB 1 If you fling something, you throw it with a lot of force. ▶ NOUN 2 a short period of unrestricted enjoyment and activity.

flint flints
NOUN Flint is a hard greyish-black form of quartz. It produces a spark when struck with steel.

flip flips flipping flipped
VERB 1 If you flip something, you turn or move it quickly and sharply EG He flipped over the first page. 2 If you flip something, you hit it sharply with your finger or thumb.

flippant
ADJECTIVE showing an inappropriate lack of seriousness EG a flippant attitude to money.
flippancy NOUN

flipper flippers
NOUN 1 one of the broad, flat limbs of sea animals, for example seals or penguins, used for swimming. 2 Flippers are broad, flat pieces of rubber that you can attach to your feet to help you swim.

flirt flirts flirting flirted
VERB 1 If you flirt with someone, you behave as if you are sexually attracted to them but without serious intentions. 2 If you flirt with an idea, you consider it without seriously intending to do anything about it. ▶ NOUN 3 someone who often flirts with people.
flirtation NOUN, **flirtatious** ADJECTIVE

flit flits flitting flitted
VERB To flit somewhere is to fly or move there with quick, light movements.

float floats floating floated
VERB **1** Something that floats is supported by water. **2** Something that floats through the air moves along gently, supported by the air. **3** If a company is floated, shares are sold to the public for the first time and the company gains a listing on the stock exchange. ▶ NOUN **4** a light object that floats and either supports something or someone or regulates the level of liquid in a tank or cistern. **5** In Australian English, a float is also a vehicle for transporting horses.

flock flocks flocking flocked
NOUN **1** a group of birds, sheep, or goats. ▶ VERB **2** If people flock somewhere, they go there in large numbers.

flog flogs flogging flogged
VERB **1** AN INFORMAL USE If you flog something, you sell it. **2** To flog someone is to beat them with a whip or stick.
flogging NOUN

flood floods flooding flooded
NOUN **1** a large amount of water covering an area that is usually dry. **2** A flood of something is a large amount of it suddenly occurring EG *a flood of angry language.* ▶ VERB **3** If liquid floods an area, or if a river floods, the water or liquid overflows, covering the surrounding area. **4** If people or things flood into a place, they come there in large numbers EG *Refugees have flooded into Austria in the last few months.*
■ (sense 1) deluge, spate, torrent
■ (sense 2) stream, torrent

floodgates
PHRASE To **open the floodgates** is suddenly to give a lot of people the opportunity to do something they could not do before.

floodlight floodlights
NOUN a very powerful outdoor lamp used to light up public buildings and sports grounds.

floodlit ADJECTIVE

floor floors flooring floored
NOUN **1** the part of a room you walk on. **2** one of the levels in a building EG *the top floor of a factory.* **3** the ground at the bottom of a valley, forest, or the sea. ▶ VERB **4** If a remark or question floors you, you are completely unable to deal with it or answer it.

floorboard floorboards
NOUN one of the long planks of wood from which a floor is made.

flop flops flopping flopped
VERB **1** If someone or something flops, they fall loosely and rather heavily. **2** AN INFORMAL USE Something that flops fails. ▶ NOUN **3** AN INFORMAL USE something that is completely unsuccessful.

floppy floppier floppiest
ADJECTIVE tending to hang downwards in a rather loose way EG *a floppy, outsize jacket.*
■ droopy, limp

floppy disk floppy disks; also spelt floppy disc
NOUN a small flexible magnetic disk on which computer data is stored.

floral
ADJECTIVE patterned with flowers or made from flowers EG *floral cotton dresses.*

florid
Rhymes with "horrid" ADJECTIVE **1** highly elaborate and extravagant EG *florid language.* **2** having a red face.

florist florists
NOUN a person or shop selling flowers.

floss
NOUN Dental floss is soft silky threads or fibre which you use to clean between your teeth.

flotation flotations
NOUN **1** The flotation of a business is the issuing of shares in order to launch it or to raise money. **2** Flotation is the act of floating.

flotilla flotillas

A
B
C
D
E
F
G
H
I
J
K
L
M
N
O
P
Q
R
S
T
U
V
W
X
Y
Z

Said "flot-**til**-la" NOUN a small fleet or group of small ships.
🔲 from Spanish *flotilla* meaning 'little fleet'

flotsam
NOUN Flotsam is rubbish or wreckage floating at sea or washed up on the shore.

flounce flounces flouncing flounced
VERB **1** If you flounce somewhere, you walk there with exaggerated movements suggesting that you are feeling angry or impatient about something EG *She flounced out of the office.* ▶ NOUN **2** a big frill around the bottom of a dress or skirt.

flounder flounders floundering floundered
VERB **1** To flounder is to struggle to move or stay upright, for example in water or mud. **2** If you flounder in a conversation or situation, you find it difficult to decide what to say or do. ▶ NOUN **3** a type of edible flatfish.

flour
NOUN Flour is a powder made from finely ground grain, usually wheat, and used for baking and cooking.
floured ADJECTIVE, **floury** ADJECTIVE

flourish flourishes flourishing flourished
VERB **1** Something that flourishes develops or functions successfully or healthily. **2** If you flourish something, you wave or display it so that people notice it. ▶ NOUN **3** a bold sweeping or waving movement.

flout flouts flouting flouted
VERB If you flout a convention or law, you deliberately disobey it.
☑ Be careful not to confuse *flout* with *flaunt*, which means 'display obviously'.

flow flows flowing flowed
VERB **1** If something flows, it moves or happens in a steady continuous stream. ▶ NOUN **2** A flow of something is a steady continuous

movement of it; also the rate at which it flows EG *a steady flow of complaints.*

flower flowers flowering flowered
NOUN **1** the part of a plant containing the reproductive organs from which the fruit or seeds develop. ▶ VERB **2** When a plant flowers, it produces flowers.

flowery
ADJECTIVE Flowery language is full of elaborate expressions.

flown
the past participle of **fly**.

flu
NOUN Flu is an illness similar to a very bad cold, which causes headaches, sore throat, weakness, and aching muscles. Flu is short for 'influenza'.

fluctuate fluctuates fluctuating fluctuated
VERB Something that fluctuates is irregular and changeable EG *fluctuating between feeling well and not so well.*

flue flues
NOUN a pipe which takes fumes and smoke away from a stove or boiler.

fluent
ADJECTIVE **1** able to speak a foreign language correctly and without hesitation. **2** able to express yourself clearly and without hesitation.
fluently ADVERB

fluff fluffs fluffing fluffed
NOUN **1** Fluff is soft, light, woolly threads or fibres bunched together. ▶ VERB **2** If you fluff something up or out, you brush or shake it to make it seem larger and lighter EG *Fluff the rice up with a fork before serving.*
fluffy ADJECTIVE

fluid fluids
NOUN **1** a liquid. ▶ ADJECTIVE **2** Fluid movement is smooth and flowing. **3** A fluid arrangement or plan is flexible and without a fixed

structure.

fluidity NOUN

fluke flukes
NOUN an accidental success or piece of good luck.

flung
the past tense of **fling**.

fluorescent
Said "floo-er-ess-nt" ADJECTIVE
1 having a very bright appearance when light is shone on it, as if it is shining itself EG *fluorescent yellow dye*. **2** A fluorescent light is in the form of a tube and shines with a hard bright light.

fluoride
NOUN Fluoride is a mixture of chemicals that is meant to prevent tooth decay.

flurry flurries
NOUN a short rush of activity or movement.

flush flushes flushing flushed
NOUN **1** A flush is a rosy red colour EG *The flowers are cream with a pink flush*. **2** In cards, a flush is a hand all of one suit. ▶ VERB **3** If you flush, your face goes red. **4** If you flush a toilet or something such as a pipe, you force water through it to clean it. ▶ ADJECTIVE **5** AN INFORMAL USE Someone who is flush has plenty of money. **6** Something that is flush with a surface is level with it or flat against it.

flustered
ADJECTIVE If you are flustered, you feel confused, nervous, and rushed.

flute flutes
NOUN a musical wind instrument consisting of a long metal tube with holes and keys. It is held sideways to the mouth and played by blowing across a hole in its side.

fluted
ADJECTIVE decorated with long grooves.

flutter flutters fluttering fluttered
VERB **1** If something flutters, it flaps or waves with small, quick movements. ▶ NOUN **2** If you are in a flutter, you are excited and nervous. **3** AN INFORMAL USE If you have a flutter, you have a small bet.

flux
NOUN Flux is a state of constant change EG *stability in a world of flux*.

fly flies flying flew flown
NOUN **1** an insect with two pairs of wings. **2** The front opening on a pair of trousers is the fly or the flies. **3** The fly or fly sheet of a tent is either a flap at the entrance or an outer layer providing protection from rain. ▶ VERB **4** When a bird, insect, or aircraft flies, it moves through the air. **5** If someone or something flies, they move or go very quickly. **6** If you fly at someone or let fly at them, you attack or criticize them suddenly and aggressively.
flying ADJECTIVE OR NOUN, **flyer** NOUN

fly-fishing
NOUN Fly-fishing is a method of fishing using imitation flies as bait.

flying fox flying foxes
NOUN **1** a large bat that eats fruit, found in Australia and Africa. **2** In Australia and New Zealand, a cable car used to carry people over rivers and gorges.

flying saucer flying saucers
NOUN a large disc-shaped spacecraft which some people claim to have seen.

flyover flyovers
NOUN a structure carrying one road over another at a junction or intersection.

foal foals foaling foaled
NOUN **1** a young horse. ▶ VERB
2 When a female horse foals, she gives birth.

foam foams foaming foamed
NOUN **1** Foam is a mass of tiny bubbles. **2** Foam is light spongy material used, for example, in furniture or packaging. ▶ VERB
3 When something foams, it forms a mass of small bubbles.

A
B
C
D
E
F
G
H
I
J
K
L
M
N
O
P
Q
R
S
T
U
V
W
X
Y
Z

▤ (sense 1) bubbles, froth

fob off fobs off fobbing off fobbed off
VERB; AN INFORMAL USE If you fob someone off, you provide them with something that is not very good or not adequate.

focus focuses or focusses focusing or focussing focused or focussed; focuses or foci
VERB 1 If you focus your eyes or an instrument on an object, you adjust them so that the image is clear. ▸ NOUN 2 The focus of something is its centre of attention EG *The focus of the conversation had moved around during the meal.*
focal ADJECTIVE
☑ When you add the verb endings to *focus*, you can either add them straight to *focus* (*focuses*, *focusing*, *focused*), or you can put another *s* at the end of *focus* before adding the endings (*focusses*, *focussing*, *focussed*). Either way is correct, but the first way is much more common. The plural of the noun is either *focuses* or *foci*, but *focuses* is the commoner.

fodder
NOUN Fodder is food for farm animals or horses.

foe foes
NOUN an enemy.

foetus foetuses
Said "fee-tus"; *also spelt* fetus
NOUN an unborn child or animal in the womb.
foetal ADJECTIVE

fog fogs fogging fogged
NOUN 1 Fog is a thick mist of water droplets suspended in the air. ▸ VERB 2 If glass fogs up, it becomes clouded with steam or condensation.
foggy ADJECTIVE

foil foils foiling foiled
VERB 1 If you foil someone's attempt at something, you prevent them from succeeding. ▸ NOUN 2 Foil is thin, paper-like sheets of metal

used to wrap food. **3** Something that is a good foil for something else contrasts with it and makes its good qualities more noticeable. **4** a thin, light sword with a button on the tip, used in fencing.

foist foists foisting foisted
VERB If you foist something on someone, you force or impose it on them.

fold folds folding folded
VERB 1 If you fold something, you bend it so that one part lies over another. **2** AN INFORMAL USE If a business folds, it fails and closes down. **3** In cooking, if you fold one ingredient into another, you mix it in gently. ▸ NOUN **4** a crease or bend in paper or cloth. **5** a small enclosed area for sheep.
▤ (sense 1) bend, crease, double over

folder folders
NOUN a thin piece of folded cardboard for keeping loose papers together.

foliage
NOUN Foliage is leaves and plants.

folk folks
NOUN 1 Folk or folks are people.
▸ ADJECTIVE **2** Folk music, dance, or art is traditional or representative of the ordinary people of an area.

folklore
NOUN Folklore is the traditional stories and beliefs of a community.

follicle follicles
NOUN a small sac or cavity in the body EG *hair follicles.*

follow follows following followed
VERB 1 If you follow someone, you move along behind them. If you follow a path or a sign, you move along in that direction.
2 Something that follows a particular thing happens after it. **3** Something that follows is true or logical as a result of something else being the case EG *Just because she is pretty, it doesn't follow that she can sing.* **4** If you follow instructions or

advice, you do what you are told. **5** If you follow an explanation or the plot of a story, you understand each stage of it.

follower followers
NOUN The followers of a person or belief are the people who support them.
◪ adherent, supporter

folly follies
NOUN Folly is a foolish act or foolish behaviour.
◪ foolishness, stupidity

fond fonder fondest
ADJECTIVE **1** If you are fond of someone or something, you like them. **2** A fond hope or belief is thought of with happiness but is unlikely to happen.
fondly ADVERB, **fondness** NOUN
◪ (sense 1) affectionate, loving

fondle fondles fondling fondled
VERB To fondle something is to stroke it affectionately.

font fonts
NOUN a large stone bowl in a church that holds the water for baptisms.

food foods
NOUN Food is any substance consumed by an animal or plant to provide energy.
◪ fare, nourishment

food chain food chains
NOUN a series of living things which are linked because each one feeds on the next one in the series. For example, a plant may be eaten by a rabbit which may be eaten by a fox.

foodstuff foodstuffs
NOUN anything used for food.

food technology
NOUN Food technology is the study of foods and what they consist of, and their effect on the body.

fool fools fooling fooled
NOUN **1** someone who behaves in a silly and unintelligent way. **2** a dessert made from fruit, eggs, cream, and sugar whipped together. ▸ VERB **3** If you fool

someone, you deceive or trick them.

foolhardy
ADJECTIVE foolish and involving too great a risk.

foolish
ADJECTIVE very silly or unwise.
foolishly ADVERB, **foolishness** NOUN

foolproof
ADJECTIVE Something that is foolproof is so well designed or simple to use that it cannot fail.

foot feet
NOUN **1** the part of your body at the end of your leg. **2** the bottom, base, or lower end of something EG *the foot of the mountain.* **3** a unit of length equal to 12 inches or about 30.5 centimetres. **4** In poetry, a foot is the basic unit of rhythm containing two or three syllables.
▸ ADJECTIVE **5** A foot brake, pedal, or pump is operated by your foot.

footage
NOUN Footage is a length of film EG *library footage of prison riots.*

football footballs
NOUN **1** Football is any game in which the ball can be kicked, such as soccer, Australian Rules, rugby union, and American football. **2** a ball used in any of these games.
footballer NOUN

foothills
PLURAL NOUN Foothills are hills at the base of mountains.

foothold footholds
NOUN **1** a place where you can put your foot when climbing. **2** a position from which further progress can be made.

footing
NOUN **1** Footing is a secure grip by or for your feet EG *He missed his footing and fell flat.* **2** a footing is the basis or nature of a relationship or situation EG *Steps to put the nation on a war footing.*

footman footmen
NOUN a male servant in a large

A B C D E F G H I J K L M N O P Q R S T U V W X Y Z

house who wears uniform.

footnote footnotes
NOUN a note at the bottom of a page or an additional comment giving extra information.

footpath footpaths
NOUN a path for people to walk on.

footprint footprints
NOUN a mark left by a foot or shoe.

footstep footsteps
NOUN the sound or mark made by someone walking.

for
PREPOSITION **1** meant to be given to or used by a particular person, or done in order to help or benefit them EG *private beaches for their exclusive use*. **2** 'For' is used when explaining the reason, cause, or purpose of something EG *This is my excuse for going to Italy*. **3** You use 'for' to express a quantity, time, or distance EG *I'll play for ages... the only house for miles around*. **4** If you are for something, you support it or approve of it EG *votes for or against independence*.

forage forages foraging foraged
VERB When a person or animal forages, they search for food.

foray forays
NOUN **1** a brief attempt to do or get something EG *her first foray into acting*. **2** an attack or raid by soldiers.

forbid forbids forbidding forbade forbidden
VERB If you forbid someone to do something, you order them not to do it.
forbidden ADJECTIVE

force forces forcing forced
VERB **1** To force someone to do something is to make them do it. **2** To force something is to use violence or great strength to move or open it. ▶ NOUN **3** The use of force is the use of violence or great strength. **4** The force of something is its strength or power EG *The force*

of the explosion shook buildings. **5** a person or thing that has a lot of influence or effect EG *She became the dominant force in tennis*. **6** an organized group of soldiers or police. **7** In physics, force is a pushing or pulling influence that changes a body from a state of rest to one of motion, or changes its rate of motion. ▶ PHRASE **8** A law or rule that is **in force** is currently valid and must be obeyed.
■ (sense 1) compel, drive, make

forceful
ADJECTIVE powerful and convincing EG *a forceful, highly political lawyer*.
forcefully ADVERB

forceps
PLURAL NOUN Forceps are a pair of long tongs or pincers used by a doctor or surgeon.

forcible
ADJECTIVE **1** involving physical force or violence. **2** convincing and making a strong impression EG *a forcible reminder*.
forcibly ADVERB

ford fords fording forded
NOUN **1** a shallow place in a river where it is possible to cross on foot or in a vehicle. ▶ VERB **2** To ford a river is to cross it on foot or in a vehicle.

fore
PHRASE Someone or something that comes **to the fore** becomes important or popular.

forearm forearms
NOUN the part of your arm between your elbow and your wrist.

forebear forebears
NOUN Your forebears are your ancestors.

foreboding forebodings
NOUN a strong feeling of approaching disaster.

forecast forecasts forecasting forecast or forecasted
NOUN **1** a prediction of what will happen, especially a statement

about what the weather will be like. ▶ VERB **2** To forecast an event is to predict what will happen.

forecourt forecourts
NOUN an open area at the front of a petrol station or large building.

forefather forefathers
NOUN Your forefathers are your ancestors.

forefinger forefingers
NOUN the finger next to your thumb.

forefront
NOUN The forefront of something is the most important and progressive part of it.

forego foregoes foregoing forewent foregone; also spelt forgo
VERB If you forego something pleasant, you give it up or do not insist on having it.

foregoing
A FORMAL PHRASE You can say **the foregoing** when talking about something that has just been said EG *The foregoing discussion has highlighted the difficulties.*

foregone conclusion foregone conclusions
NOUN A foregone conclusion is a result or conclusion that is bound to happen.

foreground
NOUN In a picture, the foreground is the part that seems nearest to you.

forehand forehands
NOUN OR ADJECTIVE a stroke in tennis, squash, or badminton made with the palm of your hand facing in the direction that you hit the ball.

forehead foreheads
NOUN the area at the front of your head, above your eyebrows and below your hairline.

foreign
ADJECTIVE **1** belonging to or involving countries other than your own EG *foreign coins... foreign travel.* **2** unfamiliar or uncharacteristic EG *Such daft*

enthusiasm was foreign to him. **3** A foreign object has got into something, usually by accident, and should not be there EG *a foreign object in my eye.*
foreigner NOUN
■ (sense 2) alien, unfamiliar

foreman foremen
NOUN **1** a person in charge of a group of workers, for example on a building site. **2** The foreman of a jury is the spokesman.

foremost
ADJECTIVE The foremost of a group of things is the most important or the best.

forensic
ADJECTIVE **1** relating to or involving the scientific examination of objects involved in a crime.
2 relating to or involving the legal profession.

forerunner forerunners
NOUN The forerunner of something is the person who first introduced or achieved it, or the first example of it.

foresee foresees foreseeing foresaw foreseen
VERB If you foresee something, you predict or expect that it will happen.
foreseeable ADJECTIVE

foresight
NOUN Foresight is the ability to know what is going to happen in the future.

foreskin foreskins
NOUN A man's foreskin is the fold of skin covering the end of his penis.

forest forests
NOUN a large area of trees growing close together.

forestry
NOUN Forestry is the study and work of growing and maintaining forests.

foretaste foretastes
NOUN a slight taste or experience of something in advance.

foretell foretells foretelling

A B C D E F G H I J K L M N O P Q R S T U V W X Y Z

A B C D E F G H I J K L M N O P Q R S T U V W X Y Z

foretold
VERB If you foretell something, you predict that it will happen.

forever
ADVERB permanently or continually.

forewarn forewarns forewarning forewarned
VERB If you forewarn someone, you warn them in advance about something.

foreword forewords
NOUN an introduction in a book.

forfeit forfeits forfeiting forfeited
VERB 1 If you forfeit something, you have to give it up as a penalty.
▶ NOUN 2 something that you have to give up or do as a penalty.

forge forges forging forged
NOUN 1 a place where a blacksmith works making metal goods by hand. ▶ VERB 2 To forge metal is to hammer and bend it into shape while hot. 3 To forge a relationship is to create a strong and lasting relationship. 4 Someone who forges money, documents, or paintings makes illegal copies of them. 5 To forge ahead is to progress quickly.

forgery forgeries
NOUN Forgery is the crime of forging money, documents, or paintings; also something that has been forged.
forger NOUN

forget forgets forgetting forgot forgotten
VERB 1 If you forget something, you fail to remember or think about it. 2 If you forget yourself, you behave in an unacceptable, uncontrolled way.
forgetful ADJECTIVE

forget-me-not forget-me-nots
NOUN a small plant with tiny blue flowers.

forgive forgives forgiving forgave forgiven
VERB If you forgive someone for doing something bad, you stop feeling angry and resentful towards them.
forgiveness NOUN, **forgiving** ADJECTIVE
■ absolve, excuse, pardon

forgo
another spelling of **forego**.

fork forks forking forked
NOUN 1 a pronged instrument used for eating food. 2 a large garden tool with three or four prongs. 3 a y-shaped junction or division in a road, river, or branch. ▶ VERB 4 To fork something is to move or turn it with a fork.
fork out VERB; AN INFORMAL USE If you fork out for something, you pay for it, often unwillingly.

forlorn
ADJECTIVE 1 lonely, unhappy, and uncared for. 2 desperate and without any expectation of success EG *a forlorn fight for a draw*.
forlornly ADVERB

form forms forming formed
NOUN 1 A particular form of something is a type or kind of it EG *a new form of weapon*. 2 The form of something is the shape or pattern of something EG *a brooch in the form of a bright green lizard*. 3 a sheet of paper with questions and spaces for you to fill in the answers. 4 a class in a school. ▶ VERB 5 The things that form something are the things it consists of EG *events that were to form the basis of her novel*. 6 When someone forms something or when it forms, it is created, organized, or started.

formal
ADJECTIVE 1 correct, serious, and conforming to accepted conventions EG *a very formal letter of apology*. 2 official and publicly recognized EG *the first formal agreement of its kind*.
formally ADVERB

formaldehyde
Said "for-**mal**-di-hide" NOUN Formaldehyde is a poisonous, strong-smelling gas, used for

preserving specimens in biology.

formality formalities
NOUN an action or process that is carried out as part of an official procedure.

format formats
NOUN the way in which something is arranged or presented.

formation formations
NOUN **1** The formation of something is the process of developing and creating it. **2** the pattern or shape of something.

formative
ADJECTIVE having an important and lasting influence on character and development EG *the formative days of his young manhood*.

former
ADJECTIVE **1** happening or existing before now or in the past EG *a former tennis champion*. ▶ NOUN **2** You use 'the former' to refer to the first of two things just mentioned EG *If I had to choose between happiness and money, I would have the former*.
formerly ADVERB

formidable
ADJECTIVE very difficult to deal with or overcome, and therefore rather frightening or impressive EG *formidable enemies*.
⬜ from Latin *formido* meaning 'terror'
◼ daunting, intimidating

formula formulae or formulas
NOUN **1** a group of letters, numbers, and symbols which stand for a mathematical or scientific rule. **2** a list of quantities of substances that when mixed make another substance, for example in chemistry. **3** a plan or set of rules for dealing with a particular problem EG *my secret formula for keeping in trim*.

formulate formulates formulating formulated
VERB If you formulate a plan or thought, you create it and express it in a clear and precise way.

fornication
NOUN; A FORMAL WORD Fornication is the sin of having sex with someone when you are not married to them.

forsake forsakes forsaking forsook forsaken
VERB To forsake someone or something is to give up or abandon them.

fort forts
NOUN **1** a strong building built for defence. ▶ PHRASE **2** If you **hold the fort** for someone, you manage their affairs while they are away.

forte fortes
Said "for-tay" **1** In music, forte is an instruction to play or sing something loudly. ▶ NOUN **2** If something is your forte, you are particularly good at doing it.
◼ (sense 2) speciality, strong point

forth
ADVERB **1** out and forward from a starting place EG *Christopher Columbus set forth on his epic voyage of discovery*. **2** into view EG *he brought forth a slim volume of his newly published verse*.

forthcoming
ADJECTIVE **1** planned to happen soon EG *their forthcoming holiday*. **2** given or made available EG *Medical aid might be forthcoming*. **3** willing to give information EG *He was not too forthcoming about this*.

forthright
ADJECTIVE Someone who is forthright is direct and honest about their opinions and feelings.

fortification fortifications
NOUN Fortifications are buildings, walls, and ditches used to protect a place.

fortitude
NOUN Fortitude is calm and patient courage.

fortnight fortnights
NOUN a period of two weeks.
fortnightly ADVERB OR ADJECTIVE

fortress fortresses

A B C D E F G H I J K L M N O P Q R S T U V W X Y Z

NOUN a castle or well-protected town built for defence.

fortuitous
*Said "for-***tyoo***-it-uss"* ADJECTIVE happening by chance or good luck EG *a fortuitous winning goal.*

fortunate
ADJECTIVE **1** Someone who is fortunate is lucky. **2** Something that is fortunate brings success or advantage.
fortunately ADVERB

fortune fortunes
NOUN **1** Fortune or good fortune is good luck. **2** A fortune is a large amount of money. ▶ PHRASE **3** If someone **tells your fortune**, they predict your future.

forty forties
the number 40.
fortieth

forum forums
NOUN **1** a place or meeting in which people can exchange ideas and discuss public issues. **2** a square in Roman towns where people met to discuss business and politics.

forward forwards forwarding forwarded
ADVERB OR ADJECTIVE **1** Forward or forwards means in the front or towards the front EG *A photographer moved forward to capture the moment.* **2** Forward means in or towards a future time EG *a positive atmosphere of looking forward and making fresh starts.* **3** Forward or forwards also means developing or progressing EG *The new committee would push forward government plans.* ▶ ADVERB **4** If someone or something is put forward, they are suggested as being suitable for something. ▶ VERB **5** If you forward a letter that you have received, you send it on to the person to whom it is addressed at their new address. ▶ NOUN **6** In a game such as football or hockey, a forward is a player in an attacking position.
▤ (sense 3) ahead, on

fossick fossicks fossicking fossicked
VERB **1** In Australian and New Zealand English, to fossick for gold nuggets or precious stones is to look for them in rivers or old mines. **2** In Australian and New Zealand English, to fossick for something is to search for it.

fossil fossils
NOUN the remains or impression of an animal or plant from a previous age, preserved in rock.
fossilize VERB

fossil fuel fossil fuels
NOUN Fossil fuels are fuels such as coal, oil, and natural gas, which have been formed by rotting animals and plants from millions of years ago.

foster fosters fostering fostered
VERB **1** If someone fosters a child, they are paid to look after the child for a period, but do not become its legal parent. **2** If you foster something such as an activity or an idea, you help its development and growth by encouraging people to do or think it EG *to foster and maintain this goodwill.*
foster child NOUN, **foster home** NOUN, **foster parent** NOUN

fought
the past tense and past participle of fight.

foul fouler foulest; fouls fouling fouled
ADJECTIVE **1** Something that is foul is very unpleasant, especially because it is dirty, wicked, or obscene. ▶ VERB **2** To foul something is to make it dirty, especially with faeces EG *Dogs must not be allowed to foul the pavement.* ▶ NOUN **3** In sport, a foul is an act of breaking the rules.

found founds founding founded
1 Found is the past tense and past participle of **find.** ▶ VERB **2** If someone founds an organization or institution, they start it and set it up.

foundation foundations
NOUN **1** The foundation of a belief or way of life is the basic ideas or attitudes on which it is built. **2** a solid layer of concrete or bricks in the ground, on which a building is built to give it a firm base. **3** an organization set up by money left in someone's will for research or charity.

founder founders foundering foundered
NOUN **1** The founder of an institution or organization is the person who sets it up. ▶ VERB **2** If something founders, it fails.

foundry foundries
NOUN a factory where metal is melted and cast.

fountain fountains
NOUN an ornamental structure consisting of a jet of water forced into the air by a pump.

fountain pen fountain pens
NOUN a pen which is supplied with ink from a container inside the pen.

four fours
1 the number 4. ▶ PHRASE **2** If you are **on all fours**, you are on your hands and knees.

four-poster four-posters
NOUN a bed with a tall post at each corner supporting a canopy and curtains.

fourteen
the number 14.
fourteenth

fourth
The fourth item in a series is the one counted as number four.

fowl fowls
NOUN a bird such as chicken or duck that is kept or hunted for its meat or eggs.

fox foxes foxing foxed
NOUN **1** a dog-like wild animal with reddish-brown fur, a pointed face and ears, and a thick tail. ▶ VERB **2** If something foxes you, it is too confusing or puzzling for you to understand.

foxglove foxgloves
NOUN a plant with a tall spike of purple or white trumpet-shaped flowers.

foxhound foxhounds
NOUN a dog trained for hunting foxes.

foyer foyers
Said "**foy-ay**" NOUN a large area just inside the main doors of a cinema, hotel, or public building.

fracas
Said "**frak-ah**" NOUN a rough noisy quarrel or fight.

fraction fractions
NOUN **1** In arithmetic, a fraction is a part of a whole number. **2** a tiny proportion or amount of something EG *an area a fraction of the size of London.*
fractional ADJECTIVE, **fractionally** ADVERB

fractious
ADJECTIVE When small children are fractious, they become upset or angry very easily, often because they are tired.

fracture fractures fracturing fractured
NOUN **1** a crack or break in something, especially a bone. ▶ VERB **2** If something fractures, it breaks.

fragile
ADJECTIVE easily broken or damaged EG *fragile glass... a fragile relationship.*
fragility NOUN
■ breakable, delicate, frail

fragment fragments fragmenting fragmented
NOUN **1** a small piece or part of something. ▶ VERB **2** If something fragments, it breaks into small pieces or different parts.
fragmentation NOUN, **fragmented** ADJECTIVE

fragmentary
ADJECTIVE made up of small or unconnected pieces EG *fragmentary notes in a journal.*

fragrance fragrances

NOUN a sweet or pleasant smell.
■ aroma, perfume, scent

fragrant
ADJECTIVE Something that is fragrant smells sweet or pleasant.

frail frailer frailest
ADJECTIVE 1 Someone who is frail is not strong or healthy. 2 Something that is frail is easily broken or damaged.
frailty NOUN

frame frames framing framed
NOUN 1 the structure surrounding a door, window, or picture. 2 an arrangement of connected bars over which something is built. 3 The frames of a pair of glasses are the wire or plastic parts that hold the lenses. 4 Your frame is your body EG *his large frame*. 5 one of the many separate photographs of which a cinema film is made up.
▶ VERB 6 To frame a picture is to put it into a frame EG *I've framed pictures I've pulled out of magazines*. 7 The language something is framed in is the language used to express it.

framework frameworks
NOUN 1 a structure acting as a support or frame. 2 a set of rules, beliefs, or ideas which you use to decide what to do.

franc francs
NOUN the main unit of currency in France, Belgium, Switzerland, and some other countries. A franc is worth 100 centimes.

franchise franchises
NOUN 1 The franchise is the right to vote in an election EG *a franchise that gave the vote to less than 2% of the population*. 2 the right given by a company to someone to allow them to sell its goods or services.

frank franker frankest
ADJECTIVE If you are frank, you say things in an open and honest way.
frankly ADVERB, **frankness** NOUN
■ candid, honest, open

frantic
ADJECTIVE If you are frantic, you

behave in a wild, desperate way because you are anxious or frightened.
frantically ADVERB
▥ from Greek *phrenitikis* meaning 'delirious'

fraternal
ADJECTIVE 'Fraternal' is used to describe friendly actions and feelings between groups of people EG *an affectionate fraternal greeting*.

fraternity fraternities
NOUN 1 Fraternity is friendship between groups of people. 2 a group of people with something in common EG *the golfing fraternity*.

fraud frauds
NOUN 1 Fraud is the crime of getting money by deceit or trickery. 2 something that deceives people in an illegal or immoral way. 3 Someone who is not what they pretend to be.

fraudulent
ADJECTIVE dishonest or deceitful EG *fraudulent cheques*.

fraught
ADJECTIVE If something is fraught with problems or difficulties, it is full of them EG *Modern life was fraught with hazards*.

fray frays fraying frayed
VERB 1 If cloth or rope frays, its threads or strands become worn and it is likely to tear or break.
▶ NOUN 2 a fight or argument.

freak freaks
NOUN 1 someone whose appearance or behaviour is very unusual.
▶ ADJECTIVE OR NOUN 2 A freak event is very unusual and unlikely to happen EG *a freak allergy to peanuts*.

freckle freckles
NOUN Freckles are small, light brown spots on someone's skin, especially their face.
freckled ADJECTIVE

free freer freest; frees freeing freed
ADJECTIVE 1 not controlled or limited

EG *the free flow of aid... free trade.*
2 Someone who is free is no longer a prisoner. **3** To be free of something unpleasant is not to have it EG *She wanted her aunt's life to be free of worry.* **4** If someone is free, they are not busy or occupied. If a place, seat, or machine is free, it is not occupied or not being used EG *Are you free for dinner?* **5** If something is free, you can have it without paying for it. ▶ VERB **6** If you free something that is fastened or trapped, you release it EG *a campaign to free captive animals.* **7** When a prisoner is freed, he or she is released.

▤ (sense 2) at liberty, liberated
▤ (sense 5) complimentary, gratis
▤ (sense 7) liberate, release

freedom
NOUN **1** If you have the freedom to do something, you have the scope or are allowed to do it EG *We have the freedom to decide our own futures.* **2** When prisoners gain their freedom, they escape or are released. **3** When there is freedom from something unpleasant, people are not affected by it EG *freedom from guilt.*

▤ (sense 2) liberty, release

freehold freeholds
NOUN the right to own a house or piece of land for life without conditions.

freelance
ADJECTIVE OR ADVERB A freelance journalist or photographer is not employed by one organization, but is paid for each job he or she does.

freely
ADVERB Freely means without restriction EG *the pleasure of being able to walk about freely.*

free-range
ADJECTIVE Free-range eggs are laid by hens that can move and feed freely on an area of open ground.

freestyle
NOUN Freestyle refers to sports competitions, especially swimming, in which competitors can use any style or method.

freeway freeways
NOUN In Australia, South Africa, and the United States, a road-designed for fast-moving traffic.

free will
PHRASE If you do something **of your own free will**, you do it by choice and not because you are forced to.

freeze freezes freezing froze frozen
VERB **1** When a liquid freezes, it becomes solid because it is very cold. **2** If you freeze, you suddenly become still and quiet, because there is danger. **3** If you freeze food, you put it in a freezer to preserve it. **4** When wages or prices are frozen, they are officially prevented from rising. ▶ NOUN **5** an official action taken to prevent wages or prices from rising. **6** a period of freezing weather.

freezer freezers
NOUN a large refrigerator which freezes and stores food for a long time.

freezing
ADJECTIVE extremely cold.

freight
NOUN Freight is goods moved by lorries, ships, or other transport; also the moving of these goods.

French
ADJECTIVE **1** belonging or relating to France. ▶ NOUN **2** French is the main language spoken in France, and is also spoken by many people in Belgium, Switzerland, and Canada.

French bean French beans
NOUN French beans are green pods eaten as a vegetable, which grow on a climbing plant with white or mauve flowers.

French horn French horns
NOUN a brass musical wind instrument consisting of a tube wound in a circle.

A B C D E F G H I J K L M N O P Q R S T U V W X Y Z

Frenchman Frenchmen
NOUN a man who comes from France.
Frenchwoman NOUN

french window french windows
NOUN French windows are glass doors that lead into a garden or onto a balcony.

frenetic
ADJECTIVE Frenetic behaviour is wild and excited.

frenzy frenzies
NOUN If someone is in a frenzy, their behaviour is wild and uncontrolled.
frenzied ADJECTIVE

frequency frequencies
NOUN **1** The frequency of an event is how often it happens EG *He was not known to call anyone with great frequency.* **2** The frequency of a sound or radio wave is the rate at which it vibrates.

frequent frequents frequenting frequented
ADJECTIVE **1** often happening EG *His visits were frequent... They were at frequent intervals.* ▶ VERB **2** If you frequent a place, you go there often.
frequently ADVERB

fresco frescoes
NOUN a picture painted on a plastered wall while the plaster is still wet.
📖 from Italian *fresco* meaning 'fresh'

fresh fresher freshest
ADJECTIVE **1** A fresh thing replaces a previous one, or is added to it EG *footprints filled in by fresh snow... fresh evidence.* **2** Fresh food is newly made or obtained, and not tinned or frozen. **3** Fresh water is not salty, for example the water in a stream. **4** If the weather is fresh, it is fairly cold and windy. **5** If you are fresh from something, you have experienced it recently EG *a teacher fresh from college.*
freshly ADVERB, **freshness** NOUN

freshwater
ADJECTIVE **1** A freshwater lake or pool contains water that is not salty. **2** A freshwater creature lives in a river, lake, or pool that is not salty.

fret frets fretting fretted
VERB **1** If you fret about something, you worry about it. ▶ NOUN **2** The frets on a stringed instrument, such as a guitar, are the metal ridges across its neck.
fretful ADJECTIVE

Freudian slip Freudian slips
NOUN something that you say or do that reveals your unconscious thoughts.

friar friars
NOUN a member of a Catholic religious order.

friction
NOUN **1** Friction is the force that stops things from moving freely when they rub against each other. **2** Friction between people is disagreement and quarrels.

Friday Fridays
NOUN the day between Thursday and Saturday.
📖 from Old English *Frigedæg* meaning 'Freya's day'. Freya was the Norse goddess of love

fridge fridges
NOUN the same as a **refrigerator**.

friend friends
NOUN Your friends are people you know well and like to spend time with.
▤ chum, companion, mate, pal

friendly friendlier friendliest
ADJECTIVE **1** If you are friendly to someone, you behave in a kind and pleasant way to them. **2** People who are friendly with each other like each other and enjoy spending time together.
friendliness NOUN
▤ (sense 1) amicable, cordial, genial

friendship friendships
NOUN **1** Your friendships are the special relationships that you have

with your friends. **2** Friendship is the state of being friends with someone.

■ (sense 2) friendliness, goodwill

frieze friezes
NOUN a strip of decoration along the top of a wall.

frigate frigates
NOUN a small, fast warship.

fright
NOUN Fright is a sudden feeling of fear.

frighten frightens frightening frightened
VERB If something frightens you, it makes you afraid.
frightened ADJECTIVE, **frightening** ADJECTIVE

frightful
ADJECTIVE very bad or unpleasant EG *a frightful bully*.

frigid
ADJECTIVE Frigid behaviour is cold and unfriendly EG *frigid stares*.

frill frills
NOUN a strip of cloth with many folds, attached to something as a decoration.
frilly ADJECTIVE

fringe fringes
NOUN **1** the hair that hangs over a person's forehead. **2** a decoration on clothes and other objects, consisting of a row of hanging strips or threads. **3** The fringes of a place are the parts farthest from its centre EG *the western fringe of the Amazon basin*.
fringed ADJECTIVE

frisk frisks frisking frisked
VERB; AN INFORMAL USE If someone frisks you, they search you quickly with their hands to see if you are hiding a weapon in your clothes.

frisky friskier friskiest
ADJECTIVE A frisky animal or child is energetic and wants to have fun.

fritter fritters frittering frittered
NOUN **1** Fritters consist of food dipped in batter and fried EG *apple fritters*. ▶ VERB **2** If you fritter away your time or money, you waste it on unimportant things.
🏛 from Latin *frigere* meaning 'to fry'

frivolous
ADJECTIVE Someone who is frivolous behaves in a silly or light-hearted way, especially when they should be serious or sensible.
frivolity NOUN
■ flippant, silly

frizzy frizzier frizziest
ADJECTIVE Frizzy hair has stiff, wiry curls.

frock frocks
NOUN; AN OLD-FASHIONED WORD a dress.

frog frogs
NOUN a small amphibious creature with smooth skin, prominent eyes, and long back legs which it uses for jumping.

frolic frolics frolicking frolicked
VERB When animals or children frolic, they run around and play in a lively way.
🏛 from Dutch *vrolijk* meaning 'joyful'
■ frisk, play, romp

from
PREPOSITION **1** You use 'from' to say what the source, origin, or starting point of something is EG *a call from a public telephone... people from a city 100 miles away*. **2** If you take something from an amount, you reduce the amount by that much EG *A sum of money was wrongly taken from his account*. **3** You also use 'from' when stating the range of something EG *a score from one to five*.

frond fronds
NOUN Fronds are long feathery leaves.

front fronts fronting fronted
NOUN **1** The front of something is the part that faces forward. **2** In a war, the front is the place where two armies are fighting. **3** In meteorology, a front is the line where a mass of cold air meets a

A
B
C
D
E
F
G
H
I
J
K
L
M
N
O
P
Q
R
S
T
U
V
W
X
Y
Z

A B C D E F G H I J K L M N O P Q R S T U V W X Y Z

mass of warm air. **4** A front is an outward appearance, often one that is false EG *I put up a brave front... He's no more than a respectable front for some very dubious happenings.* ▶ PHRASE **5 In front** means ahead or further forward. **6** If you do something **in front of** someone, you do it when they are present.
frontal ADJECTIVE

frontage frontages
NOUN The frontage of a building is the wall that faces a street.

frontier frontiers
NOUN a border between two countries.

frontispiece frontispieces
NOUN a picture opposite the title page of a book.

frost frosts
NOUN When there is a frost, the temperature outside falls below freezing.

frostbite
NOUN Frostbite is damage to your fingers, toes, or ears caused by extreme cold.

frosty frostier frostiest
ADJECTIVE **1** If it is frosty, the temperature outside is below freezing point. **2** If someone is frosty, they are unfriendly or disapproving.

froth froths frothing frothed
NOUN **1** Froth is a mass of small bubbles on the surface of a liquid. ▶ VERB **2** If a liquid froths, small bubbles appear on its surface.
frothy ADJECTIVE

frown frowns frowning frowned
VERB **1** If you frown, you move your eyebrows closer together, because you are annoyed, worried, or concentrating. ▶ NOUN **2** a cross expression on someone's face.

froze
the past tense of **freeze**.

frozen
1 Frozen is the past participle of **freeze**. ▶ ADJECTIVE **2** If you say are

frozen, you mean you are extremely cold.
■ chilled, ice-cold, icy

fructose
*Said "****fruck-toes****"* NOUN Fructose is a type of sugar found in many fruits and in honey.

frugal
ADJECTIVE **1** Someone who is frugal spends very little money. **2** A frugal meal is small and cheap.
frugality NOUN
■ (sense 1) economical, thrifty

fruit fruits
NOUN **1** the part of a plant that develops after the flower and contains the seeds. Many fruits are edible. ▶ PLURAL NOUN **2** The fruits of something are its good results EG *It will be a few years before the fruits of this work are apparent.*

fruitful
ADJECTIVE Something that is fruitful has good and useful results EG *a fruitful experience.*

fruitless
ADJECTIVE Something that is fruitless does not achieve anything EG *a fruitless effort.*

fruit machine fruit machines
NOUN a coin-operated gambling machine which pays out money when a particular series of symbols, usually fruit, appears on a screen.

fruit salad fruit salads
NOUN a mixture of pieces of different fruits served in a juice as a dessert.

fruity fruitier fruitiest
ADJECTIVE Something that is fruity smells or tastes of fruit.

frustrate frustrates frustrating frustrated
VERB **1** If something frustrates you, it prevents you doing what you want and makes you upset and angry EG *Everyone gets frustrated with their work.* **2** To frustrate something such as a plan is to prevent it EG *She hopes to frustrate the engagement of her son.*

frustrated ADJECTIVE, **frustrating** ADJECTIVE, **frustration** NOUN
■ (sense 2) foil, thwart

fry fries frying fried
VERB When you fry food, you cook it in a pan containing hot fat or oil.

fuchsia fuchsias
Said "fyoo-sha" NOUN a plant or small bush with pink, purple, or white flowers that hang downwards.

fudge fudges fudging fudged
NOUN **1** Fudge is a soft brown sweet made from butter, milk, and sugar.
▶ VERB **2** If you fudge something, you avoid making clear or definite decisions or statements about it EG *He was carefully fudging his message.*

fuel fuels fuelling fuelled
NOUN **1** Fuel is a substance such as coal or petrol that is burned to provide heat or power. ▶ VERB **2** A machine or vehicle that is fuelled by a substance works by burning the substance as a fuel EG *power stations fuelled by wood.*

fug
NOUN A fug is an airless, smoky atmosphere.

fugitive fugitives
Said "fyoo-jit-tiv" NOUN someone who is running away or hiding, especially from the police.

fulcrum fulcrums or fulcra
NOUN the point at which something is balancing or pivoting.

fulfil fulfils fulfilling fulfilled
VERB **1** If you fulfil a promise, hope, or duty, you carry it out or achieve it. **2** If something fulfils you, it gives you satisfaction.
fulfilling ADJECTIVE, **fulfilment** NOUN

full fuller fullest
ADJECTIVE **1** containing or having as much as it is possible to hold EG *His room is full of posters.* **2** complete or whole EG *They had taken a full meal... a full 20 years later.* **3** loose and made from a lot of fabric EG *full sleeves.* **4** rich and strong EG *a full,*

fruity wine. ▶ ADVERB **5** completely and directly EG *Turn the taps full on.*
▶ PHRASE **6** Something that has been done or described **in full** has been dealt with completely.
fullness NOUN, **fully** ADVERB
■ (sense 1) filled, loaded, packed

full-blooded
ADJECTIVE having great commitment and enthusiasm EG *a full-blooded sprint for third place.*

full-blown
ADJECTIVE complete and fully developed EG *a full-blown love of music.*

full moon full moons
NOUN the moon when it appears as a complete circle.

full stop full stops
NOUN the punctuation mark (.) used at the end of a sentence and after an abbreviation or initial.

What does the Full Stop do?

The **full stop** (.) marks the end of any sentence which is not a question or an exclamation.

The train is leaving.

A full stop is also used after an abbreviation or initial.

etc. Dr. Jenkins J.R. Hartley

A full stop is also used after an expression that stands by itself but is not a complete sentence.

Good morning.

---

full-time
ADJECTIVE **1** involving work for the whole of each normal working week. ▶ NOUN **2** In games such as football, full time is the end of the match.

fully-fledged
ADJECTIVE completely developed EG *I was a fully-fledged and mature human being.*

fulsome
ADJECTIVE exaggerated and elaborate, and often sounding insincere EG *His most fulsome praise was reserved for his*

A B C D E F G H I J K L M N O P Q R S T U V W X Y Z

mother.

fumble fumbles fumbling fumbled
VERB If you fumble, you feel or
handle something clumsily.

fume fumes fuming fumed
NOUN 1 Fumes are
unpleasant-smelling gases and
smoke, often toxic, that are
produced by burning and by some
chemicals. ▶ VERB 2 If you are
fuming, you are very angry.

fun
NOUN 1 Fun is pleasant, enjoyable
and light-hearted activity. ▶ PHRASE
2 If you **make fun** of someone, you
tease them or make jokes about
them.

**function functions functioning
functioned**
NOUN 1 The function of something
is its purpose or role EG *The proper
function of criticism is to bring about
change for the better.* 2 a large formal
dinner, reception, or party. ▶ VERB
3 When something functions, it
operates or works.

functional
ADJECTIVE 1 relating to the way
something works. 2 designed for
practical use rather than for
decoration or attractiveness EG
*Feminine clothing has never been
designed to be functional.* 3 working
properly EG *fully functional smoke
alarms.*

fund funds funding funded
NOUN 1 an amount of available
money, usually for a particular
purpose EG *a pension fund.* 2 A fund
of something is a lot of it EG *He had
a fund of hilarious tales on the subject.*
▶ VERB 3 Someone who funds
something provides money for it EG
*research funded by pharmaceutical
companies.*
■ (sense 3) finance, subsidize

fundamental fundamentals
ADJECTIVE 1 basic and central EG *the
fundamental right of freedom of
choice... fundamental changes.* ▶ NOUN
2 The fundamentals of something

are its most basic and important
parts EG *teaching small children the
fundamentals of road safety.*

funeral funerals
Said "fyoo-ner-al" NOUN a ceremony
or religious service for the burial or
cremation of a dead person.

funereal
Said "few-nee-ree-al" ADJECTIVE
depressing and gloomy.

fungicide fungicides
NOUN a chemical used to kill or
prevent fungus.

fungus fungi or funguses
NOUN a plant such as a mushroom
or mould that does not have leaves
and grows on other living things.
fungal ADJECTIVE

funk funks funking funked
VERB 1 AN OLD-FASHIONED INFORMAL USE If
you funk something, you fail to do
it because of fear. ▶ NOUN 2 Funk is a
style of music with a strong
rhythm based on jazz and blues.

**funnel funnels funnelling
funnelled**
NOUN 1 an open cone narrowing to
a tube, used to pour substances
into containers. 2 a metal chimney
on a ship or steam engine. ▶ VERB
3 If something is funnelled
somewhere, it is directed through a
narrow space into that place.

funny funnier funniest
ADJECTIVE 1 strange or puzzling EG *You
get a lot of funny people coming into
the libraries.* 2 causing amusement
or laughter EG *a funny old film.*
funnily ADVERB
■ (sense 1) odd, peculiar, strange
■ (sense 2) amusing, comical,
humorous

fur furs
NOUN 1 Fur is the soft thick body
hair of many animals. 2 a coat
made from an animal's fur.
furry ADJECTIVE

furious
ADJECTIVE 1 extremely angry.
2 involving great energy, effort, or

speed EG *the furious speed of technological development.*
furiously ADVERB

furlong furlongs
NOUN a unit of length equal to 220 yards or about 201.2 metres. Furlong originally referred to the length of the average furrow.

furnace furnaces
NOUN a container for a very large, hot fire used, for example, in the steel industry for melting ore.

furnish furnishes furnishing furnished
VERB **1** If you furnish a room, you put furniture into it. **2** A FORMAL USE If you furnish someone with something, you supply or provide it for them.

furnishings
PLURAL NOUN The furnishings of a room or house are the furniture and fittings in it.

furniture
NOUN Furniture is movable objects such as tables, chairs and wardrobes.

furore
Said "fyoo-**roh**-ree" NOUN an angry and excited reaction or protest.
from Italian *furore* meaning 'rage'

furrow furrows furrowing furrowed
NOUN **1** a long, shallow trench made by a plough. ▶ VERB **2** When someone furrows their brow, they frown.

further furthers furthering furthered
1 a comparative form of **far**.
▶ ADJECTIVE **2** additional or more EG *There was no further rain.* ▶ VERB **3** If you further something, you help it to progress EG *He wants to further his acting career.*
(sense 3) advance, promote

further education
NOUN Further education is education at a college after leaving

school, but not at a university.

furthermore
ADVERB; A FORMAL USE used to introduce additional information EG *There is no record of such a letter. Furthermore it is company policy never to send such letters.*

furthest
a superlative form of **far**.

furtive
ADJECTIVE secretive, sly, and cautious EG *a furtive smile.*
furtively ADVERB

fury
NOUN Fury is violent or extreme anger.

fuse fuses fusing fused
NOUN **1** a safety device in a plug or electrical appliance consisting of a piece of wire which melts to stop the electric current if a fault occurs. **2** a long cord attached to some types of simple bomb which is lit to detonate. ▶ VERB **3** When an electrical appliance fuses, it stops working because the fuse has melted to protect it. **4** If two things fuse, they join or become combined EG *Christianity slowly fused with existing beliefs.*

fuselage fuselages
Said "**fyoo**-zil-ahj" NOUN the main part of an aeroplane or rocket.

fusion
NOUN **1** Fusion is what happens when two substances join by melting together. **2** Fusion is also nuclear fusion.

fuss fusses fussing fussed
NOUN **1** Fuss is unnecessarily anxious or excited behaviour. ▶ VERB **2** If someone fusses, they behave with unnecessary anxiety and concern for unimportant things.
(sense 1) bother, commotion, palaver

fussy fussier fussiest
ADJECTIVE **1** likely to fuss a lot EG *He was unusually fussy about keeping things perfect.* **2** with too much

A
B
C
D
E
F
G
H
I
J
K
L
M
N
O
P
Q
R
S
T
U
V
W
X
Y
Z

elaborate detail or decoration EG *fussy chiffon evening wear.*
■ (sense 1) finicky, particular

futile
ADJECTIVE having no chance of success EG *a futile attempt to calm the storm.*
futility NOUN
■ useless, vain

future futures
NOUN **1** The future is the period of time after the present. **2** Something that has a future is likely to succeed EG *She sees no future in a modelling career.* ▶ ADJECTIVE **3** relating to or occurring at a time after the present EG *to predict future events.* **4** The future tense of a verb is the form used to express something that will happen in the future.

Talking about the Future
There is no simple future tense in English. When we talk about an event that will happen in the future, we usually use **compound tenses**.
The auxiliary verbs *will* and *shall* are used before the basic form of the verb to show that an action will happen.
 *His father **will cook** the dinner.*
 *I **shall cook** the dinner.*

You can also talk about the future by putting the verbs *will have* or *shall have* before the verb, and adding the ending *-ed*. This form shows that an action will be completed in the future.
 *His father **will have cooked** the dinner.*
 *I **shall have cooked** the dinner.*

You can also talk about the future by using the phrase *be about to* or *be going to* in front of the dictionary form of the verb. This shows that the action will take place very soon.
 *He **is about to cook** the dinner.*
 *I **am going to cook** the dinner.*

You can sometimes use a form of the present tense to talk about future events, but only if the sentence contains a clear reference to the future.
 *His father **is cooking** the dinner tonight.*
 *The plane **leaves** at three o'clock.*

Also look at the grammar box at **tense**.

futuristic
ADJECTIVE very modern and strange, as if belonging to a time in the future EG *futuristic cars.*

fuzz
NOUN **1** Fuzz is short fluffy hair. ▶ PLURAL NOUN **2** AN INFORMAL USE The fuzz are the police.

g
an abbreviation for 'grams'.

gabble gabbles gabbling gabbled
VERB If you gabble, you talk so fast that it is difficult for people to understand you.

gable gables
NOUN Gables are the triangular parts at the top of the outside walls at each end of a house.

gadget gadgets
NOUN a small machine or tool.
gadgetry NOUN
■ contraption, device

Gaelic
Said "gay-lik" NOUN Gaelic is a language spoken in some parts of Scotland and Ireland.

gaffe gaffes
Said "gaf" NOUN a social blunder or mistake.

gaffer gaffers
NOUN; AN INFORMAL WORD a boss.

gag gags gagging gagged
NOUN 1 a strip of cloth that is tied round someone's mouth to stop them speaking. 2 AN INFORMAL USE a joke told by a comedian. ▶ VERB 3 To gag someone means to put a gag round their mouth. 4 If you gag, you choke and nearly vomit.

gaggle gaggles
NOUN 1 a group of geese. 2 AN INFORMAL USE a noisy group EG a gaggle of schoolboys.
🔟 from Old German gagen meaning 'to cry like a goose'

gaiety
Said "gay-yet-tee" NOUN Gaiety is liveliness and fun.

gaily
ADVERB in a happy and cheerful way.

gain gains gaining gained
VERB 1 If you gain something, you get it gradually EG I spent years at night school trying to gain qualifications. 2 If you gain from a

situation, you get some advantage from it. 3 If you gain on someone, you gradually catch them up.
▶ NOUN 4 an increase EG a gain in speed. 5 an advantage that you get for yourself EG People use whatever influence they have for personal gain.

gait gaits
NOUN Someone's gait is their way of walking EG an awkward gait.

gala galas
NOUN a special public celebration or performance EG the Olympics' opening gala.

galah galahs
NOUN 1 an Australian cockatoo with a pink breast and a grey back and wings. 2 AN INFORMAL USE In Australian English, a galah is also a stupid person.

galaxy galaxies
NOUN an enormous group of stars that extends over many millions of miles.
galactic ADJECTIVE

gale gales
NOUN an extremely strong wind.

gall galls galling galled
Rhymes with "ball" NOUN 1 If someone has the gall to do something, they have enough courage or impudence to do it EG He even has the gall to visit her. ▶ VERB 2 If something galls you, it makes you extremely annoyed.

gallant
ADJECTIVE 1 brave and honourable EG They have put up a gallant fight for pensioners' rights. 2 polite and considerate towards women.
gallantly ADVERB, **gallantry** NOUN

gall bladder gall bladders
NOUN an organ in your body which stores bile and which is next to your liver.

galleon galleons
NOUN a large sailing ship used in the

A B C D E F **G** H I J K L M N O P Q R S T U V W X Y Z

sixteenth and seventeenth centuries.

gallery galleries
NOUN **1** a building or room where works of art are shown. **2** In a theatre or large hall, the gallery is a raised area at the back or sides EG *the public gallery in Parliament.*

galley galleys
NOUN **1** a kitchen in a ship or aircraft. **2** a ship, driven by oars, used in ancient and medieval times.

Gallic
Said "gal-lik" ADJECTIVE; A FORMAL OR LITERARY WORD French.

gallon gallons
NOUN a unit of liquid volume equal to eight pints or about 4.55 litres.

gallop gallops galloping galloped
VERB **1** When a horse gallops, it runs very fast, so that during each stride all four feet are off the ground at the same time. ▶ NOUN **2** a very fast run.

gallows
NOUN A gallows is a framework on which criminals used to be hanged.

gallstone gallstones
NOUN a small painful lump that can develop in your gall bladder.

galore
ADJECTIVE in very large numbers EG *chocolates galore.*
🏛 from Irish Gaelic *go leór* meaning 'to sufficiency'

galoshes
PLURAL NOUN Galoshes are waterproof rubber shoes which you wear over your ordinary shoes to stop them getting wet.

galvanized or **galvanised**
ADJECTIVE Galvanized metal has been coated with zinc by an electrical process to protect it from rust.

gambit gambits
NOUN something which someone does to gain an advantage in a situation EG *Commentators are calling the plan a clever political gambit.*
🏛 from Italian *gambetto* meaning

'a tripping up'

gamble gambles gambling gambled
VERB **1** When people gamble, they bet money on the result of a game or race. **2** If you gamble something, you risk losing it in the hope of gaining an advantage EG *The company gambled everything on the new factory.* ▶ NOUN **3** If you take a gamble, you take a risk in the hope of gaining an advantage.
gambler NOUN, **gambling** NOUN
▤ (sense 1) bet, wager

game games
NOUN **1** an enjoyable activity with a set of rules which is played by individuals or teams against each other. **2** an enjoyable imaginative activity played by small children EG *childhood games of cowboys and Indians.* **3** You might describe something as a game when it is designed to gain advantage EG *the political game.* **4** Game is wild animals or birds that are hunted for sport or for food. ▶ PLURAL NOUN **5** Games are sports played at school or in a competition. ▶ ADJECTIVE **6** AN INFORMAL USE Someone who is game is willing to try something unusual or difficult.
gamely ADVERB
▤ (sense 1) amusement, pastime

gamekeeper gamekeepers
NOUN a person employed to look after game animals and birds on a country estate.

gammon
NOUN Gammon is cured meat from a pig, similar to bacon.

gamut
Said "gam-mut" NOUN; A FORMAL WORD The gamut of something is the whole range of things that can be included in it EG *the whole gamut of human emotions.*

gander ganders
NOUN a male goose.

gang gangs ganging ganged
NOUN **1** a group of people who join

together for some purpose, for example to commit a crime. ▶ VERB **2** AN INFORMAL USE If people gang up on you, they join together to oppose you.

gangplank gangplanks
NOUN a plank used for boarding and leaving a ship or boat.

gangrene
Said "gang-green" NOUN Gangrene is decay in the tissues of part of the body, caused by inadequate blood supply.
gangrenous ADJECTIVE
▥ from Greek *gangraina* meaning 'ulcer' or 'festering sore'

gangster gangsters
NOUN a violent criminal who is a member of a gang.

gannet gannets
NOUN a large sea bird which dives to catch fish.

gaol
another spelling of **jail**.

gap gaps
NOUN **1** a space between two things or a hole in something solid. **2** A gap between things, people, or ideas is a great difference between them EG *the gap between fantasy and reality*.
▤ (sense 1) hole, opening, space

gape gapes gaping gaped
VERB **1** If you gape at someone or something, you stare at them with your mouth open in surprise.
2 Something that gapes is wide open EG *gaping holes in the wall*.

garage garages
NOUN **1** a building where a car can be kept. **2** a place where cars are repaired and where petrol is sold.

garb
NOUN; A FORMAL WORD Someone's garb is their clothes EG *his usual garb of a dark suit*.

garbage
NOUN Garbage is rubbish, especially household rubbish.
▥ from Anglo-French *garbelage*

meaning 'removal of discarded matter'

garbled
ADJECTIVE Garbled messages are jumbled and the details may be wrong.

garden gardens
NOUN **1** an area of land next to a house, where flowers, fruit, or vegetables are grown. ▶ PLURAL NOUN **2** Gardens are a type of park in a town or around a large house.
gardening NOUN

gardener gardeners
NOUN a person who looks after a garden as a job or as a hobby.

gargle gargles gargling gargled
VERB When you gargle, you rinse the back of your throat by putting some liquid in your mouth and making a bubbling sound without swallowing the liquid.

gargoyle gargoyles
NOUN a stone carving below the roof of an old building, in the shape of an ugly person or animal.

garish
Said "gair-rish" ADJECTIVE bright and harsh to look at EG *garish bright red boots*.

garland garlands
NOUN a circle of flowers and leaves which is worn around the neck or head.

garlic
NOUN Garlic is the small white bulb of an onion-like plant which has a strong taste and smell and is used in cooking.

garment garments
NOUN a piece of clothing.

garnet garnets
NOUN a type of gemstone, usually red in colour.

garnish garnishes garnishing garnished
NOUN **1** something such as a a sprig of parsley, that is used in cooking for decoration. ▶ VERB **2** To garnish food means to decorate it with a

A
B
C
D
E
F
G
H
I
J
K
L
M
N
O
P
Q
R
S
T
U
V
W
X
Y
Z

garnish.

garret garrets
NOUN an attic.

garrison garrisons
NOUN a group of soldiers stationed in a town in order to guard it; also used of the buildings in which these soldiers live.

garrotte garrottes garrotting garrotted
Said "gar-**rot**"; also spelt **garotte**
VERB To garrotte someone means to strangle them with a piece of wire.

garter garters
NOUN a piece of elastic worn round the top of a stocking or sock to stop it slipping.

gas gases; gasses gassing gassed
NOUN **1** any airlike substance that is not liquid or solid, such as oxygen or the gas used as a fuel in heating. **2** In American English, gas is petrol. ▸ VERB **3** To gas people or animals means to kill them with poisonous gas.
☑ The plural of the noun *gas* is *gases*. The verb forms of *gas* are spelt with a double *s*.

gas chamber gas chambers
NOUN a room in which people or animals are killed with poisonous gas.

gash gashes gashing gashed
NOUN **1** a long, deep cut. ▸ VERB **2** If you gash something, you make a long, deep cut in it.

gas mask gas masks
NOUN a large mask with special filters attached which people wear over their face to protect them from poisonous gas.

gasoline
NOUN In American English, gasoline is petrol.

gasp gasps gasping gasped
VERB **1** If you gasp, you quickly draw in your breath through your mouth because you are surprised or in pain. ▸ NOUN **2** a sharp intake of breath through the mouth.

gastric
ADJECTIVE occurring in the stomach or involving the stomach EG *gastric pain*.

gate gates
NOUN **1** a barrier which can open and shut and is used to close the entrance to a garden or field. **2** The gate at a sports event is the number of people who have attended it.

gateau gateaux
Said "**gat**-toe" NOUN a rich layered cake with cream in it.

gatecrash gatecrashes gatecrashing gatecrashed
VERB If you gatecrash a party, you go to it when you have not been invited.

gateway gateways
NOUN **1** an entrance through a wall or fence where there is a gate. **2** Something that is considered to be the entrance to a larger or more important thing can be described as the gateway to the larger thing EG *New York is the great gateway to America*.

gather gathers gathering gathered
VERB **1** When people gather, they come together in a group. **2** If you gather a number of things, you bring them together in one place. **3** If something gathers speed or strength, it gets faster or stronger. **4** If you gather something, you learn it, often from what someone says.
▤ (sense 1) assemble, congregate
▤ (sense 2) amass, assemble, collect

gathering gatherings
NOUN a meeting of people who have come together for a particular purpose.

gauche
Said "gohsh" ADJECTIVE; A FORMAL WORD
socially awkward.
▥ from French *gauche* meaning 'left-handed'

gaudy gaudier gaudiest
Said "**gaw**-dee" ADJECTIVE very

colourful in a vulgar way.

■ bright, flashy, garish

gauge gauges gauging gauged
Said "gayj" VERB **1** If you gauge something, you estimate it or calculate it EG *He gauged the wind at over 30 knots.* ▸ NOUN **2** a piece of equipment that measures the amount of something EG *a rain gauge.* **3** something that is used as a standard by which you judge a situation EG *They see profit as a gauge of efficiency.* **4** On railways, the gauge is the distance between the two rails on a railway line.

gaunt
ADJECTIVE A person who looks gaunt is thin and bony.

gauntlet gauntlets
NOUN **1** Gauntlets are long thick gloves worn for protection, for example by motorcyclists. ▸ PHRASE **2** If you **throw down the gauntlet**, you challenge someone. **3** If you **run the gauntlet**, you have an unpleasant experience in which you are attacked or criticized by people.

gave
the past tense of **give**.

gay gayer gayest; gays
ADJECTIVE **1** Someone who is gay is homosexual. **2** AN OLD-FASHIONED USE Gay people or places are lively and full of fun. ▸ NOUN **3** a homosexual person.

☑ The most common meaning of *gay* now is 'homosexual'. In some older books it may have its old-fashioned meaning of 'lively and full of fun'. The noun *gaiety* is related to this older meaning of *gay*. The noun that means 'the state of being homosexual' is *gayness*.

gaze gazes gazing gazed
VERB If you gaze at something, you look steadily at it for a long time.

gazelle gazelles
NOUN a small antelope found in Africa and Asia.

gazette gazettes

NOUN a newspaper or journal.

GB
an abbreviation for **Great Britain**.

GCSE GCSEs
In Britain, the GCSE is an examination taken by school students aged fifteen and sixteen. GCSE is an abbreviation for 'General Certificate of Secondary Education'.

gear gears gearing geared
NOUN **1** a piece of machinery which controls the rate at which energy is converted into movement. Gears in vehicles control the speed and power of the vehicle. **2** The gear for an activity is the clothes and equipment that you need for it. ▸ VERB **3** If someone or something is geared to a particular event or purpose, they are prepared for it.

geese
the plural of **goose**.

gel gels gelling gelled
Said "jel" NOUN **1** a smooth soft jelly-like substance EG *shower gel.* ▸ VERB **2** If a liquid gels, it turns into a gel. **3** If a vague thought or plan gels, it becomes more definite.

gelatine or **gelatin**
Said "jel-lat-tin" NOUN a clear tasteless substance, obtained from meat and bones, used to make liquids firm and jelly-like.

gelding geldings
Said "gel-ding" NOUN a horse which has been castrated.

gem gems
NOUN **1** a jewel or precious stone. **2** You can describe something or someone that is extremely good or beautiful as a gem EG *A gem of a novel.*

Gemini
Said "jem-in-nye" NOUN Gemini is the third sign of the zodiac, represented by a pair of twins. People born between May 21st and June 20th are born under this sign.

gemsbok gemsbok or **gemsboks**

A
B
C
D
E
F
G
H
I
J
K
L
M
N
O
P
Q
R
S
T
U
V
W
X
Y
Z

also spelt **gemsbuck**

NOUN In South African English, a gemsbok is an oryx, a type of large antelope with straight horns.

gen

NOUN; AN INFORMAL WORD The gen on something is information about it.

gender genders

NOUN **1** Gender is the sex of a person or animal EG *the female gender*. **2** the classification of nouns as masculine, feminine, and neuter in certain languages.

What is Gender?

When we talk about the "gender" of a noun, we mean whether it is referred to as *he, she,* or *it*. There are three genders:
masculine (things referred to as *he*),
feminine (things referred to as *she*), and
neuter (things referred to as *it*).

Masculine nouns refer to male people and animals.

  The boy put on his coat. ➤ *boy is masculine*

Feminine nouns denote female people and animals.

  The girl put on her coat. ➤ *girl is feminine*

It is customary to refer to countries and vehicles as if they were feminine.

  The ship came into view, her sails swelling in the breeze.

Neuter nouns refer to inanimate objects and abstract ideas.

  The kettle will switch itself off. ➤ *kettle is neuter*

Common nouns may be either masculine or feminine. Other words in the sentence may tell us if they are male or female.

  The doctor parked his car.
  The doctor parked her car.

---

gene genes

Said "jeen" NOUN one of the parts of a living cell which controls the physical characteristics of an organism and which are passed on from one generation to the next.

general generals

ADJECTIVE **1** relating to the whole of something or to most things in a group EG *your general health.* **2** true, suitable, or relevant in most situations EG *the general truth of science.* **3** including or involving a wide range of different things EG *a general hospital.* **4** having complete responsibility over a wide area of work or a large number of people EG *the general secretary.* ▶ NOUN **5** an army officer of very high rank. ▶ PHRASE **6 In general** means usually.

generally ADVERB
目 (sense 1) overall
目 (sense 2) common, universal, widespread

general election general elections

NOUN an election for a new government, which all the people of a country may vote in.

generalize generalizes generalizing generalized; also spelt **generalise**

VERB To generalize means to say that something is true in most cases, ignoring minor details.

generalization NOUN

general practitioner general practitioners

NOUN a doctor who works in the community rather than in a hospital.

generate generates generating generated

VERB To generate something means to create or produce it EG *using wind power to generate electricity.*

generation generations

NOUN all the people of about the same age; also the period of time between one generation and the next, usually considered to be about 25-30 years.

generator generators

NOUN a machine which produces electricity from another form of energy such as wind or water power.

generic

ADJECTIVE A generic term is a name that applies to all the members of a group of similar things.

generous
ADJECTIVE **1** A generous person is very willing to give money or time. **2** Something that is generous is very large EG *a generous waist.*
generously ADVERB, **generosity** NOUN
▤ (sense 1) lavish, liberal
▤ (sense 2) abundant, ample, lavish

genesis
NOUN; A FORMAL WORD The genesis of something is its beginning.

genetics
NOUN Genetics is the science of the way that characteristics are passed on from generation to generation by means of genes.
genetic ADJECTIVE, **genetically** ADVERB

genial
ADJECTIVE cheerful, friendly, and kind.
genially ADVERB

genie genies
Said "jee-nee" NOUN a magical being that obeys the wishes of the person who controls it.
▥ from Arabic *jinni* meaning 'demon'

genitals
PLURAL NOUN The genitals are the reproductive organs. Technical name: genitalia.
genital ADJECTIVE

genius geniuses
NOUN **1** a highly intelligent, creative, or talented person. **2** Genius is great intelligence, creativity, or talent EG *a poet of genius.*

genocide
Said "jen-nos-side" NOUN; A FORMAL WORD Genocide is the systematic murder of all members of a particular race or group.

genre genres
Said "jahn-ra" NOUN; A FORMAL WORD particular style in literature or art.

genteel
ADJECTIVE very polite and refined.

Gentile Gentiles
Said "jen-tile" NOUN a person who is not Jewish.

gentility
NOUN Gentility is excessive politeness and refinement.

gentle gentler gentlest
ADJECTIVE mild and calm; not violent or rough EG *a gentle man.*
gently ADVERB, **gentleness** NOUN

gentleman gentlemen
NOUN a man who is polite and well-educated; also a polite way of referring to any man.
gentlemanly ADJECTIVE

gentry
PLURAL NOUN The gentry are people from the upper classes.

genuine
Said "jen-yoo-in" ADJECTIVE **1** real and not false or pretend EG *a genuine smile... genuine silver.* **2** A genuine person is sincere and honest.
genuinely ADVERB, **genuineness** NOUN

genus genera
Said "jee-nuss" NOUN In biology, a genus is a class of animals or closely related plants.

geography
NOUN Geography is the study of the physical features of the earth, together with the climate, natural resources and population in different parts of the world.
geographic OR **geographical** ADJECTIVE, **geographically** ADVERB

geology
NOUN Geology is the study of the earth's structure, especially the layers of rock and soil that make up the surface of the earth.
geological ADJECTIVE, **geologist** NOUN

geometric OR **geometrical**
ADJECTIVE **1** consisting of regular lines and shapes, such as squares, triangles, and circles EG *bold geometric designs.* **2** involving geometry.

geometry
NOUN Geometry is the branch of mathematics that deals with lines, angles, curves, and spaces.

Georgian
ADJECTIVE belonging to or typical of the time from 1714 to 1830, when George I to George IV reigned in Britain.

geranium geraniums
NOUN a garden plant with red, pink, or white flowers.

gerbil gerbils
Said "jer-bil" NOUN a small rodent with long back legs, often kept as a pet.

geriatric
Said "jer-ree-at-rik" ADJECTIVE
1 relating to the medical care of old people EG *a geriatric nurse*.
2 Someone or something that is geriatric is very old EG *a geriatric donkey*. ▸ NOUN **3** an old person, especially as a patient.
geriatrics NOUN

germ germs
NOUN **1** a very small organism that causes disease. **2** A FORMAL USE The germ of an idea or plan is the beginning of it.

German Germans
ADJECTIVE **1** belonging or relating to Germany. ▸ NOUN **2** someone who comes from Germany. **3** German is the main language spoken in Germany and Austria and is also spoken by many people in Switzerland.

Germanic
ADJECTIVE **1** typical of Germany or the German people. **2** The Germanic group of languages includes English, Dutch, German, Danish, Swedish, and Norwegian.

German measles
NOUN German measles is a contagious disease that gives you a sore throat and red spots.

germinate germinates germinating germinated
VERB **1** When a seed germinates, it starts to grow. **2** When an idea or plan germinates, it starts to develop.
germination NOUN

gerrymander gerrymanders gerrymandering gerrymandered
VERB To gerrymander is to change political boundaries in an area so that a particular party or politician gets a bigger share of votes in an election.

gestation
Said "jes-tay-shn" NOUN; A TECHNICAL WORD Gestation is the time during which a foetus is growing inside its mother's womb.

gesticulate gesticulates gesticulating gesticulated
Said "jes-stik-yoo-late" VERB If you gesticulate, you move your hands and arms around while you are talking.
gesticulation NOUN

gesture gestures gesturing gestured
NOUN **1** a movement of your hands or head that conveys a message or feeling. **2** an action symbolizing something EG *a gesture of support*.
▸ VERB **3** If you gesture, you move your hands or head in order to communicate a message or feeling.

get gets getting got
VERB **1** Get often means the same as become EG *People draw the curtains once it gets dark.* **2** If you get into a particular situation, you put yourself in that situation EG *We are going to get into a hopeless muddle.* **3** If you get something done, you do it or you persuade someone to do it EG *You can get your homework done in time.* **4** If you get somewhere, you go there EG *I must get home.* **5** If you get something, you fetch it or are given it EG *I'll get us all a cup of coffee... I got your message.* **6** If you get a joke or get the point of something, you understand it. **7** If you get a train, bus, or plane, you travel on it EG *You can get a bus.*
▦ (sense 1) become, grow
▦ (sense 5) acquire, obtain, procure
get across VERB If you get an idea across, you make people understand it.

get at VERB **1** If someone is getting at you, they are criticizing you in an unkind way. **2** If you ask someone what they are getting at, you are asking them to explain what they mean.

get away with VERB If you get away with something dishonest, you are not found out or punished for doing it.

get by VERB If you get by, you have just enough money to live on.

get on VERB **1** If two people get on well together, they like each other's company. **2** If you get on with a task, you do it.

get over with VERB If you want to get something unpleasant over with, you want it to be finished quickly.

get through VERB **1** If you get through to someone, you make them understand what you are saying. **2** If you get through to someone on the telephone, you succeed in talking to them.

getaway getaways
NOUN an escape made by criminals.

get-together get-togethers
NOUN; AN INFORMAL WORD an informal meeting or party.

geyser geysers
Said "gee-zer" NOUN a spring through which hot water and steam gush up in spurts.
🔲 from Old Norse *geysa* meaning 'to gush'

Ghanaian Ghanaians
Said "gah-**nay**-an" ADJECTIVE
1 belonging or relating to Ghana.
▶ NOUN **2** someone who comes from Ghana.

ghastly ghastlier ghastliest
ADJECTIVE extremely horrible and unpleasant EG *a ghastly crime... ghastly food.*

gherkin gherkins
NOUN a small pickled cucumber.

ghetto ghettoes or ghettos
NOUN a part of a city where many poor people of a particular race live.

🔲 from Italian *borghetto* meaning 'settlement outside the city walls'

ghost ghosts
NOUN the spirit of a dead person, believed to haunt people or places.
🟰 phantom, spectre, spirit

ghoulish
Said "**gool**-ish" ADJECTIVE very interested in unpleasant things such as death and murder.

giant giants
NOUN **1** a huge person in a myth or legend. ▶ ADJECTIVE **2** much larger than other similar things EG *giant prawns... a giant wave.*

gibberish
NOUN Gibberish is speech that makes no sense at all.

gibbon gibbons
NOUN an ape with very long arms.

gibe gibes; also spelt jibe
NOUN an insulting remark.

giddy giddier giddiest
ADJECTIVE If you feel giddy, you feel unsteady on your feet usually because you are ill.
giddily ADVERB

gift gifts
NOUN **1** a present. **2** a natural skill or ability EG *a gift for comedy.*

gifted
ADJECTIVE having a special ability EG *gifted tennis players.*

gig gigs
NOUN a rock or jazz concert.

gigantic
ADJECTIVE extremely large.

giggle giggles giggling giggled
VERB **1** To giggle means to laugh in a nervous or embarrassed way. ▶ NOUN **2** a short, nervous laugh.
giggly ADJECTIVE

gilded
ADJECTIVE Something which is gilded is covered with a thin layer of gold.

gill gills
NOUN **1** *Said* "gil" The gills of a fish are the organs on its sides which it uses for breathing. **2** *Said* "jil" a

A
B
C
D
E
F
G
H
I
J
K
L
M
N
O
P
Q
R
S
T
U
V
W
X
Y
Z

unit of liquid volume equal to one quarter of a pint or about 0.142 litres.

gilt gilts
NOUN **1** a thin layer of gold.
▶ ADJECTIVE **2** covered with a thin layer of gold EG *a gilt writing-table.*

gimmick gimmicks
NOUN a device that is not really necessary but is used to attract interest EG *All pop stars need a good gimmick.*
gimmicky ADJECTIVE

gin
NOUN Gin is a strong, colourless alcoholic drink made from grain and juniper berries.

ginger
NOUN **1** Ginger is a plant root with a hot, spicy flavour, used in cooking.
▶ ADJECTIVE **2** bright orangey-brown EG *ginger hair.*

gingerbread
NOUN Gingerbread is a sweet, ginger-flavoured cake.

gingerly
ADVERB If you move gingerly, you move cautiously EG *They walked gingerly down the stairs.*

gingham
NOUN Gingham is checked cotton cloth.
▦ from Malay *ginggang* meaning 'striped cloth'

gipsy
another spelling of **gypsy.**

giraffe giraffes
NOUN a tall, four-legged African mammal with a very long neck.
▦ from Arabic *zarafah* meaning 'giraffe'

girder girders
NOUN a large metal beam used in the construction of a bridge or a building.

girdle girdles
NOUN a woman's corset.

girl girls
NOUN a female child.
girlish ADJECTIVE, **girlhood** NOUN

girlfriend girlfriends
NOUN Someone's girlfriend is the woman or girl with whom they are having a romantic or sexual relationship.

giro giros
Said "jie-roh" NOUN **1** Giro is a system of transferring money from one account to another through a bank or post office. **2** In Britain, a cheque received regularly from the government by unemployed or sick people.

girth
NOUN The girth of something is the measurement round it.

gist
Said "jist" NOUN the general meaning or most important points in a piece of writing or speech.

give gives giving gave given
VERB **1** If you give someone something, you hand it to them or provide it for them EG *I gave her a tape... George gave me my job.* **2** 'Give' is also used to express physical actions and speech EG *He gave a fierce smile... Rosa gave a lovely performance.* **3** If you give a party or a meal, you are the host at it. **4** If something gives, it collapses under pressure. ▶ NOUN **5** If material has give, it will bend or stretch when pulled or put under pressure.
▶ PHRASE **6** You use **give or take** to indicate that an amount you are mentioning is not exact EG *About two years, give or take a month or so.*
7 If something **gives way** to something else, it is replaced by it.
8 If something **gives way**, it collapses.
▤ (sense 1) grant, present, provide
give in VERB If you give in, you admit that you are defeated.
give out VERB If something gives out, it stops working EG *the electricity gave out.*
give up VERB **1** If you give something up, you stop doing it EG *I can't give up my job.* **2** If you give up, you admit that you cannot do

something. **3** If you give someone up, you let the police know where they are hiding.

given
1 the past participle of **give**.
▶ ADJECTIVE **2** fixed or specified EG *My style can change at any given moment.*

glacé
Said "glass-say" ADJECTIVE Glacé fruits are fruits soaked and coated with sugar EG *glacé cherries.*

glaciation
Said "glay-see-ay-shn" NOUN In geography, glaciation is the condition of being covered with sheet ice.

glacier glaciers
Said "glass-yer" NOUN a huge frozen river of slow-moving ice.

glad gladder gladdest
ADJECTIVE happy and pleased EG *They'll be glad to get away from it all.*
gladly ADVERB, **gladness** NOUN

glade glades
NOUN a grassy space in a forest.

gladiator gladiators
NOUN In ancient Rome, gladiators were slaves trained to fight in arenas to provide entertainment.
⊞ from Latin *gladius* meaning 'sword'

gladiolus gladioli
NOUN a garden plant with spikes of brightly coloured flowers on a long stem.

glamour
NOUN The glamour of a fashionable or attractive person or place is the charm and excitement that they have EG *the glamour of Paris.*
glamorous ADJECTIVE

glance glances glancing glanced
VERB **1** If you glance at something, you look at it quickly. **2** If one object glances off another, it hits it at an angle and bounces away in another direction. ▶ NOUN **3** a quick look.

gland glands
NOUN an organs in your body, such

as the thyroid gland and the sweat glands, which either produce chemical substances for your body to use, or which help to get rid of waste products from your body.
glandular ADJECTIVE

glare glares glaring glared
VERB **1** If you glare at someone, you look at them angrily. ▶ NOUN **2** a hard, angry look. **3** Glare is extremely bright light.

glass glasses
NOUN **1** Glass is a hard, transparent substance that is easily broken, used to make windows and bottles. **2** a container for drinking out of, made from glass.

glasses
PLURAL NOUN Glasses are two lenses in a frame, which some people wear over their eyes to improve their eyesight.

glassy
ADJECTIVE **1** smooth and shiny like glass EG *glassy water.* **2** A glassy look shows no feeling or expression.

glaze glazes glazing glazed
NOUN **1** A glaze on pottery or on food is a smooth shiny surface.
▶ VERB **2** To glaze pottery or food means to cover it with a glaze. **3** To glaze a window means to fit a sheet of glass into a window frame.
glaze over VERB If your eyes glaze over, they lose all expression, usually because you are bored.

glazed
ADJECTIVE Someone who has a glazed expression looks bored.

gleam gleams gleaming gleamed
VERB **1** If something gleams, it shines and reflects light. ▶ NOUN **2** a pale shining light.

glean gleans gleaning gleaned
VERB To glean information means to collect it from various sources.

glee
NOUN; AN OLD-FASHIONED WORD Glee is joy and delight.
gleeful ADJECTIVE, **gleefully** ADVERB

A
B
C
D
E
F
G
H
I
J
K
L
M
N
O
P
Q
R
S
T
U
V
W
X
Y
Z

311

glen glens

NOUN a deep, narrow valley, especially in Scotland or Ireland.

glide glides gliding glided

VERB 1 To glide means to move smoothly EG *cygnets gliding up the stream*. 2 When birds or aeroplanes glide, they float on air currents.

glider gliders

NOUN an aeroplane without an engine, which flies by floating on air currents.

glimmer glimmers glimmering glimmered

NOUN 1 a faint, unsteady light. 2 A glimmer of a feeling or quality is a faint sign of it EG *a glimmer of intelligence*.

glimpse glimpses glimpsing glimpsed

NOUN 1 a brief sight of something EG *They caught a glimpse of their hero*. ▶ VERB 2 If you glimpse something, you see it very briefly.

glint glints glinting glinted

VERB 1 If something glints, it reflects quick flashes of light. ▶ NOUN 2 a quick flash of light. 3 A glint in someone's eye is a brightness expressing some emotion EG *A glint of mischief in her blue-grey eyes*.

glisten glistens glistening glistened

Said "gliss-sn" VERB If something glistens, it shines or sparkles.

glitter glitters glittering glittered

VERB 1 If something glitters, it shines in a sparkling way EG *a glittering crown*. ▶ NOUN 2 Glitter is sparkling light.

gloat gloats gloating gloated

VERB If you gloat, you cruelly show your pleasure about your own success or someone else's failure EG *Their rivals were gloating over their triumph*.

global

ADJECTIVE concerning the whole world EG *a global tour*.

global warming

NOUN an increase in the world's overall temperature believed to be caused by the greenhouse effect.

globe globes

NOUN 1 a ball-shaped object, especially one with a map of the earth on it. 2 You can refer to the world as the globe. 3 In South African, Australian, and New Zealand English, a globe is an electric light bulb.

gloom

NOUN 1 Gloom is darkness or dimness. 2 Gloom is also a feeling of unhappiness or despair.

gloomy ADJECTIVE, **gloomily** ADVERB

glorify glorifies glorifying glorified

VERB If you glorify someone or something, you make them seem better than they really are EG *Their aggressive music glorifies violence*.

glorification NOUN

glorious

ADJECTIVE 1 beautiful and impressive to look at EG *glorious beaches*. 2 very pleasant and giving a feeling of happiness EG *glorious sunshine*. 3 involving great fame and success EG *a glorious career*.

gloriously ADVERB

glory glories glorying gloried

NOUN 1 Glory is fame and admiration for an achievement. 2 something considered splendid or admirable EG *the true glories of the Alps*. ▶ VERB 3 If you glory in something, you take great delight in it.

glory box glory boxes

NOUN; AN OLD-FASHIONED WORD In Australian and New Zealand English, a chest in which a young woman stores household goods and linen for her marriage.

gloss glosses glossing glossed

NOUN 1 Gloss is a bright shine on a surface. 2 Gloss is also an attractive appearance which may hide less attractive qualities EG *to put a positive gloss on the events*. 3 If you gloss over a problem or fault, you try to ignore it or deal with it very quickly.

glossary glossaries
NOUN a list of explanations of specialist words, usually found at the back of a book.

glossy glossier glossiest
ADJECTIVE **1** smooth and shiny EG *glossy lipstick*. **2** Glossy magazines and photographs are produced on expensive, shiny paper.
■ (sense 1) lustrous, shiny

glove gloves
NOUN Gloves are coverings which you wear over your hands for warmth or protection.

glow glows glowing glowed
VERB **1** If something glows, it shines with a dull, steady light EG *A light glowed behind the curtains*. **2** If you are glowing, you look very happy or healthy. ▶ NOUN **3** a dull, steady light. **4** a strong feeling of pleasure or happiness.

glower glowers glowering glowered
Rhymes with "**shower**" VERB If you glower, you stare angrily.
■ glare, scowl

glowing
ADJECTIVE A glowing description praises someone or something very highly EG *a glowing character reference*.

glucose
NOUN Glucose is a type of sugar found in plants and that animals and people make in their bodies from food to provide energy.

glue glues gluing or **glueing glued**
NOUN **1** a substance used for sticking things together. ▶ VERB **2** If you glue one object to another, you stick them together using glue.

glum glummer glummest
ADJECTIVE miserable and depressed.
glumly ADVERB

glut gluts
NOUN a greater quantity of things than is needed.

gluten
Said "**gloo-ten**" NOUN a sticky protein found in cereal grains, such as wheat.

glutton gluttons
NOUN **1** a person who eats too much. **2** If you are a glutton for something, such as punishment or hard work, you seem very eager for it.
gluttony NOUN

gnarled
Said "**narld**" ADJECTIVE old, twisted, and rough EG *gnarled fingers*.

gnat gnats
Said "**nat**" NOUN a tiny flying insect that bites.

gnaw gnaws gnawing gnawed
Said "**naw**" VERB **1** To gnaw something means to bite at it repeatedly. **2** If a feeling gnaws at you, it keeps worrying you EG *a question gnawed at him*.

gnome gnomes
Said "**nome**" NOUN a tiny old man in fairy stories.

gnu gnus
Said "**noo**" NOUN a large African antelope.

go goes going went gone
VERB **1** If you go somewhere, you move or travel there. **2** You can use 'go' to mean become EG *She felt she was going mad*. **3** You can use 'go' to describe the state that someone or something is in EG *Our arrival went unnoticed*. **4** If something goes well, it is successful. If it goes badly, it is unsuccessful. **5** If you are going to do something, you will do it. **6** If a machine or clock goes, it works and is not broken. **7** You use 'go' before giving the sound something makes or before quoting a song or saying EG *The bell goes ding-dong*. **8** If something goes on something or to someone, it is allotted to them. **9** If one thing goes with another, they are appropriate together. **10** If one number goes into another, it can be divided into it. **11** If you go back

A B C D E F **G** H I J K L M N O P Q R S T U V W X Y Z

on a promise or agreement, you do not do what you promised or agreed. **12** If someone goes for you, they attack you. **13** If you go in for something, you decide to do it as your job. **14** If you go out with someone, you have a romantic relationship with them. **15** If you go over something, you think about it or discuss it carefully. ▶ NOUN **16** an attempt at doing something. ▶ PHRASE **17** If someone is always **on the go**, they are always busy and active. **18** To go means remaining EG *I've got one more year of my course to go.*

go down VERB **1** If something goes down well, people like it. If it goes down badly, they do not like it. **2** If you go down with an illness, you catch it.

go off VERB **1** If you go off someone or something, you stop liking them. **2** If a bomb goes off, it explodes.

go on VERB **1** If you go on doing something, you continue to do it. **2** If you go on about something, you keep talking about it in a rather boring way. **3** Something that is going on is happening.

go through VERB **1** If you go through an unpleasant event, you experience it. **2** If a law or agreement goes through, it is approved and becomes official. **3** If you go through with something, you do it even though it is unpleasant.

goad goads goading goaded
VERB If you goad someone, you encourage them to do something by making them angry or excited EG *He had goaded the man into near violence.*

go-ahead
NOUN If someone gives you the go-ahead for something, they give you permission to do it.

goal goals
NOUN **1** the space, in games like football or hockey, into which the

players try to get the ball in order to score a point. **2** an instance of this. **3** Your goal is something that you hope to achieve.

goalkeeper goalkeepers
NOUN the player, in games like soccer or hockey, who stands in the goal and tries to stop the other team from scoring.

goanna goannas
NOUN a large Australian lizard.

goat goats
NOUN an animal, like a sheep, with shaggy hair, a beard, and horns.

go-away bird go-away birds
NOUN In South Africa, a go-away bird is a grey lourie, a type of bird which lives in open grassland.

gob gobs
NOUN; AN INFORMAL USE Your gob is your mouth.

gobble gobbles gobbling gobbled
VERB **1** If you gobble food, you eat it very quickly. **2** When a turkey gobbles, it makes a loud gurgling sound.
■ devour, guzzle, wolf

gobbledygook or gobbledegook
NOUN Gobbledygook is language that is impossible to understand because it is so formal or complicated.

goblet goblets
NOUN a glass with a long stem.

goblin goblins
NOUN an ugly, mischievous creature in fairy stories.

god gods
PROPER NOUN **1** The name God is given to the being who is worshipped by Christians, Jews, and Muslims as the creator and ruler of the world. ▶ NOUN **2** any of the beings that are believed in many religions to have power over an aspect of life or a part of the world EG *Dionysus, the Greek god of wine.* **3** If someone is your god, you

admire them very much. ▶ PLURAL NOUN **4** In a theatre, the gods are the highest seats farthest from the stage.

godchild godchildren
NOUN If you are someone's godchild, they agreed to be responsible for your religious upbringing when you were baptized in a Christian church.
goddaughter NOUN, **godson** NOUN

goddess goddesses
NOUN a female god.

godparent godparents
NOUN A person's godparent is someone who agrees to be responsible for their religious upbringing when they are baptized in a Christian church.
godfather NOUN, **godmother** NOUN

godsend godsends
NOUN something that comes unexpectedly and helps you very much.

goggles
PLURAL NOUN Goggles are special glasses that fit closely round your eyes to protect them.

going
NOUN The going is the conditions that affect your ability to do something EG *He found the going very slow indeed.*

gold
NOUN **1** Gold is a valuable, yellow-coloured metal. It is used for making jewellery and as an international currency. **2** 'Gold' is also used to mean things that are made of gold. ▶ ADJECTIVE **3** bright yellow.

golden
ADJECTIVE **1** gold in colour EG *golden syrup.* **2** made of gold EG *a golden chain.* **3** excellent or ideal EG *a golden hero.*

golden rule golden rules
NOUN a very important rule to remember in order to be able to do something successfully.

golden wedding golden weddings
NOUN A married couple's golden wedding is their fiftieth wedding anniversary.

goldfish
NOUN a small orange-coloured fish, often kept in ponds or bowls.

goldsmith goldsmiths
NOUN a person whose job is making jewellery out of gold.

golf
NOUN Golf is a game in which players use special clubs to hit a small ball into holes that are spread out over a large area of grassy land.
golfer NOUN

golf course golf courses
NOUN an area of grassy land where people play golf.

gondola gondolas
*Said "**gon-dol-la**"* NOUN a long narrow boat used in Venice, which is propelled with a long pole.

gone
the past participle of go.

gong gongs
NOUN a flat, circular piece of metal that is hit with a hammer to make a loud sound, often as a signal for something.

good better best; goods
ADJECTIVE **1** pleasant, acceptable, or satisfactory EG *good news... a good film.* **2** skilful or successful EG *good at art.* **3** kind, thoughtful, and loving EG *She was grateful to him for being so good to her.* **4** well-behaved EG *Have the children been good?* **5** used to emphasize something EG *a good few million pounds.* ▶ NOUN **6** Good is moral and spiritual justice and rightness EG *the forces of good and evil.* **7** Good also refers to anything that is desirable or beneficial as opposed to harmful EG *The break has done me good.* ▶ PLURAL NOUN **8** Goods are objects that people own or that are sold in shops EG *leather goods.*
▶ PHRASE **9** For good means for ever. **10** As good as means almost EG *The*

A B C D E F G H I J K L M N O P Q R S T U V W X Y Z

election is as good as decided.

☑ *Good* is an adjective, and should not be used as an adverb. You should say that *a person did well* not *did good*.

goodbye

You say goodbye when you are leaving someone or ending a telephone conversation.

Good Friday

NOUN Good Friday is the Friday before Easter, when Christians remember the crucifixion of Christ.

good-natured

ADJECTIVE friendly, pleasant and even-tempered.

goodness

NOUN 1 Goodness is the quality of being kind. ▶ INTERJECTION 2 People say 'Goodness!' or 'My goodness!' when they are surprised.

goodwill

NOUN Goodwill is kindness and helpfulness EG *Messages of goodwill were exchanged.*

goody goodies

NOUN 1 AN INFORMAL WORD Goodies are enjoyable things, often food. 2 You can call a hero in a film or book a goody.

goose geese

NOUN a fairly large bird with webbed feet and a long neck.

gooseberry gooseberries

NOUN a round, green berry that grows on a bush and has a sharp taste.

gore gores goring gored

VERB 1 If an animal gores someone, it wounds them badly with its horns or tusks. ▶ NOUN 2 Gore is clotted blood from a wound.

gorge gorges gorging gorged

NOUN 1 a deep, narrow valley. ▶ VERB 2 If you gorge yourself, you eat a lot of food greedily.

gorgeous

ADJECTIVE extremely pleasant or attractive EG *a gorgeous man.*

gorilla gorillas

NOUN a very large, ape with very dark fur.

🔟 from *Gorillai*, the Greek name for an African tribe with hairy bodies

gorse

NOUN Gorse is a dark green wild shrub that has sharp prickles and small yellow flowers.

gory gorier goriest

ADJECTIVE Gory situations involve people being injured in horrible ways.

gosling goslings

Said "goz-ling" NOUN a young goose.

gospel gospels

NOUN 1 The Gospels are the four books in the New Testament which describe the life and teachings of Jesus Christ. 2 a set of ideas that someone strongly believes in EG *the so-called gospel of work.* ▶ ADJECTIVE 3 Gospel music is a style of religious music popular among Black Christians in the United States.

gossip gossips gossiping gossiped

NOUN 1 Gossip is informal conversation, often concerning people's private affairs. 2 Someone who is a gossip enjoys talking about other people's private affairs. ▶ VERB 3 If you gossip, you talk informally with someone, especially about other people.

got

1 Got is the past tense and past participle of get. 2 You can use 'have got' instead of the more formal 'have' when talking about possessing things EG *The director has got a map.* 3 You can use 'have got to' instead of the more formal 'have to' when talking about something that must be done EG *He has got to win.*

gouge gouges gouging gouged

Said "gowj" VERB 1 If you gouge a hole in something, you make a hole in it with a pointed object. 2 If you gouge something out, you force it out of position with your fingers or a sharp tool.

gourd gourds
Said "goord" NOUN a large fruit with a hard outside.

gourmet gourmets
Said "goor-may" NOUN a person who enjoys good food and drink and knows a lot about it.

gout
NOUN Gout is a disease which causes someone's joints to swell painfully, especially in their toes.

govern governs governing governed
VERB 1 To govern a country means to control it. 2 Something that governs a situation influences it EG *Our thinking is as much governed by habit as by behaviour.*

governess governesses
NOUN a woman who is employed to teach the children in a family and who lives with the family.

government governments
NOUN 1 The government is the group of people who govern a country. 2 Government is the control and organization of a country.
governmental ADJECTIVE

governor governors
NOUN 1 a person who controls and organizes a state or an institution. 2 In Australia, the Governor is the representative of the King or Queen in a State.

governor-general governors-general
NOUN the chief representative of the King or Queen in Australia, New Zealand, and other Commonwealth countries.

gown gowns
NOUN 1 a long, formal dress. 2 a long, dark cloak worn by people such as judges and lawyers.

GP
an abbreviation for **general**

practitioner.

grab grabs grabbing grabbed
VERB 1 If you grab something, you take it or pick it up roughly. 2 If you grab an opportunity, you take advantage of it eagerly. 3 AN INFORMAL USE If an idea grabs you, it excites you. ▶ NOUN 4 A grab at an object is an attempt to grab it.
■ (senses 1 & 2) grasp, seize, snatch

grace graces gracing graced
NOUN 1 Grace is an elegant way of moving. 2 Grace is also a pleasant, kind way of behaving. 3 Grace is also a short prayer of thanks said before a meal. 4 Dukes and archbishops are addressed as 'Your Grace' and referred to as 'His Grace'. ▶ VERB 5 Something that graces a place makes it more attractive. 6 If someone important graces an event, they kindly agree to be present at it.
graceful ADJECTIVE, **gracefully** ADVERB
■ (sense 1) elegance, poise

gracious
ADJECTIVE 1 kind, polite, and pleasant. 2 'Good gracious' is an exclamation of surprise.
graciously ADVERB

grade grades grading graded
VERB 1 To grade things means to arrange them according to quality. ▶ NOUN 2 The grade of something is its quality. 3 the mark that you get for an exam or piece of written work. 4 Your grade in a company or organization is your level of importance or your rank.

gradient gradients
NOUN a slope or the steepness of a slope.

gradual
ADJECTIVE happening or changing slowly over a long period of time.

gradually
ADVERB happening or changing slowly over a long period of time.

graduate graduates graduating graduated
NOUN 1 a person who has completed

A
B
C
D
E
F
G
H
I
J
K
L
M
N
O
P
Q
R
S
T
U
V
W
X
Y
Z

a first degree at a university or college. ▶ VERB **2** When students graduate, they complete a first degree at a university or college. **3** To graduate from one thing to another means to progress gradually towards the second thing.
graduation NOUN

graffiti
Said "graf-**fee**-tee" NOUN Graffiti is slogans or drawings scribbled on walls.
⌸ from Italian *graffiare* meaning 'to scratch a surface'
☑ Although *graffiti* is a plural in Italian, the language it comes from, in English it can be used as a singular noun or a plural noun.

graft grafts grafting grafted
NOUN **1** a piece of living tissue which is used to replace by surgery a damaged or unhealthy part of a person's body. **2** AN INFORMAL USE Graft is hard work. ▶ VERB **3** To graft one thing to another means to attach it.

grain grains
NOUN **1** a cereal plant, such as wheat, that is grown as a crop and used for food. **2** Grains are seeds of a cereal plant. **3** A grain of sand or salt is a tiny particle of it. **4** The grain of a piece of wood is the pattern of lines made by the fibres in it. ▶ PHRASE **5** If something **goes against the grain**, you find it difficult to accept because it is against your principles.
▤ (sense 3) bit, granule, particle

gram grams; also spelt **gramme**
NOUN a unit of weight equal to one thousandth of a kilogram.

grammar
NOUN Grammar is the rules of a language relating to the ways you can combine words to form sentences.

grammar school grammar schools
NOUN **1** a secondary school for pupils of high academic ability.

2 In Australia, a private school, usually one controlled by a church.

grammatical
ADJECTIVE **1** relating to grammar EG *grammatical knowledge.* **2** following the rules of grammar correctly EG *grammatical sentences.*
grammatically ADVERB

gran grans
NOUN; AN INFORMAL WORD Your gran is your grandmother.

granary granaries
NOUN **1** a building for storing grain. ▶ ADJECTIVE **2** A TRADEMARK Granary bread contains whole grains of wheat.'

grand grander grandest
ADJECTIVE **1** magnificent in appearance and size EG *a grand house.* **2** very important EG *the grand scheme of your life.* **3** AN INFORMAL USE very pleasant or enjoyable EG *It was a grand day.* **4** A grand total is the final complete amount. ▶ NOUN **5** AN INFORMAL USE a thousand pounds or dollars.
grandly ADVERB
▤ (sense 1) impressive, magnificent, splendid

grandad grandads
NOUN; AN INFORMAL WORD Your grandad is your grandfather.

grandchild grandchildren
NOUN Someone's grandchildren are the children of their son or daughter.

granddaughter granddaughters
NOUN Someone's granddaughter is the daughter of their son or daughter.

grandeur
Said "grand-yer" NOUN Grandeur is great beauty and magnificence.

grandfather grandfathers
NOUN Your grandfather is your father's father or your mother's father.

grandfather clock grandfather clocks
NOUN a clock in a tall wooden case

that stands on the floor.

grandiose
Said "**gran**-dee-ose" ADJECTIVE intended to be very impressive, but seeming ridiculous EG *a grandiose gesture of love*.

grandma grandmas
NOUN; AN INFORMAL WORD Your grandma is your grandmother.

grandmother grandmothers
NOUN Your grandmother is your father's mother or your mother's mother.

grandparent grandparents
NOUN Your grandparents are your parents' parents.

grand piano grand pianos
NOUN a large flat piano with horizontal strings.

grandson grandsons
NOUN Someone's grandson is the son of their son or daughter.

grandstand grandstands
NOUN a structure with a roof and seats for spectators at a sports ground.

granite
Said "**gran**-nit" NOUN Granite is a very hard rock used in building.

granny grannies
NOUN; AN INFORMAL WORD Your granny is your grandmother.

grant grants granting granted
NOUN **1** an amount of money that an official body gives to someone for a particular purpose EG *a grant to carry out repairs*. ▶ VERB **2** If you grant something to someone, you allow them to have it. **3** If you grant that something is true, you admit that it is true. ▶ PHRASES **4** If you take **something for granted**, you believe it without thinking about it. If you take **someone for granted**, you benefit from them without showing that you are grateful.

granule granules
NOUN a very small piece of something EG *granules of salt*.

grape grapes
NOUN a small green or purple fruit, eaten raw or used to make wine.

grapefruit grapefruits
NOUN a large, round, yellow citrus fruit.

grapevine grapevines
NOUN **1** a climbing plant which grapes grow on. **2** If you hear some news on the grapevine, it has been passed on from person to person, usually unofficially or secretly.

graph graphs
NOUN a diagram in which a line shows how two sets of numbers or measurements are related.

graphic graphics
ADJECTIVE **1** A graphic description is very detailed and lifelike. **2** relating to drawing or painting. ▶ PLURAL NOUN **3** Graphics are drawings and pictures composed of simple lines and strong colours EG *computerized graphics*.
graphically ADVERB

grapple grapples grappling grappled
VERB **1** If you grapple with someone, you struggle with them while fighting. **2** If you grapple with a problem, you try hard to solve it.

grasp grasps grasping grasped
VERB **1** If you grasp something, you hold it firmly. **2** If you grasp an idea, you understand it. ▶ NOUN **3** a firm hold. **4** Your grasp of something is your understanding of it.

grass grasses
NOUN Grass is the common green plant that grows on lawns and in parks.
grassy ADJECTIVE

grasshopper grasshoppers
NOUN an insect with long back legs which it uses for jumping and making a high-pitched sound.

grate grates grating grated
NOUN **1** a framework of metal bars in a fireplace. ▶ VERB **2** To grate food

means to shred it into small pieces by rubbing it against a grater. **3** When something grates on something else, it rubs against it making a harsh sound. **4** If something grates on you, it irritates you.

grateful
ADJECTIVE If you are grateful for something, you are glad you have it and want to thank the person who gave it to you.
gratefully ADVERB
≡ appreciative, thankful

grater graters
NOUN a small metal tool used for grating food.

gratify gratifies gratifying gratified
VERB **1** If you are gratified by something, you are pleased by it. **2** If you gratify a wish or feeling, you satisfy it.

grating gratings
NOUN **1** a metal frame with bars across it fastened over a hole in a wall or in the ground. ▶ ADJECTIVE **2** A grating sound is harsh and unpleasant EG *grating melodies*.

gratis
*Said "***grah-tis***"* ADVERB OR ADJECTIVE free EG *food and drink supplied gratis*.

gratitude
NOUN Gratitude is the feeling of being grateful.
≡ appreciation, thankfulness

gratuitous
*Said "***grat-yoo-it-tuss***"* ADJECTIVE unnecessary EG *a gratuitous attack*.
gratuitously ADVERB

grave graves; graver gravest
*Rhymes with "***save***"* NOUN **1** a place where a corpse is buried. ▶ ADJECTIVE **2** A FORMAL USE very serious EG *grave danger*.

grave
*Said "***grahv***"* ADJECTIVE In French and some other languages, a grave accent is a line sloping downwards from left to right placed over a

vowel to indicate a change in pronunciation, as in the word *lèvre*.

gravel
NOUN Gravel is small stones used for making roads and paths.

gravestone gravestones
NOUN a large stone placed over someone's grave, with their name on it.

graveyard graveyards
NOUN an area of land where corpses are buried.

gravitate gravitates gravitating gravitated
VERB When people gravitate towards something, they go towards it because they are attracted by it.

gravitation
NOUN Gravitation is the force which causes objects to be attracted to each other.

gravity
NOUN **1** Gravity is the force that makes things fall when you drop them. **2** A FORMAL USE The gravity of a situation is its seriousness.

gravy
NOUN Gravy is a brown sauce made from meat juices.

graze grazes grazing grazed
VERB **1** When animals graze, they eat grass. **2** If something grazes a part of your body, it scrapes against it, injuring you slightly. ▶ NOUN **3** a slight injury caused by something scraping against your skin.

grease greases greasing greased
NOUN **1** Grease is an oily substance used for lubricating machines. **2** Grease is also melted animal fat, used in cooking. **3** Grease is also an oily substance produced by your skin and found in your hair. ▶ VERB **4** If you grease something, you lubricate it with grease.
greasy ADJECTIVE

great greater greatest
ADJECTIVE **1** very large EG *a great sea... great efforts*. **2** very important EG *a great artist*. **3** AN INFORMAL USE very

good EG *Paul had a great time.*
greatly ADVERB, **greatness** NOUN

Great Britain
NOUN Great Britain is the largest of
the British Isles, consisting of
England, Scotland, and Wales.

Great Dane Great Danes
NOUN a very large dog with short
hair.

great-grandfather
great-grandfathers
NOUN Your great-grandfather is your
father's or mother's grandfather.

great-grandmother
great-grandmothers
NOUN Your great-grandmother is
your father's or mother's
grandmother.

greed
NOUN Greed is a desire for more of
something than you really need.

greedy greedier greediest
ADJECTIVE wanting more of
something than you really need.
greedily ADVERB, **greediness** NOUN
■ grasping, insatiable, voracious

Greek Greeks
ADJECTIVE **1** belonging or relating to
Greece. ▶ NOUN **2** someone who
comes from Greece. **3** Greek is the
main language spoken in Greece.

green greener greenest; greens
ADJECTIVE OR NOUN **1** Green is a colour
between yellow and blue on the
spectrum. ▶ NOUN **2** an area of grass
in the middle of a village. **3** A
putting green or bowling green is a
grassy area on which putting or
bowls is played. **4** an area of
smooth short grass around each
hole on a golf course. ▶ PLURAL NOUN
5 Greens are green vegetables.
▶ ADJECTIVE **6** 'Green' is used to
describe political movements
which are concerned with
environmental issues. **7** AN INFORMAL
USE Someone who is green is young
and inexperienced.

greenery
NOUN Greenery is a lot of trees,
bushes, or other green plants
together in one place.

greenfly
NOUN Greenfly are small green
insects that damage plants.

greengrocer greengrocers
NOUN a shopkeeper who sells
vegetables and fruit.

greenhouse greenhouses
NOUN a glass building in which
people grow plants that need to be
kept warm.

greenhouse effect
NOUN the gradual rise in
temperature in the earth's
atmosphere due to heat being
absorbed from the sun and being
trapped by gases such as carbon
dioxide in the air around the earth.

green paper green papers
NOUN In Britain, Australia, and New
Zealand, a report published by the
government containing proposals
to be discussed before decisions are
made about them.

greenstone
NOUN a type of jade found in New
Zealand and used for making
ornaments, weapons, and tools.

greet greets greeting greeted
VERB **1** If you greet someone, you say
something friendly like 'hello' to
them when you meet them. **2** If
you greet something in a particular
way, you react to it in that way EG
He was greeted with deep suspicion.
■ (sense 1) hail, salute

greeting greetings
NOUN something friendly that you
say to someone when you meet
them EG *Her greeting was warm.*

gregarious
Said "grig-air-ee-uss" ADJECTIVE; A
FORMAL WORD Someone who is
gregarious enjoys being with other
people.

grenade grenades
NOUN a small bomb, containing
explosive or tear gas, which can be
thrown.

A
B
C
D
E
F
G
H
I
J
K
L
M
N
O
P
Q
R
S
T
U
V
W
X
Y
Z

A
B
C
D
E
F
G
H
I
J
K
L
M
N
O
P
Q
R
S
T
U
V
W
X
Y
Z

🗌 from Spanish *granada* meaning 'pomegranate'

grevillea grevilleas
NOUN an evergreen Australian tree or shrub.

grew
the past tense of **grow**.

grey greyer greyest; greys greying greyed
ADJECTIVE OR NOUN **1** Grey is a colour between black and white. ▶ ADJECTIVE **2** dull and boring EG *He's a bit of a grey man*. ▶ VERB **3** If someone is greying, their hair is going grey.
greyness NOUN

greyhound greyhounds
NOUN a thin dog with long legs that can run very fast.

grid grids
NOUN **1** a pattern of lines crossing each other to form squares. **2** The grid is the network of wires and cables by which electricity is distributed throughout a country.

grief
NOUN **1** Grief is extreme sadness. ▶ PHRASE **2** If someone or something **comes to grief**, they fail or are injured.
🗌 (sense 1) heartache, sadness, sorrow

grievance grievances
NOUN a reason for complaining.

grieve grieves grieving grieved
VERB **1** If you grieve, you are extremely sad, especially because someone has died. **2** If something grieves you, it makes you feel very sad.
🗌 (sense 1) lament, mourn

grievous
ADJECTIVE; A FORMAL WORD extremely serious EG *grievous damage*.
grievously ADVERB

grill grills grilling grilled
NOUN **1** a part on a cooker where food is cooked by strong heat from above. **2** a metal frame on which you cook food over a fire. ▶ VERB **3** If you grill food, you cook it on or under a grill. **4** AN INFORMAL USE If you grill someone, you ask them a lot of questions in a very intense way.

grille grilles
Rhymes with "pill" NOUN a metal framework over a window or piece of machinery, used for protection.

grim grimmer grimmest
ADJECTIVE **1** If a situation or piece of news is grim, it is very unpleasant and worrying EG *There are grim times ahead*. **2** Grim places are unattractive and depressing. **3** If someone is grim, they are very serious or stern.
grimly ADVERB

grimace grimaces grimacing grimaced
Said "grim-mace" NOUN **1** a twisted facial expression indicating disgust or pain. ▶ VERB **2** When someone grimaces, they make a grimace.

grime
NOUN Grime is thick dirt which gathers on the surface of something.
grimy ADJECTIVE

grin grins grinning grinned
VERB **1** If you grin, you smile broadly. ▶ NOUN **2** a broad smile. ▶ PHRASE **3** If you **grin and bear it**, you accept a difficult situation without complaining.

grind grinds grinding ground
VERB **1** If you grind something such as pepper, you crush it into a fine powder. **2** If you grind your teeth, you rub your upper and lower teeth together. ▶ PHRASE **3** If something **grinds to a halt**, it stops EG *Progress ground to a halt*.
🗌 (sense 1) crush, powder, pulverize

grip grips gripping gripped
VERB **1** If you grip something, you hold it firmly. ▶ NOUN **2** a firm hold. **3** a handle on a bat or a racket. **4** Your grip on a situation is your control over it. ▶ PHRASE **5** If you **get to grips with** a situation or problem, you start to deal with it effectively.

grisly grislier grisliest
ADJECTIVE very nasty and horrible EG *a grisly murder scene.*

grit grits gritting gritted
NOUN **1** Grit consists of very small stones. It is put on icy roads to make them less slippery. ▶ VERB **2** When workmen grit an icy road, they put grit on it. ▶ PHRASE **3** To **grit your teeth** means to decide to carry on in a difficult situation.
gritty ADJECTIVE

grizzled
ADJECTIVE Grizzled hair is grey. A grizzled person has grey hair.

grizzly bear grizzly bears
NOUN a large, greyish-brown bear from North America.

groan groans groaning groaned
VERB **1** If you groan, you make a long, low sound of pain, unhappiness, or disapproval. ▶ NOUN **2** the sound you make when you groan.

grocer grocers
NOUN a shopkeeper who sells many kinds of food and other household goods.

grocery groceries
NOUN **1** a grocer's shop. ▶ PLURAL NOUN **2** Groceries are the goods that you buy in a grocer's shop.

grog
NOUN; AN INFORMAL WORD In Australian and New Zealand English, grog is any alcoholic drink.

groin groins
NOUN the area where your legs join the main part of your body at the front.

groom grooms grooming groomed
NOUN **1** someone who looks after horses in a stable. **2** At a wedding, the groom is the bridegroom. ▶ VERB **3** To groom an animal means to clean its fur. **4** If you groom someone for a job, you prepare them for it by teaching them the skills they will need.

groove grooves
NOUN a deep line cut into a surface.
grooved ADJECTIVE

grope gropes groping groped
VERB **1** If you grope for something you cannot see, you search for it with your hands. **2** If you grope for something such as the solution to a problem, you try to think of it.

gross grosser grossest; grosses grossing grossed
ADJECTIVE **1** extremely bad EG *a gross betrayal.* **2** Gross speech or behaviour is very rude. **3** Gross things are ugly EG *gross holiday outfits.* **4** Someone's gross income is their total income before any deductions are made. **5** The gross weight of something is its total weight including the weight of its container. ▶ VERB **6** If you gross an amount of money, you earn that amount in total.
grossly ADVERB

grotesque
Said "groh-tesk" ADJECTIVE
1 exaggerated and absurd EG *It was the most grotesque thing she had ever heard.* **2** very strange and ugly EG *grotesque animal puppets.*
grotesquely ADVERB
▣ from Old Italian *pittura grottesca* meaning 'cave paintings'

grotto grottoes or grottos
NOUN a small cave that people visit because it is attractive.

ground grounds grounding grounded
NOUN **1** The ground is the surface of the earth. **2** a piece of land that is used for a particular purpose EG *the training ground.* **3** The ground covered by a book or course is the range of subjects it deals with. ▶ PLURAL NOUN **4** The grounds of a large building are the land belonging to it and surrounding it. **5** A FORMAL USE The grounds for something are the reasons for it EG *genuine grounds for caution.* ▶ VERB **6** A FORMAL USE If something is grounded

A B C D E F **G** H I J K L M N O P Q R S T U V W X Y Z

in something else, it is based on it. **7** If an aircraft is grounded, it has to remain on the ground. **8** Ground is the past tense and past participle of **grind**.

ground floor ground floors

NOUN The ground floor of a building is the floor that is approximately level with the ground.

grounding

NOUN If you have a grounding in a skill or subject, you have had basic instruction in it.

groundless

ADJECTIVE not based on reason or evidence EG *groundless accusations*.

group groups grouping grouped

NOUN **1** A group of things or people is a number of them that are linked together in some way. **2** a number of musicians who perform pop music together. ▶ VERB **3** When things or people are grouped together, they are linked together in some way.

■ (sense 1) band, bunch, crowd, set

grouping groupings

NOUN a number of things or people that are linked together in some way.

grouse grouse

NOUN a fat brown or grey bird, often shot for sport.

grove groves

NOUN; A LITERARY WORD a group of trees growing close together.

grovel grovels grovelling grovelled

VERB If you grovel, you behave in an unpleasantly humble way towards someone you regard as important.

grow grows growing grew grown

VERB **1** To grow means to increase in size or amount. **2** If a tree or plant grows somewhere, it is alive there. **3** When people grow plants, they plant them and look after them. **4** If a man grows a beard or moustache, he lets it develop by

not shaving. **5** If you grow to have a particular feeling, you eventually have it. **6** If one thing grows from another, it develops from it. **7** AN INFORMAL USE If something grows on you, you gradually get to like it.

■ (sense 1) expand, get bigger, increase

grow up VERB When a child grows up, he or she becomes an adult.

growl growls growling growled

VERB **1** When an animal growls, it makes a low rumbling sound, usually because it is angry. **2** If you growl something, you say it in a low, rough, rather angry voice. ▶ NOUN **3** the sound an animal makes when it growls.

grown-up grown-ups

NOUN **1** AN INFORMAL USE an adult. ▶ ADJECTIVE **2** Someone who is grown-up is adult, or behaves like an adult.

growth growths

NOUN **1** When there is a growth in something, it gets bigger EG *the growth of the fishing industry*. **2** Growth is the process by which something develops to its full size. **3** an abnormal lump that grows inside or on a person, animal, or plant.

■ (sense 1) expansion, increase

grub grubs

NOUN **1** a wormlike insect that has just hatched from its egg. **2** AN INFORMAL USE Grub is food.

grubby grubbier grubbiest

ADJECTIVE rather dirty.

grudge grudges grudging grudged

NOUN **1** If you have a grudge against someone, you resent them because they have harmed you in the past. ▶ VERB **2** If you grudge someone something, you give it to them unwillingly, or are displeased that they have it.

grudging

ADJECTIVE done or felt unwillingly EG *grudging admiration*.

A
B
C
D
E
F
G
H
I
J
K
L
M
N
O
P
Q
R
S
T
U
V
W
X
Y
Z

grudgingly ADVERB

gruel
NOUN Gruel is oatmeal boiled in water or milk.

gruelling
ADJECTIVE difficult and tiring EG *a gruelling race*.

gruesome
ADJECTIVE shocking and horrible EG *gruesome pictures*.

gruff gruffer gruffest
ADJECTIVE If someone's voice is gruff, it sounds rough and unfriendly.

grumble grumbles grumbling grumbled
VERB 1 If you grumble, you complain in a bad-tempered way. ▶ NOUN 2 a bad-tempered complaint.

grumpy grumpier grumpiest
ADJECTIVE bad-tempered and fed-up.
■ ill-tempered, irritable

grunt grunts grunting grunted
VERB 1 If a person or a pig grunts, they make a short, low, gruff sound. ▶ NOUN 2 the sound a person or a pig makes when they grunt.

guarantee guarantees guaranteeing guaranteed
VERB 1 If something or someone guarantees something, they make certain that it will happen EG *Money may not guarantee success*. ▶ NOUN 2 If something is a guarantee of something else, it makes it certain that it will happen. 3 a written promise that if a product develops a fault it will be replaced or repaired free.
guarantor NOUN
■ (sense 1) ensure, promise
■ (sense 2) assurance, pledge, promise

guard guards guarding guarded
VERB 1 If you guard a person or object, you stay near to them either to protect them or to make sure they do not escape. 2 If you guard against something, you are careful to avoid it happening. ▶ NOUN 3 a person or group of people who guard a person, object, or place. 4 a railway official in charge of a train. 5 Any object which covers something to prevent it causing harm can be called a guard EG *a fire guard*.
■ (sense 1) defend, protect, watch over
■ (sense 3) protector, sentry, watchman

guardian guardians
NOUN 1 someone who has been legally appointed to look after an orphaned child. 2 A guardian of something is someone who protects it EG *a guardian of the law*.
guardianship NOUN

guernsey guernseys
NOUN 1 In Australian and New Zealand English, a jersey. 2 a sleeveless top worn by an Australian Rules football player.

guerrilla guerrillas
Said "ger-ril-la"; also spelt **guerilla**
NOUN a member of a small unofficial army fighting an official army.
🏛 from Spanish *guerrilla* meaning 'little war'

guess guesses guessing guessed
VERB 1 If you guess something, you form or express an opinion that it is the case, without having much information. ▶ NOUN 2 an attempt to give the correct answer to something without having much information.
■ (sense 1) conjecture, suppose
■ (sense 2) conjecture, speculation, supposition

guest guests
NOUN 1 someone who stays at your home or who attends an occasion because they have been invited. 2 The guests in a hotel are the people staying there.

guffaw
NOUN a loud, coarse laugh.

guidance
NOUN Guidance is help and advice.

guide guides guiding guided
NOUN 1 someone who shows you

round places, or leads the way through difficult country. **2** a book which gives you information or instructions EG *a Sydney street guide*. **3** A Guide is a girl who is a member of an organization that encourages discipline and practical skills. ▶ VERB **4** If you guide someone in a particular direction, you lead them in that direction. **5** If you are guided by something, it influences your actions or decisions.

guidebook guidebooks
NOUN a book which gives information about a place.

guide dog guide dogs
NOUN a dog that has been trained to lead a blind person.

guideline guidelines
NOUN a piece of advice about how something should be done.

guild guilds
NOUN a society of people EG *the Screen Writers' Guild*.

guile
Rhymes with "mile" NOUN Guile is cunning and deceit.
guileless ADJECTIVE

guillotine guillotines
Said "gil-lot-teen" NOUN a machine used for beheading people, especially in the past in France.

guilt
NOUN **1** Guilt is an unhappy feeling of having done something wrong. **2** Someone's guilt is the fact that they have done something wrong EG *The law will decide their guilt*.

guilty guiltier guiltiest
ADJECTIVE **1** If you are guilty of doing something wrong, you did it EG *He was guilty of theft*. **2** If you feel guilty, you are unhappy because you have done something wrong.
guiltily ADVERB

guinea guineas
Said "gin-ee" NOUN an old British unit of money, worth 21 shillings.

guinea pig guinea pigs
NOUN **1** a small furry animal without a tail, often kept as a pet. **2** a person used to try something out on EG *a guinea pig for a new drug*.

guise guises
Rhymes with "prize" NOUN a misleading appearance EG *political statements in the guise of religious talk*.

guitar guitars
NOUN a musical instrument with six strings which are strummed or plucked.
guitarist NOUN

gulf gulfs
NOUN **1** a very large bay. **2** a wide gap or difference between two things or people.

gull gulls
NOUN a sea bird with long wings, white and grey or black feathers, and webbed feet.
🔲 from Welsh *gwylan*

gullet gullets
NOUN the tube that goes from your mouth to your stomach.

gullible
ADJECTIVE easily tricked.
gullibility NOUN
▤ credulous, naive

gully gullies
NOUN a long, narrow valley.

gulp gulps gulping gulped
VERB **1** If you gulp food or drink, you swallow large quantities of it. **2** If you gulp, you swallow air, because you are nervous. ▶ NOUN **3** A gulp of food or drink is a large quantity of it swallowed at one time.

gum gums
NOUN **1** Gum is a soft flavoured substance that people chew but do not swallow. **2** Gum is also glue for sticking paper. **3** Your gums are the firm flesh in which your teeth are set.

gumboot gumboots
NOUN Gumboots are long waterproof boots.

gumtree gumtrees
NOUN a eucalyptus, or other tree

which produces gum.

gun guns
NOUN a weapon which fires bullets or shells.

gunpowder
NOUN Gunpowder is an explosive powder made from a mixture of potassium nitrate and other substances.

gunshot gunshots
NOUN the sound of a gun being fired.

gunyah gunyahs
NOUN In Australia, a hut or shelter in the bush.

guppy guppies
NOUN a small, brightly coloured tropical fish.

gurdwara
NOUN a Sikh place of worship.
▥ from Sanskrit *guru* meaning 'teacher' + *dvāra* meaning 'door'

gurgle gurgles gurgling gurgled
VERB 1 To gurgle means to make a bubbling sound. ▸ NOUN 2 a bubbling sound.

guru gurus
Said "**goo**-rooh" NOUN a spiritual leader and teacher, especially in India.
▥ from Sanskrit *guruh* meaning 'weighty' or 'of importance'

gush gushes gushing gushed
VERB 1 When liquid gushes from something, it flows out of it in large quantities. 2 When people gush, they express admiration or pleasure in an exaggerated way.
gushing ADJECTIVE
▤ (sense 1) flow, pour, spurt, stream

gust gusts
NOUN a sudden rush of wind.
gusty ADJECTIVE

gusto
NOUN Gusto is energy and enthusiasm EG *Her gusto for life was amazing.*

gut guts gutting gutted
PLURAL NOUN 1 Your guts are your internal organs, especially your intestines. ▸ VERB 2 To gut a dead fish means to remove its internal organs. 3 If a building is gutted, the inside of it is destroyed, especially by fire. ▸ NOUN 4 AN INFORMAL USE Guts is courage.
▤ (sense 1) entrails, innards, intestines

gutter gutters
NOUN 1 the edge of a road next to the pavement, where rain collects and flows away. 2 a channel fixed to the edge of a roof, where rain collects and flows away.
guttering NOUN

guttural
Said "**gut**-ter-al" ADJECTIVE Guttural sounds are produced at the back of a person's throat and are often considered to be unpleasant.

guy guys
NOUN 1 AN INFORMAL USE a man or boy. 2 a crude model of Guy Fawkes, that is burnt on top of a bonfire on Guy Fawkes Day (November 5).
▥ short for *Guy* Fawkes, who plotted to blow up the British Houses of Parliament

guzzle guzzles guzzling guzzled
VERB To guzzle something means to drink or eat it quickly and greedily.

gym gyms
NOUN 1 a gymnasium. 2 Gym is gymnastics.

gymkhana gymkhanas
Said "jim-**kah**-na" NOUN an event in which people take part in horse-riding contests.
▥ from Hindi *gend-khana* literally meaning 'ball house', because it is where sports were held

gymnasium gymnasiums
NOUN a room with special equipment for physical exercises.
▥ from Greek *gumnazein* meaning 'to exercise naked'

gymnast gymnasts
NOUN someone who is trained in gymnastics.
gymnastic ADJECTIVE

A
B
C
D
E
F
G
H
I
J
K
L
M
N
O
P
Q
R
S
T
U
V
W
X
Y
Z

A
B
C
D
E
F
G
H
I
J
K
L
M
N
O
P
Q
R
S
T
U
V
W
X
Y
Z

gymnastics
NOUN Gymnastics is physical exercises, especially ones using equipment such as bars and ropes.

gynaecology or **gynecology**
Said "gie-nak-kol-loj-ee" NOUN Gynaecology is the branch of medical science concerned with the female reproductive system. **gynaecologist** NOUN, **gynaecological** ADJECTIVE

gypsy gypsies; also spelt **gipsy**
NOUN a member of a race of people who travel from place to place in caravans.
▥ from 'Egyptian', because people used to think gypsies came from Egypt

gyrate gyrates gyrating gyrated
Said "jy-rate" VERB To gyrate means to move round in a circle.

Hh Hh

habit habits
NOUN **1** something that you do often EG *He got into the habit of eating out.* **2** something that you keep doing and find it difficult to stop doing EG *a 20-a-day smoking habit.* **3** A monk's or nun's habit is a garment like a loose dress.
habitual ADJECTIVE, **habitually** ADVERB

habitat habitats
NOUN the natural home of a plant or animal.

hack hacks hacking hacked
VERB **1** If you hack at something, you cut it using rough strokes.
▶ NOUN **2** a writer or journalist who produces work fast without worrying about quality.

hacker hackers
NOUN; AN INFORMAL WORD someone who uses a computer to break into the computer system of a company or government.

hackles
PLURAL NOUN **1** A dog's hackles are the hairs on the back of its neck which rise when it is angry. ▶ PHRASE **2** Something that **makes your hackles rise** makes you angry.

hackneyed
ADJECTIVE A hackneyed phrase is meaningless because it has been used too often.
■ clichéd, unoriginal

hacksaw hacksaws
NOUN a small saw with a narrow blade set in a frame.

haddock
NOUN an edible sea fish.

haemoglobin
Said "hee-moh-gloh-bin" NOUN Haemoglobin is a substance in red blood cells which carries oxygen round the body.

haemorrhage
Said "hem-er-rij" NOUN A haemorrhage is serious bleeding especially inside a person's body.

haemorrhoids
Said "hem-er-roydz" PLURAL NOUN Haemorrhoids are painful lumps around the anus that are caused by swollen veins.

hag hags
NOUN; AN OFFENSIVE WORD an ugly old woman.

haggard
ADJECTIVE A person who is haggard looks very tired and ill.

haggis
NOUN Haggis is a Scottish dish made of the internal organs of a sheep, boiled together with oatmeal and spices in a skin.

haggle haggles haggling haggled
VERB If you haggle with someone, you argue with them, usually about the cost of something.

hail hails hailing hailed
NOUN **1** Hail is frozen rain. **2** A hail of things is a lot of them falling together EG *a hail of bullets... a hail of protest.* ▶ VERB **3** When it is hailing, frozen rain is falling. **4** If someone hails you, they call you to attract your attention or greet you EG *He hailed a taxi.*

hair hairs
NOUN Hair consists of the long, threadlike strands that grow from the skin of animals and humans.

haircut haircuts
NOUN the cutting of someone's hair; also the style in which it is cut.

hairdo hairdos
NOUN a hairstyle.

hairdresser hairdressers
NOUN someone who is trained to cut and style people's hair; also a shop where this is done.
hairdressing NOUN OR ADJECTIVE

hairline hairlines
NOUN **1** the edge of the area on your forehead where your hair grows.

A B C D E F G H I J K L M N O P Q R S T U V W X Y Z

329

A
B
C
D
E
F
G
H
I
J
K
L
M
N
O
P
Q
R
S
T
U
V
W
X
Y
Z

▶ ADJECTIVE **2** A hairline crack is so fine that you can hardly see it.

hairpin hairpins
NOUN **1** a U-shaped wire used to hold hair in position. ▶ ADJECTIVE **2** A hairpin bend is a U-shaped bend in the road.

hair-raising
ADJECTIVE very frightening or exciting.

hairstyle hairstyles
NOUN Someone's hairstyle is the way in which their hair is arranged or cut.

hairy hairier hairiest
ADJECTIVE **1** covered in a lot of hair. **2** AN INFORMAL USE difficult, exciting, and rather frightening EG *He had lived through many hairy adventures.*

hajj
*Rhymes with "**badge**"* NOUN The hajj is the pilgrimage to Mecca that every Muslim must make at least once in their life if they are healthy and wealthy enough to do so.
🔳 from Arabic *hajj* pilgrimage

haka haka or hakas
NOUN **1** In New Zealand, a haka is a ceremonial Maori dance made up of various postures and accompanied by a chant. **2** an imitation of this dance performed by New Zealand sports teams before matches as a challenge.

hake hakes
NOUN an edible sea fish related to the cod.

hakea hakeas
NOUN a large Australian shrub with bright flowers and hard, woody fruit.

halcyon
*Said "**hal-see-on**"* ADJECTIVE **1** A LITERARY WORD peaceful, gentle, and calm EG *halcyon colours of yellow and turquoise.* ▶ PHRASE **2 Halcyon days** are a happy and carefree time in the past EG *halcyon days in the sun.*

half halves
NOUN, ADJECTIVE, OR ADVERB **1** Half refers

to one of two equal parts that make up a whole EG *the two halves of the brain... They chatted for another half hour... The bottle was only half full.* ▶ ADVERB **2** You can use 'half' to say that something is only partly true EG *I half expected him to explode in anger.*

half-baked
ADJECTIVE; AN INFORMAL WORD
Half-baked ideas or plans have not been properly thought out.

half board
NOUN Half board at a hotel includes breakfast and dinner but not lunch.

half-brother half-brothers
NOUN Your half-brother is the son of either your mother or your father but not of your other parent.

half-hearted
ADJECTIVE showing no real effort or enthusiasm.

half-pie
ADJECTIVE; AN INFORMAL WORD In New Zealand English, half-pie means incomplete or not properly done EG *finished in a half-pie way.*

half-sister half-sisters
NOUN Your half-sister is the daughter of either your mother or your father but not of your other parent.

half-timbered
ADJECTIVE A half-timbered building has a framework of wooden beams showing in the walls.

half-time
NOUN Half-time is a short break between two parts of a game when the players have a rest.

halfway
ADVERB at the middle of the distance between two points in place or time EG *He stopped halfway down the ladder... halfway through the term.*

halibut halibuts
NOUN a large edible flat fish.

hall halls
NOUN **1** the room just inside the front entrance of a house which

leads into other rooms. **2** a large room or building used for public events EG *a concert hall*.

hallmark hallmarks
NOUN **1** The hallmark of a person or group is their most typical quality EG *A warm, hospitable welcome is the hallmark of island people*. **2** an official mark on gold or silver indicating the quality of the metal.

hallowed
Said "**hal**-lode" ADJECTIVE respected as being holy EG *hallowed ground*.

Halloween
NOUN Halloween is October 31st, and is celebrated by children dressing up, often as ghosts and witches.
🔲 from Old English *halig* + *æfen* meaning 'holy evening', the evening before All Saints' Day

hallucinate hallucinates hallucinating hallucinated
Said "hal-**loo**-sin-ate" VERB If you hallucinate, you see strange things in your mind because of illness or drugs.
hallucination NOUN, **hallucinatory** ADJECTIVE
🔲 from Latin *alucinari* meaning 'to wander in thought'

halo haloes or halos
NOUN a circle of light around the head of a holy figure.
🔲 from Greek *halos* meaning 'disc shape of the sun or moon'

halt halts halting halted
VERB **1** To halt when moving means to stop. **2** To halt development or action means to stop it. ▶ NOUN **3** a short standstill.

halter halters
NOUN a strap fastened round a horse's head so that it can be led easily.

halve halves halving halved
Said "hahv" VERB **1** If you halve something, you divide it into two equal parts. **2** To halve something also means to reduce its size or amount by half.

ham hams
NOUN **1** Ham is meat from the hind leg of a pig, salted and cured. **2** a bad actor who exaggerates emotions and gestures. **3** someone who is interested in amateur radio.

hamburger hamburgers
NOUN a flat disc of minced meat, seasoned and fried; often eaten in a bread roll.
🔲 named after its city of origin *Hamburg* in Germany

hammer hammers hammering hammered
NOUN **1** a tool consisting of a heavy piece of metal at the end of a handle, used for hitting nails into things. ▶ VERB **2** If you hammer something, you hit it repeatedly, with a hammer or with your fist. **3** If you hammer an idea into someone, you keep repeating it and telling them about it. **4** AN INFORMAL USE If you hammer someone, you criticize or attack them severely.

hammock hammocks
NOUN a piece of net or canvas hung between two supports and used as a bed.

hamper hampers hampering hampered
NOUN **1** a rectangular wicker basket with a lid, used for carrying food. ▶ VERB **2** If you hamper someone, you make it difficult for them to move or progress.
🟰 (sense 2) handicap, hinder, impede

hamster hamsters
NOUN a small furry rodent which is often kept as a pet.
☑ There is no *p* in *hamster*.

hamstring hamstrings
NOUN Your hamstring is a tendon behind your knee joining your thigh muscles to the bones of your lower leg.

hand hands handing handed
NOUN **1** Your hand is the part of your body beyond the wrist, with four fingers and a thumb. **2** Your

A
B
C
D
E
F
G
H
I
J
K
L
M
N
O
P
Q
R
S
T
U
V
W
X
Y
Z

hand is also your writing style.
3 The hand of someone in a situation is their influence or the part they play in it EG *He had a hand in its design.* **4** If you give someone a hand, you help them to do something. **5** When an audience gives someone a big hand, they applaud. **6** The hands of a clock or watch are the pointers that point to the numbers. **7** In cards, your hand is the cards you are holding. ▶ VERB **8** If you hand something to someone, you give it to them. ▶ PHRASES **9** Something that is at **hand, to hand,** or **on hand** is available, close by, and ready for use. **10** You use **on the one hand** to introduce the first part of an argument or discussion with two different points of view. **11** You use **on the other hand** to introduce the second part of an argument or discussion with two different points of view. **12** If you do something **by hand,** you do it using your hands rather than a machine.
hand down VERB Something that is handed down is passed from one generation to another.

handbag **handbags**
NOUN a small bag used mainly by women to carry money and personal items.

handbook **handbooks**
NOUN a book giving information and instructions about something.

handcuff **handcuffs**
NOUN Handcuffs are two metal rings linked by a chain which are locked around a prisoner's wrists.

handful **handfuls**
NOUN **1** A handful of something is the amount of it you can hold in your hand EG *He picked up a handful of seeds.* **2** a small quantity EG *Only a handful of people knew.* **3** Someone who is a handful is difficult to control EG *He is a bit of a handful.*

handicap **handicaps** **handicapping**

handicapped
NOUN **1** a physical or mental disability. **2** something that makes it difficult for you to achieve something. **3** In sport, a handicap is a disadvantage or advantage given to competitors according to their skill, in order to give them an equal chance of winning. ▶ VERB **4** If something handicaps someone, it makes it difficult for them to achieve something.
■ (sense 1) disability, impairment

handicraft **handicrafts**
NOUN Handicrafts are activities such as embroidery or pottery which involve making things with your hands; also the items produced.

handiwork
NOUN Your handiwork is something that you have done or made yourself.

handkerchief **handkerchiefs**
NOUN a small square of fabric used for blowing your nose.

handle **handles** **handling** **handled**
NOUN **1** The handle of an object is the part by which it is held or controlled. **2** a small lever used to open and close a door or window. ▶ VERB **3** If you handle an object, you hold it in your hands to examine it. **4** If you handle something, you deal with it or control it EG *I have learned how to handle pressure.*

handlebar **handlebars**
NOUN Handlebars are the bar and handles at the front of a bicycle, used for steering.

handout **handouts**
NOUN **1** a gift of food, clothing, or money given to a poor person. **2** a piece of paper giving information about something.

hand-picked
ADJECTIVE carefully chosen EG *a hand-picked team of bodyguards.*

handset **handsets**
NOUN The handset of a telephone is the part that you speak into and

listen with.

handshake handshakes
NOUN the grasping and shaking of a
person's hand by another person.

handsome
ADJECTIVE **1** very attractive in
appearance. **2** large and generous EG
a handsome profit.
handsomely ADVERB
■ (sense 1) attractive, good-looking

handwriting
NOUN Someone's handwriting is
their style of writing as it looks on
the page.

handy handier handiest
ADJECTIVE **1** conveniently near. **2** easy
to handle or use. **3** skilful.

hang hangs hanging hung
VERB **1** If you hang something
somewhere, you attach it to a high
point. If it is hanging there, it is
attached by its top to something EG
*His jacket hung from a hook behind the
door.* **2** If a future event or
possibility is hanging over you, it
worries or frightens you EG *She has
an eviction notice hanging over her.*
3 When you hang wallpaper, you
stick it onto a wall. **4** To hang
someone means to kill them by
suspending them by a rope around
the neck. ▶ PHRASE **5** When you **get
the hang of something**, you
understand it and are able to do it.
hang about OR **hang around** VERB **1** AN
INFORMAL USE To hang about or hang
around means to wait somewhere.
2 To hang about or hang around
with someone means to spend a lot
of time with them.
hang on VERB **1** If you hang on to
something, you hold it tightly or
keep it. **2** AN INFORMAL USE To hang on
means to wait.
hang up VERB When you hang up,
you put down the receiver to end a
telephone call.
☑ When *hang* means 'kill someone
by suspending them by a rope'
(sense 4), the past tense and past
participle are *hanged*: *he was hanged*

for murder in 1959.

hangar hangars
NOUN a large building where aircraft
are kept.

hanger hangers
NOUN a coat hanger.

hanger-on hangers-on
NOUN an unwelcome follower of an
important person.

hang-glider hang-gliders
NOUN an unpowered aircraft
consisting of a large frame covered
in fabric, from which the pilot
hangs in a harness.

hangi hangi OR hangis
Said "hung-ee" NOUN In New
Zealand, a Maori oven made from a
hole in the ground lined with hot
stones.

hangover hangovers
NOUN a feeling of sickness and
headache after drinking too much
alcohol.

hang-up hang-ups
NOUN A hang-up about something is
a continual feeling of
embarrassment or fear about it.

hanker hankers hankering
hankered
VERB If you hanker after something,
you continually want it.
hankering NOUN

hanky hankies
NOUN a handkerchief.

Hanukkah OR **Chanukah**
Said "hah-na-ka" NOUN Hanukkah is
an eight-day Jewish festival of
lights.
■ a Hebrew word meaning literally
'a dedication'

haphazard
Said "hap-haz-ard" ADJECTIVE not
organized or planned.
haphazardly ADVERB
■ from Old Norse *hap* meaning
'chance' and Arabic *az-zahr*
meaning 'gaming dice'

hapless
ADJECTIVE; A LITERARY WORD unlucky.

A B C D E F G H I J K L M N O P Q R S T U V W X Y Z

A B C D E F G **H** I J K L M N O P Q R S T U V W X Y Z

happen happens happening happened

VERB **1** When something happens, it occurs or takes place. **2** If you happen to do something, you do it by chance.

happening NOUN

■ (sense 1) come about, occur, take place

happiness

NOUN a feeling of great contentment or pleasure.

happy happier happiest

ADJECTIVE **1** feeling, showing, or producing contentment or pleasure EG *a happy smile... a happy atmosphere.* **2** satisfied that something is right EG *I wasn't very happy about the layout.* **3** willing EG *I would be happy to help.* **4** fortunate or lucky EG *a happy coincidence.*

happily ADVERB

■ (sense 1) blissful, content, glad, joyful

happy-go-lucky

ADJECTIVE carefree and unconcerned.

harangue harangues haranguing harangued

Said "har-**rang**" NOUN **1** a long, forceful, passionate speech. ▶ VERB **2** To harangue someone means to talk to them at length passionately and forcefully about something.

🔲 from Old Italian *aringa* meaning 'public speech'

harass harasses harassing harassed

Said "har-rass" VERB If someone harasses you, they trouble or annoy you continually.

harassed ADJECTIVE, harassment NOUN

harbinger harbingers

Said "har-bin-jer" NOUN a person or thing that announces or indicates the approach of a future event EG *others see the shortage of cash as a harbinger of bankruptcy.*

harbour harbours harbouring harboured

NOUN **1** a protected area of deep water where boats can be moored.

▶ VERB **2** To harbour someone means to hide them secretly in your house. **3** If you harbour a feeling, you have it for a long time EG *She's still harbouring great bitterness.*

🔲 from Old English *here* + *beorg* meaning 'army shelter'

hard harder hardest

ADJECTIVE OR ADVERB **1** Something that is hard is firm, solid, or stiff EG *a hard piece of cheese... The ground was baked hard.* **2** requiring a lot of effort EG *hard work... They tried hard to attract tourists.* ▶ ADJECTIVE **3** difficult EG *These are hard times.* **4** Someone who is hard has no kindness or pity EG *Don't be hard on him.* **5** A hard colour or voice is harsh and unpleasant. **6** Hard evidence or facts can be proved to be true. **7** Hard water contains a lot of lime and does not easily produce a lather. **8** Hard drugs are very strong illegal drugs. **9** Hard drink is strong alcohol. ▶ ADVERB **10** An event that follows hard upon something takes place immediately afterwards.

hardness NOUN

■ (sense 1) firm, rigid, solid, stiff

hard and fast

ADJECTIVE fixed and not able to be changed EG *hard and fast rules.*

hardback hardbacks

NOUN a book with a stiff cover.

hard core

NOUN The hard core in an organization is the group of people who most resist change.

harden hardens hardening hardened

VERB To harden means to become hard or get harder.

hardening NOUN, hardened ADJECTIVE

hard labour

NOUN physical work which is difficult and tiring, used in some countries as a punishment for a crime.

hardly

ADVERB **1** almost not or not quite EG *I could hardly believe it.* **2** certainly not

EG *It's hardly a secret.*

☑ You should not use *hardly* with a negative word like *not* or *no: he could hardly hear her* not *he could not hardly hear her.*

hard-nosed
ADJECTIVE tough, practical, and realistic.

hard of hearing
ADJECTIVE not able to hear properly.

hardship hardships
NOUN Hardship is a time or situation of suffering and difficulty.

hard shoulder hard shoulders
NOUN the area at the edge of a motorway where a driver can stop in the event of a breakdown.

hard up
ADJECTIVE; AN INFORMAL EXPRESSION having hardly any money.

hardware
NOUN 1 Hardware is tools and equipment for use in the home and garden. 2 Hardware is also computer machinery rather than computer programs.

hard-wearing
ADJECTIVE strong, well-made, and long-lasting.

hardwood hardwoods
NOUN strong, hard wood from a tree such as an oak; also the tree itself.

hardy hardier hardiest
ADJECTIVE tough and able to endure very difficult or cold conditions EG *a hardy race of pioneers.*

hare hares haring hared
NOUN 1 an animal like a large rabbit, but with longer ears and legs. ▶ VERB 2 To hare about means to run very fast EG *He hared off down the corridor.*

harem harems
Said "har-reem" NOUN a group of wives or mistresses of one man, especially in Muslim societies; also the place where these women live.

hark harks harking harked
VERB 1 AN OLD-FASHIONED USE To hark means to listen. 2 To hark back to something in the past means to

refer back to it or recall it.

harlequin
Said "har-lik-win" ADJECTIVE having many different colours.

harm harms harming harmed
VERB 1 To harm someone or something means to injure or damage them. ▶ NOUN 2 Harm is injury or damage.
■ (sense 1) damage, hurt, injure

harmful
ADJECTIVE having a bad effect on something EG *Whilst most stress is harmful, some is beneficial.*

harmless
ADJECTIVE 1 safe to use or be near. 2 unlikely to cause problems or annoyance EG *He's harmless really.*
harmlessly ADVERB

harmonic
ADJECTIVE using musical harmony.

harmonica harmonicas
NOUN a small musical instrument which you play by blowing and sucking while moving it across your lips.

harmonious
Said "har-moh-nee-uss" ADJECTIVE 1 showing agreement, peacefulness, and friendship EG *a harmonious relationship.* 2 consisting of parts which blend well together making an attractive whole EG *harmonious interior decor.*
harmoniously ADVERB

harmony harmonies
NOUN 1 Harmony is a state of peaceful agreement and cooperation EG *the promotion of racial harmony.* 2 In music, harmony is the pleasant combination of two or more notes played at the same time.

harness harnesses harnessing harnessed
NOUN 1 a set of straps and fittings fastened round a horse so that it can pull a vehicle, or fastened round someone's body to attach something EG *a safety harness.* ▶ VERB 2 If you harness something, you

A
B
C
D
E
F
G
H
I
J
K
L
M
N
O
P
Q
R
S
T
U
V
W
X
Y
Z

bring it under control to use it EG *harnessing public opinion.*

harp harps harping harped
NOUN **1** a musical instrument consisting of a triangular frame with vertical strings which you pluck with your fingers. ▸ VERB **2** If someone harps on something, they keep talking about it, especially in a boring way.

harpoon harpoons
NOUN a barbed spear attached to a rope, thrown or fired from a gun and used for catching whales or large fish.

harpsichord harpsichords
NOUN a musical instrument like a small piano, with strings which are plucked when the keys are pressed.

harrowing
ADJECTIVE very upsetting or disturbing EG *a harrowing experience.*

harsh harsher harshest
ADJECTIVE severe, difficult, and unpleasant EG *harsh weather conditions... harsh criticism.*
harshly ADVERB, **harshness** NOUN
▣ hard, severe, tough

harvest harvests harvesting harvested
NOUN **1** the cutting and gathering of a crop; also the ripe crop when it is gathered and the time of gathering. ▸ VERB **2** To harvest food means to gather it when it is ripe.
harvester NOUN
▣ from Old German *herbist* meaning 'autumn'

has-been has-beens
NOUN; AN INFORMAL EXPRESSION a person who is no longer important or successful.

hash
PHRASE **1** If you **make a hash of** a job, you do it badly. ▸ NOUN **2** Hash is a dish made of small pieces of meat and vegetables cooked together. **3** AN INFORMAL USE Hash is also hashish.

hashish

Said "**hash**-eesh" NOUN Hashish is a drug made from the hemp plant. It is usually smoked, and is illegal in many countries.
▣ from Arabic *hashish* meaning 'hemp' or 'dried grass'

hassle hassles hassling hassled
NOUN **1** AN INFORMAL WORD Something that is a hassle is difficult or causes trouble. ▸ VERB **2** If you hassle someone, you annoy them by repeatedly asking them to do something.

haste
NOUN Haste is doing something quickly, especially too quickly.

hasten hastens hastening hastened
Said "**hay**-sn" VERB To hasten means to move quickly or do something quickly.

hasty hastier hastiest
ADJECTIVE done or happening suddenly and quickly, often without enough care or thought.
hastily ADVERB

hat hats
NOUN a covering for the head.

hatch hatches hatching hatched
VERB **1** When an egg hatches, or when a bird or reptile hatches, the egg breaks open and the young bird or reptile emerges. **2** To hatch a plot means to plan it. ▸ NOUN **3** a covered opening in a floor or wall.

hatchback hatchbacks
NOUN a car with a door at the back which opens upwards.

hatchet hatchets
NOUN **1** a small axe. ▸ PHRASE **2** To **bury the hatchet** means to resolve a disagreement and become friends again.

hate hates hating hated
VERB **1** If you hate someone or something, you have a strong dislike for them. ▸ NOUN **2** Hate is a strong dislike.
▣ (sense 1) detest, loathe

hatred

Said "**hay**-trid" NOUN Hatred is an extremely strong feeling of dislike.

hat trick hat tricks

NOUN In sport, a hat trick is three achievements, for example when a footballer scores three goals in a match EG *Crawford completed his hat trick in the 60th minute.*

haughty haughtier haughtiest

*Rhymes with "**naughty**"* ADJECTIVE showing excessive pride EG *He behaved in a haughty manner.*
haughtily ADVERB
▤ disdainful, proud, supercilious

haul hauls hauling hauled

VERB **1** To haul something somewhere means to pull it with great effort. ▸ NOUN **2** a quantity of something obtained EG *a good haul of fish.* ▸ PHRASE **3** Something that you describe as **a long haul** takes a lot of time and effort to achieve EG *So women began the long haul to equality.*

haulage

*Said "**hawl**-lij"* NOUN Haulage is the business or cost of transporting goods by road.

haunches

PLURAL NOUN Your haunches are your buttocks and the tops of your legs EG *He squatted on his haunches.*

haunt haunts haunting haunted

VERB **1** If a ghost haunts a place, it is seen or heard there regularly. **2** If a memory or a fear haunts you, it continually worries you. ▸ NOUN **3** A person's favourite haunt is a place they like to visit often.

haunted

ADJECTIVE **1** regularly visited by a ghost EG *a haunted house.* **2** very worried or troubled EG *a haunted expression.*

haunting

ADJECTIVE extremely beautiful or sad so that it makes a lasting impression on you EG *haunting landscapes.*

have has having had

VERB **1** Have is an auxiliary verb, used to form the past tense or to express completed actions EG *They have never met... I have lost it.* **2** If you have something, you own or possess it EG *We have two tickets for the concert.* **3** If you have something, you experience it, it happens to you, or you are affected by it EG *I have an idea!... He had a marvellous time.* **4** To have a child or baby animal means to give birth to it EG *When is she having the baby?* ▸ PHRASES **5** If you **have to** do something, you must do it. If you **had better** do something, you ought to do it.

haven havens

*Said "**hay**-ven"* NOUN a safe place.

havoc

NOUN **1** Havoc is disorder and confusion. ▸ PHRASE **2** To **play havoc** with something means to cause great disorder and confusion EG *Food allergies often play havoc with the immune system.*

hawk hawks hawking hawked

NOUN **1** a bird of prey with short rounded wings and a long tail. ▸ VERB **2** To hawk goods means to sell them by taking them around from place to place.

hawthorn hawthorns

NOUN a small, thorny tree producing white blossom and red berries.

hay

NOUN Hay is grass which has been cut and dried and is used as animal feed.

hay fever

NOUN Hay fever is an allergy to pollen and grass, causing sneezing and watering eyes.

haystack haystacks

NOUN a large, firmly built pile of hay, usually covered and left out in the open.

hazard hazards hazarding hazarded

NOUN **1** something which could be dangerous to you. ▸ VERB **2** If you

A B C D E F G **H** I J K L M N O P Q R S T U V W X Y Z

hazard something, you put it at risk EG *hazarding the health of his crew.* ▸ PHRASE **3** If you **hazard a guess**, you make a guess.

hazardous ADJECTIVE

🏛 from Arabic *az-zahr* meaning 'gaming dice'

haze

NOUN If there is a haze, you cannot see clearly because there is moisture or smoke in the air.

hazel hazels

NOUN **1** a small tree producing edible nuts. ▸ ADJECTIVE **2** greenish brown in colour.

hazy hazier haziest

ADJECTIVE dim or vague EG *hazy sunshine... a hazy memory.*

he

PRONOUN 'He' is used to refer to a man, boy, or male animal or to any person whose sex is not mentioned.

head heads heading headed

NOUN **1** Your head is the part of your body which has your eyes, brain, and mouth in it. **2** Your head is also your mind and mental abilities EG *He has a head for figures.* **3** The head of something is the top, start, or most important end EG *at the head of the table.* **4** The head of a group or organization is the person in charge. **5** The head on beer is the layer of froth on the top. **6** The head on a computer or tape recorder is the part that can read or write information. **7** When you toss a coin, the side called heads is the one with the head on it. ▸ VERB **8** To head a group or organization means to be in charge EG *Bryce heads the help organization.* **9** To head in a particular direction means to move in that direction EG *She is heading for a breakdown.* **10** To head a ball means to hit it with your head. ▸ PHRASE **11** If you **lose your head**, you panic. **12** If you say that someone is **off their head**, you mean that they are mad or very stupid. **13** If something is **over**

someone's head, it is too difficult for them to understand. **14** If you **can't make head nor tail of something**, you cannot understand it.

head off VERB If you head off someone or something, you make them change direction or prevent something from happening EG *He hopes to head off a public squabble.*

headache headaches

NOUN **1** a pain in your head. **2** Something that is a headache is causing a lot of difficulty or worry EG *Delays in receiving money owed is a major headache for small firms.*

header headers

NOUN A header in soccer is hitting the ball with your head.

heading headings

NOUN a piece of writing that is written or printed at the top of a page.

headland headlands

NOUN a narrow piece of land jutting out into the sea.

headlight headlights

NOUN The headlights on a motor vehicle are the large powerful lights at the front.

headline headlines

NOUN **1** A newspaper headline is the title of a newspaper article printed in large, bold type. **2** The headlines are the main points of the radio or television news.

headmaster headmasters

NOUN a man who is the head teacher of a school.

headmistress headmistresses

NOUN a woman who is the head teacher of a school.

headphones

PLURAL NOUN Headphones are a pair of small speakers which you wear over your ears to listen to a radio without other people hearing.

headquarters

NOUN The headquarters of an organization is the main place or from which it is run.

headroom

NOUN Headroom is the amount of space below a roof or surface under which an object must pass or fit.

headstone headstones

NOUN a large stone standing at one end of a grave and showing the name of the person buried there.

headstrong

ADJECTIVE determined to do something in your own way and ignoring other people's advice.

head teacher head teachers

NOUN the teacher who is in charge of a school.

headway

PHRASE If you are **making headway**, you are making progress.

headwind headwinds

NOUN a wind blowing in the opposite direction to the way you are travelling.

heady

ADJECTIVE extremely exciting EG *the heady days of the civil rights era.*

heal heals healing healed

VERB If something heals or if you heal it, it becomes healthy or normal again EG *He had a nasty wound which had not healed properly.*
healer NOUN

health

NOUN Health is the normally good condition of someone's body and the extent to which it is free from illness EG *Vitamins are essential for health.*
🏛 from Old English *hælth* a toast drunk to a person's wellbeing
🔲 fitness, wellbeing

health food health foods

NOUN food which is free from added chemicals and is considered to be good for your health.

healthy healthier healthiest

ADJECTIVE **1** Someone who is healthy is fit and strong and does not have any diseases. **2** Something that is healthy is good for you EG *a healthy*

diet. **3** An organization or system that is healthy is successful EG *a healthy economy.*
healthily ADVERB
🔲 (sense 1) fit, well

heap heaps heaping heaped

NOUN **1** a pile of things. **2** AN INFORMAL USE Heaps of something means plenty of it EG *His performance earned him heaps of praise.* ▸ VERB **3** If you heap things, you pile them up.
4 To heap something such as praise on someone means to give them a lot of it.
🔲 (sense 1) mass, mound, pile

hear hears hearing heard

VERB **1** When you hear sounds, you are aware of them because they reach your ears. **2** When you hear from someone, they write to you or phone you. **3** When a judge hears a case, he or she listens to it in court in order to make a decision on it.
▸ PHRASE **4** If you say that you **won't hear** of something, you mean you refuse to allow it.
hear out VERB If you hear someone out, you listen to all they have to say without interrupting.

hearing hearings

NOUN **1** Hearing is the sense which makes it possible for you to be aware of sounds EG *My hearing is poor.* **2** a court trial or official meeting to hear facts about an incident. **3** If someone gives you a hearing, they let you give your point of view and listen to you.

hearsay

NOUN Hearsay is information that you have heard from other people rather than something that you know personally to be true.

hearse hearses

Rhymes with "verse" NOUN a large car that carries the coffin at a funeral.

heart hearts

NOUN **1** the organ in your chest that pumps the blood around your body. **2** Your heart is also thought

339

of as the centre of your emotions. **3** Heart is courage, determination, or enthusiasm EG *They were losing heart.* **4** The heart of something is the most central and important part of it. **5** a shape similar to a heart, used especially as a symbol of love. **6** Hearts is one of the four suits in a pack of playing cards. It is marked by a red heart-shaped symbol.

heartache heartaches
NOUN Heartache is very great sadness and emotional suffering.

heart attack heart attacks
NOUN a serious medical condition in which the heart suddenly beats irregularly or stops completely.

heartbreak heartbreaks
NOUN Heartbreak is great sadness and emotional suffering.
heartbreaking ADJECTIVE

heartbroken
ADJECTIVE very sad and emotionally upset EG *She was heartbroken at his death.*

heartburn
NOUN Heartburn is a painful burning sensation in your chest, caused by indigestion.

heartening
ADJECTIVE encouraging or uplifting EG *heartening news.*

heart failure
NOUN Heart failure is a serious condition in which someone's heart does not work as well as it should, sometimes stopping completely.

heartfelt
ADJECTIVE sincerely and deeply felt EG *Our heartfelt sympathy goes out to you.*

hearth hearths
Said "harth" NOUN the floor of a fireplace.

heartless
ADJECTIVE cruel and unkind.

heart-rending
ADJECTIVE causing great sadness and pity EG *a heart-rending story.*

heart-throb heart-throbs
NOUN someone who is attractive to a lot of people.

heart-to-heart heart-to-hearts
NOUN a discussion in which two people talk about their deepest feelings.

hearty heartier heartiest
ADJECTIVE **1** cheerful and enthusiastic EG *hearty congratulations.* **2** strongly felt EG *a hearty dislike for her teacher.* **3** A hearty meal is large and satisfying.
heartily ADVERB

heat heats heating heated
NOUN **1** Heat is warmth or the quality of being hot; also the temperature of something that is warm or hot. **2** Heat is strength of feeling, especially of anger or excitement. **3** a contest or race in a competition held to decide who will play in the final. ▶ VERB **4** To heat something means to raise its temperature. ▶ PHRASE **5** When a female animal is **on heat**, she is ready for mating.
heater NOUN

heath heaths
NOUN an area of open land covered with rough grass or heather.

heathen heathens
NOUN; AN OLD-FASHIONED WORD someone who does not believe in one of the established religions.

heather
NOUN a plant with small purple or white flowers that grows wild on hills and moorland.

heating
NOUN Heating is the equipment used to heat a building; also the process and cost of running the equipment to provide heat.

heatwave heatwaves
NOUN a period of time during which the weather is much hotter than usual.

heave heaves heaving heaved
VERB **1** To heave something means

to move or throw it with a lot of effort. **2** If your stomach heaves, you vomit or suddenly feel sick. **3** If you heave a sigh, you sigh loudly. ▶ NOUN **4** If you give something a heave, you move or throw it with a lot of effort.

heaven heavens

NOUN **1** a place of happiness where God is believed to live and where good people are believed to go when they die. **2** If you describe a situation or place as heaven, you mean that it is wonderful EG *The cake was pure heaven.* ▶ PHRASE **3** You say 'Good heavens' to express surprise.

heavenly

ADJECTIVE **1** relating to heaven EG *a heavenly choir.* **2** AN INFORMAL USE wonderful EG *his heavenly blue eyes.*

heavy heavier heaviest; heavies

ADJECTIVE **1** great in weight or force EG *How heavy are you?... a heavy blow.* **2** great in degree or amount EG *heavy casualties.* **3** solid and thick in appearance EG *heavy shoes.* **4** using a lot of something quickly EG *The van is heavy on petrol.* **5** serious and difficult to deal with or understand EG *It all got a bit heavy when the police arrived... a heavy speech.* **6** Food that is heavy is solid and difficult to digest EG *a heavy meal.* **7** When it is heavy, the weather is hot, humid, and still. **8** Someone with a heavy heart is very sad. ▶ NOUN **9** AN INFORMAL USE a large, strong man employed to protect someone or something.
heavily ADVERB, **heaviness** NOUN

heavy-duty

ADJECTIVE Heavy-duty equipment is strong and hard-wearing.

heavy-handed

ADJECTIVE showing a lack of care or thought and using too much authority EG *heavy-handed police tactics.*

heavyweight heavyweights

NOUN **1** a boxer in the heaviest weight group. **2** an important person with a lot of influence.

Hebrew Hebrews

Said "**hee**-broo" NOUN **1** Hebrew is an ancient language now spoken in Israel, where it is the official language. **2** In the past, the Hebrews were Hebrew-speaking Jews who lived in Israel. ▶ ADJECTIVE **3** relating to the Hebrews and their customs.
🔲 from Hebrew *ibhri* meaning 'one from beyond (the river)'

heckle heckles heckling heckled

VERB If members of an audience heckle a speaker, they interrupt and shout rude remarks.
heckler NOUN

hectare hectares

NOUN a unit for measuring areas of land, equal to 10,000 square metres or about 2.471 acres.

hectic

ADJECTIVE involving a lot of rushed activity EG *a hectic schedule.*

hedge hedges hedging hedged

NOUN **1** a row of bushes forming a barrier or boundary. ▶ VERB **2** If you hedge against something unpleasant happening, you protect yourself. **3** If you hedge, you avoid answering a question or dealing with a problem. ▶ PHRASE **4** If you **hedge your bets**, you support two or more people or courses of action to avoid the risk of losing a lot.

hedgehog hedgehogs

NOUN a small, brown animal with sharp spikes covering its back.

hedonism

Said "**hee**-dn-izm" NOUN Hedonism is the belief that gaining pleasure is the most important thing in life.
hedonistic ADJECTIVE

heed heeds heeding heeded

VERB **1** If you heed someone's advice, you pay attention to it. ▶ NOUN **2** If you take or pay heed to something, you give it careful attention.
▣ (sense 1) listen to, mind, pay

attention to

heel heels heeling heeled
NOUN **1** the back part of your foot.
2 The heel of a shoe or sock is the
part that fits over your heel. ▶ VERB
3 To heel a pair of shoes means to
put a new piece on the heel.
▶ PHRASE **4** A person or place that
looks **down at heel** looks untidy
and in poor condition.

heeler heelers
NOUN In Australia, a dog that herds
cattle by biting at their heels.

hefty heftier heftiest
ADJECTIVE of great size, force, or
weight EG *a hefty fine... hefty volumes.*

height heights
NOUN **1** The height of an object is its
measurement from the bottom to
the top. **2** a high position or place
EG *Their nesting rarely takes place at
any great height.* **3** The height of
something is its peak, or the time
when it is most successful or
intense EG *the height of the tourist
season... at the height of his career.*

heighten heightens heightening
heightened
VERB If something heightens a
feeling or experience, it increases
its intensity.

heinous
Said "hay-nuss" *or* "hee-nuss"
ADJECTIVE evil and terrible EG *heinous
crimes.*

heir heirs
Said "air" NOUN A person's heir is
the person who is entitled to
inherit their property or title.

heiress heiresses
Said "air-iss" NOUN a female with
the right to inherit property or a
title.

heirloom heirlooms
Said "air-loom" NOUN something
belonging to a family that has been
passed from one generation to
another.

helicopter helicopters
NOUN an aircraft with rotating

blades above it which enable it to
take off vertically, hover, and fly.
📖 from Greek *heliko + pteron*
meaning 'spiral wing'

helium
Said "hee-lee-um" NOUN Helium is a
gas that is lighter than air and that
is used to fill balloons.

hell
NOUN **1** Hell is the place where souls
of evil people are believed to go to
be punished after death. **2** AN
INFORMAL USE If you say that
something is hell, you mean it is
very unpleasant. ▶ INTERJECTION
3 'Hell' is also a swearword.

hell-bent
ADJECTIVE determined to do
something whatever the
consequences.

hellish
ADJECTIVE; AN INFORMAL WORD very
unpleasant.

hello
INTERJECTION You say 'Hello' as a
greeting or when you answer the
phone.

helm helms
NOUN **1** The helm on a boat is the
position from which it is steered
and the wheel or tiller. ▶ PHRASE **2** At
the helm means in a position of
leadership or control.

helmet helmets
NOUN a hard hat worn to protect the
head.

help helps helping helped
VERB **1** To help someone means to
make something easier or better for
them. ▶ NOUN **2** If you need or give
help, you need or give assistance.
3 someone or something that helps
you EG *He really is a good help.*
▶ PHRASE **4** If you **help yourself** to
something, you take it. **5** If you
can't help something, you cannot
control it or change it EG *I can't help
feeling sorry for him.*
helper NOUN

helpful

ADJECTIVE **1** If someone is helpful, they help you by doing something for you. **2** Something that is helpful makes a situation more pleasant or easier to tolerate.
helpfully ADVERB
▤ (sense 1) cooperative, supportive
▤ (sense 2) beneficial, useful

helping helpings
NOUN an amount of food that you get in a single serving.

helpless
ADJECTIVE **1** unable to cope on your own EG *a helpless child.* **2** weak or powerless EG *helpless despair.*
helplessly ADVERB, **helplessness** NOUN

hem hems hemming hemmed
NOUN **1** The hem of a garment is an edge which has been turned over and sewn in place. ▶ VERB **2** To hem something means to make a hem on it.
hem in VERB If someone is hemmed in, they are surrounded and prevented from moving.

hemisphere hemispheres
Said "hem-iss-feer" NOUN one half of the earth, the brain, or a sphere.

hemp
NOUN Hemp is a tall plant, some varieties of which are used to make rope, and others to produce the drug cannabis.

hen hens
NOUN a female chicken; also any female bird.

hence
ADVERB **1** A FORMAL WORD for this reason EG *It sells more papers, hence more money is made.* **2** from now or from the time mentioned EG *The convention is due to start two weeks hence.*

henceforth
ADVERB; A FORMAL WORD from this time onward EG *His life henceforth was to revolve around her.*

henchman henchmen
NOUN The henchmen of a powerful person are the people employed to

do violent or dishonest work for that person.

hepatitis
NOUN Hepatitis is a serious infectious disease causing inflammation of the liver.

her
PRONOUN OR ADJECTIVE 'Her' is used to refer to a woman, girl or female animal that has already been mentioned, or to show that something belongs to a particular female.

herald heralds heralding heralded
NOUN **1** In the past, a herald was a messenger. ▶ VERB **2** Something that heralds a future event is a sign of that event.

herb herbs
NOUN a plant whose leaves are used in medicine or to flavour food.
herbal ADJECTIVE, **herbalist** NOUN

herbivore herbivores
NOUN an animal that eats only plants.

herd herds herding herded
NOUN **1** a large group of animals. ▶ VERB **2** To herd animals or people means to make them move together as a group.

here
ADVERB **1** at, to, or in the place where you are, or the place mentioned or indicated. ▶ PHRASE **2** Here and there means in various unspecified places EG *dense forests broken here and there by small towns.*

hereafter
ADVERB; A FORMAL WORD after this time or point EG *the South China Morning Post (referred to hereafter as SCMP).*

hereby
ADVERB; A FORMAL WORD used in documents and statements to indicate that a declaration is official EG *All leave is hereby cancelled.*

hereditary
ADJECTIVE passed on to a child from a parent EG *a hereditary disease.*

heredity

343

NOUN Heredity is the process by which characteristics are passed from parents to their children through the genes.

herein

ADVERB; A FORMAL WORD in this place or document.

heresy heresies

Said "herr-ess-ee" NOUN Heresy is belief or behaviour considered to be wrong because it disagrees with what is generally accepted, especially with regard to religion. **heretic** NOUN, **heretical** ADJECTIVE

herewith

ADVERB; A FORMAL WORD with this letter or document EG *I herewith return your cheque.*

heritage

NOUN the possessions or traditions that have been passed from one generation to another.

hermit hermits

NOUN a person who lives alone with a simple way of life, especially for religious reasons.

📖 from Greek *erēmitēs* meaning 'living in the desert'

hernia hernias

Said "her-nee-a" NOUN a medical condition in which part of the intestine sticks through a weak point in the surrounding tissue.

hero heroes

NOUN **1** the main male character in a book, film, or play. **2** a person who has done something brave or good.

heroic

ADJECTIVE brave, courageous, and determined.
heroically ADVERB

heroin

Said "herr-oh-in" NOUN Heroin is a powerful drug formerly used as an anaesthetic and now taken illegally by some people for pleasure.

heroine heroines

Said "herr-oh-in" NOUN **1** the main female character in a book, film, or play. **2** a woman who has done

something brave or good.

heroism

Said "herr-oh-i-zm" NOUN Heroism is great courage and bravery.

heron herons

NOUN a wading bird with very long legs and a long beak and neck.

herpes

Said "her-peez" NOUN Herpes is a virus which causes painful red spots on the skin.

herring herrings

NOUN a silvery fish that lives in large shoals in northern seas.

hers

PRONOUN 'Hers' refers to something that belongs to or relates to a woman, girl, or female animal.

herself

PRONOUN **1** 'Herself' is used when the same woman, girl, or female animal does an action and is affected by it EG *She pulled herself out of the water.* **2** 'Herself' is used to emphasize 'she'.

hertz

NOUN A hertz is a unit of frequency equal to one cycle per second.

hesitant

ADJECTIVE If you are hesitant, you do not do something immediately because you are uncertain or worried.
hesitantly ADVERB
▦ irresolute, uncertain, unsure

hesitate hesitates hesitating hesitated

VERB To hesitate means to pause or show uncertainty.
hesitation NOUN

hessian

NOUN Hessian is a thick, rough fabric used for making sacks.

heterosexual heterosexuals

Said "het-roh-seks-yool" ADJECTIVE **1** involving a sexual relationship between a man and a woman EG *heterosexual couples.* ▶ NOUN **2** a person who is sexually attracted to people of the opposite sex.

hewn

ADJECTIVE carved from a substance EG *a cave, hewn out of the hillside.*

hexagon hexagons

NOUN a shape with six straight sides.
hexagonal ADJECTIVE

heyday

*Said "**hay**-day"* NOUN The heyday of a person or thing is the period when they are most successful or popular EG *Hollywood in its heyday.*

hi

INTERJECTION 'Hi!' is an informal greeting.

hiatus hiatuses

*Said "high-**ay**-tuss"* NOUN; A FORMAL WORD a pause or gap.

hibernate hibernates hibernating hibernated

VERB Animals that hibernate spend the winter in a state like deep sleep.
hibernation NOUN
▩ from Latin *hibernare* meaning 'to spend the winter'

hibiscus hibiscuses

*Said "hie-**bis**-kuss"* NOUN a type of tropical shrub with brightly coloured flowers.

hiccup hiccups hiccupping hiccupped

*Said "**hik**-kup"* NOUN **1** Hiccups are short, uncontrolled choking sounds in your throat that you sometimes get if you have been eating or drinking too quickly. **2** AN INFORMAL USE a minor problem. ▶ VERB **3** When you hiccup, you make these little choking sounds.

hide hides hiding hid hidden

VERB **1** To hide something means to put it where it cannot be seen, or to prevent it from being discovered EG *He was unable to hide his disappointment.* ▶ NOUN **2** the skin of a large animal.
▣ (sense 1) conceal, disguise

hideous

*Said "**hid**-ee-uss"* ADJECTIVE extremely ugly or unpleasant.
hideously ADVERB

hideout hideouts

NOUN a hiding place.

hierarchy hierarchies

*Said "**high**-er-ar-kee"* NOUN a system in which people or things are ranked according to how important they are.
hierarchical ADJECTIVE

hi-fi hi-fis

NOUN a set of stereo equipment on which you can play compact discs and tapes.

high higher highest; highs

ADJECTIVE OR ADVERB **1** tall or a long way above the ground. **2** great in degree, quantity, or intensity EG *high interest rates... There is a high risk of heart disease.* **3** towards the top of a scale of importance or quality EG *high fashion.* **4** close to the top of a range of sound or notes EG *the human voice reaches a very high pitch.*
▶ ADJECTIVE **5** AN INFORMAL USE Someone who is high on a drug is affected by having taken it. ▶ NOUN **6** a high point or level EG *Morale reached a new high.* **7** AN INFORMAL USE Someone who is on a high is in a very excited and optimistic mood.
▣ (sense 1) lofty, tall, towering

highbrow

ADJECTIVE concerned with serious, intellectual subjects.

higher education

NOUN Higher education is education at universities and colleges.

high jump

NOUN The high jump is an athletics event involving jumping over a high bar.

highlands

PLURAL NOUN Highlands are mountainous or hilly areas of land.

highlight highlights highlighting highlighted

VERB **1** If you highlight a point or problem, you emphasize and draw attention to it. ▶ NOUN **2** The highlight of something is the most interesting part of it EG *His show was the highlight of the Festival.* **3** a lighter

A B C D E F G **H** I J K L M N O P Q R S T U V W X Y Z

area of a painting, showing where light shines on things. **4** Highlights are also light-coloured streaks in someone's hair.

highly
ADVERB **1** extremely EG *It is highly unlikely I'll be able to replace it.* **2** towards the top of a scale of importance, admiration, or respect EG *She thought highly of him... highly qualified personnel.*

high-minded
ADJECTIVE Someone who is high-minded has strong moral principles.

Highness
'Highness' is used in titles and forms of address for members of the royal family other than a king or queen EG *Her Royal Highness, Princess Alexandra.*

high-pitched
ADJECTIVE A high-pitched sound is high and often rather shrill.

high-rise
ADJECTIVE High-rise buildings are very tall.

high school high schools
NOUN a secondary school.

high technology
NOUN High technology is the development and use of advanced electronics and computers.

high tide
NOUN On a coast, high tide is the time, usually twice a day, when the sea is at its highest level.

highway highways
NOUN a road along which vehicles have the right to pass.

highwayman highwaymen
NOUN In the past, highwaymen were robbers on horseback who used to rob travellers.

hijack hijacks hijacking hijacked
VERB If someone hijacks a plane or vehicle, they illegally take control of it during a journey.
hijacking NOUN

hike hikes hiking hiked
NOUN **1** a long country walk. ▶ VERB **2** To hike means to walk long distances in the country.

hilarious
ADJECTIVE very funny.
hilariously ADVERB
■ funny, humorous, uproarious

hilarity
NOUN Hilarity is great amusement and laughter EG *His antics caused great hilarity.*

hill hills
NOUN a rounded area of land higher than the land surrounding it.
hilly ADJECTIVE

hillbilly hillbillies
NOUN someone who lives in the country away from other people, especially in remote areas in the southern United States.

hilt hilts
NOUN The hilt of a sword or knife is its handle.

him
PRONOUN You use 'him' to refer to a man, boy, or male animal that has already been mentioned, or to any person whose sex is not known.

himself
PRONOUN **1** 'Himself' is used when the same man, boy, or male animal does an action and is affected by it EG *He discharged himself from hospital.* **2** 'Himself' is used to emphasize 'he'.

hind hinds
Rhymes with "**blind**" ADJECTIVE **1** used to refer to the back part of an animal EG *the hind legs.* ▶ NOUN **2** a female deer.

hinder hinders hindering hindered
Said "**hin-der**" VERB If you hinder someone or something, you get in their way and make something difficult for them.

Hindi
Said "**hin-dee**" NOUN Hindi is a language spoken in northern India.
🏛 from Old Persian *Hindu* meaning 'the river Indus'

hindrance hindrances
NOUN **1** Someone or something that is a hindrance causes difficulties or is an obstruction. **2** Hindrance is the act of hindering someone or something.

hindsight
NOUN Hindsight is the ability to understand an event after it has actually taken place EG *With hindsight, I realized how strange he'd been.*

Hindu Hindus
Said "hin-doo" NOUN a person who believes in Hinduism, an Indian religion which has many gods and believes that people have another life on earth after death.

hinge hinges hinging hinged
NOUN **1** the movable joint which attaches a door or window to its frame. ▶ VERB **2** Something that hinges on a situation or event depends entirely on that situation or event EG *Victory or defeat hinged on her final putt.*

hint hints hinting hinted
NOUN **1** a suggestion, clue, or helpful piece of advice. ▶ VERB **2** If you hint at something, you suggest it indirectly.
■ (sense 1) clue, indication, suggestion
■ (sense 2) imply, insinuate, suggest

hinterland hinterlands
NOUN The hinterland of a coastline or a port is the area of land behind it or around it.

hip hips
NOUN Your hips are the two parts at the sides of your body between your waist and your upper legs.

hippo hippos
NOUN; AN INFORMAL WORD a hippopotamus.

hippopotamus hippopotamuses
or **hippopotami**
NOUN a large African animal with thick wrinkled skin and short legs, that lives near rivers.

▦ from Greek *hippo* + *potamos* meaning 'river horse'

hippy hippies; also spelt **hippie**
NOUN In the 1960s and 1970s hippies were people who rejected conventional society and tried to live a life based on peace and love .

hire hires hiring hired
VERB **1** If you hire something, you pay money to be able to use it for a period of time. **2** If you hire someone, you pay them to do a job for you. ▶ PHRASE **3** Something that is **for hire** is available for people to hire.

hirsute
Said "hir-syoot" ADJECTIVE; A FORMAL WORD hairy.

his
ADJECTIVE OR PRONOUN 'His' refers to something that belongs or relates to a man, boy, or male animal that has already been mentioned, or to any person whose sex is not known.

hiss hisses hissing hissed
VERB **1** To hiss means to make a long 's' sound, especially to show disapproval or aggression. ▶ NOUN **2** a long 's' sound.

histogram histograms
NOUN a graph consisting of rectangles of varying sizes, that shows the frequency of values of a quantity.

historian historians
NOUN a person who studies and writes about history.

historic
ADJECTIVE important in the past or likely to be seen as important in the future.

historical
ADJECTIVE **1** occurring in the past, or relating to the study of the past EG *historical events.* **2** describing or representing the past EG *historical novels.*
historically ADVERB

history histories
NOUN History is the study of the

A
B
C
D
E
F
G
H
I
J
K
L
M
N
O
P
Q
R
S
T
U
V
W
X
Y
Z

past. A history is a record of the past EG *The village is steeped in history... my family history.*

histrionic histrionics

Said "hiss-tree-on-ik" ADJECTIVE **1** Histrionic behaviour is very dramatic and full of exaggerated emotion EG *The setting was unbelievably histrionic.* **2** A FORMAL USE relating to drama and acting EG *a young man of marked histrionic ability.* ▶ PLURAL NOUN **3** Histrionics are histrionic behaviour.

hit hits hitting hit

VERB **1** To hit someone or something means to strike them forcefully, usually causing hurt or damage. **2** To hit a ball or other object means to make it move by hitting it with something. **3** If something hits you, it affects you badly and suddenly EG *The recession has hit the tourist industry hard.* **4** If something hits a particular point or place, it reaches it EG *The book hit Britain just at the right time.* **5** If you hit on an idea or solution, you suddenly think of it. ▶ NOUN **6** a person or thing that is popular and successful. **7** the action of hitting something EG *Give it a good hard hit with the hammer.* ▶ PHRASE **8** AN INFORMAL USE If you **hit it off** with someone, you become friendly with them the first time you meet them.

hit and miss

ADJECTIVE happening in an unplanned or unpredictable way.

hit-and-run

ADJECTIVE A hit-and-run car accident is one in which the person who has caused the damage drives away without stopping.

hitch hitches hitching hitched

NOUN **1** a slight problem or difficulty EG *The whole process was completed without a hitch.* ▶ VERB **2** AN INFORMAL USE If you hitch, you travel by getting lifts from passing vehicles EG *America is no longer a safe place to hitch round.*

hitchhiking

NOUN Hitchhiking is travelling by getting free lifts from passing vehicles.

hi tech

ADJECTIVE designed using the most modern methods and equipment, especially electronic equipment.

hither

AN OLD-FASHIONED WORD ▶ ADVERB **1** used to refer to movement towards the place where you are. ▶ PHRASE **2** Something that moves **hither and thither** moves in all directions.

hitherto

ADVERB; A FORMAL WORD until now EG *What he was aiming at had not hitherto been attempted.*

HIV

NOUN HIV is a virus that reduces people's resistance to illness and can cause AIDS. HIV is an abbreviation for 'human immunodeficiency virus'.

hive hives hiving hived

NOUN **1** a beehive. **2** A place that is a hive of activity is very busy with a lot of people working hard. ▶ VERB **3** If part of something such as a business is hived off, it is transferred to new ownership EG *The company is poised to hive off its music interests.*

hoard hoards hoarding hoarded

VERB **1** To hoard things means to save them even though they may no longer be useful. ▶ NOUN **2** a store of things that has been saved or hidden.

⬛ (sense 1) save, stockpile, store
⬛ (sense 2) cache, stash, store
✔ Do not confuse *hoard* with *horde*.

hoarding hoardings

NOUN a large advertising board by the side of the road.

hoarse hoarser hoarsest

ADJECTIVE A hoarse voice sounds rough and unclear.
hoarsely ADVERB

hoax hoaxes hoaxing hoaxed
NOUN **1** a trick or an attempt to
deceive someone. ▶ VERB **2** To hoax
someone means to trick or deceive
them.

hob hobs
NOUN a surface on top of a cooker
which can be heated in order to
cook things.

hobble hobbles hobbling hobbled
VERB **1** If you hobble, you walk
awkwardly because of pain or
injury. **2** If you hobble an animal,
you tie its legs together to restrict
its movement.

hobby hobbies
NOUN something that you do for
enjoyment in your spare time.

hock hocks
NOUN The hock of a horse or other
animal is the angled joint in its
back leg.

hockey
NOUN Hockey is a game in which
two teams use long sticks with
curved ends to try to hit a small
ball into the other team's goal.

hoe hoes hoeing hoed
NOUN **1** a long-handled gardening
tool with a small square blade, used
to remove weeds and break up the
soil. ▶ VERB **2** To hoe the ground
means to use a hoe on it.

hog hogs hogging hogged
NOUN **1** a castrated male pig. ▶ VERB
2 AN INFORMAL USE If you hog
something, you take more than
your share of it, or keep it for too
long. ▶ PHRASE **3** AN INFORMAL USE If you
go the whole hog, you do
something completely or
thoroughly in a bold or
extravagant way.

hoist hoists hoisting hoisted
VERB **1** To hoist something means to
lift it, especially using a crane or
other machinery. ▶ NOUN **2** a
machine for lifting heavy things.

hokey-pokey
NOUN In New Zealand, hokey-pokey

is a kind of brittle toffee.

hold holds holding held
VERB **1** To hold something means to
carry or keep it in place, usually
with your hand or arms.
2 Someone who holds power,
office, or an opinion has it or
possesses it. **3** If you hold
something such as a meeting or an
election, you arrange it and cause it
to happen. **4** If something holds, it
is still available or valid EG *The offer
still holds*. **5** If you hold someone
responsible for something, you
consider them responsible for it.
6 If something holds a certain
amount, it can contain that
amount EG *The theatre holds 150
people*. **7** If you hold something
such as theatre tickets, a telephone
call, or the price of something, you
keep or reserve it for a period of
time EG *The line is engaged — will you
hold?* **8** To hold something down
means to keep it or to keep it under
control EG *How could I have children
and hold down a job like this?* **9** If you
hold on to something, you
continue it or keep it even though
it might be difficult EG *They are keen
to hold on to their culture*. **10** To hold
something back means to prevent
it, keep it under control, or not
reveal it EG *She failed to hold back the
tears*. ▶ NOUN **11** If someone or
something has a hold over you,
they have power, control, or
influence over you EG *The party has a
considerable hold over its own leader*.
12 a way of holding something or
the act of holding it EG *He grabbed
the rope and got a hold on it*. **13** the
place where cargo or luggage is
stored in a ship or a plane.

holdall holdalls
NOUN a large, soft bag for carrying
clothing.

hole holes holing holed
NOUN **1** an opening or hollow in
something. **2** AN INFORMAL USE If you
are in a hole, you are in a difficult
situation. **3** AN INFORMAL USE A hole in

A B C D E F G H I J K L M N O P Q R S T U V W X Y Z

a theory or argument is a weakness or error in it. **4** In golf, a hole is one of the small holes into which you have to hit the ball. ▶ VERB **5** When you hole the ball in golf, you hit the ball into one of the holes.

▣ (sense 1) aperture, gap, opening

Holi
NOUN Holi is a Hindu festival celebrated in spring.

▥ from *Holika*, a legendary female demon

holiday holidays holidaying holidayed
NOUN **1** a period of time spent away from home for enjoyment. **2** a time when you are not working or not at school. ▶ VERB **3** When you holiday somewhere, you take a holiday there EG *She is currently holidaying in Italy.*

▥ from Old English *haligdæg* meaning 'holy day'

holidaymaker holidaymakers
NOUN a person who is away from home on holiday.

holiness
NOUN **1** Holiness is the state or quality of being holy. **2** 'Your Holiness' and 'His Holiness' are titles used to address or refer to the Pope or to leaders of some other religions.

hollow hollows hollowing hollowed
ADJECTIVE **1** Something that is hollow has space inside it rather than being solid. **2** An opinion or situation that is hollow has no real value or worth EG *a hollow gesture.* **3** A hollow sound is dull and has a slight echo EG *the hollow sound of his footsteps on the stairs.* ▶ NOUN **4** a hole in something or a part of a surface that is lower than the rest EG *It is a pleasant village in a lush hollow.* ▶ VERB **5** To hollow means to make a hollow EG *They hollowed out crude dwellings from the soft rock.*

holly
NOUN Holly is an evergreen tree or

shrub with spiky leaves. It often has red berries in winter.

holocaust holocausts
Said "hol-o-kawst" NOUN **1** a large-scale destruction or loss of life, especially the result of war or fire. **2** The Holocaust was the mass murder of the Jews in Europe by the Nazis during World War II.

▥ from Greek *holos* + *kaustos* meaning 'completely burnt'

holster holsters
NOUN a holder for a hand gun, worn at the side of the body or under the arm.

holy holier holiest
ADJECTIVE **1** relating to God or to a particular religion EG *the holy city.* **2** Someone who is holy is religious and leads a pure and good life.

▣ (sense 1) hallowed, sacred
▣ (sense 2) devout, pious

homage
Said "hom-ij" NOUN Homage is an act of respect and admiration EG *The thronging crowds paid homage to their assassinated president.*

home homes
NOUN **1** Your home is the building or place in which you live and feel you belong. **2** a building in which elderly or ill people live and are looked after EG *He has been confined to a nursing home since his stroke.* ▶ ADJECTIVE **3** connected with or involving your home or country EG *He gave them his home phone number... The government is expanding the home market.*

▣ (sense 1) abode, dwelling, residence

homeland homelands
NOUN Your homeland is your native country.

homeless
ADJECTIVE **1** having nowhere to live. ▶ PLURAL NOUN **2** The homeless are people who have nowhere to live. **homelessness** NOUN

homely
ADJECTIVE simple, ordinary and

comfortable EG *The room was small and homely.*

homeopathy
Said "home-ee-op-path-ee" NOUN Homeopathy is a way of treating illness by means of tiny amounts of a substance that would normally cause illness in a healthy person.
homeopathic ADJECTIVE

homeowner **homeowners**
NOUN a person who owns the home in which he or she lives.

homesick
ADJECTIVE unhappy because of being away from home and missing family and friends.

homespun
ADJECTIVE simple and uncomplicated EG *The book is simple homespun philosophy.*

homestead **homesteads**
NOUN a house and its land and other buildings, especially a farm.

home truth **home truths**
NOUN Home truths are unpleasant facts about yourself that you are told by someone else.

homeward or **homewards**
ADJECTIVE OR ADVERB towards home EG *the homeward journey.*

homework
NOUN **1** Homework is school work given to pupils to be done in the evening at home. **2** Homework is also research and preparation EG *You certainly need to do your homework before buying a horse.*

homicide **homicides**
NOUN Homicide is the crime of murder.
homicidal ADJECTIVE

homing
ADJECTIVE A homing device is able to guide itself to a target. An animal with a homing instinct is able to guide itself home.

homophone **homophones**
NOUN Homophones are words with different meanings which are pronounced in the same way but are spelt differently. For example, 'write' and 'right' are homophones.

homo sapiens
*Said "hoh-moh **sap**-ee-enz"* NOUN; A FORMAL EXPRESSION Homo sapiens is the scientific name for human beings.
📖 from Latin *homo* meaning 'man' and *sapiens* meaning 'wise'

homosexual **homosexuals**
NOUN **1** a person who is sexually attracted to someone of the same sex. ▶ ADJECTIVE **2** sexually attracted to people of the same sex EG *a homosexual relationship.*
homosexuality NOUN

hone **hones** **honing** **honed**
VERB **1** If you hone a tool, you sharpen it. **2** If you hone a quality or ability, you develop and improve it EG *He had a sharply honed sense of justice.*

honest
ADJECTIVE truthful and trustworthy.
honestly ADVERB
▤ honourable, trustworthy, truthful

honesty
NOUN Honesty is the quality of being truthful and trustworthy.
▤ honour, integrity, truthfulness

honey
NOUN **1** Honey is a sweet, edible, sticky substance produced by bees. **2** Honey means 'sweetheart' or 'darling' EG *What is it, honey?*

honeycomb **honeycombs**
NOUN a wax structure consisting of rows of six-sided cells made by bees for storage of honey and the eggs.

honeyeater **honeyeaters**
NOUN a small Australian bird that feeds on nectar from flowers.

honeymoon **honeymoons**
NOUN a holiday taken by a couple who have just got married.

honeysuckle
NOUN Honeysuckle is a climbing plant with fragrant pink or cream flowers.

hongi

A B C D E F G H I J K L M N O P Q R S T U V W X Y Z

Said "hong-ee" NOUN In New Zealand, hongi is a Maori greeting in which people touch noses.

honk honks honking honked
NOUN 1 a short, loud sound like that made by a car horn or a goose. ▶ VERB 2 When something honks, it makes a short, loud sound.

honorary
ADJECTIVE An honorary title or job is given as a mark of respect, and does not involve the usual qualifications or work EG *She was awarded an honorary degree.*

honour honours honouring honoured
NOUN 1 Your honour is your good reputation and the respect that other people have for you EG *This is a war fought by men totally without honour.* 2 an award or privilege given as a mark of respect. 3 Honours is a class of university degree which is higher than a pass or ordinary degree. ▶ PHRASE 4 If something is done in honour of someone, it is done out of respect for them EG *Egypt celebrated frequent minor festivals in honour of the dead.* ▶ VERB 5 If you honour someone, you give them special praise or attention, or an award. 6 If you honour an agreement or promise, you do what was agreed or promised EG *There is enough cash to honour the existing pledges.*

honourable
ADJECTIVE worthy of respect or admiration EG *He should do the honourable thing and resign.*

hood hoods
NOUN 1 a loose covering for the head, usually part of a coat or jacket. 2 a cover on a piece of equipment or vehicle, usually curved and movable EG *The mechanic had the hood up to work on the engine.*
hooded ADJECTIVE

hoof hooves or hoofs
NOUN the hard bony part of certain animals' feet.

hook hooks hooking hooked
NOUN 1 a curved piece of metal or plastic that is used for catching, holding, or hanging things EG *picture hooks.* 2 a curving movement, for example of the fist in boxing, or of a golf ball. ▶ VERB 3 If you hook one thing onto another, you attach it there using a hook. ▶ PHRASE 4 If you are let off the hook, something happens so that you avoid punishment or a difficult situation.

hooked
ADJECTIVE addicted to something; also obsessed by something EG *hooked on alcohol... I'm hooked on exercise.*

hooligan hooligans
NOUN a destructive and violent young person.
hooliganism NOUN
▣ delinquent, ruffian, yob

hoop hoops
NOUN a large ring, often used as a toy.

hooray
INTERJECTION another spelling of **hurray.**

hoot hoots hooting hooted
VERB 1 To hoot means to make a long 'oo' sound like an owl EG *hooting with laughter.* 2 If a car horn hoots, it makes a loud honking noise. ▶ NOUN 3 a sound like that made by an owl or a car horn.

hoover hoovers hoovering hoovered
NOUN 1 A TRADEMARK a vacuum cleaner. ▶ VERB 2 When you hoover, you use a vacuum cleaner to clean the floor.

hooves
a plural of **hoof.**

hop hops hopping hopped
VERB 1 If you hop, you jump on one foot. 2 When animals or birds hop, they jump with two feet together. 3 AN INFORMAL USE If you hop into or

out of something, you move there quickly and easily EG *You only have to hop on the ferry to get there.* ▶ NOUN **4** a jump on one leg. **5** Hops are flowers of the hop plant, which are dried and used for making beer.

hope hopes hoping hoped
VERB **1** If you hope that something will happen or hope that it is true, you want it to happen or be true. ▶ NOUN **2** Hope is a wish or feeling of desire and expectation EG *There was little hope of recovery.*
hopeful ADJECTIVE, **hopefully** ADVERB
☑ Some people do not like the use of *hopeful* to mean 'it is hoped', for example *hopefully, we can get a good result on Saturday*. Although it is very common in speech, it should be avoided in written work.

hopeless
ADJECTIVE **1** having no hope EG *She shook her head in hopeless bewilderment.* **2** certain to fail or be unsuccessful. **3** unable to do something well EG *I'm hopeless at remembering birthdays.*
hopelessly ADVERB, **hopelessness** NOUN

hopper hoppers
NOUN a large, funnel-shaped container for storing things such as grain or sand.

horde hordes
Rhymes with "bored" NOUN a large group or number of people or animals EG *hordes of tourists.*
☑ Do not confuse *horde* with *hoard*.

horizon horizons
Said "hor-eye-zn" NOUN **1** the distant line where the sky seems to touch the land or sea. **2** Your horizons are the limits of what you want to do or are interested in EG *Travel broadens your horizons.* ▶ PHRASE **3** If something is **on the horizon**, it is almost certainly going to happen or be done in the future EG *Political change was on the horizon.*

horizontal
Said "hor-riz-zon-tl" ADJECTIVE flat and level with the ground or with a line considered as a base EG *a patchwork of vertical and horizontal black lines.*
horizontally ADVERB

hormone hormones
NOUN a chemical made by one part of your body that stimulates or has a specific effect on another part of your body.
hormonal ADJECTIVE

horn horns
NOUN **1** one of the hard, pointed growths on the heads of animals such as goats. **2** a musical instrument made of brass, consisting of a pipe or that is narrow at one end and wide at the other. **3** On vehicles, a horn is a warning device which makes a loud noise.

hornet hornets
NOUN a type of very large wasp.

horoscope horoscopes
Said "hor-ros-kope" NOUN a prediction about what is going to happen to someone, based on the position of the stars when they were born.
🔲 from Greek *hora* + *skopos* meaning 'hour observer'

horrendous
ADJECTIVE very unpleasant and shocking EG *horrendous injuries.*

horrible
ADJECTIVE **1** disagreeable and unpleasant EG *A horrible nausea rose within him.* **2** causing shock, fear, or disgust EG *horrible crimes.*
horribly ADVERB
🔳 (sense 1) disagreeable, nasty, unpleasant
🔳 (sense 2) dreadful, ghastly, shocking

horrid
ADJECTIVE very unpleasant indeed EG *We were all so horrid to him.*

horrific
ADJECTIVE so bad or unpleasant that people are horrified EG *a horrific attack.*

A
B
C
D
E
F
G
H
I
J
K
L
M
N
O
P
Q
R
S
T
U
V
W
X
Y
Z

horrify horrifies horrifying horrified

VERB If something horrifies you, it makes you feel dismay or disgust EG *a crime trend that will horrify parents.*
horrifying ADJECTIVE

horror horrors

NOUN 1 a strong feeling of alarm, dismay, and disgust EG *He gazed in horror at the knife.* 2 If you have a horror of something, you fear it very much EG *He had a horror of fire.*

horse horses

NOUN 1 a large animal with a mane and long tail, on which people can ride. 2 a piece of gymnastics equipment with four legs, used for jumping over.

horsepower

NOUN Horsepower is a unit used for measuring how powerful an engine is, equal to about 746 watts.

horseradish

NOUN Horseradish is the white root of a plant made into a hot-tasting sauce, often served cold with beef.

horseshoe horseshoes

NOUN a U-shaped piece of metal, nailed to the hard surface of a horse's hoof to protect it; also anything of this shape, often regarded as a good luck symbol.

horsey or **horsy**

ADJECTIVE 1 very keen on horses and riding. 2 having a face similar to that of a horse.

horticulture

NOUN Horticulture is the study and practice of growing flowers, fruit, and vegetables.
horticultural ADJECTIVE

hose hoses hosing hosed

NOUN 1 a long flexible tube through which liquid or gas can be passed EG *He left the garden hose on.* ▶ VERB 2 If you hose something, you wash or water it using a hose EG *The street cleaners need to hose the square down.*

hosiery

Said "hoze-yer-ee" NOUN Hosiery consists of tights, socks, and similar items, especially in shops.

hospice hospices

Said "hoss-piss" NOUN a hospital which provides care for people who are dying.

hospitable

ADJECTIVE friendly, generous, and welcoming to guests or strangers.
hospitality NOUN

hospital hospitals

NOUN a place where sick and injured people are treated and cared for.

host hosts hosting hosted

NOUN 1 The host of an event is the person that welcomes guests and provides food or accommodation for them EG *He is a most generous host who takes his guests to the best restaurants in town.* 2 a plant or animal with smaller plants or animals living on or in it. 3 A host of things is a large number of them EG *a host of close friends.* 4 In the Christian church, the Host is the consecrated bread used in Mass or Holy Communion. ▶ VERB 5 To host an event means to organize it or act as host at it.

hostage hostages

NOUN a person who is illegally held prisoner and threatened with injury or death unless certain demands are met by other people.

hostel hostels

NOUN a large building in which people can stay or live EG *a hostel for battered women.*

hostess hostesses

NOUN a woman who welcomes guests or visitors and provides food or accommodation for them.

hostile

ADJECTIVE 1 unfriendly, aggressive, and unpleasant EG *a hostile audience.* 2 relating to or involving the enemies of a country EG *hostile territory.*
hostility NOUN

hot hotter hottest

ADJECTIVE 1 having a high temperature EG *a hot climate*. **2** very spicy and causing a burning sensation in your mouth EG *a hot curry*. **3** new, recent, and exciting EG *hot news from tinseltown*. **4** dangerous or difficult to deal with EG *Animal testing is a hot issue*.
hotly ADVERB

hotbed hotbeds
NOUN A hotbed of some type of activity is a place that seems to encourage it EG *The city was a hotbed of rumour*.

hot dog hot dogs
NOUN a sausage served in a roll split lengthways.

hotel hotels
NOUN a building where people stay, paying for their room and meals.

hothouse hothouses
NOUN **1** a large heated greenhouse. **2** a place or situation of intense intellectual or emotional activity EG *a hothouse of radical socialist ideas*.

hot seat
NOUN; AN INFORMAL EXPRESSION Someone who is in the hot seat has to make difficult decisions for which they will be held responsible.

hound hounds hounding hounded
NOUN **1** a dog, especially one used for hunting or racing. ▶ VERB **2** If someone hounds you, they constantly pursue or trouble you.

hour hours
NOUN **1** a unit of time equal to 60 minutes, of which there are 24 in a day. **2** The hour for something is the time when it happens EG *The hour for launching approached*. **3** The hour is also the time of day EG *What are you doing up at this hour?* **4** an important or difficult time EG *The hour has come... He is the hero of the hour*. ▶ PLURAL NOUN **5** The hours that you keep are the times that you usually go to bed and get up.
hourly ADJECTIVE OR ADVERB

house houses housing housed
NOUN **1** a building where a person or family lives. **2** a building used for a particular purpose EG *an auction house... the opera house*. **3** In a theatre or cinema, the house is the part where the audience sits; also the audience itself EG *The show had a packed house calling for more*. ▶ VERB **4** To house something means to keep it or contain it EG *The west wing housed a store of valuable antiques*.

houseboat houseboats
NOUN a small boat which people live on that is tied up at a particular place on a river or canal.

household households
NOUN **1** all the people who live as a group in a house or flat. ▶ PHRASE **2** Someone who is **a household name** is very well-known.
householder NOUN

housekeeper housekeepers
NOUN a person who is employed to do the cooking and cleaning in a house.

House of Commons
NOUN The House of Commons is the more powerful of the two parts of the British Parliament. Its members are elected by the public.

House of Lords
NOUN The House of Lords is the less powerful of the two parts of the British Parliament. Its members are unelected and come from noble families or are appointed by the Queen as an honour for a life of public service.

House of Representatives
1 NOUN In Australia, the House of Representatives is the larger of the two parts of the Federal Parliament. **2** In New Zealand, the House of Representatives is the Parliament.

housewife housewives
NOUN a married woman who does the chores in her home, and does not have a paid job.

housing
NOUN Housing is the buildings in which people live EG *the serious housing shortage*.

A B C D E F G H I J K L M N O P Q R S T U V W X Y Z

hovel hovels
NOUN a small hut or house that is dirty or badly in need of repair.

hover hovers hovering hovered
VERB **1** When a bird, insect, or aircraft hovers, it stays in the same position in the air. **2** If someone is hovering they are hesitating because they cannot decide what to do EG *He was hovering nervously around the sick animal.*

hovercraft hovercraft or hovercrafts
NOUN a vehicle which can travel over water or land supported by a cushion of air.

how
ADVERB **1** 'How' is used to ask about, explain, or refer to the way in which something is done, known, or experienced EG *How did this happen?... He knew how quickly rumours could spread.* **2** 'How' is used to ask about or refer to a measurement or quantity EG *How much is it for the weekend?... I wonder how old he is.* **3** 'How' is used to emphasize the following word or statement EG *How odd!*

however
ADVERB **1** You use 'however' when you are adding a comment that seems to contradict or contrast with what has just been said EG *For all his compassion, he is, however, surprisingly restrained.* **2** You use 'however' to say that something makes no difference to a situation EG *However hard she tried, nothing seemed to work.*

howl howls howling howled
VERB **1** To howl means to make a long, loud wailing noise such as that made by a dog when it is upset EG *A distant coyote howled at the moon... The wind howled through the trees.* ▶ NOUN **2** a long, loud wailing noise.

HQ
an abbreviation for **headquarters**.

hub hubs

NOUN **1** the centre part of a wheel. **2** the most important or active part of a place or organization EG *The kitchen is the hub of most households.*

hubbub
NOUN Hubbub is great noise or confusion EG *the general hubbub of conversation.*

huddle huddles huddling huddled
VERB **1** If you huddle up or are huddled, you are curled up with your arms and legs close to your body. **2** When people or animals huddle together, they sit or stand close to each other, often for warmth. ▶ NOUN **3** A huddle of people or things is a small group of them.

hue hues
NOUN **1** A LITERARY USE a colour or a particular shade of a colour. ▶ PHRASE **2** If people raise a **hue and cry**, they are very angry about something and protest.

huff
PHRASE If you are **in a huff**, you are sulking or offended about something.
huffy ADJECTIVE

hug hugs hugging hugged
VERB **1** If you hug someone, you put your arms round them and hold them close to you. **2** To hug the ground or a stretch of water or land means to keep very close to it EG *The road hugs the coast for hundreds of miles.* ▶ NOUN **3** If you give someone a hug, you hold them close to you.
▣ from Old Norse *hugga* meaning 'to comfort' or 'console'

huge huger hugest
ADJECTIVE extremely large in amount, size, or degree EG *a huge success... a huge crowd.*
hugely ADVERB
▣ enormous, gigantic, vast

hui hui or huis
Said "**hoo-ee**" NOUN **1** In New Zealand, a meeting of Maori people. **2** AN INFORMAL USE In New Zealand English, a party.

A B C D E F G H I J K L M N O P Q R S T U V W X Y Z

hulk hulks
NOUN **1** a large, heavy person or thing. **2** the body of a ship that has been wrecked or abandoned.
hulking ADJECTIVE

hull hulls
NOUN The hull of a ship is the main part of its body that sits in the water.

hum hums humming hummed
VERB **1** To hum means to make a continuous low noise EG *The generator hummed faintly.* **2** If you hum, you sing with your lips closed. ▶ NOUN **3** a continuous low noise EG *the hum of the fridge.*

human humans
ADJECTIVE **1** relating to, concerning, or typical of people EG *Intolerance appears deeply ingrained in human nature.* ▶ NOUN **2** a person.
humanly ADVERB

human being human beings
NOUN a person.

humane
ADJECTIVE showing kindness and sympathy towards others EG *Medicine is regarded as the most humane of professions.*
humanely ADVERB

humanism
NOUN Humanism is the belief in mankind's ability to achieve happiness and fulfilment without the need for religion.

humanitarian humanitarians
NOUN **1** a person who works for the welfare of mankind. ▶ ADJECTIVE **2** concerned with the welfare of mankind EG *humanitarian aid.*
humanitarianism NOUN

humanity
NOUN **1** Humanity is people in general EG *I have faith in humanity.* **2** Humanity is also the condition of being human EG *He denies his humanity.* **3** Someone who has humanity is kind and sympathetic.

human rights
PLURAL NOUN Human rights are the rights of individuals to freedom and justice.

humble humbler humblest; humbles humbling humbled
ADJECTIVE **1** A humble person is modest and thinks that he or she has very little value. **2** Something that is humble is small or not very important EG *Just a splash of wine will transform a humble casserole.* ▶ VERB **3** To humble someone means to make them feel humiliated.
humbly ADVERB, **humbled** ADJECTIVE
■ (sense 1) modest, unassuming

humbug humbugs
NOUN **1** a hard black and white striped sweet that tastes of peppermint. **2** Humbug is speech or writing that is obviously dishonest or untrue EG *hypocritical humbug.*

humdrum
ADJECTIVE ordinary, dull, and uninteresting EG *humdrum domestic tasks.*

humid
ADJECTIVE If it is humid, the air feels damp, heavy, and warm.

humidity
NOUN Humidity is the amount of moisture in the air, or the state of being humid.

humiliate humiliates humiliating humiliated
VERB To humiliate someone means to make them feel ashamed or appear stupid to other people.
humiliation NOUN
■ embarrass, mortify, shame

humility
NOUN Humility is the quality of being modest and humble.

hummingbird hummingbirds
NOUN a small bird with powerful wings that make a humming noise as they beat.

humour humours humouring humoured
NOUN **1** Humour is the quality of being funny EG *They discussed it with*

A
B
C
D
E
F
G
H
I
J
K
L
M
N
O
P
Q
R
S
T
U
V
W
X
Y
Z

tact and humour. **2** Humour is also the ability to be amused by certain things eg *Helen's got a peculiar sense of humour.* **3** Someone's humour is the mood they are in eg *He hasn't been in a good humour lately.* ▶ VERB **4** If you humour someone, you are especially kind to them and do whatever they want.

humorous ADJECTIVE

■ (sense 1) comedy, funniness, wit

hump humps humping humped
NOUN **1** a small, rounded lump or mound eg *a camel's hump.* ▶ VERB **2** AN INFORMAL USE If you hump something heavy, you carry or move it with difficulty.

hunch hunches hunching hunched
NOUN **1** a feeling or suspicion about something, not based on facts or evidence. ▶ VERB **2** If you hunch your shoulders, you raise them and lean forwards.

hunchback hunchbacks
NOUN; AN OLD-FASHIONED WORD someone who has a large hump on their back.

hundred hundreds
the number 100.
hundredth

Hungarian Hungarians
Said "hung-gair-ee-an" ADJECTIVE **1** belonging or relating to Hungary. ▶ NOUN **2** someone who comes from Hungary. **3** Hungarian is the main language spoken in Hungary.

hunger hungers hungering hungered
NOUN **1** Hunger is the need to eat or the desire to eat. **2** A hunger for something is a strong need or desire for it eg *a hunger for winning.* ▶ VERB **3** If you hunger for something, you want it very much.

hunger strike hunger strikes
NOUN a refusal to eat anything at all, especially by prisoners, as a form of protest.

hungry hungrier hungriest
ADJECTIVE needing or wanting to eat eg *People are going hungry.*

hungrily ADVERB

hunk hunks
NOUN A hunk of something is a large piece of it.

hunt hunts hunting hunted
VERB **1** To hunt means to chase wild animals to kill them for food or for sport. **2** If you hunt for something, you search for it. ▶ NOUN **3** the act of hunting eg *Police launched a hunt for an abandoned car.*

hunter NOUN, **hunting** ADJECTIVE OR NOUN

huntaway huntaways
NOUN In Australia and New Zealand, a dog trained to drive sheep forward.

hurdle hurdles
NOUN **1** one of the frames or barriers that you jump over in an athletics race called hurdles eg *She won the four hundred metre hurdles.* **2** a problem or difficulty eg *Several hurdles exist for anyone seeking to do postgraduate study.*

hurl hurls hurling hurled
VERB **1** To hurl something means to throw it with great force. **2** If you hurl insults at someone, you insult them aggressively and repeatedly.

hurray or **hurrah** or **hooray**
INTERJECTION an exclamation of excitement or approval.

hurricane hurricanes
NOUN a violent wind or storm.

hurry hurries hurrying hurried
VERB **1** To hurry means to move or do something as quickly as possible eg *She hurried through the empty streets.* **2** To hurry something means to make it happen more quickly eg *You can't hurry nature.* ▶ NOUN **3** Hurry is the speed with which you do something quickly eg *He was in a hurry to leave.*

hurried ADJECTIVE, **hurriedly** ADVERB
■ (sense 1) dash, fly, rush
■ (sense 3) haste, rush

hurt hurts hurting hurt
VERB **1** To hurt someone means to cause them physical pain. **2** If a

part of your body hurts, you feel pain there. **3** If you hurt yourself, you injure yourself. **4** To hurt someone also means to make them unhappy by being unkind or thoughtless towards them EG *I didn't want to hurt his feelings.* ▶ ADJECTIVE **5** If someone feels hurt, they feel unhappy because of someone's unkindness towards them EG *He felt hurt by all the lies.*
hurtful ADJECTIVE

hurtle hurtles hurtling hurtled
VERB To hurtle means to move or travel very fast indeed, especially in an uncontrolled way.

husband husbands
NOUN A woman's husband is the man she is married to.

husbandry
NOUN **1** Husbandry is the art or skill of farming. **2** Husbandry is also the art or skill of managing something carefully and economically.

hush hushes hushing hushed
VERB **1** If you tell someone to hush, you are telling them to be quiet. **2** To hush something up means to keep it secret, especially something dishonest involving important people EG *The government has hushed up a series of scandals.* ▶ NOUN **3** If there is a hush, it is quiet and still EG *A graveyard hush fell over the group.*
hushed ADJECTIVE

husk husks
NOUN Husks are the dry outer coverings of grain or seed.

husky huskier huskiest; huskies
ADJECTIVE **1** A husky voice is rough or hoarse. ▶ NOUN **2** a large, strong dog with a thick coat, often used to pull sledges across snow.

hustle hustles hustling hustled
VERB To hustle someone means to make them move by pushing and jostling them EG *The guards hustled him out of the car.*

hut huts
NOUN a small, simple building, with one or two rooms.

hutch hutches
NOUN a wooden box with wire mesh at one side, in which small pets can be kept.

hyacinth hyacinths
Said "high-as-sinth" NOUN a spring flower with many small, bell-shaped flowers.

hybrid hybrids
NOUN **1** a plant or animal that has been bred from two different types of plant or animal. **2** anything that is a mixture of two other things.

hydra hydras or hydrae
NOUN a microscopic freshwater creature that has a slender tubular body and tentacles round the mouth.

hydrangea hydrangeas
Said "high-drain-ja" NOUN a garden shrub with large clusters of pink or blue flowers.

hydraulic
Said "high-drol-lik" ADJECTIVE operated by water or other fluid which is under pressure.

hydrogen
NOUN Hydrogen is the lightest gas and the simplest chemical element.

hyena hyenas
Said "high-ee-na"; also spelt hyaena
NOUN a wild doglike animal of Africa and Asia that hunts in packs.

hygiene
Said "high-jeen" NOUN Hygiene is the practice of keeping yourself and your surroundings clean, especially to stop the spread of disease.
hygienic ADJECTIVE

hymn hymns
NOUN a Christian song in praise of God.

hyperactive
ADJECTIVE A hyperactive person is unable to relax and is always in a state of restless activity.

hyperbole
Said "high-per-bol-lee" NOUN

A
B
C
D
E
F
G
H
I
J
K
L
M
N
O
P
Q
R
S
T
U
V
W
X
Y
Z

Hyperbole is a style of speech or writing which uses exaggeration.

hypertension
NOUN Hypertension is a medical condition in which a person has high blood pressure.

hyphen hyphens
NOUN a punctuation mark used to join together words or parts of words, as for example in the word 'left-handed'.
hyphenate VERB, **hyphenation** NOUN

What does the Hyphen do?
The **hyphen** (-) separates the different parts of certain words. A hyphen is often used when there would otherwise be an awkward combination of letters, or confusion with another word.
Anna was re-elected president.
She adopted a no-nonsense approach.
In printed texts, the hyphen also divides a word that will not fit at the end of a line and has to be continued on the next line.

hypnosis
Said "hip-**noh**-siss" NOUN Hypnosis is an artificially produced state of relaxation in which the mind is very receptive to suggestion.
📖 from Greek *hupnos* meaning 'sleep'

hypnotize hypnotizes hypnotizing hypnotized; also spelt **hypnotise**
VERB To hypnotize someone means to put them into a state in which they seem to be asleep but can respond to questions and suggestions.
hypnotic ADJECTIVE, **hypnotism** NOUN, **hypnotist** NOUN

hypochondriac hypochondriacs
Said "high-pok-**kon**-dree-ak" NOUN a person who continually worries

about their health, being convinced that they are ill when there is actually nothing wrong with them.

hypocrisy hypocrisies
NOUN Hypocrisy is pretending to have beliefs or qualities that you do not really have, so that you seem a better person than you are.
hypocritical ADJECTIVE, **hypocrite** NOUN

hypodermic hypodermics
NOUN a medical instrument with a hollow needle, used for giving people injections, or taking blood samples.

hypothermia
NOUN Hypothermia is a condition in which a person is very ill because their body temperature has been unusually low for a long time.

hypothesis hypotheses
NOUN an explanation or theory which has not yet been proved to be correct.

hypothetical
ADJECTIVE based on assumption rather than on fact or reality.

hysterectomy hysterectomies
Said "his-ter-**rek**-tom-ee" NOUN an operation to remove a woman's womb.

hysteria
Said "hiss-**teer**-ee-a" NOUN Hysteria is a state of uncontrolled excitement or panic.

hysterical
ADJECTIVE 1 Someone who is hysterical is in a state of uncontrolled excitement or panic.
2 AN INFORMAL USE Something that is hysterical is extremely funny.
hysterically ADVERB, **hysterics** NOUN
▤ (sense 1) frantic, frenzied

I

PRONOUN A speaker or writer uses 'I' to refer to himself or herself EG *I like the colour*.

ibis ibises
Said "eye-biss" NOUN a large wading bird with a long, thin, curved bill that lives in warm countries.

ice ices icing iced
NOUN **1** Ice is water that has frozen solid. **2** an ice cream. ▶ VERB **3** If you ice cakes, you cover them with icing. **4** If something ices over or ices up, it becomes covered with a layer of ice. ▶ PHRASE **5** If you do something to **break the ice**, you make people feel relaxed and comfortable.

Ice Age Ice Ages
NOUN a period of time lasting thousands of years when a lot of the earth's surface was covered with ice.

iceberg icebergs
NOUN a large mass of ice floating in the sea.
🔲 from Dutch *ijsberg* meaning 'ice mountain'

icecap icecaps
NOUN a layer of ice and snow that permanently covers the North or South Pole.

ice cream ice creams
NOUN Ice cream is a very cold sweet food made from frozen cream.

ice cube ice cubes
NOUN Ice cubes are small cubes of ice put in drinks to make them cold.

ice hockey
NOUN Ice hockey is a type of hockey played on ice, with two teams of six skaters.

Icelandic
NOUN Icelandic is the main language spoken in Iceland.

ice-skate ice-skates ice-skating ice-skated
NOUN **1** a boot with a metal blade on the bottom, which you wear when skating on ice. ▶ VERB **2** If you ice-skate, you move about on ice wearing ice-skates.

icicle icicles
Said "eye-sik-kl" NOUN a piece of ice shaped like a pointed stick that hangs down from a surface.

icing
NOUN Icing is a mixture of powdered sugar and water or egg whites, used to decorate cakes.

icon icons
Said "eye-kon" NOUN **1** In the Orthodox Churches, an icon is a holy picture of Christ, the Virgin Mary, or a saint. **2** a picture on a computer screen representing a program that can be activated by moving the cursor over it.
🔲 from Greek *eikōn* meaning 'likeness' or 'image'

icy icier iciest
ADJECTIVE **1** Something which is icy is very cold EG *an icy wind*. **2** An icy road has ice on it.
icily ADVERB

id
NOUN In psychology, your id is your basic instincts and unconscious thoughts.

idea ideas
NOUN **1** a plan, suggestion, or thought that you have after thinking about a problem. **2** an opinion or belief EG *old-fashioned ideas about women*. **3** An idea of something is what you know about it EG *They had no idea of their position*.
◨ (sense 1) impression, thought
◨ (sense 2) belief, notion, opinion

ideal ideals
NOUN **1** a principle or idea that you try to achieve because it seems perfect to you. **2** Your ideal of something is the person or thing

that seems the best example of it.
▶ ADJECTIVE **3** The ideal person or thing is the best possible person or thing for the situation.

idealism
Said "eye-dee-il-izm" NOUN Idealism is behaviour that is based on a person's ideals.
idealist NOUN, **idealistic** ADJECTIVE

idealize idealizes idealizing idealized; also spelt **idealise**
VERB If you idealize someone or something, you regard them as being perfect.
idealization NOUN

ideally
ADVERB **1** If you say that ideally something should happen, you mean that you would like it to happen but you know that it is not possible. **2** Ideally means perfectly EG *The hotel is ideally placed for business travellers.*

identical
ADJECTIVE exactly the same EG *identical twins.*
identically ADVERB

identification
NOUN **1** The identification of someone or something is the act of identifying them. **2** Identification is a document such as a driver's licence or passport, which proves who you are.

identify identifies identifying identified
VERB **1** To identify someone or something is to recognize them or name them. **2** If you identify with someone, you understand their feelings and ideas.
identifiable ADJECTIVE

identity identities
NOUN the characteristics that make you who you are.

ideology ideologies
NOUN a set of political beliefs.
ideological ADJECTIVE, **ideologically** ADVERB

idiom idioms

NOUN a group of words whose meaning together is different from all the words taken individually. For example, 'It is raining cats and dogs' is an idiom.
📖 from Greek *idiōma* meaning 'special phraseology'

idiosyncrasy idiosyncrasies
Said "id-ee-oh-**sing**-krass-ee" NOUN Someone's idiosyncrasies are their own habits and likes or dislikes.
idiosyncratic ADJECTIVE

idiot idiots
NOUN someone who is stupid or foolish.
📖 from Greek *idiōtēs* meaning 'ignorant person'
🔲 fool, halfwit, moron

idiotic
ADJECTIVE extremely foolish or silly.
🔲 foolish, senseless, stupid

idle idles idling idled
ADJECTIVE If you are idle, you are doing nothing.
idleness NOUN, **idly** ADVERB
📖 from Saxon *idal* meaning 'worthless' or 'empty'

idol idols
Said "eye-doll" NOUN **1** a famous person who is loved and admired by fans. **2** a picture or statue which is worshipped as if it were a god.
📖 from Greek *eidōlon* meaning 'image' or 'phantom'

idyll idylls
Said "id-ill" NOUN a situation which is peaceful and beautiful.
idyllic ADJECTIVE

i.e
i.e. means 'that is', and is used before giving more information. It is an abbreviation for the Latin expression 'id est'.

if
CONJUNCTION **1** on the condition that EG *I shall stay if I can.* **2** whether EG *I asked my friend if she wanted to come shopping.*

igloo igloos
NOUN a dome-shaped house built

out of blocks of snow by the Inuit, or Eskimo people.

🔲 from *igdlu*, an Eskimo word meaning 'house'

igneous
Said "**ig**-nee-uss" ADJECTIVE; A TECHNICAL WORD Igneous rocks are formed by hot liquid rock cooling and going hard.

🔲 from Latin *igneus* meaning 'fiery'

ignite ignites igniting ignited
VERB If you ignite something or if it ignites, it starts burning.

🔲 from Latin *ignis* meaning 'fire'

ignition ignitions
NOUN In a car, the ignition is the part of the engine where the fuel is ignited.

ignominious
ADJECTIVE shameful or considered wrong.

ignominiously ADVERB, **ignominy** NOUN

ignoramus ignoramuses
Said "ig-nor-**ray**-muss" NOUN an ignorant person.

🔲 from the character *Ignoramus*, an uneducated lawyer in a 17th-century play by Ruggle. In Latin *ignoramus* means 'we do not know'

ignorant
ADJECTIVE **1** If you are ignorant of something, you do not know about it EG *He was completely ignorant of the rules.* **2** Someone who is ignorant does not know about things in general EG *I thought of asking, but didn't want to seem ignorant.*

ignorantly ADVERB, **ignorance** NOUN
🔳 (sense 1) unaware, unconscious, uninformed

ignore ignores ignoring ignored
VERB If you ignore someone or something, you deliberately do not take any notice of them.

iguana iguanas
Said "ig-**wah**-na" NOUN a large, tropical lizard.

ill ills
ADJECTIVE **1** unhealthy or sick.

2 harmful or unpleasant EG *ill effects.* ▸ PLURAL NOUN **3** Ills are difficulties or problems.

🔲 from Norse *illr* meaning 'bad'
🔳 (sense 1) sick, unhealthy, unwell

ill at ease
PHRASE If you feel **ill at ease**, you feel unable to relax.

illegal
ADJECTIVE forbidden by the law.

illegally ADVERB, **illegality** NOUN
🔳 criminal, illicit, unlawful

illegible
Said "il-**lej**-i-bl" ADJECTIVE Writing which is illegible is unclear and very difficult to read.

illegitimate
Said "il-lij-**it**-tim-it" ADJECTIVE A person who is illegitimate was born to parents who were not married at the time.

illegitimacy NOUN

ill-fated
ADJECTIVE doomed to end unhappily EG *his ill-fated attempt on the world record.*

illicit
Said "il-**liss**-it" ADJECTIVE not allowed by law or not approved of by society EG *illicit drugs.*

illiterate
ADJECTIVE unable to read or write.

illiteracy NOUN

illness illnesses
NOUN **1** Illness is the experience of being ill. **2** a particular disease EG *the treatment of common illnesses.*

🔳 (sense 2) ailment, disease, malady, sickness

illogical
ADJECTIVE An illogical feeling or action is not reasonable or sensible.

illogically ADVERB

ill-treat ill-treats ill-treating ill-treated
VERB If you ill-treat someone or something you hurt or damage them or treat them cruelly.

ill-treatment NOUN

illuminate illuminates illuminating

A
B
C
D
E
F
G
H
I
J
K
L
M
N
O
P
Q
R
S
T
U
V
W
X
Y
Z

illuminated
VERB To illuminate something is to shine light on it to make it easier to see.

illumination illuminations
NOUN **1** Illumination is lighting. **2** Illuminations are the coloured lights put up to decorate a town, especially at Christmas.

illusion illusions
NOUN **1** a false belief which you think is true EG *Their hopes proved to be an illusion.* **2** something which you think you see clearly but does not really exist EG *Painters create the illusion of space.*

illusory
Said "ill-**yoo**-ser-ee" ADJECTIVE seeming to be true, but actually false EG *an illusory truce.*

illustrate illustrates illustrating illustrated
VERB **1** If you illustrate a point, you explain it or make it clearer, often by using examples. **2** If you illustrate a book, you put pictures in it.
illustrator NOUN, **illustrative** ADJECTIVE

illustration illustrations
NOUN **1** an example or a story which is used to make a point clear. **2** a picture in a book.

illustrious
ADJECTIVE An illustrious person is famous and respected.

ill will
NOUN Ill will is a feeling of hostility.

image images
NOUN **1** a mental picture of someone or something. **2** the appearance which a person, group, or organization presents to the public.

imagery
NOUN The imagery of a poem or book is the descriptive language used.

imaginary
ADJECTIVE Something that is imaginary exists only in your mind, not in real life.

imagination imaginations
NOUN the ability to form new and exciting ideas.

imaginative
ADJECTIVE Someone who is imaginative can easily form new or exciting ideas in their mind.
imaginatively ADVERB

imagine imagines imagining imagined
VERB **1** If you imagine something, you form an idea of it in your mind, or you think you have seen or heard it but you have not really. **2** If you imagine that something is the case, you believe it is the case EG *I imagine that's what you aim to do.*
imaginable ADJECTIVE
▤ (sense 1) conceive, envisage, picture, visualize
▤ (sense 2) believe, suppose, think

imam
Said "ih-**mam**" NOUN a person who leads a group in prayer in a mosque.

imbalance imbalances
NOUN If there is an imbalance between things, they are unequal EG *the imbalance between rich and poor.*

imbecile imbeciles
Said "im-**bis**-seel" NOUN a stupid person.
▥ from Latin *imbecillus* meaning 'physically or mentally feeble'

imitate imitates imitating imitated
VERB To imitate someone or something is to copy them.
imitator NOUN, **imitative** ADJECTIVE
▤ copy, mimic

imitation imitations
NOUN a copy of something else.

immaculate
Said "im-**mak**-yoo-lit" ADJECTIVE **1** completely clean and tidy EG *The flat was immaculate.* **2** without any mistakes at all EG *his usual immaculate guitar accompaniment.*
immaculately ADVERB

immaterial
ADJECTIVE Something that is

immaterial is not important.

immature
ADJECTIVE **1** Something that is immature has not finished growing or developing. **2** A person who is immature does not behave in a sensible adult way.
immaturity NOUN

immediate
ADJECTIVE **1** Something that is immediate happens or is done without delay. **2** Your immediate relatives and friends are the ones most closely connected or related to you.

immediately
ADVERB **1** If something happens immediately it happens right away. **2** Immediately means very near in time or position EG *immediately behind the house.*

immemorial
ADJECTIVE If something has been happening from time immemorial, it has been happening longer than anyone can remember.

immense
ADJECTIVE very large or huge.
immensely ADVERB, **immensity** NOUN

immerse immerses immersing immersed
VERB **1** If you are immersed in an activity you are completely involved in it. **2** If you immerse something in a liquid, you put it into the liquid so that it is completely covered.
immersion NOUN

immigrant immigrants
NOUN someone who has come to live permanently in a new country.
immigrate VERB, **immigration** NOUN

imminent
ADJECTIVE If something is imminent, it is going to happen very soon.
imminently ADVERB, **imminence** NOUN
▪ coming, impending, near

immobile
ADJECTIVE not moving.
immobility NOUN

immoral
ADJECTIVE If you describe someone or their behaviour as immoral, you mean that they do not fit in with most people's idea of what is right and proper.
immorality NOUN
☑ Do not confuse *immoral* and *amoral*. You use *immoral* to talk about people who are aware of moral standards, but go against them. *Amoral* applies to people with no moral standards.

immortal
ADJECTIVE **1** Something that is immortal is famous and will be remembered for a long time EG *Emily Bronte's immortal love story.* **2** In stories, someone who is immortal will never die.
immortality NOUN

immovable or immoveable
ADJECTIVE Something that is immovable is fixed and cannot be moved.
immovably ADVERB

immune
Said "im-yoon" ADJECTIVE **1** If you are immune to a particular disease, you cannot catch it. **2** If someone or something is immune to something, they are able to avoid it or are not bound by it EG *The captain was immune to prosecution.*
immunity NOUN

immune system
NOUN Your body's immune system consists of your white blood cells, which fight disease by producing antibodies or germs to kill germs which come into your body.

imp imps
NOUN a small mischievous creature in fairy stories.
impish ADJECTIVE

impact impacts
NOUN **1** The impact that someone or something has is the impression that they make or the effect that they have. **2** Impact is the action of one object hitting another, usually

with a lot of force EG *The aircraft crashed into a ditch, exploding on impact.*

impair impairs impairing impaired
VERB To impair something is to damage it so that it stops working properly EG *Travel had made him weary and impaired his judgement.*

impale impales impaling impaled
VERB If you impale something, you pierce it with a sharp object.

impart imparts imparting imparted
VERB; A FORMAL WORD To impart information to someone is to pass it on to them.

impartial
ADJECTIVE Someone who is impartial has a fair and unbiased view of something.
impartially ADVERB, **impartiality** NOUN
■ fair, neutral, objective

impasse
Said "am-pass" NOUN a difficult situation in which it is impossible to find a solution.
▥ from French *impasse* meaning 'dead end'

impassioned
ADJECTIVE full of emotion EG *an impassioned plea.*

impassive
ADJECTIVE showing no emotion.
impassively ADVERB

impatient
ADJECTIVE 1 Someone who is impatient becomes annoyed easily or is quick to lose their temper when things go wrong. 2 If you are impatient to do something, you are eager and do not want to wait EG *He was impatient to get back.*
impatiently ADVERB, **impatience** NOUN

impeccable
Said "im-pek-i-bl" ADJECTIVE excellent, without any faults.
impeccably ADVERB

impede impedes impeding impeded
VERB If you impede someone, you

make their progress difficult.

impediment impediments
NOUN something that makes it difficult to move, develop, or do something properly EG *a speech impediment.*

impelled
ADJECTIVE If you feel impelled to do something, you feel strongly that you must do it.

impending
ADJECTIVE; A FORMAL WORD You use 'impending' to describe something that is going to happen very soon EG *a sense of impending doom.*

impenetrable
ADJECTIVE impossible to get through.

imperative
ADJECTIVE 1 Something that is imperative is extremely urgent or important. ▶ NOUN 2 In grammar, an imperative is the form of a verb that is used for giving orders.

imperfect
ADJECTIVE 1 Something that is imperfect has faults or problems.
▶ NOUN 2 In grammar, the imperfect is a tense used to describe continuous or repeated actions which happened in the past.
imperfectly ADVERB, **imperfection** NOUN
■ (sense 1) faulty, flawed

imperial
ADJECTIVE 1 Imperial means relating to an empire or an emperor or empress EG *the Imperial Palace.* 2 The imperial system of measurement is the measuring system which uses inches, feet, and yards, ounces and pounds, and pints and gallons.

imperialism
NOUN Imperialism is a system of rule in which a rich and powerful nation controls other nations.
imperialist ADJECTIVE OR NOUN

imperious
ADJECTIVE proud and domineering EG *an imperious manner.*
imperiously ADVERB

impersonal

ADJECTIVE Something that is impersonal makes you feel that individuals and their feelings do not matter EG *impersonal cold rooms.*
impersonally ADVERB

■ detached, dispassionate, inhuman

impersonate **impersonates impersonating impersonated**
VERB If you impersonate someone, you pretend to be that person.
impersonation NOUN, **impersonator** NOUN

impertinent
ADJECTIVE disrespectful and rude EG *impertinent questions.*
impertinently ADVERB, **impertinence** NOUN

impetuous
ADJECTIVE If you are impetuous, you act quickly without thinking EG *an impetuous gamble.*
impetuously ADVERB, **impetuosity** NOUN

impetus
NOUN 1 An impetus is the stimulating effect that something has on a situation, which causes it to develop more quickly. 2 In physics, impetus is the force that starts an object moving and resists changes in speed or direction.

impinge **impinges impinging impinged**
VERB If something impinges on your life, it has an effect on you and influences you EG *My private life doesn't impinge on my professional life.*

implacable
Said "im-plak-a-bl" ADJECTIVE Someone who is implacable is being harsh and refuses to change their mind.
implacably ADVERB

implant **implants implanting implanted**
VERB 1 To implant something into a person's body is to put it there, usually by means of an operation. ▶ NOUN 2 something that has been implanted into someone's body.

implausible

ADJECTIVE very unlikely EG *implausible stories.*
implausibly ADVERB

implement **implements implementing implemented**
VERB 1 If you implement something such as a plan, you carry it out EG *The government has failed to implement promised reforms.* ▶ NOUN 2 An implement is a tool.
implementation NOUN

implicate **implicates implicating implicated**
VERB If you are implicated in a crime, you are shown to be involved in it.

implication **implications**
NOUN something that is suggested or implied but not stated directly.

implicit
Said "im-pliss-it" ADJECTIVE
1 expressed in an indirect way EG *implicit criticism.* 2 If you have an implicit belief in something, you have no doubts about it EG *He had implicit faith in the noble intentions of the Emperor.*
implicitly ADVERB

implore **implores imploring implored**
VERB If you implore someone to do something, you beg them to do it.

imply **implies implying implied**
VERB If you imply that something is the case, you suggest it in an indirect way.

import **imports importing imported**
VERB 1 If you import something from another country, you bring it into your country or have it sent there. ▶ NOUN 2 a product that is made in another country and sent to your own country for use there.
importation NOUN, **importer** NOUN

important
ADJECTIVE 1 Something that is important is very valuable, necessary, or significant. 2 An important person has great influence or power.

A
B
C
D
E
F
G
H
I
J
K
L
M
N
O
P
Q
R
S
T
U
V
W
X
Y
Z

A B C D E F G H I J K L M N O P Q R S T U V W X Y Z

importantly ADVERB, **importance** NOUN
■ (sense 1) momentous, significant

impose imposes imposing
imposed
VERB 1 If you impose something on
people, you force it on them EG *The
allies had imposed a ban on all flights
over Iraq.* 2 If someone imposes on
you, they unreasonably expect you
to do something for them.
imposition NOUN

imposing
ADJECTIVE having an impressive
appearance or manner EG *an
imposing building.*

impossible
ADJECTIVE Something that is
impossible cannot happen, be
done, or be believed.
impossibly ADVERB, **impossibility** NOUN

imposter imposters; also spelt
impostor
NOUN a person who pretends to be
someone else in order to get things
they want.

impotent
ADJECTIVE 1 Someone who is
impotent has no power to
influence people or events. 2 A
man who is impotent is unable to
have or maintain an erection
during sexual intercourse.
impotently ADVERB, **impotence** NOUN

impound impounds impounding
impounded
VERB If something you own is
impounded, the police or other
officials take it.

impoverished
ADJECTIVE Someone who is
impoverished is poor.

impractical
ADJECTIVE not practical, sensible, or
realistic.

impregnable
ADJECTIVE A building or other
structure that is impregnable is so
strong that it cannot be broken
into or captured.

impregnated

ADJECTIVE If something is
impregnated with a substance, it
has absorbed the substance so that
it spreads right through it EG *sponges
impregnated with detergent and water.*

impresario impresarios
Said "im-pris-**sar**-ee-oh" NOUN a
person who manages theatrical or
musical events or companies.

impress impresses impressing
impressed
VERB 1 If you impress someone, you
make them admire or respect you.
2 If you impress something on
someone, you make them
understand the importance of it.

impression impressions
NOUN 1 An impression of someone
or something is the way they look
or seem to you. 2 If you **make an
impression**, you have a strong
effect on people you meet.

impressionable
ADJECTIVE easy to influence EG
impressionable teenagers.

impressionism
NOUN Impressionism is a style of
painting which is concerned with
the impressions created by light
and shapes, rather than with exact
details.
impressionist NOUN

impressive
ADJECTIVE If something is impressive,
it impresses you EG *an impressive
display of old-fashioned American cars.*

imprint imprints imprinting
imprinted
NOUN 1 If something leaves an
imprint on your mind, it has a
strong and lasting effect. 2 the
mark left by the pressure of one
object on another. ▶ VERB 3 If
something is imprinted on your
memory, it is firmly fixed there.

imprison imprisons imprisoning
imprisoned
VERB If you are imprisoned, you are
locked up, usually in a prison.
imprisonment NOUN

improbable

ADJECTIVE not probable or likely to happen.

improbably ADVERB

■ doubtful, unlikely

impromptu

Said "im-**prompt**-yoo" ADJECTIVE An impromptu action is one done without planning or organization.

▦ from Latin *in promptu* meaning 'in readiness'

■ improvised, off the cuff, unprepared

improper

ADJECTIVE **1** rude or shocking EG *improper behaviour.* **2** illegal or dishonest EG *improper dealings.* **3** not suitable or correct EG *an improper diet.*

improperly ADVERB

improve improves improving improved

VERB If something improves or if you improve it, it gets better or becomes more valuable.

improvement NOUN

■ better, enhance

improvise improvises improvising improvised

VERB **1** If you improvise something, you make or do something without planning in advance, and with whatever materials are available. **2** When musicians or actors improvise, they make up the music or words as they go along.

improvised ADJECTIVE, **improvisation** NOUN

impudent

ADJECTIVE If someone is impudent, they behave or speak disrespectfully.

impudently ADVERB, **impudence** NOUN

impulse impulses

NOUN a strong urge to do something EG *She felt a sudden impulse to confide in her.*

impulsive

ADJECTIVE If you are impulsive, you do things suddenly, without thinking about them carefully.

impulsively ADVERB

in

PREPOSITION OR ADVERB 'In' is used to indicate position, direction, time, and manner EG *boarding schools in England... in the past few years.*

in-

PREFIX **1** In- is added to the beginning of some words to form a word with the opposite meaning EG *insincere.* **2** In- also means in, into, or in the course of EG *infiltrate.*

inability

NOUN a lack of ability to do something.

inaccessible

ADJECTIVE impossible or very difficult to reach.

inadequate

ADJECTIVE **1** If something is inadequate, there is not enough of it, or it is not good enough in quality for a particular purpose. **2** If someone feels inadequate, they feel they do not possess the skills necessary to do a particular job or to cope with life in general.

inadequately ADVERB, **inadequacy** NOUN

■ (sense 1) insufficient, meagre

inadvertent

ADJECTIVE not intentional EG *the murder had been inadvertent.*

inadvertently ADVERB

inane

ADJECTIVE silly or stupid.

inanely ADVERB, **inanity** NOUN

inanimate

ADJECTIVE An inanimate object is not alive.

inappropriate

ADJECTIVE not suitable for a particular purpose or occasion EG *It was quite inappropriate to ask such questions.*

inappropriately ADVERB

■ out of place, unfitting, unsuitable

inarticulate

ADJECTIVE If you are inarticulate, you are unable to express yourself well or easily in speech.

inasmuch

A B C D E F G H I J K L M N O P Q R S T U V W X Y Z

CONJUNCTION 'Inasmuch as' means to the extent that EG *She's giving herself a hard time inasmuch as she feels guilty.*

inaudible
ADJECTIVE not loud enough to be heard.
inaudibly ADVERB

inaugurate inaugurates inaugurating inaugurated
Said "in-**awg**-yoo-rate" VERB **1** To inaugurate a new scheme is to start it. **2** To inaugurate a new leader is to officially establish them in their new position in a special ceremony EG *Albania's Orthodox Church inaugurated its first archbishop in 25 years.*
inauguration NOUN, **inaugural** ADJECTIVE

inborn
ADJECTIVE An inborn quality is one that you were born with.

incandescent
ADJECTIVE Something which is incandescent gives out light when it is heated.
incandescence NOUN
📖 from Latin *candescere* meaning 'to glow white'

incapable
ADJECTIVE **1** Someone who is incapable of doing something is not able to do it EG *He is incapable of changing a fuse.* **2** An incapable person is weak and helpless.

incarcerate incarcerates incarcerating incarcerated
Said "in-**kar**-ser-rate" VERB To incarcerate someone is to lock them up.
incarceration NOUN

Incarnation
NOUN The Incarnation is the Christian belief that God took human form in Jesus Christ.

incendiary
Said "in-**send**-yer-ee" ADJECTIVE An incendiary weapon is one which sets fire to things EG *incendiary bombs.*

incense
NOUN Incense is a spicy substance which is burned to create a sweet smell, especially during religious services.

incensed
ADJECTIVE If you are incensed by something, it makes you extremely angry.

incentive incentives
NOUN something that encourages you to do something.
📖 from Latin *incentivus* meaning 'the beginning of a song'

inception
NOUN; A FORMAL WORD The inception of a project is the start of it.

incessant
ADJECTIVE continuing without stopping EG *her incessant talking.*
incessantly ADVERB

incest
NOUN Incest is the crime of two people who are closely related having sex with each other.
incestuous ADJECTIVE

inch inches inching inched
NOUN **1** a unit of length equal to about 2.54 centimetres. ▶ VERB **2** To inch forward is to move forward slowly.
📖 from Latin *uncia* meaning 'twelfth part'; there are twelve inches to the foot

incident incidents
NOUN an event EG *a shooting incident.*

incidental
ADJECTIVE occurring as a minor part of something EG *vivid incidental detail.*
incidentally ADVERB

incinerate incinerates incinerating incinerated
VERB If you incinerate something, you burn it.
incineration NOUN

incinerator incinerators
NOUN a furnace for burning rubbish.

incipient
ADJECTIVE beginning to happen or

appear EG *incipient panic*.

incision incisions
NOUN a sharp cut, usually made by a surgeon operating on a patient.

incisive
ADJECTIVE Incisive language is clear and forceful..

incite incites inciting incited
VERB If you incite someone to do something, you encourage them to do it by making them angry or excited.
incitement NOUN
≣ encourage, provoke, spur

inclination inclinations
NOUN If you have an inclination to do something, you want to do it.

incline inclines inclining inclined
VERB **1** If you are inclined to behave in a certain way, you often behave that way or you want to behave that way. ▶ NOUN **2** a slope.

include includes including included
VERB If one thing includes another, it has the second thing as one of its parts.
including PREPOSITION
≣ contain, incorporate

inclusion
NOUN The inclusion of one thing in another is the act of making it part of the other thing.

inclusive
ADJECTIVE A price that is inclusive includes all the goods and services that are being offered, with no extra charge for any of them.

incognito
Said "in-kog-**nee**-toe" ADVERB If you are travelling incognito, you are travelling in disguise.
▥ from Latin *in-* + *cognitus* meaning 'not known'

incoherent
ADJECTIVE If someone is incoherent, they are talking in an unclear or rambling way.
incoherently ADVERB, **incoherence** NOUN

income incomes

NOUN the money a person earns.

income tax
NOUN Income tax is a part of someone's salary which they have to pay regularly to the government.

incoming
ADJECTIVE coming in EG *incoming trains... an incoming phone call*.

incomparable
ADJECTIVE Something that is incomparable is so good that it cannot be compared with anything else.
incomparably ADVERB
≣ matchless, unequalled, unparalleled

incompatible
ADJECTIVE Two things or people are incompatible if they are unable to live or exist together because they are completely different.
incompatibility NOUN

incompetent
ADJECTIVE Someone who is incompetent does not have the ability to do something properly.
incompetently ADVERB, **incompetence** NOUN

incomplete
ADJECTIVE not complete or finished.
incompletely ADVERB

incomprehensible
ADJECTIVE not able to be understood.

inconceivable
ADJECTIVE impossible to believe.

inconclusive
ADJECTIVE not leading to a decision or to a definite result.

incongruous
ADJECTIVE Something that is incongruous seems strange because it does not fit in to a place or situation.
incongruously ADVERB

inconsequential
ADJECTIVE Something that is inconsequential is not very important.

inconsistent
ADJECTIVE Someone or something

A B C D E F G H I J K L M N O P Q R S T U V W X Y Z

371

which is inconsistent is unpredictable and behaves differently in similar situations.
inconsistently ADVERB, **inconsistency** NOUN

inconspicuous
ADJECTIVE not easily seen or obvious.
inconspicuously ADVERB

incontinent
ADJECTIVE Someone who is incontinent is unable to control their bladder or bowels.

inconvenience inconveniences inconveniencing inconvenienced
NOUN **1** If something causes inconvenience, it causes difficulty or problems. ▶ VERB **2** To inconvenience someone is to cause them difficulty or problems.
inconvenient ADJECTIVE, **inconveniently** ADVERB

incorporate incorporates incorporating incorporated
VERB If something is incorporated into another thing, it becomes part of that thing.
incorporation NOUN

incorrect
ADJECTIVE wrong or untrue.
incorrectly ADVERB

increase increases increasing increased
VERB **1** If something increases, it becomes larger in amount. ▶ NOUN **2** A rise in the number, level, or amount of something.
increasingly ADVERB

incredible
ADJECTIVE totally amazing or impossible to believe.
incredibly ADVERB
▪ amazing, unbelievable

incredulous
ADJECTIVE If you are incredulous, you are unable to believe something because it is very surprising or shocking.
incredulously ADVERB, **incredulity** NOUN

increment increments
NOUN the amount by which

something increases, or a regular increase in someone's salary.
incremental ADJECTIVE

incriminate incriminates incriminating incriminated
VERB If something incriminates you, it suggests that you are involved in a crime.

incubate incubates incubating incubated
Said "in-kyoo-bate" VERB When eggs incubate, they are kept warm until they are ready to hatch.
incubation NOUN

incubator incubators
NOUN a piece of hospital equipment in which sick or weak newborn babies are kept warm.

incumbent incumbents
A FORMAL WORD ▶ ADJECTIVE **1** If it is incumbent on you to do something, it is your duty to do it. ▶ NOUN **2** the person in a particular official position.

incur incurs incurring incurred
VERB If you incur something unpleasant, you cause it to happen.

incurable
ADJECTIVE **1** An incurable disease is one which cannot be cured. **2** An incurable habit is one which cannot be changed EG *an incurable romantic*.
incurably ADVERB

indebted
ADJECTIVE If you are indebted to someone, you are grateful to them.

indecent
ADJECTIVE Something that is indecent is shocking or rude, usually because it concerns nakedness or sex.
indecently ADVERB, **indecency** NOUN

indeed
ADVERB You use 'indeed' to strengthen a point that you are making EG *The desserts are very good indeed*.
▣ from Middle English *in dede* meaning 'in fact'

indefatigable

Said "in-dif-**fat**-ig-a-bl" ADJECTIVE
People who never get tired of doing something are indefatigable.

indefinite
ADJECTIVE 1 If something is indefinite, no time to finish has been decided EG *an indefinite strike*. 2 Indefinite also means vague or not exact EG *indefinite words and pictures*.
indefinitely ADVERB

indefinite article indefinite articles
NOUN the grammatical term for 'a' and 'an'.

indelible
ADJECTIVE unable to be removed EG *indelible ink*.
indelibly ADVERB

indemnity
NOUN; A FORMAL WORD Indemnity is protection against damage or loss.

indentation indentations
NOUN a dent or a groove in a surface or on the edge of something.

independent
ADJECTIVE 1 Something that is independent happens or exists separately from other people or things EG *Results are assessed by an independent panel*. 2 Someone who is independent does not need other people's help EG *a fiercely independent woman*.
independently ADVERB, **independence** NOUN
■ (sense 1) autonomous, self-governing

indeterminate
ADJECTIVE not certain or definite EG *some indeterminate point in the future*.

index indexes
NOUN an alphabetical list at the back of a book, referring to items in the book.

index finger index fingers
NOUN your first finger, next to your thumb.

Indian Indians
ADJECTIVE 1 belonging or relating to India. ▶ NOUN 2 someone who comes from India. 3 someone descended from the people who lived in North, South, or Central America before Europeans arrived.

indicate indicates indicating indicated
VERB 1 If something indicates something, it shows that it is true EG *a gesture which clearly indicates his relief*. 2 If you indicate something to someone, you point to it. 3 If you indicate a fact, you mention it. 4 If the driver of a vehicle indicates, they give a signal to show which way they are going to turn.
■ (sense 1) denote, show, signify

indication indications
NOUN a sign of what someone feels or what is likely to happen.

indicative
ADJECTIVE 1 If something is indicative of something else, it is a sign of that thing EG *Clean, pink tongues are indicative of a good, healthy digestion*. ▶ NOUN 2 If a verb is used in the indicative, it is in the form used for making statements.

indicator indicators
NOUN 1 something which tells you what something is like or what is happening. 2 A car's indicators are the lights at the front and back which are used to show when it is turning left or right. 3 a substance used in chemistry that shows if another substance is an acid or alkali by changing colour when it comes into contact with it.

indict indicts indicting indicted
Said "in-**dite**" VERB; A FORMAL WORD To indict someone is to charge them officially with a crime.
indictment NOUN, **indictable** ADJECTIVE

indifferent
ADJECTIVE 1 If you are indifferent to something, you have no interest in it. 2 If something is indifferent, it is of a poor quality or low standard EG *a pair of rather indifferent paintings*.

A B C D E F G H I J K L M N O P Q R S T U V W X Y Z

indifferently ADVERB, **indifference** NOUN

indigenous
Said "in-**dij**-in-uss" ADJECTIVE If something is indigenous to a country, it comes from that country EG *a plant indigenous to Asia.*

indigestion
NOUN Indigestion is a pain you get when you find it difficult to digest food.

indignant
ADJECTIVE If you are indignant, you feel angry about something that you think is unfair.
indignantly ADVERB

indignation
NOUN Indignation is anger about something that you think is unfair.

indignity **indignities**
NOUN something that makes you feel embarrassed or humiliated EG *the indignity of having to flee angry protesters.*

indigo
NOUN OR ADJECTIVE dark violet-blue.

indirect
ADJECTIVE Something that is indirect is not done or caused directly by a particular person or thing, but by someone or something else.
indirectly ADVERB
⊟ circuitous, roundabout

indiscriminate
ADJECTIVE not involving careful thought or choice EG *an indiscriminate bombing campaign.*
indiscriminately ADVERB

indispensable
ADJECTIVE If something is indispensable, you cannot do without it EG *A good pair of walking shoes is indispensable.*

indistinct
ADJECTIVE not clear EG *indistinct voices.*

individual **individuals**
ADJECTIVE **1** relating to one particular person or thing EG *Each family needs individual attention.* **2** Someone who is individual behaves quite differently from the way other

people behave. ▸ NOUN **3** a person, different from any other person EG *wealthy individuals.*
individually ADVERB

individualist **individualists**
NOUN someone who likes to do things in their own way.
individualistic ADJECTIVE

individuality
NOUN If something has individuality, it is different from all other things, and therefore is very interesting and noticeable.

indomitable
ADJECTIVE; A FORMAL WORD impossible to overcome EG *an indomitable spirit.*

Indonesian **Indonesians**
Said "in-don-**nee**-zee-an" ADJECTIVE **1** belonging or relating to Indonesia. ▸ NOUN **2** someone who comes from Indonesia. **3** Indonesian is the official language of Indonesia.

indoor
ADJECTIVE situated or happening inside a building.

indoors
ADVERB If something happens indoors, it takes place inside a building.

induce **induces inducing induced**
VERB **1** To induce a state is to cause it EG *His manner was rough and suspicious but he did not induce fear.* **2** If you induce someone to do something, you persuade them to do it.

inducement **inducements**
NOUN something offered to encourage someone to do something.

indulge **indulges indulging indulged**
VERB **1** If you indulge in something, you allow yourself to do something that you enjoy. **2** If you indulge someone, you let them have or do what they want, often in a way that is not good for them.

indulgence **indulgences**

NOUN **1** something you allow yourself to have because it gives you pleasure. **2** Indulgence is the act of indulging yourself or another person.

indulgent
ADJECTIVE If you are indulgent, you treat someone with special kindness EG *a rich, indulgent father.*
indulgently ADJECTIVE

industrial
ADJECTIVE relating to industry.

industrial action
NOUN Industrial action is action such as striking taken by workers in protest over pay or working conditions.

industrialist industrialists
NOUN a person who owns or controls a lot of factories.

Industrial Revolution
NOUN The Industrial Revolution took place in Britain in the late eighteenth and early nineteenth century, when machines began to be used more in factories and more goods were produced as a result.

industrious
ADJECTIVE An industrious person works very hard.

industry industries
NOUN **1** Industry is the work and processes involved in manufacturing things in factories. **2** all the people and processes involved in manufacturing a particular thing.

inedible
ADJECTIVE too nasty or poisonous to eat.

inefficient
ADJECTIVE badly organized, wasteful, and slow EG *a corrupt and inefficient administration.*
inefficiently ADVERB, **inefficiency** NOUN

inept
ADJECTIVE without skill EG *an inept lawyer.*
ineptitude NOUN

inequality inequalities

NOUN a difference in size, status, wealth, or position, between different things, groups, or people.

inert
ADJECTIVE Something that is inert does not move and appears lifeless EG *an inert body lying on the floor.*

inertia
Said "in-**ner**-sha" NOUN If you have a feeling of inertia, you feel very lazy and unwilling to do anything.

inevitable
ADJECTIVE certain to happen.
inevitably ADVERB, **inevitability** NOUN

inexhaustible
ADJECTIVE Something that is inexhaustible will never be used up EG *an inexhaustible supply of ideas.*

inexorable
ADJECTIVE; A FORMAL WORD Something that is inexorable cannot be prevented from continuing EG *the inexorable increase in the number of cars.*
inexorably ADVERB

inexpensive
ADJECTIVE not costing much.

inexperienced
ADJECTIVE lacking experience of a situation or activity EG *inexperienced drivers.*
inexperience NOUN
■ new, raw, unpractised

inexplicable
ADJECTIVE If something is inexplicable, you cannot explain it EG *For some inexplicable reason I still felt uneasy.*
inexplicably ADVERB

inextricably
ADVERB If two or more things are inextricably linked, they cannot be separated.

infallible
ADJECTIVE never wrong EG *No machine is infallible.*
infallibility NOUN

infamous
Said "**in**-fe-muss" ADJECTIVE well-known because of something

A
B
C
D
E
F
G
H
I
J
K
L
M
N
O
P
Q
R
S
T
U
V
W
X
Y
Z

bad or evil EG *a book about the country's most infamous murder cases.*

infant infants
NOUN **1** a baby or very young child. ▶ ADJECTIVE **2** designed for young children EG *an infant school.*
infancy NOUN, **infantile** ADJECTIVE
⬛ from Latin *infans* meaning 'unable to speak'

infantry
NOUN In an army, the infantry are soldiers who fight on foot rather than in tanks or on horses.

infatuated
ADJECTIVE If you are infatuated with someone, you have such strong feelings of love or passion that you cannot think sensibly about them.
infatuation NOUN

infect infects infecting infected
VERB To infect someone or something is to cause disease in them.

infection infections
NOUN **1** a disease caused by germs EG *a chest infection.* **2** Infection is the state of being infected EG *a very small risk of infection.*

infectious
ADJECTIVE spreading from one person to another EG *an infectious disease.*
▤ catching, contagious

infer infers inferring inferred
VERB If you infer something, you work out that it is true on the basis of information that you already have.
inference NOUN
✔ Do not use *infer* to mean the same as *imply.*

inferior inferiors
ADJECTIVE **1** having a lower position or worth less than something else EG *inferior quality cassette tapes.* ▶ NOUN **2** Your inferiors are people in a lower position than you.
inferiority NOUN

infernal
ADJECTIVE very unpleasant EG *an infernal bore.*

⬛ from Latin *infernus* meaning 'hell'

inferno infernos
NOUN a very large dangerous fire.

infertile
ADJECTIVE **1** Infertile soil is of poor quality and plants cannot grow well in it. **2** Someone who is infertile cannot have children.

infested
ADJECTIVE Something that is infested has a large number of animals or insects living on it and causing damage EG *The flats are damp and infested with rats.*
infestation NOUN

infidelity infidelities
NOUN Infidelity is being unfaithful to your husband, wife, or lover.

infighting
NOUN Infighting is quarrelling or rivalry between members of the same organization.

infiltrate infiltrates infiltrating infiltrated
VERB If people infiltrate an organization, they gradually enter it in secret to spy on its activities.
infiltration NOUN

infinite
ADJECTIVE without any limit or end EG *an infinite number of possibilities.*
infinitely ADVERB
▤ limitless, never-ending

infinitive infinitives
NOUN In grammar, the infinitive is the base form of the verb. It often has 'to' in front of it, for example 'to go' or 'to see'.

infinity
NOUN **1** Infinity is a number that is larger than any other number and can never be given an exact value. **2** Infinity is also an unreachable point, further away than any other point EG *skies stretching on into infinity.*

infirmary infirmaries
NOUN a hospital.

inflamed

ADJECTIVE If part of your body is inflamed, it is red and swollen, usually because of infection.

inflammable
ADJECTIVE An inflammable material burns easily.
☑ Although *inflammable* and *flammable* both mean 'likely to catch fire', *flammable* is used more often as people sometimes think that *inflammable* means 'not likely to catch fire'.

inflammation
NOUN Inflammation is painful redness or swelling of part of the body.

inflammatory
ADJECTIVE Inflammatory actions are likely to make people very angry.

inflate inflates inflating inflated
VERB When you inflate something, you fill it with air or gas to make it swell.
inflatable ADJECTIVE

inflation
NOUN Inflation is an increase in the price of goods and services in a country.
inflationary ADJECTIVE

inflection inflections; also spelt inflexion
NOUN a change in the form of a word that shows its grammatical function, for example a change that makes a noun plural.

inflexible
ADJECTIVE fixed and unable to be altered EG *an inflexible routine*.

inflict inflicts inflicting inflicted
VERB If you inflict something unpleasant on someone, you make them suffer it.

influence influences influencing influenced
NOUN 1 Influence is power that a person has over other people. 2 An influence is also the effect that someone or something has EG *under the influence of alcohol*. ▶ VERB 3 To influence someone or something

means to have an effect on them.
▥ from Latin *influentia* meaning 'power flowing from the stars'
▤ (sense 1) hold, power, pull

influential
ADJECTIVE Someone who is influential has a lot of influence over people.

influenza
NOUN; A FORMAL WORD Influenza is flu.

influx
NOUN a steady arrival of of people or things EG *a large influx of tourists*.

inform informs informing informed
VERB 1 If you inform someone of something, you tell them about it. 2 If you inform on a person, you tell the police about a crime they have committed.
informant NOUN
▤ (sense 1) notify, tell
▤ (sense 2) betray, grass, shop

informal
ADJECTIVE relaxed and casual EG *an informal meeting*.
informally ADVERB, **informality** NOUN

information
NOUN If you have information on or about something, you know something about it.
▤ data, facts

informative
ADJECTIVE Something that is informative gives you useful information.

informer informers
NOUN someone who tells the police that another person has committed a crime.

infrastructure infrastructures
NOUN The infrastructure of a country consists of things like factories, schools, and roads, which show how much money the country has and how strong its economy is.

infringe infringes infringing infringed
VERB 1 If you infringe a law, you

A
B

break it. **2** To infringe people's rights is to not allow them the rights to which they are entitled.
infringement NOUN

C
D

infuriate infuriates infuriating infuriated
VERB If someone infuriates you, they make you very angry.
infuriating ADJECTIVE

E
F
G
H

infuse infuses infusing infused
VERB **1** If you infuse someone with a feeling such as enthusiasm or joy, you fill them with it. **2** If you infuse a substance such as a herb or medicine, you pour hot water onto it and leave it for the water to absorb the flavour.
infusion NOUN

I

ingenious
Said "in-**jeen**-yuss" ADJECTIVE very clever and using new ideas EG *his ingenious invention.*
ingeniously ADVERB

J
K
L

ingenuity
Said "in-jen-**yoo**-it-ee" NOUN Ingenuity is cleverness and skill at inventing things or working out plans.

M
N
O

ingot ingots
NOUN a brick-shaped lump of metal, especially gold.

P

ingrained
ADJECTIVE If habits and beliefs are ingrained, they are difficult to change or destroy.

Q
R

ingredient ingredients
NOUN Ingredients are the things that something is made from, especially in cookery.

S
T

inhabit inhabits inhabiting inhabited
VERB If you inhabit a place, you live there.

U
V

inhabitant inhabitants
NOUN The inhabitants of a place are the people who live there.
▤ citizen, dweller, resident

W
X
Y

inhale inhales inhaling inhaled
VERB When you inhale, you breathe in.

Z

inhalation NOUN

inherent
ADJECTIVE Inherent qualities or characteristics in something are a natural part of it EG *her inherent common sense.*
inherently ADVERB

inherit inherits inheriting inherited
VERB **1** If you inherit money or property, you receive it from someone who has died. **2** If you inherit a quality or characteristic from a parent or ancestor, it is passed on to you at birth.
inheritance NOUN, **inheritor** NOUN

inhibit inhibits inhibiting inhibited
VERB If you inhibit someone from doing something, you prevent them from doing it.

inhibited
ADJECTIVE People who are inhibited find it difficult to relax and to show their emotions.

inhibition inhibitions
NOUN Inhibitions are feelings of fear or embarrassment that make it difficult for someone to relax and to show their emotions.

inhospitable
ADJECTIVE **1** An inhospitable place is unpleasant or difficult to live in. **2** If someone is inhospitable, they do not make people who visit them feel welcome.

inhuman
ADJECTIVE not human or not behaving like a human EG *the inhuman killing of their enemies.*

inhumane
ADJECTIVE extremely cruel.
inhumanity NOUN

inimitable
ADJECTIVE If you have an inimitable characteristic, no-one else can imitate it EG *her inimitable sense of style.*

initial initials
Said "in-**nish**-l" ADJECTIVE **1** first, or at the beginning EG *Shock and dismay*

were my initial reactions. ▶ NOUN **2** the first letter of a name.
initially ADVERB

initiate initiates initiating initiated
Said "in-**nish**-ee-ate" VERB **1** If you initiate something, you make it start or happen. **2** If you initiate someone into a group or club, you allow them to become a member of it, usually by means of a special ceremony.
initiation NOUN

initiative initiatives
Said "in-**nish**-at-ive" NOUN **1** an attempt to get something done. **2** If you have initiative, you decide what to do and then do it, without needing the advice of other people.

inject injects injecting injected
VERB **1** If a doctor or nurse injects you with a substance, they use a needle and syringe to put the substance into your body. **2** If you inject something new into a situation, you add it.
injection NOUN

injunction injunctions
NOUN an order issued by a court of law to stop someone doing something.

injure injures injuring injured
VERB To injure someone is to damage part of their body.
injury NOUN

injustice injustices
NOUN **1** Injustice is unfairness and lack of justice. **2** If you do someone an injustice, you judge them too harshly.

ink
NOUN Ink is the coloured liquid used for writing or printing.

inkling inklings
NOUN a vague idea about something.

inlaid
ADJECTIVE decorated with small pieces of wood, metal, or stone EG *decorative plates inlaid with brass.*
inlay NOUN

inland

ADVERB OR ADJECTIVE towards or near the middle of a country, away from the sea.

in-law in-laws
NOUN Your in-laws are members of your husband's or wife's family.

inlet inlets
NOUN a narrow bay.

inmate inmates
NOUN someone who lives in a prison or psychiatric hospital.

inn inns
NOUN a small old country pub or hotel.

innards
PLURAL NOUN The innards of something are its inside parts.

innate
ADJECTIVE An innate quality is one that you were born with EG *an innate sense of fairness.*
innately ADVERB

inner
ADJECTIVE contained inside a place or object EG *an inner room.*

innermost
ADJECTIVE deepest and most secret EG *our innermost feelings.*

innings
NOUN In cricket, an innings is a period when a particular team is batting.

innocent
ADJECTIVE **1** not guilty of a crime. **2** without experience of evil or unpleasant things EG *an innocent child.*
innocently ADVERB, **innocence** NOUN

innocuous
Said "in-**nok**-yoo-uss" ADJECTIVE not harmful.

innovation innovations
NOUN a completely new idea, product, or system of doing things.

innuendo innuendos or innuendoes
Said "in-yoo-**en**-doe" NOUN an indirect reference to something rude or unpleasant.

A B C D E F G H I J K L M N O P Q R S T U V W X Y Z

379

A
B
C
D
E
F
G
H
I
J
K
L
M
N
O
P
Q
R
S
T
U
V
W
X
Y
Z

🏛 from Latin *innuendo* meaning 'by hinting', from *innuere* meaning 'to convey by a nod'

innumerable
ADJECTIVE too many to be counted EG *innumerable cups of tea*.

input inputs
NOUN **1** Input consists of all the money, information, and other resources that are put into a job, project, or company to make it work. **2** In computing, input is information which is fed into a computer.

inquest inquests
NOUN an official inquiry to find out what caused a person's death.

inquire inquires inquiring inquired; also spelt **enquire**
VERB If you inquire about something, you ask for information about it.
inquiring ADJECTIVE, **inquiry** NOUN

inquisition inquisitions
NOUN an official investigation, especially one which is very thorough and uses harsh methods of questioning.

inquisitive
ADJECTIVE Someone who is inquisitive is keen to find out about things.
inquisitively ADVERB

inroads
PLURAL NOUN If something makes inroads on or into something, it starts affecting it.

insane
ADJECTIVE Someone who is insane is mad.
insanely ADVERB, **insanity** NOUN

insatiable
Said "in-**saysh**-a-bl" ADJECTIVE A desire or urge that is insatiable is very great EG *an insatiable curiosity*.
insatiably ADVERB

inscribe inscribes inscribing inscribed
VERB If you inscribe words on an object, you write or carve them on

it.

inscription inscriptions
NOUN the words that are written or carved on something.

inscrutable
Said "in-**skroot**-a-bl" ADJECTIVE Someone who is inscrutable does not show what they are really thinking.

insect insects
NOUN a small creature with six legs, and usually wings.

insecticide insecticides
NOUN a poisonous chemical used to kill insects.

insecure
ADJECTIVE **1** If you are insecure, you feel unsure of yourself and doubt whether other people like you. **2** Something that is insecure is not safe or well protected EG *People still feel their jobs are insecure*.
insecurity NOUN

insensitive
ADJECTIVE If you are insensitive, you do not notice when you are upsetting people.
insensitivity NOUN

insert inserts inserting inserted
VERB If you insert an object into something, you put it inside.
insertion NOUN

inshore
ADJECTIVE at sea but close to the shore EG *inshore boats*.

inside insides
ADVERB, PREPOSITION, OR ADJECTIVE
1 Inside refers to the part of something which is surrounded by the main part and is often hidden EG *Tom had to stay inside and work... inside the house... an inside pocket*.
▶ PLURAL NOUN **2** Your insides are the parts inside your body. ▶ PHRASE
3 Inside out means with the inside part facing outwards.
✔ Do not use *of* after *inside*. You should write *she was waiting inside the school* and not *inside of the school*.

insider insiders
NOUN a person who is involved in a situation and so knows more about it than other people.

insidious
ADJECTIVE Something that is insidious is unpleasant and develops slowly without being noticed EG *the insidious progress of the disease.*
insidiously ADVERB

insight insights
NOUN If you gain insight into a problem, you gradually get a deep and accurate understanding of it.

insignia
Said "in-sig-nee-a" NOUN the badge or a sign of a particular organization.

insignificant
ADJECTIVE small and unimportant.
insignificance NOUN

insinuate insinuates insinuating insinuated
VERB If you insinuate something unpleasant, you hint about it.
insinuation NOUN

insipid
ADJECTIVE 1 An insipid person or activity is dull and boring. 2 Food that is insipid has very little taste.
■ (sense 1) bland, colourless, uninteresting

insist insists insisting insisted
VERB If you insist on something, you demand it forcefully.
insistent ADJECTIVE, **insistence** NOUN

insolent
ADJECTIVE very rude and disrespectful.
insolently ADVERB, **insolence** NOUN

insoluble
Said "in-soll-yoo-bl" ADJECTIVE
1 impossible to solve EG *an insoluble problem.* 2 unable to dissolve EG *substances which are insoluble in water.*

insolvent
ADJECTIVE unable to pay your debts.
insolvency NOUN

insomnia
NOUN Insomnia is difficulty in sleeping.
insomniac NOUN

inspect inspects inspecting inspected
VERB To inspect something is to examine it carefully to check that everything is all right.
inspection NOUN

inspector inspectors
NOUN 1 someone who inspects things. 2 a police officer just above a sergeant in rank.

inspire inspires inspiring inspired
VERB 1 If something inspires you, it gives you new ideas and enthusiasm to do something. 2 To inspire an emotion in someone is to make them feel this emotion.
inspired ADJECTIVE, **inspiring** ADJECTIVE, **inspiration** NOUN

instability
NOUN Instability is a lack of stability in a place EG *political instability.*

install installs installing installed
VERB 1 If you install a piece of equipment in a place, you put it there so it is ready to be used. 2 To install someone in an important job is to officially give them that position. 3 If you install yourself in a place, you settle there and make yourself comfortable.
installation NOUN

instalment instalments
NOUN 1 If you pay for something in instalments, you pay small amounts of money regularly over a period of time. 2 one of the parts of a story or television series.

instance instances
NOUN 1 a particular example or occurrence of an event, situation, or person EG *a serious instance of corruption.* ▶ PHRASE 2 You use **for instance** to give an example of something you are talking about.

instant instants
NOUN 1 a moment or short period of time EG *In an instant they were gone.*
▶ ADJECTIVE 2 immediate and without delay EG *The record was an instant*

success.

instantly ADVERB

instantaneous

ADJECTIVE happening immediately and without delay EG *The applause was instantaneous.*

instantaneously ADVERB

instead

ADVERB in place of something EG *Take the stairs instead of the lift.*

instigate instigates instigating instigated

VERB Someone who instigates a situation makes it happen.

instigation NOUN, **instigator** NOUN

instil instils instilling instilled

VERB If you instil an idea or feeling into someone, you make them feel or think it.

instinct instincts

NOUN a natural tendency to do something EG *My first instinct was to protect myself.*

instinctive ADJECTIVE, **instinctively** ADVERB

institute institutes instituting instituted

NOUN **1** an organization for teaching or research. ▶ VERB **2** A FORMAL USE If you institute a rule or system, you introduce it.

institution institutions

NOUN **1** a custom or system regarded as an important tradition within a society EG *The family is an institution to be cherished.* **2** a large, important organization, for example a university or bank.

institutional ADJECTIVE

instruct instructs instructing instructed

VERB **1** If you instruct someone to do something, you tell them to do it. **2** If someone instructs you in a subject or skill, they teach you about it.

instructor NOUN, **instructive** ADJECTIVE, **instruction** NOUN

instrument instruments

NOUN **1** a tool or device used for a particular job EG *a special instrument*

which cut through the metal. **2** A musical instrument is an object, such as a piano or flute, played to make music.

instrumental

ADJECTIVE **1** If you are instrumental in doing something, you help to make it happen. **2** Instrumental music is performed using only musical instruments, and not voices.

insufficient

ADJECTIVE not enough for a particular purpose.

insufficiently ADVERB

insular

Said "inss-yoo-lar" ADJECTIVE Someone who is insular is unwilling to meet new people or to consider new ideas.

insularity NOUN

insulate insulates insulating insulated

VERB If you insulate something, you cover it with a layer to keep it warm or to stop electricity passing through it.

insulation NOUN, **insulator** NOUN

insulin

Said "inss-yoo-lin" NOUN Insulin is a substance which controls the level of sugar in the blood. People who have diabetes do not produce insulin naturally and have to take regular doses of it.

insult insults insulting insulted

VERB **1** If you insult someone, you offend them by being rude to them. ▶ NOUN **2** a rude remark which offends you.

insulting ADJECTIVE

▤ (sense 1) abuse, affront, offend
▤ (sense 2) abuse, affront, offence

insure insures insuring insured

VERB **1** If you insure something or yourself, you pay money regularly to a company so that if there is an accident or damage, the company will pay for medical treatment or repairs. **2** If you do something to insure against something unpleasant happening, you do it to prevent the unpleasant thing from happening or to protect yourself if it does happen.

insurance NOUN

insurrection insurrections
NOUN a violent action taken against the rulers of a country.

intact
ADJECTIVE complete, and not changed or damaged in any way EG *The rear of the aircraft remained intact when it crashed.*

intake intakes
NOUN A person's intake of food, drink, or air is the amount they take in.

integral
ADJECTIVE If something is an integral part of a whole thing, it is an essential part.

integrate integrates integrating integrated
VERB **1** If a person integrates into a group, they become part of it. **2** To integrate things is to combine them so that they become closely linked or form one thing EG *his plan to integrate the coal and steel industries.*
integration NOUN

integrity
NOUN **1** Integrity is the quality of being honest and following your principles. **2** The integrity of a group of people is their being united as one whole.

intellect intellects
NOUN Intellect is the ability to understand ideas and information.

intellectual intellectuals
ADJECTIVE **1** involving thought, ideas, and understanding EG *an intellectual exercise.* ▶ NOUN **2** someone who enjoys thinking about complicated ideas.
intellectually ADVERB

intelligence
NOUN A person's intelligence is their ability to understand and learn

things quickly and well.
intelligent ADJECTIVE, **intelligently** ADVERB
■ brains, intellect, understanding

intelligentsia
Said "in-tell-lee-jent-sya" NOUN The intelligentsia are intellectual people, considered as a group.

intelligible
ADJECTIVE able to be understood EG *very few intelligible remarks.*

intend intends intending intended
VERB **1** If you intend to do something, you have decided or planned to do it EG *She intended to move back to Cape Town.* **2** If something is intended for a particular use, you have planned that it should have this use EG *The booklet is intended to be kept handy.*

intense
ADJECTIVE **1** very great in strength or amount EG *intense heat.* **2** If a person is intense, they take things very seriously and have very strong feelings.
intensely ADVERB, **intensity** NOUN

intensify intensifies intensifying intensified
VERB To intensify something is to make it greater or stronger.

intensive
ADJECTIVE involving a lot of energy or effort over a very short time EG *an intensive training course.*

intent intents
NOUN **1** A FORMAL USE A person's intent is their purpose or intention.
▶ ADJECTIVE **2** If you are intent on doing something, you are determined to do it.
intently ADVERB

intention intentions
NOUN If you have an intention to do something, you have a plan of what you are going to do.

intentional
ADJECTIVE If something is intentional, it is done on purpose.
intentionally ADVERB

inter-

A
B
C
D
E
F
G
H
I
J
K
L
M
N
O
P
Q
R
S
T
U
V
W
X
Y
Z

383

PREFIX Inter- means between EG *inter-school competitions.*

interact interacts interacting interacted
VERB The way two people or things interact is the way they work together, communicate, or react with each other.
interaction NOUN, **interactive** ADJECTIVE

intercept intercepts intercepting intercepted
Said "in-ter-**sept**" VERB If you intercept someone or something that is going from one place to another, you stop them.

interchange interchanges
NOUN An interchange is the act or process of exchanging things or ideas.
interchangeable ADJECTIVE

intercom intercoms
NOUN a device consisting of a microphone and a loudspeaker, which you use to speak to people in another room.

intercourse
NOUN Intercourse or sexual intercourse is the act of having sex.

interest interests interesting interested
NOUN **1** If you have an interest in something or if something is of interest, you want to learn or hear more about it. **2** Your interests are your hobbies. **3** If you have an interest in something being done, you want it to be done because it will benefit you. **4** Interest is an extra payment made to the lender by someone who has borrowed a sum of money, or by a bank or company to someone who has invested money in them. Interest is worked out as a percentage of the sum of money borrowed or invested. ▶ VERB **5** Something that interests you attracts your attention so that you want to learn or hear more about it.
interesting ADJECTIVE, **interestingly** ADVERB, **interested** ADJECTIVE

interface interfaces
NOUN The interface between two subjects or systems is the area in which they affect each other or are linked.

interfere interferes interfering interfered
VERB **1** If you interfere in a situation, you try to influence it, although it does not really concern you.
2 Something that interferes with a situation has a damaging effect on it.
interference NOUN, **interfering** ADJECTIVE
▥ from Old French *s'entreferir* meaning 'to collide'
▤ (sense 1) butt in, intrude, meddle

interim
ADJECTIVE intended for use only until something permanent is arranged EG *an interim government.*
▥ from Latin *interim* meaning 'meanwhile'

interior interiors
NOUN **1** the inside part of something. ▶ ADJECTIVE **2** Interior means inside EG *They painted the interior walls white.*

interjection interjections
NOUN a word or phrase spoken suddenly to express surprise, pain, or anger.

What is an Interjection?

An interjection is a word that expresses a strong emotion, such as anger, surprise, or excitement. Interjections often stand alone rather than as part of a sentence.

Some interjections express greetings.
Hello.   Congratulations!

Some interjections express agreement or disagreement.
Indeed.   No.

Some interjections express pain, anger, or annoyance.
Ouch!   Blast!

Some interjections express approval, pleasure, or excitement.
Bravo!   Hooray!

Some interjections express surprise or relief.
Wow!   Phew!

Sometimes an interjection is more like a noise than a word.
Sh! Psst!

A group of words can be used together as an interjection.
Happy birthday! Hey presto!

When an interjection does occur within a sentence, it is usually separated by commas or dashes.
*I turned the key and, **bingo**, the engine started.*

interlude interludes
*Rhymes with "**rude**"* NOUN a short break from an activity.

intermediary intermediaries
Said "in-ter-meed-yer-ee" NOUN someone who tries to get two groups of people to come to an agreement.

intermediate
ADJECTIVE An intermediate level occurs in the middle, between two other stages EG *intermediate students.*

interminable
ADJECTIVE If something is interminable, it goes on for a very long time EG *an interminable wait for the bus.*
interminably ADVERB

intermission intermissions
NOUN an interval between two parts of a film or play.

intermittent
ADJECTIVE happening only occasionally.
intermittently ADVERB

internal
ADJECTIVE happening inside a person, place, or object.
internally ADVERB

international internationals
ADJECTIVE 1 involving different countries. ▶ NOUN 2 a sports match between two countries.
internationally ADVERB

Internet
NOUN The Internet is a worldwide communication system which people use through computers.

interplay
NOUN The interplay between two things is the way they react with one another.

interpret interprets interpreting interpreted
VERB 1 If you interpret what someone says or does, you decide what it means. 2 If you interpret a foreign language that someone is speaking, you translate it.
interpretation NOUN, **interpreter** NOUN

interrogate interrogates interrogating interrogated
VERB If you interrogate someone, you question them thoroughly to get information from them.
interrogation NOUN, **interrogator** NOUN
☰ cross-examine, question

interrupt interrupts interrupting interrupted
VERB 1 If you interrupt someone, you start talking while they are talking. 2 If you interrupt a process or activity, you stop it continuing for a time.
interruption NOUN

intersect intersects intersecting intersected
VERB When two roads intersect, they cross each other.
intersection NOUN

interspersed
ADJECTIVE If something is interspersed with things, these things occur at various points in it.

interval intervals
NOUN 1 the period of time between two moments or dates. 2 a short break during a play or concert.
☰ (sense 2) break, interlude, intermission

intervene intervenes intervening intervened
VERB If you intervene in a situation, you step in to prevent conflict between people.
intervention NOUN
☰ mediate, step in

intervening
ADJECTIVE An intervening period of

A B C D E F G H I J K L M N O P Q R S T U V W X Y Z

385

A
B
C
D
E
F
G
H
I
J
K
L
M
N
O
P
Q
R
S
T
U
V
W
X
Y
Z

time is one which separates two events.

interview interviews
NOUN **1** a meeting at which someone asks you questions about yourself to see if you are suitable for a particular job. **2** a conversation in which a journalist asks a famous person questions. ▶ VERB **3** If you interview someone, you ask them questions about themselves.

intestine intestines
NOUN Your intestines are a long tube which carries food from your stomach through to your bowels, and in which the food is digested.
intestinal ADJECTIVE

intimate intimates intimating intimated
ADJECTIVE **1** If two people are intimate, there is a close relationship between them. **2** An intimate matter is very private and personal. **3** An intimate knowledge of something is very deep and detailed. ▶ VERB **4** If you intimate something, you hint at it EG *He did intimate that he is considering legal action.*
intimately ADVERB, **intimacy** NOUN, **intimation** NOUN

intimidate intimidates intimidating intimidated
VERB If you intimidate someone, you frighten them in a threatening way.
intimidated ADJECTIVE, **intimidating** ADJECTIVE, **intimidation** NOUN

into
PREPOSITION **1** If something goes into something else, it goes inside it. **2** If you bump or crash into something, you hit it. **3** AN INFORMAL USE If you are into something, you like it very much EG *Nowadays I'm really into healthy food.*

intolerable
ADJECTIVE If something is intolerable, it is so bad that it is difficult to put up with it.

intolerably ADVERB

intonation
NOUN Your intonation is the way that your voice rises and falls as you speak.

intoxicated
ADJECTIVE If someone is intoxicated, they are drunk.
intoxicating ADJECTIVE, **intoxication** NOUN

intra-
PREFIX Intra- means within or inside EG *intra-European conflicts.*
from Latin *intra* meaning 'within'

intractable
ADJECTIVE; A FORMAL WORD stubborn and difficult to deal with or control.

intransitive
ADJECTIVE An intransitive verb is one that does not have a direct object. For example, 'sings' is intransitive in 'She sings', but not in 'She sings a song'.

intravenous
Said "in-trav-vee-nuss" ADJECTIVE Intravenous foods or drugs are given to sick people through their veins.
intravenously ADVERB

intrepid
ADJECTIVE not worried by danger EG *an intrepid explorer.*
intrepidly ADVERB

intricate
ADJECTIVE Something that is intricate has many fine details EG *walls and ceilings covered with intricate patterns.*
intricately ADVERB, **intricacy** NOUN

intrigue intrigues intriguing intrigued
NOUN **1** Intrigue is the making of secret plans, often with the intention of harming other people EG *political intrigue.* ▶ VERB **2** If something intrigues you, you are fascinated by it and curious about it.
intriguing ADJECTIVE

intrinsic
ADJECTIVE; A FORMAL WORD The intrinsic

qualities of something are its basic qualities.
intrinsically ADVERB

introduce introduces introducing introduced
VERB **1** If you introduce one person to another, you tell them each other's name so that they can get to know each other. **2** When someone introduces a radio or television show, they say a few words at the beginning to tell you about it. **3** If you introduce someone to something, they learn about it for the first time.
introductory ADJECTIVE

introduction introductions
NOUN **1** The introduction of someone or something is the act of presenting them for the first time. **2** a piece of writing at the beginning of a book, which usually tells you what the book is about.
■ (sense 2) foreword, opening, preface

introvert introverts
NOUN someone who spends more time thinking about their private feelings than about the world around them, and who often finds it difficult to talk to others.
introverted ADJECTIVE

intrude intrudes intruding intruded
VERB To intrude on someone or something is to disturb them EG *I don't want to intrude on your parents.*
intruder NOUN, **intrusion** NOUN, **intrusive** ADJECTIVE
■ butt in, trespass

intuition intuitions
Said "int-yoo-**ish**-n" NOUN Your intuition is a feeling you have about something that you cannot explain EG *My intuition is right about him.*
intuitive ADJECTIVE, **intuitively** ADVERB

Inuit Inuits; also spelt **Innuit**
NOUN an Eskimo who comes from North America or Greenland.

inundated

ADJECTIVE If you are inundated by letters or requests, you receive so many that you cannot deal with them all.

invade invades invading invaded
VERB **1** If an army invades a country, it enters it by force. **2** If someone invades your privacy, they disturb you when you want to be alone.
invader NOUN, **invasion** NOUN

invalid invalids
Said "**in**-va-lid" NOUN someone who is so ill that they need to be looked after by someone else.
▥ from Latin *invalidus* meaning 'infirm'

invalid
Said "in-**val**-id" ADJECTIVE **1** If an argument or result is invalid, it is not acceptable because it is based on a mistake. **2** If a law, marriage, or election is invalid, it is illegal because it has not been carried out properly.
invalidate VERB
▥ from Latin *invalidus* meaning 'without legal force'

invalidity
Said "in-va-**lid**-dit-ee" NOUN Invalidity is the condition of being very ill for a very long time.

invaluable
ADJECTIVE extremely useful EG *This book contains invaluable tips.*

invariably
ADVERB If something invariably happens, it almost always happens.

invective
NOUN; A FORMAL WORD Invective is abusive language used by someone who is angry.

invent invents inventing invented
VERB **1** If you invent a device or process, you are the first person to think of it or to use it. **2** If you invent a story or an excuse, you make it up.
inventor NOUN, **invention** NOUN, **inventive** ADJECTIVE, **inventiveness** NOUN
■ (sense 1) conceive, create, devise

A B C D E F G H I J K L M N O P Q R S T U V W X Y Z

387

A B C D E F G H I J K L M N O P Q R S T U V W X Y Z

inventory inventories
NOUN a written list of all the objects in a place.

inverse
ADJECTIVE; A FORMAL WORD If there is an inverse relationship between two things, one decreases as the other increases.

invertebrate invertebrates
NOUN; A TECHNICAL WORD a creature which does not have a spine.

inverted
ADJECTIVE upside down or back to front.

inverted comma inverted commas
NOUN Inverted commas are the punctuation marks " " or ' ', used to show where speech begins and ends.

What do Inverted Commas do?

Inverted commas or **quotation marks** (" " or ' ') mark the beginning and end of a speaker's exact words or thoughts.

"I would like some more," said Matthew.

Inverted commas are not used when a speaker's words are reported indirectly rather than in their exact form.

Matthew said that he would like some more.

Inverted commas can also be used to indicate the title of a book, piece of music, etc.

The class had been reading "The Little Prince".

Inverted commas are also used to draw attention to the fact that a word or phrase is being used in an unusual way, or that a word itself is the subject of discussion.

Braille allows a blind person to "see" with the fingers.
What rhymes with "orange"?

---

invest invests investing invested
VERB **1** If you invest money, you pay it into a bank or buy shares so that you will receive a profit. **2** If you invest in something useful, you buy it because it will help you do something better. **3** If you invest money, time, or energy in something, you try to make it a success.
investor NOUN, **investment** NOUN

investigate investigates investigating investigated
VERB To investigate something is to try to find out all the facts about it.
investigator NOUN, **investigation** NOUN
▣ examine, look into, study

inveterate
ADJECTIVE having lasted for a long time and not likely to stop EG *an inveterate gambler*.

invincible
ADJECTIVE unable to be defeated.
invincibility NOUN

invisible
ADJECTIVE If something is invisible, you cannot see it, because it is hidden, very small, or imaginary.
invisibly ADVERB, **invisibility** NOUN

invite invites inviting invited
VERB **1** If you invite someone to an event, you ask them to come to it. **2** If you invite someone to do something, you ask them to do it EG *Andrew has been invited to speak at the conference.*
inviting ADJECTIVE, **invitation** NOUN

invoice invoices
NOUN a bill for services or goods.

invoke invokes invoking invoked
VERB **1** A FORMAL WORD If you invoke a law, you use it to justify what you are doing. **2** If you invoke certain feelings, you cause someone to have these feelings.
▥ from Latin *invocare* meaning 'to call upon'

involuntary
ADJECTIVE sudden and uncontrollable.
involuntarily ADVERB

involve involves involving involved
VERB If a situation involves someone or something, it includes them as a necessary part.
involvement NOUN

inward or **inwards**

ADJECTIVE **1** Your inward thoughts and feelings are private. ▶ ADJECTIVE OR ADVERB **2** If something moves inward or inwards, it moves towards the inside or centre of something.
inwardly ADVERB

iodine
Said "eye-oh-deen" NOUN Iodine is a bluish-black substance used in medicine and photography.

ion ions
Said "eye-on". NOUN Ions are electrically charged atoms.

iota
NOUN an extremely small amount EG *He did not have an iota of proof.*

IQ IQs
NOUN Your IQ is your level of intelligence shown by the results of a special test. IQ is an abbreviation for 'intelligence quotient'.

Iranian Iranians
*Said "ir-**rain**-ee-an"* ADJECTIVE **1** belonging or relating to Iran. ▶ NOUN **2** someone who comes from Iran. **3** Iranian is the main language spoken in Iran. It is also known as Farsi.

Iraqi Iraqis
*Said "ir-**ah**-kee"* ADJECTIVE **1** belonging or relating to Iraq. ▶ NOUN **2** someone who comes from Iraq.

irate
Said "eye-rate" ADJECTIVE very angry.

iris irises
Said "eye-riss" NOUN **1** the round, coloured part of your eye. **2** a tall plant with long leaves and large blue, yellow, or white flowers.
▣ from Greek *iris* meaning 'rainbow' or 'coloured circle'

Irish
ADJECTIVE **1** belonging or relating to the Irish Republic, or to the whole of Ireland. ▶ NOUN **2** Irish or Irish Gaelic is a language spoken in some parts of Ireland.

Irishman Irishmen

NOUN a man who comes from Ireland.
Irishwoman NOUN

irk irks irking irked
VERB If something irks you, it annoys you.
irksome ADJECTIVE

iron irons ironing ironed
NOUN **1** Iron is a hard dark metal used to make steel, and things like gates and fences. Small amounts of iron are found in blood. **2** a device which heats up and which you rub over clothes to remove creases.
▶ VERB **3** If you iron clothes, you use a hot iron to remove creases from them.
ironing NOUN
iron out VERB If you iron out difficulties, you solve them.

Iron Age
NOUN The Iron Age was a time about three thousand years ago when people first started to make tools out of iron.

ironbark ironbarks
NOUN an Australian eucalypt with a hard, rough bark.

irony
Said "eye-ron-ee" NOUN **1** Irony is a form of humour in which you say the opposite of what you really mean EG *This group could be described, without irony, as the fortunate ones.* **2** There is irony in a situation when there is an unexpected or unusual connection between things or events EG *It's a sad irony of life: once you are lost, a map is useless.*
ironic or **ironical** ADJECTIVE, **ironically** ADVERB

irrational
ADJECTIVE Irrational feelings are not based on logical reasons EG *irrational fears.*
irrationally ADVERB, **irrationality** NOUN

irregular
ADJECTIVE Something that is irregular is not smooth or straight, or does not form a regular pattern EG *irregular walls.*

irregularly ADVERB, **irregularity** NOUN
≡ haphazard, random, variable

irrelevant
ADJECTIVE not directly connected with a subject EG *He either ignored questions or gave irrelevant answers.*
irrelevance NOUN

irrepressible
ADJECTIVE Someone who is irrepressible is lively and cheerful.

irresistible
ADJECTIVE **1** unable to be controlled EG *an irresistible urge to yawn.* **2** extremely attractive EG *Women always found him irresistible.*
irresistibly ADVERB

irrespective
ADJECTIVE If you say something will be done irrespective of certain things, you mean it will be done without taking those things into account.

irresponsible
ADJECTIVE An irresponsible person does things without considering the consequences EG *an irresponsible driver.*
irresponsibly ADVERB, **irresponsibility** NOUN
≡ careless, reckless, thoughtless

irrigate **irrigates** **irrigating** **irrigated**
VERB To irrigate land is to supply it with water brought through pipes or ditches.
irrigated ADJECTIVE, **irrigation** NOUN

irritate **irritates** **irritating** **irritated**
VERB **1** If something irritates you, it annoys you. **2** If something irritates part of your body, it makes it tender, sore, or itchy.
irritable ADJECTIVE, **irritant** NOUN, **irritation** NOUN
≡ (sense 1) annoy, get on one's nerves

is
the third person, present tense of be.

Islam
Said "iz-lahm" NOUN Islam is the Muslim religion, which teaches that there is only one God, Allah, and Mohammed is his prophet. The holy book of Islam is the Koran.
Islamic ADJECTIVE
📖 from Arabic *islam* meaning 'surrender to God'

island **islands**
Said "eye-land" NOUN a piece of land surrounded on all sides by water.
islander NOUN

isle **isles**
Rhymes with "mile" NOUN; A LITERARY WORD an island.

isolate **isolates** **isolating** **isolated**
VERB **1** If something isolates you or if you isolate yourself, you are set apart from other people. **2** If you isolate something, you separate it from everything else.
isolated ADJECTIVE, **isolation** NOUN

isosceles
Said "eye-soss-il-eez" ADJECTIVE An isosceles triangle has two sides of the same length.
📖 from Greek *iso-* meaning 'equal' and *skelos* meaning 'leg'

Israeli **Israelis**
Said "iz-rail-ee" ADJECTIVE
1 belonging or relating to Israel.
▶ NOUN **2** someone who comes from Israel.

issue **issues** **issuing** **issued**
Said "ish-yoo" NOUN **1** an important subject that people are talking about. **2** a particular edition of a newspaper or magazine. ▶ VERB **3** If you issue a statement or a warning, you say it formally and publicly. **4** If someone issues something, they officially give it EG *Staff were issued with plastic cards.*
≡ (sense 4) distribute, give out

isthmus **isthmuses**
NOUN a narrow strip of land connecting two larger areas.

it
PRONOUN **1** 'It' is used to refer to something that has already been mentioned, or to a situation or fact

EG *It was a difficult decision.* **2** 'It' is used to refer to people or animals whose sex is not known EG *If a baby is thirsty, it feeds more often.* **3** You use 'it' to make statements about the weather, time, or date EG *It's noon.*

Italian Italians

ADJECTIVE **1** belonging or relating to Italy. ▶ NOUN **2** someone who comes from Italy. **3** Italian is the main language spoken in Italy.

italics

PLURAL NOUN Italics are letters printed in a special sloping way, and are often used to emphasize something. All the examples in this dictionary are in italics.

italic ADJECTIVE

itch itches itching itched

VERB **1** When your skin itches, it has an unpleasant feeling and you want to scratch it. **2** If you are itching to do something, you are impatient to do it. ▶ NOUN **3** an unpleasant feeling on your skin that you want to scratch.

itchy ADJECTIVE

📖 from Old English *giccean* meaning 'to itch'

item items

NOUN **1** one of a collection or list of objects. **2** a newspaper or magazine article.

◼ (sense 2) article, feature, piece

itinerary itineraries

NOUN a plan of a journey, showing a route to follow and places to visit.

its

ADJECTIVE OR PRONOUN 'Its' refers to something belonging to or relating to things, children, or animals that have already been mentioned EG *The lion lifted its head.*

☑ Many people are confused about the difference between *its* and *it's*. *Its*, without the apostrophe, is the possessive form of *it*: *the cat has hurt its paw. It's*, with the apostrophe, is a short form of *it is* or *it has*: *it's green; it's been snowing again.*

itself

PRONOUN **1** 'Itself' is used when the same thing, child, or animal does an action and is affected by it EG *Paris prides itself on its luxurious hotels.* **2** 'Itself' is used to emphasize 'it'.

ivory

NOUN **1** Ivory is the valuable creamy-white bone which forms the tusk of an elephant. It is used to make ornaments. ▶ NOUN OR ADJECTIVE **2** creamy-white.

ivy

NOUN Ivy is an evergreen plant which creeps along the ground and up walls.

iwi iwi or iwis

NOUN In New Zealand, a Maori tribe.

Jj Jj

jab jabs jabbing jabbed
VERB **1** To jab something means to poke at it roughly. ▶ NOUN **2** a sharp or sudden poke. **3** AN INFORMAL USE an injection.

jabiru jabirus
NOUN a white-and-green Australian stork with red legs.

jack jacks jacking jacked
NOUN **1** a piece of equipment for lifting heavy objects, especially for lifting a car when changing a wheel. **2** In a pack of cards, a jack is a card whose value is between a ten and a queen. ▶ VERB **3** To jack up an object means to raise it, especially by using a jack.

jackal jackals
NOUN a wild animal related to the dog.

jackaroo jackaroos; also spelt **jackeroo**
NOUN In Australia, a young person learning the work of a sheep or cattle station.

jackdaw jackdaws
NOUN a bird like a small crow with black and grey feathers.

jacket jackets
NOUN **1** a short coat. **2** an outer covering for something EG *a book jacket*. **3** The jacket of a baked potato is its skin.

jackpot jackpots
NOUN In a gambling game, the jackpot is the top prize.

jack up jacks up jacking up jacked up
VERB; AN INFORMAL TERM In New Zealand English, to jack up is to organize or prepare something.

jade
NOUN Jade is a hard green stone used for making jewellery and ornaments.

jagged
ADJECTIVE sharp and spiky.

◼ serrated, spiked, uneven

jaguar jaguars
NOUN a large member of the cat family with spots on its back.

jail jails jailing jailed; also spelt **gaol**
NOUN **1** a building where people convicted of a crime are locked up. ▶ VERB **2** To jail someone means to lock them up in a jail.
◼ (sense 1) nick, penitentiary, prison

jailer jailers; also spelt **gaoler**
NOUN a person who is in charge of the prisoners in a jail.

jam jams jamming jammed
NOUN **1** a food, made by boiling fruit and sugar together until it sets. **2** a situation where there are so many things or people that it is impossible to move EG *a traffic jam.* ▶ AN INFORMAL PHRASE **3** If someone is in a jam, they are in a difficult situation. ▶ VERB **4** If people or things are jammed into a place, they are squeezed together so closely that they can hardly move. **5** To jam something somewhere means to push it there roughly EG *He jammed his foot on the brake.* **6** If something is jammed, it is stuck or unable to work properly. **7** To jam a radio signal means to interfere with it and prevent it from being received clearly.
◼ (sense 3) fix, predicament, tight spot

Jamaican Jamaicans
Said "jam-**may**-kn" ADJECTIVE
1 belonging or relating to Jamaica. ▶ NOUN **2** someone who comes from Jamaica.

jamboree jamborees
NOUN a gathering of large numbers of people enjoying themselves.

Jandal Jandals
NOUN; A TRADEMARK In New Zealand, a sandal with a strap between the big

toe and other toes and over the foot.

jangle jangles jangling jangled
VERB **1** If something jangles, it makes a harsh metallic ringing noise. ▶ NOUN **2** the sound made by metal objects striking against each other.

janitor janitors
NOUN the caretaker of a building.

January
NOUN January is the first month of the year. It has 31 days.
📖 from Latin *Januarius* meaning 'the month of Janus', named after a Roman god

Japanese
ADJECTIVE **1** belonging or relating to Japan. ▶ NOUN **2** someone who comes from Japan. **3** Japanese is the main language spoken in Japan.

jar jars jarring jarred
NOUN **1** a glass container with a wide top used for storing food. ▶ VERB **2** If something jars on you, you find it unpleasant or annoying.

jargon
NOUN Jargon consists of words that are used in special or technical ways by particular groups of people, often making the language difficult to understand.

jarrah jarrahs
NOUN an Australian eucalypt tree that produces wood used for timber.

jasmine
NOUN Jasmine is a climbing plant with small sweet-scented white flowers.

jaundice
NOUN Jaundice is an illness affecting the liver, in which the skin and the whites of the eyes become yellow.

jaundiced
ADJECTIVE unenthusiastic and pessimistic EG *He takes a rather jaundiced view of politicians.*

jaunt jaunts
NOUN a journey or trip you go on for pleasure.

jaunty jauntier jauntiest
ADJECTIVE expressing cheerfulness and self-confidence EG *a jaunty tune.*
jauntily ADVERB

javelin javelins
NOUN a long spear that is thrown in sports competitions.

jaw jaws
NOUN **1** A person's or animal's jaw is the bone in which the teeth are set. **2** A person's or animal's mouth and teeth are their jaws.

jay jays
NOUN a kind of noisy chattering bird.

jazz jazzes jazzing jazzed
NOUN **1** Jazz is a style of popular music with a forceful rhythm.
▶ VERB **2** AN INFORMAL USE To jazz something up means to make it more colourful or exciting.

jazzy jazzier jazziest
ADJECTIVE; AN INFORMAL WORD bright and showy.

jealous
ADJECTIVE **1** If you are jealous, you feel bitterness towards someone who has something that you would like to have. **2** If you are jealous of something you have, you feel you must try to keep it from other people.
jealously ADVERB, **jealousy** NOUN
= (sense 1) covetous, envious
= (sense 2) possessive

jeans
PLURAL NOUN Jeans are casual denim trousers.

jeep jeeps
NOUN; A TRADEMARK a small road vehicle with four-wheel drive.

jeer jeers jeering jeered
VERB **1** If you jeer at someone, you insult them in a loud, unpleasant way. ▶ NOUN **2** Jeers are rude and insulting remarks.
jeering ADJECTIVE

Jehovah
Said "ji-**hove**-ah" PROPER NOUN
Jehovah is the name of God in the Old Testament.

393

🔲 from adding vowels to the Hebrew *JHVH*, the sacred name of God

jelly jellies
NOUN **1** a clear, sweet food eaten as a dessert. **2** a type of clear, set jam.

jellyfish jellyfishes
NOUN a sea animal with a clear soft body and tentacles which may sting.

jeopardize jeopardizes jeopardizing jeopardized
Said "jep-par-dyz"; *also spelt* jeopardise
VERB To jeopardize something means to do something which puts it at risk of failing EG *Elaine jeopardized her health.*

jeopardy
NOUN If someone or something is in jeopardy, they are at risk of failing or of being destroyed.

jerk jerks jerking jerked
VERB **1** To jerk something means to give it a sudden, sharp pull. **2** If something jerks, it moves suddenly and sharply. ▶ NOUN **3** a sudden sharp movement. **4** AN INFORMAL USE If you call someone a jerk, you mean they are stupid.
jerky ADJECTIVE, **jerkily** ADVERB

jerkin jerkins
NOUN a short sleeveless jacket.

jersey jerseys
NOUN **1** a knitted garment for the upper half of the body. **2** Jersey is a type of knitted woollen or cotton fabric used to make clothing.

jest jests jesting jested
NOUN **1** a joke. ▶ VERB **2** To jest means to speak jokingly.

jester jesters
NOUN In the past, a jester was a man who was kept to amuse the king or queen.

jet jets jetting jetted
NOUN **1** a plane which is able to fly very fast. **2** a stream of liquid, gas, or flame forced out under pressure. **3** Jet is a hard black stone, usually

highly polished and used in jewellery and ornaments. ▶ VERB **4** To jet somewhere means to fly there in a plane, especially a jet.

jet boat jet boats
NOUN In New Zealand, a motor boat that is powered by a jet of water at the rear.

jet lag
NOUN Jet lag is a feeling of tiredness or confusion that people have after a long flight across different time zones.

jettison jettisons jettisoning jettisoned
VERB If you jettison something, you throw it away because you no longer want it.

jetty jetties
NOUN a wide stone wall or wooden platform at the edge of the sea or a river, where boats can be moored.

Jew Jews
Said "joo" NOUN a person who practises the religion of Judaism, or who is of Hebrew descent.
Jewish ADJECTIVE
🔲 from *Judah*, the name of a Jewish patriarch

jewel jewels
NOUN a precious stone used to decorate valuable ornaments or jewellery.
jewelled ADJECTIVE

jeweller jewellers
NOUN a person who makes jewellery or who sells and repairs jewellery and watches.

jewellery
NOUN Jewellery consists of ornaments that people wear, such as rings or necklaces, made of valuable metals and sometimes decorated with precious stones.

jib jibs
NOUN a small sail towards the front of a sailing boat.

jibe
another spelling of gibe.

jig jigs jigging jigged

NOUN **1** a type of lively folk dance.
▶ VERB **2** If you jig, you dance around in a lively bouncy manner.

jiggle jiggles jiggling jiggled
VERB If you jiggle something, you move it around with quick jerky movements.

jigsaw jigsaws
NOUN a puzzle consisting of a picture on cardboard that has been cut up into small pieces, which have to be put together again.

jilt jilts jilting jilted
VERB If you jilt someone, you suddenly break off your relationship with them.
jilted ADJECTIVE

jingle jingles jingling jingled
NOUN **1** a short, catchy phrase or rhyme set to music and used to advertise something on radio or television. **2** the sound of something jingling. ▶ VERB **3** When something jingles, it makes a tinkling sound like small bells.

jinks
PLURAL NOUN High jinks is boisterous and mischievous behaviour.

jinx jinxes
NOUN someone or something that is thought to bring bad luck EG *He was beginning to think he was a jinx.*

jinxed
ADJECTIVE If something is jinxed it is considered to be unlucky EG *I think this house is jinxed.*

jitters
PLURAL NOUN; AN INFORMAL WORD If you have got the jitters, you are feeling very nervous.
jittery ADJECTIVE

job jobs
NOUN **1** the work that someone does to earn money. **2** a duty or responsibility EG *It is a captain's job to lead from the front.* ▶ PHRASE **3** If something is **just the job**, it is exactly right or exactly what you wanted.
▤ (sense 1) employment,

occupation, work

job centre job centres
NOUN a government office where people can find out about job vacancies.

jobless
ADJECTIVE without any work.

jockey jockeys jockeying jockeyed
NOUN **1** someone who rides a horse in a race. ▶ VERB **2** To jockey for a position means to manoeuvre in order to gain an advantage over other people.

jocular
ADJECTIVE A jocular comment is intended to make people laugh.

jodhpurs
Said "**jod**-purz" PLURAL NOUN Jodhpurs are close-fitting trousers worn when riding a horse.
▦ from *Jodhpur*, the name of a town in N. India

joey joeys
NOUN; AN INFORMAL WORD In Australian English, a young kangaroo or other young animal.

jog jogs jogging jogged
VERB **1** To jog means to run slowly and rhythmically, often as a form of exercise. **2** If you jog something, you knock it slightly so that it shakes or moves. **3** If someone or something jogs your memory, they remind you of something. ▶ NOUN **4** a slow run.
jogger NOUN, **jogging** NOUN

join joins joining joined
VERB **1** When two things join, or when one thing joins another, they come together. **2** If you join a club or organization, you become a member of it or start taking part in it. **3** To join two things means to fasten them. ▶ NOUN **4** a place where two things are fastened together.
▤ (senses 1 & 3) connect, link, unite
▤ (sense 2) enlist, enrol, sign up
join up VERB If someone joins up, they become a member of the

A B C D E F G H I J K L M N O P Q R S T U V W X Y Z

armed forces.

joiner joiners
NOUN a person who makes wooden window frames, doors, and furniture.

joinery
NOUN Joinery is the work done by a joiner.

joint joints jointing jointed
ADJECTIVE **1** shared by or belonging to two or more people EG *a joint building society account.* ▶ NOUN **2** a part of the body where two bones meet and are joined together so that they can move, for example a knee or hip. **3** a place where two things are fixed together. **4** a large piece of meat suitable for roasting. **5** AN INFORMAL USE any place of entertainment, such as a nightclub or pub. ▶ VERB **6** To joint meat means to cut it into large pieces according to where the bones are.
jointly ADVERB, **jointed** ADJECTIVE

joist joists
NOUN a large beam used to support floors or ceilings.

joke jokes joking joked
NOUN **1** something that you say or do to make people laugh, such as a funny story. **2** anything that you think is ridiculous and not worthy of respect EG *The decision was a joke.* ▶ VERB **3** If you are joking, you are teasing someone.
jokingly ADVERB
▤ (sense 1) gag, jest
▤ (sense 3) jest, kid

joker jokers
NOUN In a pack of cards, a joker is an extra card that does not belong to any of the four suits, but is used in some games.

jolly jollier jolliest
ADJECTIVE **1** happy, cheerful, and pleasant. ▶ ADVERB **2** AN INFORMAL USE Jolly also means very EG *jolly good fun.*

jolt jolts jolting jolted
VERB **1** To jolt means to move or shake roughly and violently. **2** If

you are jolted by something, it gives you an unpleasant surprise.
▶ NOUN **3** a sudden jerky movement. **4** an unpleasant shock or surprise.

jostle jostles jostling jostled
VERB To jostle means to push roughly against people in a crowd.

jot jots jotting jotted
VERB **1** If you jot something down, you write it quickly in the form of a short informal note. ▶ NOUN **2** a very small amount.
jotting NOUN

jotter jotters
NOUN a pad or notebook.

joule joules
Rhymes with "school" NOUN a unit of energy or work.

journal journals
NOUN **1** a magazine that deals with a particular subject, trade, or profession. **2** a diary which someone keeps regularly.

journalism
NOUN Journalism is the work of collecting, writing, and publishing news in newspapers, magazines, and on television and radio.
journalist NOUN, **journalistic** ADJECTIVE

journey journeys journeying journeyed
NOUN **1** the act of travelling from one place to another. ▶ VERB **2** A FORMAL USE To journey somewhere means to travel there EG *He intended to journey up the Amazon.*

joust jousts
NOUN In medieval times, a joust was a competition between knights fighting on horseback, using lances.

jovial
ADJECTIVE cheerful and friendly.
jovially ADVERB, **joviality** NOUN

joy joys
NOUN **1** Joy is a feeling of great happiness. **2** AN INFORMAL USE Joy also means success or luck EG *Any joy with your insurance claim?* **3** something that makes you happy or gives you pleasure.

joyful
ADJECTIVE **1** causing pleasure and happiness. **2** Someone who is joyful is extremely happy.
joyfully ADVERB

joyous
ADJECTIVE; A FORMAL WORD joyful.
joyously ADVERB

joyride joyrides
NOUN a drive in a stolen car for pleasure.
joyriding NOUN, **joyrider** NOUN

joystick joysticks
NOUN a lever in an aircraft which the pilot uses to control height and direction.

jube jubes
NOUN; AN INFORMAL WORD In Australian and New Zealand English, a fruit-flavoured jelly sweet.

jubilant
ADJECTIVE feeling or expressing great happiness or triumph.
jubilantly ADVERB

jubilation
NOUN Jubilation is a feeling of great happiness and triumph.

jubilee jubilees
NOUN a special anniversary of an event such as a coronation EG *Queen Elizabeth's Silver Jubilee in 1977.*
🔲 from Hebrew *yobhel* meaning 'ram's horn'; rams' horns were blown during festivals and celebrations

Judaism
Said "joo-day-i-zm" NOUN Judaism is the religion of the Jewish people. It is based on a belief in one God, and draws its laws and authority from the Old Testament.
Judaic ADJECTIVE

judder judders juddering juddered
VERB To judder means to shake and vibrate noisily and violently.

judder bar judder bars
NOUN In New Zealand English, a bump built across a road to stop drivers from going too fast. In Britain it is called a sleeping policeman.

judge judges judging judged
NOUN **1** the person in a law court who decides how the law should be applied to people who appear in the court. **2** someone who decides the winner in a contest or competition. ▶ VERB **3** If you judge someone or something, you form an opinion about them based on the evidence that you have. **4** To judge a contest or competition means to decide on the winner.
judgment or **judgement** NOUN
■ (sense 2) adjudicator, referee, umpire
■ (sense 4) adjudicate, referee, umpire
☑ *Judgment* and *judgement* are both correct spellings.

judicial
ADJECTIVE relating to judgment or to justice EG *a judicial review.*

judiciary
NOUN The judiciary is the branch of government concerned with justice and the legal system.

judicious
ADJECTIVE sensible and showing good judgment.
judiciously ADVERB

judo
NOUN Judo is a sport in which two people try to force each other to the ground using special throwing techniques.

jug jugs
NOUN a container with a lip or spout used for holding or serving liquids.

juggernaut juggernauts
NOUN a large heavy lorry.
🔲 from Hindi *Jagannath*, the name of a huge idol of the god Krishna, which every year is wheeled through the streets of Puri in India

juggle juggles juggling juggled
VERB To juggle means to throw objects into the air, catching them in sequence, and tossing them up

A B C D E F G H I J K L M N O P Q R S T U V W X Y Z

again so there are several in the air at one time.

juggler NOUN

jugular jugulars

NOUN The jugular or jugular vein is one of the veins in the neck which carry blood from the head back to the heart.

juice juices

NOUN 1 Juice is the liquid that can be squeezed or extracted from fruit or other food. 2 Juices in the body are fluids EG *gastric juices*.

juicy juicier juiciest

ADJECTIVE 1 Juicy food has a lot of juice in it. 2 Something that is juicy is interesting, exciting, or scandalous EG *a juicy bit of gossip*.

jukebox jukeboxes

NOUN a large record player found in cafés and pubs which automatically plays a selected record when coins are inserted.

July

NOUN July is the seventh month of the year. It has 31 days.

from Latin *Julius*, the month of July, named after Julius Caesar by the Romans

jumble jumbles jumbling jumbled

NOUN 1 an untidy muddle of things. 2 Jumble consists of articles for a jumble sale. ▶ VERB 3 To jumble things means to mix them up untidily.

jumble sale jumble sales

NOUN an event at which cheap second-hand clothes and other articles are sold to raise money, usually for a charity.

jumbo jumbos

NOUN 1 A jumbo or jumbo jet is a large jet aeroplane that can carry several hundred passengers.
▶ ADJECTIVE 2 very large EG *jumbo packs of elastic bands*.

from *Jumbo*, the name of a famous 19th-century elephant

jumbuck jumbucks

NOUN; AN OLD-FASHIONED WORD In

Australian English, a sheep.

jump jumps jumping jumped

VERB 1 To jump means to spring off the ground using your leg muscles. 2 To jump something means to spring off the ground and move over or across it. 3 If you jump at something such as an opportunity, you accept it eagerly. 4 If you jump on someone, you criticize them suddenly and forcefully. 5 If someone jumps, they make a sudden sharp movement of surprise. 6 If an amount or level jumps, it suddenly increases. ▶ NOUN 7 a spring into the air, sometimes over an object.
(senses 1 & 7) bound, leap, spring

jumper jumpers

NOUN a knitted garment for the top half of the body.

jumpy jumpier jumpiest

ADJECTIVE nervous and worried.

junction junctions

NOUN a place where roads or railway lines meet or cross.

June

NOUN June is the sixth month of the year. It has 30 days.

from Latin *Junius*, the month of June, probably from the name of an important Roman family

jungle jungles

NOUN 1 a dense tropical forest. 2 a tangled mass of plants or other objects.

junior juniors

ADJECTIVE 1 Someone who is junior to other people has a lower position in an organization. 2 Junior also means younger. 3 relating to childhood EG *a junior school*. ▶ NOUN 4 someone who holds an unimportant position in an organization.

juniper junipers

NOUN an evergreen shrub with purple berries used in cooking and medicine.

junk junks

NOUN **1** Junk is old or second-hand articles which are sold cheaply or thrown away. **2** If you think something is junk, you think it is worthless rubbish. **3** a Chinese sailing boat with a flat bottom and square sails.

junk food
NOUN Junk food is food low in nutritional value which is eaten as well as or instead of proper meals.

junkie junkies
NOUN; AN INFORMAL WORD a drug addict.

Jupiter
NOUN Jupiter is the largest planet in the solar system and the fifth from the sun.

jurisdiction
NOUN **1** A FORMAL WORD Jurisdiction is the power or right of the courts to apply laws and make legal judgments EG *The Court held that it did not have the jurisdiction to examine the merits of the case.* **2** Jurisdiction is power or authority EG *The airport was under French jurisdiction.*

juror jurors
NOUN a member of a jury.

jury juries
NOUN a group of people in a court of law who have been selected to listen to the facts of a case on trial, and to decide whether the accused person is guilty or not.

just
ADJECTIVE **1** fair and impartial EG *She arrived at a just decision.* **2** morally right or proper EG *a just reward.* ▶ ADVERB **3** If something has just happened, it happened a very short time ago. **4** If you just do

something, you do it by a very small amount EG *They only just won.* **5** simply or only EG *It was just an excuse not to mow the lawn.* **6** exactly EG *It's just what she wanted.* ▶ PHRASE **7** In South African English, **just now** means in a little while.
justly ADVERB

justice justices
NOUN **1** Justice is fairness and reasonableness. **2** The system of justice in a country is the way in which laws are maintained by the courts. **3** a judge or magistrate.

justify justifies justifying justified
VERB If you justify an action or idea, you prove or explain why it is reasonable or necessary.
justification NOUN, **justifiable** ADJECTIVE

jut juts jutting jutted
VERB If something juts out, it sticks out beyond or above a surface or edge.
■ project, protrude, stick out

jute
NOUN Jute is a strong fibre made from the bark of an Asian plant, used to make rope and sacking.

juvenile juveniles
ADJECTIVE **1** suitable for young people. **2** childish and rather silly EG *a juvenile game.* ▶ NOUN **3** a young person not old enough to be considered an adult.

juxtapose juxtaposes juxtaposing juxtaposed
VERB If you juxtapose things or ideas, you put them close together, often to emphasize the difference between them.
juxtaposition NOUN

A
B
C
D
E
F
G
H
I
J
K
L
M
N
O
P
Q
R
S
T
U
V
W
X
Y
Z

Kk Kk

kaffir kaffirs or **kaffir**
NOUN; A VERY OFFENSIVE WORD In South African English, a kaffir is a Black person.

kaleidoscope kaleidoscopes
Said "kal-**eye**-dos-skope" NOUN a toy consisting of a tube with a hole at one end. When you look through the hole and twist the other end of the tube, you can see a changing pattern of colours.
📖 from Greek *kalos* meaning 'beautiful', *eidos* meaning 'shape', and *skopein* meaning 'to look at'

kamikaze
NOUN In the Second World War, a kamikaze was a Japanese pilot who flew an aircraft loaded with explosives directly into an enemy target knowing he would be killed doing so.
📖 from Japanese *kami* meaning 'divine' + *kaze* meaning 'wind'

kangaroo kangaroos
NOUN a large Australian animal with very strong back legs which it uses for jumping.

karate
Said "kar-**rat**-ee" NOUN Karate is a sport in which people fight each other using only their hands, elbows, feet, and legs.
📖 from Japanese *kara* + *te* meaning 'empty hand'

karma
NOUN In Buddhism and Hinduism, karma is actions you take which affect you in your present and future lives.

Karoo Karoos; also spelt **Karroo**
NOUN In South Africa, the Karoos are areas of very dry land.

karri karris
NOUN an Australian eucalypt that produces a dark red wood used for building.

katipo katipo or **katipos**
NOUN a small, poisonous spider with a red or orange stripe on its back, found in New Zealand.

kauri kauri or **kauris**
NOUN a large tree found in New Zealand which produces wood used for building and making furniture.

kayak kayaks
Said "ky-ak" NOUN a covered canoe with a small opening for the person sitting in it, originally used by Eskimos.

kea kea or **keas**
Said "kay-ah" NOUN 1 a large, greenish parrot found in New Zealand. 2 In New Zealand, Keas are the youngest members of the Scouts.

kebab kebabs
NOUN pieces of meat or vegetable stuck on a stick and grilled.

keel keels keeling keeled
NOUN 1 the specially shaped bottom of a ship which supports the sides and sits in the water. ▶ VERB 2 If someone or something keels over, they fall down sideways.

keen keener keenest
ADJECTIVE 1 Someone who is keen shows great eagerness and enthusiasm. 2 If you are keen on someone or something, you are attracted to or fond of them. 3 Keen senses let you see, hear, smell, and taste things very clearly or strongly.
keenly ADVERB, **keenness** NOUN
▤ (sense 1) avid, eager, enthusiastic

keep keeps keeping kept
VERB 1 To keep someone or something in a particular condition means to make them stay in that condition EG *We'll walk to keep warm.* 2 If you keep something, you have it and look after it. 3 If you keep doing something, you do it repeatedly or continuously EG *I kept phoning the hospital.* 4 If you keep a promise,

you do what you promised to do.
5 If you keep a secret, you do not tell anyone else. **6** If you keep a diary, you write something in it every day. **7** If you keep someone from going somewhere, you delay them so that they are late. **8** To keep someone means to provide them with money, food, and clothing. ▶ NOUN **9** Your keep is the cost of the food you eat, your housing, and your clothing EG *He does not contribute towards his keep.* **10** the main tower inside the walls of a castle.
目 (sense 2) hold, maintain, preserve

keep up VERB If you keep up with other people, you move or work at the same speed as they do.

keeper keepers
NOUN **1** a person whose job is to look after the animals in a zoo. **2** a goalkeeper in soccer or hockey.

keeping
NOUN **1** If something is in your keeping, it has been given to you to look after for a while. ▶ PHRASE **2** If one thing is **in keeping with** another, the two things are suitable or appropriate together.

keepsake keepsakes
NOUN something that someone gives you to remind you of a particular person or event.
目 memento, souvenir

keg kegs
NOUN a small barrel.

kelpie kelpies; also spelt **kelpy**
NOUN a smooth-haired Australian sheepdog with upright ears.

kennel kennels
NOUN **1** a shelter for a dog. **2** A kennels is a place where dogs can be kept for a time, or where they are bred.

Kenyan Kenyans
Said "**keen**-yan" ADJECTIVE
1 belonging or relating to Kenya.
▶ NOUN **2** someone who comes from Kenya.

kerb kerbs
NOUN the raised edge at the point where a pavement joins onto a road.

kernel kernels
NOUN the part of a nut that is inside the shell.

kerosene
NOUN Kerosene is the same as paraffin.

kestrel kestrels
NOUN a type of small falcon.

ketchup
NOUN Ketchup is a cold sauce, usually made from tomatoes.

kettle kettles
NOUN a metal container with a spout, in which you boil water.

key keys keying keyed
NOUN **1** a shaped piece of metal that fits into a hole so that you can unlock a door, wind something that is clockwork, or start a car.
2 The keys on a typewriter, piano, or cash register are the buttons that you press to use it. **3** an explanation of the symbols used in a map or diagram. **4** In music, a key is a scale of notes. ▶ VERB **5** If you key in information on a computer keyboard, you type it.

keyboard keyboards
NOUN a row of levers or buttons on a piano, typewriter, or computer.

kg
an abbreviation for 'kilograms'.

khaki
Said "**kah**-kee" NOUN **1** Khaki is a strong yellowish-brown material, used especially for military uniforms. ▶ NOUN OR ADJECTIVE **2** yellowish-brown.
▥ from Urdu *kaki* meaning 'dusty'

khanda khandas
Said "**kun**-dah" NOUN a sword used by Sikhs in the Amrit ceremony.

kia ora
Said "ki-**or**-ah" In New Zealand, 'kia ora' is a Maori greeting.

kibbutz kibbutzim

Said "kib-**boots**" NOUN a place of work in Israel, for example a farm or factory, where the workers live together and share all the duties and income.

kick kicks kicking kicked
VERB **1** If you kick something, you hit it with your foot. ▶ NOUN **2** If you give something a kick, you hit it with your foot. **3** AN INFORMAL USE If you get a kick out of doing something, you enjoy doing it very much.

kick off VERB When players kick off, they start a soccer or rugby match.
kick-off NOUN

kid kids kidding kidded
NOUN **1** AN INFORMAL USE a child. **2** a young goat. ▶ VERB **3** If you kid people, you tease them by deceiving them in fun.

kidnap kidnaps kidnapping kidnapped
VERB To kidnap someone is to take them away by force and demand a ransom in exchange for returning them.
kidnapper NOUN, **kidnapping** NOUN
■ abduct, seize

kidney kidneys
NOUN Your kidneys are two organs in your body that remove waste products from your blood.

kill kills killing killed
VERB **1** To kill a person, animal, or plant is to make them die. **2** If something is killing you, it is causing you severe pain or discomfort EG *My arms are killing me.* ▶ NOUN **3** The kill is the moment when a hunter kills an animal.
killer NOUN
■ (sense 1) murder, slay

kiln kilns
NOUN an oven for baking china or pottery until it becomes hard and dry.

kilo kilos
NOUN a kilogram.

kilogram kilograms
NOUN a unit of weight equal to 1000 grams.

kilohertz
NOUN a unit of measurement of radio waves equal to one thousand hertz.

kilometre kilometres
NOUN a unit of distance equal to one thousand metres.

kilowatt kilowatts
NOUN a unit of power equal to one thousand watts.

kilt kilts
NOUN a tartan skirt worn by men as part of Scottish Highland dress.

kimono kimonos
NOUN a long, loose garment with wide sleeves and a sash, worn in Japan.

kin
PLURAL NOUN Your kin are your relatives.
■ family, kindred, relatives

kind kinds; kinder kindest
NOUN **1** A particular kind of thing is something of the same type or sort as other things EG *that kind of film.* ▶ ADJECTIVE **2** Someone who is kind is considerate and generous towards other people.
kindly ADVERB, **kindness** NOUN
■ (sense 1) class, sort, type
■ (sense 2) considerate, generous
☑ When you use *kind* in its singular form, the adjective before it should be singular: *that kind of dog.* When you use the plural form *kinds*, the adjective before it should be plural: *those kinds of dog; those kinds of dogs.*

kindergarten kindergartens
NOUN a school for children who are too young to go to primary school.
⌂ from German *Kinder* + *Garten* meaning 'children's garden'

kindle kindles kindling kindled
VERB **1** If you kindle a fire, you light it. **2** If something kindles a feeling in you, it causes you to have that feeling.

kindling

NOUN Kindling is bits of dry wood or paper that you use to start a fire.

kindred

ADJECTIVE If you say that someone is a kindred spirit, you mean that they have the same interests or opinions as you.

kinetic energy

NOUN Kinetic energy is the energy that is produced when something moves.

king kings

NOUN **1** a man who is the head of state in a country, and who inherited his position from his parents. **2** a chess piece which can only move one square at a time. **3** In a pack of cards, a king is a card with a picture of a king on it.

kingdom kingdoms

NOUN **1** a country that is governed by a king or queen. **2** The divisions of the natural world are called kingdoms EG *the animal kingdom*.

kingfisher kingfishers

NOUN a brightly coloured bird that lives near water and feeds on fish.

king-size or **king-sized**

ADJECTIVE larger than the normal size EG *a king-size bed*.

kink kinks

NOUN a dent or curve in something which is normally straight.

kinky

ADJECTIVE; AN INFORMAL WORD having peculiar sexual tastes.

kinship

NOUN Kinship is a family relationship to other people.

kiosk kiosks

Said "kee-osk" NOUN a covered stall on a street where you can buy newspapers, sweets, or cigarettes. 🏛 from Turkish *kösk* meaning 'pavilion'

kip kips kipping kipped

AN INFORMAL WORD ▶ NOUN **1** a period of sleep. ▶ VERB **2** When you kip, you sleep.

kipper kippers

NOUN a smoked herring.

kirk kirks

NOUN In Scotland, a kirk is a church.

kiss kisses kissing kissed

VERB **1** When you kiss someone, you touch them with your lips as a sign of love or affection. ▶ NOUN **2** When you give someone a kiss, you kiss them.

kiss of life

NOUN The kiss of life is a method of reviving someone by blowing air into their lungs.

kit kits

NOUN **1** a collection of things that you use for a sport or other activity. **2** a set of parts that you put together to make something.

kitchen kitchens

NOUN a room used for cooking and preparing food.

kite kites

NOUN **1** a frame covered with paper or cloth which is attached to a piece of string, and which you fly in the air. **2** a shape with four sides, with two pairs of the same length, and none of the sides parallel to each other. **3** a large bird of prey with a long tail and long wings.

kitset kitsets

NOUN In New Zealand English, a set of parts which you have to put together yourself to make an item such as a house or a piece of furniture.

kitten kittens

NOUN a young cat.

kitty kitties

NOUN a fund of money that has been given by a group of people who will use it to pay for or do things together.

kiwi kiwi or **kiwis**

Said "kee-wee" NOUN **1** a type of bird found in New Zealand. Kiwis cannot fly. **2** someone who comes from New Zealand. The plural of this sense is 'kiwis'.

kiwi fruit kiwi fruits

NOUN a fruit with a brown hairy skin and green flesh.

kloof kloofs
NOUN In South Africa, a kloof is a narrow valley.

km
an abbreviation for 'kilometres'.

knack
NOUN an ability to do something difficult whilst making it look easy EG *the knack of making friends*.

knead kneads kneading kneaded
VERB If you knead dough, you press it and squeeze it with your hands before baking it.

knee knees
NOUN the joint in your leg between your ankle and your hip.

kneecap kneecaps
NOUN Your kneecaps are the bones at the front of your knees.

kneel kneels kneeling knelt
VERB When you kneel, you bend your legs and lower your body until your knees are touching the ground.

knell knells
NOUN; A LITERARY WORD the sound of a bell rung to announce a death or at a funeral.

knickers
PLURAL NOUN Knickers are underpants worn by women and girls.

knick-knacks
PLURAL NOUN Knick-knacks are small ornaments.

knife knives; knifes knifing knifed
NOUN 1 a sharp metal tool that you use to cut things. ▶ VERB 2 To knife someone is to stab them with a knife.

knight knights knighting knighted
NOUN 1 a man who has been given the title 'Sir' by the King or Queen. 2 In medieval Europe, a knight was a man who served a monarch or lord as a mounted soldier. 3 a chess piece that is usually in the shape of a horse's head. ▶ VERB 4 To knight a man is to give him the title 'Sir'.

knighthood NOUN

knit knits knitting knitted
VERB 1 If you knit a piece of clothing, you make it by working lengths of wool together, either using needles held in the hand, or with a machine. 2 If you knit your brows, you frown.
knitting NOUN

knob knobs
NOUN 1 a round handle. 2 a round switch on a machine EG *the knobs of a radio*.

knobkerrie knobkerries
NOUN In South Africa, a knobkerrie is a club or stick with a rounded end.

knock knocks knocking knocked
VERB 1 If you knock on something, you strike it with your hand or fist. 2 If you knock a part of your body against something, you bump into it quite forcefully. 3 AN INFORMAL USE To knock someone is to criticize them. ▶ NOUN 4 a firm blow on something solid EG *There was a knock at the door*.
knock out VERB To knock someone out is to hit them so hard that they become unconscious.

knocker knockers
NOUN a metal lever attached to a door, which you use to knock on the door.

knockout knockouts
NOUN 1 a punch in boxing which knocks a boxer unconscious. 2 a competition in which competitors are eliminated in each round until only the winner is left.

knoll knolls
Rhymes with "roll" NOUN; A LITERARY WORD a gently sloping hill with a rounded top.

knot knots knotting knotted
NOUN 1 a fastening made by looping a piece of string around itself and pulling the ends tight. 2 a small lump visible on the surface of a piece of wook. 3 A knot of people is a small group of them. 4 A TECHNICAL

use a unit of speed used for ships and aircraft. ▶ VERB **5** If you knot a piece of string, you tie a knot in it.

know knows knowing knew known
VERB **1** If you know a fact, you have it in your mind and you do not need to learn it. **2** People you know are not strangers because you have met them and spoken to them. ▶ AN INFORMAL PHRASE **3** If you are **in the know**, you are one of a small number of people who share a secret.

know-how
NOUN Know-how is the ability to do something that is quite difficult or technical.

knowing
ADJECTIVE A knowing look is one that shows that you know or understand something that other people do not.
knowingly ADVERB

knowledge
NOUN Knowledge is all the information and facts that you know.

knowledgeable
ADJECTIVE Someone who is knowledgeable knows a lot about a subject EG *She was very knowledgeable about Irish mythology.*

knuckle knuckles
NOUN Your knuckles are the joints at the end of your fingers where they join your hand.

koala koalas
NOUN an Australian animal with grey fur and small tufted ears. Koalas live in trees and eat eucalyptus leaves.

kohanga reo or kohanga
kohanga reo
NOUN In New Zealand, an infant class where children are taught in Maori.
📖 a Maori term meaning 'language nest'

koppie koppies

Said "kop-i"; also spelt **kopje**
NOUN In South Africa, a koppie is a small hill with no other hills around it.

Koran or Qur'an
Said "kaw-**rahn**" NOUN The Koran is the holy book of Islam.
📖 from Arabic *kara'a* meaning 'to read'

Korean Koreans
Said "kor-**ree**-an" ADJECTIVE **1** relating or belonging to Korea. ▶ NOUN **2** someone who comes from Korea. **3** Korean is the main language spoken in Korea.

kosher
Said "koh-sher" ADJECTIVE Kosher food has been specially prepared to be eaten according to Jewish law.
📖 from Hebrew *kasher* meaning 'right' or 'proper'

kowhai kowhai or kowhais
Said "ko-wigh" a small New Zealand tree with clusters of yellow flowers.

kraal kraals
NOUN In South Africa, a kraal is a village in which a tribe lives and which is often surrounded by a fence.

kudu kudus; also spelt koodoo
NOUN a large African antelope with curled horns.

kumara or kumera kumara or kumaras
Said "**koo**-mih-rah" NOUN In New Zealand English, a kumara is a sweet potato, a vegetable with yellow or orange flesh.

kumquat kumquats
NOUN a very small round or oval citrus fruit.

kung fu
Said "kung **foo**" NOUN Kung fu is a Chinese style of fighting which involves using your hands and feet.

kura kaupapa Maori kura kaupapa Maori
Said "**koo**-ra kow-puh-puh" NOUN In New Zealand, a primary school

A
B
C
D
E
F
G
H
I
J
K
L
M
N
O
P
Q
R
S
T
U
V
W
X
Y
Z

where teaching is based on Maori language and culture.

Kurd Kurds

NOUN The Kurds are a group of people who live mainly in eastern Turkey, northern Iraq, and western Iran.

Kurdish

ADJECTIVE **1** belonging or relating to the Kurds EG *Kurdish culture.* ▶ NOUN **2** Kurdish is the language spoken by the Kurds.

I

an abbreviation for 'litres'.

lab labs

NOUN; AN INFORMAL WORD a laboratory.

label labels labelling labelled

NOUN **1** a piece of paper or plastic attached to something as an identification. ▶ VERB **2** If you label something, you put a label on it.

laboratory laboratories

NOUN a place where scientific experiments are carried out.

laborious

ADJECTIVE needing a lot of effort or time.
laboriously ADVERB

Labor Party

NOUN In Australia, the Labor Party is one of the major political parties.

labour labours labouring laboured

NOUN **1** Labour is hard work. **2** The workforce of a country or industry is sometimes called its labour EG *unskilled labour*. **3** In Britain, the Labour Party is a political party that believes that the government should provide free health care and education for everyone. **4** New Zealand, the Labour Party is one of the main political parties. **5** Labour is also the last stage of pregnancy when a woman gives birth to a baby. ▶ VERB **6** AN OLD-FASHIONED USE To labour means to work hard.
labourer NOUN
▤ (sense 1) toil, work
▤ (sense 6) slave, toil, work

labrador labradors

NOUN a large dog with short black or golden hair.

labyrinth labyrinths

Said "**lab-er-inth**" NOUN a complicated series of paths or passages.

lace laces lacing laced

NOUN **1** Lace is a very fine decorated cloth made with a lot of holes in it.

2 Laces are cords with which you fasten your shoes. ▶ VERB **3** When you lace up your shoes, you tie a bow in the laces. **4** To lace someone's food or drink means to put a small amount of alcohol, a drug, or poison in it EG *black coffee laced with vodka*.
lacy ADJECTIVE

lack lacks lacking lacked

NOUN **1** If there is a lack of something, it is not present when or where it is needed. ▶ VERB **2** If something is lacking, it is not present when or where it is needed. **3** If someone or something is lacking something, they do not have it or do not have enough of it EG *Francis was lacking in stamina*.
▤ (sense 1) absence, scarcity, shortage

lacklustre

Said "**lak-luss-ter**" ADJECTIVE dull and unexciting.

laconic

Said "**lak-kon-ik**" ADJECTIVE using very few words.
▥ from Greek *Lakonikas* meaning 'Spartan'. The Spartans were famous for using few words

lacquer lacquers

Said "**lak-er**" NOUN Lacquer is thin, clear paint that you put on wood to protect it and make it shiny.

lacrosse

NOUN Lacrosse is an outdoor ball game in which two teams try to score goals using long sticks with nets on the end of them.
▥ from Canadian French *la crosse* meaning 'the hooked stick'

lad lads

NOUN a boy or young man.

ladder ladders laddering laddered

NOUN **1** a wooden or metal frame used for climbing which consists of horizontal steps fixed to two vertical poles. **2** If your stockings or tights have a ladder in them, they have a vertical, ladder-like tear in them. ▶ VERB **3** If you ladder your stockings or tights, you get a ladder in them.

laden
Said "lay-den" ADJECTIVE To be laden with something means to be carrying a lot of it EG *bushes laden with ripe fruit.*

ladle ladles ladling ladled
NOUN **1** a long-handled spoon with a deep, round bowl, which you use to serve soup. ▶ VERB **2** If you ladle out food, you serve it with a ladle.

lady ladies
NOUN **1** a woman, especially one who is considered to be well mannered. **2** Lady is a title used in front of the name of a woman from the nobility, such as a lord's wife.

ladybird ladybirds
NOUN a small flying beetle with a round red body patterned with black spots.

lady-in-waiting ladies-in-waiting
NOUN a woman who acts as companion to a queen or princess.

ladylike
ADJECTIVE behaving in a polite and socially correct way.

Ladyship Ladyships
NOUN You address a woman who has the title 'Lady' as 'Your Ladyship'.

lag lags lagging lagged
VERB **1** To lag behind means to make slower progress than other people or processes. **2** To lag pipes or water tanks means to wrap cloth round them to prevent the water inside freezing in cold weather.

lager lagers
NOUN Lager is light-coloured beer.
▥ from German *Lagerbier* meaning 'beer for storing'

lagoon lagoons
NOUN an area of water separated from the sea by reefs or sand.

laid
the past tense and past participle of **lay.**

lain
the past participle of some meanings of **lie.**

lair lairs
NOUN a place where a wild animal lives.

laird lairds
Rhymes with "**dared**" NOUN a landowner in Scotland.

lake lakes
NOUN an area of fresh water surrounded by land.

lama lamas
NOUN a Buddhist priest or monk.

lamb lambs
NOUN **1** a young sheep. **2** Lamb is the meat from a lamb.

lame
ADJECTIVE **1** Someone who is lame has an injured leg and cannot walk easily. **2** A lame excuse is unconvincing.
lamely ADVERB, **lameness** NOUN
▣ (sense 2) feeble, flimsy, weak

lament laments lamenting lamented
VERB **1** To lament something means to express sorrow or regret about it.
▶ NOUN **2** an expression of sorrow or regret. **3** a song or poem expressing grief at someone's death.

lamentable
ADJECTIVE disappointing and regrettable.

laminated
ADJECTIVE consisting of several thin sheets or layers stuck together EG *laminated glass.*

lamp lamps
NOUN a device that produces light.

lamppost lampposts
NOUN a tall column in a street, with a lamp at the top.

lampshade lampshades
NOUN a decorative covering over an electric light bulb which prevents

the bulb giving out too harsh a
light.

lance lances lancing lanced
VERB **1** To lance a boil or abscess
means to stick a sharp instrument
into it in order to release the fluid.
▸ NOUN **2** a long spear that used to
be used by soldiers on horseback.

land lands landing landed
NOUN **1** Land is an area of ground.
2 Land is also the part of the earth
that is not covered by water. **3** a
country EG *our native land.* ▸ VERB
4 When a plane lands, it arrives
back on the ground after a flight.
5 If you land something you have
been trying to get, you succeed in
getting it EG *She eventually landed a
job with a local radio station.* **6** To
land a fish means to catch it while
fishing. **7** If you land someone with
something unpleasant, you cause
them to have to deal with it.

landing landings
NOUN **1** a flat area in a building at
the top of a flight of stairs. **2** The
landing of an aeroplane is its
arrival back on the ground after a
flight EG *a smooth landing.*

landlady landladies
NOUN a woman who owns a house
or small hotel and who lets rooms
to people.

landlord landlords
NOUN a man who owns a house or
small hotel and who lets rooms to
people.

landmark landmarks
NOUN **1** a noticeable feature in a
landscape, which you can use to
check your position. **2** an
important stage in the
development of something EG *The
play is a landmark in Japanese theatre.*

landscape landscapes
NOUN **1** The landscape is the view
over an area of open land. **2** a
painting of the countryside.

landslide landslides
NOUN **1** a large amount of loose
earth and rocks falling down a

mountain side. **2** a victory in an
election won by a large number of
votes.

lane lanes
NOUN **1** a narrow road, especially in
the country. **2** one of the strips on
a road marked with lines to guide
drivers.

language languages
NOUN **1** the system of words that the
people of a country use to
communicate with each other.
2 Your language is the style in
which you express yourself EG *His
language is often obscure.* **3** Language
is the study of the words and
grammar of a particular language.
■ (sense 2) expression, speech

languid
Said "**lang**-gwid" ADJECTIVE slow and
lacking energy.
languidly ADVERB

languish languishes languishing
languished
VERB If you languish, you endure an
unpleasant situation for a long
time EG *Many languished in poverty.*

lanky lankier lankiest
ADJECTIVE Someone who is lanky is
tall and thin and moves rather
awkwardly.

lantana lantanas
NOUN In Australia, a shrub with
yellow or orange flowers which is
regarded as a pest in some areas.

lantern lanterns
NOUN a lamp in a metal frame with
glass sides.

lap laps lapping lapped
NOUN **1** Your lap is the flat area
formed by your thighs when you
are sitting down. **2** one circuit of a
running track or racecourse. ▸ VERB
3 When an animal laps up liquid, it
drinks using its tongue to get the
liquid into its mouth. **4** If you lap
someone in a race, you overtake
them when they are still on the
previous lap. **5** When water laps
against something, it gently moves
against it in little waves.

lapel lapels
Said "lap-**el**" NOUN a flap which is joined on to the collar of a jacket or coat.

lapse lapses lapsing lapsed
NOUN **1** a moment of bad behaviour by someone who usually behaves well. **2** a slight mistake. **3** a period of time between two events. ▶ VERB **4** If you lapse into a different way of behaving, you start behaving that way EG *The offenders lapsed into a sullen silence.* **5** If a legal document or contract lapses, it is not renewed on the date when it expires.

lard
NOUN Lard is fat from a pig, used in cooking.

larder larders
NOUN a room in which you store food, often next to a kitchen.

large larger largest
ADJECTIVE **1** Someone or something that is large is much bigger than average. ▶ PHRASE **2** If a prisoner is at large, he or she has escaped from prison.

largely
ADVERB to a great extent EG *The public are largely unaware of this.*

lark larks
NOUN **1** a small brown bird with a distinctive song. **2** If you do something for a lark, you do it in a high-spirited or mischievous way for fun.

larrikin larrikins
NOUN; AN INFORMAL WORD In Australian and New Zealand English, a young person who behaves in a wild or irresponsible way.

larva larvae
NOUN an insect, which looks like a short, fat worm, at the stage before it becomes an adult.

laryngitis
Said "lar-in-**jie**-tiss" NOUN Laryngitis is an infection of the throat which causes you to lose your voice.

larynx larynxes or **larynges**

NOUN the part of your throat containing the vocal cords, through which air passes between your nose and lungs.

lasagne
Said "laz-**zan**-ya" NOUN Lasagne is an Italian dish made with wide flat sheets of pasta, meat, and cheese sauce.
▥ from Latin *lasanum* meaning 'cooking pot'

laser lasers
NOUN a machine that produces a powerful concentrated beam of light which is used to cut very hard materials and in some kinds of surgery.
▥ from the first letters of 'Light Amplification by Stimulated Emission of Radiation'

lash lashes lashing lashed
NOUN **1** Your lashes are the hairs growing on the edge of your eyelids. **2** a strip of leather at the end of a whip. **3** Lashes are blows struck with a whip.
lash out VERB To lash out at someone means to criticize them severely.

lass lasses
NOUN a girl or young woman.

lasso lassoes or **lassos** lassoing lassoed
Said "las-**soo**" NOUN **1** a length of rope with a noose at one end, used by cowboys to catch cattle and horses. ▶ VERB **2** To lasso an animal means to catch it by throwing the noose of a lasso around its neck.

last lasts lasting lasted
ADJECTIVE **1** The last thing or event is the most recent one EG *last year.* **2** The last thing that remains is the only one left after all the others have gone EG *The last family left in 1950.* ▶ ADVERB **3** If you last did something on a particular occasion, you have not done it since then EG *They last met in Rome.* **4** The thing that happens last in a sequence of events is the final one EG *He added the milk last.* ▶ VERB **5** If

something lasts, it continues to exist or happen EG *Her speech lasted fifty minutes.* **6** To last also means to remain in good condition EG *The mixture will last for up to 2 weeks in the fridge.* ▶ PHRASE **7 At last** means after a long time.
lastly ADVERB

last-ditch
ADJECTIVE A last-ditch attempt to do something is a final attempt to succeed when everything else has failed.

latch latches latching latched
NOUN **1** a simple door fastening consisting of a metal bar which falls into a hook. **2** a type of door lock which locks automatically when you close the door and which has to be opened with a key. ▶ VERB **3** AN INFORMAL USE If you latch onto someone or something, you become attached to them.

late later latest
ADJECTIVE OR ADVERB **1** Something that happens late happens towards the end of a period of time EG *the late evening... late in the morning.* **2** If you arrive late, or do something late, you arrive or do it after the time you were expected to. ▶ ADJECTIVE **3** A late event happens after the time when it usually takes place EG *a late breakfast.* **4** A FORMAL USE Late means dead EG *my late grandmother.*
■ (sense 2) belated, overdue, tardy

lately
ADVERB Events that happened lately happened recently.

latent
ADJECTIVE A latent quality is hidden at the moment, but may emerge in the future EG *a latent talent for art.*

lateral
ADJECTIVE relating to the sides of something, or moving in a sideways direction.

lathe lathes
NOUN a machine which holds and turns a piece of wood or metal against a tool to cut and shape it.

lather lathers
NOUN Lather is the foam that you get when you rub soap in water.

Latin Latins
NOUN **1** Latin is the language of ancient Rome. ▶ NOUN OR ADJECTIVE **2** Latins are people who speak languages closely related to Latin, such as French, Italian, Spanish, and Portuguese.

Latin America
NOUN Latin America consists of the countries in North, South, and Central America where Spanish or Portuguese is the main language.
Latin American ADJECTIVE

latitude latitudes
NOUN The latitude of a place is its distance north or south of the equator measured in degrees.

latrine latrines
Said "lat-**reen**" NOUN a hole or trench in the ground used as a toilet at a camp.

latter
ADJECTIVE OR NOUN **1** You use 'latter' to refer to the second of two things that are mentioned EG *They were eating sandwiches and cakes (the latter bought from Mrs Paul's bakery).*
▶ ADJECTIVE **2** 'Latter' also describes the second or end part of something EG *The latter part of his career.*
✓ You use *latter* to talk about the second of two items. To talk about the last of three or more items you should use *last-named.*

latterly
ADVERB; A FORMAL WORD Latterly means recently EG *It's only latterly that this has become an issue.*

lattice lattices
NOUN a structure made of strips which cross over each other diagonally leaving holes in between.

laudable
ADJECTIVE; A FORMAL WORD deserving praise EG *It is a laudable enough aim.*

laugh laughs laughing laughed
VERB **1** When you laugh, you make a noise which shows that you are amused or happy. ▶ NOUN **2** the noise you make when you laugh.
laughter NOUN

laughable
ADJECTIVE quite absurd.

laughing stock
NOUN someone who has been made to seem ridiculous.

launch launches launching launched
VERB **1** To launch a ship means to send it into the water for the first time. **2** To launch a rocket means to send it into space. **3** When a company launches a new product, they have an advertising campaign to promote it as they start to sell it. ▶ NOUN **4** a motorboat.

launch pad launch pads
NOUN A launch pad, or a launching pad, is the place from which space rockets take off.

launder launders laundering laundered
VERB; AN OLD-FASHIONED WORD To launder clothes, sheets, or towels means to wash and iron them.

laundry laundries
NOUN **1** a business that washes and irons clothes and sheets. **2** Laundry is also the dirty clothes and sheets that are being washed, or are about to be washed.

laurel laurels
NOUN an evergreen tree with shiny leaves.

lava
NOUN Lava is the very hot liquid rock that comes shooting out of an erupting volcano, and becomes solid as it cools.

lavatory lavatories
NOUN a toilet.

lavender
NOUN **1** Lavender is a small bush with bluish-pink flowers that have a strong, pleasant scent. ▶ ADJECTIVE

2 bluish-pink.

lavish lavishes lavishing lavished
ADJECTIVE **1** If you are lavish, you are very generous with your time, money, or gifts. **2** A lavish amount is a large amount. ▶ VERB **3** If you lavish money or affection on someone, you give them a lot of it.
lavishly ADVERB

law laws
NOUN **1** The law is the system of rules developed by the government of a country, which regulate what people may and may not do and deals with people who break these rules. **2** The law is also the profession of people such as lawyers, whose job involves the application of the laws of a country. **3** one of the rules established by a government or a religion, which tells people what they may or may not do. **4** a scientific fact which allows you to explain how things work in the physical world.
lawful ADJECTIVE, **lawfully** ADVERB

law-abiding
ADJECTIVE obeying the law and not causing any trouble.

lawless
ADJECTIVE having no regard for the law.

lawn lawns
NOUN an area of cultivated grass.

lawnmower lawnmowers
NOUN a machine for cutting grass.

lawsuit lawsuits
NOUN a civil court case between two people, as opposed to the police prosecuting someone for a criminal offence.

lawyer lawyers
NOUN a person who is qualified in law, and whose job is to advise people about the law and represent them in court.

lax
ADJECTIVE careless and not keeping up the usual standards EG *a lax*

accounting system.

laxative laxatives
NOUN something that you eat or drink to stop you being constipated.

lay lays laying laid
VERB **1** When you lay something somewhere, you put it down so that it lies there. **2** If you lay the table, you put cutlery on the table ready for a meal. **3** When a bird lays an egg, it produces the egg out of its body. **4** If you lay a trap for someone, you create a situation in which you will be able to catch them out. **5** If you lay emphasis on something, you refer to it in a way that shows you think it is very important. **6** If you lay odds on something, you bet that it will happen. ▶ ADJECTIVE **7** You use 'lay' to describe people who are involved with a Christian church but are not members of the clergy EG *a lay preacher.* **8** Lay is the past tense of some senses of **lie**.
lay off VERB **1** When workers are laid off, their employers tell them not to come to work for a while because there is a shortage of work. **2** AN INFORMAL USE If you tell someone to lay off, you want them to stop doing something annoying.
lay on VERB If you lay on a meal or entertainment, you provide it.
☑ People often get confused about *lay* and *lie*. The verb *lay* takes an object: *lay the table please; the Queen laid a wreath.* The verb *lie* does not take an object: *the book was lying on the table; I'm going to lie down.*

lay-by lay-bys
NOUN **1** an area by the side of a main road where motorists can stop for a short while. **2** In Australia and New Zealand, lay-by is a system where you pay a deposit on an item in a shop so that it will be kept for you until you pay the rest of the price.

layer layers
NOUN a single thickness of something EG *layers of clothing.*

layman laymen
NOUN **1** someone who does not have specialized knowledge of a subject EG *a layman's guide to computers.* **2** someone who belongs to the church but is not a member of the clergy.

layout layouts
NOUN The layout of something is the pattern in which it is arranged.

laze lazes lazing lazed
VERB If you laze, you relax and do no work EG *We spent a few days lazing around by the pool.*

lazy lazier laziest
ADJECTIVE idle and unwilling to work.
lazily ADVERB, **laziness** NOUN
■ idle, indolent, slothful

lb
an abbreviation for 'pounds' EG *3lb of sugar.*

lbw
In cricket lbw is an abbreviation for 'leg before wicket', which is a way of dismissing a batsman when his legs prevent the ball from hitting the wicket.

leach leaches leaching leached
VERB When minerals are leached from rocks, they are dissolved by water which filters through the rock.

lead leads leading led
Rhymes with "feed" VERB **1** If you lead someone somewhere, you go in front of them in order to show them the way. **2** If one thing leads to another, it causes the second thing to happen. **3** a person who leads a group of people is in charge of them. ▶ NOUN **4** a length of leather or chain attached to a dog's collar, so that the dog can be kept under control. **5** If the police have a lead, they have a clue which might help them to solve a crime.
leading ADJECTIVE
■ (sense 1) conduct, escort, guide

lead
Rhymes with "fed" NOUN Lead is a soft, grey, heavy metal.

A B C D E F G H I J K L M N O P Q R S T U V W X Y Z

413

leaden

Said "**led-en**" ADJECTIVE **1** dark grey EG *a leaden sky.* **2** heavy and slow-moving.

leader leaders

NOUN **1** someone who is in charge of a country, an organization, or a group of people. **2** the person who is winning in a competition or race. **3** a newspaper article that expresses the newspaper's opinions.

leadership

NOUN **1** the group of people in charge of an organization. **2** Leadership is the ability to be a good leader.

leaf leaves; leafs leafing leafed

NOUN **1** the flat green growth on the end of a twig or branch of a tree or other plant. ▶ VERB **2** If you leaf through a book, magazine, or newspaper, you turn the pages over quickly.

leafy ADJECTIVE

leaflet leaflets

NOUN a piece of paper with information or advertising printed on it.

league leagues

Said "**leeg**" NOUN **1** a group of countries, clubs, or people who have joined together for a particular purpose or because they share a common interest EG *the League of Red Cross Societies... the Australian Football League.* **2** a unit of distance used in former times, equal to about 3 miles.

leak leaks leaking leaked

VERB **1** If a pipe or container leaks, it has a hole which lets gas or liquid escape. **2** If liquid or gas leaks, it escapes from a pipe or container. **3** If someone in an organization leaks information, they give the information to someone who is not supposed to have it EG *The letter was leaked to the press.* ▶ NOUN **4** If a pipe or container has a leak, it has a hole which lets gas or liquid escape. **5** If there is a leak in an organization, someone inside the organization is giving information to people who are not supposed to have it.

leaky ADJECTIVE

leakage leakages

NOUN an escape of gas or liquid from a pipe or container.

lean leans leaning leant or leaned; leaner leanest

VERB **1** When you lean in a particular direction, you bend your body in that direction. **2** When you lean on something, you rest your body against it for support. **3** If you lean on someone, you depend on them. **4** If you lean towards particular ideas, you approve of them and follow them EG *parents who lean towards strictness.* ▶ ADJECTIVE **5** having little or no fat EG *lean cuts of meat.* **6** A lean period is a time when food or money is in short supply.

leap leaps leaping leapt or leaped

VERB **1** If you leap somewhere, you jump over a long distance or high in the air. ▶ NOUN **2** a jump over a long distance or high in the air.

leap year leap years

NOUN a year, occurring every four years, in which there are 366 days.

learn learns learning learnt or learned

VERB **1** When you learn something, you gain knowledge or a skill through studying or training. **2** If you learn of something, you find out about it EG *She had first learnt of the bomb attack that morning.*

learner NOUN

■ (sense 2) discover, find out, hear

learned

Said "**ler-nid**" ADJECTIVE A learned person has a lot of knowledge gained from years of study.

learning

NOUN Learning is knowledge that has been acquired through serious study.

lease leases leasing leased

NOUN **1** an agreement which allows someone to use a house or flat in return for rent. ▶ VERB **2** To lease property to someone means to allow them to use it in return for rent.

leash leashes
NOUN a length of leather or chain attached to a dog's collar so that the dog can be controlled.

least
NOUN **1** The least is the smallest possible amount of something. ▶ ADJECTIVE OR ADVERB **2** Least is a superlative form of **little**. ▶ PHRASE **3** You use **at least** to show that you are referring to the minimum amount of something, and that you think the true amount is greater EG *At least 200 hundred people were injured*.

leather
NOUN Leather is the tanned skin of some animals, used to make shoes and clothes.
leathery ADJECTIVE

leave leaves leaving left
VERB **1** When you leave a place, you go away from it. **2** If you leave someone somewhere, they stay behind after you go away. **3** If you leave a job or organization, you stop being part of it EG *He left his job shortly after Christmas*. **4** If someone leaves money or possessions to someone, they arrange for them to be given to them after their death. **5** In subtraction, when you take one number from another, it leaves a third number. ▶ NOUN **6** a period of holiday or absence from a job. ■ (sense 1) depart, exit, go

Lebanese
ADJECTIVE **1** belonging or relating to Lebanon. ▶ NOUN **2** someone who comes from Lebanon.

lecherous
ADJECTIVE constantly thinking about sex.

lectern lecterns
NOUN a sloping desk which people use to rest books or notes on.

lecture lectures lecturing lectured
NOUN **1** a formal talk intended to teach people about a particular subject. **2** a talk intended to tell someone off. ▶ VERB **3** Someone who lectures teaches in a college or university.

lecturer lecturers
NOUN a teacher in a college or university.

led
the past tense and past participle of **lead**.

ledge ledges
NOUN a narrow shelf on the side of a cliff or rock face, or on the outside of a building, directly under a window.

ledger ledgers
NOUN a book in which accounts are kept.

lee
NOUN **1** the sheltered side of a place EG *the lee of the mountain*. ▶ ADJECTIVE **2** the side of a ship away from the wind.

leech leeches
NOUN a small worm that lives in water and feeds by sucking the blood from other animals.

leek leeks
NOUN a long vegetable of the onion family, which is white at one end and has green leaves at the other.

leer leers leering leered
VERB **1** To leer at someone means to smile at them in an unpleasant or sexually suggestive way. ▶ NOUN **2** an unpleasant or sexually suggestive smile.

leeway
NOUN If something gives you some leeway, it allows you more flexibility in your plans, for example by giving you time to finish an activity.

left
NOUN **1** The left is one of two sides of something. For example, on a

A B C D E F G H I J K L M N O P Q R S T U V W X Y Z

page, English writing begins on the left. **2** People and political groups who hold socialist or communist views are referred to as the Left. **3** Left is the past tense and past participle of **leave**. ▶ ADJECTIVE OR ADVERB **4** Left means on or towards the left side of something EG *Turn left down Govan Road.*

left-handed

ADJECTIVE OR ADVERB Someone who is left-handed does things such as writing with their left hand.

leftist leftists

NOUN OR ADJECTIVE someone who holds left-wing political views.

leftovers

PLURAL NOUN The leftovers are the bits of uneaten food that remain at the end of a meal.

left-wing

ADJECTIVE believing more strongly in socialism, or less strongly in capitalism or conservatism, than other members of the same party or group.
left-winger NOUN

leg legs

NOUN **1** Your legs are the two limbs which stretch from your hips to your feet. **2** The legs of a pair of trousers are the parts that cover your legs. **3** The legs of an object such as a table are the parts which rest on the floor and support the object's weight. **4** A leg of a journey is one part of it. **5** one of two matches played between two sports teams EG *He will miss the second leg of their UEFA Cup tie.*

legacy legacies

NOUN **1** property or money that someone gets in the will of a person who has died. **2** something that exists as a result of a previous event or time EG *the legacy of a Catholic upbringing.*
■ (sense 1) bequest, inheritance

legal

ADJECTIVE **1** relating to the law EG *the Dutch legal system.* **2** allowed by the

law EG *The strike was perfectly legal.*
legally ADVERB

legal aid

NOUN Legal aid is a system which provides the services of a lawyer free, or very cheaply, to people who cannot afford the full fees.

legality

NOUN The legality of an action means whether or not it is allowed by the law EG *They challenged the legality of the scheme.*

legalize legalizes legalizing legalized; also spelt legalise

VERB To legalize something that is illegal means to change the law so that it becomes legal.
legalization NOUN

legend legends

NOUN **1** an old story which was once believed to be true, but which is probably untrue. **2** If you refer to someone or something as a legend, you mean they are very famous EG *His career has become a legend.*
legendary ADJECTIVE

leggings

PLURAL NOUN **1** Leggings are very close-fitting trousers made of stretch material, worn mainly by young women. **2** Leggings are also a waterproof covering worn over ordinary trousers to protect them.

legible

ADJECTIVE Writing that is legible is clear enough to be read.

legion legions

NOUN **1** In ancient Rome, a legion was a military unit of between 3000 and 6000 soldiers. **2** a large military force EG *the French Foreign Legion.* **3** Legions of people are large numbers of them.

legislate legislates legislating legislated

VERB; A FORMAL WORD When a government legislates, it creates new laws.

legislation

NOUN Legislation is a law or set of

laws created by a government.

legislative
ADJECTIVE relating to the making of new laws EG *a legislative council*.

legislator legislators
NOUN; A FORMAL WORD a person involved in making or passing laws.

legislature
NOUN; A FORMAL WORD the parliament in a country, which is responsible for making new laws.

legitimate
Said "lij-it-tim-it" ADJECTIVE Something that is legitimate is reasonable or acceptable according to existing laws or standards EG *a legitimate charge for parking the car*.
legitimacy NOUN, **legitimately** ADVERB

leisure
Rhymes with "**measure**" NOUN
1 Leisure is time during which you do not have to work, and can do what you enjoy doing. ▶ PHRASES **2** If you do something **at leisure**, or **at your leisure**, you do it at a convenient time.

leisurely
ADJECTIVE OR ADVERB A leisurely action is done in an unhurried and calm way.

lekker
ADJECTIVE; A SLANG WORD **1** In South African English, lekker means pleasant. **2** In South African English, lekker can also mean tasty.

lemming lemmings
NOUN a small rodent which lives in cold, northern countries. Lemmings were believed in the past to jump off cliffs to their death in large numbers.

lemon lemons
NOUN **1** a yellow citrus fruit with a sour taste. ▶ ADJECTIVE **2** pale yellow.

lemonade
NOUN a sweet, fizzy drink made from lemons, water, and sugar.

lend lends lending lent
VERB **1** If you lend someone something, you give it to them for a period of time and then they give it back to you. **2** If a bank lends money, it gives the money to someone and the money has to be repaid in the future, usually with interest. ▶ PHRASE **3** If you **lend someone a hand**, you help them.
lender NOUN

length lengths
NOUN **1** The length of something is the horizontal distance from one end to the other. **2** The length of an event or activity is the amount of time it lasts for. **3** The length of something is also the fact that it is long rather than short EG *Despite its length, it is a rewarding read*. **4** a long piece of something.

lengthen lengthens lengthening lengthened
VERB To lengthen something means to make it longer.
■ elongate, extend, prolong

lengthways or **lengthwise**
ADVERB If you measure something lengthways, you measure the horizontal distance from one end to the other.

lengthy lengthier lengthiest
ADJECTIVE Something that is lengthy lasts for a long time.

lenient
ADJECTIVE If someone in authority is lenient, they are less severe than expected.
leniently ADVERB, **leniency** NOUN

lens lenses
NOUN **1** a curved piece of glass designed to focus light in a certain way, for example in a camera, telescope, or pair of glasses. **2** The lens in your eye is the part behind the iris, which focuses light.

lent
1 the past tense and past participle of **lend**. ▶ NOUN **2** Lent is the period of forty days leading up to Easter, during which Christians give up something they enjoy.

lentil lentils
NOUN Lentils are small dried red or

brown seeds which are cooked and eaten in soups and curries.

Leo

NOUN Leo is the fifth sign of the zodiac, represented by a lion. People born between July 23rd and August 22nd are born under this sign.

leopard leopards

NOUN a wild Asian or African big cat, with yellow fur and black or brown spots.

leotard leotards

Said "**lee-eh-tard**" NOUN a tight-fitting costume covering the body and legs, which is worn for dancing or exercise.

leper lepers

NOUN someone who has leprosy.

▣ from Greek *lepros* meaning 'scaly'

leprosy

NOUN Leprosy is an infectious disease which attacks the skin and nerves, and which can lead to fingers or toes dropping off.

lesbian lesbians

NOUN a homosexual woman. **lesbianism** NOUN

lesion lesions

Said "**lee-shen**" NOUN a wound or injury.

less

ADJECTIVE OR ADVERB **1** Less means a smaller amount, or not as much in quality EG *They left less than three weeks ago... She had become less frightened of him now.* **2** Less is a comparative form of **little**.

▶ PREPOSITION **3** You use 'less' to show that you are subtracting one number from another EG *Eight less two leaves six.*

☑ You use *less* to talk about things that can't be counted: *less time*. When you are talking about amounts that can be counted you should use *fewer*.

-less

SUFFIX -less means without EG *tasteless*

tomatoes... jobless people.

lessen lessens lessening lessened

VERB If something lessens, it is reduced in amount, size, or quality. ▣ decrease, diminish, reduce

lesser

ADJECTIVE smaller in importance or amount than something else.

lesson lessons

NOUN **1** a fixed period of time during which a class of pupils is taught by a teacher. **2** an experience that makes you understand something important which you had not realized before.

lest

CONJUNCTION; AN OLD-FASHIONED WORD as a precaution in case something unpleasant or unwanted happens EG *I was afraid to open the door lest he should follow me.*

let lets letting let

VERB **1** If you let someone do something, you allow them to do it. **2** If someone lets a house or flat that they own, they rent it out. **3** You can say 'let's' or 'let us' when you want to suggest doing something with someone else EG *Let's go.* **4** If you let yourself in for something, you agree to do it although you do not really want to.

let off VERB **1** If someone in authority lets you off, they do not punish you for something you have done wrong. **2** If you let off a firework or explosive, you light it or detonate it.

lethal

Said "**lee-thal**" ADJECTIVE able to kill someone EG *a lethal weapon.*

lethargic

Said "**lith-ar-jik**" ADJECTIVE If you feel lethargic, you have no energy or enthusiasm.

lethargy

Said "**leth-ar-jee**" NOUN Lethargy is a lack of energy and enthusiasm.

letter letters

NOUN **1** Letters are written symbols which go together to make words. **2** a piece of writing addressed to someone, and usually sent through the post.

letter box letter boxes
NOUN **1** an oblong gap in the front door of a house or flat, through which letters are delivered. **2** a large metal container in the street, where you post letters.

lettering
NOUN Lettering is writing, especially when you are describing the type of letters used EG *bold lettering*.

lettuce lettuces
NOUN a vegetable with large green leaves eaten raw in salad.

leukaemia or **leukemia**
Said "loo-kee-mee-a" NOUN Leukaemia is a serious illness which affects the blood.

level levels levelling levelled
ADJECTIVE **1** A surface that is level is smooth, flat, and parallel to the ground. ▶ VERB **2** To level a piece of land means to make it flat. **3** If you level a criticism at someone, you say or write something critical about them. ▶ ADVERB **4** If you draw level with someone, you get closer to them so that you are moving next to them. ▶ NOUN **5** a point on a scale which measures the amount, importance, or difficulty of something. **6** The level of a liquid is the height it comes up to in a container.
■ (sense 5) grade, position, stage
level off or **level out** VERB If something levels off or levels out, it stops increasing or decreasing EG *Profits are beginning to level off*.

level crossing level crossings
NOUN a place where road traffic is allowed to drive across a railway track.

level-headed
ADJECTIVE Someone who is level-headed is sensible and calm in emergencies.

lever levers
NOUN **1** a handle on a machine that you pull in order to make the machine work. **2** a long bar that you wedge underneath a heavy object and press down on to make the object move.

leverage
NOUN Leverage is knowledge or influence that you can use to make someone do something.

leveret leverets
NOUN a young hare.

levy levies levying levied
Said "lev-ee" NOUN **1** A FORMAL WORD an amount of money that you pay in tax. ▶ VERB **2** When a government levies a tax, it makes people pay the tax and organizes the collection of the money.

lewd
Rhymes with "**rude**" ADJECTIVE sexually coarse and crude.

liability liabilities
NOUN **1** Someone's liability is their responsibility for something they have done wrong. **2** In business, a company's liabilities are its debts. **3** AN INFORMAL USE If you describe someone as a liability, you mean that they cause a lot of problems or embarrassment.

liable
ADJECTIVE **1** If you say that something is liable to happen, you mean that you think it will probably happen. **2** If you are liable for something you have done, you are legally responsible for it.
☑ It used to be wrong to use *liable* to mean 'probable or likely', but that use is now considered correct.

liaise liaises liaising liaised
Said "lee-aze" VERB To liaise with someone or an organization means to cooperate with them and keep them informed.

liaison liaisons
Said "lee-aze-on" NOUN Liaison is communication between two organizations or two sections of an

A B C D E F G H I J K L M N O P Q R S T U V W X Y Z

organization.

liar liars
NOUN a person who tells lies.

libel libels libelling libelled
Said "lie-bel" NOUN **1** Libel is something written about someone which is not true, and for which the writer can be made to pay damages in court. ▶ VERB **2** To libel someone means to write or say something untrue about them.
libellous ADJECTIVE

liberal liberals
NOUN **1** someone who believes in political progress, social welfare, and individual freedom. ▶ ADJECTIVE **2** Someone who is liberal is tolerant of a wide range of behaviour, standards, or opinions. **3** To be liberal with something means to be generous with it. **4** A liberal quantity of something is a large amount of it.
liberally ADVERB, **liberalism** NOUN
🔟 from Latin *liberalis* meaning 'of freedom'

Liberal Democrat Liberal Democrats
NOUN In Britain, a member or supporter of the Liberal Democrats, a political party that believes that individuals should have more rights and freedom.

liberate liberates liberating liberated
VERB To liberate people means to free them from prison or from an unpleasant situation.
liberation NOUN, **liberator** NOUN

liberty
NOUN Liberty is the freedom to choose how you want to live, without government restrictions.

libido libidos
Said "lib-bee-doe" NOUN Someone's libido is their sexual drive.
🔟 from Latin *libido* meaning 'desire'

Libra
NOUN Libra is the seventh sign of the zodiac, represented by a pair of scales. People born between September 23rd and October 22nd are born under this sign.

librarian librarians
NOUN a person who works in, or is in charge of, a library.

library libraries
NOUN **1** a building in which books are kept for people to come and read or borrow. **2** a collection of books, records, or videos.

Libyan Libyans
ADJECTIVE **1** belonging or relating to Libya. ▶ NOUN **2** someone who comes from Libya.

lice
the plural of **louse**.

licence licences
NOUN **1** an official document which entitles you to carry out a particular activity, for example to drive a car. **2** Licence is the freedom to do what you want, especially when other people consider that it is being used irresponsibly.
✓ The noun *licence* ends in *ce*.

license licenses licensing licensed
VERB To license an activity means to give official permission for it to be carried out.
✓ The verb *license* ends in *se*.

lichen lichens
Said "lie-ken" NOUN Lichen is a green, moss-like growth on rocks or tree trunks.

lick licks licking licked
VERB **1** If you lick something, you move your tongue over it. ▶ NOUN **2** the action of licking.

lid lids
NOUN the top of a container, which you open in order to reach what is inside.

lie lies lying lay lain
VERB **1** To lie somewhere means to rest there horizontally. **2** If you say where something lies, you are describing where it is EG *The farm lies between two valleys.*

☑ The past tense of this verb *lie* is *lay*. Do not confuse it with the verb *lay* meaning 'put'.

lie lies lying lied
VERB **1** To lie means to say something that is not true. ▶ NOUN **2** something you say which is not true.

lieu
Said "**lyoo**" PHRASE If one thing happens **in lieu** of another, it happens instead of it.

lieutenant lieutenants
Said "**lef-ten-ent**" NOUN a junior officer in the army or navy.
▦ from Old French *lieutenant* meaning literally 'holding a place'

life lives
NOUN **1** Life is the quality of being able to grow and develop, which is present in people, plants, and animals. **2** Your life is your existence from the time you are born until the time you die. **3** The life of a machine is the period of time for which it is likely to work. **4** If you refer to the life in a place, you are talking about the amount of activity there EG *The town was full of life*. **5** If criminals are sentenced to life, they are sent to prison for the rest of their lives, or until they are granted parole.

life assurance
NOUN Life assurance is an insurance which provides a sum of money in the event of the policy holder's death.

lifeblood
NOUN The lifeblood of something is the most essential part of it.

lifeboat lifeboats
NOUN **1** a boat kept on shore, which is sent out to rescue people who are in danger at sea. **2** a small boat kept on a ship, which is used if the ship starts to sink.

life expectancy life expectancies
NOUN Your life expectancy is the number of years you can expect to live.

lifeguard lifeguards
NOUN a person whose job is to rescue people who are in difficulty in the sea or in a swimming pool.

life jacket life jackets
NOUN a sleeveless inflatable jacket that keeps you afloat in water.

lifeless
ADJECTIVE **1** Someone who is lifeless is dead. **2** If you describe a place or person as lifeless, you mean that they are dull and unexciting.

lifelike
ADJECTIVE A picture or sculpture that is lifelike looks very real or alive.

lifeline lifelines
NOUN **1** something which helps you to survive or helps an activity to continue. **2** a rope thrown to someone who is in danger of drowning.

lifelong
ADJECTIVE existing throughout someone's life EG *He had a lifelong interest in music.*

lifesaver lifesavers
NOUN In Australia and New Zealand, a person whose job is to rescue people who are in difficulty in the sea.

life span life spans
NOUN **1** Someone's life span is the length of time during which they are alive. **2** The life span of a product or organization is the length of time it exists or is useful.

lifetime lifetimes
NOUN Your lifetime is the period of time during which you are alive.

lift lifts lifting lifted
VERB **1** To lift something means to move it to a higher position. **2** When fog or mist lifts, it clears away. **3** To lift a ban on something means to remove it. **4** AN INFORMAL USE To lift things means to steal them. ▶ NOUN **5** a machine like a large box which carries passengers from one floor to another in a building. **6** If you give someone a

A
B
C
D
E
F
G
H
I
J
K
L
M
N
O
P
Q
R
S
T
U
V
W
X
Y
Z

lift, you drive them somewhere in a car or on a motorcycle.
■ (sense 1) elevate, raise

ligament ligaments
NOUN a piece of tough tissue in your body which connects your bones.

light lights lighting lighted or lit; lighter lightest
NOUN 1 Light is brightness from the sun, moon, fire, or lamps, that enables you to see things. 2 a lamp or other device that gives out brightness. 3 If you give someone a light, you give them a match or lighter to light their cigarette. ▶ ADJECTIVE 4 A place that is light is bright because of the sun or the use of lamps. 5 A light colour is pale. 6 A light object does not weigh much. 7 A light task is fairly easy. 8 Light books or music are entertaining and are not intended to be serious. ▶ VERB 9 To light a place means to cause it to be filled with light. 10 To light a fire means to make it start burning. 11 To light upon something means to find it by accident.
lightly ADVERB, lightness NOUN

lighten lightens lightening lightened
VERB 1 When something lightens, it becomes less dark. 2 To lighten a load means to make it less heavy.

lighter lighters
NOUN a device for lighting a cigarette or cigar.

light-headed
ADJECTIVE If you feel light-headed, you feel slightly dizzy or drunk.

light-hearted
ADJECTIVE Someone who is light-hearted is cheerful and has no worries.
■ blithe, carefree, happy-go-lucky

lighthouse lighthouses
NOUN a tower by the sea, which sends out a powerful light to guide ships and warn them of danger.

lighting
NOUN The lighting in a room or building is the way that it is lit.

lightning
NOUN Lightning is the bright flashes of light in the sky which are produced by natural electricity during a thunder storm.

lightweight lightweights
NOUN 1 a boxer in one of the lighter weight groups. ▶ ADJECTIVE 2 Something that is lightweight does not weigh very much EG a lightweight jacket.

light year light years
NOUN a unit of distance equal to the distance that light travels in a year.

likable or **likeable**
ADJECTIVE Someone who is likable is very pleasant and friendly.

like likes liking liked
PREPOSITION 1 If one thing is like another, it is similar to it. ▶ NOUN 2 'The like' means other similar things of the sort just mentioned EG nappies, prams, cots, and the like. ▶ PHRASE 3 If you feel like something, you want to do it or have it EG I feel like a walk. ▶ VERB 4 If you like something or someone, you find them pleasant.

-like
SUFFIX -like means resembling or similar to EG a balloonlike object.

likelihood
NOUN If you say that there is a likelihood that something will happen, you mean that you think it will probably happen.

likely likelier likeliest
ADJECTIVE Something that is likely will probably happen or is probably true.

liken likens likening likened
VERB If you liken one thing to another, you say that they are similar.

likeness likenesses
NOUN If two things have a likeness to each other, they are similar in appearance.

likewise

ADVERB Likewise means similarly EG *She sat down and he did likewise.*

liking

NOUN If you have a liking for someone or something, you like them.

lilac

NOUN **1** a shrub with large clusters of pink, white, or mauve flowers. ▶ ADJECTIVE **2** pale mauve.

lilt lilts

NOUN A lilt in someone's voice is a pleasant rising and falling sound in it.

lilting ADJECTIVE

lily lilies

NOUN a plant with trumpet-shaped flowers of various colours.

limb limbs

NOUN **1** Your limbs are your arms and legs. **2** The limbs of a tree are its branches. ▶ PHRASE **3** If you have gone out on a limb, you have said or done something risky.

limber up limbers up limbering up limbered up

VERB If you limber up, you stretch your muscles before doing a sport.

limbo

NOUN **1** If you are in limbo, you are in an uncertain situation over which you feel you have no control. **2** The limbo is a West Indian dance in which the dancer has to pass under a low bar while leaning backwards.

▣ sense **1** is from Latin *in limbo* meaning 'on the border (of Hell)'

lime limes

NOUN **1** a small, green citrus fruit, rather like a lemon. **2** A lime tree is a large tree with pale green leaves. **3** Lime is a chemical substance that is used in cement and as a fertilizer.

limelight

NOUN If someone is in the limelight, they are getting a lot of attention.

limerick limericks

NOUN an amusing nonsense poem of five lines.

limestone

NOUN Limestone is a white rock which is used for building and making cement.

limit limits limiting limited

NOUN **1** a boundary or an extreme beyond which something cannot go EG *the speed limit.* ▶ VERB **2** To limit something means to prevent it from becoming bigger, spreading, or making progress EG *He did all he could to limit the damage.*

limitation limitations

NOUN **1** The limitation of something is the reducing or controlling of it. **2** If you talk about the limitations of a person or thing, you are talking about the limits of their abilities.

limited

ADJECTIVE Something that is limited is rather small in amount or extent EG *a limited number of bedrooms.*

limousine limousines

Said "lim-o-zeen" NOUN a large, luxurious car, usually driven by a chauffeur.

limp limps limping limped; limper limpest

VERB **1** If you limp, you walk unevenly because you have hurt your leg or foot. ▶ NOUN **2** an uneven way of walking. ▶ ADJECTIVE **3** Something that is limp is soft and floppy, and not stiff or firm EG *a limp lettuce.*

limpet limpets

NOUN a shellfish with a pointed shell, that attaches itself very firmly to rocks.

line lines lining lined

NOUN **1** a long, thin mark. **2** a number of people or things positioned one behind the other. **3** a route along which someone or something moves EG *a railway line.* **4** In a piece of writing, a line is a number of words together EG *I often used to change my lines as an actor.* **5** Someone's line of work is the kind of work they do. **6** The line someone takes is the attitude they have towards something EG *He took a hard line with terrorism*. **7** In a shop or business, a line is a type of product EG *That line has been discontinued*. ▶ VERB **8** To line something means to cover its inside surface or edge with something EG *Cottages lined the edge of the harbour*.

line up VERB **1** When people line up, they stand in a line. **2** When you line something up, you arrange it for a special occasion EG *A tour is being lined up for July*.

lineage lineages
Said "lin-ee-ij" NOUN Someone's lineage is all the people from whom they are directly descended.

linear
Said "lin-ee-ar" ADJECTIVE arranged in a line or in a strict sequence, or happening at a constant rate.

line dancing
NOUN a type of dancing performed by rows of people to country music.

linen
NOUN **1** Linen is a type of cloth made from a plant called flax. **2** Linen is also household goods made of cloth, such as sheets and tablecloths.

liner liners
NOUN a large passenger ship that makes long journeys.

linesman linesmen
NOUN an official at a sports match who watches the lines of the field or court and indicates when the ball goes outside them.

linger lingers lingering lingered
VERB To linger means to remain for a long time EG *Economic problems lingered in the background*.

lingerie
Said "lan-jer-ee" NOUN Lingerie is women's nightwear and underclothes.

lingo lingoes
NOUN; AN INFORMAL WORD a foreign language.

linguist linguists
NOUN someone who studies foreign languages or the way in which language works.

lining linings
NOUN any material used to line the inside of something.

link links linking linked
NOUN **1** a relationship or connection between two things EG *the link between sunbathing and skin cancer*. **2** a physical connection between two things or places EG *a high-speed rail link between the cities*. **3** one of the rings in a chain. ▶ VERB **4** To link people, places, or things means to join them together.
linkage NOUN

lino
NOUN Lino is the same as linoleum.

linoleum
NOUN Linoleum is a floor covering with a shiny surface.

lint
NOUN Lint is soft cloth made from linen, used to dress wounds.

lion lions
NOUN a large member of the cat family which comes from Africa. Lions have light brown fur, and the male has a long mane. A female lion is called a lioness.

lip lips
NOUN **1** Your lips are the edges of your mouth. **2** The lip of a jug is the slightly pointed part through which liquids are poured out.

lip-read lip-reads lip-reading lip-read
VERB To lip-read means to watch someone's lips when they are talking in order to understand what they are saying. Deaf people often lip-read.

lipstick lipsticks
NOUN Lipstick is a coloured substance which women wear on their lips.

liqueur liqueurs

Said "lik-**yoor**" NOUN a strong sweet alcoholic drink, usually drunk after a meal.

liquid liquids
NOUN **1** any substance which is not a solid or a gas, and which can be poured. ▶ ADJECTIVE **2** Something that is liquid is in the form of a liquid EG *liquid nitrogen*. **3** In commerce and finance a person's or company's liquid assets are the things that can be sold quickly to raise cash.

liquidate liquidates liquidating liquidated
VERB **1** To liquidate a company means to close it down and to use its assets to pay off its debts. **2** AN INFORMAL USE To liquidate a person means to murder them.
liquidation NOUN, **liquidator** NOUN

liquor
NOUN Liquor is any strong alcoholic drink.

liquorice
Said "**lik-ker-iss**" NOUN Liquorice is a root used to flavour sweets; also the sweets themselves.

lira lire
NOUN the unit of currency in Italy.

lisp lisps lisping lisped
NOUN **1** Someone who has a lisp pronounces the sounds 's' and 'z' like 'th'. ▶ VERB **2** To lisp means to speak with a lisp.

list lists listing listed
NOUN **1** a set of words or items written one below the other. ▶ VERB **2** If you list a number of things, you make a list of them.

listen listens listening listened
VERB If you listen to something, you hear it and pay attention to it.
listener NOUN

listless
ADJECTIVE lacking energy and enthusiasm.
listlessly ADVERB
🔲 from Old English *list* meaning 'desire'

lit

a past tense and past participle of **light**.

litany litanies
NOUN **1** a part of a church service in which the priest says or chants prayers and the people give responses. **2** something, especially a list of things, that is repeated often or in a boring or insincere way EG *a tedious litany of complaints*.

literacy
NOUN Literacy is the ability to read and write.
literate ADJECTIVE

literal
ADJECTIVE **1** The literal meaning of a word is its most basic meaning. **2** A literal translation from a foreign language is one that has been translated exactly word for word.
literally ADVERB
☑ Be careful where you use *literally*. It can emphasize something without changing the meaning: *the house was literally only five minutes walk away*. However, it can make nonsense of some things: *he literally swept me off my feet*. This sentence is ridiculous unless *he* actually took a broom and swept the speaker over.

literary
ADJECTIVE connected with literature EG *literary critics*.

literature
NOUN **1** Literature consists of novels, plays, and poetry. **2** The literature on a subject is everything that has been written about it.

lithe
ADJECTIVE supple and graceful.

litmus
NOUN In chemistry, litmus is a substance that turns red under acid and blue under alkali conditions.

litmus test litmus tests
NOUN something which is regarded as a simple and accurate test of a particular thing, such as a person's attitude to an issue EG *The conflict was seen as a litmus test of Britain's*

will to remain a major power.

litre litres

NOUN a unit of liquid volume equal to about 1.76 pints.

litter litters littering littered

NOUN **1** Litter is rubbish in the street and other public places. **2** Cat litter is a gravelly substance you put in a container where you want your cat to urinate and defecate. **3** a number of baby animals born at the same time to the same mother. ▶ VERB **4** If things litter a place, they are scattered all over it.

little less lesser least

ADJECTIVE **1** small in size or amount. ▶ NOUN OR ADVERB **2** A little is a small amount or degree EG *Would you like a little fruit juice?* **3** Little also means not much EG *He has little to say.*

live lives living lived

VERB **1** If you live in a place, that is where your home is. **2** To live means to be alive. **3** If something lives up to your expectations, it is as good as you thought it would be. ▶ ADJECTIVE OR ADVERB **4** Live television or radio is broadcast while the event is taking place EG *a live football match... The concert will go out live.* ▶ ADJECTIVE **5** Live animals or plants are alive, rather than dead or artificial EG *a live spider.* **6** Something is live if it is directly connected to an electricity supply EG *Careful — those wires are live.* **7** Live bullets or ammunition have not yet been exploded.

live down VERB If you cannot live down a mistake or failure, you cannot make people forget it.

livelihood livelihoods

NOUN Someone's livelihood is their job or the source of their income.

lively

ADJECTIVE full of life and enthusiasm EG *lively conversation.*

liveliness NOUN

■ brisk, energetic, vigorous

liven livens livening livened

VERB To liven things up means to

make them more lively or interesting.

liver livers

NOUN **1** Your liver is a large organ in your body which cleans your blood and helps digestion. **2** Liver is also the liver of some animals, which may be cooked and eaten.

🏛 from Greek *liparos* meaning 'fat'

livestock

NOUN Livestock is farm animals.

livid

ADJECTIVE **1** extremely angry. **2** dark purple or bluish EG *livid bruises.*

living

ADJECTIVE **1** If someone is living, they are alive EG *her only living relative.* ▶ NOUN **2** The work you do for a living is the work you do in order to earn money to live.

living room living rooms

NOUN the room where people relax and entertain in their homes.

lizard lizards

NOUN a long, thin, dry-skinned reptile found in hot, dry countries.

llama llamas

NOUN a South American animal related to the camel.

load loads loading loaded

NOUN **1** something being carried. **2** AN INFORMAL USE Loads means a lot EG *loads of work.* ▶ VERB **3** To load a vehicle or animal means to put a large number of things into it or onto it.

loaf loaves; loafs loafing loafed

NOUN **1** a large piece of bread baked in a shape that can be cut into slices. ▶ VERB **2** To loaf around means to be lazy and not do any work.

loan loans loaning loaned

NOUN **1** a sum of money that you borrow. **2** the act of borrowing or lending something EG *I am grateful to Jane for the loan of her book.* ▶ VERB **3** If you loan something to someone, you lend it to them.

loath

Rhymes with **"both"** ADJECTIVE If you are loath to do something, you are very unwilling to do it.
☑ Do not confuse *loath* with *loathe*.

loathe loathes loathing loathed
VERB To loathe someone or something means to feel strong dislike for them.
loathing NOUN, **loathsome** ADJECTIVE
☑ Do not confuse *loathe* with *loath*.

lob lobs lobbing lobbed
VERB **1** If you lob something, you throw it high in the air. ▶ NOUN **2** In tennis, a lob is a stroke in which the player hits the ball high in the air.

lobby lobbies lobbying lobbied
NOUN **1** The lobby in a building is the main entrance area with corridors and doors leading off it. **2** a group of people trying to persuade an organization that something should be done EG *the environmental lobby*. ▶ VERB **3** To lobby an MP or an organization means to try to persuade them to do something, for example by writing them lots of letters.

lobe lobes
NOUN **1** The lobe of your ear is the rounded soft part at the bottom. **2** any rounded part of something EG *the frontal lobe of the brain*.

lobster lobsters
NOUN an edible shellfish with two front claws and eight legs.

local locals
ADJECTIVE **1** Local means in, near, or belonging to the area in which you live EG *the local newspaper*. **2** A local anaesthetic numbs only one part of your body and does not send you to sleep. ▶ NOUN **3** The locals are the people who live in a particular area. **4** AN INFORMAL USE Someone's local is the pub nearest their home.
locally ADVERB
▤ (sense 1) provincial, regional

locality localities
NOUN an area of a country or city EG *a large map of the locality*.

localized or **localised**
ADJECTIVE existing or happening in only one place EG *localized pain*.

locate locates locating located
VERB **1** To locate someone or something means to find out where they are. **2** If something is located in a place, it is in that place.

location locations
NOUN **1** a place, or the position of something. **2** In South Africa, a location was a small town where only Black people or Coloured people were allowed to live. ▶ PHRASE **3** If a film is made on location, it is made away from a studio.
▤ (sense 1) place, position

loch lochs
NOUN In Scottish English, a loch is a lake.

lock locks locking locked
VERB **1** If you lock something, you close it and fasten it with a key. **2** If something locks into place, it moves into place and becomes firmly fixed there. ▶ NOUN **3** a device on something which fastens it and prevents it from being opened except with a key. **4** A lock on a canal is a place where the water level can be raised or lowered to allow boats to go between two parts of the canal which have different water levels. **5** A lock of hair is a small bunch of hair.

locker lockers
NOUN a small cupboard for your personal belongings, for example in a changing room.

locket lockets
NOUN a piece of jewellery consisting of a small case which you can keep a photograph in, and which you wear on a chain round your neck.

locksmith locksmiths
NOUN a person who makes or mends locks.

locomotive locomotives
NOUN a railway engine.

locust locusts

NOUN an insect like a large grasshopper, which travels in huge swarms and eats crops.

lodge lodges lodging lodged
NOUN **1** a small house in the grounds of a large country house, or a small house used for holidays. ▶ VERB **2** If you lodge in someone else's house, you live there and pay them rent. **3** If something lodges somewhere, it gets stuck there EG *The bullet lodged in his pelvis.* **4** If you lodge a complaint, you formally make it.

lodger lodgers
NOUN a person who lives in someone's house and pays rent.

lodgings
PLURAL NOUN If you live in lodgings, you live in someone else's house and pay them rent.

loft lofts
NOUN the space immediately under the roof of a house, often used for storing things.

lofty loftier loftiest
ADJECTIVE **1** very high EG *a lofty hall.* **2** very noble and important EG *lofty ideals.* **3** proud and superior EG *her lofty manner.*

log logs logging logged
NOUN **1** a thick branch or piece of tree trunk which has fallen or been cut down. **2** the captain's official record of everything that happens on board a ship. ▶ VERB **3** If you log something, you officially make a record of it, for example in a ship's log. **4** To log into a computer system means to gain access to it, usually by giving your name and password. To log out means to finish using the system.

logic
NOUN Logic is a way of reasoning involving a series of statements, each of which must be true if the statement before it is true.

logical
ADJECTIVE **1** A logical argument uses logic. **2** A logical course of action or decision is sensible or reasonable in the circumstances EG *the logical conclusion.*
logically ADVERB

logistics
NOUN; A FORMAL WORD The logistics of a complicated undertaking is the skilful organization of it.

logo logos
Said "loh-goh" NOUN The logo of an organization is a special design that is put on all its products.
🔲 from Greek *logos* meaning 'word'

-logy
SUFFIX -logy is used to form words that refer to the study of something EG *biology... geology.*

loin loins
NOUN **1** AN OLD-FASHIONED USE Your loins are the front part of your body between your waist and your thighs, especially your sexual parts. **2** Loin is a piece of meat from the back or sides of an animal EG *loin of pork.*

loiter loiters loitering loitered
VERB To loiter means stand about idly with no real purpose.

loll lolls lolling lolled
VERB **1** If you loll somewhere, you sit or lie there in an idle, relaxed way. **2** If your head or tongue lolls, it hangs loosely.

lollipop lollipops
NOUN a hard sweet on the end of a stick.

lolly lollies
NOUN **1** a lollipop. **2** a piece of flavoured ice or ice cream on a stick. **3** In Australian and New Zealand English, a sweet.

lolly scramble lolly scrambles
NOUN In New Zealand, a lolly scramble is a lot of sweets thrown on the ground for children to pick up.

lone
ADJECTIVE A lone person or thing is the only one in a particular place EG *a lone climber.*

≡ single, solitary

lonely lonelier loneliest
ADJECTIVE **1** If you are lonely, you are unhappy because you are alone. **2** A lonely place is an isolated one which very few people visit EG *a lonely hillside.*
loneliness NOUN

loner loners
NOUN a person who likes to be alone.

lonesome
ADJECTIVE lonely and sad.

long longer longest; longs longing longed
ADJECTIVE OR ADVERB **1** continuing for a great amount of time EG *There had been no rain for a long time... The equipment will not last much longer.*
▶ ADJECTIVE **2** great in length or distance EG *a long dress... a long road.*
▶ PHRASE **3** If something **no longer** happens, it does not happen any more. **4 Before long** means soon. **5** If one thing is true **as long as** another thing is true, it is true only if the other thing is true. ▶ VERB **6** If you long for something, you want it very much.
longing NOUN

longevity
Said "lon-jev-it-ee" NOUN; A FORMAL WORD Longevity is long life.

longhand
NOUN If you write something in longhand, you do it in your own handwriting rather than using shorthand or a typewriter.

longitude longitudes
NOUN The longitude of a place is its distance east or west of a line passing through Greenwich, measured in degrees.

long jump
NOUN The long jump is an athletics event in which you jump as far as possible after taking a long run.

long-range
ADJECTIVE **1** able to be used over a great distance EG *long-range artillery.* **2** extending a long way into the future EG *a long-range weather forecast.*

long-sighted
ADJECTIVE If you are long-sighted, you have difficulty seeing things that are close.

long-standing
ADJECTIVE having existed for a long time EG *a long-standing tradition.*

long-suffering
ADJECTIVE very patient EG *her long-suffering husband.*

long-term
ADJECTIVE extending a long way into the future EG *a long-term investment.*

long-winded
ADJECTIVE long and boring EG *a long-winded letter.*

loo loos
NOUN; AN INFORMAL WORD a toilet.

look looks looking looked
VERB **1** If you look at something, you turn your eyes towards it so that you can see it. **2** If you look for someone or something, you try to find them. **3** If you look at a subject or situation, you study it or judge it. **4** If you look down on someone, you think that they are inferior to you. **5** If you are looking forward to something, you want it to happen because you think you will enjoy it. **6** If you look up to someone, you admire and respect them. **7** If you describe the way that something looks, you are describing its appearance. ▶ NOUN **8** If you have a look at something, you look at it. **9** The look on your face is the expression on it. **10** If you talk about someone's looks, you are talking about how attractive they are. ▶ INTERJECTION **11** You say 'look out' to warn someone of danger.
≡ (sense 1) gaze, glance, see, watch
≡ (sense 8) glance, glimpse, peek
≡ (sense 9) appearance, expression
look after VERB If you look after someone or something, you take care of them.
look up VERB **1** To look up

information means to find it out in a book. **2** If you **look** someone **up**, you go to see them after not having seen them for a long time. **3** If a situation is looking up, it is improving.

lookalike **lookalikes**
NOUN a person who looks very like someone else EG *an Elvis lookalike*.

lookout **lookouts**
NOUN **1** someone who is watching for danger, or a place where they watch for danger. ▸ PHRASE **2** If you are **on the lookout** for something, you are watching for it or waiting expectantly for it.

loom **looms** **looming** **loomed**
NOUN **1** a machine for weaving cloth. ▸ VERB **2** If something looms in front of you, it suddenly appears as a tall, unclear, and sometimes frightening shape. **3** If a situation or event is looming, it is likely to happen soon and is rather worrying.

loony **loonies**
AN INFORMAL WORD ▸ ADJECTIVE **1** People or behaviour can be described as loony if they are mad or eccentric. ▸ NOUN **2** a mad or eccentric person.

loop **loops** **looping** **looped**
NOUN **1** a curved or circular shape in something long such as a piece of string. ▸ VERB **2** If you loop rope or string around an object, you place it in a loop around the object.

loophole **loopholes**
NOUN a small mistake or omission in the law which allows you to do something that the law really intends that you should not do.

loose **looser** **loosest**
ADJECTIVE **1** If something is loose, it is not firmly held, fixed, or attached. **2** Loose clothes are rather large and do not fit closely. ▸ ADVERB **3** To set animals loose means to set them free after they have been tied up or kept in a cage.
loosely ADVERB
☑ The adjective and adverb *loose* is

spelt with two *o*s. Do not confuse it with the verb *lose*.

loosen **loosens** **loosening** **loosened**
VERB To loosen something means to make it looser.

loot **loots** **looting** **looted**
VERB **1** To loot shops and houses means to steal goods from them during a battle or riot. **2** Loot is stolen money or goods.
▥ from Hindi *lut*
▤ (sense 1) pillage, plunder, ransack
▤ (sense 2) booty, plunder, spoils

lop **lops** **lopping** **lopped**
VERB If you lop something off, you cut it off with one quick stroke.

lopsided
ADJECTIVE Something that is lopsided is uneven because its two sides are different sizes or shapes.

lord **lords**
NOUN **1** a nobleman. **2** Lord is a title used in front of the names of some noblemen, and of bishops, archbishops, judges, and some high-ranking officials EG *the Lord Mayor of London*. **3** In Christianity, Lord is a name given to God and Jesus Christ.

Lordship **Lordships**
NOUN You address a lord, judge, or bishop as Your Lordship.

lore
NOUN The lore of a place, people, or subject is all the traditional knowledge and stories about it.

lorikeet **lorikeets**
NOUN a type of small parrot found in Australia.

lorry **lorries**
NOUN a large vehicle for transporting goods by road.

lory **lories**
Said "**law**-ree" NOUN a small, brightly coloured parrot found in Australia.

lose **loses** **losing** **lost**
VERB **1** If you lose something, you

cannot find it, or you no longer have it because it has been taken away from you EG *I lost my airline ticket.* **2** If you lose a relative or friend, they die EG *She lost her brother in the war.* **3** If you lose a fight or an argument, you are beaten. **4** If a business loses money, it is spending more money than it is earning.

loser NOUN

☑ The verb *lose* is spelt with one *o*. Do not confuse it with the adjective and adverb *loose*.

loss losses
NOUN **1** The loss of something is the losing of it. ▸ PHRASE **2** If you are **at a loss**, you do not know what to do.

lost
ADJECTIVE **1** If you are lost, you do not know where you are. **2** If something is lost, you cannot find it. **3** Lost is the past tense and past participle of **lose**.

lot lots
NOUN **1** A lot of something, or lots of something, is a large amount of it. **2** A lot means very much or very often EG *I love him a lot.* **3** an amount of something or a number of things EG *He bet all his wages and lost the lot.* **4** In an auction, a lot is one of the things being sold.
▤ (sense 1) abundance, load(s), plenty

lotion lotions
NOUN a liquid that you put on your skin to protect or soften it EG *suntan lotion.*

lottery lotteries
NOUN a method of raising money by selling tickets by which a winner is selected at random.

lotus lotuses
NOUN a large water lily, found in Africa and Asia.

loud louder loudest
ADJECTIVE OR ADVERB **1** A loud noise has a high volume of sound EG *a loud explosion.* **2** If you describe clothing as loud, you mean that it is too

bright EG *a loud tie.*
loudly ADVERB

loudspeaker loudspeakers
NOUN a piece of equipment that makes your voice louder when you speak into a microphone connected to it.

lounge lounges lounging lounged
NOUN **1** a room in a house or hotel with comfortable chairs where people can relax. **2** The lounge or lounge bar in a pub or hotel is a more expensive and comfortably furnished bar. ▸ VERB **3** If you lounge around, you lean against something or sit or lie around in a lazy and comfortable way.

louse lice
NOUN Lice are small insects that live on people's bodies EG *head lice.*

lousy lousier lousiest
ADJECTIVE; AN INFORMAL WORD **1** of bad quality or very unpleasant EG *The weather is lousy.* **2** ill or unhappy.

lout louts
NOUN a young man who behaves in an impolite or aggressive way.

lovable or **loveable**
ADJECTIVE having very attractive qualities and therefore easy to love EG *a lovable black mongrel.*

love loves loving loved
VERB **1** If you love someone, you have strong emotional feelings of affection for them. **2** If you love something, you like it very much EG *We both love fishing.* **3** If you would love to do something, you want very much to do it EG *I would love to live there.* ▸ NOUN **4** Love is a strong emotional feeling of affection for someone or something. **5** In tennis, love is a score of zero. ▸ PHRASE **6** If you are **in love** with someone, you feel strongly attracted to them romantically or sexually. **7** When two people **make love**, they have sex.
loving ADJECTIVE, **lovingly** ADVERB
▤ (sense 1) adore, dote on

love affair love affairs

love life love lives
NOUN a person's romantic and sexual relationships.

lovely lovelier loveliest
ADJECTIVE very beautiful, attractive, and pleasant.
loveliness NOUN

lover lovers
NOUN 1 A person's lover is someone that they have a sexual relationship with but are not married to. 2 Someone who is a lover of something, for example art or music, is very fond of it.

low lower lowest
ADJECTIVE OR ADVERB 1 Something that is low is close to the ground, or measures a short distance from the ground to the top EG *a low stool*. 2 'Low' is used to describe people who are considered not respectable EG *mixing with low company*. ▶ NOUN 3 a level or amount that is less than before EG *Sales hit a new low*.

lowboy lowboys
NOUN In Australian and New Zealand English, a small wardrobe or chest of drawers.

lower lowers lowering lowered
VERB To lower something means to move it downwards or to make it less in value or amount.

lowlands
PLURAL NOUN Lowlands are an area of flat, low land.
lowland ADJECTIVE

lowly lowlier lowliest
ADJECTIVE low in importance, rank or status.

low tide
NOUN On a coast, low tide is the time, usually twice a day, when the sea is at its lowest level.

loyal
ADJECTIVE firm in your friendship or support for someone or something.
loyally ADVERB, **loyalty** NOUN

loyalist loyalists
NOUN a person who remains firm in their support for a government or ruler.

lozenge lozenges
NOUN 1 a type of sweet with medicine in it, which you suck to relieve a sore throat or cough. 2 a diamond shape.

LP LPs
NOUN a long-playing record. LP is short for 'long-playing record'.

LSD
NOUN LSD is a very powerful drug which causes hallucinations. LSD is an abbreviation for 'lysergic acid diethylamide'.

Ltd
an abbreviation for 'limited'; used after the names of limited companies.

lubra lubras
NOUN an Australian Aboriginal woman.

lubricate lubricates lubricating lubricated
VERB To lubricate something such as a machine means to put oil or an oily substance onto it, so that it moves smoothly and friction is reduced.
lubrication NOUN, **lubricant** NOUN

lucid
ADJECTIVE 1 Lucid writing or speech is clear and easy to understand. 2 Someone who is lucid after having been ill or delirious is able to think clearly again.

luck
NOUN Luck is anything that seems to happen by chance and not through your own efforts.
▤ chance, fortune

luckless
ADJECTIVE unsuccessful or unfortunate EG *We reduced our luckless opponents to shattered wrecks*.

lucky luckier luckiest
ADJECTIVE 1 Someone who is lucky has a lot of good luck. 2 Something

NOUN a romantic and often sexual relationship between two people who are not married to each other.

that is lucky happens by chance and has good effects or consequences.

luckily ADVERB

lucrative

ADJECTIVE Something that is lucrative earns you a lot of money EG *a lucrative sponsorship deal*.

ludicrous

ADJECTIVE completely foolish, unsuitable, or ridiculous.

lug lugs lugging lugged

VERB If you lug a heavy object around, you carry it with difficulty.

luggage

NOUN Your luggage is the bags and suitcases that you take with you when you travel.

lukewarm

ADJECTIVE **1** slightly warm EG *a mug of lukewarm tea*. **2** not very enthusiastic or interested EG *The report was given a polite but lukewarm response*.

lull lulls lulling lulled

NOUN **1** a pause in something, or a short time when it is quiet and nothing much happens EG *There was a temporary lull in the fighting*. ▶ VERB **2** If you are lulled into feeling safe, someone or something causes you to feel safe at a time when you are not safe EG *We had been lulled into a false sense of security*.

lullaby lullabies

NOUN a song used for sending a baby or child to sleep.

lumber lumbers lumbering lumbered

NOUN **1** Lumber is wood that has been roughly cut up. **2** Lumber is also old unwanted furniture and other items. ▶ VERB **3** If you lumber around, you move heavily and clumsily. **4** AN INFORMAL USE If you are lumbered with something, you are given it to deal with even though you do not want it EG *Women are still lumbered with the housework*.

luminary luminaries

NOUN; A LITERARY WORD a person who is famous or an expert in a particular subject.

luminous

ADJECTIVE Something that is luminous glows in the dark, usually because it has been treated with a special substance EG *The luminous dial on her clock*.

luminosity NOUN

lump lumps lumping lumped

NOUN **1** A lump of something is a solid piece of it, of any shape or size EG *a big lump of dough*. **2** a bump on the surface of something. ▶ VERB **3** If you lump people or things together, you combine them into one group or consider them as being similar in some way.

lumpy ADJECTIVE

lump sum lump sums

NOUN a large sum of money given or received all at once.

lunacy

NOUN **1** Lunacy is extremely foolish or eccentric behaviour. **2** AN OLD-FASHIONED USE Lunacy is also severe mental illness.

lunar

ADJECTIVE relating to the moon.
🏛 from Latin *luna* meaning 'moon'

lunatic lunatics

NOUN **1** If you call someone a lunatic, you mean that they are very foolish EG *He drives like a lunatic!* **2** someone who is insane. ▶ ADJECTIVE **3** Lunatic behaviour is very stupid, foolish, or dangerous.

lunch lunches lunching lunched

NOUN **1** a meal eaten in the middle of the day. ▶ VERB **2** When you lunch, you eat lunch.

luncheon luncheons

Said "lun-shen" NOUN; A FORMAL WORD Luncheon is lunch.

lung lungs

NOUN Your lungs are the two organs inside your ribcage with which you breathe.

lunge lunges lunging lunged

A
B
C
D
E
F
G
H
I
J
K
L
M
N
O
P
Q
R
S
T
U
V
W
X
Y
Z

NOUN **1** a sudden forward movement EG *He made a lunge for her.* ▶ VERB **2** To lunge means to make a sudden movement in a particular direction.

lurch lurches lurching lurched
VERB **1** To lurch means to make a sudden, jerky movement. ▶ NOUN **2** a sudden, jerky movement.

lure lures luring lured
VERB **1** To lure someone means to attract them into going somewhere or doing something. ▶ NOUN **2** something that you find very attractive.

lurid
Said "loo-rid" ADJECTIVE **1** involving a lot of sensational detail EG *lurid stories in the press.* **2** very brightly coloured or patterned.

lurk lurks lurking lurked
VERB To lurk somewhere means to remain there hidden from the person you are waiting for.

luscious
ADJECTIVE very tasty EG *luscious fruit.*

lush lusher lushest
ADJECTIVE In a lush field or garden, the grass or plants are healthy and growing thickly.

lust lusts lusting lusted
NOUN **1** Lust is a very strong feeling of sexual desire for someone. **2** A lust for something is a strong desire to have it EG *a lust for money.* ▶ VERB **3** To lust for or after someone means to desire them sexually. **4** If you lust for or after something, you have a very strong desire to possess it EG *She lusted after fame.*

lustre
Said "lus-ter" NOUN Lustre is soft shining light reflected from the surface of something EG *the lustre of silk.*

lute lutes
NOUN an old-fashioned stringed musical instrument which is plucked like a guitar.

luxuriant
ADJECTIVE Luxuriant plants, trees, and gardens are large, healthy and growing strongly.

luxurious
ADJECTIVE very expensive and full of luxury.
luxuriously ADVERB
▣ opulent, splendid, sumptuous

luxury luxuries
NOUN **1** Luxury is great comfort in expensive and beautiful surroundings EG *a life of luxury.* **2** something that you enjoy very much but do not have very often, usually because it is expensive.
▣ (sense 1) extravagance, indulgence, treat

lying
NOUN **1** Lying is telling lies. **2** Lying is also the present participle of **lie**.

lynch lynches lynching lynched
VERB If a crowd lynches someone, it kills them in a violent way without first holding a legal trial.

lynx lynxes
NOUN a wildcat with a short tail and tufted ears.

lyre lyres
NOUN a stringed instrument rather like a small harp, which was used in ancient Greece.

lyric lyrics
NOUN **1** The lyrics of a song are the words. ▶ ADJECTIVE **2** Lyric poetry is written in a simple and direct style, and is usually about love.

lyrical
ADJECTIVE poetic and romantic.

m
an abbreviation for 'metres' or 'miles'.

macabre
Said "mak-**kahb**-ra" ADJECTIVE A macabre event is strange and horrible EG *a macabre horror story*.

macadamia macadamias
Said "ma-ka-**dame**-ee-a" NOUN an Australian tree, also grown in New Zealand, that produces edible nuts.

macaroni
NOUN Macaroni is short hollow tubes of pasta.
📖 an Italian word; from Greek *makaria* meaning 'food made from barley'

macaroon macaroons
NOUN a sweet biscuit flavoured with almonds or coconut.

mace maces
NOUN an ornamental pole carried by an official during ceremonies as a symbol of authority.

machete machetes
Said "mash-**ett**-ee" NOUN a large, heavy knife with a big blade.

machine machines machining machined
NOUN **1** a piece of equipment which uses electricity or power from an engine to make it work. ▶ VERB **2** If you machine something, you make it or work on it using a machine.

machine-gun machine-guns
NOUN a gun that works automatically, firing bullets one after the other.

machinery
NOUN Machinery is machines in general.

machismo
Said "mak-**kiz**-moe" NOUN Machismo is exaggerated aggressive male behaviour.

macho
Said "**mat**-shoh" ADJECTIVE A man who is described as macho behaves in an aggressively masculine way.
📖 from Spanish *macho* meaning 'male'

mackerel mackerels
NOUN a sea fish with blue and silver stripes.

mackintosh mackintoshes
NOUN a raincoat made from specially treated waterproof cloth.

mad madder maddest
ADJECTIVE **1** Someone who is mad has a mental illness which often causes them to behave in strange ways. **2** If you describe someone as mad, you mean that they are very foolish EG *He said we were mad to share a flat*. **3** AN INFORMAL USE Someone who is mad is angry. **4** If you are mad about someone or something, you like them very much EG *Alan was mad about golf*.
madness NOUN, **madman** NOUN
▤ (sense 1) crazy, deranged, insane
▤ (sense 2) daft, foolish

madam
'Madam' is a very formal way of addressing a woman.

maddening
ADJECTIVE irritating or frustrating EG *She had many maddening habits*.

madly
ADVERB If you do something madly, you do it in a fast, excited way.

madrigal madrigals
NOUN a song sung by several people without instruments.

Mafia
NOUN The Mafia is a large crime organization operating in Sicily, Italy, and the USA.

magazine magazines
NOUN **1** a weekly or monthly publication with articles and photographs. **2** a compartment in a gun for cartridges.
📖 from Arabic *makhzan* meaning

'storehouse'

magenta
Said "maj-jen-ta" NOUN OR ADJECTIVE
dark reddish-purple.

maggot maggots
NOUN a creature that looks like a
small worm and lives on decaying
things. Maggots turn into flies.

magic
NOUN **1** In fairy stories, magic is a
special power that can make
impossible things happen. **2** Magic
is the art of performing tricks to
entertain people.
magical ADJECTIVE, **magically** ADVERB

magician magicians
NOUN **1** a person who performs
tricks as entertainment. **2** In fairy
stories, a magician is a man with
magical powers.

magistrate magistrates
NOUN an official who acts as a judge
in a law court that deals with less
serious crimes.

magnanimous
ADJECTIVE generous and forgiving.

magnate magnates
NOUN someone who is very rich and
powerful in business.

magnet magnets
NOUN a piece of iron which attracts
iron or steel towards it, and which
points towards north if allowed to
swing freely.
magnetic ADJECTIVE, **magnetism** NOUN

magnificent
ADJECTIVE extremely beautiful or
impressive.
magnificently ADVERB, **magnificence**
NOUN

magnify magnifies magnifying
magnified
VERB When a microscope or lens
magnifies something, it makes it
appear bigger than it actually is.
magnification NOUN

magnifying glass magnifying
glasses
NOUN a lens which makes things
appear bigger than they really are.

magnitude
NOUN The magnitude of something
is its great size or importance.

magnolia magnolias
NOUN a tree which has large white or
pink flowers in spring.

magpie magpies
NOUN a large black and white bird
with a long tail.

mahogany
NOUN Mahogany is a hard reddish
brown wood used for making
furniture.

maid maids
NOUN a female servant.

maiden maidens
NOUN **1** A LITERARY USE a young woman.
▶ ADJECTIVE **2** first EG *a maiden voyage.*

maiden name maiden names
NOUN the surname a woman had
before she married.

mail mails mailing mailed
NOUN **1** Your mail is the letters and
parcels delivered to you by the post
office. ▶ VERB **2** If you mail a letter,
you send it by post.

mail order
NOUN Mail order is a system of
buying goods by post.

maim maims maiming maimed
VERB To maim someone is to injure
them very badly for life.

main mains
ADJECTIVE **1** most important EG *the
main event.* ▶ NOUN **2** The mains are
large pipes or wires that carry gas,
water or electricity.
mainly ADVERB
▤ (sense 1) chief, major, principal

mainframe mainframes
NOUN a large computer which can
be used by many people at the
same time.

mainland
NOUN The mainland is the main part
of a country in contrast to islands
around its coast.

mainstay
NOUN The mainstay of something is

the most important part of it.

mainstream

NOUN The mainstream is the most ordinary and conventional group of people or ideas in a society.

maintain maintains maintaining maintained

VERB 1 If you maintain something, you keep it going or keep it at a particular rate or level EG *I wanted to maintain our friendship.* 2 If you maintain someone, you provide them regularly with money for what they need. 3 To maintain a machine or a building is to keep it in good condition. 4 If you maintain that something is true, you believe it is true and say so.

maintenance

NOUN 1 Maintenance is the process of keeping something in good condition. 2 Maintenance is also money that a person sends regularly to someone to provide for the things they need.

maize

NOUN Maize is a tall plant which produces sweet corn.

majesty majesties

1 You say 'His Majesty' when you are talking about a king, and 'Her Majesty' when you are talking about a queen. ▶ NOUN 2 Majesty is great dignity and impressiveness.
majestic ADJECTIVE, **majestically** ADVERB

major majors

ADJECTIVE 1 more important or more significant than other things EG *There were over fifty major injuries.* ▶ NOUN 2 an army officer of the rank immediately above captain.

majority majorities

NOUN 1 The majority of people or things in a group is more than half of the group. 2 In an election, the majority is the difference between the number of votes gained by the winner and the number gained by the runner-up.

☑ You should use *majority* only to talk about things that can be

counted: *the majority of car owners.* To talk about an amount that cannot be counted you should use *most*: *most of the harvest was saved.*

make makes making made

VERB 1 To make something is to produce or construct it, or to cause it to happen. 2 To make something is to do it EG *He was about to make a speech.* 3 To make something is to prepare it EG *I'll make some salad dressing.* 4 If someone makes you do something, they force you to do it EG *Mum made me clean the bathroom.* ▶ NOUN 5 The make of a product is the name of the company that manufactured it EG *'What make of car do you drive?' — 'Toyota'.*
■ (sense 1) create, fashion, form, produce
■ (sense 5) brand, kind, type

make up VERB 1 If a number of things make up something, they form that thing. 2 If you make up a story, you invent it. 3 If you make yourself up, you put make-up on. 4 If two people make it up, they become friends again after a quarrel.

make-up

NOUN 1 Make-up is coloured creams and powders which women put on their faces to make themselves look more attractive. 2 Someone's make-up is their character or personality.

making

NOUN 1 The making of something is the act or process of creating or producing it. ▶ PHRASE 2 When you describe someone as something in the making, you mean that they are gradually becoming that thing EG *a captain in the making.*

maladjusted

ADJECTIVE A maladjusted person has psychological or behaviour problems.

malaise

Said "mal-**laze**" NOUN; A FORMAL WORD Malaise is a feeling of

A B C D E F G H I J K L M N O P Q R S T U V W X Y Z

A
B
C
D
E
F
G
H
I
J
K
L
M
N
O
P
Q
R
S
T
U
V
W
X
Y
Z

dissatisfaction or unhappiness.

malaria
Said "mal-**lay**-ree-a" NOUN Malaria is a tropical disease caught from mosquitoes which causes fever and shivering.

Malaysian Malaysians
ADJECTIVE **1** belonging or relating to Malaysia. ▶ NOUN **2** someone who comes from Malaysia.

male males
NOUN **1** a person or animal belonging to the sex that cannot give birth or lay eggs. ▶ ADJECTIVE **2** concerning or affecting men rather than women.

male chauvinist male chauvinists
NOUN a man who thinks that men are better than women.

malevolent
Said "mal-**lev**-oh-lent" ADJECTIVE; A FORMAL WORD wanting or intending to cause harm.
malevolence NOUN
▣ malicious, spiteful, vindictive

malfunction malfunctions malfunctioning malfunctioned
VERB **1** If a machine malfunctions, it fails to work properly. ▶ NOUN **2** the failure of a machine to work properly.

malice
NOUN Malice is a desire to cause harm to people.

malicious
ADJECTIVE Malicious talk or behaviour is intended to harm someone.

malign maligns maligning maligned
VERB; A FORMAL WORD To malign someone is to say unpleasant and untrue things about them.

malignant
ADJECTIVE **1** harmful and cruel. **2** A malignant disease or tumour could cause death if it is allowed to continue.

mallard mallards
NOUN a kind of wild duck. The male has a green head.

mallee mallees
NOUN a eucalypt that grows close to the ground in dry areas of Australia.

mallet mallets
NOUN a wooden hammer with a square head.

malnutrition
NOUN Malnutrition is not eating enough healthy food.

malpractice
NOUN If someone such as a doctor or lawyer breaks the rules of their profession, their behaviour is called malpractice.

malt
NOUN Malt is roasted grain, usually barley, that is used in making beer and whisky.

mammal mammals
NOUN Animals that give birth to live babies and feed their young with milk from the mother's body are called mammals. Human beings, dogs, and whales are all mammals.

mammoth mammoths
ADJECTIVE **1** very large indeed EG *a mammoth outdoor concert*. ▶ NOUN **2** a huge animal that looked like a hairy elephant with long tusks. Mammoths became extinct a long time ago.

man men; mans manning manned
NOUN **1** an adult male human being.
▶ PLURAL NOUN **2** Human beings in general are sometimes referred to as men EG *All men are equal*. ▶ VERB **3** To man something is to be in charge of it or operate it EG *Two officers were manning the radar screens*.
▣ (sense 1) bloke, chap, guy
▣ (sense 2) humanity, mankind

mana
NOUN Mana is authority and influence such as that held by a New Zealand Maori chief.

manacle manacles
NOUN Manacles are metal rings or clamps attached to a prisoner's wrists or ankles.

manage manages managing

managed
VERB **1** If you manage to do
something, you succeed in doing it
EG *We managed to find somewhere to
sit.* **2** If you manage an
organization or business, you are
responsible for controlling it.
■ (sense 1) accomplish, succeed

manageable
ADJECTIVE able to be dealt with.

management
NOUN **1** The management of a
business is the controlling and
organizing of it. **2** The people who
control an organization are called
the management.
■ (sense 1) administration,
control, running

manager managers
NOUN a person responsible for
running a business or organization
EG *a bank manager.*
☑ In business, the word *manager*
can apply to either a man or a
woman.

manageress manageresses
NOUN a woman responsible for
running a business or organization.

**managing director managing
directors**
NOUN a company director who is
responsible for the way the
company is managed.

mandarin mandarins
NOUN a type of small orange which
is easy to peel.

mandate mandates
NOUN; A FORMAL WORD A government's
mandate is the authority it has to
carry out particular policies as a
result of winning an election.

mandatory
ADJECTIVE If something is mandatory,
there is a law or rule stating that it
must be done EG *a mandatory life
sentence for murder.*

mandir mandirs
*Said "**mun-dir**"* NOUN a Hindu
temple.
🏛 a Hindi word

mandolin mandolins
NOUN a musical instrument like a
small guitar with a deep, rounded
body.

mane manes
NOUN the long hair growing from
the neck of a lion or horse.

manger mangers
NOUN a feeding box in a barn or
stable.

**mangle mangles mangling
mangled**
VERB **1** If something is mangled, it is
crushed and twisted. ▶ NOUN **2** an
old-fashioned piece of equipment
consisting of two large rollers
which squeeze water out of wet
clothes.

mango mangoes or **mangos**
NOUN a sweet yellowish fruit which
grows in tropical countries.

manhole manholes
NOUN a covered hole in the ground
leading to a drain or sewer.

manhood
NOUN Manhood is the state of being
a man rather than a boy.

mania manias
NOUN **1** a strong liking for
something EG *my wife's mania for
plant collecting.* **2** a mental illness.
🏛 from Greek *mania* meaning
'madness'

maniac maniacs
NOUN a mad person who is violent
and dangerous.

manic
ADJECTIVE energetic and excited EG *a
manic attack.*

manicure manicures
NOUN a special treatment for the
hands and nails.
manicurist NOUN

**manifest manifests manifesting
manifested**
A FORMAL WORD ▶ ADJECTIVE **1** obvious or
easily seen EG *his manifest
enthusiasm.* ▶ VERB **2** To manifest
something is to make people aware
of it EG *Fear can manifest itself in*

A
B
C
D
E
F
G
H
I
J
K
L
M
N
O
P
Q
R
S
T
U
V
W
X
Y
Z

A
B
C
D
E
F
G
H
I
J
K
L
M
N
O
P
Q
R
S
T
U
V
W
X
Y
Z

many ways.

manifestation manifestations
NOUN; A FORMAL WORD A manifestation of something is a sign that it is happening or exists EG *The illness may be a manifestation of stress.*

manifesto manifestoes or manifestos
NOUN a published statement of the aims and policies of a political party.

manipulate manipulates manipulating manipulated
VERB 1 To manipulate people or events is to control or influence them to produce a particular result. 2 If you manipulate a piece of equipment, you control it in a skilful way. **manipulation** NOUN, **manipulator** NOUN, **manipulative** ADJECTIVE

mankind
NOUN 'Mankind' is used to refer to all human beings EG *a threat to mankind.*

manly manlier manliest
ADJECTIVE having qualities that are typically masculine EG *He laughed a deep, manly laugh.*

manna
NOUN If something appears like manna from heaven, it appears suddenly as if by a miracle and helps you in a difficult situation.

manner manners
NOUN 1 The manner in which you do something is the way you do it. 2 Your manner is the way in which you behave and talk EG *his kind manner.* ▶ PLURAL NOUN 3 If you have good manners, you behave very politely.

mannerism mannerisms
NOUN a gesture or a way of speaking which is characteristic of a person.

manoeuvre manoeuvres manoeuvring manoeuvred
Said "man-**noo**-ver" VERB 1 If you manoeuvre something into a place, you skilfully move it there EG *It took*

expertise to manoeuvre the boat so close to the shore. ▶ NOUN 2 a clever move you make in order to change a situation to your advantage.

manor manors
NOUN a large country house with land.

manpower
NOUN Workers can be referred to as manpower.

mansion mansions
NOUN a very large house.

manslaughter
NOUN; A LEGAL WORD Manslaughter is the accidental killing of a person.

mantelpiece mantelpieces
NOUN a shelf over a fireplace.

mantle mantles
NOUN; A LITERARY WORD To take on the mantle of something is to take on responsibility for it EG *He has taken over the mantle of England's greatest living poet.*

mantra mantras
NOUN a word or short piece of sacred text or prayer continually repeated to help concentration.

manual manuals
ADJECTIVE 1 Manual work involves physical strength rather than mental skill. 2 operated by hand rather than by electricity or by motor EG *a manual typewriter.* ▶ NOUN 3 an instruction book which tells you how to use a machine. **manually** ADVERB

manufacture manufactures manufacturing manufactured
VERB 1 To manufacture goods is to make them in a factory. ▶ NOUN 2 The manufacture of goods is the making of them in a factory. **manufacturer** NOUN

manure
NOUN Manure is animal faeces used to fertilize the soil.

manuscript manuscripts
NOUN a handwritten or typed document, especially a version of a book before it is printed.

Manx

ADJECTIVE belonging or relating to
the Isle of Man.

many

ADJECTIVE **1** If there are many people
or things, there are a large number
of them. **2** You also use 'many' to
ask how great a quantity is or to
give information about it EG *How
many tickets do you require?* ▶ PRONOUN
3 a large number of people or
things EG *Many are too weak to walk.*

Maori Maoris

NOUN **1** someone descended from
the people who lived in New
Zealand before Europeans arrived.
2 Maori is a language spoken by
Maoris.

map maps mapping mapped

NOUN **1** a detailed drawing of an area
as it would appear if you saw it
from above. ▶ VERB **2** If you map out
a plan, you work out in detail what
you will do.

maple maples

NOUN a tree that has large leaves
with five points.

mar mars marring marred

VERB To mar something is to spoil it
EG *The game was marred by violence.*

marae marae or maraes

Said "ma-rye" In New Zealand, a
Maori meeting house; also the
enclosed space in front of it.

marathon marathons

NOUN **1** a race in which people run
26 miles along roads. ▶ ADJECTIVE **2** A
marathon task is a large one that
takes a long time.

marble marbles

NOUN **1** Marble is a very hard, cold
stone which is often polished to
show the coloured patterns in it.
2 Marbles is a children's game
played with small coloured glass
balls. These balls are also called
marbles.

march marches marching marched

NOUN **1** March is the third month of
the year. It has 31 days. **2** an
organized protest in which a large
group of people walk somewhere
together. ▶ VERB **3** When soldiers
march, they walk with quick
regular steps in time with each
other. **4** To march somewhere is to
walk quickly in a determined way
EG *He marched out of the room.*
🏛 sense 1 is from Latin *Martius*
(month) of Mars, the Roman god of
war

mare mares

NOUN an adult female horse.

margarine

Said "**mar**-jar-reen" NOUN Margarine
is a substance that is similar to
butter but is made from vegetable
oil and animal fats.

margin margins

NOUN **1** If you win a contest by a
large or small margin, you win it by
a large or small amount. **2** an extra
amount that allows you more
freedom in doing something EG *a
small margin of error.* **3** the blank
space at each side on a written or
printed page.

marginal

ADJECTIVE **1** small and not very
important EG *a marginal increase.* **2** A
marginal seat or constituency is a
political constituency where the
previous election was won by a
very small majority.
marginally ADVERB

marigold marigolds

NOUN a type of yellow or orange
garden flower.

marijuana

Said "mar-rih-**hwan**-a" NOUN
Marijuana is an illegal drug which
is smoked in cigarettes.

marina marinas

NOUN a harbour for pleasure boats
and yachts.

marinate marinates marinating marinated; also spelt marinade

VERB To marinate food is to soak it
in a mixture of oil and vinegar to
flavour it before cooking.

A
B
C
D
E
F
G
H
I
J
K
L
M
N
O
P
Q
R
S
T
U
V
W
X
Y
Z

marine marines
NOUN **1** a soldier who serves with the navy. ▸ ADJECTIVE **2** relating to or involving the sea EG *marine life*.

marital
ADJECTIVE relating to or involving marriage EG *marital problems*.

maritime
ADJECTIVE relating to the sea and ships EG *maritime trade*.

marjoram
NOUN Marjoram is a herb with small, rounded leaves and tiny, pink flowers.

mark marks marking marked
NOUN **1** a small stain or damaged area on a surface EG *I can't get this mark off the curtain*. **2** a written or printed symbol EG *He made a few marks with his pen*. **3** a letter or number showing how well you have done in homework or in an exam. **4** The mark or Deutsche Mark is the main unit of currency in Germany. A mark is worth 100 pfennigs. ▸ VERB **5** If something marks a surface, it damages it in some way. **6** If you mark something, you write a symbol on it or identify it in some other way. **7** When a teacher marks your work, he or she decides how good it is and gives it a mark. **8** To mark something is to be a sign of it EG *The accident marked a tragic end to the day*. **9** In soccer or hockey, if you mark your opposing player, you stay close to them, trying to prevent them from getting the ball.

marked
ADJECTIVE very obvious EG *a marked improvement*.
markedly ADVERB

market markets marketing marketed
NOUN **1** a place where goods or animals are bought and sold. **2** a place with many small stalls selling different goods. **3** The market for a product is the number of people who want to buy it EG *the market for cars*. ▸ VERB **4** To market a product is to sell it in an organized way.
▤ (sense 1) bazaar, fair, mart

marketing
NOUN Marketing is the part of a business concerned with the way a product is sold.

market research
NOUN Market research is research into what people want and buy.

marksman marksmen
NOUN someone who can shoot very accurately.

marlin marlins
NOUN a large fish found in tropical seas which has a very long upper jaw.

marmalade
NOUN Marmalade is a jam made from citrus fruit, usually eaten at breakfast.
▥ from Latin *marmelo* meaning 'quince'

maroon
NOUN OR ADJECTIVE dark reddish-purple.

marooned
ADJECTIVE If you are marooned in a place, you are stranded there and cannot leave it.

marquee marquees
Said "mar-kee" NOUN a very large tent used at a fair or other outdoor entertainment.

marquis marquises
Said "mar-kwiss"; also spelt **marquess**
NOUN a male member of the nobility of the rank between duke and earl.

marriage marriages
NOUN **1** the relationship between a husband and wife. **2** Marriage is the act of marrying someone.
▤ (sense 1) matrimony, wedlock

marrow marrows
NOUN a long, thick green vegetable with cream-coloured flesh.

marry marries marrying married
VERB **1** When a man and a woman marry, they become each other's

husband and wife during a special ceremony. **2** When a clergyman or registrar marries a couple, he or she is in charge of their marriage ceremony.

married ADJECTIVE

Mars

NOUN Mars is the planet in the solar system which is fourth from the sun.

marsh marshes

NOUN an area of land which is permanently wet.

marshal marshals marshalling marshalled

VERB **1** If you marshal things or people, you gather them together and organize them EG *Shipping was being marshalled into convoys.* ▶ NOUN **2** an official who helps to organize a public event.

marshmallow marshmallows

NOUN a soft, spongy, pink or white sweet.

marsupial marsupials

Said "mar-**syoo**-pee-al" NOUN an animal that carries its young in a pouch. Koala bears and kangaroos are marsupials.

📖 from Greek *marsupion* meaning 'purse'

martial

Said "**mar**-shal" ADJECTIVE relating to or involving war or soldiers EG *martial music.*

martial arts

PLURAL NOUN The martial arts are the techniques of self-defence that come from the Far East, for example karate or judo.

Martian Martians

Said "**mar**-shan" NOUN an imaginary creature from the planet Mars.

martyr martyrs martyring martyred

NOUN **1** someone who suffers or is killed rather than change their beliefs. ▶ VERB **2** If someone is martyred, they are killed because of their beliefs.

martyrdom NOUN

marvel marvels marvelling marvelled

VERB **1** If you marvel at something, it fills you with surprise or admiration EG *Modern designers can only marvel at his genius.* ▶ NOUN **2** something that makes you feel great surprise or admiration EG *a marvel of high technology.*

marvellous

ADJECTIVE wonderful or excellent.

marvellously ADVERB

Marxism

NOUN Marxism is a political philosophy based on the writings of Karl Marx. It states that society will develop towards communism through the struggle between different social classes.

Marxist ADJECTIVE OR NOUN

marzipan

NOUN Marzipan is a paste made of almonds, sugar, and egg. It is put on top of cakes or used to make small sweets.

mascara

NOUN Mascara is a substance that can be used to colour eyelashes and make them look longer.

mascot mascots

NOUN a person, animal, or toy which is thought to bring good luck EG *Celtic's mascot, Hoopy the Huddle Hound.*

masculine

ADJECTIVE **1** typical of men, rather than women EG *the masculine world of motorsport.* **2** belonging to a particular class of nouns in some languages, such as French, German, and Latin.

masculinity NOUN

What is Masculine?

Masculine nouns refer to male people and animals.

The boy put on his coat. ➤ *boy is* **masculine**

Common nouns may be either masculine

A
B
C
D
E
F
G
H
I
J
K
L
M
N
O
P
Q
R
S
T
U
V
W
X
Y
Z

or feminine. Other words in the sentence may tell us if they are male or female.

The doctor parked his car.

The doctor parked her car.

Also look at the grammar boxes at **gender**, **feminine** and **neuter**.

mash mashes mashing mashed
VERB If you mash vegetables, you crush them after they have been cooked.

mask masks masking masked
NOUN **1** something you wear over your face for protection or disguise EG *a surgical mask*. ▶ VERB **2** If you mask something, you cover it so that it is protected or cannot be seen.

masochist masochists
Said "**mass**-so-kist" NOUN someone who gets pleasure from their own suffering.
masochism NOUN
🏛 named after the Austrian novelist Leopold von Sacher Masoch (1836-1895), who wrote about masochism.

mason masons
NOUN a person who is skilled at making things with stone.

masonry
NOUN Masonry is pieces of stone which form part of a wall or building.

masquerade masquerades masquerading masqueraded
Said "mass-ker-**raid**" VERB If you masquerade as something, you pretend to be it EG *He masqueraded as a doctor.*

mass masses massing massed
NOUN **1** a large amount of something. **2** The masses are the ordinary people in society considered as a group EG *opera for the masses.* **3** In physics, the mass of an object is the amount of physical matter that it has. **4** In the Roman Catholic Church, Mass is a religious service in which people share bread and wine in remembrance of the death and resurrection of Jesus Christ.
▶ ADJECTIVE **5** involving a large number of people EG *mass unemployment.* ▶ VERB **6** When people mass, they gather together in a large group.

massacre massacres massacring massacred
Said "**mass**-ik-ker" NOUN **1** the killing of a very large number of people in a violent and cruel way.
▶ VERB **2** To massacre people is to kill large numbers of them in a violent and cruel way.

massage massages massaging massaged
VERB **1** To massage someone is to rub their body in order to help them relax or to relieve pain.
▶ NOUN **2** A massage is treatment which involves rubbing the body.

massive
ADJECTIVE extremely large EG *a massive iceberg.*
massively ADVERB

mass-produce mass-produces mass-producing mass-produced
VERB To mass-produce something is to make it in large quantities EG *They began mass-producing cameras after the war.*

mast masts
NOUN the tall upright pole that supports the sails of a boat.

master masters mastering mastered
NOUN **1** a man who has authority over others, such as the employer of servants, or the owner of slaves or animals. **2** If you are master of a situation, you have control over it EG *He was master of his own destiny.* **3** a male teacher at some schools.
▶ VERB **4** If you master a difficult situation, you succeed in controlling it. **5** If you master something, you learn how to do it properly EG *She found it easy to master the typewriter.*

masterful

ADJECTIVE showing control and
authority.

masterly
ADJECTIVE extremely clever or well
done EG *a masterly exhibition of
batting.*

**mastermind masterminds
masterminding masterminded**
VERB **1** If you mastermind a
complicated activity, you plan and
organize it. ▶ NOUN **2** The
mastermind behind something is
the person responsible for planning
it.

masterpiece masterpieces
NOUN an extremely good painting or
other work of art.

**masturbate masturbates
masturbating masturbated**
VERB If someone masturbates, they
stroke or rub their own genitals in
order to get sexual pleasure.
masturbation NOUN

mat mats
NOUN **1** a small round or square
piece of cloth, card, or plastic that
is placed on a table to protect it
from plates or glasses. **2** a small
piece of carpet or other thick
material that is placed on the floor.

matador matadors
NOUN a man who fights and tries to
kill bulls in a bullfight.
▥ from Spanish *matar* meaning 'to
kill'

match matches matching matched
NOUN **1** an organized game of
football, cricket, or some other
sport. **2** a small, thin stick of wood
that produces a flame when you
strike it against a rough surface.
▶ VERB **3** If one thing matches
another, the two things look the
same or have similar qualities.

mate mates mating mated
NOUN **1** AN INFORMAL USE Your mates
are your friends. **2** The first mate
on a ship is the officer who is next
in importance to the captain. **3** An
animal's mate is its sexual partner.
▶ VERB **4** When a male and female

animal mate, they come together
sexually in order to breed.

material materials
NOUN **1** Material is cloth. **2** a
substance from which something is
made EG *the materials to make red dye.*
3 The equipment for a particular
activity can be referred to as
materials EG *building materials.*
4 Material for a book, play, or film
is the information or ideas on
which it is based. ▶ ADJECTIVE
5 involving possessions and money
EG *concerned with material comforts.*
materially ADVERB

materialism
NOUN Materialism is thinking that
money and possessions are the
most important things in life.
materialistic ADJECTIVE

**materialize materializes
materializing materialized**; also
spelt **materialise**
VERB If something materializes, it
actually happens or appears EG
*Fortunately, the attack did not
materialize.*

maternal
ADJECTIVE relating to or involving a
mother EG *her maternal instincts.*

maternity
ADJECTIVE relating to or involving
pregnant women and birth EG *a
maternity hospital.*

mathematics
NOUN Mathematics is the study of
numbers, quantities, and shapes.
mathematical ADJECTIVE, **mathematically**
ADVERB, **mathematician** NOUN

maths
NOUN Maths is mathematics.

Matilda
NOUN; AN OLD-FASHIONED INFORMAL WORD
In Australia, Matilda is the pack of
belongings carried by a swagman
in the bush. The word is now used
only in the phrase 'waltzing
Matilda', meaning to travel in the
bush with few possessions.

matinee matinees

A
B
C
D
E
F
G
H
I
J
K
L
M
N
O
P
Q
R
S
T
U
V
W
X
Y
Z

Said "**mat-in-nay**"; *also spelt* **matinée**
NOUN an afternoon performance of a play or film.

matrimony
NOUN; A FORMAL WORD Matrimony is marriage.
matrimonial ADJECTIVE

matrix matrices
Said "**may-trix**" NOUN 1 A FORMAL USE the framework in which something grows and develops. 2 In maths, a matrix is a set of numbers or elements set out in rows and columns.

matron matrons
NOUN In a hospital, a senior nurse in charge of all the nursing staff used to be known as matron.

matt
ADJECTIVE A matt surface is dull rather than shiny EG *matt black plastic.*

matted
ADJECTIVE Hair that is matted is tangled with the strands sticking together.

matter matters mattering mattered
NOUN 1 something that you have to deal with. 2 Matter is any substance EG *The atom is the smallest divisible particle of matter.* 3 Books and magazines are reading matter.
▶ VERB 4 If something matters to you, it is important. ▶ PHRASE 5 If you ask **What's the matter?**, you are asking what is wrong.
■ (sense 1) affair, business, situation, subject

matter-of-fact
ADJECTIVE showing no emotion.

matting
NOUN Matting is thick woven material such as rope or straw, used as a floor covering.

mattress mattresses
NOUN a large thick pad filled with springs or feathers that is put on a bed to make it comfortable.

mature matures maturing matured
VERB 1 When a child or young animal matures, it becomes an adult. 2 When something matures, it reaches complete development.
▶ ADJECTIVE 3 Mature means fully developed and emotionally balanced.
maturely ADVERB, **maturity** NOUN

maudlin
ADJECTIVE Someone who is maudlin is sad and sentimental when they are drunk.

maul mauls mauling mauled
VERB If someone is mauled by an animal, they are savagely attacked and badly injured by it.

mausoleum mausoleums
Said "**maw-sal-lee-um**" NOUN a building which contains the grave of a famous person.

mauve
Rhymes with "**grove**" NOUN OR ADJECTIVE pale purple.

maxim maxims
NOUN a short saying which gives a rule for good or sensible behaviour EG *Instant action: that's my maxim.*

maximize maximizes maximizing maximized; *also spelt* **maximise**
VERB To maximize something is to make it as great or effective as possible EG *Their objective is to maximize profits.*

maximum
ADJECTIVE 1 The maximum amount is the most that is possible EG *the maximum recommended intake.* ▶ NOUN 2 The maximum is the most that is possible EG *a maximum of fifty men.*

may
VERB 1 If something may happen, it is possible that it will happen EG *It may happen quite soon.* 2 If someone may do something, they are allowed to do it EG *Please may I be excused?* 3 You can use 'may' when saying that, although something is true, something else is also true EG *This may be true, but it is only part of*

the story. **4** A FORMAL USE You also use
'may' to express a wish that
something will happen EG *May you
live to be a hundred.* ▸ NOUN **5** May is
the fifth month of the year. It has
31 days.

📷 sense 5 is probably from *Maia*, a
Roman goddess

✅ It used to be that you used *may*
instead of *can* when asking for or
giving someone permission to do
something: *you may leave the table.*
Nowadays *may* is usually only used
in polite questions: *may I open the
window?*

maybe

ADVERB You use 'maybe' when you
are stating a possibility that you are
not certain about EG *Maybe I should
lie about my age.*

mayhem

NOUN You can refer to a confused
and chaotic situation as mayhem EG
*There was complete mayhem in the
classroom.*

mayonnaise

Said "may-on-**nayz**" NOUN
Mayonnaise is a thick salad
dressing made with egg yolks and
oil.

mayor mayors

NOUN a person who has been elected
to lead and represent the people of
a town.

maze mazes

NOUN a system of complicated
passages which it is difficult to find
your way through EG *a maze of dark
tunnels.*

MBE MBEs

NOUN a British honour granted by
the King or Queen. MBE is an
abbreviation for 'Member of the
Order of the British Empire' EG *Ally
McCoist, MBE.*

MD

an abbreviation for 'Doctor of
Medicine' or 'Managing Director'.

me

PRONOUN A speaker or writer uses
'me' to refer to himself or herself.

meadow meadows

NOUN a field of grass.

meagre

Said "**mee**-ger" ADJECTIVE very small
and poor EG *his meagre pension.*

meal meals

NOUN an occasion when people eat,
or the food they eat at that time.

mealie mealies; also spelt mielie

NOUN In South African English,
mealie is maize or an ear of maize.

mean means meaning meant;
meaner meanest

VERB **1** If you ask what something
means, you want it explained to
you. **2** If you mean what you say,
you are serious EG *The boss means
what he says.* **3** If something means
a lot to you, it is important to you.
4 If one thing means another, it
shows that the second thing is true
or will happen EG *Major roadworks
will mean long delays.* **5** If you mean
to do something, you intend to do
it EG *I meant to phone you, but didn't
have time.* **6** If something is meant
to be true, it is supposed to be true
EG *I found a road that wasn't meant to
be there.* ▸ ADJECTIVE **7** Someone who
is mean is unwilling to spend
much money. **8** Someone who is
mean is unkind or cruel EG *He
apologized for being so mean to her.*
▸ NOUN **9** A means of doing
something is a method or object
which makes it possible EG *The tests
were marked by means of a computer.*
▸ PLURAL NOUN **10** Someone's means
are their money and income EG *He's
obviously a man of means.* ▸ NOUN
11 In mathematics, the mean is the
average of a set of numbers.
meanness NOUN

📋 (sense 5) aim, intend, plan
📋 (sense 7) miserly, parsimonious,
stingy, tight-fisted

meander meanders meandering
meandered

Said "mee-**an**-der" VERB If a road or
river meanders, it has a lot of bends
in it.

A B C D E F G H I J K L M N O P Q R S T U V W X Y Z

A
B
C
D
E
F
G
H
I
J
K
L
M
N
O
P
Q
R
S
T
U
V
W
X
Y
Z

meaning meanings

NOUN **1** The meaning of a word, expression, or gesture is what it refers to or expresses. **2** The meaning of what someone says, or of a book or a film, is the thoughts or ideas that it is intended to express. **3** If something has meaning, it seems to be worthwhile and to have real purpose.

meaningful ADJECTIVE, **meaningfully** ADVERB, **meaningless** ADJECTIVE

■ (sense 1) gist, sense, significance

means test means tests

NOUN a check of a person's money and income to see whether they need money or benefits from the government or other organization.

meantime

PHRASE **In the meantime** means in the period of time between two events EG *I'll call the nurse; in the meantime, you must rest.*

meanwhile

ADVERB **1** Meanwhile means while something else is happening. ▶ NOUN **2** Meanwhile also means the time between two events.

measles

NOUN Measles is an infectious illness in which you have red spots on your skin.

measly

ADJECTIVE; AN INFORMAL WORD very small or inadequate EG *a measly ten cents.*

measure measures measuring measured

VERB **1** When you measure something, you find out how big it is by using a ruler or tape measure. **2** If something measures a particular distance, its length or depth is that distance EG *slivers of glass measuring a few millimetres across.* ▶ NOUN **3** A measure of something is a certain amount of it EG *There has been a measure of agreement.* **4** a unit in which size, speed, or depth is expressed. **5** Measures are actions carried out

to achieve a particular result EG *Tough measures are needed to maintain order.*

measurement NOUN

measured

ADJECTIVE careful and deliberate EG *walking at the same measured pace.*

measurement measurements

NOUN **1** the result that you obtain when you measure something. **2** Measurement is the activity of measuring something. **3** Your measurements are the sizes of your chest, waist, and hips that you use to buy the correct size of clothes.

meat meats

NOUN Meat is the flesh of animals that is cooked and eaten.

meaty ADJECTIVE

Mecca

NOUN **1** Mecca is the holiest city of Islam, to which many Muslims make pilgrimages. **2** If a place is a mecca for people of a particular kind, many of them go there because it is of special interest to them EG *The island is a mecca for bird lovers.*

☑ Most Muslims dislike this form and use the Arabic *Makkah.*

mechanic mechanics

NOUN **1** a person who repairs and maintains engines and machines. ▶ PLURAL NOUN **2** The mechanics of something are the way in which it works or is done EG *the mechanics of accounting.* ▶ NOUN **3** Mechanics is also the scientific study of movement and the forces that affect objects.

mechanical

ADJECTIVE **1** A mechanical device has moving parts and is used to do a physical task. **2** A mechanical action is done automatically without thinking about it EG *He gave a mechanical smile.*

mechanically ADVERB

mechanism mechanisms

NOUN **1** a part of a machine that does a particular task EG *a locking* *mechanism.* **2** part of your behaviour that is automatic EG *the body's defence mechanisms.*

medal medals
NOUN a small disc of metal given as an award for bravery or as a prize for sport.

medallion medallions
NOUN a round piece of metal worn as an ornament on a chain round the neck.

medallist medallists
NOUN a person who has won a medal in sport EG *a gold medallist at the Olympics.*

meddle meddles meddling meddled
VERB To meddle is to interfere and try to change things without being asked.

media
PLURAL NOUN You can refer to the television, radio, and newspapers as the media.
☑ Although *media* is a plural noun, it is becoming more common for it to be used as a singular: *the media is obsessed with violence.*

mediaeval
another spelling of **medieval.**

median medians
Said "mee-dee-an" ADJECTIVE **1** The median value of a set is the middle value when the set is arranged in order. ▶ NOUN **2** In geometry, a straight line drawn from one of the angles of a triangle to the midpoint of the opposite side.

mediate mediates mediating mediated
VERB If you mediate between two groups, you try to settle a dispute between them.
mediation NOUN, **mediator** NOUN

medical medicals
ADJECTIVE **1** relating to the prevention and treatment of illness and injuries. ▶ NOUN **2** a thorough examination of your body by a doctor.

medically ADVERB
medication medications
NOUN Medication is a substance that is used to treat illness.

medicinal
ADJECTIVE relating to the treatment of illness EG *a valuable medicinal herb.*

medicine medicines
NOUN **1** Medicine is the treatment of illness and injuries by doctors and nurses. **2** a substance that you drink or swallow to help cure an illness.

medieval or **mediaeval**
Said "med-dee-ee-vul" ADJECTIVE relating to the period between about 1100 AD and 1500 AD, especially in Europe.
🔳 from Latin *medium aevum* meaning 'the middle age'

mediocre
Said "meed-dee-oh-ker" ADJECTIVE of rather poor quality EG *a mediocre string of performances.*
mediocrity NOUN

meditate meditates meditating meditated
VERB **1** If you meditate on something, you think about it very deeply. **2** If you meditate, you remain in a calm, silent state for a period of time, often as part of a religious training.
meditation NOUN

Mediterranean
NOUN **1** The Mediterranean is the large sea between southern Europe and northern Africa. ▶ ADJECTIVE **2** relating to or typical of the Mediterranean or the European countries adjoining it.

medium mediums or media
ADJECTIVE **1** If something is of medium size or degree, it is neither large nor small EG *a medium sized hotel.* ▶ NOUN **2** a means that you use to communicate something EG *the medium of television.* **3** a person who claims to be able to speak to the dead and to receive messages from them.

medley medleys

NOUN **1** a mixture of different things creating an interesting effect. **2** a number of different songs or tunes sung or played one after the other.

meek meeker meekest

ADJECTIVE A meek person is timid and does what other people say.

meekly ADVERB

≣ submissive, timid

meet meets meeting met

VERB **1** If you meet someone, you happen to be in the same place as them. **2** If you meet a visitor you go to be with them when they arrive. **3** When a group of people meet, they gather together for a purpose. **4** If something meets a need, it can fulfil it EG *services intended to meet the needs of the elderly.* **5** If something meets with a particular reaction, it gets that reaction from people EG *I was met with silence.*

meeting meetings

NOUN **1** an event in which people discuss proposals and make decisions together. **2** what happens when you meet someone.

megabyte megabytes

NOUN a unit of storage in a computer, equal to 1 048 576 bytes.

melaleuca melaleucas

Said "mel-a-**loo**-ka" NOUN an Australian tree or shrub that has black branches and a white trunk.

melancholy

ADJECTIVE OR NOUN If you feel melancholy, you feel sad.

mêlée mêlées

Said "**mel**-lay" NOUN a situation where there are a lot of people rushing around.

mellow mellower mellowest; mellows mellowing mellowed

ADJECTIVE **1** Mellow light is soft and golden. **2** A mellow sound is smooth and pleasant to listen to EG *his mellow clarinet.* ▶ VERB **3** If someone mellows, they become more pleasant or relaxed EG *He*

certainly hasn't mellowed with age.

melodic

ADJECTIVE relating to melody.

melodious

ADJECTIVE pleasant to listen to EG *soft melodious music.*

melodrama melodramas

NOUN a story or play in which people's emotions are exaggerated.

melodramatic

ADJECTIVE behaving in an exaggerated, emotional way.

≣ histrionic, overdramatic, theatrical

melody melodies

NOUN a tune.

melon melons

NOUN a large, juicy fruit with a green or yellow skin and many seeds inside.

melt melts melting melted

VERB **1** When something melts or when you melt it, it changes from a solid to a liquid because it has been heated. **2** If something melts, it disappears EG *The crowd melted away... Her inhibitions melted.*

member members

NOUN **1** A member of a group is one of the people or things belonging to the group EG *members of the family.* **2** A member of an organization is a person who has joined the organization. ▶ ADJECTIVE **3** A country belonging to an international organization is called a member country or a member state.

Member of Parliament Members of Parliament

NOUN a person who has been elected to represent people in a country's parliament.

membership

NOUN **1** Membership of an organization is the state of being a member of it. **2** The people who belong to an organization are its membership.

membrane membranes

NOUN a very thin piece of skin or tissue which connects or covers plant or animal organs or cells EG *the nasal membrane.*

memento mementos
NOUN an object which you keep because it reminds you of a person or a special occasion EG *a lasting memento of their romance.*

memo memos
NOUN a note from one person to another within the same organization. Memo is short for 'memorandum'.

memoirs
Said "mem-wahrz" PLURAL NOUN If someone writes their memoirs, they write a book about their life and experiences.

memorable
ADJECTIVE If something is memorable, it is likely to be remembered because it is special or unusual EG *a memorable victory.*
memorably ADVERB

memorandum memorandums or memoranda
NOUN a memo.

memorial memorials
NOUN **1** a structure built to remind people of a famous person or event EG *a war memorial.* ▶ ADJECTIVE **2** A memorial event or prize is in honour of someone who has died, so that they will be remembered.

memory memories
NOUN **1** Your memory is your ability to remember things. **2** something you remember about the past EG *memories of their school days.* **3** the part in which information is stored in a computer.
■ (sense 1) recall, recollection, remembrance

men
the plural of **man.**

menace menaces menacing menaced
NOUN **1** someone or something that is likely to cause serious harm EG *the*

menace of drugs in sport. **2** Menace is the quality of being threatening EG *an atmosphere of menace.* ▶ VERB **3** If someone or something menaces you, they threaten to harm you.
menacingly ADVERB

menagerie menageries
Said "men-naj-er-ree" NOUN a collection of different wild animals.
▦ from French *menagerie* meaning 'household management', which used to include the care of domestic animals

mend mends mending mended
VERB If you mend something that is broken, you repair it.

menial
ADJECTIVE Menial work is boring and tiring and the people who do it have low status.

meningitis
NOUN Meningitis is a serious infectious illness which affects your brain and spinal cord.

menopause
NOUN The menopause is the time during which a woman gradually stops menstruating. This usually happens when she is about fifty.

menorah menorahs
Said "mi-naw-rah" NOUN a candelabra that usually has seven parts and is used in Jewish temples.

menstruate menstruates menstruating menstruated
VERB When a woman menstruates, blood comes from her womb. This normally happens once a month.
menstruation NOUN, **menstrual** ADJECTIVE

mental
ADJECTIVE **1** relating to the process of thinking or intelligence EG *mental arithmetic.* **2** relating to the health of the mind EG *mental health.*
mentally ADVERB

mentality mentalities
NOUN an attitude or way of thinking EG *the traditional military mentality.*

mention mentions mentioning

A
B
C
D
E
F
G
H
I
J
K
L
M
N
O
P
Q
R
S
T
U
V
W
X
Y
Z

mentioned
VERB **1** If you mention something, you talk about it briefly. ▶ NOUN **2** a brief comment about someone or something EG *He made no mention of his criminal past.*
■ (sense 1) bring up, refer to, touch upon

mentor mentors
NOUN Someone's mentor is a person who teaches them and gives them advice.

menu menus
NOUN **1** a list of the foods you can eat in a restaurant. **2** a list of different options shown on a computer screen which the user must choose from.

mercenary mercenaries
NOUN **1** a soldier who is paid to fight for a foreign country. ▶ ADJECTIVE **2** Someone who is mercenary is mainly interested in getting money.

merchandise
NOUN; A FORMAL WORD Merchandise is goods that are sold EG *He had left me with more merchandise than I could sell.*

merchant merchants
NOUN a trader who imports and exports goods EG *a coal merchant.*

merchant navy
NOUN The merchant navy is the boats and sailors involved in carrying goods for trade.

merciful
ADJECTIVE **1** considered to be fortunate as a relief from suffering EG *Death came as a merciful release.* **2** showing kindness and forgiveness.
mercifully ADVERB
■ (sense 2) compassionate, humane, kind

merciless
ADJECTIVE showing no kindness or forgiveness.
mercilessly ADVERB
■ cruel, heartless, ruthless

mercury
NOUN **1** Mercury is a silver-coloured

452

metallic element that is liquid at room temperature. It is used in thermometers. **2** Mercury is also the planet in the solar system which is nearest to the sun.

mercy mercies
NOUN If you show mercy, you show kindness and forgiveness and do not punish someone as severely as you could.
■ compassion, kindness, pity

mere merest
ADJECTIVE used to emphasize how unimportant or small something is EG *It's a mere 7-minute journey by boat.*
merely ADVERB

merge merges merging merged
VERB When two things merge, they combine together to make one thing EG *The firms merged in 1983.*
merger NOUN

meringue meringues
Said "mer-**rang**" NOUN a type of crisp, sweet cake made with egg whites and sugar.

merino merinos
Said "mer-**ree**-no" NOUN a breed of sheep, common in Australia and New Zealand, with long, fine wool.

merit merits meriting merited
NOUN **1** If something has merit, it is good or worthwhile. **2** The merits of something are its advantages or good qualities. ▶ VERB **3** If something merits a particular treatment, it deserves that treatment EG *He merits a place in the team.*

mermaid mermaids
NOUN In stories, a mermaid is a woman with a fish's tail instead of legs, who lives in the sea.

merry merrier merriest
ADJECTIVE happy and cheerful EG *He was, for all his shyness, a merry man.*
merrily ADVERB

merry-go-round merry-go-rounds
NOUN a large rotating platform with models of animals or vehicles on it, on which children ride at a fair.

mesh

NOUN Mesh is threads of wire or plastic twisted together like a net EG *a fence made of wire mesh.*

mess messes messing messed

NOUN **1** something untidy. **2** a situation which is full of problems and trouble. **3** a room or building in which members of the armed forces eat EG *the officers' mess.* ▶ VERB **4** If you mess about or mess around, you do things without any particular purpose. **5** If you mess something up, you spoil it or do it wrong.

messy ADJECTIVE

message messages

NOUN **1** a piece of information or a request that you send someone or leave for them. **2** an idea that someone tries to communicate to people, for example in a play or a speech EG *the story's anti-drugs message.*

messenger messengers

NOUN someone who takes a message to someone for someone else.

■ courier, emissary, envoy

Messiah

Said "miss-**eye**-ah" PROPER NOUN **1** For Jews, the Messiah is the king of the Jews who will be sent by God. **2** For Christians, the Messiah is Jesus Christ.

🔲 from Hebrew *mashiach* meaning 'anointed'

Messrs

Said "**mes**-serz" Messrs is the plural of **Mr**. It is often used in the names of businesses EG *Messrs Brown and Humberley, Solicitors.*

met

the past tense and past participle of **meet**.

metabolism metabolisms

NOUN Your metabolism is the chemical processes in your body that use food for growth and energy.

metabolic ADJECTIVE

metal metals

NOUN Metal is a chemical element such as iron, steel, copper, or lead. Metals are good conductors of heat and electricity.

metallic ADJECTIVE

metamorphic

ADJECTIVE Metamorphic rock is rock that has been altered from its original state by heat or pressure.

metamorphosis metamorphoses

Said "met-am-**mor**-fiss-iss" NOUN; A FORMAL WORD When a metamorphosis occurs, a person or thing changes into something completely different EG *the metamorphosis of a larva into an insect.*

metaphor metaphors

NOUN an imaginative way of describing something as another thing, and so suggesting that it has the typical qualities of that other thing. For example, if you wanted to say that someone is shy, you might say they are a mouse.

metaphorical ADJECTIVE, **metaphorically** ADVERB

meteor meteors

NOUN a piece of rock or metal that burns very brightly when it enters the earth's atmosphere from space.

meteoric

ADJECTIVE A meteoric rise to power or success happens very quickly.

meteorite meteorites

NOUN a piece of rock from space that has landed on earth.

meteorological

ADJECTIVE relating to or involving the weather or weather forecasting.

meteorology NOUN

meter meters

NOUN a device that measures and records something EG *a gas meter.*

methane

Said "**mee**-thane" NOUN Methane is a colourless gas with no smell that is found in coal gas and produced by decaying vegetable matter. It burns easily and can be used as a fuel.

A
B
C
D
E
F
G
H
I
J
K
L
M
N
O
P
Q
R
S
T
U
V
W
X
Y
Z

method methods
NOUN a particular way of doing something EG *the traditional method of making wine.*

methodical
ADJECTIVE Someone who is methodical does things carefully and in an organized way.
methodically ADVERB

Methodist Methodists
NOUN OR ADJECTIVE someone who belongs to the Methodist Church, a Protestant church whose members worship God in a way begun by John Wesley and his followers.

meticulous
ADJECTIVE A meticulous person does things very carefully and with great attention to detail.
meticulously ADVERB

metre metres
NOUN 1 a unit of length equal to 100 centimetres. 2 In poetry, metre is the rhythmic arrangement of words and syllables.

metric
ADJECTIVE relating to the system of measurement that uses metres, grams, and litres.

metropolis metropolises
NOUN a very large city.
🔤 from Greek *mētēr* + *polis* meaning 'mother city'

metropolitan
ADJECTIVE relating or belonging to a large, busy city EG *metropolitan districts.*

mettle
NOUN If you are on your mettle, you are ready to do something as well as you can because you know you are being tested or challenged.

mew mews mewing mewed
VERB 1 When a cat mews, it makes a short high-pitched noise. ▶ NOUN 2 the short high-pitched sound that a cat makes. 3 A mews is a quiet yard or street surrounded by houses.

Mexican Mexicans

ADJECTIVE 1 belonging or relating to Mexico. ▶ NOUN 2 someone who comes from Mexico.

mg
an abbreviation for 'milligrams'.

mice
the plural of **mouse**.

micro-
PREFIX very small.

microchip microchips
NOUN a small piece of silicon on which electronic circuits for a computer are printed.

microphone microphones
NOUN a device that is used to make sounds louder or to record them on a tape recorder.

microprocessor microprocessors
NOUN a microchip which can be programmed to do a large number of tasks or calculations.

microscope microscopes
NOUN a piece of equipment which magnifies very small objects so that you can study them.

microscopic
ADJECTIVE very small indeed EG *microscopic parasites.*

microwave microwaves
NOUN A microwave or microwave oven is a type of oven which cooks food very quickly by radiation.

mid-
PREFIX 'Mid-' is used to form words that refer to the middle part of a place or period of time EG *mid-Atlantic... the mid-70s.*

midday
NOUN Midday is twelve o'clock in the middle of the day.

middle middles
NOUN 1 The middle of something is the part furthest from the edges, ends, or outside surface. ▶ ADJECTIVE 2 The middle one in a series or a row is the one that has an equal number of people or things each side of it EG *the middle house.*

middle age

NOUN Middle age is the period of your life when you are between about 40 and 60 years old.
middle-aged ADJECTIVE

Middle Ages
PLURAL NOUN In European history, the Middle Ages were the period between about 1100 AD and 1500 AD.

middle class middle classes
NOUN The middle classes are the people in a society who are not working class or upper class, for example managers and lawyers.

Middle East
NOUN The Middle East consists of Iran and the countries in Asia to the west and south-west of Iran.

Middle English
NOUN Middle English was the English language from about 1100 AD until about 1450 AD.

middle-of-the-road
ADJECTIVE Middle-of-the-road opinions are moderate.

middle school middle schools
NOUN In England and Wales, a middle school is for children aged between about 8 and 12.

middling
ADJECTIVE of average quality or ability.

midge midges
NOUN a small flying insect which can bite people.

midget midgets
NOUN a very short person.

midnight
NOUN Midnight is twelve o'clock at night.

midriff midriffs
NOUN the middle of your body between your waist and your chest.

midst
NOUN If you are in the midst of a crowd or an event, you are in the middle of it.

midsummer
ADJECTIVE relating to the period in the middle of summer EG *a lovely midsummer morning in July.*

midway
ADVERB in the middle of a distance or period of time EG *They scored midway through the second half.*

midwife midwives
NOUN a nurse who is trained to help women at the birth of a baby.
midwifery NOUN

might
VERB **1** If you say something might happen, you mean that it is possible that it will happen EG *I might stay a while.* **2** If you say that someone might do something, you are suggesting that they do it EG *You might like to go and see it.* **3** Might is also the past tense of **may.** ▶ NOUN **4** A LITERARY USE Might is strength or power EG *the full might of the Navy.*
☑ You can use *might* or *may* to make a very polite request: *might I ask a favour?; may I ask a favour?*

mightily
ADVERB; A LITERARY WORD to a great degree or extent EG *I was mightily relieved by the decision.*

mighty mightier mightiest
ADJECTIVE; A LITERARY WORD very powerful or strong EG *a mighty army on the march.*

migraine migraines
Said "mee-grane" NOUN a severe headache that makes you feel very ill.
🔠 from Latin *hemicrania* meaning 'pain in half the head'

migrate migrates migrating migrated
VERB **1** If people migrate, they move from one place to another, especially to find work. **2** When birds or animals migrate, they move at a particular season to a different place, usually to breed or to find new feeding grounds EG *the birds migrate each year to Mexico.*
migration NOUN, **migratory** ADJECTIVE, **migrant** NOUN OR ADJECTIVE

mike mikes
NOUN; AN INFORMAL WORD a

A
B
C
D
E
F
G
H
I
J
K
L
M
N
O
P
Q
R
S
T
U
V
W
X
Y
Z

A
B
C
D
E
F
G
H
I
J
K
L
M
N
O
P
Q
R
S
T
U
V
W
X
Y
Z

microphone.

mild milder mildest

ADJECTIVE **1** Something that is mild is not strong and does not have any powerful or damaging effects EG *a mild shampoo.* **2** Someone who is mild is gentle and kind. **3** Mild weather is warmer than usual EG *The region has mild winters and hot summers.* **4** Mild emotions or attitudes are not very great or extreme EG *mild surprise.*

mildly ADVERB

mildew

NOUN Mildew is a soft white fungus that grows on things when they are warm and damp.

mile miles

NOUN a unit of distance equal to 1760 yards or about 1.6 kilometres. 📖 from Latin *milia passuum* meaning 'a thousand paces'

mileage mileages

NOUN **1** Your mileage is the distance that you have travelled, measured in miles. **2** The amount of mileage that you get out of something is how useful it is to you.

militant militants

ADJECTIVE **1** A militant person is very active in trying to bring about extreme political or social change EG *a militant socialist.* ▶ NOUN **2** a person who tries to bring about extreme political or social change.

militancy NOUN

military

ADJECTIVE **1** related to or involving the armed forces of a country EG *military bases.* ▶ NOUN **2** The military are the armed forces of a country.

militarily ADVERB

militia militias

*Said "mil-**lish**-a"* NOUN an organization that operates like an army but whose members are not professional soldiers.

milk milks milking milked

NOUN **1** Milk is the white liquid produced by female cows, goats, and some other animals to feed

their young. People drink milk and use it to make butter, cheese, and yogurt. **2** Milk is also the white liquid that a baby drinks from its mother's breasts. ▶ VERB **3** When someone milks a cow or a goat, they get milk from it by pulling its udders. **4** If you milk a situation, you get as much personal gain from it as possible EG *They milked money from a hospital charity.*

milk tooth milk teeth

NOUN Your milk teeth are your first teeth which fall out and are replaced by the permanent set.

milky milkier milkiest

ADJECTIVE **1** pale creamy white EG *milky white skin.* **2** containing a lot of milk EG *a large mug of milky coffee.*

Milky Way

NOUN The Milky Way is a strip of stars clustered closely together, appearing as a pale band in the sky.

mill mills

NOUN **1** a building where grain is crushed to make flour. **2** a factory for making materials such as steel, wool, or cotton. **3** a small device for grinding coffee or spices into powder EG *a pepper mill.*

millennium millennia or **millenniums**

NOUN; A FORMAL WORD a period of 1000 years.

millennium bug

NOUN a computer software problem caused by the change of date at the start of the year 2000.

miller millers

NOUN the person who operates a flour mill.

milligram milligrams

NOUN a unit of weight equal to one thousandth of a gram.

millilitre millilitres

NOUN a unit of liquid volume equal to one thousandth of a litre.

millimetre millimetres

NOUN a unit of length equal to a tenth of a centimetre or one thousandth of a metre.

million millions
the number 1,000,000.
millionth

millionaire millionaires
NOUN a very rich person who has property worth millions of pounds or dollars.

millstone millstones
PHRASE If something is **a millstone round your neck**, it is an unpleasant problem or responsibility you cannot escape from.

mime mimes miming mimed
NOUN **1** Mime is the use of movements and gestures to express something or to tell a story without using speech. ▶ VERB **2** If you mime something, you describe or express it using mime.

mimic mimics mimicking mimicked
VERB **1** If you mimic someone's actions or voice, you imitate them in an amusing way. ▶ NOUN **2** a person who can imitate other people.
mimicry NOUN

minaret minarets
NOUN a tall, thin tower on a mosque.

mince minces mincing minced
NOUN **1** Mince is meat which has been chopped into very small pieces in a mincer. ▶ VERB **2** If you mince meat, you chop it into very small pieces. **3** To mince about is to walk with small quick steps in an affected, effeminate way.

mind minds minding minded
NOUN **1** Your mind is your ability to think, together with all the thoughts you have and your memory. ▶ PHRASE **2** If you **change your mind**, you change a decision that you have made or an opinion that you have. ▶ VERB **3** If you do not mind something, you are not annoyed by it or bothered about it. **4** If you say that you wouldn't mind something, you mean that you would quite like it EG *I wouldn't*

mind a drink. **5** If you mind a child or mind something for someone, you look after it for a while EG *My mother is minding the office*.

mindful
ADJECTIVE; A FORMAL WORD If you are mindful of something, you think about it carefully before taking action EG *mindful of their needs*.

mindless
ADJECTIVE **1** Mindless actions are regarded as stupid and destructive EG *mindless violence*. **2** A mindless job or activity is simple and repetitive.

mine mines mining mined
PRONOUN **1** 'Mine' refers to something belonging or relating to the person who is speaking or writing EG *a friend of mine*. ▶ NOUN **2** a series of holes or tunnels in the ground from which diamonds, coal, or other minerals are dug out EG *a diamond mine*. **3** a bomb hidden in the ground or underwater, which explodes when people or things touch it. ▶ VERB **4** To mine diamonds, coal, or other minerals is to obtain these substances from underneath the ground.
miner NOUN, mining NOUN

minefield minefields
NOUN an area of land or water where mines have been hidden.

mineral minerals
NOUN a substance such as tin, salt, or coal that is formed naturally in rocks and in the earth EG *rich mineral deposits*.

mineral water
NOUN Mineral water is water which comes from a natural spring.

minestrone
Said "min-nes-**strone**-ee" NOUN Minestrone is soup containing small pieces of vegetable and pasta.
▧ from Italian *minestrare* meaning 'to serve'

minesweeper minesweepers
NOUN a ship for clearing away underwater mines.

A
B
C
D
E
F
G
H
I
J
K
L
M
N
O
P
Q
R
S
T
U
V
W
X
Y
Z

mingle mingles mingling mingled
VERB If things mingle, they become
mixed together EG *His cries mingled*
with theirs.

mini-
PREFIX 'Mini-' is used to form nouns
referring to something smaller or
less important than similar things
EG *a TV mini-series.*

miniature miniatures
Said "min-nit-cher" ADJECTIVE **1** a
tiny copy of something much
larger. ▶ NOUN **2** a very small
detailed painting, often of a person.

minibus minibuses
NOUN a van with seats in the back
which is used as a small bus.

minimal
ADJECTIVE very small in quality,
quantity, or degree EG *He has*
minimal experience.
minimally ADVERB

minimize minimizes minimizing
minimized; also spelt **minimise**
VERB If you minimize something,
you reduce it to the smallest
amount possible EG *His route was*
changed to minimize jet lag.

minimum
ADJECTIVE **1** The minimum amount is
the smallest amount that is
possible EG *a minimum wage.* ▶ NOUN
2 The minimum is the smallest
amount that is possible EG *a*
minimum of three weeks.

minister ministers
NOUN **1** A minister is a person who is
in charge of a particular
government department EG
Portugal's deputy foreign minister. **2** A
minister in a Protestant church is a
member of the clergy.

ministerial
ADJECTIVE relating to a government
minister or ministry EG *ministerial*
duties.

ministry ministries
NOUN **1** a government department
that deals with a particular area of
work EG *the Ministry of Defence.*

2 Members of the clergy can be
referred to as the ministry EG *Her son*
is in the ministry.

mink minks
NOUN Mink is an expensive fur used
to make coats or hats.

minnow minnows
NOUN a very small freshwater fish.

minor minors
ADJECTIVE **1** not as important or
serious as other things EG *a minor*
injury. ▶ NOUN **2** A FORMAL USE a young
person under the age of 18 EG *laws*
concerning the employment of minors.

minority minorities
NOUN **1** The minority of people or
things in a group is a number of
them forming less than half of the
whole EG *Only a minority of people*
want this. **2** A minority is a group of
people of a particular race or
religion living in a place where
most people are of a different race
or religion EG *ethnic minorities.*

minstrel minstrels
NOUN a singer and entertainer in
medieval times.

mint mints minting minted
NOUN **1** Mint is a herb used for
flavouring in cooking. **2** a
peppermint-flavoured sweet. **3** The
mint is the place where the official
coins of a country are made. ▶ VERB
4 When coins or medals are
minted, they are made. ▶ ADJECTIVE
5 If something is in mint
condition, it is in very good
condition, like new.

minus
1 You use 'minus' to show that one
number is being subtracted from
another EG *Ten minus six equals four.*
▶ ADJECTIVE **2** 'Minus' is used when
talking about temperatures below
0°C or 0°F.

minuscule
Said "min-nus-kyool" ADJECTIVE very
small indeed.

minute minutes minuting minuted
Said "min-nit" NOUN **1** a unit of

time equal to sixty seconds. **2** The minutes of a meeting are the written records of what was said and decided. ▶ VERB **3** To minute a meeting is to write the official notes of it.

minute
*Said "my-**nyoot**"* ADJECTIVE extremely small EG *a minute amount of pesticide.*
minutely ADVERB

minutiae
*Said "my-**nyoo**-shee-aye"* PLURAL NOUN; A FORMAL WORD Minutiae are small, unimportant details.

miracle miracles
NOUN **1** a wonderful and surprising event, believed to have been caused by God. **2** any very surprising and fortunate event EG *My father got a job. It was a miracle.*
miraculous ADJECTIVE, **miraculously** ADVERB

mirage mirages
*Said "mir-**ahj**"* NOUN an image which you can see in the distance in very hot weather, but which does not actually exist.

mire
NOUN; A LITERARY WORD Mire is swampy ground or mud.

mirror mirrors mirroring mirrored
NOUN **1** a piece of glass which reflects light and in which you can see your reflection. ▶ VERB **2** To mirror something is to have similar features to it EG *His own shock was mirrored on her face.*

mirth
NOUN; A LITERARY WORD Mirth is great amusement and laughter.

misbehave misbehaves misbehaving misbehaved
VERB If a child misbehaves, he or she is naughty or behaves badly.
misbehaviour NOUN

miscarriage miscarriages
NOUN **1** If a woman has a miscarriage she gives birth to a baby before it is properly formed

and it dies. **2** A miscarriage of justice is a wrong decision made by a court, which causes an innocent person to be punished.

miscellaneous
ADJECTIVE A miscellaneous group is made up of people or things that are different from each other.

mischief
NOUN Mischief is eagerness to have fun by teasing people or playing tricks.
mischievous ADJECTIVE

misconception misconceptions
NOUN a wrong idea about something EG *Another misconception is that cancer is infectious.*

misconduct
NOUN Misconduct is bad or unacceptable behaviour by a professional person EG *The Football Association found him guilty of misconduct.*

misdemeanour misdemeanours
*Said "miss-dem-**mee**-ner"* NOUN; A FORMAL WORD an act that is shocking or unacceptable.

miser misers
NOUN a person who enjoys saving money but hates spending it.
miserly ADJECTIVE

miserable
ADJECTIVE **1** If you are miserable, you are very unhappy. **2** If a place or a situation is miserable, it makes you feel depressed EG *a miserable little flat.*
miserably ADVERB
▤ (sense 1) dejected, unhappy, wretched
▤ (sense 2) gloomy, wretched

misery miseries
NOUN Misery is great unhappiness.

misfire misfires misfiring misfired
VERB If a plan misfires, it goes wrong.

misfit misfits
NOUN a person who is not accepted by other people because of being rather strange or eccentric.

misfortune misfortunes

A
B
C
D
E
F
G
H
I
J
K
L
M
N
O
P
Q
R
S
T
U
V
W
X
Y
Z

459

NOUN an unpleasant occurrence that is regarded as bad luck EG *I had the misfortune to fall off my bike.*

misgiving misgivings

NOUN If you have misgivings, you are worried or unhappy about something EG *I had misgivings about his methods.*

misguided

ADJECTIVE A misguided opinion or action is wrong because it is based on a misunderstanding or bad information.

misinform misinforms misinforming misinformed

VERB If you are misinformed, you are given wrong or inaccurate information.

misinformation NOUN

misinterpret misinterprets misinterpreting misinterpreted

VERB To misinterpret something is to understand it wrongly EG *You completely misinterpreted what I wrote.*

misjudge misjudges misjudging misjudged

VERB If you misjudge someone or something, you form an incorrect idea or opinion about them.

mislay mislays mislaying mislaid

VERB If you mislay something, you lose it because you have forgotten where you put it.

mislead misleads misleading misled

VERB To mislead someone is to make them believe something which is not true.

misplaced

ADJECTIVE A misplaced feeling is inappropriate or directed at the wrong thing or person EG *misplaced loyalty.*

misprint misprints

NOUN a mistake such as a spelling mistake in something that has been printed.

misrepresent misrepresents misrepresenting misrepresented

VERB To misrepresent someone is to give an inaccurate or misleading account of what they have said or done.

misrepresentation NOUN

miss misses missing missed

VERB **1** If you miss something, you do not notice it EG *You can't miss it. It's on the second floor.* **2** If you miss someone or something, you feel sad that they are no longer with you EG *The boys miss their father.* **3** If you miss a chance or opportunity, you fail to take advantage of it. **4** If you miss a bus, plane, or train, you arrive too late to catch it. **5** If you miss something, you fail to hit it when you aim at it EG *His shot missed the target and went wide.*
▶ NOUN **6** an act of missing something that you were aiming at. **7** 'Miss' is used before the name of an unmarried woman or girl as a form of address EG *Did you know Miss Smith?*

missile missiles

NOUN a weapon that moves long distances through the air and explodes when it reaches its target; also used of any object thrown as a weapon.

mission missions

NOUN **1** an important task that you have to do. **2** a group of people who have been sent to a foreign country to carry out an official task EG *He became head of the Israeli mission.* **3** a journey made by a military aeroplane or space rocket to carry out a task. **4** If you have a mission, there is something that you believe it is your duty to try to achieve. **5** the workplace of a group of Christians who are working for the Church.

missionary missionaries

NOUN a Christian who has been sent to a foreign country to work for the Church.

missive missives

NOUN; AN OLD-FASHIONED WORD a letter or message.

mist mists misting misted
NOUN **1** Mist consists of a large number of tiny drops of water in the air, which make it hard to see clearly. ▶ VERB **2** If your eyes mist, you cannot see very far because there are tears in your eyes. **3** If glass mists over or mists up, it becomes covered with condensation so that you cannot see through it.

mistake mistakes mistaking mistook mistaken
NOUN **1** an action or opinion that is wrong or is not what you intended. ▶ VERB **2** If you mistake someone or something for another person or thing, you wrongly think that they are the other person or thing EG *I mistook him for the owner of the house.* ▤ (sense 1) blunder, error, miscalculation, slip

mistaken
ADJECTIVE **1** If you are mistaken about something, you are wrong about it. **2** If you have a mistaken belief or opinion, you believe something which is not true.
mistakenly ADVERB

mister
A man is sometimes addressed in a very informal way as 'mister' EG *Where do you live, mister?*

mistletoe
Said "mis-sel-toe" NOUN Mistletoe is a plant which grows on trees and has white berries on it. It is used as a Christmas decoration.

mistook
the past tense of **mistake**.

mistreat mistreats mistreating mistreated
VERB To mistreat a person or animal is to treat them badly and make them suffer.

mistress mistresses
NOUN **1** A married man's mistress is a woman who is not his wife and who he is having a sexual relationship with. **2** A school mistress is a female teacher. **3** A

servant's mistress is the woman who is the servant's employer.

mistrust mistrusts mistrusting mistrusted
VERB **1** If you mistrust someone, you do not feel that you can trust them. ▶ NOUN **2** Mistrust is a feeling that you cannot trust someone.

misty mistier mistiest
ADJECTIVE full of or covered with mist.

misunderstand misunderstands misunderstanding misunderstood
VERB If you misunderstand someone, you do not properly understand what they say or do EG *He misunderstood the problem.* ▶ VERB

misunderstanding misunderstandings
NOUN If two people have a misunderstanding, they have a slight quarrel or disagreement.

misuse misuses misusing misused
NOUN **1** The misuse of something is the incorrect or dishonest use of it EG *the misuse of public money.* ▶ VERB **2** To misuse something is to use it incorrectly or dishonestly.

mite mites
NOUN a very tiny creature that lives in the fur of animals.

mitigating
ADJECTIVE; A FORMAL WORD Mitigating circumstances make a crime easier to understand, and perhaps justify it.

mitten mittens
NOUN Mittens are gloves which have one section that covers your thumb and another section for the rest of your fingers together.

mix mixes mixing mixed
VERB If you mix things, you combine them or shake or stir them together. ▤ blend, combine, merge, mingle
mix up VERB If you mix up two things or people, you confuse them EG *People often mix us up and greet us by each other's names.*

mixed

461

mixed up

ADJECTIVE **1** If you are mixed up, you are confused EG *I'm mixed up about which country I want to play for.* **2** If you are mixed up in a crime or a scandal, you are involved in it.

mixer mixers

NOUN a machine used for mixing things together EG *a cement mixer.*

mixture mixtures

NOUN several different things mixed together a substance that consists of other substances which have been stirred or shaken together EG *Spoon the mixture into serving glasses.*
■ blend, medley, mix

mix-up mix-ups

NOUN a mistake in something that was planned EG *a mix-up with the bookings.*

ml

an abbreviation for 'millilitres'.

mm

an abbreviation for 'millimetres'.

moa moa or **moas**

NOUN a large, flightless bird that lived in New Zealand and which became extinct in the late 18th century.

moan moans moaning moaned

VERB **1** If you moan, you make a low, miserable sound because you are in pain or suffering. **2** AN INFORMAL USE If you moan about something, you complain about it. ▶ NOUN **3** a low cry of pain or misery.

moat moats

NOUN a wide, water-filled ditch around a building such as a castle.

mob mobs mobbing mobbed

NOUN **1** a large, disorganized crowd of people EG *A violent mob attacked*

the team bus. ▶ VERB **2** If a lot of people mob someone, they crowd around the person in a disorderly way EG *The band was mobbed by over a thousand fans.*
🔲 from Latin *mobile vulgus* meaning 'the fickle public'

mobile mobiles

ADJECTIVE **1** able to move or be moved freely and easily EG *a mobile phone.* **2** If you are mobile, you are able to travel or move to another place EG *a mobile workforce.* ▶ NOUN **3** a decoration consisting of several small objects which hang from threads and move around when a breeze blows. **4** a mobile phone.
mobility NOUN

moccasin moccasins

NOUN Moccasins are flat, soft leather shoes with a raised seam above the toe.
🔲 from *mocussin*, a North American Indian word meaning 'shoe'

mock mocks mocking mocked

VERB **1** If you mock someone, you say something scornful or imitate their foolish behaviour. ▶ ADJECTIVE **2** not genuine EG *mock surprise... a mock Tudor house.* **3** A mock examination is one that you do as a practice before the real examination.
■ (sense 1) laugh at, make fun of, ridicule

mockery

NOUN Mockery is the expression of scorn or ridicule of someone.
■ derision, ridicule

mode modes

NOUN **1** A mode of life or behaviour is a particular way of living or behaving. **2** In mathematics, the mode is the biggest in a set of groups.

model models modelling modelled

NOUN OR ADJECTIVE **1** a copy of a something that shows what it looks like or how it works EG *a model*

---

the **ADJECTIVE 1** consisting of several things of the same general kind EG *a mixed salad.* **2** involving people from two or more different races EG *mixed marriages.* **3** Mixed education or accommodation is for both males and females EG *a mixed comprehensive.*

aircraft. ▸ NOUN **2** Something that is described as, for example, a model of clarity or a model of perfection, is extremely clear or absolutely perfect. **3** a type or version of a machine EG *Which model of washing machine did you choose?* **4** a person who poses for a painter or a photographer. **5** a person who wears the clothes that are being displayed at a fashion show. ▸ ADJECTIVE **6** Someone who is described as, for example, a model wife or a model student is an excellent wife or student. ▸ VERB **7** If you model yourself on someone, you copy their behaviour because you admire them. **8** To model clothes is to display them by wearing them. **9** To model shapes or figures is to make them out of clay or wood.

■ (sense 2) example, ideal, pattern

modem modems
Said "moe-dem" NOUN a piece of equipment that links a computer to the telephone system so that data can be transferred from one machine to another via the telephone line.

moderate moderates moderating moderated
ADJECTIVE **1** Moderate views are not extreme, and usually favour gradual changes rather than major ones. **2** A moderate amount of something is neither large not small. ▸ NOUN **3** a person whose political views are not extreme. ▸ VERB **4** If you moderate something or if it moderates, it becomes less extreme or violent EG *The weather moderated.*

moderately ADVERB

moderation
NOUN Moderation is control of your behaviour that stops you acting in an extreme way EG *a man of fairness and moderation.*

modern
ADJECTIVE **1** relating to the present time EG *modern society.* **2** new and

involving the latest ideas and equipment EG *modern technology.*

modernity NOUN
■ (sense 1) contemporary, current, present-day

modernize modernizes modernizing modernized; also spelt **modernise**
VERB To modernize something is to introduce new methods or equipment to it.

modest
ADJECTIVE **1** quite small in size or amount. **2** Someone who is modest does not boast about their abilities or possessions. **3** shy and easily embarrassed.

modestly ADVERB, **modesty** NOUN

modification modifications
NOUN a small change made to improve something EG *Modifications to the undercarriage were made.*

modify modifies modifying modified
VERB If you modify something, you change it slightly in order to improve it.

module modules
NOUN **1** one of the parts which when put together form a whole unit or object EG *The college provides modules for trainees.* **2** a part of a spacecraft which can do certain things away from the main body EG *the lunar module.*

modular ADJECTIVE

mohair
NOUN Mohair is very soft, fluffy wool obtained from angora goats.

moist moister moistest
ADJECTIVE slightly wet.

moisten moistens moistening moistened
VERB If you moisten something, you make it slightly wet.

moisture
NOUN Moisture is tiny drops of water in the air or on the ground.

molar molars
NOUN Your molars are the large

A B C D E F G H I J K L M N O P Q R S T U V W X Y Z

teeth at the back of your mouth.

mole moles

NOUN **1** a dark, slightly raised spot on your skin. **2** a small animal with black fur. Moles live in tunnels underground. **3** AN INFORMAL USE a member of an organization who is working as a spy for a rival organization.

molecule molecules

NOUN the smallest amount of a substance that can exist.

molecular ADJECTIVE

molest molests molesting molested

VERB To molest a child is to touch the child in a sexual way. This is illegal.

molester NOUN

mollify mollifies mollifying mollified

VERB To mollify someone is to do something to make them less upset or angry.

mollusc molluscs

NOUN an animal with a soft body and no backbone. Snails, slugs, clams, and mussels are all molluscs.

molten

ADJECTIVE Molten rock or metal has been heated to a very high temperature and has become a thick liquid.

moment moments

NOUN **1** a very short period of time EG *He paused for a moment.* **2** The moment at which something happens is the point in time at which it happens EG *At that moment, the doorbell rang.* ▶ PHRASE **3** If something is happening **at the moment**, it is happening now.

■ (sense 1) instant, second

momentary

ADJECTIVE Something that is momentary lasts for only a few seconds EG *a momentary lapse of concentration.*

momentarily ADVERB

☑ Some Americans say *momentarily* when they mean 'very soon', rather than 'for a moment'.

momentous

ADJECTIVE; A FORMAL WORD very important, often because of its future effect EG *a momentous occasion.*

momentum

NOUN **1** Momentum is the ability that something has to keep developing EG *The campaign is gaining momentum.* **2** Momentum is also the ability that an object has to continue moving as a result of the speed it already has.

monarch monarchs

Said "mon-nark" NOUN a queen, king, or other royal person who reigns over a country.

monarchy monarchies

NOUN a system in which a queen or king reigns in a country.

monastery monasteries

NOUN a building in which monks live.

monastic ADJECTIVE

Monday Mondays

NOUN Monday is the day between Sunday and Tuesday.

▦ from Old English *monandæg* meaning 'moon's day'

money

NOUN Money is the coins or banknotes that you use to buy something.

mongrel mongrels

NOUN a dog with parents of different breeds.

monitor monitors monitoring monitored

VERB **1** If you monitor something, you regularly check its condition and progress EG *Her health will be monitored daily.* ▶ NOUN **2** a machine used to check or record things. **3** the visual display unit of a computer. **4** a school pupil chosen to do special duties by the teacher.

monk monks

NOUN a member of a male religious community.

monkey monkeys

NOUN an animal which has a long tail and climbs trees. Monkeys live in hot countries.

mono-
PREFIX 'Mono-' is used at the beginning of nouns and adjectives that have 'one' as part of their meaning EG *monopoly... monogamy*.

monocle monocles
NOUN a glass lens worn in front of one eye only and held in place by the curve of the eye socket.

monogamy
NOUN; A FORMAL WORD Monogamy is the custom of being married to only one person at a time.
monogamous ADJECTIVE

monologue monologues
Said "mon-nol-og" NOUN a long speech by one person during a play or a conversation.

monopoly monopolies
NOUN control of most of an industry by one or a few large firms.

monotone monotones
NOUN a tone which does not vary EG *He droned on in a boring monotone*.

monotonous
ADJECTIVE having a regular pattern which is very dull and boring EG *monotonous work*.
monotony NOUN

monotreme monotremes
NOUN an Australian mammal that has a single opening in its body.

monounsaturated
ADJECTIVE Monounsaturated oils are made mainly from vegetable fats and are considered to be healthier than saturated oils.
monounsaturate NOUN

monsoon monsoons
NOUN the season of very heavy rain in South-east Asia.

monster monsters
NOUN 1 a large, imaginary creature that looks very frightening. 2 a cruel or frightening person.
▶ ADJECTIVE 3 extremely large EG *a monster truck*.

🔲 from Latin *monstrum* meaning 'omen' or 'warning'

monstrosity monstrosities
NOUN something that is large and extremely ugly EG *a concrete monstrosity in the middle of the city*.

monstrous
ADJECTIVE extremely shocking or unfair EG *a monstrous crime*.
monstrously ADVERB

montage montages
Said "mon-tahj" NOUN a picture or film consisting of a combination of several different items arranged to produce an unusual effect.

month months
NOUN one of the twelve periods that a year is divided into.

monthly monthlies
ADJECTIVE Monthly describes something that happens or appears once a month EG *monthly staff meetings*.

monument monuments
NOUN a large stone structure built to remind people of a famous person or event EG *a monument to the dead*.

monumental
ADJECTIVE 1 A monumental building or sculpture is very large and important. 2 very large or extreme EG *We face a monumental task*.

moo moos mooing mooed
VERB When a cow moos, it makes a long, deep sound.

mood moods
NOUN the way you are feeling at a particular time EG *She was in a really cheerful mood*.
🔳 humour, state of mind, temper

moody moodier moodiest
ADJECTIVE 1 Someone who is moody is depressed or unhappy EG *Tony, despite his charm, could sulk and be moody*. 2 Someone who is moody often changes their mood for no apparent reason.
🔳 (sense 1) morose, sulky, sullen
🔳 (sense 2) mercurial, temperamental

A B C D E F G H I J K L M N O P Q R S T U V W X Y Z

moon moons

NOUN The moon is an object moving round the earth which you see as a shining circle or crescent in the sky at night. Some other planets have moons.

moonlight moonlights moonlighting moonlighted

NOUN 1 Moonlight is the light that comes from the moon at night. ▸ VERB 2 AN INFORMAL USE If someone is moonlighting, they have a second job that they have not informed the tax office about.
moonlit ADJECTIVE

moor moors mooring moored

NOUN 1 a high area of open land. ▸ VERB 2 If a boat is moored, it is attached to the land with a rope.

mooring moorings

NOUN a place where a boat can be tied.

moose

NOUN a large North American deer with flat antlers.

moot moots mooting mooted

VERB; A FORMAL WORD When something is mooted, it is suggested for discussion EG The project was first mooted in 1988.

mop mops mopping mopped

NOUN 1 a tool for washing floors, consisting of a sponge or string head attached to a long handle. 2 a large amount of loose or untidy hair. ▸ VERB 3 To mop a floor is to clean it with a mop. 4 To mop a surface is to wipe it with a dry cloth to remove liquid.

mope mopes moping moped

VERB If you mope, you feel miserable and not interested in anything.

moped mopeds

Said "moe-ped" NOUN a type of small motorcycle.

mopoke mopokes

NOUN a small, spotted owl found in Australia and New Zealand. In New Zealand it is called a **morepork**.

moral morals

PLURAL NOUN 1 Morals are values based on beliefs about the correct and acceptable way to behave. ▸ ADJECTIVE 2 concerned with whether behaviour is right or acceptable EG moral values.
morality NOUN, **morally** ADVERB

morale

Said "mor-rahl" NOUN Morale is the amount of confidence and optimism that you have EG The morale of the troops was high.

morbid

ADJECTIVE having a great interest in unpleasant things, especially death.

more

ADJECTIVE OR PRONOUN 1 More means a greater number or extent than something else EG He's got more chips than me... I've got more than you. 2 used to refer to an additional thing or amount of something EG He found some more clues. ▸ ADVERB 3 to a greater degree or extent EG more amused than concerned. 4 You can use 'more' in front of adjectives and adverbs to form comparatives EG You look more beautiful than ever.

moreover

ADVERB used to introduce a piece of information that supports or expands the previous statement EG They have accused the government of corruption. Moreover, they have named names.

morepork moreporks

NOUN In New Zealand English, the same as a mopoke.

morgue morgues

Said "morg" NOUN a building where dead bodies are kept before being buried or cremated.

moribund

ADJECTIVE no longer having a useful function and about to come to an end EG a moribund industry.

morning mornings

NOUN 1 the early part of the day until lunchtime. 2 the part of the day between midnight and noon EG He was born at three in the morning.

Moroccan Moroccans
*Said "mor-***rok***-an"* ADJECTIVE
1 belonging or relating to Morocco.
▶ NOUN **2** someone who comes from
Morocco.

moron morons
NOUN; AN INFORMAL WORD a very stupid
person.
moronic ADJECTIVE

morose
ADJECTIVE miserable and
bad-tempered.

morphine
NOUN Morphine is a drug which is
used to relieve pain.

Morse or **Morse code**
NOUN Morse or Morse code is a code
used for sending messages in which
each letter is represented by a series
of dots and dashes.

morsel morsels
NOUN a small piece of food.

mortal mortals
ADJECTIVE **1** unable to live forever EG
Remember that you are mortal. **2** A
mortal wound is one that causes
death. ▶ NOUN **3** an ordinary person.

mortality
NOUN **1** Mortality is the fact that all
people must die. **2** Mortality also
refers to the number of people who
die at any particular time EG *a low
infant mortality rate.*

mortar mortars
NOUN **1** a short cannon which fires
missiles high into the air for a short
distance. **2** Mortar is a mixture of
sand, water, and cement used to
hold bricks firmly together.

mortgage mortgages mortgaging
mortgaged
*Said "mor-***gij***"* NOUN **1** a loan which
you get from a bank or a building
society in order to buy a house.
▶ VERB **2** If you mortgage your
house, you use it as a guarantee to
a company in order to borrow
money from them. They can take
the house from you if you do not
pay back the money you have
borrowed.

mortifying
ADJECTIVE embarrassing or
humiliating EG *There were some
mortifying setbacks.*

mortuary mortuaries
NOUN a special room in a hospital
where dead bodies are kept before
being buried or cremated.

mosaic mosaics
*Said "moe-***zay***-yik"* NOUN a design
made of small coloured stones or
pieces of coloured glass set into
concrete or plaster.

Moslem
another spelling of **Muslim.**

mosque mosques
*Said "***mosk***"* NOUN a building where
Muslims go to worship.
▦ from Arabic *masjid* meaning
'temple'

mosquito mosquitoes or
mosquitos
*Said "moss-***skee***-toe"* NOUN
Mosquitoes are small insects which
bite people in order to suck their
blood.
▦ from Spanish *mosquito* meaning
'little fly'

moss mosses
NOUN Moss is a soft, low-growing,
green plant which grows on damp
soil or stone.
mossy ADJECTIVE

most
ADJECTIVE OR PRONOUN **1** Most of a
group of things or people means
nearly all of them EG *Most people
don't share your views.* **2** The most
means a larger amount than
anyone or anything else EG *She has
the most talent.* ▶ ADVERB **3** You can
use 'most' in front of adjectives or
adverbs to form superlatives EG *the
most beautiful women in the world.*

mostly
ADVERB 'Mostly' is used to show that
a statement is generally true EG *Her
friends are mostly men.*

MOT MOTs

A
B
C
D
E
F
G
H
I
J
K
L
M
N
O
P
Q
R
S
T
U
V
W
X
Y
Z

NOUN In Britain, an annual test for road vehicles to check that they are safe to drive.

motel motels
NOUN a hotel providing overnight accommodation for people in the middle of a car journey.

moth moths
NOUN an insect like a butterfly which usually flies at night.

mother mothers mothering mothered
NOUN **1** Your mother is the woman who gave birth to you. **2** Your mother could also be the woman who has looked after you and brought you up. ▶ VERB **3** To mother someone is to look after them and bring them up.

motherhood
NOUN Motherhood is the state of being a mother.

mother-in-law mothers-in-law
NOUN Someone's mother-in-law is the mother of their husband or wife.

motif motifs
Said "moe-**teef**" NOUN a design which is used as a decoration.

motion motions motioning motioned
NOUN **1** Motion is the process of continually moving or changing position EG the motion of the ship. **2** an action or gesture EG Apply with a brush using circular motions. **3** a proposal which people discuss and vote on at a meeting. ▶ VERB **4** If you motion to someone, you make a movement with your hand in order to show them what they should do EG I motioned him to proceed.

motionless
ADJECTIVE not moving at all EG He sat motionless.

motivate motivates motivating motivated
VERB **1** If you are motivated by something, it makes you behave in a particular way EG He is motivated by

duty rather than ambition. **2** If you motivate someone, you make them feel determined to do something.
motivated ADJECTIVE, motivation NOUN
■ (sense 1) drive, inspire, prompt

motive motives
NOUN a reason or purpose for doing something EG There was no motive for the attack.

motley
ADJECTIVE A motley collection is made up of people or things of very different types.

motor motors
NOUN **1** a part of a vehicle or a machine that uses electricity or fuel to produce movement so that the machine can work. ▶ ADJECTIVE **2** concerned with or relating to vehicles with a petrol or diesel engine EG the motor industry.

motorcycle motorcycles
NOUN a two-wheeled vehicle with an engine which is ridden like a bicycle.

motoring
ADJECTIVE relating to cars and driving EG a motoring correspondent.

motorist motorists
NOUN a person who drives a car.

motorway motorways
NOUN a wide road built for fast travel over long distances.

mottled
ADJECTIVE covered with patches of different colours EG mottled leaves.

motto mottoes or mottos
NOUN a short sentence or phrase that is a rule for good or sensible behaviour.

mould moulds moulding moulded
VERB **1** To mould someone or something is to influence and change them so they develop in a particular way EG Early experiences mould our behaviour for life. **2** To mould a substance is to make it into a particular shape EG Mould the mixture into flat round cakes. ▶ NOUN **3** a container used to make

something into a particular shape
EG *a jelly mould*. **4** Mould is a soft
grey or green substance that can
form on old food or damp walls.
mouldy ADJECTIVE

moult moults moulting moulted
VERB When an animal or bird
moults, it loses its hair or feathers
so new ones can grow.

mound mounds
NOUN **1** a small man-made hill. **2** a
large, untidy pile EG *a mound of
blankets*.

mount mounts mounting
mounted
VERB **1** To mount a campaign or
event is to organize it and carry it
out. **2** If something is mounting, it
is increasing EG *Economic problems
are mounting*. **3** A FORMAL USE To
mount something is to go to the
top of it EG *He mounted the steps*. **4** If
you mount a horse, you climb on
its back. **5** If you mount an object
in a particular place, you fix it
there to display it. ▶ NOUN **6** 'Mount'
is also used as part of the name of a
mountain EG *Mount Everest*.

mountain mountains
NOUN **1** a very high piece of land
with steep sides. **2** a large amount
of something EG *mountains of
paperwork*.

mountaineer mountaineers
NOUN a person who climbs
mountains.

mountainous
ADJECTIVE A mountainous area has a
lot of mountains.

mourn mourns mourning
mourned
VERB **1** If you mourn for someone
who has died, you are very sad and
think about them a lot. **2** If you
mourn something, you are sad
because you no longer have it EG *He
mourned the end of his marriage*.

mourner mourners
NOUN a person who attends a
funeral.

mournful
ADJECTIVE very sad.

mourning
NOUN If someone is in mourning,
they wear special black clothes or
behave in a quiet and restrained
way because a member of their
family has died.

mouse mice
NOUN **1** a small rodent with a long
tail. **2** a small device moved by
hand to control the position of the
cursor on a computer screen.

mousse mousses
Said "moos" NOUN Mousse is a light,
fluffy food made from whipped
eggs and cream.

moustache moustaches
Said "mus-stahsh" NOUN A man's
moustache is hair growing on his
upper lip.
▣ from Greek *mustax* meaning
'upper lip'

mouth mouths mouthing
mouthed
NOUN **1** your lips, or the space
behind them where your tongue
and teeth are. **2** The mouth of a
cave or a hole is the entrance to it.
3 The mouth of a river is the place
where it flows into the sea. ▶ VERB
4 If you mouth something, you
form words with your lips without
making any sound EG *He mouthed
'Thank you' to the jurors*.
mouthful NOUN

mouthpiece mouthpieces
NOUN **1** the part you speak into on a
telephone. **2** the part of a musical
instrument you put to your mouth.
3 The mouthpiece of an
organization is the person who
publicly states its opinions and
policies.

movable
ADJECTIVE Something that is movable
can be moved from one place to
another.

move moves moving moved
VERB **1** To move means to go to a
different place or position. To

A B C D E F G H I J K L M N O P Q R S T U V W X Y Z

move something means to change its place or position. **2** If you move, or move house, you go to live in a different house. **3** If something moves you, it causes you to feel a deep emotion EG *Her story moved us to tears.* ▸ NOUN **4** a change from one place or position to another EG *We were watching his every move.* **5** an act of moving house. **6** the act of putting a piece or counter in a game in a different position EG *It's your move next.*

🔳 (sense 1) budge, go, shift, stir

movement movements
NOUN **1** Movement involves changing position or going from one place to another. ▸ PLURAL NOUN **2** A FORMAL USE Your movements are everything you do during a period of time EG *They asked him for an account of his movements during the previous morning.* ▸ NOUN **3** a group of people who share the same beliefs or aims EG *the peace movement.* **4** one of the major sections of a piece of classical music.

moving
ADJECTIVE Something that is moving makes you feel deep sadness or emotion.
movingly ADVERB

mow mows mowing mowed mown
VERB **1** To mow grass is to cut it with a lawnmower. **2** To mow down a large number of people is to kill them all violently.

mower mowers
NOUN a machine for cutting grass.

MP MPs
NOUN a person who has been elected to represent people in a country's parliament. MP is an abbreviation for 'Member of Parliament'.

mpg
an abbreviation for 'miles per gallon'.

mph
an abbreviation for 'miles per hour'.

Mr

*Said "**miss**-ter"* 'Mr' is used before a man's name when you are speaking or referring to him.

Mrs
*Said "**miss**-iz"* 'Mrs' is used before the name of a married woman when you are speaking or referring to her.

Ms
*Said "**miz**"* 'Ms' is used before a woman's name when you are speaking or referring to her. Ms does not specify whether a woman is married or not.

much
ADVERB **1** You use 'much' to emphasize that something is true to a great extent EG *I feel much better now.* **2** If something does not happen much, it does not happen very often. ▸ ADJECTIVE OR PRONOUN **3** You use 'much' to ask questions or give information about the size or amount of something EG *How much money do you need?*

muck mucks mucking mucked
NOUN **1** AN INFORMAL USE Muck is dirt or some other unpleasant substance. **2** Muck is also manure. ▸ VERB **3** AN INFORMAL USE If you muck about, you behave stupidly and waste time.
mucky ADJECTIVE

mucus
*Said "**myoo**-kuss"* NOUN Mucus is a liquid produced in parts of your body, for example in your nose.

mud
NOUN Mud is wet, sticky earth.

muddle muddles muddling muddled
NOUN **1** A muddle is a state of disorder or untidiness EG *Our finances are in a muddle.* ▸ VERB **2** If you muddle things, you mix them up.

🔳 (sense 2) jumble, mix up

muddy muddier muddiest
ADJECTIVE **1** covered in mud. **2** A muddy colour is dull and not clear EG *a mottled, muddy brown.*

muesli

Said "myooz-lee" NOUN Muesli is a mixture of chopped nuts, cereal flakes, and dried fruit that you can eat for breakfast with milk.

muffin muffins

NOUN a small, round cake which you eat hot.

muffled

ADJECTIVE A muffled sound is quiet or difficult to hear EG *a muffled explosion.*

mug mugs mugging mugged

NOUN **1** a large, deep cup. **2** AN INFORMAL USE someone who is stupid and easily deceived. ▶ VERB **3** AN INFORMAL USE If someone mugs you, they attack you in order to steal your money.
mugging NOUN, **mugger** NOUN

muggy muggier muggiest

ADJECTIVE Muggy weather is unpleasantly warm and damp.

mule mules

NOUN the offspring of a female horse and a male donkey.

mulga

NOUN **1** Mulga are acacia shrubs that are found in the desert regions of Australia. **2** AN INFORMAL USE In Australian English, mulga is also the bush or outback.

mull mulls mulling mulled

VERB If you mull something over, you think about it for a long time before making a decision.

mullet mullets

NOUN a common edible fish found in Australian and New Zealand waters.

mulloway mulloways

NOUN a large edible fish found in Australian waters.

multi-

PREFIX 'Multi-' is used to form words that refer to something that has many parts or aspects EG *a multistorey car park.*

multinational multinationals

NOUN a very large company with branches in many countries.

multiple multiples

ADJECTIVE **1** having or involving many different functions or things EG *He died from multiple injuries in the crash.* ▶ NOUN **2** The multiples of a number are other numbers that it will divide into exactly. For example, 6, 9, and 12 are multiples of 3.

multiple sclerosis

Said "skler-roe-siss" NOUN Multiple sclerosis is a serious disease which attacks the nervous system, affecting your ability to move.

multiplication

NOUN **1** Multiplication is the process of multiplying one number by another. **2** The multiplication of things is a large increase in their number EG *the multiplication of universities.*

multiplicity

NOUN If there is a multiplicity of things, there is a large number or variety of them.

multiply multiplies multiplying multiplied

VERB **1** When something multiplies, it increases greatly in number EG *The trip wore on and the hazards multiplied.* **2** When you multiply one number by another, you calculate the total you would get if you added the first number to itself a particular number of times. For example, two multiplied by three is equal to two plus two plus two, which equals six.

multitude multitudes

NOUN; A FORMAL WORD a very large number of people or things.

mum mums

NOUN; AN INFORMAL WORD Your mum is your mother.

mumble mumbles mumbling mumbled

VERB If you mumble, you speak very quietly and indistinctly.

mummy mummies

NOUN **1** AN INFORMAL USE, USED ESPECIALLY BY CHILDREN Your mummy is your mother. **2** a dead body which was preserved long ago by being rubbed with special oils and wrapped in cloth.

mumps

NOUN Mumps is a disease that causes painful swelling in the neck glands.

munch munches munching munched

VERB If you munch something, you chew it steadily and thoroughly.

mundane

ADJECTIVE very ordinary and not interesting or unusual EG *a mundane job*.

municipal

Said "myoo-**nis**-si-pl" ADJECTIVE belonging to a city or town which has its own local government EG *a municipal golf course*.

▥ from Latin *municipium* meaning 'free town'

munitions

PLURAL NOUN Munitions are bombs, guns, and other military supplies.

mural murals

NOUN a picture painted on a wall.

murder murders murdering murdered

NOUN **1** Murder is the deliberate killing of a person. ▶ VERB **2** To murder someone is to kill them deliberately.

murderer NOUN

▤ (sense 1) homicide, killing

murderous

ADJECTIVE **1** likely to murder someone EG *murderous gangsters*. **2** A murderous attack or other action results in the death of many people EG *murderous acts of terrorism*.

murky murkier murkiest

ADJECTIVE dark or dirty and unpleasant EG *He rushed through the murky streets*.

murmur murmurs murmuring murmured

VERB **1** If you murmur, you say

something very softly. ▶ NOUN **2** something that someone says which can hardly be heard.

muscle muscles muscling muscled

NOUN **1** Your muscles are pieces of flesh which you can expand or contract in order to move parts of your body. ▶ VERB **2** AN INFORMAL USE If you muscle in on something, you force your way into a situation in which you are not welcome.

▥ from Latin *musculus* meaning 'little mouse', because muscles were thought to look like mice

muscular

Said "**musk**-yool-lar" ADJECTIVE **1** involving or affecting your muscles EG *muscular strength*. **2** Someone who is muscular has strong, firm muscles.

muse muses musing mused

VERB; A LITERARY USE To muse is to think about something for a long time.

museum museums

NOUN a building where many interesting or valuable objects are kept and displayed.

mush

NOUN A mush is a thick, soft paste.

mushroom mushrooms mushrooming mushroomed

NOUN **1** a fungus with a short stem and a round top. Some types of mushroom are edible. ▶ VERB **2** If something mushrooms, it appears and grows very quickly EG *The mill towns mushroomed into cities*.

mushy mushier mushiest

ADJECTIVE **1** Mushy fruits or vegetables are too soft EG *mushy tomatoes*. **2** AN INFORMAL USE Mushy stories are too sentimental.

music

NOUN **1** Music is a pattern of sounds performed by people singing or playing instruments. **2** Music is also the written symbols that represent musical sounds EG *I taught myself to read music*.

musical musicals
ADJECTIVE **1** relating to playing or studying music EG *a musical instrument.* ▶ NOUN **2** a play or film that uses songs and dance to tell the story.
musically ADVERB

musician musicians
NOUN a person who plays a musical instrument as their job or hobby.

musk
NOUN Musk is a substance with a strong, sweet smell. It is used to, make perfume.
musky ADJECTIVE

musket muskets
NOUN an old-fashioned gun with a long barrel.

Muslim Muslims; also spelt Moslem
NOUN **1** a person who believes in Islam and lives according to its rules. ▶ ADJECTIVE **2** relating to Islam.

muslin
NOUN Muslin is a very thin cotton material.

mussel mussels
NOUN Mussels are a kind of shellfish with black shells.

must
VERB **1** If something must happen, it is very important or necessary that it happens EG *You must be over 18.* **2** If you tell someone they must do something, you are suggesting that they do it EG *You must try this pudding: it's delicious.* ▶ NOUN **3** something that is absolutely necessary EG *The museum is a must for all visitors.*

mustard
NOUN Mustard is a spicy-tasting yellow or brown paste made from seeds.

muster musters mustering mustered
VERB If you muster something such as energy or support, you gather it together EG *as much calm as he could muster.*

mutate mutates mutating mutated
VERB; A TECHNICAL WORD If something mutates, its structure or appearance alters in some way EG *Viruses react to change and can mutate fast.*
mutation NOUN, **mutant** NOUN OR ADJECTIVE

mute
ADJECTIVE; A FORMAL WORD not giving out sound or speech EG *mute amazement.*

muted
ADJECTIVE **1** Muted colours or sounds are soft and gentle. **2** A muted reaction is not very strong.

muti
Said "moo-ti" NOUN; AN INFORMAL WORD In South African English, muti is medicine.

mutilate mutilates mutilating mutilated
VERB **1** If someone is mutilated, their body is badly injured EG *His leg was badly mutilated.* **2** If you mutilate something, you deliberately damage or spoil it EG *Almost every book had been mutilated.*
mutilation NOUN

mutiny mutinies
NOUN A mutiny is a rebellion against someone in authority.

mutter mutters muttering muttered
VERB To mutter is to speak in a very low and perhaps cross voice EG *Rory muttered something under his breath.*

mutton
NOUN Mutton is the meat of an adult sheep.

muttonbird muttonbirds
NOUN a seabird in the Pacific Ocean that is often hunted for its flesh, which is said to taste like mutton.

mutual
ADJECTIVE used to describe something that two or more people do to each other or share EG *They had a mutual interest in rugby.*
☑ It used to be that *mutual* could

A
B
C
D
E
F
G
H
I
J
K
L
M
N
O
P
Q
R
S
T
U
V
W
X
Y
Z

473

A B C D E F G H I J K L M N O P Q R S T U V W X Y Z

only be used of something that was shared between two people or groups. Nowadays you can use it to mean 'shared between two or more people or groups'.

mutually

ADVERB Mutually describes a situation in which two or more people feel the same way about each other EG *a mutually supportive relationship.*

muzzle muzzles muzzling muzzled

NOUN **1** the nose and mouth of an animal. **2** a cover or a strap for a dog's nose and mouth to prevent it from biting. **3** the open end of a gun through which the bullets come out. ▶ VERB **4** To muzzle a dog is to put a muzzle on it.

my

ADJECTIVE 'My' refers to something belonging or relating to the person speaking or writing EG *I held my breath.*

mynah bird mynah birds

NOUN a tropical bird which can mimic speech and sounds.

myriad myriads

Said "**mir-ree-ad**" NOUN OR ADJECTIVE; A LITERARY WORD a very large number of people or things.

myrrh

Rhymes with "**purr**" NOUN Myrrh is a fragrant substance used in perfume and incense.

myself

PRONOUN **1** 'Myself' is used when the person speaking or writing does an action and is affected by it EG *I was ashamed of myself.* **2** 'Myself' is also used to emphasize 'I' EG *I find it a bit odd myself.*

mysterious

ADJECTIVE **1** strange and not well

understood. **2** secretive about something EG *Stop being so mysterious.*

mysteriously ADVERB

▤ (sense 2) enigmatic, secretive

mystery mysteries

NOUN something that is not understood or known about.

mystic mystics

NOUN **1** a religious person who spends long hours meditating. ▶ ADJECTIVE **2** Mystic means the same as mystical.

mystical

ADJECTIVE involving spiritual powers and influences EG *a mystical experience.*

mysticism NOUN

mystify mystifies mystifying mystified

VERB If something mystifies you, you find it impossible to understand.

mystique

Said "**mis-steek**" NOUN Mystique is an atmosphere of mystery and importance associated with a particular person or thing.

myth myths

NOUN **1** an untrue belief or explanation. **2** a story which was made up long ago to explain natural events and religious beliefs EG *Viking myths.*

mythical

ADJECTIVE imaginary, untrue, or existing only in myths EG *a mythical beast.*

mythology

NOUN Mythology refers to stories that have been made up in the past to explain natural events or justify religious beliefs.

mythological ADJECTIVE

naartjie naartjies
Said "nar-chi" NOUN In South
African English, a tangerine.

nag nags nagging nagged
VERB **1** If you nag someone, you
keep complaining to them about
something. **2** If something nags at
you, it keeps worrying you.

nail nails nailing nailed
NOUN **1** a small piece of metal with a
sharp point at one end, which you
hammer into objects to hold them
together. **2** Your nails are the thin
hard areas covering the ends of
your fingers and toes. ▸ VERB **3** If
you nail something somewhere,
you fit it there using a nail.

naive or **naïve**
Said "ny-eev" ADJECTIVE foolishly
believing that things are easier or
less complicated than they really
are.
naively ADVERB, **naivety** NOUN

naked
ADJECTIVE **1** not wearing any clothes
or not covered by anything.
2 shown openly EG *naked aggression.*
nakedness NOUN

name names naming named
NOUN **1** a word that you use to
identify a person, place, or thing.
2 Someone's name is also their
reputation EG *My only wish now is to
clear my name.* ▸ VERB **3** If you name
someone or something, you give
them a name or you say their
name. **4** If you name a price or a
date, you say what you want it to
be.

nameless
ADJECTIVE You describe someone or
something as nameless when you
do not know their name, or when a
name has not yet been given to
them.

namely
ADVERB that is; used to introduce
more detailed information about
what you have just said EG *The state
stripped them of their rights, namely
the right to own land.*

namesake namesakes
NOUN Your namesake is someone
with the same name as you EG
*Audrey Hepburn and her namesake
Katharine.*

nanny nannies
NOUN a woman whose job is looking
after young children.

nap naps napping napped
NOUN **1** a short sleep. ▸ VERB **2** When
you nap, you have a short sleep.

nape napes
NOUN The nape of your neck is the
back of it.

napkin napkins
NOUN a small piece of cloth or paper
used to wipe your hands and
mouth after eating.

nappy nappies
NOUN a piece of towelling or paper
worn round a baby's bottom.

narcotic narcotics
NOUN a drug which makes you
sleepy and unable to feel pain.
🏛 from Greek *narkoun* meaning
'to make numb'

narrate narrates narrating
narrated
VERB If you narrate a story, you tell
it.
narration NOUN, **narrator** NOUN

narrative narratives
Said "nar-rat-tiv" NOUN a story or an
account of events.

narrow narrower narrowest;
narrows narrowing narrowed
ADJECTIVE **1** having a small distance
from one side to the other EG *a
narrow stream.* **2** concerned only
with a few aspects of something
and ignoring the important points
EG *people with a narrow point of view.*
3 A narrow escape or victory is one
that you only just achieve. ▸ VERB

4 To narrow means to become less wide EG *The road narrowed.*
narrowly ADVERB

narrow-minded
ADJECTIVE unwilling to consider new ideas or opinions.
■ bigoted, intolerant

nasal
Said "**nay**-zal" ADJECTIVE **1** relating to the nose EG *the nasal passages.*
2 Nasal sounds are made by breathing out through your nose as you speak.

nasty nastier nastiest
ADJECTIVE very unpleasant EG *a nasty shock.*
nastily ADVERB, **nastiness** NOUN

nation nations
NOUN a large group of people sharing the same history and language and usually inhabiting a particular country.

national nationals
ADJECTIVE **1** relating to the whole of a country EG *a national newspaper.*
2 typical of a particular country EG *women in Polish national dress.* ▸ NOUN
3 A national of a country is a citizen of that country EG *Turkish nationals.*
nationally ADVERB

national anthem national anthems
NOUN A country's national anthem is its official song.

nationalism
NOUN **1** Nationalism is a desire for the independence of a country; also a political movement aiming to achieve such independence.
2 Nationalism is also love of your own country.
nationalist NOUN, **nationalistic** ADJECTIVE

nationality nationalities
NOUN Nationality is the fact of belonging to a particular country.

nationalize nationalizes
nationalizing nationalized; also spelt **nationalise**
VERB To nationalize an industry means to bring it under the control and ownership of the state.
nationalization NOUN

National Party
NOUN In Australia and New Zealand, the National Party is a major political party.

national service
NOUN National service is a compulsory period of service in the armed forces.

nationwide
ADJECTIVE OR ADVERB happening all over a country EG *a nationwide search.*

native natives
ADJECTIVE **1** Your native country is the country where you were born.
2 Your native language is the language that you first learned to speak. **3** Animals or plants that are native to a place live or grow there naturally and have not been brought there by people. ▸ NOUN **4** A native of a place is someone who was born there.

Nativity
NOUN In Christianity, the Nativity is the birth of Christ or the festival celebrating this.

natter natters nattering nattered
VERB; AN INFORMAL WORD If you natter, you talk about unimportant things.

natural naturals
ADJECTIVE **1** normal and to be expected EG *It was only natural that he was tempted.* **2** not trying to pretend or hide anything EG *Caitlin's natural manner reassured her.*
3 existing or happening in nature EG *natural disasters.* **4** A natural ability is one you were born with. **5** Your natural mother or father is your real mother or father and not someone who has adopted you.
▸ NOUN **6** someone who is born with a particular ability EG *She's a natural at bridge.* **7** In music, a natural is a note that is not a sharp or a flat. It is represented by the symbol (♮).
naturally ADVERB
■ (sense 4) inborn, inherent, innate

nature natures

NOUN **1** Nature is animals, plants, and all the other things in the world not made by people. **2** The nature of a person or thing is their basic character EG *She liked his warm, generous nature.*

🏛 from Latin *natura* meaning 'birth'

naughty naughtier naughtiest

ADJECTIVE **1** behaving badly. **2** rude or indecent EG *naughty films.*
naughtiness NOUN

nausea

Said "naw-zee-ah" NOUN Nausea is a feeling in your stomach that you are going to be sick.
nauseous ADJECTIVE

nautical

Said "naw-tik-kl" ADJECTIVE relating to ships or navigation.

naval

ADJECTIVE relating to or having a navy EG *naval officers... naval bases.*

navel navels

NOUN the small hollow on the front of your body just below your waist.

navigate navigates navigating navigated

VERB **1** When someone navigates, they work out the direction in which a ship, plane, or car should go, using maps and sometimes instruments. **2** To navigate a stretch of water means to travel safely across it EG *It was the first time I had navigated the ocean.*
navigation NOUN, **navigator** NOUN

navy navies

NOUN **1** the part of a country's armed forces that fights at sea.
▶ ADJECTIVE **2** dark blue.

Nazi Nazis

Said "naht-see" NOUN The Nazis were members of the National Socialist German Workers' Party, which was led by Adolf Hitler.

NB

You write NB to draw attention to what you are going to write next.

NB is an abbreviation for the Latin 'nota bene', which means 'note well'.

near nearer nearest; nears nearing neared

PREPOSITION OR ADVERB **1** not far from.
▶ ADJECTIVE **2** You can also use 'near' to mean almost EG *a night of near disaster.* ▶ VERB **3** When you are nearing something, you are approaching it and will soon reach it EG *The dog began to bark as he neared the porch.*

nearby

ADJECTIVE OR ADVERB only a short distance away.

nearly

ADVERB not completely but almost.

neat neater neatest

ADJECTIVE **1** tidy and smart. **2** A neat alcoholic drink does not have anything added to it EG *a small glass of neat vodka.*
neatly ADVERB, **neatness** NOUN

necessarily

ADVERB Something that is not necessarily the case is not always or inevitably the case.

necessary

ADJECTIVE **1** Something that is necessary is needed or must be done. **2** A FORMAL USE Necessary also means certain or inevitable EG *a necessary consequence of war.*
▤ (sense 1) essential, needed, requisite

necessity necessities

NOUN **1** Necessity is the need to do something EG *There is no necessity for any of this.* **2** Necessities are things needed in order to live.

neck necks

NOUN **1** the part of your body which joins your head to the rest of your body. **2** the long narrow part at the top of a bottle.

necklace necklaces

NOUN **1** a piece of jewellery which a woman wears around her neck.
2 In South Africa, a name for a tyre

A B C D E F G H I J K L M N O P Q R S T U V W X Y Z

filled with petrol which is placed round a person's neck and set on fire in order to kill that person.

nectar
NOUN Nectar is a sweet liquid produced by flowers and attractive to insects.

nectarine nectarines
NOUN a kind of peach with a smooth skin.

née
Rhymes with "day" 'Née' is used to indicate what a woman's surname was before she got married EG *Sara Black, née Wells.*

need needs needing needed
VERB 1 If you need something, you believe that you must have it or do it. ▶ NOUN 2 Your needs are the things that you need to have. 3 a strong feeling that you must have or do something EG *I just felt the need to write about it.*
■ (sense 2) necessity, requirement

needle needles needling needled
NOUN 1 a small thin piece of metal with a pointed end and a hole at the other, which is used for sewing. 2 Needles are also long thin pieces of steel or plastic, used for knitting. 3 the small pointed part in a record player that touches the record and picks up the sound signals. 4 the part of a syringe which a doctor or nurse sticks into your body. 5 the thin piece of metal or plastic on a dial which moves to show a measurement. 6 The needles of a pine tree are its leaves. ▶ VERB 7 AN INFORMAL USE If someone needles you, they annoy or provoke you.

needless
ADJECTIVE unnecessary.
needlessly ADVERB

needy needier neediest
ADJECTIVE very poor.

negative negatives
ADJECTIVE 1 A negative answer means 'no'. 2 Someone who is negative sees only problems and disadvantages EG *Why are you so*

negative about everything? 3 If a medical or scientific test is negative, it shows that something has not happened or is not present EG *The pregnancy test came back negative.* 4 A negative number is less than zero. ▶ NOUN 5 the image that is first produced when you take a photograph.
negatively ADVERB

neglect neglects neglecting neglected
VERB 1 If you neglect something, you do not look after it properly. 2 A FORMAL USE If you neglect to do something, you fail to do it EG *He had neglected to give her his address.* ▶ NOUN 3 Neglect is failure to look after something or someone properly EG *Most of her plants died from neglect.*
neglectful ADJECTIVE

negligent
ADJECTIVE not taking enough care EG *her negligent driving.*
negligence NOUN

negligible
ADJECTIVE very small and unimportant EG *a negligible amount of fat.*

negotiable
ADJECTIVE able to be changed or agreed by discussion EG *All contributions are negotiable.*

negotiate negotiates negotiating negotiated
VERB 1 When people negotiate, they have formal discussions in order to reach an agreement about something. 2 If you negotiate an obstacle, you manage to get over it or round it.
negotiation NOUN, **negotiator** NOUN

Negro Negroes
NOUN; AN OLD-FASHIONED USE a person with black skin who comes from Africa or whose ancestors came from Africa.

neigh neighs neighing neighed
Rhymes with "day" VERB 1 When a horse neighs, it makes a loud

high-pitched sound. ▶ NOUN **2** a loud sound made by a horse.

neighbour neighbours

NOUN **1** Your neighbour is someone who lives next door to you or near you. **2** Your neighbour is also someone standing or sitting next to you EG *I got chatting with my neighbour in the studio.*

neighbourhood neighbourhoods

NOUN a district where people live EG *a safe neighbourhood.*

neighbouring

ADJECTIVE situated nearby EG *schools in neighbouring areas.*

neither

ADJECTIVE OR PRONOUN used to indicate that a negative statement refers to two or more things or people EG *It's neither a play nor a musical... Neither of them spoke.*

☑ When *neither* is followed by a plural noun, the verb can be plural too: *neither of these books are useful.* When you have two singular subjects the verb should be singular too: *neither Jack nor John has done the work.*

neo-

PREFIX new or modern EG *neo-fascism.*

nephew nephews

NOUN Someone's nephew is the son of their sister or brother.

Neptune

NOUN Neptune is the planet in the solar system which is eighth from the sun.

🏛 from *Neptune*, the Roman god of the sea

nerve nerves

NOUN **1** a long thin fibre that sends messages between your brain and other parts of your body. **2** If you talk about someone's nerves, you are referring to how able they are to remain calm in a difficult situation EG *It needs confidence and strong nerves.* **3** Nerve is courage EG *O'Meara held his nerve to sink the putt.* **4** AN INFORMAL USE Nerve is boldness or rudeness EG *He had the nerve to*

swear at me. ▶ AN INFORMAL PHRASE **5** If someone **gets on your nerves**, they irritate you.

nerve-racking

ADJECTIVE making you feel very worried and tense EG *a nerve-racking experience.*

nervous

ADJECTIVE **1** worried and frightened. **2** A nervous illness affects your emotions and mental health.
nervously ADVERB, **nervousness** NOUN
☰ (sense 1) apprehensive, edgy, jumpy

nervous breakdown nervous breakdowns

NOUN an illness in which someone suffers from deep depression and needs psychiatric treatment.

nervous system nervous systems

NOUN Your nervous system is the nerves in your body together with your brain and spinal cord.

nest nests nesting nested

NOUN **1** a place that a bird makes to lay its eggs in; also a place that some insects and other animals make to rear their young in. ▶ VERB **2** When birds nest, they build a nest and lay eggs in it.

nestle nestles nestling nestled

Said "**ness-sl**" VERB If you nestle somewhere, you settle there comfortably, often pressing up against someone else EG *A new puppy nestled in her lap.*

nestling nestlings

NOUN a young bird that has not yet learned to fly and so has not left the nest.

net nets

NOUN **1** a piece of material made of threads woven together with small spaces in between. **2** The net is the same as the **Internet.** ▶ ADJECTIVE **3** A net result or amount is final, after everything has been considered EG *a net profit of 171 million.* **4** The net weight of something is its weight without its wrapping.

479

A
B
C
D
E
F
G
H
I
J
K
L
M
N
O
P
Q
R
S
T
U
V
W
X
Y
Z

netball
NOUN Netball is a game played by two teams of seven players in which each team tries to score goals by throwing a ball through a net at the top of a pole.

netting
NOUN Netting is material made of threads or metal wires woven together with small spaces in between.

nettle nettles
NOUN a wild plant covered with little hairs that sting.

network networks
NOUN **1** a large number of lines or roads which cross each other at many points EG *a small network of side roads*. **2** A network of people or organizations is a large number of them that work together as a system EG *the public telephone network*. **3** A television network is a group of broadcasting stations that all transmit the same programmes at the same time. **4** a group of computers connected to each other.

neuron neurons
NOUN a cell that is part of the nervous system and conducts messages to and from the brain.

neurone neurones
NOUN the same as a **neuron**.

neurosis neuroses
Said "nyoor-roh-siss" NOUN Neurosis is mental illness which causes people to have strong and unreasonable fears and worries.

neurotic
Said "nyoor-rot-ik" ADJECTIVE having strong and unreasonable fears and worries EG *He was almost neurotic about being followed.*

neuter neuters neutering neutered
Said "nyoo-ter" VERB **1** When an animal is neutered, its reproductive organs are removed. ▶ ADJECTIVE **2** In some languages, a neuter noun or pronoun is one which is not masculine or feminine.

> ### What is Neuter?
> **Neuter nouns** refer to inanimate objects and abstract ideas.
> *The kettle will switch itself off.* ➤ *kettle is* **neuter**
> Also look at the grammar boxes at **gender**, **masculine** and **feminine**.

---

neutral neutrals
ADJECTIVE **1** People who are neutral do not support either side in a disagreement or war. **2** The neutral wire in an electric plug is the one that is not earth or live. **3** A neutral colour is not definite or striking, for example pale grey. **4** In chemistry, a neutral substance is neither acid nor alkaline. ▶ NOUN **5** a person or country that does not support either side in a disagreement or war. **6** Neutral is the position between the gears of a vehicle in which the gears are not connected to the engine and so the vehicle cannot move.
neutrality NOUN

neutron neutrons
NOUN an atomic particle that has no electrical charge.

never
ADVERB at no time in the past, present, or future.
☑ Do not use *never* to mean 'not' in writing. You should say *I didn't see her* not *I never saw her*.

nevertheless
ADVERB in spite of what has just been said EG *They dress rather plainly but nevertheless look quite smart.*

new newer newest
ADJECTIVE **1** recently made or created EG *a new house... a new plan*. **2** only recently discovered EG *a new virus*. **3** not used or owned before EG *We've got a new car*. **4** different or unfamiliar EG *a name which was new to me*.
☰ (sense 1) latest, modern, recent

newcomer newcomers
NOUN someone who has recently

arrived in a place.

newly
ADVERB recently EG *the newly born baby*.

new moon new moons
NOUN The moon is a new moon when it is a thin crescent shape at the start of its four-week cycle.

news
NOUN News is information about things that have happened.

newsagent newsagents
NOUN a person or shop that sells newspapers and magazines.

newspaper newspapers
NOUN a publication, on large sheets of paper, that is produced regularly and contains news and articles.

newt newts
NOUN a small amphibious creature with a moist skin, short legs, and a long tail.
🔲 from a mistaken division of Middle English *an ewt*

New Testament
NOUN The New Testament is the second part of the Bible, which deals with the life of Jesus Christ and with the early Church.

New Year
NOUN New Year is the time when people celebrate the start of a year.

New Zealander New Zealanders
NOUN someone who comes from New Zealand.

next
ADJECTIVE OR ADVERB **1** coming immediately after something else EG *They lived in the next street.* ▶ PHRASE **2** If one thing is **next to** another, it is at the side of it.
■ (sense 1) following, subsequent

next door
ADJECTIVE OR ADVERB in the house next to yours.

NHS
In Britain, an abbreviation for 'National Health Service'.

nib nibs
NOUN the pointed end of a pen.

nibble nibbles nibbling nibbled
VERB **1** When you nibble something, you take small bites of it. ▶ NOUN **2** a small bite of something.

nice nicer nicest
ADJECTIVE pleasant or attractive.
nicely ADVERB

nicety niceties
Said "nigh-se-tee" NOUN a small detail EG *the social niceties*.

niche niches
Said "neesh" NOUN **1** a hollow area in a wall. **2** If you say that you have found your niche, you mean that you have found a job or way of life that is exactly right for you.

nick nicks nicking nicked
VERB **1** If you nick something, you make a small cut in its surface EG *He nicked his chin.* **2** AN INFORMAL USE To nick something also means to steal it. ▶ NOUN **3** a small cut in the surface of something.

nickel
NOUN Nickel is a silver-coloured metal that is used in making steel.

nickname nicknames nicknaming nicknamed
NOUN **1** an informal name given to someone. ▶ VERB **2** If you nickname someone, you give them a nickname.
🔲 from Middle English *an ekename* meaning 'an additional name'

nicotine
NOUN Nicotine is an addictive substance found in tobacco.

niece nieces
NOUN Someone's niece is the daughter of their sister or brother.

nifty
ADJECTIVE neat and pleasing or cleverly done.

Nigerian Nigerians
Said "nie-jeer-ee-an" ADJECTIVE **1** belonging or relating to Nigeria. ▶ NOUN **2** someone who comes from Nigeria.

niggle niggles niggling niggled

A B C D E F G H I J K L M N O P Q R S T U V W X Y Z

VERB **1** If something niggles you, it worries you slightly. ▶ NOUN **2** a small worry that you keep thinking about.

night nights
NOUN Night is the time between sunset and sunrise when it is dark.

nightclub nightclubs
NOUN a place where people go late in the evening to drink and dance.

nightdress nightdresses
NOUN a loose dress that a woman or girl wears to sleep in.

nightfall
NOUN Nightfall is the time of day when it starts to get dark.

nightie nighties
NOUN; AN INFORMAL WORD a nightdress.

nightingale nightingales
NOUN a small brown European bird, the male of which sings very beautifully, especially at night.

nightly
ADJECTIVE OR ADVERB happening every night EG *the nightly news programme*.

nightmare nightmares
NOUN a very frightening dream; also used of any very unpleasant or frightening situation EG *The meal itself was a nightmare*.
nightmarish ADJECTIVE
⌂ from *night* + Middle English *mare* meaning 'evil spirit'

nil
NOUN Nil means zero or nothing. It is used especially in sports scores.

nimble nimbler nimblest
ADJECTIVE **1** able to move quickly and easily. **2** able to think quickly and cleverly.
nimbly ADVERB

nine
the number 9.
ninth

nineteen
the number 19.
nineteenth

ninety nineties
the number 90.

ninetieth

nip nips nipping nipped
VERB **1** AN INFORMAL USE If you nip somewhere, you go there quickly. **2** To nip someone or something means to pinch or them slightly. ▶ NOUN **3** a light pinch.

nipple nipples
NOUN Your nipples are the two small pieces of projecting flesh on your chest. Babies suck milk through the nipples on their mothers' breasts.

nirvana
Said "neer-**vah**-na" NOUN Nirvana is the ultimate state of spiritual enlightenment which can be achieved in the Hindu and Buddhist religions.

nit nits
NOUN Nits are the eggs of a kind of louse that sometimes lives in people's hair.

nitrogen
NOUN Nitrogen is a chemical element usually found as a gas. It forms about 78% of the earth's atmosphere.

no
INTERJECTION **1** used to say that something is not true or to refuse something. ▶ ADJECTIVE **2** none at all or not at all EG *She gave no reason... You're no friend of mine.* ▶ ADVERB **3** used with a comparative to mean 'not' EG *no later than 24th July*.

no.
a written abbreviation for **number**.

nobility
NOUN **1** Nobility is the quality of being noble EG *the unmistakable nobility of his character.* **2** The nobility of a society are all the people who have titles and high social rank.

noble nobler noblest; nobles
ADJECTIVE **1** honest and brave, and deserving admiration. **2** very impressive EG *broad cheekbones which gave them a noble appearance.* ▶ NOUN **3** a member of the nobility.

A
B
C
D
E
F
G
H
I
J
K
L
M
N
O
P
Q
R
S
T
U
V
W
X
Y
Z

nobly ADVERB

nobleman noblemen
NOUN a man who is a member of the nobility.
noblewoman NOUN

nobody nobodies
PRONOUN **1** not a single person.
▶ NOUN **2** Someone who is a nobody is not at all important.
✓ *Nobody* and *no-one* mean the same.

nocturnal
ADJECTIVE **1** happening at night EG *a nocturnal journey through New York.*
2 active at night EG *a nocturnal animal.*

nod nods nodding nodded
VERB **1** When you nod, you move your head up and down, usually to show agreement. ▶ NOUN **2** a movement of your head up and down.
nod off VERB If you nod off, you fall asleep.

noise noises
NOUN a sound, especially one that is loud or unpleasant.
■ din, racket, sound

noisy noisier noisiest
ADJECTIVE making a lot of noise or full of noise EG *a noisy crowd.*
noisily ADVERB, **noisiness** NOUN

nomad nomads
NOUN a person who belongs to a tribe which travels from place to place rather than living in just one place.
nomadic ADJECTIVE

nominal
ADJECTIVE **1** Something that is nominal is supposed to have a particular identity or status, but in reality does not have it EG *the nominal leader of his party.* **2** A nominal amount of money is very small compared to the value of something EG *I am prepared to sell my shares at a nominal price.*
nominally ADVERB

nominate nominates nominating

nominated
VERB If you nominate someone for a job or position, you formally suggest that they have it.
nomination NOUN
■ name, propose, suggest

non-
PREFIX not EG *non-smoking.*

nonchalant
Said "non-shal-nt" ADJECTIVE seeming calm and not worried.
nonchalance NOUN, **nonchalantly** ADVERB

noncommissioned officer noncommissioned officers
NOUN an officer such as a sergeant or corporal who has been promoted from the lower ranks.

nondescript
ADJECTIVE dull and uninteresting in appearance EG *a nondescript coat.*

none
PRONOUN not a single thing or person, or not even a small amount of something.

nonplussed
ADJECTIVE confused and unsure about how to react.

nonsense
NOUN Nonsense is foolish and meaningless words or behaviour.
nonsensical ADJECTIVE

nonstop
ADJECTIVE OR ADVERB continuing without any pauses or breaks EG *nonstop excitement.*

noodle noodles
NOUN Noodles are a kind of pasta shaped into long, thin pieces.

nook nooks
NOUN; A LITERARY WORD a small sheltered place.

noon
NOUN Noon is midday.

no-one or **no one**
PRONOUN not a single person.
✓ *No-one* and *nobody* mean the same.

noose nooses
NOUN a loop at the end of a piece of

483

A
B
C
D
E
F
G
H
I
J
K
L
M
N
O
P
Q
R
S
T
U
V
W
X
Y
Z

rope, with a knot that tightens when the rope is pulled.

nor

CONJUNCTION used after 'neither' or after a negative statement, to add something else that the negative statement applies to EG *They had neither the time nor the money for the sport.*

norm

NOUN If something is the norm, it is the usual and expected thing EG *cultures where large families are the norm.*

▣ from Latin *norma* meaning 'carpenter's rule'

normal

ADJECTIVE usual and ordinary EG *I try to lead a normal life.*

normality NOUN

▤ conventional, ordinary, usual·

normally

ADVERB 1 usually EG *I don't normally like dancing.* 2 in a way that is normal EG *The foetus is developing normally.*

north

NOUN 1 The north is the direction to your left when you are looking towards the place where the sun rises. 2 The north of a place or country is the part which is towards the north when you are in the centre. ▶ ADVERB OR ADJECTIVE 3 North means towards the north EG *The helicopter took off and headed north.* ▶ ADJECTIVE 4 A north wind blows from the north.

North America

NOUN North America is the third largest continent, consisting of Canada, the United States, and Mexico.

North American ADJECTIVE

north-east

NOUN, ADVERB, OR ADJECTIVE North-east is halfway between north and east.

north-easterly

ADJECTIVE 1 North-easterly means to or towards the north-east. 2 A north-easterly wind blows from the north-east.

north-eastern

ADJECTIVE in or from the north-east.

northerly

ADJECTIVE 1 Northerly means to or towards the north EG *travelling in a northerly direction.* 2 A northerly wind blows from the north.

northern

ADJECTIVE in or from the north EG *the mountains of northern Italy.*

North Pole

NOUN The North Pole is the most northerly point of the earth's surface.

northward or **northwards**

ADVERB 1 Northward or northwards means towards the north EG *We continued northwards.* ▶ ADJECTIVE 2 The northward part of something is the north part.

north-west

NOUN, ADVERB, OR ADJECTIVE North-west is halfway between north and west.

north-westerly

ADJECTIVE 1 North-westerly means to or towards the north-west. 2 A north-westerly wind blows from the north-west.

north-western

ADJECTIVE in or from the north-west.

Norwegian Norwegians

Said "nor-wee-jn" ADJECTIVE 1 belonging or relating to Norway. ▶ NOUN 2 someone who comes from Norway. 3 Norwegian is the main language spoken in Norway.

nose noses

NOUN 1 the part of your face above your mouth which you use for smelling and breathing. 2 the front part of a car or plane.

nostalgia

Said "nos-**tal**-ja" NOUN Nostalgia is a feeling of affection for the past, and sadness that things have changed.

nostalgic ADJECTIVE

nostril nostrils

NOUN Your nostrils are the two

openings in your nose which you breathe through.

nosy nosier nosiest; also spelt **nosey**

ADJECTIVE trying to find out about things that do not concern you.

not

ADVERB used to make a sentence negative, to refuse something, or to deny something.

What does Not do?

You can turn most sentences into negatives if you want to express the opposite meaning.

You can usually make a sentence into a negative by adding the word *not*.
*Robbie was **not** feeling tired.*

If a sentence already contains an auxiliary verb, such as *have*, *will*, *be*, or *must*, the word *not* should go after this verb.
*She has **not** gone to the shops.*

If the sentence does not already contain an auxiliary verb, a form of the verb *do* is added, and the word *not* is placed after this.
*We **do not** expect to win.*

In spoken and informal English, the ending *-n't* may be added to an auxiliary verb in place of *not*.
*She **hasn't** gone to the shops.*

---

notable

ADJECTIVE important or interesting EG *The production is notable for some outstanding performances.*
notably ADVERB

notch notches

NOUN a small V-shaped cut in a surface.

▣ from a mistaken division of Middle English *an otch*

note notes noting noted

NOUN **1** a short letter. **2** a written piece of information that helps you to remember something EG *You should make a note of that.* **3** In music, a note is a musical sound of a particular pitch, or a written symbol that represents it. **4** a banknote. **5** an atmosphere,

feeling, or quality EG *There was a note of regret in his voice... I'm determined to close on an optimistic note.* ▶ VERB **6** If you note a fact, you become aware of it or you mention it EG *I noted that the rain had stopped.* ▶ PHRASE **7** If you **take note** of something, you pay attention to it EG *The world hardly took note of this crisis.*

note down VERB If you note something down, you write it down so that you will remember it.

notebook notebooks

NOUN a small book for writing notes in.

noted

ADJECTIVE well-known and admired EG *a noted Hebrew scholar.*

nothing

PRONOUN not anything EG *There was nothing to do.*

▣ nil, nought, zero

☑ *Nothing* is usually followed by a singular verb: *nothing was in the bag.* If the expression *nothing but* is followed by a plural noun, the verb should be plural too: *a large room where nothing but souvenirs were sold.*

notice notices noticing noticed

VERB **1** If you notice something, you become aware of it. ▶ NOUN **2** Notice is attention or awareness EG *I'm glad he brought it to my notice.* **3** a written announcement. **4** Notice is also advance warning about something EG *We were lucky to get you at such short notice.* ▶ PHRASE **5** If you **hand in your notice**, you tell your employer that you intend to leave your job after a fixed period of time.

▣ (sense 1) detect, observe, perceive

noticeable

ADJECTIVE obvious and easy to see EG *a noticeable improvement.*
noticeably ADVERB

noticeboard noticeboards

NOUN a board for notices.

notify notifies notifying notified

VERB To notify someone of

A B C D E F G H I J K L M N O P Q R S T U V W X Y Z

something means to officially inform them of it EG *You must notify us of any change of address.*

notification NOUN

notion notions
NOUN an idea or belief.

notorious
ADJECTIVE well-known for something bad EG *The area has become notorious for violence against tourists.*

notoriously ADVERB, **notoriety** NOUN

notwithstanding
PREPOSITION; A FORMAL WORD in spite of EG *Notwithstanding his age, Sikorski had an important job.*

nougat
Said "noo-gah" NOUN Nougat is a kind of chewy sweet containing nuts and sometimes fruit.

📖 from Provençal *noga* meaning 'nut'

nought
the number 0.

noun nouns
NOUN a word which refers to a person, thing, or idea. Examples of nouns are 'president', 'table', 'sun', and 'beauty'.

What is a Noun?

A noun is a word that labels a person, a thing or an idea. In any sentence, the nouns will tell you which people or things are involved. They are sometimes called "naming words".

Common nouns are words which indicate every example of a certain type of thing. They begin with small letters.

girl   city   picture

Proper nouns are words which give the name of a particular person, place, or object. They begin with capital letters.

Anna Jamieson   Los Angeles   The Mona Lisa

Some common nouns are **concrete nouns**. These are words that indicate things that you *can* touch.

cat   pen   apple

Other common nouns are **abstract nouns**. These are words that indicate things that you *cannot* touch.

beauty   ambition   popularity

Some common nouns are **collective nouns**. These are words that indicate a group or collection of things.

pack   bunch   flock

---

nourish nourishes nourishing nourished
Said "nur-rish" VERB To nourish people or animals means to provide them with food.

nourishing
ADJECTIVE Food that is nourishing makes you strong and healthy.

nourishment
NOUN Nourishment is food that your body needs in order to remain healthy EG *poor nourishment.*

novel novels
NOUN 1 a book that tells an invented story. ▶ ADJECTIVE 2 new and interesting EG *a very novel experience.*

novelist novelists
NOUN a person who writes novels.

novelty novelties
NOUN 1 Novelty is the quality of being new and interesting EG *The novelty had worn off.* 2 something new and interesting EG *Steam power was still a bit of a novelty.* 3 a small, unusual object sold as a gift or souvenir.

November
NOUN November is the eleventh month of the year. It has 30 days.

📖 from Latin *November* meaning 'the ninth month'

novice novices
NOUN 1 someone who is not yet experienced at something. 2 someone who is preparing to become a monk or nun.

now
ADVERB 1 at the present time or moment. ▶ CONJUNCTION 2 as a result or consequence of a particular fact EG *Things have got better now there is a new board.* ▶ PHRASE 3 Just now means very recently EG *I drove Brenda back to the camp just now.* 4 If

something happens **now and then**, it happens sometimes but not regularly.

nowadays
ADVERB at the present time EG *Nowadays most fathers choose to be present at the birth.*

nowhere
ADVERB not anywhere.

noxious
Said "nok-shus" ADJECTIVE harmful or poisonous EG *a noxious gas.*

nozzle nozzles
NOUN a spout fitted onto the end of a pipe or hose to control the flow of a liquid.

nuance nuances
Said "nyoo-ahnss" NOUN a small difference in sound, colour, or meaning EG *the nuances of his music.*

nubile
Said "nyoo-bile" ADJECTIVE A woman who is nubile is young and sexually attractive.
🔟 from Latin *nubere* meaning 'to take a husband'

nuclear
ADJECTIVE **1** relating to the energy produced when the nuclei of atoms are split EG *nuclear power... the nuclear industry.* **2** relating to weapons that explode using the energy released by atoms EG *nuclear war.* **3** relating to the structure and behaviour of the nuclei of atoms EG *nuclear physics.*

nuclear reactor nuclear reactors
NOUN A nuclear reactor is a device which is used to obtain nuclear energy.

nucleus nuclei
Said "nyoo-klee-uss" NOUN **1** the central part of an atom or cell. **2** The nucleus of something is the basic central part of it to which other things are added EG *They have retained the nucleus of the team that won the World Cup.*
🔟 from Latin *nucleus* meaning 'kernel'

nude nudes
ADJECTIVE **1** naked. ▶ NOUN **2** a picture or statue of a naked person.
nudity NOUN

nudge nudges nudging nudged
VERB **1** If you nudge someone, you push them gently, usually with your elbow. ▶ NOUN **2** a gentle push.

nudist nudists
NOUN a person who believes in wearing no clothes.

nugget nuggets
NOUN a small rough lump of something, especially gold.

nuisance nuisances
NOUN someone or something that is annoying or inconvenient.
▣ bother, inconvenience, problem

null
PHRASE **Null and void** means not legally valid EG *Other documents were declared to be null and void.*

nulla-nulla nulla-nullas
NOUN a thick heavy stick used as a weapon by Australian Aborigines.

numb numbs numbing numbed
ADJECTIVE **1** unable to feel anything EG *My legs felt numb... numb with grief.* ▶ VERB **2** If something numbs you, it makes you unable to feel anything EG *The cold numbed my fingers.*

numbat numbats
NOUN a small Australian marsupial with a long snout and tongue and strong claws which it uses for hunting and eating insects.

number numbers numbering numbered
NOUN **1** a word or a symbol used for counting or calculating. **2** Someone's number is the series of numbers that you dial when you telephone them. **3** A number of things is a quantity of them EG *Adrian has introduced me to a large number of people.* **4** a song or piece of music. ▶ VERB **5** If things number a particular amount, there are that many of them EG *At that time London's population numbered about*

460,000. **6** If you number something, you give it a number EG *The picture is signed and numbered by the artist.* **7** To be numbered among a particular group means to belong to it EG *Only the best are numbered among their champions.*
▇ (sense 1) digit, figure, numeral

What do Numbers do?

Numbers tell you how many of a thing there are.

Cardinal numbers tell you the total number of a thing.
Three figures huddled in the doorway.

Ordinal numbers tell you the order of something. They often end with the letters *-th.*
Her sixth novel was the most successful yet.

---

numeral numerals
NOUN a symbol that represents a number EG *a wristwatch with Roman numerals.*

numerical
ADJECTIVE expressed in numbers or relating to numbers EG *a numerical value.*

numerous
ADJECTIVE existing or happening in large numbers.

nun nuns
NOUN a woman who has taken religious vows and lives in a convent.

nurse nurses nursing nursed
NOUN **1** a person whose job is to look after people who are ill. ▶ VERB **2** If you nurse someone, you look after them when they are ill. **3** If you nurse a feeling, you feel it strongly for a long time EG *He nursed a grudge against the USA.*

nursery nurseries
NOUN **1** a place where young children are looked after while their parents are working. **2** a room

in which young children sleep and play. **3** a place where plants are grown and sold.

nursery school nursery schools
NOUN a school for children from three to five years old.

nursing home nursing homes
NOUN a privately run hospital, especially for old people.

nurture nurtures nurturing nurtured
VERB; A FORMAL WORD If you nurture a young child or a plant, you look after it carefully.

nut nuts
NOUN **1** a fruit with a hard shell and an edible centre that grows on certain trees. **2** a piece of metal with a hole in the middle which a bolt screws into.

nutmeg
NOUN Nutmeg is a spice used for flavouring in cooking.

nutrient nutrients
NOUN Nutrients are substances that help plants or animals to grow EG *the nutrients in the soil.*

nutrition
NOUN Nutrition is the food that you eat, considered from the point of view of how it helps you to grow and remain healthy EG *The effects of poor nutrition are evident.*
nutritionist NOUN

nutritious
ADJECTIVE containing substances that help you to grow and remain healthy.

nutty nuttier nuttiest
ADJECTIVE **1** AN INFORMAL USE mad or very foolish. **2** tasting of nuts.

nylon nylons
NOUN **1** Nylon is a type of strong artificial material EG *nylon stockings.* **2** Nylons are stockings or tights.

oaf oafs

NOUN a clumsy and stupid person.
📖 from Old Norse *alfr* meaning 'elf'

oak oaks

NOUN a large tree which produces acorns. It has a hard wood which is often used to make furniture.

OAP OAPs

NOUN In Britain, a man over the age of 65 or a woman over the age of 60 who receives a pension. OAP is an abbreviation for 'old age pensioner'.

oar oars

NOUN a wooden pole with a wide, flat end, used for rowing a boat.

oasis oases

Said "oh-**ay**-siss" NOUN a small area in a desert where water and plants are found.

oat oats

NOUN Oats are a type of grain.

oath oaths

NOUN a formal promise, especially a promise to tell the truth in a court of law.
📕 pledge, promise, vow

oatmeal

NOUN Oatmeal is a rough flour made from oats.

OBE OBEs

NOUN a British honour awarded by the King or Queen. OBE is an abbreviation for 'Officer of the Order of the British Empire'.

obedient

ADJECTIVE If you are obedient, you do what you are told to do.
obediently ADVERB, **obedience** NOUN

obelisk obelisks

NOUN a stone pillar built in honour of a person or an event.

obese

Said "oh-**bees**" ADJECTIVE extremely fat.
obesity NOUN
📖 from Latin *ob-* meaning 'much'

and *edere* meaning 'to eat'

obey obeys obeying obeyed

VERB If you obey a person or an order, you do what you are told to do.

obituary obituaries

NOUN a piece of writing about the life and achievements of someone who has just died.

object objects objecting objected

NOUN **1** anything solid that you can touch or see, and that is not alive. **2** an aim or purpose. **3** The object of your feelings or actions is the person that they are directed towards. **4** In grammar, the object of a verb or preposition is the word or phrase which follows it and describes the person or thing affected. ▶ VERB **5** If you object to something, you dislike it or disapprove of it.
📕 (sense 5) oppose, protest, take exception

objection objections

NOUN If you have an objection to something, you dislike it or disapprove of it.

objectionable

ADJECTIVE unpleasant and offensive.

objective objectives

NOUN **1** an aim EG *The protection of the countryside is their main objective.*
▶ ADJECTIVE **2** If you are objective, you are not influenced by personal feelings or prejudices EG *an objective approach.*
objectively ADVERB, **objectivity** NOUN

obligation obligations

NOUN something that you must do because it is your duty.

obligatory

Said "ob-**lig**-a-tree" ADJECTIVE required by a rule or law EG *Religious education was made obligatory.*

oblige obliges obliging obliged

VERB **1** If you are obliged to do

A B C D E F G H I J K L M N O P Q R S T U V W X Y Z

something, you have to do it. **2** If you oblige someone, you help them.
obliging ADJECTIVE

oblique
Said "o-**bleek**" ADJECTIVE **1** An oblique remark is not direct, and is therefore difficult to understand. **2** An oblique line slopes at an angle.

obliterate obliterates obliterating obliterated
VERB To obliterate something is to destroy it completely.
obliteration NOUN

oblivion
NOUN Oblivion is unconsciousness or complete unawareness of your surroundings.
oblivious ADJECTIVE, **obliviously** ADVERB

oblong oblongs
NOUN **1** a four-sided shape with two parallel short sides, two parallel long sides, and four right angles.
▶ ADJECTIVE **2** shaped like an oblong.

obnoxious
Said "ob-**nok**-shuss" ADJECTIVE extremely unpleasant.

oboe oboes
NOUN a woodwind musical instrument with a double reed.
oboist NOUN
🔲 from French *haut bois* meaning literally 'high wood', a reference to the instrument's pitch

obscene
ADJECTIVE indecent and likely to upset people EG *obscene pictures*.
obscenely ADVERB, **obscenity** NOUN
■ filthy, indecent, pornographic

obscure obscures obscuring obscured
ADJECTIVE **1** Something that is obscure is known by only a few people EG *an obscure Mongolian dialect*. **2** Something obscure is difficult to see or to understand EG *The news was shrouded in obscure language*. ▶ VERB **3** To obscure something is to make it difficult to see or understand EG *His view was obscured by trees*.

obscurity NOUN
■ (sense 2) cryptic, unclear, vague

observance
NOUN The observance of a law or custom is the practice of obeying or following it.

observant
ADJECTIVE Someone who is observant notices things that are not easy to see.

observation observations
NOUN **1** Observation is the act of watching carefully EG *Success hinges on close observation*. **2** something that you have seen or noticed. **3** a remark. **4** Observation is the ability to notice things that are not easy to see.

observatory observatories
NOUN a room or building containing telescopes and other equipment for studying the sun, moon, and stars.

observe observes observing observed
VERB **1** To observe something is to watch it carefully. **2** To observe something is to notice it. **3** If you observe that something is the case, you make a comment about it. **4** To observe a law or custom is to obey or follow it.
observer NOUN, **observable** ADJECTIVE

obsession obsessions
NOUN If someone has an obsession about something, they cannot stop thinking about that thing.
obsessional ADJECTIVE, **obsessed** ADJECTIVE, **obsessive** ADJECTIVE

obsolete
ADJECTIVE out of date and no longer used.
■ outmoded, passé

obstacle obstacles
NOUN something which is in your way and makes it difficult to do something.
■ difficulty, stumbling block

obstetrics
NOUN Obstetrics is the branch of medicine concerned with

pregnancy and childbirth.
obstetrician NOUN

obstinate
ADJECTIVE Someone who is obstinate is stubborn and unwilling to change their mind.
obstinately ADVERB, **obstinacy** NOUN

obstruct obstructs obstructing obstructed
VERB If something obstructs a road or path, it blocks it.
obstruction NOUN, **obstructive** ADJECTIVE

obtain obtains obtaining obtained
VERB If you obtain something, you get it.
obtainable ADJECTIVE

obtrusive
ADJECTIVE noticeable in an unpleasant way EG *a remarkably obtrusive cigar*.

obtuse
ADJECTIVE 1 Someone who is obtuse is stupid or slow to understand things. 2 An obtuse angle is an angle between 90° and 180°.

obvious
ADJECTIVE easy to see or understand.
obviously ADVERB
■ clear, evident, plain

occasion occasions occasioning occasioned
NOUN 1 a time when something happens. 2 an important event. 3 An occasion for doing something is an opportunity for doing it.
▶ VERB 4 A FORMAL USE To occasion something is to cause it EG *damage occasioned by fire*.

occasional
ADJECTIVE happening sometimes but not often EG *an occasional outing*.
occasionally ADVERB

occult
NOUN The occult is the knowledge and study of supernatural and magical forces or powers.

occupancy
NOUN The occupancy of a building is the act of living or working in it.

occupant occupants

NOUN The occupants of a building are the people who live or work in it.

occupation occupations
NOUN 1 a job or profession. 2 a hobby or something you do for pleasure. 3 The occupation of a country is the act of invading it and taking control of it.
occupational ADJECTIVE

occupy occupies occupying occupied
VERB 1 The people who occupy a building are the people who live or work there. 2 When people occupy a place, they move into it and take control of it EG *Demonstrators occupied the building*. 3 To occupy a position in a system or plan is to have that position EG *His phone-in show occupies a daytime slot*. 4 If something occupies you, you spend your time doing it EG *That problem occupies me night and day*.
occupier NOUN

occur occurs occurring occurred
VERB 1 If something occurs, it happens or exists EG *The second attack occurred at a swimming pool*. 2 If something occurs to you, you suddenly think of it.
✓ If an event has been planned, you should not say that it *occurred* or *happened*: *the wedding took place on Saturday*. Only something unexpected *occurs* or *happens*: *an accident has occurred; the burglary happened last night*.

occurrence occurrences
NOUN 1 an event. 2 The occurrence of something is the fact that it happens or exists EG *the occurrence of diseases*.

ocean oceans
NOUN 1 A LITERARY USE the sea. 2 The five oceans are the five very large areas of sea EG *the Atlantic Ocean*.
oceanic ADJECTIVE

o'clock
ADVERB You use 'o'clock' after the number of the hour to say what

A
B
C
D
E
F
G
H
I
J
K
L
M
N
O
P
Q
R
S
T
U
V
W
X
Y
Z

the time is.

octagon octagons
NOUN a shape with eight straight
sides.
octagonal ADJECTIVE

octave octaves
NOUN the difference in pitch
between the first note and the
eighth note of a musical scale.

October
NOUN October is the tenth month of
the year. It has 31 days.
🏛 from Latin *october* meaning 'the
eighth month'

octopus octopuses
NOUN a sea creature with eight long
tentacles which it uses to catch
food.
🏛 from Greek *okto* + *pous* meaning
'eight feet'

odd odder oddest; odds
ADJECTIVE 1 Something odd is strange
or unusual. 2 Odd things do not
match each other EG *odd socks*.
3 Odd numbers are numbers that
cannot be divided exactly by two.
▶ ADVERB 4 You use 'odd' after a
number to say that it is
approximate EG *I've written twenty
odd plays*. ▶ PLURAL NOUN 5 In
gambling, the probability of
something happening is called the
odds EG *The odds are against the record
being beaten*.
oddly ADVERB, **oddness** NOUN

oddity oddities
NOUN something very strange.

oddments
PLURAL NOUN Oddments are things
that are left over after other things
have been used.

odds and ends
PLURAL NOUN You can refer to a
collection of small unimportant
things as odds and ends.

ode odes
NOUN a poem written in praise of
someone or something.

odious
ADJECTIVE extremely unpleasant.

odour odours
NOUN; A FORMAL WORD a strong smell.
odorous ADJECTIVE

odyssey odysseys
Said "**od**-i-see" NOUN a long and
eventful journey.

oesophagus oesophaguses
Said "ee-**sof**-fag-uss" NOUN the tube
that carries food from your throat
to your stomach.

oestrogen
another spelling of **estrogen**.

of
PREPOSITION 1 consisting of or
containing EG *a collection of short
stories... a cup of tea*. 2 used when
naming something or describing a
characteristic of something EG *the
city of Canberra... a woman of great
power and influence*. 3 belonging to
or connected with EG *a friend of
Rachel... the cover of the book*.
✓ Where *of* means 'belonging to',
it can be replaced by an
apostrophe: *the cover of the book* is
the same as *the book's cover*.

off
PREPOSITION OR ADVERB 1 indicating
movement away from or out of a
place EG *They had just stepped off the
plane... She got up and marched off*.
2 indicating separation or distance
from a place EG *some islands off the
coast of Australia... The whole crescent
has been fenced off*. 3 not working EG
It was Frank's night off. ▶ ADVERB OR
ADJECTIVE 4 not switched on EG *He
turned the radio off... the off switch*.
▶ ADJECTIVE 5 cancelled or postponed
EG *The concert was off*. 6 Food that is
off has gone sour or bad.
▶ PREPOSITION 7 not liking or not
using something EG *He went right off
alcohol*.
✓ Do not use *of* after *off*. You
should say *he stepped off the bus* not
he stepped off of the bus. It is very
informal to use *off* where you mean
'from': *they bought milk off a farmer*
instead of *they bought milk from a
farmer*. Always use *from* in written

work.

offal

NOUN Offal is liver, kidneys, and other parts of animals, which can be eaten.

offence offences

NOUN **1** a crime EG *a drink-driving offence.* ▶ PHRASES **2** If something **gives offence**, it upsets people. If you **take offence**, you are upset by someone or something.

offend offends offending offended

VERB **1** If you offend someone, you upset them. **2** A FORMAL USE To offend or to offend a law is to commit a crime.

offender NOUN

offensive offensives

ADJECTIVE **1** Something offensive is rude and upsetting EG *offensive behaviour.* **2** Offensive actions or weapons are used in attacking someone. ▶ NOUN **3** an attack EG *a full-scale offensive against the rebels.*

offensively ADVERB

offer offers offering offered

VERB **1** If you offer something to someone, you ask them if they would like it. ▶ NOUN **2** something that someone says they will give you or do for you if you want them to EG *He refused the offer of a drink.* **3** a specially low price for a product in a shop EG *You will need a voucher to qualify for the special offer.*

offering offerings

NOUN something that is offered or given to someone.

offhand

ADJECTIVE **1** If someone is offhand, they are unfriendly and slightly rude. ▶ ADVERB **2** If you know something offhand, you know it without having to think very hard EG *I couldn't tell you offhand how long he's been here.*

office offices

NOUN **1** a room where people work at desks. **2** a government department EG *the Office of Fair Trading.* **3** a place where people can go for information, tickets, or other services. **4** Someone who holds office has an important job or position in government or in an organization.

officer officers

NOUN a person with a position of authority in the armed forces, the police, or a government organization.

official officials

ADJECTIVE **1** approved by the government or by someone in authority EG *the official figures.* **2** done or used by someone in authority as part of their job EG *official notepaper.* ▶ NOUN **3** a person who holds a position of authority in an organization.

officially ADVERB

officialdom

NOUN You can refer to officials in government or other organizations as officialdom, especially when you find them unhelpful and unfriendly.

officiate officiates officiating officiated

VERB To officiate at a ceremony is to be in charge and perform the official part of the ceremony.

offing

PHRASE If something is **in the offing**, it is likely to happen soon EG *A change is in the offing.*

off-licence off-licences

NOUN a shop which sells alcoholic drinks.

offset offsets offsetting offset

VERB If one thing is offset by another thing, its effect is reduced or cancelled out by that thing EG *This tedium can be offset by watching the television.*

offshoot offshoots

NOUN something that has developed from another thing EG *The technology we use is an offshoot of the motor industry.*

A
B
C
D
E
F
G
H
I
J
K
L
M
N
O
P
Q
R
S
T
U
V
W
X
Y
Z

offshore

ADJECTIVE OR ADVERB in or from the part of the sea near the shore EG *an offshore wind... a wreck fifteen kilometres offshore.*

offside

ADJECTIVE **1** If a soccer, rugby, or hockey player is offside, they have broken the rules by moving too far forward. ▶ NOUN **2** the side of a vehicle that is furthest from the pavement.

offspring

NOUN A person's or animal's offspring are their children.

often

ADVERB happening many times or a lot of the time.

ogle ogles ogling ogled

Said "oh-gl" VERB To ogle someone is to stare at them in a way that indicates a sexual interest.

ogre ogres

Said "oh-gur" NOUN a cruel, frightening giant in a fairy story.

ohm ohms

Rhymes with "home" NOUN In physics, an ohm is a unit used to measure electrical resistance.

oil oils oiling oiled

NOUN **1** Oil is a thick, sticky liquid used as a fuel and for lubrication. **2** Oil is also a thick, greasy liquid made from plants or animals EG *cooking oil... bath oil.* ▶ VERB **3** If you oil something, you put oil in it or on it.

oil painting oil paintings

NOUN a picture that has been painted with thick paints made from coloured powder and a kind of oil.

oilskin oilskins

NOUN a piece of clothing made from a thick, waterproof material, worn especially by fishermen.

oily

ADJECTIVE Something that is oily is covered with or contains oil EG *an oily rag... oily skin.*

ointment ointments

NOUN a smooth, thick substance that you put on sore skin to heal it.

okay or **OK**

ADJECTIVE OR ADVERB; AN INFORMAL WORD
Okay means all right EG *Tell me if this sounds okay.*
■ acceptable, all right, satisfactory

old older oldest

ADJECTIVE **1** having lived or existed for a long time EG *an old lady... old clothes.* **2** 'Old' is used to give the age of someone or something EG *This photo is five years old.* **3** 'Old' also means former EG *my old art teacher.*

olden

PHRASE In the olden days means long ago.

Old English

NOUN Old English was the English language from the fifth century AD until about 1100. Old English is also known as Anglo-Saxon.

old-fashioned

ADJECTIVE **1** Something which is old-fashioned is no longer fashionable EG *old-fashioned shoes.* **2** Someone who is old-fashioned believes in the values and standards of the past.
■ (sense 1) dated, outmoded, passé

Old Norse

NOUN Old Norse was a language spoken in Scandinavia and Iceland from about 700 AD to about 1350 AD. Many English words are derived from Old Norse.

Old Testament

NOUN The Old Testament is the first part of the Christian Bible. It is also the holy book of the Jewish religion and contains writings which relate to the history of the Jews.

oleander oleanders

NOUN an evergreen shrub with fragrant white, pink, or purple flowers.

olive olives

NOUN **1** a small green or black fruit containing a stone. Olives are usually pickled and eaten as a snack or crushed to produce oil. ▶ ADJECTIVE OR NOUN **2** dark yellowish-green.

-ology
SUFFIX -ology is used to form words that refer to the study of something EG *biology... geology.*
📖 from Greek *logos* meaning 'reason', 'speech', or 'discourse'

Olympic Games
Said "ol-**lim**-pik" PLURAL NOUN The Olympic Games are a set of sporting contests held in a different city every four years.

ombudsman ombudsmen
NOUN The ombudsman is a person who investigates complaints against the government or a public organization.

omelette omelettes
Said "**om**-lit" NOUN a dish made by beating eggs together and cooking them in a flat pan.

omen omens
NOUN something that is thought to be a sign of what will happen in the future EG *John saw this success as a good omen for his trip.*
📗 portent, sign

ominous
ADJECTIVE suggesting that something unpleasant is going to happen EG *an ominous sign.*
ominously ADVERB
📗 sinister, threatening

omission omissions
NOUN **1** something that has not been included or done EG *There are some striking omissions in the survey.* **2** Omission is the act of not including or not doing something EG *controversy over the omission of female novelists.*

omit omits omitting omitted
VERB **1** If you omit something, you do not include it. **2** A FORMAL USE If you omit to do something, you do not do it.

omnibus omnibuses
NOUN **1** a book containing a collection of stories or articles by the same author or about the same subject. ▶ ADJECTIVE **2** An omnibus edition of a radio or television show contains two or more programmes that were originally broadcast separately.

omnipotent
Said "om-**nip**-a-tent" ADJECTIVE having very great or unlimited power EG *omnipotent emperors.*
omnipotence NOUN

omnivore
NOUN An omnivore is an animal that eats all kinds of food, including meat and plants.
omnivorous ADJECTIVE

on
PREPOSITION **1** touching or attached to something EG *The woman was sitting on the sofa.* **2** If you are on a bus, plane, or train, you are inside it. **3** If something happens on a particular day, that is when it happens EG *It is his birthday on Monday.* **4** If something is done on an instrument or machine, it is done using that instrument or machine EG *He preferred to play on his computer.* **5** A book or talk on a particular subject is about that subject. ▶ ADVERB **6** If you have a piece of clothing on, you are wearing it. ▶ ADJECTIVE **7** A machine or switch that is on is working. **8** If an event is on, it is happening or taking place EG *The race is definitely on.*

once
ADVERB **1** If something happens once, it happens one time only. **2** If something was once true, it was true in the past, but is no longer true. ▶ CONJUNCTION **3** If something happens once another thing has happened, it happens immediately afterwards EG *Once you get used to working for yourself, it's tough working for anybody else.* ▶ PHRASES **4** If you do something **at once**, you do it

immediately. If several things happen **at once**, they all happen at the same time.

one ones

1 One is the number 1. ▶ ADJECTIVE 2 If you refer to the one person or thing of a particular kind, you mean the only person or thing of that kind EG *My one aim is to look after the horses well.* 3 One also means 'a'; used when emphasizing something EG *They got one almighty shock.* ▶ PRONOUN 4 One refers to a particular thing or person EG *Alf Brown's business was a good one.* 5 One also means people in general EG *One likes to have the opportunity to chat.*

one-off one-offs

NOUN something that happens or is made only once.

onerous

Said "ohn-er-uss" ADJECTIVE; A FORMAL WORD difficult or unpleasant EG *an onerous task.*

oneself

PRONOUN 'Oneself' is used when you are talking about people in general EG *One could hardly hear oneself talk.*

one-sided

ADJECTIVE 1 If an activity or relationship is one-sided, one of the people has a lot more success or involvement than the other EG *a one-sided contest.* 2 A one-sided argument or report considers the facts or a situation from only one point of view.

one-way

ADJECTIVE 1 One-way streets are streets along which vehicles can drive in only one direction. 2 A one-way ticket is one that you can use to travel to a place, but not to travel back again.

ongoing

ADJECTIVE continuing to happen EG *an ongoing process of learning.*

onion onions

NOUN a small, round vegetable with a brown, papery skin and a very strong taste.

onlooker onlookers

NOUN someone who is watching an event.

only

ADVERB 1 You use 'only' to indicate the one thing or person involved EG *Only Keith knows whether he will continue.* 2 You use 'only' to emphasize that something is unimportant or small EG *He's only a little boy.* 3 You can use 'only' to introduce something which happens immediately after something else EG *She had thought of one plan, only to discard it for another.* ▶ ADJECTIVE 4 If you talk about the only thing or person, you mean that there are no others EG *their only hit single.* 5 If you are an only child, you have no brothers or sisters. ▶ CONJUNCTION 6 'Only' also means but or except EG *He was like you, only blond.* ▶ PHRASE 7 **Only too** means extremely EG *I would be only too happy to swap places.*

onomatopoeia

Said "on-o-mat-o-**pee**-a" NOUN Onomatopoeia is the use of words which sound like the thing that they represent. 'Hiss' and 'buzz' are examples of onomatopoeia.
📖 from Greek *onoma* meaning 'name' and *poiein* meaning 'to make'

onset

NOUN The onset of something unpleasant is the beginning of it EG *the onset of war.*

onslaught onslaughts

Said "on-slawt" NOUN a violent attack.

onto or **on to**

PREPOSITION If you put something onto an object, you put it on it.

onus

Rhymes with "**bonus**" NOUN; A FORMAL WORD If the onus is on you to do something, it is your duty to do it.

onwards or **onward**

ADVERB 1 continuing to happen from

a particular time EG *He could not speak a word from that moment onwards.* **2** travelling forwards EG *Duncliffe escorted the pair onwards to his own room.*

onyx
Said "**on-iks**" NOUN Onyx is a semiprecious stone used for making ornaments and jewellery.

ooze oozes oozing oozed
VERB When a thick liquid oozes, it flows slowly EG *The cold mud oozed over her new footwear.*

opal opals
NOUN a pale or whitish semiprecious stone used for making jewellery.

opaque
Said "**oh-pake**" ADJECTIVE If something is opaque, you cannot see through it EG *opaque glass windows.*

open opens opening opened
VERB **1** When you open something, or when it opens, you move it so that it is no longer closed EG *She opened the door.* **2** When a shop or office opens, people are able to go in. **3** To open something also means to start it EG *He tried to open a bank account.* ▶ ADJECTIVE **4** Something that is open is not closed or fastened EG *an open box of chocolates.* **5** If you have an open mind, you are willing to consider new ideas or suggestions. **6** Someone who is open is honest and frank. **7** When a shop or office is open, people are able to go in. **8** An open area of sea or land is a large, empty area EG *open country.* **9** If something is open to you, it is possible for you to do it EG *There is no other course open to us but to fight it out.* **10** If a situation is still open, it is still being considered EG *Even if the case remains open, the full facts may never be revealed.* ▶ PHRASE **11** In the open means outside. **12** In the open also means not secret.
openly ADVERB

opening openings

ADJECTIVE **1** Opening means coming first EG *the opening day of the season.* ▶ NOUN **2** The opening of a book or film is the first part of it. **3** a hole or gap. **4** an opportunity EG *The two men circled around, looking for an opening to attack.*
■ (sense 3) aperture, gap, hole

open-minded
ADJECTIVE willing to consider new ideas and suggestions.

open-plan
ADJECTIVE An open-plan office or building has very few dividing walls inside.

opera operas
NOUN a play in which the words are sung rather than spoken.
operatic ADJECTIVE
🏛 from Latin *opera* meaning 'works'

operate operates operating operated
VERB **1** To operate is to work EG *We are shocked at the way that businesses operate.* **2** When you operate a machine, you make it work. **3** When surgeons operate, they cut open a patient's body to remove or repair a damaged part.

operation operations
NOUN **1** a complex, planned event EG *a full-scale military operation.* **2** a form of medical treatment in which a surgeon cuts open a patient's body to remove or repair a damaged part. ▶ PHRASE **3** If something is in operation, it is working or being used EG *The system is in operation from April to the end of September.*

operational
ADJECTIVE working or able to be used EG *an operational aircraft.*

operative
ADJECTIVE Something that is operative is working or having an effect.

operator operators
NOUN **1** someone who works at a telephone exchange or on a

A B C D E F G H I J K L M N O P Q R S T U V W X Y Z

A
B
C
D
E
F
G
H
I
J
K
L
M
N
O
P
Q
R
S
T
U
V
W
X
Y
Z

switchboard. **2** someone who operates a machine EG *a computer operator*. **3** someone who runs a business EG *a tour operator*.

opinion opinions
NOUN a belief or view.
■ belief, judgment, view

opinionated
ADJECTIVE Someone who is opinionated has strong views and refuses to accept that they might be wrong.

opium
NOUN Opium is a drug made from the seeds of a poppy. It is used in medicine to relieve pain.
🔳 from Latin *opium* meaning 'poppy juice'

opponent opponents
NOUN someone who is against you in an argument or a contest.

opportune
ADJECTIVE; A FORMAL WORD happening at a convenient time EG *The king's death was opportune for the prince*.

opportunism
NOUN Opportunism is taking advantage of any opportunity to gain money or power for yourself.
opportunist NOUN

opportunity opportunities
NOUN a chance to do something.

oppose opposes opposing opposed
VERB If you oppose something, you disagree with it and try to prevent it.

opposed
ADJECTIVE **1** If you are opposed to something, you disagree with it EG *He was totally opposed to bullying in schools*. **2** Opposed also means opposite or very different EG *two opposed schools of thought*. ▶ PHRASE **3** If you refer to one thing **as opposed to** another, you are emphasizing that it is the first thing rather than the second which concerns you EG *Real spectators, as opposed to invited guests, were hard to*

spot.

opposite opposites
PREPOSITION OR ADVERB **1** If one thing is opposite another, it is facing it EG *the shop opposite the station... the house opposite*. ▶ ADJECTIVE **2** The opposite part of something is the part farthest away from you EG *the opposite side of town*. **3** If things are opposite, they are completely different EG *I take the opposite view to you*. ▶ NOUN **4** If two things are completely different, they are opposites.
■ (sense 4) antithesis, contrary, reverse

opposition
NOUN **1** If there is opposition to something, people disagree with it and try to prevent it. **2** The political parties who are not in power are referred to as the Opposition. **3** In a game or sports event, the opposition is the person or team that you are competing against.

oppressed
ADJECTIVE People who are oppressed are treated cruelly or unfairly.
oppress VERB, **oppression** NOUN, **oppressor** NOUN

oppressive
ADJECTIVE **1** If the weather is oppressive, it is hot and humid. **2** An oppressive situation makes you feel depressed or concerned EG *The silence became oppressive*. **3** An oppressive system treats people cruelly or unfairly EG *Married women were subject to oppressive laws*.
oppressively ADVERB

opt opts opting opted
VERB If you opt for something, you choose it. If you opt out of something, you choose not to be involved in it.

optical
ADJECTIVE **1** concerned with vision, light, or images EG *an optical scanner*. **2** relating to the appearance of things EG *an optical illusion*.

optic ADJECTIVE

optician opticians
NOUN someone who tests people's eyes, and makes and sells glasses and contact lenses.

optimism
NOUN Optimism is a feeling of hopefulness about the future.
optimist NOUN, **optimistic** ADJECTIVE, **optimistically** ADVERB

optimum
ADJECTIVE the best that is possible EG *Six is the optimum number of participants for a good meeting.*

option options
NOUN a choice between two or more things.
optional ADJECTIVE

opulent
Said "op-yool-nt" ADJECTIVE grand and expensive-looking EG *an opulent seafront estate.*

opus opera
NOUN an artistic work, especially a piece of music.

or
CONJUNCTION **1** used to link two different things EG *I didn't know whether to laugh or cry.* **2** used to introduce a warning EG *Do what I say or else I will fire.*

oracle oracles
NOUN **1** In ancient Greece, an oracle was a place where a priest or priestess made predictions about the future. **2** a prophecy made by a priest or other person with great authority or wisdom.

oral orals
ADJECTIVE **1** spoken rather than written EG *oral history.* **2** Oral describes things that are used in your mouth or done with your mouth EG *an oral vaccine.* ▶ NOUN **3** an examination that is spoken rather than written.
orally ADVERB
■ (sense 1) spoken, verbal

orange oranges
NOUN **1** a round citrus fruit that is juicy and sweet and has a thick reddish-yellow skin. ▶ ADJECTIVE OR NOUN **2** reddish-yellow.
▣ from Sanskrit *naranga* meaning 'orange'

orang-utan orang-utans; also spelt **orang-utang**
NOUN a large ape with reddish-brown hair.

orator orators
NOUN someone who is good at making speeches.

oratory
NOUN Oratory is the art and skill of making formal public speeches.

orbit orbits orbiting orbited
NOUN **1** the curved path followed by an object going round a planet or the sun. ▶ VERB **2** If something orbits a planet or the sun, it goes round and round it.

orchard orchards
NOUN a piece of land where fruit trees are grown.

orchestra orchestras
Said "or-kess-tra" NOUN a large group of musicians who play musical instruments together.
orchestral ADJECTIVE
▣ from Greek *orkhestra* meaning 'the area in a theatre reserved for musicians'

orchestrate orchestrates orchestrating orchestrated
VERB **1** To orchestrate something is to organize it very carefully in order to produce a particular result. **2** To orchestrate a piece of music is to rewrite it so that it can be played by an orchestra.
orchestration NOUN

orchid orchids
Said "or-kid" NOUN Orchids are plants with beautiful and unusual flowers.

ordain ordains ordaining ordained
VERB When someone is ordained, they are made a member of the clergy.

ordeal ordeals

A B C D E F G H I J K L M N O P Q R S T U V W X Y Z

NOUN a difficult and extremely unpleasant experience EG *the ordeal of being arrested and charged with attempted murder.*
■ hardship, torture, tribulation

order orders ordering ordered
NOUN **1** a command given by someone in authority. **2** If things are arranged or done in a particular order, they are arranged or done in that sequence EG *in alphabetical order.* **3** Order is a situation in which everything is in the correct place or done at the correct time. **4** something that you ask to be brought to you or sent to you. ▶ VERB **5** To order someone to do something is to tell them firmly to do it. **6** When you order something, you ask for it to be brought or sent to you. ▶ PHRASE **7** If you do something **in order to** achieve a particular thing, you do it because you want to achieve that thing.

orderly
ADJECTIVE Something that is orderly is well organized or arranged.
■ methodical, well-organized

ordinarily
ADVERB If something ordinarily happens, it usually happens.

ordinary
ADJECTIVE Ordinary means not special or different in any way.
■ conventional, normal, usual

ordination
NOUN When someone's ordination takes place, they are made a member of the clergy.

ordnance
NOUN Weapons and other military supplies are referred to as ordnance.

ore ores
NOUN Ore is rock or earth from which metal can be obtained.

oregano
Said "or-rig-**garh**-no" NOUN Oregano is a herb used for flavouring in cooking.

organ organs
NOUN **1** Your organs are parts of your body that have a particular function, for example your heart or lungs. **2** a large musical instrument with pipes of different lengths through which air is forced. It has various keyboards which are played like a piano.

organic
ADJECTIVE **1** Something that is organic is produced by or found in plants or animals EG *decaying organic matter.* **2** Organic food is produced without the use of artificial fertilizers or pesticides.
organically ADVERB

organism organisms
NOUN any living animal or plant.

organist organists
NOUN someone who plays the organ.

organization organizations; also spelt **organisation**
NOUN **1** any group or business. **2** The organization of something is the act of planning and arranging it.
organizational ADJECTIVE
■ (sense 1) body, company, group

organize organizes organizing organized; also spelt **organise**
VERB **1** If you organize an event, you plan and arrange it. **2** If you organize things, you arrange them in a sensible order.
organized ADJECTIVE, **organizer** NOUN

orgasm orgasms
NOUN the moment of greatest pleasure and excitement during sexual activity.

orgy orgies
Said "**or**-jee" NOUN **1** a wild, uncontrolled party involving a lot of drinking and sexual activity. **2** You can refer to a period of intense activity as an orgy of that activity EG *an orgy of violence.*
▥ from Greek *orgia* meaning 'nocturnal festival'

orient
NOUN; A LITERARY USE The Orient is eastern and south-eastern Asia.

oriental
ADJECTIVE relating to eastern or south-eastern Asia.

orientated
ADJECTIVE If someone is interested in a particular thing, you can say that they are orientated towards it EG *These men are very career-orientated.*

orientation
NOUN You can refer to an organization's activities and aims as its orientation EG *Poland's political and military orientation.*

oriented
ADJECTIVE Oriented means the same as orientated.

orienteering
NOUN Orienteering is a sport in which people run from one place to another in the countryside, using a map and compass to guide them.

origin origins
NOUN 1 You can refer to the beginning or cause of something as its origin or origins. 2 You can refer to someone's family background as their origin or origins EG *She was of Swedish origin.*
■ (sense 1) root, source

original originals
ADJECTIVE 1 Original describes things that existed at the beginning, rather than being added later, or things that were the first of their kind to exist EG *the original owner of the cottage.* 2 Original means imaginative and clever EG *a stunningly original idea.* ▶ NOUN 3 a work of art or a document that is the one that was first produced, and not a copy.
originally ADVERB, originality NOUN

originate originates originating originated
VERB When something originates, or you originate it, it begins to happen or exist.
originator NOUN

ornament ornaments
NOUN a small, attractive object that you display in your home or that you wear in order to look attractive.

ornamental
ADJECTIVE designed to be attractive rather than useful EG *an ornamental lake.*

ornamentation
NOUN Ornamentation is decoration on a building, a piece of furniture, or a work of art.

ornate
ADJECTIVE Something that is ornate has a lot of decoration on it.

ornithology
NOUN Ornithology is the study of birds.
ornithologist NOUN
圖 from Greek *ornis* meaning 'bird' and *-logia* meaning 'study of'

orphan orphans orphaning orphaned
NOUN 1 a child whose parents are dead. ▶ VERB 2 If a child is orphaned, its parents die.

orphanage orphanages
NOUN a place where orphans are looked after.

orthodox
ADJECTIVE 1 Orthodox beliefs or methods are the ones that most people have or use and that are considered standard. 2 People who are orthodox believe in the older, more traditional ideas of their religion or political party. 3 The Orthodox church is the part of the Christian church which separated from the western European church in the 11th century and is the main church in Greece and Russia.
orthodoxy NOUN

osmosis
Said "oz-**moh**-siss" NOUN; A TECHNICAL USE Osmosis is the process by which a liquid moves through a semipermeable membrane from a weaker solution to a more concentrated one.

osprey ospreys
Said "**oss**-pree" NOUN a large bird of

prey which catches fish with its feet.

ostensibly

ADVERB If something is done ostensibly for a reason, that seems to be the reason for it EG *Byrnes submitted his resignation, ostensibly on medical grounds.*

ostentatious

ADJECTIVE **1** Something that is ostentatious is intended to impress people, for example by looking expensive EG *ostentatious sculptures.* **2** People who are ostentatious try to impress other people with their wealth or importance.

ostentatiously ADVERB, **ostentation** NOUN

ostrich ostriches

NOUN The ostrich is the largest bird in the world. Ostriches cannot fly.

other others

ADJECTIVE OR PRONOUN **1** Other people or things are different people or things EG *All the other children had gone home... One of the cabinets came from the palace; the other is a copy.*
▶ PHRASES **2 The other day** or **the other week** means recently EG *She had bought four pairs of shoes the other day.*

otherwise

ADVERB **1** You use 'otherwise' to say a different situation would exist if a particular fact or occurrence was not the case EG *You had to learn to swim pretty quickly, otherwise you sank.* **2** 'Otherwise' means apart from the thing mentioned EG *She had written to her daughter, but otherwise refused to take sides.* **3** 'Otherwise' also means in a different way EG *The majority voted otherwise.*

otter otters

NOUN a small, furry animal with a long tail. Otters swim well and eat fish.

ouch

INTERJECTION You say ouch when you suddenly feel pain.

ought

Said "awt" VERB If you say that someone ought to do something, you mean that they should do it EG *He ought to see a doctor.*

☑ Do not use *did* and *had* with *ought*: *He ought not to come* is correct: *he didn't ought to come* is not correct.

ounce ounces

NOUN a unit of weight equal to one sixteenth of a pound or about 28.35 grams.

our

ADJECTIVE 'Our' refers to something belonging or relating to the speaker or writer and one or more other people EG *We recently sold our house.*

ours

PRONOUN 'Ours' refers to something belonging or relating to the speaker or writer and one or more other people EG *a friend of ours from Korea.*

ourselves

PRONOUN **1** 'Ourselves' is used when the same speaker or writer and one or more other people do an action and are affected by it EG *We haven't damaged ourselves too badly.* **2** 'Ourselves' is used to emphasize 'we'.

oust ousts ousting ousted

VERB If you oust someone, you force them out of a job or a place EG *Cole was ousted from the board.*

out

ADVERB **1** towards the outside of a place EG *Two dogs rushed out of the house.* **2** not at home EG *She was out when I rang last night.* **3** in the open air EG *They are playing out in bright sunshine.* **4** no longer shining or burning EG *The lights went out.*
▶ ADJECTIVE **5** on strike EG *1000 construction workers are out in sympathy.* **6** unacceptable or unfashionable EG *Miniskirts are out.* **7** incorrect EG *Logan's timing was out in the first two rounds.*

out-and-out

ADJECTIVE entire or complete EG *an out-and-out lie.*

outback

NOUN In Australia, the outback is the remote parts where very few people live.

outboard motor outboard motors

NOUN a motor that can be fixed to the back of a small boat.

outbreak outbreaks

NOUN If there is an outbreak of something unpleasant, such as war, it suddenly occurs.

outburst outbursts

NOUN **1** a sudden, strong expression of an emotion, especially anger EG *John broke into an angry outburst about how unfairly the work was divided.* **2** a sudden occurrence of violent activity EG *an outburst of gunfire.*

outcast outcasts

NOUN someone who is rejected by other people.

outclassed

ADJECTIVE If you are outclassed, you are much worse than your opponent at a particular activity.

outcome outcomes

NOUN a result EG *the outcome of the election.*

outcrop outcrops

NOUN a large piece of rock that sticks out of the ground.

outcry outcries

NOUN If there is an outcry about something, a lot of people are angry about it EG *a public outcry over alleged fraud.*

outdated

ADJECTIVE no longer in fashion.

outdo outdoes outdoing outdid outdone

VERB If you outdo someone, you do a particular thing better than they do.

outdoor

ADJECTIVE happening or used outside EG *outdoor activities.*

outdoors

ADVERB outside EG *It was too chilly to sit outdoors.*

outer

ADJECTIVE The outer parts of something are the parts furthest from the centre EG *the outer door of the office.*

outer space

NOUN Outer space is everything beyond the Earth's atmosphere.

outfit outfits

NOUN **1** a set of clothes. **2** AN INFORMAL USE an organization.

outgoing outgoings

ADJECTIVE **1** Outgoing describes someone who is leaving a job or place EG *the outgoing President.* **2** Someone who is outgoing is friendly and not shy. ▶ PLURAL NOUN **3** Your outgoings are the amount of money that you spend.

outgrow outgrows outgrowing outgrew outgrown

VERB **1** If you outgrow a piece of clothing, you grow too big for it. **2** If you outgrow a way of behaving, you stop it because you have grown older and more mature.

outhouse outhouses

NOUN a small building in the grounds of a house to which it belongs.

outing outings

NOUN a trip made for pleasure.

outlandish

ADJECTIVE very unusual or odd EG *outlandish clothes.*

outlaw outlaws outlawing outlawed

VERB **1** If something is outlawed, it is made illegal. ▶ NOUN **2** In the past, an outlaw was a criminal.

outlay outlays

NOUN an amount of money spent on something EG *a cash outlay of 300 dollars.*

outlet outlets

NOUN **1** An outlet for your feelings or ideas is a way of expressing them. **2** a hole or pipe through which water or air can flow away. **3** a shop which sells goods made by

A B C D E F G H I J K L M N O P Q R S T U V W X Y Z

A
B
C
D
E
F
G
H
I
J
K
L
M
N
O
P
Q
R
S
T
U
V
W
X
Y
Z

a particular manufacturer.

outline outlines outlining outlined
VERB **1** If you outline a plan or idea,
you explain it in a general way.
2 You say that something is
outlined when you can see its
shape because there is a light
behind it. ▶ NOUN **3** a general
explanation or description of
something. **4** The outline of
something is its shape.

outlive outlives outliving outlived
VERB To outlive someone is to live
longer than they do.

outlook
NOUN **1** Your outlook is your general
attitude towards life. **2** The outlook
of a situation is the way it is likely
to develop EG *The Japanese economy's
outlook is uncertain.*

outlying
ADJECTIVE Outlying places are far
from cities.

outmoded
ADJECTIVE old-fashioned and no
longer useful EG *an outmoded form of
transport.*

outnumber outnumbers
outnumbering outnumbered
VERB If there are more of one group
than of another, the first group
outnumbers the second.

out of
PREPOSITION **1** If you do something
out of a particular feeling, you are
motivated by that feeling EG *Out of
curiosity she went along.* **2** 'Out of'
also means from EG *old instruments
made out of wood.* **3** If you are out of
something, you no longer have any
of it EG *I do hope we're not out of fuel
again.* **4** If you are out of the rain,
sun, or wind, you are sheltered
from it. **5** You also use 'out of' to
indicate proportion. For example,
one out of five means one in every
five.

out of date
ADJECTIVE old-fashioned and no
longer useful.

out of doors
ADVERB outside EG *Sometimes we eat out
of doors.*

outpatient outpatients
NOUN Outpatients are people who
receive treatment in hospital
without staying overnight.

outpost outposts
NOUN a small collection of buildings
a long way from a main centre EG *a
remote mountain outpost.*

output outputs
NOUN **1** Output is the amount of
something produced by a person or
organization. **2** The output of a
computer is the information that it
produces.

outrage outrages outraging
outraged
VERB **1** If something outrages you, it
angers and shocks you EG *I was
outraged at what had happened to her.*
▶ NOUN **2** Outrage is a feeling of
anger and shock. **3** something very
shocking or violent.
outrageous ADJECTIVE, **outrageously**
ADVERB

outright
ADJECTIVE **1** absolute EG *an outright
rejection.* ▶ ADVERB **2** in an open and
direct way EG *Have you asked him
outright?* **3** completely and totally EG
I own the company outright.

outset
NOUN The outset of something is the
beginning of it EG *the outset of his
journey.*

outshine outshines outshining
outshone
VERB If you outshine someone, you
perform better than they do.

outside
NOUN **1** The outside of something is
the part which surrounds or
encloses the rest of it. ▶ ADVERB,
ADJECTIVE, OR PREPOSITION **2** Outside
means not inside EG *houses just
outside the airport... He stood outside
and shouted... an outside toilet.*
3 Outside also means not included
in something EG *outside office hours.*

☑ Do not use *of* after *outside*. You should write *she was waiting outside the school* and not *outside of the school*.

outsider outsiders
NOUN **1** someone who does not belong to a particular group. **2** a competitor considered unlikely to win in a race.

outsize or **outsized**
ADJECTIVE much larger than usual EG *outsize feet*.

outskirts
PLURAL NOUN The outskirts of a city or town are the parts around the edge of it.

outspoken
ADJECTIVE Outspoken people give their opinions openly, even if they shock other people.

outstanding
ADJECTIVE **1** extremely good EG *The collection contains hundreds of outstanding works of art.* **2** Money that is outstanding is still owed EG *an outstanding mortgage of 46,000 pounds.*

outstretched
ADJECTIVE If your arms are outstretched, they are stretched out as far as possible.

outstrip outstrips outstripping outstripped
VERB If one thing outstrips another thing, it becomes bigger or more successful or moves faster than the other thing.

outward
ADJECTIVE OR ADVERB **1** Outward means away from a place or towards the outside EG *the outward journey.*
▶ ADJECTIVE **2** The outward features of someone are the ones they appear to have, rather than the ones they actually have EG *He never showed any outward signs of the stress he was under.*
outwardly ADVERB

outwards
ADVERB away from a place or towards

the outside EG *The door opened outwards.*

outweigh outweighs outweighing outweighed
VERB If you say that the advantages of something outweigh its disadvantages, you mean that the advantages are more important than the disadvantages.

outwit outwits outwitting outwitted
VERB If you outwit someone, you use your intelligence to defeat them.

oval ovals
NOUN **1** a round shape, similar to a circle but wider in one direction than the other. ▶ ADJECTIVE **2** shaped like an oval EG *an oval table.*

ovary ovaries
Said "oh-var-ree" NOUN A woman's ovaries are the two organs in her body that produce eggs.

ovation ovations
NOUN a long burst of applause.

oven ovens
NOUN the part of a cooker that you use for baking or roasting food.

over overs
PREPOSITION **1** Over something means directly above it or covering it EG *the picture over the fireplace... He put his hands over his eyes.* **2** A view over an area is a view across that area EG *The pool and terrace look out over the sea.* **3** If something is over a road or river it is on the opposite side of the road or river. **4** Something that is over a particular amount is more than that amount. **5** 'Over' indicates a topic which is causing concern EG *An American was arguing over the bill.* **6** If something happens over a period of time, it happens during that period EG *I went to New Zealand over Christmas.* ▶ ADVERB OR PREPOSITION **7** If you lean over, you bend your body in a particular direction EG *He bent over and rummaged in a drawer... She was hunched over her typewriter.* ▶ ADVERB **8** 'Over' is used to indicate a

505

position eg *over by the window... Come over here.* **9** If something rolls or turns over, it is moved so that its other side is facing upwards eg *He flipped over the envelope.* ▶ ADJECTIVE **10** Something that is over is completely finished. ▶ PHRASE **11** All over a place means everywhere in that place eg *studios all over America.* ▶ NOUN **12** In cricket, an over is a set of six balls bowled by a bowler from the same end of the pitch.

over-
PREFIX to too great an extent or too much eg *overprotective parents... overindulging in chocolate and sweets.*

overall overalls
ADJECTIVE OR ADVERB **1** Overall means taking into account all the parts or aspects of something eg *The overall quality of pupils' work had shown a marked improvement... Overall, things are not really too bad.* ▶ PLURAL NOUN **2** Overalls are a piece of clothing that looks like trousers and a jacket combined. You wear overalls to protect your other clothes when you are working. ▶ NOUN **3** An overall is a piece of clothing like a coat that you wear to protect your other clothes when you are working.

overawed
ADJECTIVE If you are overawed by something, you are very impressed by it and a little afraid of it.

overbearing
ADJECTIVE trying to dominate other people eg *Mozart had a difficult relationship with his overbearing father.*

overboard
ADVERB If you fall overboard, you fall over the side of a ship into the water.

overcast
ADJECTIVE If it is overcast, the sky is covered by cloud.

overcoat overcoats
NOUN a thick, warm coat.

overcome overcomes overcoming overcame overcome
VERB **1** If you overcome a problem or a feeling, you manage to deal with it or control it. ▶ ADJECTIVE **2** If you are overcome by a feeling, you feel it very strongly.

overcrowded
ADJECTIVE If a place is overcrowded, there are too many things or people in it.

overdo overdoes overdoing overdid overdone
VERB If you overdo something, you do it too much or in an exaggerated way eg *It is important never to overdo new exercises.*

overdose overdoses
NOUN a larger dose of a drug than is safe.

overdraft overdrafts
NOUN an agreement with a bank that allows someone to spend more money than they have in their account.

overdrawn
ADJECTIVE If someone is overdrawn, they have taken more money from their bank account than the account has in it.

overdrive
NOUN Overdrive is an extra, higher gear in a vehicle, which is used at high speeds to reduce engine wear and save petrol.

overdue
ADJECTIVE If someone or something is overdue, they are late eg *The payments are overdue.*

overestimate overestimates overestimating overestimated
VERB If you overestimate something, you think that it is bigger, more important, or better than it really is eg *We had overestimated his popularity.*

overflow overflows overflowing overflowed overflown
VERB If a liquid overflows, it spills over the edges of its container. If a river overflows, it flows over its banks.

overgrown

ADJECTIVE A place that is overgrown is covered with weeds because it has not been looked after EG *an overgrown path.*

overhang overhangs overhanging overhung
VERB If one thing overhangs another, it sticks out sideways above it EG *old trees whose branches overhang a footpath.*

overhaul overhauls overhauling overhauled
VERB **1** If you overhaul something, you examine it thoroughly and repair any faults. ▶ NOUN **2** If you give something an overhaul, you examine it and repair or improve it.

overhead overheads
ADVERB OR ADJECTIVE **1** Overhead means above you EG *seagulls flying overhead.* ▶ PLURAL NOUN **2** The overheads of a business are the costs of running it.

overhear overhears overhearing overheard
VERB If you overhear someone's conversation, you hear what they are saying to someone else.

overjoyed
ADJECTIVE extremely pleased EG *Colm was overjoyed to see me.*
■ delighted, over the moon

overlaid
ADJECTIVE If something is overlaid by something else, it is covered by it.

overland
ADJECTIVE OR ADVERB travelling across land rather than going by sea or air EG *an overland trek to India... Wray was returning to England overland.*

overlander overlanders
NOUN In Australian history, an overlander was a man who drove cattle or sheep long distances through the outback.

overlap overlaps overlapping overlapped
VERB If one thing overlaps another, one part of it covers part of the other thing.

overleaf
ADVERB on the next page EG *Write to us at the address shown overleaf.*

overload overloads overloading overloaded
VERB If you overload someone or something, you give them too much to do or to carry.

overlook overlooks overlooking overlooked
VERB **1** If a building or window overlooks a place, it has a view over that place. **2** If you overlook something, you ignore it or do not notice it.

overly
ADVERB excessively EG *I'm not overly fond of jazz.*

overnight
ADJECTIVE OR ADVERB **1** during the night EG *Further rain was forecast overnight.* **2** sudden or suddenly EG *an overnight success... Good players don't become bad ones overnight.* ▶ ADJECTIVE **3** for use when you go away for one or two nights EG *an overnight bag.*

overpower overpowers overpowering overpowered
VERB **1** If you overpower someone, you seize them despite their struggles, because you are stronger than them. **2** If a feeling overpowers you, it affects you very strongly.
overpowering ADJECTIVE

overrate overrates overrating overrated
VERB If you overrate something, you think that it is better or more important than it really is.
overrated ADJECTIVE

overreact overreacts overreacting overreacted
VERB If you overreact, you react in an extreme way.

overriding
ADJECTIVE more important than anything else EG *an overriding duty.*

overrule overrules overruling overruled

A B C D E F G H I J K L M N O P Q R S T U V W X Y Z

VERB To overrule a person or their decisions is to decide that their decisions are incorrect.

■ countermand, override, reverse

overrun overruns overrunning overran overrun

VERB **1** If an army overruns a country, it occupies it very quickly. **2** If animals or plants overrun a place, they spread quickly over it. **3** If an event overruns, it continues for longer than it was meant to.

overseas

ADJECTIVE OR ADVERB **1** abroad EG *an overseas tour... travelling overseas*. ▶ ADJECTIVE **2** from abroad EG *overseas students*.

oversee oversees overseeing oversaw overseen

VERB To oversee a job is to make sure it is done properly.
overseer NOUN

overshadow overshadows overshadowing overshadowed

VERB If something is overshadowed, it is made unimportant by something else that is better or more important.

oversight oversights

NOUN something which you forget to do or fail to notice.

overspill

NOUN OR ADJECTIVE Overspill refers to the rehousing of people from overcrowded cities in smaller towns EG *an East End overspill... overspill estates*.

overstate overstates overstating overstated

VERB If you overstate something, you exaggerate its importance.

overstep oversteps overstepping overstepped

PHRASE If you **overstep the mark**, you behave in an unacceptable way.

overt

ADJECTIVE open and obvious EG *overt signs of stress*.
overtly ADVERB

overtake overtakes overtaking

overtook overtaken

VERB If you overtake someone, you pass them because you are moving faster than them.

overthrow overthrows overthrowing overthrew overthrown

VERB If a government is overthrown, it is removed from power by force.

overtime

NOUN **1** Overtime is time that someone works in addition to their normal working hours. ▶ ADVERB **2** If someone works overtime, they do work in addition to their normal working hours.

overtones

PLURAL NOUN If something has overtones of an emotion or attitude, it suggests it without showing it openly EG *the political overtones of the trial*.

overture overtures

NOUN **1** a piece of music that is the introduction to an opera or play. **2** If you make overtures to someone, you approach them because you want to start a friendly or business relationship with them.

overturn overturns overturning overturned

VERB **1** To overturn something is to turn it upside down or onto its side. **2** If someone overturns a legal decision, they change it by using their higher authority.

overview overviews

NOUN a general understanding or description of a situation.

overweight

ADJECTIVE too fat, and therefore unhealthy EG *overweight businessmen*.

overwhelm overwhelms overwhelming overwhelmed

VERB **1** If you are overwhelmed by something, it affects you very strongly EG *The priest appeared overwhelmed by the news*. **2** If one group of people overwhelm another, they gain complete control or victory over them.

overwhelming ADJECTIVE,
overwhelmingly ADVERB

overwork overworks
overworking overworked
VERB If you overwork, you work too
hard.

overwrought
Said "oh-ver-**rawt**" ADJECTIVE
extremely upset EG *He didn't get
angry or overwrought.*

ovulate ovulates ovulating
ovulated
Said "**ov**-yool-late" VERB When a
woman or female animal ovulates,
she produces ova or eggs from her
ovary.

ovum ova
Said "**oh**-vum" NOUN a reproductive
cell of a woman or female animal.
The ovum is fertilized by a male
sperm to produce young.
🏛 a Latin word meaning 'egg'

owe owes owing owed
VERB **1** If you owe someone money,
they have lent it to you and you
have not yet paid it back. **2** If you
owe a quality or skill to someone,
they are responsible for giving it to
you EG *He owes his success to his
mother.* **3** If you say that you owe
someone gratitude·or loyalty, you
mean that you deserve it from you.

owl owls
NOUN Owls are birds of prey that
hunt at night. They have large eyes
and short, hooked beaks.

own owns owning owned
ADJECTIVE **1** If something is your
own, it belongs to you or is
associated with you EG *She stayed in
her own house.* ▶ VERB **2** If you own
something, it belongs to you.
▶ PHRASE **3** On your own means
alone.

owner owners
NOUN The owner of something is the
person it belongs to.

ownership
NOUN If you have ownership of
something, you own it EG *He shared
the ownership of a sailing dinghy.*

ox oxen
NOUN Oxen are cattle which are
used for carrying or pulling things.

oxide oxides
NOUN a compound of oxygen and
another chemical element.

oxidize oxidizes oxidizing
oxidized; also spelt oxidise
VERB When a substance oxidizes, it
changes chemically by reacting
with oxygen.
oxidation NOUN

oxygen
NOUN Oxygen is a colourless gas in
the air. It makes up about 21% of
the Earth's atmosphere. All animals
and plants need oxygen to live,
and things cannot burn without it.

oxymoron oxymora or oxymorons
NOUN two words that contradict
each other placed beside each
other, for example 'deafening
silence'.

oyster oysters
NOUN Oysters are large, flat shellfish.
Some oysters can be eaten, and
others produce pearls.
🏛 from Greek *ostrakon* meaning
'shell'

oz
an abbreviation for 'ounces'.

ozone
NOUN Ozone is a form of oxygen
that is poisonous and has a strong
smell. There is a layer of ozone
high above the Earth's surface.

ozone layer
NOUN The ozone layer is that part of
the Earth's atmosphere that
protects living things from the
harmful radiation of the sun.

A
B
C
D
E
F
G
H
I
J
K
L
M
N
O
P
Q
R
S
T
U
V
W
X
Y
Z

Pp Pp

p
1 p is an abbreviation for 'pence'.
2 p is also a written abbreviation
for 'page'. The plural is pp.

pa pa or **pas**
NOUN In New Zealand, a Maori
village or settlement.

pace paces pacing paced
NOUN **1** The pace of something is the
speed at which it moves or
happens. **2** a step; also used as a
measurement of distance. ▶ VERB **3** If
you pace up and down, you
continually walk around because
you are anxious or impatient.

pacemaker pacemakers
NOUN a small electronic device put
into someone's heart to control
their heartbeat.

Pacific
Said "pas-**sif**-ik" NOUN The Pacific is
the ocean separating South and
North America from Asia and
Australia.

pacifist pacifists
NOUN someone who is opposed to
all violence and war.
pacifism NOUN

pacify pacifies pacifying pacified
VERB If you pacify someone who is
angry, you calm them.
■ appease, calm, placate

pack packs packing packed
VERB **1** If you pack, you put things
neatly into a suitcase, bag, or box.
2 If people pack into a place, it
becomes crowded with them.
▶ NOUN **3** a bag or rucksack carried
on your back. **4** a packet or
collection of something EG *a pack of
cigarettes*. **5** A pack of playing cards
is a complete set. **6** A pack of dogs
or wolves is a group of them.
pack up VERB If you pack up your
belongings, you put them in a bag
because you are leaving.

package packages
NOUN **1** a small parcel. **2** a set of

proposals or offers presented as a
whole EG *a package of beauty
treatments*.
packaged ADJECTIVE

packaging
NOUN Packaging is the container or
wrapping in which an item is sold
or sent.

packed
ADJECTIVE very full EG *The church was
packed with people*.

packet packets
NOUN a thin cardboard box or paper
container in which something is
sold.

pact pacts
NOUN a formal agreement or treaty.

pad pads padding padded
NOUN **1** a thick, soft piece of
material. **2** a number of pieces of
paper fixed together at one end.
3 The pads of an animal such as a
cat or dog are the soft, fleshy parts
on the bottom of its paws. **4** a flat
surface from which helicopters take
off or rockets are launched. ▶ VERB
5 If you pad something, you put a
pad inside it or over it to protect it
or change its shape. **6** If you pad
around, you walk softly.
padding NOUN

paddle paddles paddling paddled
NOUN **1** a short pole with a broad
blade at one or both ends, used to
move a small boat or a canoe. ▶ VERB
2 If someone paddles a boat, they
move it using a paddle. **3** If you
paddle, you walk in shallow water.

paddock paddocks
NOUN a small field where horses are
kept.

paddy paddies
NOUN A paddy or paddy field is an
area in which rice is grown.

**padlock padlocks padlocking
padlocked**
NOUN **1** a lock made up of a metal

case with a U-shaped bar attached to it, which can be put through a metal loop and then closed. It is unlocked by turning a key in the lock on the case. ▶ VERB **2** If you padlock something, you lock it with a padlock.

padre padres
Said "pah-dray" NOUN a priest, especially a chaplain to the armed forces.
📖 from Italian or Spanish *padre* meaning 'father'

paediatrician paediatricians
Said "pee-dee-ya-trish-n"; also spelt pediatrician
NOUN a doctor who specializes in treating children.
📖 from Greek *pais* meaning 'child' and *iatros* meaning 'physician'

paediatrics
Said "pee-dee-ya-triks"; also spelt pediatrics
NOUN Paediatrics is the area of medicine which deals with children's diseases.
paediatric ADJECTIVE

pagan pagans
Said "pay-gan" ADJECTIVE **1** involving beliefs and worship outside the main religions of the world EG *pagan myths and cults.* ▶ NOUN **2** someone who believes in a pagan religion.
paganism NOUN

page pages paging paged
NOUN **1** one side of one of the pieces of paper in a book or magazine; also the sheet of paper itself. **2** In medieval times, a page was a young boy servant who was learning to be a knight. ▶ VERB **3** To page someone is to send a signal or message to a small electronic device which they are carrying.

pageant pageants
Said "paj-jent" NOUN a grand, colourful show or parade.

pagoda pagodas
NOUN a tall, elaborately decorated Buddhist or Hindu temple.

pail pails
NOUN a bucket.

pain pains paining pained
NOUN **1** Pain is an unpleasant feeling of physical hurt or deep unhappiness. ▶ VERB **2** If something pains you, it makes you very unhappy.
painless ADJECTIVE, **painlessly** ADVERB
🔲 (sense 1) ache, hurt, pang, twinge

painful
ADJECTIVE causing emotional or physical pain.
painfully ADVERB

painkiller painkillers
NOUN a drug that reduces or stops pain.

painstaking
ADJECTIVE very careful and thorough EG *years of painstaking research.*

paint paints painting painted
NOUN **1** Paint is a coloured liquid used to decorate buildings, or to make a picture. ▶ VERB **2** If you paint something or paint a picture of it, you make a picture of it using paint. **3** When you paint something such as a wall, you cover it with paint.
painter NOUN, **painting** NOUN

pair pairs pairing paired
NOUN **1** two things of the same type or that do the same thing EG *a pair of earrings.* **2** You use 'pair' when referring to certain objects which have two main matching parts EG *a pair of scissors.* ▶ VERB **3** When people pair off, they become grouped in pairs. **4** If you pair up with someone, you agree to do something together.
☑ The verb following *pair* can be singular or plural. If *pair* refers to a unit, the verb is singular: *a pair of good shoes is essential.* If *pair* refers to two individual things, the verb is plural: *the pair are said to dislike each other.*

pakeha pakeha or pakehas
Said "pa-ki-ha" NOUN In New Zealand English, someone who is of European rather than Maori

A B C D E F G H I J K L M N O P Q R S T U V W X Y Z

descent.

Pakistani Pakistanis
Said "pah-kiss-tah-nee" ADJECTIVE
1 belonging or relating to Pakistan.
▶ NOUN **2** someone who comes from
Pakistan.

pal pals
NOUN; AN INFORMAL WORD a friend.

palace palaces
NOUN a large, grand house,
especially the official home of a
king or queen.

palagi palagi or palagis
Said "pa-lang-ee" NOUN a Samoan
name for a New Zealander of
European descent.

palatable
ADJECTIVE Palatable food tastes
pleasant.

palate palates
Said "pall-lat" NOUN **1** the top of the
inside of your mouth. **2** Someone's
palate is their ability to judge good
food and wine EG *dishes to tempt
every palate*.

pale paler palest
ADJECTIVE rather white and without
much colour or brightness.

Palestinian Palestinians
NOUN an Arab from the region
formerly called Palestine situated
between the River Jordan and the
Mediterranean.

palette palettes
NOUN a flat piece of wood on which
an artist mixes colours.

pall palls palling palled
Rhymes with "fall" VERB **1** If
something palls, it becomes less
interesting or less enjoyable EG *This
record palls after ten minutes*. ▶ NOUN
2 a thick cloud of smoke. **3** a cloth
covering a coffin.

palm palms
NOUN **1** A palm or palm tree is a
tropical tree with no branches and
a crown of long leaves. **2** the flat
surface of your hand which your
fingers bend towards.

Palm Sunday

NOUN Palm Sunday is the Sunday
before Easter.

palpable
ADJECTIVE obvious and easily sensed
EG *Happiness was palpable in the air*.
palpably ADVERB
▣ from Latin *palpabilis* meaning
'able to be touched'

paltry
Said "pawl-tree" ADJECTIVE A paltry
sum of money is a very small
amount.
▤ insignificant, trifling, trivial

pamper pampers pampering
pampered
VERB If you pamper someone, you
give them too much kindness and
comfort.

pamphlet pamphlets
NOUN a very thin book in paper
covers giving information about
something.

pan pans panning panned
NOUN **1** a round metal container
with a long handle, used for
cooking things in on top of a
cooker. ▶ VERB **2** When a film
camera pans, it moves in a wide
sweep. **3** AN INFORMAL USE To pan
something is to criticize it strongly.

panacea panaceas
Said "pan-nass-see-ah" NOUN
something that is supposed to cure
everything.

panache
Said "pan-nash" NOUN Something
that is done with panache is done
confidently and stylishly.

pancake pancakes
NOUN a thin, flat piece of fried batter
which can be served with savoury
or sweet fillings.

pancreas pancreases
Said "pang-kree-ass" NOUN an organ
in the body situated behind the
stomach. It helps the body to
digest food.

panda pandas
NOUN A panda or giant panda is a
large animal rather like a bear that

lives in China. It has black fur with large patches of white.

panda car panda cars
NOUN In Britain, a police patrol car.

pandemonium
Said "pan-dim-**moan**-ee-um" NOUN Pandemonium is a state of noisy confusion EG *scenes of pandemonium*.
🏛 from *Pandemonium*, the capital of Hell in Milton's 'Paradise Lost'

pander panders pandering pandered
VERB If you pander to someone, you do everything they want.

pane panes
NOUN a sheet of glass in a window or door.

panel panels
NOUN 1 a small group of people who are chosen to do something EG *a panel of judges*. 2 a flat piece of wood that is part of a larger object EG *door panels*. 3 A control panel is a surface containing switches and instruments to operate a machine.
panelled ADJECTIVE

panelling
NOUN Panelling is rectangular pieces of wood covering an inside wall.

pang pangs
NOUN a sudden strong feeling of sadness or pain.

panic panics panicking panicked
NOUN 1 Panic is a sudden overwhelming feeling of fear or anxiety. ▶ VERB 2 If you panic, you become so afraid or anxious that you cannot act sensibly.

panorama panoramas
NOUN an extensive view over a wide area of land EG *a fine panorama over the hills*.
panoramic ADJECTIVE

pansy pansies
NOUN a small garden flower with large round petals.

pant pants panting panted
VERB If you pant, you breathe quickly and loudly through your mouth.

panther panthers
NOUN a large wild animal belonging to the cat family, especially the black leopard.

pantomime pantomimes
NOUN a musical play, usually based on a fairy story and performed at Christmas.

pantry pantries
NOUN a small room where food is kept.
🏛 from Old French *paneterie* meaning 'bread store'

pants
PLURAL NOUN 1 Pants are a piece of underwear with holes for your legs and elastic around the waist or hips. 2 Pants are also trousers.

papaya papayas
NOUN a fruit with sweet yellow flesh that grows in the West Indies and tropical Australia.

paper papers papering papered
NOUN 1 Paper is a material made from wood pulp and used for writing on or wrapping things. 2 a newspaper. ▶ PLURAL NOUN 3 Papers are official documents, for example a passport for identification. ▶ NOUN 4 part of a written examination. ▶ VERB 5 If you paper a wall, you put wallpaper on it.
🏛 from *pupyrus*, the plant from which paper was made in ancient Egypt, Greece, and Rome

paperback paperbacks
NOUN a book with a thin cardboard cover.

paperwork
NOUN Paperwork is the part of a job that involves dealing with letters and records.

papier-mâché
Said "pap-yay **mash**-shay" NOUN Papier-mâché is a hard substance made from mashed wet paper mixed with glue and moulded when moist to make things such as bowls and ornaments.
🏛 from French *papier-mâché* meaning literally 'chewed paper'

A
B
C
D
E
F
G
H
I
J
K
L
M
N
O
P
Q
R
S
T
U
V
W
X
Y
Z

paprika

NOUN Paprika is a red powder made from a kind of pepper.

▥ a Hungarian word

par

PHRASE 1 Something that is **on a par** with something else is similar in quality or amount EG *This match was on a par with the German Cup Final.* 2 Something that is **below par** or **under par** is below its normal standard. ▶ NOUN 3 In golf, par is the number of strokes which it is thought a good player should take for a hole or all the holes on a particular golf course.

parable parables

NOUN a short story which makes a moral or religious point.

parachute parachutes

Said "**par**-rash-oot" NOUN a circular piece of fabric attached by lines to a person or package so that they can fall safely to the ground from an aircraft.

parade parades parading paraded

NOUN 1 a line of people or vehicles standing or moving together as a display. ▶ VERB 2 When people parade, they walk together in a group as a display.

Paradise

NOUN According to some religions, Paradise is a wonderful place where good people go when they die.

▥ from Greek *paradeisos* meaning 'garden'

paradox paradoxes

NOUN something that contains two ideas that seem to contradict each other EG *the paradox of having to drink in order to stay sober.*

paradoxical ADJECTIVE

paraffin

NOUN Paraffin is a strong-smelling liquid which is used as a fuel.

paragon paragons

NOUN someone whose behaviour is perfect in some way EG *a paragon of elegance.*

paragraph paragraphs

NOUN a section of a piece of writing. Paragraphs begin on a new line.

parallel parallels

NOUN 1 Something that is a parallel to something else has similar qualities or features to it. ▶ ADJECTIVE 2 If two lines are parallel, they are the same distance apart along the whole of their length.

parallelogram parallelograms

NOUN a four-sided shape in which each side is parallel to the opposite side.

paralyse paralyses paralysing paralysed

VERB If something paralyses you, it causes loss of feeling and movement in your body.

▤ freeze, immobilize, numb

paralysis

Said "par-**ral**-liss-iss" NOUN Paralysis is loss of the power to move.

paramedic paramedics

Said "par-ram-**med**-dik" NOUN a person who does some types of medical work, for example for the ambulance service.

parameter parameters

Said "par-**ram**-met-ter" NOUN a limit which affects the way something is done EG *the general parameters set by the president.*

paramilitary

ADJECTIVE A paramilitary organization has a military structure but is not the official army of a country.

paramount

ADJECTIVE more important than anything else EG *Safety is paramount.*

paranoia

Said "par-ran-**noy**-ah" NOUN Paranoia is a mental illness in which someone believes that other people are trying to harm them.

paranoid

Said "**par**-ran-noyd" ADJECTIVE Someone who is paranoid believes wrongly that other people are trying to harm them.

parapet **parapets**
NOUN a low wall along the edge of a bridge or roof.
📖 from Italian *parapetto* meaning 'chest-high wall'

paraphernalia
Said "par-raf-fan-**ale**-yah" NOUN Someone's paraphernalia is all their belongings or equipment.
📖 from Latin *parapherna* meaning 'personal property of a married woman'

paraphrase **paraphrases**
paraphrasing **paraphrased**
NOUN **1** A paraphrase of a piece of writing or speech is the same thing said in a different way EG *a paraphrase of the popular song.* ▶ VERB **2** If you paraphrase what someone has said, you express it in a different way.

parasite **parasites**
NOUN a small animal or plant that lives on or inside a larger animal or plant.
parasitic ADJECTIVE
📖 from Greek *parasitos* meaning 'someone who eats at someone else's table'

parasol **parasols**
NOUN an object like an umbrella that provides shelter from the sun.

paratroops or **paratroopers**
PLURAL NOUN Paratroops are soldiers trained to be dropped by parachute.

parcel **parcels** **parcelling** **parcelled**
NOUN **1** something wrapped up in paper. ▶ VERB **2** If you parcel something up, you make it into a parcel.

parched
ADJECTIVE **1** If the ground is parched, it is very dry and in need of water. **2** If you are parched, you are very thirsty.

parchment
NOUN Parchment is thick yellowish paper of very good quality.

pardon **pardons** **pardoning**
pardoned
1 You say **pardon** or **beg your pardon** to express surprise or apology, or when you have not heard what someone has said.
▶ VERB **2** If you pardon someone, you forgive them for doing something wrong.

pare **pares** **paring** **pared**
VERB When you pare fruit or vegetables, you cut off the skin.

parent **parents**
NOUN Your parents are your father and mother.
parental ADJECTIVE

parentage
NOUN A person's parentage is their parents and ancestors.

parish **parishes**
NOUN an area with its own church and clergyman, and often its own elected council.

parishioner **parishioners**
NOUN A clergyman's parishioners are the people who live in his parish and attend his church.

parity
NOUN; A FORMAL WORD If there is parity between things, they are equal EG *By 1943 the USA had achieved a rough parity of power with the British.*

park **parks** **parking** **parked**
NOUN **1** a public area with grass and trees. **2** a private area of grass and trees around a large country house.
▶ VERB **3** When someone parks a vehicle, they drive it into a position where it can be left.
parked ADJECTIVE, **parking** NOUN

parliament **parliaments**
NOUN the group of elected representatives who make the laws of a country.
parliamentary ADJECTIVE

parlour **parlours**
NOUN; AN OLD-FASHIONED WORD a sitting room.
📖 from Old French *parleur* meaning 'room for talking to visitors (in a convent)'

A
B
C
D
E
F
G
H
I
J
K
L
M
N
O
P
Q
R
S
T
U
V
W
X
Y
Z

515

parochial
Said "par-**roe**-key-yal" ADJECTIVE
concerned only with local matters
EG *narrow parochial interests.*

parody parodies parodying parodied
NOUN **1** an amusing imitation of the style of an author or of a familiar situation. ▸ VERB **2** If you parody something, you make a parody of it.
◪ (sense 1) send-up, spoof, takeoff

parole
NOUN When prisoners are given parole, they are released early on condition that they behave well.
▥ from French *parole d'honneur* meaning 'word of honour'

parrot parrots
NOUN a brightly coloured tropical bird with a curved beak.

parry parries parrying parried
VERB **1** If you parry a question, you cleverly avoid answering it EG *My searching questions are simply parried with evasions.* **2** If you parry a blow, you push aside your attacker's arm to defend yourself.

parsley
NOUN Parsley is a herb with curly leaves used for flavouring in cooking.

parsnip parsnips
NOUN a long, pointed, cream-coloured root vegetable.

parson parsons
NOUN a vicar or other clergyman.

part parts parting parted
NOUN **1** one of the pieces or aspects of something. **2** one of the roles in a play or film, played by an actor or actress. **3** Someone's part in something is their involvement in it EG *He was jailed for eleven years for his part in the plot.* ▸ PHRASE **4** If you **take part** in an activity, you do it together with other people. ▸ VERB **5** If things that are next to each other part, they move away from each other. **6** If two people part, they leave each other.

◪ (sense 1) bit, component, constituent, piece

partake partakes partaking partook partaken
VERB; A FORMAL WORD If you partake of food, you eat it EG *She partook of the refreshments offered.*

partial
ADJECTIVE **1** not complete or whole EG *a partial explanation... partial success.* **2** liking something very much EG *I'm very partial to marigolds.* **3** supporting one side in a dispute, rather than being fair and unbiased.
partially ADVERB

participate participates participating participated
VERB If you participate in an activity, you take part in it.
participant NOUN, **participation** NOUN
◪ be involved in, join in, take part

participle participles
NOUN In grammar, a participle is a form of a verb used with an auxiliary verb in compound tenses and often as an adjective. English has two participles: the past participle, which describes a completed action, and the present participle, which describes a continuing action. For example in 'He has gone', 'gone' is a past participle and in 'She was winning', 'winning' is a present participle.

particle particles
NOUN a very small piece of something.

particular particulars
ADJECTIVE **1** relating or belonging to only one thing or person EG *That particular place is dangerous.* **2** especially great or intense EG *Pay particular attention to the forehead.* **3** Someone who is particular has high standards and is not easily satisfied. ▸ PLURAL NOUN **4** Particulars are facts or details.
particularly ADVERB

parting partings

NOUN an occasion when one person leaves another.

partisan partisans
ADJECTIVE **1** favouring or supporting one person or group EG *a partisan crowd*. ▶ NOUN **2** a member of an unofficial armed force fighting to free their country from enemy occupation EG *Norwegian partisans*.

partition partitions partitioning partitioned
NOUN **1** a screen separating one part of a room or vehicle from another. **2** Partition is the division of a country into independent areas. ▶ VERB **3** To partition something is to divide it into separate parts.

partly
ADVERB to some extent but not completely.

partner partners partnering partnered
NOUN **1** Someone's partner is the person they are married to or are living with. **2** Your partner is the person you are doing something with, for example in a dance or a game. **3** Business partners are joint owners of their business. ▶ VERB **4** If you partner someone, you are their partner for a game or social occasion.
partnership NOUN

part of speech parts of speech
NOUN a particular grammatical class of word, such as 'noun' or 'adjective'.

What is a Part of Speech?

Every word in the dictionary can be classified into a group. These groups are known as **parts of speech**. If we know which group a word belongs to, we can understand what sort of idea the word represents, and how it can be combined with other words to produce meaningful statements.

You can check the part of speech of any word by looking it up in the dictionary. The part of speech is given after the main entry word. The most common parts of speech in this dictionary are noun, verb, adjective, adverb, pronoun, preposition, interjection and conjunction. There are grammar boxes for all of these.

---

partook
the past tense of **partake**.

partridge partridges
NOUN a brown game bird with a round body and a short tail.

part-time
ADJECTIVE involving work for only a part of each normal working day or week.

party parties
NOUN **1** a social event held for people to enjoy themselves. **2** an organization whose members share the same political beliefs and campaign for election to government. **3** a group who are doing something together. **4** ʌ FORMAL USE one of the people involved in a legal agreement or dispute.

pass passes passing passed
VERB **1** To pass something is to move past it. **2** To pass in a particular direction is to move in that direction EG *We passed through the gate.* **3** If you pass something to someone, you hand it to them or transfer it to them. **4** If you pass a period of time doing something, you spend it that way EG *He hoped to pass the long night in meditation.* **5** When a period of time passes, it happens and finishes. **6** If you pass a test, you are considered to be of an acceptable standard. **7** When a new law or proposal is passed, it is formally approved. **8** When a judge passes sentence on someone, the judge states what the punishment will be. **9** If you pass the ball in a ball game, you throw, kick, or hit it to another player in your team. ▶ NOUN **10** the transfer of the ball in a ball game to another player in the same team. **11** an official document that allows you to go

somewhere. **12** a narrow route between mountains.

■ (sense 1) go past, overtake

■ (sense 5) elapse, go by, lapse

pass away or **pass on** VERB Someone who has passed away has died.

pass out VERB If someone passes out, they faint.

passable

ADJECTIVE of an acceptable standard EG *a passable imitation of his dad.*

passage passages

NOUN **1** a long, narrow corridor or space that connects two places. **2** a section of a book or piece of music.

passé

Said "pas-say" ADJECTIVE no longer fashionable.

passenger passengers

NOUN a person travelling in a vehicle, aircraft, or ship.

passer-by passers-by

NOUN someone who is walking past someone or something.

passing

ADJECTIVE lasting only for a short time EG *a passing phase.*

■ brief, fleeting, momentary

passion passions

NOUN Passion is a very strong feeling, especially of sexual attraction.

■ emotion, fervour, intensity

passionate

ADJECTIVE expressing very strong feelings about something.

passionately ADVERB

■ emotional, fervent, intense

passive

ADJECTIVE **1** remaining calm and showing no feeling when provoked. ▶ NOUN **2** In grammar, the passive or passive voice is the form of the verb in which the person or thing to which an action is being done is the grammatical subject of the sentence, and is given more emphasis as a result. For example, the passive of *The committee rejected your application* is *Your application*

was rejected by the committee.

passively ADVERB, **passivity** NOUN

■ (sense 1) inactive, submissive

The Passive Voice

The **passive** voice and the **active** voice are two different ways of presenting information in a sentence. The **passive** always uses a form of the auxiliary verb *to be* with the past participle of the verb. When a sentence is in the passive voice, the subject of the verb is affected by the action, rather than doing it.

*The cat **is being fed** by Anna.*

*The mouse **was chased** by a cat.*

It usually sounds more natural to use the active rather than the passive. However, it is sometimes better to use the passive if you want to avoid giving blame or if the name of the subject is not known.

The book has been mislaid.

We are being followed.

Also look at the grammar box at **active**.

Passover

NOUN The Passover is an eight day Jewish festival held in spring.

passport passports

NOUN an official identification document which you need to show when you travel abroad.

password passwords

NOUN **1** a secret word known to only a few people. It allows people on the same side to recognize a friend. **2** a word you need to know to get into some computer files.

past

NOUN **1** The past is the period of time before the present. ▶ ADJECTIVE **2** Past things are things that happened or existed before the present EG *the past 30 years.*

▶ PREPOSITION OR ADVERB **3** You use 'past' when you are telling the time EG *It was ten past eleven.* **4** If you go past something, you move towards it and continue until you are on the other side EG *They drove rapidly past their cottage.* ▶ PREPOSITION **5** Something that is past a place is

situated on the other side of it EG
It's just past the church there.

pasta
NOUN Pasta is a dried mixture of
flour, eggs, and water, formed into
different shapes.

paste pastes pasting pasted
NOUN **1** Paste is a soft, rather sticky
mixture that can be easily spread EG
tomato paste. ▶ VERB **2** If you paste
something onto a surface, you stick
it with glue.

pastel
ADJECTIVE Pastel colours are pale and
soft.

pasteurized
Said "past-yoor-ized"; also spelt
pasteurised
ADJECTIVE Pasteurized milk has been
treated with a special heating
process to kill bacteria.

pastime pastimes
NOUN a hobby or something you do
just for pleasure.
■ activity, hobby, recreation

pastor pastors
NOUN a clergyman in charge of a
congregation.

pastoral
ADJECTIVE **1** characteristic of peaceful
country life and landscape EG
pastoral scenes. **2** relating to the
duties of the clergy in caring for
the needs of their parishioners EG *a
pastoral visit.*

past participle past participles
NOUN In grammar, the past
participle of a verb is the form,
usually ending in 'ed' or 'en', that
is used to make some past tenses
and the passive. For example
'killed' in 'She has killed the
goldfish' and 'broken' in 'My leg
was broken' are past participles.

pastry pastries
NOUN **1** Pastry is a mixture of flour,
fat, and water, rolled flat and used
for making pies. **2** a small cake.

past tense
NOUN In grammar, the past tense is

the tense of a verb that you use
mainly to refer to things that
happened or existed before the
time of writing or speaking.

Talking about the Past

You can talk about events that have already
happened by using **simple past tenses** or
compound tenses.

The **simple past tense** is formed without
any auxiliary verbs. It is usually formed by
taking the dictionary form of the verb and
adding the ending *-ed*. (If the verb already
ends in *-e*, then you only need to add *-d*.)
    I **cooked** the dinner.
    She **liked** fish.

You can also use **compound tenses** to talk
about actions that have happened.

One compound past tense is formed by
using *was* or *were* in front of the main verb,
and adding the ending *-ing*. This shows that
an action happening in the past was
continuous.
    I **was cooking** the dinner.
    We **were dining**.

Notice that if the verb ends in *e*, the *e* is
dropped.

Another compound past tense is formed by
using a form of the verb *to have* in front of
the main verb, and adding the ending *-ed*.
This shows that an action has been
completed.
    I **have cooked** the dinner.
    We **have dined**.

Notice that if the verb already ends in *e* you
don't need to add one.

Another compound past tense is formed by
using *had* in front of the main verb, and
adding the ending *-ed*. This form shows
that an action in the past had been
completed before something else took place.
    I **had cooked** the dinner.
    We **had dined**.

Another compound past tense is formed by
using *did* in front of the basic form of the
verb. This can add emphasis.
    We **did enjoy** that!

---

pasture pastures
NOUN Pasture is an area of grass on
which farm animals graze.

519

A
B
C
D
E
F
G
H
I
J
K
L
M
N
O
P
Q
R
S
T
U
V
W
X
Y
Z

A B C D E F G H I J K L M N O P Q R S T U V W X Y Z

pasty pasties
ADJECTIVE **1** *Rhymes with "hasty"* Someone who is pasty looks pale and unhealthy. ▶ NOUN **2** *Said "pass-tee"* a small pie containing meat and vegetables.

pat pats patting patted
VERB **1** If you pat something, you tap it lightly with your hand held flat. ▶ NOUN **2** a small lump of butter.

patch patches patching patched
NOUN **1** a piece of material used to cover a hole in something. **2** an area of a surface that is different in appearance from the rest EG *a bald patch.* ▶ VERB **3** If you patch something, you mend it by fixing a patch over the hole.
patch up VERB If you patch something up, you mend it hurriedly or temporarily.

patchwork
ADJECTIVE **1** A patchwork quilt is made from many small pieces of material sewn together. ▶ NOUN **2** Something that is a patchwork is made up of many parts.

patchy patchier patchiest
ADJECTIVE Something that is patchy is unevenly spread or incomplete in parts EG *patchy fog on the hills.*

pâté
Said "pa-tay" NOUN Pâté is a mixture of meat, fish, or vegetables blended into a paste and spread on bread or toast.

patent patents patenting patented
NOUN **1** an official right given to an inventor to be the only person or company allowed to make or sell a new product. ▶ VERB **2** If you patent something, you obtain a patent for it. ▶ ADJECTIVE **3** obvious EG *This was patent nonsense.*
patently ADVERB

paternal
ADJECTIVE relating to a father EG *paternal pride.*

paternity
NOUN Paternity is the state or fact of being a father.

path paths
NOUN **1** a strip of ground for people to walk on. **2** Your path is the area ahead of you and the direction in which you are moving.

pathetic
ADJECTIVE **1** If something is pathetic, it makes you feel pity. **2** Pathetic also means very poor or unsuccessful EG *a pathetic attempt.*
pathetically ADVERB
■ (sense 1) heart-rending, moving, sad

pathological
ADJECTIVE extreme and uncontrollable EG *a pathological fear of snakes.*
pathologically ADVERB

pathology
NOUN Pathology is the study of diseases and the way they develop.
pathologist NOUN

pathos
Said "pay-thoss" NOUN Pathos is a quality in literature or art that causes great sadness or pity.

pathway pathways
NOUN a path.

patience
NOUN Patience is the ability to stay calm in a difficult or irritating situation.
■ forbearance, tolerance

patient patients
ADJECTIVE **1** If you are patient, you stay calm in a difficult or irritating situation. ▶ NOUN **2** a person receiving medical treatment from a doctor or in a hospital.
patiently ADVERB

patio patios
NOUN a paved area close to a house.

patriarch patriarchs
Said "pay-tree-ark" NOUN the male head of a family or tribe.
patriarchal ADJECTIVE

patrician
ADJECTIVE; A FORMAL WORD belonging to a family of high rank.

patriot patriots

NOUN someone who loves their country and feels very loyal towards it.

patriotic ADJECTIVE, **patriotism** NOUN

patrol patrols patrolling patrolled

VERB **1** When soldiers, police, or guards patrol an area, they walk or drive around to make sure there is no trouble. ▸ NOUN **2** a group of people patrolling an area.

🏛 from French *patouiller* meaning 'to flounder in mud'

patron patrons

NOUN **1** a person who supports or gives money to artists, writers, or musicians. **2** The patrons of a hotel, pub, or shop are the people who use it.

patronage NOUN

patronize patronizes patronizing patronized; also spelt **patronise**

VERB **1** If someone patronizes you, they treat you kindly, but in a way that suggests that you are less intelligent than them or inferior to them. **2** If you patronize a hotel, pub, or shop, you are a customer there.

patronizing ADJECTIVE

patron saint patron saints

NOUN The patron saint of a group of people or place is a saint who is believed to look after them.

patter patters pattering pattered

VERB **1** If something patters on a surface, it makes quick, light, tapping sounds. ▸ NOUN **2** a series of light tapping sounds EG *a patter of light rain.*

pattern patterns

NOUN **1** a decorative design of repeated shapes. **2** The pattern of something is the way it is usually done or happens EG *a perfectly normal pattern of behaviour.* **3** a diagram or shape used as a guide for making something, for example clothes.

patterned ADJECTIVE

paunch paunches

NOUN If a man has a paunch, he has a fat stomach.

pauper paupers

NOUN; AN OLD-FASHIONED WORD a very poor person.

pause pauses pausing paused

VERB **1** If you pause, you stop what you are doing for a short time. ▸ NOUN **2** a short period when you stop what you are doing. **3** a short period of silence.

pave paves paving paved

VERB When an area of ground is paved, it is covered with flat blocks of stone or concrete.

pavement pavements

NOUN a path with a hard surface at the side of a road.

pavilion pavilions

NOUN a building at a sports ground where players can wash and change.

paw paws pawing pawed

NOUN **1** The paws of an animal such as a cat or bear are its feet with claws and soft pads. ▸ VERB **2** If an animal paws something, it hits it or scrapes at it with its paws.

pawn pawns pawning pawned

VERB **1** If you pawn something, you leave it with a pawnbroker in exchange for money. ▸ NOUN **2** the smallest and least valuable playing piece in chess.

pawnbroker pawnbrokers

NOUN a dealer who lends money in return for personal property left with him or her, which may be sold if the loan is not repaid on time.

pawpaw pawpaws

NOUN the same as a **papaya**.

pay pays paying paid

VERB **1** When you pay money to someone, you give it to them because you are buying something or owe it to them. **2** If it pays to do something, it is to your advantage to do it EG *They say it pays to advertise.* **3** If you pay for something

A
B
C
D
E
F
G
H
I
J
K
L
M
N
O
P
Q
R
S
T
U
V
W
X
Y
Z

A
B
C
D
E
F
G
H
I
J
K
L
M
N
O
P
Q
R
S
T
U
V
W
X
Y
Z

that you have done, you suffer as a result. **4** If you pay attention to something, you give it your attention. **5** If you pay a visit to someone, you visit them. ▶ NOUN **6** Someone's pay is their salary or wages.
■ (sense 1) give, reimburse, settle

payable
ADJECTIVE **1** An amount of money that is payable has to be paid or can be paid EG *All fees are payable in advance.* **2** If a cheque is made payable to you, you are the person who should receive the money.

payment payments
NOUN **1** Payment is the act of paying money. **2** a sum of money paid.

payroll payrolls
NOUN Someone who is on an organization's payroll is employed and paid by them.

PC PCs
NOUN **1** In Britain, a police constable. **2** a personal computer.

PE
NOUN PE is a lesson in which gymnastics or sports are taught. PE is an abbreviation for 'physical education'.

pea peas
NOUN Peas are small round green seeds that grow in pods and are eaten as a vegetable.

peace
NOUN **1** Peace is a state of undisturbed calm and quiet. **2** When a country is at peace, it is not at war.
peaceable ADJECTIVE
■ (sense 1) stillness, tranquillity

peaceful
ADJECTIVE quiet and calm.
peacefully ADVERB
■ serene, tranquil

peach peaches
NOUN **1** a soft, round fruit with yellow flesh and a yellow and red skin. ▶ ADJECTIVE **2** pale pinky-orange.

peacock peacocks

NOUN a large bird with green and blue feathers. The male has a long tail which it can spread out in a fan.

peak peaks peaking peaked
NOUN **1** The peak of an activity or process is the point at which it is strongest or most successful. **2** the pointed top of a mountain. ▶ VERB **3** When something peaks, it reaches its highest value or its greatest level of success.
peaked ADJECTIVE
■ (sense 1) climax, culmination, high point

peal peals pealing pealed
NOUN **1** A peal of bells is the musical sound made by bells ringing one after another. ▶ VERB **2** When bells peal, they ring one after the other.

peanut peanuts
NOUN Peanuts are small oval nuts that grow under the ground.

pear pears
NOUN a fruit which is narrow at the top and wide and rounded at the bottom.

pearl pearls
NOUN a hard, round, creamy-white object used in jewellery. Pearls grow inside the shell of an oyster.

peasant peasants
NOUN a person who works on the land, especially in a poor country.

peat
NOUN Peat is dark-brown decaying plant material found in cool, wet regions. Dried peat can be used as fuel.

pebble pebbles
NOUN a smooth, round stone.

peck pecks pecking pecked
VERB **1** If a bird pecks something, it bites at it quickly with its beak. **2** If you peck someone on the cheek, you give them a quick kiss. ▶ NOUN **3** a quick bite by a bird. **4** a quick kiss on the cheek.

peculiar
ADJECTIVE **1** strange and perhaps unpleasant. **2** relating or belonging

only to a particular person or thing
eg *a gesture peculiar to her.*
peculiarly ADVERB, **peculiarity** NOUN

pedal pedals pedalling pedalled
NOUN **1** a control lever on a machine
or vehicle that you press with your
foot. ▶ VERB **2** When you pedal a
bicycle, you push the pedals round
with your feet to move along.

pedantic
ADJECTIVE If a person is pedantic,
they are too concerned with
unimportant details and traditional
rules.

**peddle peddles peddling
peddled**
VERB Someone who peddles
something sells it.

pedestal pedestals
NOUN a base on which a statue
stands.

pedestrian pedestrians
NOUN **1** someone who is walking.
▶ ADJECTIVE **2** Pedestrian means
ordinary and rather dull eg *a
pedestrian performance.*

**pedestrian crossing pedestrian
crossings**
NOUN a specially marked place
where you can cross the road safely.

pediatrician
another spelling of **paediatrician**.

pediatrics
another spelling of **paediatrics**.

pedigree pedigrees
ADJECTIVE **1** A pedigree animal is
descended from a single breed and
its ancestors are known and
recorded. ▶ NOUN **2** Someone's
pedigree is their background or
ancestry.

peek peeks peeking peeked
VERB **1** If you peek at something,
you have a quick look at it eg *I
peeked round the corner.* ▶ NOUN **2** a
quick look at something.

peel peels peeling peeled
NOUN **1** The peel of a fruit is the skin
when it has been removed. ▶ VERB
2 When you peel fruit or

vegetables, you remove the skin.
3 If a surface is peeling, it is coming
off in thin layers.
peelings PLURAL NOUN

peep peeps peeping peeped
VERB **1** If you peep at something,
you have a quick look at it. **2** If
something peeps out from behind
something else, a small part of it
becomes visible eg *a handkerchief
peeping out of his breast pocket.* ▶ NOUN
3 a quick look at something.

peer peers peering peered
VERB **1** If you peer at something, you
look at it very hard. ▶ NOUN **2** a
member of the nobility. **3** Your
peers are the people who are of the
same age and social status as
yourself.

peerage peerages
NOUN **1** The peers in a country are
called the peerage. **2** A peerage is
also the rank of being a peer.

peer group peer groups
NOUN Your peer group is the people
who are of the same age and social
status as yourself.

peerless
ADJECTIVE so magnificent or perfect
that nothing can equal it eg *peerless
wines.*

peewee peewees
NOUN a small black-and-white
Australian bird with long, thin legs.

peg pegs pegging pegged
NOUN **1** a plastic or wooden clip
used for hanging wet clothes on a
line. **2** a hook on a wall where you
can hang things. ▶ VERB **3** If you peg
clothes on a line, you fix them
there with pegs. **4** If a price is
pegged at a certain level, it is fixed
at that level.

peggy square peggy squares
NOUN In New Zealand, a small
square of knitted wool which is
sewn together with others to make
a rug.

pejorative
Said "pej-**jor**-ra-tiv" ADJECTIVE A

A
B
C
D
E
F
G
H
I
J
K
L
M
N
O
P
Q
R
S
T
U
V
W
X
Y
Z

pejorative word expresses criticism.

pekinese pekineses
Said "pee-kin-**eez**"; also spelt
pekingese
NOUN a small long-haired dog with a
flat nose.

pelican pelicans
NOUN a large water bird with a
pouch beneath its beak in which it
stores fish.

pellet pellets
NOUN a small ball of paper, lead, or
other material.

pelt pelts pelting pelted
VERB **1** If you pelt someone with
things, you throw the things with
force at them. **2** If you pelt along,
you run very fast. ▶ NOUN **3** the skin
and fur of an animal.

pelvis pelvises
NOUN the wide, curved group of
bones at hip-level at the base of
your spine.
pelvic ADJECTIVE

pen pens penning penned
NOUN **1** a long, thin instrument used
for writing with ink. **2** a small
fenced area in which farm animals
are kept for a short time. ▶ VERB **3** A
LITERARY USE If someone pens a letter
or article, they write it. **4** If you are
penned in or penned up, you have
to remain in an uncomfortably
small area.
📖 from Latin *penna* meaning
'feather'; pens used to be made
from feathers

penal
ADJECTIVE relating to the punishment
of criminals.

penalize penalizes penalizing
penalized; also spelt **penalise**
VERB If you are penalized, you are
made to suffer some disadvantage
as a punishment for something.

penalty penalties
NOUN **1** a punishment or
disadvantage that someone is made
to suffer. **2** In soccer, a penalty is a
free kick at goal that is given to the
attacking team if the defending
team have committed a foul near
their goal.

penance
NOUN If you do penance, you do
something unpleasant to show that
you are sorry for something wrong
that you have done.

pence
a plural form of **penny**.

penchant
Said "**pon**-shon" NOUN; A FORMAL WORD
If you have a penchant for
something, you have a particular
liking for it EG *a penchant for crime.*

pencil pencils
NOUN a long thin stick of wood with
graphite in the centre, used for
drawing or writing.

pendant pendants
NOUN a piece of jewellery attached
to a chain and worn round the
neck.

pending
A FORMAL WORD ▶ ADJECTIVE
1 Something that is pending is
waiting to be dealt with or will
happen soon. ▶ PREPOSITION
2 Something that is done pending
a future event is done until the
event happens EG *The army should
stay in the west pending a future war.*

pendulum pendulums
NOUN a rod with a weight at one end
in a clock which swings regularly
from side to side to control the
clock.

penetrate penetrates penetrating
penetrated
VERB To penetrate an area that is
difficult to get into is to succeed in
getting into it.
penetration NOUN

penetrating
ADJECTIVE **1** loud and high-pitched EG
a penetrating voice. **2** having or
showing deep understanding EG
penetrating questions.

pen friend pen friends
NOUN someone living in a different

place or country whom you write to regularly, although you may never have met each other.

penguin penguins
NOUN a black and white bird with webbed feet and small wings like flippers.

penicillin
NOUN Penicillin is a powerful antibiotic obtained from fungus and used to treat infections.

peninsula peninsulas
NOUN an area of land almost surrounded by water.

penis penises
NOUN A man's penis is the part of his body that he uses when urinating and having sexual intercourse.

penitent
ADJECTIVE Someone who is penitent is deeply sorry for having done something wrong.
penitence NOUN

penknife penknives
NOUN a small knife with a blade that folds back into the handle.

pennant pennants
NOUN a triangular flag, especially one used by ships as a signal.

penniless
ADJECTIVE Someone who is penniless has no money.

penny pennies or pence
NOUN a unit of currency in Britain and some other countries. In Britain a penny is worth one-hundredth of a pound.

pension pensions
Said "pen-shn" NOUN a regular sum of money paid to an old or retired person.

pensioner pensioners
NOUN an old retired person who gets a pension paid by the state.

pensive
ADJECTIVE deep in thought.
■ dreamy, meditative, thoughtful

pentagon pentagons

NOUN a shape with five straight sides.

pentathlon pentathlons
Said "pen-**tath**-lon" NOUN a sports contest in which athletes compete in five different events.

penthouse penthouses
NOUN a luxurious flat at the top of a building.

pent-up
ADJECTIVE Pent-up emotions have been held back for a long time without release.
■ bottled up, suppressed

penultimate
ADJECTIVE The penultimate thing in a series is the one before the last.

peony peonies
Said "**pee**-yon-ee" NOUN a garden plant with large pink, white, or red flowers.

people peoples peopling peopled
PLURAL NOUN **1** People are men, women, and children. ▶ NOUN **2** all the men, women, and children of a particular country or race. ▶ VERB **3** If an area is peopled by a particular group, that group of people live there.
■ (sense 1) humanity, mankind, persons
■ (sense 2) nation, population, race

pepper peppers
NOUN **1** Pepper is a hot-tasting powdered spice used for flavouring in cooking. **2** a hollow green, red, or yellow vegetable, with sweet-flavoured flesh.

peppermint peppermints
NOUN Peppermint is a plant with a strong taste. It is used for making sweets and in medicine.

per
PREPOSITION 'Per' is used to mean 'each' when expressing rates and ratios EG The class meets two evenings per week.

perceive perceives perceiving perceived
VERB If you perceive something that is not obvious, you see it or realize

A B C D E F G H I J K L M N O P Q R S T U V W X Y Z

A
B
C
D
E
F
G
H
I
J
K
L
M
N
O
P
Q
R
S
T
U
V
W
X
Y
Z

it.

≡ notice, see, spot

per cent

PHRASE You use **per cent** to talk about amounts as a proportion of a hundred. An amount that is 10 per cent (10%) of a larger amount is equal to 10 hundredths of the larger amount EG *86 per cent of Americans believe Presley is alive.*

🏛 from Latin *per* meaning 'each' and *centum* meaning 'hundred'

percentage percentages

NOUN a fraction expressed as a number of hundredths EG *the high percentage of failed marriages.*

perceptible

ADJECTIVE Something that is perceptible can be seen EG *a barely perceptible nod.*

perception perceptions

NOUN 1 Perception is the recognition of things using the senses, especially the sense of sight. 2 Someone who has perception realizes or notices things that are not obvious. 3 Your perception of something or someone is your understanding of them.

perceptive

ADJECTIVE Someone who is perceptive realizes or notices things that are not obvious.

perceptively ADVERB

≡ astute, observant, sharp

perch perches perching perched

VERB 1 If you perch on something, you sit on the edge of it. 2 When a bird perches on something, it stands on it. ▶ NOUN 3 a short rod for a bird to stand on. 4 an edible freshwater fish.

percolator percolators

NOUN a special pot for making and serving coffee.

percussion

NOUN OR ADJECTIVE Percussion instruments are musical instruments that you hit to produce sounds.

percussionist NOUN

perennial

ADJECTIVE continually occurring or never ending EG *The damp cellar was a perennial problem.*

perfect perfects perfecting perfected

ADJECTIVE 1 of the highest standard and without fault EG *His English was perfect.* 2 complete or absolute EG *They have a perfect right to say so.* 3 In English grammar, the perfect tense of a verb is formed with the present tense of 'have' and the past participle of the main verb EG *I have lost my home.* ▶ VERB 4 If you perfect something, you make it as good as it can possibly be.

perfectly ADVERB, **perfection** NOUN

≡ (sense 1) faultless, flawless

≡ (sense 4) improve, refine

perfectionist perfectionists

NOUN someone who always tries to do everything perfectly.

perforated

ADJECTIVE Something that is perforated has had small holes made in it.

perforation NOUN

perform performs performing performed

VERB 1 To perform a task or action is to do it. 2 To perform is to act, dance, or play music in front of an audience.

performer NOUN

performance performances

NOUN 1 an entertainment provided for an audience. 2 The performance of a task or action is the doing of it. 3 Someone's or something's performance is how successful they are EG *the poor performance of the American economy.*

perfume perfumes

NOUN 1 Perfume is a pleasant-smelling liquid which women put on their bodies. 2 The perfume of something is its pleasant smell.

perfumed ADJECTIVE

perfunctory

ADJECTIVE done quickly without interest or care EG *a perfunctory kiss*.

perhaps
ADVERB You use 'perhaps' when you are not sure whether something is true or possible.

peril perils
NOUN; A FORMAL WORD Peril is great danger.
perilous ADJECTIVE, **perilously** ADVERB

perimeter perimeters
NOUN The perimeter of an area or figure is the whole of its outer edge.

period periods
NOUN **1** a particular length of time. **2** one of the parts the day is divided into at school. **3** A woman's period is the monthly bleeding from her womb. ▶ ADJECTIVE **4** relating to a historical period of time EG *period furniture*.
periodic ADJECTIVE, **periodically** ADVERB

periodical periodicals
NOUN a magazine.

peripheral
Said "per-**rif**-fer-ral" ADJECTIVE **1** of little importance in comparison with other things EG *a peripheral activity*. **2** on or relating to the edge of an area.

periphery peripheries
NOUN The periphery of an area is its outside edge.

perish perishes perishing perished
VERB **1** A FORMAL USE If someone or something perishes, they are killed or destroyed. **2** If fruit or fabric perishes, it rots.
perishable ADJECTIVE

perjury
NOUN; A FORMAL OR LEGAL WORD If someone commits perjury, they tell a lie in court while under oath.
perjure VERB

perk perks perking perked
NOUN **1** an extra, such as a company car, offered by an employer in addition to a salary. Perk is an abbreviation of 'perquisite'. ▶ VERB

2 AN INFORMAL EXPRESSION When someone perks up, they become more cheerful.
perky ADJECTIVE

perm perms perming permed
NOUN **1** If you have a perm, your hair is curled and treated with chemicals to keep the curls for several months. ▶ VERB **2** To perm someone's hair means to put a perm in it.

permanent
ADJECTIVE lasting for ever, or present all the time.
permanently ADVERB, **permanence** NOUN

permeate permeates permeating permeated
VERB To permeate something is to spread through it and affect every part of it EG *The feeling of failure permeates everything I do*.

permissible
ADJECTIVE allowed by the rules.
▤ allowable, permitted

permission
NOUN If you have permission to do something, you are allowed to do it.
▤ authorization, go-ahead

permissive
ADJECTIVE A permissive society allows things which some people disapprove of, especially freedom in sexual behaviour.
permissiveness NOUN

permit permits permitting permitted
VERB **1** To permit something is to allow it or make it possible. ▶ NOUN **2** an official document which says that you are allowed to do something.
▤ (sense 1) allow, give permission, let

permutation permutations
NOUN one possible arrangement of a number of things.

pernicious
ADJECTIVE; A FORMAL WORD very harmful EG *the pernicious influence of television*.

A B C D E F G H I J K L M N O P Q R S T U V W X Y Z

527

A
B
C
D
E
F
G
H
I
J
K
L
M
N
O
P
Q
R
S
T
U
V
W
X
Y
Z

peroxide
NOUN Peroxide is a chemical used for bleaching hair or as an antiseptic.

perpendicular
ADJECTIVE upright, or at right angles to a horizontal line.
📖 from Latin *perpendiculum* meaning 'plumb line'

perpetrate perpetrates perpetrating perpetrated
VERB; A FORMAL WORD To perpetrate a crime is to commit it.
perpetrator NOUN

perpetual
ADJECTIVE never ending EG *a perpetual toothache*.
perpetually ADVERB, **perpetuity** NOUN

perpetuate perpetuates perpetuating perpetuated
VERB To perpetuate a situation or belief is to cause it to continue EG *The television series will perpetuate the myths*.

perplexed
ADJECTIVE If you are perplexed, you are puzzled and do not know what to do.

persecute persecutes persecuting persecuted
VERB To persecute someone is to treat them with continual cruelty and unfairness.
persecution NOUN, **persecutor** NOUN
▦ pick on, victimize

persevere perseveres persevering persevered
VERB If you persevere, you keep trying to do something and do not give up.
perseverance NOUN
▦ carry on, continue, keep going

Persian
Said "**per**-shn" ADJECTIVE OR NOUN an old word for **Iranian**, used especially when referring to the older forms of the language.

persimmon persimmons
NOUN a sweet, red, tropical fruit.

persist persists persisting

persisted
VERB 1 If something undesirable persists, it continues to exist. 2 If you persist in doing something, you continue in spite of opposition or difficulty.
persistence NOUN, **persistent** ADJECTIVE

person people or persons
NOUN 1 a man, woman, or child.
2 In grammar, the first person is the speaker (I), the second person is the person being spoken to (you), and the third person is anyone else being referred to (he, she, they).
▦ (sense 1) human being, individual
☑ The usual plural of *person* is *people*. *Persons* is much less common, and is used only in formal or official English.

personal
ADJECTIVE 1 Personal means belonging or relating to a particular person rather than to people in general EG *my personal feeling*.
2 Personal matters relate to your feelings, relationships, and health which you may not wish to discuss with other people.
personally ADVERB
▦ (sense 1) individual, own, private

personality personalities
NOUN 1 Your personality is your character and nature. 2 a famous person in entertainment or sport.

personify personifies personifying personified
VERB Someone who personifies a particular quality seems to be a living example of it EG *Louis personified the romance of the times* If you personify a thing or concept, you write or speak of it as if it has human abilities or qualities, for example 'The sun is trying to come out'.
personification NOUN

personnel
Said "per-son-**nell**" NOUN The personnel of an organization are the people who work for it.

perspective perspectives
NOUN A particular perspective is one way of thinking about something.

perspiration
NOUN Perspiration is the moisture that appears on your skin when you are hot or frightened.

perspire perspires perspiring perspired
VERB If someone perspires, they sweat.

persuade persuades persuading persuaded
VERB If someone persuades you to do something or persuades you that something is true, they make you do it or believe it by giving you very good reasons.
persuasion NOUN, **persuasive** ADJECTIVE
≣ convince, talk into

pertaining
ADJECTIVE; A FORMAL WORD If information or questions are pertaining to a place or thing, they are about that place or thing EG *issues pertaining to women*.

pertinent
ADJECTIVE especially relevant to the subject being discussed EG *He asks pertinent questions*.

perturbed
ADJECTIVE Someone who is perturbed is worried.

Peruvian Peruvians
Said "per-roo-vee-an" ADJECTIVE
1 belonging or relating to Peru.
▶ NOUN 2 someone who comes from Peru.

pervade pervades pervading pervaded
VERB Something that pervades a place is present and noticeable throughout it EG *a fear that pervades the community*.
pervasive ADJECTIVE

perverse
ADJECTIVE Someone who is perverse deliberately does things that are unreasonable or harmful.
perversely ADVERB, **perversity** NOUN

pervert perverts perverting perverted
VERB 1 A FORMAL USE To pervert something is to interfere with it so that it is no longer what it should be EG *a conspiracy to pervert the course of justice*. ▶ NOUN 2 a person whose sexual behaviour is disgusting or harmful.
perversion NOUN
📖 from Latin *pervertere* meaning 'to turn the wrong way'

perverted
ADJECTIVE 1 Someone who is perverted has disgusting or unacceptable behaviour or ideas, especially sexual behaviour or ideas. 2 Something that is perverted is completely wrong EG *a perverted sense of value*.

peseta pesetas
Said "pes-say-ta" NOUN the main unit of currency in Spain.

peso pesos
Said "pay-soh" NOUN the main unit of currency in several South American countries.

pessimism
NOUN Pessimism is the tendency to believe that bad things will happen.
pessimist NOUN, **pessimistic** ADJECTIVE

pest pests
NOUN 1 an insect or small animal which damages plants or food supplies. 2 someone who keeps bothering or annoying you.

pester pesters pestering pestered
VERB If you pester someone, you keep bothering them or asking them to do something.
≣ annoy, badger, hassle

pesticide pesticides
NOUN Pesticides are chemicals sprayed onto plants to kill insects and grubs.

pet pets petting petted
NOUN 1 a tame animal kept at home.
▶ ADJECTIVE 2 Someone's pet theory or pet project is something that

they particularly support or feel strongly about. ▶ VERB **3** If you pet a person or animal, you stroke them affectionately.

petal petals
NOUN The petals of a flower are the coloured outer parts.

peter out peters out petering out petered out
VERB If something peters out, it gradually comes to an end.

petite
Said "pet-**teet**" ADJECTIVE A woman who is petite is small and slim.

petition petitions petitioning petitioned
NOUN **1** a document demanding official action which is signed by a lot of people. **2** an formal request to a court for legal action to be taken. ▶ VERB **3** If you petition someone in authority, you make a formal request to them EG *I petitioned the Chinese government for permission to visit its country.*

petrified
ADJECTIVE If you are petrified, you are very frightened.

petrol
NOUN Petrol is a liquid obtained from petroleum and used as a fuel for motor vehicles.

petroleum
NOUN Petroleum is thick, dark oil found under the earth or under the sea bed.
▥ from Latin *petra* meaning 'rock' and *oleum* meaning 'oil'

petticoat petticoats
NOUN a piece of women's underwear like a very thin skirt.

petty pettier pettiest
ADJECTIVE **1** Petty things are small and unimportant. **2** Petty behaviour consists of doing small things which are selfish and unkind.

petulant
ADJECTIVE showing unreasonable and childish impatience or anger.

petulantly ADVERB, **petulance** NOUN

petunia petunias
Said "pit-**yoon**-nee-ah" NOUN a garden plant with large trumpet-shaped flowers.

pew pews
NOUN a long wooden seat with a back, which people sit on in church.

pewter
NOUN Pewter is a silvery-grey metal made from a mixture of tin and lead.

pH
NOUN The pH of a solution or of the soil is a measurement of how acid or alkaline it is. Acid solutions have a pH of less than 7 and alkaline solutions have a pH greater than 7. pH is an abbreviation for 'potential hydrogen'.

phalanger phalangers
Said "fal-**lan**-jer" NOUN an Australian marsupial with thick fur and a long tail. In Australia and New Zealand, it is also called a possum.

phallus phalluses
NOUN a penis or a symbolic model of a penis.
phallic ADJECTIVE

phantom phantoms
NOUN **1** a ghost. ▶ ADJECTIVE **2** imagined or unreal EG *a phantom pregnancy.*

pharaoh pharaohs
Said "**fair**-oh" NOUN The pharaohs were kings of ancient Egypt.

pharmaceutical
Said "far-mass-**yoo**-tik-kl" ADJECTIVE connected with the industrial production of medicines.

pharmacist pharmacists
NOUN a person who is qualified to prepare and sell medicines.

pharmacy pharmacies
NOUN a shop where medicines are sold.

phase phases phasing phased
NOUN **1** a particular stage in the development of something. ▶ VERB

2 To phase something is to cause it to happen gradually in stages.

PhD PhDs
NOUN a degree awarded to someone who has done advanced research in a subject. PhD is an abbreviation for 'Doctor of Philosophy'.

pheasant pheasants
NOUN a large, long-tailed game bird.

phenomenal
Said "fin-**nom**-in-nal" ADJECTIVE extraordinarily great or good.
phenomenally ADVERB

phenomenon phenomena
NOUN something that happens or exists, especially something remarkable or something being considered in a scientific way EG *a well-known geographical phenomenon.*
☑ The word *phenomenon* is singular. The plural form is *phenomena.*

philanthropist philanthropists
Said "fil-**lan**-throp-pist" NOUN someone who freely gives help or money to people in need.
philanthropic ADJECTIVE, **philanthropy** NOUN

philistine philistines
NOUN If you call someone a philistine, you mean that they do not like art, literature, or music.

philosophical or **philosophic**
ADJECTIVE Someone who is philosophical does not get upset when disappointing things happen.

philosophy philosophies
NOUN **1** Philosophy is the study or creation of ideas about existence, knowledge or beliefs. **2** a set of beliefs that a person has.
philosopher NOUN
⬛ from Greek *philosophos* meaning 'lover of wisdom'

phlegm
Said "**flem**" NOUN Phlegm is a thick mucus which you get in your throat when you have a cold.

phobia phobias
NOUN an great fear or hatred of something EG *The man had a phobia about flying.*
phobic ADJECTIVE

phoenix phoenixes
Said "**fee**-niks" NOUN an imaginary bird which, according to myth, burns itself to ashes every five hundred years and rises from the fire again.

phone phones phoning phoned
NOUN **1** a piece of electronic equipment which allows you to speak to someone in another place by keying in or dialling their number. ▶ VERB **2** If you phone someone, you key in or dial their number and speak to them using a phone.

phoney phonier phoniest; also spelt **phony**
ADJECTIVE; AN INFORMAL WORD false and intended to deceive.

photo photos
NOUN; AN INFORMAL WORD a photograph.

photocopier photocopiers
NOUN a machine which makes instant copies of documents by photographing them.

photocopy photocopies photocopying photocopied
NOUN **1** a copy of a document produced by a photocopier. ▶ VERB **2** If you photocopy a document, you make a copy of it using a photocopier.

photogenic
ADJECTIVE Someone who is photogenic always looks nice in photographs.

photograph photographs photographing photographed
NOUN **1** a picture made using a camera. ▶ VERB **2** When you photograph someone, you take a picture of them by using a camera.
photographer NOUN, **photography** NOUN

photographic
ADJECTIVE connected with photography.

photosynthesis

A
B
C
D
E
F
G
H
I
J
K
L
M
N
O
P
Q
R
S
T
U
V
W
X
Y
Z

NOUN Photosynthesis is the process by which the action of sunlight on the chlorophyll in plants produces the substances that keep the plants alive.

phrasal verb phrasal verbs
NOUN a verb such as 'take over' or 'break in', which is made up of a verb and an adverb or preposition.

phrase phrases phrasing phrased
NOUN **1** a group of words considered as a unit. ▶ VERB **2** If you phrase something in a particular way, you choose those words to express it EG *I should have phrased that better.*

What is a Phrase?

A **phrase** is a group of words which combine together but is not usually capable of standing on its own to describe an idea or situation. It requires additional words to form a meaningful sentence.
> *She drank **a cup of tea**.*
> *I **was reading** a book.*

Some phrases act as nouns.
> ***A stack of newspapers** lay on the floor.*
> ***My sister's friend** lives in Canada.*

Some phrases act as verbs. Verb phrases often contain an auxiliary verb. They may also contain adverbs.
> *She **was always complaining** about the buses.*
> *He **used to play** the piano.*

Some phrases act as adjectives. When words combine to act as an adjective, they are usually hyphenated if they occur before the noun.
> *The food here is **of the highest quality**.*
> *He asked for an **up-to-the-minute** report.*

Some phrases act as adverbs. Adverb phrases often begin with a preposition.
> *She disappeared **in the blink of an eye**.*
> *They played **with great gusto**.*

Some phrases are acceptable as substitutes for sentences. Although they do not contain a subject and a verb, they can be understood on their own.
> *Happy Birthday!   Good morning.   All right?*

physical
ADJECTIVE **1** concerning the body

rather than the mind. **2** relating to things that can be touched or seen, especially with regard to their size or shape EG *the physical characteristics of their machinery.*
physically ADVERB

physical education
NOUN Physical education consists of the sport that you do at school.

physician physicians
NOUN a doctor.

physics
NOUN Physics is the scientific study of matter, energy, gravity, electricity, heat, and sound.
physicist NOUN

physiology
NOUN Physiology is the scientific study of the way the bodies of living things work.

physiotherapy
NOUN Physiotherapy is medical treatment which involves exercise and massage.
physiotherapist NOUN

physique physiques
*Said "fiz-**zeek**"* NOUN A person's physique is the shape and size of their body.

pi
*Rhymes with "**fly**"* NOUN Pi is a number, approximately 3.142 and symbolized by the Greek letter π. Pi is the ratio of the circumference of a circle to its diameter.

piano pianos
NOUN a large musical instrument with a row of black and white keys. When the keys are pressed, little hammers hit wires to produce the different notes.
pianist NOUN
🏛 originally called 'pianoforte', from Italian *gravecembalo col piano e forte* meaning 'harpsichord with soft and loud (sounds)'

piccolo piccolos
NOUN a high-pitched wind instrument like a small flute.
🏛 from Italian *piccolo* meaning

'small'

pick picks picking picked
VERB **1** To pick something is to choose it. **2** If you pick a flower or fruit, or pick something from a place, you remove it with your fingers. **3** If someone picks a lock, they open it with a piece of wire instead of a key. ▶ NOUN **4** a pickaxe.
pick on VERB If you pick on someone, you criticize them unfairly or treat them unkindly.
pick up VERB If you pick someone or something up, you collect them from the place where they are waiting.

pickaxe pickaxes
NOUN a tool consisting of a curved pointed iron bar attached in the middle to a long handle.

picket pickets picketing picketed
VERB **1** When a group of people picket a place of work, they stand outside to persuade other workers to join a strike. ▶ NOUN **2** someone who is picketing a place.

pickings
PLURAL NOUN Pickings are goods or money that can be obtained very easily EG *rich pickings*.

pickle pickles pickling pickled
NOUN **1** Pickle or pickles consists of vegetables or fruit preserved in vinegar or salt water. ▶ VERB **2** To pickle food is to preserve it in vinegar or salt water.

pickpocket pickpockets
NOUN a thief who steals from people's pockets or handbags.

picnic picnics picnicking picnicked
NOUN **1** a meal eaten out of doors.
▶ VERB **2** People who are picnicking are having a picnic.

pictorial
ADJECTIVE relating to or using pictures EG *a pictorial record of the railway*.

picture pictures picturing pictured
NOUN **1** a drawing, painting, or photograph of someone or something. **2** If you have a picture of something in your mind, you have an idea or impression of it.
▶ PLURAL NOUN **3** If you go to the pictures, you go to see a film at the cinema. ▶ VERB **4** If someone is pictured in a newspaper or magazine, a photograph of them is printed in it. **5** If you picture something, you think of it and imagine it clearly EG *That is how I always picture him.*

picturesque
Said "pik-chur-**esk**" ADJECTIVE A place that is picturesque is very attractive and unspoiled.

pie pies
NOUN a dish of meat, vegetables, or fruit covered with pastry.

piece pieces piecing pieced
NOUN **1** a portion or part of something. **2** something that has been written or created, such as a work of art or a musical composition. **3** a coin EG *a 50 pence piece*. ▶ VERB **4** If you piece together a number of things, you gradually put them together to make something complete.

piecemeal
ADVERB OR ADJECTIVE done gradually and at irregular intervals EG *a piecemeal approach to career management*.

pier piers
NOUN a large structure which sticks out into the sea at a seaside town, and which people can walk along.

pierce pierces piercing pierced
VERB If a sharp object pierces something, it goes through it, making a hole.
▤ penetrate, puncture

piercing
ADJECTIVE **1** A piercing sound is high-pitched and unpleasant. **2** Someone with piercing eyes seems to look at you very intensely.
▤ (sense 1) penetrating, shrill

piety

A

Said "pie-it-tee" NOUN Piety is strong and devout religious belief or behaviour.

pig pigs
NOUN a farm animal kept for its meat. It has pinkish skin, short legs, and a snout.

pigeon pigeons
NOUN a largish bird with grey feathers, often seen in towns.

pigeonhole pigeonholes
NOUN one of the sections in a frame on a wall where letters can be left.

piggyback piggybacks
NOUN If you give someone a piggyback, you carry them on your back, supporting them under their knees.

piglet piglets
NOUN a young pig.

pigment pigments
NOUN a substance that gives something a particular colour.
pigmentation NOUN

pigsty pigsties
NOUN a hut with a small enclosed area where pigs are kept.

pigtail pigtails
NOUN a length of plaited hair.

pike pikes
NOUN 1 a large freshwater fish of northern countries with strong teeth. 2 a medieval weapon consisting of a pointed metal blade attached to a long pole.

pilchard pilchards
NOUN a small sea fish.

pile piles piling piled
NOUN 1 a quantity of things lying one on top of another. 2 the soft surface of a carpet consisting of many threads standing on end. ▶ PLURAL NOUN 3 Piles are painful swellings that appear in the veins inside or just outside a person's anus. ▶ VERB 4 If you pile things somewhere, you put them one on top of the other.

pile-up pile-ups
NOUN; AN INFORMAL WORD a road accident involving several vehicles.

pilfer pilfers pilfering pilfered
VERB Someone who pilfers steals small things over a period of time.
🔳 from Old French *pelfre* meaning 'booty'

pilgrim pilgrims
NOUN a person who travels to a holy place for religious reasons.
pilgrimage NOUN

pill pills
NOUN 1 a small, hard tablet of medicine that you swallow. 2 The pill is a type of drug that women can take regularly to prevent pregnancy.
🔳 from Latin *pilula* meaning 'little ball'

pillage pillages pillaging pillaged
VERB If a group of people pillage a place, they steal from it using violence.

pillar pillars
NOUN 1 a tall, narrow, solid structure, usually supporting part of a building. 2 Someone who is described as a pillar of a particular group is an active and important member of it EG *a pillar of the Church.*

pillar box pillar boxes
NOUN a red cylinder or box in which you post letters.

pillory pillories pillorying pilloried
VERB If someone is pilloried, they are criticized severely by a lot of people.

pillow pillows
NOUN a rectangular cushion which you rest your head on when you are in bed.

pillowcase pillowcases
NOUN a cover for a pillow which can be removed and washed.

pilot pilots piloting piloted
NOUN 1 a person who is trained to fly an aircraft. 2 a person who goes on board ships to guide them through local waters to a port. ▶ VERB 3 To pilot something is to control its movement or to guide it. ▶ ADJECTIVE 4 a small test of a

scheme or product, done to see if it would be successful.

pimp pimps
NOUN a man who finds clients for prostitutes and takes a large part of their earnings.

pimple pimples
NOUN a small spot on the skin.
pimply ADJECTIVE

pin pins pinning pinned
NOUN **1** a thin, pointed piece of metal used to fasten together things such as pieces of fabric or paper. ▶ VERB **2** If you pin something somewhere, you fasten it there with a pin or a drawing pin. **3** If someone pins you in a particular position, they hold you there so that you cannot move. **4** If you try to pin something down, you try to get or give a clear and exact description of it or statement about it.

pinafore pinafores
NOUN a dress with no sleeves, worn over a blouse.

pincers
PLURAL NOUN **1** Pincers are a tool used for gripping and pulling things. They consist of two pieces of metal hinged in the middle. **2** The pincers of a crab or lobster are its front claws.

pinch pinches pinching pinched
VERB **1** If you pinch something, you squeeze it between your thumb and first finger. **2** AN INFORMAL USE If someone pinches something, they steal it. ▶ NOUN **3** A pinch of something is the amount that you can hold between your thumb and first finger EG *a pinch of salt*.

pinched
ADJECTIVE If someone's face is pinched, it looks thin and pale.

pine pines pining pined
NOUN **1** A pine or pine tree is an evergreen tree with very thin leaves. ▶ VERB **2** If you pine for something, you are sad because you cannot have it.

pineapple pineapples
NOUN a large, oval fruit with sweet, yellow flesh and a thick, lumpy brown skin.

ping-pong
NOUN the same as **table tennis**.

pink pinker pinkest
ADJECTIVE pale reddish-white.

pinnacle pinnacles
NOUN **1** a tall pointed piece of stone or rock. **2** The pinnacle of something is its best or highest level EG *the pinnacle of his career*.

pinpoint pinpoints pinpointing pinpointed
VERB If you pinpoint something, you explain or discover exactly what or where it is.

pinstripe
ADJECTIVE Pinstripe cloth has very narrow vertical stripes.

pint pints
NOUN a unit of liquid volume equal to one eighth of a gallon or about 0.568 litres.

pioneer pioneers pioneering pioneered
Said "pie-on-ear" NOUN **1** Someone who is a pioneer in a particular activity is one of the first people to develop it. ▶ VERB **2** Someone who pioneers a new process or invention is the first person to develop it.

pious
Said "pie-uss" ADJECTIVE very religious and moral.

pip pips
NOUN Pips are the hard seeds in a fruit.

pipe pipes piping piped
NOUN **1** a long, hollow tube through which liquid or gas can flow. **2** an object used for smoking tobacco. It consists of a small hollow bowl attached to a tube. ▶ VERB **3** To pipe a liquid or gas somewhere is to transfer it through a pipe.

pipeline pipelines
NOUN a large underground pipe that

A B C D E F G H I J K L M N O **P** Q R S T U V W X Y Z

carries oil or gas over a long distance.

piper pipers
NOUN a person who plays the bagpipes.

piping
NOUN Piping consists of pipes and tubes.

piranha piranhas
Said "pir-**rah**-nah" NOUN a small, fierce fish with sharp teeth.
🏛 a Portuguese word

pirate pirates
NOUN Pirates were sailors who attacked and robbed other ships.

pirouette pirouettes
Said "pir-roo-**et**" NOUN In ballet, a pirouette is a fast spinning step done on the toes.

Pisces
Said "**pie**-seez" NOUN Pisces is the twelfth sign of the zodiac, represented by two fish. People born between February 19th and March 20th are born under this sign.
🏛 the plural of Latin *piscis* meaning 'a fish'

pistol pistols
NOUN a small gun held in the hand.

piston pistons
NOUN a cylinder or disc that slides up and down inside a tube. Pistons make parts of engines move.

pit pits
NOUN **1** a large hole in the ground. **2** a small hollow in the surface of something. **3** a coal mine.

pitch pitches pitching pitched
NOUN **1** an area of ground marked out for playing a game such as football. **2** The pitch of a sound is how high or low it is. **3** Pitch is a black substance used in road tar and also for waterproofing boats and roofs. ▶ VERB **4** If you pitch something somewhere, you throw it with a lot of force. **5** If you pitch something at a particular level of difficulty, you set it at that level EG

Any film must be pitched at a level to suit its intended audience. **6** When you pitch a tent, you fix it in an upright position.

pitcher pitchers
NOUN a large jug.

pitfall pitfalls
NOUN The pitfalls of a situation are its difficulties or dangers.

pith
NOUN the white substance between the outer skin and the flesh of an orange or lemon.

pitiful
ADJECTIVE Someone or something that is pitiful is in such a sad or weak situation that you feel pity for them.

pittance
NOUN a very small amount of money.

pitted
ADJECTIVE covered in small hollows EG *Nails often become pitted.*

pity pities pitying pitied
VERB **1** If you pity someone, you feel very sorry for them. ▶ NOUN **2** Pity is a feeling of being sorry for someone. **3** If you say that it is a pity about something, you are expressing your disappointment about it.

pivot pivots pivoting pivoted
VERB **1** If something pivots, it balances or turns on a central point EG *The keel pivots on a large stainless steel pin.* ▶ NOUN **2** the central point on which something balances or turns.
pivotal ADJECTIVE

pixie pixies
NOUN an imaginary little creature in fairy stories.

pizza pizzas
Said "**peet**-sah" NOUN a flat piece of dough covered with cheese, tomato, and other savoury food.

placard placards
NOUN a large notice carried at a demonstration or displayed in a

public place.

placate placates placating placated
VERB If you placate someone, you stop them feeling angry by doing something to please them.

place places placing placed
NOUN **1** any point, building, or area. **2** the position where something belongs EG *She set the holder in its place on the table.* **3** a space at a table set with cutlery where one person can eat. **4** If you have a place in a group or at a college, you are a member or are accepted as a student. **5** a particular point or stage in a sequence of things EG *second place in the race.* ▶ PHRASE **6** When something **takes place**, it happens. ▶ VERB **7** If you place something somewhere, you put it there. **8** If you place an order, you order something.
■ (sense 1) location, site, spot

placebo placebos
Said "plas-**see**-boh" NOUN a harmless, inactive substance given to a patient in place of a drug.

placenta placentas
Said "plas-**sen**-tah" NOUN The placenta is the mass of veins and tissues in the womb of a pregnant woman or animal. It gives the foetus food and oxygen.

placid
ADJECTIVE calm and not easily excited or upset.
placidly ADVERB
■ even-tempered, unexcitable

plagiarism
Said "**play**-jer-rizm" NOUN Plagiarism is copying someone else's work or ideas and pretending that it is your own.
plagiarist NOUN, **plagiarize** VERB
▥ from Latin *plagiarus* meaning 'plunderer'

plague plagues plaguing plagued
Said "**playg**" NOUN **1** Plague is a very infectious disease that kills large numbers of people. **2** A plague of

unpleasant things is a large number of them occurring at the same time EG *a plague of rats.* ▶ VERB **3** If problems plague you, they keep causing you trouble.

plaice
NOUN an edible European flat fish.

plaid plaids
Said "**plad**" NOUN Plaid is woven material with a tartan design.

plain plainer plainest; plains
ADJECTIVE **1** very simple in style with no pattern or decoration EG *plain walls.* **2** obvious and easy to recognize or understand EG *plain language.* **3** A person who is plain is not at all beautiful or attractive.
▶ ADVERB **4** You can use 'plain' before a noun or adjective to emphasize it EG *You were just plain stupid.* ▶ NOUN **5** a large, flat area of land with very few trees.
plainly ADVERB
■ (sense 1) bare, simple, unadorned

plaintiff plaintiffs
NOUN a person who has brought a court case against another person.

plait plaits plaiting plaited
VERB **1** If you plait three lengths of hair or rope together, you twist them over each other in turn to make one thick length. ▶ NOUN **2** a length of hair that has been plaited.

plan plans planning planned
NOUN **1** a method of achieving something that has been worked out beforehand. **2** a detailed diagram or drawing of something that is to be made. ▶ VERB **3** If you plan something, you decide in detail what it is to be and how to do it. **4** If you are planning to do something, you intend to do it EG *They plan to marry in the summer.*
■ (sense 1) scheme, strategy
■ (sense 3) devise, scheme, think out
■ (sense 4) intend, mean, propose

plane planes planing planed
NOUN **1** a vehicle with wings and engines that enable it to fly. **2** a flat

surface. **3** You can refer to a particular level of something as a particular plane EG *to take the rock and roll concert to a higher plane.* **4** a tool with a flat bottom with a sharp blade in it. You move it over a piece of wood to remove thin pieces from the surface. ▶ VERB **5** If you plane a piece of wood, you smooth its surface with a plane.

planet planets
NOUN a round object in space which moves around the sun or a star and is lit by light from it.
planetary ADJECTIVE

plank planks
NOUN a long rectangular piece of wood.

plankton
NOUN Plankton is a layer of tiny plants and animals that live just below the surface of a sea or lake.

plant plants planting planted
NOUN **1** a living thing that grows in the earth and has stems, leaves, and roots. **2** a factory or power station EG *a giant bottling plant.* ▶ VERB **3** When you plant a seed or plant, you put it into the ground. **4** If you plant something somewhere, you put it there firmly or secretly.

plantation plantations
NOUN **1** a large area of land where crops such as tea, cotton, or sugar are grown. **2** a large number of trees planted together.

plaque plaques
Rhymes with "black" NOUN **1** a flat piece of metal which is fixed to a wall and has an inscription in memory of a famous person or event. **2** Plaque is a substance which forms around your teeth and consists of bacteria, saliva, and food.

plasma
Said "plaz-mah" NOUN Plasma is the clear fluid part of blood.

plaster plasters plastering plastered
NOUN **1** Plaster is a paste made of sand, lime, and water, which is used to form a smooth surface for inside walls and ceilings. **2** a strip of sticky material with a small pad, used for covering cuts on your body. ▶ VERB **3** To plaster a wall is to cover it with a layer of plaster. ▶ PHRASE **4** If your arm or leg is in **plaster**, it has a plaster cast on it to protect a broken bone.
plasterer NOUN

plastered
ADJECTIVE **1** If something is plastered to a surface, it is stuck there. **2** If something is plastered with things, they are all over its surface.

plastic plastics
NOUN **1** Plastic is a substance made by a chemical process that can be moulded when soft to make a wide range of objects. ▶ ADJECTIVE **2** made of plastic.

plastic surgery
NOUN Plastic surgery is surgery to replace or repair damaged skin or to improve a person's appearance by changing the shape of their features.

plate plates
NOUN **1** a flat dish used to hold food. **2** a flat piece of metal or other hard material used for various purposes in machinery or building EG *heavy steel plates used in shipbuilding.*

plateau plateaus or **plateaux**
Rhymes with "snow" NOUN a large area of high and fairly flat land.

plated
ADJECTIVE Metal that is plated is covered with a thin layer of silver or gold.

platform platforms
NOUN **1** a raised structure on which someone or something can stand. **2** the raised area in a railway station where passengers get on and off trains.

platinum
NOUN Platinum is a valuable silver-coloured metal.

platitude platitudes
NOUN a statement made as if it were significant but which has become meaningless or boring because it has been used so many times before.

platonic
ADJECTIVE A platonic relationship is simply one of friendship and does not involve sexual attraction.
🔲 from the name of the Greek philospher Plato

platoon platoons
NOUN a small group of soldiers, commanded by a lieutenant.

platter platters
NOUN a large serving plate.

platypus platypuses
NOUN A platypus or duck-billed platypus is an Australian mammal which lives in rivers. It has brown fur, webbed feet, and a snout like a duck.
🔲 from Greek *platus* meaning 'flat' and *pous* meaning 'foot'

plaudits
PLURAL NOUN; A FORMAL WORD Plaudits are expressions of admiration.

plausible
ADJECTIVE An explanation that is plausible seems likely to be true.
plausibility NOUN

play plays playing played
VERB 1 When children play, they take part in games or use toys.
2 When you play a sport or match, you take part in it. 3 If an actor plays a character in a play or film, he or she performs that role. 4 If you play a musical instrument, you produce music from it. 5 If you play a record or tape, you listen to it. ▶ NOUN 6 a piece of drama performed in the theatre or on television.
player NOUN

playboy playboys
NOUN a rich man who spends his time enjoying himself.

playful

ADJECTIVE 1 friendly and light-hearted EG *a playful kiss on the tip of his nose.* 2 lively EG *a playful puppy.*
playfully ADVERB

playground playgrounds
NOUN a special area for children to play in.

playgroup playgroups
NOUN an informal kind of school for very young children where they learn by playing.

playing card playing cards
NOUN Playing cards are cards printed with numbers or pictures which are used to play various games.

playing field playing fields
NOUN an area of grass where people play sports.

playwright playwrights
NOUN a person who writes plays.

plaza plazas
Said "plah-za" NOUN an open square in a city.

plea pleas
NOUN 1 an emotional request EG *a plea for help.* 2 In a court of law, someone's plea is their statement that they are guilty or not guilty.

plead pleads pleading pleaded
VERB 1 If you plead with someone, you ask them in an intense emotional way to do something.
2 When a person pleads guilty or not guilty, they state in court that they are guilty or not guilty of a crime.

pleasant
ADJECTIVE enjoyable, likable, or attractive.
pleasantly ADVERB
▤ agreeable, nice, pleasing

please pleases pleasing pleased
1 You say please when you are asking someone politely to do something. ▶ VERB 2 If something pleases you, it makes you feel happy and satisfied.
pleased ADJECTIVE
▤ (sense 2) delight, gladden, satisfy

pleasing
ADJECTIVE attractive, satisfying, or enjoyable EG *a pleasing appearance*.

pleasure pleasures
NOUN **1** Pleasure is a feeling of happiness, satisfaction, or enjoyment. **2** an activity that you enjoy.
pleasurable ADJECTIVE

pleat pleats
NOUN a permanent fold in fabric made by folding one part over another.

plebiscite plebiscites
Said "pleb-iss-ite" NOUN; A FORMAL WORD a vote on a matter of national importance in which all the voters in a country can take part.
⬛ from Latin *plebiscitum* meaning 'decree of the people'

pledge pledges pledging pledged
NOUN **1** a solemn promise. ▶ VERB **2** If you pledge something, you promise that you will do it or give it.

plentiful
ADJECTIVE existing in large numbers or amounts and readily available EG *Fruit and vegetables were plentiful*.
plentifully ADVERB

plenty
NOUN If there is plenty of something, there is a lot of it.

plethora
Said "pleth-thor-ah" NOUN A plethora of something is an amount that is greater than you need.

pleurisy
Said "ploor-ris-see" NOUN Pleurisy is a serious illness in which a person's lungs become inflamed and breathing is difficult.

pliable
ADJECTIVE **1** If something is pliable, you can bend it without breaking it. **2** Someone who is pliable can be easily influenced or controlled.
▤ (sense 1) bendy, flexible, supple

pliers
PLURAL NOUN Pliers are a small tool with metal jaws for holding small objects and bending wire.

plight
NOUN Someone's plight is the very difficult or dangerous situation that they are in EG *the plight of the refugees*.

plinth plinths
NOUN a block of stone on which a statue or pillar stands.

plod plods plodding plodded
VERB If you plod somewhere, you walk there slowly and heavily.

plonk plonks plonking plonked
VERB If you plonk something down, you put it down heavily and carelessly.

plop plops plopping plopped
NOUN **1** a gentle sound made by something light dropping into a liquid. ▶ VERB **2** If something plops into a liquid, it drops into it with a gentle sound.

plot plots plotting plotted
NOUN **1** a secret plan made by a group of people. **2** The plot of a novel or play is the story. **3** a small piece of land. ▶ VERB **4** If people plot to do something, they plan it secretly EG *His family is plotting to disinherit him*. **5** If someone plots the course of a plane or ship on a map, or plots a graph, they mark the points in the correct places.
▤ (sense 1) conspiracy, scheme
▤ (sense 4) conspire, plan, scheme

plough ploughs ploughing ploughed
Rhymes with "cow" NOUN **1** a large farming tool that is pulled across a field to turn the soil over before planting seeds. ▶ VERB **2** When someone ploughs land, they use a plough to turn over the soil.

ploy ploys
NOUN a clever plan or way of behaving in order to get something that you want.

pluck plucks plucking plucked
VERB **1** To pluck a fruit or flower is to remove it with a sharp pull. **2** To pluck a chicken or other dead bird means to pull its feathers out before cooking it. **3** When you pluck a stringed instrument, you pull the strings and let them go.
▸ NOUN **4** Pluck is courage.
plucky ADJECTIVE

plug plugs plugging plugged
NOUN **1** a plastic object with metal prongs that can be pushed into a socket to connect an appliance to the electricity supply. **2** a disc of rubber or metal with which you block up the hole in a sink or bath.
▸ VERB **3** If you plug a hole, you block it with something.

plum plums
NOUN a small fruit with a smooth red or yellow skin and a large stone in the middle.

plumage
Said "ploom-mage" NOUN A bird's plumage is its feathers.

plumber plumbers
NOUN a person who connects and repairs water pipes.
🏛 from Old French *plommier* meaning 'worker in lead'

plumbing
NOUN The plumbing in a building is the system of water pipes, sinks, and toilets.

plume plumes
NOUN a large, brightly coloured feather.

plummet plummets plummeting plummeted
VERB If something plummets, it falls very quickly EG *Sales have plummeted.*

plump plumper plumpest
ADJECTIVE rather fat EG *a small plump baby.*
▣ chubby, podgy, tubby

plunder plunders plundering plundered
VERB If someone plunders a place, they steal things from it.

plunge plunges plunging plunged
VERB **1** If something plunges, it falls suddenly. **2** If you plunge an object into something, you push it in quickly. **3** If you plunge into an activity or state, you suddenly become involved in it or affected by it EG *The United States had just plunged into the war.* ▸ NOUN **4** a sudden fall.
▣ (sense 1) dive, drop, fall, plummet

Plunket Society
NOUN In New Zealand, the Plunket Society was an organization for the care of mothers and babies. It is now called the Royal New Zealand Society for the Health of Women and Children.

plural plurals
NOUN the form of a word that is used to refer to two or more people or things, for example the plural of 'chair' is 'chairs', and the plural of 'mouse' is 'mice'.

What is a Plural?

Most nouns can exist in either the singular or plural.

The **singular** form of the noun is used to mean only one instance of a thing. This is the main form given in the dictionary.
one book   a raven

The **plural** form of the noun is used to mean more than one instance of a thing. The plural form is given in the dictionary in smaller type after the main form.
two books   some ravens

The plural form of the noun is usually formed by adding the letter -s to the singular.
book ➤ books   raven ➤ ravens

Words that end in -s, -z, -x, -ch, or -sh in the singular are made plural by adding the letters -es.
cross ➤ crosses   box ➤ boxes

Words that end in a consonant + -y in the singular are made plural by removing the -y and adding -ies.
pony ➤ ponies   party ➤ parties

Words that end in -ife in the singular are

made plural by removing the *-fe* and adding *-ves*.

knife ➤ knives life ➤ lives

Some words that end in *-f* in the singular are made plural by removing the *-f* and adding *-ves*. Other words that end in *-f* in the singular are made plural by simply adding *-s*.

hoof ➤ hooves roof ➤ roofs

BE CAREFUL not to use an apostrophe (') when you add an *-s* to make a plural.

Irregular Plurals

Some words that have come to English from a foreign language have plurals that do not end in *-s*.

Some words that came into English from French have plurals ending in *-x*.

bureau ➤ bureaux gateau ➤ gateaux

Some words that came into English from Italian have plurals ending in *-i*.

paparazzo ➤ paparazzi graffito ➤ graffiti

Some words that came into English from Hebrew have plurals ending in *-im*.

cherub ➤ cherubim kibbutz ➤ kibbutzim

Some words that came into English from Latin have plurals ending in *-i*, *-a*, or *-ae*.

cactus ➤ cacti medium ➤ media
formula ➤ formulae

Some words that came into English from Ancient Greek have plurals ending in *-a*.

phenomenon ➤ phenomena criterion ➤ criteria

The plural forms of a few words are not formed according to any regular rule. However, there are very few words like this. Here are some of the most common ones: child, children; deer, deer; fish, fish or fishes; foot, feet; man, men; mouse, mice; ox, oxen; sheep, sheep; woman, women.

pluralism

NOUN Pluralism is the belief that it is possible for different social and religious groups to live together peacefully while keeping their own beliefs and traditions.

pluralist ADJECTIVE OR NOUN

plural noun plural nouns

NOUN In this dictionary, 'plural noun' is the name given to a noun that is normally used only in the plural, for example 'scissors' or 'police'.

plus

1 You use 'plus' to show that one number is being added to another EG *Two plus two equals four.* ▶ ADJECTIVE **2** slightly more than the number mentioned EG *a career of 25 years plus.* ▶ PREPOSITION **3** You can use 'plus' when you mention an additional item EG *He wrote a history of Scotland plus a history of British literature.*

☑ Although you can use *plus* to mean 'additionally' in spoken language, you should avoid it in written work: *plus, you could win a holiday in Florida.*

plush

ADJECTIVE very expensive and smart EG *a plush hotel.*

Pluto

NOUN Pluto is the smallest planet in the solar system and the furthest from the sun.

ply plies plying plied

VERB **1** If you ply someone with things or questions, you keep giving them things or asking them questions. **2** To ply a trade is to do a particular job as your work. ▶ NOUN **3** Ply is the thickness of wool or thread, measured by the number of strands it is made from.

plywood

NOUN Plywood is wooden board made from several thin sheets of wood glued together under pressure.

p.m.

used to specify times between 12 noon and 12 midnight, eg *He went to bed at 9 p.m.* It is an abbreviation for the Latin phrase 'post meridiem', which means 'after noon'.

pneumatic

Said "new-**mat**-ik" ADJECTIVE operated by or filled with compressed air EG *a pneumatic drill.*
🏛 from Latin *pneumaticus*

meaning 'of air or wind'

pneumonia
Said "new-**moan**-ee-ah" NOUN
Pneumonia is a serious disease which affects a person's lungs and makes breathing difficult.

poach poaches poaching poached
VERB **1** If someone poaches animals from someone else's land, they illegally catch the animals for food. **2** When you poach food, you cook it gently in hot liquid.
poacher NOUN

pocket pockets
NOUN **1** a small pouch that forms part of a piece of clothing. **2** A pocket of something is a small area of it EG *There are still pockets of resistance.*

pocket money
NOUN Pocket money is an amount of money given regularly to children by their parents.

pod pods
NOUN a long narrow seed container that grows on plants such as peas or beans.

poddy poddies
NOUN In Australian English, a calf or lamb that is being fed by hand.

podium podiums
NOUN a small platform, often one on which someone stands to make a speech.

poem poems
NOUN a piece of writing in which the words are arranged in short rhythmic lines, often with a rhyme.

poet poets
NOUN a person who writes poems.

poetic
ADJECTIVE **1** very beautiful and expressive EG *a pure and poetic love.* **2** relating to poetry.
poetically ADVERB

poetry
NOUN Poetry is poems, considered as a form of literature.

poignant
Said "**poyn**-yant" ADJECTIVE

Something that is poignant has a strong emotional effect on you, often making you feel sad EG *a moving and poignant moment.*
poignancy NOUN

point points pointing pointed
NOUN **1** an opinion or fact expressed by someone EG *You've made a good point.* **2** a quality EG *Tact was never her strong point.* **3** the purpose or meaning something has EG *He completely missed the point in most of his argument.* **4** a position or time EG *At some point during the party, a fight erupted.* **5** a single mark in a competition. **6** the thin, sharp end of something such as a needle or knife. **7** The points of a compass are the 32 directions indicated on it. **8** The decimal point in a number is the dot separating the whole number from the fraction. **9** On a railway track, the points are the levers and rails which enable a train to move from one track to another. ▶ VERB **10** If you point at something, you stick out your finger to show where it is. **11** If something points in a particular direction, it faces that way.

point-blank
ADJECTIVE **1** Something that is shot at point-blank range is shot with a gun held very close to it. ▶ ADVERB **2** If you say something point-blank, you say it directly without explanation or apology.

pointed
ADJECTIVE **1** A pointed object has a thin, sharp end. **2** Pointed comments express criticism.
pointedly ADVERB

pointer pointers
NOUN a piece of information which helps you to understand something EG *Here are a few pointers to help you make a choice.*

pointless
ADJECTIVE Something that is pointless has no purpose.
pointlessly ADVERB

A B C D E F G H I J K L M N O P Q R S T U V W X Y Z

A
B
C
D
E
F
G
H
I
J
K
L
M
N
O
P
Q
R
S
T
U
V
W
X
Y
Z

point of view points of view
NOUN Your point of view is your opinion about something or your attitude towards it.

poise
NOUN Someone who has poise is calm and dignified.

poised
ADJECTIVE If you are poised to do something, you are ready to do it at any moment.

poison poisons poisoning poisoned
NOUN **1** Poison is a substance that can kill people or animals if they swallow it or absorb it. ▸ VERB **2** To poison someone is to try to kill them with poison.
poisonous ADJECTIVE

poke pokes poking poked
VERB **1** If you poke someone or something, you push at them quickly with your finger or a sharp object. **2** Something that pokes out of another thing appears from underneath or behind it EG *roots poking out of the earth*.
■ (sense 1) dig, jab, prod

poker pokers
NOUN **1** Poker is a card game in which the players make bets on the cards dealt to them. **2** a long metal rod used for moving coals or logs in a fire.

polar
ADJECTIVE relating to the area around the North and South Poles.

polar bear polar bears
NOUN a large white bear which lives in the area around the North Pole.

pole poles
NOUN **1** a long rounded piece of wood or metal. **2** The earth's poles are the two opposite ends of its axis EG *the North Pole*.

Pole Poles
NOUN someone who comes from Poland.

pole vault
NOUN The pole vault is an athletics event in which contestants jump over a high bar using a long flexible pole to lift themselves into the air.

police polices policing policed
PLURAL NOUN **1** The police are the people who are officially responsible for making sure that people obey the law. ▸ VERB **2** To police an area is to keep law and order there by means of the police or an armed force.

policeman policemen
NOUN a man who is a member of a police force.
policewoman NOUN

policy policies
NOUN **1** a set of plans, especially in politics or business EG *the new economic policy*. **2** An insurance policy is a document which shows an agreement made with an insurance company.

polio
NOUN Polio is an infectious disease that is caused by a virus and often results in paralysis. Polio is short for 'poliomyelitis'.

polish polishes polishing polished
VERB **1** If you polish something, you put polish on it or rub it with a cloth to make it shine. ▸ NOUN **2** Polish is a substance that you put on an object to clean it and make it shine EG *shoe polish*.
polished ADJECTIVE

Polish
Said "pole-ish" ADJECTIVE
1 belonging or relating to Poland. ▸ NOUN **2** Polish is the main language spoken in Poland.

polite
ADJECTIVE Someone who is polite has good manners and behaves considerately towards other people.
politely ADVERB, **politeness** NOUN
■ civil, courteous, well-mannered

politician politicians
NOUN a person involved in the government of a country.

politics

NOUN Politics is the activity and planning concerned with achieving power and control in a country or organization.

political ADJECTIVE, **politically** ADVERB

polka polkas

NOUN a fast dance in which couples dance together in circles around the room.

poll polls polling polled

NOUN **1** a survey in which people are asked their opinions about something. ▶ PLURAL NOUN **2** A political election can be referred to as the polls. ▶ VERB **3** If you are polled on something, you are asked your opinion about it as part of a survey.

pollen

NOUN Pollen is a fine yellow powder produced by flowers in order to fertilize other flowers of the same species.

pollinate pollinates pollinating pollinated

VERB To pollinate a plant is to fertilize it with pollen.

pollination NOUN

pollutant pollutants

NOUN a substance that causes pollution.

pollute pollutes polluting polluted

VERB To pollute water or air is to make it dirty and dangerous to use or live in.

pollution NOUN, **polluted** ADJECTIVE
≡ contaminate, foul, poison

polo

NOUN Polo is a game played between two teams of players on horseback. The players use wooden hammers with long handles to hit a ball.

polo-necked

ADJECTIVE A polo-necked jumper has a deep fold of material at the neck.

polyester

NOUN Polyester is a man-made fibre, used especially to make clothes.

polygamy

Said "pol-lig-gam-ee" NOUN Polygamy is having more than one wife at the same time.

polygamous ADJECTIVE

polystyrene

NOUN Polystyrene is a very light plastic, used especially as insulating material or to make containers.

polythene

NOUN Polythene is a type of plastic that is used to make thin sheets or bags.

polyunsaturated

ADJECTIVE Polyunsaturated oils and margarines are made mainly from vegetable fats and are considered to be healthier than saturated oils.

polyunsaturate NOUN

pomegranate pomegranates

NOUN a round fruit with a thick reddish skin. It contains a lot of small seeds.
🏛 from Latin *pomum granatum* meaning 'apple full of seeds'

pomp

NOUN Pomp is the use of ceremony, fine clothes, and decorations on special occasions EG *Sir Patrick was buried with much pomp.*

pompous

ADJECTIVE behaving in a way that is too serious and self-important.

pomposity NOUN

pond ponds

NOUN a small, usually man-made area of water.

ponder ponders pondering pondered

VERB If you ponder, you think about something deeply EG *He was pondering the problem when Phillipson drove up.*
≡ consider, mull over, think

ponderous

ADJECTIVE dull, slow, and serious EG *the ponderous commentary.*

pong pongs

NOUN; AN INFORMAL WORD an unpleasant smell.

A B C D E F G H I J K L M N O P Q R S T U V W X Y Z

pontiff pontiffs
NOUN; A FORMAL WORD The pontiff is the Pope.

pony ponies
NOUN a small horse.

ponytail ponytails
NOUN a hairstyle in which long hair is tied at the back of the head and hangs down like a tail.

pony trekking
NOUN Pony trekking is a leisure activity in which people ride across country on ponies.

poodle poodles
NOUN a type of dog with curly hair.

pool pools pooling pooled
NOUN 1 a small area of still water. 2 Pool is a game in which players try to hit coloured balls into pockets around the table using long sticks called cues. 3 A pool of people, money, or things is a group or collection used or shared by several people. ▸ PLURAL NOUN 4 The pools are a competition in which people try to guess the results of football matches. ▸ VERB 5 If people pool their resources, they gather together the things they have so that they can be shared or used by all of them.

poor poorer poorest
ADJECTIVE 1 Poor people have very little money and few possessions. 2 Poor places are inhabited by people with little money and show signs of neglect. 3 You use 'poor' to show sympathy EG Poor you! 4 'Poor' also means of a low quality or standard EG a poor performance.
▤ (sense 1) impoverished, penniless, poverty-stricken

poorly
ADJECTIVE 1 feeling unwell or ill. ▸ ADVERB 2 badly EG a poorly planned operation.

pop pops popping popped
NOUN 1 Pop is modern music played and enjoyed especially by young people. 2 You can refer to fizzy, nonalcoholic drinks as pop. 3 a short, sharp sound. ▸ VERB 4 If something pops, it makes a sudden sharp sound. 5 If you pop something somewhere, you put it there quickly EG I'd just popped the pie in the oven. 6 If you pop somewhere, you go there quickly EG His mother popped out to buy him an ice cream.

popcorn
NOUN Popcorn is a snack consisting of grains of maize heated until they puff up and burst.

Pope Popes
NOUN The Pope is the head of the Roman Catholic Church.
▤ from Latin *Papa* meaning 'bishop' or 'father'

poplar poplars
NOUN a type of tall thin tree.

poppy poppies
NOUN a plant with a large red flower on a hairy stem.

populace
NOUN; A FORMAL WORD The populace of a country is its people.

popular
ADJECTIVE 1 liked or approved of by a lot of people. 2 involving or intended for ordinary people EG the popular press.
popularly ADVERB, **popularity** NOUN, **popularize** VERB
▤ (sense 1) fashionable, well-liked

populate populates populating populated
VERB The people or animals that populate an area live there.

population populations
NOUN The population of a place is the people who live there, or the number of people living there.

porcelain
NOUN Porcelain is a delicate, hard material used to make crockery and ornaments.

porch porches
NOUN a covered area at the entrance to a building.

porcupine porcupines

NOUN a large rodent with long spines covering its body.
📖 from Old French *porc d'espins* meaning 'pig with spines'

pore pores poring pored
NOUN **1** The pores in your skin or on the surface of a plant are very small holes which allow moisture to pass through. ▶ VERB **2** If you pore over a piece of writing or a diagram, you study it carefully.

pork
NOUN Pork is meat from a pig which has not been salted or smoked.

pornography
NOUN Pornography refers to magazines and films that are designed to cause sexual excitement by showing naked people and sexual acts.
pornographic ADJECTIVE
📖 from Greek *pornos* meaning 'prostitute' and *graphein* meaning 'to write'

porpoise porpoises
Said "**por**-pus" NOUN a sea mammal related to the dolphin.
📖 from Latin *porcus* meaning 'pig' and *piscis* meaning 'fish'

porridge
NOUN Porridge is a thick, sticky food made from oats cooked in water or milk.

port ports
NOUN **1** a town or area which has a harbour or docks. **2** Port is a kind of strong, sweet red wine. ▶ ADJECTIVE **3** The port side of a ship is the left side when you are facing the front.

portable
ADJECTIVE designed to be easily carried EG *a portable television*.

porter porters
NOUN **1** a person whose job is to be in charge of the entrance of a building, greeting and directing visitors. **2** A porter in a railway station or hospital is a person whose job is to carry or move things.

portfolio portfolios
NOUN a thin, flat case for carrying papers.
📖 from Italian *portafoglio* meaning 'carrier for papers'

porthole portholes
NOUN a small window in the side of a ship or aircraft.

portion portions
NOUN a part or amount of something EG *a portion of fresh fruit*.
▣ bit, part, piece

portrait portraits
NOUN a picture or photograph of someone.

portray portrays portraying portrayed
VERB When an actor, artist, or writer portrays someone or something, they represent or describe them.
portrayal NOUN

Portuguese
Said "**por**-tyoo-**geez**" ADJECTIVE **1** belonging or relating to Portugal. ▶ NOUN **2** someone who comes from Portugal. **3** Portuguese is the main language spoken in Portugal and Brazil.

pose poses posing posed
VERB **1** If something poses a problem, it is the cause of the problem. **2** If you pose a question, you ask it. **3** If you pose as someone else, you pretend to be that person in order to deceive people. ▶ NOUN **4** a way of standing, sitting, or lying EG *Mr Clark assumes a pose for the photographer*.
▣ (sense 4) attitude, posture

poser posers
NOUN **1** someone who behaves or dresses in an exaggerated way in order to impress people. **2** a difficult problem.

posh posher poshest
ADJECTIVE **1** AN INFORMAL WORD smart, fashionable, and expensive EG *a posh restaurant*. **2** upper class EG *the man with the posh voice*.

position positions positioning

A B C D E F G H I J K L M N O P Q R S T U V W X Y Z

A
B
C
D
E
F
G
H
I
J
K
L
M
N
O
P
Q
R
S
T
U
V
W
X
Y
Z

positioned

NOUN **1** The position of someone or something is the place where they are. **2** When someone or something is in a particular position, they are sitting or lying in that way EG *I raised myself to a sitting position*. **3** a job or post in an organization. **4** The position that you are in at a particular time is the situation that you are in EG *This puts the president in a difficult position.*
▶ VERB **5** To position something somewhere is to put it there EG *Llewelyn positioned a cushion behind Joanna's back.*

positive

ADJECTIVE **1** completely sure about something EG *I was positive he'd known about that money*. **2** confident and hopeful EG *I felt very positive about everything*. **3** showing approval or encouragement EG *I anticipate a positive response*. **4** providing definite proof of the truth or identity of something EG *positive evidence*. **5** A positive number is greater than zero.
positively ADVERB
◼ (sense 4) absolute, certain, definite

possess possesses possessing possessed

VERB **1** If you possess something, you own it or have it. **2** If a feeling or belief possesses you, it strongly influences you EG *Absolute terror possessed her.*
possessor NOUN

possession possessions

NOUN **1** If something is in your possession or if you are in possession of it, you have it. **2** Your possessions are the things that you own or that you have with you.
◼ (sense 2) belongings, property

possessive

ADJECTIVE **1** A person who is possessive about someone or something wants to keep them to themselves. ▶ NOUN **2** In grammar, the possessive is the form of a

noun or pronoun used to show possession EG *my car... That's hers.*

What is the Possessive?

The possessive case is formed by adding an apostrophe (') and the letter s to the dictionary form of the word.

The **possessive** is used when a noun indicates a person or thing that owns another person or thing.
   The **cat's** fur was wet.
   The **doctor's** cat was called Joey.

If the noun is plural and already ends in -s, the possessive is formed by simply adding an apostrophe.
   The vet often trims **cats'** claws.
   Doctors' surgeries make me nervous.

The possessive can also be shown by using the word of in front of the noun. This is usually used when you are talking about something that is not alive or cannot be touched.
   We climbed to the top **of the hill**.
   He is a master **of disguise**.

When a possessive is not followed by another noun, it refers to the place where that person lives or works.
   I am going to stay at my **aunt's**.
   I bought a loaf at the **baker's**.

---

possibility possibilities

NOUN something that might be true or might happen EG *the possibility of a ban*.
◼ chance, likelihood, probability

possible

ADJECTIVE **1** likely to happen or able to be done. **2** likely or capable of being true or correct.
possibly ADVERB
◼ (sense 1) feasible, practicable

possum possums

NOUN In Australian and New Zealand English, a possum is a phalanger, a marsupial with thick fur and a long tail.

post posts posting posted

NOUN **1** The post is the system by which letters and parcels are collected and delivered. **2** a job or official position in an organization.

3 a strong upright pole fixed into the ground EG *They are tied to a post.*
▶ VERB **4** If you post a letter, you send it to someone by putting it into a postbox. **5** If you are posted somewhere, you are sent by your employers to work there.
postal ADJECTIVE

post-
PREFIX after a particular time or event EG *his postwar career.*

postage
NOUN Postage is the money that you pay to send letters and parcels by post.

postal order postal orders
NOUN a piece of paper representing a sum of money which you can buy at a post office.

postcard postcards
NOUN a card, often with a picture on one side, which you write on and send without an envelope.

postcode postcodes
NOUN a short sequence of letters and numbers at the end of an address which helps the post office to sort the mail.

poster posters
NOUN a large notice or picture that is stuck on a wall as an advertisement or for decoration.

posterior posteriors
NOUN; A HUMOROUS USE A person's posterior is their bottom.

posterity
NOUN; A FORMAL WORD You can refer to the future and the people who will be alive then as posterity EG *to record the voyage for posterity.*
📖 from Latin *posteritas* meaning 'future generations'

posthumous
Said "**poss-tyum-uss**" ADJECTIVE happening or awarded after a person's death EG *a posthumous medal.*
posthumously ADVERB

postman postmen
NOUN someone who collects and

delivers letters and parcels sent by post.

postmortem postmortems
NOUN a medical examination of a dead body to find out how the person died.

post office post offices
NOUN **1** The Post Office is the national organization responsible for postal services. **2** a building where you can buy stamps and post letters.

postpone postpones postponing postponed
VERB If you postpone an event, you arrange for it to take place at a later time than was originally planned.
postponement NOUN
🔲 put off, shelve

posture postures
NOUN Your posture is the position or manner in which you hold your body.

posy posies
NOUN a small bunch of flowers.

pot pots
NOUN a deep round container; also used to refer to its contents.

potato potatoes
NOUN a white vegetable that has a brown or red skin and grows underground.

potent
ADJECTIVE effective or powerful EG *a potent cocktail.*
potency NOUN

potential
ADJECTIVE **1** capable of becoming the thing mentioned EG *potential customers... potential sources of finance.* ▶ NOUN **2** Your potential is your ability to achieve success in the future.
potentially ADVERB

potential energy
NOUN Potential energy is the energy stored in something.

pothole potholes
NOUN **1** a hole in the surface of a road caused by bad weather or

traffic. **2** an underground cavern.

potion potions
NOUN a drink containing medicine, poison, or supposed magical powers.
📖 from Latin *potio* meaning 'a drink'

potted
ADJECTIVE Potted meat or fish is cooked and put into a small sealed container to preserve it.

potter potters pottering pottered
NOUN **1** a person who makes pottery.
▶ VERB **2** If you potter about, you pass the time doing pleasant, unimportant things.

pottery
NOUN **1** Pottery is pots, dishes, and other items made from clay and fired in a kiln. **2** Pottery is also the craft of making pottery.

potty potties; pottier pottiest
NOUN **1** a bowl which a small child can sit on and use instead of a toilet. ▶ ADJECTIVE **2** AN INFORMAL USE crazy or foolish.

pouch pouches
NOUN **1** a small, soft container with a fold-over top EG *a tobacco pouch*. **2** Animals like kangaroos have a pouch, which is a pocket of skin in which they carry their young.

poultry
NOUN Chickens, turkeys, and other birds kept for their meat or eggs are referred to as poultry.

pounce pounces pouncing pounced
VERB If an animal or person pounces on something, they leap and grab it.

pound pounds pounding pounded
NOUN **1** The pound is the main unit of currency in Britain and in some other countries. **2** a unit of weight equal to 16 ounces or about 0.454 kilograms. ▶ VERB **3** If you pound something, you hit it repeatedly with your fist EG *Someone was*

pounding on the door. **4** If you pound a substance, you crush it into a powder or paste EG *Wooden mallets were used to pound the meat.* **5** If your heart is pounding, it is beating very strongly and quickly. **6** If you pound somewhere, you run there with heavy noisy steps.

pour pours pouring poured
VERB **1** If you pour a liquid out of a container, you make it flow out by tipping the container. **2** If something pours somewhere, it flows there quickly and in large quantities EG *Sweat poured down his face.* **3** When it is raining heavily, you can say that it is pouring.

pout pouts pouting pouted
VERB If you pout, you stick out your lips or bottom lip.

poverty
NOUN Poverty is the state of being very poor.
🗏 destitution, pennilessness, want

powder powders powdering powdered
NOUN **1** Powder consists of many tiny particles of a solid substance.
▶ VERB **2** If you powder a surface, you cover it with powder.
powdery ADJECTIVE

power powers powering powered
NOUN **1** Someone who has power has a lot of control over people and activities. **2** Someone who has the power to do something has the ability to do it EG *the power of speech.* **3** The power of something is the physical strength that it has to move things. **4** Power is energy obtained, for example, by burning fuel or using the wind or waves. **5** In physics, power is the energy transferred from one thing to another in one second. It is measured in watts. ▶ VERB **6** Something that powers a machine provides the energy for it to work.
powerful ADJECTIVE, **powerfully** ADVERB

A B C D E F G H I J K L M N O P Q R S T U V W X Y Z

◨ (sense 3) force, strength

powerless

ADJECTIVE unable to control or influence events EG *I was powerless to save her.*

◨ helpless, impotent, incapable

power station power stations

NOUN a place where electricity is generated.

practicable

ADJECTIVE If a task or plan is practicable, it can be carried out successfully EG *a practicable option.*

practical practicals

ADJECTIVE **1** The practical aspects of something are those that involve experience and real situations rather than ideas or theories EG *the practical difficulties of teaching science.* **2** sensible and likely to be effective EG *practical low-heeled shoes.* **3** Someone who is practical is able to deal effectively and sensibly with problems. ▶ NOUN **4** an examination in which you make or perform something rather than simply write.

practicality NOUN

◨ (sense 2) functional, utilitarian

practically

ADVERB **1** almost but not completely or exactly EG *The house was practically a wreck.* **2** in a practical way EG *practically minded.*

practice practices

NOUN **1** You can refer to something that people do regularly as a practice EG *the practice of kissing hands.* **2** Practice is regular training or exercise EG *I need more practice.* **3** A doctor's or lawyer's practice is his or her business.

☑ The noun *practice* ends in *ice.*

practise practises practising practised

VERB **1** If you practise something, you do it regularly in order to improve. **2** People who practise a religion, custom, or craft regularly take part in the activities associated with it EG *a practising Buddhist.*

3 Someone who practises medicine or law works as a doctor or lawyer.

☑ The verb *practise* ends in *ise.*

practised

ADJECTIVE Someone who is practised at doing something is very skilful at it EG *a practised performer.*

practitioner practitioners

NOUN You can refer to someone who works in a particular profession as a practitioner EG *a medical practitioner.*

pragmatic

ADJECTIVE A pragmatic way of considering or doing something is a practical rather than theoretical way EG *He is pragmatic about the risks involved.*

pragmatically ADVERB, **pragmatism** NOUN

prairie prairies

NOUN a large area of flat, grassy land in North America.

praise praises praising praised

VERB **1** If you praise someone or something, you express strong approval of their qualities or achievements. ▶ NOUN **2** Praise is what is said or written in approval of someone's qualities or achievements.

◨ (sense 1) acclaim, approve, compliment

◨ (sense 2) acclaim, approval, commendation

pram prams

NOUN a baby's cot on wheels.

prance prances prancing pranced

VERB Someone who is prancing around is walking with exaggerated movements.

prank pranks

NOUN a childish trick.

prattle prattles prattling prattled

VERB If someone prattles on, they talk a lot without saying anything important.

prawn prawns

NOUN a small, pink, edible shellfish with a long tail.

pray prays praying prayed

VERB When someone prays, they

speak to God to give thanks or to ask for help.

prayer prayers

NOUN **1** Prayer is the activity of praying. **2** the words said when someone prays.

pre-

PREFIX before a particular time or event EG *the pre-Christmas rush*.

preach preaches preaching preached

VERB When someone preaches, they give a short talk on a religious or moral subject as part of a church service.

preacher NOUN

precarious

ADJECTIVE **1** If your situation is precarious, you may fail in what you are doing at any time. **2** Something that is precarious is likely to fall because it is not well balanced or secured.

precariously ADVERB

■ (sense 2) insecure, shaky, unsafe

precaution precautions

NOUN an action that is intended to prevent something from happening EG *It's still worth taking precautions against accidents.*

precautionary ADJECTIVE

precede precedes preceding preceded

VERB **1** Something that precedes another thing happens or occurs before it. **2** If you precede someone somewhere, you go in front of them.

preceding ADJECTIVE

precedence

Said "press-id-ens" NOUN If something takes precedence over other things, it is the most important thing and should be dealt with first.

precedent precedents

NOUN An action or decision that is regarded as a precedent is used as a guide in taking similar action or decisions later.

precinct precincts

NOUN **1** A shopping precinct is a pedestrian shopping area. ▶ PLURAL NOUN **2** The precincts of a place are its buildings and land.

precious

ADJECTIVE Something that is precious is valuable or very important and should be looked after or used carefully.

precipice precipices

Said "press-sip-piss" NOUN a very steep rock face.

precipitate precipitates precipitating precipitated

VERB; A FORMAL USE If something precipitates an event or situation, it causes it to happen suddenly.

precipitation

NOUN; A FORMAL WORD Precipitation is rain, snow, or hail; used especially when stating the amount that falls during a particular period.

precise

ADJECTIVE exact and accurate in every detail EG *precise measurements*.

precisely ADVERB, **precision** NOUN

preclude precludes precluding precluded

VERB; A FORMAL WORD If something precludes an event or situation, it prevents it from happening EG *The meal precluded serious conversation.*

precocious

ADJECTIVE Precocious children behave in a way that seems too advanced for their age.

preconceived

ADJECTIVE Preconceived ideas about something have been formed without any real experience or information.

preconception NOUN

precondition preconditions

NOUN If something is a precondition for another thing, it must happen before the second thing can take place.

precursor precursors

NOUN A precursor of something that

exists now is a similar thing that existed at an earlier time EG *real tennis, an ancient precursor of the modern game.*

predator predators
Said "pred-dat-tor" NOUN an animal that kills and eats other animals.
predatory ADJECTIVE

predecessor predecessors
NOUN Someone's predecessor is a person who used to do their job before.

predetermined
ADJECTIVE decided in advance or controlled by previous events rather than left to chance.

predicament predicaments
NOUN a difficult situation.
■ dilemma, fix, jam

predict predicts predicting predicted
VERB If someone predicts an event, they say that it will happen in the future.
prediction NOUN
■ forecast, foretell, prophesy

predominant
ADJECTIVE more important or more noticeable than anything else in a particular set of people or things EG *Yellow is the predominant colour in the house.*
predominantly ADVERB
■ chief, main, prevailing

predominate predominates predominating predominated
VERB If one type of person or thing predominates, it is the most common, frequent, or noticeable EG *Fresh flowers predominate in the bouquet.*
predominance NOUN

pre-eminent
ADJECTIVE recognized as being the most important in a particular group EG *the pre-eminent experts in the area.*
pre-eminence NOUN

pre-empt pre-empts pre-empting pre-empted

VERB; A FORMAL WORD If you pre-empt something, you prevent it by doing something else which makes it pointless or impossible EG *a wish to pre-empt any further publicity.*

preen preens preening preened
VERB When a bird preens its feathers, it cleans them using its beak.

preface prefaces
Said "pref-fiss" NOUN an introduction at the beginning of a book explaining what the book is about or why it was written.

prefect prefects
NOUN a pupil who has special duties at a school.
▥ from Latin *praefectus* meaning 'someone put in charge'

prefer prefers preferring preferred
VERB If you prefer one thing to another, you like it better than the other thing.
preferable ADJECTIVE, **preferably** ADVERB

preference preferences
Said "pref-fer-enss" NOUN **1** If you have a preference for something, you like it more than other things EG *a preference for white.* **2** When making a choice, if you give preference to one type of person or thing, you try to choose that type.

preferential
ADJECTIVE A person who gets preferential treatment is treated better than others.

prefix prefixes
NOUN a letter or group of letters added to the beginning of a word to make a new word, for example 'semi-', 'pre-', and 'un-'.

pregnant
ADJECTIVE A woman who is pregnant has a baby developing in her womb.
pregnancy NOUN

prehistoric
ADJECTIVE existing at a time in the past before anything was written

A B C D E F G H I J K L M N O P Q R S T U V W X Y Z

A B C D E F G H I J K L M N O P Q R S T U V W X Y Z

down.

prejudice prejudices
NOUN Prejudice is an unreasonable and unfair dislike of, or preference for, a particular type of person or thing.
prejudiced ADJECTIVE, **prejudicial** ADJECTIVE

preliminary
ADJECTIVE Preliminary activities take place before something starts, in preparation for it EG *the preliminary rounds of the competition.*
■ first, initial, preparatory

prelude preludes
NOUN Something that is an introduction to a more important event can be described as a prelude to that event.

premature
ADJECTIVE happening too early, or earlier than expected EG *premature baldness.*
prematurely ADVERB

premeditated
ADJECTIVE planned in advance EG *a premeditated attack.*

premier premiers
NOUN **1** The leader of a government is sometimes referred to as the premier. **2** In Australia, the leader of a State government. ▶ ADJECTIVE **3** considered to be the best or most important EG *Wellington's premier jewellers.*

premiere premieres
Said "**prem-mee-er**" NOUN the first public performance of a new play or film.

premise premises
Said "**prem-iss**" PLURAL NOUN **1** The premises of an organization are all the buildings it occupies on one site. ▶ NOUN **2** a statement which you suppose is true and use as the basis for an idea or argument.

premium premiums
NOUN an extra sum of money that has to be paid EG *Paying a premium for space is worthwhile.*

premonition premonitions
Said "prem-on-**ish**-on" NOUN a feeling that something unpleasant is going to happen.
■ (sense 1) feeling, foreboding, presentiment

preoccupation preoccupations
NOUN If you have a preoccupation with something, it is very important to you and you keep thinking about it.

preoccupied
ADJECTIVE Someone who is preoccupied is deep in thought or totally involved with something.

preparatory
ADJECTIVE Preparatory activities are done before doing something else in order to prepare for it.

prepare prepares preparing prepared
VERB If you prepare something, you make it ready for a particular purpose or event EG *He was preparing the meal.*
preparation NOUN

prepared
ADJECTIVE If you are prepared to do something, you are willing to do it.

preposition prepositions
NOUN a word such as 'by', 'for', 'into', or 'with', which usually has a noun as its object.

What is a Preposition?

A preposition is a word that is used before a noun or pronoun to relate it to other words.

Prepositions may tell you the **place** of something in relation to another thing.
*She saw the cat **in** the garden.*
*The cat was sheltering **under** a bench.*

Prepositions may indicate **movement**.
*The train came **into** the station.*
*We pushed **through** the crowd.*

Prepositions may indicate **time**.
*They will arrive **on** Friday.*
*They will stay **for** two days.*

---

preposterous
ADJECTIVE extremely unreasonable

and ridiculous eg *a preposterous statement.*

prerequisite prerequisites
Said "pree-**rek**-wiz-zit" NOUN; A FORMAL WORD Something that is a prerequisite for another thing must happen or exist before the other thing is possible eg *Self-esteem is a prerequisite for a happy life.*

prerogative prerogatives
Said "prir-**rog**-at-tiv" NOUN; A FORMAL WORD Something that is the prerogative of a person is their special privilege or right.

prescribe prescribes prescribing prescribed
VERB When a doctor prescribes treatment, he or she states what treatment a patient should have.

prescription prescriptions
NOUN a piece of paper on which the doctor has written the name of a medicine needed by a patient.

presence
NOUN 1 Someone's presence in a place is the fact of their being there eg *His presence made me happy.* 2 If you are in someone's presence, you are in the same place as they are. 3 Someone who has presence has an impressive appearance or manner.

present presents presenting presented
ADJECTIVE *Said* "**prez**-ent" 1 If someone is present somewhere, they are there eg *He had been present at the birth of his son.* 2 A present situation is one that exists now rather than in the past or the future. ▸ NOUN *Said* "**prez**-ent" 3 The present is the period of time that is taking place now. 4 something that you give to someone for them to keep. ▸ VERB *Said* "pri-**zent**" 5 If you present someone with something, you give it to them eg *She presented a bravery award to the girl.* 6 Something that presents a difficulty or a challenge causes it or provides it. 7 The person who

presents a radio or television show introduces each part or each guest.
presentation NOUN, **presenter** NOUN
■ (sense 2) contemporary, current, existing

presentable
ADJECTIVE neat or attractive and suitable for people to see.

present-day
ADJECTIVE existing or happening now eg *present-day farming practices.*

presently
ADVERB 1 If something will happen presently, it will happen soon eg *I'll finish the job presently.* 2 Something that is presently happening is happening now eg *Some progress is presently being made.*

present participle present participles
NOUN In grammar, the present participle of an English verb is the form that ends in '-ing'. It is used to form some tenses, and can be used to form adjectives and nouns from a verb.

present tense
NOUN In grammar, the present tense is the tense of a verb that you use mainly to talk about things that happen or exist at the time of writing or speaking.

Talking about the Present

You can talk about events that are happening now by using **simple tenses** or **compound tenses**.

The **simple present tense** is formed by using the verb on its own, without any auxiliary verbs. For the first and second person, and for all plural forms, the simple present tense of the verb is the same as the main form given in the dictionary.
*I **cook** the dinner.*

For the third person singular, however, you need to add an -*s* to the dictionary form to make the simple present tense.
*He **cooks** the dinner.*

You can also talk about an event that is happening in the present by using **compound tenses**. Compound tenses are

A B C D E F G H I J K L M N O P Q R S T U V W X Y Z

A B C D E F G

formed by adding an auxiliary verb to a form of the main verb.

The most common compound present tense is formed by putting a form of the verb *to be* in front of the main verb, and adding the ending *-ing*. This shows that the action is going on at the present time and is continuous.

*I **am listening** to the radio.*

You can also talk about the present using a form of the verb *to do* in front of the basic form of the verb. This can add emphasis.

*I **do like** fish.*

preservative preservatives
NOUN a substance or chemical that stops things decaying.

preserve preserves preserving preserved
VERB **1** If you preserve something, you take action so that it remains as it is. **2** If you preserve food, you treat it to prevent it from decaying. ▶ NOUN **3** Preserves are foods such as jam or chutney that have been made with a lot of sugar or vinegar.
preservation NOUN

preside presides presiding presided
VERB A person who presides over a formal event is in charge of it.

president presidents
NOUN **1** In a country which has no king or queen, the president is the elected leader EG *the President of the United States of America.* **2** The president of an organization is the person who has the highest position.
presidency NOUN, **presidential** ADJECTIVE

press presses pressing pressed
VERB **1** If you press something, you push it or hold it firmly against something else EG *Lisa pressed his hand... Press the blue button.* **2** If you press clothes, you iron them. **3** If you press for something, you try hard to persuade someone to agree to it EG *She was pressing for improvements to the education system.* **4** If you press charges, you make an accusation against someone which has to be decided in a court of law. ▶ NOUN **5** Newspapers and the journalists who work for them are called the press.

press conference press conferences
NOUN When someone gives a press conference, they have a meeting to answer questions put by reporters.

pressing
ADJECTIVE Something that is pressing needs to be dealt with immediately EG *pressing needs.*

pressure pressures pressuring pressured
NOUN **1** Pressure is the force that is produced by pushing on something. **2** If you are under pressure, you have too much to do and not enough time, or someone is trying hard to persuade you to do something. ▶ VERB **3** If you pressure someone, you try hard to persuade them to do something.

pressurize pressurizes pressurizing pressurized; also spelt **pressurise**
VERB If you pressurize someone, you try hard to persuade them to do something.

prestige
Said "press-**teezh**" NOUN If you have prestige, people admire you because of your position.
prestigious ADJECTIVE
▤ honour, standing, status

presumably
ADVERB If you say that something is presumably the case, you mean you assume that it is EG *Your audience, presumably, are younger.*

presume presumes presuming presumed
Said "priz-**yoom**" VERB If you presume something, you think that it is the case although you have no proof.
presumption NOUN
▤ assume, believe, suppose

presumptuous

ADJECTIVE Someone who behaves in a presumptuous way does things that they have no right to do.

pretence pretences
NOUN a way of behaving that is false and intended to deceive people.

pretend pretends pretending pretended
VERB If you pretend that something is the case, you try to make people believe that it is, although in fact it is not EG *Latimer pretended not to notice.*
▣ affect, feign, sham

pretender pretenders
NOUN A pretender to a throne or title is someone who claims it but whose claim is being questioned.

pretension pretensions
NOUN Someone with pretensions claims that they are more important than they really are.

pretentious
ADJECTIVE Someone or something that is pretentious is trying to seem important when in fact they are not.

pretext pretexts
NOUN a false reason given to hide the real reason for doing something.

pretty prettier prettiest
ADJECTIVE 1 attractive in a delicate way. ▶ ADVERB 2 AN INFORMAL USE quite or rather EG *He spoke pretty good English.*
prettily ADVERB, **prettiness** NOUN

prevail prevails prevailing prevailed
VERB 1 If a custom or belief prevails in a particular place, it is normal or most common there EG *This attitude has prevailed in Britain for many years.* 2 If someone or something prevails, they succeed in their aims EG *In recent years better sense has prevailed.*
prevailing ADJECTIVE

prevalent
ADJECTIVE very common or

widespread EG *the hooliganism so prevalent today.*
prevalence NOUN

prevent prevents preventing prevented
VERB If you prevent something, you stop it from happening or being done.
preventable ADJECTIVE, **prevention** NOUN
▣ avert, forestall, stop

preventive or **preventative**
ADJECTIVE intended to help prevent things such as disease or crime EG *preventive health care.*

preview previews
NOUN an opportunity to see something, such as a film or exhibition, before it is shown to the public.

previous
ADJECTIVE happening or existing before something else in time or position EG *previous reports... the previous year.*
previously ADVERB
▣ earlier, former, preceding

prey preys preying preyed
Rhymes with "say" NOUN 1 The creatures that an animal hunts and eats are called its prey. ▶ VERB 2 An animal that preys on a particular kind of animal lives by hunting and eating it.

price prices pricing priced
NOUN 1 The price of something is the amount of money you have to pay to buy it. ▶ VERB 2 To price something at a particular amount is to fix its price at that amount.
▣ (sense 1) charge, cost, expense

priceless
ADJECTIVE Something that is priceless is so valuable that it is difficult to work out how much it is worth.

pricey pricier priciest
ADJECTIVE; AN INFORMAL WORD expensive.

prick pricks pricking pricked
VERB 1 If you prick something, you stick a sharp pointed object into it. ▶ NOUN 2 a small, sharp pain caused

A B C D E F G H I J K L M N O P Q R S T U V W X Y Z

when something pricks you.

prickle prickles prickling prickled
NOUN **1** Prickles are small sharp points or thorns on plants. ▶ VERB **2** If your skin prickles, it feels as if a lot of sharp points are being stuck into it.
prickly ADJECTIVE

pride prides priding prided
NOUN **1** Pride is a feeling of satisfaction you have when you have done something well. **2** Pride is also a feeling of being better than other people. ▶ VERB **3** If you pride yourself on a quality or skill, you are proud of it EG *She prides herself on punctuality.*
▣ (sense 1) gratification, pleasure, satisfaction

priest priests
NOUN **1** a member of the clergy in some Christian Churches. **2** In many non-Christian religions, a priest is a man who has special duties in the place where people worship.
priestly ADJECTIVE

priesthood
NOUN The priesthood is the position of being a priest.

prim primmer primmest
ADJECTIVE Someone who is prim always behaves very correctly and is easily shocked by anything rude.
▣ priggish, prudish, strait-laced

primaeval
another spelling of **primeval**.

primarily
ADVERB You use 'primarily' to indicate the main or most important feature of something EG *I still rated people primarily on their looks.*

primary
ADJECTIVE 'Primary' is used to describe something that is extremely important for someone or something EG *the primary aim of his research.*

primary colour primary colours

NOUN In art, the primary colours are red, yellow, and blue, from which other colours can be obtained by mixing.

primary school primary schools
NOUN a school for children aged up to 11.

primate primates
NOUN **1** an archbishop. **2** a member of the group of animals which includes humans, monkeys, and apes.

prime primes priming primed
ADJECTIVE **1** main or most important EG *a prime cause of brain damage.* **2** of the best quality EG *in prime condition.*
▶ NOUN **3** Someone's prime is the stage when they are at their strongest, most active, or most successful. ▶ VERB **4** If you prime someone, you give them information about something in advance to prepare them EG *We are primed for every lesson.*
▣ (sense 3) height, heyday, peak

prime minister prime ministers
NOUN The prime minister is the leader of the government.

primeval or **primaeval**
Said "pry-mee-vl" ADJECTIVE belonging to a very early period in the history of the world.

primitive
ADJECTIVE **1** connected with a society that lives very simply without industries or a writing system EG *the primitive peoples of the world.* **2** very simple, basic, or old-fashioned EG *a very small primitive cottage.*

primrose primroses
NOUN a small plant that has pale yellow flowers in spring.
▥ from Latin *prima rosa* meaning 'first rose'

prince princes
NOUN a male member of a royal family, especially the son of a king or queen.
princely ADJECTIVE
▥ from Latin *princeps* meaning 'chief' or 'ruler'

A B C D E F G H I J K L M N O P Q R S T U V W X Y Z

princess princesses
NOUN a female member of a royal family, usually the daughter of a king or queen, or the wife of a prince.

principal principals
ADJECTIVE **1** main or most important EG *the principal source of food.* ▶ NOUN **2** the person in charge of a school or college.

principally ADVERB
☑ Do not confuse *principal* with *principle*: *my principal objection.*

principality principalities
NOUN a country ruled by a prince.

principle principles
NOUN **1** a belief you have about the way you should behave EG *a woman of principle.* **2** a general rule or scientific law which explains how something happens or works EG *the principle of evolution in nature.*
☰ (sense 1) precept, standard, rule
☑ Do not confuse *principle* with *principal*: *a man with no principles.*

print prints printing printed
VERB **1** To print a newspaper or book is to reproduce it in large quantities using a mechanical or electronic copying process. **2** If you print when you are writing, you do not join the letters together. ▶ NOUN **3** The letters and numbers on the pages of a book or newspaper are referred to as the print. **4** a photograph, or a printed copy of a painting. **5** Footprints and fingerprints can be referred to as prints.

printer NOUN

print-out print-outs
NOUN a printed copy of information from a computer.

prior priors
ADJECTIVE **1** planned or done at an earlier time EG *I have a prior engagement.* ▶ PHRASE **2** Something that happens **prior to** a particular time or event happens before it. ▶ NOUN **3** a monk in charge of a small group of monks in a priory.

prioress NOUN

priority priorities
NOUN something that needs to be dealt with first EG *The priority is building homes.*

priory priories
NOUN a place where a small group of monks live under the charge of a prior.

prise prises prising prised
VERB If you prise something open or away from a surface, you force it open or away EG *She prised his fingers loose.*

prism prisms
NOUN an object made of clear glass with many flat sides. It separates light passing through it into the colours of the rainbow.

prison prisons
NOUN a building where criminals are kept in captivity.

prisoner prisoners
NOUN someone who is kept in prison or held in captivity against their will.

pristine
Said "**priss-teen**" ADJECTIVE; A FORMAL WORD very clean or new and in perfect condition.

private privates
ADJECTIVE **1** for the use of one person rather than people in general EG *a private bathroom.* **2** taking place between a small number of people and kept secret from others EG *a private conversation.* **3** owned or run by individuals or companies rather than by the state EG *a private company.* ▶ NOUN **4** a soldier of the lowest rank.

privacy NOUN, **privately** ADVERB

private school private schools
NOUN a school that does not receive money from the government, and parents pay for their children to attend.

privatize privatizes privatizing privatized; also spelt **privatise**
VERB If the government privatizes a

A B C D E F G H I J K L M N O P Q R S T U V W X Y Z

A
B
C
D
E
F
G
H
I
J
K
L
M
N
O
P
Q
R
S
T
U
V
W
X
Y
Z

state-owned industry or organization, it allows it to be bought and owned by a private individual or group.

privilege privileges
NOUN a special right or advantage given to a person or group EG *the privileges of monarchy*.
privileged ADJECTIVE

privy
ADJECTIVE; A FORMAL USE If you are privy to something secret, you have been told about it.

prize prizes prizing prized
NOUN **1** a reward given to the winner of a competition or game. ▶ ADJECTIVE **2** of the highest quality or standard EG *his prize dahlia*. ▶ VERB **3** Something that is prized is wanted and admired for its value or quality.
▣ (sense 1) award, reward, trophy

pro pros
NOUN **1** AN INFORMAL USE a professional. ▶ PHRASE **2** The **pros and cons** of a situation are its advantages and disadvantages.
▣ sense 2 is from Latin *pro* meaning 'for' and *contra* meaning 'against'

pro-
PREFIX supporting or in favour of EG *pro-democracy protests*.

probability probabilities
NOUN **1** The probability of something happening is how likely it is to happen EG *the probability of success*. **2** If something is a probability, it is likely to happen EG *The probability is that you will be feeling better*.
▣ (sense 1) chance(s), likelihood, odds

probable
ADJECTIVE Something that is probable is likely to be true or correct, or likely to happen EG *the most probable outcome*.

probably
ADVERB Something that is probably the case is likely but not certain.

probation
NOUN Probation is a period of time during which a person convicted of a crime is supervised by a probation officer instead of being sent to prison.
probationary ADJECTIVE

probe probes probing probed
VERB **1** If you probe, you ask a lot of questions to discover the facts about something. ▶ NOUN **2** a long thin instrument used by doctors and dentists when examining a patient.

problem problems
NOUN **1** an unsatisfactory situation that causes difficulties. **2** a puzzle or question that you solve using logical thought or mathematics.
problematic ADJECTIVE
▣ (sense 1) difficulty, predicament

procedure procedures
NOUN a way of doing something, especially the correct or usual way EG *It's standard procedure*.
procedural ADJECTIVE

proceed proceeds proceeding proceeded
VERB **1** If you proceed to do something, you start doing it, or continue doing it EG *She proceeded to tell them*. **2** A FORMAL USE If you proceed in a particular direction, you move in that direction EG *The taxi proceeded along a lonely road*. ▶ PLURAL NOUN **3** The proceeds from a fund-raising event are the money obtained from it.

proceedings
PLURAL NOUN **1** You can refer to an organized and related series of events as the proceedings EG *She was determined to see the proceedings from start to finish*. **2** Legal proceedings are legal action taken against someone.

process processes processing processed
NOUN **1** a series of actions intended to achieve a particular result or change. ▶ PHRASE **2** If you are in the

process of doing something, you have started doing it but have not yet finished. ▶ VERB 3 When something such as food or information is processed, it is treated or dealt with.

procession processions
NOUN a group of people or vehicles moving in a line, often as part of a ceremony.

proclaim proclaims proclaiming proclaimed
VERB If someone proclaims something, they announce it or make it known EG *You have proclaimed your innocence.*
proclamation NOUN

procure procures procuring procured
VERB; A FORMAL WORD If you procure something, you obtain it.

prod prods prodding prodded
VERB If you prod something, you give it a push with your finger or with something pointed.

prodigy prodigies
Said "prod-dij-ee" NOUN someone who shows an extraordinary natural ability at an early age.

produce produces producing produced
VERB 1 To produce something is to make it or cause it EG *a white wine produced mainly from black grapes.* 2 If you produce something from somewhere, you bring it out so it can be seen. ▶ NOUN 3 Produce is food that is grown to be sold EG *fresh produce.*

producer producers
NOUN The producer of a record, film, or show is the person in charge of making it or putting it on.

product products
NOUN 1 something that is made to be sold EG *high-quality products.* 2 In maths, the product of two or more numbers or quantities is the result of multiplying them together.

production productions

NOUN 1 Production is the process of manufacturing or growing something in large quantities EG *modern methods of production.*
2 Production is also the amount of goods manufactured or food grown by a country or company EG *Production has fallen by 13.2%.* 3 A production of a play, opera, or other show is a series of performances of it.

productive
ADJECTIVE 1 To be productive means to produce a large number of things EG *Farms were more productive in these areas.* 2 If something such as a meeting is productive, good or useful things happen as a result of it.
■ (sense 2) beneficial, useful, worthwhile

productivity
NOUN Productivity is the rate at which things are produced or dealt with.

profane
ADJECTIVE; A FORMAL WORD showing disrespect for a religion or religious things EG *profane language.*

profess professes professing professed
VERB 1 A FORMAL WORD If you profess to do or have something, you claim to do or have it. 2 If you profess a feeling or opinion, you express it EG *He professes a lasting affection for Trinidad.*

profession professions
NOUN 1 a type of job that requires advanced education or training.
2 You can use 'profession' to refer to all the people who have a particular profession EG *the medical profession.*

professional professionals
ADJECTIVE 1 Professional means relating to the work of someone who is qualified in a particular profession EG *I think you need professional advice.* 2 Professional also describes activities when they

A B C D E F G H I J K L M N O P Q R S T U V W X Y Z

are done to earn money rather than as a hobby EG *professional football*. **3** A professional piece of work is of a very high standard. ▶ NOUN **4** a person who has been trained in a profession. **5** someone who plays a sport to earn money rather than as a hobby.

professor professors
NOUN the senior teacher in a department of a British university.
professorial ADJECTIVE

proficient
ADJECTIVE If you are proficient at something, you can do it well.
proficiency NOUN

profile profiles
NOUN **1** Your profile is the outline of your face seen from the side. **2** A profile of someone is a short description of their life and character.
🔲 from Italian *profilare* meaning 'to sketch lightly'

profit profits profiting profited
NOUN **1** When someone sells something, the profit is the amount they gain by selling it for more than it cost them to buy or make. ▶ VERB **2** If you profit from something, you gain or benefit from it.
profitable ADJECTIVE
🟰 (sense 1) gain, proceeds, return

profound
ADJECTIVE **1** great in degree or intensity EG *a profound need to please*. **2** showing great and deep intellectual understanding EG *a profound question*.
profoundly ADVERB, **profundity** NOUN

profuse
Said "prof-**yooss**" ADJECTIVE very large in quantity or number EG *There were profuse apologies for his absence*.
profusely ADVERB

program programs programming programmed
NOUN **1** a set of instructions that a computer follows to perform a

particular task. ▶ VERB **2** When someone programs a computer, they write a program and put it into the computer.
programmer NOUN

programme programmes
NOUN **1** a planned series of events EG *a programme of official engagements*. **2** a particular piece presented as a unit on television or radio, such as a play, show, or discussion. **3** a booklet giving information about a play, concert, or show that you are attending.
🟰 (sense 1) agenda, plan, schedule

progress progresses progressing progressed
NOUN **1** Progress is the process of gradually improving or getting near to achieving something EG *Gerry is now making some real progress towards fitness*. **2** The progress of something is the way in which it develops or continues EG *news on the progress of the war*. ▶ PHRASE **3** Something that is **in progress** is happening EG *A cricket match was in progress*. ▶ VERB **4** If you progress, you become more advanced or skilful. **5** To progress is to continue EG *As the evening progressed, sadness turned to rage*.
progression NOUN
🟰 (sense 1) advance, headway
🟰 (sense 2) course, movement

progressive
ADJECTIVE **1** having modern ideas about how things should be done. **2** happening gradually EG *a progressive illness*.

prohibit prohibits prohibiting prohibited
VERB If someone prohibits something, they forbid it or make it illegal.
prohibition NOUN
✅ You *prohibit* a person *from* doing something.

prohibitive
ADJECTIVE If the cost of something is prohibitive, it is so high that

A
B
C
D
E
F
G
H
I
J
K
L
M
N
O
P
Q
R
S
T
U
V
W
X
Y
Z

people cannot afford it.

project projects projecting projected
NOUN **1** a carefully planned attempt to achieve something or to study something over a period of time.
▶ VERB **2** Something that is projected is planned or expected to happen in the future EG *The population aged 65 or over is projected to increase.* **3** To project an image onto a screen is to make it appear there using equipment such as a projector. **4** Something that projects sticks out beyond a surface or edge.
projection NOUN

projector projectors
NOUN a piece of equipment which produces a large image on a screen by shining light through a photographic slide or film strip.

proletariat
NOUN; A FORMAL WORD Working-class people are sometimes referred to as the proletariat.
proletarian ADJECTIVE

proliferate proliferates proliferating proliferated
VERB If things proliferate, they quickly increase in number.
proliferation NOUN
🏛 from Latin *prolifer* meaning 'having children'

prolific
ADJECTIVE producing a lot of something EG *this prolific artist.*

prologue prologues
NOUN a speech or section that introduces a play or book.

prolong prolongs prolonging prolonged
VERB If you prolong something, you make it last longer.
prolonged ADJECTIVE

prom proms
NOUN; AN INFORMAL WORD a concert at which some of the audience stand.

promenade promenades
Said "prom-min-ahd" NOUN a road or path next to the sea at a seaside resort.
🏛 a French word, from *se promener* meaning 'to go for a walk'

prominent
ADJECTIVE **1** Prominent people are important. **2** Something that is prominent is very noticeable EG *a prominent nose.*
prominence NOUN, **prominently** ADVERB

promiscuous
Said "prom-**misk**-yoo-uss" ADJECTIVE Someone who is promiscuous has sex with many different people.
promiscuity NOUN

promise promises promising promised
VERB **1** If you promise to do something, you say that you will definitely do it. **2** Something that promises to have a particular quality shows signs that it will have that quality EG *This promised to be a very long night.* ▶ NOUN **3** a statement made by someone that they will definitely do something EG *He made a promise to me.* **4** Someone or something that shows promise seems likely to be very successful.
promising ADJECTIVE
🟰 (sense 1) guarantee, pledge, vow
🟰 (sense 3) guarantee, oath, vow

promontory promontories
Said "prom-mon-tree" NOUN an area of high land sticking out into the sea.

promote promotes promoting promoted
VERB **1** If someone promotes something, they try to make it happen or become more popular EG *to promote their latest film.* **2** If someone is promoted, they are given a more important job at work.
promoter NOUN, **promotion** NOUN

prompt prompts prompting prompted
VERB **1** If something prompts someone to do something, it makes

them decide to do it EG *Curiosity prompted him to push at the door.* **2** If you prompt someone when they stop speaking, you tell them what to say next or encourage them to continue. ▶ ADVERB **3** exactly at the time mentioned EG *Wednesday morning at 10.40 prompt.* ▶ ADJECTIVE **4** A prompt action is done without any delay EG *a prompt reply.*

promptly ADVERB

prone

ADJECTIVE **1** If you are prone to something, you have a tendency to be affected by it or to do it EG *She is prone to depression.* **2** If you are prone, you are lying flat and face downwards EG *lying prone on the grass.*

▤ (sense 1) inclined, liable, subject

prong prongs

NOUN The prongs of a fork are the long, narrow, pointed parts.

pronoun pronouns

NOUN In grammar, a pronoun is a word that is used to replace a noun. 'He', 'she', and 'them' are all pronouns.

What is a Pronoun?

A **pronoun** is a word that is used in place of a noun. Pronouns may be used instead of naming a person or thing.

Personal pronouns replace the subject or object of a sentence.
* **She** caught a fish.
* The nurse reassured **him**.

Reflexive pronouns replace the object when it is the same person or thing as the subject.
* Matthew saw **himself** in the mirror.

Demonstrative pronouns replace the subject or object when you want to show where something is.
* **That** is a nice jacket.
* Have you seen **this**?

Possessive pronouns replace the subject or object when you want to show who owns it.
* The blue car is **mine**.
* **Hers** is a strange story.

Relative pronouns replace a noun to link two different parts of the sentence.
* Do you know the man **who** lives next door?
* I watched a programme **that** I had recorded yesterday.

Interrogative pronouns ask questions.
* **What** are you doing?

Indefinite pronouns replace a subject or object to talk about a broad or vague range of people or things.
* **Everybody** knew the exercise was a waste of time.
* **Some** say he cheats at cards.

Also look at the grammar box at **relative pronoun**.

---

pronounce pronounces pronouncing pronounced

VERB When you pronounce a word, you say it.

☑ There is an *o* before the *u* in *pronounce*. Compare this spelling with *pronunciation*.

pronounced

ADJECTIVE very noticeable EG *He talks with a pronounced lowland accent.*

pronouncement pronouncements

NOUN a formal statement.

pronunciation pronunciations

Said "pron-nun-see-ay-shn" NOUN the way a word is usually said.

☑ There is no *o* before the *u* in *pronunciation*. Compare this spelling with *pronounce*.

proof

NOUN If you have proof of something, you have evidence which shows that it is true or exists.

▤ confirmation, evidence, verification

prop props propping propped

VERB **1** If you prop an object somewhere, you support it or rest it against something EG *The barman propped himself against the counter.* ▶ NOUN **2** a stick or other object used to support something. **3** The props in a play are all the objects and furniture used by the actors.

propaganda

NOUN Propaganda is exaggerated or false information that is published or broadcast in order to influence people.

propagate propagates propagating propagated
VERB **1** If people propagate an idea, they spread it to try to influence many other people. **2** If you propagate plants, you grow more of them from an original one.
propagation NOUN

propel propels propelling propelled
VERB To propel something is to cause it to move in a particular direction.

propeller propellers
NOUN a device on a boat or aircraft with rotating blades which make the boat or aircraft move.

propensity propensities
NOUN; A FORMAL WORD a tendency to behave in a particular way.

proper
ADJECTIVE **1** real and satisfactory EG *He was no nearer having a proper job.* **2** correct or suitable EG *Put things in their proper place.*
properly ADVERB

proper noun proper nouns
NOUN the name of a person, place, or institution.

property properties
NOUN **1** A person's property is the things that belong to them. **2** a building and the land belonging to it. **3** a characteristic or quality EG *Mint has powerful healing properties.*

prophecy prophecies
NOUN a statement about what someone believes will happen in the future.
☑ The noun *prophecy* ends in *cy.*

prophesy prophesies prophesying prophesied
VERB If someone prophesies something, they say it will happen.
☑ The verb *prophesy* ends in *sy.*

prophet prophets

NOUN a person who predicts what will happen in the future.

prophetic
ADJECTIVE correctly predicting what will happen EG *It was a prophetic warning.*

proportion proportions
NOUN **1** A proportion of an amount or group is a part of it EG *a tiny proportion of the population.* **2** The proportion of one amount to another is its size in comparison with the other amount EG *the highest proportion of single women to men.*
▶ PLURAL NOUN **3** You can refer to the size of something as its proportions EG *a red umbrella of vast proportions.*

proportional or **proportionate**
ADJECTIVE If one thing is proportional to another, it remains the same size in comparison with the other EG *proportional increases in profit.*
proportionally or **proportionately** ADVERB

proportional representation
NOUN Proportional representation is a system of voting in elections in which the number of representatives of each party is in proportion to the number of people who voted for it.

proposal proposals
NOUN a plan that has been suggested EG *business proposals.*

propose proposes proposing proposed
VERB **1** If you propose a plan or idea, you suggest it. **2** If you propose to do something, you intend to do it EG *And how do you propose to do that?* **3** When someone proposes a toast to a particular person, they ask people to drink a toast to that person. **4** If someone proposes to another person, they ask that person to marry them.

proposition propositions
NOUN **1** a statement expressing a theory or opinion. **2** an offer or suggestion EG *I made her a proposition.*

proprietor proprietors

A B C D E F G H I J K L M N O P Q R S T U V W X Y Z

NOUN The proprietor of a business is the owner.

propriety
NOUN; A FORMAL WORD Propriety is social or moral acceptability EG *a model of propriety*.

propulsion
NOUN Propulsion is the power that moves something.

prose
NOUN Prose is ordinary written language in contrast to poetry.
🏛 from Latin *prosa oratorio* meaning 'straightforward speech'

prosecute prosecutes prosecuting prosecuted
VERB If someone is prosecuted, they are charged with a crime and have to stand trial.
prosecutor NOUN

prosecution
NOUN The lawyers who try to prove that a person on trial is guilty are called the prosecution.

prospect prospects prospecting prospected
NOUN 1 If there is a prospect of something happening, there is a possibility that it will happen EG *There was little prospect of going home.* 2 Someone's prospects are their chances of being successful in the future. ▶ VERB 3 If someone prospects for gold or oil, they look for it.
prospector NOUN

prospective
ADJECTIVE 'Prospective' is used to say that someone wants to be or is likely to be something. For example, the prospective owner of something is the person who wants to own it.

prospectus prospectuses
NOUN a booklet giving details about a college or a company.

prosper prospers prospering prospered
VERB When people or businesses prosper, they are successful and make a lot of money.
prosperous ADJECTIVE, **prosperity** NOUN

prostitute prostitutes
NOUN a person, usually a woman, who has sex with men in exchange for money.
prostitution NOUN

prostrate
ADJECTIVE lying face downwards on the ground.

protagonist protagonists
NOUN; A FORMAL WORD 1 Someone who is a protagonist of an idea or movement is a leading supporter of it. 2 a main character in a play or story.
🏛 from Greek *prōtagonistēs* meaning 'main actor in a play'

protea proteas
NOUN an evergreen African shrub with colourful flowers.

protect protects protecting protected
VERB To protect someone or something is to prevent them from being harmed or damaged.
protection NOUN, **protective** ADJECTIVE

protégé protégés
*Said "**proh**-tij-ay"* NOUN Someone who is the protégé of an older, more experienced person is helped and guided by that person.

protein proteins
NOUN Protein is a substance that is found in meat, eggs, and milk and that is needed by bodies for growth.

protest protests protesting protested
VERB 1 If you protest about something, you say or demonstrate publicly that you disagree with it EG *They protested against the killing of a teenager.* ▶ NOUN 2 a demonstration or statement showing that you disagree with something.

Protestant Protestants
NOUN OR ADJECTIVE a member of one of the Christian Churches which separated from the Catholic Church in the sixteenth century.

protestation protestations
NOUN a strong declaration that
something is true or not true EG *his
protestations of love.*

protocol
NOUN Protocol is the system of rules
about the correct way to behave in
formal situations.

proton protons
NOUN a particle which forms part of
the nucleus of an atom and has a
positive electrical charge.

prototype prototypes
NOUN a first model of something
that is made so that the design can
be tested and improved.

protracted
ADJECTIVE lasting longer than usual EG
a protracted dispute.

protractor protractors
NOUN a flat, semicircular piece of
plastic used for measuring angles.

protrude protrudes protruding
protruded
VERB; A FORMAL WORD If something is
protruding from a surface or edge,
it is sticking out.
protrusion NOUN

proud prouder proudest
ADJECTIVE **1** feeling pleasure and
satisfaction at something you own
or have achieved EG *I was proud of
our players today.* **2** having great
dignity and self-respect EG *too proud
to ask for money.*
proudly ADVERB

prove proves proving proved or
proven
VERB **1** To prove that something is
true is to provide evidence that it is
definitely true EG *A letter from
Kathleen proved that he lived there.* **2** If
something proves to be the case, it
becomes clear that it is so EG *His first
impressions of her proved wrong.*
■ (sense 1) confirm, show, verify

proverb proverbs
NOUN a short sentence which gives
advice or makes a comment about
life.

proverbial ADJECTIVE

provide provides providing
provided
VERB **1** If you provide something for
someone, you give it to them or
make it available for them. **2** If you
provide for someone, you give
them the things they need.
■ (sense 1) furnish, supply

provided or **providing**
CONJUNCTION If you say that
something will happen provided
something else happens, you mean
that the first thing will happen
only if the second thing does.
✓ *Provided* is followed by *that*, but
providing is not: *I'll come, providing
he doesn't; you can go, provided that
you phone as soon as you get there.*

providence
NOUN Providence is God or a force
which is believed to arrange the
things that happen to us.

province provinces
NOUN **1** one of the areas into which
some large countries are divided,
each province having its own
administration. **2** You can refer to
the parts of a country which are
not near the capital as the
provinces.
▥ from Latin *provincia* meaning 'a
conquered territory'

provincial
ADJECTIVE **1** connected with the parts
of a country outside the capital EG *a
provincial theatre.* **2** narrow-minded
and unsophisticated.

provision provisions
NOUN **1** The provision of something
is the act of making it available to
people EG *the provision of health care.*
▶ PLURAL NOUN **2** Provisions are
supplies of food.

provisional
ADJECTIVE A provisional arrangement
has not yet been made definite and
so might be changed.

proviso provisos
Said "prov-**eye**-zoh" NOUN a
condition in an agreement.

A B C D E F G H I J K L M N O P Q R S T U V W X Y Z

provocation provocations
NOUN an act done deliberately to annoy someone.

provocative
ADJECTIVE **1** intended to annoy people or make them react EG *a provocative speech*. **2** intended to make someone feel sexual desire EG *provocative poses*.

provoke provokes provoking provoked
VERB **1** If you provoke someone, you deliberately try to make them angry. **2** If something provokes an unpleasant reaction, it causes it EG *illness provoked by tension or worry*.

prow prows
NOUN the front part of a boat.

prowess
NOUN Prowess is outstanding ability EG *his prowess at tennis*.

prowl prowls prowling prowled
VERB If a person or animal prowls around, they move around quietly and secretly, as if hunting.

proximity
NOUN; A FORMAL WORD Proximity is nearness to someone or something.

proxy
PHRASE If you do something by **proxy**, someone else does it on your behalf EG *voting by proxy*.

prude prudes
NOUN someone who is too easily shocked by sex or nudity.
prudish ADJECTIVE
📖 from Old French *prode femme* meaning 'respectable woman'

prudent
ADJECTIVE behaving in a sensible and cautious way EG *It is prudent to plan ahead.*
prudence NOUN, **prudently** ADVERB

prune prunes pruning pruned
NOUN **1** a dried plum. ▶ VERB **2** When someone prunes a tree or shrub, they cut back some of the branches.

pry pries prying pried
VERB If someone is prying, they are trying to find out about something secret or private.

PS
PS is written before an additional message at the end of a letter. PS is an abbreviation for 'postscript'.

psalm psalms
Said "**sahm**" NOUN one of the 150 songs, poems, and prayers which together form the Book of Psalms in the Bible.

pseudo-
Said "**syoo**-doh" PREFIX 'Pseudo-' is used to form adjectives and nouns indicating that something is not what it is claimed to be EG *pseudo-scientific theories*.

pseudonym pseudonyms
Said "**syoo**-doe-nim" NOUN a name an author uses rather than their real name.

psyche psyches
Said "**sigh**-kee" NOUN your mind and your deepest feelings.

psychiatry
NOUN Psychiatry is the branch of medicine concerned with mental illness.
psychiatrist NOUN, **psychiatric** ADJECTIVE

psychic
ADJECTIVE having unusual mental powers such as the ability to read people's minds or predict the future.

psychoanalysis
NOUN Psychoanalysis is the examination and treatment of someone who is mentally ill by encouraging them to talk about their feelings and past events in order to discover the cause of the illness.
psychoanalyst NOUN, **psychoanalyse** VERB

psychology
NOUN Psychology is the scientific study of the mind and of the reasons for people's behaviour.
psychological ADJECTIVE, **psychologist** NOUN

psychopath psychopaths
NOUN a mentally ill person who

behaves violently without feeling guilt.

psychopathic ADJECTIVE

psychosis psychoses
Said "sigh-koe-siss" NOUN a severe mental illness.
psychotic ADJECTIVE

pterodactyl pterodactyls
Said "ter-rod-dak-til" NOUN Pterodactyls were flying reptiles in prehistoric times.
📖 from Greek *pteron* meaning 'wing' and *daktulos* meaning 'finger'

PTO
PTO is an abbreviation for 'please turn over'. It is written at the bottom of a page to indicate that the writing continues on the other side.

pub pubs
NOUN a building where people go to buy and drink alcoholic or soft drinks and talk with their friends.

puberty
Said "pyoo-ber-tee" NOUN Puberty is the stage when a person's body changes from that of a child into that of an adult.

pubic
Said "pyoo-bik" ADJECTIVE relating to the area around and above a person's genitals.

public
NOUN 1 You can refer to people in general as the public. ▶ ADJECTIVE 2 relating to people in general EG *There was some public support for the idea.* 3 provided for everyone to use, or open to anyone EG *public transport.*
publicly ADVERB

publican publicans
NOUN a person who owns or manages a pub.

publication publications
NOUN 1 The publication of a book is the act of printing it and making it available. 2 a book or magazine EG *medical publications.*

publicity
NOUN Publicity is information or advertisements about an item or event.

publicize publicizes publicizing publicized; *also spelt* **publicise**
VERB When someone publicizes a fact or event, they advertise it and make it widely known.

public school public schools
NOUN In Britain, a public school is a school that is privately run and that charges fees for the pupils to attend.

public servant public servants
NOUN In Australia and New Zealand, someone who works in the public service.

public service
NOUN In Australia and New Zealand, the public service is the government departments responsible for the administration of the country.

publish publishes publishing published
VERB When a company publishes a book, newspaper, or magazine, they print copies of it and distribute it.
publisher NOUN, **publishing** NOUN

pudding puddings
NOUN 1 a sweet cake mixture cooked with fruit or other flavouring and served hot. 2 You can refer to the sweet course of a meal as the pudding.

puddle puddles
NOUN a small shallow pool of liquid.

puerile
Said "pyoo-rile" ADJECTIVE Puerile behaviour is silly and childish.
📖 from Latin *puerilis*, from *puer* meaning 'boy'

puff puffs puffing puffed
VERB 1 To puff a cigarette or pipe is to smoke it. 2 If you are puffing, you are breathing loudly and quickly with your mouth open. 3 If something puffs out or puffs up, it

A
B
C
D
E
F
G
H
I
J
K
L
M
N
O
P
Q
R
S
T
U
V
W
X
Y
Z

NOUN **4** a small amount of air or smoke that is released.

puffin puffins
NOUN a black and white sea bird with a large brightly coloured beak.

pug pugs
NOUN a small, short-haired dog with a flat nose.

puja
Said "**poo**-jah" NOUN Puja is a variety of practices which make up Hindu worship.

puke pukes puking puked
VERB; AN INFORMAL WORD If someone pukes, they vomit.

pull pulls pulling pulled
VERB **1** When you pull something, you hold it and move it towards you. **2** When something is pulled by a vehicle or animal, it is attached to it and moves along behind it EG *Four oxen can pull a single plough.* **3** When you pull a curtain or blind, you move it so that it covers or uncovers the window. **4** If you pull a muscle, you injure it by stretching it too far or too quickly. **5** When a vehicle pulls away, pulls out, or pulls in, it moves in that direction. ▶ NOUN **6** The pull of something is its attraction or influence EG *the pull of the past.*
pull down VERB When a building is pulled down, it is deliberately destroyed.
pull out VERB If you pull out of something, you leave it or decide not to continue with it EG *The German government has pulled out of the project.*
pull through VERB When someone pulls through, they recover from a serious illness.

pulley pulleys
NOUN a device for lifting heavy weights. The weight is attached to a rope which passes over a wheel or series of wheels.

pullover pullovers
NOUN a woollen piece of clothing that covers the top part of your body.

pulmonary
ADJECTIVE; A FORMAL WORD relating to the lungs or to the veins and arteries carrying blood between the lungs and the heart.

pulp
NOUN If something is turned into a pulp, it is crushed until it is soft and moist.

pulpit pulpits
Said "**pool**-pit" NOUN the small raised platform in a church where a member of the clergy stands to preach.

pulse pulses pulsing pulsed
NOUN **1** Your pulse is the regular beating of blood through your body, the rate of which you can feel at your wrists and elsewhere. **2** The seeds of beans, peas, and lentils are called pulses when they are used for food. ▶ VERB **3** If something is pulsing, it is moving or vibrating with rhythmic, regular movements EG *She could feel the blood pulsing in her eardrums.*

puma pumas
Said "**pyoo**-mah" NOUN a wild animal belonging to the cat family.

pumice
Said "**pum**-miss" NOUN Pumice stone is very light-weight grey stone that can be used to soften areas of hard skin.

pummel pummels pummelling pummelled
VERB If you pummel something, you beat it with your fists.

pump pumps pumping pumped
NOUN **1** a machine that is used to force a liquid or gas to move in a particular direction. **2** Pumps are light shoes with flat soles which people wear for sport or leisure. ▶ VERB **3** To pump a liquid or gas somewhere is to force it to flow in that direction, using a pump. **4** If you pump money into something,

you put a lot of money into it.

pumpkin pumpkins
NOUN a very large, round, orange vegetable.

pun puns
NOUN a clever and amusing use of words so that what you say has two different meanings, such as *my dog's a champion boxer.*

punch punches punching punched
VERB 1 If you punch someone, you hit them hard with your fist. ▸ NOUN 2 a hard blow with the fist. 3 a tool used for making holes. 4 Punch is a drink made from a mixture of wine, spirits, and fruit.

punctual
ADJECTIVE arriving at the correct time.
punctually ADVERB, punctuality NOUN
◼ on time, prompt

punctuate punctuates punctuating punctuated
VERB 1 Something that is punctuated by a particular thing is interrupted by it at intervals EG *a grey day punctuated by bouts of rain.* 2 When you punctuate a piece of writing, you put punctuation into it.

punctuation
NOUN The marks in writing such as full stops, question marks, and commas are called punctuation or punctuation marks.

What does Punctuation do?

Punctuation marks are essential parts of written language. They help the reader to understand what is being read.

Look at the grammar boxes at **apostrophe, bracket, colon, comma, dash, exclamation mark, full stop, hyphen, inverted comma, question mark,** and **semicolon**.

---

puncture punctures puncturing punctured
NOUN 1 If a tyre has a puncture, a small hole has been made in it and

it has become flat. ▸ VERB 2 To puncture something is to make a small hole in it.

pungent
ADJECTIVE having a strong, unpleasant smell or taste.
pungency NOUN

punish punishes punishing punished
VERB To punish someone who has done something wrong is to make them suffer because of it.
◼ chastise, discipline, penalize

punishment punishments
NOUN something unpleasant done to someone because they have done something wrong.

punitive
Said "pyoo-nit-tiv" ADJECTIVE harsh and intended to punish people EG *punitive military action.*

Punjabi Punjabis
Said "pun-jah-bee" ADJECTIVE
1 belonging or relating to the Punjab, a state in north-western India. ▸ NOUN 2 someone who comes from the Punjab. 3 Punjabi is a language spoken in the Punjab.

punk
NOUN Punk or punk rock is an aggressive style of rock music.

punt punts
NOUN a long, flat-bottomed boat. You move it along by pushing a pole against the river bottom.

puny punier puniest
ADJECTIVE very small and weak.

pup pups
NOUN a young dog. Some other young animals such as seals are also called pups.

pupil pupils
NOUN 1 The pupils at a school are the children who go there. 2 Your pupils are the small, round, black holes in the centre of your eyes.

puppet puppets
NOUN a doll or toy animal that is moved by pulling strings or by putting your hand inside its body.

A
B
C
D
E
F
G
H
I
J
K
L
M
N
O
P
Q
R
S
T
U
V
W
X
Y
Z

A B C D E F G H I J K L M N O P Q R S T U V W X Y Z

puppy puppies
NOUN a young dog.

purchase purchases purchasing purchased
VERB **1** When you purchase something, you buy it. ▶ NOUN **2** something you have bought.
purchaser NOUN

pure purer purest
ADJECTIVE **1** Something that is pure is not mixed with anything else EG *pure wool... pure white.* **2** Pure also means clean and free from harmful substances EG *The water is pure enough to drink.* **3** People who are pure have not done anything considered to be sinful. **4** Pure also means complete and total EG *a matter of pure luck.*
purity NOUN
■ (sense 2) clean, uncontaminated
■ (sense 3) chaste, innocent, virtuous

purée purées
Said "pyoo-ray" NOUN a food which has been mashed or blended to a thick, smooth consistency.

purely
ADVERB involving only one feature and not including anything else EG *purely professional.*

Purgatory
NOUN Roman Catholics believe that Purgatory is a place where spirits of the dead are sent to suffer for their sins before going to Heaven.

purge purges purging purged
VERB To purge something is to remove undesirable things from it EG *to purge the country of criminals.*

purify purifies purifying purified
VERB To purify something is to remove all dirty or harmful substances from it.
purification NOUN

purist purists
NOUN someone who believes that something should be done in a particular, correct way EG *a football purist.*

puritan puritans
NOUN someone who believes in strict moral principles and avoids physical pleasures.
puritanical ADJECTIVE

purple
NOUN OR ADJECTIVE reddish-blue.

purport purports purporting purported
Said "pur-**port**" VERB; A FORMAL WORD Something that purports to be or have a particular thing is claimed to be or have it EG *a country which purports to disapprove of smokers.*

purpose purposes
NOUN **1** The purpose of something is the reason for it EG *the purpose of the meeting.* **2** If you have a particular purpose, this is what you want to achieve EG *To make music is my purpose in life.* ▶ PHRASE **3** If you do something **on purpose**, you do it deliberately.
purposely ADVERB, **purposeful** ADJECTIVE

purr purrs purring purred
VERB When a cat purrs, it makes a low vibrating sound because it is contented.

purse purses pursing pursed
NOUN **1** a small leather or fabric container for carrying money.
▶ VERB **2** If you purse your lips, you move them into a tight, rounded shape.

purser pursers
NOUN the officer responsible for the paperwork and the welfare of passengers on a ship.

pursue pursues pursuing pursued
VERB **1** If you pursue an activity or plan, you do it or make efforts to achieve it EG *I decided to pursue a career in photography.* **2** If you pursue someone, you follow them to try to catch them.
pursuer NOUN, **pursuit** NOUN

purveyor purveyors
NOUN; A FORMAL WORD A purveyor of goods or services is a person who sells them or provides them.

pus

NOUN Pus is a thick yellowish liquid that forms in an infected wound.

push pushes pushing pushed

VERB **1** When you push something, you press it using force in order to move it. **2** If you push someone into doing something, you force or persuade them to do it EG *His mother pushed him into auditioning for a part.* **3** AN INFORMAL USE Someone who pushes drugs sells them illegally.

■ (sense 1) shove, thrust

push off VERB; AN INFORMAL EXPRESSION If you tell someone to push off, you are telling them rudely to go away.

pushchair pushchairs

NOUN a small folding chair on wheels in which a baby or toddler can be wheeled around.

pusher pushers

NOUN; AN INFORMAL WORD someone who sells illegal drugs.

pushing

PREPOSITION Someone who is pushing a particular age is nearly that age EG *pushing sixty.*

pushover

NOUN; AN INFORMAL WORD **1** something that is easy. **2** someone who is easily persuaded or defeated.

pushy pushier pushiest

ADJECTIVE; AN INFORMAL WORD behaving in a forceful and determined way.

pussy pussies

NOUN; AN INFORMAL USE a cat.

put puts putting put

VERB **1** When you put something somewhere, you move it into that place or position. **2** If you put an idea or remark in a particular way, you express it that way EG *I think you've put that very well.* **3** To put someone or something in a particular state or situation means to cause them to be in it EG *It puts us both in an awkward position.* **4** You can use 'put' to express an estimate of the size or importance of something EG *Her wealth is now put at 290 million.*

■ (sense 1) place, position, set

put down VERB **1** To put someone down is to criticize them and make them appear foolish. **2** If an animal is put down, it is killed because it is very ill or dangerous.

put off VERB **1** If you put something off, you delay doing it. **2** To put someone off is to discourage them.

put out VERB **1** If you put a fire out or put the light out, you make it stop burning or shining. **2** If you are put out, you are annoyed or upset.

put up VERB **1** If you put up resistance to something, you argue or fight against it EG *She put up a tremendous struggle.* **2** If you put up with something, you tolerate it even though you disagree with it or dislike it.

putt putts

NOUN In golf, a putt is a gentle stroke made when the ball is near the hole.

putting

NOUN Putting is a game played on a small grass course with no obstacles. You hit a ball gently with a club so that it rolls towards one of a series of holes around the course.

putty

NOUN Putty is a paste used to fix panes of glass into frames.

puzzle puzzles puzzling puzzled

VERB **1** If something puzzles you, it confuses you and you do not understand it EG *There was something about her that puzzled me.* ▶ NOUN **2** A puzzle is a game or question that requires a lot of thought to complete or solve.

puzzled ADJECTIVE, **puzzlement** NOUN

■ (sense 1) baffle, mystify, perplex

PVC

NOUN PVC is a plastic used for making clothing, pipes, and many other things. PVC is an abbreviation for 'polyvinyl chloride'.

pygmy pygmies

Said "pig-mee"; also spelt **pigmy**
NOUN a very small person, especially
one who belongs to a racial group
in which all the people are small.
📖 from Greek *pugmaios* meaning
'undersized'

pyjamas
PLURAL NOUN Pyjamas are loose
trousers and a jacket or top that
you wear in bed.
📖 from Persian *pay jama* meaning
'leg clothing'

pylon pylons
NOUN a very tall metal structure
which carries overhead electricity
cables.

pyramid pyramids

NOUN **1** a three-dimensional shape
with a flat base and flat triangular
sides sloping upwards to a point.
2 The Pyramids are ancient stone
structures built over the tombs of
Egyptian kings and queens.

pyre pyres
NOUN a high pile of wood on which
a dead body or religious offering is
burned.

python pythons
NOUN a large snake that kills animals
by squeezing them with its body.
📖 from Greek *Puthon,* a huge
mythical serpent

quack quacks quacking quacked
VERB When a duck quacks, it makes a loud harsh sound.

quad quads
Said "kwod" NOUN Quad is the same as quadruplet.

quadrangle quadrangles
Said "kwod-rang-gl" NOUN a courtyard with buildings all round it.

quadri-
PREFIX Quadri- means four.

quadrilateral quadrilaterals
Said "kwod-ril-lat-ral" NOUN a shape with four straight sides.

quadruped quadrupeds
Said "kwod-roo-ped" NOUN any animal with four legs.

quadruple quadruples quadrupling quadrupled
Said "kwod-roo-pl" VERB When an amount or number quadruples, it becomes four times as large as it was.

quadruplet quadruplets
Said "kwod-roo-plet" NOUN Quadruplets are four children born at the same time to the same mother.

quagmire quagmires
Said "kwag-mire" NOUN a soft, wet area of land which you sink into if you walk on it.

quail quails quailing quailed
NOUN 1 a type of small game bird with a round body and short tail. ▶ VERB 2 If you quail, you feel or look afraid.

quaint quainter quaintest
ADJECTIVE attractively old-fashioned or unusual EG quaint customs.
quaintly ADVERB

quake quakes quaking quaked
VERB If you quake, you shake and tremble because you are very frightened.

Quaker Quakers
NOUN a member of a Christian group, the Society of Friends.

qualification qualifications
NOUN 1 Your qualifications are your skills and achievements, especially as officially recognized at the end of a course of training or study. 2 something you add to a statement to make it less strong EG It is a good novel and yet cannot be recommended without qualification.

qualify qualifies qualifying qualified
VERB 1 When you qualify, you pass the examinations that you need to pass to do a particular job. 2 If you qualify a statement, you add a detail or explanation to make it less strong EG I would qualify that by putting it into context. 3 If you qualify for something, you become entitled to have it EG You qualify for a discount.
qualified ADJECTIVE

quality qualities
NOUN 1 The quality of something is how good it is EG The quality of food is very poor. 2 a characteristic EG These qualities are essential for success.

qualm qualms
Said "kwahm" NOUN If you have qualms about what you are doing, you worry that it might not be right.

quandary quandaries
Said "kwon-dree" NOUN If you are in a quandary, you cannot decide what to do.

quantity quantities
NOUN 1 an amount you can measure or count EG a small quantity of alcohol. 2 Quantity is the amount of something that there is EG emphasis on quantity rather than quality.

quarantine
Said "kwor-an-teen" NOUN If an animal is in quarantine, it is kept away from other animals for a time

A
B
C
D
E
F
G
H
I
J
K
L
M
N
O
P
Q
R
S
T
U
V
W
X
Y
Z

A
B
C
D
E
F
G
H
I
J
K
L
M
N
O
P
Q
R
S
T
U
V
W
X
Y
Z

because it might have an infectious disease.

🏛 from Italian *quarantina* meaning 'forty days'

quarrel quarrels quarrelling quarrelled

NOUN **1** an angry argument. ▶ VERB **2** If people quarrel, they have an angry argument.

■ (sense 1) argument, disagreement, fight

■ (sense 2) argue, disagree, fall out

quarry quarries quarrying quarried

Said "kwor-ree" NOUN **1** a place where stone is removed from the ground by digging or blasting. **2** A person's or animal's quarry is the animal that they are hunting. ▶ VERB **3** To quarry stone means to remove it from a quarry by digging or blasting.

🏛 sense 2 is from Middle English *quirre* meaning 'entrails given to the hounds to eat'

quart quarts

Said "kwort" NOUN a unit of liquid volume equal to two pints or about 1.136 litres.

quarter quarters

NOUN **1** one of four equal parts. **2** an American coin worth 25 cents. **3** You can refer to a particular area in a city as a quarter EG *the French quarter*. **4** You can use 'quarter' to refer vaguely to a particular person or group of people EG *You are very popular in certain quarters*. ▶ PLURAL NOUN **5** A soldier's or a servant's quarters are the rooms that they live in.

quarterly quarterlies

ADJECTIVE OR ADVERB **1** Quarterly means happening regularly every three months EG *my quarterly report*. ▶ NOUN **2** a magazine or journal published every three months.

quartet quartets

Said "kwor-tet" NOUN a group of four musicians who sing or play together; also a piece of music

written for four instruments or singers.

quartz

NOUN Quartz is a kind of hard, shiny crystal used in making very accurate watches and clocks.

quash quashes quashing quashed

Said "kwosh" VERB To quash a decision or judgment means to reject it officially EG *The judges quashed their convictions*.

quasi-

Said "kway-sie" PREFIX Quasi- means resembling something but not actually being that thing EG *a quasi-religious order*.

🏛 a Latin word meaning 'as if'

quaver quavers quavering quavered

Said "kway-ver" VERB If your voice quavers, it sounds unsteady, usually because you are nervous.

quay quays

Said "kee" NOUN a place where boats are tied up and loaded or unloaded.

queasy queasier queasiest

Said "kwee-zee" ADJECTIVE feeling slightly sick.

queen queens

NOUN **1** a female monarch or a woman married to a king. **2** a female bee or ant which can lay eggs. **3** In chess, the queen is the most powerful piece, which can move in any direction. **4** In a pack of cards, a queen is a card with a picture of a queen on it.

queen mother queen mothers

NOUN the widow of a king and the mother of the reigning monarch.

queer queerer queerest

ADJECTIVE Queer means very strange.

quell quells quelling quelled

VERB **1** To quell a rebellion or riot means to put an end to it by using force. **2** If you quell a feeling such as fear or grief, you stop yourself from feeling it EG *trying to quell the loneliness*.

quench quenches quenching

quenched

VERB If you quench your thirst, you have a drink so that you are no longer thirsty.

query queries querying queried

Said "qweer-ree" NOUN **1** a question. ▶ VERB **2** If you query something, you ask about it because you think it might not be right EG *No-one queried my decision.*

quest quests

NOUN a long search for something.

question questions questioning questioned

NOUN **1** a sentence which asks for information. **2** If there is some question about something, there is doubt about it. **3** a problem that needs to be discussed EG *Can we get back to the question of the car?* ▶ VERB **4** If you question someone, you ask them questions. **5** If you question something, you express doubts about it EG *He never stopped questioning his own beliefs.* ▶ PHRASE **6** If something is **out of the question**, it is impossible.

目 (sense 1) inquiry, query
目 (sense 5) challenge, dispute

What is a Question?

Questions are used to ask for information.

A question has a question mark at the end of the sentence.
  What is your name?

Questions are often introduced by a questioning word such as *what, who, where, when, why,* or *how.*
  Where do you live?

If a sentence does not already contain an auxiliary verb, a form of the auxiliary verb *do* may be placed at the start to turn it into a question.
  Does Anna have a sister?

If there is already an auxiliary verb in the sentence, you can turn it into a question by reversing the word order so the auxiliary verb comes before the subject instead of after it.
  Are you going to the swimming baths?
  Must they keep doing that?

A question can also be made by adding a phrase, such as *isn't it?* or *don't you?*, on to the end of a statement.
  *It is hot today, **isn't it?***
  *You like chocolate, **don't you?***

questionable

ADJECTIVE possibly not true or not honest.

question mark question marks

NOUN the punctuation mark (?) which is used at the end of a question.

What does the Question Mark do?

The **question mark** (?) marks the end of a question.
  When is the train leaving?

After an indirect question or a polite request, a full stop is used rather than a question mark.
  Anna asked when the train was leaving.
  Will you please send me an application form.

---

questionnaire questionnaires

NOUN a list of questions which asks for information for a survey.

queue queues queuing or queueing queued

Said "kyoo" NOUN **1** a line of people or vehicles waiting for something. ▶ VERB **2** When people queue, they stand in a line waiting for something.

quibble quibbles quibbling quibbled

VERB **1** If you quibble, you argue about something unimportant. ▶ NOUN **2** a minor objection.

quiche quiches

Said "keesh" NOUN a tart with a savoury filling.
目 a French word, originally from German *Kuchen* meaning 'cake'

quick quicker quickest

ADJECTIVE **1** moving with great speed. **2** lasting only a short time EG *a quick chat.* **3** happening without any delay EG *a quick response.* **4** intelligent and able to

A B C D E F G H I J K L M N O P Q R S T U V W X Y Z

A
B
C
D
E
F
G
H
I
J
K
L
M
N
O
P
Q
R
S
T
U
V
W
X
Y
Z

understand things easily.
quickly ADVERB

quicksand quicksands
NOUN an area of deep wet sand that you sink into if you walk on it.

quid
NOUN; AN INFORMAL WORD In British English, a pound in money.

quiet quieter quietest
ADJECTIVE **1** Someone or something that is quiet makes very little noise or no noise at all. **2** Quiet also means peaceful EG *a quiet evening at home*. **3** A quiet event happens with very little fuss or publicity EG *a quiet wedding*. ▶ NOUN **4** Quiet is silence.
quietly ADVERB
▦ (sense 1) silent, soft

quieten quietens quietening quietened
VERB To quieten someone means to make them become quiet.

quill quills
NOUN **1** a pen made from a feather. **2** A bird's quills are the large feathers on its wings and tail. **3** A porcupine's quills are its spines.

quilt quilts
NOUN A quilt for a bed is a cover, especially a cover that is padded.

quilted
ADJECTIVE Quilted clothes or coverings are made of thick layers of material sewn together.

quin quins
NOUN Quin is the same as **quintuplet**.

quince quinces
NOUN an acid-tasting fruit used for making jam and marmalade.

quintessential
ADJECTIVE; A FORMAL WORD A person or thing that is quintessential seems to represent the basic nature of something in a pure, concentrated form EG *It was the quintessential Hollywood party*.

quintet quintets
Said "kwin-**tet**" NOUN a group of five musicians who sing or play

together; also a piece of music written for five instruments or singers.

quintuplet quintuplets
Said "kwin-**tyoo**-plit" NOUN Quintuplets are five children born at the same time to the same mother.

quip quips quipping quipped
NOUN **1** an amusing or clever remark. ▶ VERB **2** To quip means to make an amusing or clever remark.

quirk quirks
NOUN **1** an odd habit or characteristic EG *an interesting quirk of human nature*. **2** an unexpected event or development EG *a quirk of fate*.
quirky ADJECTIVE

quit quits quitting quit
VERB If you quit something, you leave it or stop doing it EG *Leigh quit his job as a salesman*.

quite
ADVERB **1** fairly but not very EG *quite old*. **2** completely EG *Jane lay quite still*. ▶ PHRASE **3** You use **quite a** to emphasize that something is large or impressive EG *It was quite a party*.
☑ You should be careful about using *quite*. It can mean 'completely': *quite amazing*. It can also mean 'fairly but not very': *quite friendly*.

quiver quivers quivering quivered
VERB **1** If something quivers, it trembles. ▶ NOUN **2** a trembling movement EG *a quiver of panic*.

quiz quizzes quizzing quizzed
NOUN **1** a game in which the competitors are asked questions to test their knowledge. ▶ VERB **2** If you quiz someone, you question them closely about something.

quizzical
Said "**kwiz**-ik-kl" ADJECTIVE amused and questioning EG *a quizzical smile*.

quota quotas
NOUN a number or quantity of something which is officially

allowed EG *a quota of three foreign players allowed in each team.*

quotation quotations
NOUN an extract from a book or speech which is quoted.

What is a Quotation?

There are two ways of writing what people say. You can write down the exact words that are spoken. This is called **direct speech**. The second way is to write down the meaning of what they say without using the exact words. This is called **indirect speech** or **reported speech**.

When you use direct speech, the exact words spoken go into quotation marks.

Robbie said, "Thank you very much for the prize."

The sentence will contain a main verb which indicates speaking, such as *say, tell, ask,* or *answer.* The words contained in quotation marks begin with a capital letter. If there is no other punctuation, they are separated from the rest of the sentence by a comma.

"This is the best picture," said the judge.

When you use indirect or reported speech, there is a subordinate clause which reports the meaning of what was said.

*The judge said **that Robbie's picture was the best**.*

When the reported words are a statement, the clause that reports them is usually introduced by *that*. The main clause usually contains a verb such as *say, tell, explain,* or *reply.*

*The judge said **that** Robbie should win first prize.*

Sometimes the word *that* can be left out.

The judge said Robbie should win first prize.

quote quotes quoting quoted
VERB **1** If you quote something that someone has written or said, you repeat their exact words. **2** If you quote a fact, you state it because it supports what you are saying.
▶ NOUN **3** an extract from a book or speech. **4** an estimate of how much a piece of work will cost.

Qur'an
another spelling of **Koran**.

Rr Rr

RAAF

In Australia, an abbreviation for 'Royal Australian Air Force'.

rabbi rabbis

Said "rab-by" NOUN a Jewish religious leader.

🏛 from Hebrew *rabh* + *-i* meaning 'my master'

rabbit rabbits

NOUN a small animal with long ears.

rabble

NOUN a noisy, disorderly crowd.

rabid

ADJECTIVE **1** used to describe someone with strong views that you do not approve of EG *a rabid Nazi.* **2** A rabid dog or other animal has rabies.

rabies

Said "ray-beez" NOUN Rabies is an infectious disease which causes people and animals, especially dogs, to go mad and die.

raccoon raccoons; also spelt racoon

NOUN a small North American animal with a long striped tail.

race races racing raced

NOUN **1** a competition to see who is fastest, for example in running or driving. **2** one of the major groups that human beings can be divided into according to their physical features. ▶ VERB **3** If you race someone, you compete with them in a race. **4** If you race something or if it races, it goes at its greatest rate EG *Her heart raced uncontrollably.* **5** If you race somewhere, you go there as quickly as possible EG *The hares raced away out of sight.*

racing NOUN

racecourse racecourses

NOUN a grass track, sometimes with jumps, along which horses race.

racehorse racehorses

NOUN a horse trained to run in races.

racial

ADJECTIVE relating to the different races that people belong to EG *racial harmony.*

racially ADVERB

racism or **racialism**

NOUN Racism or racialism is the treatment of some people as inferior because of their race.

racist NOUN OR ADJECTIVE

rack racks racking racked

NOUN **1** a piece of equipment for holding things or hanging things on. ▶ VERB **2** If you are racked by something, you suffer because of it EG *She was racked by guilt.* ▶ AN INFORMAL PHRASE **3** If you **rack your brains**, you try hard to think of or remember something.

racket rackets

NOUN **1** If someone is making a racket, they are making a lot of noise. **2** an illegal way of making money EG *a drugs racket.* **3** Racket is another spelling of **racquet**.

racquet racquets; also spelt **racket**

NOUN a bat with strings across it used in tennis and similar games.

🏛 from Arabic *rahat* meaning 'palm of the hand'

radar

NOUN Radar is equipment used to track ships or aircraft that are out of sight by using radio signals that are reflected back from the object and shown on a screen.

🏛 from *RA(dio) D(etecting) A(nd) R(anging)*

radiant

ADJECTIVE **1** Someone who is radiant is so happy that it shows in their face. **2** glowing brightly.

radiance NOUN

radiate radiates radiating radiated

VERB **1** If things radiate from a place, they form a pattern like lines spreading out from the centre of a circle. **2** If you radiate a quality or emotion, it shows clearly in your face and behaviour EG *He radiated health.*

radiation

NOUN Radiation is the stream of particles given out by a radioactive substance.

radiator radiators

NOUN **1** a hollow metal device for heating a room, usually connected to a central heating system. **2** the part of a car that is filled with water to cool the engine.

radical radicals

NOUN **1** Radicals are people who think there should be great changes in society, and try to make them happen. ▶ ADJECTIVE **2** very significant, important, or basic EG *a radical change in the law.*
radically ADVERB, **radicalism** NOUN

radii

the plural of **radius.**

radio radios radioing radioed

NOUN **1** Radio is a system of sending sound over a distance by transmitting electrical signals. **2** Radio is also the broadcasting of programmes to the public by radio. **3** a piece of equipment for listening to radio programmes. ▶ VERB **4** To radio someone means to send them a message by radio EG *The pilot radioed that a fire had started.*

radioactive

ADJECTIVE giving off powerful and harmful rays.
radioactivity NOUN

radiotherapy

NOUN Radiotherapy is the treatment of diseases such as cancer using radiation.
radiotherapist NOUN

radish radishes

NOUN a small salad vegetable with a red skin and white flesh and a hot taste.

radium

NOUN Radium is a radioactive element which is used in the treatment of cancer.

radius radii

NOUN The radius of a circle is the length of a straight line drawn from its centre to its circumference.

RAF

In Britain, an abbreviation for 'Royal Air Force'.

raffia

NOUN Raffia is a material made from palm leaves and used for making mats and baskets.

raffle raffles

NOUN a competition in which people buy numbered tickets and win a prize if they have the ticket that is chosen.

raft rafts

NOUN a floating platform made from long pieces of wood tied together.

rafter rafters

NOUN Rafters are the sloping pieces of wood that support a roof.

rag rags

NOUN **1** a piece of old cloth used to clean or wipe things. **2** If someone is dressed in rags, they are wearing old torn clothes.

rage rages raging raged

NOUN **1** Rage is great anger. ▶ VERB **2** To rage about something means to speak angrily about it. **3** If something such as a storm or battle is raging, it is continuing with great force or violence EG *The fire still raged out of control.*
■ (sense 1) anger, fury, wrath

ragged

ADJECTIVE Ragged clothes are old and torn.

raid raids raiding raided

VERB **1** To raid a place means to enter it by force to attack it or steal something. ▶ NOUN **2** the raiding of a building or a place EG *an armed raid on a bank.*

rail rails

NOUN **1** a fixed horizontal bar used as a support or for hanging things on. **2** Rails are the steel bars which

A
B
C
D
E
F
G
H
I
J
K
L
M
N
O
P
Q
R
S
T
U
V
W
X
Y
Z

A B C D E F G H I J K L M N O P Q R S T U V W X Y Z

trains run along. **3** Rail is the railway considered as a means of transport EG *I plan to go by rail.*

railing railings
NOUN Railings are a fence made from metal bars.

railway railways
NOUN a route along which trains travel on steel rails.

rain rains raining rained
NOUN **1** Rain is water falling from the clouds in small drops. ▶ VERB **2** When it is raining, rain is falling.
rainy ADJECTIVE

rainbird rainbirds
NOUN a bird whose call is believed to be a sign that it will rain.

rainbow rainbows
NOUN an arch of different colours that sometimes appears in the sky after it has been raining.

raincoat raincoats
NOUN a waterproof coat.

rainfall
NOUN Rainfall is the amount of rain that falls in a place during a particular period.

rainforest rainforests
NOUN a dense forest of tall trees in a tropical area where there is a lot of rain.

rainwater
NOUN Rainwater is rain that has been stored.

raise raises raising raised
VERB **1** If you raise something, you make it higher EG *She went to the window and raised the blinds... a drive to raise standards of literacy.* **2** If you raise your voice, you speak more loudly. **3** To raise money for a cause means to get people to donate money towards it. **4** To raise a child means to look after it until it is grown up. **5** If you raise a subject, you mention it.

raisin raisins
NOUN Raisins are dried grapes.

rake rakes raking raked
NOUN a garden tool with a row of

metal teeth and a long handle.
rake up VERB If you rake up something embarrassing from the past, you remind someone about it.

rally rallies rallying rallied
NOUN **1** a large public meeting held to show support for something. **2** a competition in which vehicles are raced over public roads. **3** In tennis or squash, a rally is a continuous series of shots exchanged by the players. ▶ VERB **4** When people rally to something, they gather together to continue a struggle or to support something.

ram rams ramming rammed
VERB **1** If one vehicle rams another, it crashes into it. **2** To ram something somewhere means to push it there firmly EG *He rammed his key into the lock.* ▶ NOUN **3** an adult male sheep.

RAM
NOUN In computing, RAM is a storage space which can be filled with data but which loses its contents when the machine is switched off. RAM stands for 'random access memory'.

Ramadan
NOUN Ramadan is the ninth month of the Muslim year, during which Muslims eat and drink nothing during daylight.
📖 from Arabic *Ramadan* meaning literally 'the hot month'

ramble rambles rambling rambled
NOUN **1** a long walk in the countryside. ▶ VERB **2** To ramble means to go for a ramble. **3** To ramble also means to talk in a confused way EG *He then started rambling and repeating himself.*
rambler NOUN

ramification ramifications
NOUN The ramifications of a decision or plan are all its consequences and effects.

ramp ramps
NOUN a sloping surface connecting two different levels.

rampage rampages rampaging rampaged
VERB **1** To rampage means to rush about wildly causing damage. ▶ PHRASE **2** To **go on the rampage** means to rush about in a wild or violent way.
■ (sense 1) go berserk, run amok

rampant
ADJECTIVE If something such as crime or disease is rampant, it is growing or spreading uncontrollably.

rampart ramparts
NOUN Ramparts are earth banks, often with a wall on top, built to protect a castle or city.

ramshackle
ADJECTIVE A ramshackle building is in very poor condition.

ranch ranches
NOUN a large farm where cattle or horses are reared, especially in the USA.
▥ from Mexican Spanish *rancho* meaning 'small farm'

rancid
Said "**ran**-sid" ADJECTIVE Rancid food has gone bad.
▥ from Latin *rancere* meaning 'to stink'

rancour
Said "**rang**-kur" NOUN; A FORMAL WORD Rancour is bitter hatred.
rancorous ADJECTIVE

rand
NOUN The rand is the main unit of currency in South Africa.

random
ADJECTIVE **1** A random choice or arrangement is not based on any definite plan. ▶ PHRASE **2** If you do something **at random**, you do it without any definite plan EG *He chose his victims at random*.
randomly ADVERB
■ (sense 1) chance, haphazard, incidental

range ranges ranging ranged
NOUN **1** The range of something is the maximum distance over which it can reach things or detect things EG *This mortar has a range of 15,000 metres.* **2** a number of different things of the same kind EG *A wide range of colours are available.* **3** a set of values on a scale EG *The average age range is between 35 and 55.* **4** A range of mountains is a line of them. **5** A rifle range or firing range is a place where people practise shooting at targets. ▶ VERB **6** When a set of things ranges between two points, they vary within these points on a scale EG *prices ranging between 370 and 1200 pounds.*
■ (sense 2) series, variety

ranger rangers
NOUN someone whose job is to look after a forest or park.

rank ranks ranking ranked
NOUN **1** Someone's rank is their official level in a job or profession. **2** The ranks are the ordinary members of the armed forces, rather than the officers. **3** The ranks of a group are its members EG *We welcomed five new members to our ranks.* **4** a row of people or things. ▶ VERB **5** To rank as something means to have that status or position on a scale EG *His dismissal ranks as the worst humiliation he has ever known.* ▶ ADJECTIVE **6** complete and absolute EG *rank stupidity.* **7** having a strong, unpleasant smell EG *the rank smell of unwashed clothes.*

ransack ransacks ransacking ransacked
VERB To ransack a place means to disturb everything and leave it in a mess, in order to search for or steal something.
▥ from Old Norse *rann* meaning 'house' and *saka* meaning 'to search'

ransom ransoms
NOUN money that is demanded to free someone who has been kidnapped.

rant rants ranting ranted
VERB To rant means to talk loudly in

an excited or angry way.

rap raps rapping rapped
· VERB **1** If you rap something, you hit it with a series of quick blows.
▶ NOUN **2** a quick knock or blow on something eg *A rap on the door signalled his arrival.* **3** Rap is a style of poetry spoken to music with a strong rhythmic beat.

rape rapes raping raped
VERB **1** If a man rapes a woman, he violently forces her to have sex with him against her will. ▶ NOUN **2** Rape is the act or crime of raping a woman eg *victims of rape.* **3** Rape is a plant with yellow flowers that is grown as a crop for oil and fodder.
rapist NOUN

rapid rapids
ADJECTIVE **1** happening or moving very quickly eg *rapid industrial expansion... He took a few rapid steps.*
▶ PLURAL NOUN **2** An area of a river where the water moves extremely fast over rocks is referred to as rapids.
rapidly ADVERB, **rapidity** NOUN

rapier rapiers
NOUN a long thin sword with a sharp point.

rapport
Said "rap-**por**" NOUN; A FORMAL WORD If there is a rapport between two people, they find it easy to understand each other's feelings and attitudes.

rapt
ADJECTIVE If you are rapt, you are so interested in something that you are not aware of other things eg *sitting with rapt attention in front of the screen.*

rapture
NOUN Rapture is a feeling of extreme delight.
rapturous ADJECTIVE, **rapturously** ADVERB

rare rarer rarest
ADJECTIVE **1** Something that is rare is not common or does not happen often eg *a rare flower... Such major disruptions are rare.* **2** Rare meat has

been lightly cooked.
rarely ADVERB

rarefied
Said "**rare**-if-eyed" ADJECTIVE seeming to have little connection with ordinary life eg *He grew up in a rarefied literary atmosphere.*

raring
ADJECTIVE If you are raring to do something, you are very eager to do it.

rarity rarities
NOUN **1** something that is interesting or valuable because it is unusual. **2** The rarity of something is the fact that it is not common.

rascal rascals
NOUN If you refer to someone as a rascal, you mean that they do bad or mischievous things.

rash rashes
ADJECTIVE **1** If you are rash, you do something hasty and foolish.
▶ NOUN **2** an area of red spots that appear on your skin when you are ill or have an allergy. **3** A rash of events is a lot of them happening in a short time eg *a rash of strikes.*
rashly ADVERB
📰 (sense 1) foolhardy, reckless

rasher rashers
NOUN a thin slice of bacon.

rasp rasps rasping rasped
VERB **1** To rasp means to make a harsh unpleasant sound. ▶ NOUN **2** a coarse file with rows of raised teeth, used for smoothing wood or metal.

raspberry raspberries
NOUN a small soft red fruit that grows on a bush.

rat rats
NOUN a long-tailed animal which looks like a large mouse.

rate rates rating rated
NOUN **1** The rate of something is the speed or frequency with which it happens eg *New diet books appear at the rate of nearly one a week.* **2** The rate of interest is its level eg *a further*

cut in interest rates. **3** Rates are a local tax paid by people who own buildings. ▶ PHRASE **4** If you say at **this rate** something will happen, you mean it will happen if things continue in the same way EG *At this rate we'll be lucky to get home before six.* **5** You say **at any rate** when you want to add to or amend what you have just said EG *He is the least appealing character, to me at any rate.* ▶ VERB **6** The way you rate someone or something is your opinion of them EG *He was rated as one of England's top young players.*

rather
ADVERB **1** Rather means to a certain extent EG *We got along rather well... The reality is rather more complex.* ▶ PHRASE **2** If you **would rather** do a particular thing, you would prefer to do it. **3** If you do one thing **rather than** another, you choose to do the first thing instead of the second.
■ (sense 1) quite, relatively, somewhat
■ (sense 2) preferably, sooner

ratify ratifies ratifying ratified
VERB; A FORMAL WORD To ratify a written agreement means to approve it formally, usually by signing it.
ratification NOUN

rating ratings
NOUN **1** a score based on the quality or status of something. **2** The ratings are statistics showing how popular each television programme is.

ratio ratios
NOUN a relationship which shows how many times one thing is bigger than another EG *The adult to child ratio is 1 to 6.*

ration rations rationing rationed
NOUN **1** Your ration of something is the amount you are allowed to have. **2** Rations are the food given each day to a soldier or member of an expedition. ▶ VERB **3** When

something is rationed, you are only allowed a limited amount of it, because there is a shortage.

rational
ADJECTIVE When people are rational, their judgments are based on reason rather than emotion.
rationally ADVERB, **rationality** NOUN

rationale
Said "rash-on-nahl" NOUN The rationale for a course of action or for a belief is the set of reasons on which it is based.

rattle rattles rattling rattled
VERB **1** When something rattles, it makes short, regular knocking sounds. **2** If something rattles you, it upsets you EG *He was obviously rattled by events.* ▶ NOUN **3** the noise something makes when it rattles. **4** a baby's toy which makes a noise when it is shaken.

rattlesnake rattlesnakes
NOUN a poisonous American snake.

raucous
Said "raw-kuss" ADJECTIVE A raucous voice is loud and rough.

ravage ravages ravaging ravaged
A FORMAL WORD ▶ VERB **1** To ravage something means to seriously harm or damage it EG *a country ravaged by floods.* ▶ NOUN **2** The ravages of something are its damaging effects EG *the ravages of two world wars.*

rave raves raving raved
VERB **1** If someone raves, they talk in an angry, uncontrolled way EG *He started raving about being treated badly.* **2** AN INFORMAL USE If you rave about something, you talk about it very enthusiastically. ▶ ADJECTIVE **3** AN INFORMAL USE If something gets a rave review, it is praised enthusiastically. ▶ NOUN **4** AN INFORMAL USE a large party with electronic dance music.

raven ravens
NOUN **1** a large black bird with a deep, harsh call. ▶ ADJECTIVE **2** Raven hair is black and shiny.

A B C D E F G H I J K L M N O P Q R S T U V W X Y Z

ravenous

ADJECTIVE very hungry.

ravine ravines

NOUN a deep, narrow valley with steep sides.

raving ravings

ADJECTIVE 1 If someone is raving, they are mad EG *a raving lunatic.*
▶ NOUN 2 Someone's ravings are crazy things they write or say.

ravioli

Said "rav-ee-oh-lee" NOUN Ravioli consists of small squares of pasta filled with meat and served with a sauce.

ravishing

ADJECTIVE Someone or something that is ravishing is very beautiful EG *a ravishing landscape.*

raw

ADJECTIVE 1 Raw food is uncooked.
2 A raw substance is in its natural state EG *raw sugar.* 3 If part of your body is raw, the skin has come off or been rubbed away. 4 Someone who is raw is too young or too new in a job or situation to know how to behave.

raw material raw materials

NOUN Raw materials are the natural substances used to make something.

ray rays

NOUN 1 a beam of light or radiation.
2 A ray of hope is a small amount that makes an unpleasant situation seem slightly better. 3 a large sea fish with eyes on the top of its body, and a long tail.

raze razes razing razed

VERB To raze a building, town, or forest means to completely destroy it EG *The town was razed to the ground during the occupation.*

razor razors

NOUN a tool that people use for shaving.

razor blade razor blades

NOUN a small, sharp, flat piece of metal fitted into a razor for shaving.

re-

PREFIX 'Re-' is used to form nouns and verbs that refer to the repetition of an action or process. For example, to reread something means to read it again, and to remarry means to marry again.

reach reaches reaching reached

VERB 1 When you reach a place, you arrive there. 2 When you reach for something, you stretch out your arm to it. 3 If something reaches a place or point, it extends as far as that place or point EG *She has a cloak that reaches to the ground.* 4 If something or someone reaches a stage or level, they get to it EG *Unemployment has reached record levels.* 5 To reach an agreement or decision means to succeed in achieving it. ▶ PHRASE 6 If a place is **within reach**, you can get there EG *a cycle route well within reach of most people.* 7 If something is **out of reach**, you cannot get it to it by stretching out your arm EG *Store out of reach of children.*

react reacts reacting reacted

VERB 1 When you react to something, you behave in a particular way because of it EG *He reacted badly to the news.* 2 If one substance reacts with another, a chemical change takes place when they are put together.

reaction reactions

NOUN 1 Your reaction to something is what you feel, say, or do because of it EG *Reaction to the visit is mixed.* 2 Your reactions are your ability to move quickly in response to something that happens EG *Squash requires fast reactions.* 3 If there is a reaction against something, it becomes unpopular EG *a reaction against Christianity.* 4 In a chemical reaction, a chemical change takes place when two substances are put together.

reactionary reactionaries

ADJECTIVE 1 Someone who is reactionary tries to prevent

political or social change. ▶ NOUN
2 Reactionaries are reactionary
people.

reactor reactors
NOUN a device which is used to
produce nuclear energy.

read reads reading read
VERB **1** When you read, you look at
something written and follow it or
say it aloud. **2** If you can read
someone's moods or mind, you can
judge what they are feeling or
thinking. **3** When you read a meter
or gauge, you look at it and record
the figure on it. **4** If you read a
subject at university, you study it.

reader readers
NOUN **1** The readers of a newspaper
or magazine are the people who
read it regularly. **2** At a university, a
reader is a senior lecturer just
below the rank of professor.

readership
NOUN The readership of a newspaper
or magazine consists of the people
who read it regularly.

readily
ADVERB **1** willingly and eagerly EG *She
readily agreed to see Alex.* **2** easily
done or quickly obtainable EG *Help
is readily available.*

reading readings
NOUN **1** Reading is the activity of
reading books. **2** The reading on a
meter or gauge is the figure or
measurement it shows.

readjust readjusts readjusting
readjusted
Said "ree-aj-**just**" VERB **1** If you
readjust, you adapt to a new
situation. **2** If you readjust
something, you alter it to a
different position.

ready
ADJECTIVE **1** having reached the
required stage, or prepared for
action or use EG *In a few days time the
plums will be ready to eat.* **2** willing or
eager to do something EG *She says
she's not ready for marriage.* **3** If you
are ready for something, you need

it EG *I'm ready for bed.* **4** easily
produced or obtained EG *ready cash.*
readiness NOUN

ready-made
ADJECTIVE already made and therefore
able to be used immediately.

reaffirm reaffirms reaffirming
reaffirmed
VERB To reaffirm something means
to state it again EG *He reaffirmed his
support for the campaign.*

real
ADJECTIVE **1** actually existing and not
imagined or invented. **2** genuine
and not imitation EG *Who's to know
if they're real guns?* **3** true or actual
and not mistaken EG *This was the
real reason for her call.*
■ (sense 1) authentic, genuine, true

real estate
NOUN Real estate is property in the
form of land and buildings rather
than personal possessions.

realism
NOUN Realism is the recognition of
the true nature of a situation EG *a
triumph of muddled thought over
realism and common sense.*
realist NOUN

realistic
ADJECTIVE **1** recognizing and
accepting the true nature of a
situation. **2** representing things in a
way that is true to real life EG *His
novels are more realistic than his short
stories.*
realistically ADVERB

reality
NOUN **1** Reality is the real nature of
things, rather than the way
someone imagines it EG *Fiction and
reality were increasingly blurred.* **2** If
something has become reality, it
actually exists or is actually
happening.
■ (sense 1) fact, truth

realize realizes realizing realized;
also spelt **realise**
VERB **1** If you realize something, you
become aware of it. **2** A FORMAL USE If
your hopes or fears are realized,

A
B
C
D
E
F
G
H
I
J
K
L
M
N
O
P
Q
R
S
T
U
V
W
X
Y
Z

what you hoped for or feared actually happens EG *Our worst fears were realized*. **3** To realize a sum of money means to receive it as a result of selling goods or shares.
realization NOUN

really
ADVERB **1** used to add emphasis to what is being said EG *I'm not really surprised*. **2** used to indicate that you are talking about the true facts about something EG *What was really going on?*
☑ If you want to emphasize an adjective you should always use *really* rather than *real*: *really interesting*.

realm realms
Said "relm" NOUN; A FORMAL WORD **1** You can refer to any area of thought or activity as a realm EG *the realm of politics*. **2** a country with a king or queen EG *defence of the realm*.

reap reaps reaping reaped
VERB **1** To reap a crop such as corn means to cut and gather it. **2** When people reap benefits or rewards, they get them as a result of hard work or careful planning.
reaper NOUN

reappear reappears reappearing reappeared
VERB When people or things reappear, you can see them again, because they have come back EG *The stolen ring reappeared three years later in a pawn shop*.
reappearance NOUN

reappraisal reappraisals
NOUN; A FORMAL WORD If there is a reappraisal, people think about something and decide whether they want to change it EG *a reappraisal of the government's economic policies*.

rear rears rearing reared
NOUN **1** The rear of something is the part at the back. ▶ VERB **2** To rear children or young animals means to bring them up until they are able to look after themselves.

3 When a horse rears, it raises the front part of its body, so that its front legs are in the air.

rear admiral rear admirals
NOUN a senior officer in the navy.

rearrange rearranges rearranging rearranged
VERB To rearrange something means to organize or arrange it in a different way.

reason reasons reasoning reasoned
NOUN **1** The reason for something is the fact or situation which explains why it happens or which causes it to happen. **2** If you have reason to believe or feel something, there are definite reasons why you believe it or feel it EG *He had every reason to be upset*. **3** Reason is the ability to think and make judgments. ▶ VERB **4** If you reason that something is true, you decide it is true after considering all the facts. **5** If you reason with someone, you persuade them to accept sensible arguments.
▪ (sense 1) cause, motive
▪ (sense 3) rationality, sense(s), understanding

reasonable
ADJECTIVE **1** Reasonable behaviour is fair and sensible. **2** If an explanation is reasonable, there are good reasons for thinking it is correct. **3** A reasonable amount is a fairly large amount. **4** A reasonable price is fair and not too high.
reasonably ADVERB

reasoning
NOUN Reasoning is the process by which you reach a conclusion after considering all the facts.

reassess reassesses reassessing reassessed
VERB If you reassess something, you consider whether it still has the same value or importance.
reassessment NOUN

reassure reassures reassuring reassured

VERB If you reassure someone, you say or do things that make them less worried.

reassurance NOUN

rebate rebates

NOUN money paid back to someone who has paid too much tax or rent.

rebel rebels rebelling rebelled

NOUN **1** Rebels are people who are fighting their own country's army to change the political system. **2** Someone who is a rebel rejects society's values and behaves differently from other people. ▸ VERB **3** To rebel means to fight against authority and reject accepted values.

rebellion rebellions

NOUN A rebellion is organized and often violent opposition to authority.

■ mutiny, revolution, uprising

rebellious

ADJECTIVE unwilling to obey and likely to rebel against authority.

rebuff rebuffs rebuffing rebuffed

VERB **1** If you rebuff someone, you reject what they offer EG *She rebuffed their offers of help.* ▸ NOUN **2** a rejection of an offer.

rebuild rebuilds rebuilding rebuilt

VERB When a town or building is rebuilt, it is built again after being damaged or destroyed.

rebuke rebukes rebuking rebuked

Said "rib-**yook**" VERB To rebuke someone means to speak severely to them about something they have done.

recall recalls recalling recalled

VERB **1** To recall something means to remember it. **2** If you are recalled to a place, you are ordered to return there. **3** If a company recalls products, it asks people to return them because they are faulty.

recap recaps recapping recapped

VERB To recap means to repeat and summarize the main points of an explanation or discussion.

recapture recaptures recapturing recaptured

VERB **1** When you recapture a pleasant feeling, you experience it again EG *She may never recapture that past assurance.* **2** When soldiers recapture a place, they capture it from the people who took it from them. **3** When animals or prisoners are recaptured, they are caught after they have escaped.

recede recedes receding receded

VERB **1** When something recedes, it moves away into the distance. **2** If a man's hair is receding, he is starting to go bald at the front.

receipt receipts

Said "ris-**seet**" NOUN **1** a piece of paper confirming that money or goods have been received. **2** In a shop or theatre, the money received is often called the receipts EG *Box-office receipts were down last month.* **3** A FORMAL USE The receipt of something is the receiving of it EG *You have to sign here and acknowledge receipt.*

receive receives receiving received

VERB **1** When you receive something, someone gives it to you, or you get it after it has been sent to you. **2** To receive something also means to have it happen to you EG *injuries she received in a car crash.* **3** When you receive visitors or guests, you welcome them. **4** If something is received in a particular way, that is how people react to it EG *The decision has been received with great disappointment.*

receiver receivers

NOUN the part of a telephone you hold near to your ear and mouth.

recent

ADJECTIVE Something recent happened a short time ago.

recently ADVERB

reception receptions

NOUN **1** In a hotel or office,

reception is the place near the entrance where appointments or enquiries are dealt with. **2** a formal party. **3** The reception someone or something gets is the way people react to them eg *Her tour met with a rapturous reception.* **4** If your radio or television gets good reception, the sound or picture is clear.

receptionist receptionists

NOUN The receptionist in a hotel or office deals with people when they arrive, answers the telephone, and arranges appointments.

receptive

ADJECTIVE Someone who is receptive to ideas or suggestions is willing to consider them.

recess recesses

NOUN **1** a period when no work is done by a committee or parliament eg *the Christmas recess.* **2** a place where part of a wall has been built further back than the rest.

recession recessions

NOUN a period when a country's economy is less successful and more people become unemployed.

recharge recharges recharging recharged

VERB To recharge a battery means to charge it with electricity again after it has been used.

recipe recipes

Said "res-sip-ee" NOUN **1** a list of ingredients and instructions for cooking something. **2** If something is a recipe for disaster or for success, it is likely to result in disaster or success.

recipient recipients

NOUN The recipient of something is the person receiving it.

reciprocal

ADJECTIVE A reciprocal agreement involves two people, groups, or countries helping each other in a similar way eg *a reciprocal agreement on trade.*

reciprocate reciprocates

reciprocating reciprocated

VERB If you reciprocate someone's feelings or behaviour, you feel or behave in the same way towards them.

recital recitals

NOUN a performance of music or poetry, usually by one person.

recite recites reciting recited

VERB If you recite a poem or something you have learnt, you say it aloud.

recitation NOUN

reckless

ADJECTIVE showing a complete lack of care about danger or damage eg *a reckless tackle.*

recklessly ADVERB, **recklessness** NOUN

reckon reckons reckoning reckoned

VERB **1** AN INFORMAL USE If you reckon that something is true, you think it is true eg *I reckoned he was still fond of her.* **2** AN INFORMAL USE If someone reckons to do something, they claim or expect to do it eg *Officers on the case are reckoning to charge someone shortly.* **3** To reckon an amount means to calculate it. **4** If you reckon on something, you rely on it happening when making your plans eg *He reckons on being world champion.* **5** If you had not reckoned with something, you had not expected it and therefore were unprepared when it happened eg *Giles had not reckoned with the strength of Sally's feelings.*

reckoning reckonings

NOUN a calculation eg *There were a thousand or so, by my reckoning.*

reclaim reclaims reclaiming reclaimed

VERB **1** When you reclaim something, you collect it after leaving it somewhere or losing it. **2** To reclaim land means to make it suitable for use, for example by draining it.

reclamation NOUN

recline reclines reclining reclined

VERB To recline means to lie or lean back at an angle EG *a photo of him reclining on his bed.*

recluse recluses
NOUN Someone who is a recluse lives alone and avoids other people.
reclusive ADJECTIVE

recognize recognizes recognizing recognized; also spelt recognise
VERB **1** If you recognize someone or something, you realize that you know who or what they are EG *The receptionist recognized me at once.* **2** To recognize something also means to accept and acknowledge it EG *The RAF recognized him as an outstanding pilot.*
recognition NOUN, **recognizable** ADJECTIVE, **recognizably** ADVERB
■ (sense 1) identify, know, place

recommend recommends recommending recommended
VERB If you recommend something to someone, you praise it and suggest they try it.
recommendation NOUN

reconcile reconciles reconciling reconciled
VERB **1** To reconcile two things that seem to oppose one another, means to make them work or exist together successfully EG *The designs reconciled style with comfort.* **2** When people are reconciled, they become friendly again after a quarrel. **3** If you reconcile yourself to an unpleasant situation, you accept it.
reconciliation NOUN

reconnaissance
Said "rik-**kon**-iss-sanss" NOUN Reconnaissance is the gathering of military information by soldiers, planes, or satellites.

reconsider reconsiders reconsidering reconsidered
VERB To reconsider something means to think about it again to decide whether to change it.
reconsideration NOUN

reconstruct reconstructs reconstructing reconstructed

VERB **1** To reconstruct something that has been damaged means to build it again. **2** To reconstruct a past event means to get a complete description of it from small pieces of information.
reconstruction NOUN

record records recording recorded
NOUN **1** If you keep a record of something, you keep a written account or store information in a computer EG *medical records.* **2** a round, flat piece of plastic on which music has been recorded. **3** an achievement which is the best of its type. **4** Your record is what is known about your achievements or past activities EG *He had a distinguished war record.* ▶ VERB **5** If you record information, you write it down or put it into a computer. **6** To record sound means to put it on tape, record, or compact disc. ▶ ADJECTIVE **7** higher, lower, better, or worse than ever before EG *Profits were at a record level.*
■ (sense 1) document, file, register
■ (sense 5) note, register, write down

recorder recorders
NOUN a small woodwind instrument.

recording recordings
NOUN A recording of something is a record, tape, or video of it.

recount recounts recounting recounted
VERB **1** If you recount a story, you tell it. ▶ NOUN **2** a second count of votes in an election when the result is very close.

recoup recoups recouping recouped
Said "rik-**koop**" VERB If you recoup money that you have spent or lost, you get it back.

recourse
NOUN; A FORMAL WORD If you have recourse to something, you use it to help you EG *The members settled their differences without recourse to war.*

A
B
C
D
E
F
G
H
I
J
K
L
M
N
O
P
Q
R
S
T
U
V
W
X
Y
Z

recover recovers recovering recovered

VERB **1** To recover from an illness or unhappy experience means to get well again or get over it. **2** If you recover a lost object or your ability to do something, you get it back.

recovery NOUN

▪ (sense 1) convalesce, get better, recuperate

▪ (sense 2) regain, retrieve

recreate recreates recreating recreated

VERB To recreate something means to succeed in making it happen or exist again EG *a museum that faithfully recreates an old farmhouse.*

recreation recreations

Said "rek-kree-**ay**-shn" NOUN Recreation is all the things that you do for enjoyment in your spare time.

recreational ADJECTIVE

recrimination recriminations

NOUN Recriminations are accusations made by people about each other.

recruit recruits recruiting recruited

VERB **1** To recruit people means to get them to join a group or help with something. ▸ NOUN **2** someone who has joined the army or some other organization.

recruitment NOUN

rectangle rectangles

NOUN a four-sided shape with four right angles.

rectangular ADJECTIVE

rectify rectifies rectifying rectified

VERB; A FORMAL WORD If you rectify something that is wrong, you put it right.

rector rectors

NOUN a Church of England priest in charge of a parish.

rectory rectories

NOUN a house where a rector lives.

rectum rectums

NOUN; A MEDICAL WORD the bottom end of the tube down which waste food passes out of your body.

rectal ADJECTIVE

recuperate recuperates recuperating recuperated

VERB When you recuperate, you gradually recover after being ill or injured.

recuperation NOUN

recur recurs recurring recurred

VERB If something recurs, it happens or occurs again EG *His hamstring injury recurred after the first game.*

recurrence NOUN, **recurrent** ADJECTIVE

recurring

ADJECTIVE happening or occurring many times EG *a recurring dream.*

recycle recycles recycling recycled

VERB To recycle used products means to process them so that they can be used again EG *recycled glass.*

red redder reddest; reds

NOUN OR ADJECTIVE **1** Red is the colour of blood or of a ripe tomato.

▸ ADJECTIVE **2** Red hair is between orange and brown in colour.

redback redbacks

NOUN a small Australian spider with a poisonous bite.

redcurrant redcurrants

NOUN Redcurrants are very small, bright red fruits that grow in bunches on a bush.

redeem redeems redeeming redeemed

VERB **1** If a feature redeems an unpleasant thing or situation, it makes it seem less bad. **2** If you redeem yourself, you do something that gives people a good opinion of you again. **3** If you redeem something, you get it back by paying for it. **4** In Christianity, to redeem someone means to free them from sin by giving them faith in Jesus Christ.

redemption

NOUN Redemption is the state of

being redeemed.

red-handed

PHRASE To **catch someone red-handed** means to catch them doing something wrong.

red-hot

ADJECTIVE Red-hot metal has been heated to such a high temperature that it has turned red.

redress redresses redressing redressed

A FORMAL WORD ▸ VERB **1** To redress a wrong means to put it right. ▸ NOUN **2** If you get redress for harm done to you, you are compensated for it.

red tape

NOUN Red tape is official rules and procedures that seem unnecessary and cause delay.

reduce reduces reducing reduced

VERB **1** To reduce something means to make it smaller in size or amount. **2** You can use 'reduce' to say that someone or something is changed to a weaker or inferior state EG *She reduced them to tears... The village was reduced to rubble.*
■ (sense 1) cut, decrease, lessen

reduction reductions

NOUN When there is a reduction in something, it is made smaller.

redundancy redundancies

NOUN **1** Redundancy is the state of being redundant. **2** The number of redundancies is the number of people made redundant.

redundant

ADJECTIVE **1** When people are made redundant, they lose their jobs because there is no more work for them or no money to pay them. **2** When something becomes redundant, it is no longer needed.

reed reeds

NOUN **1** Reeds are hollow stemmed plants that grow in shallow water or wet ground. **2** a thin piece of cane or metal inside some wind instruments which vibrates when air is blown over it.

reef reefs

NOUN a long line of rocks or coral close to the surface of the sea.

reek reeks reeking reeked

VERB **1** To reek of something means to smell strongly and unpleasantly of it. ▸ NOUN **2** If there is a reek of something, there is a strong unpleasant smell of it.

reel reels reeling reeled

NOUN **1** a cylindrical object around which you wrap something; often part of a device which you turn as a control. **2** a fast Scottish dance.
▸ VERB **3** When someone reels, they move unsteadily as if they are going to fall. **4** If your mind is reeling, you are confused because you have too much to think about.
reel off VERB If you reel off information, you repeat it from memory quickly and easily.

re-elect re-elects re-electing re-elected

VERB When someone is re-elected, they win an election again and are able to stay in power.

refer refers referring referred

VERB **1** If you refer to something, you mention it. **2** If you refer to a book or record, you look at it to find something out. **3** When a problem or issue is referred to someone, they are formally asked to deal with it EG *The case was referred to the European Court.*
🏛 from Latin *referre* meaning 'to carry back'
☑ The word *refer* contains the sense 'back' in its meaning. Therefore, you should not use *back* after *refer*: *this refers to what has already been said* not *refers back*.

referee referees

NOUN **1** the official who controls a football game or a boxing or wrestling match. **2** someone who gives a reference to a person who is applying for a job.

reference references

NOUN **1** A reference to something or

593

A
B
C
D
E
F
G
H
I
J
K
L
M
N
O
P
Q
R
S
T
U
V
W
X
Y
Z

someone is a mention of them.
2 Reference is the act of referring to
something or someone for
information or advice EG *He makes
that decision without reference to her.*
3 a number or name that tells you
where to find information or
identifies a document. **4** If
someone gives you a reference
when you apply for a job, they
write a letter about your abilities.

referendum **referendums** or
referenda
NOUN a vote in which all the people
in a country are officially asked
whether they agree with a policy or
proposal.

refine **refines** **refining** **refined**
VERB To refine a raw material such as
oil or sugar means to process it to
remove impurities.

refined
ADJECTIVE very polite and
well-mannered.

refinement **refinements**
NOUN **1** Refinements are minor
improvements. **2** Refinement is
politeness and good manners.

refinery **refineries**
NOUN a factory where substances
such as oil or sugar are refined.

reflect **reflects** **reflecting**
reflected
VERB **1** If something reflects an
attitude or situation, it shows what
it is like EG *His off-duty hobbies
reflected his maritime interests.* **2** If
something reflects light or heat,
the light or heat bounces off it.
3 When something is reflected in a
mirror or water, you can see its
image in it. **4** When you reflect,
you think about something.
reflective ADJECTIVE, **reflectively** ADVERB

reflection **reflections**
NOUN **1** If something is a reflection
of something else, it shows what it
is like EG *This is a terrible reflection of
the times.* **2** an image in a mirror or
water. **3** Reflection is the process by
which light and heat are bounced

off a surface. **4** Reflection is also
thought EG *After days of reflection she
decided to leave.*

reflex **reflexes**
NOUN **1** A reflex or reflex action is a
sudden uncontrollable movement
that you make as a result of
pressure or a blow. **2** If you have
good reflexes, you respond very
quickly when something
unexpected happens. ▶ ADJECTIVE **3** A
reflex angle is between 180° and
360°.

reflexive **reflexives**
ADJECTIVE OR NOUN In grammar, a
reflexive verb or pronoun is one
that refers back to the subject of
the sentence EG *She washed herself.*

reform **reforms** **reforming**
reformed
NOUN **1** Reforms are major changes
to laws or institutions EG *a
programme of economic reform.* ▶ VERB
2 When laws or institutions are
reformed, major changes are made
to them. **3** When people reform,
they stop committing crimes or
doing other unacceptable things.
reformer NOUN

Reformation
NOUN The Reformation was a
religious and political movement
in Europe in the 16th century that
began as an attempt to reform the
Roman Catholic Church, but
ended in the establishment of the
Protestant Churches.

refraction
NOUN Refraction is the bending of a
ray of light, for example when it
enters water or glass.

refrain **refrains** **refraining**
refrained
VERB **1** A FORMAL USE If you refrain
from doing something, you do not
do it EG *Please refrain from smoking in
the hall.* ▶ NOUN **2** The refrain of a
song is a short, simple part,
repeated many times.

refresh **refreshes** **refreshing**
refreshed

VERB **1** If something **refreshes** you when you are hot or tired, it makes you feel cooler or more energetic EG *A glass of fruit juice will refresh you.*
▶ PHRASE **2** To **refresh someone's memory** means to remind them of something they had forgotten.

refreshing
ADJECTIVE You say that something is refreshing when it is pleasantly different from what you are used to EG *She is a refreshing contrast to her father.*

refreshment refreshments
NOUN Refreshments are drinks and small amounts of food provided at an event.

refrigerator refrigerators
NOUN an electrically cooled container in which you store food to keep it fresh.

refuel refuels refuelling refuelled
VERB When an aircraft or vehicle is refuelled, it is filled with more fuel.

refuge refuges
NOUN **1** a place where you go for safety. **2** If you take refuge, you go somewhere for safety or behave in a way that will protect you EG *They took refuge in a bomb shelter... Father Rowan took refuge in silence.*
■ (sense 1) haven, sanctuary, shelter

refugee refugees
NOUN Refugees are people who have been forced to leave their country and live elsewhere.

refund refunds refunding refunded
NOUN **1** money returned to you because you have paid too much for something or because you have returned goods. ▶ VERB **2** To refund someone's money means to return it to them after they have paid for something with it.

refurbish refurbishes refurbishing refurbished
VERB; A FORMAL WORD To refurbish a building means to decorate it and repair damage.

refurbishment NOUN

refusal refusals
NOUN A refusal is when someone says firmly that they will not do, allow, or accept something.

refuse refuses refusing refused
Said "rif-yooz" VERB **1** If you refuse to do something, you say or decide firmly that you will not do it. **2** If someone refuses something, they do not allow it or do not accept it EG *The United States has refused him a visa... He offered me a second drink which I refused.*

refuse
Said "ref-yoos" NOUN Refuse is rubbish or waste.

refute refutes refuting refuted
VERB; A FORMAL WORD To refute a theory or argument means to prove that it is wrong.
☑ *Refute* does not mean the same as *deny*. If you *refute* something, you provide evidence to show that it is not true. If you *deny* something, you say that it is not true.

regain regains regaining regained
VERB To regain something means to get it back.

regal
ADJECTIVE very grand and suitable for a king or queen EG *regal splendour.*
regally ADVERB

regard regards regarding regarded
VERB **1** To regard someone or something in a particular way means to think of them in that way or have that opinion of them EG *We all regard him as a friend... Many disapprove of the tax, regarding it as unfair.* **2** A LITERARY USE To regard someone in a particular way also means to look at them in that way EG *She regarded him curiously for a moment.* ▶ NOUN **3** If you have a high regard for someone, you have a very good opinion of them.
▶ PHRASES **4 Regarding**, **as regards**, **with regard to**, and **in regard to**

are all used to indicate what you are talking or writing about EG *There was always some question regarding education... As regards the war, he believed in victory at any price.* **5** 'Regards' is used in various expressions to express friendly feelings EG *Give my regards to your husband.*

regardless
PREPOSITION OR ADVERB done or happening in spite of something else EG *He led from the front, regardless of the danger.*

regatta regattas
NOUN a race meeting for sailing or rowing boats.

regency regencies
NOUN a period when a country is ruled by a regent.

regenerate regenerates regenerating regenerated
VERB; A FORMAL WORD To regenerate something means to develop and improve it after it has been declining EG *a scheme to regenerate the docks area of the city.*
regeneration NOUN

regent regents
NOUN someone who rules in place of a king or queen who is ill or too young to rule.

reggae
NOUN Reggae is a type of music, originally from the West Indies, with a strong beat.

regime regimes
Said "ray-jeem" NOUN a system of government, and the people who are ruling a country EG *a communist regime.*

regiment regiments
NOUN a large group of soldiers commanded by a colonel.
regimental ADJECTIVE

regimented
ADJECTIVE very strictly controlled EG *the regimented life of the orphanage.*
regimentation NOUN

region regions

NOUN **1** a large area of land. **2** You can refer to any area or part as a region EG *the pelvic region.* ▶ PHRASE **3 In the region of** means approximately EG *The scheme will cost in the region of six million.*
regional ADJECTIVE, **regionally** ADVERB
■ (sense 1) area, district, territory

register registers registering registered
NOUN **1** an official list or record of things EG *the electoral register.* **2** A TECHNICAL USE a style of speaking or writing used in particular circumstances or social occasions. ▶ VERB **3** When something is registered, it is recorded on an official list EG *The car was registered in my name.* **4** If an instrument registers a measurement, it shows it. **5** If your face registers a feeling, it expresses it.
registration NOUN

registrar registrars
NOUN **1** a person who keeps official records of births, marriages, and deaths. **2** At a college or university, the registrar is a senior administrative official. **3** a senior hospital doctor.

registration number registration numbers
NOUN the sequence of letters and numbers on the front and back of a motor vehicle that identify it.

registry registries
NOUN a place where official records are kept.

registry office registry offices
NOUN a place where births, marriages, and deaths are recorded, and where people can marry without a religious ceremony.

regret regrets regretting regretted
VERB **1** If you regret something, you are sorry that it happened. **2** You can say that you regret something as a way of apologizing EG *We regret any inconvenience to passengers.* ▶ NOUN **3** If you have regrets, you are

sad or sorry about something.
regretful ADJECTIVE, **regretfully** ADVERB
■ (sense 1) repent, rue

regrettable
ADJECTIVE unfortunate and
undesirable EG *a regrettable accident*.
regrettably ADVERB

regular regulars
ADJECTIVE **1** even and equally spaced
EG *soft music with a regular beat*.
2 Regular events or activities
happen often and according to a
pattern, for example each day or
each week EG *The trains to London are
fairly regular*. **3** If you are a regular
customer or visitor somewhere,
you go there often. **4** usual or
normal EG *I was filling in for the
regular bartender*. **5** having a well
balanced appearance EG *a regular
geometrical shape*. ▶ NOUN **6** People
who go to a place often are known
as its regulars.
regularly ADVERB, **regularity** NOUN
■ (sense 1) even, steady, uniform

regulate regulates regulating
regulated
VERB To regulate something means
to control the way it operates EG
*Sweating helps to regulate the body's
temperature*.
regulator NOUN

regulation regulations
NOUN **1** Regulations are official rules.
2 Regulation is the control of
something EG *regulation of the betting
industry*.

regurgitate regurgitates
regurgitating regurgitated
Said "rig-gur-jit-tate" VERB To
regurgitate food means to bring it
back from the stomach before it is
digested.

rehabilitate rehabilitates
rehabilitating rehabilitated
VERB To rehabilitate someone who
has been ill or in prison means to
help them lead a normal life.
rehabilitation NOUN

rehearsal rehearsals
NOUN a practice of a performance in
preparation for the actual event.

rehearse rehearses rehearsing
rehearsed
VERB To rehearse a performance
means to practise it in preparation
for the actual event.

reign reigns reigning reigned
Said "rain" VERB **1** When a king or
queen reigns, he or she rules a
country. **2** You can say that
something reigns when it is a
noticeable feature of a situation or
period of time EG *Panic reigned after
his assassination*. ▶ NOUN **3** The reign
of a king or queen is the period
during which he or she reigns.

rein reins
NOUN **1** Reins are the thin leather
straps which you hold when you
are riding a horse. ▶ PHRASE **2** To
keep a tight rein on someone or
something means to control them
firmly.

reincarnation
NOUN People who believe in
reincarnation believe that when
you die, you are born again as
another creature.

reindeer
NOUN Reindeer are deer with large
antlers, that live in northern
regions.

reinforce reinforces reinforcing
reinforced
VERB **1** To reinforce something
means to strengthen it EG *a
reinforced steel barrier*. **2** If something
reinforces an idea or claim, it
provides evidence to support it.

reinforcement reinforcements
NOUN **1** Reinforcements are
additional soldiers sent to join an
army in battle. **2** Reinforcement is
the reinforcing of something.

reinstate reinstates reinstating
reinstated
VERB **1** To reinstate someone means
to give them back a position they
have lost. **2** To reinstate something
means to bring it back EG *Parliament
voted against reinstating capital*

A
B
C
D
E
F
G
H
I
J
K
L
M
N
O
P
Q
R
S
T
U
V
W
X
Y
Z

punishment.
reinstatement NOUN

reiterate reiterates reiterating
reiterated
Said "ree-**it**-er-ate" VERB; A FORMAL
WORD If you reiterate something,
you say it again.
reiteration NOUN

reject rejects rejecting rejected
VERB **1** If you reject a proposal or
request, you do not accept it or
agree to it. **2** If you reject a belief,
political system, or way of life, you
decide that it is not for you. ▶ NOUN
3 a product that cannot be used,
because there is something wrong
with it.
rejection NOUN
■ (sense 1) decline, refuse, turn
down

rejoice rejoices rejoicing rejoiced
VERB To rejoice means to be very
pleased about something EG *The
whole country rejoiced after his
downfall.*

rejoin rejoins rejoining rejoined
VERB If you rejoin someone, you go
back to them soon after leaving
them EG *She rejoined her friends in the
bar.*

rejuvenate rejuvenates
rejuvenating rejuvenated
Said "ree-**joo**-vin-ate" VERB To
rejuvenate someone means to
make them feel young again.
rejuvenation NOUN

relapse relapses
NOUN If a sick person has a relapse,
their health suddenly gets worse
after improving.

relate relates relating related
VERB **1** If something relates to
something else, it is connected or
concerned with it EG *The statistics
relate only to western Germany.* **2** If
you can relate to someone, you can
understand their thoughts and
feelings. **3** To relate a story means
to tell it.

relation relations
NOUN **1** If there is a relation between

two things, they are similar or
connected in some way EG *This
theory bears no relation to reality.*
2 Your relations are the members
of your family. **3** Relations between
people are their feelings and
behaviour towards each other EG
*Relations between husband and wife
had not improved.*

relationship relationships
NOUN **1** The relationship between
two people or groups is the way
they feel and behave towards each
other. **2** a close friendship,
especially one involving romantic
or sexual feelings. **3** The
relationship between two things is
the way in which they are
connected EG *the relationship between
slavery and the sugar trade.*

relative relatives
ADJECTIVE **1** compared to other things
or people of the same kind EG *The
fighting resumed after a period of
relative calm... He is a relative novice.*
2 You use 'relative' when
comparing the size or quality of
two things EG *the relative strengths of
the British and German forces.* ▶ NOUN
3 Your relatives are the members
of your family.

relative pronoun relative
pronouns
NOUN a pronoun that replaces a
noun that links two parts of a
sentence.

What is a Relative Pronoun?

Relative pronouns are used to replace a
noun which links two different parts of a
sentence. The relative pronouns are *who,
whom, whose, which,* and *that.*

Relative pronouns always refer back to a
word in the earlier part of the sentence. The
word they refer to is called the
antecedent. (In the examples that follow,
the antecedents are underlined.)
*I have a friend who lives in Rome.
We could go to a place that I know.*

The forms *who, whom,* and *whose* are used
when the antecedent is a person. *Who*

indicates the subject of the verb, while *whom* indicates the object of the verb.

It was <u>the same person</u> **who** saw me yesterday.

It was <u>the person</u> **whom** I saw yesterday.

The distinction between *who* and *whom* is often ignored in everyday English, and *who* is often used as the object.

It was <u>the person</u> **who** I saw yesterday.

Whom is used immediately after a preposition. However, if the preposition is separated from the relative pronoun, *who* is usually used.

He is <u>a man</u> **in** whom I have great confidence.

He is <u>a man</u> **who** I have great confidence **in**.

Whose is the possessive form of the relative pronoun. It can refer to things as well as people.

Anna has <u>a sister</u> **whose** name is Rosie.

I found <u>a book</u> **whose** pages were torn.

Which is only used when the antecedent is not a person.

We took <u>the road</u> **which** leads to the sea.

That refers to things or people. It is never used immediately after a preposition, but it can be used if the preposition is separated from the relative pronoun.

It was <u>a film</u> **that** I had little interest **in**.

relax relaxes relaxing relaxed
VERB **1** If you relax, you become calm and your muscles lose their tension. **2** If you relax your hold, you hold something less tightly. **3** To relax something also means to make it less strict or controlled EG *The rules governing student conduct were relaxed.*
relaxation NOUN
■ (sense 1) rest, take it easy, unwind
■ (sense 2) lessen, loosen, slacken

relay relays relaying relayed
NOUN **1** A relay race or relay is a race between teams, with each team member running one part of the race. ▶ VERB **2** To relay a television or radio signal means to send it on. **3** If you relay information, you tell it to someone else.

release releases releasing released
VERB **1** To release someone or something means to set them free or remove restraints from them. **2** To release something also means to issue it or make it available EG *He is releasing an album of love songs.* ▶ NOUN **3** When the release of someone or something takes place, they are set free. **4** A press release or publicity release is an official written statement given to reporters. **5** A new release is a new record or video that has just become available.

relegate relegates relegating relegated
VERB To relegate something or someone means to give them a less important position or status.
relegation NOUN

relent relents relenting relented
VERB If someone relents, they agree to something they had previously not allowed.

relentless
ADJECTIVE never stopping and never becoming less intense EG *the relentless rise of business closures.*
relentlessly ADVERB

relevant
ADJECTIVE If something is relevant, it is connected with and is appropriate to what is being discussed EG *We have passed all relevant information on to the police.*
relevance NOUN
■ appropriate, pertinent, significant

reliable
ADJECTIVE **1** Reliable people and things can be trusted to do what you want. **2** If information is reliable, you can assume that it is correct.
reliably ADVERB, **reliability** NOUN

reliant
ADJECTIVE If you are reliant on someone or something, you depend on them EG *They are not*

wholly reliant on charity.
reliance NOUN

relic relics
NOUN **1** Relics are objects or customs that have survived from an earlier time. **2** an object regarded as holy because it is thought to be connected with a saint.

relief
NOUN **1** If you feel relief, you are glad and thankful because a bad situation is over or has been avoided. **2** Relief is also money, food, or clothing provided for poor or hungry people.

relief map relief maps
NOUN a map showing the shape of mountains and hills by shading.

relieve relieves relieving relieved
VERB **1** If something relieves an unpleasant feeling, it makes it less unpleasant EG *Drugs can relieve much of the pain.* **2** A FORMAL USE If you relieve someone, you do their job or duty for a period. **3** If someone is relieved of their duties, they are dismissed from their job. **4** If you relieve yourself, you urinate.

religion religions
NOUN **1** Religion is the belief in a god or gods and all the activities connected with such beliefs. **2** a system of religious belief.

religious
ADJECTIVE **1** connected with religion EG *religious worship.* **2** Someone who is religious has a strong belief in a god or gods.
▪ (sense 2) devout, pious

religiously
ADVERB If you do something religiously, you do it regularly as a duty EG *He stuck religiously to the rules.*

relinquish relinquishes relinquishing relinquished
Said "ril-**ling**-kwish" VERB; A FORMAL WORD If you relinquish something, you give it up.

relish relishes relishing relished
VERB **1** If you relish something, you enjoy it EG *He relished the idea of getting some cash.* ▸ NOUN **2** Relish is enjoyment EG *He told me with relish of the wonderful times he had.* **3** Relish is also a savoury sauce or pickle.

relive relives reliving relived
VERB If you relive a past experience, you remember it and imagine it happening again.

relocate relocates relocating relocated
VERB If people or businesses are relocated, they are moved to a different place.
relocation NOUN

reluctant
ADJECTIVE If you are reluctant to do something, you are unwilling to do it.
reluctance NOUN

reluctantly
ADVERB If you do something reluctantly, you do it although you do not want to.

rely relies relying relied
VERB **1** If you rely on someone or something, you need them and depend on them EG *She has to rely on hardship payments.* **2** If you can rely on someone to do something, you can trust them to do it EG *They can always be relied on to turn up.*

remain remains remaining remained
VERB **1** If you remain in a particular place or state, you stay there or stay the same and do not change EG *The three men remained silent.*
2 Something that remains still exists or is left over EG *Huge amounts of weapons remain to be collected.*
▸ PLURAL NOUN **3** The remains of something are the parts that are left after most of it has been destroyed EG *the remains of an ancient mosque.* **4** You can refer to a dead body as remains EG *More human remains have been unearthed today.*
▪ (sense 3) debris, remnants

remainder
NOUN The remainder of something

is the part that is left EG *He gulped down the remainder of his coffee.*

remand **remands remanding remanded**
VERB **1** If a judge remands someone who is accused of a crime, the trial is postponed and the person is ordered to come back at a later date. ▶ PHRASE **2** If someone is on **remand**, they are in prison waiting for their trial to begin.

remark **remarks remarking remarked**
VERB **1** If you remark on something, you mention it or comment on it EG *She had remarked on the boy's improvement.* ▶ NOUN **2** something you say, often in a casual way.

remarkable
ADJECTIVE impressive and unexpected EG *It was a remarkable achievement.*
remarkably ADVERB
◼ extraordinary, outstanding, wonderful

remarry **remarries remarrying remarried**
VERB If someone remarries, they get married again.

remedial
ADJECTIVE **1** Remedial activities are to help someone improve their health after they have been ill. **2** Remedial exercises are designed to improve someone's ability in something EG *the remedial reading class.*

remedy **remedies remedying remedied**
NOUN **1** a way of dealing with a problem EG *a remedy for colic.* ▶ VERB **2** If you remedy something that is wrong, you correct it EG *We have to remedy the situation immediately.*

remember **remembers remembering remembered**
VERB **1** If you can remember someone or something from the past, you can bring them into your mind or think about them. **2** If you remember to do something, you do it when you intended to EG *Ben had remembered to book reservations.*

◼ (sense 1) recall, recollect

remembrance
NOUN If you do something in remembrance of a dead person, you are showing that they are remembered with respect and affection.

remind **reminds reminding reminded**
VERB **1** If someone reminds you of a fact, they say something to make you think about it EG *Remind me to buy a bottle of wine, will you?* **2** If someone reminds you of another person, they look similar and make you think of them.

reminder **reminders**
NOUN **1** If one thing is a reminder of another, the first thing makes you think of the second EG *a reminder of better times.* **2** a note sent to tell someone they have forgotten to do something.

reminiscent
ADJECTIVE Something that is reminiscent of something else reminds you of it.

remission
NOUN When prisoners get remission for good behaviour, their sentences are reduced.

remit **remits**
NOUN; A FORMAL WORD The remit of a person or committee is the subject or task they are responsible for EG *Their remit is to research into a wide range of health problems.*

remittance **remittances**
NOUN; A FORMAL WORD payment for something sent through the post.

remnant **remnants**
NOUN a small part of something left after the rest has been used or destroyed.

remorse
NOUN; A FORMAL WORD Remorse is a strong feeling of guilt.
remorseful ADJECTIVE
◼ contrition, regret, repentance

remote **remoter remotest**

A B C D E F G H I J K L M N O P Q R S T U V W X Y Z

601

ADJECTIVE 1 Remote areas are far away from places where most people live. **2** far away in time EG *the remote past.* **3** If you say a person is remote, you mean they do not want to be friendly EG *She is severe, solemn, and remote.* **4** If there is only a remote possibility of something happening, it is unlikely to happen.

remoteness NOUN

remote control
NOUN Remote control is a system of controlling a machine or vehicle from a distance using radio or electronic signals.

remotely
ADVERB used to emphasize a negative statement EG *He isn't remotely keen.*

removal
NOUN **1** The removal of something is the act of taking it away. **2** A removal company transports furniture from one building to another.

remove removes removing removed
VERB **1** If you remove something from a place, you take it off or away. **2** If you are removed from a position of authority, you are not allowed to continue your job. **3** If you remove an undesirable feeling or attitude, you get rid of it EG *Most of her fears had been removed.*

removable ADJECTIVE

■ (sense 1) extract, take away, withdraw

Renaissance
Said "ren-**nay**-sonss" NOUN The Renaissance was a period from the 14th to 16th centuries in Europe when there was a great revival in the arts and learning.

■ a French word, meaning literally 'rebirth'

renal
ADJECTIVE; A TECHNICAL WORD concerning the kidneys EG *renal failure.*

rename renames renaming renamed
VERB If you rename something, you give it a new name.

render renders rendering rendered
VERB You can use 'render' to say that something is changed into a different state EG *The bomb was quickly rendered harmless.*

rendezvous
Said "**ron**-day-voo" NOUN **1** a meeting EG *Baxter arranged a six o'clock rendezvous.* **2** a place where you have arranged to meet someone EG *The pub became a popular rendezvous for office workers.*

rendition renditions
NOUN; A FORMAL WORD a performance of a play, poem, or piece of music.

renew renews renewing renewed
VERB **1** To renew an activity or relationship means to begin it again. **2** To renew a licence or contract means to extend the period of time for which it is valid.

renewal NOUN

renounce renounces renouncing renounced
VERB; A FORMAL WORD If you renounce something, you reject it or give it up.

renunciation NOUN

renovate renovates renovating renovated
VERB If you renovate an old building or machine, you repair it and restore it to good condition.

renovation NOUN

renowned
ADJECTIVE well-known for something good EG *He is not renowned for his patience.*

renown NOUN

rent rents renting rented
VERB **1** If you rent something, you pay the owner a regular sum of money in return for being able to use it. ▶ NOUN **2** Rent is the amount of money you pay regularly to rent land or accommodation.

rental

ADJECTIVE **1** concerned with the renting out of goods and services EG *Scotland's largest video rental company.* ▶ NOUN **2** Rental is the amount of money you pay when you rent something.

rep reps
NOUN; AN INFORMAL WORD a travelling salesperson. Rep is an abbreviation for representative.

repair repairs repairing repaired
NOUN **1** something you do to mend something that is damaged or broken. ▶ VERB **2** If you repair something, you mend it.

repay repays repaying repaid
VERB **1** To repay money means to give it back to the person who lent it. **2** If you repay a favour, you do something to help the person who helped you.
repayment NOUN

repeal repeals repealing repealed
VERB If the government repeals a law, it cancels it so that it is no longer valid.

repeat repeats repeating repeated
VERB **1** If you repeat something, you say, write, or do it again. **2** If you repeat what someone has said, you tell someone else about it EG *I trust you not to repeat that to anyone.* ▶ NOUN **3** something which is done or happens again EG *the number of repeats shown on TV.*
repeated ADJECTIVE, **repeatedly** ADVERB

repel repels repelling repelled
VERB **1** If something repels you, you find it horrible and disgusting. **2** When soldiers repel an attacking force, they successfully defend themselves against it. **3** When a magnetic pole repels an opposite pole, it forces the opposite pole away.
■ (sense 1) disgust, revolt, sicken

repellent repellents
ADJECTIVE **1** A FORMAL USE horrible and disgusting EG *I found him repellent.* ▶ NOUN **2** Repellents are chemicals used to keep insects or other creatures away.

repent repents repenting repented
VERB; A FORMAL WORD If you repent, you are sorry for something bad you have done.
repentance NOUN, **repentant** ADJECTIVE

repercussion repercussions
NOUN The repercussions of an event are the effects it has at a later time.

repertoire repertoires
Said "rep-et-twar" NOUN A performer's repertoire is all the pieces of music or dramatic parts he or she has learned and can perform.

repertory repertories
NOUN **1** Repertory is the practice of performing a small number of plays in a theatre for a short time, using the same actors in each play. **2** In Australian, New Zealand and South African English, repertory is the same as **repertoire.**

repetition repetitions
NOUN If there is a repetition of something, it happens again EG *We don't want a repetition of last week's fiasco.*

repetitive
ADJECTIVE A repetitive activity involves a lot of repetition and is boring EG *dull and repetitive work.*

replace replaces replacing replaced
VERB **1** When one thing replaces another, the first thing takes the place of the second. **2** If you replace something that is damaged or lost, you get a new one. **3** If you replace something, you put it back where it was before EG *She replaced the receiver.*
■ (sense 1) supersede, supplant

replacement replacements
NOUN **1** The replacement for someone or something is the person or thing that takes their place. **2** The replacement of a person or thing happens when

603

A
B
C
D
E
F
G
H
I
J
K
L
M
N
O
P
Q
R
S
T
U
V
W
X
Y
Z

they are replaced by another person or thing.

replay replays replaying replayed
VERB **1** If a match is replayed, the teams play it again. **2** If you replay a tape or film, you play it again EG *Replay the first few seconds of the tape please.* ▶ NOUN **3** a match that is played for a second time.

replenish replenishes replenishing replenished
VERB; A FORMAL WORD If you replenish something, you make it full or complete again.

replica replicas
NOUN an accurate copy of something EG *a replica of Columbus's ship.*
replicate VERB

reply replies replying replied
VERB **1** If you reply to something, you say or write an answer. ▶ NOUN **2** what you say or write when you answer someone.

report reports reporting reported
VERB **1** If you report that something has happened, you tell someone about it or give an official account of it EG *He reported the theft to the police.* **2** To report someone to an authority means to make an official complaint about them. **3** If you report to a person or place, you go there and say you have arrived.
▶ NOUN **4** an account of an event or situation.
■ (sense 4) account, description

reported speech
NOUN a report of what someone said that gives the content of the speech without repeating the exact words.

reporter reporters
NOUN someone who writes news articles or broadcasts news reports.

repossess repossesses repossessing repossessed
VERB If a shop or company repossesses goods that have not been paid for, they take them back.

represent represents representing represented
VERB **1** If you represent someone, you act on their behalf EG *lawyers representing relatives of the victims.* **2** If a sign or symbol represents something, it stands for it. **3** To represent something in a particular way means to describe it in that way EG *The popular press tends to represent him as a hero.*

representation representations
NOUN **1** Representation is the state of being represented by someone EG *Was there any student representation?* **2** You can describe a picture or statue of someone as a representation of them.

representative representatives
NOUN **1** a person chosen to act on behalf of another person or a group. ▶ ADJECTIVE **2** A representative selection is typical of the group it belongs to EG *The photos chosen are not representative of his work.*

repress represses repressing repressed
VERB **1** If you repress a feeling, you succeed in not showing or feeling it EG *I couldn't repress my anger any longer.* **2** To repress people means to restrict their freedom and control them by force.
repression NOUN

repressive
ADJECTIVE Repressive governments use force and unjust laws to restrict and control people.

reprieve reprieves reprieving reprieved
Said "rip-**preev**" VERB **1** If someone who has been sentenced to death is reprieved, their sentence is changed and they are not killed.
▶ NOUN **2** a delay before something unpleasant happens EG *The zoo won a reprieve from closure.*

reprimand reprimands reprimanding reprimanded
VERB **1** If you reprimand someone, you officially tell them that they

should not have done something.
▶ NOUN **2** something said or written by a person in authority when they are reprimanding someone.

reprisal reprisals
NOUN Reprisals are violent actions taken by one group of people against another group that has harmed them.

reproach reproaches reproaching reproached
A FORMAL WORD ▶ NOUN **1** If you express reproach, you show that you feel sad and angry about what someone has done EG *a long letter of reproach.*
▶ VERB **2** If you reproach someone, you tell them, rather sadly, that they have done something wrong.
reproachful ADJECTIVE

reproduce reproduces reproducing reproduced
VERB **1** To reproduce something means to make a copy of it.
2 When living things reproduce, they produce more of their own kind EG *Bacteria reproduce by splitting into two.*

reproduction reproductions
NOUN **1** a modern copy of a painting or piece of furniture.
2 Reproduction is the process by which a living thing produces more of its kind EG *the study of animal reproduction.*

reproductive
ADJECTIVE relating to the reproduction of living things EG *the female reproductive system.*

reptile reptiles
NOUN a cold-blooded animal, such as a snake or a lizard, which has scaly skin and lays eggs.
reptilian ADJECTIVE
▥ from Latin *reptilis* meaning 'creeping'

republic republics
NOUN a country which has a president rather than a king or queen.
republican NOUN OR ADJECTIVE,
republicanism NOUN

▥ from Latin *res publica* meaning literally 'public thing'

repulse repulses repulsing repulsed
VERB **1** If you repulse someone who is being friendly, you put them off by behaving coldly towards them EG *He repulses friendly advances.* **2** To repulse an attacking force means to fight it and cause it to retreat. **3** If something repulses you, you find it horrible and disgusting and want to avoid it.

repulsion
NOUN **1** Repulsion is a strong feeling of disgust. **2** Repulsion is a force separating two objects, such as the force between two like electric charges.

repulsive
ADJECTIVE horrible and disgusting.

reputable
ADJECTIVE known to be good and reliable EG *a well-established and reputable firm.*

reputation reputations
NOUN The reputation of something or someone is the opinion that people have of them EG *The college had a good reputation.*
▣ name, renown, standing

reputed
ADJECTIVE If something is reputed to be true, some people say that it is true EG *the reputed tomb of Christ.*
reputedly ADVERB

request requests requesting requested
VERB **1** If you request something, you ask for it politely or formally.
▶ NOUN **2** If you make a request for something, you request it.

requiem requiems
Said "rek-wee-em" NOUN **1** A requiem or requiem mass is a mass celebrated for someone who has recently died. **2** a piece of music for singers and an orchestra, originally written for a requiem mass EG *Mozart's Requiem.*
▥ from Latin *requies* meaning 'rest'

require **requires requiring required**

VERB **1** If you require something, you need it. **2** If you are required to do something, you have to do it because someone says you must EG *The rules require employers to provide safety training.*

requirement **requirements**

NOUN something that you must have or must do EG *A good degree is a requirement for entry.*

requisite **requisites**

A FORMAL WORD ▶ ADJECTIVE **1** necessary for a particular purpose EG *She filled in the requisite paperwork.* ▶ NOUN **2** something that is necessary for a particular purpose.

rescue **rescues rescuing rescued**

VERB **1** If you rescue someone, you save them from a dangerous or unpleasant situation. ▶ NOUN **2** Rescue is help which saves someone from a dangerous or unpleasant situation.
rescuer NOUN

research **researches researching researched**

NOUN **1** Research is work that involves studying something and trying to find out facts about it. ▶ VERB **2** If you research something, you try to discover facts about it.
researcher NOUN

resemblance

NOUN If there is a resemblance between two things, they are similar to each other EG *There was a remarkable resemblance between them.*
■ likeness, similarity

resemble **resembles resembling resembled**

VERB To resemble something means to be similar to it.

resent **resents resenting resented**

VERB If you resent something, you feel bitter and angry about it.
resentment NOUN

resentful

ADJECTIVE bitter and angry EG *He felt very resentful about losing his job.*

resentfully ADVERB

reservation **reservations**

NOUN **1** If you have reservations about something, you are not sure that it is right. **2** If you make a reservation, you book a place in advance. **3** an area of land set aside for American Indian peoples EG *a Cherokee reservation.*

reserve **reserves reserving reserved**

VERB **1** If something is reserved for a particular person or purpose, it is kept specially for them. ▶ NOUN **2** a supply of something for future use. **3** In sport, a reserve is someone who is available to play in case one of the team is unable to play. **4** A nature reserve is an area of land where animals, birds, or plants are officially protected. **5** If someone shows reserve, they keep their feelings hidden.
reserved ADJECTIVE
■ (sense 1) put by, save, set aside

reservoir **reservoirs**

Said "rez-ev-wahr" NOUN a lake used for storing water before it is supplied to people.

reshuffle **reshuffles**

NOUN a reorganization of people or things.

reside **resides residing resided**

Said "riz-**zide**" VERB; A FORMAL WORD If a quality resides in something, the quality is in that thing.

residence **residence**

NOUN; A FORMAL WORD a house.

resident **residents**

NOUN **1** A resident of a house or area is someone who lives there. ▶ ADJECTIVE **2** If someone is resident in a house or area, they live there.

residential

ADJECTIVE **1** A residential area contains mainly houses rather than offices or factories. **2** providing accommodation EG *residential care for the elderly.*

residue **residues**

NOUN a small amount of something that remains after most of it has gone EG *an increase in toxic residues found in drinking water.*
residual ADJECTIVE

resign resigns resigning resigned
VERB **1** If you resign from a job, you formally announce that you are leaving it. **2** If you resign yourself to an unpleasant situation, you realize that you have to accept it.
resigned ADJECTIVE

resignation resignations
NOUN **1** Someone's resignation is a formal statement of their intention to leave a job. **2** Resignation is the reluctant acceptance of an unpleasant situation or fact.

resilient
ADJECTIVE able to recover quickly from unpleasant or damaging events.
resilience NOUN

resin resins
NOUN **1** Resin is a sticky substance produced by some trees. **2** Resin is also a substance produced chemically and used to make plastics.

resist resists resisting resisted
VERB **1** If you resist something, you refuse to accept it and try to prevent it EG *The pay squeeze will be fiercely resisted by the unions.* **2** If you resist someone, you fight back against them.
■ (sense 1) fight, oppose

resistance resistances
NOUN **1** Resistance to something such as change is a refusal to accept it. **2** Resistance to an attack consists of fighting back EG *The demonstrators offered no resistance.* **3** Your body's resistance to germs or disease is its power to remain unharmed by them. **4** Resistance is also the power of a substance to resist the flow of an electrical current through it.

resistant
ADJECTIVE **1** opposed to something

and wanting to prevent it EG *People were very resistant to change.* **2** If something is resistant to a particular thing, it is not harmed or affected by it EG *Certain insects are resistant to this spray.*

resolute
Said "rez-ol-loot" ADJECTIVE; A FORMAL WORD Someone who is resolute is determined not to change their mind.
resolutely ADVERB

resolution resolutions
NOUN **1** Resolution is determination. **2** If you make a resolution, you promise yourself to do something. **3** a formal decision taken at a meeting. **4** A FORMAL USE The resolution of a problem is the solving of it.

resolve resolves resolving resolved
VERB **1** If you resolve to do something, you firmly decide to do it. **2** If you resolve a problem, you find a solution to it. ▶ NOUN **3** Resolve is absolute determination.

resonance resonances
NOUN **1** Resonance is sound produced by an object vibrating as a result of another sound nearby. **2** Resonance is also a deep, clear, and echoing quality of sound.

resonate resonates resonating resonated
VERB If something resonates, it vibrates and produces a deep, strong sound.

resort resorts resorting resorted
VERB **1** If you resort to a course of action, you do it because you have no alternative. ▶ NOUN **2** a place where people spend their holidays. ▶ PHRASE **3** If you do something as a last resort, you do it because you can find no other way of solving a problem.

resounding
ADJECTIVE **1** loud and echoing EG *a resounding round of applause.* **2** A resounding success is a great

A B C D E F G H I J K L M N O P Q R S T U V W X Y Z

A
B
C
D
E
F
G
H
I
J
K
L
M
N
O
P
Q
R
S
T
U
V
W
X
Y
Z

success.

resource resources
NOUN The resources of a country, organization, or person are the materials, money, or skills they have.

resourceful
ADJECTIVE A resourceful person is good at finding ways of dealing with problems.
resourcefulness NOUN

respect respects respecting respected
VERB **1** If you respect someone, you have a good opinion of their character or ideas. **2** If you respect someone's rights or wishes, you do not do things that they would not like, or would consider wrong EG *It is about time they started respecting the law.* ▶ NOUN **3** If you have respect for someone, you respect them. ▶ PHRASE **4** You can say in this respect to refer to a particular feature EG *At least in this respect we are equals.*

respectable
ADJECTIVE **1** considered to be acceptable and morally correct EG *respectable families.* **2** adequate or reasonable EG *a respectable rate of economic growth.*
respectability NOUN, **respectably** ADVERB

respectful
ADJECTIVE showing respect for someone EG *Our children are always respectful to their elders.*
respectfully ADVERB

respective
ADJECTIVE belonging or relating individually to the people or things just mentioned EG *They went into their respective rooms to pack.*

respectively
ADVERB in the same order as the items just mentioned EG *They finished first and second respectively.*

respiration
NOUN; A TECHNICAL WORD Your respiration is your breathing.

respiratory
ADJECTIVE; A TECHNICAL WORD relating to breathing EG *respiratory diseases.*

respite
NOUN; A FORMAL WORD a short rest from something unpleasant.

respond responds responding responded
VERB When you respond to something, you react to it by doing or saying something.

respondent respondents
NOUN **1** a person who answers a questionnaire or a request for information. **2** In a court case, the respondent is the defendant.

response responses
NOUN Your response to an event is your reaction or reply to it EG *There has been no response to his remarks yet.*

responsibility responsibilities
NOUN **1** If you have responsibility for something, it is your duty to deal with it or look after it EG *The garden was to have been his responsibility.* **2** If you accept responsibility for something that has happened, you agree that you caused it or were to blame EG *We must all accept responsibility for our own mistakes.*

responsible
ADJECTIVE **1** If you are responsible for something, it is your duty to deal with it and you are to blame if it goes wrong. **2** If you are responsible to someone, that person is your boss and tells you what you have to do. **3** A responsible person behaves properly and sensibly without needing to be supervised. **4** A responsible job involves making careful judgments about important matters.
responsibly ADVERB
≡ (sense 1) accountable, answerable, liable

responsive
ADJECTIVE **1** quick to show interest and pleasure. **2** taking notice of events and reacting in an

appropriate way EG *The course is responsive to students' needs.*

rest rests resting rested
NOUN **1** The rest of something is all the remaining parts of it. **2** If you have a rest, you sit or lie quietly and relax. ▶ VERB **3** If you rest, you relax and do not do anything active for a while.

restaurant restaurants
Said "rest-ront" NOUN a place where you can buy and eat a meal.
🏛 a French word; from *restaurer* meaning 'to restore'

restaurateur restaurateurs
Said "rest-er-a-tur" NOUN someone who owns or manages a restaurant.

restful
ADJECTIVE Something that is restful helps you feel calm and relaxed.

restless
ADJECTIVE finding it hard to remain still or relaxed because of boredom or impatience.
restlessness NOUN, **restlessly** ADVERB

restore restores restoring restored
VERB **1** To restore something means to cause it to exist again or to return to its previous state EG *He was anxious to restore his reputation.* **2** To restore an old building or work of art means to clean and repair it.
restoration NOUN
■ (sense 2) refurbish, renovate

restrain restrains restraining restrained
VERB To restrain someone or something means to hold them back or prevent them from doing what they want to.

restrained
ADJECTIVE behaving in a controlled way.

restraint restraints
NOUN **1** Restraints are rules or conditions that limit something EG *wage restraints.* **2** Restraint is calm, controlled behaviour.

restrict restricts restricting

restricted
VERB **1** If you restrict something, you prevent it becoming too large or varied. **2** To restrict people or animals means to limit their movement or actions.
restrictive ADJECTIVE

restriction restrictions
NOUN a rule or situation that limits what you can do EG *financial restrictions.*

result results resulting resulted
NOUN **1** The result of an action or situation is the situation that is caused by it EG *As a result of the incident he got a two-year suspension.* **2** The result is also the final marks, figures, or situation at the end of an exam, calculation, or contest EG *election results... The result was calculated to three decimal places.*
▶ VERB **3** If something results in a particular event, it causes that event to happen. **4** If something results from a particular event, it is caused by that event EG *The fire had resulted from carelessness.*
resultant ADJECTIVE
■ (sense 1) consequence, outcome, upshot

resume resumes resuming resumed
Said "riz-yoom" VERB If you resume an activity or position, you return to it after a break.
resumption NOUN

resurgence
NOUN If there is a resurgence of an attitude or activity, it reappears and grows stronger.
resurgent ADJECTIVE

resurrect resurrects resurrecting resurrected
VERB If you resurrect something, you make it exist again after it has disappeared or ended.
resurrection NOUN

Resurrection
NOUN In Christian belief, the Resurrection is the coming back to life of Jesus Christ three days after

he had been killed.

resuscitate resuscitates
resuscitating resuscitated
Said "ris-**suss**-it-tate" VERB If you
resuscitate someone, you make
them conscious again after an
accident.
resuscitation NOUN

retail
NOUN The retail price is the price at
which something is sold in the
shops.
retailer NOUN

retain retains retaining retained
VERB To retain something means to
keep it.
retention NOUN

retaliate retaliates retaliating
retaliated
VERB If you retaliate, you do
something to harm or upset
someone because they have already
acted in a similar way against you.
retaliation NOUN

retarded
ADJECTIVE If someone is retarded,
their mental development is much
less advanced than average.

rethink rethinks rethinking
rethought
VERB If you rethink something, you
think about how it should be
changed EG *We have to rethink our
strategy.*

reticent
ADJECTIVE Someone who is reticent is
unwilling to tell people about
things.
reticence NOUN

retina retinas
NOUN the light-sensitive part at the
back of your eyeball, which
receives an image and sends it to
your brain.

retinue retinues
NOUN a group of helpers or friends
travelling with an important
person.

retire retires retiring retired
VERB **1** When older people retire,

they give up work. **2** A FORMAL USE If
you retire, you leave to go into
another room, or to bed EG *She
retired early with a good book.*
retired ADJECTIVE, **retirement** NOUN

retort retorts retorting retorted
VERB **1** To retort means to reply
angrily. ▶ NOUN **2** a short, angry
reply.

retract retracts retracting
retracted
VERB **1** If you retract something you
have said, you say that you did not
mean it. **2** When something is
retracted, it moves inwards or
backwards EG *The undercarriage was
retracted shortly after takeoff.*
retraction NOUN, **retractable** ADJECTIVE

retreat retreats retreating
retreated
VERB **1** To retreat means to move
backwards away from something or
someone. **2** If you retreat from
something difficult or unpleasant,
you avoid doing it. ▶ NOUN **3** If an
army moves away from the enemy,
this is referred to as a retreat. **4** a
quiet place that you can go to rest
or do things in private.

retribution
NOUN; A FORMAL WORD Retribution is
punishment EG *the threat of
retribution.*

retrieve retrieves retrieving
retrieved
VERB If you retrieve something, you
get it back.
retrieval NOUN

retriever retrievers
NOUN a large dog often used by
hunters to bring back birds and
animals which have been shot.

retrospect
NOUN When you consider
something in retrospect, you think
about it afterwards and often have
a different opinion from the one
you had at the time EG *In retrospect, I
probably shouldn't have resigned.*

retrospective
ADJECTIVE **1** concerning things that

happened in the past. **2** taking effect from a date in the past.
retrospectively ADVERB

return returns returning returned
VERB **1** When you return to a place, you go back after you have been away. **2** If you return something to someone, you give it back to them. **3** When you return a ball during a game, you hit it back to your opponent. **4** When a judge or jury returns a verdict, they announce it. ▶ NOUN **5** Your return is your arrival back at a place. **6** The return on an investment is the profit or interest you get from it. **7** a ticket for the journey to a place and back again. ▶ PHRASE **8** If you do something **in return** for a favour, you do it to repay the favour.

reunion reunions
NOUN a party or meeting for people who have not seen each other for a long time.

reunite reunites reuniting reunited
VERB If people are reunited, they meet again after they have been separated for some time.

rev revs revving revved
AN INFORMAL WORD ▶ VERB **1** When you rev the engine of a vehicle, you press the accelerator to increase the engine speed. ▶ NOUN **2** The speed of an engine is measured in revolutions per minute, referred to as revs EG *I noticed that the engine revs had dropped.*

Rev or **Revd**
abbreviations for **Reverend.**

revamp revamps revamping revamped
VERB To revamp something means to improve or repair it.

reveal reveals revealing revealed
VERB **1** To reveal something means to tell people about it EG *They were not ready to reveal any of the details.* **2** If you reveal something that has been hidden, you uncover it.

revel revels revelling revelled

VERB If you revel in a situation, you enjoy it very much.
revelry NOUN

revelation revelations
NOUN **1** a surprising or interesting fact made known to people. **2** If an experience is a revelation, it makes you realize or learn something.

revenge revenges revenging revenged
NOUN **1** Revenge involves hurting someone who has hurt you. ▶ VERB **2** If you revenge yourself on someone who has hurt you, you hurt them in return.
▣ (sense 1) retaliation, vengeance
▣ (sense 2) avenge, retaliate

revenue revenues
NOUN Revenue is money that a government, company, or organization receives EG *government tax revenues.*

revered
ADJECTIVE If someone is revered, he or she is respected and admired EG *He is still revered as the father of the nation.*

reverence
NOUN Reverence is a feeling of great respect.

Reverend
Reverend is a title used before the name of a member of the clergy EG *the Reverend George Young.*

reversal reversals
NOUN If there is a reversal of a process or policy, it is changed to the opposite process or policy.

reverse reverses reversing reversed
VERB **1** When someone reverses a process, they change it to the opposite process EG *They won't reverse the decision to increase prices.* **2** If you reverse the order of things, you arrange them in the opposite order. **3** When you reverse a car, you drive it backwards. ▶ NOUN **4** The reverse is the opposite of what has just been said or done. ▶ ADJECTIVE **5** Reverse means opposite

A
B
C
D
E
F
G
H
I
J
K
L
M
N
O
P
Q
R
S
T
U
V
W
X
Y
Z

A
B
C
D
E
F
G
H
I
J
K
L
M
N
O
P
Q
R
S
T
U
V
W
X
Y
Z

to what is usual or to what has just been described.

reversible

ADJECTIVE Reversible clothing can be worn with either side on the outside.

revert reverts reverting reverted
VERB; A FORMAL WORD To revert to a former state or type of behaviour means to go back to it.

review reviews reviewing reviewed
NOUN **1** an article or an item on television or radio, giving an opinion of a new book or play. **2** When there is a review of a situation or system, it is examined to decide whether changes are needed. ▶ VERB **3** To review a play or book means to write an account expressing an opinion of it. **4** To review something means to examine it to decide whether changes are needed.

reviewer NOUN
▤ (sense 2) examination, survey
▤ (sense 4) reassess, reconsider, revise

revise revises revising revised
VERB **1** If you revise something, you alter or correct it. **2** When you revise for an examination, you go over your work to learn things thoroughly.

revision NOUN

revive revives reviving revived
VERB **1** When a feeling or practice is revived, it becomes active or popular again. **2** When you revive someone who has fainted, they become conscious again.

revival NOUN

revolt revolts revolting revolted
NOUN **1** a violent attempt by a group of people to change their country's political system. ▶ VERB **2** When people revolt, they fight against the authority that governs them. **3** If something revolts you, it is so horrible that you feel disgust.

revolting

ADJECTIVE horrible and disgusting EG *The smell in the cell was revolting.*

revolution revolutions
NOUN **1** a violent attempt by a large group of people to change the political system of their country. **2** an important change in an area of human activity EG *the Industrial Revolution.* **3** one complete turn in a circle.

revolutionary revolutionaries
ADJECTIVE **1** involving great changes EG *a revolutionary new cooling system.* ▶ NOUN **2** a person who takes part in a revolution.

revolve revolves revolving revolved
VERB **1** If something revolves round something else, it centres on that as the most important thing EG *My job revolves around the telephone.* **2** When something revolves, it turns in a circle around a central point EG *The moon revolves round the earth.*

revolver revolvers
NOUN a small gun held in the hand.

revulsion
NOUN Revulsion is a strong feeling of disgust or disapproval.

reward rewards rewarding rewarded
NOUN **1** something you are given because you have done something good. ▶ VERB **2** If you reward someone, you give them a reward.

rewarding
ADJECTIVE Something that is rewarding gives you a lot of satisfaction.

rewind rewinds rewinding rewound
VERB If you rewind a tape on a tape recorder or video, you make the tape go backwards.

rhapsody rhapsodies
Said "**rap**-sod-ee" NOUN a short piece of music which is very passionate and flowing.

rhetoric

NOUN Rhetoric is speech or writing that is intended to impress people.

rhetorical

ADJECTIVE **1** A rhetorical question is one which is asked in order to make a statement rather than to get an answer. **2** Rhetorical language is intended to be grand and impressive.

rheumatism

Said "room-at-izm" NOUN Rheumatism is an illness that makes your joints and muscles stiff and painful.
rheumatic ADJECTIVE

rhino rhinos

NOUN; AN INFORMAL WORD a rhinoceros.

rhinoceros rhinoceroses

NOUN a large African or Asian animal with one or two horns on its nose.
📖 from Greek *rhin* meaning 'of the nose' and *keras* meaning 'horn'

rhododendron rhododendrons

NOUN an evergreen bush with large coloured flowers.

rhombus rhombuses or rhombi

NOUN a shape with four equal sides and no right angles.

rhubarb

NOUN Rhubarb is a plant with long red stems which can be cooked with sugar and eaten.

rhyme rhymes rhyming rhymed

VERB **1** If two words rhyme, they have a similar sound EG *Sally rhymes with valley.* ▶ NOUN **2** a word that rhymes with another. **3** a short poem with rhyming lines.

rhythm rhythms

NOUN **1** Rhythm is a regular movement or beat. **2** a regular pattern of changes, for example, in the seasons.
rhythmic ADJECTIVE, **rhythmically** ADVERB

rib ribs

NOUN Your ribs are the curved bones that go from your backbone to your chest.
ribbed ADJECTIVE

ribbon ribbons

NOUN a long, narrow piece of cloth used for decoration.

rice

NOUN Rice is a tall grass that produces edible grains. Rice is grown in warm countries on wet ground.

rich richer richest; riches

ADJECTIVE **1** Someone who is rich has a lot of money and possessions. **2** Something that is rich in something contains a large amount of it EG *Liver is particularly rich in vitamin A.* **3** Rich food contains a large amount of fat, oil, or sugar. **4** Rich colours, smells, and sounds are strong and pleasant. ▶ PLURAL NOUN **5** Riches are valuable possessions or large amounts of money EG *the oil riches of the Middle East.*
richness NOUN

richly

ADVERB **1** If someone is richly rewarded, they are rewarded well with something valuable. **2** If you feel strongly that someone deserves something, you can say it is richly deserved.

rick ricks

NOUN a large pile of hay or straw.

rickets

NOUN Rickets is a disease that causes soft bones in children if they do not get enough vitamin D.

rickety

ADJECTIVE likely to collapse or break EG *a rickety wooden jetty.*

rickshaw rickshaws

NOUN a hand-pulled cart used in Asia for carrying passengers.

ricochet ricochets ricocheting or ricochetting ricocheted or ricochetted

Said "rik-osh-ay" VERB When a bullet ricochets, it hits a surface and bounces away from it.

rid rids ridding rid

PHRASE **1** When you get rid of

A
B
C
D
E
F
G
H
I
J
K
L
M
N
O
P
Q
R
S
T
U
V
W
X
Y
Z

something you do not want, you remove or destroy it. ▶ VERB **2** A FORMAL USE To rid a place of something unpleasant means to succeed in removing it.

riddle riddles

NOUN **1** a puzzle which seems to be nonsense, but which has an entertaining solution. **2** Something that is a riddle puzzles and confuses you.

🔲 (sense 2) enigma, mystery

riddled

ADJECTIVE full of something undesirable EG *The report was riddled with errors.*

🔲 from Old English *hriddel* meaning 'sieve'

ride rides riding rode ridden

VERB **1** When you ride a horse or a bike, you sit on it and control it as it moves along. **2** When you ride in a car, you travel in it. ▶ NOUN **3** a journey on a horse or bike or in a vehicle.

rider riders

NOUN **1** a person riding on a horse or bicycle. **2** an additional statement which changes or puts a condition on what has already been said.

ridge ridges

NOUN **1** a long, narrow piece of high land. **2** a raised line on a flat surface.

ridicule ridicules ridiculing ridiculed

VERB **1** To ridicule someone means to make fun of them in an unkind way. ▶ NOUN **2** Ridicule is unkind laughter and mockery.

ridiculous

ADJECTIVE very foolish.

ridiculously ADVERB

rife

ADJECTIVE; A FORMAL WORD very common EG *Unemployment was rife.*

rifle rifles rifling rifled

NOUN **1** a gun with a long barrel. ▶ VERB **2** When someone rifles something, they make a quick search through it to steal things.

rift rifts

NOUN **1** a serious quarrel between friends that damages their friendship. **2** a split in something solid, especially in the ground.

rig rigs rigging rigged

VERB **1** If someone rigs an election or contest, they dishonestly arrange for a particular person to succeed. ▶ NOUN **2** a large structure used for extracting oil or gas from the ground or sea bed.

rig up VERB If you rig up a device or structure, you make it quickly and fix it in place EG *They had even rigged up a makeshift aerial.*

right rights righting righted

ADJECTIVE OR ADVERB **1** correct and in accordance with the facts EG *That clock never tells the right time... That's absolutely right.* **2** 'Right' means on or towards the right side of something. ▶ ADJECTIVE **3** The right choice or decision is the best or most suitable one. **4** The right people or places are those that have influence or are socially admired EG *He was always to be seen in the right places.* **5** The right side of something is the side intended to be seen and to face outwards. ▶ NOUN **6** 'Right' is used to refer to principles of morally correct behaviour EG *At least he knew right from wrong.* **7** If you have a right to do something, you are morally or legally entitled to do it. **8** The right is one of the two sides of something. For example, when you look at the word 'to', the 'o' is to the right of the 't'. **9** The Right refers to people who support the political ideas of capitalism and conservatism rather than socialism. ▶ ADVERB **10** 'Right' is used to emphasize a precise place EG *I'm right here.* **11** 'Right' means immediately EG *I had to decide right then.* ▶ VERB **12** If you right something, you correct it or put it back in an upright position.

rightly ADVERB
■ (sense 3) appropriate, proper, suitable
■ (sense 7) prerogative, privilege

right angle right angles
NOUN an angle of 90°.

righteous
ADJECTIVE Righteous people behave in a way that is morally good and religious.

rightful
ADJECTIVE Someone's rightful possession is one which they have a moral or legal right to.
rightfully ADVERB

right-handed
ADJECTIVE OR ADVERB Someone who is right-handed does things such as writing and painting with their right hand.

right-wing
ADJECTIVE believing more strongly in capitalism or conservatism, or less strongly in socialism, than other members of the same party or group.
right-winger NOUN

rigid
ADJECTIVE 1 Rigid laws or systems cannot be changed and are considered severe. 2 A rigid object is stiff and does not bend easily.
rigidly ADVERB, **rigidity** NOUN
■ (sense 1) inflexible, strict

rigorous
ADJECTIVE very careful and thorough.
rigorously ADVERB

rigour rigours
NOUN; A FORMAL WORD The rigours of a situation are the things which make it hard or unpleasant EG *the rigours of childbirth.*

rim rims
NOUN the outside or top edge of an object such as a wheel or a cup.

rimu rimu or **rimus**
Said "**ree-moo**" NOUN A New Zealand tree with narrow, pointed leaves, which produces wood used for furniture.

rind rinds
NOUN Rind is the thick outer skin of fruit, cheese, or bacon.

ring rings ringing rang rung
VERB 1 If you ring someone, you phone them. 2 When a bell rings, it makes a clear, loud sound. 3 To ring something means to draw a circle around it. 4 If something is ringed with something else, it has that thing all the way around it EG *The courthouse was ringed with police.*
▶ NOUN 5 the sound made by a bell. 6 a small circle of metal worn on your finger. 7 an object or group of things in the shape of a circle. 8 At a boxing match or circus, the ring is the place where the fight or performance takes place. 9 an organized group of people who are involved in an illegal activity EG *an international spy ring.*
☑ The past tense of *ring* is *rang*, and the past participle is *rung*. Do not confuse these words: *she rang the bell; I had rung the police.*

ringbark ringbarks ringbarking ringbarked
VERB If you ringbark a tree, you kill it by cutting away a strip of bark from around its trunk.

ringer ringers
NOUN 1 a person or thing that is almost identical to another. 2 In Australian English, someone who works on a sheep farm. 3 In Australian and New Zealand English, the fastest shearer in a woolshed.

ring-in ring-ins
NOUN; AN INFORMAL WORD 1 In Australian English, a person or thing that is not normally a member of a particular group. 2 In Australian and New Zealand English, someone who is brought in at the last minute as a replacement for someone else.

ringleader ringleaders
NOUN the leader of a group of troublemakers or criminals.

A
B
C
D
E
F
G
H
I
J
K
L
M
N
O
P
Q
R
S
T
U
V
W
X
Y
Z

rink rinks

NOUN a large indoor area for ice-skating or roller-skating.

rinse rinses rinsing rinsed

VERB **1** When you rinse something, you wash it in clean water. ▸ NOUN **2** a liquid you can put on your hair to give it a different colour.

riot riots rioting rioted

NOUN **1** When there is a riot, a crowd of people behave noisily and violently. ▸ VERB **2** To riot means to behave noisily and violently. ▸ PHRASE **3** To **run riot** means to behave in a wild and uncontrolled way.

rip rips ripping ripped

VERB **1** When you rip something, you tear it violently. **2** If you rip something away, you remove it quickly and violently. ▸ NOUN **3** a long split in cloth or paper.

rip off VERB; AN INFORMAL EXPRESSION If someone rips you off, they cheat you by charging you too much money.

RIP

RIP is an abbreviation often written on gravestones, meaning 'rest in peace'.

ripe riper ripest

ADJECTIVE **1** When fruit or grain is ripe, it is fully developed and ready to be eaten. **2** If a situation is ripe for something to happen, it is ready for it.

ripeness NOUN

ripen ripens ripening ripened

VERB When crops ripen, they become ripe.

ripper rippers

NOUN; AN INFORMAL WORD In Australia and New Zealand English, an excellent person or thing.

ripple ripples rippling rippled

NOUN **1** Ripples are little waves on the surface of calm water. **2** If there is a ripple of laughter or applause, people laugh or applaud gently for a short time. ▸ VERB **3** When the surface of water ripples, little waves appear on it.

rise rises rising rose risen

VERB **1** If something rises, it moves upwards. **2** A FORMAL USE When you rise, you stand up. **3** To rise also means to get out of bed. **4** When the sun rises, it first appears. **5** The place where a river rises is where it begins. **6** If land rises, it slopes upwards. **7** If a sound or wind rises, it becomes higher or stronger. **8** If an amount rises, it increases. **9** If you rise to a challenge or a remark, you respond to it rather than ignoring it EG *He rose to the challenge with enthusiasm.* **10** When people rise up, they start fighting against people in authority. ▸ NOUN **11** an increase. **12** Someone's rise is the process by which they become more powerful or successful EG *his rise to fame.*

■ (sense 1) ascend, climb, go up

riser risers

NOUN An early riser is someone who likes to get up early in the morning.

risk risks risking risked

NOUN **1** a chance that something unpleasant or dangerous might happen. ▸ VERB **2** If you risk something unpleasant, you do something knowing that the unpleasant thing might happen as a result EG *If he doesn't play, he risks losing his place in the team.* **3** If you risk someone's life, you put them in a dangerous situation in which they might be killed.

risky ADJECTIVE

▥ from Italian *rischiare* meaning 'to be in danger'

rite rites

NOUN a religious ceremony.

ritual rituals

NOUN **1** a series of actions carried out according to the custom of a particular society or group EG *This is the most ancient of the Buddhist rituals.* ▸ ADJECTIVE **2** Ritual activities happen as part of a tradition or ritual EG *fasting and ritual dancing.*

ritualistic ADJECTIVE

rival rivals rivalling rivalled
NOUN **1** Your rival is the person you are competing with. ▸ VERB **2** If something rivals something else, it is of the same high standard or quality EG *As a holiday destination, South Africa rivals Kenya for weather.*
■ (sense 1) adversary, opponent

rivalry rivalries
NOUN Rivalry is active competition between people.

river rivers
NOUN a natural feature consisting of water flowing for a long distance between two banks.

rivet rivets
NOUN a short, round pin with a flat head which is used to fasten sheets of metal together.

riveting
ADJECTIVE If you find something riveting, you find it fascinating and it holds your attention EG *I find tennis riveting.*

road roads
NOUN a long piece of hard ground specially surfaced so that people and vehicles can travel along it easily.

road rage
NOUN Road rage is aggressive behaviour by a driver as a reaction to the behaviour of another driver.

road train road trains
NOUN In Australia, a line of linked trailers pulled by a truck, used for transporting cattle or sheep.

roadworks
PLURAL NOUN Roadworks are repairs being done on a road.

roam roams roaming roamed
VERB If you roam around, you wander around without any particular purpose EG *Hens were roaming around the yard.*

roar roars roaring roared
VERB **1** If something roars, it makes a very loud noise. **2** To roar with laughter or anger means to laugh or shout very noisily. **3** When a lion roars, it makes a loud, angry sound. ▸ NOUN **4** a very loud noise.

roast roasts roasting roasted
VERB **1** When you roast meat or other food, you cook it using dry heat in an oven or over a fire.
▸ ADJECTIVE **2** Roast meat has been roasted. ▸ NOUN **3** a piece of meat that has been roasted.

rob robs robbing robbed
VERB **1** If someone robs you, they steal your possessions. **2** If you rob someone of something they need or deserve, you deprive them of it EG *He robbed me of my childhood.*

robber robbers
NOUN Robbers are people who steal money or property using force or threats EG *bank robbers.*
robbery NOUN

robe robes
NOUN a long, loose piece of clothing which covers the body EG *He knelt in his white robes before the altar.*

robin robins
NOUN a small bird with a red breast.

robot robots
NOUN a machine which is programmed to move and perform tasks automatically.
▥ from Czech *robota* meaning 'work'

robust
ADJECTIVE very strong and healthy.
robustly ADVERB

rock rocks rocking rocked
NOUN **1** Rock is the hard mineral substance that forms the surface of the earth. **2** a large piece of rock EG *She picked up a rock and threw it into the lake.* **3** Rock or rock music is music with simple tunes and a very strong beat. **4** Rock is also a sweet shaped into long, hard sticks, sold in holiday resorts. ▸ VERB **5** When something rocks or when you rock it, it moves regularly backwards and forwards or from side to side EG *She rocked the baby.* **6** If something rocks people, it shocks and upsets

them EG *Palermo was rocked by a crime wave.* **7** If someone's marriage or relationship is **on the rocks**, it is unsuccessful and about to end.

rock and roll
NOUN Rock and roll is a style of music with a strong beat that was especially popular in the 1950s.

rocket rockets rocketing rocketed
NOUN **1** a space vehicle, usually shaped like a long pointed tube. **2** an explosive missile EG *They fired rockets into a number of government buildings.* **3** a firework that explodes when it is high in the air. ▸ VERB **4** If prices rocket, they increase very quickly.

rocking chair rocking chairs
NOUN a chair on two curved pieces of wood that rocks backwards and forwards when you sit in it.

rock melon rock melons
NOUN In Australian, New Zealand, and American English a rock melon is a cantaloupe, a melon with orange flesh and a hard, lumpy skin.

rocky
ADJECTIVE covered with rocks.

rod rods
NOUN a long, thin pole or bar, usually made of wood or metal EG *a fishing rod.*

rodent rodents
NOUN a small mammal with sharp front teeth which it uses for gnawing.
🏛 from Latin *rodere* meaning 'to gnaw'

rodeo rodeos
NOUN a public entertainment in which cowboys show different skills.

roe
NOUN Roe is the eggs of a fish.

rogue rogues
NOUN **1** You can refer to a man who behaves dishonestly as a rogue. ▸ ADJECTIVE **2** a vicious animal that

lives apart from its herd or pack.

role roles; also spelt **rôle**
NOUN **1** Someone's role is their position and function in a situation or society. **2** An actor's role is the character that he or she plays EG *her first leading role.*

roll rolls rolling rolled
VERB **1** When something rolls or when you roll it, it moves along a surface, turning over and over. **2** When vehicles roll along, they move EG *Tanks rolled into the village.* **3** If you roll your eyes, you make them turn up or go from side to side. **4** If you roll something flexible into a cylinder or ball, you wrap it several times around itself EG *He rolled up the bag with the money in it.* ▸ NOUN **5** A roll of paper or cloth is a long piece of it that has been rolled into a tube EG *a roll of film.* **6** a small, rounded, individually baked piece of bread. **7** an official list of people's names EG *the electoral roll.* **8** A roll on a drum is a long, rumbling sound made on it.

roll-call roll-calls
NOUN If you take a roll-call, you call a register of names to see who is present.

roller rollers
NOUN **1** a cylinder that turns round in a machine or piece of equipment. **2** Rollers are tubes which you can wind your hair around to make it curly.

Rollerblade Rollerblades
NOUN; A TRADEMARK Rollerblades are roller-skates which have the wheels set in one straight line on the bottom of the boot.

roller-coaster roller-coasters
NOUN a pleasure ride at a fair, consisting of a small railway that goes up and down very steep slopes.

roller-skate roller-skates roller-skating roller-skated
NOUN **1** Roller-skates are shoes with four small wheels underneath.

A B C D E F G H I J K L M N O P Q R S T U V W X Y Z

▶ VERB **2** If you roller-skate, you move along wearing roller-skates.

rolling pin rolling pins

NOUN a wooden cylinder used for rolling pastry dough to make it flat.

ROM

NOUN In computing, ROM is a storage device that holds data permanently and cannot be altered by the programmer. ROM stands for 'read only memory'.

Roman Catholic Roman Catholics

ADJECTIVE **1** relating or belonging to the branch of the Christian church that accepts the Pope in Rome as its leader. ▶ NOUN **2** someone who belongs to the Roman Catholic church.

Roman Catholicism NOUN

romance romances

NOUN **1** a relationship between two people who are in love with each other. **2** Romance is the pleasure and excitement of doing something new and unusual EG *the romance of foreign travel*. **3** a novel about a love affair.

Romanian Romanians

Said "roe-may-nee-an"; *also spelt* **Rumanian**
ADJECTIVE **1** belonging or relating to Romania. ▶ NOUN **2** someone who comes from Romania. **3** Romanian is the main language spoken in Romania.

romantic romantics

ADJECTIVE OR NOUN **1** A romantic person has ideas that are not realistic, for example about love or about ways of changing society EG *a romantic idealist*. ▶ ADJECTIVE **2** connected with sexual love EG *a romantic relationship*. **3** Something that is romantic is beautiful in a way that strongly affects your feelings EG *It is one of the most romantic ruins in Scotland*. **4** Romantic describes a style of music, literature, and art popular in Europe in the late 18th and early 19th centuries, which emphasized feeling and imagination rather than order and form .

romantically ADVERB, **romanticism** NOUN

rondavel rondavels

NOUN In South Africa, a rondavel is a small circular building with a conical roof.

roo roos

NOUN; AN INFORMAL WORD In Australian English, a kangaroo.

roof roofs

NOUN **1** The roof of a building or car is the covering on top of it. **2** The roof of your mouth or of a cave is the highest part.

roofing

NOUN Roofing is material used for covering roofs.

rooftop rooftops

NOUN the outside part of the roof of a building.

rook rooks

NOUN **1** a large black bird. **2** a chess piece which can move any number of squares in a straight but not diagonal line.

room rooms

NOUN **1** a separate section in a building, divided from other rooms by walls. **2** If there is plenty of room, there is a lot of space EG *There wasn't enough room for his gear*.

roost roosts roosting roosted

NOUN **1** a place where birds rest or build their nests. ▶ VERB **2** When birds roost, they settle somewhere for the night.

root roots rooting rooted

NOUN **1** The roots of a plant are the parts that grow under the ground. **2** The root of a hair is the part beneath the skin. **3** You can refer to the place or culture that you grew up in as your roots. **4** The root of something is its original cause or basis EG *We got to the root of the problem*. ▶ VERB **5** To root through things means to search through them, pushing them aside EG *She rooted through his bag*.

A
B
C
D
E
F
G
H
I
J
K
L
M
N
O
P
Q
R
S
T
U
V
W
X
Y
Z

root out VERB If you root something or someone out, you find them and force them out EG *a major drive to root out corruption.*

rooted
ADJECTIVE developed from or strongly influenced by something EG *songs rooted in traditional African music.*

rope ropes roping roped
NOUN **1** a thick, strong length of twisted cord. ▶ VERB **2** If you rope one thing to another, you tie them together with rope.

rosary rosaries
NOUN a string of beads that Catholics use for counting prayers.

rose roses
NOUN **1** a large garden flower which has a pleasant smell and grows on a bush with thorns. ▶ NOUN OR ADJECTIVE **2** reddish-pink.

rosella rosellas
NOUN a brightly coloured Australian parrot.

rosemary
NOUN Rosemary is a herb with fragrant spiky leaves, used for flavouring in cooking.

rosette rosettes
NOUN a large badge of coloured ribbons gathered into a circle, which is worn as a prize in a competition or to support a political party.

Rosh Hashanah or **Rosh Hashana**
NOUN the festival celebrating the Jewish New Year.
🔲 a Hebrew phrase meaning 'head of the year'

roster rosters
NOUN a list of people who take it in turn to do a particular job EG *He put himself first on the new roster for domestic chores.*

rostrum rostrums or **rostra**
NOUN a raised platform on which someone stands to speak to an audience or conduct an orchestra.
🔲 from Latin *rostrum* meaning

'ship's prow'; Roman orators' platforms were decorated with the prows of captured ships

rosy rosier rosiest
ADJECTIVE **1** reddish-pink. **2** If a situation seems rosy, it is likely to be good or successful. **3** If a person looks rosy, they have pink cheeks and look healthy.

rot rots rotting rotted
VERB **1** When food or wood rots, it decays and can no longer be used. **2** When something rots another substance, it causes it to decay EG *Sugary drinks rot your teeth.* ▶ NOUN **3** Rot is the condition that affects things when they rot EG *The timber frame was not protected against rot.*
🔲 (sense 1) decay, decompose

rota rotas
NOUN a list of people who take turns to do a particular job.

rotate rotates rotating rotated
VERB When something rotates, it turns with a circular movement EG *He rotated the camera 180°.*
rotation NOUN

rotor rotors
NOUN **1** The rotor is the part of a machine that turns. **2** The rotors or rotor blades of a helicopter are the four long flat pieces of metal on top of it which rotate and lift it off the ground.

rotten
ADJECTIVE **1** decayed and no longer of use EG *The front bay window is rotten.* **2** AN INFORMAL USE of very poor quality EG *I think it's a rotten idea.* **3** AN INFORMAL USE very unfair, unkind, or unpleasant EG *That's a rotten thing to say!*

rouble roubles
Said "**roo**-bl" NOUN the main unit of currency in Russia.
🔲 In Russian *rubl* means literally 'silver bar'

rough rougher roughest; roughs
Said "**ruff**" ADJECTIVE **1** uneven and not smooth. **2** not using enough care or gentleness EG *Don't be so*

rough or you'll break it. **3** difficult or unpleasant EG *Teachers have been given a rough time.* **4** approximately correct EG *At a rough guess it is five times more profitable.* **5** If the sea is rough, there are large waves because of bad weather. **6** A rough town or area has a lot of crime or violence. ▶ NOUN OR ADJECTIVE **7** A rough or a rough sketch is a drawing or description that shows the main features but does not show the details. **8** On a golf course, the rough is the part of the course next to a fairway where the grass has not been cut.

roughly ADVERB, **roughness** NOUN

roulette

*Said "roo-**let**"* NOUN Roulette is a gambling game in which a ball is dropped onto a revolving wheel with numbered holes in it.

round rounder roundest; rounds rounding rounded

ADJECTIVE **1** Something round is shaped like a ball or a circle. **2** complete or whole EG *round numbers.* ▶ PREPOSITION OR ADVERB **3** If something is round something else, it surrounds it. **4** The distance round something is the length of its circumference or boundary EG *I'm about two inches larger round the waist.* **5** You can refer to an area near a place as the area round it EG *There's nothing to do round here.* ▶ PREPOSITION **6** If something moves round you, it keeps moving in a circle with you in the centre. **7** When someone goes to the other side of something, they have gone round it. ▶ ADVERB OR PREPOSITION **8** If you go round a place, you go to different parts of it to look at it EG *We went round the museum.* ▶ ADVERB **9** If you turn or look round, you turn so you are facing in a different direction. **10** When someone comes round, they visit you EG *He came round with a bottle of wine.* ▶ NOUN **11** one of a series of events EG *After round three, two Americans*

shared the lead. **12** If you buy a round of drinks, you buy a drink for each member of the group you are with.

■ (sense 1) globular, spherical

round up VERB If you round up people or animals, you gather them together.

roundabout roundabouts

NOUN **1** a meeting point of several roads with a circle in the centre which vehicles have to travel around. **2** a circular platform which rotates and which children can ride on in a playground. **3** the same as a merry-go-round.

rounded

ADJECTIVE curved in shape, without any points or sharp edges.

round-the-clock

ADJECTIVE happening continuously.

rouse rouses rousing roused

VERB **1** If someone rouses you, they wake you up. **2** If you rouse yourself to do something, you make yourself get up and do it. **3** If something rouses you, it makes you feel very emotional and excited.

rouseabout rouseabouts

NOUN In Australian and New Zealand English, an unskilled worker who does odd jobs, especially on a farm.

rout routs routing routed

Rhymes with "out" VERB To rout your opponents means to defeat them completely and easily.

route routes

Said "root" NOUN a way from one place to another.

routine routines

ADJECTIVE **1** Routine activities are done regularly. ▶ NOUN **2** the usual way or order in which you do things. **3** a boring repetition of tasks.

routinely ADVERB

roving

ADJECTIVE **1** wandering or roaming EG

A
B
C
D
E
F
G
H
I
J
K
L
M
N
O
P
Q
R
S
T
U
V
W
X
Y
Z

roving gangs of youths. **2** not restricted to any particular location or area EG *a roving reporter.*

row rows rowing rowed
Rhymes with "snow" NOUN **1** A row of people or things is several of them arranged in a line. ▶ VERB **2** When you row a boat, you use oars to make it move through the water.

row rows rowing rowed
Rhymes with "now" NOUN **1** a serious argument. **2** If someone is making a row, they are making too much noise. ▶ VERB **3** If people are rowing, they are quarrelling noisily.

rowdy rowdier rowdiest
ADJECTIVE rough and noisy.

royal royals
ADJECTIVE **1** belonging to or involving a queen, a king, or a member of their family. **2** 'Royal' is used in the names of organizations appointed or supported by a member of a royal family. ▶ NOUN **3** AN INFORMAL USE Members of the royal family are sometimes referred to as the royals.
■ (sense 1) imperial, regal

royalist royalists
NOUN someone who supports their country's royal family.

royalty royalties
NOUN **1** The members of a royal family are sometimes referred to as royalty. **2** Royalties are payments made to authors and musicians from the sales of their books or records.

rub rubs rubbing rubbed
VERB If you rub something, you move your hand or a cloth backwards and forwards over it.
rub out VERB To rub out something written means to remove it by rubbing it with a rubber or a cloth.

rubber rubbers
NOUN **1** Rubber is a strong, elastic substance used for making tyres, boots, and other products. **2** a small piece of rubber used to rub

out pencil mistakes.

rubbish
NOUN **1** Rubbish is unwanted things or waste material. **2** You can refer to nonsense or something of very poor quality as rubbish.
■ (sense 1) garbage, refuse, trash, waste
■ (sense 2) garbage, nonsense, twaddle

rubble
NOUN Bits of old brick and stone are referred to as rubble.

rubric rubrics
Said "roo-brik" NOUN; A FORMAL WORD a set of instructions at the beginning of an official document.

ruby rubies
NOUN a type of red jewel.

rucksack rucksacks
NOUN a bag with shoulder straps for carrying things on your back.

rudder rudders
NOUN a piece of wood or metal at the back of a boat or plane which is moved to make the boat or plane turn.

rude ruder rudest
ADJECTIVE **1** not polite.
2 embarrassing or offensive because of reference to sex or other bodily functions EG *rude jokes.*
3 unexpected and unpleasant EG *a rude awakening.*
rudely ADVERB, **rudeness** NOUN
■ (sense 1) discourteous, ill-mannered, impolite, uncivil

rudimentary
ADJECTIVE; A FORMAL WORD very basic and undeveloped EG *He had only a rudimentary knowledge of French.*

rudiments
PLURAL NOUN When you learn the rudiments of something, you learn only the simplest and most basic things about it.
▥ from Latin *rudimentum* meaning 'beginning'

ruff ruffs
NOUN **1** a stiff circular collar with

A
B
C
D
E
F
G
H
I
J
K
L
M
N
O
P
Q
R
S
T
U
V
W
X
Y
Z

many pleats in it, worn especially in the 16th century. **2** a thick band of fur or feathers around the neck of a bird or animal.

ruffle ruffles ruffling ruffled
VERB **1** If you ruffle someone's hair, you move your hand quickly backwards and forwards over their head. **2** If something ruffles you, it makes you annoyed or upset. ▸ NOUN **3** Ruffles are small folds made in a piece of material for decoration.

rug rugs
NOUN **1** a small, thick carpet. **2** a blanket which you can use to cover your knees or for sitting on outdoors.

rugby
NOUN Rugby is a game played by two teams, who try to kick and throw an oval ball to their opponents' end of the pitch. Rugby League is played with 13 players in each side, Rugby Union is played with 15 players in each side.

rugged
ADJECTIVE **1** rocky, wild, and unsheltered EG *the rugged west coast of Ireland*. **2** having strong features EG *his rugged good looks*.

rugger
NOUN Rugger is the same as rugby.

ruin ruins ruining ruined
VERB **1** If you ruin something, you destroy or spoil it completely. **2** If someone is ruined, they have lost all their money. ▸ NOUN **3** Ruin is the state of being destroyed or completely spoilt. **4** A ruin or the ruins of something refers to the parts that are left after it has been severely damaged EG *the ruins of a thirteenth-century monastery*.

rule rules ruling ruled
NOUN **1** Rules are statements which tell you what you are allowed to do. ▸ VERB **2** To rule a country or group of people means to have power over it and be in charge of its affairs. **3** A FORMAL USE When

someone in authority rules on a particular matter, they give an official decision about it. ▸ PHRASE **4 As a rule**, means usually or generally EG *As a rule, I eat my meals in front of the TV.*
■ (sense 1) law, regulation

rule out VERB **1** If you rule out an idea or course of action, you reject it. **2** If one thing rules out another, it prevents it from happening or being possible EG *The accident ruled out a future for him in football*.

ruler rulers
NOUN **1** a person who rules a country. **2** a long, flat piece of wood or plastic with straight edges marked in centimetres or inches, used for measuring or drawing straight lines.

rum
NOUN Rum is a strong alcoholic drink made from sugar cane juice.

Rumanian
Said "roo-**may**-nee-an" another spelling of **Romanian**.

rumble rumbles rumbling rumbled
VERB **1** If something rumbles, it makes a continuous low noise EG *Another train rumbled past the house.*
▸ NOUN **2** a continuous low noise EG *the distant rumble of traffic*.

rummage rummages rummaging rummaged
VERB If you rummage somewhere, you search for something, moving things about carelessly.

rumour rumours rumoured
NOUN **1** a story that people are talking about, which may or may not be true. ▸ VERB **2** If something is rumoured, people are suggesting that it is has happened.
🏛 from Latin *rumor* meaning 'common talk'
■ (sense 1) gossip, hearsay, story

rump rumps
NOUN **1** An animal's rump is its rear end. **2** Rump or rump steak is meat cut from the rear end of a cow.

run runs running ran

VERB **1** When you run, you move quickly, leaving the ground during each stride. **2** If you run away from a place, you leave it suddenly and secretly. **3** If you say that a road or river runs in a particular direction, you are describing its course. **4** If you run your hand or an object over something, you move it over it. **5** If someone runs in an election, they stand as a candidate EG *He announced he would run for President.* **6** If you run a business or an activity, you are in charge of it. **7** If you run an experiment, a computer program, or tape, you start it and let it continue EG *He ran a series of computer checks.* **8** To run a car means to have it and use it. **9** If you run someone somewhere in a car, you drive them there EG *Could you run me up to town?* **10** If you run water, you turn on a tap to make it flow EG *We heard him running the kitchen tap.* **11** If your nose is running, it is producing a lot of mucus. **12** If the dye in something runs, the colour comes out when it is washed. **13** If a feeling runs through your body, it affects you quickly and strongly. **14** If an amount is running at a particular level, it is at that level EG *Inflation is currently running at 2.6%.* **15** If someone or something is running late, they have taken more time than was planned. **16** If an event or contract runs for a particular time, it lasts for that time. ▶ NOUN **17** If you go for a run, you run for pleasure or exercise. **18** a journey somewhere EG *It was quite a run to the village.* **19** If a play or show has a run of a particular length of time, it is on for that time. **20** A run of success or failure is a series of successes or failures. **21** In cricket or baseball, a player scores one run by running between marked places on the pitch after hitting the ball.

≡ (sense 1) dash, race, sprint
≡ (sense 2) bolt, flee

run out VERB If you run out of something, you have no more left.
run over VERB If someone is run over, they are hit by a moving vehicle.

runaway runaways

NOUN a person who has escaped from a place or left it secretly and hurriedly.

rundown

ADJECTIVE **1** tired and not well. **2** neglected and in poor condition. ▶ NOUN **3** AN INFORMAL USE If you give someone the rundown on a situation, you tell them the basic, important facts about it.

rung rungs

NOUN The rungs on a ladder are the bars that form the steps.

runner runners

NOUN **1** a person who runs, especially as a sport. **2** a person who takes messages or runs errands. **3** A runner on a plant such as a strawberry is a long shoot from which a new plant develops. **4** The runners on drawers and ice skates are the thin strips on which they move.

runner bean runner beans

NOUN Runner beans are long green pods eaten as a vegetable, which grow on a climbing plant.

runner-up runners-up

NOUN a person or team that comes second in a race or competition.

running

ADJECTIVE **1** continuing without stopping over a period of time EG *a running commentary.* **2** Running water is flowing rather than standing still.

runny runnier runniest

ADJECTIVE **1** more liquid than usual EG *Warm the honey until it becomes runny.* **2** If someone's nose or eyes are runny, liquid is coming out of them.

runt runts

NOUN The runt of a litter of animals is the smallest and weakest.

runway runways

NOUN a long strip of ground used by aeroplanes for taking off or landing.

rupee rupees

Said "roo-pee" NOUN the main unit of currency in India, Pakistan, and some other countries.

rupture ruptures rupturing ruptured

NOUN **1** a severe injury in which part of your body tears or bursts open. ▸ VERB **2** To rupture part of the body means to cause it to tear or burst EG *a ruptured spleen.*

rural

ADJECTIVE relating to or involving the countryside.

ruse ruses

NOUN; A FORMAL WORD an action which is intended to trick someone.

rush rushes rushing rushed

VERB **1** To rush means to move fast or do something quickly. **2** If you rush someone into doing something, you make them do it without allowing them enough time to think. ▸ NOUN **3** If you are in a rush, you are busy and do not have enough time to do things. **4** If there is a rush for something, there is a sudden increase in demand for it EG *There was a rush for tickets.* **5** Rushes are plants with long, thin stems that grow near water.

rush hour rush hours

NOUN The rush hour is one of the busy parts of the day when most people are travelling to or from work.

rusk rusks

NOUN a hard, dry biscuit given to babies.

Russian Russians

ADJECTIVE **1** belonging or relating to Russia. ▸ NOUN **2** someone who comes from Russia. **3** Russian is the main language spoken in Russia.

rust rusts rusting rusted

NOUN **1** Rust is a reddish-brown substance that forms on iron or steel which has been in contact with water and which is decaying gradually. ▸ NOUN OR ADJECTIVE **2** reddish-brown. ▸ VERB **3** When a metal object rusts, it becomes covered in rust.

rustic

ADJECTIVE simple in a way considered to be typical of the countryside EG *a rustic old log cabin.*

rustle rustles rustling rustled

VERB When something rustles, it makes soft sounds as it moves. **rustling** ADJECTIVE OR NOUN

rusty rustier rustiest

ADJECTIVE **1** affected by rust EG *a rusty iron gate.* **2** If someone's knowledge is rusty, it is not as good as it used to be because they have not used it for a long time EG *My German is a bit rusty these days.*

rut ruts

NOUN **1** a deep, narrow groove in the ground made by the wheels of a vehicle. ▸ PHRASE **2** If someone is in a rut, they have become fixed in their way of doing things.

ruthless

ADJECTIVE very harsh or cruel EG *a ruthless drug dealer.* **ruthlessness** NOUN, **ruthlessly** ADVERB

rye

NOUN Rye is a type of grass that produces light brown grain.

A B C D E F G H I J K L M N O P Q R S T U V W X Y Z

625

Ss Ss

Sabbath

NOUN The Sabbath is the day of the week when members of some religious groups, especially Jews and Christians, do not work.

📖 from Hebrew *shabbath* meaning 'to rest'

sable sables

NOUN a very expensive fur used for making coats and hats; also the wild animal from which this fur is obtained.

sabotage sabotages sabotaging sabotaged

Said "**sab**-ot-ahj" NOUN **1** Sabotage is the deliberate damaging of things such as machinery and railway lines. ▶ VERB **2** If something is sabotaged, it is deliberately damaged.

saboteur NOUN

📖 from French *saboter* meaning 'to spoil through clumsiness'

sabre sabres

NOUN **1** a heavy curved sword. **2** a light sword used in fencing.

saccharine or **saccharin**

Said "**sak**-er-rine" NOUN Saccharine is a chemical used instead of sugar to sweeten things.

sachet sachets

Said "**sash**-ay" NOUN a small closed packet, containing a small amount of something such as sugar or shampoo.

sack sacks sacking sacked

NOUN **1** a large bag made of rough material used for carrying or storing goods. ▶ VERB **2** AN INFORMAL USE If someone is sacked, they are dismissed from their job by their employer. ▶ PHRASE **3** AN INFORMAL USE If someone **gets the sack**, they are sacked by their employer.

🔲 (sense 2) dismiss, fire

sacrament sacraments

NOUN an important Christian ceremony such as communion,
baptism, or marriage.

sacred

Said "**say**-krid" ADJECTIVE holy, or connected with religion or religious ceremonies EG *sacred ground*.

sacrifice sacrifices sacrificing sacrificed

Said "**sak**-riff-ice" VERB **1** If you sacrifice something valuable or important, you give it up. **2** To sacrifice an animal means to kill it as an offering to a god. ▶ NOUN **3** the killing of an animal as an offering to a god or gods.

sacrificial ADJECTIVE

🔲 (sense 1) forfeit, give up

sacrilege

Said "**sak**-ril-ij" NOUN Sacrilege is behaviour that shows great disrespect for something holy.

sacrilegious ADJECTIVE

sacrosanct

Said "**sak**-roe-sangkt" ADJECTIVE regarded as too important to be criticized or changed EG *Freedom of the press is sacrosanct*.

sad sadder saddest

ADJECTIVE **1** If you are sad, you feel unhappy. **2** Something sad makes you feel unhappy EG *a sad story*.

sadly ADVERB, **sadness** NOUN

🔲 (sense 1) low, melancholy, unhappy

sadden saddens saddening saddened

VERB If something saddens you, it makes you feel sad.

saddle saddles saddling saddled

NOUN **1** a leather seat that you sit on when you are riding a horse. **2** The saddle on a bicycle is the seat. ▶ VERB **3** If you saddle a horse, you put a saddle on it.

sadism

Said "**say**-diz-m" NOUN Sadism is the obtaining of pleasure, especially sexual pleasure, from making people suffer pain or humiliation.

sadist NOUN, **sadistic** ADJECTIVE
🏛 from the Marquis de Sade (1740-1814), who got his pleasure in this way

safari safaris
NOUN an expedition for hunting or observing wild animals.
🏛 from Swahili *safari* meaning 'journey'

safari park safari parks
NOUN a large park where wild animals such as lions and elephants roam freely.

safe safer safest; safes
ADJECTIVE **1** Something that is safe does not cause harm or danger. **2** If you are safe, you are not in any danger. **3** If it is safe to say something, you can say it with little risk of being wrong. ▶ NOUN **4** a strong metal box with special locks, in which you can keep valuable things.
safely ADVERB, **safety** NOUN
■ (sense 2) out of danger, secure

safeguard safeguards safeguarding safeguarded
VERB **1** To safeguard something means to protect it. ▶ NOUN **2** a rule or law designed to protect something or someone.

safekeeping
NOUN If something is given to you for safekeeping, it is given to you to look after.

sag sags sagging sagged
VERB When something sags, it hangs down loosely or sinks downwards in the middle.
sagging ADJECTIVE

saga sagas
Said "**sah**-ga" NOUN a very long story, usually with many different adventures EG *a saga of rivalry, honour and love.*
🏛 from Old Norse *saga* meaning 'story'

sage sages
NOUN **1** A LITERARY USE a very wise person. **2** Sage is also a herb used for flavouring in cooking.

🏛 sense 1 is from Latin *sapere* meaning 'to be wise'; sense 2 is from Latin *salvus* meaning 'healthy', because of the supposed medicinal properties of the plant

Sagittarius
Said "saj-it-**tair**-ee-uss" NOUN Sagittarius is the ninth sign of the zodiac, represented by a creature half-horse, half-man holding a bow and arrow. People born between November 22nd and December 21st are born under this sign.
🏛 from Latin *sagittarius* meaning 'archer'

sail sails sailing sailed
NOUN **1** Sails are large pieces of material attached to a ship's mast. The wind blows against the sail and moves the ship. ▶ VERB **2** When a ship sails, it moves across water. **3** If you sail somewhere, you go there by ship.

sailor sailors
NOUN a member of a ship's crew.

saint saints
NOUN a person who after death is formally recognized by a Christian Church as deserving special honour because of having lived a very holy life.
🏛 from Latin *sanctus* meaning 'holy'

saintly
ADJECTIVE behaving in a very good or holy way.

sake sakes
PHRASE **1** If you do something for someone's sake, you do it to help or please them. **2** You use for the sake of to say why you are doing something EG *a one-off expedition for interest's sake.*

salad salads
NOUN a mixture of raw vegetables.
🏛 from Old Provençal *salar* meaning 'to season with salt'

salami
Said "sal-**lah**-mee" NOUN Salami is a kind of spicy sausage.

A B C D E F G H I J K L M N O P Q R S T U V W X Y Z

627

salary salaries
NOUN a regular monthly payment to an employee.
🏛 from Latin *salarium* meaning 'money given to soldiers to buy salt'

sale sales
NOUN 1 The sale of goods is the selling of them. 2 an occasion when a shop sells things at reduced prices. ▶ PLURAL NOUN 3 The sales of a product are the numbers that are sold.

salesman salesmen
NOUN someone who sells products for a company.
saleswoman NOUN

salient
Said "say-lee-ent" ADJECTIVE; A FORMAL WORD The salient points or facts are the important ones.

saliva
Said "sal-**live**-a" NOUN Saliva is the watery liquid in your mouth that helps you chew and digest food.

sallow
ADJECTIVE Sallow skin is pale and unhealthy.

salmon salmons or **salmon**
Said "sam-on" NOUN a large edible silver-coloured fish with pink flesh.

salmonella
Said "sal-mon-**nell**-a" NOUN Salmonella is a kind of bacteria which can cause severe food poisoning.

salon salons
NOUN a place where hairdressers work.

saloon saloons
NOUN 1 a car with a fixed roof and a separate boot. 2 In America, a place where alcoholic drinks are sold and drunk.

salt salts
NOUN 1 Salt is a white substance found naturally in sea water. It is used to flavour and preserve food. 2 a chemical compound formed from an acid base.

salty saltier saltiest
ADJECTIVE containing salt or tasting of salt.

salute salutes saluting saluted
NOUN 1 a formal sign of respect. Soldiers give a salute by raising their right hand to their forehead. ▶ VERB 2 If you salute someone, you give them a salute.

salvage salvages salvaging salvaged
VERB 1 If you salvage things, you save them, for example from a wrecked ship or a destroyed building. ▶ NOUN 2 You refer to things saved from a wrecked ship or destroyed building as salvage.

salvation
NOUN 1 When someone's salvation takes place, they are saved from harm or evil. 2 To be someone's salvation means to save them from harm or evil.

salvo salvos or **salvoes**
NOUN the firing of several guns or missiles at the same time.

same
ADJECTIVE OR PRONOUN 1 If two things are the same, they look like one another. 2 Same means just one thing and not two different ones EG *They were born in the same town.*

Samoan Samoans
ADJECTIVE 1 belonging or relating to Samoa. ▶ NOUN 2 someone who comes from Samoa.

sample samples sampling sampled
NOUN 1 A sample of something is a small amount of it that you can try or test EG *a sample of new wine.* ▶ VERB 2 If you sample something, you try it EG *I sampled his cooking.*

samurai
Said "sam-oor-eye" NOUN A samurai was a member of an ancient Japanese warrior class.

sanctimonious
Said "sank-tim-**moan**-ee-uss" ADJECTIVE pretending to be very religious and virtuous.

sanction sanctions sanctioning sanctioned

VERB **1** To sanction something means to officially approve of it or allow it. ▶ NOUN **2** Sanction is official approval of something. **3** a severe punishment or penalty intended to make people obey the law. **4** Sanctions are sometimes taken by countries against a country that has broken international law.

sanctity

NOUN If you talk about the sanctity of something, you are saying that it should be respected because it is very important EG *the sanctity of marriage*.

sanctuary sanctuaries

NOUN **1** a place where you are safe from harm or danger. **2** a place where wildlife is protected EG *a bird sanctuary*.

sand sands sanding sanded

NOUN **1** Sand consists of tiny pieces of stone. Beaches are made of sand. ▶ VERB **2** If you sand something, you rub sandpaper over it to make it smooth.

sandal sandals

NOUN Sandals are light shoes with straps, worn in warm weather.

sandpaper

NOUN Sandpaper is strong paper with a coating of sand on it, used for rubbing surfaces to make them smooth.

sandshoe sandshoes

NOUN In British, Australian, and New Zealand English, a light canvas shoe with a rubber sole.

sandstone

NOUN Sandstone is a type of rock formed from sand, often used for building.

sandwich sandwiches sandwiching sandwiched

NOUN **1** two slices of bread with a filling between them. ▶ VERB **2** If one thing is sandwiched between two others, it is in a narrow space between them EG *a small shop sandwiched between a bar and an office.*

▣ sense 1 is named after the 4th Earl of Sandwich (1718-1792), for whom they were invented so that he could eat and gamble at the same time

sandy sandier sandiest

ADJECTIVE **1** A sandy area is covered with sand. **2** Sandy hair is light orange-brown.

sane saner sanest

ADJECTIVE **1** If someone is sane, they have a normal and healthy mind. **2** A sane action is sensible and reasonable.

sanguine

Said "**sang**-gwin" ADJECTIVE; A FORMAL WORD cheerful and confident.

sanitary

ADJECTIVE Sanitary means concerned with keeping things clean and hygienic EG *improving the sanitary conditions*.

sanitary towel sanitary towels

NOUN Sanitary towels are pads of thick, soft material which women wear during their periods.

sanitation

NOUN Sanitation is the process of keeping places clean and hygienic, especially by providing a sewage system and clean water supply.

sanity

NOUN Your sanity is your ability to think and act normally and reasonably.

sap saps sapping sapped

VERB **1** If something saps your strength or confidence, it gradually weakens and destroys it. ▶ NOUN **2** Sap is the watery liquid in plants.

sapling saplings

NOUN a young tree.

sapphire sapphires

NOUN a blue precious stone.

sarcastic

ADJECTIVE saying or doing the opposite of what you really mean in order to mock or insult someone

A
B
C
D
E
F
G
H
I
J
K
L
M
N
O
P
Q
R
S
T
U
V
W
X
Y
Z

EG *a sarcastic remark.*
sarcasm NOUN, **sarcastically** ADVERB
📖 from Greek *sarkazein* meaning 'to tear the flesh'

sarcophagus **sarcophagi** or **sarcophaguses**
Said "sar-**kof**-fag-uss" NOUN a stone coffin used in ancient times.

sardine **sardines**
NOUN a small edible sea fish.

sardonic
ADJECTIVE mocking or scornful EG *a sardonic grin.*
sardonically ADVERB

sari **saris**
Said "sah-ree" NOUN a piece of clothing worn especially by Indian women, consisting of a long piece of material folded around the body.
📖 a Hindi word

sarmie **sarmies**
NOUN; A SLANG WORD In South African English, a sarmie is a sandwich.

sartorial
ADJECTIVE; A FORMAL WORD relating to clothes EG *sartorial elegance.*

sash **sashes**
NOUN a long piece of cloth worn round the waist or over one shoulder.
📖 from Arabic *shash* meaning 'muslin'

Satan
NOUN Satan is the Devil.
📖 from Hebrew *satan* meaning 'to plot against'

satanic
Said "sa-**tan**-ik" ADJECTIVE caused by or influenced by Satan EG *satanic forces.*

satchel **satchels**
NOUN a leather or cloth bag with a long strap.

satellite **satellites**
NOUN **1** an spacecraft sent into orbit round the earth to collect information or as part of a communications system. **2** a natural object in space that moves round a planet or star.

satin **satins**
NOUN Satin is a kind of smooth, shiny silk.

satire **satires**
NOUN Satire is the use of mocking or ironical humour, especially in literature, to show how foolish or wicked some people are.
satirical ADJECTIVE

satisfaction
NOUN Satisfaction is the feeling of pleasure you get when you do something you wanted or needed to do.

satisfactory
ADJECTIVE acceptable or adequate EG *a satisfactory explanation.*
satisfactorily ADVERB

satisfy **satisfies** **satisfying** **satisfied**
VERB **1** To satisfy someone means to give them enough of something to make them pleased or contented. **2** To satisfy someone that something is the case means to convince them of it. **3** To satisfy the requirements for something means to fulfil them.
satisfied ADJECTIVE
▪ (sense 1) content, indulge, please

satisfying
ADJECTIVE Something that is satisfying gives you a feeling of pleasure and fulfilment.

satsuma **satsumas**
Said "sat-**soo**-ma" NOUN a fruit like a small orange.

saturated
ADJECTIVE **1** very wet. **2** If a place is saturated with things, it is completely full of them.
saturation NOUN

Saturday **Saturdays**
NOUN the day between Friday and Sunday.
📖 from Latin *Saturni dies* meaning 'day of Saturn'

Saturn
NOUN Saturn is the planet in the

solar system which is sixth from the sun.

sauce sauces
NOUN a liquid eaten with food to give it more flavour.

saucepan saucepans
NOUN a deep metal cooking pot with a handle and a lid.

saucer saucers
NOUN a small curved plate for a cup.

saucy saucier sauciest
ADJECTIVE cheeky in an amusing way.

Saudi Saudis
Rhymes with "cloudy" ADJECTIVE
1 belonging or relating to Saudi Arabia. ▶ NOUN **2** someone who comes from Saudi Arabia.

sauna saunas
Said "saw-na" NOUN If you have a sauna, you go into a very hot room in order to sweat, then have a cold bath or shower.
▥ a Finnish word

saunter saunters sauntering sauntered
VERB To saunter somewhere means to walk there slowly and casually.

sausage sausages
NOUN a mixture of minced meat and herbs formed into a tubular shape and served cooked.

sauté sautés sautéing or sautéeing sautéed
Said "soh-tay" VERB To sauté food means to fry it quickly in a small amount of oil or butter.

savage savages savaging savaged
ADJECTIVE **1** cruel and violent EG *savage fighting.* ▶ NOUN **2** If you call someone a savage, you mean that they are violent and uncivilized.
▶ VERB **3** If an animal savages you, it attacks you and bites you.
savagely ADVERB
▦ (sense 1) brutal, cruel, vicious

savagery
NOUN Savagery is cruel and violent behaviour.

save saves saving saved

VERB **1** If you save someone, you rescue them or help to keep them safe EG *He saved my life.* **2** If you save something, you keep it so that you can use it later EG *He'd saved up enough money for the deposit.* **3** To save time, money, or effort means to prevent it from being wasted EG *You could have saved us the trouble.*
▶ PREPOSITION **4** A FORMAL USE Save means except EG *I was alone in the house save for a very old woman.*

saving savings
NOUN **1** a reduction in the amount of time or money used. ▶ PLURAL NOUN **2** Your savings are the money you have saved.

saviour saviours
NOUN **1** If someone saves you from danger, you can refer to them as your saviour. ▶ PROPER NOUN **2** In Christianity, the Saviour is Jesus Christ.

savour savours savouring savoured
VERB If you savour something, you take your time with it and enjoy it fully EG *These spirits should be sipped and savoured like fine whiskies.*

savoury
ADJECTIVE **1** Savoury is salty or spicy. **2** Something that is not very savoury is not very pleasant or respectable EG *the less savoury places.*

saw saws sawing sawed sawn
1 Saw is the past tense of see.
▶ NOUN **2** a tool, with a blade with sharp teeth along one edge, for cutting wood. ▶ VERB **3** If you saw something, you cut it with a saw.

sawdust
NOUN Sawdust is the fine powder produced when you saw wood.

saxophone saxophones
NOUN a curved metal wind instrument often played in jazz bands.
▥ named after Adolphe Sax (1814-1894), who invented the instrument

say says saying said

saying

VERB **1** When you say something, you speak words. **2** 'Say' is used to give an example EG *a maximum fee of, say, a million.* ▶ NOUN **3** If you have a say in something, you can give your opinion and influence decisions.

■ (sense 1) remark, speak, utter

saying sayings

NOUN a well-known sentence or phrase that tells you something about human life.

■ adage, proverb

scab scabs

NOUN a hard, dry covering that forms over a wound.

scabby ADJECTIVE

scaffolding

NOUN Scaffolding is a framework of poles and boards that is used by workmen to stand on while they are working on the outside structure of a building.

scald scalds scalding scalded

Said "skawld" VERB **1** If you scald yourself, you burn yourself with very hot liquid or steam. ▶ NOUN **2** a burn caused by scalding.

scale scales scaling scaled

NOUN **1** The scale of something is its size or extent EG *the sheer scale of the disaster.* **2** a set of levels or numbers used for measuring things. **3** The scale of a map, plan, or model is the relationship between the size of something in the map, plan, or model and its size in the real world EG *a scale of 1:10,000.* **4** an upward or downward sequence of musical notes. **5** The scales of a fish or reptile are the small pieces of hard skin covering its body. ▶ PLURAL NOUN **6** Scales are a piece of equipment used for weighing things. ▶ VERB **7** If you scale something high, you climb it.

scalene

ADJECTIVE A scalene triangle has sides which are all of different lengths.

scallop scallops

NOUN Scallops are edible shellfish with two flat fan-shaped shells.

scalp scalps scalping scalped

NOUN **1** Your scalp is the skin under the hair on your head. **2** the piece of skin and hair removed when someone is scalped. ▶ VERB **3** To scalp someone means to remove the skin and hair from their head in one piece.

scalpel scalpels

NOUN a knife with a thin, sharp blade, used by surgeons.

scamper scampers scampering scampered

VERB To scamper means to move quickly and lightly.

scampi

PLURAL NOUN Scampi are large prawns often eaten fried in breadcrumbs.

scan scans scanning scanned

VERB **1** If you scan something, you look at all of it carefully EG *I scanned the horizon to the north-east.* **2** If a machine scans something, it examines it by means of a beam of light or X-rays. ▶ NOUN **3** an examination or search by a scanner EG *a brain scan.*

scandal scandals

NOUN a situation or event that people think is shocking and immoral.

scandalous ADJECTIVE

Scandinavia

Said "skan-din-**nay**-vee-a" NOUN Scandinavia is the name given to a group of countries in Northern Europe, including Norway, Sweden, Denmark, and sometimes Finland and Iceland.

Scandinavian NOUN OR ADJECTIVE

scanner scanners

NOUN a machine which is used to examine, identify, or record things by means of a beam of light or X-rays.

scant scanter scantest

ADJECTIVE If something receives scant attention, it does not receive enough attention.

scapegoat scapegoats
NOUN If someone is made a scapegoat, they are blamed for something, although it may not be their fault.

scar scars scarring scarred
NOUN **1** a mark left on your skin after a wound has healed. **2** a permanent effect on someone's mind that results from a very unpleasant experience EG *the scars of war.* ▶ VERB **3** If an injury scars you, it leaves a permanent mark on your skin. **4** If an unpleasant experience scars you, it has a permanent effect on you.

scarce scarcer scarcest
ADJECTIVE If something is scarce, there is not very much of it.
scarcity NOUN

scarcely
ADVERB Scarcely means hardly EG *I can scarcely hear her.*
☑ As *scarcely* already has a negative sense, it is followed by *ever* or *any*, and not by *never* or *no*.

scare scares scaring scared
VERB **1** If something scares you, it frightens you. ▶ NOUN **2** If something gives you a scare, it scares you. **3** If there is a scare about something, a lot of people are worried about it EG *an AIDS scare.*
scared ADJECTIVE
▤ (sense 1) alarm, frighten, startle

scarecrow scarecrows
NOUN an object shaped like a person put in a field to scare birds away.

scarf scarfs or scarves
NOUN a piece of cloth worn round your neck or head to keep you warm.

scarlet
NOUN OR ADJECTIVE bright red.

scary scarier scariest
ADJECTIVE; AN INFORMAL WORD frightening.

scathing
Said "skayth-ing" ADJECTIVE harsh and scornful EG *They were scathing about his job.*

scatter scatters scattering scattered
VERB **1** To scatter things means to throw or drop them all over an area. **2** If people scatter, they suddenly move away in different directions.
▤ (sense 1) sprinkle, strew, throw about

scattering
NOUN A scattering of things is a small number of them spread over a large area EG *the scattering of islands.*

scavenge scavenges scavenging scavenged
VERB If you scavenge for things, you search for them among waste and rubbish.
scavenger NOUN

scenario scenarios
Said "sin-**nar**-ee-oh" NOUN **1** The scenario of a film or play is a summary of its plot. **2** the way a situation could possibly develop in the future EG *the worst possible scenario.*

scene scenes
NOUN **1** part of a play or film in which a series of events happen in one place. **2** Pictures and views are sometimes called scenes EG *a village scene.* **3** The scene of an event is the place where it happened. **4** an area of activity EG *the music scene.*

scenery
NOUN **1** In the countryside, you can refer to everything you see as the scenery. **2** In a theatre, the scenery is the painted cloth on the stage which represents the place where the action is happening.

scenic
ADJECTIVE A scenic place or route has nice views.

scent scents scenting scented
NOUN **1** a smell, especially a pleasant one. **2** Scent is perfume. ▶ VERB **3** When an animal scents something, it becomes aware of it

by smelling it.

sceptic sceptics
Said "skep-tik" NOUN someone who has doubts about things that other people believe.
sceptical ADJECTIVE, **scepticism** NOUN

sceptre sceptres
Said "sep-ter" NOUN an ornamental rod carried by a king or queen as a symbol of power.

schedule schedules scheduling scheduled
Said "shed-yool" NOUN 1 a plan that gives a list of events or tasks, together with the times at which each thing should be done. ▶ VERB 2 If something is scheduled to happen, it has been planned and arranged EG *Their journey was scheduled for the beginning of May.*

schema schemata
Said "skee-ma" NOUN 1 A TECHNICAL WORD an outline of a plan or theory. 2 a mental model which the mind uses to understand new experiences or to view the world.

scheme schemes scheming schemed
NOUN 1 a plan or arrangement EG *a five-year development scheme.* ▶ VERB 2 When people scheme, they make secret plans.

schism schisms
Said "skizm" NOUN a split or division within a group or organization.

schizophrenia
Said "skit-soe-free-nee-a" NOUN Schizophrenia is a serious mental illness which prevents someone relating their thoughts and feelings to what is happening around them.
schizophrenic NOUN OR ADJECTIVE
▥ from Greek *skhizein* meaning 'to split' and *phren* meaning 'mind'

scholar scholars
NOUN 1 a person who studies an academic subject and knows a lot about it. 2 In South African English, a scholar is a school pupil.

scholarly
ADJECTIVE having or showing a lot of knowledge.

scholarship scholarships
NOUN 1 If you get a scholarship to a school or university, your studies are paid for by the school or university or by some other organization. 2 Scholarship is academic study and knowledge.

school schools schooling schooled
NOUN 1 a place where children are educated. 2 University departments and colleges are sometimes called schools EG *My oldest son is in medical school.* 3 You can refer to a large group of dolphins or fish as a school. ▶ VERB 4 When someone is schooled in something, they are taught it EG *They were schooled in the modern techniques.*

schoolchild schoolchildren
NOUN Schoolchildren are children who go to school.
schoolboy NOUN, **schoolgirl** NOUN

schooling
NOUN Your schooling is the education you get at school.

schooner schooners
NOUN a sailing ship.

science sciences
NOUN 1 Science is the study of the nature and behaviour of natural things and the knowledge obtained about them. 2 a branch of science, for example physics or biology.

science fiction
NOUN Stories about events happening in the future or in other parts of the universe are called science fiction.

scientific
ADJECTIVE 1 relating to science or to a particular science EG *scientific knowledge.* 2 done in a systematic way, using experiments or tests EG *this scientific method.*
scientifically ADVERB

scientist scientists
NOUN an expert in one of the

sciences who does work connected with it.

scintillating
Said **"sin-til-late-ing"** ADJECTIVE lively and witty EG *scintillating conversation.*

scissors
PLURAL NOUN Scissors are a cutting tool with two sharp blades.

scoff scoffs scoffing scoffed
VERB **1** If you scoff, you speak in a scornful, mocking way about something. **2** AN INFORMAL USE If you scoff food, you eat it quickly and greedily.

scold scolds scolding scolded
VERB If you scold someone, you tell them off.
📇 rebuke, reprimand, tell off

scone scones
Said **"skon"** or **"skone"** NOUN Scones are small cakes made from flour and fat and usually eaten with butter.

scoop scoops scooping scooped
VERB **1** If you scoop something up, you pick it up using a spoon or the palm of your hand. ▶ NOUN **2** an object like a large spoon which is used for picking up food such as ice cream.

scooter scooters
NOUN **1** a small, light motorcycle. **2** a simple cycle which a child rides by standing on it and pushing the ground with one foot.

scope
NOUN **1** If there is scope for doing something, the opportunity to do it exists. **2** The scope of something is the whole subject area which it deals with or includes.

scorch scorches scorching scorched
VERB To scorch something means to burn it slightly.

scorching
ADJECTIVE extremely hot EG *another scorching summer.*

score scores scoring scored
VERB **1** If you score in a game, you

get a goal, run, or point. **2** To score in a game also means to record the score obtained by the players. **3** If you score a success or victory, you achieve it. **4** To score a surface means to cut a line into it. ▶ NOUN **5** The score in a game is the number of goals, runs, or points obtained by the two teams. **6** Scores of things means very many of them EG *Ros entertained scores of celebrities.* **7** AN OLD-FASHIONED USE A score is twenty. **8** The score of a piece of music is the written version of it.
scorer NOUN

scorn scorns scorning scorned
NOUN **1** Scorn is great contempt EG *a look of scorn.* ▶ VERB **2** A FORMAL USE If you scorn something, you refuse to accept it.

scornful
ADJECTIVE showing contempt EG *his scornful comment.*
scornfully ADVERB
📇 contemptuous, disdainful, sneering

Scorpio
NOUN Scorpio is the eighth sign of the zodiac, represented by a scorpion. People born between October 23rd and November 21st are born under this sign.
🔲 from Latin *scorpio* meaning 'scorpion'

scorpion scorpions
NOUN an animal that looks like a small lobster, with a long tail with a poisonous sting on the end.

Scot Scots
NOUN **1** a person who comes from Scotland. ▶ ADJECTIVE **2** Scots means the same as **Scottish.**

scotch scotches
NOUN Scotch is whisky made in Scotland.

Scotsman Scotsmen
NOUN a man who comes from Scotland.
Scotswoman NOUN

Scottish

A
B
C
D
E
F
G
H
I
J
K
L
M
N
O
P
Q
R
S
T
U
V
W
X
Y
Z

ADJECTIVE belonging or relating to Scotland.

scoundrel scoundrels
NOUN; AN OLD-FASHIONED WORD a man who cheats and deceives people.

scour scours scouring scoured
VERB **1** If you scour a place, you look all over it in order to find something EG *The police scoured the area.* **2** If you scour something such as a pan, you clean it by rubbing it with something rough.

scourge scourges
Rhymes with "urge" NOUN something that causes a lot of suffering EG *hay fever, that scourge of summer.*

scout scouts scouting scouted
NOUN **1** a boy who is a member of the Scout Association, an organization for boys which aims to develop character and responsibility. **2** someone who is sent to an area to find out the position of an enemy army. ▶ VERB **3** If you scout around for something, you look around for it.

scowl scowls scowling scowled
VERB **1** If you scowl, you frown because you are angry EG *They were scowling at me.* ▶ NOUN **2** an angry expression.

scrabble scrabbles scrabbling scrabbled
VERB If you scrabble at something, you scrape at it with your hands or feet.
▥ from Old Dutch *schrabbelen* meaning 'to scrape repeatedly'

scramble scrambles scrambling scrambled
VERB **1** If you scramble over something, you climb over it using your hands to help you. ▶ NOUN **2** a motorcycle race over rough ground.

scrap scraps scrapping scrapped
NOUN **1** A scrap of something is a very small piece of it EG *a scrap of cloth.* ▶ PLURAL NOUN **2** Scraps are pieces of leftover food. ▶ ADJECTIVE OR NOUN **3** Scrap metal or scrap is metal

from old machinery or cars that can be re-used. ▶ VERB **4** If you scrap something, you get rid of it EG *They considered scrapping passport controls.*

scrapbook scrapbooks
NOUN a book in which you stick things such as pictures or newspaper articles.

scrape scrapes scraping scraped
VERB **1** If you scrape something off a surface, you remove it by pulling a rough or sharp object over it EG *to scrape the fallen snow off the track.* **2** If something scrapes, it makes a harsh noise by rubbing against something EG *his shoes scraping across the stone ground.*

scratch scratches scratching scratched
VERB **1** To scratch something means to make a small cut on it accidentally EG *They were always getting scratched by cats.* **2** If you scratch, you rub your skin with your nails because it is itching. ▶ NOUN **3** a small cut.

scratchcard scratchcards
NOUN a ticket in a competition with a surface that you scratch off to show whether or not you have won a prize.

scrawl scrawls scrawling scrawled
VERB **1** If you scrawl something, you write it in a careless and untidy way. ▶ NOUN **2** You can refer to careless and untidy writing as a scrawl.

scrawny scrawnier scrawniest
ADJECTIVE thin and bony EG *a small scrawny man.*

scream screams screaming screamed
VERB **1** If you scream, you shout or cry in a loud, high-pitched voice. ▶ NOUN **2** a loud, high-pitched cry.
▤ cry, shriek, yell

screech screeches screeching screeched
VERB **1** To screech means to make an unpleasant high-pitched noise EG *The car wheels screeched.* ▶ NOUN **2** an

unpleasant high-pitched noise.

screen screens screening screened
NOUN **1** a flat vertical surface on which a picture is shown EG *a television screen*. **2** a vertical panel used to separate different parts of a room or to protect something. ▶ VERB **3** To screen a film or television programme means to show it. **4** If you screen someone, you put something in front of them to protect them.

screenplay screenplays
NOUN The screenplay of a film is the script.

screw screws screwing screwed
NOUN **1** a small, sharp piece of metal used for fixing things together or for fixing something to a wall. ▶ VERB **2** If you screw things together, you fix them together using screws. **3** If you screw something onto something else, you fix it there by twisting it round and round EG *He screwed the top on the ink bottle*.
screw up VERB If you screw something up, you twist it or squeeze it so that it no longer has its proper shape EG *Amy screwed up her face*.

screwdriver screwdrivers
NOUN A tool for turning screws.

scribble scribbles scribbling scribbled
VERB **1** If you scribble something, you write it quickly and roughly. **2** To scribble also means to make meaningless marks EG *When Caroline was five she scribbled on a wall*. ▶ NOUN **3** You can refer to something written or drawn quickly and roughly as a scribble.

scrimp scrimps scrimping scrimped
VERB If you scrimp, you live cheaply and spend as little money as you can.

script scripts
NOUN The script of a play or film is

the written version of it.

scripture scriptures
NOUN Scripture refers to sacred writings, especially the Bible.
scriptural ADJECTIVE

scroll scrolls
NOUN a long roll of paper or parchment with writing on it.

scrounge scrounges scrounging scrounged
VERB; AN INFORMAL WORD If you scrounge something, you get it by asking for it rather than by earning or buying it.
scrounger NOUN
■ cadge, sponge

scrub scrubs scrubbing scrubbed
VERB **1** If you scrub something, you clean it with a stiff brush and water. ▶ NOUN **2** If you give something a scrub, you scrub it. **3** Scrub consists of low trees and bushes.

scruff
NOUN The scruff of your neck is the back of your neck or collar.

scruffy scruffier scruffiest
ADJECTIVE dirty and untidy EG *four scruffy youths*.
■ tatty, unkempt

scrum scrums
NOUN When rugby players form a scrum, they form a group and push against each other with their heads down in an attempt to get the ball.

scrunchie scrunchies
NOUN a loop of elastic loosely covered with material which is used to hold hair in a ponytail.

scruple scruples
Said "skroo-pl" NOUN Scruples are moral principles that make you unwilling to do something that seems wrong EG *The West must drop its scruples and fight back*.

scrupulous
ADJECTIVE **1** always doing what is honest or morally right. **2** paying very careful attention to detail EG *a long and scrupulous search*.

scrupulously ADVERB

scrutiny
NOUN If something is under scrutiny, it is being observed very carefully.

scuba diving
NOUN Scuba diving is the sport of swimming underwater with tanks of compressed air on your back.

scuff scuffs scuffing scuffed
VERB 1 If you scuff your feet, you drag them along the ground when you are walking. 2 If you scuff your shoes, you mark them by scraping or rubbing them.

scuffle scuffles scuffling scuffled
NOUN 1 a short, rough fight. ▶ VERB 2 When people scuffle, they fight roughly.

scullery sculleries
NOUN a small room next to a kitchen where washing and cleaning are done.

sculpt sculpts sculpting sculpted
VERB When something is sculpted, it is carved or shaped in stone, wood, or clay.

sculptor sculptors
NOUN someone who makes sculptures.

sculpture sculptures
NOUN 1 a work of art produced by carving or shaping stone or clay. 2 Sculpture is the art of making sculptures.

scum
NOUN Scum is a layer of a dirty substance on the surface of a liquid.

scurrilous
Said "skur-ril-luss" ADJECTIVE abusive and damaging to someone's good name EG scurrilous stories.

scurry scurries scurrying scurried
VERB To scurry means to run quickly with short steps.

scurvy
NOUN Scurvy is a disease caused by a lack of vitamin C.

scuttle scuttles scuttling scuttled

VERB 1 To scuttle means to run quickly. 2 To scuttle a ship means to sink it deliberately by making holes in the bottom. ▶ NOUN 3 a container for coal.

scythe scythes
NOUN a tool with a long handle and a curved blade used for cutting grass or grain.

sea seas
NOUN 1 The sea is the salty water that covers much of the earth's surface. 2 A sea of people or things is a very large number of them EG a sea of red flags.

seagull seagulls
NOUN Seagulls are common white, grey, and black birds that live near the sea.

seahorse seahorses
NOUN a small fish which swims upright, with a head that resembles a horse's head.

seal seals sealing sealed
NOUN 1 an official mark on a document which shows that it is genuine. 2 a piece of wax fixed over the opening of a container. 3 a large mammal with flippers, that lives partly on land and partly in the sea. ▶ VERB 4 If you seal an envelope, you stick down the flap. 5 If you seal an opening, you cover it securely so that air, gas, or liquid cannot get through.

sea lion sea lions
NOUN a type of large seal.

seam seams
NOUN 1 a line of stitches joining two pieces of cloth. 2 A seam of coal is a long, narrow layer of it beneath the ground.

seaman seamen
NOUN a sailor.

seance seances
Said "say-ahnss"; also spelt séance
NOUN a meeting in which people try to communicate with the spirits of dead people.

search searches searching

searched

VERB **1** If you search for something, you look for it in several places. **2** If a person is searched their body and clothing is examined to see if they are hiding anything. ▶ NOUN **3** an attempt to find something.

▤ (sense 1) hunt, look, scour
▤ (sense 3) look, hunt, quest

searching

ADJECTIVE intended to discover the truth about something EG *searching questions*.

searchlight searchlights

NOUN a powerful light whose beam can be turned in different directions.

searing

ADJECTIVE A searing pain is very sharp.

seashore

NOUN The seashore is the land along the edge of the sea.

seasick

ADJECTIVE feeling sick because of the movement of a boat.

seasickness NOUN

seaside

NOUN The seaside is an area next to the sea.

season seasons seasoning seasoned

NOUN **1** The seasons are the periods into which a year is divided and which have their own typical weather conditions. The seasons are spring, summer, autumn, and winter. **2** a period of the year when something usually happens EG *the football season... the hunting season*.
▶ VERB **3** If you season food, you add salt, pepper, or spices to it.

seasonal

ADJECTIVE happening during one season or one time of the year EG *seasonal work*.

seasoned

ADJECTIVE very experienced EG *a seasoned professional*.

seasoning

NOUN Seasoning is flavouring such

as salt and pepper.

season ticket season tickets

NOUN a train or bus ticket that you can use as many times as you like within a certain period.

seat seats seating seated

NOUN **1** something you can sit on. **2** The seat of a piece of clothing is the part that covers your bottom. **3** If someone wins a seat in parliament, they are elected. ▶ VERB **4** If you seat yourself somewhere, you sit down. **5** If a place seats a particular number of people, it has enough seats for that number EG *The theatre seats 570 people*.

seat belt seat belts

NOUN a strap that you fasten across your body for safety when travelling in a car or an aircraft.

seating

NOUN The seating in a place is the number or arrangement of seats there.

seaweed

NOUN Plants that grow in the sea are called seaweed.

secateurs

Said "sek-at-**turz**" PLURAL NOUN Secateurs are small shears for pruning garden plants.

secluded

ADJECTIVE quiet and hidden from view EG *a secluded beach*.

seclusion NOUN

second seconds seconding seconded

ADJECTIVE **1** The second item in a series is the one counted as number two. ▶ NOUN **2** one of the sixty parts that a minute is divided into.
▶ PLURAL NOUN **3** Seconds are goods that are sold cheaply because they are slightly faulty. ▶ VERB **4** If you second a proposal, you formally agree with it so that it can be discussed or voted on. **5** If you are seconded somewhere, you are sent there temporarily to work.

secondly ADVERB

☑ Senses 1-4 are pronounced

A
B
C
D
E
F
G
H
I
J
K
L
M
N
O
P
Q
R
S
T
U
V
W
X
Y
Z

seck-ond, but sense 5 is pronounced sick-*kond*.

secondary

ADJECTIVE **1** Something that is secondary is less important than something else. **2** Secondary education is education for pupils between the ages of eleven and eighteen.

secondary school secondary schools

NOUN a school for pupils between the ages of eleven and eighteen.

second-class

ADJECTIVE **1** Second-class things are regarded as less important than other things of the same kind EG *He has been treated as a second-class citizen.* ▶ ADJECTIVE OR ADVERB **2** Second-class services are cheaper and therefore slower or less comfortable than first-class ones.

second cousin second cousins

NOUN Your second cousins are the children of your parents' cousins.

second-hand

ADJECTIVE OR ADVERB **1** Something that is second-hand has already been owned by someone else EG *a second-hand car.* **2** If you hear a story second-hand, you hear it indirectly, rather than from the people involved.

second-rate

ADJECTIVE of poor quality EG *a second-rate movie.*

secret secrets

ADJECTIVE **1** Something that is secret is told to only a small number of people and hidden from everyone else EG *a secret meeting.* ▶ NOUN **2** a fact told to only a small number of people and hidden from everyone else.

secretly ADVERB, **secrecy** NOUN
■ (sense 1) confidential, concealed, hidden

secret agent secret agents

NOUN a spy.

secretary secretaries

NOUN **1** a person employed by an organization to keep records, write letters, and do office work. **2** Ministers in charge of some government departments are also called secretaries EG *the Health Secretary.*

secretarial ADJECTIVE

secrete secretes secreting secreted

Said "sik-**kreet**" VERB **1** When part of a plant or animal secretes a liquid, it produces it. **2** A FORMAL USE If you secrete something somewhere, you hide it.

secretion NOUN

secretive

ADJECTIVE Secretive people tend to hide their feelings and intentions.
■ reticent, tight-lipped

secret service

NOUN A country's secret service is the government department in charge of espionage.

sect sects

NOUN a religious or political group which has broken away from a larger group.

sectarian

Said "sek-**tair**-ee-an" ADJECTIVE strongly supporting a particular sect EG *sectarian violence.*

section sections

NOUN A section of something is one of the parts it is divided into EG *this section of the motorway.*
■ part, portion, segment

sector sectors

NOUN **1** A sector of something, especially a country's economy, is one part of it EG *the private sector.* **2** A sector of a circle is one of the two parts formed when you draw two straight lines from the centre to the circumference.

secular

ADJECTIVE having no connection with religion EG *secular education.*

secure secures securing secured

VERB **1** A FORMAL USE If you secure

something, you manage to get it EG *They secured the rights to her story.* **2** If you secure a place, you make it safe from harm or attack. **3** To secure something also means to fasten it firmly EG *One end was secured to the pier.* ▶ ADJECTIVE **4** If a place is secure, it is tightly locked or well protected. **5** If an object is secure, it is firmly fixed in place. **6** If you feel secure, you feel safe and confident.
securely ADVERB

security

NOUN OR ADJECTIVE **1** Security means all the precautions taken to protect a place EG *Security forces arrested one member.* ▶ NOUN **2** A feeling of security is a feeling of being safe.

sedate sedates sedating sedated
Said "sid-**date**" ADJECTIVE **1** quiet and dignified. ▶ VERB **2** To sedate someone means to give them a drug to calm them down or make them sleep.
sedately ADVERB

sedative sedatives
Said "**sed**-at-tiv" NOUN **1** a drug that calms you down or makes you sleep. ▶ ADJECTIVE **2** having a calming or soothing effect EG *antihistamines which have a sedative effect.*
sedation NOUN

sedentary
Said "**sed**-en-tree" ADJECTIVE A sedentary occupation is one in which you spend most of your time sitting down.

sediment

NOUN **1** Sediment is solid material that settles at the bottom of a liquid EG *a bottle of beer with sediment in it is usually a guarantee of quality.* **2** Sediment is also small particles of rock that have been worn down and deposited together by water, ice, and wind.

sedimentary

ADJECTIVE Sedimentary rocks are formed from fragments of shells or rocks that have become compressed. Sandstone and limestone are sedimentary rocks.

seduce seduces seducing seduced
VERB **1** To seduce someone means to persuade them to have sex. **2** If you are seduced into doing something, you are persuaded to do it because it seems very attractive.

seductive

ADJECTIVE **1** A seductive person is sexually attractive. **2** Something seductive is very attractive and tempting.
seductively ADVERB

see sees seeing saw seen
VERB **1** If you see something, you are looking at it or you notice it. **2** If you see someone, you visit them or meet them EG *I went to see my dentist.* **3** If you see someone to a place, you accompany them there. **4** To see something also means to realize or understand it EG *I see what you mean.* **5** If you say you will see what is happening, you mean you will find out. **6** If you say you will see if you can do something, you mean you will try to do it. **7** If you see that something is done, you make sure that it is done. **8** If you see to something, you deal with it. **9** 'See' is used to say that an event takes place during a particular period of time EG *The next couple of years saw two momentous developments.*
▶ PHRASES **10** AN INFORMAL USE **Seeing that** or **seeing as** means because EG *I took John for lunch, seeing as it was his birthday.* ▶ NOUN **11** A bishop's see is his diocese.
◾ (sense 1) notice, perceive, spot

seed seeds
NOUN **1** The seeds of a plant are the small, hard parts from which new plants can grow. **2** The seeds of a feeling or process are its beginning or origins EG *the seeds of mistrust.*

seedling seedlings
NOUN a young plant grown from a seed.

seedy seedier seediest

ADJECTIVE untidy and shabby EG *a seedy hotel*.

seek seeks seeking sought
VERB; A FORMAL WORD **1** To seek something means to try to find it, obtain it, or achieve it EG *The police were still seeking information*. **2** If you seek to do something, you try to do it EG *De Gaulle sought to reunite the country*.

seem seems seeming seemed
VERB If something seems to be the case, it appears to be the case or you think it is the case EG *He seemed such a quiet chap*.

seeming
ADJECTIVE appearing to be real or genuine EG *this seeming disregard for human life*.
seemingly ADVERB

seep seeps seeping seeped
VERB If a liquid or gas seeps through something, it flows through very slowly.

seesaw seesaws
NOUN a long plank, supported in the middle, on which two children sit, one on each end, and move up and down in turn.

seething
ADJECTIVE If you are seething about something, you are very angry but it does not show.

segment segments
NOUN **1** A segment of something is one part of it. **2** The segments of an orange or grapefruit are the sections which you can divide it into. **3** A segment of a circle is one of the two parts formed when you draw a straight line across it.

segregate segregates segregating segregated
VERB To segregate two groups of people means to keep them apart from each other.
segregated ADJECTIVE, **segregation** NOUN

seize seizes seizing seized
VERB **1** If you seize something, you grab it firmly EG *He seized the phone*.

2 To seize a place or to seize control of it means to take control of it quickly and suddenly. **3** If you seize an opportunity, you take advantage of it. **4** If you seize on something, you immediately show great interest in it EG *MPs have seized on a new report*.

seizure seizures
Said "seez-yer" NOUN **1** a sudden violent attack of an illness, especially a heart attack or a fit. **2** If there is a seizure of power, a group of people suddenly take control using force.

seldom
ADVERB not very often EG *They seldom speak to each other*.

select selects selecting selected
VERB If you select something, you choose it. ▶ ADJECTIVE **2** of good quality EG *a select gentlemen's club*.
selector NOUN

selection selections
NOUN **1** Selection is the choosing of people or things EG *the selection of parliamentary candidates*. **2** A selection of people or things is a set of them chosen from a larger group. **3** The selection of goods in a shop is the range of goods available EG *a good selection of wines*.

selective
ADJECTIVE choosing things carefully EG *I am selective about what I eat*.
selectively ADVERB

self selves
NOUN Your self is your basic personality or nature EG *Hershey is her normal dependable self*.

self-
PREFIX **1** done to yourself or by yourself EG *self-help... self-control*. **2** doing something automatically EG *a self-loading rifle*.

self-assured
ADJECTIVE behaving in a way that shows confidence in yourself.

self-centred
ADJECTIVE thinking only about

yourself and not about other
people.

self-confessed
ADJECTIVE admitting to having bad
habits or unpopular opinions EG *a
self-confessed liar.*

self-confident
ADJECTIVE confident of your own
abilities or worth.
self-confidence NOUN

self-conscious
ADJECTIVE nervous and easily
embarrassed, and worried about
what other people think of you.
self-consciously ADVERB

self-control
NOUN Self-control is the ability to
restrain yourself and not show your
feelings.

self-defence
NOUN Self-defence is the use of
special physical techniques to
protect yourself when someone
attacks you.

self-employed
ADJECTIVE working for yourself and
organizing your own finances,
rather than working for an
employer.

self-esteem
NOUN Your self-esteem is your good
opinion of yourself.

self-evident
ADJECTIVE Self-evident facts are
completely obvious and need no
proof or explanation.

self-indulgent
ADJECTIVE allowing yourself to do or
have things you enjoy, especially as
a treat.

self-interest
NOUN If you do something out of
self-interest, you do it for your own
benefit rather than to help other
people.

selfish
ADJECTIVE caring only about yourself,
and not about other people.
selfishly ADVERB, **selfishness** NOUN

selfless

ADJECTIVE putting other people's
interests before your own.

self-made
ADJECTIVE rich and successful
through your own efforts EG *a
self-made man.*

self-raising
ADJECTIVE Self-raising flour contains
baking powder to make it rise.

self-respect
NOUN Self-respect is a feeling of
confidence and pride in your own
abilities and worth.

self-righteous
ADJECTIVE convinced that you are
better or more virtuous than other
people.
self-righteousness NOUN
◼ holier-than-thou, sanctimonious

self-service
ADJECTIVE A self-service shop or
restaurant is one where you serve
yourself.

self-sufficient
ADJECTIVE **1** producing or making
everything you need, and so not
needing to buy things. **2** able to
live in a way in which you do not
need other people.

sell sells selling sold
VERB **1** If you sell something, you let
someone have it in return for
money. **2** If a shop sells something,
it has it available for people to buy
EG *a tobacconist that sells stamps.* **3** If
something sells, people buy it EG
This book will sell.
◼ (sense 2) deal in, retail, stock
sell out VERB If a shop has sold out of
something, it has sold it all.
seller NOUN

Sellotape
NOUN; A TRADEMARK Sellotape is a
transparent sticky tape.

semblance
NOUN If there is a semblance of
something, it seems to exist,
although it might not really exist EG
*an effort to restore a semblance of
normality.*

A
B
C
D
E
F
G
H
I
J
K
L
M
N
O
P
Q
R
S
T
U
V
W
X
Y
Z

semen
Said "see-men" NOUN Semen is the liquid containing sperm produced by a man's or male animal's sex organs.

semi-
PREFIX half or partly EG *semiskilled workers*.

semicircle semicircles
NOUN a half of a circle, or something with this shape.
semicircular ADJECTIVE

semicolon semicolons
NOUN the punctuation mark (;), used to separate different parts of a sentence or to indicate a pause.

What does the Semicolon do?

The **semicolon** (;) and the **colon** (:) are often confused and used incorrectly.

The **semicolon** is stronger than a comma, but weaker than a full stop. It can be used to mark the break between two main clauses, especially where there is balance or contrast between them.

I'm not that interested in jazz; I prefer classical music.

The semicolon can also be used instead of a comma to separate clauses or items in a long list.

They did not enjoy the meal: the food was cold; the service was poor; and the music was too loud.

Also look at the grammar box at **colon**.

---

semidetached
ADJECTIVE A semidetached house is joined to another house on one side.

semifinal semifinals
NOUN The semifinals are the two matches in a competition played to decide who plays in the final.
semifinalist NOUN

seminar seminars
NOUN a meeting of a small number of university students or teachers to discuss a particular topic.

Senate Senates
NOUN The Senate is the smaller, more important of the two councils in the government of some countries, for example Australia, Canada, and the USA.

senator senators
NOUN a member of a Senate.

send sends sending sent
VERB 1 If you send something to someone, you arrange for it to be delivered to them. 2 To send a radio signal or message means to transmit it. 3 If you send someone somewhere, you tell them to go there or arrange for them to go. 4 If you send for someone, you send a message asking them to come and see you. 5 If you send off for something, you write and ask for it to be sent to you. 6 To send people or things in a particular direction means to make them move in that direction EG *It should have sent him tumbling from the saddle*.
■ (sense 1) direct, dispatch, forward

senile
ADJECTIVE If old people become senile, they become confused and cannot look after themselves.
senility NOUN

senior seniors
ADJECTIVE 1 The senior people in an organization or profession have the highest and most important jobs.
▶ NOUN 2 Someone who is your senior is older than you.
seniority NOUN

senior citizen senior citizens
NOUN an elderly person, especially one receiving an old-age pension.

sensation sensations
NOUN 1 a feeling, especially a physical feeling. 2 If something is a sensation, it causes great excitement and interest.

sensational
ADJECTIVE 1 causing great excitement and interest. 2 AN INFORMAL USE extremely good EG *a sensational party*.
sensationally ADVERB

sense senses sensing sensed

NOUN **1** Your senses are the physical abilities of sight, hearing, smell, touch, and taste. **2** a feeling EG *a sense of guilt.* **3** A sense of a word is one of its meanings. **4** Sense is the ability to think and behave sensibly. ▶ VERB **5** If you sense something, you become aware of it. ▶ PHRASE **6** If something **makes sense**, you can understand it or it seems sensible EG *It makes sense to find out as much as you can.*

senseless
ADJECTIVE **1** A senseless action has no meaning or purpose EG *senseless destruction.* **2** If someone is senseless, they are unconscious.

sensibility sensibilities
NOUN Your sensibility is your ability to experience deep feelings EG *a man of sensibility rather than reason.*

sensible
ADJECTIVE showing good sense and judgment.
sensibly ADVERB
■ prudent, rational, wise

sensitive
ADJECTIVE **1** If you are sensitive to other people's feelings, you understand them. **2** If you are sensitive about something, you are worried or easily upset about it EG *He was sensitive about his height.* **3** A sensitive subject or issue needs to be dealt with carefully because it can make people angry or upset. **4** Something that is sensitive to a particular thing is easily affected or harmed by it.
sensitively ADVERB, **sensitivity** NOUN

sensor sensors
NOUN an instrument which reacts to physical conditions such as light or heat.

sensual
Said "senss-yool" ADJECTIVE
1 showing or suggesting a liking for sexual pleasures EG *He was a very sensual person.* **2** giving pleasure to your physical senses rather than to your mind EG *the sensual rhythm of*

his voice.
sensuality NOUN

sensuous
ADJECTIVE giving pleasure through the senses.
sensuously ADVERB

sentence sentences sentencing sentenced
NOUN **1** a group of words which make a statement, question, or command. When written down a sentence begins with a capital letter and ends with a full stop. **2** In a law court, a sentence is a punishment given to someone who has been found guilty. ▶ VERB **3** When a guilty person is sentenced, they are told officially what their punishment will be.

What is a Sentence?

The different types of word can go together to make sentences. A sentence is a group of words which expresses an idea or describes a situation.

Sentences begin with a **capital letter**.
The child was sleeping.

Sentences usually end with a **full stop**.
Anna lives in Lisbon.

If a sentence is a question, it ends with a **question mark** instead of a full stop.
Where is my purse?

If a sentence is an exclamation of surprise, anger, or excitement, it ends with an **exclamation mark** instead of a full stop.
You must be joking!

Sentences have a **subject**, which indicates a person or thing. The rest of the sentence usually says something about the subject. The subject is usually the first word or group of words in a sentence.
Anna laughed.
Robbie likes bananas.

Most sentences have a **verb**. The verb says what the subject of the sentence is doing or what is happening to the subject. The verb usually follows immediately after the subject.
Matthew smiled.

Simple Sentences, Compound Sentences, and Complex Sentences
Simple sentences consist of only one

A B C D E F G H I J K L M N O P Q R S T U V W X Y Z

main clause, and no subordinate clause.
Anna fed the cat.

The **subject** of a simple sentence is the person or thing that the sentence is about. It usually comes at the start of the sentence. The subject may be a noun, a pronoun, or a noun phrase.
We often go to the cinema.

The remaining part of the sentence is called the **predicate**. The predicate says something about the subject.
*Anna **likes to go swimming**.*
*She **is a strong swimmer**.*
*A ginger cat **was sitting on the stair**.*

Compound sentences consist of two or more main clauses joined together by a conjunction. Both clauses are equally important.
Anna likes to go swimming, but Matthew likes to go fishing.

Complex sentences consist of a main clause with one or more subordinate clauses joined to it.

Numerous subordinate clauses can be added to a main clause.
***After looking at all the pictures**, the judges gave the first prize, **which was a silver trophy**, to Robbie, **because his work was the best**.*

sentiment sentiments
NOUN **1** a feeling, attitude, or opinion EG *I doubt my parents share my sentiments.* **2** Sentiment consists of feelings such as tenderness or sadness EG *There's no room for sentiment in business.*

sentimental
ADJECTIVE **1** feeling or expressing tenderness or sadness to an exaggerated extent EG *sentimental love stories.* **2** relating to a person's emotions EG *things of sentimental value.*
sentimentality NOUN
▤ (sense 1) emotional, romantic, slushy

sentinel sentinels
NOUN; AN OLD-FASHIONED WORD a sentry.

sentry sentries
NOUN a soldier who keeps watch and

guards a camp or building.

separate separates separating separated
ADJECTIVE **1** If something is separate from something else, the two things are not connected. ▶ VERB **2** To separate people or things means to cause them to be apart from each other. **3** If people or things separate, they move away from each other. **4** If a married couple separate, they decide to live apart.
separately ADVERB, separation NOUN
▤ (sense 2) divide, split, part
▤ (sense 3) diverge, part, part company

sepia
Said "see-pee-a" ADJECTIVE OR NOUN deep brown, like the colour of old photographs.
▥ from Latin *sepia* meaning 'cuttlefish', because the brown dye is obtained from the ink of this fish

September
NOUN September is the ninth month of the year. It has 30 days.
▥ from Latin *September* meaning 'the seventh month'

septic
ADJECTIVE If a wound becomes septic, it becomes infected with poison.

sepulchre sepulchres
Said "sep-pul-ka" NOUN; A LITERARY WORD a large tomb.

sequel sequels
NOUN **1** A sequel to a book or film is another book or film which continues the story. **2** The sequel to an event is a result or consequence of it EG *There's a sequel to my egg story.*

sequence sequences
NOUN **1** A sequence of events is a number of them coming one after the other EG *the whole sequence of events that had brought me to this place.* **2** The sequence in which things are arranged is the order in which they are arranged EG *Do things in the right sequence.*

sequin sequins

NOUN Sequins are small, shiny, coloured discs sewn on clothes to decorate them.

Serbian Serbians
ADJECTIVE **1** belonging to or relating to Serbia. ▶ NOUN **2** someone who comes from Serbia. **3** Serbian is the form of Serbo-Croat spoken in Serbia.

Serbo-Croat
Said "ser-boh-kroh-at" NOUN Serbo-Croat is the main language spoken in Serbia and Croatia.

serenade serenades serenading serenaded
VERB **1** If you serenade someone you love, you sing or play music to them outside their window. ▶ NOUN **2** a song sung outside a woman's window by a man who loves her.

serene
ADJECTIVE peaceful and calm EG *She had a serene air.*
serenely ADVERB, **serenity** NOUN

serf serfs
NOUN Serfs were servants in medieval Europe who had to work on their master's land and could not leave without his permission.

sergeant sergeants
NOUN **1** a noncommissioned officer of middle rank in the army or air force. **2** a police officer just above a constable in rank.

sergeant major sergeant majors
NOUN a noncommissioned army officer of the highest rank.

serial serials
NOUN a story which is broadcast or published in a number of parts over a period of time EG *a television serial.*

serial number serial numbers
NOUN An object's serial number is a number you can see on it which identifies it and distinguishes it from other objects of the same kind.

series
NOUN **1** A series of things is a number of them coming one after the other EG *a series of loud explosions.* **2** A radio or television series is a set of programmes with the same title.
■ (sense 1) sequence, set, succession

serious
ADJECTIVE **1** A serious problem or situation is very bad and worrying. **2** Serious matters are important and should be thought about carefully. **3** If you are serious about something, you are sincere about it EG *You are really serious about having a baby.* **4** People who are serious are thoughtful, quiet, and do not laugh much.
seriousness NOUN
■ (sense 1) grave, severe
■ (sense 4) grave, solemn

seriously
ADVERB **1** You say seriously to emphasize that you mean what you say EG *Seriously, though, something must be done.* ▶ PHRASE **2** If you **take something seriously**, you regard it as important.

sermon sermons
NOUN a talk on a religious or moral subject given as part of a church service.

serpent serpents
NOUN; A LITERARY WORD a snake.

serrated
ADJECTIVE having a row of V-shaped points along the edge, like a saw EG *green serrated leaves.*

servant servants
NOUN someone who is employed to work in another person's house.

serve serves serving served
VERB **1** If you serve a country, an organization, or a person, you do useful work for them. **2** To serve as something means to act or be used as that thing EG *the room that served as their office.* **3** If something serves people in a particular place, it provides them with something they need EG *a recycling plant which*

A B C D E F G H I J K L M N O P Q R S T U V W X Y Z

serves the whole of the county. **4** If you serve food or drink to people, you give it to them. **5** To serve customers in a shop means to help them and provide them with what they want. **6** To serve a prison sentence or an apprenticeship means to spend time doing it. **7** When you serve in tennis or badminton, you throw the ball or shuttlecock into the air and hit it over the net to start playing. ▶ NOUN **8** the act of serving in tennis or badminton.

service **services servicing serviced**

NOUN **1** a system organized to provide something for the public EG *the bus service*. **2** Some government organizations are called services EG *the diplomatic service*. **3** The services are the army, the navy, and the air force. **4** If you give your services to a person or organization, you work for them or help them in some way EG *services to the community*. **5** In a shop or restaurant, service is the process of being served. **6** a religious ceremony. **7** When it is your service in a game of tennis or badminton, it is your turn to serve. ▶ PLURAL NOUN **8** Motorway services consist of a garage, restaurant, shop, and toilets. ▶ VERB **9** When a machine or vehicle is serviced, it is examined and adjusted so that it will continue working efficiently.

serviceman **servicemen**

NOUN a man in the army, navy, or air force.
servicewoman NOUN

service station **service stations**

NOUN a garage that sells petrol, oil, spare parts, and snacks.

servile

ADJECTIVE too eager to obey people.
servility NOUN
◼ obsequious, subservient

serving **servings**

NOUN **1** a helping of food. ▶ ADJECTIVE **2** A serving spoon or dish is used for serving food.

session **sessions**

NOUN **1** a meeting of an official group EG *the emergency session of the Indiana Supreme Court*. **2** a period during which meetings are held regularly EG *the end of the parliamentary session*. **3** The period during which an activity takes place can also be called a session EG *a drinking session*.

set **sets setting set**

NOUN **1** Several things make a set when they belong together or form a group EG *a set of weights*. **2** In maths, a set is a collection of numbers or other things which are treated as a group. **3** A television set is a television. **4** The set for a play or film is the scenery or furniture on the stage or in the studio. **5** In tennis, a set is a group of six or more games. There are usually several sets in a match. ▶ VERB **6** If something is set somewhere, that is where it is EG *The house was set back from the beach.* **7** When the sun sets, it goes below the horizon. **8** When you set the table, you prepare it for a meal by putting plates and cutlery on it. **9** When you set a clock or a control, you adjust it to a particular point or position. **10** If you set someone a piece of work or a target, you give it to them to do or to achieve. **11** When something such as jelly or cement sets, it becomes firm or hard. ▶ ADJECTIVE **12** Something that is set is fixed and not varying EG *a set charge*. **13** If you are set to do something, you are ready or likely to do it. **14** If you are set on doing something, you are determined to do it. **15** If a play or story is set at a particular time or in a particular place, the events in it take place at that time or in that place.
◼ (sense 12) fixed, hard and fast, inflexible
set about VERB If you set about doing

something, you start doing it.

set back VERB If something sets back a project or scheme, it delays it.

set off VERB **1** When you set off, you start a journey. **2** To set something off means to cause it to start.

set out VERB **1** When you set out, you start a journey. **2** If you set out to do something, you start trying to do it.

set up VERB If you set something up, you make all the necessary preparations for it EG *We have done all we can about setting up a system of communication.*

setback settbacks
NOUN something that delays or hinders you.

settee settees
NOUN a long comfortable seat for two or three people to sit on.

setter setters
NOUN a long-haired breed of dog originally used in hunting.

setting settings
NOUN **1** The setting of something is its surroundings or circumstances EG *The Irish setting made the story realistic.* **2** The settings on a machine are the different positions to which the controls can be adjusted.

settle settles settling settled
VERB **1** To settle an argument means to put an end to it EG *The dispute was settled.* **2** If something is settled, it has all been decided and arranged. **3** If you settle on something or settle for it, you choose it EG *We settled for orange juice and coffee.* **4** When you settle a bill, you pay it. **5** If you settle in a place, you make it your permanent home. **6** If you settle yourself somewhere, you sit down and make yourself comfortable. **7** If something settles, it sinks slowly down and comes to rest EG *A black dust settled on the walls.*

settle down VERB **1** When someone settles down, they start living a quiet life in one place, especially when they get married. **2** To settle down means to become quiet or calm.

settlement settlements
NOUN **1** an official agreement between people who have been involved in a conflict EG *the last chance for a peaceful settlement.* **2** a place where people have settled and built homes.

settler settlers
NOUN someone who settles in a new country EG *the first settlers in Cuba.*

seven
the number 7.

seventeen
the number 17.
seventeenth

seventh sevenths
1 The seventh item in a series is the one counted as number seven.
▶ NOUN **2** one of seven equal parts.

seventy seventies
the number 70.
seventieth

sever severs severing severed
VERB **1** To sever something means to cut it off or cut right through it. **2** If you sever a connection with someone or something, you end it completely EG *She severed her ties with England.*

several
ADJECTIVE OR PRONOUN Several people or things means a small number of them.

severe
ADJECTIVE **1** extremely bad or unpleasant EG *severe stomach pains.* **2** stern and harsh EG *Perhaps I was too severe with that young man.*
severely ADVERB, **severity** NOUN

sew sews sewing sewed sewn
Said "so" VERB When you sew things together, you join them using a needle and thread.
sewing NOUN

sewage
NOUN Sewage is dirty water and

A B C D E F G H I J K L M N O P Q R S T U V W X Y Z

waste which is carried away in sewers.

sewer sewers
NOUN an underground channel that carries sewage to a place where it is treated to make it harmless.

sewerage
NOUN Sewerage is the system by which sewage is carried away and treated.

sex sexes
NOUN **1** The sexes are the two groups, male and female, into which people and animals are divided. **2** The sex of a person or animal is their characteristic of being either male or female. **3** Sex is the physical activity by which people and animals produce young.

sexism
NOUN Sexism is discrimination against the members of one sex, usually women.
sexist ADJECTIVE OR NOUN

sextet sextets
NOUN a group of six musicians who sing or play together; also a piece of music written for six instruments or singers.

sextuplet sextuplets
NOUN Sextuplets are six children born at the same time to the same mother.

sexual
ADJECTIVE **1** connected with the act of sex or with people's desire for sex EG *sexual attraction*. **2** relating to the difference between males and females EG *sexual equality*. **3** relating to the biological process by which people and animals produce young EG *sexual reproduction*.
sexually ADVERB

sexual intercourse
NOUN Sexual intercourse is the physical act of sex between two people.

sexuality
Said "seks-yoo-**al**-it-ee" NOUN A person's sexuality is their ability to experience sexual feelings.

sexy sexier sexiest
ADJECTIVE sexually attractive or exciting EG *these sexy blue eyes*.

shabby shabbier shabbiest
ADJECTIVE **1** old and worn in appearance EG *a shabby overcoat*. **2** dressed in old, worn-out clothes EG *a shabby figure crouching in a doorway*. **3** behaving in a mean or unfair way EG *shabby treatment*.
shabbily ADVERB
■ (sense 1) tatty, threadbare, worn

shack shacks
NOUN a small hut.

shackle shackles shackling shackled
NOUN **1** In the past, shackles were two metal rings joined by a chain fastened around a prisoner's wrists or ankles. ▶ VERB **2** To shackle someone means to put shackles on them. **3** A LITERARY USE If you are shackled by something, it restricts or hampers you.

shade shades shading shaded
NOUN **1** Shade is an area of darkness and coolness which the sun does not reach EG *The table was in the shade*. **2** a lampshade. **3** The shades of a colour are its different forms. For example, olive green is a shade of green. ▶ VERB **4** If a place is shaded by trees or buildings, they prevent the sun from shining on it. **5** If you shade your eyes, you put your hand in front of them to protect them from a bright light.

shadow shadows shadowing shadowed
NOUN **1** the dark shape made when an object prevents light from reaching a surface. **2** Shadow is darkness caused by light not reaching a place. ▶ VERB **3** To shadow someone means to follow them and watch them closely.

shadow cabinet
NOUN The shadow cabinet consists of the leaders of the main opposition party, each of whom is

concerned with a particular policy.

shadowy
ADJECTIVE **1** A shadowy place is dark and full of shadows. **2** A shadowy figure or shape is difficult to see because it is dark or misty.

shady shadier shadiest
ADJECTIVE A shady place is sheltered from sunlight by trees or buildings.

shaft shafts
NOUN **1** a vertical passage, for example one for a lift or one in a mine. **2** A shaft of light is a beam of light. **3** A shaft in a machine is a rod which revolves and transfers movement in the machine EG *the drive shaft.*

shake shakes shaking shook shaken
VERB **1** To shake something means to move it quickly from side to side or up and down. **2** If something shakes, it moves from side to side or up and down with small, quick movements. **3** If your voice shakes, it trembles because you are nervous or angry. **4** If something shakes you, it shocks and upsets you. **5** When you shake your head, you move it from side to side in order to say 'no'. ▶ NOUN **6** If you give something a shake, you shake it. ▶ PHRASE **7** When you **shake hands** with someone, you grasp their hand as a way of greeting them. ■ (sense 2) quiver, tremble, vibrate

shaky shakier shakiest
ADJECTIVE rather weak and unsteady EG *Confidence in the economy is still shaky.*
shakily ADVERB

shall
VERB **1** If I say I shall do something, I mean that I intend to do it. **2** If I say something shall happen, I am emphasizing that it will definitely happen, or I am ordering it to happen EG *There shall be work and security!* **3** 'Shall' is also used in questions when you are asking what to do, or making a suggestion

EG *Shall we sit down... Shall I go and check for you?*

shallow shallower shallowest; shallows
ADJECTIVE **1** Shallow means not deep. **2** Shallow also means not involving serious thought or sincere feelings EG *a well-meaning but shallow man.* ▶ PLURAL NOUN **3** The shallows are the shallow part of a river or lake.

sham shams
NOUN **1** Something that is a sham is not real or genuine. ▶ ADJECTIVE **2** not real or genuine EG *a sham display of affection.*

shambles
NOUN If an event is a shambles, it is confused and badly organized.

shame shames shaming shamed
NOUN **1** Shame is the feeling of guilt or embarrassment you get when you know you have done something wrong or foolish. **2** To bring shame on someone means to

make people lose respect for them EG *the scenes that brought shame to English soccer.* **3** If you say something is a shame, you mean you are sorry about it EG *It's a shame you can't come round.* ▶ INTERJECTION **4** AN INFORMAL EXPRESSION In South African English, you say 'Shame!' to show sympathy. ▶ VERB **5** If something shames you, it makes you feel ashamed. **6** If you shame someone into doing something, you force them to do it by making them feel ashamed not to EG *Two children shamed their parents into giving up cigarettes.*

shameful
ADJECTIVE If someone's behaviour is shameful, they ought to be ashamed of it.
shamefully ADVERB

shameless
ADJECTIVE behaving in an indecent or unacceptable way, but showing no shame EG *shameless dishonesty.*
shamelessly ADVERB
▤ barefaced, brazen, flagrant

shampoo shampoos shampooing shampooed
NOUN **1** Shampoo is a soapy liquid used for washing your hair. ▶ VERB **2** When you shampoo your hair, you wash it with shampoo.
▥ from Hindi *champna* meaning 'to knead'

shamrock shamrocks
NOUN a plant with three round leaves on each stem which is the national emblem of Ireland.
▥ from Irish Gaelic *seamrog* meaning 'little clover'

shanghai shanghais shanghaiing shanghaied
AN INFORMAL WORD ▶ VERB **1** If someone is shanghaied, they are kidnapped and forced to work on a ship. **2** If you shanghai someone, you trick or force them into doing something. ▶ NOUN **3** In Australian and New Zealand English, a catapult.

shanty shanties
NOUN **1** a small, rough hut. **2** A sea shanty is a song sailors used to sing.

shape shapes shaping shaped
NOUN **1** The shape of something is the form or pattern of its outline, for example whether it is round or square. **2** something with a definite form, for example a circle or triangle. **3** The shape of something such as an organization is its structure and size. ▶ VERB **4** If you shape an object, you form it into a particular shape EG *Shape the dough into an oblong.* **5** To shape something means to cause it to develop in a particular way EG *events that shaped the lives of some of the leading characters.*
▤ (sense 1) figure, form, outline

shapeless
ADJECTIVE not having a definite shape.

shapely shapelier shapeliest
ADJECTIVE A shapely woman has an attractive figure.

shard shards
NOUN a small fragment of pottery, glass, or metal.

share shares sharing shared
VERB **1** If two people share something, they both use it, do it, or have it EG *We shared a bottle of champagne.* **2** If you share an idea or a piece of news with someone, you tell it to them. ▶ NOUN **3** A share of something is a portion of it. **4** The shares of a company are the equal parts into which its ownership is divided. People can buy shares as an investment.
▤ (sense 3) lot, part, portion
share out VERB If you share something out, you give it out equally among a group of people.

shareholder shareholders
NOUN a person who owns shares in a company.

share-milker share-milkers
NOUN In New Zealand, someone who works on a dairy farm and shares the profit from the sale of its

produce.

shark sharks

NOUN **1** Sharks are large, powerful fish with sharp teeth. **2** a person who cheats people out of money.

sharp sharper sharpest; sharps

ADJECTIVE **1** A sharp object has a fine edge or point that is good for cutting or piercing things. **2** A sharp outline or distinction is easy to see. **3** A sharp person is quick to notice or understand things. **4** A sharp change is sudden and significant EG *a sharp rise in prices.* **5** If you say something in a sharp way, you say it firmly and rather angrily. **6** A sharp sound is short, sudden, and quite loud. **7** A sharp pain is sudden and painful. **8** A sharp taste is slightly sour. **9** A musical instrument or note that is sharp is slightly too high in pitch. ▶ ADVERB **10** If something happens at a certain time sharp, it happens at that time precisely EG *You'll begin at eight o'clock sharp.* ▶ NOUN **11** In music, a sharp is a note or key a semitone higher than that described by the same letter. It is represented by the symbol (♯).
sharply ADVERB, **sharpness** NOUN
■ (sense 3) astute, perceptive, quick-witted

sharpen sharpens sharpening sharpened

VERB **1** To sharpen an object means to make its edge or point sharper. **2** If your senses or abilities sharpen, you become quicker at noticing or understanding things.
sharpener NOUN

shatter shatters shattering shattered

VERB **1** If something shatters, it breaks into a lot of small pieces. **2** If something shatters your hopes or beliefs, it destroys them completely. **3** If you are shattered by an event or piece of news, you are shocked and upset by it.

shattered

ADJECTIVE; AN INFORMAL WORD
completely exhausted EG *He must be absolutely shattered after all his efforts.*

shattering

ADJECTIVE making you feel shocked and upset EG *a shattering event.*

shave shaves shaving shaved

VERB **1** When a man shaves, he removes hair from his face with a razor. **2** If you shave off part of a piece of wood, you cut thin pieces from it. ▶ NOUN **3** When a man has a shave, he shaves.

shaven

ADJECTIVE If part of someone's body is shaven, it has been shaved EG *a shaven head.*

shaver shavers

NOUN an electric razor.

shavings

PLURAL NOUN Shavings are small, very thin pieces of wood which have been cut from a larger piece.

shawl shawls

NOUN a large piece of woollen cloth worn round a woman's head or shoulders or used to wrap a baby in.

she

PRONOUN 'She' is used to refer to a woman or girl whose identity is clear. 'She' is also used to refer to a country, a ship, or a car.

sheaf sheaves

NOUN **1** A sheaf of papers is a bundle of them. **2** A sheaf of corn is a bundle of ripe corn tied together.

shear shears shearing sheared shorn

VERB **1** To shear a sheep means to cut the wool off it. ▶ PLURAL NOUN **2** Shears are a tool like a large pair of scissors, used especially for cutting hedges.

sheath sheaths

NOUN **1** a covering for the blade of a knife. **2** a condom.

shed sheds shedding shed

NOUN **1** a small building used for storing things. ▶ VERB **2** When an animal sheds hair or skin, some of

A B C D E F G H I J K L M N O P Q R S T U V W X Y Z

its hair or skin drops off. When a tree sheds its leaves, its leaves fall off. **3** A FORMAL USE To shed something also means to get rid of it EG *The firm is to shed 700 jobs.* **4** If a lorry sheds its load, the load falls off the lorry onto the road. **5** If you shed tears, you cry.

sheen
NOUN a gentle brightness on the surface of something.

sheep
NOUN A sheep is a farm animal with a thick woolly coat. Sheep are kept for meat and wool.
☑ The plural of *sheep* is *sheep*.

sheep-dip sheep-dips
NOUN a liquid disinfectant used to keep sheep clean and free of pests.

sheepdog sheepdogs
NOUN a breed of dog often used for controlling sheep.

sheepish
ADJECTIVE If you look sheepish, you look embarrassed because you feel shy or foolish.
sheepishly ADVERB

sheepskin
NOUN Sheepskin is the skin and wool of a sheep, used for making rugs and coats.

sheer sheerer sheerest
ADJECTIVE **1** Sheer means complete and total EG *sheer exhaustion.* **2** A sheer cliff or drop is vertical. **3** Sheer fabrics are very light and delicate.

sheet sheets
NOUN **1** a large rectangular piece of cloth used to cover a bed. **2** A sheet of paper is a rectangular piece of it. **3** A sheet of glass or metal is a large, flat piece of it.

sheik sheiks
Said "shake"; also spelt **sheikh**
NOUN an Arab chief or ruler.
▦ from Arabic *shaykh* meaning 'old man'

shelf shelves
NOUN a flat piece of wood, metal, or

glass fixed to a wall and used for putting things on.

shell shells shelling shelled
NOUN **1** The shell of an egg or nut is its hard covering. **2** The shell of a tortoise, snail, or crab is the hard protective covering on its back. **3** The shell of a building or other structure is its frame EG *The room was just an empty shell.* **4** a container filled with explosives that can be fired from a gun. ▶ VERB **5** If you shell peas or nuts, you remove their natural covering. **6** To shell a place means to fire large explosive shells at it.

shellfish shellfish or shellfishes
NOUN a small sea creature with a shell.

shelter shelters sheltering sheltered
NOUN **1** a small building made to protect people from bad weather or danger. **2** If a place provides shelter, it provides protection from bad weather or danger. ▶ VERB **3** If you shelter in a place, you stay there and are safe. **4** If you shelter someone, you provide them with a place to stay when they are in danger.

sheltered
ADJECTIVE **1** A sheltered place is protected from wind and rain. **2** If you lead a sheltered life, you do not experience unpleasant or upsetting things. **3** Sheltered accommodation is accommodation designed for old or handicapped people.

shelve shelves shelving shelved
VERB If you shelve a plan, you decide to postpone it for a while.

shepherd shepherds shepherding shepherded
NOUN **1** a person who looks after sheep. ▶ VERB **2** If you shepherd someone somewhere, you accompany them there.

sheriff sheriffs
NOUN **1** In America, a sheriff is a

person elected to enforce the law in a county. **2** In Australia, an administrative officer of the Supreme Court who carries out writs and judgments.

🔳 from Old English *scir* meaning 'shire' and *gerefa* meaning 'reeve', an official

sherry sherries
NOUN Sherry is a kind of strong wine.

🔳 from the Spanish town *Jerez* where it was first made

shield shields shielding shielded
NOUN **1** a large piece of a strong material like metal or plastic which soldiers or policeman carry to protect themselves. **2** If something is a shield against something, it gives protection from it. ▶ VERB **3** To shield someone means to protect them from something.

shift shifts shifting shifted
VERB **1** If you shift something, you move it. If something shifts, it moves EG *to shift the rubble.* **2** If an opinion or situation shifts, it changes slightly. ▶ NOUN **3** A shift in an opinion or situation is a slight change. **4** a set period during which people work in a factory EG *the night shift.*

shilling shillings
NOUN a former British, Australian, and New Zealand coin worth one-twentieth of a pound.

shimmer shimmers shimmering shimmered
VERB **1** If something shimmers, it shines with a faint, flickering light. ▶ NOUN **2** a faint, flickering light.

shin shins shinning shinned
NOUN **1** Your shin is the front part of your leg between your knee and your ankle. ▶ VERB **2** If you shin up a tree or pole, you climb it quickly by gripping it with your hands and legs.

shine shines shining shone
VERB **1** When something shines, it gives out or reflects a bright light EG

The stars shone brilliantly. **2** If you shine a torch or lamp somewhere, you point it there.

shingle shingles
NOUN **1** Shingle consists of small pebbles on the seashore. **2** Shingles are small wooden roof tiles. **3** Shingles is a disease that causes a painful red rash, especially around the waist.

shining
ADJECTIVE **1** Shining things are very bright, usually because they are reflecting light EG *shining stainless steel tables.* **2** A shining example of something is a very good or typical example of that thing EG *a shining example of courage.*

🟩 (sense 1) bright, gleaming

shiny shinier shiniest
ADJECTIVE Shiny things are bright and look as if they have been polished EG *a shiny brass plate.*

ship ships shipping shipped
NOUN **1** a large boat which carries passengers or cargo. ▶ VERB **2** If people or things are shipped somewhere, they are transported there.

shipment shipments
NOUN **1** a quantity of goods that are transported somewhere EG *a shipment of olive oil.* **2** The shipment of goods is the transporting of them.

shipping
NOUN **1** Shipping is the transport of cargo on ships. **2** You can also refer to ships generally as shipping EG *Attention all shipping!*

shipwreck shipwrecks
NOUN When there is a shipwreck, a ship is destroyed in an accident at sea EG *He was drowned in a shipwreck.*

shipyard shipyards
NOUN a place where ships are built and repaired.

shiralee shiralees
NOUN; AN OLD-FASHIONED WORD In Australian English, the bundle of

A
B
C
D
E
F
G
H
I
J
K
L
M
N
O
P
Q
R
S
T
U
V
W
X
Y
Z

A
B
C
D
E
F
G
H
I
J
K
L
M
N
O
P
Q
R
S
T
U
V
W
X
Y
Z

possessions carried by a swagman.

shire shires
NOUN **1** AN OLD-FASHIONED USE In Britain, a county. **2** In Australia, a rural district with its own local council.

shirk shirks shirking shirked
VERB To shirk a task means to avoid doing it.

shirt shirts
NOUN a piece of clothing worn on the upper part of the body, having a collar, sleeves, and buttons down the front.

shiver shivers shivering shivered
VERB **1** When you shiver, you tremble slightly because you are cold or scared. ▶ NOUN **2** a slight trembling caused by cold or fear.

shoal shoals
NOUN A shoal of fish is a large group of them swimming together.

shock shocks shocking shocked
NOUN **1** If you have a shock, you have a sudden upsetting experience. **2** Shock is a person's emotional and physical condition when something very unpleasant or upsetting has happened to them. **3** In medicine, shock is a serious physical condition in which the blood cannot circulate properly because of an injury. **4** a slight movement in something when it is hit by something else EG *The straps help to absorb shocks.* **5** A shock of hair is a thick mass of it. ▶ VERB **6** If something shocks you, it upsets you because it is unpleasant and unexpected EG *I was shocked by his appearance.* **7** You can say that something shocks you when it offends you because it is rude or immoral.
shocked ADJECTIVE
▤ (sense 6) appal, horrify
▤ (sense 7) disgust, scandalize

shocking
ADJECTIVE **1** AN INFORMAL USE very bad EG *It's been a shocking year.* **2** rude or immoral EG *a shocking video.*

shoddy shoddier shoddiest

ADJECTIVE badly made or done EG *a shoddy piece of work.*

shoe shoes shoeing shod
NOUN **1** Shoes are strong coverings for your feet. They cover most of your foot, but not your ankle. ▶ VERB **2** To shoe a horse means to fix horseshoes onto its hooves.

shoestring
NOUN If you do something on a shoestring, you do it using very little money.

shoot shoots shooting shot
VERB **1** To shoot a person or animal means to kill or injure them by firing a gun at them. **2** To shoot an arrow means to fire it from a bow. **3** If something shoots in a particular direction, it moves there quickly and suddenly EG *They shot back into Green Street.* **4** When a film is shot, it is filmed EG *The whole film was shot in California.* **5** In games such as football or hockey, to shoot means to kick or hit the ball towards the goal. ▶ NOUN **6** an occasion when people hunt animals or birds with guns. **7** a plant that is beginning to grow, or a new part growing from a plant.

shooting shootings
NOUN an incident in which someone is shot.

shooting star shooting stars
NOUN a meteor.

shop shops shopping shopped
NOUN **1** a place where things are sold. **2** a place where a particular type of work is done EG *a bicycle repair shop.* ▶ VERB **3** When you shop, you go to the shops to buy things.
shopper NOUN

shopkeeper shopkeepers
NOUN someone who owns or manages a small shop.

shoplifting
NOUN Shoplifting is stealing goods from shops.
shoplifter NOUN

shopping

NOUN Your shopping is the goods you have bought from the shops.

shop steward shop stewards
NOUN a trade union member elected to represent the workers in a factory or office.

shore shores shoring shored
NOUN **1** The shore of a sea, lake, or wide river is the land along the edge of it. ▶ VERB **2** If you shore something up, you reinforce it or strengthen it EG *a short-term solution to shore up the worst defence in the League.*

shoreline shorelines
NOUN the edge of a sea, lake, or wide river.

shorn
1 Shorn is the past participle of **shear**. ▶ ADJECTIVE **2** Grass or hair that is shorn is cut very short.

short shorter shortest; shorts
ADJECTIVE **1** not lasting very long. **2** small in length, distance, or height EG *a short climb... the short road.* **3** If you are short with someone, you speak to them crossly. **4** If you have a short temper, you get angry very quickly. **5** If you are short of something, you do not have enough of it. **6** If a name is short for another name, it is a short version of it. ▶ PLURAL NOUN **7** Shorts are trousers with short legs. ▶ ADVERB **8** If you stop short of a place, you do not quite reach it. ▶ PHRASE **9** Short of is used to say that a level or amount has not quite been reached EG *a hundred votes short of a majority.*
■ (sense 3) abrupt, curt, sharp

shortage shortages
NOUN If there is a shortage of something, there is not enough of it.

shortbread
NOUN Shortbread is a crumbly biscuit made from flour and butter. ▥ from an old-fashioned use of *short* meaning 'crumbly'

short circuit short circuits

NOUN a fault in an electrical system when two points accidentally become connected and the electricity travels directly between them rather than through the complete circuit.

shortcoming shortcomings
NOUN Shortcomings are faults or weaknesses.

shortcut shortcuts
NOUN **1** a quicker way of getting somewhere than the usual route. **2** a quicker way of doing something EG *Stencils have been used as a shortcut to hand painting.*

shorten shortens shortening shortened
VERB If you shorten something or if it shortens, it becomes shorter EG *This might help to shorten the conversation.*

shortfall shortfalls
NOUN If there is a shortfall in something, there is less than you need.

shorthand
NOUN Shorthand is a way of writing in which signs represent words or syllables. It is used to write down quickly what someone is saying.

short-list short-lists short-listing short-listed
NOUN **1** a list of people selected from a larger group, from which one person is finally selected for a job or prize. ▶ VERB **2** If someone is short-listed for a job or prize, they are put on a short-list.

shortly
ADVERB **1** Shortly means soon EG *I'll be back shortly.* **2** If you speak to someone shortly, you speak to them in a cross and impatient way.

short-sighted
ADJECTIVE **1** If you are short-sighted, you cannot see things clearly when they are far away. **2** A short-sighted decision does not take account of the way things may develop in the future.

A
B
C
D
E
F
G
H
I
J
K
L
M
N
O
P
Q
R
S
T
U
V
W
X
Y
Z

short-term
ADJECTIVE happening or having an effect within a short time or for a short time.

shot shots
1 Shot is the past tense and past participle of **shoot**. ▸ NOUN **2** the act of firing a gun. **3** Someone who is a good shot can shoot accurately. **4** In football, golf, and tennis, a shot is the act of kicking or hitting the ball. **5** a photograph or short film sequence EG *I'd like to get some shots of the river.* **6** AN INFORMAL USE If you have a shot at something, you try to do it.

shotgun shotguns
NOUN a gun that fires a lot of small pellets all at once.

shot put
NOUN In athletics, the shot put is an event in which the contestants throw a heavy metal ball called a shot as far as possible.
shot putter NOUN

should
VERB **1** You use 'should' to say that something ought to happen EG *Ward should have done better.* **2** You also use 'should' to say that you expect something to happen EG *He should have heard by now.* **3** A FORMAL USE You can use 'should' to announce that you are about to do or say something EG *I should like to express my thanks to the Professor.* **4** 'Should' is used in conditional sentences EG *If they should discover the fact, what use would the knowledge be to them?* **5** 'Should' is sometimes used in 'that' clauses EG *It is inevitable that you should go.* **6** If you say that you should think something, you mean that it is probably true EG *I should think that's unlikely.*

shoulder shoulders shouldering shouldered
NOUN **1** Your shoulders are the parts of your body between your neck and the tops of your arms. ▸ VERB

2 If you shoulder something heavy, you put it across one of your shoulders to carry it. **3** If you shoulder the responsibility or blame for something, you accept it.

shoulder blade shoulder blades
NOUN Your shoulder blades are the two large, flat bones in the upper part of your back, below your shoulders.

shout shouts shouting shouted
NOUN **1** a loud call or cry. ▸ VERB **2** If you shout something, you say it very loudly EG *He shouted something to his brother.*
■ call, cry, yell

shove shoves shoving shoved
VERB **1** If you shove someone or something, you push them roughly EG *He shoved his wallet into a back pocket.* ▸ NOUN **2** a rough push.
shove off VERB; AN INFORMAL USE If you tell someone to shove off, you are telling them angrily and rudely to go away.

shovel shovels shovelling shovelled
NOUN **1** a tool like a spade, used for moving earth or snow. ▸ VERB **2** If you shovel earth or snow, you move it with a shovel.

show shows showing showed shown
VERB **1** To show that something exists or is true means to prove it EG *The survey showed that 29 per cent would now approve the treaty.* **2** If a picture shows something, it represents it EG *The painting shows supporters and crowd scenes.* **3** If you show someone something, you let them see it EG *Show me your passport.* **4** If you show someone to a room or seat, you lead them there. **5** If you show someone how to do something, you demonstrate it to them. **6** If something shows, it is visible. **7** If something shows a quality or characteristic, you can see that it has it EG *Her sketches and watercolours showed promise.* **8** If you

show your feelings, you let people see them EG *She was flustered, but too proud to show it.* **9** If you show affection or mercy, you behave in an affectionate or merciful way EG *the first person who showed me some affection.* **10** To show a film or television programme means to let the public see it. ▶ NOUN **11** a form of light entertainment at the theatre or on television. **12** an exhibition EG *the Napier Antiques Show.* **13** A show of a feeling or attitude is behaviour in which you show it EG *a show of optimism.*
▶ PHRASE **14** If something is on **show**, it is being exhibited for the public to see.
▤ (sense 1) demonstrate, prove
▤ (sense 7) display, indicate, reveal
▤ (sense 12) display, exhibition
show off VERB; AN INFORMAL USE If someone is showing off, they are trying to impress people.
show up VERB **1** AN INFORMAL USE If you show up, you arrive at a place where you are expected. **2** If something shows up, it can be seen clearly EG *Her bones were too soft to show up on an X-ray.*

show business
NOUN Show business is entertainment in the theatre, films, and television.

showdown showdowns
NOUN; AN INFORMAL WORD a major argument or conflict intended to end a dispute.

shower showers showering showered
NOUN **1** a device which sprays you with water so that you can wash yourself. **2** If you have a shower, you wash yourself by standing under a shower. **3** a short period of rain. **4** You can refer to a lot of things falling at once as a shower EG *a shower of confetti.* ▶ VERB **5** If you shower, you have a shower. **6** If you are showered with a lot of things, they fall on you.

showing showings

NOUN A showing of a film or television programme is a presentation of it so that the public can see it.

showjumping
NOUN Showjumping is a horse-riding competition in which the horses jump over a series of high fences.

show-off show-offs
NOUN; AN INFORMAL WORD someone who tries to impress people with their knowledge or skills.

showroom showrooms
NOUN a shop where goods such as cars or electrical appliances are displayed.

showy showier showiest
ADJECTIVE large or bright and intended to impress people EG *a showy house.*
▤ flamboyant, flashy, ostentatious

shrapnel
NOUN Shrapnel consists of small pieces of metal scattered from an exploding shell.
▦ named after General Henry **Shrapnel** (1761-1842), who invented it

shred shreds shredding shredded
VERB **1** If you shred something, you cut or tear it into very small pieces. ▶ NOUN **2** A shred of paper or material is a small, narrow piece of it. **3** If there is not a shred of something, there is absolutely none of it EG *He was left without a shred of self-esteem.*

shrew shrews
Said "shroo" NOUN a small mouse-like animal with a long pointed nose.

shrewd shrewder shrewdest
ADJECTIVE Someone who is shrewd is intelligent and makes good judgments.
shrewdly ADVERB, **shrewdness** NOUN
▤ astute, clever, sharp

shriek shrieks shrieking shrieked
NOUN **1** a high-pitched scream. ▶ VERB

A B C D E F G H I J K L M N O P Q R S T U V W X Y Z

2 If you shriek, you make a high-pitched scream.

shrift

NOUN If you give someone or something short shrift, you pay very little attention to them.
📖 from Old English *scrift* meaning 'confession'; 'short shrift' referred to the short time allowed to prisoners before they were put to death to make their confession

shrill shriller shrillest

ADJECTIVE A shrill sound is unpleasantly high-pitched and piercing.
shrilly ADVERB

shrimp shrimps

NOUN a small edible shellfish with a long tail and many legs.

shrine shrines

NOUN a place of worship associated with a sacred person or object.

shrink shrinks shrinking shrank shrunk

VERB **1** If something shrinks, it becomes smaller. **2** If you shrink from something, you move away from it because you are afraid of it.
shrinkage NOUN

shrivel shrivels shrivelling shrivelled

VERB When something shrivels, it becomes dry and withered.

shroud shrouds shrouding shrouded

NOUN **1** a cloth in which a dead body is wrapped before it is buried. ▶ VERB **2** If something is shrouded in darkness or fog, it is hidden by it.

shrub shrubs

NOUN a low, bushy plant.

shrug shrugs shrugging shrugged

VERB **1** If you shrug your shoulders, you raise them slightly as a sign of indifference. ▶ NOUN **2** If you give a shrug of your shoulders, you shrug them.

shrunken

ADJECTIVE; A FORMAL USE Someone or something that is shrunken has become smaller than it used to be EG *a shrunken old man*.

shudder shudders shuddering shuddered

VERB **1** If you shudder, you tremble with fear or horror. **2** If a machine or vehicle shudders, it shakes violently. ▶ NOUN **3** a shiver of fear or horror.

shuffle shuffles shuffling shuffled

VERB **1** If you shuffle, you walk without lifting your feet properly off the ground. **2** If you shuffle about, you move about and fidget because you feel uncomfortable or embarrassed. **3** If you shuffle a pack of cards, you mix them up before you begin a game. ▶ NOUN **4** the way someone walks when they shuffle.

shun shuns shunning shunned

VERB If you shun someone or something, you deliberately avoid them.

shunt shunts shunting shunted

VERB; AN INFORMAL WORD If you shunt people or things to a place, you move them there EG *You are shunted from room to room*.

shut shuts shutting shut

VERB **1** If you shut something, you close it. **2** When a shop or pub shuts, it is closed and you can no longer go into it. ▶ ADJECTIVE **3** If something is shut, it is closed.
shut up VERB; AN INFORMAL EXPRESSION If you shut up, you stop talking.

shutter shutters

NOUN Shutters are hinged wooden or metal covers fitted on the outside or inside of a window.

shuttle shuttles

ADJECTIVE **1** A shuttle service is an air, bus, or train service which makes frequent journeys between two places. ▶ NOUN **2** a plane used in a shuttle service.

shuttlecock shuttlecocks

NOUN the feathered object used as a ball in the game of badminton.

shy shyer shyest; shies shying

shied

ADJECTIVE **1** A shy person is nervous and uncomfortable in the company of other people. ▶ VERB **2** When a horse shies, it moves away suddenly because something has frightened it. **3** If you shy away from doing something, you avoid doing it because you are afraid or nervous.

shyly ADVERB, **shyness** NOUN

☰ (sense 1) bashful, self-conscious, timid

sibling siblings

NOUN; A FORMAL WORD Your siblings are your brothers and sisters.

sick sicker sickest

ADJECTIVE **1** If you are sick, you are ill. **2** If you feel sick, you feel as if you are going to vomit. If you are sick, you vomit. **3** AN INFORMAL USE If you are sick of doing something, you feel you have been doing it too long. **4** AN INFORMAL USE A sick joke or story deals with death or suffering in an unpleasantly frivolous way. ▶ PHRASE **5** If something **makes you sick**, it makes you angry.

sickness NOUN

☰ (sense 2) nauseous, queasy

sicken sickens sickening sickened

VERB If something sickens you, it makes you feel disgusted.

sickening ADJECTIVE

sickle sickles

NOUN a tool with a short handle and a curved blade used for cutting grass or grain.

sickly sicklier sickliest

ADJECTIVE **1** A sickly person or animal is weak and unhealthy. **2** Sickly also means very unpleasant to smell or taste.

side sides siding sided

NOUN **1** Side refers to a position to the left or right of something EG *the two armchairs on either side of the fireplace.* **2** The sides of a boundary or barrier are the two areas it separates EG *this side of the border.* **3** Your sides are the parts of your body from your armpits down to your hips. **4** The sides of something are its outside surfaces, especially the surfaces which are not its front or back. **5** The sides of a hill or valley are the parts that slope. **6** The two sides in a war, argument, or relationship are the two people or groups involved. **7** A particular side of something is one aspect of it EG *the sensitive, caring side of human nature.* ▶ ADJECTIVE **8** situated on a side of a building or vehicle EG *the side door.* **9** A side road is a small road leading off a larger one. **10** A side issue is an issue that is less important than the main one. ▶ VERB **11** If you side with someone in an argument, you support them.

sideboard sideboards

NOUN **1** a long, low cupboard for plates and glasses. ▶ PLURAL NOUN **2** A man's sideboards are his sideburns.

sideburns

PLURAL NOUN A man's sideburns are areas of hair growing on his cheeks in front of his ears.

🏛 from a 19th century US army general called *Burnside* who wore his whiskers like this

side effect side effects

NOUN The side effects of a drug are the effects it has in addition to its main effects.

sidekick sidekicks

NOUN; AN INFORMAL WORD Someone's sidekick is their close friend who spends a lot of time with them.

sideline sidelines

NOUN an extra job in addition to your main job.

sideshow sideshows

NOUN Sideshows are stalls at a fairground.

sidestep sidesteps sidestepping sidestepped

VERB If you sidestep a difficult problem or question, you avoid dealing with it.

sidewalk sidewalks

NOUN In American English, a

A B C D E F G H I J K L M N O P Q R S T U V W X Y Z

sidewalk is a pavement.

sideways
ADVERB from or towards the side of something or someone.

siding sidings
NOUN a short railway track beside the main tracks, where engines and carriages are left when not in use.

sidle sidles sidling sidled
VERB If you sidle somewhere, you walk there cautiously and slowly, as if you do not want to be noticed.

siege sieges
Said "seej" NOUN a military operation in which an army surrounds a place and prevents food or help from reaching the people inside.

sieve sieves sieving sieved
Said "siv" NOUN 1 a kitchen tool made of mesh, used for sifting or straining things. ▶ VERB 2 If you sieve a powder or liquid, you pass it through a sieve.

sift sifts sifting sifted
VERB 1 If you sift a powdery substance, you pass it through a sieve to remove lumps. 2 If you sift through something such as evidence, you examine it all thoroughly.

sigh sighs sighing sighed
VERB 1 When you sigh, you let out a deep breath. ▶ NOUN 2 the breath you let out when you sigh.

sight sights sighting sighted
NOUN 1 Sight is the ability to see EG *His sight was so poor that he could not follow the cricket.* 2 something you see EG *It was a ghastly sight.* ▶ PLURAL NOUN 3 Sights are interesting places which tourists visit. ▶ VERB 4 If you sight someone or something, you see them briefly or suddenly EG *He had been sighted in Cairo.* ▶ PHRASES 5 If something is **in sight**, you can see it. If it is **out of sight**, you cannot see it.

sighted
ADJECTIVE Someone who is sighted can see.

sighting sightings
NOUN A sighting of something rare or unexpected is an occasion when it is seen.

sightseeing
NOUN Sightseeing is visiting the interesting places that tourists usually visit.
sightseer NOUN

sign signs signing signed
NOUN 1 a mark or symbol that always has a particular meaning, for example in mathematics or music. 2 a gesture with a particular meaning. 3 A sign can also consist of words, a picture, or a symbol giving information or a warning. 4 If there are signs of something, there is evidence that it exists or is happening EG *We are now seeing the first signs of recovery.* ▶ VERB 5 If you sign a document, you write your name on it EG *He hurriedly signed the death certificate.* 6 If you sign, you communicate by using sign language.
■ (sense 2) gesture, signal
sign on VERB 1 If you sign on for a job or course, you officially agree to do it by signing a contract. 2 When people sign on, they officially state that they are unemployed and claim benefit from the state.
sign up VERB If you sign up for a job or course, you officially agree to do it by signing a contract.

signal signals signalling signalled
NOUN 1 a gesture, sound, or action intended to give a message to someone. 2 A railway signal is a piece of equipment beside the track which tells train drivers whether to stop or not. ▶ VERB 3 If you signal to someone, you make a gesture or sound to give them a message.

signature signatures
NOUN If you write your signature, you write your name the way you usually write it.

significant

ADJECTIVE **1** A significant amount is a large amount. **2** Something that is significant is important EG *a significant victory*.

significance NOUN, **significantly** ADVERB

signify signifies signifying signified

VERB A sign or gesture that signifies something has a particular meaning EG *They signified a desire to leave*.

sign language

NOUN Sign language is a way of communicating using your hands, used especially by deaf people.

signpost signposts

NOUN a road sign with information on it such as the name of a town and how far away it is.

Sikh Sikhs

Said "seek" NOUN a person who believes in Sikhism, an Indian religion which separated from Hinduism in the sixteenth century and which teaches that there is only one God.

📖 from Hindi *sikh* meaning 'disciple'

silence silences silencing silenced

NOUN **1** Silence is quietness. **2** Someone's silence about something is their failure or refusal to talk about it. ▶ VERB **3** To silence someone or something means to stop them talking or making a noise.

silent

ADJECTIVE **1** If you are silent, you are not saying anything. **2** If you are silent about something, you do not tell people about it. **3** When something is silent, it makes no noise. **4** A silent film has only pictures and no sound.

silently ADVERB

▣ (sense 1) dumb, mute, speechless

silhouette silhouettes

Said "sil-loo-ett" NOUN the outline of a dark shape against a light background.

silhouetted ADJECTIVE

silicon

NOUN Silicon is an element found in sand, clay, and stone. It is used to make parts of computers.

silk silks

NOUN Silk is a fine, soft cloth made from a substance produced by silkworms.

📖 from Chinese *ssu* meaning 'silk'

silkworm silkworms

NOUN Silkworms are the larvae of a particular kind of moth.

silky silkier silkiest

ADJECTIVE smooth and soft.

sill sills

NOUN a ledge at the bottom of a window.

silly sillier silliest

ADJECTIVE foolish or childish.

▣ daft, foolish, stupid

silt

NOUN Silt is fine sand or soil which is carried along by a river.

silver

NOUN **1** Silver is a valuable greyish-white metallic element used for making jewellery and ornaments. **2** Silver is also coins made from silver or from silver-coloured metal EG *a handful of silver*. ▶ ADJECTIVE OR NOUN **3** greyish-white.

silver beet silver beets

NOUN a type of beet grown in Australia and New Zealand.

silver fern

NOUN a tall fern that is found in New Zealand. It is the symbol of New Zealand national sports teams.

silverfish silverfishes or silverfish

NOUN a small silver insect with no wings that eats paper and clothing.

silver jubilee silver jubilees

NOUN the 25th anniversary of an important event.

silver medal silver medals

NOUN a medal made from silver awarded to the competitor who

A B C D E F G H I J K L M N O P Q R S T U V W X Y Z

comes second in a competition.

silver wedding silver weddings

NOUN A couple's silver wedding is the 25th anniversary of their wedding.

silvery

ADJECTIVE having the appearance or colour of silver EG *the silvery moon.*

similar

ADJECTIVE **1** If one thing is similar to another, or if two things are similar, they are like each other. **2** In maths, two triangles are similar if the angles in one correspond exactly to the angles in the other.

similarly ADVERB

☑ Be careful when deciding whether to use *similar* or *same*. *Similar* means 'alike but not identical', and *same* means 'identical'. Do not put *as* after *similar*: *her dress was similar to mine.*

similarity similarities

NOUN If there is a similarity between things, they are similar in some way.

🔳 likeness, resemblance

simile similes

Said "**sim-ill-ee**" NOUN an expression in which a person or thing is described as being similar to someone or something else. Examples of similes are *She runs like a deer* and *He's as white as a sheet.*

simmer simmers simmering simmered

VERB When food simmers, it cooks gently at just below boiling point.

simple simpler simplest

ADJECTIVE **1** Something that is simple is uncomplicated and easy to understand or do. **2** Simple also means plain and not elaborate in style EG *a simple coat.* **3** A simple way of life is uncomplicated. **4** Someone who is simple is mentally retarded. **5** You use 'simple' to emphasize that what you are talking about is the only important thing EG *simple*

stubbornness.

simplicity NOUN

simple-minded

ADJECTIVE naive and unsophisticated EG *simple-minded pleasures.*

simplify simplifies simplifying simplified

VERB To simplify something means to make it easier to do or understand.

simplification NOUN

simplistic

ADJECTIVE too simple or naive EG *a rather simplistic approach to the subject.*

simply

ADVERB **1** Simply means merely EG *It was simply a question of making the decision.* **2** You use 'simply' to emphasize what you are saying EG *It is simply not true.* **3** If you say or write something simply, you do it in a way that makes it easy to understand.

simulate simulates simulating simulated

VERB To simulate something means to imitate it EG *The wood has been painted to simulate stone.*

simulation NOUN

simultaneous

ADJECTIVE Things that are simultaneous happen at the same time.

simultaneously ADVERB

sin sins sinning sinned

NOUN **1** Sin is wicked and immoral behaviour. ▶ VERB **2** To sin means to do something wicked and immoral.

🔳 (sense 1) evil, iniquity, wrongdoing

🔳 (sense 2) lapse, transgress

since

PREPOSITION, CONJUNCTION, OR ADVERB

1 Since means from a particular time until now EG *I've been waiting patiently since half past three.* ▶ ADVERB **2** Since also means at some time after a particular time in the past EG *They split up and he has since remarried.* ▶ CONJUNCTION **3** Since also means because EG *I'm forever on a*

diet, since I put on weight easily.
☑ Do not put *ago* before *since*, as it is not needed: *it is ten years since she wrote her book* not *ten years ago since.*

sincere
ADJECTIVE If you are sincere, you say things that you really mean EG *a sincere expression of friendliness.*
sincerity NOUN
☰ genuine, honest

sincerely
ADVERB **1** If you say or feel something sincerely, you mean it or feel it genuinely. ▶ PHRASE **2** You write **Yours sincerely** before your signature at the end of a formal letter.

sinew sinews
Said "sin-yoo" NOUN a tough cord in your body that connects a muscle to a bone.

sinful
ADJECTIVE wicked and immoral.

sing sings singing sang sung
VERB **1** When you sing, you make musical sounds with your voice, usually producing words that fit a tune. **2** When birds or insects sing, they make pleasant sounds.
singer NOUN
☑ The past tense of *sing* is *sang*, and the past participle is *sung*. Do not confuse these words: *the team sang the national anthem; we have sung together many times.*

singe singes singeing singed
VERB **1** To singe something means to burn it slightly so that it goes brown but does not catch fire. ▶ NOUN **2** a slight burn.

single singles singling singled
ADJECTIVE **1** Single means only one and not more EG *A single shot was fired.* **2** People who are single are not married. **3** A single bed or bedroom is for one person. **4** A single ticket is a one-way ticket. ▶ NOUN **5** a recording of one or two short pieces of music on a small record, CD, or cassette. **6** Singles is a game of tennis, badminton, or

squash between just two players.
single out VERB If you single someone out from a group, you give them special treatment EG *He'd been singled out for some special award.*

single-handed
ADVERB If you do something single-handed, you do it on your own, without any help.

single-minded
ADJECTIVE A single-minded person has only one aim and is determined to achieve it.

singly
ADVERB If people do something singly, they do it on their own or one by one.

singular
NOUN **1** In grammar, the singular is the form of a word that refers to just one person or thing. ▶ ADJECTIVE **2** A FORMAL USE unusual and remarkable EG *her singular beauty.*
singularity NOUN, **singularly** ADVERB

sinister
ADJECTIVE seeming harmful or evil EG *something cold and sinister about him.*
🏛 from Latin *sinister* meaning 'left-hand side', because the left side was considered unlucky

sink sinks sinking sank sunk
NOUN **1** a basin with taps supplying water, usually in a kitchen or bathroom. ▶ VERB **2** If something sinks, it moves downwards, especially through water EG *An Indian cargo ship sank in icy seas.* **3** To sink a ship means to cause it to sink by attacking it. **4** If an amount or value sinks, it decreases. **5** If you sink into an unpleasant state, you gradually pass into it EG *He sank into black despair.* **6** To sink something sharp into an object means to make it go deeply into it EG *The tiger sank its teeth into his leg.*
sink in VERB When a fact sinks in, you fully understand it or realize it EG *The truth was at last sinking in.*

sinner sinners
NOUN someone who has committed

A
B
C
D
E
F
G
H
I
J
K
L
M
N
O
P
Q
R
S
T
U
V
W
X
Y
Z

A
B
C
D
E
F
G
H
I
J
K
L
M
N
O
P
Q
R
S
T
U
V
W
X
Y
Z

a sin.

sinus sinuses

NOUN Your sinuses are the air passages in the bones of your skull, just behind your nose.

sip sips sipping sipped

VERB **1** If you sip a drink, you drink it by taking a small amount at a time. ▶ NOUN **2** a small amount of drink that you take into your mouth.

siphon siphons siphoning siphoned

Said "sigh-fn"; also spelt **syphon**
VERB If you siphon off a liquid, you draw it out of a container through a tube and transfer it to another place.

sir

NOUN **1** Sir is a polite, formal way of addressing a man. **2** Sir is also the title used in front of the name of a knight or baronet.

siren sirens

NOUN a warning device, for example on a police car, which makes a loud, wailing noise.
📖 the Sirens in Greek mythology were sea nymphs who had beautiful voices and sang in order to lure sailors to their deaths on the rocks where the nymphs lived

sirloin

NOUN Sirloin is a prime cut of beef from the lower part of a cow's back.
📖 from Old French *sur* meaning 'above' and *longe* meaning 'loin'

sis or **sies**

Said "siss" INTERJECTION; AN INFORMAL EXPRESSION In South African English, you say 'Sis!' to show disgust.

sister sisters

NOUN **1** Your sister is a girl or woman who has the same parents as you. **2** a member of a female religious order. **3** In a hospital, a sister is a senior nurse who supervises a ward. ▶ ADJECTIVE **4** Sister means closely related to something or very similar to it EG *Citroen and its sister company Peugeot.*

sisterhood

NOUN Sisterhood is a strong feeling of companionship between women.

sister-in-law sisters-in-law

NOUN Your sister-in-law is the wife of your brother, the sister of your husband or wife, or the woman married to your wife's or husband's brother.

sit sits sitting sat

VERB **1** If you are sitting, your weight is supported by your buttocks rather than your feet. **2** When you sit or sit down somewhere, you lower your body until you are sitting. **3** If you sit an examination, you take it. **4** A FORMAL USE When a parliament, law court, or other official body sits, it meets and officially carries out its work.

sitcom sitcoms

NOUN; AN INFORMAL WORD a television comedy series which shows characters in amusing situations that are similar to everyday life.
📖 shortened from *situation comedy*

site sites siting sited

NOUN **1** a piece of ground where a particular thing happens or is situated EG *a building site.* ▶ VERB **2** If something is sited in a place, it is built or positioned there.

sitting sittings

NOUN **1** one of the times when a meal is served. **2** one of the occasions when a parliament or law court meets and carries out its work.

sitting room sitting rooms

NOUN a room in a house where people sit and relax.

situated

ADJECTIVE If something is situated somewhere, that is where it is EG *a town situated 45 minutes from Geneva.*

situation situations

NOUN **1** what is happening in a particular place at a particular time EG *the political situation.* **2** The situation of a building or town is its surroundings EG *a beautiful* *situation*.

■ (sense 1) circumstances, condition, state of affairs

Siva

PROPER NOUN Siva is a Hindu god and is one of the Trimurti.

▥ from a Sanskrit word meaning 'auspicious'

six

Six is the number 6.

sixteen

the number 16.

sixteenth

sixth sixths

1 The sixth item in a series is the one counted as number six. ▶ NOUN **2** one of six equal parts.

sixth sense

NOUN You say that someone has a sixth sense when they know something instinctively, without having any evidence of it.

sixty sixties

the number 60.

sixtieth

sizable or **sizeable**

ADJECTIVE fairly large EG *a sizable amount of money*.

size sizes

NOUN **1** The size of something is how big or small it is EG *the size of the audience*. **2** The size of something is also the fact that it is very large EG *the sheer size of Australia*. **3** one of the standard graded measurements of clothes and shoes.

■ (sense 1) dimensions, magnitude, proportions

sizzle sizzles sizzling sizzled

VERB If something sizzles, it makes a hissing sound like the sound of frying food.

sjambok sjamboks

Said "**sham-bok**" NOUN In South African English, a sjambok is a long whip made from animal hide.

skate skates skating skated

NOUN **1** Skates are ice skates or roller skates. **2** a flat edible sea fish. ▶ VERB

3 If you skate, you move about on ice wearing ice skates. **4** If you skate round a difficult subject, you avoid discussing it.

skateboard skateboards

NOUN a narrow board on wheels which you stand on and ride for fun.

skeleton skeletons

NOUN Your skeleton is the framework of bones in your body.

sketch sketches sketching sketched

NOUN **1** a quick, rough drawing. **2** A sketch of a situation or incident is a brief description of it. **3** a short, humorous piece of acting, usually forming part of a comedy show. ▶ VERB **4** If you sketch something, you draw it quickly and roughly.

sketchy sketchier sketchiest

ADJECTIVE giving only a rough description or account EG *Details surrounding his death are sketchy*.

skew or **skewed**

Said "**skyoo**" ADJECTIVE in a slanting position, rather than straight or upright.

skewer skewers skewering skewered

NOUN **1** a long metal pin used to hold pieces of food together during cooking. ▶ VERB **2** If you skewer something, you push a skewer through it.

ski skis skiing skied

NOUN **1** Skis are long pieces of wood, metal, or plastic that you fasten to special boots so you can move easily on snow. ▶ VERB **2** When you ski, you move on snow wearing skis, especially as a sport.

▥ from Old Norse *skith* meaning 'snowshoes'

skid skids skidding skidded

VERB If a vehicle skids, it slides in an uncontrolled way, for example because the road is wet or icy.

skilful

ADJECTIVE If you are skilful at

A B C D E F G H I J K L M N O P Q R S T U V W X Y Z

something, you can do it very well.
skilfully ADVERB
■ able, expert, proficient

skill skills
NOUN **1** Skill is the knowledge and ability that enables you to do something well. **2** a type of work or technique which requires special training and knowledge.
■ (sense 1) ability, expertise, proficiency

skilled
ADJECTIVE **1** A skilled person has the knowledge and ability to do something well. **2** Skilled work is work which can only be done by people who have had special training.

skim skims skimming skimmed
VERB **1** If you skim something from the surface of a liquid, you remove it. **2** If something skims a surface, it moves along just above it EG *seagulls skimming the waves.*

skimmed milk
NOUN Skimmed milk has had the cream removed.

skin skins skinning skinned
NOUN **1** Your skin is the natural covering of your body. An animal skin is the skin and fur of a dead animal. **2** The skin of a fruit or vegetable is its outer covering. **3** a solid layer which forms on the surface of a liquid. ▶ VERB **4** If you skin a dead animal, you remove its skin. **5** If you skin a part of your body, you accidentally graze it.

skinny skinnier skinniest
ADJECTIVE extremely thin.

skip skips skipping skipped
VERB **1** If you skip along, you move along jumping from one foot to the other. **2** If you skip something, you miss it out or avoid doing it EG *It is all too easy to skip meals.* ▶ NOUN **3** Skips are the movements you make when you skip. **4** a large metal container for holding rubbish and rubble.

skipper skippers

NOUN; AN INFORMAL WORD The skipper of a ship or boat is its captain.
▥ from Old Dutch *schipper* meaning 'shipper'

skirmish skirmishes
NOUN a short, rough fight.

skirt skirts skirting skirted
NOUN **1** A woman's skirt is a piece of clothing which fastens at her waist and hangs down over her legs.
▶ VERB **2** Something that skirts an area is situated around the edge of it. **3** If you skirt something, you go around the edge of it EG *We skirted the town.* **4** If you skirt a problem, you avoid dealing with it EG *He was skirting the real question.*
▥ from Old Norse *skyrta* meaning 'shirt'

skirting skirtings
NOUN A skirting or skirting board is a narrow strip of wood running along the bottom of a wall in a room.

skite skites skiting skited
AN INFORMAL WORD ▶ VERB **1** In Australian and New Zealand English, to skite is to talk in a boastful way about something that you own or that you have done.
▶ NOUN **2** In Australian and New Zealand English, someone who boasts.

skittle skittles
NOUN Skittles is a game in which players roll a ball and try to knock down wooden objects called skittles.

skull skulls
NOUN Your skull is the bony part of your head which surrounds your brain.

skunk skunks
NOUN a small black and white animal from North America which gives off an unpleasant smell when it is frightened.
▥ a North American Indian word

sky skies
NOUN The sky is the space around the earth which you can see when

you look upwards.

from Old Norse *sky* meaning 'cloud'

skylight skylights
NOUN a window in a roof or ceiling.

skyline skylines
NOUN The skyline is the line where the sky meets buildings or the ground EG *the New York City skyline*.

skyscraper skyscrapers
NOUN a very tall building.

slab slabs
NOUN a thick, flat piece of something.

slack slacker slackest; slacks
ADJECTIVE **1** Something that is slack is loose and not firmly stretched or positioned. **2** A slack period is one in which there is not much work to do. ▶ NOUN **3** The slack in a rope is the part that hangs loose. ▶ PLURAL NOUN **4** Slacks are casual trousers.
slackness NOUN

slacken slackens slackening slackened
VERB **1** If something slackens, it becomes slower or less intense EG *The rain had slackened to a drizzle*. **2** To slacken also means to become looser EG *Her grip slackened on Arnold's arm*.

slag slags slagging slagged
NOUN **1** Slag is the waste material left when ore has been melted down to remove the metal EG *a slag heap*. ▶ VERB **2** AN INFORMAL USE To slag someone off means to criticize them in an unpleasant way, usually behind their back.

slalom slaloms
Said "**slah**-lom" NOUN a skiing competition in which the competitors have to twist and turn quickly to avoid obstacles.
from Norwegian *slad + lom* meaning 'sloping path'

slam slams slamming slammed
VERB **1** If you slam a door or if it slams, it shuts noisily and with great force. **2** If you slam

something down, you throw it down violently EG *She slammed the phone down*.

slander slanders slandering slandered
NOUN **1** Slander is something untrue and malicious said about someone. ▶ VERB **2** To slander someone means to say untrue and malicious things about them.
slanderous ADJECTIVE
(sense 1) defamation, smear

slang
NOUN Slang consists of very informal words and expressions.

slant slants slanting slanted
VERB **1** If something slants, it slopes EG *The back can be adjusted to slant into the most comfortable position*. **2** If news or information is slanted, it is presented in a biased way. ▶ NOUN **3** a slope. **4** A slant on a subject is one way of looking at it, especially a biased one.

slap slaps slapping slapped
VERB **1** If you slap someone, you hit them with the palm of your hand. **2** If you slap something onto a surface, you put it there quickly and noisily. ▶ NOUN **3** If you give someone a slap, you slap them.
from German *Schlappe* an imitation of the sound

slash slashes slashing slashed
VERB **1** If you slash something, you make a long, deep cut in it. **2** AN INFORMAL USE To slash money means to reduce it greatly EG *Car makers could be forced to slash prices*. ▶ NOUN **3** a diagonal line that separates letters, words, or numbers, for example in the number 340/21/K.

slat slats
NOUN Slats are the narrow pieces of wood or metal plastic in things such as Venetian blinds.
slatted ADJECTIVE

slate slates slating slated
NOUN **1** Slate is a dark grey rock that splits easily into thin layers. **2** Slates are small, flat pieces of

slate used for covering roofs. ▶ VERB **3** AN INFORMAL USE If critics slate a play, film, or book, they criticize it severely.

slaughter slaughters slaughtering slaughtered
VERB **1** To slaughter a large number of people means to kill them unjustly or cruelly. **2** To slaughter farm animals means to kill them for meat. ▶ NOUN **3** Slaughter is the killing of many people.
≡ (sense 3) carnage, massacre, murder

slave slaves slaving slaved
NOUN **1** someone who is owned by another person and must work for them. ▶ VERB **2** If you slave for someone, you work very hard for them.
slavery NOUN
⌂ from Latin *Sclavus* meaning 'a Slav', because the Slavonic races were frequently conquered and made into slaves

slay slays slaying slew slain
VERB; A LITERARY WORD To slay someone means to kill them.

sleazy sleazier sleaziest
ADJECTIVE A sleazy place looks dirty, run-down, and not respectable.

sled sleds
NOUN a sledge.

sledge sledges
NOUN a vehicle on runners used for travelling over snow.

sledgehammer sledgehammers
NOUN a large, heavy hammer.

sleek sleeker sleekest
ADJECTIVE **1** Sleek hair is smooth and shiny. **2** Someone who is sleek looks rich and dresses elegantly.

sleep sleeps sleeping slept
NOUN **1** Sleep is the natural state of rest in which your eyes are closed and you are inactive and unconscious. **2** If you have a sleep, you sleep for a while EG *He'll be ready for a sleep soon.* ▶ VERB **3** When you sleep, you rest in a state of

sleep. ▶ PHRASE **4** If a sick or injured animal **is put to sleep**, it is painlessly killed.
≡ (sense 2) doze, nap, slumber

sleeper sleepers
NOUN **1** You use 'sleeper' to say how deeply someone sleeps EG *I'm a very heavy sleeper.* **2** a bed on a train, or a train which has beds on it.
3 Railway sleepers are the large beams that support the rails of a railway track.

sleeping bag sleeping bags
NOUN a large, warm bag for sleeping in, especially when you are camping.

sleeping pill sleeping pills
NOUN A sleeping pill or a sleeping tablet is a pill which you take to help you sleep.

sleepout sleepouts
NOUN **1** In Australia, an area of veranda or porch which has been closed off to be used as a bedroom. **2** In New Zealand, a small building outside a house, used for sleeping.

sleepwalk sleepwalks sleepwalking sleepwalked
VERB If you sleepwalk, you walk around while you are asleep.

sleepy sleepier sleepiest
ADJECTIVE **1** tired and ready to go to sleep. **2** A sleepy town or village is very quiet.
sleepily ADVERB, **sleepiness** NOUN

sleet
NOUN Sleet is a mixture of rain and snow.

sleeve sleeves
NOUN The sleeves of a piece of clothing are the parts that cover your arms.
sleeveless ADJECTIVE

sleigh sleighs
Said "slay" NOUN a sledge.

slender
ADJECTIVE **1** attractively thin and graceful. **2** small in amount or degree EG *the first slender hopes of peace.*

■ (sense 1) slim, willowy

sleuth sleuths
Said "slooth" NOUN; AN OLD-FASHIONED
WORD a detective.
🏛 a shortened form of
sleuthhound, a tracker dog, from
Old Norse *sloth* meaning 'track'

slew slews slewing slewed
1 Slew is the past tense of **slay**.
▶ VERB **2** If a vehicle slews, it slides
or skids EG *The bike slewed into the
crowd.*

slice slices slicing sliced
NOUN **1** A slice of cake, bread, or
other food is a piece of it cut from a
larger piece. **2** a kitchen tool with a
broad, flat blade EG *a fish slice.* **3** In
sport, a slice is a stroke in which
the player makes the ball go to one
side, rather than straight ahead.
▶ VERB **4** If you slice food, you cut it
into thin pieces. **5** To slice through
something means to cut or move
through it quickly, like a knife EG
The ship sliced through the water.

slick slicker slickest; slicks
ADJECTIVE **1** A slick action is done
quickly and smoothly EG *slick
passing and strong running.* **2** A slick
person speaks easily and
persuasively but is not sincere EG *a
slick TV presenter.* ▶ NOUN **3** An oil
slick is a layer of oil floating on the
surface of the sea or a lake.

slide slides sliding slid
VERB **1** When something slides, it
moves smoothly over or against
something else. ▶ NOUN **2** a small
piece of photographic film which
can be projected onto a screen so
that you can see the picture. **3** a
small piece of glass on which you
put something that you want to
examine through a microscope.
4 In a playground, a slide is a
structure with a steep, slippery
slope for children to slide down.

slight slighter slightest; slights
slighting slighted
ADJECTIVE **1** Slight means small in
amount or degree EG *a slight dent.*

2 A slight person has a slim body.
▶ PHRASE **3** Not in the slightest
means not at all EG *This doesn't
surprise me in the slightest.* ▶ VERB **4** If
you slight someone, you insult
them by behaving rudely towards
them. ▶ NOUN **5** A slight is rude or
insulting behaviour.
slightly ADVERB

slim slimmer slimmest; slims
slimming slimmed
ADJECTIVE **1** A slim person is
attractively thin. **2** A slim object is
thinner than usual EG *a slim book.*
3 If there is only a slim chance that
something will happen, it is
unlikely to happen. ▶ VERB **4** If you
are slimming, you are trying to lose
weight.
slimmer NOUN

slime
NOUN Slime is an unpleasant, thick,
slippery substance.
🏛 from Old English *slim* meaning
'soft sticky mud'

slimy slimier slimiest
ADJECTIVE **1** covered in slime. **2** Slimy
people are friendly and pleasant in
an insincere way EG *a slimy business
partner.*

sling slings slinging slung
VERB **1** AN INFORMAL USE If you sling
something somewhere, you throw
it there. **2** If you sling a rope
between two points, you attach it
so that it hangs loosely between
them. ▶ NOUN **3** a piece of cloth tied
round a person's neck to support a
broken or injured arm. **4** a device
made of ropes or cloth used for
carrying things.

slip slips slipping slipped
VERB **1** If you slip, you accidentally
slide and lose your balance. **2** If
something slips, it slides out of
place accidentally EG *One of the
knives slipped from her grasp.* **3** If you
slip somewhere, you go there
quickly and quietly EG *She slipped out
of the house.* **4** If you slip something
somewhere, you put it there

quickly and quietly. **5** If something slips to a lower level or standard, it falls to that level or standard EG *The shares slipped to an all-time low.*
▸ NOUN **6** a small mistake. **7** A slip of paper is a small piece of paper. **8** a piece of underclothing worn under a dress or skirt.

slipped disc slipped discs
NOUN a painful condition in which one of the discs in your spine has moved out of its proper position.

slipper slippers
NOUN Slippers are loose, soft shoes that you wear indoors.

slippery
ADJECTIVE **1** smooth, wet, or greasy, and difficult to hold or walk on.
2 You describe a person as slippery when they cannot be trusted.

slippery dip slippery dips
NOUN; AN INFORMAL WORD In Australian English, a children's slide at a playground or funfair.

slip rail slip rails
NOUN In Australian and New Zealand English, a rail in a fence that can be slipped out of place to make an opening.

slipstream slipstreams
NOUN The slipstream of a car or plane is the flow of air directly behind it.

slit slits slitting slit
VERB **1** If you slit something, you make a long, narrow cut in it.
▸ NOUN **2** a long, narrow cut or opening.

slither slithers slithering slithered
VERB To slither somewhere means to move there by sliding along the ground in an uneven way EG *The snake slithered into the water.*

sliver slivers
NOUN a small, thin piece of something.

slob slobs
NOUN; AN INFORMAL WORD a lazy, untidy person.

slog slogs slogging slogged

VERB; AN INFORMAL WORD If you slog at something, you work hard and steadily at it EG *They are still slogging away at algebra.*

slogan slogans
NOUN a short, easily-remembered phrase used in advertising or by a political party.
📖 from Gaelic *sluagh-ghairm* meaning 'war cry'
🔲 catch-phrase, motto

slop slops slopping slopped
VERB **1** If a liquid slops, it spills over the edge of a container in a messy way. ▸ PLURAL NOUN **2** You can refer to dirty water or liquid waste as slops.

slope slopes sloping sloped
NOUN **1** a flat surface that is at an angle, so that one end is higher than the other. **2** The slope of something is the angle at which it slopes. ▸ VERB **3** If a surface slopes, it is at an angle. **4** If something slopes, it leans to one side rather than being upright EG *sloping handwriting.*
🔲 (sense 1) incline, slant, tilt
🔲 (sense 2) gradient, inclination

sloppy sloppier sloppiest
ADJECTIVE; AN INFORMAL WORD **1** very messy or careless EG *two sloppy performances.* **2** foolishly sentimental EG *some sloppy love story.*
sloppily ADVERB, **sloppiness** NOUN

slot slots slotting slotted
NOUN **1** a narrow opening in a machine or container, for example for putting coins in. ▸ VERB **2** When you slot something into something else, you put it into a space where it fits.

sloth sloths
Rhymes with "growth" NOUN **1** A FORMAL USE Sloth is laziness. **2** a South and Central American animal that moves very slowly and hangs upside down from the branches of trees.

slouch slouches slouching slouched
VERB If you slouch, you stand or sit

with your shoulders and head drooping forwards.

slouch hat slouch hats
NOUN a hat with a wide, flexible brim, especially an Australian army hat with the left side of the brim turned up.

Slovak Slovaks
ADJECTIVE **1** belonging to or relating to Slovakia. ▶ NOUN **2** someone who comes from Slovakia. **3** Slovak is the language spoken in Slovakia.

slow slower slowest; slows slowing slowed
ADJECTIVE **1** moving, happening, or doing something with very little speed EG *His progress was slow.*
2 Someone who is slow is not very clever. **3** If a clock or watch is slow, it shows a time earlier than the correct one. ▶ VERB **4** If something slows, slows down, or slows up, it moves or happens more slowly.
slowly ADVERB, **slowness** NOUN

slow motion
NOUN Slow motion is movement which is much slower than normal, especially in a film EG *It all seemed to happen in slow motion.*

sludge
NOUN Sludge is thick mud or sewage.

slug slugs
NOUN **1** a small, slow-moving creative with a slimy body, like a snail without a shell. **2** AN INFORMAL USE A slug of a strong alcoholic drink is a mouthful of it.

sluggish
ADJECTIVE moving slowly and without energy EG *the sluggish waters.*

sluice sluices sluicing sluiced
Said "sloose" NOUN **1** a channel which carries water, with an opening called a sluicegate which can be opened or closed to control the flow of water. ▶ VERB **2** If you sluice something, you wash it by pouring water over it EG *He had sluiced his hands under a tap.*
📖 from Latin *exclusa aqua* meaning 'water shut out'

slum slums
NOUN a poor, run-down area of a city.

slumber slumbers slumbering slumbered
A LITERARY WORD ▶ NOUN **1** Slumber is sleep. ▶ VERB **2** When you slumber, you sleep.

slump slumps slumping slumped
VERB **1** If an amount or a value slumps, it falls suddenly by a large amount. **2** If you slump somewhere, you fall or sit down heavily EG *He slumped against the side of the car.* ▶ NOUN **3** a sudden, severe drop in an amount or value EG *the slump in house prices.* **4** a time when there is economic decline and high unemployment.

slur slurs slurring slurred
NOUN **1** an insulting remark. ▶ VERB **2** When people slur their speech, they do not say their words clearly, often because they are drunk or ill.

slurp slurps slurping slurped
VERB If you slurp a drink, you drink it noisily.
📖 from Old Dutch *slorpen* meaning 'to sip'

slush
NOUN **1** Slush is wet melting snow. **2** AN INFORMAL USE You can refer to sentimental love stories as slush.
slushy ADJECTIVE

slut sluts
NOUN; AN OFFENSIVE WORD a dirty, untidy woman, or one considered to be immoral.

sly slyer or **slier** slyest or **sliest**
ADJECTIVE **1** A sly expression or remark shows that you know something other people do not know EG *a sly smile.* **2** A sly person is cunning and good at deceiving people.
slyly ADVERB
📧 (sense 2) crafty, cunning, devious

smack smacks smacking smacked
VERB **1** If you smack someone, you hit them with your open hand. **2** If something smacks of something

A
B
C
D
E
F
G
H
I
J
K
L
M
N
O
P
Q
R
S
T
U
V
W
X
Y
Z

else, it reminds you of it EG *His tale smacks of fantasy.* ▶ NOUN **3** If you give someone a smack, you smack them. **4** a loud, sharp noise EG *He landed with a smack on the tank.*

small smaller smallest; smalls
ADJECTIVE **1** Small means not large in size, number, or amount. **2** Small means not important or significant EG *small changes.* ▶ NOUN **3** The small of your back is the narrow part where your back curves slightly inwards.
▤ (sense 1) little, tiny
▤ (sense 2) insignificant, minor, trivial

smallpox
NOUN Smallpox is a serious contagious disease that causes a fever and a rash.

small talk
NOUN Small talk is conversation about unimportant things.

smart smarter smartest; smarts smarting smarted
ADJECTIVE **1** A smart person is clean and neatly dressed. **2** Smart means clever EG *a smart idea.* **3** A smart movement is quick and sharp. ▶ VERB **4** If a wound smarts, it stings. **5** If you are smarting from criticism or unkindness, you are feeling upset by it.
smartly ADVERB

smarten smartens smartening smartened
VERB If you smarten something up, you make it look neater and tidier.

smash smashes smashing smashed
VERB **1** If you smash something, you break it into a lot of pieces by hitting it or dropping it. **2** To smash through something such as a wall means to go through it by breaking it. **3** To smash against something means to hit it with great force EG *An immense wave smashed against the hull.* ▶ NOUN **4** AN INFORMAL USE If a play or film is a smash or a smash hit, it is very

successful. **5** a car crash. **6** In tennis, a smash is a stroke in which the player hits the ball downwards very hard.

smashing
ADJECTIVE; AN INFORMAL WORD If you describe something as smashing, you mean you like it very much.

smattering
NOUN A smattering of knowledge or information is a very small amount of it EG *a smattering of Russian.*

smear smears smearing smeared
NOUN **1** a dirty, greasy mark on a surface EG *a smear of pink lipstick.* **2** an untrue and malicious rumour. ▶ VERB **3** If something smears a surface, it makes dirty, greasy marks on it EG *The blade was chipped and smeared.* **4** If you smear a surface with a greasy or sticky substance, you spread a layer of the substance over the surface.

smell smells smelling smelled or **smelt**
NOUN **1** The smell of something is a quality it has which you perceive through your nose EG *a smell of damp wood.* **2** Your sense of smell is your ability to smell things. ▶ VERB **3** If something smells or if you can smell it, it has a quality you can perceive through your nose EG *He smelled of tobacco and garlic.* **4** If you can smell something such as danger or trouble, you feel it is present or likely to happen.
▤ (sense 1) odour, scent

smelly smellier smelliest
ADJECTIVE having a strong, unpleasant smell.

smelt smelts smelting smelted
VERB To smelt a metal ore means to heat it until it melts, so that the metal can be extracted.

smile smiles smiling smiled
VERB **1** When you smile, the corners of your mouth move outwards and slightly upwards because you are pleased or amused. ▶ NOUN **2** the expression you have when you

smile.

smirk smirks smirking smirked

VERB **1** When you smirk, you smile in a sneering or sarcastic way EG *The boy smirked and turned the volume up.* ▶ NOUN **2** a sneering or sarcastic smile.

smith smiths

NOUN someone who makes things out of iron, gold, or another metal.

smitten

ADJECTIVE If you are smitten with someone or something, you are very impressed with or enthusiastic about them EG *They were totally smitten with each other.*

smock smocks

NOUN a loose garment like a long blouse.

smog

NOUN Smog is a mixture of smoke and fog which occurs in some industrial cities.

smoke smokes smoking smoked

NOUN **1** Smoke is a mixture of gas and small particles sent into the air when something burns. ▶ VERB **2** If something is smoking, smoke is coming from it. **3** When someone smokes a cigarette or pipe, they suck smoke from it into their mouth and blow it out again. **4** To smoke fish or meat means to hang it over burning wood so that the smoke preserves it and gives it a pleasant flavour EG *smoked bacon.* **smoker** NOUN, **smoking** NOUN

smoky smokier smokiest

ADJECTIVE A smoky place is full of smoke.

smooth smoother smoothest; smooths smoothing smoothed

ADJECTIVE **1** A smooth surface has no roughness and no holes in it. **2** A smooth liquid or mixture has no lumps in it. **3** A smooth movement or process happens evenly and steadily EG *smooth acceleration.* **4** Smooth also means successful and without problems EG *staff responsible for the smooth running of the hall.* ▶ VERB **5** If you smooth something, you move your hands over it to make it smooth and flat. **smoothly** ADVERB, **smoothness** NOUN

smother smothers smothering smothered

VERB **1** If you smother a fire, you cover it with something to put it out. **2** To smother a person means to cover their face with something so that they cannot breathe. **3** To smother someone also means to give them too much love and protection EG *She loved her own children, almost smothering them with love.* **4** If you smother an emotion, you control it so that people do not notice it EG *They tried to smother their glee.*

smothered

ADJECTIVE completely covered with something EG *a spectacular trellis smothered in climbing roses.*

smoulder smoulders smouldering smouldered

VERB **1** When something smoulders, it burns slowly, producing smoke but no flames. **2** If a feeling is smouldering inside you, you feel it very strongly but do not show it EG *smouldering with resentment.*

smudge smudges smudging smudged

NOUN **1** a dirty or blurred mark or a smear on something. ▶ VERB **2** If you smudge something, you make it dirty or messy by touching it or marking it.

smug smugger smuggest

ADJECTIVE Someone who is smug is very pleased with how good or clever they are. **smugly** ADVERB, **smugness** NOUN

smuggle smuggles smuggling smuggled

VERB To smuggle things or people into or out of a place means to take them there illegally or secretly.

smuggler smugglers

NOUN someone who smuggles goods illegally into a country.

A B C D E F G H I J K L M N O P Q R S T U V W X Y Z

A B C D E F G H I J K L M N O P Q R S T U V W X Y Z

snack snacks
NOUN a light, quick meal.

snag snags snagging snagged
NOUN **1** a small problem or disadvantage EG *There is one snag: it is not true.* ▸ VERB **2** If you snag your clothing, you damage it by catching it on something sharp. ▸ NOUN; AN INFORMAL USE **3** In Australian and New Zealand English, a sausage.

snail snails
NOUN a small, slow-moving creature with a long, shiny body and a shell on its back.

snail mail
NOUN; AN INFORMAL USE the conventional postal system, as opposed to email.

snake snakes snaking snaked
NOUN **1** a long, thin, scaly reptile with no legs. ▸ VERB **2** Something that snakes moves in long winding curves EG *The queue snaked out of the shop.*

snap snaps snapping snapped
VERB **1** If something snaps or if you snap it, it breaks with a sharp cracking noise. **2** If you snap something into a particular position, you move it there quickly with a sharp sound. **3** If an animal snaps at you, it shuts its jaws together quickly as if to bite you. **4** If someone snaps at you, they speak in a sharp, unfriendly way. **5** If you snap someone, you take a quick photograph of them. ▸ NOUN **6** the sound of something snapping. **7** AN INFORMAL USE a photograph taken quickly and casually. ▸ ADJECTIVE **8** A snap decision or action is taken suddenly without careful thought.

snapper snappers
NOUN a fish with edible pink flesh, found in waters around Australia and New Zealand.

snapshot snapshots
NOUN a photograph taken quickly and casually.

snare snares snaring snared
NOUN **1** a trap for catching birds or small animals. ▸ VERB **2** To snare an animal or bird means to catch it using a snare.

snarl snarls snarling snarled
VERB **1** When an animal snarls, it bares its teeth and makes a fierce growling noise. **2** If you snarl, you say something in a fierce, angry way. ▸ NOUN **3** the noise an animal makes when it snarls.

snatch snatches snatching snatched
VERB **1** If you snatch something, you reach out for it quickly and take it. **2** If you snatch an amount of time or an opportunity, you quickly make use of it. ▸ NOUN **3** If you make a snatch at something, you reach out for it quickly to try to take it. **4** A snatch of conversation or song is a very small piece of it.

sneak sneaks sneaking sneaked
VERB **1** If you sneak somewhere, you go there quietly trying not to be seen or heard. **2** If you sneak something somewhere, you take it there secretly. ▸ NOUN **3** AN INFORMAL USE someone who tells people in authority that someone else has done something wrong.

sneaker sneakers
NOUN Sneakers are casual shoes with rubber soles.

sneaking
ADJECTIVE If you have a sneaking feeling about something or someone, you have this feeling rather reluctantly EG *I had a sneaking suspicion that she was enjoying herself.*

sneaky sneakier sneakiest
ADJECTIVE; AN INFORMAL WORD Someone who is sneaky does things secretly rather than openly.

sneer sneers sneering sneered
VERB **1** If you sneer at someone or something, you show by your expression and your comments that you think they are stupid or inferior. ▸ NOUN **2** the expression on

someone's face when they sneer.

sneeze sneezes sneezing sneezed
VERB **1** When you sneeze, you suddenly take in breath and blow it down your nose noisily, because there is a tickle in your nose. ▶ NOUN **2** an act of sneezing.

snide
ADJECTIVE A snide comment or remark criticizes someone in a nasty and unfair way.

sniff sniffs sniffing sniffed
VERB **1** When you sniff, you breathe in air through your nose hard enough to make a sound. **2** If you sniff something, you smell it by sniffing. **3** You can say that a person sniffs at something when they do not think very much of it EG *Bessie sniffed at his household arrangements*. ▶ NOUN **4** the noise you make when you sniff. **5** A sniff of something is a smell of it EG *a sniff at the flowers*.

snigger sniggers sniggering sniggered
VERB **1** If you snigger, you laugh quietly and disrespectfully EG *They were sniggering at her accent*. ▶ NOUN **2** a quiet, disrespectful laugh.

snip snips snipping snipped
VERB **1** If you snip something, you cut it with scissors or shears in a single quick action. ▶ NOUN **2** a small cut made by scissors or shears.

snippet snippets
NOUN A snippet of something such as information or news is a small piece of it.

snob snobs
NOUN **1** someone who admires upper-class people and looks down on lower-class people. **2** someone who believes that they are better than other people.
snobbery NOUN, **snobbish** ADJECTIVE

snooker
NOUN Snooker is a game played on a large table covered with smooth green cloth. Players score points by hitting different coloured balls into side pockets using a long stick called a cue.

snoop snoops snooping snooped
VERB; AN INFORMAL WORD Someone who is snooping is secretly looking round a place to find out things.
📖 from Dutch *snoepen* meaning 'to eat furtively'

snooze snoozes snoozing snoozed
AN INFORMAL WORD ▶ VERB **1** If you snooze, you sleep lightly for a short time, especially during the day. ▶ NOUN **2** a short, light sleep.

snore snores snoring snored
VERB **1** When a sleeping person snores, they make a loud noise each time they breathe. ▶ NOUN **2** the noise someone makes when they snore.

snorkel snorkels
NOUN a tube you can breathe through when you are swimming just under the surface of the sea.
snorkelling NOUN
📖 from German *Schnorchel*, originally an air pipe for a submarine

snort snorts snorting snorted
VERB **1** When people or animals snort, they force breath out through their nose in a noisy way EG *Sarah snorted with laughter*. ▶ NOUN **2** the noise you make when you snort.

snout snouts
NOUN An animal's snout is its nose.

snow snows snowing snowed
NOUN **1** Snow consists of flakes of ice crystals which fall from the sky in cold weather. ▶ VERB **2** When it snows, snow falls from the sky.

snowball snowballs snowballing snowballed
NOUN **1** a ball of snow for throwing. ▶ VERB **2** When something such as a project snowballs, it grows rapidly.

snowdrift snowdrifts
NOUN a deep pile of snow formed by the wind.

snowdrop snowdrops
NOUN a small white flower which appears in early spring.

snowman snowmen
NOUN a large mound of snow moulded into the shape of a person.

snub snubs snubbing snubbed
VERB 1 To snub someone means to behave rudely towards them, especially by making an insulting remark or ignoring them. ▶ NOUN 2 an insulting remark or a piece of rude behaviour. ▶ ADJECTIVE 3 A snub nose is short and turned-up.
■ (sense 2) affront, insult, slap in the face

snuff
NOUN Snuff is powdered tobacco which people take by sniffing it up their noses.

snug
ADJECTIVE A snug place is warm and comfortable. If you are snug, you are warm and comfortable.
snugly ADVERB

snuggle snuggles snuggling snuggled
VERB If you snuggle somewhere, you cuddle up more closely to something or someone.

so
ADVERB 1 'So' is used to refer back to what has just been mentioned EG Had he locked the car? If so, where were the keys? 2 'So' is used to mean also EG He laughed, and so did Jarvis. 3 'So' can be used to mean 'therefore' EG It's a bit expensive, so I don't think I will get one. 4 'So' is used when you are talking about the degree or extent of something EG Why are you so cruel? 5 'So' is used before words like 'much' and 'many' to say that there is a definite limit to something EG There are only so many questions that can be asked about the record. ▶ CONJUNCTION 6 'So that' and 'so as' are used to introduce the reason for doing something EG to die so that you might live.

soak soaks soaking soaked
VERB 1 To soak something or leave it to soak means to put it in a liquid and leave it there. 2 When a liquid soaks something, it makes it very wet. 3 When something soaks up a liquid, the liquid is drawn up into it.
■ (sense 2) saturate, wet

soaked
ADJECTIVE extremely wet.

soaking
ADJECTIVE If something is soaking, it is very wet.

soap soaps
NOUN Soap is a substance made of natural oils and fats and used for washing yourself.
soapy ADJECTIVE

soap opera soap operas
NOUN a popular television drama serial about people's daily lives.

soar soars soaring soared
VERB 1 If an amount soars, it quickly increases by a great deal EG Property prices soared. 2 If something soars into the air, it quickly goes up into the air.
soaring ADJECTIVE

sob sobs sobbing sobbed
VERB 1 When someone sobs, they cry in a noisy way, breathing in short breaths. ▶ NOUN 2 the noise made when you cry.

sober soberer soberest; sobers sobering sobered
ADJECTIVE 1 If someone is sober, they are not drunk. 2 Sober also means serious and thoughtful. 3 Sober colours are plain and rather dull. ▶ VERB 4 To sober up means to become sober after being drunk.
soberly ADVERB

sobering
ADJECTIVE Something which is sobering makes you serious and thoughtful EG the sobering lesson of the last year.

so-called
ADJECTIVE You use 'so-called' to say that the name by which something

is called is incorrect or misleading
EG *so-called environmentally-friendly
products.*

soccer

NOUN Soccer is a game played by
two teams of eleven players kicking
a ball in an attempt to score goals.
📖 formed from ***Association
Football***

sociable

ADJECTIVE Sociable people are
friendly and enjoy talking to other
people.
sociability NOUN
■ friendly, gregarious, outgoing

social

ADJECTIVE **1** to do with society or life
within a society EG *women from
similar social backgrounds.* **2** to do
with leisure activities that involve
meeting other people.
socially ADVERB

socialism

NOUN Socialism is the political belief
that the state should own
industries on behalf of the people
and that everyone should be equal.
socialist ADJECTIVE OR NOUN

socialize socializes socializing socialized; also spelt socialise

VERB When people socialize, they
meet other people socially, for
example at parties.

social security

NOUN Social security is a system by
which the government pays money
regularly to people who have no
other income or only a very small
income.

social work

NOUN Social work involves giving
help and advice to people with
serious financial or family
problems.
social worker NOUN

society societies

NOUN **1** Society is the people in a
particular country or region EG *a
major problem in society.* **2** an
organization for people who have
the same interest or aim EG *the
school debating society.* **3** Society is
also rich, upper-class, fashionable
people.
■ (sense 1) civilization, culture

sociology

NOUN Sociology is the study of
human societies and the
relationships between groups in
these societies.
sociological ADJECTIVE, **sociologist** NOUN

sock socks

NOUN Socks are pieces of clothing
covering your foot and ankle.
📖 from Old English *socc* meaning
'light shoe'

socket sockets

NOUN **1** a place on a wall or on a
piece of electrical equipment into
which you can put a plug or bulb.
2 Any hollow part or opening into
which another part fits can be
called a socket EG *eye sockets.*

sod

NOUN; A LITERARY USE The sod is the
surface of the ground, together
with the grass and roots growing in
it.

soda sodas

NOUN **1** Soda is the same as **soda
water**. **2** Soda is also sodium in the
form of crystals or a powder, and is
used for baking or cleaning.

soda water soda waters

NOUN Soda water is fizzy water used
for mixing with alcoholic drinks or
fruit juice.

sodden

ADJECTIVE soaking wet.

sodium

NOUN Sodium is a silvery-white
chemical element which combines
with other chemicals. Salt is a
sodium compound.

sofa sofas

NOUN a long comfortable seat with a
back and arms for two or three
people.
📖 from Arabic ***suffah*** meaning 'an
upholstered raised platform'

soft softer softest

A
B
C
D
E
F
G
H
I
J
K
L
M
N
O
P
Q
R
S
T
U
V
W
X
Y
Z

A B C D E F G H I J K L M N O P Q R S T U V W X Y Z

ADJECTIVE **1** Something soft is not hard, stiff, or firm. **2** Soft also means very gentle EG *a soft breeze*. **3** A soft sound or voice is quiet and not harsh. **4** A soft colour or light is not bright.
softly ADVERB

soft drink soft drinks
NOUN any cold, nonalcoholic drink.

soften softens softening softened
VERB **1** If something is softened or softens, it becomes less hard, stiff, or firm. **2** If you soften, you become more sympathetic and less critical EG *Phillida softened as she spoke*.

software
NOUN Computer programs are known as software.

soggy soggier soggiest
ADJECTIVE unpleasantly wet or full of water.
▣ from American dialect *sog* meaning 'marsh'

soil soils soiling soiled
NOUN **1** Soil is the top layer on the surface of the earth in which plants grow. ▶ VERB **2** If you soil something, you make it dirty.
soiled ADJECTIVE
▤ (sense 1) earth, ground

solace
NOUN; A LITERARY WORD Solace is something that makes you feel less sad EG *I found solace in writing*.

solar
ADJECTIVE **1** relating or belonging to the sun. **2** using the sun's light and heat as a source of energy EG *a solar-powered calculator*.

solar system
NOUN The solar system is the sun and all the planets, comets, and asteroids that orbit round it.

solder solders soldering soldered
VERB **1** To solder two pieces of metal together means to join them with molten metal. ▶ NOUN **2** Solder is the soft metal used for soldering.

soldier soldiers

NOUN a person in an army.

sole soles soling soled
ADJECTIVE **1** The sole thing or person of a particular type is the only one of that type. ▶ NOUN **2** The sole of your foot or shoe is the underneath part. **3** a flat sea-water fish which you can eat. ▶ VERB **4** When a shoe is soled, a sole is fitted to it.

solely
ADVERB If something involves solely one thing, it involves that thing and nothing else.

solemn
ADJECTIVE Solemn means serious rather than cheerful or humorous.
solemnly ADVERB, **solemnity** NOUN

solicitor solicitors
NOUN a lawyer who gives legal advice and prepares legal documents and cases.

solid solids
ADJECTIVE **1** A solid substance or object is hard or firm, and not in the form of a liquid or gas. **2** You say that something is solid when it is not hollow EG *solid steel*. **3** You say that a structure is solid when it is strong and not likely to fall down EG *solid fences*. **4** You use 'solid' to say that something happens for a period of time without interruption EG *I cried for two solid days*. ▶ NOUN **5** a solid substance or object.
solidly ADVERB

solidarity
NOUN If a group of people show solidarity, they show unity and support for each other.

soliloquy soliloquies
Said "sol-lill-ok-wee" NOUN a speech in a play made by a character who is alone on the stage.
▣ from Latin *solus* meaning 'alone' and *loqui* meaning 'to speak'

solitary
ADJECTIVE **1** A solitary activity is one that you do on your own. **2** A solitary person or animal spends a

lot of time alone. **3** If there is a solitary person or object somewhere, there is only one.

solitary confinement
NOUN A prisoner in solitary confinement is being kept alone in a prison cell.

solitude
NOUN Solitude is the state of being alone.
■ isolation, seclusion

solo solos
NOUN **1** a piece of music played or sung by one person alone.
▶ ADJECTIVE **2** A solo performance or activity is done by one person alone EG *my first solo flight*. ▶ ADVERB **3** Solo means alone EG *to sail solo around the world*.

soloist soloists
NOUN a person who performs a solo.

solstice solstices
NOUN one of the two times in the year when the sun is at its furthest point south or north of the equator.
🔲 from Latin *sol* meaning 'sun' and *sistere* meaning 'to stand still'

soluble
ADJECTIVE A soluble substance is able to dissolve in liquid.

solution solutions
NOUN **1** a way of dealing with a problem or difficult situation EG *a quick solution to our problem*. **2** The solution to a riddle or a puzzle is the answer. **3** a liquid in which a solid substance has been dissolved.

solve solves solving solved
VERB If you solve a problem or a question, you find a solution or answer to it.
■ answer, resolve, work out

solvent solvents
ADJECTIVE **1** If a person or company is solvent, they have enough money to pay all their debts. ▶ NOUN **2** a liquid that can dissolve other substances.
solvency NOUN

Somali Somalis
ADJECTIVE **1** belonging or relating to Somalia. ▶ NOUN **2** The Somalis are a group of people who live in Somalia. **3** Somali is the language spoken by Somalis.

sombre
ADJECTIVE **1** Sombre colours are dark and dull. **2** A sombre person is serious, sad, or gloomy.

some
1 You use 'some' to refer to a quantity or number when you are not stating the quantity or number exactly EG *There's some money on the table*. **2** You use 'some' to emphasize that a quantity or number is fairly large EG *She had been there for some days*. ▶ ADVERB **3** You use 'some' in front of a number to show that it is not exact EG *a fishing village some seven miles north*.

somebody
PRONOUN Somebody means someone.
☑ *Somebody* and *someone* mean the same.

some day
ADVERB Some day means at a date in the future that is unknown or that has not yet been decided.

somehow
ADVERB **1** You use 'somehow' to say that you do not know how something was done or will be done EG *You'll find a way of doing it somehow*. **2** You use 'somehow' to say that you do not know the reason for something EG *Somehow it didn't feel quite right*.

someone
PRONOUN You use 'someone' to refer to a person without saying exactly who you mean.
☑ *Someone* and *somebody* mean the same.

somersault somersaults
NOUN a forwards or backwards roll in which the head is placed on the ground and the body is brought

A
B
C
D
E
F
G
H
I
J
K
L
M
N
O
P
Q
R
S
T
U
V
W
X
Y
Z

A B C D E F G H I J K L M N O P Q R S T U V W X Y Z

over it.

⌨ from Old Provençal *sobre* meaning 'over' and *saut* meaning 'jump'

something

PRONOUN You use 'something' to refer to anything that is not a person without saying exactly what you mean.

sometime

ADVERB **1** at a time in the future or the past that is unknown or that has not yet been fixed EG *He has to find out sometime.* ▶ ADJECTIVE **2** A FORMAL USE 'Sometime' is used to say that a person had a particular job or role in the past EG *a sometime actress, dancer and singer.*

sometimes

ADVERB occasionally, rather than always or never.

somewhat

ADVERB to some extent or degree EG *The future seemed somewhat bleak.*

somewhere

ADVERB **1** 'Somewhere' is used to refer to a place without stating exactly where it is EG *There has to be a file somewhere.* **2** 'Somewhere' is used when giving an approximate amount, number, or time EG *somewhere between the winter of 1989 and the summer of 1991.*

son sons

NOUN Someone's son is their male child.

sonar

NOUN Sonar is equipment on a ship which calculates the depth of the sea or the position of an underwater object using sound waves.

⌨ from *So(und) Na(vigation) R(anging)*

sonata sonatas

NOUN a piece of classical music, usually in three or more movements, for piano or for another instrument with or without piano.

song songs

NOUN a piece of music with words that are sung to the music.

son-in-law sons-in-law

NOUN Someone's son-in-law is the husband of their daughter.

sonnet sonnets

NOUN a poem with 14 lines, in which lines rhyme according to fixed patterns.

⌨ from Old Provençal *sonet* meaning 'little poem'

soon sooner soonest

ADVERB If something is going to happen soon, it will happen in a very short time.

soot

NOUN Soot is black powder which rises in the smoke from a fire.

sooty ADJECTIVE

soothe soothes soothing soothed

VERB **1** If you soothe someone who is angry or upset, you make them calmer. **2** Something that soothes pain makes the pain less severe.

soothing ADJECTIVE

sophisticated

ADJECTIVE **1** Sophisticated people have refined or cultured tastes or habits. **2** A sophisticated machine or device is made using advanced and complicated methods.

sophistication NOUN

▤ (sense 1) cultured, urbane

soppy soppier soppiest

ADJECTIVE; AN INFORMAL WORD silly or foolishly sentimental.

soprano sopranos

NOUN a woman, girl, or boy with a singing voice in the highest range of musical notes.

sorcerer sorcerers

Said "sor-ser-er" NOUN a person who performs magic by using the power of evil spirits.

sorceress sorceresses

NOUN a female sorcerer.

sorcery

NOUN Sorcery is magic that uses the power of evil spirits.

sordid

ADJECTIVE **1** dishonest or immoral EG *a rather sordid business.* **2** dirty, unpleasant, or depressing EG *the sordid guest house.*
■ (sense 2) seedy, sleazy, squalid

sore sorer sorest; sores

ADJECTIVE **1** If part of your body is sore, it causes you pain and discomfort. **2** A LITERARY USE 'Sore' is used to emphasize something EG *The President is in sore need of friends.*
▶ NOUN **3** a painful place where your skin has become infected.
sorely ADVERB, **soreness** NOUN
■ (sense 1) painful, sensitive, tender

sorghum

Said "saw-gum" NOUN a type of tropical grass that is grown for hay, grain, and syrup.

sorrow sorrows

NOUN **1** Sorrow is deep sadness or regret. **2** Sorrows are things that cause sorrow EG *the sorrows of this world.*

sorry sorrier sorriest

ADJECTIVE **1** If you are sorry about something, you feel sadness, regret, or sympathy because of it EG *I was so sorry to hear about your husband.* **2** 'Sorry' is used to describe people and things that are in a bad physical or mental state EG *She was in a pretty sorry state when we found her.*
■ (sense 1) apologetic, contrite, regretful

sort sorts sorting sorted

NOUN **1** The different sorts of something are the different types of it. ▶ VERB **2** To sort things means to arrange them into different groups or sorts.
■ (sense 1) kind, type, variety
sort out VERB If you sort out a problem or misunderstanding, you deal with it and find a solution to it.
☑ When you use *sort* in its singular form, the adjective before it should

also be singular: *that sort of car.* When you use the plural form *sorts*, the adjective before it should be plural: *those sorts of shop; those sorts of shops.*

SOS

NOUN An SOS is a signal that you are in danger and need help.

so-so

ADJECTIVE neither good nor bad EG *The food is so-so.*

soufflé soufflés

Said "soo-flay"; also spelt **souffle**
NOUN a light, fluffy food made from beaten egg whites and other ingredients that is baked in the oven.

sought

the past tense and past participle of seek.

soul souls

NOUN **1** A person's soul is the spiritual part of them that is supposed to continue after their body is dead. **2** People also use 'soul' to refer to a person's mind, character, thoughts, and feelings. **3** 'Soul' can be used to mean person EG *There was not a soul there.* **4** Soul is a type of pop music.

sound sounds sounding sounded; sounder soundest

NOUN **1** Sound is everything that can be heard. **2** A particular sound is something that you hear. **3** The sound of someone or something is the impression you have of them EG *I like the sound of your father's grandfather.* ▶ VERB **4** If something sounds or if you sound it, it makes a noise. **5** To sound something deep, such as a well or the sea, means to measure how deep it is using a weighted line or sonar.
▶ ADJECTIVE **6** in good condition EG *a guarantee that a house is sound.* **7** reliable and sensible EG *The logic behind the argument seems sound.*
soundly ADVERB

sound bite sound bites

NOUN a short and memorable

sentence or phrase extracted from a longer speech for use on radio or television.

sound effect sound effects
NOUN Sound effects are sounds created artificially to make a play more realistic, especially a radio play.

soundproof
ADJECTIVE If a room is soundproof, sound cannot get into it or out of it.

soup soups
NOUN Soup is liquid food made by boiling meat, fish, or vegetables in water.

sour sours souring soured
ADJECTIVE **1** If something is sour, it has a sharp, acid taste. **2** Sour milk has an unpleasant taste because it is no longer fresh. **3** A sour person is bad-tempered and unfriendly.
▶ VERB **4** If a friendship, situation, or attitude sours or if something sours it, it becomes less friendly, enjoyable, or hopeful.

source sources
NOUN **1** The source of something is the person, place, or thing that it comes from EG *the source of his confidence.* **2** The source of a river or stream is the place where it begins.

sour grapes
PLURAL NOUN You describe someone's behaviour as sour grapes when they say something is worthless but secretly want it and cannot have it.

south
NOUN **1** The south is the direction to your right when you are looking towards the place where the sun rises. **2** The south of a place or country is the part which is towards the south when you are in the centre. ▶ ADVERB OR ADJECTIVE **3** South means towards the south EG *The taxi headed south... the south end of the site.* ▶ ADJECTIVE **4** A south wind blows from the south.

South America
NOUN South America is the fourth largest continent. It has the Pacific Ocean on its west side, the Atlantic on the east, and the Antarctic to the south. South America is joined to North America by the Isthmus of Panama.
South American ADJECTIVE

south-east
NOUN, ADVERB, OR ADJECTIVE South-east is halfway between south and east.

south-easterly
ADJECTIVE **1** South-easterly means to or towards the south-east. **2** A south-easterly wind blows from the south-east.

south-eastern
ADJECTIVE in or from the south-east.

southerly
ADJECTIVE **1** Southerly means to or towards the south. **2** A southerly wind blows from the south.

southern
ADJECTIVE in or from the south.

Southern Cross
NOUN The Southern Cross is a small group of stars which can be seen from the southern part of the earth, and which is represented on the national flags of Australia and New Zealand.

South Pole
NOUN The South Pole is the place on the surface of the earth that is farthest towards the south.

southward or **southwards**
ADVERB **1** Southward or southwards means towards the south EG *the dusty road which led southwards.*
▶ ADJECTIVE **2** The southward part of something is the south part.

south-west
NOUN, ADVERB, OR ADJECTIVE South-west is halfway between south and west.

south-westerly
ADJECTIVE **1** South-westerly means to or towards the south-west. **2** A south-westerly wind blows from the south-west.

south-western
ADJECTIVE in or from the south-west.

souvenir souvenirs

NOUN something you keep to remind you of a holiday, place, or event.

🔲 from French *se souvenir* meaning 'to remember'

sovereign sovereigns

Said "sov-rin" NOUN **1** a king, queen, or royal ruler of a country. **2** In the past, a sovereign was a British gold coin worth one pound. ▶ ADJECTIVE **3** A sovereign state or country is independent and not under the authority of any other country.

sovereignty

Said "sov-rin-tee" NOUN Sovereignty is the political power that a country has to govern itself.

Soviet Soviets

Said "soe-vee-et" ADJECTIVE **1** belonging or relating to the country that used to be the Soviet Union. ▶ NOUN **2** The people and the government of the country that used to be the Soviet Union were sometimes referred to as the Soviets.

sow sows sowing sowed sown

Said "soh" VERB **1** To sow seeds or sow an area of land with seeds means to plant them in the ground. **2** To sow undesirable feelings or attitudes means to cause them EG *You have sown discontent.*

sow sows

Rhymes with "**now**" NOUN an adult female pig.

soya

NOUN Soya flour, margarine, oil, and milk are made from soya beans.

🔲 from Chinese *chiang yu* meaning 'paste sauce'

soya bean soya beans

NOUN Soya beans are a type of edible Asian bean.

spa spas

NOUN a place where water containing minerals bubbles out of the ground, at which people drink or bathe in the water to improve their health.

🔲 from the Belgian town *Spa*

where there are mineral springs

space spaces spacing spaced

NOUN **1** Space is the area that is empty or available in a place, building, or container. **2** Space is the area beyond the earth's atmosphere surrounding the stars and planets. **3** a gap between two things EG *the space between the tables.* **4** Space can also refer to a period of time EG *two incidents in the space of a week.* ▶ VERB **5** If you space a series of things, you arrange them with gaps between them.

spaceman spacemen

NOUN someone who travels in space.

spaceship spaceships

NOUN a spacecraft that carries people through space.

space shuttle space shuttles

NOUN a spacecraft designed to be used many times for travelling out into space and back again.

spacious

ADJECTIVE having or providing a lot of space EG *the spacious living room.*

▣ capacious, commodious, roomy

spade spades

NOUN **1** a tool with a flat metal blade and a long handle used for digging. **2** Spades is one of the four suits in a pack of playing cards. It is marked by a black symbol in the shape of a heart-shaped leaf with a stem.

spaghetti

Said "spag-get-ee" NOUN Spaghetti consists of long, thin pieces of pasta.

span spans spanning spanned

NOUN **1** the period of time during which something exists or functions EG *looking back today over a span of forty years.* **2** The span of something is the total length of it from one end to the other. ▶ VERB **3** If something spans a particular length of time, it lasts throughout that time EG *a career that spanned 50 years.* **4** A bridge that spans something stretches right across it.

A
B
C
D
E
F
G
H
I
J
K
L
M
N
O
P
Q
R
S
T
U
V
W
X
Y
Z

A
B
C
D
E
F
G
H
I
J
K
L
M
N
O
P
Q
R
S
T
U
V
W
X
Y
Z

spangle spangles spangling spangled
VERB **1** If something is spangled, it is covered with small, sparkling objects. ▸ NOUN **2** Spangles are small sparkling pieces of metal or plastic used to decorate clothing or hair.

Spaniard Spaniards
Said "**span-yard**" NOUN someone who comes from Spain.

spaniel spaniels
NOUN a dog with long drooping ears and a silky coat.
📖 from Old French *espaigneul* meaning 'Spanish dog'

Spanish
ADJECTIVE **1** belonging or relating to Spain. ▸ NOUN **2** Spanish is the main language spoken in Spain, and is also spoken by many people in Central and South America.

spank spanks spanking spanked
VERB If a child is spanked, it is punished by being slapped, usually on its leg or bottom.

spanner spanners
NOUN a tool with a specially shaped end that fits round a nut to turn it.

spar spars sparring sparred
VERB **1** When boxers spar, they hit each other with light punches for practice. **2** To spar with someone also means to argue with them, but not in an unpleasant or serious way. ▸ NOUN **3** a strong pole that a sail is attached to on a yacht or ship.

spare spares sparing spared
ADJECTIVE **1** extra to what is needed EG *What does she do in her spare time?* ▸ NOUN **2** a thing that is extra to what is needed. ▸ VERB **3** If you spare something for a particular purpose, you make it available EG *Few troops could be spared to go abroad.* **4** If someone is spared an unpleasant experience, they are prevented from suffering it EG *The capital was spared the misery of an all-out train strike.*

sparing

ADJECTIVE If you are sparing with something, you use it in very small quantities.
sparingly ADVERB

spark sparks sparking sparked
NOUN **1** a tiny, bright piece of burning material thrown up by a fire. **2** a small flash of light caused by electricity. **3** A spark of feeling is a small amount of it EG *that tiny spark of excitement.* ▸ VERB **4** If something sparks, it throws out sparks. **5** If one thing sparks another thing off, it causes the second thing to start happening EG *The tragedy sparked off a wave of sympathy among staff.*

sparkle sparkles sparkling sparkled
VERB **1** If something sparkles, it shines with a lot of small, bright points of light. ▸ NOUN **2** Sparkles are small, bright points of light.
sparkling ADJECTIVE
📊 (sense 1) gleam, glitter, twinkle

sparrow sparrows
NOUN a common, small bird with brown and grey feathers.

sparse sparser sparsest
ADJECTIVE small in number or amount and spread out over an area EG *the sparse audience.*
sparsely ADVERB

spartan
ADJECTIVE A spartan way of life is very simple with no luxuries EG *spartan accommodation.*
📖 from *Sparta*, a city in Ancient Greece, whose inhabitants were famous for their discipline, military skill, and stern and plain way of life

spasm spasms
NOUN **1** a sudden tightening of the muscles. **2** a sudden, short burst of something EG *a spasm of fear.*

spasmodic
ADJECTIVE happening suddenly for short periods of time at irregular intervals EG *spasmodic movements.*

spastic spastics
ADJECTIVE **1** A spastic person is born

with a disability which makes it difficult for them to control their muscles. ▶ NOUN **2** a spastic person.
📖 from Greek *spasmos* meaning 'cramp' or 'convulsion'

spate
NOUN A spate of things is a large number of them that happen or appear in a rush EG *a recent spate of first novels from older writers.*

spatial
Said "spay-shl" ADJECTIVE to do with size, area, or position.

spatter spatters spattering spattered
VERB **1** If something spatters a surface, it covers the surface with drops of liquid. ▶ NOUN **2** A spatter of something is a small amount of it in drops or tiny pieces.

spawn spawns spawning spawned
NOUN **1** Spawn is a jelly-like substance containing the eggs of fish or amphibians. ▶ VERB **2** When fish or amphibians spawn, they lay their eggs. **3** If something spawns something else, it causes it EG *The depressed economy spawned the riots.*

speak speaks speaking spoke spoken
VERB **1** When you speak, you use your voice to say words. **2** If you speak a foreign language, you know it and can use it.
📑 (sense 1) say, talk, utter
speak out VERB To speak out about something means to publicly state an opinion about it.

speaker speakers
NOUN **1** a person who is speaking, especially someone making a speech. **2** A speaker on a radio or hi-fi is a loudspeaker.

spear spears spearing speared
NOUN **1** a weapon consisting of a long pole with a sharp point. ▶ VERB **2** To spear something means to push or throw a spear or other pointed object into it.

spearhead spearheads

spearheading spearheaded
VERB If someone spearheads a campaign, they lead it.

spec specs
AN INFORMAL WORD ▶ PLURAL NOUN
1 Someone's specs are their glasses.
▶ PHRASE **2** If you do something on spec, you do it hoping for a result but without any certainty EG *He turned up at the same event on spec.*

special
ADJECTIVE **1** Something special is more important or better than other things of its kind. **2** Special describes someone who is officially appointed, or something that is needed for a particular purpose EG *Karen actually had to get special permission to go there.* **3** Special also describes something that belongs or relates to only one particular person, group, or place EG *the special needs of the chronically sick.*

specialist specialists
NOUN **1** someone who has a particular skill or who knows a lot about a particular subject EG *a skin specialist.* ▶ ADJECTIVE **2** having a skill or knowing a lot about a particular subject EG *a specialist teacher.*
specialism NOUN

speciality specialities
NOUN A person's speciality is something they are especially good at or know a lot about EG *Roses are her speciality.*

specialize specializes specializing specialized; also spelt specialise
VERB If you specialize in something, you make it your speciality EG *a shop specializing in ceramics.*
specialization NOUN

specialized or specialised
ADJECTIVE developed for a particular purpose or trained in a particular area of knowledge EG *a specialized sales team.*

specially
ADVERB If something has been done specially for a particular person or purpose, it has been done only for

A B C D E F G H I J K L M N O P Q R S T U V W X Y Z

that person or purpose.

species

Said "spee-sheez" NOUN A class of plants or animals whose members have the same characteristics and are able to breed with each other.

specific

ADJECTIVE **1** particular EG *specific areas of difficulty*. **2** precise and exact EG *She will ask for specific answers.*
specifically ADVERB

specification specifications

NOUN a detailed description of what is needed for something, such as the necessary features in the design of something EG *I like to build it to my own specifications.*

specify specifies specifying specified

VERB To specify something means to state or describe it precisely EG *In his will he specified that these documents were never to be removed.*

specimen specimens

NOUN A specimen of something is an example or small amount of it which gives an idea of what the whole is like EG *a specimen of your writing.*

speck specks

NOUN a very small stain or amount of something.

speckled

ADJECTIVE Something that is speckled is covered in very small marks or spots.

spectacle spectacles

PLURAL NOUN **1** Someone's spectacles are their glasses. ▶ NOUN **2** a strange or interesting sight or scene EG *an astonishing spectacle*. **3** a grand and impressive event or performance.

spectacular spectaculars

ADJECTIVE **1** Something spectacular is very impressive or dramatic. ▶ NOUN **2** a grand and impressive show or performance.
■ (sense 1) impressive, sensational, stunning

spectator spectators

NOUN a person who is watching something.
■ observer, onlooker, watcher

spectra

the plural of **spectrum**.

spectre spectres

NOUN **1** a frightening idea or image EG *the spectre of war*. **2** a ghost.

spectrum spectra or **spectrums**

NOUN **1** The spectrum is the range of different colours produced when light passes through a prism or a drop of water. A rainbow shows the colours in a spectrum. **2** A spectrum of opinions or emotions is a range of them.

speculate speculates speculating speculated

VERB If you speculate about something, you think about it and form opinions about it.
speculation NOUN

speculative

ADJECTIVE **1** A speculative piece of information is based on guesses and opinions rather than known facts. **2** Someone with a speculative expression seems to be trying to guess something EG *His mother regarded him with a speculative eye.*

speech speeches

NOUN **1** Speech is the ability to speak or the act of speaking. **2** a formal talk given to an audience. **3** In a play, a speech is a group of lines spoken by one of the characters.
■ (sense 2) address, talk

speechless

ADJECTIVE Someone who is speechless is unable to speak for a short time because something has shocked them.

speed speeds speeding sped or **speeded**

NOUN **1** The speed of something is the rate at which it moves or happens. **2** Speed is very fast movement or travel. ▶ VERB **3** If you speed somewhere, you move or travel there quickly. **4** Someone who is speeding is driving a vehicle

faster than the legal speed limit.
■ (sense 2) rapidity, swiftness,
velocity

speedboat speedboats
NOUN a small, fast motorboat.

speed limit speed limits
NOUN The speed limit is the
maximum speed at which vehicles
are legally allowed to drive on a
particular road.

speedway
NOUN Speedway is the sport of
racing lightweight motorcycles on
special tracks.

speedy speedier speediest
ADJECTIVE done very quickly.
speedily ADVERB

spell spells spelling spelt or
spelled
VERB 1 When you spell a word, you
name or write its letters in order.
2 When letters spell a word, they
form that word when put together
in a particular order. 3 If something
spells a particular result, it suggests
that this will be the result EG *This
haphazard method could spell disaster
for you.* ▶ NOUN 4 A spell of
something is a short period of it EG
a spell of rough weather. 5 a word or
sequence of words used to perform
magic.
spell out VERB If you spell something
out, you explain it in detail EG *I
don't have to spell it out, do I?*

spellbound
ADJECTIVE so fascinated by something
that you cannot think about
anything else EG *She had sat
spellbound through the film.*

spelling spellings
NOUN The spelling of a word is the
correct order of letters in it.

spend spends spending spent
VERB 1 When you spend money, you
buy things with it. 2 To spend time
or energy means to use it.

spent
ADJECTIVE 1 Spent describes things
which have been used and

therefore cannot be used again EG
spent matches. 2 If you are spent,
you are exhausted and have no
energy left.

sperm sperms
NOUN a cell produced in the sex
organ of a male animal which can
enter a female animal's egg and
fertilize it.

spew spews spewing spewed
VERB 1 When things spew from
something or when it spews them
out, they come out of it in large
quantities. 2 AN INFORMAL USE To spew
up means to vomit.

sphere spheres
NOUN 1 a perfectly round object,
such as a ball. 2 An area of activity
or interest can be referred to as a
sphere of activity or interest.
spherical ADJECTIVE

sphinx sphinxes
Said "sfingks" NOUN In mythology,
the sphinx was a monster with a
person's head and a lion's body.

spice spices spicing spiced
NOUN 1 Spice is powder or seeds
from a plant added to food to give
it flavour. 2 Spice is something
which makes life more exciting EG
Variety is the spice of life. ▶ VERB 3 To
spice food means to add spice to it.
4 If you spice something up, you
make it more exciting or lively.

spicy spicier spiciest
ADJECTIVE strongly flavoured with
spices.

spider spiders
NOUN a small insect-like creature
with eight legs that spins webs to
catch insects for food.
▥ from Old English *spinnan*
meaning 'to spin'

spike spikes
NOUN 1 a long pointed piece of
metal. 2 The spikes on a sports
shoe are the pointed pieces of
metal attached to the sole. 3 Some
other long pointed objects are
called spikes EG *beautiful pink flower
spikes.*

A
B
C
D
E
F
G
H
I
J
K
L
M
N
O
P
Q
R
S
T
U
V
W
X
Y
Z

A
B
C
D
E
F
G
H
I
J
K
L
M
N
O
P
Q
R
S
T
U
V
W
X
Y
Z

spiky spikier spikiest
ADJECTIVE Something spiky has sharp points.

spill spills spilling spilled or spilt
VERB **1** If you spill something or if it spills, it accidentally falls or runs out of a container. **2** If people or things spill out of a place, they come out of it in large numbers.

spillage spillages
NOUN the spilling of something, or something that has been spilt EG *the oil spillage in the Shetlands.*

spin spins spinning spun
VERB **1** If something spins, it turns quickly around a central point. **2** When spiders spin a web, they give out a sticky substance and make it into a web. **3** When people spin, they make thread by twisting together pieces of fibre using a machine. **4** If your head is spinning, you feel dizzy or confused. ▶ NOUN **5** a rapid turn around a central point EG *a golf club which puts more spin on the ball.*

spinach
Said "**spin**-ij" NOUN Spinach is a vegetable with large green leaves.

spinal
ADJECTIVE to do with the spine.

spine spines
NOUN **1** Your spine is your backbone. **2** Spines are long, sharp points on an animal's body or on a plant.

spinifex
NOUN Spinifex is a coarse, spiny Australian grass.

spinning wheel spinning wheels
NOUN a wooden machine for spinning flax or wool.

spin-off spin-offs
NOUN something useful that unexpectedly results from an activity.

spinster spinsters
NOUN a woman who has never married.
🏛 originally a person whose

occupation was spinning; later, the official label of an unmarried woman

spiral spirals spiralling spiralled
NOUN **1** a continuous curve which winds round and round, with each curve above or outside the previous one. ▶ ADJECTIVE **2** in the shape of a spiral EG *a spiral staircase.* ▶ VERB **3** If something spirals, it moves up or down in a spiral curve EG *The aircraft spiralled down.* **4** If an amount or level spirals, it rises or falls quickly at an increasing rate EG *Prices have spiralled recently.*

spire spires
NOUN The spire of a church is the tall cone-shaped structure on top.

spirit spirits spiriting spirited
NOUN **1** Your spirit is the part of you that is not physical and that is connected with your deepest thoughts and feelings. **2** The spirit of a dead person is a nonphysical part that is believed to remain alive after death. **3** a supernatural being, such as a ghost. **4** Spirit is liveliness, energy, and self-confidence EG *a band full of spirit.* **5** Spirit can refer to an attitude EG *his old fighting spirit.* ▶ PLURAL NOUN **6** Spirits can describe how happy or unhappy someone is EG *in good spirits.* **7** Spirits are strong alcoholic drinks such as whisky and gin. ▶ VERB **8** If you spirit someone or something into or out of a place, you get them in or out quickly and secretly.

spirited
ADJECTIVE showing energy and courage.

spirit level spirit levels
NOUN a device for finding out if a surface is level, consisting of a bubble of air sealed in a tube of liquid in a wooden or metal frame.

spiritual spirituals
ADJECTIVE **1** to do with people's thoughts and beliefs, rather than their bodies and physical

surroundings. **2** to do with people's religious beliefs EG *spiritual guidance.*
▶ NOUN **3** a religious song originally sung by Black slaves in America.
spiritually ADVERB, **spirituality** NOUN

spit spits spitting spat
NOUN **1** Spit is saliva. **2** a long stick made of metal or wood which is pushed through a piece of meat so that it can be hung over a fire and cooked. **3** a long, flat, narrow piece of land sticking out into the sea.
▶ VERB **4** If you spit, you force saliva or some other substance out of your mouth. **5** When it is spitting, it is raining very lightly.

spite spites spiting spited
PHRASE **1** In spite of is used to introduce a statement which makes the rest of what you are saying seem surprising EG *In spite of all the gossip, Virginia stayed behind.* ▶ VERB **2** If you do something to spite someone, you do it deliberately to hurt or annoy them. ▶ NOUN **3** If you do something out of spite, you do it to spite someone.

spiteful
ADJECTIVE A spiteful person does or says nasty things to people deliberately to hurt them.
= malicious, nasty, vindictive

spitting image
NOUN If someone is the spitting image of someone else, they look just like them.

splash splashes splashing splashed
VERB **1** If you splash around in water, your movements disturb the water in a noisy way. **2** If liquid splashes something, it scatters over it in a lot of small drops. ▶ NOUN **3** A splash is the sound made when something hits or falls into water. **4** A splash of liquid is a small quantity of it that has been spilt on something.

splatter splatters splattering splattered
VERB When something is splattered

with a substance, the substance is splashed all over it EG *fur coats splattered with paint.*

spleen spleens
NOUN Your spleen is an organ near your stomach which controls the quality of your blood.

splendid
ADJECTIVE **1** very good indeed EG *a splendid career.* **2** beautiful and impressive EG *a splendid old mansion.*
splendidly ADVERB
= (sense 2) grand, magnificent

splendour splendours
NOUN **1** If something has splendour, it is beautiful and impressive.
▶ PLURAL NOUN **2** The splendours of something are its beautiful and impressive features.

splint splints
NOUN a long piece of wood or metal fastened to a broken limb to hold it in place.

splinter splinters splintering splintered
NOUN **1** a thin, sharp piece of wood or glass which has broken off a larger piece. ▶ VERB **2** If something splinters, it breaks into thin, sharp pieces.

split splits splitting split
VERB **1** If something splits or if you split it, it divides into two or more parts. **2** If something such as wood or fabric splits, a long crack or tear appears in it. **3** If people split something, they share it between them. ▶ NOUN **4** A split in a piece of wood or fabric is a crack or tear. **5** A split between two things is a division or difference between them EG *the split between rugby league and rugby union.*
= (sense 1) break, divide, separate
= (sense 5) division, schism
split up VERB If two people split up, they end their relationship or marriage.

split second
NOUN an extremely short period of time.

A B C D E F G H I J K L M N O P Q R S T U V W X Y Z

A B C D E F G H I J K L M N O P Q R S T U V W X Y Z

splitting
ADJECTIVE A splitting headache is very painful.

splutter splutters spluttering spluttered
VERB **1** If someone splutters, they speak in a confused way because they are embarrassed. **2** If something splutters, it makes a series of short, sharp sounds.

spoil spoils spoiling spoiled or spoilt
VERB **1** If you spoil something, you prevent it from being successful or satisfactory. **2** To spoil children means to give them everything they want, with harmful effects on their character. **3** To spoil someone also means to give them something nice as a treat. ▶ PLURAL NOUN **4** Spoils are valuable things obtained during war or as a result of violence EG *the spoils of war*.

▣ (sense 1) mess up, ruin, wreck
▣ (sense 2) overindulge, pamper

spoilsport spoilsports
NOUN someone who spoils people's fun.

spoke spokes
NOUN The spokes of a wheel are the bars which connect the hub to the rim.

spokesperson spokespersons
NOUN someone who speaks on behalf of another person or a group.
spokesman NOUN, **spokeswoman** NOUN

sponge sponges sponging sponged
NOUN **1** a sea creature with a body made up of many cells. **2** part of the very light skeleton of a sponge, used for bathing and cleaning. **3** A sponge or sponge cake is a very light cake. ▶ VERB **4** If you sponge something, you clean it by wiping it with a wet sponge.

sponsor sponsors sponsoring sponsored
VERB **1** To sponsor something, such as an event or someone's training, means to support it financially EG *The visit was sponsored by the London Natural History Society.* **2** If you sponsor someone who is doing something for charity, you agree to give them a sum of money for the charity if they manage to do it. **3** If you sponsor a proposal or suggestion, you officially put it forward and support it EG *the MP who sponsored the Bill.* ▶ NOUN **4** a person or organization sponsoring something or someone.
sponsorship NOUN

spontaneous
ADJECTIVE **1** Spontaneous acts are not planned or arranged, but are done because you feel like it. **2** A spontaneous event happens because of processes within something rather than being caused by things outside it EG *spontaneous bleeding.*
spontaneously ADVERB, **spontaneity** NOUN

spoof spoofs
NOUN something such as an article or television programme that seems to be about a serious matter but is actually a joke.

spooky spookier spookiest
ADJECTIVE eerie and frightening.

spool spools
NOUN a cylindrical object onto which thread, tape, or film can be wound.

spoon spoons
NOUN an object shaped like a small shallow bowl with a long handle, used for eating, stirring, and serving food.

spoonful spoonfuls or spoonsful
NOUN the amount held by a spoon.

sporadic
ADJECTIVE happening at irregular intervals EG *a few sporadic attempts at keeping a diary.*
sporadically ADVERB

spore spores
NOUN; A TECHNICAL WORD Spores are cells produced by bacteria and

nonflowering plants such as fungi which develop into new bacteria or plants.

sporran sporrans
NOUN a large purse made of leather or fur, worn by a Scotsman over his kilt.
▣ from Scottish Gaelic *sporan* meaning 'purse'

sport sports sporting sported
NOUN **1** Sports are games and other enjoyable activities which need physical effort and skill. **2** You say that someone is a sport when they accept defeat or teasing cheerfully EG *Be a sport, Minister!* ▸ VERB **3** If you sport something noticeable or unusual, you wear it EG *A German boy sported a ponytail.*

sporting
ADJECTIVE **1** relating to sport. **2** behaving in a fair and decent way.

sports car sports cars
NOUN a low, fast car, usually with room for only two people.

sportsman sportsmen
NOUN a man who takes part in sports and is good at them.

sportswoman sportswomen
NOUN a woman who takes part in sports and is good at them.

sporty sportier sportiest
ADJECTIVE **1** A sporty car is fast and flashy. **2** A sporty person is good at sports.

spot spots spotting spotted
NOUN **1** Spots are small, round, coloured areas on a surface. **2** Spots on a person's skin are small lumps, usually caused by an infection or allergy. **3** A spot of something is a small amount of it EG *spots of rain.* **4** A place can be called a spot EG *the most beautiful spot in the garden.* ▸ VERB **5** If you spot something, you notice it. ▸ PHRASE **6** If you do something **on the spot**, you do it immediately.

spot check spot checks
NOUN a random examination made

without warning on one of a group of things or people EG *spot checks by road safety officers.*

spotless
ADJECTIVE perfectly clean.
spotlessly ADVERB
▤ clean, immaculate, impeccable

spotlight spotlights spotlighting spotlit or spotlighted
NOUN **1** a powerful light which can be directed to light up a small area. ▸ VERB **2** If something spotlights a situation or problem, it draws the public's attention to it EG *a national campaign to spotlight the problem.*

spot-on
ADJECTIVE; AN INFORMAL EXPRESSION exactly correct or accurate.

spotted
ADJECTIVE Something spotted has a pattern of spots on it.

spotter spotters
NOUN a person whose hobby is looking out for things of a particular kind EG *a train spotter.*

spotty spottier spottiest
ADJECTIVE Someone who is spotty has spots or pimples on their skin, especially on their face.

spouse spouses
NOUN Someone's spouse is the person they are married to.

spout spouts spouting spouted
VERB **1** When liquid or flame spouts out of something, it shoots out in a long stream. **2** When someone spouts what they have learned, they say it in a boring way. ▸ NOUN **3** a tube with a lip-like end for pouring liquid EG *a teapot with a long spout.*

sprain sprains spraining sprained
VERB **1** If you sprain a joint, you accidentally damage it by twisting it violently. ▸ NOUN **2** the injury caused by spraining a joint.

sprawl sprawls sprawling sprawled
VERB **1** If you sprawl somewhere, you sit or lie there with your legs

and arms spread out. **2** A place that sprawls is spread out over a large area EG *a Monday market which sprawls all over town.* ▶ NOUN **3** anything that spreads in an untidy and uncontrolled way EG *a sprawl of skyscrapers.*
sprawling ADJECTIVE

spray sprays spraying sprayed
NOUN **1** Spray consists of many drops of liquid splashed or forced into the air EG *The salt spray stung her face.* **2** Spray is also a liquid kept under pressure in a can or other container EG *hair spray.* **3** a piece of equipment for spraying liquid EG *a garden spray.* **4** A spray of flowers or leaves consists of several of them on one stem. ▶ VERB **5** To spray a liquid over something means to cover it with drops of the liquid.

spread spreads spreading spread
VERB **1** If you spread something out, you open it out or arrange it so that it can be seen or used easily EG *He spread the map out on his knees.* **2** If you spread a substance on a surface, you put a thin layer on the surface. **3** If something spreads, it gradually reaches or affects more people EG *The news spread quickly.* **4** If something spreads over a period of time, it happens regularly or continuously over that time EG *His four international appearances were spread over eight years.* **5** If something such as work is spread, it is distributed evenly. ▶ NOUN **6** The spread of something is the extent to which it gradually reaches or affects more people EG *the spread of Buddhism.* **7** A spread of ideas, interests, or other things is a wide variety of them. **8** soft food put on bread EG *cheese spread.*

spread-eagled
ADJECTIVE Someone who is spread-eagled is lying with their arms and legs spread out.

spreadsheet spreadsheets
NOUN a computer program that is used for entering and arranging

figures, used mainly for financial planning.

spree sprees
NOUN a period of time spent doing something enjoyable EG *a shopping spree.*

sprig sprigs
NOUN **1** a small twig with leaves on it. **2** In Australian and New Zealand English, sprigs are studs on the sole of a football boot.

sprightly sprightlier sprightliest
ADJECTIVE lively and active.

spring springs springing sprang sprung
NOUN **1** Spring is the season between winter and summer. **2** a coil of wire which returns to its natural shape after being pressed or pulled. **3** a place where water comes up through the ground. **4** an act of springing EG *With a spring he had opened the door.* ▶ VERB **5** To spring means to jump upwards or forwards EG *Martha sprang to her feet.* **6** If something springs in a particular direction, it moves suddenly and quickly EG *The door sprang open.* **7** If one thing springs from another, it is the result of it EG *The failures sprang from three facts.*

springboard springboards
NOUN **1** a flexible board on which a diver or gymnast jumps to gain height. **2** If something is a springboard for an activity or enterprise, it makes it possible for it to begin.

springbok springboks
NOUN **1** a small South African antelope which moves in leaps. **2** a Springbok is a person who has represented South Africa in a sports team.

spring-clean spring-cleans spring-cleaning spring-cleaned
VERB To spring-clean a house means to clean it thoroughly throughout.

spring onion spring onions
NOUN a small onion with long green shoots, often eaten raw in salads.

sprinkle **sprinkles sprinkling sprinkled**
VERB If you sprinkle a liquid or powder over something, you scatter it over it.

sprinkling **sprinklings**
NOUN A sprinkling of something is a small quantity of it EG *a light sprinkling of snow*.

sprint **sprints sprinting sprinted**
NOUN **1** a short, fast race. ▶ VERB **2** To sprint means to run fast over a short distance.

sprinter **sprinters**
NOUN an athlete who runs fast over short distances.

sprite **sprites**
NOUN a type of fairy.

sprout **sprouts sprouting sprouted**
VERB **1** When something sprouts, it grows. **2** If things sprout up, they appear rapidly EG *Their houses sprouted up in that region.* ▶ NOUN **3** Sprouts are the same as **brussels sprouts.**

spruce **spruces; sprucer sprucest; spruces sprucing spruced**
NOUN **1** an evergreen tree with needle-like leaves. ▶ ADJECTIVE **2** Someone who is spruce is very neat and smart. ▶ VERB **3** To spruce something up means to make it neat and smart.

spunk **spunks**
NOUN; AN INFORMAL WORD **1** AN OLD-FASHIONED USE Spunk is courage. **2** In Australian and New Zealand English, someone who is good-looking.

spur **spurs spurring spurred**
VERB **1** If something spurs you to do something or spurs you on, it encourages you to do it. ▶ NOUN **2** Something that acts as a spur encourages a person to do something. **3** Spurs are sharp metal points attached to the heels of a rider's boots and used to urge a horse on. ▶ PHRASE **4** If you do something **on the spur of the**

moment, you do it suddenly, without planning it.

spurious
Said "**spyoor**-ee-uss" ADJECTIVE not genuine or real.

spurn **spurns spurning spurned**
VERB If you spurn something, you refuse to accept it EG *You spurned his last offer.*

spurt **spurts spurting spurted**
VERB **1** When a liquid or flame spurts out of something, it comes out quickly in a thick, powerful stream. ▶ NOUN **2** A spurt of liquid or flame is a thick powerful stream of it EG *a small spurt of blood.* **3** A spurt of activity or effort is a sudden, brief period of it.

spy **spies spying spied**
NOUN **1** a person sent to find out secret information about a country or organization. ▶ VERB **2** Someone who spies tries to find out secret information about another country or organization. **3** If you spy on someone, you watch them secretly. **4** If you spy something, you notice it.

squabble **squabbles squabbling squabbled**
VERB **1** When people squabble, they quarrel about something trivial. ▶ NOUN **2** a quarrel.

squad **squads**
NOUN a small group chosen to do a particular activity EG *the fraud squad.* 🏛 from Old Spanish *escuadra* meaning 'square', because of the square formation used by soldiers

squadron **squadrons**
NOUN a section of one of the armed forces, especially the air force. 🏛 from Italian *squadrone* meaning 'soldiers drawn up in a square formation'

squalid
ADJECTIVE **1** dirty, untidy, and in bad condition. **2** Squalid activities are unpleasant and often dishonest.

squall **squalls**

NOUN a brief, violent storm.

squalor
NOUN Squalor consists of bad or dirty conditions or surroundings.

squander squanders squandering squandered
VERB To squander money or resources means to waste them EG *They have squandered huge amounts of money.*

square squares squaring squared
NOUN 1 a shape with four equal sides and four right angles. 2 In a town or city, a square is a flat, open place, bordered by buildings or streets. 3 The square of a number is the number multiplied by itself. For example, the square of 3, written 3^2, is 3×3. ▶ ADJECTIVE 4 shaped like a square EG *her delicate square face.* 5 'Square' is used before units of length when talking about the area of something EG $24m^2$. 6 'Square' is used after units of length when you are giving the length of each side of something square EG *a towel measuring a foot square.* ▶ VERB 7 If you square a number, you multiply it by itself.

squarely
ADVERB 1 Squarely means directly rather than indirectly or at an angle EG *I looked squarely in the mirror.* 2 If you approach a subject squarely, you consider it fully, without trying to avoid unpleasant aspects of it.

square root square roots
NOUN A square root of a number is a number that makes the first number when it is multiplied by itself. For example, the square roots of 25 are 5 and –5.

squash squashes squashing squashed
VERB 1 If you squash something, you press it, so that it becomes flat or loses its shape. ▶ NOUN 2 If there is a squash in a place, there are a lot of people squashed in it. 3 Squash is a game in which two players hit a small rubber ball against the walls of a court using rackets. 4 Squash is a drink made from fruit juice, sugar, and water.

squat squats squatting squatted; squatter squattest
VERB 1 If you squat down, you crouch, balancing on your feet with your legs bent. 2 A person who squats in an unused building lives there as a squatter. ▶ NOUN 3 a building used by squatters. ▶ ADJECTIVE 4 short and thick.

squatter squatters
NOUN 1 a person who lives in an unused building without permission and without paying rent. 2 In Australian English, someone who owns a large amount of land for sheep or cattle farming. 3 In Australia and New Zealand in the past, someone who rented land from the King or Queen.

squawk squawks squawking squawked
VERB 1 When a bird squawks, it makes a loud, harsh noise. ▶ NOUN 2 a loud, harsh noise made by a bird.

squeak squeaks squeaking squeaked
VERB 1 If something squeaks, it makes a short high-pitched sound. ▶ NOUN 2 a short, high-pitched sound.
squeaky ADJECTIVE

squeal squeals squealing squealed
VERB 1 When things or people squeal, they make long, high-pitched sounds. ▶ NOUN 2 a long, high-pitched sound.

squeamish
ADJECTIVE easily upset by unpleasant sights or situations.

squeeze squeezes squeezing squeezed
VERB 1 When you squeeze something, you press it firmly from two sides. 2 If you squeeze something into a small amount of

A B C D E F G H I J K L M N O P Q R S T U V W X Y Z

time or space, you manage to fit it in. ▶ NOUN **3** If you give something a squeeze, you squeeze it EG *She gave my hand a quick squeeze.* **4** If getting into something is a squeeze, it is just possible to fit into it EG *It would take four comfortably, but six would be a squeeze.*

squelch squelches squelching squelched
VERB **1** To squelch means to make a wet, sucking sound. ▶ NOUN **2** a wet, sucking sound.

squid squids
NOUN a sea creature with a long soft body and many tentacles.

squiggle squiggles
NOUN a wriggly line.

squint squints squinting squinted
VERB **1** If you squint at something, you look at it with your eyes screwed up. ▶ NOUN **2** If someone has a squint, their eyes look in different directions from each other.

squire squires
NOUN In a village, the squire was a gentleman who owned a large house with a lot of land.

squirm squirms squirming squirmed
VERB If you squirm, you wriggle and twist your body about, usually because you are nervous or embarrassed.

squirrel squirrels
NOUN a small furry animal with a long bushy tail.
▥ from Greek *skia* meaning 'shadow' and *oura* meaning 'tail'

squirt squirts squirting squirted
VERB **1** If a liquid squirts, it comes out of a narrow opening in a thin, fast stream. ▶ NOUN **2** a thin, fast stream of liquid.

Sri Lankan Sri Lankans
Said "sree-**lang**-kan" ADJECTIVE **1** belonging or relating to Sri Lanka. ▶ NOUN **2** someone who comes from Sri Lanka.

stab stabs stabbing stabbed
VERB **1** To stab someone means to wound them by pushing a knife into their body. **2** To stab at something means to push at it sharply with your finger or with something long and narrow.
▶ PHRASE **3** AN INFORMAL USE If you **have a stab** at something, you try to do it. ▶ NOUN **4** You can refer to a sudden unpleasant feeling as a stab of something EG *He felt a stab of guilt.*

stable stables
ADJECTIVE **1** not likely to change or come to an end suddenly EG *I am in a stable relationship.* **2** firmly fixed or balanced and not likely to move, wobble, or fall. ▶ NOUN **3** a building in which horses are kept.
stability NOUN, **stabilize** VERB

staccato
Said "stak-**kah**-toe" ADJECTIVE consisting of a series of short, sharp, separate sounds.

stack stacks stacking stacked
NOUN **1** A stack of things is a pile of them, one on top of the other.
▶ PLURAL NOUN **2** AN INFORMAL USE If someone has stacks of something, they have a lot of it. ▶ VERB **3** If you stack things, you arrange them one on top of the other in a pile.

stadium stadiums
NOUN a sports ground with rows of seats around it.
▥ from Greek *stadion* meaning 'racecourse'

staff staffs staffing staffed
NOUN **1** The staff of an organization are the people who work for it.
▶ VERB **2** To staff an organization means to find and employ people to work in it. **3** If an organization is staffed by particular people, they are the people who work for it.

stag stags
NOUN an adult male deer.

stage stages staging staged
NOUN **1** a part of a process that lasts for a period of time. **2** In a theatre, the stage is a raised platform where

A
B
C
D
E
F
G
H
I
J
K
L
M
N
O
P
Q
R
S
T
U
V
W
X
Y
Z

A B C D E F G H I J K L M N O P Q R S T U V W X Y Z

the actors or entertainers perform. **3** You can refer to the profession of acting as the stage. ▶ VERB **4** If someone stages a play or event, they organize it and present it or take part in it.
☰ (sense 1) period, phase, point

stagecoach stagecoaches
NOUN a large carriage pulled by horses which used to carry passengers and mail.

stagger staggers staggering staggered
VERB **1** If you stagger, you walk unsteadily because you are ill or drunk. **2** If something staggers you, it amazes you. **3** If events are staggered, they are arranged so that they do not all happen at the same time.
staggering ADJECTIVE
☰ (sense 1) lurch, reel, totter

stagnant
ADJECTIVE Stagnant water is not flowing and is unhealthy and dirty.

stag night stag nights
NOUN a party for a man who is about to get married, which only men go to.

staid
ADJECTIVE serious and dull.

stain stains staining stained
NOUN **1** a mark on something that is difficult to remove. ▶ VERB **2** If a substance stains something, the thing becomes marked or coloured by it.

stained glass
NOUN Stained glass is coloured pieces of glass held together with strips of lead.

stainless steel
NOUN Stainless steel is a metal made from steel and chromium which does not rust.

stair stairs
NOUN Stairs are a set of steps inside a building going from one floor to another.

staircase staircases

NOUN a set of stairs.

stairway stairways
NOUN a set of stairs.

stake stakes staking staked
PHRASE **1** If something is **at stake**, it might be lost or damaged if something else is not successful EG *The whole future of the company was at stake.* ▶ PLURAL NOUN **2** The stakes involved in something are the things that can be lost or gained. ▶ VERB **3** If you say you would stake your money, life, or reputation on the success or truth of something, you mean you would risk it EG *He is prepared to stake his own career on this.* ▶ NOUN **4** If you have a stake in something such as a business, you own part of it and its success is important to you. **5** a pointed wooden post that can be hammered into the ground and used as a support.

stale staler stalest
ADJECTIVE **1** Stale food or air is no longer fresh. **2** If you feel stale, you have no new ideas and are bored.
☰ (sense 1) fusty, musty, old

stalemate
NOUN **1** Stalemate is a situation in which neither side in an argument or contest can win. **2** In chess, stalemate is a situation in which a player cannot make any move permitted by the rules, so that the game ends and no-one wins.

stalk stalks stalking stalked
Said "stawk" NOUN **1** The stalk of a flower or leaf is its stem. ▶ VERB **2** To stalk a person or animal means to follow them quietly in order to catch, kill, or observe them. **3** If someone stalks into a room, they walk in a stiff, proud, or angry way.

stall stalls stalling stalled
NOUN **1** a large table containing goods for sale or information. ▶ PLURAL NOUN **2** In a theatre, the stalls are the seats at the lowest level, in front of the stage. ▶ VERB **3** When a vehicle stalls, the engine

suddenly stops. **4** If you **stall** when someone asks you to do something, you try to avoid doing it until a later time.

stallion stallions
NOUN an adult male horse that can be used for breeding.

stamina
NOUN Stamina is the physical or mental energy needed to do something for a very long time.

stammer stammers stammering stammered
VERB **1** When someone stammers, they speak with difficulty, repeating words and sounds and hesitating awkwardly. ▶ NOUN **2** Someone who has a stammer tends to stammer when they speak.

stamp stamps stamping stamped
NOUN **1** a small piece of gummed paper which you stick on a letter or parcel before posting it. **2** a small block with a pattern cut into it, which you press onto an inky pad and make a mark with it on paper; also the mark made by the stamp. **3** If something bears the stamp of a particular quality or person, it shows clear signs of that quality or of the person's style or characteristics. ▶ VERB **4** If you stamp a piece of paper, you make a mark on it using a stamp. **5** If you stamp, you lift your foot and put it down hard on the ground.
stamp out VERB To stamp something out means to put an end to it EG *the battle to stamp out bullying in schools.*

stampede stampedes stampeding stampeded
VERB **1** When a group of animals stampede, they run in a wild, uncontrolled way. ▶ NOUN **2** a group of animals stampeding.
▣ from Spanish *estampida* meaning 'crash' or 'din'

stance stances
NOUN Your stance on a particular matter is your attitude and way of dealing with it EG *He takes no particular stance on animal rights.*

stand stands standing stood
VERB **1** If you are standing, you are upright, your legs are straight, and your weight is supported by your feet. When you stand up, you get into a standing position. **2** If something stands somewhere, that is where it is EG *The house stands alone on the top of a small hill.* **3** If you stand something somewhere, you put it there in an upright position EG *Stand the containers on bricks.* **4** If a decision or offer stands, it is still valid EG *My offer still stands.* **5** You can use 'stand' when describing the state or condition of something EG *Youth unemployment stands at 35%.* **6** If a letter stands for a particular word, it is an abbreviation for that word. **7** If you say you will not stand for something, you mean you will not tolerate it. **8** If something can stand a situation or test, it is good enough or strong enough not to be damaged by it. **9** If you cannot stand something, you cannot bear it EG *I can't stand that woman.* **10** If you stand in an election, you are one of the candidates. ▶ PHRASE **11** When someone **stands trial**, they are tried in a court of law. ▶ NOUN **12** a stall or very small shop outdoors or in a large public building. **13** a large structure at a sports ground, where the spectators sit to watch what is happening. **14** a piece of furniture designed to hold something EG *an umbrella stand.*
stand by VERB **1** If you stand by to provide help or take action, you are ready to do it if necessary. **2** If you stand by while something happens, you do nothing to stop it.
stand down VERB If someone stands down, they resign from their job or position.
stand in VERB If you stand in for someone, you take their place while they are ill or away.

stand out VERB If something stands out, it can be easily noticed or is more important than other similar things.

stand up VERB **1** If something stands up to rough treatment, it remains undamaged or unharmed. **2** If you stand up to someone who is criticizing or attacking you, you defend yourself.

standard standards
NOUN **1** a level of quality or achievement that is considered acceptable EG *The work is not up to standard.* ▶ PLURAL NOUN **2** Standards are moral principles of behaviour. ▶ ADJECTIVE **3** usual, normal, and correct EG *The practice became standard procedure for most motor companies.*

standard English
NOUN Standard English is the form of English taught in schools, used in text books and broadsheet newspapers, and spoken and written by most educated people.

standardize standardizes standardizing standardized; also spelt **standardise**
VERB To standardize things means to change them so that they all have a similar set of features EG *We have decided to standardize our equipment.*

stand-by stand-bys
NOUN **1** something available for use when you need it EG *a useful stand-by.* ▶ ADJECTIVE **2** A stand-by ticket is a cheap ticket that you buy just before a theatre performance or a flight if there are any seats left.

stand-in stand-ins
NOUN someone who takes a person's place while the person is ill or away EG *stand-in teachers.*

standing
ADJECTIVE **1** permanently in existence or used regularly EG *a standing joke.* ▶ NOUN **2** A person's standing is their status and reputation. **3** 'Standing' is used to say how long something has existed EG *a*

friend of 20 years' standing.

standpoint standpoints
NOUN If you consider something from a particular standpoint, you consider it from that point of view EG *from a military standpoint.*

standstill
NOUN If something comes to a standstill, it stops completely.

stanza stanzas
NOUN a verse of a poem.
🔲 from Italian *stanza* meaning 'stopping place'

staple staples stapling stapled
NOUN **1** Staples are small pieces of wire that hold sheets of paper firmly together. ▶ VERB **2** If you staple sheets of paper, you fasten them together with staples.
▶ ADJECTIVE **3** A staple food forms a regular and basic part of someone's everyday diet.

star stars starring starred
NOUN **1** a large ball of burning gas in space that appears as a point of light in the sky at night. **2** a shape with four, five, or more points sticking out in a regular pattern. **3** Famous actors, sports players, and musicians are referred to as stars. ▶ PLURAL NOUN **4** The horoscope in a newspaper or magazine can be referred to as the stars EG *I'm a Virgo, but don't read my stars every day.*
▶ VERB **5** If an actor or actress stars in a film or if the film stars that person, he or she has one of the most important parts in it.

starboard
ADJECTIVE OR NOUN The starboard side of a ship is the right-hand side when you are facing the front.
🔲 from Old English *steorbord* meaning 'steering side', because boats were formerly steered with a paddle over the right-hand side

starch starches starching starched
NOUN **1** Starch is a substance used for stiffening fabric such as cotton and linen. **2** Starch is a carbohydrate found in foods such

as bread and potatoes. ▶ VERB **3** To starch fabric means to stiffen it with starch.

stare stares staring stared
VERB **1** If you stare at something, you look at it for a long time. ▶ NOUN **2** a long fixed look at something.
■ (sense 1) gawp, gaze, goggle

starfish starfishes or starfish
NOUN a flat, star-shaped sea creature with five limbs.

stark starker starkest
ADJECTIVE **1** harsh, unpleasant and plain EG *the stark choice*. ▶ PHRASE **2** If someone is **stark-naked**, they have no clothes on at all.

starling starlings
NOUN a common European bird with shiny dark feathers.

start starts starting started
VERB **1** To start means to begin. To start doing something means to begin doing it EG *School starts next week... Suzy started crying*. **2** If you start a machine or car, you operate the controls to make it work. **3** If you start, your body suddenly jerks because of surprise or fear. ▶ NOUN **4** The start of something is the point or time at which it begins. **5** If you do something with a start, you do it with a sudden jerky movement because of surprise or fear EG *I awoke with a start*.

starter starters
NOUN a small quantity of food served as the first part of a meal.

startle startles startling startled
VERB If something sudden and unexpected startles you, it surprises you and makes you slightly frightened.
startled ADJECTIVE, **startling** ADJECTIVE

starve starves starving starved
VERB **1** If people are starving, they are suffering from a serious lack of food and are likely to die. **2** To starve a person or animal means to prevent them from having any food. **3** AN INFORMAL USE If you say

you are starving, you mean you are very hungry. **4** If someone or something is starved of something they need, they are suffering because they are not getting enough of it EG *The hospital was starved of cash*.
starvation NOUN

stash stashes stashing stashed
VERB; AN INFORMAL WORD If you stash something away in a secret place, you store it there to keep it safe.

state states stating stated
NOUN **1** The state of something is its condition, what it is like, or its circumstances. **2** Countries are sometimes referred to as states EG *the state of Denmark*. **3** Some countries are divided into regions called states which make some of their own laws EG *the State of Vermont*. **4** You can refer to the government or administration of a country as the state. ▶ PHRASE **5** If you are **in a state**, you are nervous or upset and unable to control your emotions. ▶ ADJECTIVE **6** A state ceremony involves the ruler or leader of a country. ▶ VERB **7** If you state something, you say it or write it, especially in a formal way.

state house state houses
NOUN In New Zealand, a house built and owned by the government and rented out.

stately home stately homes
NOUN In Britain, a very large old house which belongs to an upper-class family.

statement statements
NOUN **1** something you say or write when you give facts or information in a formal way. **2** a document provided by a bank showing all the money paid into and out of an account during a period of time.

state school state schools
NOUN a school maintained and financed by the government in which education is free.

statesman statesmen

NOUN an important and experienced politician.

static

ADJECTIVE **1** never moving or changing EG *The temperature remains fairly static.* ▶ NOUN **2** Static is an electrical charge caused by friction. It builds up in metal objects.

station stations stationing stationed

NOUN **1** a building and platforms where trains stop for passengers. **2** A bus or coach station is a place where some buses start their journeys. **3** A radio station is the frequency on which a particular company broadcasts. **4** In Australian and New Zealand English, a large sheep or cattle farm. **5** AN OLD-FASHIONED USE A person's station is their position or rank in society. ▶ VERB **6** Someone who is stationed somewhere is sent there to work or do a particular job EG *Her husband was stationed in Vienna.*

stationary

ADJECTIVE not moving EG *a stationary car.*
■ fixed, motionless

stationery

NOUN Stationery is paper, pens, and other writing equipment.

statistic statistics

NOUN **1** Statistics are facts obtained by analysing numerical information. **2** Statistics is the branch of mathematics that deals with the analysis of numerical information.
statistical ADJECTIVE

statistician statisticians

Said "stat-iss-**tish**-an" NOUN a person who studies or works with statistics.

statue statues

NOUN a sculpture of a person.

stature

NOUN **1** Someone's stature is their height and size. **2** Someone's stature is also their importance and reputation EG *the desire to gain international stature.*

status statuses

Said "**stay**-tuss" NOUN **1** A person's status is their position and importance in society. **2** Status is also the official classification given to someone or something EG *I am not sure what your legal status is.*
■ (sense 1) position, prestige, standing

status quo

Said "**stay**-tuss **kwoh**" NOUN The status quo is the situation that exists at a particular time EG *They want to keep the status quo.*
▦ a Latin expression, meaning literally 'the state in which'

statute statutes

NOUN a law.
statutory ADJECTIVE

staunch stauncher staunchest

ADJECTIVE A staunch supporter is a strong and loyal supporter.

stave staves staving staved

NOUN **1** In music, a stave is the five lines that music is written on. ▶ VERB **2** If you stave something off, you try to delay or prevent it.

stay stays staying stayed

VERB **1** If you stay in a place, you do not move away from it EG *She stayed in bed until noon.* **2** If you stay at a hotel or a friend's house, you spend some time there as a guest or visitor. **3** If you stay in a particular state, you continue to be in it EG *I stayed awake the first night.* **4** In Scottish and South African English, to stay in a place can also mean to live there. ▶ NOUN **5** a short time spent somewhere EG *a very pleasant stay in Cornwall.*
■ (sense 1) linger, remain

stead

NOUN; A FORMAL WORD Something that will stand someone in good stead will be useful to them in the future.

steady steadier steadiest; steadies steadying steadied

ADJECTIVE **1** continuing or developing gradually without major interruptions or changes EG *a steady rise in profits.* **2** firm and not shaking or wobbling EG *O'Brien held out a steady hand.* **3** A steady look or voice is calm and controlled. **4** Someone who is steady is sensible and reliable. ▶ VERB **5** When you steady something, you hold on to prevent it from shaking or wobbling. **6** When you steady yourself, you control and calm yourself.

steadily ADVERB

▣ (sense 2) firm, secure, stable

steak steaks

NOUN **1** Steak is good-quality beef without much fat. **2** A fish steak is a large piece of fish.

▥ from Old Norse *steik* meaning 'roast'

steal steals stealing stole stolen

VERB **1** To steal something means to take it without permission and without intending to return it. **2** To steal somewhere means to move there quietly and secretively.

▣ (sense 1) nick, purloin, take

stealth

Rhymes with "**health**" NOUN If you do something with stealth, you do it quietly and secretively.

stealthy ADJECTIVE, **stealthily** ADVERB

steam steams steaming steamed

NOUN **1** Steam is the hot vapour formed when water boils. ▶ ADJECTIVE **2** Steam engines are operated using steam as a means of power. ▶ VERB **3** If something steams, it gives off steam. **4** To steam food means to cook it in steam.

steamy ADJECTIVE

steam-engine steam-engines

NOUN any engine that uses the energy of steam to produce mechanical work.

steamer steamers

NOUN **1** a ship powered by steam. **2** a container with small holes in the bottom in which you steam food.

steed steeds

NOUN; A LITERARY WORD a horse.

steel steels steeling steeled

NOUN **1** Steel is a very strong metal containing mainly iron with a small amount of carbon. ▶ VERB **2** To steel yourself means to prepare to deal with something unpleasant.

steel band steel bands

NOUN a group of people who play music on special metal drums.

steep steeper steepest; steeps steeping steeped

ADJECTIVE **1** A steep slope rises sharply and is difficult to go up. **2** A steep increase is large and sudden. ▶ VERB **3** To steep something in a liquid means to soak it thoroughly.

steeply ADVERB

▣ (sense 1) precipitous, sheer

steeped

ADJECTIVE If a person or place is steeped in a particular quality, they are deeply affected by it EG *an industry steeped in tradition.*

steeple steeples

NOUN a tall pointed structure on top of a church tower.

steeplechase steeplechases

NOUN a long horse race in which the horses jump over obstacles such as hedges and water jumps.

▥ originally a race with a church steeple in sight as the goal

steer steers steering steered

VERB **1** To steer a vehicle or boat means to control it so that it goes in the right direction. **2** To steer someone towards a particular course of action means to influence and direct their behaviour or thoughts. ▶ NOUN **3** a castrated bull.

▣ (sense 1) direct, guide, pilot

stem stems stemming stemmed

NOUN **1** The stem of a plant is the long thin central part above the ground that carries the leaves and flowers. **2** The stem of a glass is the long narrow part connecting the bowl to the base. ▶ VERB **3** If a problem stems from a particular situation, that situation is the

A
B
C
D
E
F
G
H
I
J
K
L
M
N
O
P
Q
R
S
T
U
V
W
X
Y
Z

original starting point or cause of the problem. **4** If you stem the flow of something, you restrict it or stop it from spreading EG *to stem the flow of refugees.*

stench stenches

NOUN a very strong, unpleasant smell.

stencil stencils stencilling stencilled

NOUN **1** a thin sheet with a cut-out pattern through which ink or paint passes to form the pattern on the surface below. ▸ VERB **2** To stencil a design on a surface means to create it using a stencil.

📖 from Middle English *stanselen* meaning 'to decorate with bright colours'

step steps stepping stepped

NOUN **1** If you take a step, you lift your foot and put it down somewhere else. **2** one of a series of actions that you take in order to achieve something. **3** a raised flat surface, usually one of a series that you can walk up or down. ▸ VERB **4** If you step in a particular direction, you move your foot in that direction. **5** If someone steps down or steps aside from an important position, they resign.

step-

PREFIX If a word like 'father' or 'sister' has 'step-' in front of it, it shows that the family relationship has come about because a parent has married again EG *stepfather... stepsister.*

stepping stone stepping stones

NOUN **1** Stepping stones are a line of large stones that you walk on to cross a shallow river. **2** a job or event that is regarded as a stage in your progress, especially in your career.

stereo stereos

ADJECTIVE **1** A stereo recording or music system is one in which the sound is directed through two speakers. ▸ NOUN **2** a piece of

equipment that reproduces sound from records, tapes, or CDs directing the sound through two speakers.

stereotype stereotypes stereotyping stereotyped

NOUN **1** a fixed image or set of characteristics that people consider to represent a particular type of person or thing EG *the stereotype of the polite, industrious Japanese.* ▸ VERB **2** If you stereotype someone, you assume they are a particular type of person and will behave in a particular way.

sterile

ADJECTIVE **1** Sterile means completely clean and free from germs. **2** A sterile person or animal is unable to produce offspring.

sterility NOUN

🔲 (sense 1) germ-free, sterilized

sterilize sterilizes sterilizing sterilized; also spelt **sterilise**

VERB **1** To sterilize something means to make it completely clean and free from germs, usually by boiling it or treating it with an antiseptic. **2** If a person or animal is sterilized, they have an operation that makes it impossible for them to produce offspring.

sterling

NOUN **1** Sterling is the money system of Great Britain. ▸ ADJECTIVE **2** excellent in quality EG *Volunteers are doing sterling work.*

stern sterner sternest; sterns

ADJECTIVE **1** very serious and strict EG *a stern father... a stern warning.* ▸ NOUN **2** The stern of a boat is the back part.

steroid steroids

NOUN Steroids are chemicals that occur naturally in your body. Sometimes sportsmen illegally take them as drugs to improve their performance.

stethoscope stethoscopes

NOUN a device used by doctors to listen to a patient's heart and breathing, consisting of earpieces connected to a hollow tube and a small disc.

🔲 from Greek *stēthos* meaning 'chest' and *skopein* meaning 'to look at'

stew stews stewing stewed
NOUN **1** a dish of small pieces of savoury food cooked together slowly in a liquid. ▶ VERB **2** To stew meat, vegetables, or fruit means to cook them slowly in a liquid.

🔲 from Middle English *stuen* meaning 'to take a very hot bath'

steward stewards
NOUN **1** a man who works on a ship or plane looking after passengers and serving meals. **2** a person who helps to direct the public at a race, march, or other event.

🔲 from Old English *stigweard* meaning 'hall protector'

stewardess stewardesses
NOUN a woman who works on a ship or plane looking after passengers and serving meals.

stick sticks sticking stuck
NOUN **1** a long, thin piece of wood. **2** A stick of something is a long, thin piece of it EG *a stick of celery*. ▶ VERB **3** If you stick a long or pointed object into something, you push it in. **4** If you stick one thing to another, you attach it with glue or sticky tape. **5** If one thing sticks to another, it becomes attached and is difficult to remove. **6** If a movable part of something sticks, it becomes fixed and will no longer move or work properly EG *My gears keep sticking*. **7** AN INFORMAL USE If you stick something somewhere, you put it there. **8** If you stick by someone, you continue to help and support them. **9** If you stick to something, you keep to it and do not change to something else EG *He should have stuck to the old ways of doing things*. **10** When people stick together, they stay together and support each other.

stick out VERB **1** If something sticks out, it projects from something else. **2** To stick out also means to be very noticeable.

stick up VERB **1** If something sticks up, it points upwards from a surface. **2** AN INFORMAL USE If you stick up for a person or principle, you support or defend them.

sticker stickers
NOUN a small piece of paper or plastic with writing or a picture on it, that you stick onto a surface.

sticking plaster sticking plasters
NOUN a small piece of fabric that you stick over a cut or sore to protect it.

stick insect stick insects
NOUN an insect with a long cylindrical body and long legs, which looks like a twig.

sticky stickier stickiest
ADJECTIVE **1** A sticky object is covered with a substance that can stick to other things EG *sticky hands*. **2** Sticky paper or tape has glue on one side so that you can stick it to a surface. **3** AN INFORMAL USE A sticky situation is difficult or embarrassing to deal with. **4** Sticky weather is unpleasantly hot and humid.

stiff stiffer stiffest
ADJECTIVE **1** Something that is stiff is firm and not easily bent. **2** If you feel stiff, your muscles or joints ache when you move. **3** Stiff behaviour is formal and not friendly or relaxed. **4** Stiff also means difficult or severe EG *stiff competition for places*. **5** A stiff drink contains a large amount of alcohol. **6** A stiff breeze is blowing strongly. ▶ ADVERB **7** AN INFORMAL USE If you are bored stiff or scared stiff, you are very bored or very scared.
stiffly ADVERB, **stiffness** NOUN

stiffen stiffens stiffening stiffened
VERB **1** If you stiffen, you suddenly stop moving and your muscles become tense EG *I stiffened with tension*. **2** If your joints or muscles stiffen, they become sore and

difficult to bend or move. **3** If
fabric or material is stiffened, it is
made firmer so that it does not
bend easily.

stifle stifles stifling stifled
Said "sty-fl" VERB **1** If the
atmosphere stifles you, you feel
you cannot breathe properly. **2** To
stifle something means to stop it
from happening or continuing EG
Martin stifled a yawn.
stifling ADJECTIVE

stigma stigmas
NOUN If something has a stigma
attached to it, people consider it
unacceptable or a disgrace EG *the
stigma of mental illness.*

stile stiles
NOUN a step on either side of a wall
or fence to enable you to climb
over.

stiletto stilettos
NOUN Stilettos are women's shoes
with very high, narrow heels.
🔲 from Italian *stilo* meaning
'dagger', because of the shape of
the heels

still stiller stillest; stills
ADVERB **1** If a situation still exists, it
has continued to exist and it exists
now. **2** If something could still
happen, it might happen although
it has not happened yet. **3** 'Still'
emphasizes that something is the
case in spite of other things EG
*Whatever you think of him, he's still
your father.* ▶ ADVERB OR ADJECTIVE **4** Still
means staying in the same position
without moving EG *Sit still... The air
was still.* ▶ ADJECTIVE **5** A still place is
quiet and peaceful with no signs of
activity. ▶ NOUN **6** a photograph
taken from a cinema film or video.
stillness NOUN

stillborn
ADJECTIVE A stillborn baby is dead
when it is born.

stilt stilts
NOUN **1** Stilts are long upright poles
on which a building is built, for
example on wet land. **2** Stilts are

also two long pieces of wood or
metal on which people balance and
walk.

stilted
ADJECTIVE formal, unnatural, and
rather awkward EG *a stilted
conversation.*

stimulant stimulants
NOUN a drug or other substance that
makes your body work faster,
increasing your heart rate and
making it difficult to sleep.

**stimulate stimulates stimulating
stimulated**
VERB **1** To stimulate something
means to encourage it to begin or
develop EG *to stimulate discussion.* **2** If
something stimulates you, it gives
you new ideas and enthusiasm.
stimulating ADJECTIVE, **stimulation** NOUN
▤ (sense 1) arouse, encourage,
inspire

stimulus stimuli
NOUN something that causes a
process or event to begin or
develop.

sting stings stinging stung
VERB **1** If a creature or plant stings
you, it pricks your skin and injects
a substance which causes pain. **2** If
a part of your body stings, you feel
a sharp tingling pain there. **3** If
someone's remarks sting you, they
make you feel upset and hurt.
▶ NOUN **4** A creature's sting is the
part it stings you with.
▤ (sense 2) hurt, smart

stink stinks stinking stank stunk
VERB **1** Something that stinks smells
very unpleasant. ▶ NOUN **2** a very
unpleasant smell.
▤ (sense 2) pong, stench

stint stints
NOUN a period of time spent doing a
particular job EG *a three-year stint in
the army.*

**stipulate stipulates stipulating
stipulated**
VERB; A FORMAL WORD If you stipulate
that something must be done, you
state clearly that it must be done.

stipulation NOUN

stir stirs stirring stirred
VERB **1** When you stir a liquid, you move it around using a spoon or a stick. **2** To stir means to move slightly. **3** If something stirs you, it makes you feel strong emotions EG *The power of the singing stirred me.*
▶ NOUN **4** If an event causes a stir, it causes general excitement or shock EG *two books which have caused a stir.*

stirring stirrings
ADJECTIVE **1** causing excitement, emotion, and enthusiasm EG *a stirring account of the action.* ▶ NOUN **2** If there is a stirring of emotion, people begin to feel it.

stirrup stirrups
NOUN Stirrups are two metal loops hanging by leather straps from a horse's saddle, which you put your feet in when riding.

stitch stitches stitching stitched
VERB **1** When you stitch pieces of material together, you use a needle and thread to sew them together. **2** To stitch a wound means to use a special needle and thread to hold the edges of skin together. ▶ NOUN **3** one of the pieces of thread that can be seen where material has been sewn. **4** one of the pieces of thread that can be seen where a wound has been stitched EG *He had eleven stitches in his lip.* **5** If you have a stitch, you feel a sharp pain at the side of your abdomen, usually because you have been running or laughing.

stoat stoats
NOUN a small wild animal with a long body and brown fur.

stock stocks stocking stocked
NOUN **1** Stocks are shares bought as an investment in a company; also the amount of money raised by the company through the issue of shares. **2** A shop's stock is the total amount of goods it has for sale. **3** If you have a stock of things, you have a supply ready for use. **4** The

stock an animal or person comes from is the type of animal or person they are descended from EG *She was descended from Scots Highland stock.* **5** Stock is farm animals. **6** Stock is a liquid made from boiling meat, bones, or vegetables together in water. Stock is used as a base for soups, stews, and sauces.
▶ VERB **7** A shop that stocks particular goods keeps a supply of them to sell. **8** If you stock a shelf or cupboard, you fill it with food or other things. ▶ ADJECTIVE **9** A stock expression or way of doing something is one that is commonly used.
stock up VERB If you stock up with something, you buy a supply of it.

stockbroker stockbrokers
NOUN A stockbroker is a person whose job is to buy and sell shares for people who want to invest money.

stock exchange stock exchanges
NOUN a place where there is trading in stocks and shares EG *the New York Stock Exchange.*

stocking stockings
NOUN Stockings are long pieces of thin clothing that cover a woman's leg.

stockman stockmen
NOUN a man who looks after sheep or cattle on a farm.

stock market stock markets
NOUN The stock market is the organization and activity involved in buying and selling stocks and shares.

stockpile stockpiles stockpiling stockpiled
VERB **1** If someone stockpiles something, they store large quantities of it for future use.
▶ NOUN **2** a large store of something.

stocktaking
NOUN Stocktaking is the counting and checking of all a shop's or business's goods.

stocky stockier stockiest

A B C D E F G H I J K L M N O P Q R S T U V W X Y Z

A B C D E F G H I J K L M N O P Q R S T U V W X Y Z

ADJECTIVE A stocky person is rather short, but broad and solid-looking.

stoke stokes stoking stoked
VERB To stoke a fire means to keep it burning by moving or adding fuel.

stomach stomachs stomaching stomached
NOUN **1** Your stomach is the organ inside your body where food is digested. **2** You can refer to the front part of your body below your waist as your stomach. ▶ VERB **3** If you cannot stomach something, you strongly dislike it and cannot accept it.

stone stones stoning stoned
NOUN **1** Stone is the hard solid substance found in the ground and used for building. **2** A small piece of rock. **3** The stone in a fruit such as a plum or cherry is the large seed in the centre. **4** a unit of weight equal to 14 pounds or about 6.35 kilograms. **5** You can refer to a jewel as a stone EG *a diamond ring with three stones*. ▶ VERB **6** To stone something or someone means to throw stones at them.

stoned
ADJECTIVE; AN INFORMAL WORD affected by drugs.

stony stonier stoniest
ADJECTIVE **1** Stony ground is rough and contains a lot of stones or rocks. **2** If someone's expression is stony, it shows no friendliness or sympathy.

stool stools
NOUN **1** a seat with legs but no back or arms. **2** a lump of faeces.

stoop stoops stooping stooped
VERB **1** If you stoop, you stand or walk with your shoulders bent forwards. **2** If you would not stoop to something, you would not disgrace yourself by doing it.

stop stops stopping stopped
VERB **1** If you stop doing something, you no longer do it. **2** If an activity or process stops, it comes to an end or no longer happens. **3** If a

machine stops, it no longer functions or it is switched off. **4** To stop something means to prevent it. **5** If people or things that are moving stop, they no longer move. **6** If you stop somewhere, you stay there for a short while. ▶ PHRASE **7** To **put a stop to** something means to prevent it from happening or continuing. ▶ NOUN **8** a place where a bus, train, or other vehicle stops during a journey. **9** If something that is moving comes to a stop, it no longer moves.
■ (sense 1) cease, desist, halt

stoppage stoppages
NOUN If there is a stoppage, people stop work because of a disagreement with their employer.

stopper stoppers
NOUN a piece of glass or cork that fits into the neck of a jar or bottle.

stopwatch stopwatches
NOUN a watch that can be started and stopped by pressing buttons, which is used to time events.

storage
NOUN The storage of something is the keeping of it somewhere until it is needed.

store stores storing stored
NOUN **1** a shop. **2** A store of something is a supply kept for future use. **3** a place where things are kept while they are not used. ▶ VERB **4** When you store something somewhere, you keep it there until it is needed. ▶ PHRASE **5** Something that is in store for you is going to happen to you in the future.
■ (sense 1) hoard, stockpile, supply

storeroom storerooms
NOUN a room where things are kept until they are needed.

storey storeys
NOUN A storey of a building is one of its floors or levels.

stork storks
NOUN a very large white and black bird with long red legs and a long bill.

storm storms storming stormed

NOUN **1** When there is a storm, there is heavy rain, a strong wind, and often thunder and lightning. **2** If something causes a storm, it causes an angry or excited reaction EG *His words caused a storm of protest.* ▸ VERB **3** If someone storms out, they leave quickly, noisily, and angrily. **4** To storm means to say something in a loud, angry voice EG *'It's a fiasco!' he stormed.* **5** If people storm a place, they attack it.
stormy ADJECTIVE

story stories

NOUN **1** a description of imaginary people and events written or told to entertain people. **2** The story of something or someone is an account of the important events that have happened to them EG *his life story.*
▤ anecdote, tale, yarn

stout stouter stoutest

ADJECTIVE **1** rather fat. **2** thick, strong, and sturdy EG *stout walking shoes.* **3** determined, firm, and strong EG *He can outrun the stoutest opposition.*
stoutly ADVERB

stove stoves

NOUN a piece of equipment for heating a room or for cooking.

stow stows stowing stowed

VERB **1** If you stow something somewhere or stow it away, you store it until it is needed. **2** If someone stows away in a ship or plane, they hide in it to go somewhere secretly without paying.

straddle straddles straddling straddled

VERB **1** If you straddle something, you stand or sit with one leg on either side of it. **2** If something straddles a place, it crosses it, linking different parts together EG *The town straddles a river.*

straight straighter straightest

ADJECTIVE OR ADVERB **1** continuing in the same direction without curving or bending EG *the straight path... Amy*

stared straight ahead of her. **2** upright or level rather than sloping or bent EG *Keep your arms straight.* ▸ ADVERB **3** immediately and directly EG *We will go straight to the hotel.* ▸ ADJECTIVE **4** neat and tidy EG *Get this room straight.* **5** honest, frank, and direct EG *They wouldn't give me a straight answer.* **6** A straight choice involves only two options.

straightaway

ADVERB If you do something straightaway, you do it immediately.

straighten straightens straightening straightened

VERB **1** To straighten something means to remove any bends or curves from it. **2** To straighten something also means to make it neat and tidy. **3** To straighten out a confused situation means to organize and deal with it.

straightforward

ADJECTIVE **1** easy and involving no problems. **2** honest, open, and frank.

strain strains straining strained

NOUN **1** Strain is worry and nervous tension. **2** If a strain is put on something, it is affected by a strong force which may damage it. **3** You can refer to an aspect of someone's character, remarks, or work as a strain EG *There was a strain of bitterness in his voice.* **4** You can refer to distant sounds of music as strains of music. **5** A particular strain of plant is a variety of it EG *strains of rose.* ▸ VERB **6** To strain something means to force it or use it more than is reasonable or normal. **7** If you strain a muscle, you injure it by moving awkwardly. **8** To strain food means to pour away the liquid from it.
▤ (sense 1) anxiety, stress
▤ (sense 6) overexert, tax

strained

ADJECTIVE **1** worried and anxious. **2** If a relationship is strained, people feel unfriendly and do not trust each other.

strait straits

NOUN **1** You can refer to a narrow strip of sea as a strait or the straits EG *the Straits of Hormuz.* ▶ PLURAL NOUN **2** If someone is in a bad situation, you can say they are in difficult straits.

straitjacket straitjackets

NOUN A special jacket used to tie the arms of a violent person tightly around their body.

strait-laced

ADJECTIVE having a very strict and serious attitude to moral behaviour.

strand strands

NOUN **1** A strand of thread or hair is a single long piece of it. **2** You can refer to a part of a situation or idea as a strand of it EG *the different strands of the problem.*

stranded

ADJECTIVE If someone or something is stranded somewhere, they are stuck and cannot leave.

strange stranger strangest

ADJECTIVE **1** unusual or unexpected. **2** not known, seen, or experienced before EG *alone in a strange country.*
strangely ADVERB, **strangeness** NOUN
≡ (sense 1) curious, odd, peculiar
≡ (sense 2) alien, new, unfamiliar

stranger strangers

NOUN **1** someone you have never met before. **2** If you are a stranger to a place or situation, you have not been there or experienced it before.

strangle strangles strangling strangled

VERB To strangle someone means to kill them by squeezing their throat.
strangulation NOUN

strangled

ADJECTIVE A strangled sound is unclear and muffled.

stranglehold strangleholds

NOUN To have a stranglehold on something means to have control

over it and prevent it from developing.

strap straps strapping strapped

NOUN **1** a narrow piece of leather or cloth, used to fasten or hold things together. ▶ VERB **2** To strap something means to fasten it with a strap.

strapping

ADJECTIVE tall, strong, and healthy-looking.

strata

the plural of **stratum**.

strategic

Said "strat-tee-jik" ADJECTIVE planned or intended to achieve something or to gain an advantage EG *a strategic plan.*
strategically ADVERB

strategy strategies

NOUN **1** a plan for achieving something. **2** Strategy is the skill of planning the best way to achieve something, especially in war.
strategist NOUN

stratum strata

NOUN The strata in the earth's surface are the different layers of rock.

straw straws

NOUN **1** Straw is the dry, yellowish stalks from cereal crops. **2** a hollow tube of paper or plastic which you use to suck a drink into your mouth. ▶ PHRASE **3** If something is **the last straw**, it is the latest in a series of bad events and makes you feel you cannot stand any more.

strawberry strawberries

NOUN a small red fruit with tiny seeds in its skin.

stray strays straying strayed

VERB **1** When people or animals stray, they wander away from where they should be. **2** If your thoughts stray, you stop concentrating. ▶ ADJECTIVE **3** A stray dog or cat is one that has wandered away from home. **4** Stray things are separated from the main group of things of their kind EG *a stray piece of lettuce.* ▶ NOUN **5** a stray dog or cat.

streak **streaks streaking streaked**
NOUN **1** a long mark or stain. **2** If someone has a particular streak, they have that quality in their character. **3** A lucky or unlucky streak is a series of successes or failures. ▶ VERB **4** If something is streaked with a colour, it has lines of the colour in it. **5** To streak somewhere means to move there very quickly.
streaky ADJECTIVE

stream **streams streaming streamed**
NOUN **1** a small river. **2** You can refer to a steady flow of something as a stream EG *a constant stream of people.* **3** In a school, a stream is a group of children of the same age and ability. ▶ VERB **4** To stream somewhere means to move in a continuous flow in large quantities EG *Rain streamed down the windscreen.*

streamer **streamers**
NOUN a long, narrow strip of coloured paper used for decoration.

streamline **streamlines streamlining streamlined**
VERB **1** To streamline a vehicle, aircraft, or boat means to improve its shape so that it moves more quickly and efficiently. **2** To streamline an organization means to make it more efficient by removing parts of it.

street **streets**
NOUN a road in a town or village, usually with buildings along it.

strength **strengths**
NOUN **1** Your strength is your physical energy and the power of your muscles. **2** Strength can refer to the degree of someone's confidence or courage. **3** You can refer to power or influence as strength EG *The campaign against factory closures gathered strength.* **4** Someone's strengths are their good qualities and abilities. **5** The

strength of an object is the degree to which it can stand rough treatment. **6** The strength of a substance is the amount of other substances that it contains EG *coffee with sugar and milk in it at the correct strength.* **7** The strength of a feeling or opinion is the degree to which it is felt or supported. **8** The strength of a relationship is its degree of closeness or success. **9** The strength of a group is the total number of people in it. ▶ PHRASE **10** If people do something **in strength**, a lot of them do it together EG *The press were here in strength.*
▤ (sense 1) might, muscle
▤ (sense 3) force, intensity, power

strengthen **strengthens strengthening strengthened**
VERB **1** To strengthen something means to give it more power, influence, or support and make it more likely to succeed. **2** To strengthen an object means to improve it or add to its structure so that it can withstand rough treatment.
▤ fortify, reinforce

strenuous
Said "**stren-yoo-uss**" ADJECTIVE involving a lot of effort or energy.
strenuously ADVERB

stress **stresses stressing stressed**
NOUN **1** Stress is worry and nervous tension. **2** Stresses are strong physical forces applied to an object. **3** Stress is emphasis put on a word or part of a word when it is pronounced, making it slightly louder. ▶ VERB **4** If you stress a point, you emphasize it and draw attention to its importance.
stressful ADJECTIVE
▤ (sense 1) anxiety, pressure, strain
▤ (sense 3) accent, emphasis
▤ (sense 4) accentuate, emphasize

stretch **stretches stretching stretched**
VERB **1** Something that stretches over an area extends that far. **2** When you stretch, you hold out

A
B
C
D
E
F
G
H
I
J
K
L
M
N
O
P
Q
R
S
T
U
V
W
X
Y
Z

part of your body as far as you can. **3** To stretch something soft or elastic means to pull it to make it longer or bigger. ▸ NOUN **4** A stretch of land or water is an area of it. **5** A stretch of time is a period of time.

stretcher stretchers
NOUN a long piece of material with a pole along each side, used to carry an injured person.

strewn
ADJECTIVE If things are strewn about, they are scattered about untidily EG *The costumes were strewn all over the floor.*

stricken
ADJECTIVE severely affected by something unpleasant.

strict stricter strictest
ADJECTIVE **1** Someone who is strict controls other people very firmly. **2** A strict rule must always be obeyed absolutely. **3** The strict meaning of something is its precise and accurate meaning. **4** You can use 'strict' to describe someone who never breaks the rules or principles of a particular belief EG *a strict Muslim.*
  ▤ (sense 1) severe, stern
  ▤ (sense 2) stringent

strictly
ADVERB **1** Strictly means only for a particular purpose EG *I was in it strictly for the money.* ▸ PHRASE **2** You say **strictly speaking** to correct a statement or add more precise information EG *Somebody pointed out that, strictly speaking, electricity was a discovery, not an invention.*

stride strides striding strode stridden
VERB **1** To stride along means to walk quickly with long steps.
  ▸ NOUN **2** a long step; also the length of a step.

strident
Said "**stry-dent**" ADJECTIVE loud, harsh, and unpleasant.

strife
NOUN; A FORMAL WORD Strife is trouble, conflict, and disagreement.

strike strikes striking struck
NOUN **1** If there is a strike, people stop working as a protest. **2** A hunger strike is a refusal to eat anything as a protest. A rent strike is a refusal to pay rent. **3** a military attack EG *the threat of American air strikes.* ▸ VERB **4** To strike someone or something means to hit them. **5** If an illness, disaster, or enemy strikes, it suddenly affects or attacks someone. **6** If a thought strikes you, it comes into your mind. **7** If you are struck by something, you are impressed by it. **8** When a clock strikes, it makes a sound to indicate the time. **9** To strike a deal with someone means to come to an agreement with them. **10** If someone strikes oil or gold, they discover it in the ground. **11** If you strike a match, you rub it against something to make it burst into flame.
strike off VERB If a professional person is struck off for bad behaviour, their name is removed from an official register and they are not allowed to practise their profession.
strike up VERB To strike up a conversation or friendship means to begin it.

striker strikers
NOUN **1** Strikers are people who are refusing to work as a protest. **2** In soccer, a player whose function is to attack and score goals.

striking
ADJECTIVE very noticeable because of being unusual or very attractive.
strikingly ADVERB

string strings stringing strung
NOUN **1** String is thin cord made of twisted threads. **2** You can refer to a row or series of similar things as a string of them EG *a string of islands... a string of injuries.* **3** The strings of a musical instrument are tightly stretched lengths of wire or nylon which vibrate to produce the notes.

▶ PLURAL NOUN **4** The section of an orchestra consisting of stringed instruments is called the strings.
string along VERB; AN INFORMAL USE To string someone along means to deceive them.
string out VERB **1** If things are strung out, they are spread out in a long line. **2** To string something out means to make it last longer than necessary.

stringed
ADJECTIVE A stringed instrument is one with strings, such as a guitar or violin.

stringent
ADJECTIVE Stringent laws conditions are very severe or are strictly controlled EG *stringent financial checks*.

stringy-bark stringy-barks
NOUN any Australian eucalypt that has bark that peels off in long, tough strands.

strip strips stripping stripped
NOUN **1** A strip of something is a long, narrow piece of it. **2** A comic strip is a series of drawings which tell a story. **3** A sports team's strip is the clothes worn by the team when playing a match. ▶ VERB **4** If you strip, you take off all your clothes. **5** To strip something means to remove whatever is covering its surface. **6** To strip someone of their property or rights means to take their property or rights away from them officially.

stripe stripes
NOUN Stripes are long, thin lines, usually of different colours.
striped ADJECTIVE

stripper strippers
NOUN an entertainer who does striptease.

striptease
NOUN Striptease is a form of entertainment in which someone takes off their clothes gradually to music.

strive strives striving strove

striven
VERB If you strive to do something, you make a great effort to achieve it.

stroke strokes stroking stroked
VERB **1** If you stroke something, you move your hand smoothly and gently over it. ▶ NOUN **2** If someone has a stroke, they suddenly lose consciousness as a result of a blockage or rupture in a blood vessel in the brain. A stroke can result in damage to speech and paralysis. **3** The strokes of a brush or pen are the movements that you make with it. **4** The strokes of a clock are the sounds that indicate the hour. **5** A swimming stroke is a particular style of swimming.
▶ PHRASE **6** If you have **a stroke of luck**, then you are lucky and something good happens to you.

stroll strolls strolling strolled
VERB **1** To stroll along means to walk slowly in a relaxed way. ▶ NOUN **2** a slow, pleasurable walk.
■ amble, saunter, walk

stroller strollers
NOUN In Australian English, a stroller is a pushchair.

strong stronger strongest
ADJECTIVE **1** Someone who is strong has powerful muscles. **2** You also say that someone is strong when they are confident and have courage. **3** Strong objects are able to withstand rough treatment. **4** Strong also means great in degree or intensity EG *a strong wind*. **5** A strong argument or theory is supported by a lot of evidence. **6** If a group or organization is strong, it has a lot of members or influence. **7** You can use 'strong' to say how many people there are in a group EG *The audience was about two dozen strong*. **8** Your strong points are the things you are good at. **9** A strong economy or currency is stable and successful. **10** A strong liquid or drug contains a lot of a particular substance. ▶ ADVERB **11** If someone

A B C D E F G H I J K L M N O P Q R S T U V W X Y Z

or something is still going strong, they are still healthy or working well after a long time.

strongly ADVERB

= (sense 1) muscular, powerful

= (sense 4) acute, intense

stronghold strongholds

NOUN **1** a place that is held and defended by an army. **2** A stronghold of an attitude or belief is a place in which the attitude or belief is strongly held EG *Europe's last stronghold of male dominance.*

structure structures structuring structured

NOUN **1** The structure of something is the way it is made, built, or organized. **2** something that has been built or constructed. **3** If something has structure, it is properly organized EG *The days have no real structure.* ▸ VERB **4** To structure something means to arrange it into an organized pattern or system.

structural ADJECTIVE, **structurally** ADVERB

= (sense 1) arrangement, construction, make-up

struggle struggles struggling struggled

VERB **1** If you struggle to do something, you try hard to do it in difficult circumstances. **2** When people struggle, they twist and move violently during a fight. ▸ NOUN **3** Something that is a struggle is difficult to achieve and takes a lot of effort. **4** a fight.

strum strums strumming strummed

VERB To strum a guitar means to play it by moving your fingers backwards and forwards across all the strings.

strut struts strutting strutted

VERB **1** To strut means to walk in a stiff, proud way with your chest out and your head high. ▸ NOUN **2** a piece of wood or metal which strengthens or supports part of a building or structure.

Stuart Stuarts

NOUN Stuart was the family name of the monarchs who ruled Scotland from 1371 to 1714 and England from 1603 to 1714.

stub stubs stubbing stubbed

NOUN **1** The stub of a pencil or cigarette is the short piece that remains when the rest has been used. **2** The stub of a cheque or ticket is the small part that you keep. ▸ VERB **3** If you stub your toe, you hurt it by accidentally kicking something.

stubble

NOUN **1** The short stalks remaining in the ground after a crop is harvested are called stubble. **2** If a man has stubble on his face, he has very short hair growing there because he has not shaved recently.

stubborn

ADJECTIVE **1** Someone who is stubborn is determined not to change their opinion or course of action. **2** A stubborn stain is difficult to remove.

stubbornly ADVERB, **stubbornness** NOUN

= (sense 1) inflexible, obstinate, pig-headed

stuck

ADJECTIVE **1** If something is stuck in a particular position, it is fixed or jammed and cannot be moved EG *His car's stuck in a snowdrift.* **2** If you are stuck, you are unable to continue what you were doing because it is too difficult. **3** If you are stuck somewhere, you are unable to get away.

stuck-up

ADJECTIVE; AN INFORMAL WORD proud and conceited.

stud studs

NOUN **1** a small piece of metal fixed into something. **2** A male horse or other animal that is kept for stud is kept for breeding purposes.

studded

ADJECTIVE decorated with small pieces of metal or precious stones.

student students

NOUN a person studying at university or college.

studied
ADJECTIVE A studied action or response has been carefully planned and is not natural EG *She sipped her glass of white wine with studied boredom.*

studio studios
NOUN **1** a room where a photographer or painter works. **2** a room containing special equipment where records, films, or radio or television programmes are made.

studious
Said "styoo-dee-uss" ADJECTIVE spending a lot of time studying.

studiously
ADVERB carefully and deliberately EG *She was studiously ignoring me.*

study studies studying studied
VERB **1** If you study a particular subject, you spend time learning about it. **2** If you study something, you look at it carefully EG *He studied the map in silence.* ▶ NOUN **3** Study is the activity of studying a subject EG *the serious study of medieval archaeology.* **4** Studies are subjects which are studied EG *media studies.* **5** a piece of research on a particular subject EG *a detailed study of the world's most violent people.* **6** a room used for writing and studying.

stuff stuffs stuffing stuffed
NOUN **1** You can refer to a substance or group of things as stuff. ▶ VERB **2** If you stuff something somewhere, you push it there quickly and roughly. **3** If you stuff something with a substance or objects, you fill it with the substance or objects.

stuffing
NOUN Stuffing is a mixture of small pieces of food put inside poultry or a vegetable before it is cooked.

stuffy stuffier stuffiest
ADJECTIVE **1** very formal and old-fashioned. **2** If it is stuffy in a room, there is not enough fresh air. ▤ (sense 2) airless, close, fusty

stumble stumbles stumbling stumbled
VERB **1** If you stumble while you are walking or running, you trip and almost fall. **2** If you stumble when speaking, you make mistakes when pronouncing the words. **3** If you stumble across something or stumble on it, you find it unexpectedly.

stump stumps stumping stumped
NOUN **1** a small part of something that is left when the rest has been removed EG *the stump of a dead tree.* **2** In cricket, the stumps are the three upright wooden sticks that support the bails, forming the wicket. ▶ VERB **3** If a question or problem stumps you, you cannot think of an answer or solution.

stun stuns stunning stunned
VERB **1** If you are stunned by something, you are very shocked by it. **2** To stun a person or animal means to knock them unconscious with a blow to the head.

stunning
ADJECTIVE very beautiful or impressive EG *a stunning first novel.*

stunt stunts stunting stunted
NOUN **1** an unusual or dangerous and exciting action that someone does to get publicity or as part of a film. ▶ VERB **2** To stunt the growth or development of something means to prevent it from developing as it should.

stupendous
ADJECTIVE very large or impressive EG *a stupendous amount of money.*

stupid stupider stupidest
ADJECTIVE showing lack of good judgment or intelligence and not at all sensible.
stupidity NOUN
▤ foolish, obtuse, unintelligent

sturdy sturdier sturdiest
ADJECTIVE strong and firm and unlikely to be damaged or injured

A
B
C
D
E
F
G
H
I
J
K
L
M
N
O
P
Q
R
S
T
U
V
W
X
Y
Z

A B C D E F G H I J K L M N O P Q R S T U V W X Y Z

EG *a sturdy chest of drawers.*

sturgeon
Said "stur-jon" NOUN a large edible fish, the eggs of which are also eaten and are known as caviar.

stutter stutters stuttering stuttered
NOUN 1 Someone who has a stutter finds it difficult to speak smoothly and often repeats sounds through being unable to complete a word. ▶ VERB 2 When someone stutters, they hesitate or repeat sounds when speaking.

sty sties
NOUN a pigsty.

stye styes
NOUN an infection in the form of a small red swelling on a person's eyelid.

style styles styling styled
NOUN 1 The style of something is the general way in which it is done or presented, often showing the attitudes of the people involved. 2 A person or place that has style is smart, elegant, and fashionable. 3 The style of something is its design EG *new windows that fit in with the style of the house.* ▶ VERB 4 To style a piece of clothing or a person's hair means to design and create its shape.
▤ (sense 2) elegance, flair, panache

stylish
ADJECTIVE smart, elegant, and fashionable.
stylishly ADVERB
▤ chic, smart

suave
Said "swahv" ADJECTIVE charming, polite, and confident EG *a suave Italian.*

sub-
PREFIX 1 'Sub-' is used at the beginning of words that have 'under' as part of their meaning EG *submarine.* 2 'Sub-' is also used to form nouns that refer to the parts into which something is divided EG *Subsection 2 of section 49... a*

particular subgroup of citizens.

subconscious
NOUN 1 Your subconscious is the part of your mind that can influence you without your being aware of it. ▶ ADJECTIVE 2 happening or existing in someone's subconscious and therefore not directly realized or understood by them EG *a subconscious fear of rejection.*
subconsciously ADVERB

subcontinent subcontinents
NOUN a large mass of land, often consisting of several countries, and forming part of a continent EG *the Indian subcontinent.*

subdue subdues subduing subdued
VERB 1 If soldiers subdue a group of people, they bring them under control by using force EG *It would be quite impossible to subdue the whole continent.* 2 To subdue a colour, light, or emotion means to make it less bright or strong.
▤ (sense 1) control, overcome, quell

subdued
ADJECTIVE 1 rather quiet and sad. 2 not very noticeable or bright.

subject subjects subjecting subjected
NOUN 1 The subject of writing or a conversation is the thing or person being discussed. 2 In grammar, the subject is the word or words representing the person or thing doing the action expressed by the verb. For example, in the sentence 'My cat keeps catching birds', 'my cat' is the subject. 3 an area of study. 4 The subjects of a country are the people who live there. ▶ VERB 5 To subject someone to something means to make them experience it EG *He was subjected to constant interruption.* ▶ ADJECTIVE 6 Someone or something that is subject to something is affected by it EG *He was subject to attacks at various times.*

subjective

ADJECTIVE influenced by personal feelings and opinion rather than based on fact or rational thought.

subjunctive

NOUN In grammar, the subjunctive or subjunctive mood is one of the forms a verb can take. It is used to express attitudes such as wishing and doubting.

sublime

ADJECTIVE Something that is sublime is wonderful and affects people emotionally EG *sublime music*.

submarine submarines

NOUN a ship that can travel beneath the surface of the sea.

submerge submerges submerging submerged

VERB 1 To submerge means to go beneath the surface of a liquid. 2 If you submerge yourself in an activity, you become totally involved in it.

submission submissions

NOUN 1 Submission is a state in which someone accepts the control of another person EG *Now he must beat us into submission*. 2 The submission of a proposal or application is the act of sending it for consideration.

submissive

ADJECTIVE behaving in a quiet, obedient way.

submit submits submitting submitted

VERB 1 If you submit to something, you accept it because you are not powerful enough to resist it. 2 If you submit an application or proposal, you send it to someone for consideration.

subordinate subordinates subordinating subordinated

NOUN 1 A person's subordinate is someone who is in a less important position than them. ▶ ADJECTIVE 2 If one thing is subordinate to another, it is less important EG *Non-elected officials are subordinate to elected leaders*. ▶ VERB 3 To

subordinate one thing to another means to treat it as being less important.

subscribe subscribes subscribing subscribed

VERB 1 If you subscribe to a particular belief or opinion, you support it or agree with it. 2 If you subscribe to a magazine, you pay to receive regular copies.
subscriber NOUN

subscription subscriptions

NOUN a sum of money that you pay regularly to belong to an organization or to receive regular copies of a magazine.

subsequent

ADJECTIVE happening or coming into existence at a later time than something else EG *the December uprising and the subsequent political violence*.
subsequently ADVERB

subservient

ADJECTIVE Someone who is subservient does whatever other people want them to do.

subside subsides subsiding subsided

VERB 1 To subside means to become less intense or quieter EG *Her excitement suddenly subsided*. 2 If water or the ground subsides, it sinks to a lower level.

subsidence

NOUN If a place is suffering from subsidence, parts of the ground have sunk to a lower level.

subsidiary subsidiaries

Said "sub-sid-yer-ee" NOUN 1 a company which is part of a larger company. ▶ ADJECTIVE 2 treated as being of less importance and additional to another thing EG *Drama is offered as a subsidiary subject*.

subsidize subsidizes subsidizing subsidized; also spelt subsidise

VERB To subsidize something means to provide part of the cost of it EG *He feels the government should do much more to subsidize films*.

A B C D E F G H I J K L M N O P Q R S T U V W X Y Z

subsidized ADJECTIVE

subsidy subsidies
NOUN a sum of money paid to help support a company or provide a public service.

substance substances
NOUN **1** Anything which is a solid, a powder, a liquid, or a paste can be referred to as a substance. **2** If a speech or piece of writing has substance, it is meaningful or important EG *a good speech, but there was no substance.*
■ (sense 1) material, stuff

substantial
ADJECTIVE **1** very large in degree or amount EG *a substantial pay rise.* **2** large and strongly built EG *a substantial stone building.*

substantially
ADVERB Something that is substantially true is generally or mostly true.

substitute substitutes substituting substituted
VERB **1** To substitute one thing for another means to use it instead of the other thing or to put it in the other thing's place. ▶ NOUN **2** If one thing is a substitute for another, it is used instead of it or put in its place.
substitution NOUN
■ (sense 1) exchange, replace
■ (sense 2) alternative, replacement, surrogate

subterfuge subterfuges
Said "sub-ter-fyooj" NOUN Subterfuge is the use of deceitful or dishonest methods.
▥ from Latin *subterfugere* meaning 'to escape by stealth'

subtitle subtitles
NOUN A film with subtitles has a printed translation of the dialogue at the bottom of the screen.

subtle subtler subtlest
Said "sut-tl" ADJECTIVE **1** very fine, delicate, or small in degree EG *a subtle change.* **2** using indirect methods to achieve something.

subtly ADVERB, **subtlety** NOUN

subtract subtracts subtracting subtracted
VERB If you subtract one number from another, you take away the first number from the second.
subtraction NOUN

suburb suburbs
NOUN an area of a town or city that is away from its centre.

suburban
ADJECTIVE **1** relating to a suburb or suburbs. **2** dull and conventional.

suburbia
NOUN You can refer to the suburbs of a city as suburbia.

subversive subversives
ADJECTIVE **1** intended to destroy or weaken a political system EG *subversive activities.* ▶ NOUN **2** Subversives are people who try to destroy or weaken a political system.
subversion NOUN

subvert subverts subverting subverted
VERB; A FORMAL WORD To subvert something means to cause it to weaken or fail EG *a cunning campaign to subvert the music industry.*

subway subways
NOUN **1** a footpath that goes underneath a road. **2** an underground railway.

succeed succeeds succeeding succeeded
VERB **1** To succeed means to achieve the result you intend. **2** To succeed someone means to be the next person to have their job. **3** If one thing succeeds another, it comes after it in time EG *The explosion was succeeded by a crash.*
succeeding ADJECTIVE
■ (sense 1) be successful, do well, make it

success successes
NOUN **1** Success is the achievement of something you have been trying to do. **2** Someone who is a success

has achieved an important position or made a lot of money.

successful ADJECTIVE, **successfully** ADVERB

succession successions
NOUN **1** A succession of things is a number of them occurring one after the other. **2** When someone becomes the next person to have an important position, you can refer to this event as their succession to this position EG *his succession to the throne.* ▶ PHRASE **3** If something happens a number of weeks, months, or years in succession, it happens that number of times without a break EG *Borg won Wimbledon five years in succession.*

successive
ADJECTIVE occurring one after the other without a break EG *three successive victories.*

successor successors
NOUN Someone's successor is the person who takes their job when they leave.

succinct
Said "suk-**singkt**" ADJECTIVE expressing something clearly and in very few words.
succinctly ADVERB

succulent
ADJECTIVE Succulent food is juicy and delicious.

succumb succumbs succumbing succumbed
VERB If you succumb to something, you are unable to resist it any longer EG *She never succumbed to his charms.*

such
ADJECTIVE OR PRONOUN **1** You use 'such' to refer to the person or thing you have just mentioned, or to someone or something similar EG *Naples or Palermo or some such place.* ▶ PHRASE **2** You can use **such as** to introduce an example of something EG *herbal teas such as camomile.* **3** You can use **such as it is** to indicate that something is not

great in quality or quantity EG *The action, such as it is, is set in Egypt.* **4** You can use **such and such** when you want to refer to something that is not specific EG *A good trick is to ask whether they have seen such and such a film.* ▶ ADJECTIVE **5** 'Such' can be used for emphasizing EG *I have such a terrible sense of guilt.*

suchlike
ADJECTIVE OR PRONOUN used to refer to things similar to those already mentioned EG *shampoos, talcs, toothbrushes, and suchlike.*

suck sucks sucking sucked
VERB **1** If you suck something, you hold it in your mouth and pull at it with your cheeks and tongue, usually to get liquid out of it. **2** To suck something in a particular direction means to draw it there with a powerful force. **3** AN INFORMAL USE To suck up to someone means to do things to please them in order to obtain praise or approval.

sucker suckers
NOUN **1** AN INFORMAL USE If you call someone a sucker, you mean that they are easily fooled or cheated. **2** Suckers are pads on the bodies of some animals and insects which they use to cling to a surface.

suckle suckles suckling suckled
VERB When a mother suckles a baby, she feeds it with milk from her breast.

sucrose
Said "**syoo**-kroze" NOUN; A TECHNICAL WORD Sucrose is sugar in crystalline form found in sugar cane and sugar beet.

suction
NOUN **1** Suction is the force involved when a substance is drawn or sucked from one place to another. **2** Suction is the process by which two surfaces stick together when the air between them is removed EG *They stay there by suction.*

Sudanese
Said "soo-dan-**neez**" ADJECTIVE

A B C D E F G H I J K L M N O P Q R S T U V W X Y Z

1 belonging or relating to the Sudan. ▶ NOUN **2** someone who comes from the Sudan.

sudden

ADJECTIVE happening quickly and unexpectedly EG *a sudden cry*.
suddenly ADVERB, **suddenness** NOUN

sue sues suing sued

VERB To sue someone means to start a legal case against them, usually to claim money from them.

suede

Said "swayd" NOUN Suede is a thin, soft leather with a rough surface.
📖 from French *gants de Suède* meaning 'gloves from Sweden'

suffer suffers suffering suffered

VERB **1** If someone is suffering pain, or suffering as a result of an unpleasant situation, they are badly affected by it. **2** If something suffers as a result of neglect or an unfavourable situation, its condition or quality becomes worse EG *The bus service is suffering*.
sufferer NOUN, **suffering** NOUN

suffice suffices sufficing sufficed

VERB; A FORMAL WORD If something suffices, it is enough or adequate for a purpose.

sufficient

ADJECTIVE If a supply or quantity is sufficient for a purpose, there is enough of it available.
sufficiently ADVERB

suffix suffixes

NOUN A suffix is a group of letters which is added to the end of a word to form a new word, for example '-ology' or '-itis'.

suffocate suffocates suffocating suffocated

VERB To suffocate means to die as a result of having too little air or oxygen to breathe.
suffocation NOUN

suffrage

NOUN Suffrage is the right to vote in political elections.

suffragette suffragettes

NOUN a woman who, at the beginning of the 20th century, campaigned for women to be given the right to vote.

suffused

ADJECTIVE; A LITERARY WORD If something is suffused with light or colour, light or colour has gradually spread over it.

sugar

NOUN Sugar is a sweet substance used to sweeten food and drinks.

suggest suggests suggesting suggested

VERB **1** If you suggest a plan or idea to someone, you mention it as a possibility for them to consider. **2** If something suggests a particular thought or impression, it makes you think in that way or gives you that impression EG *Nothing you say suggests he is mentally ill*.
■ (sense 1) advocate, propose, recommend
■ (sense 2) hint, imply

suggestion suggestions

NOUN **1** a plan or idea that is mentioned as a possibility for someone to consider. **2** A suggestion of something is a very slight indication or faint sign of it EG *a suggestion of dishonesty*.
■ (sense 1) proposal, recommendation

suggestive

ADJECTIVE **1** Something that is suggestive of a particular thing gives a slight hint or sign of it. **2** Suggestive remarks or gestures make people think about sex.
■ (sense 2) risqué, smutty

suicidal

ADJECTIVE **1** People who are suicidal want to kill themselves. **2** Suicidal behaviour is so dangerous that it is likely to result in death EG *a mad suicidal attack*.

suicide

NOUN People who commit suicide deliberately kill themselves.
📖 from Latin *sui* meaning 'of

oneself' and *caedere* meaning 'to kill'

suit suits suiting suited
NOUN **1** a matching jacket and trousers or skirt. **2** In a court of law, a suit is a legal action taken by one person against another. **3** one of four different types of card in a pack of playing cards. The four suits are hearts, clubs, diamonds, and spades. ▶ VERB **4** If a situation or course of action suits you, it is appropriate or acceptable for your purpose. **5** If a piece of clothing or a colour suits you, you look good when you are wearing it. **6** If you do something to suit yourself, you do it because you want to and without considering other people.

suitable
ADJECTIVE right or acceptable for a particular purpose or occasion.
suitability NOUN, **suitably** ADVERB
≡ appropriate, apt, fitting

suitcase suitcases
NOUN a case in which you carry your clothes when you are travelling.

suite suites
Said "**sweet**" NOUN **1** In a hotel, a suite is a set of rooms. **2** a set of matching furniture or bathroom fittings.

suited
ADJECTIVE right or appropriate for a particular purpose or person EG *He is well suited to be minister for the arts.*

suitor suitors
NOUN; AN OLD-FASHIONED WORD A woman's suitor is a man who wants to marry her.

sulk sulks sulking sulked
VERB Someone who is sulking is showing their annoyance by being silent and moody.
sulky ADJECTIVE

sullen
ADJECTIVE behaving in a bad-tempered and disagreeably silent way EG *a sullen and resentful workforce.*

sulphur
NOUN Sulphur is a pale yellow nonmetallic element which burns with a very unpleasant smell.

sultan sultans
NOUN In some Muslim countries, the ruler of the country is called the sultan.
🏛 from Arabic *sultan* meaning 'rule'

sultana sultanas
NOUN **1** a dried grape. **2** the wife of a sultan.

sum sums summing summed
NOUN **1** an amount of money. **2** In arithmetic, a sum is a calculation. **3** The sum of something is the total amount of it.
sum up VERB If you sum something up, you briefly describe its main points.

summarize summarizes summarizing summarized; also spelt **summarise**
VERB To summarize something means to give a short account of its main points.

summary summaries
NOUN **1** A summary of something is a short account of its main points. ▶ ADJECTIVE **2** A summary action is done without delay or careful thought EG *Summary executions are common.*
summarily ADVERB
≡ (sense 1) précis, résumé, synopsis

summer summers
NOUN Summer is the season between spring and autumn.

summit summits
NOUN **1** The summit of a mountain is its top. **2** a meeting between leaders of different countries to discuss particular issues.

summon summons summoning summoned
VERB **1** If someone summons you, they order you to go to them. **2** If you summon up strength or energy, you make a great effort to be strong or energetic.

A B C D E F G H I J K L M N O P Q R S T U V W X Y Z

summons summonses

NOUN **1** an official order to appear in court. **2** an order to go to someone EG *The result was a summons to headquarters.*

sumptuous

ADJECTIVE Something that is sumptuous is magnificent and obviously very expensive.

sum total

NOUN The sum total of a number of things is all of them added or considered together.

sun suns sunning sunned

NOUN **1** The sun is the star providing heat and light for the planets revolving around it in our solar system. **2** You refer to heat and light from the sun as sun EG *We need a bit of sun.* ▶ VERB **3** If you sun yourself, you sit in the sunshine.

sunbathe sunbathes sunbathing sunbathed

VERB If you sunbathe, you sit in the sunshine to get a suntan.

sunburn

NOUN Sunburn is sore red skin on someone's body due to too much exposure to the rays of the sun. **sunburnt** ADJECTIVE

sundae sundaes

*Said "sun-*day" NOUN a dish of ice cream with cream and fruit or nuts.

Sunday Sundays

NOUN Sunday is the day between Saturday and Monday.

from Old English *sunnandæg* meaning 'day of the sun'

Sunday school Sunday schools

NOUN Sunday school is a special class held on Sundays to teach children about Christianity.

sundial sundials

NOUN an object used for telling the time, consisting of a pointer which casts a shadow on a flat base marked with the hours.

sundry

ADJECTIVE **1** 'Sundry' is used to refer to several things or people of various sorts EG *sundry journalists and lawyers.* ▶ PHRASE **2** All and sundry means everyone.

sunflower sunflowers

NOUN a tall plant with very large yellow flowers.

sunglasses

PLURAL NOUN Sunglasses are spectacles with dark lenses that you wear to protect your eyes from the sun.

sunken

ADJECTIVE **1** having sunk to the bottom of the sea, a river, or lake EG *sunken ships.* **2** A sunken object or area has been constructed below the level of the surrounding area EG *a sunken garden.* **3** curving inwards EG *Her cheeks were sunken.*

sunlight

NOUN Sunlight is the bright light produced when the sun is shining. **sunlit** ADJECTIVE

sunny sunnier sunniest

ADJECTIVE When it is sunny, the sun is shining.

sunrise sunrises

NOUN Sunrise is the time in the morning when the sun first appears, and the colours produced in the sky at that time.

sunset sunsets

NOUN Sunset is the time in the evening when the sun disappears below the horizon, and the colours produced in the sky at that time.

sunshine

NOUN Sunshine is the bright light produced when the sun is shining.

sunstroke

NOUN Sunstroke is an illness caused by spending too much time in hot sunshine.

suntan suntans

NOUN If you have a suntan, the sun has turned your skin brown. **suntanned** ADJECTIVE

super

ADJECTIVE very nice or very good EG *a super party.*

super-

PREFIX 'Super-' is used to describe something that is larger or better than similar things EG *a European superstate*.

📖 from Latin *super* meaning 'above'

superb

ADJECTIVE very good indeed.
superbly ADVERB

supercilious

Said "soo-per-**sill**-ee-uss" ADJECTIVE If you are supercilious, you behave in a scornful way towards other people because you think they are inferior to you.

superego

NOUN; A TECHNICAL WORD Your superego is the part of your mind that controls your ideas of right and wrong and produces feelings of guilt.

superficial

ADJECTIVE **1** involving only the most obvious or most general aspects of something EG *a superficial knowledge of music*. **2** not having a deep, serious, or genuine interest in anything EG *a superficial and rather silly woman*. **3** Superficial wounds are not very deep or severe.
superficially ADVERB

superfluous

Said "soo-per-**floo**-uss" ADJECTIVE; A FORMAL WORD unnecessary or no longer needed.

superhuman

ADJECTIVE having much greater power or ability than is normally expected of humans EG *superhuman strength*.

superimpose superimposes superimposing superimposed
VERB To superimpose one image on another means to put the first image on top of the other so that they are seen as one image.

superintendent superintendents
NOUN **1** a police officer above the rank of inspector. **2** a person whose job is to be responsible for a particular thing EG *the superintendent of prisons*.

superior superiors
ADJECTIVE **1** better or of higher quality than other similar things. **2** in a position of higher authority than another person. **3** showing too much pride and self-importance EG *Jerry smiled in a superior way*. ▶ NOUN **4** Your superiors are people who are in a higher position than you in society or an organization.
superiority NOUN

superlative superlatives
Said "soo-per-**lat**-tiv" NOUN **1** In grammar, the superlative is the form of an adjective which indicates that the person or thing described has more of a particular quality than anyone or anything else. For example, 'quickest', 'best', and 'easiest' are all superlatives.
▶ ADJECTIVE **2** A FORMAL USE very good indeed EG *a superlative performance*.

What is a Superlative?

Many adjectives have three different forms. These are known as the **positive**, the **comparative**, and the **superlative**. The comparative and superlative are used when you make comparisons.

The **positive** form of an adjective is given as the entry in the dictionary. It is used when there is no comparison between different objects.
    *Matthew is **tall**.*

The **superlative** form is usually made by adding the ending -est to the positive form of the adjective. It shows that something possesses a quality to a greater extent than all the others in its class or group.
    *Matthew is the **tallest** boy in his class.*

You can also express superlatives by using the words *most* or *least* with the positive (not the superlative) form of the adjective.
    *Matthew is the **most energetic** member of the family.*

Also look at the grammar box at **comparative**.

---

supermarket supermarkets

A
B
C
D
E
F
G
H
I
J
K
L
M
N
O
P
Q
R
S
T
U
V
W
X
Y
Z

NOUN a shop selling food and household goods arranged so that you can help yourself and pay for everything at a till by the exit.

supernatural
ADJECTIVE **1** Something that is supernatural, for example ghosts or witchcraft, cannot be explained by normal scientific laws. ▶ NOUN **2** You can refer to supernatural things as the supernatural.

superpower superpowers
NOUN a very powerful and influential country such as the USA.

supersede supersedes superseding superseded
Said "soo-per-**seed**" VERB If something supersedes another thing, it replaces it because it is more modern EG *New York superseded Paris as the centre for modern art.*

supersonic
ADJECTIVE A supersonic aircraft can travel faster than the speed of sound.

superstar superstars
NOUN You can refer to a very famous entertainer or sports player as a superstar.

superstition superstitions
NOUN Superstition is a belief in things like magic and powers that bring good or bad luck.
superstitious ADJECTIVE
from Latin *superstitio* meaning 'dread of the supernatural'

supervise supervises supervising supervised
VERB To supervise someone means to check and direct what they are doing to make sure that they do it correctly.
supervision NOUN, **supervisor** NOUN
oversee, superintend

supper suppers
NOUN Supper is a meal eaten in the evening or a snack eaten before you go to bed.

supplant supplants supplanting supplanted

VERB; A FORMAL WORD To supplant someone or something means to take their place EG *By the 1930s the wristwatch had supplanted the pocket watch.*

supple
ADJECTIVE able to bend and move easily.

supplement supplements supplementing supplemented
VERB **1** To supplement something means to add something to it to improve it EG *Many village men supplemented their wages by fishing for salmon.* ▶ NOUN **2** something that is added to something else to improve it.

supplementary
ADJECTIVE added to something else to improve it EG *supplementary doses of vitamin E.*

supplier suppliers
NOUN a firm which provides particular goods.

supply supplies supplying supplied
VERB **1** To supply someone with something means to provide it or send it to them. ▶ NOUN **2** A supply of something is an amount available for use EG *the world's supply of precious metals.* ▶ PLURAL NOUN **3** Supplies are food and equipment for a particular purpose.

support supports supporting supported
VERB **1** If you support someone, you agree with their aims and want them to succeed. **2** If you support someone who is in difficulties, you are kind, encouraging, and helpful to them. **3** If something supports an object, it is underneath it and holding it up. **4** To support someone or something means to prevent them from falling by holding them. **5** To support someone financially means to provide them with money. ▶ NOUN **6** an object that is holding something up. **7** Financial support

is money that is provided for someone or something.

supporter NOUN, **supportable** ADJECTIVE

supportive

ADJECTIVE A supportive person is encouraging and helpful to someone who is in difficulties.

suppose supposes supposing supposed

VERB **1** If you suppose that something is the case, you think that it is likely EG *I supposed that would be too obvious.* ▶ PHRASE **2** You can say **I suppose** when you are not entirely certain or enthusiastic about something EG *Yes, I suppose he could come.* **3** If something **is supposed** to be done, it should be done EG *You are supposed to report it to the police.* **4** If something **is supposed** to happen, it is planned or expected to happen EG *It was supposed to be this afternoon.* **5** Something that **is supposed** to be the case is generally believed or thought to be so EG *Wimbledon is supposed to be the best tournament of them all.* ▶ CONJUNCTION **6** You can use 'suppose' or 'supposing' when you are considering or suggesting a possible situation or action EG *Supposing he were to break down under interrogation?*

supposed

ADJECTIVE 'Supposed' is used to express doubt about something that is generally believed EG *the supposed culprit.*

supposedly ADVERB

supposition suppositions

NOUN something that is believed or assumed to be true EG *the supposition that science requires an ordered universe.*

suppress suppresses suppressing suppressed

VERB **1** If an army or government suppresses an activity, it prevents people from doing it. **2** If someone suppresses a piece of information, they prevent it from becoming generally known. **3** If you suppress your feelings, you stop yourself expressing them.

suppression NOUN

■ (sense 1) crush, quell, stop

supremacy

Said "soo-**prem**-mass-ee" NOUN If a group of people has supremacy over others, it is more powerful than the others.

supreme

ADJECTIVE **1** 'Supreme' is used as part of a title to indicate the highest level of an organization or system EG *the Supreme Court.* **2** 'Supreme' is used to emphasize the greatness of something EG *the supreme achievement of the human race.*

supremely ADVERB

■ (sense 2) greatest, highest, paramount

surcharge surcharges

NOUN an additional charge.

sure surer surest

ADJECTIVE **1** If you are sure about something, you have no doubts about it. **2** If you are sure of yourself, you are very confident. **3** If something is sure to happen, it will definitely happen. **4** Sure means reliable or accurate EG *a sure sign that something is wrong.* ▶ PHRASE **5** If you **make sure** about something, you check it or take action to see that it is done. ▶ INTERJECTION **6** Sure is an informal way of saying 'yes' EG *'Can I come too?' — 'Sure'.*

surely

ADVERB 'Surely' is used to emphasize the belief that something is the case EG *Surely these people here knew that?*

surf surfs surfing surfed

VERB **1** When you surf, you go surfing. **2** When you surf the Internet, you go from website to website reading the information. ▶ NOUN **3** Surf is the white foam that forms on the top of waves when they break near the shore.

surface surfaces surfacing

surfaced

NOUN **1** The surface of something is the top or outside area of it. **2** The surface of a situation is what can be seen easily rather than what is hidden or not immediately obvious. ▶ VERB **3** If someone surfaces, they come up from under water to the surface.

surfboard surfboards

NOUN a long narrow lightweight board used for surfing.

surf club surf clubs

NOUN In Australia, a surf club is an organization of lifesavers in charge of safety on a particular beach, and which often provides leisure facilities.

surfeit

Said "sur-fit" NOUN If there is a surfeit of something, there is too much of it.

surfing

NOUN Surfing is a sport which involves riding towards the shore on the top of a large wave while standing on a surfboard.

surge surges surging surged

NOUN **1** a sudden great increase in the amount of something EG *a surge of panic*. ▶ VERB **2** If something surges, it moves suddenly and powerfully EG *The soldiers surged forwards*.

surgeon surgeons

NOUN a doctor who performs operations.

surgery surgeries

NOUN **1** Surgery is medical treatment involving cutting open part of the patient's body to treat the damaged part. **2** The room or building where a doctor or dentist works is called a surgery. **3** A period of time during which a doctor is available to see patients is called surgery EG *evening surgery*.

surgical

ADJECTIVE used in or involving a medical operation EG *surgical gloves*.
surgically ADVERB

surly surlier surliest

ADJECTIVE rude and bad-tempered.
surliness NOUN

surmise surmises surmising surmised

VERB; A FORMAL WORD To surmise something means to guess it EG *I surmised it was of French manufacture*.

surmount surmounts surmounting surmounted

VERB **1** To surmount a difficulty means to manage to solve it. **2** A FORMAL USE If something is surmounted by a particular thing, that thing is on top of it EG *The island is surmounted by a huge black castle*.

surname surnames

NOUN Your surname is your last name which you share with other members of your family.

surpass surpasses surpassing surpassed

VERB; A FORMAL WORD To surpass someone or something means to be better than them.

surplus surpluses

NOUN If there is a surplus of something there is more of it than is needed.
■ excess, surfeit

surprise surprises surprising surprised

NOUN **1** an unexpected event.
2 Surprise is the feeling caused when something unexpected happens. ▶ VERB **3** If something surprises you, it gives you a feeling of surprise. **4** If you surprise someone, you do something they were not expecting.
surprising ADJECTIVE

surreal

ADJECTIVE very strange and dreamlike.

surrender surrenders surrendering surrendered

VERB **1** To surrender means to stop fighting and agree that the other side has won. **2** If you surrender to a temptation or feeling, you let it take control of you. **3** To surrender

something means to give it up to someone else EG *The gallery director surrendered his keys.* ▶ NOUN
4 Surrender is a situation in which one side in a fight agrees that the other side has won and gives in.
▣ (sense 1) give in, submit, yield
▣ (sense 4) capitulation, submission

surreptitious
Said "sur-rep-tish-uss" ADJECTIVE A surreptitious action is done secretly or so that no-one will notice EG *a surreptitious glance.*
surreptitiously ADVERB

surrogate surrogates
ADJECTIVE **1** acting as a substitute for someone or something. ▶ NOUN **2** a person or thing that acts as a substitute.

surround surrounds surrounding surrounded
VERB **1** To surround someone or something means to be situated all around them. ▶ NOUN **2** The surround of something is its outside edge or border.
▣ (sense 1) encircle, enclose

surrounding surroundings
ADJECTIVE **1** The surrounding area of a particular place is the area around it EG *the surrounding countryside.*
▶ PLURAL NOUN **2** You can refer to the area and environment around a place or person as their surroundings EG *very comfortable surroundings.*

surveillance
Said "sur-vay-lanss" NOUN Surveillance is the close watching of a person's activities by the police or army.
▥ from French *surveiller* meaning 'to watch over'

survey surveys surveying surveyed
VERB **1** To survey something means to look carefully at the whole of it. **2** To survey a building or piece of land means to examine it carefully in order to make a report or plan of

its structure and features. ▶ NOUN
3 A survey of something is a detailed examination of it, often in the form of a report.
▣ (sense 1) look over, scan, view

surveyor surveyors
NOUN a person whose job is to survey buildings or land.

survival survivals
NOUN Survival is being able to continue living or existing in spite of great danger or difficulties EG *There was no hope of survival.*

survive survives surviving survived
VERB To survive means to continue to live or exist in spite of a great danger or difficulties EG *a German monk who survived the shipwreck.*
survivor NOUN

susceptible
ADJECTIVE If you are susceptible to something, you arc likcly to be influenced or affected by it EG *Elderly people are more susceptible to infection.*
susceptibility NOUN

suspect suspects suspecting suspected
VERB **1** If you suspect something, you think that it is likely or is probably true EG *I suspected that the report would be sent.* **2** If you suspect something, you have doubts about its reliability EG *He suspected her intent.* **3** If you suspect someone of doing something wrong, you think that they have done it. ▶ NOUN
4 someone who is thought to be guilty of a crime. ▶ ADJECTIVE **5** If something is suspect, it cannot be trusted or relied upon EG *a rather suspect holy man.*

suspend suspends suspending suspended
VERB **1** If something is suspended, it is hanging from somewhere EG *the television set suspended above the bar.*
2 To suspend an activity or event means to delay it or stop it for a while. **3** If someone is suspended

A
B
C
D
E
F
G
H
I
J
K
L
M
N
O
P
Q
R
S
T
U
V
W
X
Y
Z

A B C D E F G H I J K L M N O P Q R S T U V W X Y Z

from their job, they are told not to do it for a period of time, usually as a punishment.

suspender suspenders
NOUN Suspenders are fastenings which hold up a woman's stockings.

suspense
NOUN Suspense is a state of excitement or anxiety caused by having to wait for something.

suspension
NOUN **1** The suspension of something is the delaying or stopping of it. **2** A person's suspension is their removal from a job for a period of time, usually as a punishment. **3** The suspension of a vehicle consists of springs and shock absorbers which provide a smooth ride. **4** a liquid mixture in which very small bits of a solid material are contained and are not dissolved.

suspicion suspicions
NOUN **1** Suspicion is the feeling of not trusting someone or the feeling that something is wrong. **2** a feeling that something is likely to happen or is probably true EG *the suspicion that more could have been achieved*.
■ (sense 1) distrust, misgiving, scepticism

suspicious
ADJECTIVE **1** If you are suspicious of someone, you do not trust them. **2** 'Suspicious' is used to describe things that make you think that there is something wrong with a situation EG *suspicious circumstances*.
suspiciously ADVERB
■ (sense 2) dubious, questionable, suspect

sustain sustains sustaining sustained
VERB **1** To sustain something means to continue it for a period of time EG *Their team-mates were unable to sustain the challenge.* **2** If something sustains you, it gives you energy

and strength. **3** A FORMAL USE To sustain an injury or loss means to suffer it.

sustainable
ADJECTIVE **1** capable of being sustained. **2** If economic development or energy resources are sustainable they are capable of being maintained at a steady level without exhausting natural resources or causing ecological damage EG *sustainable forestry*.

sustenance
NOUN; A FORMAL WORD Sustenance is food and drink.

swab swabs swabbing swabbed
NOUN **1** a small piece of cotton wool used for cleaning a wound. ▶ VERB **2** To swab something means to clean it using a large mop and a lot of water. **3** To swab a wound means to clean it or take specimens from it using a swab.

swag swags
NOUN; AN INFORMAL WORD **1** goods or valuables, especially ones which have been gained dishonestly. **2** In Australian and New Zealand English, the bundle of possessions belonging to a tramp. **3** In Australian and New Zealand English, swags of something is lots of it.

swagger swaggers swaggering swaggered
VERB **1** To swagger means to walk in a proud, exaggerated way. ▶ NOUN **2** an exaggerated walk.

swagman swagmen
NOUN; AN INFORMAL WORD In Australia and New Zealand in the past, a tramp who carried his possessions on his back.

swallow swallows swallowing swallowed
VERB **1** If you swallow something, you make it go down your throat and into your stomach. **2** When you swallow, you move your throat muscles as if you were swallowing something, especially when you

are nervous. ▶ NOUN **3** a bird with pointed wings and a long forked tail.

swamp swamps swamping swamped
NOUN **1** an area of permanently wet land. ▶ VERB **2** If something is swamped, it is covered or filled with water. **3** If you are swamped by things, you have more than you are able to deal with EG *She was swamped with calls.*
swampy ADJECTIVE

swan swans
NOUN a large, usually white, bird with a long neck that lives on rivers or lakes.

swap swaps swapping swapped
Rhymes with "stop" VERB To swap one thing for another means to replace the first thing with the second, often by making an exchange with another person EG *Webb swapped shirts with a Leeds player.*
◼ exchange, switch, trade

swarm swarms swarming swarmed
NOUN **1** A swarm of insects is a large group of them flying together. ▶ VERB **2** When bees or other insects swarm, they fly together in a large group. **3** If people swarm somewhere, a lot of people go there quickly and at the same time EG *the crowds of office workers who swarm across the bridge.* **4** If a place is swarming with people, there are a lot of people there.

swarthy swarthier swarthiest
ADJECTIVE A swarthy person has a dark complexion.

swashbuckling
ADJECTIVE 'Swashbuckling' is used to describe people who have the exciting behaviour or appearance of pirates.
◼ from Middle English *swashbuckling* meaning 'making a noise by striking your sword against a shield'

swastika swastikas
Said "swoss-tik-ka" NOUN a symbol in the shape of a cross with each arm bent over at right angles. It was the official symbol of the Nazis in Germany, but in India it is a good luck sign.
◼ from Sanskrit *svasti* meaning 'prosperity'

swat swats swatting swatted
VERB To swat an insect means to hit it sharply in order to kill it.

swathe swathes
Rhymes with "bathe" NOUN **1** a long strip of cloth that is wrapped around something EG *swathes of white silk.* **2** A swathe of land is a long strip of it.

swathed
ADJECTIVE If someone is swathed in something, they are wrapped in it EG *She was swathed in towels.*

sway sways swaying swayed
VERB **1** To sway means to lean or swing slowly from side to side. **2** If something sways you, it influences your judgment. ▶ NOUN **3** A LITERARY USE Sway is the power to influence people EG *under the sway of more powerful neighbours.*

swear swears swearing swore sworn
VERB **1** To swear means to say words that are considered to be very rude or blasphemous. **2** If you swear to something, you state solemnly that you will do it or that it is true. **3** If you swear by something, you firmly believe that it is a reliable cure or solution EG *Some women swear by extra vitamins.*

swearword swearwords
NOUN a word which is considered to be rude or blasphemous, which people use when they are angry.

sweat sweats sweating sweated
NOUN **1** Sweat is the salty liquid produced by your sweat glands when you are hot or afraid. ▶ VERB **2** When you sweat, sweat comes through the pores in your skin in

order to lower the temperature of your body.

sweater sweaters

NOUN a knitted piece of clothing covering your upper body and arms.

sweatshirt sweatshirts

NOUN a piece of clothing made of thick cotton, covering your upper body and arms.

sweaty

ADJECTIVE covered or soaked with sweat.

swede swedes

NOUN a large round root vegetable with yellow flesh and a brownish-purple skin.

📖 from *Swedish turnip* because it was introduced from Sweden in the 18th century

Swede Swedes

NOUN someone who comes from Sweden.

Swedish

ADJECTIVE 1 belonging or relating to Sweden. ▶ NOUN 2 Swedish is the main language spoken in Sweden.

sweep sweeps sweeping swept

VERB 1 If you sweep the floor, you use a brush to gather up dust or rubbish from it. 2 To sweep things off a surface means to push them all off with a quick, smooth movement. 3 If something sweeps from one place to another, it moves there very quickly EG *A gust of wind swept over the terrace.* 4 If an attitude or new fashion sweeps a place, it spreads rapidly through it EG *a phenomenon that is sweeping America.* ▶ NOUN 5 If you do something with a sweep of your arm, you do it with a wide curving movement of your arm.

sweeping

ADJECTIVE 1 A sweeping curve or movement is long and wide. 2 A sweeping statement is based on a general assumption rather than on careful thought. 3 affecting a lot of people to a great extent EG *sweeping*

changes.

sweet sweeter sweetest; sweets

ADJECTIVE 1 containing a lot of sugar EG *a mug of sweet tea.* 2 pleasant and satisfying EG *sweet success.* 3 A sweet smell is soft and fragrant. 4 A sweet sound is gentle and tuneful. 5 attractive and delightful EG *a sweet little baby.* ▶ NOUN 6 Things such as toffees, chocolates, and mints are sweets. 7 a dessert.

sweetly ADVERB, **sweetness** NOUN

▤ (sense 5) charming, cute, delightful

sweet corn

NOUN Sweet corn is a long stalk covered with juicy yellow seeds that can be eaten as a vegetable.

sweeten sweetens sweetening sweetened

VERB To sweeten food means to add sugar or another sweet substance to it.

sweetener sweeteners

NOUN a very sweet, artificial substance that can be used instead of sugar.

sweetheart sweethearts

NOUN 1 You can call someone who you are very fond of 'sweetheart'. 2 A young person's sweetheart is their boyfriend or girlfriend.

sweet pea sweet peas

NOUN Sweet peas are delicate, very fragrant climbing flowers.

sweet tooth

NOUN If you have a sweet tooth, you like sweet food very much.

swell swells swelling swelled swollen

VERB 1 If something swells, it becomes larger and rounder EG *It causes the abdomen to swell.* 2 If an amount swells, it increases in number. ▶ NOUN 3 The regular up and down movement of the waves at sea can be called a swell.

swelling swellings

NOUN 1 an enlarged area on your body as a result of injury or illness.

2 The swelling of something is an increase in its size.

sweltering
ADJECTIVE If the weather is sweltering, it is very hot.

swerve swerves swerving swerved
VERB To swerve means to suddenly change direction to avoid colliding with something.

swift swifter swiftest; swifts
ADJECTIVE **1** happening or moving very quickly EG *a swift glance.* ▸ NOUN **2** a bird with narrow crescent-shaped wings.
swiftly ADVERB

swig swigs swigging swigged
AN INFORMAL WORD ▸ VERB **1** To swig a drink means to drink it in large mouthfuls, usually from a bottle. ▸ NOUN **2** If you have a swig of a drink, you take a large mouthful of it.

swill swills swilling swilled
VERB **1** To swill something means to pour water over it to clean it EG *Swill the can out thoroughly.* ▸ NOUN **2** Swill is a liquid mixture containing waste food that is fed to pigs.

swim swims swimming swam swum
VERB **1** To swim means to move through water using various movements with parts of the body. **2** If things are swimming, it seems as if everything you see is moving and you feel dizzy. ▸ NOUN **3** If you go for a swim, you go into water to swim for pleasure.
swimmer NOUN

swimming
NOUN Swimming is the activity of moving through water using your arms and legs.

swimming bath swimming baths
NOUN a public swimming pool.

swimming costume swimming costumes
NOUN the clothing worn by a woman when she goes swimming.

swimming pool swimming pools
NOUN a large hole that has been tiled and filled with water for swimming.

swimming trunks
PLURAL NOUN Swimming trunks are shorts worn by a man when he goes swimming.

swimsuit swimsuits
NOUN a swimming costume.

swindle swindles swindling swindled
VERB **1** To swindle someone means to deceive them to obtain money or property. ▸ NOUN **2** a trick in which someone is cheated out of money or property.
swindler NOUN
🏛 from German *Schwindler* meaning 'cheat'

swine swines
NOUN **1** AN OLD-FASHIONED USE Swine are pigs. **2** AN INFORMAL USE If you call someone a swine, you mean they are nasty and spiteful.

swing swings swinging swung
VERB **1** If something swings, it moves repeatedly from side to side from a fixed point. **2** If someone or something swings in a particular direction, they turn quickly or move in a sweeping curve in that direction. ▸ NOUN **3** a seat hanging from a frame or a branch, which moves backwards and forwards when you sit on it. **4** A swing in opinion is a significant change in people's opinion.

swipe swipes swiping swiped
VERB **1** To swipe at something means to try to hit it making a curving movement with the arm. **2** AN INFORMAL USE To swipe something means to steal it. **3** To swipe a credit card means to pass it through a machine that electronically reads the information stored in the card. ▸ NOUN **4** To take a swipe at something means to swipe at it.

A B C D E F G H I J K L M N O P Q R S T U V W X Y Z

A
B
C
D
E
F
G
H
I
J
K
L
M
N
O
P
Q
R
S
T
U
V
W
X
Y
Z

swirl swirls swirling swirled
VERB To swirl means to move quickly in circles EG *The black water swirled around his legs.*

swish swishes swishing swished
VERB 1 To swish means to move quickly through the air making a soft sound EG *The curtains swished back.* ▶ NOUN 2 the sound made when something swishes.

Swiss
ADJECTIVE 1 belonging or relating to Switzerland. ▶ NOUN 2 someone who comes from Switzerland.

switch switches switching switched
NOUN 1 a small control for an electrical device or machine. 2 a change EG *a switch in routine.* ▶ VERB 3 To switch to a different task or topic means to change to it. 4 If you switch things, you exchange one for the other.
switch off VERB To switch off a light or machine means to stop it working by pressing a switch.
switch on VERB To switch on a light or machine means to start it working by pressing a switch.

switchboard switchboards
NOUN The switchboard in an organization is the part where all telephone calls are received.

swivel swivels swivelling swivelled
VERB 1 To swivel means to turn round on a central point. ▶ ADJECTIVE 2 A swivel chair or lamp is made so that you can move the main part of it while the base remains in a fixed position.

swollen
ADJECTIVE Something that is swollen has swelled up.
▤ distended, enlarged, puffed up

swoon swoons swooning swooned
VERB; A LITERARY WORD To swoon means to faint as a result of strong emotion.

swoop swoops swooping

swooped
VERB To swoop means to move downwards through the air in a fast curving movement EG *A flock of pigeons swooped low over the square.*

swop
another spelling of **swap**.

sword swords
NOUN a weapon consisting of a very long blade with a short handle.

swordfish swordfishes or swordfish
NOUN a large sea fish with a long upper jaw.

sworn
ADJECTIVE If you make a sworn statement, you swear that everything in it is true.

swot swots swotting swotted
AN INFORMAL WORD ▶ VERB 1 To swot means to study or revise very hard. 2 If you swot up on a subject you find out as much about it as possible in a short time. ▶ NOUN 3 someone who spends too much time studying.

sycamore sycamores
Said "sik-am-mor" NOUN a tree that has large leaves with five points.

syllable syllables
NOUN a part of a word that contains a single vowel sound and is pronounced as a unit. For example, 'book' has one syllable and 'reading' has two.

syllabus syllabuses or syllabi
NOUN The subjects that are studied for a particular course or examination are called the syllabus.
☑ The plural *syllabuses* is much more common than *syllabi*.

symbol symbols
NOUN a shape, design, or idea that is used to represent something EG *The fish has long been a symbol of Christianity.*
▤ emblem, representation, sign

symbolic
ADJECTIVE Something that is symbolic

has a special meaning that is considered to represent something else EG *Six tons of ivory were burned in a symbolic ceremony.*

symbolize symbolizes
symbolizing symbolized; also spelt symbolise
VERB If a shape, design, or idea symbolizes something, it is regarded as being a symbol of it EG *In China and Japan the carp symbolizes courage.*
symbolism NOUN

symmetrical
ADJECTIVE If something is symmetrical, it has two halves which are exactly the same, except that one half is like a reflection of the other half.
symmetrically ADVERB

symmetry
NOUN Something that has symmetry is symmetrical.

sympathetic
ADJECTIVE 1 A sympathetic person shows kindness and understanding to other people. 2 If you are sympathetic to a proposal or an idea, you approve of it.

sympathize sympathizes
sympathizing sympathized; also spelt sympathise
VERB To sympathize with someone who is in difficulties means to show them understanding and care.

sympathizer sympathizers; also spelt sympathiser
NOUN People who support a particular cause can be referred to as sympathizers.

sympathy sympathies
NOUN 1 Sympathy is kindness and understanding towards someone who is in difficulties. 2 If you have sympathy with someone's ideas or actions, you agree with them.
▶ PHRASE 3 If you do something in sympathy with someone, you do it to show your support for them.
▤ (sense 1) compassion, pity

symphony symphonies

NOUN a piece of music for an orchestra, usually in four movements.
▥ from Greek *sumphōnos* meaning 'harmonious'

symptom symptoms
NOUN 1 something wrong with your body that is a sign of an illness. 2 Something that is considered to be a sign of a bad situation can be referred to as a symptom of it EG *another symptom of the racism sweeping across the country.*
symptomatic ADJECTIVE

synagogue synagogues
Said "sin-a-gog" NOUN a building where Jewish people meet for worship and religious instruction.
▥ from Greek *sunagōgē* meaning 'meeting'

synchronize synchronizes
synchronizing synchronized
Said "sing-kron-nize"; also spelt synchronise
VERB 1 To synchronize two actions means to do them at the same time and speed. 2 To synchronize watches means to set them to show exactly the same time as each other.

syndicate syndicates
NOUN an association of business people formed to carry out a particular project.

syndrome syndromes
NOUN 1 a medical condition characterized by a particular set of symptoms EG *Down's syndrome.* 2 You can refer to a typical set of characteristics as a syndrome EG *the syndrome of skipping from one wonder diet to the next.*

synod synods
NOUN a council of church leaders which meets regularly to discuss religious and moral issues.
▥ from Greek *sunodos* meaning 'meeting'

synonym synonyms
NOUN If two words have the same or a very similar meaning, they are synonyms.

A
B
C
D
E
F
G
H
I
J
K
L
M
N
O
P
Q
R
S
T
U
V
W
X
Y
Z

synonymous
ADJECTIVE **1** Two words that are synonymous have the same or very similar meanings. **2** If two things are closely associated, you can say that one is synonymous with the other EG *New York is synonymous with the Statue of Liberty*.

synopsis synopses
NOUN a summary of a book, play, or film.

syntax
NOUN The syntax of a language is its grammatical rules and the way its words are arranged.

synthetic
ADJECTIVE made from artificial substances rather than natural ones.

syphon
another spelling of **siphon**.

Syrian Syrians
Said "sirr-ee-an" ADJECTIVE
1 belonging or relating to Syria.
▶ NOUN **2** someone who comes from Syria.

syringe syringes
Said "sir-rinj" NOUN a hollow tube with a plunger and a fine hollow needle, used for injecting or extracting liquids.

syrup syrups
NOUN a thick sweet liquid made by boiling sugar with water.
🏛 from Arabic *sharab* meaning 'drink'

system systems
NOUN **1** an organized way of doing or arranging something according to a fixed plan or set of rules.
2 People sometimes refer to the government and administration of the country as the system. **3** You can also refer to a set of equipment as a system EG *an old stereo system*.
4 In biology, a system of a particular kind is the set of organs that perform that function EG *the immune system*.
▤ (sense 1) method, procedure, routine

systematic
ADJECTIVE following a fixed plan and done in an efficient way EG *a systematic study*.
systematically ADVERB

tab tabs
NOUN a small extra piece that is attached to something, for example on a curtain so it can be hung on a pole.

tabby tabbies
NOUN a cat whose fur has grey, brown, or black stripes.
📖 from Old French *tabis* meaning 'striped silk cloth'

tabernacle tabernacles
Said "**tab**-er-nak-kl" NOUN a place of Christian worship not called a church.
📖 from Latin *tabernaculum* meaning 'tent'

table tables tabling tabled
NOUN 1 a piece of furniture with a flat horizontal top supported by one or more legs. 2 a set of facts or figures arranged in rows or columns. ▶ VERB 3 If you table something such as a proposal, you say formally that you want it to be discussed.

tablecloth tablecloths
NOUN a cloth used to cover a table and keep it clean.

tablespoon tablespoons
NOUN a large spoon used for serving food; also the amount that a tablespoon contains.

tablet tablets
NOUN 1 any small, round pill made of powdered medicine. 2 a slab of stone with words cut into it.

table tennis
NOUN Table tennis is a game for two or four people in which you use bats to hit a small hollow ball over a low net across a table.

tabloid tabloids
NOUN a newspaper with small pages, short news stories, and lots of photographs.

taboo taboos
NOUN 1 a social custom that some words, subjects, or actions must be avoided because they are considered embarrassing or offensive EG *We have a powerful taboo against boasting.* 2 a religious custom that forbids people to do something. ▶ ADJECTIVE 3 forbidden or disapproved of EG *a taboo subject.*

tacit
Said "**tass**-it" ADJECTIVE understood or implied without actually being said or written.
tacitly ADVERB

taciturn
Said "**tass**-it-urn" ADJECTIVE Someone who is taciturn does not talk very much and so seems unfriendly.

tack tacks tacking tacked
NOUN 1 a short nail with a broad, flat head. 2 If you change tack, you start to use a different method for dealing with something. ▶ VERB 3 If you tack something to a surface, you nail it there with tacks. 4 If you tack a piece of fabric, you sew it with long loose stitches.

tackies or takkies
PLURAL NOUN; AN INFORMAL WORD In South African English, tackies are tennis shoes or plimsolls.

tackle tackles tackling tackled
VERB 1 If you tackle a difficult task, you start dealing with it in a determined way. 2 If you tackle someone in a game such as soccer, you try to get the ball away from them. 3 If you tackle someone about something, you talk to them about it in order to get something changed or dealt with. ▶ NOUN 4 A tackle in sport is an attempt to get the ball away from your opponent. 5 Tackle is the equipment used for fishing.
📖 (sense 1) deal with, undertake

tacky tackier tackiest
ADJECTIVE 1 slightly sticky to touch EG *The cream feels tacky to the touch.* 2 AN

INFORMAL USE badly made and in poor taste EG *tacky furniture*.

tact

NOUN Tact is the ability to see when a situation is difficult or delicate and to handle it without upsetting people.

tactful ADJECTIVE, **tactfully** ADVERB, **tactless** ADJECTIVE, **tactlessly** ADVERB

■ delicacy, diplomacy, discretion

tactic tactics

NOUN 1 Tactics are the methods you use to achieve what you want. 2 Tactics are also the ways in which troops and equipment are used in order to win a battle.

tactical ADJECTIVE, **tactically** ADVERB

tactile

ADJECTIVE involving the sense of touch.

tadpole tadpoles

NOUN Tadpoles are the larvae of frogs and toads. They are black with round heads and long tails and live in water.

🏛 from Middle English *tadde* meaning 'toad' and *pol* meaning 'head'

taffeta

Said "taf-fit-a" NOUN Taffeta is a stiff, shiny fabric that is used mainly for making women's clothes.

tag tags tagging tagged

NOUN 1 a small label made of cloth, paper, or plastic. 2 If you tag along with someone, you go with them or behind them.

tail tails tailing tailed

NOUN 1 The tail of an animal, bird, or fish is the part extending beyond the end of its body. 2 Tail can be used to mean the end part of something EG *the tail of the plane*. ▸ PLURAL NOUN 3 If a man is wearing tails, he is wearing a formal jacket which has two long pieces hanging down at the back. ▸ VERB 4 AN INFORMAL USE If you tail someone, you follow them in order to find out where they go and what they do.

▸ ADJECTIVE OR ADVERB 5 The tails side of a coin is the side which does not have a person's head.

tail off VERB If something tails off, it becomes gradually less.

tailback tailbacks

NOUN a long queue of traffic stretching back from whatever is blocking the road.

tailor tailors tailoring tailored

NOUN 1 a person who makes, alters, and repairs clothes, especially for men. ▸ VERB 2 If something is tailored for a particular purpose, it is specially designed for it.

tailor-made

ADJECTIVE suitable for a particular person or purpose, or specifically designed for them.

taint taints tainting tainted

VERB 1 To taint something is to spoil it by adding something undesirable to it. ▸ NOUN 2 an undesirable quality in something which spoils it.

taipan taipans

NOUN a large and very poisonous Australian snake.

take takes taking took taken

VERB 1 'Take' is used to show what action or activity is being done EG *Amy took a bath... She took her driving test.* 2 If something takes a certain amount of time, or a particular quality or ability, it requires it EG *He takes three hours to get ready.* 3 If you take something, you put your hand round it and hold it or carry it EG *Here, let me take your coat.* 4 If you take someone somewhere, you drive them there by car or lead them there. 5 If you take something that is offered to you, you accept it EG *He had to take the job.* 6 If you take the responsibility or blame for something, you accept responsibility or blame. 7 If you take something that does not belong to you, you steal it. 8 If you take pills or medicine, you swallow them. 9 If you can take something painful, you can bear it EG *We can't take much more of this.* **10** If you take someone's advice, you do what they say you should do. **11** If you take a person's temperature or pulse, you measure it. **12** If you take a car or train, or a road or route, you use it to go from one place to another.

take after VERB If you take after someone in your family, you look or behave like them.

take down VERB If you take down what someone is saying, you write it down.

take in VERB **1** If someone is taken in, they are deceived. **2** If you take something in, you understand it.

take off VERB When an aeroplane takes off, it leaves the ground and begins to fly.

takeoff NOUN

take over VERB To take something over means to start controlling it.

takeover NOUN

take to VERB If you take to someone or something, you like them immediately.

takeaway takeaways
NOUN **1** a shop or restaurant that sells hot cooked food to be eaten elsewhere. **2** a hot cooked meal bought from a takeaway.

takings
PLURAL NOUN Takings are the money that a shop or cinema gets from selling its goods or tickets.

talc
NOUN Talc is the same as talcum powder.

talcum powder
NOUN Talcum powder is a soft perfumed powder used for absorbing moisture on the body.

tale tales
NOUN a story.

talent talents
NOUN Talent is the natural ability to do something well.
talented ADJECTIVE
▣ ability, flair, gift

talisman talismans
Said "tal-iz-man" NOUN an object which you believe has magic powers to protect you or bring luck.
🏛 from Greek *telesma* meaning 'holy object'

talk talks talking talked
VERB **1** When you talk, you say things to someone. **2** If people talk, especially about other people's private affairs, they gossip about them EG *the neighbours might talk.* **3** If you talk on or about something, you make an informal speech about it. ▶ NOUN **4** Talk is discussion or gossip. **5** an informal speech about something.

talk down VERB If you talk down to someone, you talk to them in a way that shows that you think you are more important or clever than them.

talkative
ADJECTIVE talking a lot.
▣ chatty, garrulous, loquacious

tall taller tallest
ADJECTIVE **1** of more than average or normal height. **2** having a particular height EG *a wall ten metres tall.* ▶ PHRASE **3** If you describe something as **a tall story**, you mean that it is difficult to believe because it is so unlikely.

tally tallies tallying tallied
NOUN **1** an informal record of amounts which you keep adding to as you go along EG *He ended with a reasonable goal tally last season.* ▶ VERB **2** If numbers or statements tally, they are exactly the same or they give the same results or conclusions.

Talmud
Said "tal-mood" NOUN The Talmud consists of the books containing the ancient Jewish ceremonies and civil laws.
🏛 a Hebrew word meaning literally 'instruction'

talon talons

A B C D E F G H I J K L M N O P Q R S T U V W X Y Z

A B C D E F G H I J K L M N O P Q R S T U V W X Y Z

NOUN Talons are sharp, hooked claws, especially of a bird of prey.

tambourine tambourines
NOUN a percussion instrument made of a skin stretched tightly over a circular frame, with small round pieces of metal around the edge with the tambourine is beaten or shaken.

tame tamer tamest; tames taming tamed
ADJECTIVE **1** A tame animal or bird is not afraid of people and is not violent towards them. **2** Something that is tame is uninteresting and lacks excitement or risk EG *The report was pretty tame.* ▶ VERB **3** If you tame people or things, you bring them under control. **4** To tame a wild animal or bird is to train it to be obedient and live with humans.

tamper tampers tampering tampered
VERB If you tamper with something, you interfere or meddle with it.

tampon tampons
NOUN a firm, specially shaped piece of cotton wool that a woman places inside her vagina to absorb the blood during her period.

tan tans tanning tanned
NOUN **1** If you have a tan, your skin is darker than usual because you have been in the sun. ▶ VERB **2** To tan an animal's hide is to turn it into leather by treating it with chemicals. ▶ ADJECTIVE **3** Something that is tan is of a light yellowish-brown colour EG *a tan dress.*

tandem tandems
NOUN a bicycle designed for two riders sitting one behind the other.

tang tangs
NOUN a strong, sharp smell or flavour EG *the tang of lemon.*
tangy ADJECTIVE

tangata whenua
Said "tang-ah-tah feh-noo-ah"
NOUN Tangata whenua is a Maori term for the original Polynesian settlers in New Zealand, and their descendants.

tangent tangents
NOUN **1** A tangent of a curve is any straight line that touches the curve at one point only. ▶ PHRASE **2** If you **go off at a tangent**, you start talking or thinking about something that is not completely relevant to what has gone before.

tangerine tangerines
NOUN **1** a type of small sweet orange with a loose rind. ▶ NOUN OR ADJECTIVE **2** reddish-orange.

tangible
Said "tan-jib-bl" ADJECTIVE clear or definite enough to be easily seen or felt EG *tangible proof.*

tangle tangles tangling tangled
NOUN **1** a mass of things such as hairs or fibres knotted or coiled together and difficult to separate. ▶ VERB **2** If you are tangled in wires or ropes, you are caught or trapped in them so that it is difficult to get free.

tango tangos
NOUN A tango is a Latin American dance using long gliding steps and sudden pauses; also a piece of music composed for this dance.

taniwha taniwha or taniwhas
Said "tun-ee-fah" NOUN In New Zealand, a monster of Maori legends that lives in water.

tank tanks
NOUN **1** a large container for storing liquid or gas. **2** an armoured military vehicle which moves on tracks and is equipped with guns or rockets.

tankard tankards
NOUN a large metal mug used for drinking beer.

tanker tankers
NOUN a ship or lorry designed to carry large quantities of gas or liquid EG *a petrol tanker.*

tantalizing or **tantalising**
ADJECTIVE Something that is

tantalizing makes you feel hopeful and excited, although you know that you probably will not be able to have what you want EG *a tantalizing glimpse of riches to come.*

tantamount
ADJECTIVE If you say that something is tantamount to something else, you mean that it is almost the same as it EG *That would be tantamount to treason.*

tantrum tantrums
NOUN a noisy and sometimes violent outburst of temper, especially by a child.

Tanzanian Tanzanians
Said "tan-zan-**nee**-an" ADJECTIVE **1** belonging or relating to Tanzania. ▶ NOUN **2** someone who comes from Tanzania.

tap taps tapping tapped
NOUN **1** a device that you turn to control the flow of liquid or gas from a pipe or container. **2** the action of hitting something lightly; also the sound that this action makes. ▶ VERB **3** If you tap something or tap on it, you hit it lightly. **4** If a telephone is tapped, a device is fitted to it so that someone can listen secretly to the calls.

tap-dancing
NOUN Tap-dancing is a type of dancing in which the dancers wear special shoes with pieces of metal on the toes and heels which click against the floor.

tape tapes taping taped
NOUN **1** Tape is plastic ribbon covered with a magnetic substance and used to record sounds, pictures, and computer information. **2** a cassette or spool with magnetic tape wound round it. **3** Tape is a long, thin strip of fabric that is used for binding or fastening. **4** Tape is also a strip of sticky plastic which you use for sticking things together. ▶ VERB **5** If you tape sounds or television

pictures, you record them using a tape recorder or a video recorder. **6** If you tape one thing to another, you attach them using sticky tape.

tape measure tape measures
NOUN a strip of plastic or metal that is marked off in inches or centimetres and used for measuring things.

taper tapers tapering tapered
VERB **1** Something that tapers becomes thinner towards one end. ▶ NOUN **2** a thin candle.

tape recorder tape recorders
NOUN a machine used for recording sounds onto magnetic tape, and for playing these sounds back.

tapestry tapestries
NOUN a piece of heavy cloth with designs embroidered on it.

tar
NOUN Tar is a thick, black, sticky substance which is used in making roads.

tarantula tarantulas
Said "tar-**rant**-yoo-la" NOUN a large, hairy poisonous spider.

target targets
NOUN **1** something which you aim at when firing weapons. **2** The target of an action or remark is the person or thing at which it is directed EG *You become a target for our hatred.* **3** Your target is the result that you are trying to achieve.

tariff tariffs
NOUN **1** a tax that a government collects on imported goods. **2** any list of prices or charges.

tarmac
NOUN Tarmac is a material used for making road surfaces. It consists of crushed stones mixed with tar.
🔲 short for *tarmacadam*, from the name of John McAdam, the Scottish engineer who invented it

tarnish tarnishes tarnishing tarnished
VERB **1** If metal tarnishes, it becomes stained and loses its shine. **2** If

something tarnishes your reputation, it spoils it and causes people to lose their respect for you.

tarot
Said "tar-roh" NOUN A tarot card is one of a special pack of cards used for fortune-telling.

tarpaulin tarpaulins
NOUN a sheet of heavy waterproof material used as a protective covering.

tarragon
NOUN Tarragon is a herb with narrow green leaves used in cooking.

tarry tarries tarrying tarried
VERB; AN OLD-FASHIONED WORD To tarry is to wait, or to stay somewhere for a little longer.

tarseal
NOUN In New Zealand English, tarseal is the tarmac surface of a road.

tart tarts; tarter tartest
NOUN 1 a pastry case with a sweet filling. ▶ ADJECTIVE 2 Something that is tart is sour or sharp to taste. 3 A tart remark is unpleasant and cruel.

tartan tartans
NOUN Tartan is a woollen fabric from Scotland with checks of various colours and sizes, depending on which clan it belongs to.

tartar
NOUN Tartar is a hard, crusty substance that forms on teeth.

tarwhine tarwhines
NOUN an edible Australian marine fish, especially a sea bream.

task tasks
NOUN any piece of work which has to be done.
■ chore, duty, job

Tasmanian devil Tasmanian devils
NOUN a black-and-white marsupial of Tasmania, which eats flesh.

tassel tassels
NOUN a tuft of loose threads tied by a knot and used for decoration.

taste tastes tasting tasted
NOUN 1 Your sense of taste is your ability to recognize the flavour of things in your mouth. 2 The taste of something is its flavour. 3 If you have a taste of food or drink, you have a small amount of it to see what it is like. 4 If you have a taste for something, you enjoy it EG *a taste for publicity*. 5 If you have a taste of something, you experience it EG *my first taste of defeat*. 6 A person's taste is their choice in the things they like to buy or have around them EG *His taste in music is great*. ▶ VERB 7 When you can taste something in your mouth, you are aware of its flavour. 8 If you taste food or drink, you have a small amount of it to see what it is like. 9 If food or drink tastes of something, it has that flavour.

taste bud taste buds
NOUN Your taste buds are the little points on the surface of your tongue which enable you to taste things.

tasteful
ADJECTIVE attractive and elegant.
tastefully ADVERB

tasteless
ADJECTIVE 1 vulgar and unattractive. 2 A tasteless remark or joke is offensive. 3 Tasteless food has very little flavour.

tasty tastier tastiest
ADJECTIVE having a pleasant flavour.

tatters
PLURAL NOUN Clothes that are in tatters are badly torn.
tattered ADJECTIVE

tattoo tattoos tattooing tattooed
VERB 1 If someone tattoos you or tattoos a design on you, they draw it on your skin by pricking little holes and filling them with coloured dye. ▶ NOUN 2 a picture or design tattooed on someone's body. 3 a public military display of exercises and music.

tatty tattier tattiest

ADJECTIVE worn out or untidy and rather dirty.

taught
the past tense and past participle of teach.

taunt taunts taunting taunted
VERB **1** To taunt someone is to speak to them about their weaknesses or failures in order to make them angry or upset. ▶ NOUN **2** an offensive remark intended to make a person angry or upset.

Taurus
NOUN Taurus is the second sign of the zodiac, represented by a bull. People born between April 20th and May 20th are born under this sign.
📖 from Latin *taurus* meaning 'bull'

taut
ADJECTIVE stretched very tight EG *taut wires*.

tavern taverns
NOUN; AN OLD-FASHIONED WORD a pub.

tawdry tawdrier tawdriest
Said "taw-dree" ADJECTIVE cheap, gaudy, and of poor quality.

tawny
NOUN OR ADJECTIVE brownish-yellow.

tax taxes taxing taxed
NOUN **1** Tax is an amount of money that the people in a country have to pay to the government so that it can provide public services such as health care and education. ▶ VERB **2** If a sum of money is taxed, a certain amount of it has to be paid to the government. **3** If goods are taxed, a certain amount of their price has to be paid to the government. **4** If a person or company is taxed, they have to pay a certain amount of their income to the government. **5** If something taxes you, it makes heavy demands on you EG *They must be told not to tax your patience.*
taxation NOUN

taxi taxis taxiing taxied
NOUN **1** a car with a driver which you hire to take you to where you want to go. ▶ VERB **2** When an aeroplane taxis, it moves slowly along the runway before taking off or after landing.

tea teas
NOUN **1** Tea is the dried leaves of an evergreen shrub found in Asia. **2** Tea is a drink made by brewing the leaves of the tea plant in hot water; also a cup of this. **3** Tea is also any drink made with hot water and leaves or flowers EG *peppermint tea.* **4** Tea is a meal taken in the late afternoon or early evening.

tea bag tea bags
NOUN a small paper bag with tea leaves in it which is placed in boiling water to make tea.

teach teaches teaching taught
VERB **1** If you teach someone something, you give them instructions so that they know about it or know how to do it. **2** If you teach a subject, you help students learn about a subject at school, college, or university.
teacher NOUN, **teaching** NOUN
▤ (sense 1) educate, instruct, train, tutor

teak
NOUN Teak is a hard wood which comes from a large Asian tree.

team teams teaming teamed
NOUN **1** a group of people who play together against another group in a sport or game. ▶ VERB **2** If you team up with someone, you join them and work together with them.

teamwork
NOUN Teamwork is the ability of a group of people to work well together.

teapot teapots
NOUN a round pot with a handle, a lid, and a spout, used for brewing and pouring tea.

tear tears tearing tore torn
NOUN **1** Tears are the drops of salty liquid that come out of your eyes when you cry. **2** a hole that has

A
B
C
D
E
F
G
H
I
J
K
L
M
N
O
P
Q
R
S
T
U
V
W
X
Y
Z

been made in something. ▶ VERB **3** If you tear something, it is damaged by being pulled so that a hole appears in it. **4** If you tear somewhere, you rush there EG *He tore through busy streets in a high-speed chase.*

■ (sense 2) hole, rip, rupture

☑ When *tear* means 'a drop of salty water' (sense 1), it rhymes with *fear*. For all the other senses it rhymes with *hair*.

tearaway tearaways
NOUN someone who is wild and uncontrollable.

tearful
ADJECTIVE about to cry or crying gently.
tearfully ADVERB

tease teases teasing teased
VERB **1** If you tease someone, you deliberately make fun of them or embarrass them because it amuses you. ▶ NOUN **2** someone who enjoys teasing people.

teaspoon teaspoons
NOUN a small spoon used for stirring drinks; also the amount that a teaspoon holds.

teat teats
NOUN **1** a nipple on a female animal. **2** a piece of rubber or plastic that is shaped like a nipple and fitted to a baby's feeding bottle.

tea tree tea trees
NOUN a tree found in Australia and New Zealand with leaves that contain tannin, like tea leaves.

tech techs
NOUN; AN INFORMAL WORD a technical college.

technical
ADJECTIVE **1** involving machines, processes, and materials used in industry, transport, and communications. **2** skilled in practical and mechanical things rather than theories and ideas. **3** involving a specialized field of activity EG *I never understood the technical jargon.*

technical college technical colleges
NOUN a college where you can study subjects like technology and secretarial skills.

technicality technicalities
NOUN **1** The technicalities of a process or activity are the detailed methods used to do it. **2** an exact detail of a law or a set of rules, especially one some people might not notice EG *The verdict may have been based on a technicality.*

technically
ADVERB If something is technically true or correct, it is true or correct when you consider only the facts, rules, or laws, but may not be important or relevant in a particular situation EG *Technically, they were not supposed to drink on duty.*

technician technicians
NOUN someone whose job involves skilled practical work with scientific equipment.

technique techniques
NOUN **1** a particular method of doing something EG *these techniques of manufacture.* **2** Technique is skill and ability in an activity which is developed through training and practice EG *Jim's unique vocal technique.*

technology technologies
NOUN **1** Technology is the study of the application of science and scientific knowledge for practical purposes in industry, farming, medicine, or business. **2** a particular area of activity that requires scientific methods and knowledge EG *computer technology.*
technological ADJECTIVE, **technologically** ADVERB

teddy teddies
NOUN A teddy or teddy bear is a stuffed toy that looks like a friendly bear.

🏛 named after the American President Theodore (Teddy) Roosevelt, who hunted bears

tedious
Said "**tee**-dee-uss" ADJECTIVE boring and lasting for a long time EG *the tedious task of clearing up.*

tedium
Said "**tee**-dee-um" NOUN Tedium is the quality of being boring and lasting for a long time EG *the tedium of unemployment.*

tee tees teeing teed
NOUN **1** the small wooden or plastic peg on which a golf ball is placed before the golfer first hits it. ▶ VERB **2** To tee off is to hit the golf ball from the tee, or to start a round of golf.

teem teems teeming teemed
VERB **1** If a place is teeming with people or things, there are a lot of them moving about. **2** If it teems, it rains very heavily EG *The rain was teeming down.*

teenage
ADJECTIVE **1** aged between thirteen and nineteen. **2** typical of people aged between thirteen and nineteen EG *teenage fashion.*
teenager NOUN

teens
PLURAL NOUN Your teens are the period of your life when you are between thirteen and nineteen years old.

tee shirt
another spelling of **T-shirt**.

teeter teeters teetering teetered
VERB To teeter is to shake or sway slightly in an unsteady way and seem about to fall over.

teeth
the plural of **tooth**.

teethe teethes teething teethed
Rhymes with "**breathe**" VERB When babies are teething, their teeth are starting to come through, usually causing them pain.

teetotal
Said "**tee-toe-**tl" ADJECTIVE Someone who is teetotal never drinks alcohol.

teetotaller NOUN

tele-
PREFIX at or over a distance EG *telegraph.*
▩ from Greek *tele* meaning 'far'

telecommunications
NOUN Telecommunications is the science and activity of sending signals and messages over long distances using electronic equipment.

telegram telegrams
NOUN a message sent by telegraph.

telegraph
NOUN The telegraph is a system of sending messages over long distances using electrical or radio signals.

telepathy
Said "til-**lep**-ath-ee" NOUN Telepathy is direct communication between people's minds.
telepathic ADJECTIVE

telephone telephones telephoning telephoned
NOUN **1** a piece of electrical equipment for talking directly to someone who is in a different place. ▶ VERB **2** If you telephone someone, you speak to them using a telephone.

telephone box telephone boxes
NOUN a small shelter in the street where there is a public telephone.

telescope telescopes
NOUN a long instrument shaped like a tube which has lenses which make distant objects appear larger and nearer.

teletext
NOUN Teletext is an electronic system that broadcasts pages of information onto a television set.

televise televises televising televised
VERB If an event is televised, it is filmed and shown on television.

television televisions
NOUN a piece of electronic equipment which receives pictures

A B C D E F G H I J K L M N O P Q R S T U V W X Y Z

A
B
C
D
E
F
G
H
I
J
K
L
M
N
O
P
Q
R
S
T
U
V
W
X
Y
Z

and sounds by electrical signals over a distance.

tell tells telling told
VERB **1** If you tell someone something, you let them know about it. **2** If you tell someone to do something, you order or advise them to do it. **3** If you can tell something, you are able to judge correctly what is happening or what the situation is EG *I could tell he was scared.* **4** If an unpleasant or tiring experience begins to tell, it begins to have a serious effect EG *The pressure began to tell.*
■ (sense 1) inform, notify

teller tellers
NOUN a person who receives or gives out money in a bank. ·

telling
ADJECTIVE Something that is telling has an important effect, often because it shows the true nature of a situation EG *a telling account of the war.*

telltale
ADJECTIVE A telltale sign reveals information EG *the sad, telltale signs of a recent accident.*

telly tellies
NOUN; AN INFORMAL WORD a television.

temerity
Said "tim-**mer**-it-ee" NOUN If someone has the temerity to do something, they do it even though it upsets or annoys other people EG *She had the temerity to call him Bob.*

temp temps
NOUN; AN INFORMAL WORD a secretary who works for short periods of time in different places.

temper tempers tempering tempered
NOUN **1** Your temper is the frame of mind or mood you are in. **2** a sudden outburst of anger. ▶ PHRASE **3** If you **lose your temper**, you become very angry. ▶ VERB **4** To temper something is to make it more acceptable or suitable EG *curiosity tempered with some caution.*

temperament temperaments
Said "**tem**-pra-ment" NOUN Your temperament is your nature or personality, shown in the way you react towards people and situations EG *an artistic temperament.*

temperamental
ADJECTIVE Someone who is temperamental has moods that change often and suddenly.

temperate
ADJECTIVE A temperate place has weather that is neither extremely hot nor extremely cold.

temperature temperatures
NOUN **1** The temperature of something is how hot or cold it is. **2** Your temperature is the temperature of your body. ▶ PHRASE **3** If you **have a temperature**, the temperature of your body is higher than it should be, because you are ill.

tempest tempests
NOUN; A LITERARY WORD a violent storm.

tempestuous
Said "tem-**pest**-yoo-uss" ADJECTIVE violent or strongly emotional EG *a tempestuous relationship.*

template templates
NOUN a shape or pattern cut out in wood, metal, plastic, or card which you draw or cut around to reproduce that shape or pattern.

temple temples
NOUN **1** a building used for the worship of a god in various religions EG *a Buddhist temple.* **2** Your temples are the flat parts on each side of your forehead.

tempo tempos or tempi
NOUN **1** The tempo of something is the speed at which it happens EG *the slow tempo of change.* **2** A TECHNICAL USE The tempo of a piece of music is its speed.

temporary
ADJECTIVE lasting for only a short time.
temporarily ADVERB

tempt tempts tempting tempted
VERB **1** If you tempt someone, you try to persuade them to do something by offering them something they want. **2** If you are tempted to do something, you want to do it but you think it might be wrong or harmful EG *He was tempted to reply with sarcasm.*
■ (sense 1) entice, lure

temptation temptations
NOUN **1** Temptation is the state you are in when you want to do or have something, even though you know it might be wrong or harmful. **2** something that you want to do or have, even though you know it might be wrong or harmful EG *There is a temptation to ignore the problem.*

ten
the number 10.
tenth

tenacious
Said "tin-**nay**-shuss" ADJECTIVE determined and not giving up easily.
tenaciously ADVERB, **tenacity** NOUN

tenant tenants
NOUN someone who pays rent for the place they live in, or for land or buildings that they use.
tenancy NOUN

tend tends tending tended
VERB **1** If something tends to happen, it happens usually or often. **2** If you tend someone or something, you look after them EG *the way we tend our cattle.*
■ (sense 1) be apt to, be inclined to, be liable to

tendency tendencies
NOUN a trend or type of behaviour that happens very often EG *a tendency to be critical.*

tender tenderest; tenders tendering tendered
ADJECTIVE **1** Someone who is tender has gentle and caring feelings. **2** If someone is at a tender age, they are young and do not know very much

about life. **3** Tender meat is easy to cut or chew. **4** If a part of your body is tender, it is painful and sore. ▸ VERB **5** If someone tenders an apology or their resignation, they offer it. ▸ NOUN **6** a formal offer to supply goods or to do a job for a particular price.
■ (sense 1) affectionate, gentle, loving

tendon tendons
NOUN a strong cord of tissue which joins a muscle to a bone.

tendril tendrils
NOUN Tendrils are short, thin stems which grow on climbing plants and attach them to walls.

tenement tenements
Said "**ten**-em-ent" NOUN a large house or building divided into many flats.

tenet tenets
NOUN The tenets of a theory or belief are the main ideas it is based upon.

tenner tenners
NOUN; AN INFORMAL WORD a ten-pound or ten-dollar note.

tennis
NOUN Tennis is a game played by two or four players on a rectangular court in which a ball is hit by players over a central net.

tenor tenors
NOUN **1** a man who sings in a fairly high voice. **2** The tenor of something is the general meaning or mood that it expresses EG *the whole tenor of his poetry had changed.* ▸ ADJECTIVE **3** A tenor recorder, saxophone, or other musical instrument has a range of notes of a fairly low pitch.

tense tenser tensest; tenses tensing tensed
ADJECTIVE **1** If you are tense, you are nervous and cannot relax. **2** A tense situation or period of time is one that makes people nervous and worried. **3** If your body is tense, your muscles are tight. ▸ VERB **4** If

A
B
C
D
E
F
G
H
I
J
K
L
M
N
O
P
Q
R
S
T
U
V
W
X
Y
Z

you tense, or if your muscles tense, your muscles become tight and stiff. ▶ NOUN **5** The tense of a verb is the form which shows whether you are talking about the past, present, or future.

■ (sense 1) anxious, nervous, uptight

What is a Tense?

The "tense" of the verb tells us whether the action is in the past, the present or the future.

Some forms of the verb indicate that the action has already happened. These forms are **past tenses**.

*The captain **asked** Matthew for advice.*
*The captain **has asked** Matthew for advice.*
*The captain **was asking** Matthew for advice this morning.*
*The captain **had asked** Matthew for advice that morning.*

Some forms of the verb indicate that the action is happening at the present time. These forms are **present tenses**.

*I **see** some cause for optimism.*
*I **do see** some cause for optimism.*

Some forms of the verb indicate that the action will happen in the future. These forms are **future tenses**.

*They **will go** to Fiji in September.*
*They **will have gone** to Fiji by the end of September.*

Also look at the grammar boxes at **future**, **past tense**, and **present tense**.

tension tensions

NOUN **1** Tension is the feeling of nervousness or worry that you have when something dangerous or important is happening. **2** The tension in a rope or wire is how tightly it is stretched.

tent tents

NOUN a shelter made of canvas or nylon held up by poles and pinned down with pegs and ropes.

tentacle tentacles

NOUN The tentacles of an animal such as an octopus are the long, thin parts that it uses to feel and hold things.

tentative

ADJECTIVE acting or speaking cautiously because of being uncertain or afraid.
tentatively ADVERB

tenterhooks

PLURAL NOUN If you are on tenterhooks, you are nervous and excited about something that is going to happen.
🔟 from the hooks called *tenterhooks* which were used to stretch cloth tight while it was drying

tenuous

Said "ten-yoo-uss" ADJECTIVE If an idea or connection is tenuous, it is so slight and weak that it may not really exist or may easily cease to exist EG *a very tenuous friendship*.

tenure tenures

Said "ten-yoor" NOUN **1** Tenure is the legal right to live in a place or to use land or buildings for a period of time. **2** Tenure is the period of time during which someone holds an important job EG *His tenure ended in 1998*.

tepee tepees

Said "tee-pee" NOUN a cone-shaped tent of animal skins used by North American Indians.

tepid

ADJECTIVE Tepid liquid is only slightly warm.

term terms terming termed

NOUN **1** a fixed period of time EG *her second term of office*. **2** one of the periods of time that each year is divided into at a school or college. **3** a name or word used for a particular thing. ▶ PLURAL NOUN **4** The terms of an agreement are the conditions that have been accepted by the people involved in it. **5** If you express something in particular terms, you express it using a particular type of language or in a way that clearly shows your attitude EG *The young priest spoke of* her in glowing terms. ▶ PHRASE **6** If you **come to terms with** something difficult or unpleasant, you learn to accept it. ▶ VERB **7** To term something is to give it a name or to describe it EG *He termed my performance memorable.*

terminal terminals
ADJECTIVE **1** A terminal illness or disease cannot be cured and causes death gradually. ▶ NOUN **2** a place where vehicles, passengers, or goods begin or end a journey. **3** A computer terminal is a keyboard and a visual display unit that is used to put information into or get information out of a computer. **4** one of the parts of an electrical device through which electricity enters or leaves.
terminally ADVERB

terminate terminates terminating terminated
VERB When you terminate something or when it terminates, it stops or ends.
termination NOUN

terminology terminologies
NOUN The terminology of a subject is the set of special words and expressions used in it.

terminus terminuses
Said "ter-min-uss" NOUN a place where a bus or train route ends.

termite termites
NOUN Termites are small white insects that feed on wood.

tern terns
NOUN a small black and white sea bird with long wings and a forked tail.

terrace terraces
NOUN **1** a row of houses joined together. **2** a flat area of stone next to a building where people can sit.

terracotta
NOUN Terracotta is a type of reddish-brown unglazed pottery. 🔲 from Italian *terra cotta* meaning 'baked earth'

terrain
NOUN The terrain of an area is the type of land there EG *the region's hilly terrain.*

terrapin terrapins
NOUN a small North American freshwater turtle.

terrestrial
ADJECTIVE involving the earth or land.

terrible
ADJECTIVE **1** serious and unpleasant EG *a terrible illness.* **2** AN INFORMAL USE very bad or of poor quality EG *Paddy's terrible haircut.*

terribly
ADVERB very or very much EG *I was terribly upset.*

terrier terriers
NOUN a small, short-bodied dog.

terrific
ADJECTIVE **1** AN INFORMAL USE very pleasing or impressive EG *a terrific film.* **2** great in amount, degree, or intensity EG *a terrific blow on the head.*
terrifically ADVERB

terrify terrifies terrifying terrified
VERB If something terrifies you, it makes you feel extremely frightened.

territorial
ADJECTIVE involving or relating to the ownership of a particular area of land or water EG *a territorial dispute.*

territory territories
NOUN **1** The territory of a country is the land that it controls. **2** An animal's territory is an area which it regards as its own and defends when other animals try to enter it.

terror terrors
NOUN **1** Terror is great fear or panic. **2** something that makes you feel very frightened.

terrorism
NOUN Terrorism is the use of violence for political reasons.
terrorist NOUN OR ADJECTIVE

terrorize terrorizes terrorizing terrorized; also spelt terrorise

A B C D E F G H I J K L M N O P Q R S T U V W X Y Z

VERB If someone terrorizes you, they frighten you by threatening you or being violent to you.

terse terser tersest
ADJECTIVE A terse statement is short and rather unfriendly.

tertiary
Said "ter-shar-ee" ADJECTIVE **1** third in order or importance. **2** Tertiary education is education at university or college level.

test tests testing tested
VERB **1** When you test something, you try it to find out what it is, what condition it is in, or how well it works. **2** If you test someone, you ask them questions to find out how much they know. ▶ NOUN **3** a deliberate action or experiment to find out whether something works or how well it works. **4** a set of questions or tasks given to someone to find out what they know or can do.

testament testaments
NOUN **1** A LEGAL USE a will. **2** a copy of either the Old or the New Testament of the Bible.

test case test cases
NOUN a legal case that becomes an example for deciding other similar cases.

testicle testicles
NOUN A man's testicles are the two sex glands that produce sperm.

testify testifies testifying testified
VERB **1** When someone testifies, they make a formal statement, especially in a court of law EG *Ismay later testified at the British inquiry.* **2** To testify to something is to show that it is likely to be true EG *a consultant's certificate testifying to her good health.*

testimonial testimonials
Said "tess-tim-moh-nee-al" NOUN a statement saying how good someone or something is.

testimony testimonies
NOUN A person's testimony is a formal statement they make, especially in a court of law.

testing
ADJECTIVE Testing situations or problems are very difficult to deal with EG *It is a testing time for his team.*

testis testes
NOUN A man's testes are his testicles.

test match test matches
NOUN one of a series of international cricket or rugby matches.

testosterone
Said "tess-**toss**-ter-rone" NOUN Testosterone is a male hormone that produces male characteristics.

test tube test tubes
NOUN a small cylindrical glass container that is used in chemical experiments.

tetanus
Said "**tet**-nuss" NOUN Tetanus is a painful infectious disease caused by germs getting into wounds.

tether tethers tethering tethered
VERB **1** If you tether an animal, you tie it to a post. ▶ PHRASE **2** If you are **at the end of your tether**, you are extremely tired and have no more patience or energy left to deal with your problems.

Teutonic
Said "tyoo-**tonn**-ik" ADJECTIVE; A FORMAL WORD involving or related to German people.

text texts
NOUN **1** The text of a book is the main written part of it, rather than the pictures or index. **2** Text is any written material. **3** a book or other piece of writing used for study or an exam at school or college.
textual ADJECTIVE

textbook textbooks
NOUN a book about a particular subject for students to use.

textile textiles
NOUN a woven cloth or fabric.

texture textures
NOUN The texture of something is the way it feels when you touch it.

⊟ consistency, feel

Thai Thais
ADJECTIVE **1** belonging or relating to Thailand. ▶ NOUN **2** someone who comes from Thailand. **3** Thai is the main language spoken in Thailand.

than
PREPOSITION OR CONJUNCTION **1** You use 'than' to link two parts of a comparison EG *She was older than me.* **2** You use 'than' to link two parts of a contrast EG *Players would rather play than train.*

thank thanks thanking thanked
VERB When you thank someone, you show that you are grateful for something, usually by saying 'thank you'.

thankful
ADJECTIVE happy and relieved that something has happened.
thankfully ADVERB

thankless
ADJECTIVE A thankless job or task involves doing a lot of hard work that other people do not notice or are not grateful for EG *Referees have a thankless task.*

thanks
PLURAL NOUN **1** When you express your thanks to someone, you tell or show them how grateful you are for something. ▶ PHRASE **2** If something happened **thanks to** someone or something, it happened because of them EG *I'm as prepared as I can be, thanks to you.* ▶ INTERJECTION **3** You say 'thanks' to show that you are grateful for something.

thanksgiving
NOUN **1** Thanksgiving is an act of thanking God, especially in prayer or in a religious ceremony. **2** In the United States, Thanksgiving is a public holiday in the autumn.

thank you
You say 'thank you' to show that you are grateful to someone for something.

that those
ADJECTIVE OR PRONOUN **1** 'That' or 'those' is used to refer to things or people already mentioned or known about EG *That man was waving.* ▶ CONJUNCTION **2** 'That' is used to introduce a clause EG *I said that I was coming home.* ▶ PRONOUN **3** 'That' is also used to introduce a relative clause EG *I followed Alex to a door that led inside.*

☑ You can use either *that* or *which* in clauses known as defining clauses. These are clauses that identify the object you are talking about. In the sentence *the book that is on the table is mine, that is on the table* is a defining clause which distinguishes the book from other books that are not on the table. Some people think these types of clause should only be introduced by *that*, and *which* should be kept for nondefining clauses. These nondefining clauses add extra information about the object, but do not identify it. In the sentence *the book, which is on the table, is mine, which is on the table* is a nondefining clause which gives the reader extra detail about the book.

What does That do?

That is a relative pronoun. A relative pronoun replaces a noun which links two different parts of a sentence.

Relative pronouns always refer back to a word in the earlier part of the sentence. The word they refer to is called the **antecedent**. (In the examples that follow, the antecedents are underlined.)

*I have <u>a friend</u> **who** lives in Rome.*
*We could go to <u>a place</u> **that** I know.*

That refers to things or people. It is never used immediately after a preposition, but it can be used if the preposition is separated from the relative pronoun.

*It was <u>a film</u> **that** I had little interest **in**.*

Also look at the grammar box at **relative pronoun**.

---

thatch thatches thatching

A
B
C
D
E
F
G
H
I
J
K
L
M
N
O
P
Q
R
S
T
U
V
W
X
Y
Z

thatched
NOUN **1** Thatch is straw and reeds used to make roofs. ▶ VERB **2** To thatch a roof is to cover it with thatch.

thaw thaws thawing thawed
VERB **1** When snow or ice thaws, it melts. **2** When you thaw frozen food, or when it thaws, it becomes unfrozen. **3** When people who are unfriendly thaw, they begin to be more friendly and relaxed. ▶ NOUN **4** a period of warmer weather in winter when snow or ice melts.

the
ADJECTIVE The definite article 'the' is used when you are talking about something that is known about, that has just been mentioned, or that you are going to give details about.

The Definite Article

The word *the* is known as the **definite article**. You use it before a noun to refer to a specific example of that noun.
the kitchen table
the school I attend

The definite article *the* may be used before singular and plural nouns. However, you cannot use the indefinite article *a* or *an* before a plural noun. You need to use the word *some* in this case.
the tables   some tables
the schools   some schools

Also look at the grammar box at **a**.

---

theatre theatres
Said "theer-ter" NOUN **1** a building where plays and other entertainments are performed on a stage. **2** Theatre is work such as writing, producing, and acting in plays. **3** An operating theatre is a room in a hospital designed and equipped for surgical operations.
▥ from Greek *theatron* meaning 'viewing place'

theatrical
Said "thee-at-rik-kl" ADJECTIVE
1 involving the theatre or

performed in a theatre EG *his theatrical career*. **2** Theatrical behaviour is exaggerated, unnatural, and done for effect.
theatrically ADVERB

thee
PRONOUN; AN OLD-FASHIONED WORD Thee means you.

theft thefts
NOUN Theft is the crime of stealing.
▤ robbery, stealing

their
ADJECTIVE 'Their' refers to something belonging or relating to people or things, other than yourself or the person you are talking to, which have already been mentioned EG *It was their fault.*
☑ Be careful not to confuse *their* with *there*.

theirs
PRONOUN 'Theirs' refers to something belonging or relating to people or things, other than yourself or the person you are talking to, which have already been mentioned EG *Amy had been Helen's friend, not theirs.*

them
PRONOUN 'Them' refers to things or people, other than yourself or the people you are talking to, which have already been mentioned EG *He picked up the pillows and threw them to the floor.*

theme themes
NOUN **1** a main idea or topic in a piece of writing, painting, film, or music EG *the main theme of the book*. **2** a tune, especially one played at the beginning and end of a television or radio programme.

themselves
PRONOUN **1** 'Themselves' is used when people, other than yourself or the person you are talking to, do an action and are affected by it EG *They think they've made a fool of themselves.* **2** 'Themselves' is used to emphasize 'they' EG *He was as excited as they themselves were.*

then

ADVERB at a particular time in the past or future EG *I'd left home by then.*

theologian theologians
Said "thee-ol-**loe**-jee-an" NOUN someone who studies religion and the nature of God.

theology
NOUN Theology is the study of religion and God.
theological ADJECTIVE

theoretical
ADJECTIVE **1** based on or to do with ideas of a subject rather than the practical aspects. **2** not proved to exist or be true.
theoretically ADVERB

theory theories
NOUN **1** an idea or set of ideas that is meant to explain something EG *Darwin's theory of evolution.* **2** Theory is the set of rules and ideas that a particular subject or skill is based upon. ▶ PHRASE **3** You use **in theory** to say that although something is supposed to happen, it may not in fact happen EG *In theory, prices should rise by 2%.*
■ (sense 1) conjecture, hypothesis

therapeutic
Said "ther-ap-**yoo**-tik" ADJECTIVE **1** If something is therapeutic, it helps you to feel happier and more relaxed EG *Laughing is therapeutic.* **2** In medicine, therapeutic treatment is designed to treat a disease or to improve a person's health.

therapy
NOUN Therapy is the treatment of mental or physical illness, often without the use of drugs or operations.
therapist NOUN

there
ADVERB **1** in, at, or to that place, point, or case EG *He's sitting over there.* ▶ PRONOUN **2** 'There' is used to say that something exists or does not exist, or to draw attention to something EG *There are flowers on the table.*

☑ Be careful not to confuse *there* with *their.* A good way to remember that *there* is connected to the idea of place is by remembering the spelling of two other place words, *here* and *where.*

thereby
ADVERB; A FORMAL WORD as a result of the event or action mentioned EG *They had recruited 200 new members, thereby making the day worthwhile.*

therefore
ADVERB as a result.

thermal
ADJECTIVE **1** to do with or caused by heat EG *thermal energy.* **2** Thermal clothes are specially designed to keep you warm in cold weather.

thermometer thermometers
NOUN an instrument for measuring the temperature of a room or a person's body.

thermostat thermostats
NOUN a device used to control temperature, for example on a central heating system.

thesaurus thesauruses
Said "this-**saw**-russ" NOUN a reference book in which words with similar meanings are grouped together.
🏛 from Greek *thēsauros* meaning 'treasure'

these
the plural of **this.**

thesis theses
Said "thee-siss" NOUN a long piece of writing, based on research, that is done as part of a university degree.

they
PRONOUN **1** 'They' refers to people or things, other than you or the people you are talking to, that have already been mentioned EG *They married two years later.* **2** 'They' is sometimes used instead of 'he' or 'she' where the sex of the person is unknown or unspecified. Some people consider this to be incorrect EG *Someone could have a nasty accident*

751

A
B
C
D
E
F
G
H
I
J
K
L
M
N
O
P
Q
R
S
T
U
V
W
X
Y
Z

if they tripped over that.

thick thicker thickest

ADJECTIVE **1** Something thick has a large distance between its two opposite surfaces. **2** If something is a particular amount thick, it measures that amount between its two sides. **3** Thick means growing or grouped closely together and in large quantities EG *thick dark hair.* **4** Thick liquids contain little water and do not flow easily EG *thick soup.* **5** AN INFORMAL USE A thick person is stupid or slow to understand things.

thicken thickens thickening thickened

VERB If something thickens, it becomes thicker EG *The clouds thickened.*

thicket thickets

NOUN a small group of trees growing closely together.

thief thieves

NOUN a person who steals.

thieving

NOUN Thieving is the act of stealing.

thigh thighs

NOUN Your thighs are the top parts of your legs, between your knees and your hips.

thimble thimbles

NOUN a small metal or plastic cap that you put on the end of your finger to protect it when you are sewing.

thin thinner thinnest; thins thinning thinned

ADJECTIVE **1** Something that is thin is much narrower than it is long. **2** A thin person or animal has very little fat on their body. **3** Thin liquids contain a lot of water EG *thin soup.* ▶ VERB **4** If you thin something such as paint or soup, you add water or other liquid to it.
■ (sense 2) lean, skinny, slim

thing things

NOUN **1** an object, rather than a plant, an animal, a human being. ▶ PLURAL NOUN **2** Your things are your

clothes or possessions.
■ (sense 1) article, object

think thinks thinking thought

VERB **1** When you think about ideas or problems, you use your mind to consider them. **2** If you think something, you have the opinion that it is true or the case EG *I think she has a secret boyfriend.* **3** If you think of something, you remember it or it comes into your mind. **4** If you think a lot of someone or something, you admire them or think they are good.

third thirds

1 The third item in a series is the one counted as number three. ▶ NOUN **2** one of three equal parts.

Third World

NOUN The poorer countries of Africa, Asia, and South America can be referred to as the Third World.

thirst thirsts

NOUN **1** If you have a thirst, you feel a need to drink something. **2** A thirst for something is a very strong desire for it EG *a thirst for money.*
thirsty ADJECTIVE, **thirstily** ADVERB

thirteen

the number 13.
thirteenth

thirty thirties

the number 30.
thirtieth

this these

ADJECTIVE OR PRONOUN **1** 'This' is used to refer to something or someone that is nearby or has just been mentioned EG *This is Robert.* **2** 'This' is used to refer to the present time or place EG *I've been on holiday this week.*

thistle thistles

NOUN a wild plant with prickly-edged leaves and purple flowers.

thong thongs

NOUN a long narrow strip of leather.

thorn thorns

NOUN one of many sharp points growing on some plants and trees.

thorny thornier thorniest
ADJECTIVE **1** covered with thorns. **2** A thorny subject or question is difficult to discuss or answer.

thorough
Said "**thur-ruh**" ADJECTIVE **1** done very carefully and completely EG *a thorough examination.* **2** A thorough person is very careful in what they do and make sure that nothing has been missed out.
thoroughly ADVERB

thoroughbred thoroughbreds
NOUN an animal that has parents that are of the same high quality breed.

thoroughfare thoroughfares
NOUN a main road in a town.

those
the plural of **that**.

thou
PRONOUN; AN OLD-FASHIONED WORD Thou means you, when you are talking to only one person.

though
Rhymes with "**show**" CONJUNCTION **1** despite the fact that EG *Meg felt better, even though she knew it was the end.* **2** if EG *It looks as though you were right.*

thought thoughts
1 Thought is the past tense and past participle of **think**. ▶ NOUN **2** an idea that you have in your mind. **3** Thought is the activity of thinking EG *She was lost in thought.* **4** Thought is a particular way of thinking or a particular set of ideas EG *this school of thought.*
■ (sense 3) consideration, reflection, thinking

thoughtful
ADJECTIVE **1** When someone is thoughtful, they are quiet and serious because they are thinking about something. **2** A thoughtful person remembers what other people want or need, and tries to be kind to them.
thoughtfully ADVERB
■ (sense 1) meditative, pensive, reflective
■ (sense 2) caring, considerate, kind

thoughtless
ADJECTIVE A thoughtless person forgets or ignores what other people want, need, or feel.
thoughtlessly ADVERB

thousand thousands
the number 1000.
thousandth

thrash thrashes thrashing thrashed
VERB **1** To thrash someone is to beat them by hitting them with something. **2** To thrash someone in a contest or fight is to defeat them completely. **3** To thrash out a problem or an idea is to discuss it in detail until a solution is reached.

thread threads threading threaded
NOUN **1** a long, fine piece of cotton, silk, nylon, or wool. **2** The thread on something such as a screw or the top of a container is the raised spiral line of metal or plastic round it. **3** The thread of an argument or story is an idea or theme that connects the different parts of it. ▶ VERB **4** When you thread something, you pass thread, tape, or cord through it. **5** If you thread your way through people or things, you carefully make your way through them.

threadbare
ADJECTIVE Threadbare cloth or clothing is old and thin.

threat threats
NOUN **1** a statement that someone will harm you, especially if you do not do what they want. **2** anything or anyone that seems likely to harm you. **3** If there is a threat of something unpleasant happening, it is very possible that it will happen.

A
B
C
D
E
F
G
H
I
J
K
L
M
N
O
P
Q
R
S
T
U
V
W
X
Y
Z

threaten threatens threatening threatened

VERB **1** If you threaten to harm someone or threaten to do something that will upset them, you say that you will do it. **2** If someone or something threatens a person or thing, they are likely to harm them.

■ (sense 2) endanger, jeopardize

three

the number 3.

three-dimensional

ADJECTIVE A three-dimensional object or shape is not flat, but has height or depth as well as length and width.

threesome threesomes

NOUN a group of three.

threshold thresholds

Said "thresh-hold" NOUN **1** the doorway or the floor in the doorway of a building or room. **2** The threshold of something is the lowest amount, level, or limit at which something happens or changes EG *the tax threshold... His boredom threshold was exceptionally low.*

thrice

ADVERB; AN OLD-FASHIONED WORD If you do something thrice, you do it three times.

thrift

NOUN Thrift is the practice of saving money and not wasting things.

thrifty thriftier thriftiest

ADJECTIVE A thrifty person saves money and does not waste things.

thrill thrills thrilling thrilled

NOUN **1** a sudden feeling of great excitement, pleasure, or fear; also any event or experience that gives you such a feeling. ▶ VERB **2** If something thrills you, or you thrill to it, it gives you a feeling of great pleasure and excitement.

thrilled ADJECTIVE, thrilling ADJECTIVE

■ (sense 1) buzz, kick

thriller thrillers

NOUN a book, film, or play that tells an exciting story about dangerous or mysterious events.

thrive thrives thriving thrived or throve

VERB When people or things thrive, they are healthy, happy, or successful.

thriving ADJECTIVE

throat throats

NOUN **1** the back of your mouth and the top part of the passages inside your neck. **2** the front part of your neck.

throb throbs throbbing throbbed

VERB **1** If a part of your body throbs, you feel a series of strong beats or dull pains. **2** If something throbs, it vibrates and makes a loud, rhythmic noise EG *The engines throbbed.*

throes

PLURAL NOUN **1** Throes are a series of violent pangs or movements EG *death throes.* ▶ PHRASE **2** If you are **in the throes of** something, you are deeply involved in it.

thrombosis thromboses

Said "throm-boe-siss" NOUN a blood clot which blocks the flow of blood in the body. Thromboses are dangerous and often fatal.

throne thrones

NOUN **1** a ceremonial chair used by a king or queen on important official occasions. **2** The throne is a way of referring to the position of being king or queen.

throng throngs thronging thronged

NOUN **1** a large crowd of people. ▶ VERB **2** If people throng somewhere or throng a place, they go there in great numbers EG *Hundreds of city workers thronged the scene.*

throttle throttles throttling throttled

VERB To throttle someone is to kill or injure them by squeezing their throat.

through

Said "threw" PREPOSITION **1** moving all the way from one side of something to the other EG *a path through the woods.* **2** because of EG *He had been exhausted through lack of sleep.* **3** during EG *He has to work through the summer.* **4** If you go through an experience, it happens to you EG *I don't want to go through that again.* ▶ ADJECTIVE **5** If you are through with something, you have finished doing it or using it.

throughout

PREPOSITION **1** during EG *I stayed awake throughout the night.* ▶ ADVERB **2** happening or existing through the whole of a place EG *The house was painted brown throughout.*

throve

the past tense of **thrive**.

throw throws throwing threw thrown

VERB **1** When you throw something you are holding, you move your hand quickly and let it go, so that it moves through the air. **2** If you throw yourself somewhere, you move there suddenly and with force EG *We threw ourselves on the ground.* **3** To throw someone into an unpleasant situation is to put them there EG *It threw them into a panic.* **4** If something throws light or shadow on something else, it makes that thing have light or shadow on it. **5** If you throw yourself into an activity, you become actively and enthusiastically involved in it. **6** If you throw a fit or tantrum, you suddenly begin behaving in an uncontrolled way.
▣ (sense 1) chuck, fling, hurl

throwback throwbacks

NOUN something which has the characteristics of something that existed a long time ago EG *Everything about her was a throwback to the fifties.*

thrush thrushes

NOUN **1** a small brown songbird.

2 Thrush is a disease of the mouth or of the vagina, caused by a fungus.

thrust thrusts thrusting thrust

VERB **1** If you thrust something somewhere, you push or move it there quickly with a lot of force. **2** If you thrust your way somewhere, you move along, pushing between people or things. ▶ NOUN **3** a sudden forceful movement. **4** The main thrust of an activity or idea is the most important part of it EG *the general thrust of his argument.*

thud thuds thudding thudded

NOUN **1** a dull sound, usually made by a solid, heavy object hitting something soft. ▶ VERB **2** If something thuds somewhere, it makes a dull sound, usually by hitting something else.

thug thugs

NOUN a very rough and violent person.
▣ from Hindi *thag* meaning 'thief'

thumb thumbs thumbing thumbed

NOUN **1** the short, thick finger on the side of your hand. ▶ VERB **2** If someone thumbs a lift, they stand at the side of the road and stick out their thumb until a driver stops and gives them a lift.

thump thumps thumping thumped

VERB **1** If you thump someone or something, you hit them hard with your fist. **2** If something thumps somewhere, it makes a fairly loud, dull sound, usually when it hits something else. **3** When your heart thumps, it beats strongly and quickly. ▶ NOUN **4** a hard hit EG *a great thump on the back.* **5** a fairly loud, dull sound.

thunder thunders thundering thundered

NOUN **1** Thunder is a loud cracking or rumbling noise caused by expanding air which is suddenly heated by lightning. **2** Thunder is any loud rumbling noise EG *the distant thunder of bombs.* ▶ VERB **3** When it thunders, a loud cracking or rumbling noise occurs in the sky after a flash of lightning. **4** If something thunders, it makes a loud continuous noise EG *The helicopter thundered low over the trees.*

thunderbolt thunderbolts
NOUN a flash of lightning, accompanied by thunder.

thunderous
ADJECTIVE A thunderous noise is very loud EG *thunderous applause.*

Thursday Thursdays
NOUN Thursday is the day between Wednesday and Friday.
▣ from Old English *Thursdæg* meaning 'Thor's day'; Thor was the Norse god of thunder

thus
ADVERB; A FORMAL WORD **1** in this way EG *I sat thus for nearly half an hour.* **2** therefore EG *Critics were thus able to denounce him.*

thwart thwarts thwarting thwarted
VERB To thwart someone or their plans is to prevent them from doing or getting what they want.

thy
ADJECTIVE; AN OLD-FASHIONED WORD Thy means your.

thyme
Said "**time**" NOUN Thyme is a bushy herb with very small leaves.

tiara tiaras
Said "tee-ah-ra" NOUN a semicircular crown of jewels worn by a woman on formal occasions.

Tibetan Tibetans
ADJECTIVE **1** belonging or relating to Tibet. ▶ NOUN **2** someone who comes from Tibet.

tic tics
NOUN a twitching of a group of muscles, especially the muscles in the face.

tick ticks ticking ticked
NOUN **1** a written mark to show that something is correct or has been dealt with. **2** The tick of a clock is the series of short sounds it makes when it is working. **3** a tiny, blood-sucking, insect-like creature that usually lives on the bodies of people or animals. ▶ VERB **4** To tick something written on a piece of paper is to put a tick next to it. **5** When a clock ticks, it makes a regular series of short sounds as it works.
tick off VERB; AN INFORMAL EXPRESSION If you tick someone off, you speak angrily to them because they have done something wrong.
ticking NOUN

ticket tickets
NOUN a piece of paper or card which shows that you have paid for a journey or have paid to enter a place of entertainment.

tickle tickles tickling tickled
VERB **1** When you tickle someone, you move your fingers lightly over their body in order to make them laugh. **2** If something tickles you, it amuses you or gives you pleasure EG *Simon is tickled by the idea.*

tidal
ADJECTIVE to do with or produced by tides EG *a tidal estuary.*

tidal wave tidal waves
NOUN a very large wave, often caused by an earthquake, that comes over land and destroys things.

tide tides tiding tided
NOUN **1** The tide is the regular change in the level of the sea on the shore, caused by the gravitational pull of the sun and the moon. **2** The tide of opinion or fashion is what the majority of people think or do at a particular time. **3** A tide of something is a large amount of it EG *the tide of anger and bitterness.*
tide over VERB If something will tide someone over, it will help them

through a difficult period of time.

tidings

PLURAL NOUN; A FORMAL WORD Tidings
are news.

tidy tidier tidiest; tidies tidying tidied

ADJECTIVE **1** Something that is tidy is neat and arranged in an orderly way. **2** Someone who is tidy always keeps their things neat and arranged in an orderly way. **3** AN INFORMAL USE A tidy amount of money is a fairly large amount of it. ▶ VERB **4** To tidy a place is to make it neat by putting things in their proper place.

tie ties tying tied

VERB **1** If you tie one thing to another or tie it in a particular position, you fasten it using cord of some kind. **2** If you tie a knot or a bow in a piece of cord or cloth, you fasten the ends together to make a knot or bow. **3** Something or someone that is tied to something else is closely linked with it EG 40,000 jobs are tied to the project. **4** If you tie with someone in a competition or game, you have the same number of points. ▶ NOUN **5** a long, narrow piece of cloth worn around the neck under a shirt collar and tied in a knot at the front. **6** a connection or feeling that links you with a person, place, or organization EG I had very close ties with the family.
■ (sense 1) bind, fasten

tied up

ADJECTIVE If you are tied up, you are busy.

tier tiers

NOUN one of a number of rows or layers of something EG Take the stairs to the upper tier.

tiff tiffs

NOUN a small unimportant quarrel.

tiger tigers

NOUN a large meat-eating animal of the cat family. It comes from Asia and has an orange coloured coat with black stripes.

tiger snake tiger snakes

NOUN a fierce, very poisonous Australian snake with dark stripes across its back.

tight tighter tightest

ADJECTIVE **1** fitting closely EG The shoes are too tight. **2** firmly fastened and difficult to move EG a tight knot. **3** stretched or pulled so as not to be slack EG a tight cord. **4** A tight plan or arrangement allows only the minimum time or money needed to do something EG Our schedule tonight is very tight. ▶ ADVERB **5** held firmly and securely EG He held me tight.
tightly ADVERB, tightness NOUN
■ (sense 3) stretched, taut

tighten tightens tightening tightened

VERB **1** If you tighten your hold on something, you hold it more firmly. **2** If you tighten a rope or chain, or if it tightens, it is stretched or pulled until it is straight. **3** If someone tightens a rule or system, they make it stricter or more efficient.

tightrope tightropes

NOUN a tightly-stretched rope on which an acrobat balances and performs tricks.

tights

PLURAL NOUN Tights are a piece of clothing made of thin stretchy material that fit closely round a person's hips, legs, and feet.

tiki tiki or tikis

NOUN In New Zealand, a small carving of an ancestor worn as a pendant in some Maori cultures.

tile tiles tiling tiled

NOUN **1** a small flat square piece of something, for example slate or carpet, that is used to cover surfaces. ▶ VERB **2** To tile a surface is to fix tiles to it.
tiled ADJECTIVE

till tills tilling tilled

PREPOSITION OR CONJUNCTION **1** Till

means the same as until. ▶ NOUN **2** a drawer or box in a shop where money is kept, usually in a cash register. ▶ VERB **3** To till the ground is to plough it for raising crops.

tiller tillers
NOUN the handle fixed to the top of the rudder for steering a boat.

tilt tilts tilting tilted
VERB **1** If you tilt an object or it tilts, it changes position so that one end or side is higher than the other. ▶ NOUN **2** a position in which one end or side of something is higher than the other.
■ (sense 1) incline, lean, tip

timber timbers
NOUN **1** Timber is wood that has been cut and prepared ready for building and making furniture. **2** The timbers of a ship or house are the large pieces of wood that have been used to build it.

time times timing timed
NOUN **1** Time is what is measured in hours, days, and years EG *What time is it?* **2** 'Time' is used to mean a particular period or point EG *I enjoyed my time in Durban.* **3** If you say it is time for something or it is time to do it, you mean that it ought to happen or be done now EG *It is time for a change.* **4** 'Times' is used after numbers to indicate how often something happens EG *I saw my father four times a year.* **5** 'Times' is used after numbers when you are saying how much bigger, smaller, better, or worse one thing is compared to another EG *The Belgians drink three times as much beer as the French.* **6** 'Times' is used in arithmetic to link numbers that are multiplied together EG *Two times three is six.* ▶ VERB **7** If you time something for a particular time, you plan that it should happen then EG *We could not have timed our arrival better.* **8** If you time an activity or action, you measure how long it lasts.
■ (sense 2) interval, period, spell

timeless
ADJECTIVE Something timeless is so good or beautiful that it cannot be affected by the passing of time or by changes in fashion.

timely
ADJECTIVE happening at just the right time EG *a timely appearance.*
■ opportune, well-timed

timer timers
NOUN a device that measures time, especially one that is part of a machine.

timescale timescales
NOUN The timescale of an event is the length of time during which it happens.

timetable timetables
NOUN **1** a plan of the times when particular activities or jobs should be done. **2** a list of the times when particular trains, boats, buses, or aeroplanes arrive and depart.

timid
ADJECTIVE shy and having no courage or self-confidence.
timidly ADVERB, **timidity** NOUN
■ fearful, shy, timorous

timing
NOUN **1** Someone's timing is their skill in judging the right moment at which to do something. **2** The timing of an event is when it actually happens.

timpani
Said "**tim**-pan-ee" PLURAL NOUN
Timpani are large drums with curved bottoms that are played in an orchestra.

tin tins
NOUN **1** Tin is a soft silvery-white metal. **2** a metal container which is filled with food and then sealed in order to preserve the food. **3** a small metal container which may have a lid EG *a cake tin.*

tinder
NOUN Tinder is small pieces of dry wood or grass that burn easily and can be used for lighting a fire.

tinge tinges
NOUN a small amount of something
EG *a tinge of envy*.
tinged ADJECTIVE

tingle tingles tingling tingled
VERB 1 When a part of your body
tingles, you feel a slight prickling
feeling in it. ▸ NOUN 2 a slight
prickling feeling.
tingling NOUN OR ADJECTIVE

tinker tinkers tinkering tinkered
NOUN 1 a person who travels from
place to place mending metal pots
and pans or doing other small
repair jobs. ▸ VERB 2 If you tinker
with something, you make a lot of
small changes to it in order to
repair or improve it EG *All he wanted
was to tinker with engines*.

tinkle tinkles tinkling tinkled
VERB 1 If something tinkles, it makes
a sound like a small bell ringing.
▸ NOUN 2 a sound like that of a small
bell ringing.

tinned
ADJECTIVE Tinned food has been
preserved by being sealed in a tin.

tinsel
NOUN Tinsel is long threads with
strips of shiny paper attached, used
as a decoration at Christmas.

tint tints tinting tinted
NOUN 1 a small amount of a
particular colour EG *a distinct tint of
green*. ▸ VERB 2 If a person tints their
hair, they change its colour by
adding a weak dye to it.
tinted ADJECTIVE

tiny tinier tiniest
ADJECTIVE extremely small.
■ diminutive, minute

tip tips tipping tipped
NOUN 1 the end of something long
and thin EG *a fingertip*. 2 a place
where rubbish is dumped. 3 If you
give someone such as a waiter a tip,
you give them some money to
thank them for their services. 4 a
useful piece of advice or
information. ▸ VERB 5 If you tip an
object, you move it so that it is no

longer horizontal or upright. 6 If
you tip something somewhere, you
pour it there quickly or carelessly.
tipped ADJECTIVE

tipple tipples
NOUN A person's tipple is the
alcoholic drink that they normally
drink.

tipsy tipsier tipsiest
ADJECTIVE slightly drunk.

tiptoe tiptoes tiptoeing tiptoed
VERB If you tiptoe somewhere, you
walk there very quietly on your
toes.

tirade tirades
Said "tie-**rade**" NOUN a long, angry
speech in which you criticize
someone or something.
🔟 from Italian *tirata* meaning
'volley of shots'

tire tires tiring tired
VERB 1 If something tires you, it
makes you use a lot of energy so
that you want to rest or sleep. 2 If
you tire of something, you become
bored with it.
tired ADJECTIVE, **tiredness** NOUN
■ (sense 1) exhaust, fatigue, weary

tireless
ADJECTIVE Someone who is tireless
has a lot of energy and never seems
to need a rest.

tiresome
ADJECTIVE A person or thing that is
tiresome makes you feel irritated or
bored.

tiring
ADJECTIVE Something that is tiring
makes you tired.

tissue tissues
Said "**tiss**-yoo" NOUN 1 The tissue in
plants and animals consists of cells
that are similar in appearance and
function EG *scar tissue... dead tissue*.
2 Tissue is thin paper that is used
for wrapping breakable objects. 3 a
small piece of soft paper that you
use as a handkerchief.

tit tits
NOUN a small European bird EG *a blue*

tit.

titanic

ADJECTIVE very big or important.

🏛 in Greek legend, the **Titans** were a family of giants

titillate titillates titillating titillated

VERB If something titillates someone, it pleases and excites them, especially in a sexual way.

titillation NOUN

title titles

NOUN 1 the name of a book, play, or piece of music. 2 a word that describes someone's rank or job EG *My official title is Design Manager.* 3 the position of champion in a sports competition EG *the European featherweight title.*

titled

ADJECTIVE Someone who is titled has a high social rank and has a title such as 'Princess', 'Lord', 'Lady', or 'Sir'.

titter titters tittering tittered

VERB If you titter, you laugh in a way that shows you are nervous or embarrassed.

TNT

NOUN TNT is a type of powerful explosive. It is an abbreviation for 'trinitrotoluene'.

to

PREPOSITION 1 'To' is used to indicate the place that someone or something is moving towards or pointing at EG *They are going to China.* 2 'To' is used to indicate the limit of something EG *Goods to the value of 500 pounds.* 3 'To' is used in ratios and rates when saying how many units of one type there are for each unit of another EG *I only get about 30 kilometres to the gallon from it.* ▶ ADVERB 4 If you push or shut a door to, you close it but do not shut it completely.

toad toads

NOUN an amphibian that looks like a frog but has a drier skin and lives less in the water.

toadstool toadstools

NOUN a type of poisonous fungus.

toast toasts toasting toasted

NOUN 1 Toast is slices of bread made brown and crisp by cooking at a high temperature. 2 To drink a toast to someone is to drink an alcoholic drink in honour of them. ▶ VERB 3 If you toast bread, you cook it at a high temperature so that it becomes brown and crisp. 4 If you toast yourself, you sit in front of a fire so that you feel pleasantly warm. 5 To toast someone is to drink an alcoholic drink in honour of them.

🏛 from Latin *tostus* meaning 'parched'

toaster toasters

NOUN a piece of electrical equipment used for toasting bread.

tobacco

NOUN Tobacco is the dried leaves of the tobacco plant which people smoke in pipes, cigarettes, and cigars.

tobacconist tobacconists

NOUN a shop where tobacco, cigarettes, and cigars are sold.

toboggan toboggans

NOUN a flat seat with two wooden or metal runners, used for sliding over the snow.

🏛 an American Indian word

today

ADVERB OR NOUN 1 Today means the day on which you are speaking or writing. 2 Today also means the present period of history EG *the challenges of teaching in today's schools.*

toddle toddles toddling toddled

VERB To toddle is to walk in short, quick steps, as a very young child does.

toddler toddlers

NOUN a small child who has just learned to walk.

to-do to-dos

NOUN A to-do is a situation in which

people are very agitated or confused eg *It's just like him to make such a to-do about a baby.*

toe toes
NOUN **1** Your toes are the five movable parts at the end of your foot. **2** The toe of a shoe or sock is the part that covers the end of your foot.

toff toffs
NOUN; AN INFORMAL, OLD-FASHIONED WORD a rich person or one from an aristocratic family.

toffee toffees
NOUN Toffee is a sticky, chewy sweet made by boiling sugar and butter together with water.

toga togas
NOUN a long loose robe worn in ancient Rome.

together
ADVERB **1** If people do something together, they do it with each other. **2** If two things happen together, they happen at the same time. **3** If things are joined or fixed together, they are joined or fixed to each other. **4** If things or people are together, they are very near to each other.

◼ (sense 1) collectively, jointly
◼ (sense 2) concurrently, simultaneously

✅ Two nouns joined by *together with* do not make a plural subject, so the following verb is not plural: *Jones, together with his partner, has had great success.*

togetherness
NOUN Togetherness is a feeling of closeness and friendship.

toil toils toiling toiled
VERB **1** When people toil, they work hard doing unpleasant, difficult, or tiring tasks or jobs. ▶ NOUN **2** Toil is unpleasant, difficult, or tiring work.

toilet toilets
NOUN **1** a large bowl, connected by a pipe to the drains, which you use when you want to get rid of urine or faeces. **2** a small room

containing a toilet.

toiletries
PLURAL NOUN Toiletries are the things you use when cleaning and taking care of your body, such as soap and talc.

token tokens
NOUN **1** a piece of paper or card that is worth a particular amount of money and can be exchanged for goods eg *record tokens*. **2** a flat round piece of metal or plastic that can sometimes be used instead of money. **3** If you give something to someone as a token of your feelings for them, you give it to them as a way of showing those feelings.
▶ ADJECTIVE **4** If something is described as token, it shows that it is not being treated as important eg *a token contribution to your fees.*

told
Told is the past tense and past participle of **tell**.

tolerable
ADJECTIVE **1** able to be put up with. **2** fairly satisfactory or reasonable eg *a tolerable salary.*

tolerance
NOUN **1** A person's tolerance is their ability to accept or put up with something which may not be enjoyable or pleasant for them. **2** Tolerance is the quality of allowing other people to have their own attitudes or beliefs, or to behave in a particular way, even if you do not agree or approve eg *religious tolerance.*
tolerant ADJECTIVE

tolerate tolerates tolerating tolerated
VERB **1** If you tolerate things that you do not approve of or agree with, you allow them. **2** If you can tolerate something, you accept it, even though it is unsatisfactory or unpleasant.
toleration NOUN
◼ (sense 2) bear, endure, stand

toll tolls tolling tolled

NOUN **1** The death toll in an accident is the number of people who have died in it. **2** a sum of money that you have to pay in order to use a particular bridge or road. ▶ VERB **3** When someone tolls a bell, it is rung slowly, often as a sign that someone has died.

tom toms
NOUN a male cat.

tomahawk tomahawks
NOUN a small axe used by North American Indians.

tomato tomatoes
NOUN a small round red fruit, used as a vegetable and often eaten raw in salads.

tomb tombs
NOUN a large grave for one or more corpses.

tomboy tomboys
NOUN a girl who likes playing rough or noisy games.

tome tomes
NOUN; A FORMAL WORD a very large heavy book.

tomorrow
ADVERB OR NOUN **1** Tomorrow means the day after today. **2** You can refer to the future, especially the near future, as tomorrow.

ton tons
NOUN **1** a unit of weight equal to 2240 pounds or about 1016 kilograms. ▶ PLURAL NOUN **2** AN INFORMAL USE If you have tons of something, you have a lot of it.

tonal
ADJECTIVE involving the quality or pitch of a sound or of music.

tone tones toning toned
NOUN **1** Someone's tone is a quality in their voice which shows what they are thinking or feeling. **2** The tone of a musical instrument or a singer's voice is the kind of sound it has. **3** The tone of a piece of writing is its style and the ideas or opinions expressed in it EG *I was shocked at the tone of your leading*

article. **4** a lighter, darker, or brighter shade of the same colour EG *The whole room is painted in two tones of orange*.
tone down VERB If you tone down something, you make it less forceful or severe.

tone-deaf
ADJECTIVE unable to sing in tune or to recognize different tunes.

tongs
PLURAL NOUN Tongs consist of two long narrow pieces of metal joined together at one end. You press the pieces together to pick an object up.

tongue tongues
NOUN **1** Your tongue is the soft part in your mouth that you can move and use for tasting, licking, and speaking. **2** a language. **3** Tongue is the cooked tongue of an ox. **4** The tongue of a shoe or boot is the piece of leather underneath the laces.

tonic tonics
NOUN **1** Tonic or tonic water is a colourless, fizzy drink that has a slightly bitter flavour and is often mixed with alcoholic drinks. **2** a medicine that makes you feel stronger, healthier, and less tired. **3** anything that makes you feel stronger or more cheerful EG *It was a tonic just being with her*.

tonight
ADVERB OR NOUN Tonight is the evening or night that will come at the end of today.

tonne tonnes
Said "**tun**" NOUN a unit of weight equal to 1000 kilograms.

tonsil tonsils
NOUN Your tonsils are the two small, soft lumps in your throat at the back of your mouth.

tonsillitis
Said "**ton-sil-lie-tiss**" NOUN Tonsillitis is a painful swelling of your tonsils caused by an infection.

too

ADVERB **1** also or as well EG *You were there too*. **2** more than a desirable, necessary, or acceptable amount EG *a man who had taken too much to drink*.

tool tools
NOUN **1** any hand-held instrument or piece of equipment that you use to help you do a particular kind of work. **2** an object, skill, or idea that is needed or used for a particular purpose EG *You can use the survey as a bargaining tool in the negotiations*.
■ (sense 1) implement, instrument, utensil

toot toots tooting tooted
VERB If a car horn toots, it produces a short sound.

tooth teeth
NOUN **1** Your teeth are the hard enamel-covered objects in your mouth that you use for biting and chewing food. **2** The teeth of a comb, saw, or zip are the parts that stick out in a row on its edge.

toothpaste
NOUN Toothpaste is a substance which you use to clean your teeth.

top tops topping topped
NOUN **1** The top of something is its highest point, part, or surface. **2** The top of a bottle, jar, or tube is its cap or lid. **3** a piece of clothing worn on the upper half of your body. **4** a toy with a pointed end on which it spins. ▶ ADJECTIVE **5** The top thing of a series of things is the highest one EG *the top floor of the building*. ▶ VERB **6** If someone tops a poll or popularity chart, they do better than anyone else in it EG *It has topped the bestseller lists in almost every country*. **7** If something tops a particular amount, it is greater than that amount EG *The temperature topped 90°*.
■ (sense 1) apex, height, peak

top hat top hats
NOUN a tall hat with a narrow brim that men wear on special occasions.

topic topics
NOUN a particular subject that you write about or discuss.

topical
ADJECTIVE involving or related to events that are happening at the time you are speaking or writing.

topping toppings
NOUN food that is put on top of other food in order to decorate it or add to its flavour.

topple topples toppling toppled
VERB If something topples, it becomes unsteady and falls over.

top-secret
ADJECTIVE meant to be kept completely secret.

topsy-turvy
ADJECTIVE in a confused state EG *My life was truly topsy-turvy*.

Torah
NOUN The Torah is Jewish law and teaching.

torch torches
NOUN **1** a small electric light carried in the hand and powered by batteries. **2** a long stick with burning material wrapped around one end.

torment torments tormenting tormented
NOUN **1** Torment is extreme pain or unhappiness. **2** something that causes extreme pain and unhappiness EG *It's a torment to see them staring at me*. ▶ VERB **3** If something torments you, it causes you extreme unhappiness.

torn
1 Torn is the past participle of **tear**. ▶ ADJECTIVE **2** If you are torn between two or more things, you cannot decide which one to choose and this makes you unhappy EG *torn between duty and pleasure*.

tornado tornadoes or **tornados**
Said "tor-**nay**-doh" NOUN a violent storm with strong circular winds around a funnel-shaped cloud.

torpedo torpedoes torpedoing torpedoed

A B C D E F G H I J K L M N O P Q R S T U V W X Y Z

Said "tor-**pee**-doh" NOUN **1** a tube-shaped bomb that travels underwater and explodes when it hits a target. ▸ VERB **2** If a ship is torpedoed, it is hit, and usually sunk, by a torpedo.

torrent torrents
NOUN **1** When a lot of water is falling very rapidly, it can be said to be falling in torrents. **2** A torrent of speech is a lot of it directed continuously at someone EG *torrents of abuse.*

torrential
ADJECTIVE Torrential rain pours down very rapidly and in great quantities.

torrid
ADJECTIVE **1** Torrid weather is very hot and dry. **2** A torrid love affair is one in which people show very strong emotions.

torso torsos
NOUN the main part of your body, excluding your head, arms, and legs.

tortoise tortoises
NOUN a slow-moving reptile with a large hard shell over its body into which it can pull its head and legs for protection.

tortuous
ADJECTIVE **1** A tortuous road is full of bends and twists. **2** A tortuous piece of writing is long and complicated.

torture tortures torturing tortured
NOUN **1** Torture is great pain that is deliberately caused to someone to punish them or get information from them. ▸ VERB **2** If someone tortures another person, they deliberately cause that person great pain to punish them or get information. **3** To torture someone is also to cause them to suffer mentally EG *Memory tortured her.*
torturer NOUN

Tory Tories
NOUN In Britain, a member or supporter of the Conservative Party.
🔲 from Irish *toraidhe* meaning 'outlaw'

toss tosses tossing tossed
VERB **1** If you toss something somewhere, you throw it there lightly and carelessly. **2** If you toss a coin, you decide something by throwing a coin into the air and guessing which side will face upwards when it lands. **3** If you toss your head, you move it suddenly backwards, especially when you are angry, annoyed, or want your own way. **4** To toss is to move repeatedly from side to side EG *We tossed and turned and tried to sleep.*
▣ (sense 1) fling, sling, throw

tot tots totting totted
NOUN **1** a very young child. **2** a small amount of strong alcohol such as whisky. ▸ VERB **3** To tot up numbers is to add them together.

total totals totalling totalled
NOUN **1** the number you get when you add several numbers together. ▸ VERB **2** When you total a set of numbers or objects, you add them all together. **3** If several numbers total a certain figure, that is the figure you get when all the numbers are added together EG *Their debts totalled over 300,000 dollars.* ▸ ADJECTIVE **4** Total means complete EG *a total failure.*
totally ADVERB
▣ (sense 1) aggregate, sum, whole

totalitarian
Said "toe-tal-it-**tair**-ee-an" ADJECTIVE A totalitarian political system is one in which one political party controls everything and does not allow any other parties to exist.
totalitarianism NOUN

tote totes toting toted
VERB; AN INFORMAL WORD To tote a gun is to carry it.

totem pole totem poles
NOUN a long wooden pole with symbols and pictures carved and

painted on it. Totem poles are made by some North American Indians.

totter totters tottering tottered
VERB When someone totters, they walk in an unsteady way.

toucan toucans
Said "**too**-kan" NOUN a large tropical bird with a very large beak.

touch touches touching touched
VERB **1** If you touch something, you put your fingers or hand on it. **2** When two things touch, their surfaces come into contact EG *Their knees were touching.* **3** If you are touched by something, you are emotionally affected by it EG *I was touched by his thoughtfulness.* ▶ NOUN **4** Your sense of touch is your ability to tell what something is like by touching it. **5** a detail which is added to improve something EG *finishing touches.* **6** a small amount of something EG *a touch of mustard.* ▶ PHRASE **7** If you are in **touch** with someone, you are in contact with them.

touchdown touchdowns
NOUN Touchdown is the landing of an aircraft.

touching
ADJECTIVE causing feelings of sadness and sympathy.
■ moving, poignant, sad

touchy touchier touchiest
ADJECTIVE **1** If someone is touchy, they are easily upset or irritated. **2** A touchy subject is one that needs to be dealt with carefully, because it might upset or offend people.

tough tougher toughest
Said "**tuff**" ADJECTIVE **1** A tough person is strong and independent and able to put up with hardship. **2** A tough substance is difficult to break. **3** A tough task, problem, or way of life is difficult or full of hardship. **4** Tough policies or actions are strict and firm EG *tough measures against organized crime.*

toughly ADVERB, **toughness** NOUN, **toughen** VERB
■ (sense 2) durable, resilient, strong

toupee toupees
Said "**too**-pay" NOUN a small wig worn by a man to cover a bald patch on his head.

tour tours touring toured
NOUN **1** a long journey during which you visit several places. **2** a short trip round a place such as a city or famous building. ▶ VERB **3** If you tour a place, you go on a journey or a trip round it.

tourism
NOUN Tourism is the business of providing services for people on holiday, for example hotels and sightseeing trips.

tourist tourists
NOUN a person who visits places for pleasure or interest.

tournament tournaments
NOUN a sports competition in which players who win a match play further matches, until just one person or team is left.

tourniquet tourniquets
Said "**toor**-nik-kay" NOUN a strip of cloth tied tightly round a wound to stop it bleeding.

tousled
ADJECTIVE Tousled hair is untidy.

tout touts touting touted
VERB **1** If someone touts something, they try to sell it. **2** If someone touts for business or custom, they try to obtain it in a very direct way EG *volunteers who spend days touting for donations.* ▶ NOUN **3** someone who sells tickets outside a sports ground or theatre, charging more than the original price.

tow tows towing towed
VERB **1** If a vehicle tows another vehicle, it pulls it along behind it. ▶ NOUN **2** To give a vehicle a tow is to tow it. ▶ PHRASE **3** If you have someone in **tow**, they are with you because you are looking after them.

A B C D E F G H I J K L M N O P Q R S T U V W X Y Z

towards

PREPOSITION **1** in the direction of EG *He turned towards the door.* **2** about or involving EG *My feelings towards Susan have changed.* **3** as a contribution for EG *a huge donation towards the new opera house.* **4** near to EG *We sat towards the back.*

towel towels

NOUN a piece of thick, soft cloth that you use to dry yourself with.

towelling

NOUN Towelling is thick, soft cloth that is used for making towels.

tower towers towering towered

NOUN **1** a tall, narrow building, sometimes attached to a larger building such as a castle or church. ▶ VERB **2** Someone or something that towers over other people or things is much taller than them.
towering ADJECTIVE

town towns

NOUN **1** a place with many streets and buildings where people live and work. **2** Town is the central shopping and business part of a town rather than the suburbs EG *She has gone into town.*

township townships

NOUN a small town in South Africa where only Black people or Coloured people were allowed to live.

towpath towpaths

NOUN a path along the side of a canal or river.

toxic

ADJECTIVE poisonous EG *toxic waste.* from Greek *toxikon* meaning 'poison used on arrows' from *toxon* meaning 'arrow'

toxin toxins

NOUN a poison, especially one produced by bacteria and very harmful to living creatures.

toy toys toying toyed

NOUN **1** any object made to play with. ▶ VERB **2** If you toy with an idea, you consider it without being

very serious about it EG *She toyed with the idea of telephoning him.* **3** If you toy with an object, you fiddle with it EG *Jessica was toying with her glass.*

toyi-toyi or **toy-toy**

NOUN In South Africa, a toyi-toyi is a dance performed to protest about something.

trace traces tracing traced

VERB **1** If you trace something, you find it after looking for it EG *Police are trying to trace the owner.* **2** To trace the development of something is to find out or describe how it developed. **3** If you trace a drawing or a map, you copy it by covering it with a piece of transparent paper and drawing over the lines underneath. ▶ NOUN **4** a sign which shows you that someone or something has been in a place EG *No trace of his father had been found.* **5** a very small amount of something.
tracing NOUN

track tracks tracking tracked

NOUN **1** a narrow road or path. **2** a strip of ground with rails on it that a train travels along. **3** a piece of ground, shaped like a ring, which horses, cars, or athletes race around. ▶ PLURAL NOUN **4** Tracks are marks left on the ground by a person or animal EG *the deer tracks by the side of the path.* ▶ ADJECTIVE **5** In an athletics competition, the track events are the races on a running track. ▶ VERB **6** If you track animals or people, you find them by following their footprints or other signs that they have left behind.
track down VERB If you track down someone or something, you find them by searching for them.

track record track records

NOUN The track record of a person or a company is their past achievements or failures EG *the track record of the film's star.*

tracksuit tracksuits

NOUN a loose, warm suit of trousers and a top, worn for outdoor sports.

tract tracts
NOUN **1** A tract of land or forest is a large area of it. **2** a pamphlet which expresses a strong opinion on a religious, moral, or political subject. **3** a system of organs and tubes in an animal's or person's body that has a particular function EG *the digestive tract.*

traction
NOUN Traction is a form of medical treatment given to an injured limb which involves pulling it gently for long periods of time using a system of weights and pulleys.

tractor tractors
NOUN a vehicle with large rear wheels that is used on a farm for pulling machinery and other heavy loads.

trade trades trading traded
NOUN **1** Trade is the activity of buying, selling, or exchanging goods or services between people, firms, or countries. **2** Someone's trade is the kind of work they do, especially when it requires special training in practical skills EG *a joiner by trade.* ▶ VERB **3** When people, firms, or countries trade, they buy, sell, or exchange goods or services. **4** If you trade things, you exchange them EG *Their mother had traded her rings for a few potatoes.*
≡ (sense 1) business, commerce
≡ (sense 3) deal, do business, traffic

trademark trademarks
NOUN a name or symbol that a manufacturer always uses on its products. Trademarks are usually protected by law so that no-one else can use them.

trader traders
NOUN a person whose job is to trade in goods EG *a timber trader.*

tradesman tradesmen
NOUN a person, for example a shopkeeper, whose job is to sell goods.

trade union trade unions
NOUN an organization of workers that tries to improve the pay and conditions in a particular industry.

tradition traditions
NOUN a custom or belief that has existed for a long time without changing.
≡ convention, custom

traditional
ADJECTIVE **1** Traditional customs or beliefs have existed for a long time without changing EG *her traditional Indian dress.* **2** A traditional organization or institution is one in which older methods are used rather than modern ones EG *a traditional school.*
traditionally ADVERB

traditionalist traditionalists
NOUN someone who supports the established customs and beliefs of their society, and does not want to change them.

traffic traffics trafficking trafficked
NOUN **1** Traffic is the movement of vehicles or people along a route at a particular time. **2** Traffic in something such as drugs is an illegal trade in them. ▶ VERB **3** Someone who traffics in drugs or other goods buys and sells them illegally.

traffic light traffic lights
NOUN Traffic lights are the set of red, amber, and green lights at a road junction which control the flow of traffic.

traffic warden traffic wardens
NOUN a person whose job is to make sure that cars are not parked in the wrong place or for longer than is allowed.

tragedy tragedies
Said "**traj**-id-ee" NOUN **1** an event or situation that is disastrous or very sad. **2** a serious story or play, that usually ends with the death of the main character.

tragic

A
B
C
D
E
F
G
H
I
J
K
L
M
N
O
P
Q
R
S
T
U
V
W
X
Y
Z

ADJECTIVE **1** Something tragic is very sad because it involves death, suffering, or disaster EG *a tragic accident*. **2** Tragic films, plays, and books are sad and serious EG *a tragic love story*.
tragically ADVERB

trail trails trailing trailed
NOUN **1** a rough path across open country or through forests. **2** a series of marks or other signs left by someone or something as they move along. ▶ VERB **3** If you trail something or it trails, it drags along behind you as you move, or it hangs down loosely EG *a small plane trailing a banner*. **4** If someone trails along, they move slowly, without any energy or enthusiasm. **5** If a voice trails away or trails off, it gradually becomes more hesitant until it stops completely.

trailer trailers
NOUN a small vehicle which can be loaded with things and pulled behind a car.

train trains training trained
NOUN **1** a number of carriages or trucks which are pulled by a railway engine. **2** A train of thought is a connected series of thoughts. **3** A train of vehicles or people is a line or group following behind something or someone EG *a train of wives and girlfriends*. ▶ VERB **4** If you train, you learn how to do a particular job EG *She trained as a serious actress*. **5** If you train for a sports match or a race, you prepare for it by doing exercises.
training NOUN

trainee trainees
NOUN someone who is being taught how to do a job.

trainers
PLURAL NOUN Trainers are special shoes worn for running or jogging.

trait traits
NOUN a particular characteristic or tendency EG *a very English trait*.

traitor traitors

NOUN someone who betrays their country or the group which they belong to.

trajectory trajectories
Said "traj-**jek**-tor-ee" NOUN The trajectory of an object moving through the air is the curving path that it follows.

tram trams
NOUN a vehicle which runs on rails along the street and is powered by electricity from an overhead wire.

tramp tramps tramping tramped
NOUN **1** a person who has no home, no job, and very little money. **2** a long country walk EG *I took a long, wet tramp through the fine woodlands*. ▶ VERB **3** If you tramp from one place to another, you walk with slow, heavy footsteps.

trample tramples trampling trampled
VERB **1** If you trample on something, you tread heavily on it so that it is damaged. **2** If you trample on someone or on their rights or feelings, you behave in a way that shows you don't care about them.

trampoline trampolines
NOUN a piece of gymnastic equipment consisting of a large piece of strong cloth held taut by springs in a frame, on which a gymnast jumps to help them jump high.

trance trances
NOUN a mental state in which someone seems to be asleep but is conscious enough to be aware of their surroundings and to respond to questions and commands.

tranquil
Said "**trang**-kwil" ADJECTIVE calm and peaceful EG *tranquil lakes... I have a tranquil mind*.
tranquillity NOUN

tranquillizer tranquillizers; also spelt **tranquilliser**
NOUN a drug that makes people feel less anxious or nervous.

trans-
PREFIX Trans- means across, through, or beyond EG *transatlantic*.

transaction transactions
NOUN a business deal which involves buying and selling something.

transcend transcends transcending transcended
VERB If one thing transcends another, it goes beyond it or is superior to it EG *Her beauty transcends all barriers*.

transcribe transcribes transcribing transcribed
VERB If you transcribe something that is spoken or written, you write it down, copy it, or change it into a different form of writing EG *These letters were often transcribed by his wife Patti*.

transcript transcripts
NOUN a written copy of of something that is spoken.

transfer transfers transferring transferred
VERB 1 If you transfer something from one place to another, you move it EG *They transferred the money to the Swiss account*. 2 If you transfer to a different place or job, or are transferred to it, you move to a different place or job within the same organization. ▶ NOUN 3 the movement of something from one place to another. 4 a piece of paper with a design on one side which can be ironed or pressed onto cloth, paper, or china.
transferable ADJECTIVE

transfixed
ADJECTIVE If a person is transfixed by something, they are so impressed or frightened by it that they cannot move EG *Price stood transfixed at the sight of that tiny figure*.

transform transforms transforming transformed
VERB If something is transformed, it is changed completely EG *The frown is transformed into a smile*.
transformation NOUN

transfusion transfusions
NOUN A transfusion or blood transfusion is a process in which blood from a healthy person is injected into the body of another person who is badly injured or ill.

transient
Said "tran-zee-ent" ADJECTIVE Something transient does not stay or exist for very long EG *transient emotions*.
transience NOUN

transistor transistors
NOUN 1 a small electrical device in something such as a television or radio which is used to control electric currents. 2 A transistor or a transistor radio is a small portable radio.

transit
NOUN 1 Transit is the carrying of goods or people by vehicle from one place to another. ▶ PHRASE 2 People or things that are in transit are travelling or being taken from one place to another EG *damage that had occurred in transit*.

transition transitions
NOUN a change from one form or state to another EG *the transition from war to peace*.

transitional
ADJECTIVE A transitional period or stage is one during which something changes from one form or state to another.

transitive
ADJECTIVE In grammar, a transitive verb is a verb which has an object.

transitory
ADJECTIVE lasting for only a short time.

translate translates translating translated
VERB To translate something that someone has said or written is to say it or write it in a different language.
translation NOUN, **translator** NOUN

translucent

transmission

ADJECTIVE If something is translucent, light passes through it so that it seems to glow EG *translucent petals*.

transmission transmissions

NOUN **1** The transmission of something involves passing or sending it to a different place or person EG *the transmission of infectious diseases*. **2** The transmission of television or radio programmes is the broadcasting of them. **3** a broadcast.

transmit transmits transmitting transmitted

VERB **1** When a message or an electronic signal is transmitted, it is sent by radio waves. **2** To transmit something to a different place or person is to pass it or send it to the place or person EG *the clergy's role in transmitting knowledge*.
transmitter NOUN

transparency transparencies

NOUN **1** a small piece of photographic film which can be projected onto a screen.
2 Transparency is the quality that an object or substance has if you can see through it.

transparent

ADJECTIVE If an object or substance is transparent, you can see through it.
transparently ADVERB
▣ clear, limpid, see-through

transpire transpires transpiring transpired

VERB **1** A FORMAL USE When it transpires that something is the case, people discover that it is the case EG *It transpired that he had flown off on holiday*. **2** When something transpires, it happens EG *You start to wonder what transpired between them*.
☑ Some people think that it is wrong to use *transpire* to mean 'happen'. However, it is very widely used in this sense, especially in spoken English.

transplant transplants

transplanting transplanted

NOUN **1** a process of removing something from one place and putting it in another EG *a man who needs a heart transplant*. ▶ VERB **2** When something is transplanted, it is moved to a different place.

transport transports transporting transported

NOUN **1** Vehicles that you travel in are referred to as transport EG *public transport*. **2** Transport is the moving of goods or people from one place to another EG *The prices quoted include transport costs*. ▶ VERB **3** When goods or people are transported from one place to another, they are moved there.
▣ (sense 3) carry, convey, transfer

transportation

NOUN Transportation is the transporting of people and things from one place to another.

transvestite transvestites

NOUN a person who enjoys wearing clothes normally worn by people of the opposite sex.
▥ from *trans-* and Latin *vestitus* meaning 'clothed'

trap traps trapping trapped

NOUN **1** a piece of equipment or a hole that is carefully positioned in order to catch animals or birds. **2** a trick that is intended to catch or deceive someone. ▶ VERB **3** Someone who traps animals catches them using traps. **4** If you trap someone, you trick them so that they do or say something which they did not want to. **5** If you are trapped somewhere, you cannot move or escape because something is blocking your way or holding you down. **6** If you are trapped, you are in an unpleasant situation that you cannot easily change EG *I'm trapped in an unhappy marriage*.
▣ (sense 3) catch, snare
▣ (sense 4) dupe, trick

trap door trap doors

NOUN a small horizontal door in a

floor, ceiling, or stage.

trapeze trapezes
NOUN a bar of wood or metal hanging from two ropes on which acrobats and gymnasts swing and perform skilful movements.

trapezium trapeziums or trapezia
Said "trap-pee-zee-um" NOUN a four-sided shape with two sides parallel to each other.

trappings
PLURAL NOUN The trappings of a particular rank, position, or state are the clothes or equipment that go with it.

trash
NOUN 1 Trash is rubbish EG *He picks up your trash on Mondays.* 2 If you say that something such as a book, painting, or film is trash, you mean that it is not very good.

trauma traumas
Said "traw-ma" NOUN a very upsetting experience which causes great stress EG *the trauma of his mother's death.*
🏛 from Greek *trauma* meaning 'wound'

traumatic
ADJECTIVE A traumatic experience is very upsetting.

travel travels travelling travelled
VERB 1 To travel is to go from one place to another. 2 When something reaches one place from another, you say that it travels there EG *Gossip travels fast.* ▶ NOUN 3 Travel is the act of travelling EG *air travel.* ▶ PLURAL NOUN 4 Someone's travels are the journeys that they make to places a long way from their home EG *my travels in the Himalayas.*
traveller NOUN, **travelling** ADJECTIVE
▤ (sense 1) go, journey

traveller's cheque traveller's cheques
NOUN Traveller's cheques are cheques for use abroad. You buy them at home and then exchange them when you are abroad for foreign currency.

traverse traverses traversing traversed
VERB; A FORMAL WORD If you traverse an area of land or water, you go across it or over it EG *They have traversed the island from the west coast.*

travesty travesties
NOUN a very bad or ridiculous representation or imitation of something EG *British salad is a travesty of freshness.*

trawl trawls trawling trawled
VERB When fishermen trawl, they drag a wide net behind a ship in order to catch fish.

trawler trawlers
NOUN a fishing boat that is used for trawling.

tray trays
NOUN a flat object with raised edges which is used for carrying food or drinks.

treacherous
ADJECTIVE 1 A treacherous person is likely to betray you and cannot be trusted. 2 The ground or the sea can be described as treacherous when it is dangerous or unreliable EG *treacherous mountain roads.*
treacherously ADVERB
▤ (sense 1) disloyal, untrustworthy

treachery
NOUN Treachery is behaviour in which someone betrays their country or a person who trusts them.

treacle
NOUN Treacle is a thick, sweet syrup used to make cakes and toffee EG *treacle tart.*

tread treads treading trod trodden
VERB 1 If you tread on something, you walk on it or step on it. 2 If you tread something into the ground or into a carpet, you crush it in by stepping on it EG *bubblegum that has been trodden into the pavement.* ▶ NOUN 3 A person's tread

A
B
C
D
E
F
G
H
I
J
K
L
M
N
O
P
Q
R
S
T
U
V
W
X
Y
Z

is the sound they make with their feet as they walk EG *his heavy tread.*
4 The tread of a tyre or shoe is the pattern of ridges on it that stops it slipping.

treadmill treadmills
NOUN Any task or job that you must keep doing even though it is unpleasant or tiring can be referred to as a treadmill EG *My life is one constant treadmill of making music.*

treason
NOUN Treason is the crime of betraying your country, for example by helping its enemies.

treasure treasures treasuring treasured
NOUN **1** Treasure is a collection of gold, silver, jewels, or other precious objects, especially one that has been hidden EG *buried treasure.* **2** Treasures are valuable works of art EG *the finest art treasures in the world.* ▶ VERB **3** If you treasure something, you are very pleased that you have it and regard it as very precious EG *He treasures his friendship with her.*
treasured ADJECTIVE

treasurer treasurers
NOUN a person who is in charge of the finance and accounts of an organization.

Treasury
NOUN The Treasury is the government department that deals with the country's finances.

treat treats treating treated
VERB **1** If you treat someone in a particular way, you behave that way towards them. **2** If you treat something in a particular way, you deal with it that way or see it that way EG *We are now treating this case as murder.* **3** When a doctor treats a patient or an illness, he or she gives them medical care and attention. **4** If something such as wood or cloth is treated, a special substance is put on it in order to protect it or give it special properties EG *The*

carpet's been treated with a stain protector.* **5** If you treat someone, you buy or arrange something special for them which they will enjoy. ▶ NOUN **6** If you give someone a treat, you buy or arrange something special for them which they will enjoy EG *my birthday treat.*
treatment NOUN

treatise treatises
Said "tree-tiz" NOUN a long formal piece of writing about a particular subject.

treaty treaties
NOUN a written agreement between countries in which they agree to do something or to help each other.

treble trebles trebling trebled
VERB **1** If something trebles or is trebled, it becomes three times greater in number or amount. ▶ ADJECTIVE **2** Treble means three times as large or three times as strong as previously EG *Next year we can raise treble that amount.*

tree trees
NOUN a large plant with a hard woody trunk, branches, and leaves.

trek treks trekking trekked
VERB **1** If you trek somewhere, you go on a long and difficult journey. ▶ NOUN **2** a long and difficult journey, especially one made by walking.
📖 an Afrikaans word

trellis trellises
NOUN a frame made of horizontal and vertical strips of wood or metal and used to support plants.

tremble trembles trembling trembled
VERB **1** If you tremble, you shake slightly, usually because you are frightened or cold. **2** If something trembles, it shakes slightly. **3** If your voice trembles, it sounds unsteady, usually because you are frightened or upset.
trembling ADJECTIVE

tremendous
ADJECTIVE **1** large or impressive EG *It*

was a *tremendous performance*. **2** AN INFORMAL USE very good or pleasing EG *tremendous fun*.

tremendously ADVERB

tremor **tremors**
NOUN **1** a shaking movement of your body which you cannot control. **2** an unsteady quality in your voice, for example when you are upset. **3** a small earthquake.

trench **trenches**
NOUN a long narrow channel dug into the ground.

trenchant
Said "**trent**-shent" ADJECTIVE Trenchant writing or comments are bold and firmly expressed.

trend **trends**
NOUN a change towards doing or being something different.

trendy **trendier** **trendiest**
ADJECTIVE; AN INFORMAL WORD Trendy things or people are fashionable.

trepidation
NOUN; A FORMAL WORD Trepidation is fear or anxiety EG *He saw the look of trepidation on my face*.

trespass **trespasses** **trespassing** **trespassed**
VERB If you trespass on someone's land or property, you go onto it without their permission.

trespasser NOUN

tresses
PLURAL NOUN; AN OLD-FASHIONED WORD A woman's tresses are her long flowing hair.

trestle **trestles**
NOUN a wooden or metal structure that is used as one of the supports for a table.

trevally **trevallies**
NOUN an Australian and New Zealand fish that is caught for both food and sport.

tri-
PREFIX three EG *tricycle*.

trial **trials**
NOUN **1** the legal process in which a judge and jury decide whether a

person is guilty of a particular crime after listening to all the evidence about it. **2** an experiment in which something is tested EG *Trials of the drug start next month*.

triangle **triangles**
NOUN **1** a shape with three straight sides. **2** a percussion instrument consisting of a thin steel bar bent in the shape of a triangle.

triangular ADJECTIVE

triathlon **triathlons**
Said "tri-**ath**-lon" NOUN a sports contest in which athletes compete in three different events.

tribe **tribes**
NOUN a group of people of the same race, who have the same customs, religion, language, or land, especially when they are thought to be primitive.

tribal ADJECTIVE

tribulation **tribulations**
NOUN; A FORMAL WORD Tribulation is trouble or suffering EG *the tribulations of a female football star*.

tribunal **tribunals**
Said "try-**byoo**-nl" NOUN a special court or committee appointed to deal with particular problems EG *an industrial tribunal*.

tributary **tributaries**
NOUN a stream or river that flows into a larger river.

tribute **tributes**
NOUN **1** A tribute is something said or done to show admiration and respect for someone EG *Police paid tribute to her courage*. **2** If one thing is a tribute to another, it is the result of the other thing and shows how good it is EG *His success has been a tribute to hard work*.

trice
NOUN If someone does something in a trice, they do it very quickly.

trick **tricks** **tricking** **tricked**
VERB **1** If someone tricks you, they deceive you. ▶ NOUN **2** an action done to deceive someone. **3** Tricks

A
B
C
D
E
F
G
H
I
J
K
L
M
N
O
P
Q
R
S
T
U
V
W
X
Y
Z

are clever or skilful actions done in order to entertain people EG *magic tricks*.

trickery

NOUN Trickery is deception EG *He accused the Serbs of trickery*.

trickle trickles trickling trickled
VERB **1** When a liquid trickles somewhere, it flows slowly in a thin stream. **2** When people or things trickle somewhere, they move there slowly in small groups or amounts. ▶ NOUN **3** a thin stream of liquid. **4** A trickle of people or things is a small number or quantity of them.

tricky trickier trickiest
ADJECTIVE difficult to do or deal with.

tricycle tricycles
NOUN a vehicle similar to a bicycle but with two wheels at the back and one at the front.

trifle trifles trifling trifled
NOUN **1** A trifle means a little EG *He seemed a trifle annoyed*. **2** Trifles are things that are not very important or valuable. **3** a cold pudding made of layers of sponge cake, fruit, jelly, and custard. ▶ VERB **4** If you trifle with someone or something, you treat them in a disrespectful way EG *He was not to be trifled with*.

trifling
ADJECTIVE small and unimportant.

trigger triggers triggering triggered
NOUN **1** the small lever on a gun which is pulled in order to fire it. ▶ VERB **2** If something triggers an event or triggers it off, it causes it to happen.
📖 from Dutch *trekken* meaning 'to pull'

trigonometry
Said "trig-gon-**nom**-it-ree" NOUN Trigonometry is the branch of mathematics that is concerned with calculating the angles of triangles or the lengths of their sides.

trill trills trilling trilled
VERB If a bird trills, it sings with short high-pitched repeated notes.

trillion trillions
NOUN; AN INFORMAL WORD Trillions of things means an extremely large number of them. Formerly, a trillion meant a million million million.

trilogy trilogies
NOUN a series of three books or plays that have the same characters or are on the same subject.

trim trimmer trimmest; trims trimming trimmed
ADJECTIVE **1** neat, tidy, and attractive. ▶ VERB **2** To trim something is to clip small amounts off it. **3** If you trim off parts of something, you cut them off because they are not needed EG *Trim off the excess marzipan*. ▶ NOUN **4** If something is given a trim, it is cut a little EG *All styles need a trim every six to eight weeks*. **5** a decoration on something, especially along its edges EG *a fur trim*.
trimmed ADJECTIVE

trimming trimmings
NOUN Trimmings are extra parts added to something for decoration or as a luxury EG *bacon and eggs with all the trimmings*.

Trimurti
NOUN In the Hindu religion, the Trimurti are the three deities Brahma, Vishnu, and Siva.

Trinity
NOUN In the Christian religion, the Trinity is the joining of God the Father, God the Son, and God the Holy Spirit.

trinket trinkets
NOUN a cheap ornament or piece of jewellery.

trio trios
NOUN **1** a group of three musicians who sing or play together; also a piece of music written for three instruments or singers. **2** any group of three things or people together

EG *a trio of children's tales.*

trip trips tripping tripped
NOUN **1** a journey made to a place.
▶ VERB **2** If you trip, you catch your foot on something and fall over. **3** If you trip someone or trip them up, you make them fall over by making them catch their foot on something.
■ (sense 1) excursion, journey, outing

tripe
NOUN Tripe is the stomach lining of a pig, cow, or ox, which is cooked and eaten.

triple triples tripling tripled
ADJECTIVE **1** consisting of three things or three parts EG *the Triple Alliance.*
▶ VERB **2** If you triple something or if it triples, it becomes three times greater in number or size.

triplet triplets
NOUN Triplets are three children born at the same time to the same mother.

tripod tripods
Said "try-pod" NOUN a stand with three legs used to support something like a camera or telescope.

tripper trippers
NOUN a tourist or someone on an excursion.

trite
ADJECTIVE dull and unoriginal EG *his trite novels.*

triumph triumphs triumphing triumphed
NOUN **1** a great success or achievement. **2** Triumph is a feeling of great satisfaction when you win or achieve something.
▶ VERB **3** If you triumph, you win a victory or succeed in overcoming something.

triumphal
ADJECTIVE done or made to celebrate a victory or great success EG *a triumphal return to Rome.*

triumphant

ADJECTIVE Someone who is triumphant feels very happy because they have won a victory or have achieved something EG *a triumphant shout.*

trivia
PLURAL NOUN Trivia are unimportant or uninteresting things.

trivial
ADJECTIVE Something trivial is unimportant.
🔲 from Latin *trivialis* meaning 'found everywhere'

troll trolls
NOUN an imaginary creature in Scandinavian mythology that lives in caves or mountains and is believed to turn to stone at daylight.

trolley trolleys
NOUN **1** a small table on wheels. **2** a small cart on wheels used for carrying heavy objects EG *a supermarket trolley.*

trombone trombones
NOUN a brass wind instrument with a U-shaped slide which you move to produce different notes.

troop troops trooping trooped
NOUN **1** Troops are soldiers. **2** A troop of people or animals is a group of them. ▶ VERB **3** If people troop somewhere, they go there in a group.

trooper troopers
NOUN a low-ranking soldier in the cavalry.

trophy trophies
NOUN **1** a cup or shield given as a prize to the winner of a competition. **2** something you keep to remember a success or victory.
🔲 from Greek *tropē* meaning 'defeat of the enemy'

tropical
ADJECTIVE belonging to or typical of the tropics EG *a tropical island.*

tropics
PLURAL NOUN The tropics are the hottest parts of the world between

A
B
C
D
E
F
G
H
I
J
K
L
M
N
O
P
Q
R
S
T
U
V
W
X
Y
Z

two lines of latitude, the Tropic of Cancer, 23½° north of the equator, and the Tropic of Capricorn, 23½° south of the equator.

trot trots trotting trotted
VERB **1** When a horse trots, it moves at a speed between a walk and a canter, lifting its feet quite high off the ground. **2** If you trot, you run or jog using small quick steps. ▶ NOUN **3** When a horse breaks into a trot, it starts trotting.

trotter trotters
NOUN A pig's trotters are its feet.

trouble troubles troubling troubled
NOUN **1** Troubles are difficulties or problems. **2** If there is trouble, people are quarrelling or fighting EG *There was more trouble after the match.* ▶ PHRASE **3** If you are **in trouble**, you are in a situation where you may be punished because you have done something wrong. ▶ VERB **4** If something troubles you, it makes you feel worried or anxious. **5** If you trouble someone for something, you disturb them in order to ask them for it EG *Can I trouble you for milk?*
troubling ADJECTIVE, **troubled** ADJECTIVE
目 (sense 1) difficulty, problem, worry
目 (sense 5) bother, inconvenience

troublesome
ADJECTIVE causing problems or difficulties EG *a troublesome teenager.*

trough troughs
Said "troff" NOUN a long, narrow container from which animals drink or feed.

trounce trounces trouncing trounced
VERB If you trounce someone, you defeat them completely.

troupe troupes
Said "troop" NOUN a group of actors, singers, or dancers who work together and often travel around together.

trousers

PLURAL NOUN Trousers are a piece of clothing covering the body from the waist down, enclosing each leg separately.
⬚ from Gaelic *triubhas*

trout
NOUN a type of freshwater fish.

trowel trowels
NOUN **1** a small garden tool with a curved, pointed blade used for planting or weeding. **2** a small tool with a flat blade used for spreading cement or plaster.

truant truants
NOUN **1** a child who stays away from school without permission. ▶ PHRASE **2** If children **play truant**, they stay away from school without permission.
truancy NOUN

truce truces
NOUN an agreement between two people or groups to stop fighting for a short time.

truck trucks
NOUN **1** a large motor vehicle used for carrying heavy loads. **2** an open vehicle used for carrying goods on a railway.

truculent
Said "truk-yoo-lent" ADJECTIVE bad-tempered and aggressive.
truculence NOUN

trudge trudges trudging trudged
VERB **1** If you trudge, you walk with slow, heavy steps. ▶ NOUN **2** a slow tiring walk EG *the long trudge home.*

true truer truest
ADJECTIVE **1** A true story or statement is based on facts and is not made up. **2** 'True' is used to describe things or people that are genuine EG *She was a true friend.* **3** True feelings are sincere and genuine. ▶ PHRASE **4** If something **comes true**, it actually happens.
truly ADVERB
目 (sense 1) accurate, correct, factual

truffle truffles
NOUN **1** a soft, round sweet. **2** a

round mushroom-like fungus which grows underground and is considered very good to eat.

trump trumps

NOUN In a game of cards, trumps is the suit with the highest value.

trumpet trumpets trumpeting trumpeted

NOUN **1** a brass wind instrument with a narrow tube ending in a bell-like shape. ▶ VERB **2** When an elephant trumpets, it makes a sound like a very loud trumpet.

truncated

ADJECTIVE Something that is truncated is made shorter.

truncheon truncheons

Said "**trunt**-shn" NOUN a short, thick stick that policemen carry as a weapon.

trundle trundles trundling trundled

VERB If you trundle something or it trundles somewhere, it moves or rolls along slowly.

trunk trunks

NOUN **1** the main stem of a tree from which the branches and roots grow. **2** the main part of your body, excluding your head, neck, arms, and legs. **3** the long flexible nose of an elephant. **4** a large, strong case or box with a hinged lid used for storing things. ▶ PLURAL NOUN **5** A man's trunks are his bathing pants or shorts.

truss trusses trussing trussed

VERB **1** To truss someone or truss them up is to tie them up so that they cannot move. ▶ NOUN **2** a supporting belt with a pad worn by a man with a hernia.

trust trusts trusting trusted

VERB **1** If you trust someone, you believe that they are honest and will not harm you. **2** If you trust someone to do something, you believe they will do it successfully or properly. **3** If you trust someone with something, you give it to them or tell it to them EG *One*

member of the group cannot be trusted with the secret. **4** If you do not trust something, you feel that it is not safe or reliable EG *I didn't trust my arms and legs to work.* ▶ NOUN **5** Trust is the responsibility you are given to deal with or look after important or secret things EG *He had built up a position of trust.* **6** a financial arrangement in which an organization looks after and invests money for someone.
trusting ADJECTIVE

trustee trustees

NOUN someone who is allowed by law to control money or property they are keeping or investing for another person.

trustworthy

ADJECTIVE A trustworthy person is reliable and responsible and can be trusted.

trusty trustier trustiest

ADJECTIVE Trusty things and animals are considered to be reliable because they have always worked well in the past EG *a trusty black labrador.*

truth truths

NOUN **1** The truth is the facts about something, rather than things that are imagined or made up EG *I know she was telling the truth.* **2** an idea or principle that is generally accepted to be true EG *the basic truths in life.*
■ (sense 1) fact, reality

truthful

ADJECTIVE A truthful person is honest and tells the truth.
truthfully ADVERB

try tries trying tried

VERB **1** To try to do something is to make an effort to do it. **2** If you try something, you use it or do it to test how useful or enjoyable it is EG *Howard wanted me to try the wine.* **3** When a person is tried, they appear in court and a judge and jury decide if they are guilty after hearing the evidence. ▶ NOUN **4** an attempt to do something. **5** a test

of something EG *You gave it a try.*
6 In rugby, a try is scored when someone carries the ball over the goal line of the opposing team and touches the ground with it.
■ (sense 1) attempt, endeavour, strive
■ (sense 4) attempt, go, shot
☑ You can use *try to* in speech and writing: *try to get here on time for once. Try and* is very common in speech, but you should avoid it in written work: *just try and stop me!*

trying
ADJECTIVE Something or someone trying is difficult to deal with and makes you feel impatient or annoyed.

tryst **trysts**
Said "trist" NOUN an appointment or meeting, especially between lovers in a quiet, secret place.

tsar **tsars**
Said "zar"; also spelt **czar**
NOUN a Russian emperor or king between 1547 and 1917.

tsarina **tsarinas**
Said "zah-ree-na"; also spelt **czarina**
NOUN a female tsar or the wife of a tsar.

tsetse fly **tsetse flies**
Said "tset-tsee" NOUN an African fly that feeds on blood and causes serious diseases in people and animals.

T-shirt **T-shirts**; also spelt **tee shirt**
NOUN a simple short-sleeved cotton shirt with no collar.

tuatara **tuatara** or **tuataras**
Said "too-ah-tah-rah" NOUN a large, lizard-like reptile found on certain islands off the coast of New Zealand.

tub **tubs**
NOUN a wide circular container.

tuba **tubas**
NOUN a large brass musical instrument that can produce very low notes.

tubby **tubbier** **tubbiest**
ADJECTIVE rather fat.

tube **tubes**
NOUN **1** a round, hollow pipe. **2** a soft metal or plastic cylindrical container with a screw cap at one end EG *a tube of toothpaste.*
tubing NOUN

tuberculosis
Said "tyoo-ber-kyoo-**low**-siss" NOUN Tuberculosis is a serious infectious disease affecting the lungs.

tubular
ADJECTIVE in the shape of a tube.

TUC
In Britain, an abbreviation for 'Trades Union Congress', which is an association of trade unions.

tuck **tucks** **tucking** **tucked**
VERB **1** If you tuck something somewhere, you put it there so that it is safe or comfortable EG *She tucked the letter into her handbag.* **2** If you tuck a piece of fabric into or under something, you push the loose ends inside or under it to make it tidy. **3** If something is tucked away, it is in a quiet place where few people go EG *a little house tucked away in a valley.*

tucker **tuckers** **tuckering** **tuckered**
AN INFORMAL WORD ▶ NOUN **1** In Australian and New Zealand English, tucker is food. ▶ VERB **2** In Australian and New Zealand English, if you are tuckered out you are tired out.

Tudor **Tudors**
NOUN Tudor was the family name of the English monarchs who reigned from 1485 to 1603.

Tuesday **Tuesdays**
NOUN Tuesday is the day between Monday and Wednesday.
🔳 from Old English *tiwesdæg* meaning 'Tiw's day'; Tiw was the Scandinavian god of war and the sky

tuft **tufts**
NOUN A tuft of something such as

hair is a bunch of it growing closely together.

tug tugs tugging tugged
VERB **1** To tug something is to give it a quick, hard pull. ▶ NOUN **2** a quick, hard pull EG *He felt a tug at his arm.* **3** a small, powerful boat that tows large ships.

tug of war
NOUN A tug of war is a sport in which two teams test their strength by pulling against each other on opposite ends of a rope.

tuition
NOUN Tuition is the teaching of a subject, especially to one person or to a small group.

tulip tulips
NOUN a brightly coloured spring flower.
📖 from Turkish *tulbend* meaning 'turban', because of its shape

tumble tumbles tumbling tumbled
VERB **1** To tumble is to fall with a rolling or bouncing movement.
▶ NOUN **2** a fall.

tumbler tumblers
NOUN a drinking glass with straight sides.

tummy tummies
NOUN; AN INFORMAL WORD Your tummy is your stomach.

tumour tumours
Said "**tyoo**-mur" NOUN a mass of diseased or abnormal cells that has grown in a person's or animal's body.

tumultuous
ADJECTIVE A tumultuous event or welcome is very noisy because people are happy or excited.

tuna
Said "**tyoo**-na" NOUN Tuna are large fish that live in warm seas and are caught for food.

tundra
NOUN The tundra is a vast treeless Arctic region.
📖 a Russian word

tune tunes tuning tuned
NOUN **1** a series of musical notes arranged in a particular way. ▶ VERB **2** To tune a musical instrument is to adjust it so that it produces the right notes. **3** To tune an engine or machine is to adjust it so that it works well. **4** If you tune to a particular radio or television station you turn or press the controls to select the station you want to listen to or watch. ▶ PHRASE **5** If your voice or an instrument is **in tune**, it produces the right notes.

tuneful
ADJECTIVE having a pleasant and easily remembered tune.

tuner tuners
NOUN A piano tuner is a person whose job it is to tune pianos.

tunic tunics
NOUN a sleeveless garment covering the top part of the body and reaching to the hips, thighs, or knees.

Tunisian Tunisians
Said "tyoo-**niz**-ee-an" ADJECTIVE **1** belonging or relating to Tunisia.
▶ NOUN **2** someone who comes from Tunisia.

tunnel tunnels tunnelling tunnelled
NOUN **1** a long underground passage.
▶ VERB **2** To tunnel is to make a tunnel.

turban turbans
NOUN a head-covering worn by a Hindu, Muslim, or Sikh man, consisting of a long piece of cloth wound round his head.

turbine turbines
NOUN a machine or engine in which power is produced when a stream of air, gas, water, or steam pushes the blades of a wheel and makes it turn round.
📖 from Latin *turbo* meaning 'whirlwind'

turbot
Said "**tur**-bot" NOUN a large European flat fish that is caught for

food.

turbulent

ADJECTIVE **1** A turbulent period of history is one where there is much uncertainty, and possibly violent change. **2** Turbulent air or water currents make sudden changes of direction.
turbulence NOUN

tureen tureens
Said "tur-**reen**" NOUN a large dish with a lid for serving soup.

turf turves; turfs turfing turfed
NOUN Turf is short thick even grass and the layer of soil beneath it.
turf out VERB; AN INFORMAL EXPRESSION To turf someone out is to force them to leave a place.

turgid
Said "tur-jid" ADJECTIVE; A LITERARY WORD A turgid play, film, or piece of writing is difficult to understand and rather boring.

Turk Turks
NOUN someone who comes from Turkey.

turkey turkeys
NOUN a large bird kept for food; also the meat of this bird.

Turkish
ADJECTIVE **1** belonging or relating to Turkey. ▶ NOUN **2** Turkish is the main language spoken in Turkey.

turmoil
NOUN Turmoil is a state of confusion, disorder, or great anxiety EG *Europe is in a state of turmoil.*

turn turns turning turned
VERB **1** When you turn, you move so that you are facing or going in a different direction. **2** When you turn something or when it turns, it moves or rotates so that it faces in a different direction or is in a different position. **3** If you turn your attention or thoughts to someone or something, you start thinking about them or discussing them. **4** When something turns or

is turned into something else, it becomes something different EG *A hobby can be turned into a career.*
▶ NOUN **5** an act of turning something so that it faces in a different direction or is in a different position. **6** a change in the way something is happening or being done EG *Her career took a turn for the worse.* **7** If it is your turn to do something, you have the right, chance, or duty to do it. ▶ PHRASE **8 In turn** is used to refer to people, things, or actions that are in sequence one after the other.
▣ (sense 7) chance, go, opportunity

turn down VERB If you turn down someone's request or offer, you refuse or reject it.

turn up VERB **1** If someone or something turns up, they arrive or appear somewhere. **2** If something turns up, it is found or discovered.

turncoat turncoats
NOUN a person who leaves one political party or group for an opposing one.

turning turnings
NOUN a road which leads away from the side of another road.

turning point turning points
NOUN the moment when decisions are taken and events start to move in a different direction.

turnip turnips
NOUN a round root vegetable with a white or yellow skin.

turnout turnouts
NOUN The turnout at an event is the number of people who go to it.

turnover turnovers
NOUN **1** The turnover of people in a particular organization or group is the rate at which people leave it and are replaced by others. **2** The turnover of a company is the value of the goods or services sold during a particular period.

turnstile turnstiles
NOUN a revolving mechanical barrier

at the entrance to places like
football grounds or zoos.

turpentine
NOUN Turpentine is a
strong-smelling colourless liquid
used for cleaning and for thinning
paint.

turps
NOUN Turps is turpentine.

turquoise
Said "tur-kwoyz" NOUN OR ADJECTIVE
1 light bluish-green. ▶ NOUN
2 Turquoise is a bluish-green stone
used in jewellery.

turret turrets
NOUN a small narrow tower on top
of a larger tower or other buildings.

turtle turtles
NOUN a large reptile with a thick
shell covering its body and flippers
for swimming. It lays its eggs on
land but lives the rest of its life in
the sea.

tusk tusks
NOUN The tusks of an elephant, wild
boar, or walrus are the pair of long
curving pointed teeth it has.

tussle tussles
NOUN an energetic fight or argument
between two people, especially
about something they both want.

tutor tutors tutoring tutored
NOUN **1** a teacher at a college or
university. **2** a private teacher.
▶ VERB **3** If someone tutors a person
or subject, they teach that person
or subject.

tutorial tutorials
NOUN a teaching session involving a
tutor and a small group of students.

tutu tutus
Said "too-too" NOUN a short stiff
skirt worn by female ballet dancers.

TV TVs
NOUN **1** TV is television. **2** a
television set.

twang twangs twanging twanged
NOUN **1** a sound like the one made
by pulling and then releasing a
tight wire. **2** A twang is a nasal

quality in a person's voice. ▶ VERB
3 If a tight wire or string twangs or
you twang it, it makes a sound as it
is pulled and then released.

tweak tweaks tweaking tweaked
VERB **1** If you tweak something, you
twist it or pull it. ▶ NOUN **2** a short
twist or pull of something.

twee
ADJECTIVE sweet and pretty but in bad
taste or sentimental.

tweed tweeds
NOUN Tweed is a thick woollen cloth.

tweet tweets tweeting tweeted
VERB **1** When a small bird tweets, it
makes a short, high-pitched sound.
▶ NOUN **2** a short high-pitched
sound made by a small bird.

tweezers
PLURAL NOUN Tweezers are a small tool
with two arms which can be closed
together and are used for pulling
out hairs or picking up small
objects.

twelve
the number 12.
twelfth

twenty twenties
the number 20.
twentieth

twice
ADVERB Twice means two times.

**twiddle twiddles twiddling
twiddled**
VERB To twiddle something is to
twist it or turn it quickly.

twig twigs
NOUN a very small thin branch
growing from a main branch of a
tree or bush.

twilight
Said "twy-lite" NOUN **1** Twilight is
the time after sunset when it is just
getting dark. **2** The twilight of
something is the final stages of it EG
the twilight of his career.

twin twins
NOUN **1** If two people are twins, they
have the same mother and were
born on the same day. **2** 'Twin' is

A
B
C
D
E
F
G
H
I
J
K
L
M
N
O
P
Q
R
S
T
U
V
W
X
Y
Z

used to describe two similar things that are close together or happen together EG *the little twin islands*.

twine twines twining twined
NOUN **1** Twine is strong smooth string. ▸ VERB **2** If you twine one thing round another, you twist or wind it round.

twinge twinges
NOUN a sudden, unpleasant feeling EG *a twinge of jealousy*.

twinkle twinkles twinkling twinkled
VERB **1** If something twinkles, it sparkles or seems to sparkle with an unsteady light EG *Her green eyes twinkled*. ▸ NOUN **2** a sparkle or brightness that something has.

twirl twirls twirling twirled
VERB If something twirls, or if you twirl it, it spins or twists round and round.

twist twists twisting twisted
VERB **1** When you twist something you turn one end of it in one direction while holding the other end or turning it in the opposite direction. **2** When something twists or is twisted, it moves or bends into a strange shape. **3** If you twist a part of your body, you injure it by turning it too sharply or in an unusual direction EG *I've twisted my ankle*. **4** If you twist something that someone has said, you change the meaning slightly. ▸ NOUN **5** a twisting action or motion. **6** an unexpected development or event in a story or film, especially at the end EG *Each day now seemed to bring a new twist to the story*.
▣ (sense 1) coil, wind
▣ (sense 2) contort, distort

twisted
ADJECTIVE **1** Something twisted has been bent or moved into a strange shape EG *a tangle of twisted metal*. **2** If someone's mind or behaviour is twisted, it is unpleasantly abnormal EG *He's bitter and twisted*.

twit twits
NOUN; AN INFORMAL WORD a silly person.

twitch twitches twitching twitched
VERB **1** If you twitch, you make little jerky movements which you cannot control. **2** If you twitch something, you give it a little jerk in order to move it. ▸ NOUN **3** a little jerky movement.

twitter twitters twittering twittered
VERB When birds twitter, they make short high-pitched sounds.

two
the number 2.

two-faced
ADJECTIVE A two-faced person is not honest in the way they behave towards other people.

twofold
ADJECTIVE Something twofold has two equally important parts or reasons EG *Their concern was twofold: personal and political*.

twosome twosomes
Said "too-sum" NOUN two people or things that are usually seen together.

two-time two-times two-timing two-timed
VERB; AN INFORMAL EXPRESSION If you two-time your boyfriend or girlfriend, you deceive them, by having a romantic relationship with someone else without telling them.

two-up
NOUN In Australia and New Zealand, two-up is a popular gambling game in which two coins are tossed and bets are placed on whether they land heads or tails.

tycoon tycoons
NOUN a person who is successful in business and has become rich and powerful.
▣ from Chinese *ta* + *chun* meaning 'great ruler'

type types typing typed

NOUN **1** A type of something is a class of it that has common features and belongs to a larger group of related things EG *What type of dog should we get?* **2** A particular type of person has a particular appearance or quality EG *Andrea is the type who likes to play safe.* ▶ VERB **3** If you type something, you use a typewriter or word processor to write it.

typewriter typewriters
NOUN a machine with a keyboard with individual keys which are pressed to produce letters and numbers on a page.

typhoid
Said "tie-foyd" NOUN Typhoid, or typhoid fever, is an infectious disease caused by dirty water or food. It produces fever and can kill.

typhoon typhoons
NOUN a very violent tropical storm.
▥ from Chinese *tai fung* meaning 'great wind'

typhus
NOUN Typhus is an infectious disease transmitted by lice or mites. It results in fever, severe headaches, and a skin rash.

typical
ADJECTIVE showing the most usual characteristics or behaviour.
typically ADVERB
▣ characteristic, standard, usual

typify typifies typifying typified

VERB If something typifies a situation or thing, it is characteristic of it or a typical example of it EG *This story is one that typifies our times.*

typing
NOUN Typing is the work or activity of producing something on a typewriter.

typist typists
NOUN a person whose job is typing.

tyrannosaurus tyrannosauruses
*Said "tir-ran-oh-**saw**-russ"* NOUN a very large meat-eating dinosaur which walked upright on its hind legs.
▥ from Greek *turannos* meaning 'tyrant' and Latin *saurus* meaning 'lizard'

tyranny tyrannies
NOUN **1** A tyranny is cruel and unjust rule of people by a person or group EG *the evils of Nazi tyranny*. **2** You can refer to something which is not human but is harsh as tyranny EG *the tyranny of drugs*.
tyrannical ADJECTIVE

tyrant tyrants
NOUN a person who treats the people he or she has authority over cruelly and unjustly.

tyre tyres
NOUN a thick ring of rubber fitted round each wheel of a vehicle and filled with air.

A
B
C
D
E
F
G
H
I
J
K
L
M
N
O
P
Q
R
S
T
U
V
W
X
Y
Z

Uu Uu

ubiquitous
Said "yoo-**bik**-wit-tuss" ADJECTIVE
Something that is ubiquitous seems
to be everywhere at the same time
EG *the ubiquitous jeans*.
从 from Latin *ubique* meaning
'everywhere'

udder udders
NOUN the baglike organ that hangs
below a cow's body and produces
milk.

UFO UFOs
NOUN a strange object seen in the
sky, which some people believe to
be a spaceship from another
planet. UFO is an abbreviation for
'unidentified flying object'.

Ugandan Ugandans
Said "yoo-**gan**-dan" ADJECTIVE
1 belonging or relating to Uganda.
▶ NOUN **2** someone who comes from
Uganda.

ugly uglier ugliest
ADJECTIVE very unattractive in
appearance.
从 from Old Norse *uggligr* meaning
'terrifying'
目 plain, unattractive, unsightly

UK
an abbreviation for **United
Kingdom**.

ulcer ulcers
NOUN a sore area on the skin or
inside the body, which takes a long
time to heal EG *stomach ulcers*.

ulterior
Said "ul-**teer**-ee-or" ADJECTIVE If you
have an ulterior motive for doing
something, you have a hidden
reason for it.

ultimate
ADJECTIVE **1** final or eventual EG
Olympic gold is the ultimate goal.
2 most important or powerful EG *the
ultimate ambition of any player*.
▶ NOUN **3** You can refer to the best or
most advanced example of
something as the ultimate EG *This

hotel is the ultimate in luxury.
ultimately ADVERB

ultimatum ultimatums
Said "ul-tim-**may**-tum" NOUN a
warning stating that unless
someone meets your conditions,
you will take action against them.

ultra-
PREFIX 'Ultra-' is used to form
adjectives describing something as
having a quality to an extreme
degree EG *the ultra-competitive world of
sport today*.

ultramarine
NOUN OR ADJECTIVE bright blue.
从 from Latin *ultramarinus*
meaning 'beyond the sea', because
the pigment was imported from
abroad

ultrasonic
ADJECTIVE An ultrasonic sound has a
very high frequency that cannot be
heard by the human ear.

ultrasound
NOUN Ultrasound is sound which
cannot be heard by the human ear
because its frequency is too high.

ultraviolet
ADJECTIVE Ultraviolet light is not
visible to the human eye. It is a
form of radiation that causes your
skin to darken after being exposed
to the sun.

umbilical cord umbilical cords
Said "um-**bil**-lik-kl" NOUN the tube
of blood vessels which connects an
unborn baby to its mother and
through which the baby receives
nutrients and oxygen.

umbrella umbrellas
NOUN a device that you use to
protect yourself from the rain. It
consists of a folding frame covered
in cloth attached to a long stick.

**umpire umpires umpiring
umpired**
NOUN **1** The umpire in cricket or

tennis is the person who makes sure that the game is played according to the rules and who makes a decision if there is a dispute. ▶ VERB **2** If you umpire a game, you are the umpire.

umpteen
ADJECTIVE; AN INFORMAL WORD very many EG *tomatoes and umpteen other plants.*
umpteenth ADJECTIVE

un-
PREFIX Un- is added to the beginning of many words to form a word with the opposite meaning EG *an uncomfortable chair... He unlocked the door.*

unabashed
ADJECTIVE not embarrassed or discouraged by something EG *Samuel was continuing unabashed.*

unabated
ADJECTIVE OR ADVERB continuing without any reduction in intensity or amount EG *The noise continued unabated.*

unable
ADJECTIVE If you are unable to do something, you cannot do it.

unacceptable
ADJECTIVE very bad or of a very low standard.

unaccompanied
ADJECTIVE alone.

unaccustomed
ADJECTIVE If you are unaccustomed to something, you are not used to it.

unaffected
ADJECTIVE **1** not changed in any way by a particular thing EG *unaffected by the recession.* **2** behaving in a natural and genuine way EG *the most down-to-earth unaffected person I've ever met.*

unaided
ADVERB OR ADJECTIVE without help EG *He was incapable of walking unaided.*

unambiguous
ADJECTIVE An unambiguous statement has only one meaning.

unanimous

Said "yoon-**nan**-nim-mus" ADJECTIVE When people are unanimous, they all agree about something.
unanimously ADVERB, **unanimity** NOUN
🏛 from Latin *unanimus* meaning 'of one mind'

unannounced
ADJECTIVE happening unexpectedly and without warning.

unarmed
ADJECTIVE not carrying any weapons.

unassuming
ADJECTIVE modest and quiet.

unattached
ADJECTIVE An unattached person is not married and is not having a steady relationship with someone.

unattended
ADJECTIVE not being watched or looked after EG *an unattended handbag.*

unauthorized or **unauthorised**
ADJECTIVE done without official permission EG *unauthorized parking.*

unavoidable
ADJECTIVE unable to be prevented or avoided.

unaware
ADJECTIVE If you are unaware of something, you do not know about it.
☑ *Unaware* is usually followed by *of* or *that.* Do not confuse it with the adverb *unawares.*

unawares
ADVERB If something catches you unawares, it happens when you are not expecting it.
☑ Do not confuse *unawares* with the adjective *unaware.*

unbalanced
ADJECTIVE **1** with more weight or emphasis on one side than the other EG *an unbalanced load... an unbalanced relationship.* **2** slightly mad. **3** made up of parts that do not work well together EG *an unbalanced lifestyle.* **4** An unbalanced account of something is an unfair one because it

A B C D E F G H I J K L M N O P Q R S T U V W X Y Z

emphasizes some things and ignores others.

unbearable

ADJECTIVE Something unbearable is so unpleasant or upsetting that you feel you cannot stand it EG *The pain was unbearable.*
unbearably ADVERB
■ insufferable, intolerable

unbeatable

ADJECTIVE Something that is unbeatable is the best thing of its kind.

unbelievable

ADJECTIVE **1** extremely great or surprising EG *unbelievable courage.* **2** so unlikely that you cannot believe it.
unbelievably ADVERB
■ (sense 1) astonishing, incredible
■ (sense 2) far-fetched, implausible

unborn

ADJECTIVE not yet born.

unbroken

ADJECTIVE continuous or complete EG *ten days of almost unbroken sunshine.*

uncanny

ADJECTIVE strange and difficult to explain EG *an uncanny resemblance.*
🏛 from Scottish *uncanny* meaning 'unreliable' or 'not safe to deal with'

uncertain

ADJECTIVE **1** not knowing what to do EG *For a minute he looked uncertain.* **2** doubtful or not known EG *The outcome of the war was uncertain.*
uncertainty NOUN

unchallenged

ADJECTIVE accepted without any questions being asked EG *We can't let this enormous theft go unchallenged.*

uncharacteristic

ADJECTIVE not typical or usual EG *My father reacted with uncharacteristic speed.*

uncle uncles

NOUN the brother of your mother or father or the husband of your aunt.

unclean

ADJECTIVE dirty EG *unclean water.*

unclear

ADJECTIVE confusing and not obvious.

uncomfortable

ADJECTIVE **1** If you are uncomfortable, you are not physically relaxed and feel slight pain or discomfort. **2** Uncomfortable also means slightly worried or embarrassed.
uncomfortably ADVERB

uncommon

ADJECTIVE **1** not happening often or not seen often. **2** unusually great EG *She had read Cecilia's last letter with uncommon interest.*
uncommonly ADVERB

uncompromising

ADJECTIVE determined not to change an opinion or aim in any way EG *an uncompromising approach to life.*
uncompromisingly ADVERB

unconcerned

ADJECTIVE not interested in something or not worried about it.

unconditional

ADJECTIVE with no conditions or limitations EG *a full three-year unconditional guarantee.*
unconditionally ADVERB

unconscious

ADJECTIVE **1** Someone who is unconscious is asleep or in a state similar to sleep as a result of a shock, accident, or injury. **2** If you are unconscious of something, you are not aware of it.
unconsciously ADVERB

unconventional

ADJECTIVE not behaving in the same way as most other people.

unconvinced

ADJECTIVE not at all certain that something is true or right EG *Some critics remain unconvinced by the plan.*

uncouth

Said "un-kooth" ADJECTIVE bad-mannered and unpleasant.
■ boorish, coarse, vulgar

uncover uncovers uncovering uncovered

VERB **1** If you uncover a secret, you

find it out. **2** To uncover something is to remove the cover or lid from it.

undaunted
ADJECTIVE If you are undaunted by something disappointing, you are not discouraged by it.

undecided
ADJECTIVE If you are undecided, you have not yet made a decision about something.

undemanding
ADJECTIVE not difficult to do or deal with EG *undemanding work*.

undeniable
ADJECTIVE certainly true EG *undeniable evidence*.
undeniably ADVERB

under
PREPOSITION **1** below or beneath. **2** You can use 'under' to say that a person or thing is affected by a particular situation or condition EG *The country was under threat... Animals are kept under unnatural conditions.* **3** If someone studies or works under a particular person, that person is their teacher or their boss. **4** less than EG *under five kilometres... children under the age of 14.* ▶ PHRASE **5** **Under way** means already started EG *A murder investigation is already under way.*

under-
PREFIX 'Under-' is used in words that describe something as not being provided to a sufficient extent or not having happened to a sufficient extent.

underarm
ADJECTIVE **1** under your arm EG *underarm hair.* ▶ ADVERB **2** If you throw a ball underarm, you throw it without raising your arm over your shoulder.

undercarriage undercarriages
NOUN the part of an aircraft, including the wheels, that supports the aircraft when it is on the ground.

underclass
NOUN The underclass is the people in society who are the most poor and whose situation is unlikely to improve.

underclothes
PLURAL NOUN Your underclothes are the clothes that you wear under your other clothes and next to your skin.

undercover
ADJECTIVE involving secret work to obtain information EG *a police undercover operation.*

undercurrent undercurrents
NOUN a weak, partly hidden feeling that may become stronger later.

undercut undercuts undercutting undercut
VERB **1** To undercut someone's prices is to sell a product more cheaply than they do. **2** If something undercuts your attempts to achieve something, it prevents them from being effective.

underdeveloped
ADJECTIVE An underdeveloped country does not have modern industries, and usually has a low standard of living.

underdog underdogs
NOUN The underdog in a competition is the person who seems likely to lose.

underestimate underestimates underestimating underestimated
VERB If you underestimate something or someone, you do not realize how large, great, or capable they are.

underfoot
ADJECTIVE OR ADVERB under your feet EG *the icy ground underfoot.*

undergo undergoes undergoing underwent undergone
VERB If you undergo something unpleasant, it happens to you.

underground
ADJECTIVE **1** below the surface of the ground. **2** secret, unofficial, and

A B C D E F G H I J K L M N O P Q R S T U V W X Y Z

usually illegal. ▶ NOUN **3** The underground is a railway system in which trains travel in tunnels below ground.

undergrowth
NOUN Small bushes and plants growing under trees are called the undergrowth.

underhand
ADJECTIVE secret and dishonest EG *underhand behaviour.*

underlie underlies underlying underlay underlain
VERB The thing that underlies a situation is the cause or basis of it.
underlying ADJECTIVE

underline underlines underlining underlined
VERB **1** If something underlines a feeling or a problem, it emphasizes it. **2** If you underline a word or sentence, you draw a line under it.

underling underlings
NOUN someone who is less important than someone else in rank or status.

undermine undermines undermining undermined
VERB To undermine an idea, feeling, or system is to make it less strong or secure EG *You're trying to undermine my confidence again.*
🔲 from the practice in warfare of digging tunnels under enemy fortifications in order to make them collapse
🟦 subvert, weaken

underneath
PREPOSITION **1** below or beneath.
▶ ADVERB OR PREPOSITION **2** Underneath describes feelings and qualities that do not show in your behaviour EG *Alex knew that underneath she was shattered.* ▶ ADJECTIVE **3** The underneath part of something is the part that touches or faces the ground.

underpants
PLURAL NOUN Underpants are a piece of clothing worn by men and boys under their trousers.

underpass underpasses
NOUN a road or footpath that goes under a road or railway.

underpin underpins underpinning underpinned
VERB If something underpins something else, it helps it to continue by supporting and strengthening it EG *Australian skill is usually underpinned by an immense team spirit.*

underprivileged
ADJECTIVE Underprivileged people have less money and fewer opportunities than other people.

underrate underrates underrating underrated
VERB If you underrate someone, you do not realize how clever or valuable they are.

understand understands understanding understood
VERB **1** If you understand what someone says, you know what they mean. **2** If you understand a situation, you know what is happening and why. **3** If you say that you understand that something is the case, you mean that you have heard that it is the case EG *I understand that she's a lot better now.*
🟦 comprehend, follow, grasp, see

understandable
ADJECTIVE If something is understandable, people can easily understand it.
understandably ADVERB

understanding understandings
NOUN **1** If you have an understanding of something, you have some knowledge about it. **2** an informal agreement between people. ▶ ADJECTIVE **3** kind and sympathetic.
🟦 (sense 1) comprehension, grasp, perception

understatement understatements
NOUN a statement that does not say fully how true something is EG *To*

say I was pleased was an understatement.

understudy understudies
NOUN someone who has learnt a part in a play so that they can act it if the main actor or actress is ill.

undertake undertakes undertaking undertook undertaken
VERB When you undertake a task or job, you agree to do it.
undertaking NOUN

undertaker undertakers
NOUN someone whose job is to prepare bodies for burial and arrange funerals.

undertone undertones
NOUN 1 If you say something in an undertone, you say it very quietly. 2 If something has undertones of a particular kind, it indirectly suggests ideas of this kind EG *unsettling undertones of violence.*

undervalue undervalues undervaluing undervalued
VERB If you undervalue something, you think it is less important than it really is.

underwater
ADVERB OR ADJECTIVE 1 beneath the surface of the sea, a river, or a lake. ▶ ADJECTIVE 2 designed to work in water EG *an underwater camera.*

underwear
NOUN Your underwear is the clothing that you wear under your other clothes, next to your skin.

underwent
the past tense of **undergo**.

undesirable
ADJECTIVE unwelcome and likely to cause harm EG *undesirable behaviour.*

undid
the past tense of **undo**.

undisputed
ADJECTIVE definite and without any doubt EG *the undisputed champion.*

undivided
ADJECTIVE If you give something your undivided attention, you

concentrate on it totally.

undo undoes undoing undid undone
VERB 1 If you undo something that is tied up, you untie it. 2 If you undo something that has been done, you reverse the effect of it.

undoing
NOUN If something is someone's undoing, it is the cause of their failure.

undoubted
ADJECTIVE You use 'undoubted' to emphasize something EG *The event was an undoubted success.*
undoubtedly ADVERB

undress undresses undressing undressed
VERB When you undress, you take off your clothes.

undue
ADJECTIVE greater than is reasonable EG *undue violence.*
unduly ADVERB

undulating
ADJECTIVE; A FORMAL WORD moving gently up and down EG *undulating hills.*

undying
ADJECTIVE lasting forever EG *his undying love for his wife.*

unearth unearths unearthing unearthed
VERB If you unearth something that is hidden, you discover it.

unearthly
ADJECTIVE strange and unnatural.

uneasy
ADJECTIVE If you are uneasy, you feel worried that something may be wrong.
unease NOUN, **uneasily** ADVERB, **uneasiness** NOUN

unemployed
ADJECTIVE 1 without a job EG *an unemployed mechanic.* ▶ NOUN 2 The unemployed are all the people who are without a job.

unemployment
NOUN Unemployment is the state of

A
B
C
D
E
F
G
H
I
J
K
L
M
N
O
P
Q
R
S
T
U
V
W
X
Y
Z

being without a job.

unending

ADJECTIVE Something unending has continued for a long time and seems as if it will never stop EG *unending joy*.

unenviable

ADJECTIVE An unenviable situation is one that you would not like to be in.

unequal

ADJECTIVE 1 An unequal society does not offer the same opportunities and privileges to all people. 2 Unequal things are different in size, strength, or ability.

uneven

ADJECTIVE 1 An uneven surface is not level or smooth. 2 not the same or consistent EG *six lines of uneven length*.

unevenly ADVERB

uneventful

ADJECTIVE An uneventful period of time is one when nothing interesting happens.

unexpected

ADJECTIVE Something unexpected is surprising because it was not thought likely to happen.

unexpectedly ADVERB

unfailing

ADJECTIVE continuous and not weakening as time passes EG *his unfailing cheerfulness*.

unfair

ADJECTIVE not right or just.

unfairly ADVERB

unfaithful

ADJECTIVE If someone is unfaithful to their lover or the person they are married to, they have a sexual relationship with someone else.

unfamiliar

ADJECTIVE If something is unfamiliar to you, or if you are unfamiliar with it, you have not seen or heard it before.

unfit

ADJECTIVE 1 If you are unfit, your

body is not in good condition because you have not been taking enough exercise. 2 Something that is unfit for a particular purpose is not suitable for that purpose.

unfold unfolds unfolding unfolded

VERB 1 When a situation unfolds, it develops and becomes known. 2 If you unfold something that has been folded, you open it out so that it is flat.

unforeseen

ADJECTIVE happening unexpectedly.

unforgettable

ADJECTIVE Something unforgettable is so good or so bad that you are unlikely to forget it.

unforgettably ADVERB

unforgivable

ADJECTIVE Something unforgivable is so bad or cruel that it can never be forgiven or justified.

unforgivably ADVERB

unfortunate

ADJECTIVE 1 Someone who is unfortunate is unlucky. 2 If you describe an event as unfortunate, you mean that it is a pity that it happened EG *an unfortunate accident*.

unfortunately ADVERB

unfounded

ADJECTIVE Something that is unfounded has no evidence to support it EG *unfounded allegations*.

ungainly

ADJECTIVE moving in an awkward or clumsy way.

🔳 from Old Norse *ungegn* meaning 'not straight'

unhappy unhappier unhappiest

ADJECTIVE 1 sad and depressed. 2 not pleased or satisfied EG *I am unhappy at being left out*. 3 If you describe a situation as an unhappy one, you are sorry that it exists EG *an unhappy state of affairs*.

unhappily ADVERB, **unhappiness** NOUN

unhealthy

ADJECTIVE 1 likely to cause illness EG *an unhealthy lifestyle*. 2 An unhealthy person is often ill.

unheard-of

ADJECTIVE never having happened before and therefore surprising or shocking.

unhinged

ADJECTIVE Someone who is unhinged is mentally ill.

unicorn unicorns

NOUN an imaginary animal that looks like a white horse with a straight horn growing from its forehead.

🏛 from Latin *unicornis* meaning 'having one horn'

unidentified

ADJECTIVE You say that someone or something is unidentified when nobody knows who or what they are.

uniform uniforms

NOUN **1** a special set of clothes worn by people at work or school.
▶ ADJECTIVE **2** Something that is uniform does not vary but is even and regular throughout.
uniformity NOUN

unify unifies unifying unified

VERB If you unify a number of things, you bring them together.
unification NOUN

unilateral

ADJECTIVE A unilateral decision or action is one taken by only one of several groups involved in a particular situation.
unilaterally ADVERB

unimaginable

ADJECTIVE impossible to imagine or understand properly EG *a fairyland of unimaginable beauty.*

unimportant

ADJECTIVE having very little significance or importance.
🟦 insignificant, minor, trivial

uninhabited

ADJECTIVE An uninhabited place is a place where nobody lives.

uninhibited

ADJECTIVE If you are uninhibited, you behave freely and naturally and show your true feelings.

unintelligible

ADJECTIVE; A FORMAL WORD impossible to understand.

uninterested

ADJECTIVE If you are uninterested in something, you are not interested in it.

uninterrupted

ADJECTIVE continuing without breaks or interruptions EG *uninterrupted views.*

union unions

NOUN **1** an organization of workers that aims to improve the working conditions, pay, and benefits of its members. **2** When the union of two things takes place, they are joined together to become one thing.

unique

Said "yoo-neek" ADJECTIVE **1** being the only one of its kind. **2** If something is unique to one person or thing, it concerns or belongs to that person or thing only EG *trees and vegetation unique to the Canary islands.*
uniquely ADVERB, **uniqueness** NOUN
☑ Something is either *unique* or *not unique*, so you should avoid saying things like *rather unique* or *very unique.*

unisex

ADJECTIVE designed to be used by both men and women EG *unisex clothing.*

unison

NOUN If a group of people do something in unison, they all do it together at the same time.
🏛 from Latin *unisonus* meaning 'making the same musical sound'

unit units

NOUN **1** If you consider something as a unit, you consider it as a single complete thing. **2** a group of people who work together at a particular job EG *the Police Support Unit.* **3** a machine or piece of equipment which has a particular function EG *a remote control unit.* **4** A unit of measurement is a fixed standard that is used for measuring things.

unite unites uniting united
VERB If a number of people unite, they join together and act as a group.

United Kingdom
NOUN The United Kingdom consists of Great Britain and Northern Ireland.

United Nations
NOUN The United Nations is an international organization which tries to encourage peace, cooperation, and friendship between countries.

unity
NOUN Where there is unity, people are in agreement and act together for a particular purpose.

universal
ADJECTIVE concerning or relating to everyone in the world or every part of the universe EG *Music and sports programmes have a universal appeal... universal destruction.*
universally ADVERB

universe universes
NOUN The universe is the whole of space, including all the stars and planets.

university universities
NOUN a place where students study for degrees.
▥ from Latin *universitas* meaning 'group of scholars'

unjust
ADJECTIVE not fair or reasonable.
unjustly ADVERB

unjustified
ADJECTIVE If a belief or action is unjustified, there is no good reason for it.

unkempt
ADJECTIVE untidy and not looked after properly EG *unkempt hair.*

unkind

ADJECTIVE unpleasant and rather cruel.
unkindly ADVERB, **unkindness** NOUN
▤ cruel, nasty, uncharitable

unknown
ADJECTIVE **1** If someone or something is unknown, people do not know about them or have not heard of them. ▶ NOUN **2** You can refer to the things that people in general do not know about as the unknown.

unlawful
ADJECTIVE not legal EG *the unlawful use of drugs.*

unleaded
ADJECTIVE Unleaded petrol has a reduced amount of lead in it in order to reduce the pollution from cars.

unleash unleashes unleashing unleashed
VERB When a powerful or violent force is unleashed, it is released.

unless
CONJUNCTION You use 'unless' to introduce the only circumstances in which something will not take place or is not true EG *Unless it was raining, they played in the little garden.*

unlike
PREPOSITION If one thing is unlike another, the two things are different.

unlikely
ADJECTIVE **1** If something is unlikely, it is probably not true or probably will not happen. **2** strange and unexpected EG *There are riches in unlikely places.*

unlimited
ADJECTIVE If a supply of something is unlimited, you can have as much as you want or need.

unload unloads unloading unloaded
VERB If you unload things from a container or vehicle, you remove them.

unlock unlocks unlocking unlocked

verb If you unlock a door or container, you open it by turning a key in the lock.

unlucky
adjective Someone who is unlucky has bad luck.
unluckily adverb
■ hapless, unfortunate

unmarked
adjective **1** with no marks of damage or injury. **2** with no signs or marks of identification eg *unmarked police cars.*

unmistakable or **unmistakeable**
adjective Something unmistakable is so obvious that it cannot be mistaken for something else.
unmistakably adverb

unmitigated
adjective; a formal word You use 'unmitigated' to describe a situation or quality that is completely bad eg *an unmitigated disaster.*

unmoved
adjective not emotionally affected eg *He is unmoved by criticism.*

unnatural
adjective **1** strange and rather frightening because it is not usual eg *There was an unnatural stillness.* **2** artificial and not typical eg *My voice sounded high-pitched and unnatural.*
unnaturally adverb

unnerve unnerves unnerving unnerved
verb If something unnerves you, it frightens or startles you.
unnerving adjective

unobtrusive
adjective Something that is unobtrusive does not draw attention to itself.

unoccupied
adjective If a house is unoccupied, there is nobody living in it.

unofficial
adjective without the approval or permission of a person in authority

eg *unofficial strikes.*
unofficially adverb

unorthodox
adjective unusual and not generally accepted eg *an unorthodox theory.*

unpack unpacks unpacking unpacked
verb When you unpack, you take everything out of a suitcase or bag.

unpaid
adjective **1** If you do unpaid work, you do not receive any money for doing it. **2** An unpaid bill has not yet been paid.

unpalatable
adjective **1** Unpalatable food is so unpleasant that you can hardly eat it. **2** An unpalatable idea is so unpleasant that it is difficult to accept.

unparalleled
adjective greater than anything else of its kind eg *an unparalleled success.*

unpleasant
adjective **1** Something unpleasant causes you to have bad feelings, for example by making you uncomfortable or upset. **2** An unpleasant person is unfriendly or rude.

unpopular
adjective disliked by most people eg *an unpopular idea.*

unprecedented
Said "un-press-id-en-tid" adjective; a formal word Something that is unprecedented has never happened before or is the best of its kind so far.

unpredictable
adjective If someone or something is unpredictable, you never know how they will behave or react.

unprepared
adjective If you are unprepared for something, you are not ready for it and are therefore surprised or at a disadvantage when it happens.

unproductive
adjective not producing anything

A B C D E F G H I J K L M N O P Q R S T U V W X Y Z

793

A
B
C
D
E
F
G
H
I
J
K
L
M
N
O
P
Q
R
S
T
U
V
W
X
Y
Z

useful.
≡ fruitless, useless

unqualified
ADJECTIVE **1** having no qualifications
or not having the right
qualifications for a particular job EG
dangers posed by unqualified doctors.
2 total EG *an unqualified success.*

unquestionable
ADJECTIVE so obviously true or real
that nobody can doubt it EG *His
devotion is unquestionable.*
unquestionably ADVERB

unravel unravels unravelling
unravelled
VERB **1** If you unravel something
such as a twisted and knotted piece
of string, you unwind it so that it is
straight. **2** If you unravel a mystery,
you work out the answer to it.
▥ from Dutch *ravelen* meaning 'to
unpick'

unreal
ADJECTIVE so strange that you find it
difficult to believe.

unrealistic
ADJECTIVE **1** An unrealistic person
does not face the truth about
something or deal with it in a
practical way. **2** Something
unrealistic is not true to life EG *an
unrealistic picture.*

unreasonable
ADJECTIVE unfair and difficult to deal
with or justify EG *an unreasonable
request.*
unreasonably ADVERB

unrelated
ADJECTIVE Things that are unrelated
have no connection with each
other.

unrelenting
ADJECTIVE continuing in a
determined way without caring
about any hurt that is caused EG
unrelenting criticism.

unreliable
ADJECTIVE If people, machines, or
methods are unreliable, you cannot
rely on them.

unremitting
ADJECTIVE continuing without
stopping.

unrest
NOUN If there is unrest, people are
angry and dissatisfied.

unrivalled
ADJECTIVE better than anything else
of its kind EG *an unrivalled range of
health and beauty treatments.*

unroll unrolls unrolling unrolled
VERB If you unroll a roll of cloth or
paper, you open it up and make it
flat.

unruly
ADJECTIVE difficult to control or
organize EG *unruly children... unruly
hair.*

unsatisfactory
ADJECTIVE not good enough.

unsaturated
ADJECTIVE Unsaturated oils and fats
are made mainly from vegetable
fats and are considered to be
healthier than saturated oils.

unscathed
ADJECTIVE not injured or harmed as a
result of a dangerous experience.

unscrew unscrews unscrewing
unscrewed
VERB If you unscrew something, you
remove it by turning it or by
removing the screws that are
holding it.

unscrupulous
ADJECTIVE willing to behave
dishonestly in order to get what
you want.

unseemly
ADJECTIVE Unseemly behaviour is not
suitable for a particular situation
and shows a lack of control and
good manners EG *an unseemly
squabble.*

unseen
ADJECTIVE You use 'unseen' to
describe things that you cannot see
or have not seen.

unsettle unsettles unsettling
unsettled

VERB If something unsettles you, it makes you restless or worried.

unshakable or **unshakeable**
ADJECTIVE An unshakable belief is so strong that it cannot be destroyed.

unsightly
ADJECTIVE very ugly EG *an unsightly scar.*

unskilled
ADJECTIVE Unskilled work does not require any special training.

unsolicited
ADJECTIVE given or happening without being asked for.

unsound
ADJECTIVE **1** If a conclusion or method is unsound, it is based on ideas that are likely to be wrong. **2** An unsound building is likely to collapse.

unspeakable
ADJECTIVE very unpleasant.

unspecified
ADJECTIVE You say that something is unspecified when you are not told exactly what it is EG *It was being stored in some unspecified place.*

unspoken
ADJECTIVE An unspoken wish or feeling is one that is not mentioned to other people.

unstable
ADJECTIVE **1** likely to change suddenly and create difficulty or danger EG *The political situation in Moscow is unstable.* **2** not firm or fixed properly and likely to wobble or fall.

unsteady
ADJECTIVE **1** having difficulty in controlling the movement of your legs or hands EG *unsteady on her feet.* **2** not held or fixed securely and likely to fall over.
unsteadily ADVERB

unstuck
ADJECTIVE If something comes unstuck, it becomes separated from the thing that it was stuck to.

unsuccessful
ADJECTIVE If you are unsuccessful,

you do not succeed in what you are trying to do.
unsuccessfully ADVERB

unsuitable
ADJECTIVE not right or appropriate for a particular purpose.
unsuitably ADVERB

unsuited
ADJECTIVE not appropriate for a particular task or situation EG *He's totally unsuited to the job.*

unsung
ADJECTIVE You use 'unsung' to describe someone who is not appreciated or praised for their good work EG *George is the unsung hero of the club.*
🏛 from the custom of celebrating in song the exploits of heroes

unsure
ADJECTIVE uncertain or doubtful.

unsuspecting
ADJECTIVE having no idea of what is happening or going to happen EG *His horse escaped and collided with an unsuspecting cyclist.*

untangle untangles untangling untangled
VERB If you untangle something that is twisted together, you undo the twists.

untenable
ADJECTIVE; A FORMAL WORD A theory, argument, or position that is untenable cannot be successfully defended.

unthinkable
ADJECTIVE so shocking or awful that you cannot imagine it to be true.

untidy untidier untidiest
ADJECTIVE not neat or well arranged.

untie unties untying untied
VERB If you untie something, you undo the knots in the string or rope around it.

until
PREPOSITION OR CONJUNCTION **1** If something happens until a particular time, it happens before that time and stops at that time EG

A B C D E F G H I J K L M N O P Q R S T U V W X Y Z

A B C D E F G H I J K L M N O P Q R S T U V W X Y Z

The shop stayed open until midnight... She waited until her husband was asleep. **2** If something does not happen until a particular time, it does not happen before that time and only starts happening at that time EG *It didn't rain until the middle of the afternoon... It was not until they arrived that they found out who he was.*

untimely

ADJECTIVE happening too soon or sooner than expected EG *his untimely death.*

unto

PREPOSITION; AN OLD-FASHIONED WORD Unto means the same as to EG *Nation shall speak peace unto nation.*

untold

ADJECTIVE You use 'untold' to emphasize how great or extreme something is EG *The island possessed untold wealth.*

untouched

ADJECTIVE **1** not changed, moved, or damaged EG *a small village untouched by tourism.* **2** If a meal is untouched, none of it has been eaten.

untoward

ADJECTIVE unexpected and causing difficulties EG *no untoward problems.*

untrue

ADJECTIVE not true.

unused

ADJECTIVE **1** *Said* "un-**yoozd**" not yet used. **2** *Said* "un-**yoost**" If you are unused to something, you have not often done or experienced it.

unusual

ADJECTIVE Something that is unusual does not occur very often.
unusually ADVERB
▤ exceptional, extraordinary, rare

unveil unveils unveiling unveiled

VERB When someone unveils a new statue or plaque, they draw back a curtain that is covering it.

unwarranted

ADJECTIVE; A FORMAL WORD not justified or not deserved EG *unwarranted fears.*

unwelcome

ADJECTIVE not wanted EG *an unwelcome visitor... unwelcome news.*

unwell

ADJECTIVE If you are unwell, you are ill.

unwieldy

ADJECTIVE difficult to move or carry because of being large or an awkward shape.

unwilling

ADJECTIVE If you are unwilling to do something, you do not want to do it.
unwillingly ADVERB
▤ averse, loath, reluctant

unwind unwinds unwinding unwound

VERB **1** When you unwind after working hard, you relax. **2** If you unwind something that is wrapped round something else, you undo it.

unwise

ADJECTIVE foolish or not sensible.

unwitting

ADJECTIVE Unwitting describes someone who becomes involved in something without realizing what is really happening EG *her unwitting victims.*
unwittingly ADVERB

unworthy

ADJECTIVE; A FORMAL WORD Someone who is unworthy of something does not deserve it.

unwrap unwraps unwrapping unwrapped

VERB When you unwrap something, you take off the paper or covering around it.

unwritten

ADJECTIVE An unwritten law is one which is generally understood and accepted without being officially laid down.

up

ADVERB OR PREPOSITION **1** towards or in a higher place EG *He ran up the stairs... high up in the mountains.* **2** towards or in the north EG *I'm flying up to Darwin.* ▶ PREPOSITION **3** If you go up a road or river, you go along it. **4** You use 'up to' to say how large something can be or what level it has reached EG *traffic jams up to 15 kilometres long*. **5** AN INFORMAL USE If someone is up to something, they are secretly doing something they should not be doing. **6** If it is up to someone to do something, it is their responsibility. ▶ ADJECTIVE **7** If you are up, you are not in bed. **8** If a period of time is up, it has come to an end. ▶ ADVERB **9** If an amount of something goes up, it increases.

up-and-coming
ADJECTIVE Up-and-coming people are likely to be successful.

upbringing
NOUN Your upbringing is the way that your parents have taught you to behave.

update updates updating updated
VERB If you update something, you make it more modern or add new information to it EG *He had failed to update his will*.

upgrade upgrades upgrading upgraded
VERB If a person or their job is upgraded, they are given more responsibility or status and usually more money.

upheaval upheavals
NOUN a big change which causes a lot of trouble.

uphill
ADVERB **1** If you go uphill, you go up a slope. ▶ ADJECTIVE **2** An uphill task requires a lot of effort and determination.

uphold upholds upholding upheld
VERB If someone upholds a law or a decision, they support and maintain it.

upholstery
NOUN Upholstery is the soft covering on chairs and sofas that makes them comfortable.

upkeep

NOUN The upkeep of something is the continual process and cost of keeping it in good condition.

upland uplands
ADJECTIVE **1** An upland area is an area of high land. ▶ NOUN **2** Uplands are areas of high land.

uplifting
ADJECTIVE making you feel happy.

up-market
ADJECTIVE sophisticated and expensive.

upon
PREPOSITION **1** A FORMAL USE Upon means on EG *I stood upon the stair*. **2** You use 'upon' when mentioning an event that is immediately followed by another EG *Upon entering the hall he took a quick glance round*. **3** If an event is upon you, it is about to happen EG *The football season is upon us once more*.

upper uppers
ADJECTIVE **1** referring to something that is above something else, or the higher part of something EG *the upper arm*. ▶ NOUN **2** the top part of a shoe.

upper class upper classes
NOUN The upper classes are people who belong to a very wealthy or aristocratic group in a society.

uppermost
ADJECTIVE OR ADVERB **1** on top or in the highest position EG *the uppermost leaves... Lay your arms beside your body with the palms turned uppermost*. ▶ ADJECTIVE **2** most important EG *His family is now uppermost in his mind*.

upright
ADJECTIVE OR ADVERB **1** standing or sitting up straight, rather than bending or lying down. **2** behaving in a very respectable and moral way.

uprising uprisings
NOUN If there is an uprising, a large group of people begin fighting against the existing government to bring about political changes.

A
B
C
D
E
F
G
H
I
J
K
L
M
N
O
P
Q
R
S
T
U
V
W
X
Y
Z

uproar

NOUN If there is uproar or an uproar, there is a lot of shouting and noise, often because people are angry.

📖 from Dutch *oproer* meaning 'revolt'

🟰 commotion, furore, pandemonium

uproot uproots uprooting uprooted

VERB 1 If someone is uprooted, they have to leave the place where they have lived for a long time. 2 If a tree is uprooted, it is pulled out of the ground.

upset upsets upsetting upset

ADJECTIVE 1 unhappy and disappointed. ▶ VERB 2 If something upsets you, it makes you feel worried or unhappy. 3 If you upset something, you turn it over or spill it accidentally. ▶ NOUN 4 A stomach upset is a slight stomach illness caused by an infection or by something you have eaten.

upshot

NOUN The upshot of a series of events is the final result.

upside down

ADJECTIVE OR ADVERB the wrong way up.

upstage upstages upstaging upstaged

VERB If someone upstages you, they draw people's attention away from you by being more attractive or interesting.

upstairs

ADVERB 1 If you go upstairs in a building, you go up to a higher floor. ▶ NOUN 2 The upstairs of a building is its upper floor or floors.

upstart upstarts

NOUN someone who has risen too quickly to an important position and are too arrogant.

upstream

ADVERB towards the source of a river EG *They made their way upstream.*

upsurge

NOUN An upsurge of something is a sudden large increase in it.

uptake

NOUN You can say that someone is quick on the uptake if they understand things quickly.

📖 from Scottish *uptake* meaning 'to understand'

uptight

ADJECTIVE; AN INFORMAL WORD tense or annoyed.

up-to-date

ADJECTIVE 1 being the newest thing of its kind. 2 having the latest information.

up-to-the-minute

ADJECTIVE Up-to-the-minute information is the latest available information.

upturn upturns

NOUN an improvement in a situation.

upturned

ADJECTIVE 1 pointing upwards EG *rain splashing down on her upturned face.* 2 upside down EG *an upturned bowl.*

upwards

ADVERB 1 towards a higher place EG *People stared upwards and pointed.* 2 to a higher level or point on a scale EG *The world population is rocketing upwards.*

upward ADJECTIVE

uranium

Said "yoo-ray-nee-um" NOUN Uranium is a radioactive metal used to produce nuclear energy and weapons.

Uranus

NOUN Uranus is the planet in the solar system which is seventh from the sun.

📖 named after the Greek god *Ouranos* who ruled the universe

urban

ADJECTIVE relating to a town or city EG *urban development.*

urbane

ADJECTIVE well-mannered, and comfortable in social situations.

Urdu

Said "**oor**-doo" NOUN Urdu is the official language of Pakistan. It is also spoken by many people in India.

urge urges urging urged
NOUN **1** If you have an urge to do something, you have a strong wish to do it. ▶ VERB **2** If you urge someone to do something, you try hard to persuade them to do it.
◼ (sense 1) compulsion, desire, impulse
◼ (sense 2) beg, implore

urgent
ADJECTIVE needing to be dealt with as soon as possible.
urgently ADVERB, **urgency** NOUN
◼ crucial, pressing

urinal urinals
Said "yoor-**rye**-nl" NOUN a bowl or trough fixed to the wall in a men's public toilet for men to urinate in.

urinate urinates urinating urinated
Said "**yoor**-rin-ate" VERB When you urinate, you go to the toilet and get rid of urine from your body.

urine
Said "**yoor**-rin" NOUN Urine is the waste liquid that you get rid of from your body when you go to the toilet.

urn urns
NOUN a decorated container, especially one that is used to hold the ashes of a person who has been cremated.

us
PRONOUN A speaker or writer uses 'us' to refer to himself or herself and one or more other people EG *Why don't you tell us?*

US or **USA**
an abbreviation for 'United States of America'.

usage
NOUN **1** Usage is the degree to which something is used, or the way in which it is used. **2** Usage is also the way in which words are actually used EG *The terms soon entered common usage.*

use uses using used
VERB **1** If you use something, you do something with it in order to do a job or achieve something EG *May I use your phone?* **2** If you use someone, you take advantage of them by making them do things for you. ▶ NOUN **3** The use of something is the act of using it EG *the use of force.* **4** If you have the use of something, you have the ability or permission to use it. **5** If you find a use for something, you find a purpose for it.
usable or **useable** ADJECTIVE, **user** NOUN
◼ (sense 1) apply, employ, utilize
◼ (sense 3) application, employment, usage

used
VERB **1** *Said* "yoost" Something that used to be done or used to be true was done or was true in the past.
▶ PHRASE **2** If you are **used to** something, you are familiar with it and have often experienced it.
▶ ADJECTIVE **3** *Said* "yoozd" A used object has had a previous owner.

useful
ADJECTIVE If something is useful, you can use it in order to do something or to help you in some way.
usefully ADVERB, **usefulness** NOUN

useless
ADJECTIVE **1** If something is useless, you cannot use it because it is not suitable or helpful. **2** If a course of action is useless, it will not achieve what is wanted.

usher ushers ushering ushered
VERB **1** If you usher someone somewhere, you show them where to go by going with them. ▶ NOUN **2** a person who shows people where to sit at a wedding or a concert.

USSR
an abbreviation for 'Union of Soviet Socialist Republics', a country which was made up of a

lot of smaller countries including Russia, but which is now broken up.

usual
ADJECTIVE **1** happening, done, or used most often EG *his usual seat.* ▶ PHRASE **2** If you do something as usual, you do it in the way that you normally do it.
usually ADVERB
🔲 (sense 1) customary, normal, regular

usurp usurps usurping usurped
*Said "yoo-**zerp**"* VERB; A FORMAL WORD If someone usurps another person's job or title they take it when they have no right to do so.

ute utes
Said "yoot" NOUN; AN INFORMAL WORD In Australian and New Zealand English, a utility truck.

utensil utensils
*Said "yoo-**ten**-sil"* NOUN Utensils are tools EG *cooking utensils.*
🏛 from Latin *utensilis* meaning 'available for use'

uterus uteruses
Said "yoo-ter-russ" NOUN; A FORMAL WORD A woman's uterus is her womb.

utility utilities
NOUN **1** The utility of something is its usefulness. **2** a service, such as water or gas, that is provided for everyone.

utility truck utility trucks
NOUN In Australian and New Zealand English, a small motor vehicle with an open body and low sides.

utilize utilizes utilizing utilized; also spelt **utilise**
VERB; A FORMAL WORD To utilize something is to use it.
utilization NOUN

utmost
ADJECTIVE used to emphasize a particular quality EG *I have the utmost respect for Richard.*

utter utters uttering uttered
VERB **1** When you utter sounds or words, you make or say them. ▶ ADJECTIVE **2** Utter means complete or total EG *scenes of utter chaos.*
utterly ADVERB

utterance utterances
NOUN something that is said EG *his first utterance.*

v

an abbreviation for **versus**.

vacant

ADJECTIVE **1** If something is vacant, it is not occupied or being used. **2** If a job or position is vacant, no-one holds it at present. **3** A vacant look suggests that someone does not understand something or is not very intelligent.

vacancy NOUN, **vacantly** ADVERB

vacate vacates vacating vacated

VERB; A FORMAL WORD If you vacate a room or job, you leave it and it becomes available for someone else.

vacation vacations

NOUN **1** the period between academic terms at a university or college EG *the summer vacation.* **2** a holiday.

vaccinate vaccinates vaccinating vaccinated

Said "**vak-sin-ate**" VERB To vaccinate someone means to give them a vaccine, usually by injection, to protect them against a disease.

vaccination NOUN

vaccine vaccines

Said "**vak-seen**" NOUN a substance made from the germs that cause a disease and is given to people to make them immune to that disease.

📖 from Latin *vacca* meaning 'cow', because smallpox vaccine is based on cowpox, a disease of cows

vacuum vacuums vacuuming vacuumed

Said "**vak-yoom**" NOUN **1** a space containing no air, gases, or other matter. ▸ VERB **2** If you vacuum something, you clean it using a vacuum cleaner.

vacuum cleaner vacuum cleaners

NOUN an electric machine which cleans by sucking up dirt.

vagina vaginas

Said "**vaj-jie-na**" NOUN A woman's vagina is the passage that connects her outer sex organs to her womb.

📖 from Latin *vagina* meaning 'sheath'

vagrant vagrants

NOUN a person who moves from place to place, and has no home or regular job.

vagrancy NOUN

vague vaguer vaguest

Said "**vayg**" ADJECTIVE **1** If something is vague, it is not expressed or explained clearly, or you cannot see or remember it clearly EG *vague statements.* **2** Someone looks or sounds vague if they are not concentrating or thinking clearly.

vaguely ADVERB, **vagueness** NOUN

◼ (sense 1) imprecise, indefinite, unclear

vain vainer vainest

ADJECTIVE **1** A vain action or attempt is one which is not successful EG *He made a vain effort to cheer her up.* **2** A vain person is very proud of their looks, intelligence, or other qualities. ▸ PHRASE **3** If you do something in vain, you do not succeed in achieving what you intend.

vainly ADVERB

vale vales

NOUN; A LITERARY WORD a valley.

valentine valentines

NOUN **1** Your valentine is someone you love and send a card to on Saint Valentine's Day, February 14th. **2** A valentine or a valentine card is the card you send to the person you love on Saint Valentine's Day.

📖 Saint Valentine was a 3rd century martyr

valet valets

Said "**val-lit**" or "**val-lay**" NOUN a male servant who is employed to look after another man, particularly caring for his clothes.

valiant
ADJECTIVE very brave.
valiantly ADVERB

valid
ADJECTIVE **1** Something that is valid is based on sound reasoning. **2** A valid ticket or document is one which is officially accepted.
validity NOUN

validate validates validating validated
VERB If something validates a statement or claim, it proves that it is true or correct.

valley valleys
NOUN a long stretch of land between hills, often with a river flowing through it.

valour
NOUN Valour is great bravery.

valuable valuables
ADJECTIVE **1** Something that is valuable has great value. ▸ PLURAL NOUN **2** Valuables are things that you own that cost a lot of money.
■ (sense 1) costly, expensive, precious

valuation valuations
NOUN a judgment about how much money something is worth or how good it is.

value values valuing valued
NOUN **1** The value of something is its importance or usefulness EG *information of great value.* **2** The value of something you own is the amount of money that it is worth. **3** The values of a group or a person are the moral principles and beliefs that they think are important EG *the values of liberty and equality.* ▸ VERB **4** If you value something, you think it is important and you appreciate it. **5** When experts value something, they decide how much money it is worth.
valued ADJECTIVE, **valuer** NOUN

valve valves
NOUN **1** a part attached to a pipe or tube which controls the flow of gas or liquid. **2** a small flap in your heart or in a vein which controls the flow and direction of blood.

vampire vampires
NOUN In horror stories, vampires are corpses that come out of their graves at night and suck the blood of living people.

van vans
NOUN a covered vehicle larger than a car but smaller than a lorry, used for carrying goods.

vandal vandals
NOUN someone who deliberately damages or destroys things, particularly public property.
vandalize or **vandalise** VERB, **vandalism** NOUN

vane vanes
NOUN a flat blade that is part of a mechanism for using the energy of the wind or water to drive a machine.

vanguard
Said "**van-gard**" NOUN If someone is in the vanguard of something, they are in the most advanced part of it.

vanilla
NOUN Vanilla is a flavouring for food such as ice cream, which comes from the pods of a tropical plant.

vanish vanishes vanishing vanished
VERB If something vanishes, it disappears or ceases to exist EG *The moon vanished behind a cloud.*

vanity
NOUN Vanity is a feeling of excessive pride about your looks or abilities.

vanquish vanquishes vanquishing vanquished
Said "**vang-kwish**" VERB; A LITERARY WORD To vanquish someone means to defeat them completely.

vapour
NOUN Vapour is a mass of tiny drops of water or other liquids in the air, which looks like mist.

variable variables
ADJECTIVE **1** Something that is variable is likely to change at any

time. ▶ NOUN **2** In any situation, a variable is something in it that can change. **3** In maths, a variable is a symbol such as x which can represent any value or any one of a set of values.

variability NOUN

variance

NOUN If one thing is at variance with another, the two seem to contradict each other.

variant variants

NOUN **1** A variant of something has a different form from the usual one, for example *gaol* is a variant of *jail*. ▶ ADJECTIVE **2** alternative or different.

variation variations

NOUN **1** a change from the normal or usual pattern EG *a variation of the same route*. **2** a change in level, amount, or quantity EG *a large variation in demand*.

varicose veins

PLURAL NOUN Varicose veins are swollen painful veins in the legs.

varied

ADJECTIVE of different types, quantities, or sizes.

variety varieties

NOUN **1** If something has variety, it consists of things which are not all the same. **2** A variety of things is a number of different kinds of them EG *a wide variety of readers*. **3** A variety of something is a particular type of it EG *a new variety of celery*. **4** Variety is a form of entertainment consisting of short unrelated acts, such as singing, dancing, and comedy.

▤ (sense 2) assortment, mixture, range

various

ADJECTIVE Various means of several different types EG *trees of various sorts.*

variously ADVERB

▤ different, miscellaneous, sundry

☑ You should avoid putting *different* after *various*: *the disease exists in various forms* not *various*

different forms.

varnish varnishes varnishing varnished

NOUN **1** a liquid which when painted onto a surface gives it a hard clear shiny finish. ▶ VERB **2** If you varnish something, you paint it with varnish.

vary varies varying varied

VERB **1** If things vary, they change EG *Weather patterns vary greatly*. **2** If you vary something, you introduce changes in it EG *Vary your routes as much as possible.*

varied ADJECTIVE

vascular

ADJECTIVE relating to tubes or ducts that carry fluids within animals or plants.

vase vases

NOUN a glass or china jar for flowers.

vasectomy vasectomies

Said "vas-**sek**-tom-ee" NOUN an operation to sterilize a man by cutting the tube that carries the sperm.

Vaseline

NOUN; A TRADEMARK Vaseline is a soft clear jelly made from petroleum and used as an ointment or as grease.

vast

ADJECTIVE extremely large.

vastly ADVERB, **vastness** NOUN

vat vats

NOUN a large container for liquids.

VAT

NOUN In Britain, VAT is a tax which is added to the costs of making or providing goods and services. VAT is an abbreviation for 'value-added tax'.

vault vaults vaulting vaulted

Rhymes with "**salt**" NOUN **1** a strong secure room, often underneath a building, where valuables are stored, or underneath a church where people are buried. **2** an arched roof, often found in churches. ▶ VERB **3** If you vault over something, you jump over it using your hands or a pole to help.

VCR

an abbreviation for 'video cassette recorder'.

VDU VDUs

NOUN a monitor screen attached to a computer or word processor. VDU is an abbreviation for 'visual display unit'.

veal

NOUN Veal is the meat from a calf.

Veda Vedas

Said "vay-da" NOUN an ancient sacred text of the Hindu religion; also these texts as a collection.
Vedic ADJECTIVE

veer veers veering veered

VERB If something which is moving veers in a particular direction, it suddenly changes course EG *The aircraft veered sharply to one side.*

vegan vegans

Said "vee-gn" NOUN someone who does not eat any food made from animal products, such as meat, eggs, cheese, or milk.

vegetable vegetables

NOUN 1 Vegetables are edible roots or leaves such as carrots or cabbage.
▶ ADJECTIVE 2 'Vegetable' is used to refer to any plants in contrast to animals or minerals EG *vegetable life*.
🏛 from Latin *vegetabilis* meaning 'enlivening'

vegetarian vegetarians

NOUN a person who does not eat meat, poultry, or fish.
vegetarianism NOUN

vegetation

NOUN Vegetation is the plants in a particular area.

vehement

Said "vee-im-ent" ADJECTIVE Someone who is vehement has strong feelings or opinions and expresses them forcefully EG *He wrote a letter of vehement protest.*
vehemence NOUN, **vehemently** ADVERB

vehicle vehicles

Said "vee-ik-kl" NOUN 1 a machine, often with an engine, used for transporting people or goods. 2 something used to achieve a particular purpose or as a means of expression EG *The play seemed an ideal vehicle for his music.*
vehicular ADJECTIVE

veil veils

Rhymes with "male" NOUN a piece of thin, soft cloth that women sometimes wear over their heads.

vein veins

Rhymes with "rain" NOUN 1 Your veins are the tubes in your body through which your blood flows to your heart. 2 Veins are the thin lines on leaves or on insects' wings. 3 A vein of a metal or a mineral is a layer of it in rock. 4 Something that is in a particular vein is in that style or mood EG *in a more serious vein.*

veld

Said "felt" NOUN The veld is flat high grassland in Southern Africa.

veldskoen veldskoens

Said "felt-skoon" NOUN In South Africa, a veldskoen is a tough ankle-length boot.

velocity

NOUN; A TECHNICAL WORD Velocity is the speed at which something is moving in a particular direction.

velvet

NOUN Velvet is a very soft material which has a thick layer of fine short threads on one side.
velvety ADJECTIVE
🏛 from Latin *villus* meaning 'shaggy hair'

vendetta vendettas

NOUN a long-lasting bitter quarrel which results in people trying to harm each other.

vending machine vending machines

NOUN a machine which provides things such as drinks or sweets when you put money in it.

vendor vendors

NOUN a person who sells something.

veneer

NOUN **1** You can refer to a superficial quality that someone has as a veneer of that quality EG *a veneer of calm.* **2** Veneer is a thin layer of wood or plastic used to cover a surface.

venerable

ADJECTIVE **1** A venerable person is someone you treat with respect because they are old and wise. **2** Something that is venerable is impressive because it is old or important historically.

venerate venerates venerating venerated

VERB; A FORMAL WORD If you venerate someone, you feel great respect for them.

veneration NOUN

vengeance

NOUN **1** Vengeance is the act of harming someone because they have harmed you. ▶ PHRASE **2** If something happens **with a vengeance**, it happens to a much greater extent than was expected EG *It began to rain again with a vengeance.*

venison

NOUN Venison is the meat from a deer.

from Latin *venatio* meaning 'hunting'

venom

NOUN **1** The venom of a snake, scorpion, or spider is its poison. **2** Venom is a feeling of great bitterness or spitefulness towards someone EG *He was glaring at me with venom.*

venomous ADJECTIVE

vent vents venting vented

NOUN **1** a hole in something through which gases and smoke can escape and fresh air can enter EG *air vents.* ▶ VERB **2** If you vent strong feelings, you express them EG *She wanted to vent her anger upon me.* ▶ PHRASE **3** If you **give vent to** strong feelings, you express them EG *Pamela gave vent to a lot of bitterness.*

ventilate ventilates ventilating ventilated

VERB To ventilate a room means to allow fresh air into it.

ventilated ADJECTIVE

ventilation

NOUN **1** Ventilation is the process of breathing air in and out of the lungs. **2** A ventilation system supplies fresh air into a building.

ventilator ventilators

NOUN a machine that helps people breathe when they cannot breathe naturally, for example if they are very ill.

ventriloquist ventriloquists

Said "ven-**trill**-o-kwist" NOUN an entertainer who can speak without moving their lips so that the words seem to come from a dummy.

ventriloquism NOUN

from Latin *venter* meaning 'belly' and *loqui* meaning 'to speak'

venture ventures venturing ventured

NOUN **1** something new which involves the risk of failure or of losing money EG *a successful venture in television films.* ▶ VERB **2** If you venture something such as an opinion, you say it cautiously or hesitantly because you are afraid it might be foolish or wrong EG *I would not venture to agree.* **3** If you venture somewhere that might be dangerous, you go there.

▬ (sense 1) enterprise, undertaking

venue venues

Said "**ven**-yoo" NOUN The venue for an event is the place where it will happen.

Venus

NOUN Venus is the planet in the solar system which is second from the sun.

named after the Roman goddess of love

veranda verandas

Said "ver-**ran**-da"; also spelt

A
B
C
D
E
F
G
H
I
J
K
L
M
N
O
P
Q
R
S
T
U
V
W
X
Y
Z

verandah
NOUN a platform with a roof that is attached to an outside wall of a house at ground level.

verb verbs
NOUN In grammar, a verb is a word that expresses actions and states, for example 'be', 'become', 'take', and 'run'.

What Is a Verb?

A verb is a word that describes an action or a state of being. Verbs are sometimes called "doing words".

Verbs of state indicate the way things are.
Robert is a Taurus.
Anna has one sister.

Verbs of action indicate specific events that happen, have happened or will happen.
Anna visits the dentist.
The man faxed his order.

Auxiliary verbs are used in combination with other verbs to allow the user to distinguish between different times, different degrees of completion, and different amounts of certainty.
Anna will visit the dentist.
The man is faxing his order.
They may talk for up to three hours.

A **phrasal verb** consists of a verb followed by either an adverb or a preposition. The two words taken together have a special meaning which could not be deduced from their literal meanings.
The car broke down again.
When did you take up croquet?

An **impersonal verb** is a verb that does not have a subject and is only used after *it* or *there*.
It rains here every day.

Modal Verbs

Can, could, may, might, must, should, would, and *ought* are called "modal verbs". They are usually used as auxiliary verbs to change the tone of the meaning of another verb.
I wonder if you can come.

Even when they are used on their own, they *suggest* another verb.
I certainly can. (i.e. I certainly can come)

There is no difference between the third person present and the other forms of the present tense. No form of the verb ends in -s.
I can speak German.
She can speak German.

These verbs do not have a present participle or a past participle.

The verb *could* may be used as the past tense of *can*.
I could speak German when I was younger.

You can talk about past time by using *could have, may have, might have, must have, should have, would have,* and *ought to have.*
We may have taken a wrong turning.
She must have thought I was stupid.

verbal
ADJECTIVE 1 You use 'verbal' to describe things connected with words and their use EG *verbal attacks on referees.* 2 'Verbal' describes things which are spoken rather than written EG *a verbal agreement.*
verbally ADVERB

verdict verdicts
NOUN 1 In a law court, a verdict is the decision which states whether a prisoner is guilty or not guilty. 2 If you give a verdict on something, you give your opinion after thinking about it.

verge verges verging verged
NOUN 1 The verge of a road is the narrow strip of grassy ground at the side. ▶ PHRASE 2 If you are **on the verge** of something, you are going to do it soon or it is likely to happen soon EG *on the verge of crying.* ▶ VERB 3 Something that verges on something else is almost the same as it EG *dark blue that verged on purple.*

verify verifies verifying verified
VERB If you verify something, you check that it is true EG *None of his statements could be verified.*
verifiable ADJECTIVE, **verification** NOUN

veritable
ADJECTIVE You use 'veritable' to emphasize that something is really true, even if it seems as if you are exaggerating EG *a veritable jungle of shops.*

vermin

PLURAL NOUN Vermin are small animals or insects, such as rats and cockroaches, which carry disease and damage crops.

vernacular vernaculars

*Said "ver-**nak**-yoo-lar"* NOUN The vernacular of a particular country or district is the language widely spoken there.

verruca verrucas

*Said "ver-**roo**-ka"* NOUN a small hard infectious growth rather like a wart, occurring on the sole of the foot.

versatile

ADJECTIVE If someone is versatile, they have many different skills.
versatility NOUN

verse verses

NOUN 1 Verse is another word for poetry. 2 one part of a poem, song, or chapter of the Bible.

versed

ADJECTIVE If you are versed in something, you know a lot about it.

version versions

NOUN 1 A version of something is a form of it in which some details are different from earlier or later forms EG *a cheaper version of the aircraft.* 2 Someone's version of an event is their personal description of what happened.

versus

PREPOSITION 'Versus' is used to indicate that two people or teams are competing against each other.

vertebra vertebrae

*Said "**ver**-tib-bra"* NOUN Vertebrae are the small bones which form a person's or animal's backbone.

vertebrate vertebrates

NOUN Vertebrates are any creatures which have a backbone.

vertical

ADJECTIVE Something that is vertical points straight up and forms a ninety-degree angle with the surface on which it stands.

vertically ADVERB

vertigo

NOUN Vertigo is a feeling of dizziness caused by looking down from a high place.

verve

NOUN Verve is lively and forceful enthusiasm.

very

ADJECTIVE OR ADVERB 1 'Very' is used before words to emphasize them EG *very bad dreams... the very end of the book.* ▶ PHRASE 2 You use **not very** to mean that something is the case only to a small degree EG *You're not very like your sister.*
■ (sense 1) extremely, greatly, really

vessel vessels

NOUN 1 a ship or large boat. 2 A LITERARY USE any bowl or container in which a liquid can be kept. 3 a thin tube along which liquids such as blood or sap move in animals and plants.

vest vests

NOUN a piece of underwear worn for warmth on the top half of the body.

vestige vestiges

*Said "**vest**-ij"* NOUN; A FORMAL WORD If there is not a vestige of something, then there is not even a little of it left EG *They have a vestige of strength left.*

vestry vestries

NOUN The vestry is the part of the church building where a priest or minister changes into their official clothes.

vet vets vetting vetted

NOUN 1 a doctor for animals. ▶ VERB 2 If you vet someone or something, you check them carefully to see if they are acceptable EG *He refused to let them vet his speeches.*

veteran veterans

NOUN 1 someone who has served in the armed forces, particularly during a war. 2 someone who has been involved in a particular activity for a long time EG *a veteran of 25 political campaigns*.

veterinary
Said "vet-er-in-ar-ee" ADJECTIVE
'Veterinary' is used to describe the work of a vet and the medical treatment of animals.
🔲 from Latin *veterinae* meaning 'animals used for pulling carts and ploughs'

veterinary surgeon veterinary surgeons
NOUN the same as a **vet**.

veto vetoes vetoing vetoed
VERB 1 If someone in authority vetoes something, they say no to it.
▶ NOUN 2 Veto is the right that someone in authority has to say no to something EG *Dr Baker has the power of veto*.

vexed
ADJECTIVE If you are vexed, you are annoyed, worried, or puzzled.

VHF
NOUN VHF is a range of high radio frequencies. VHF is an abbreviation for 'very high frequency'.

via
PREPOSITION 1 If you go to one place via another, you travel through that place to get to your destination EG *He drove directly from Bonn via Paris*. 2 Via also means done or achieved by making use of a particular thing or person EG *to follow proceedings via newspapers or television*.

viable
Said "vy-a-bl" ADJECTIVE Something that is viable is capable of doing what it is intended to do without extra help or financial support EG *a viable business*.
viability NOUN

viaduct viaducts
NOUN a long high bridge that carries a road or railway across a valley.
🔲 from Latin *via* meaning 'road' and *ducere* meaning 'to bring'

vibrant

ADJECTIVE Something or someone that is vibrant is full of life, energy, and enthusiasm.
vibrantly ADVERB, **vibrancy** NOUN

vibrate vibrates vibrating vibrated
VERB If something vibrates, it moves a tiny amount backwards and forwards very quickly.
vibration NOUN

vicar vicars
NOUN a priest in the Church of England.

vicarage vicarages
NOUN a house where a vicar lives.

vice vices
NOUN 1 a serious moral fault in someone's character, such as greed, or a weakness, such as smoking.
2 Vice is criminal activities connected with prostitution and pornography. 3 a tool with a pair of jaws that hold an object tightly while it is being worked on.

vice-
PREFIX 'Vice-' is used before a title or position to show that the holder is the deputy of the person with that title or position EG *vice-president*.

viceregal
ADJECTIVE 1 of or concerning a viceroy. 2 In Australia and New Zealand, viceregal means of or concerning a governor or governor-general.

viceroy viceroys
NOUN A viceroy is someone who has been appointed to govern a place as a representative of a monarch.

vice versa
'Vice versa' is used to indicate that the reverse of what you have said is also true EG *Wives criticize their husbands, and vice versa*.

vicinity
Said "vis-sin-it-ee" NOUN If something is in the vicinity of a place, it is in the surrounding or nearby area.

vicious

ADJECTIVE cruel and violent.
viciously ADVERB, **viciousness** NOUN

victim victims
NOUN someone who has been harmed or injured by someone or something.

victor victors
NOUN The victor in a fight or contest is the person who wins.

Victorian
ADJECTIVE **1** Victorian describes things that happened or were made during the reign of Queen Victoria. **2** Victorian also describes people or things connected with the state of Victoria in Australia.

victory victories
NOUN a success in a battle or competition.
victorious ADJECTIVE
■ conquest, triumph, win

video videos videoing videoed
NOUN **1** Video is the recording and showing of films and events using a video recorder, video tape, and a television set. **2** a sound and picture recording which can be played back on a television set. **3** a video recorder. ▶ VERB **4** If you video something, you record it on magnetic tape for later viewing.

video recorder video recorders
NOUN A video recorder or video cassette recorder is a machine for recording and playing back programmes from television.

vie vies vying vied
VERB; A FORMAL WORD If you vie with someone, you compete to do something sooner than or better than they do.

Vietnamese
Said "vyet-nam-**meez**" ADJECTIVE **1** belonging or relating to Vietnam. ▶ NOUN **2** someone who comes from Vietnam. **3** Vietnamese is the main language spoken in Vietnam.

view views viewing viewed
NOUN **1** Your views are your personal opinions EG *his political views.* **2** everything you can see from a particular place. ▶ VERB **3** If you view something in a particular way, you think of it in that way EG *They viewed me with contempt.* ▶ PHRASE **4** You use **in view of** to specify the main fact or event influencing your actions or opinions EG *He wore a lighter suit in view of the heat.* **5** If something is on view, it is being shown or exhibited to the public.
■ (sense 2) prospect, scene, vista

viewer viewers
NOUN Viewers are the people who watch television.

viewpoint viewpoints
NOUN **1** Your viewpoint is your attitude towards something. **2** a place from which you get a good view of an area or event.

vigil vigils
Said "**vij**-jil" NOUN a period of time, especially at night, when you stay quietly in one place, for example because you are making a political protest or praying.

vigilant
ADJECTIVE careful and alert to danger or trouble.

vigilante vigilantes
Said "vij-il-**ant**-ee" NOUN Vigilantes are unofficially organized groups of people who try to protect their community and catch and punish criminals.

vigorous
ADJECTIVE energetic or enthusiastic.
vigorously ADVERB, **vigour** NOUN

Viking Vikings
NOUN The Vikings were seamen from Scandinavia who attacked villages in parts of north-western Europe from the 8th to the 11th centuries.

vile viler vilest
ADJECTIVE unpleasant or disgusting EG *a vile accusation... a vile smell.*

villa villas
NOUN a house, especially a pleasant

A B C D E F G H I J K L M N O P Q R S T U V W X Y Z

A B C D E F G H I J K L M N O P Q R S T U V W X Y Z

holiday home in a country with a warm climate.

village villages
NOUN a collection of houses and other buildings in the countryside.
villager NOUN

villain villains
NOUN someone who harms others or breaks the law.
villainous ADJECTIVE, **villainy** NOUN
■ criminal, evildoer, rogue

vindicate vindicates vindicating vindicated
VERB; A FORMAL WORD If someone is vindicated, their views or ideas are proved to be right EG *My friend's instincts have been vindicated.*

vindictive
ADJECTIVE Someone who is vindictive is deliberately hurtful towards someone, often as an act of revenge.
vindictiveness NOUN

vine vines
NOUN a trailing or climbing plant which winds itself around and over a support, especially one which produces grapes.

vinegar
NOUN Vinegar is a sharp-tasting liquid made from sour wine, beer, or cider, which is used for salad dressing.
vinegary ADJECTIVE
▥ from French *vin* meaning 'wine' and *aigre* meaning 'sour'

vineyard vineyards
NOUN an area of land where grapes are grown.

vintage vintages
ADJECTIVE 1 A vintage wine is a good quality wine which has been stored for a number of years to improve its quality. 2 Vintage describes something which is the best or most typical of its kind EG *a vintage guitar.* 3 A vintage car is one made between 1918 and 1930. ▶ NOUN 4 a grape harvest of one particular year and the wine produced from it.

vinyl
NOUN Vinyl is a strong plastic used to make things such as furniture and floor coverings.

viola violas
Said "vee-oh-la" NOUN a musical instrument like a violin, but larger and with a lower pitch.

violate violates violating violated
VERB 1 If you violate an agreement, law, or promise, you break it. 2 If you violate someone's peace or privacy, you disturb it. 3 If you violate a place, especially a holy place, you treat it with disrespect or violence.
violation NOUN

violence
NOUN 1 Violence is behaviour which is intended to hurt or kill people. 2 If you do or say something with violence, you use a lot of energy in doing or saying it, often because you are angry.

violent
ADJECTIVE 1 If someone is violent, they try to hurt or kill people. 2 A violent event happens unexpectedly and with great force. 3 Something that is violent is said, felt, or done with great force.
violently ADVERB

violet violets
NOUN 1 a plant with dark purple flowers. ▶ NOUN OR ADJECTIVE 2 bluish purple.

violin violins
NOUN a musical instrument with four strings that is held under the chin and played with a bow.
violinist NOUN

VIP VIPs
NOUN VIPs are famous or important people. VIP is an abbreviation for 'very important person'.

viper vipers
NOUN Vipers are types of poisonous snakes.

virgin virgins
NOUN 1 someone who has never had

sexual intercourse. ▶ PROPER NOUN
2 The Virgin, or the Blessed Virgin,
is a name given to Mary, the
mother of Jesus Christ. ▶ ADJECTIVE
3 Something that is virgin is fresh
and unused EG *virgin land.*
virginity NOUN

virginal virginals
ADJECTIVE **1** Someone who is virginal
looks young and innocent.
2 Something that is virginal is fresh
and clean and looks as if it has
never been used. ▶ NOUN **3** a
keyboard instrument popular in
the 16th and 17th centuries.

Virgo
NOUN Virgo is the sixth sign of the
zodiac, represented by a girl. People
born between August 23rd and
September 22nd are born under
this sign.

virile
ADJECTIVE A virile man has all the
qualities that a man is traditionally
expected to have, such as strength,
forcefulness, and sexuality.
virility NOUN

virtual
Said "**vur**-tyool" ADJECTIVE Virtual
means that something has all the
characteristics of a particular thing,
but it is not formally recognized as
being that thing EG *The country is in
a virtual state of war.*
virtually ADVERB

virtual reality
NOUN Virtual reality is a situation or
setting that has been created by a
computer and that looks real to the
person using it.

virtue virtues
NOUN **1** Virtue is thinking and doing
what is morally right and avoiding
what is wrong. **2** a good quality in
someone's character. **3** A virtue of
something is an advantage EG *the
virtue of neatness.* ▶ A FORMAL PHRASE
4 By virtue of means because of EG
*The article stuck in my mind by virtue
of one detail.*
▤ (sense 1) goodness, integrity,

morality

virtuoso virtuosos or virtuosi
Said "vur-tyoo-oh-zoh" NOUN
someone who is exceptionally
good at something, particularly
playing a musical instrument.
▥ from Italian *virtuoso* meaning
'skilled'

virtuous
ADJECTIVE behaving with or showing
moral virtue.
▤ good, moral, upright

virus viruses
Said "**vie**-russ" NOUN **1** a kind of
germ that can cause disease. **2** a
program that alters or damages the
information stored in a computer
system.
viral ADJECTIVE

visa visas
NOUN an official stamp, usually put
in your passport, that allows you to
visit a particular country.

viscount viscounts
Said "**vie**-kount" NOUN a British
nobleman.
viscountess NOUN

Vishnu
PROPER NOUN Vishnu is a Hindu god
and is one of the Trimurti.

visibility
NOUN You use 'visibility' to say how
far or how clearly you can see in
particular weather conditions.

visible
ADJECTIVE **1** able to be seen.
2 noticeable or evident EG *There was
little visible excitement.*
visibly ADVERB

vision visions
NOUN **1** Vision is the ability to see
clearly. **2** a mental picture, in
which you imagine how things
might be different EG *the vision of a
possible future.* **3** Vision is also
imaginative insight EG *a total lack of
vision and imagination.* **4** an unusual
experience that you have, in which
you see things that other people
cannot see, as a result of madness,

visionary NOUN OR ADJECTIVE divine inspiration, or taking drugs.

visit visits visiting visited
VERB **1** If you visit someone, you go to see them and spend time with them. **2** If you visit a place, you go to see it. ▶ NOUN **3** a trip to see a person or place.
visitor NOUN

visor visors
Said "vie-zor" NOUN a transparent movable shield attached to a helmet, which can be pulled down to protect the eyes or face.

visual
ADJECTIVE relating to sight EG *visual problems*.

visualize visualizes visualizing visualized
Said "viz-yool-eyes"; also spelt **visualise**
VERB If you visualize something, you form a mental picture of it.

vital
ADJECTIVE **1** necessary or very important EG *vital evidence*. **2** energetic, exciting, and full of life EG *an active and vital life outside school*.
vitally ADVERB
◪ (sense 1) essential, necessary

vitality
NOUN People who have vitality are energetic and lively.

vitamin vitamins
NOUN Vitamins are organic compounds which you need in order to remain healthy. They occur naturally in food.

vitriolic
ADJECTIVE; A FORMAL WORD Vitriolic language or behaviour is full of bitterness and hate.

vivacious
Said "viv-vay-shuss" ADJECTIVE A vivacious person is attractively lively and high-spirited.
vivacity NOUN

vivid
ADJECTIVE very bright in colour or clear in detail EG *vivid red paint... vivid memories*.
vividly ADVERB, **vividness** NOUN
◪ intense, powerful

vivisection
NOUN Vivisection is the act of cutting open living animals for medical research.

vixen vixens
NOUN a female fox.

vocabulary vocabularies
NOUN **1** Someone's vocabulary is the total number of words they know in a particular language. **2** The vocabulary of a language is all the words in it.

vocal
ADJECTIVE You say that someone is vocal if they express their opinions strongly and openly.

vocation vocations
NOUN **1** a strong wish to do a particular job, especially one which involves serving other people. **2** a profession or career.

vocational
ADJECTIVE 'Vocational' is used to describe the skills needed for a particular job or profession EG *vocational training*.

vociferous
Said "voe-sif-fer-uss" ADJECTIVE; A FORMAL WORD Someone who is vociferous speaks a lot, or loudly, because they want to make a point strongly EG *vociferous critics*.
vociferously ADVERB

vodka vodkas
NOUN a strong clear alcoholic drink which originally came from Russia.
▥ from Russian *vodka* meaning 'little water'

vogue
Said "vohg" PHRASE If something is **the vogue** or **in vogue**, it is fashionable and popular EG *Colour photographs became the vogue*.

voice voices voicing voiced
NOUN **1** Your voice is the sounds produced by your vocal cords, or

the ability to make such sounds.
▶ VERB **2** If you voice an opinion or an emotion, you say what you think or feel EG *A range of opinions were voiced.*

void voids
NOUN **1** a situation which seems empty because it has no interest or excitement EG *Cats fill a very large void in your life.* **2** a large empty hole or space EG *His feet dangled in the void.*

volatile
ADJECTIVE liable to change often and unexpectedly EG *The situation at work is volatile.*

volcanic
ADJECTIVE A volcanic region has many volcanoes or was created by volcanoes.

volcano volcanoes
NOUN a hill with an opening through which lava, gas, and ash burst out from inside the earth onto the surface.
🔳 named after *Vulcan*, the Roman god of fire

vole voles
NOUN a small mammal like a mouse with a short tail, which lives in fields and near rivers.

volition
NOUN; A FORMAL WORD If you do something of your own volition, you do it because you have decided for yourself, without being persuaded by others EG *He attended of his own volition.*

volley volleys
NOUN **1** A volley of shots or gunfire is a lot of shots fired at the same time. **2** In tennis, a volley is a stroke in which the player hits the ball before it bounces.

volleyball
NOUN Volleyball is a game in which two teams hit a large ball back and forth over a high net with their hands. The ball is not allowed to bounce on the ground.

volt volts

NOUN a unit used to measure the force of an electric current.

voltage voltages
NOUN The voltage of an electric current is its force measured in volts.

volume volumes
NOUN **1** The volume of something is the amount of space it contains or occupies. **2** The volume of something is also the amount of it that there is EG *a large volume of letters.* **3** The volume of a radio, TV, or record player is the strength of the sound that it produces. **4** a book, or one of a series of books.

voluminous
Said "vol-loo-min-uss" ADJECTIVE very large or full in size or quantity EG *voluminous skirts.*

voluntary
ADJECTIVE **1** Voluntary actions are ones that you do because you choose to do them and not because you have been forced to do them. **2** Voluntary work is done by people who are not paid for what they do.
voluntarily ADVERB

volunteer volunteers volunteering volunteered
NOUN **1** someone who does work for which they are not paid EG *a volunteer for Greenpeace.* **2** someone who chooses to join the armed forces, especially during wartime.
▶ VERB **3** If you volunteer to do something, you offer to do it rather than being forced into it. **4** If you volunteer information, you give it without being asked.

voluptuous
Said "vol-lupt-yoo-uss" ADJECTIVE A voluptuous woman has a figure which is considered to be sexually exciting.
voluptuously ADVERB, **voluptuousness** NOUN

vomit vomits vomiting vomited
VERB **1** If you vomit, food and drink comes back up from your stomach and out through your mouth.

▶ NOUN **2** Vomit is partly digested food and drink that has come back up from someone's stomach and out through their mouth.

voodoo

NOUN Voodoo is a form of magic practised in the Caribbean, especially in Haiti.

vote votes voting voted

NOUN **1** Someone's vote is their choice in an election, or at a meeting where decisions are taken. **2** When a group of people have a vote, they make a decision by allowing each person in the group to say what they would prefer. **3** In an election, the vote is the total number of people who have made their choice EG *the average Liberal vote.* **4** If people have the vote, they have the legal right to vote in an election. ▶ VERB **5** When people vote, they indicate their choice or opinion, usually by writing on a piece of paper or by raising their hand. **6** If you vote that a particular thing should happen, you are suggesting it should happen EG *I vote that we all go to Holland.*
voter NOUN

vouch vouches vouching vouched

VERB **1** If you say that you can vouch for something, you mean that you have evidence from your own experience that it is true or correct. **2** If you say that you can vouch for someone, you mean that you are sure that you can guarantee their good behaviour or support EG *Her employer will vouch for her.*

voucher vouchers

NOUN a piece of paper that can be used instead of money to pay for something.

vow vows vowing vowed

VERB **1** If you vow to do something, you make a solemn promise to do it EG *He vowed to do better in future.* ▶ NOUN **2** a solemn promise.

vowel vowels

NOUN a sound made without your tongue touching the roof of your mouth or your teeth, or one of the letters a, e, i, o, u, which represent such sounds.

voyage voyages

NOUN a long journey on a ship or in a spacecraft.
voyager NOUN

vulgar

ADJECTIVE **1** socially unacceptable or offensive EG *vulgar language.* **2** showing a lack of taste or quality EG *the most vulgar person who ever existed.*
vulgarity NOUN, **vulgarly** ADVERB

vulnerable

ADJECTIVE weak and without protection.
vulnerably ADVERB, **vulnerability** NOUN
≡ defenceless, susceptible, weak

vulture vultures

NOUN a large bird which lives in hot countries and eats the flesh of dead animals.

vying

the present participle of **vie**.

Ww Ww

wacky wackier wackiest
ADJECTIVE; AN INFORMAL WORD odd or crazy EG *wacky clothes*.

wad wads
NOUN 1 A wad of papers or banknotes is a thick bundle of them. 2 A wad of something is a lump of it EG *a wad of cotton wool*.

waddle waddles waddling waddled
VERB When a duck or a fat person waddles, they walk with short, quick steps, swaying slightly from side to side.

waddy waddies
NOUN a heavy, wooden club used by Australian Aborigines as a weapon in war.

wade wades wading waded
VERB 1 If you wade through water or mud, you walk slowly through it. 2 If you wade through a book or document, you spend a lot of time and effort reading it because you find it dull or difficult.

wader waders
NOUN Waders are long waterproof rubber boots worn by fishermen.

wafer wafers
NOUN 1 a thin, crisp, sweet biscuit often eaten with ice cream. 2 a thin disc of special bread used in the Christian service of Holy Communion.

waffle waffles waffling waffled
Said "wof-fl" VERB 1 When someone waffles, they talk or write a lot without being clear or without saying anything of importance. ▸ NOUN 2 Waffle is vague and lengthy speech or writing. 3 a thick, crisp pancake with squares marked on it often eaten with syrup poured over it.

waft wafts wafting wafted
Said "wahft" VERB If a sound or scent wafts or is wafted through the air, it moves gently through it.

wag wags wagging wagged
VERB 1 When a dog wags its tail, it shakes it repeatedly from side to side. 2 If you wag your finger, you move it repeatedly up and down.

wage wages waging waged
NOUN 1 A wage or wages is the regular payment made to someone each week for the work they do, especially for manual or unskilled work. ▸ VERB 2 If a person or country wages a campaign or war, they start it and carry it on over a period of time.

wager wagers
NOUN a bet.

wagon wagons; also spelt **waggon**
NOUN 1 a strong four-wheeled vehicle for carrying heavy loads, usually pulled by a horse or tractor. 2 Wagons are also the containers for freight pulled by a railway engine.

waif waifs
Said "wayf" NOUN a young, thin person who looks hungry and homeless.

wail wails wailing wailed
VERB 1 To wail is to cry loudly with sorrow or pain. ▸ NOUN 2 a long, unhappy cry.

waist waists
NOUN the middle part of your body where it narrows slightly above your hips.

waistcoat waistcoats
NOUN a sleeveless piece of clothing, often worn under a suit or jacket, which buttons up the front.

wait waits waiting waited
VERB 1 If you wait, you spend time, usually doing little or nothing, before something happens. 2 If something can wait, it is not urgent and can be dealt with later. 3 If you wait on people in a restaurant, it is your job to serve them food. ▸ NOUN 4 a period of

time before something happens.
▶ PHRASE **5** If you **can't wait** to do something, you are very excited and eager to do it.

waiter waiters
NOUN a man who works in a restaurant, serving people with food and drink.

waiting list waiting lists
NOUN a list of people who have asked for something which cannot be given to them immediately, for example medical treatment.

waitress waitresses
NOUN a woman who works in a restaurant, serving people with food and drink.

waive waives waiving waived
Said "**wave**" VERB If someone waives something such as a rule or a right, they decide not to insist on it being applied.

wake wakes waking woke woken
VERB **1** When you wake or when something wakes you, you become conscious again after being asleep. ▶ NOUN **2** The wake of a boat or other object moving in water is the track of waves it leaves behind it. **3** a gathering of people who have got together to mourn someone's death. ▶ PHRASE **4** If one thing follows **in the wake of** another, it follows it as a result of it, or in imitation of it EG *a project set up in the wake of last year's riots.*
■ (sense 1) awaken, rouse

wake up VERB **1** When you wake up or something wakes you up, you become conscious again after being asleep. **2** If you wake up to a dangerous situation, you become aware of it.

waken wakens wakening wakened
VERB; A LITERARY WORD When you waken someone, you wake them up.

walk walks walking walked
VERB **1** When you walk, you move along by putting one foot in front

of the other on the ground. **2** If you walk away with or walk off with something such as a prize, you win it or achieve it easily.
▶ NOUN **3** a journey made by walking EG *We'll have a quick walk.* **4** Your walk is the way you walk EG *his rolling walk.*

walk out VERB **1** If you walk out on someone, you leave them suddenly. **2** If workers walk out, they go on strike.

walkabout walkabouts
NOUN **1** an informal walk amongst crowds in a public place by royalty or by some other well-known person. **2** Walkabout is when an Australian Aborigine goes off to live and wander in the bush for a period of time.

walker walkers
NOUN a person who walks, especially for pleasure or to keep fit.

walking stick walking sticks
NOUN a wooden stick which people can lean on while walking.

Walkman
NOUN; A TRADEMARK a small cassette player with lightweight headphones, which people carry around so that they can listen to music while they are doing something like walking.

walk of life walks of life
NOUN The walk of life that you come from is the position you have in society and the kind of job you have.

walkover walkovers
NOUN; AN INFORMAL WORD a very easy victory in a competition or contest.

walkway walkways
NOUN a passage between two buildings for people to walk along.

wall walls
NOUN **1** one of the vertical sides of a building or a room. **2** a long, narrow vertical structure made of stone or brick that surrounds or divides an area of land. **3** a lining or membrane enclosing a bodily

cavity or structure EG *the wall of the womb*.

wallaby wallabies
NOUN an animal like a small kangaroo.
🔳 from *wolaba*, an Australian Aboriginal word

wallaroo wallaroos
NOUN a large, stocky kangaroo that lives in rocky or mountainous regions of Australia.

wallet wallets
NOUN a small, flat case made of leather or plastic, used for keeping paper money and sometimes credit cards.

wallop wallops walloping walloped
VERB; AN INFORMAL WORD If you wallop someone, you hit them very hard.

wallow wallows wallowing wallowed
VERB 1 If you wallow in an unpleasant feeling or situation, you allow it to continue longer than is reasonable or necessary because you are getting a kind of enjoyment from it EG *We're wallowing in misery*. 2 When an animal wallows in mud or water, it lies or rolls about in it slowly for pleasure.

wallpaper wallpapers
NOUN Wallpaper is thick coloured or patterned paper for pasting onto the walls of rooms in order to decorate them.

walnut walnuts
NOUN 1 an edible nut with a wrinkled shape and a hard, round, light-brown shell. 2 Walnut is wood from the walnut tree which is often used for making expensive furniture.
🔳 from Old English *walh-hnutu* meaning 'foreign nut'

walrus walruses
NOUN an animal which lives in the sea and which looks like a large seal with a tough skin, coarse whiskers, and two tusks.

waltz waltzes waltzing waltzed
NOUN 1 a dance which has a rhythm of three beats to the bar. ▶ VERB 2 If you waltz with someone, you dance a waltz with them. 3 AN INFORMAL USE If you waltz somewhere, you walk there in a relaxed and confident way.
🔳 from Old German *walzen* meaning 'to revolve'

wan
Rhymes with "on" ADJECTIVE pale and tired-looking.

wand wands
NOUN a long, thin rod that magicians wave when they are performing tricks and magic.

wander wanders wandering wandered
VERB 1 If you wander in a place, you walk around in a casual way. 2 If your mind wanders or your thoughts wander, you lose concentration and start thinking about other things.
wanderer NOUN
🔲 (sense 1) ramble, roam, stroll

wane wanes waning waned
VERB If a condition, attitude, or emotion wanes, it becomes gradually weaker.

wangle wangles wangling wangled
VERB; AN INFORMAL WORD If you wangle something that you want, you manage to get it by being crafty or persuasive.

want wants wanting wanted
VERB 1 If you want something, you feel a desire to have it or a need for it to happen. 2 AN INFORMAL USE If something wants doing, there is a need for it to be done EG *Her hair wants cutting*. 3 If someone is wanted, the police are searching for them EG *John was wanted for fraud*. ▶ NOUN 4 A FORMAL USE A want of something is a lack of it.

wanting
ADJECTIVE If you find something wanting or if it proves wanting, it

A
B
C
D
E
F
G
H
I
J
K
L
M
N
O
P
Q
R
S
T
U
V
W
X
Y
Z

is not as good in some way as you think it should be.

wanton

ADJECTIVE A wanton action deliberately causes unnecessary harm or waste EG *wanton destruction*.

war wars warring warred

NOUN **1** a period of fighting between countries or states when weapons are used and many people may be killed. **2** a competition between groups of people, or a campaign against something EG *a trade war... the war against crime*. ▶ VERB **3** When two countries war with each other, they are fighting a war against each other.

warring ADJECTIVE

▣ (sense 1) battle, fighting, hostilities

▣ (sense 3) battle, fight

waratah waratahs

Said "wor-ra-**tah**" NOUN an Australian shrub with dark green leaves and large clusters of crimson flowers.

warble warbles warbling warbled

VERB When a bird warbles, it sings pleasantly with high notes.

ward wards warding warded

NOUN **1** a room in a hospital which has beds for several people who need similar treatment. **2** an area or district which forms a separate part of a political constituency or local council. **3** A ward or a ward of court is a child who is officially put in the care of an adult or a court of law, because their parents are dead or because they need protection. ▶ VERB **4** If you ward off a danger or an illness, you do something to prevent it from affecting or harming you.

-ward or -wards

SUFFIX -ward and -wards form adverbs or adjectives that show the way something is moving or facing EG *homeward... westwards*.

warden wardens

NOUN **1** a person in charge of a

building or institution such as a youth hostel or prison. **2** an official who makes sure that certain laws or rules are obeyed in a particular place or activity EG *a traffic warden*.

warder warders

NOUN a person who is in charge of prisoners in a jail.

wardrobe wardrobes

NOUN **1** a tall cupboard in which you can hang your clothes. **2** Someone's wardrobe is their collection of clothes.

ware wares

NOUN **1** Ware is manufactured goods of a particular kind EG *kitchenware*. **2** Someone's wares are the things they sell, usually in the street or in a market.

warehouse warehouses

NOUN a large building where raw materials or manufactured goods are stored.

warfare

NOUN Warfare is the activity of fighting a war.

warhead warheads

NOUN the front end of a bomb or missile, where the explosives are carried.

warlock warlocks

NOUN a male witch.

warm warmer warmest; warms warming warmed

ADJECTIVE **1** Something that is warm has some heat, but not enough to be hot EG *a warm day*. **2** Warm clothes or blankets are made of a material which protects you from the cold. **3** Warm colours or sounds are pleasant and make you feel comfortable and relaxed. **4** A warm person is friendly and affectionate. ▶ VERB **5** If you warm something, you heat it up gently so that it stops being cold.

warmly ADVERB

warm up VERB If you warm up for an event or an activity, you practise or exercise gently to prepare for it.

warmth

NOUN **1** Warmth is a moderate amount of heat. **2** Someone who has warmth is friendly and affectionate.

warn warns warning warned

VERB **1** If you warn someone about a possible problem or danger, you tell them about it in advance so that they are aware of it EG *I warned him what it would be like.* **2** If you warn someone not to do something, you advise them not to do it, in order to avoid possible danger or punishment EG *I have warned her not to train for 10 days.*
■ (sense 1) alert, caution, notify
warn off VERB If you warn someone off, you tell them to go away or to stop doing something.

warning warnings

NOUN something said or written to tell people of a possible problem or danger.

warp warps warping warped

VERB **1** If something warps or is warped, it becomes bent, often because of the effect of heat or water. **2** If something warps someone's mind or character, it makes them abnormal or corrupt. **3** The warp in a piece of cloth is the stronger lengthwise threads.

warrant warrants warranting warranted

VERB **1** A FORMAL USE If something warrants a particular action, it makes the action seem necessary EG *no evidence to warrant a murder investigation.* ▶ NOUN **2** an official document which gives permission to the police to do something EG *a warrant for his arrest.*

warranty warranties

NOUN a guarantee EG *a three-year warranty.*

warren warrens

NOUN a group of holes under the ground connected by tunnels, which rabbits live in.

warrigal warrigals

Said "**wor**-rih-gl" NOUN **1** In Australian English, a dingo. **2** In Australian English, a wild horse or other wild creature. ▶ ADJECTIVE **3** In Australian English, wild or untamed.

warrior warriors

NOUN a fighting man or soldier, especially in former times.

warship warships

NOUN a ship built with guns and used for fighting in wars.

wart warts

NOUN a small, hard piece of skin which can grow on someone's face or hands.

wartime

NOUN Wartime is a period of time during which a country is at war.

wary warier wariest

ADJECTIVE cautious and on one's guard EG *Michelle is wary of marriage.*
warily ADVERB

was

a past tense of be.

wash washes washing washed

VERB **1** If you wash something, you clean it with water and soap. **2** If you wash, you clean yourself using soap and water. **3** If something is washed somewhere, it is carried there gently by water EG *The infant Arthur was washed ashore.* ▶ NOUN **4** The wash is all the clothes and bedding that are washed together at one time EG *a typical family's weekly wash.* **5** The wash in water is the disturbance and waves produced at the back of a moving boat. ▶ PHRASE **6** If you **wash your hands of** something, you refuse to have anything more to do with it.
wash up VERB **1** If you wash up, you wash the dishes, pans, and cutlery used in preparing and eating a meal. **2** If something is washed up on land, it is carried by a river or sea and left there EG *A body had been washed up on the beach.*

washer washers

NOUN **1** a thin, flat ring of metal or

plastic which is placed over a bolt before the nut is screwed on, so that it is fixed more tightly. **2** In Australian English, a small piece of towelling for washing yourself.

washing
NOUN Washing consists of clothes and bedding which need to be washed or are in the process of being washed and dried.

washing machine washing machines
NOUN a machine for washing clothes in.

washing-up
NOUN If you do the washing-up, you wash the dishes, pans, and cutlery which have been used in the cooking and eating of a meal.

wasp wasps
NOUN an insect with yellow and black stripes across its body, which can sting like a bee.

wastage
NOUN Wastage is loss and misuse of something EG *wastage of resources*.

waste wastes wasting wasted
VERB **1** If you waste time, money, or energy, you use too much of it on something that is not important or necessary. **2** If you waste an opportunity, you do not take advantage of it when it is available. **3** If you say that something is wasted on someone, you mean that it is too good, too clever, or too sophisticated for them EG *This book is wasted on us*. ▶ NOUN **4** If an activity is a waste of time, money, or energy, it is not important or necessary. **5** Waste is the use of more money or some other resource than is necessary. **6** Waste is also material that is no longer wanted, or material left over from a useful process EG *nuclear waste*. ▶ ADJECTIVE **7** unwanted and unusable in its present form EG *waste paper*. **8** Waste land is land which is not used or looked after by anyone.

▤ (sense 1) fritter away, misuse, squander
▤ (sense 5) misuse, squandering

waste away VERB If someone is wasting away, they are becoming very thin and weak because they are ill or not eating properly.

wasted
ADJECTIVE unnecessary EG *a wasted journey*.

wasteful
ADJECTIVE extravagant or causing waste by using something in a careless and inefficient way.
▤ extravagant, prodigal, spendthrift

wasteland wastelands
NOUN A wasteland is land which is of no use because it is infertile or has been misused.

wasting
ADJECTIVE A wasting disease is one that gradually reduces the strength and health of the body.

watch watches watching watched
NOUN **1** a small clock usually worn on a strap on the wrist. **2** a period of time during which a guard is kept over something. ▶ VERB **3** If you watch something, you look at it for some time and pay close attention to what is happening. **4** If you watch a situation, you pay attention to it or are aware of it EG *I had watched Jimmy's progress with interest*. **5** If you watch over someone or something, you care for them.

watch out VERB **1** If you watch out for something, you keep alert to see if it is near you EG *Watch out for more fog and ice*. **2** If you tell someone to watch out, you are warning them to be very careful.

watchdog watchdogs
NOUN **1** a dog used to guard property. **2** a person or group whose job is to make sure that companies do not act illegally or irresponsibly.

watchful
ADJECTIVE careful to notice

everything that is happening EG *the watchful eye of her father.*

watchman watchmen
NOUN a person whose job is to guard property.

water waters watering watered
NOUN **1** Water is a clear, colourless, tasteless, and odourless liquid that is necessary for all plant and animal life. **2** You use water or waters to refer to a large area of water, such as a lake or sea EG *the black waters of the lake.* ▶ VERB **3** If you water a plant or an animal, you give it water to drink. **4** If your eyes water, you have tears in them because they are hurting. **5** If your mouth waters, it produces extra saliva, usually because you think of or can smell something appetizing. **water down** VERB If you water something down, you make it weaker.

watercolour watercolours
NOUN **1** Watercolours are paints for painting pictures, which are diluted with water or put on the paper using a wet brush. **2** a picture which has been painted using watercolours.

watercress
NOUN Watercress is a small plant which grows in streams and pools. Its leaves taste hot and are eaten in salads.

waterfall waterfalls
NOUN A waterfall is water from a river or stream as it flows over the edge of a steep cliff in hills or mountains and falls to the ground below.

waterfront waterfronts
NOUN a street or piece of land next to an area of water such as a river or harbour.

watering can watering cans
NOUN a container with a handle and a long spout, which you use to water plants.

waterlogged
ADJECTIVE Land that is waterlogged is

so wet that the soil cannot contain any more water, so that some water remains on the surface of the ground.

watermelon watermelons
NOUN a large, round fruit which has a hard green skin and red juicy flesh.

waterproof waterproofs
ADJECTIVE **1** not letting water pass through EG *waterproof clothing.*
▶ NOUN **2** a coat which keeps water out.

watershed watersheds
NOUN an event or period which marks a turning point or the beginning of a new way of life EG *a watershed in European history.*

watersider watersiders
NOUN In Australian and New Zealand English, a person who loads and unloads the cargo from ships.

water-skiing
NOUN Water-skiing is the sport of skimming over the water on skis while being pulled by a boat.

water table water tables
NOUN The water table is the level below the surface of the ground at which water can be found.

watertight
ADJECTIVE **1** Something that is watertight does not allow water to pass through. **2** An agreement or an argument that is watertight has been so carefully put together that nobody should be able to find a fault in it.

waterway waterways
NOUN a canal, river, or narrow channel of sea which ships or boats can sail along.

waterworks
NOUN A waterworks is the system of pipes, filters, and tanks where the public supply of water is stored and cleaned, and from where it is distributed.

watery

ADJECTIVE **1** pale or weak EG *a watery smile*. **2** Watery food or drink contains a lot of water or is thin like water.

watt watts
Said "wot" NOUN a unit of measurement of electrical power.

wattle wattles
Said "wot-tl" NOUN an Australian acacia tree with spikes of brightly coloured flowers.

wave waves waving waved
VERB **1** If you wave your hand, you move it from side to side, usually to say hello or goodbye. **2** If you wave someone somewhere or wave them on, you make a movement with your hand to tell them which way to go. **3** If you wave something, you hold it up and move it from side to side EG *The doctor waved a piece of paper at him.* ▶ NOUN **4** a ridge of water on the surface of the sea caused by wind or by tides. **5** A wave is the form in which some types of energy such as heat, light, or sound travel through a substance. **6** A wave of sympathy, alarm, or panic is a steady increase in it which spreads through you or through a group of people. **7** an increase in a type of activity or behaviour EG *the crime wave.*
■ (sense 3) brandish, flourish

wavelength wavelengths
NOUN **1** the distance between the same point on two adjacent waves of energy. **2** the size of radio wave which a particular radio station uses to broadcast its programmes.

waver wavers wavering wavered
VERB **1** If you waver or if your confidence or beliefs waver, you are no longer as firm, confident, or sure in your beliefs EG *Ben has never wavered from his belief.* **2** If something wavers, it moves slightly EG *The gun did not waver in his hand.*

wavy wavier waviest
ADJECTIVE having waves or regular curves EG *wavy hair.*

wax waxes waxing waxed
NOUN **1** Wax is a solid, slightly shiny substance made of fat or oil and used to make candles and polish. **2** Wax is also the sticky yellow substance in your ears. ▶ VERB **3** If you wax a surface, you treat it or cover it with a thin layer of wax, especially to polish it. **4** A FORMAL USE If you wax eloquent, you talk in an eloquent way.

way ways
NOUN **1** A way of doing something is the manner of doing it EG *an excellent way of cooking meat.* **2** The ways of a person or group are their customs or their normal behaviour EG *Their ways are certainly different.* **3** The way you feel about something is your attitude to it or your opinion about it. **4** If you have a way with people or things, you are very skilful at dealing with them. **5** The way to a particular place is the route that you take to get there. **6** If you go or look a particular way, you go or look in that direction EG *She glanced the other way.* **7** If you divide something a number of ways, you divide it into that number of parts. **8** 'Way' is used with words such as 'little' or 'long' to say how far off in distance or time something is EG *They lived a long way away.* ▶ PHRASE **9** If something or someone is **in the way**, they prevent you from moving freely or seeing clearly. **10** You say **by the way** when adding something to what you are saying EG *By the way, I asked Brad to drop in.* **11** If you **go out of your way** to do something, you make a special effort to do it.
■ (sense 5) course, path, route

wayside
PHRASE If someone or something **falls by the wayside**, they fail in what they are trying to do, or become forgotten and ignored.

wayward

ADJECTIVE difficult to control and likely to change suddenly EG *your wayward husband*.

WC WCs

NOUN a toilet. WC is an abbreviation for 'water closet'.

we

PRONOUN A speaker or writer uses 'we' to refer to himself or herself and one or more other people EG *We are going to see Eddie*.

weak weaker weakest

ADJECTIVE 1 not having much strength EG *weak from lack of sleep*. 2 If something is weak, it is likely to break or fail EG *Russia's weak economy*. 3 If you describe someone as weak, you mean they are easily influenced by other people.

weakly ADVERB

▤ (sense 1) feeble, frail, puny

weaken weakens weakening weakened

VERB 1 If someone weakens something, they make it less strong or certain. 2 If someone weakens, they become less certain about something.

weakling weaklings

NOUN a person who lacks physical strength or who is weak in character or health.

weakness weaknesses

NOUN 1 Weakness is lack of moral or physical strength. 2 If you have a weakness for something, you have a great liking for it EG *a weakness for whisky*.

wealth

NOUN 1 Wealth is the large amount of money or property which someone owns. 2 A wealth of something is a lot of it EG *a wealth of information*.

▤ (sense 1) fortune, prosperity, riches

wealthy wealthier wealthiest

ADJECTIVE having a large amount of money, property, or other valuable things.

▤ affluent, rich, well-off

wean weans weaning weaned

VERB To wean a baby or animal is to start feeding it food other than its mother's milk.

weapon weapons

NOUN 1 an object used to kill or hurt people in a fight or war. 2 anything which can be used to get the better of an opponent EG *Surprise was his only weapon*.

weaponry NOUN

wear wears wearing wore worn

VERB 1 When you wear something such as clothes, make-up, or jewellery, you have them on your body or face. 2 If you wear a particular expression, it shows on your face. 3 If something wears, it becomes thinner or worse in condition. ▸ NOUN 4 You can refer to clothes that are suitable for a particular time or occasion as a kind of wear EG *beach wear*. 5 Wear is the amount or type of use that something has and which causes damage or change to it EG *signs of wear*.

wear down VERB If you wear people down, you weaken them by repeatedly doing something or asking them to do something.

wear off VERB If a feeling such as pain wears off, it gradually disappears.

wear out VERB When something wears out or when you wear it out, it is used so much that it becomes thin, weak, and no longer usable.

wear and tear

NOUN Wear and tear is the damage caused to something by normal use.

wearing

ADJECTIVE Someone or something that is wearing makes you feel extremely tired.

weary wearier weariest; wearies wearying wearied

ADJECTIVE 1 very tired. ▸ VERB 2 If you weary of something, you become tired of it.

wearily ADVERB, **weariness** NOUN

A
B
C
D
E
F
G
H
I
J
K
L
M
N
O
P
Q
R
S
T
U
V
W
X
Y
Z

weasel weasels
NOUN a small wild animal with a long, thin body and short legs.

weather weathers weathering weathered
NOUN **1** The weather is the condition of the atmosphere at any particular time and the amount of rain, wind, or sunshine occurring. ▶ VERB **2** If something such as rock or wood weathers, it changes colour or shape as a result of being exposed to the wind, rain, or sun. **3** If you weather a problem or difficulty, you come through it safely. ▶ PHRASE **4** If you are **under the weather**, you feel slightly ill.

weather forecast weather forecasts
NOUN a statement saying what the weather will be like the next day or for the next few days.

weather vane weather vanes
NOUN a metal object on the roof of a building which turns round in the wind and shows which way the wind is blowing.

weave weaves weaving wove woven
VERB **1** To weave cloth is to make it by crossing threads over and under each other, especially by using a machine called a loom. **2** If you weave your way somewhere, you go there by moving from side to side through and round the obstacles. ▶ NOUN **3** The weave of cloth is the way in which the threads are arranged and the pattern that they form EG *a tight weave*.

weaver weavers
NOUN a person who weaves cloth.

web webs
NOUN **1** a fine net of threads that a spider makes from a sticky substance which it produces in its body. **2** something that has a complicated structure or pattern EG *a web of lies*. **3** The Web is the same as the **World Wide Web**.

webbed
ADJECTIVE Webbed feet have the toes connected by a piece of skin.

website websites
NOUN a publication on the World Wide Web which contains information about a particular subject.

wed weds wedding wedded or wed
VERB; AN OLD-FASHIONED WORD If you wed someone or if you wed, you get married.

wedding weddings
NOUN a marriage ceremony.

wedge wedges wedging wedged
VERB **1** If you wedge something, you force it to remain there by holding it there tightly, or by fixing something next to it to prevent it from moving EG *I shut the shed door and wedged it with a log of wood*. ▶ NOUN **2** a piece of something such as wood, metal, or rubber with one pointed edge and one thick edge which is used to wedge something. **3** a piece of something that has a thick triangular shape EG *a wedge of cheese*.

wedlock
NOUN; AN OLD-FASHIONED WORD Wedlock is the state of being married.

Wednesday Wednesdays
NOUN Wednesday is the day between Tuesday and Thursday. 🏛 from Old English *Wodnes dæg* meaning 'Woden's day'

wee weer weest
ADJECTIVE; A SCOTTISH WORD very small.

weed weeds weeding weeded
NOUN **1** a wild plant that prevents cultivated plants from growing properly. ▶ VERB **2** If you weed a place, you remove the weeds from it.
weed out VERB If you weed out unwanted things, you get rid of them.

week weeks
NOUN **1** a period of seven days,

especially one beginning on a Sunday and ending on a Saturday. **2** A week is also the number of hours you spend at work during a week EG *a 35-hour week.* **3** The week can refer to the part of a week that does not include Saturday and Sunday EG *They are working during the week.*

weekday weekdays
NOUN any day except Saturday and Sunday.

weekend weekends
NOUN Saturday and Sunday.

weekly weeklies
ADJECTIVE OR ADVERB **1** happening or appearing once a week. ▶ NOUN **2** a newspaper or magazine that is published once a week.

weep weeps weeping wept
VERB **1** If someone weeps, they cry. **2** If something such as a wound weeps, it oozes blood or other liquid.

weevil weevils
NOUN a type of beetle which eats grain, seeds, or plants.

weft
NOUN The weft of a piece of woven material is the threads which are passed sideways in and out of the threads held in a loom.

weigh weighs weighing weighed
VERB **1** If something weighs a particular amount, that is how heavy it is. **2** If you weigh something, you measure how heavy it is using scales. **3** If you weigh facts or words, you think about them carefully before coming to a decision or before speaking. **4** If a problem weighs on you or weighs upon you, it makes you very worried.
weigh down VERB **1** If a load weighs you down, it stops you moving easily. **2** If you are weighed down by a difficulty, it is making you very worried.
weigh up VERB If you weigh up a person or a situation, you make an assessment of them.

weight weights weighting weighted
NOUN **1** The weight of something is its heaviness. **2** a metal object which has a certain known heaviness. Weights are used with sets of scales in order to weigh things. **3** any heavy object. **4** The weight of something is its large amount or importance which makes it hard to fight against or contradict EG *the weight of the law.* ▶ VERB **5** If you weight something or weight it down, you make it heavier, often so that it cannot move. ▶ PHRASE **6** If you **pull your weight**, you work just as hard as other people involved in the same activity.

weighted
ADJECTIVE A system that is weighted in favour of a particular person or group is organized in such a way that this person or group will have an advantage.

weightlifting
NOUN Weightlifting is the sport of lifting heavy weights in competition or for exercise.
weightlifter NOUN

weighty weightier weightiest
ADJECTIVE serious or important EG *a weighty problem.*

weir weirs
Rhymes with "near" NOUN a low dam which is built across a river to raise the water level, control the flow of water, or change its direction.

weird weirder weirdest
Said "weerd" ADJECTIVE strange or odd.
weirdly ADVERB
▪ bizarre, odd, strange

weirdo weirdos
Said "weer-doe" NOUN; AN INFORMAL WORD If you call someone a weirdo, you mean they behave in a strange way.

welcome welcomes welcoming welcomed

A
B
C
D
E
F
G
H
I
J
K
L
M
N
O
P
Q
R
S
T
U
V
W
X
Y
Z

VERB **1** If you welcome a visitor, you greet them in a friendly way when they arrive. **2** 'Welcome' can be said as a greeting to a visitor who has just arrived. **3** If you welcome something, you approve of it and support it EG *He welcomed the decision.* ▶ NOUN **4** a greeting to a visitor EG *a warm welcome.* ▶ ADJECTIVE **5** If someone is welcome at a place, they will be warmly received there. **6** If something is welcome, it brings pleasure or is accepted gratefully EG *a welcome rest.* **7** If you tell someone they are welcome to something or welcome to do something, you mean you are willing for them to have or to do it.

welcoming ADJECTIVE

weld welds welding welded
VERB To weld two pieces of metal together is to join them by heating their edges and fixing them together so that when they cool they harden into one piece.
welder NOUN

welfare
NOUN **1** The welfare of a person or group is their general state of health and comfort. **2** Welfare services are provided to help with people's living conditions and financial problems EG *welfare workers.*

welfare state
NOUN The welfare state is a system in which the government uses money from taxes to provide health care and education services, and to give benefits to people who are old, unemployed, or sick.

well better best; wells welling welled
ADVERB **1** If something goes well, it happens in a satisfactory way EG *The interview went well.* **2** in a good, skilful, or pleasing way EG *He draws well.* **3** thoroughly and completely EG *well established.* **4** kindly EG *We treat our employees well.* **5** If something may well or could well happen, it is likely to happen. **6** You use 'well' to emphasize an adjective, adverb, or phrase EG *He was well aware of that.* ▶ ADJECTIVE **7** If you are well, you are healthy. ▶ PHRASE **8** As well means also EG *He was a bus driver as well.* **9** As well as means in addition to EG *a meal which includes meat or fish, as well as rice.* **10** If you say you **may as well** or **might as well** do something, you mean you will do it although you are not keen to do it. ▶ NOUN **11** a hole drilled in the ground from which water, oil, or gas is obtained. ▶ VERB **12** If tears well or well up, they appear in someone's eyes.

well-advised
ADJECTIVE sensible or wise EG *Bill would be well-advised to retire.*

well-balanced
ADJECTIVE sensible and without serious emotional problems EG *a well-balanced happy teenager.*

wellbeing
NOUN Someone's wellbeing is their health and happiness.

well-earned
ADJECTIVE thoroughly deserved.

well-heeled
ADJECTIVE; AN INFORMAL WORD wealthy.

well-informed
ADJECTIVE having a great deal of knowledge about a subject or subjects.

wellington wellingtons
NOUN Wellingtons or wellington boots are long waterproof rubber boots.

well-meaning
ADJECTIVE A well-meaning person tries to be helpful but is often unsuccessful.

well-off
ADJECTIVE; AN INFORMAL WORD quite wealthy.

well-to-do
ADJECTIVE quite wealthy.

well-worn
ADJECTIVE **1** A well-worn expression or saying has been used too often

and has become boring. **2** A well-worn object or piece of clothing has been used and worn so much that it looks old and shabby.

welly **wellies**
NOUN; AN INFORMAL WORD Wellies are wellingtons.

Welsh
ADJECTIVE **1** belonging or relating to Wales. ▶ NOUN **2** Welsh is a language spoken in parts of Wales.

Welshman **Welshmen**
NOUN a man who comes from Wales.
Welshwoman NOUN

welt **welts**
NOUN a raised mark on someone's skin made by a blow from something like a whip or a stick.

welter
NOUN; A FORMAL WORD A welter of things is a large number of them that happen or appear together in a state of confusion EG *a welter of rumours*.

wench **wenches**
NOUN; AN OLD-FASHIONED WORD a woman or young girl.

wept
the past tense and past participle of weep.

were
a past tense of be.

werewolf **werewolves**
NOUN In horror stories, a werewolf is a person who changes into a wolf.
▥ from Old English *wer* + *wulf* meaning 'man wolf'

Wesak
*Said "**wess**-suck"* NOUN Wesak is the Buddhist festival celebrating the Buddha, held in May.

west
NOUN **1** The west is the direction in which you look to see the sun set. **2** The west of a place or country is the part which is towards the west when you are in the centre EG *the west of America*. **3** The West refers to the countries of North America and western and southern Europe.
▶ ADVERB OR ADJECTIVE **4** West means towards the west. ▶ ADJECTIVE **5** A west wind blows from the west.

westerly
ADJECTIVE Westerly means to or towards the west EG *France's most westerly region*.

western **westerns**
ADJECTIVE **1** in or from the west. **2** coming from or associated with the countries of North America and western and southern Europe EG *western dress*. ▶ NOUN **3** a book or film about life in the west of America in the nineteenth century.

West Indian **West Indians**
NOUN someone who comes from the West Indies.

westward or **westwards**
ADVERB Westward or westwards means towards the west EG *He stared westwards towards the clouds*.

wet **wetter** **wettest**; **wets** **wetting** **wet** or **wetted**
ADJECTIVE **1** If something is wet, it is covered in water or another liquid. **2** If the weather is wet, it is raining. **3** If something such as paint, ink, or cement is wet, it is not yet dry or solid. **4** AN INFORMAL USE If you say someone is wet, you mean they are weak and lack enthusiasm or confidence EG *Don't be so wet!* ▶ NOUN **5** In northern and central Australia, the wet is the rainy season. ▶ VERB **6** To wet something is to put water or some other liquid over it. **7** If people wet themselves or wet their beds, they urinate in their clothes or bed because they cannot control their bladder.
wetness NOUN

wet suit **wet suits**
NOUN a close-fitting rubber suit which a diver or someone taking part in water sports wears to keep his or her body warm.

whack **whacks** **whacking** **whacked**
VERB If you whack someone or

A B C D E F G H I J K L M N O P Q R S T U V W X Y Z

something, you hit them hard.

whale whales
NOUN a very large sea mammal which breathes out water through a hole on the top of its head.

whaling
NOUN Whaling is the work of hunting and killing whales for oil or food.

wharf wharves
Said "**worf**" NOUN a platform beside a river or the sea, where ships load or unload.

what
PRONOUN 1 'What' is used in questions EG *What time is it?* 2 'What' is used in indirect questions and statements EG *I don't know what you mean.* 3 'What' can be used at the beginning of a clause to refer to something with a particular quality EG *It is impossible to decide what is real and what is invented.* ▸ ADJECTIVE 4 'What' can be used at the beginning of a clause to show that you are talking about the whole amount that is available to you EG *Their spouses try to earn what money they can.* 5 You say 'what' to emphasize an opinion or reaction EG *What nonsense!* ▸ PHRASE 6 You say **what about** at the beginning of a question when you are making a suggestion or offer EG *What about a drink?*

whatever
PRONOUN 1 You use 'whatever' to refer to anything or everything of a particular type EG *He said he would do whatever he could.* 2 You use 'whatever' when you do not know the precise nature of something EG *Whatever it is, I don't like it.* ▸ CONJUNCTION 3 You use 'whatever' to mean no matter what EG *Whatever happens, you have to behave decently.* ▸ ADVERB 4 You use 'whatever' to emphasize a negative statement or a question EG *You have no proof whatever... Whatever is wrong with you?*

whatsoever
ADVERB You use 'whatsoever' to emphasize a negative statement EG *I have no memory of it whatsoever.*

wheat
NOUN Wheat is a cereal plant grown for its grain which is used to make flour.

wheel wheels wheeling wheeled
NOUN 1 a circular object which turns on a rod attached to its centre. Wheels are fixed underneath vehicles so that they can move along. 2 The wheel of a car is its steering wheel. ▸ VERB 3 If you wheel something such as a bicycle, you push it. 4 If someone or something wheels, they move round in the shape of a circle EG *Cameron wheeled around and hit him.*

wheelbarrow wheelbarrows
NOUN a small cart with a single wheel at the front, used for carrying things in the garden.

wheelchair wheelchairs
NOUN a chair with wheels in which sick, injured, or disabled people can move around.

wheeze wheezes wheezing wheezed
VERB If someone wheezes, they breathe with difficulty, making a whistling sound, usually because they have a chest complaint such as asthma.
wheezy ADJECTIVE

whelk whelks
NOUN a snail-like shellfish with a strong shell and a soft edible body.

when
ADVERB 1 You use 'when' to ask what time something happened or will happen EG *When are you leaving?* ▸ CONJUNCTION 2 You use 'when' to refer to a time in the past EG *I met him when I was sixteen.* 3 You use 'when' to introduce the reason for an opinion, comment, or question EG *How did you pass the exam when you hadn't studied for it?* 4 'When' is used to mean although EG *He drives*

when he could walk.

whence

ADVERB OR CONJUNCTION; AN OLD-FASHIONED WORD Whence means from where.
☑ You should not write *from whence* because *whence* already means 'from where'.

whenever

CONJUNCTION Whenever means at any time, or every time that something happens EG *I still go on courses whenever I can.*

where

ADVERB **1** You use 'where' to ask which place something is in, is coming from, or is going to EG *Where is Philip?* ▶ CONJUNCTION, PRONOUN, OR ADVERB **2** You use 'where' when asking about or referring to something EG *I hardly know where to begin.* ▶ CONJUNCTION **3** You use 'where' to refer to the place in which something is situated or happening EG *I don't know where we are.* **4** 'Where' can introduce a clause that contrasts with the other part of the sentence EG *A teacher will be listened to, where a parent might not.*

whereabouts

NOUN **1** The whereabouts of a person or thing is the place where they are. ▶ ADVERB **2** You use 'whereabouts' when you are asking more precisely where something is EG *Whereabouts in Canada are you from?*

whereas

CONJUNCTION Whereas introduces a comment that contrasts with the other part of the sentence EG *Her eyes were blue, whereas mine were brown.*

whereby

PRONOUN; A FORMAL WORD Whereby means by which EG *a new system whereby you pay the bill quarterly.*

whereupon

CONJUNCTION; A FORMAL WORD Whereupon means at which point EG *His enemies rejected his message, whereupon he tried again.*

wherever

CONJUNCTION **1** 'Wherever' means in every place or situation EG *Alex heard the same thing wherever he went.* **2** You use 'wherever' to show that you do not know where a place or person is EG *the nearest police station, wherever that is.*

wherewithal

NOUN If you have the wherewithal to do something, you have enough money to do it.

whet whets whetting whetted

PHRASE To whet someone's appetite for something, means to increase their desire for it.

whether

CONJUNCTION You use 'whether' when you are talking about two or more alternatives EG *I don't know whether that's true or false.*

whey

Rhymes with "day" NOUN Whey is the watery liquid that is separated from the curds in sour milk when cheese is made.

which

ADJECTIVE OR PRONOUN **1** You use 'which' to ask about alternatives or to refer to a choice between alternatives EG *Which room are you in?* ▶ PRONOUN **2** 'Which' at the beginning of a clause identifies the thing you are talking about or gives more information about it EG *certain wrongs which exist in our society.*
☑ See the usage note at *that.*

What does Which do?

Which is a relative pronoun. A relative pronoun replaces a noun which links two different parts of a sentence.

Relative pronouns always refer back to a word in the earlier part of the sentence. The word they refer to is called the **antecedent**. (In the examples that follow, the antecedents are underlined.)

I have a friend who lives in Rome.
We could go to a place that I know.

Which is only used when the antecedent is not a person.

A
B
C
D
E
F
G
H
I
J
K
L
M
N
O
P
Q
R
S
T
U
V
W
X
Y
Z

A
B
C
D
E
F
G
H
I
J
K
L
M
N
O
P
Q
R
S
T
U
V
W
X
Y
Z

*We took <u>the road</u> **which** leads to the sea.*
Also look at the grammar box at **relative pronoun**.

whichever

ADJECTIVE OR PRONOUN You use 'whichever' when you are talking about different alternatives or possibilities EG *Make your pizzas round or square, whichever you prefer.*

whiff whiffs

NOUN **1** a slight smell of something. **2** a slight sign or trace of something EG *a whiff of criticism.*

while whiles whiling whiled

CONJUNCTION **1** If something happens while something else is happening, the two things happen at the same time. **2** While also means but EG *Men tend to gaze more, while women dart quick glances.* ▶ NOUN **3** a period of time EG *a little while earlier.* ▶ PHRASE **4** If an action or activity is worth your while, it will be helpful or useful to you if you do it.

while away VERB If you while away the time in a particular way, you pass the time that way because you have nothing else to do.

whilst

CONJUNCTION Whilst means the same as while.

whim whims

NOUN a sudden desire or fancy.
≡ fancy, impulse

whimper whimpers whimpering whimpered

VERB **1** When children or animals whimper, they make soft, low, unhappy sounds. **2** If you whimper something, you say it in an unhappy or frightened way, as if you are about to cry.

whimsical

ADJECTIVE unusual and slightly playful EG *an endearing, whimsical charm.*

whine whines whining whined

VERB **1** To whine is to make a long, high-pitched noise, especially one

which sounds sad or unpleasant. **2** If someone whines about something, they complain about it in an annoying way. ▶ NOUN **3** A whine is the noise made by something or someone whining.

whinge whinges whinging or whingeing whinged

VERB If someone whinges about something, they complain about it in an annoying way.

whinny whinnies whinnying whinnied

VERB When a horse whinnies, it neighs softly.

whip whips whipping whipped

NOUN **1** a thin piece of leather or rope attached to a handle, which is used for hitting people or animals. ▶ VERB **2** If you whip a person or animal, you hit them with a whip. **3** When the wind whips something, it strikes it. **4** If you whip something out or off, you take it out or off very quickly EG *She had whipped off her glasses.* **5** If you whip cream or eggs, you beat them until they are thick and frothy or stiff.

whip up VERB If you whip up a strong emotion, you make people feel it EG *The thought whipped up his temper.*

whip bird whip birds

NOUN an Australian bird whose cry ends with a sound like the crack of a whip.

whiplash injury whiplash injuries

NOUN a neck injury caused by your head suddenly jerking forwards and then back again, for example in a car accident.

whippet whippets

NOUN a small, thin dog used for racing.

whirl whirls whirling whirled

VERB **1** When something whirls, or when you whirl it round, it turns round very fast. ▶ NOUN **2** You can refer to a lot of intense activity as a whirl of activity.

🏛 from Old Norse *hvirfla* meaning

'to turn about'

whirlpool whirlpools

NOUN a small circular area in a river or the sea where the water is moving quickly round and round so that objects floating near it are pulled into its centre.

whirlwind whirlwinds

NOUN **1** a tall column of air which spins round and round very fast. ▶ ADJECTIVE **2** more rapid than usual EG *a whirlwind tour*.

whirr whirrs whirring whirred; also spelt **whir**

VERB **1** When something such as a machine whirrs, it makes a series of low sounds so fast that it sounds like one continuous sound. ▶ NOUN **2** the noise made by something whirring.

whisk whisks whisking whisked

VERB **1** If you whisk someone or something somewhere, you take them there quickly EG *We were whisked away into a private room.* **2** If you whisk eggs or cream, you stir air into them quickly. ▶ NOUN **3** a kitchen tool used for quickly stirring air into eggs or cream.

whisker whiskers

NOUN The whiskers of an animal such as a cat or mouse are the long, stiff hairs near its mouth.

whisky whiskies

NOUN Whisky is a strong alcoholic drink made from grain such as barley.

▣ from Scottish Gaelic *uisge beatha* meaning 'water of life'

whisper whispers whispering whispered

VERB **1** When you whisper, you talk to someone very quietly, using your breath and not your throat. ▶ NOUN **2** If you talk in a whisper, you whisper.

whist

NOUN Whist is a card game for four players in which one pair of players tries to win more tricks than the other pair.

whistle whistles whistling whistled

VERB **1** When you whistle a tune or whistle, you produce a clear musical sound by forcing your breath out between your lips. **2** If something whistles, it makes a loud, high sound EG *The kettle whistled.* ▶ NOUN **3** A whistle is the sound something or someone makes when they whistle. **4** a small metal tube that you blow into to produce a whistling sound.

whit

NOUN; A FORMAL USE You say 'not a whit' or 'no whit' to emphasize that something is not the case at all EG *It does not matter one whit to the customer.*

white whiter whitest; whites

NOUN OR ADJECTIVE **1** White is the lightest possible colour. **2** Someone who is white has a pale skin and is of European origin. ▶ ADJECTIVE **3** If someone goes white, their face becomes very pale because they are afraid, shocked, or ill. **4** White coffee contains milk or cream. ▶ NOUN **5** The white of an egg is the transparent liquid surrounding the yolk.

whiteness NOUN

white-collar

ADJECTIVE White-collar workers work in offices rather than doing manual work EG *a white-collar union*.

white lie white lies

NOUN a harmless lie, especially one told to prevent someone's feelings from being hurt.

whitewash

NOUN **1** Whitewash is a mixture of lime and water used for painting walls white. **2** an attempt to hide unpleasant facts EG *the refusal to accept official whitewash in the enquiry*.

whither

ADVERB OR CONJUNCTION; AN OLD-FASHIONED WORD Whither means to what place EG *Whither shall I wander?*

whiting

NOUN a sea fish related to the cod.

whittle whittles whittling whittled
VERB If you whittle a piece of wood, you shape it by shaving or cutting small pieces off it.
whittle away or **whittle down** VERB To whittle away at something or to whittle it down means to make it smaller or less effective EG *The 250 entrants had been whittled down to 34.*

whizz whizzes whizzing whizzed; also spelt **whiz**
VERB; AN INFORMAL WORD If you whizz somewhere, you move there quickly EG *We whizzed across the road.*

who
PRONOUN 1 You use 'who' when you are asking about someone's identity EG *Who gave you that black eye?* 2 'Who' at the beginning of a clause refers to the person or people you are talking about EG *a shipyard worker who wants to be a postman.*

What does Who do?

Who is a relative pronoun. A relative pronoun replaces a noun which links two different parts of a sentence.

Relative pronouns always refer back to a word in the earlier part of the sentence. The word they refer to is called the **antecedent**. (In the examples that follow, the antecedents are underlined.)

*I have <u>a friend</u> **who** lives in Rome.*
*We could go to <u>a place</u> **that** I know.*

The forms *who*, *whom*, and *whose* are used when the antecedent is a person. *Who* indicates the subject of the verb.

*It was <u>the same person</u> **who** saw me yesterday.*
*It was <u>the person</u> **whom** I saw yesterday.*

The distinction between *who* and *whom* is often ignored in everyday English, and *who* is often used as the object.

*It was <u>the person</u> **who** I saw yesterday.*

Also look at the grammar box at **relative pronoun**.

---

whoa
Said "**woh**" INTERJECTION Whoa is a command used to slow down or stop a horse.

whoever
PRONOUN 1 'Whoever' means the person who EG *Whoever bought it for you has to make the claim.*
2 'Whoever' also means no matter who EG *I pity him, whoever he is.*
3 'Whoever' is used in questions give emphasis to who EG *Whoever thought of such a thing?*

whole wholes
NOUN OR ADJECTIVE 1 The whole of something is all of it EG *the whole of Africa... Have the whole cake.* ▶ ADVERB
2 in one piece EG *He swallowed it whole.* ▶ PHRASE 3 You use **as a whole** to emphasize that you are talking about all of something EG *The country as a whole is in a very odd mood.* 4 You say **on the whole** to mean that something is generally true EG *On the whole, we should be glad they are gone.*
wholeness NOUN

wholehearted
ADJECTIVE enthusiastic and totally sincere EG *wholehearted approval.*
wholeheartedly ADVERB

wholemeal
ADJECTIVE Wholemeal flour is made from the complete grain of the wheat plant, including the husk.

wholesale
ADJECTIVE OR ADVERB 1 Wholesale refers to the activity of buying goods cheaply in large quantities and selling them again, especially to shopkeepers EG *We buy fruit and vegetables wholesale.* ▶ ADJECTIVE
2 Wholesale also means done to an excessive extent EG *the wholesale destruction of wild plant species.*
wholesaler NOUN

wholesome
ADJECTIVE good and likely to improve your life, behaviour, or health EG *good wholesome entertainment.*

wholly
Said "**hoe-lee**" ADVERB completely.

whom

PRONOUN Whom is the object form of 'who' EG *the girl whom Albert would marry.*

What does Whom do?

Whom is a relative pronoun. A relative pronoun replaces a noun which links two different parts of a sentence.

Relative pronouns always refer back to a word in the earlier part of the sentence. The word they refer to is called the **antecedent**. (In the examples that follow, the antecedents are underlined.)

I have a friend who lives in Rome.
We could go to a place that I know.

The forms who, whom, and whose are used when the antecedent is a person. *Whom* indicates the object of the verb.

It was the same person who saw me yesterday.
It was the person whom I saw yesterday.

The distinction between *who* and *whom* is often ignored in everyday English, and *who* is often used as the object.

It was the person who I saw yesterday.

Whom is used immediately after a preposition. However, if the preposition is separated from the relative pronoun, *who* is usually used.

He is a man in whom I have great confidence.
He is a man who I have great confidence in.

Also look at the grammar box at **relative pronoun**.

whoop whoops whooping whooped

VERB **1** If you whoop, you shout loudly in a happy or excited way. ▶ NOUN **2** a loud cry of happiness or excitement EG *whoops of delight.*

whooping cough

Said "**hoop**-ing" NOUN Whooping cough is an acute infectious disease which makes people cough violently and produce a loud sound when they breathe.

whore whores

Said "**hore**" NOUN; AN OFFENSIVE WORD a prostitute, or a woman believed to act like a prostitute.

whose

PRONOUN **1** You use 'whose' to ask who something belongs to EG *Whose gun is this?* **2** You use 'whose' at the beginning of a clause which gives information about something relating or belonging to the thing or person you have just mentioned EG *a wealthy gentleman whose marriage is breaking up.*

☑ Many people are confused about the difference between *whose* and *who's*. *Whose* is used to show possession in a question or when something is being described: *whose bag is this? the person whose car is blocking the exit.* *Who's*, with the apostrophe, is a short form of *who is* or *who has: who's that girl? who's got my ruler?*

What does Whose do?

Whose is a relative pronoun. A relative pronoun replaces a noun which links two different parts of a sentence.

Relative pronouns always refer back to a word in the earlier part of the sentence. The word they refer to is called the **antecedent**. (In the examples that follow, the antecedents are underlined.)

I have a friend who lives in Rome.
We could go to a place that I know.

The forms who, whom, and whose are used when the antecedent is a person.

Whose is the possessive form of the relative pronoun. It can refer to things as well as people.

Anna has a sister whose name is Rosie.
I found a book whose pages were torn.

Also look at the grammar box at **relative pronoun**.

why

ADVERB OR PRONOUN You use 'why' when you are asking about the reason for something, or talking about it EG *Why did you do it?... He wondered why she suddenly looked happier.*

wick wicks

A
B
C
D
E
F
G
H
I
J
K
L
M
N
O
P
Q
R
S
T
U
V
W
X
Y
Z

NOUN the cord in the middle of a candle, which you set alight.

wicked
ADJECTIVE **1** very bad EG *a wicked thing to do.* **2** mischievous in an amusing or attractive way EG *a wicked sense of humour.*
wickedly ADVERB, **wickedness** NOUN
▣ from Old English *wicce* meaning 'witch'
▤ (sense 1) bad, evil, sinful

wicker
ADJECTIVE A wicker basket or chair is made from twigs, canes, or reeds that have been woven together.

wicket wickets
NOUN **1** In cricket, the wicket is one of the two sets of stumps and bails at which the bowler aims the ball. **2** The grass between the wickets on a cricket pitch is also called the wicket.

wide wider widest
ADJECTIVE **1** measuring a large distance from one side to the other. **2** If there is a wide variety, range, or selection of something, there are many different kinds of it EG *a wide range of colours.* ▶ ADVERB **3** If you open or spread something wide, you open it to its fullest extent.
widely ADVERB
▤ (sense 2) broad, extensive, large

wide-awake
ADJECTIVE completely awake.

widen widens widening widened
VERB **1** If something widens or if you widen it, it becomes bigger from one side to the other. **2** You can say that something widens when it becomes greater in size or scope EG *the opportunity to widen your outlook.*

wide-ranging
ADJECTIVE extending over a variety of different things or over a large area EG *a wide-ranging survey.*

widespread
ADJECTIVE existing or happening over a large area or to a great extent EG *the widespread use of chemicals.*
▤ common, general, universal

widow widows
NOUN a woman whose husband has died.

widowed
ADJECTIVE If someone is widowed, their husband or wife has died.

widower widowers
NOUN a man whose wife has died.

width widths
NOUN The width of something is the distance from one side or edge to the other.

wield wields wielding wielded
Said "weeld" VERB **1** If you wield a weapon or tool, you carry it and use it. **2** If someone wields power, they have it and are able to use it.

wife wives
NOUN A man's wife is the woman he is married to.

wig wigs
NOUN a false head of hair worn to cover someone's own hair or to hide their baldness.
▣ short for *periwig* from Italian *perrucca* meaning 'wig'

wiggle wiggles wiggling wiggled
VERB **1** If you wiggle something, you move it up and down or from side to side with small jerky movements. ▶ NOUN **2** a small jerky movement or line.

wigwam wigwams
NOUN a kind of tent used by North American Indians.
▣ from American Indian *wikwam* meaning 'their house'

wild wilder wildest; wilds
ADJECTIVE **1** Wild animals, birds, and plants live and grow in natural surroundings and are not looked after by people. **2** Wild land is natural and uncultivated EG *wild areas of countryside.* **3** Wild weather or sea is stormy and rough. **4** Wild behaviour is excited and uncontrolled EG *wild with excitement.* **5** A wild idea or scheme is original and crazy. ▶ NOUN **6** The wild is a free and natural state of living EG

There are about 200 left in the wild.
7 The wilds are remote areas where few people live, far away from towns.
wildly ADVERB

wilderness wildernesses
NOUN an area of natural land which is not cultivated.

wildfire
NOUN If something spreads like wildfire, it spreads very quickly.

wild-goose chase wild-goose chases
NOUN a hopeless or useless search.

wildlife
NOUN Wildlife means wild animals and plants.

Wild West
NOUN The Wild West was the western part of the United States when it was first being settled by Europeans.

wiles
PLURAL NOUN Wiles are clever or crafty tricks used to persuade people to do something.

wilful
ADJECTIVE **1** Wilful actions or attitudes are deliberate and often intended to hurt someone EG *wilful damage.* **2** Someone who is wilful is obstinate and determined to get their own way EG *a wilful little boy.*
wilfully ADVERB
■ (sense 2) headstrong, stubborn

will
VERB **1** You use 'will' to form the future tense EG *Robin will be quite annoyed.* **2** You use 'will' to say that you intend to do something EG *I will not deceive you.* **3** You use 'will' when inviting someone to do or have something EG *Will you have another coffee?* **4** You use 'will' when asking or telling someone to do something EG *Will you do me a favour?...* **5** You use 'will' to say that you are assuming something to be the case EG *As you will have gathered, I was surprised.*

The Verbs Will and Shall

The verbs *will* and *shall* have only one form. They do not have a present form ending in -s, and they do not have a present participle, a past tense, or a past participle.

These verbs are used as auxiliary verbs to form the future tense.
  *She **will** give a talk about Chinese history.*
  *We **shall** arrive on Thursday.*

People used to use *shall* to indicate the first person, and *will* to indicate the second person and the third person. However, this distinction is often ignored now.
  *I **will** see you on Sunday.*
  *I **shall** see you on Sunday.*

Shall is always used in questions involving *I* and *we. Will* is avoided in these cases.
  ***Shall** I put the cat out?*
  ***Shall** we dance?*

Will is always used when making polite requests, giving orders, and indicating persistence. *Shall* is avoided in these cases.
  ***Will** you please help me?*
  ***Will** you be quiet!*
  *She **will** keep going on about Al Pacino.*

---

will wills willing willed
VERB **1** If you will something to happen, you try to make it happen by mental effort EG *I willed my eyes to open.* **2** If you will something to someone, you leave it to them when you die EG *Penbrook Farm is willed to her.* ▶ NOUN **3** Will is the determination to do something EG *the will to win.* **4** If something is the will of a person or group, they want it to happen EG *the will of the people.* **5** a legal document in which you say what you want to happen to your money and property when you die. ▶ PHRASE **6** If you can do something **at will**, you can do it whenever you want.

willing
ADJECTIVE **1** If you are willing to do something, you will do it if someone wants you to. **2** Someone who is willing is eager and enthusiastic EG *a willing helper.*

A
B
C
D
E
F
G
H
I
J
K
L
M
N
O
P
Q
R
S
T
U
V
W
X
Y
Z

willingly ADVERB, **willingness** NOUN
■ (sense 1) game, prepared, ready

willow willows
NOUN A willow or willow tree is a tree with long, thin branches and narrow leaves that often grows near water.

wilt wilts wilting wilted
VERB **1** If a plant wilts, it droops because it needs more water or is dying. **2** If someone wilts, they gradually lose strength or confidence EG *James visibly wilted under pressure.*

wily wilier wiliest
Said "wie-lee" ADJECTIVE clever and cunning.

wimp wimps
NOUN; AN INFORMAL WORD someone who is feeble and timid.

win wins winning won
VERB **1** If you win a fight, game, or argument, you defeat your opponent. **2** If you win a prize, you get it as a reward for succeeding in something. **3** If you win something you want, such as approval or support, you succeed in getting it. ▶ NOUN **4** a victory in a game or contest.
win over VERB If you win someone over, you persuade them to support you.

wince winces wincing winced
VERB When you wince, the muscles of your face tighten suddenly because of pain, fear, or distress.

winch winches winching winched
NOUN **1** a machine used to lift heavy objects. It consists of a cylinder around which a rope or chain is wound. ▶ VERB **2** If you winch an object or person somewhere, you lift, lower, or pull them using a winch.

wind winds
Rhymes with "tinned" NOUN **1** a current of air moving across the earth's surface. **2** Your wind is the ability to breathe easily EG *Brown had recovered her wind.* **3** Wind is air

swallowed with food or drink, or gas produced in your stomach, which causes discomfort. **4** The wind section of an orchestra is the group of musicians who play wind instruments.

wind winds winding wound
Rhymes with "mind" VERB **1** If a road or river winds in a particular direction, it twists and turns in that direction. **2** When you wind something round something else, you wrap it round it several times. **3** When you wind a clock or machine or wind it up, you turn a key or handle several times to make it work.
wind up VERB **1** When you wind up something such as an activity or a business, you finish it or close it. **2** If you wind up in a particular place, you end up there.

windfall windfalls
NOUN a sum of money that you receive unexpectedly.

wind instrument wind instruments
NOUN an instrument you play by using your breath, for example a flute, an oboe, or a trumpet.

windmill windmills
NOUN a machine for grinding grain or pumping water. It is driven by vanes or sails turned by the wind.

window windows
NOUN a space in a wall or roof or in the side of a vehicle, usually with glass in it so that light can pass through and people can see in or out.

window box window boxes
NOUN a long, narrow container on a windowsill in which plants are grown.

windowsill windowsills
NOUN a ledge along the bottom of a window, either on the inside or outside of a building.

windpipe windpipes
NOUN the tube which carries air into your lungs when you breathe.

windscreen windscreens
NOUN the glass at the front of a vehicle through which the driver looks.

windsurfing
NOUN Windsurfing is the sport of moving along the surface of the sea or a lake standing on a board with a sail on it.

windswept
ADJECTIVE A windswept place is exposed to strong winds EG *a windswept beach*.

windy windier windiest
ADJECTIVE If it is windy, there is a lot of wind.

wine wines
NOUN Wine is the red or white alcoholic drink which is normally made from grapes.
🔲 from Latin *vinum* meaning 'wine'

wing wings
NOUN 1 A bird's or insect's wings are the parts of its body that it uses for flying. 2 An aeroplane's wings are the long, flat parts on each side that support it while it is in the air. 3 A wing of a building is a part which sticks out from the main part or which has been added later. 4 A wing of an organization, especially a political party, is a group within it with a particular role or particular beliefs EG *the left wing of the party*. ▶ PLURAL NOUN 5 The wings in a theatre are the sides of the stage which are hidden from the audience.
winged ADJECTIVE

wink winks winking winked
VERB 1 When you wink, you close one eye briefly, often as a signal that something is a joke or a secret. ▶ NOUN 2 the closing of your eye when you wink.

winkle winkles
NOUN a small sea-snail with a hard shell and a soft edible body.

winner winners
NOUN The winner of a prize, race, or competition is the person or thing that wins it.
🔳 champion, victor

winning
ADJECTIVE 1 The winning team or entry in a competition is the one that has won. 2 attractive and charming EG *a winning smile*. ▶ PLURAL NOUN 3 Your winnings are the money you have won in a competition or by gambling.

winter winters
NOUN Winter is the season between autumn and spring.

wintry
ADJECTIVE Something wintry has features that are typical of winter EG *the wintry dawn*.

wipe wipes wiping wiped
VERB 1 If you wipe something, you rub its surface lightly to remove dirt or liquid. 2 If you wipe dirt or liquid off something, you remove it using a cloth or your hands EG *Anne wiped the tears from her eyes*.
wipe out VERB To wipe out people or places is to destroy them completely.

wire wires wiring wired
NOUN 1 Wire is metal in the form of a long, thin, flexible thread which can be used to make or fasten things or to conduct an electric current. ▶ VERB 2 If you wire one thing to another, you fasten them together using wire. 3 If you wire something or wire it up, you connect it so that electricity can pass through it.
wired ADJECTIVE

wireless wirelesses
NOUN; AN OLD-FASHIONED WORD a radio.

wiring
NOUN The wiring in a building is the system of wires that supply electricity to the rooms.

wiry wirier wiriest
ADJECTIVE 1 Wiry people are thin but with strong muscles. 2 Wiry things are stiff and rough to the touch EG *wiry hair*.

A
B
C
D
E
F
G
H
I
J
K
L
M
N
O
P
Q
R
S
T
U
V
W
X
Y
Z

A
B
C
D
E
F
G
H
I
J
K
L
M
N
O
P
Q
R
S
T
U
V
W
X
Y
Z

wisdom

NOUN **1** Wisdom is the ability to use experience and knowledge in order to make sensible decisions or judgments. **2** If you talk about the wisdom of an action or a decision, you are talking about how sensible it is.

wisdom tooth wisdom teeth

NOUN Your wisdom teeth are the four molar teeth at the back of your mouth which grow later than other teeth.

wise wiser wisest

ADJECTIVE **1** Someone who is wise can use their experience and knowledge to make sensible decisions and judgments. ▶ PHRASE **2** If you say that someone is **none the wiser** or **no wiser**, you mean that they know no more about something than they did before EG *I left the conference none the wiser.*
■ (sense 1) judicious, prudent, sensible

wisecrack wisecracks

NOUN a clever remark, intended to be amusing but often unkind.

wish wishes wishing wished

NOUN **1** a longing or desire for something, often something difficult to achieve or obtain. **2** something desired or wanted EG *That wish came true two years later.* ▶ PLURAL NOUN **3** Good wishes are expressions of hope that someone will be happy or successful EG *best wishes on your birthday.* ▶ VERB **4** If you wish to do something, you want to do it EG *We wished to return.* **5** If you wish something were the case, you would like it to be the case, but know it is not very likely EG *I wish I were tall.*

wishbone wishbones

NOUN a V-shaped bone in the breast of most birds.

wishful thinking

NOUN If someone's hope or wish is wishful thinking, it is unlikely to come true.

wishy-washy

ADJECTIVE; AN INFORMAL WORD If a person or their ideas are wishy-washy, then their ideas are not firm or clear EG *wishy-washy reasons.*

wisp wisps

NOUN **1** A wisp of grass or hair is a small, thin, untidy bunch of it. **2** A wisp of smoke is a long, thin streak of it.
wispy ADJECTIVE

wistful

ADJECTIVE sadly thinking about something, especially something you want but cannot have EG *A wistful look came into her eyes.*
wistfully ADVERB

wit wits

NOUN **1** Wit is the ability to use words or ideas in an amusing and clever way. **2** Wit means sense EG *They haven't got the wit to realize what they're doing.* ▶ PLURAL NOUN **3** Your wits are the ability to think and act quickly in a difficult situation EG *the man who lived by his wits.* ▶ PHRASE **4** If someone is **at their wits' end**, they are so worried and exhausted by problems or difficulties that they do not know what to do.

witch witches

NOUN a woman claimed to have magic powers and to be able to use them for good or evil.

witchcraft

NOUN Witchcraft is the skill or art of using magic powers, especially evil ones.
■ black magic, sorcery, wizardry

witch doctor witch doctors

NOUN a man in some societies, especially in Africa, who appears to have magic powers.

witchetty grub witchetty grubs

NOUN a large Australian caterpillar that is eaten by Aborigines as food.

with

PREPOSITION **1** 'With' someone means in their company EG *He was at home with me.* **2** 'With' is used to show who your opponent is in a fight or competition EG *next week's game with Brazil.* 3 'With' can mean using or having EG *Apply the colour with a brush... a bloke with a moustache.* 4 'With' is used to show how someone does something or how they feel EG *She looked at him with hatred.* 5 'With' can mean concerning EG *a problem with her telephone bill.* 6 'With' is used to show support EG *Are you with us or against us?*

withdraw withdraws withdrawing withdrew withdrawn

VERB 1 If you withdraw something, you remove it or take it out EG *He withdrew the money from his bank.* 2 If you withdraw to another place, you leave where you are and go there EG *He withdrew to his study.* 3 If you withdraw from an activity, you back out of it EG *They withdrew from the conference.*

withdrawal withdrawals

NOUN 1 The withdrawal of something is the act of taking it away EG *the withdrawal of Russian troops.* 2 The withdrawal of a statement is the act of saying formally that you wish to change or deny it. 3 an amount of money you take from your bank or building society account.

withdrawal symptoms

PLURAL NOUN Withdrawal symptoms are the unpleasant effects suffered by someone who has suddenly stopped taking a drug to which they are addicted.

withdrawn

1 Withdrawn is the past participle of **withdraw**. ▶ ADJECTIVE 2 unusually shy or quiet.

wither withers withering withered

VERB 1 When something withers or withers away, it becomes weaker until it no longer exists. 2 If a plant withers, it wilts or shrivels up and dies.

withering

ADJECTIVE A withering look or remark makes you feel ashamed, stupid, or inferior.

withhold withholds withholding withheld

VERB; A FORMAL WORD If you withhold something that someone wants, you do not let them have it.

within

PREPOSITION OR ADVERB 1 'Within' means in or inside. ▶ PREPOSITION 2 'Within' can mean not going beyond certain limits EG *Stay within the budget.* 3 'Within' can mean before a period of time has passed EG *You must write back within fourteen days.*

without

PREPOSITION 1 'Without' means not having, feeling, or showing EG *Didier looked on without emotion.* 2 'Without' can mean not using EG *You can't get in without a key.* 3 'Without' can mean not in someone's company EG *He went without me.* 4 'Without' can indicate that something does not happen when something else happens EG *Stone signalled the ship, again without response.*

withstand withstands withstanding withstood

VERB When something or someone withstands a force or action, they survive it or do not give in to it EG *ships designed to withstand the North Atlantic winter.*

witness witnesses witnessing witnessed

NOUN 1 someone who has seen an event such as an accident and can describe what happened. 2 someone who appears in a court of law to say what they know about a crime or other event. 3 someone who writes their name on a document that someone else has signed, to confirm that it is really that person's signature. ▶ VERB 4 A FORMAL USE If you witness an event, you see it.

= (sense 1) bystander, observer, onlooker

witticism witticisms
Said "wit-tiss-izm" NOUN a clever and amusing remark or joke.

witty wittier wittiest
ADJECTIVE amusing in a clever way EG *this witty novel.*
wittily ADVERB

wives
the plural of **wife**.

wizard wizards
NOUN a man in a fairy story who has magic powers.

wizened
Said "wiz-nd" ADJECTIVE having a wrinkled skin, especially with age EG *a wizened old man.*

wobbegong wobbegongs
Said "wob-bi-gong" NOUN an Australian shark with a richly patterned brown-and-white skin.

wobble wobbles wobbling wobbled
VERB If something wobbles, it shakes or moves from side to side because it is loose or unsteady EG *a cyclist who wobbled into my path.*
⌂ from German *wabbeln* meaning 'waver'

wobbly
ADJECTIVE unsteady EG *a wobbly table.*

woe woes
A LITERARY WORD ▶ NOUN **1** Woe is great unhappiness or sorrow. ▶ PLURAL NOUN **2** Someone's woes are their problems or misfortunes.

wok woks
NOUN a large bowl-shaped metal pan used for Chinese-style cooking.

woke
the past tense of **wake**.

woken
the past participle of **wake**.

wolf wolves; wolfs wolfing wolfed
NOUN **1** a wild animal related to the dog. Wolves hunt in packs and kill other animals for food. ▶ VERB **2** AN

INFORMAL USE If you wolf food or wolf it down, you eat it up quickly and greedily.

woman women
NOUN **1** an adult female human being. **2** Woman can refer to women in general EG *man's inhumanity to woman.*

womanhood
NOUN Womanhood is the state of being a woman rather than a girl EG *on the verge of womanhood.*

womb wombs
Said "woom" NOUN A woman's womb is the part inside her body where her unborn baby grows.

wombat wombats
Said "wom-bat" NOUN a short-legged furry Australian animal which eats plants.

wonder wonders wondering wondered
VERB **1** If you wonder about something, you think about it with curiosity or doubt. **2** If you wonder at something, you are surprised and amazed at it EG *He wondered at her anger.* ▶ NOUN **3** Wonder is a feeling of surprise and amazement. **4** something or someone that surprises and amazes people EG *the wonders of science.*
= (sense 4) marvel, miracle, phenomenon

wonderful
ADJECTIVE **1** making you feel very happy and pleased EG *It was wonderful to be together.* **2** very impressive EG *Nature is a wonderful thing.*
wonderfully ADVERB
= (sense 2) amazing, magnificent, remarkable

wondrous
ADJECTIVE; A LITERARY WORD amazing and impressive.

wont
Rhymes with "don't" ADJECTIVE; AN OLD-FASHIONED WORD If someone is wont to do something, they do it often EG *a gesture he was wont to use*

when preaching.

woo woos wooing wooed
VERB 1 If you woo people, you try to get them to help or support you EG *attempts to woo the women's vote.* 2 AN OLD-FASHIONED USE When a man woos a woman, he tries to get her to marry him.

wood woods
NOUN 1 Wood is the substance which forms the trunks and branches of trees. 2 a large area of trees growing near each other.

wooded
ADJECTIVE covered in trees EG *a wooded area nearby.*

wooden
ADJECTIVE made of wood EG *a wooden box.*

woodland woodlands
NOUN Woodland is land that is mostly covered with trees.

woodpecker woodpeckers
NOUN a climbing bird with a long, sharp beak that it uses to drill holes into trees to find insects.

woodwind
ADJECTIVE Woodwind instruments are musical instruments such as flutes, oboes, clarinets, and bassoons, that are played by being blown into.

woodwork
NOUN 1 Woodwork refers to the parts of a house, such as stairs, doors or window-frames, that are made of wood. 2 Woodwork is the craft or skill of making things out of wood.

woodworm woodworm or woodworms
NOUN 1 Woodworm are the larvae of a kind of beetle. They make holes in wood by feeding on it. 2 Woodworm is damage caused to wood by woodworm making holes in it.

woody woodier woodiest
ADJECTIVE 1 Woody plants have hard tough stems. 2 A woody area has a lot of trees in it.

woof woofs
NOUN the sound that a dog makes when it barks.

wool wools
NOUN 1 Wool is the hair that grows on sheep and some other animals. 2 Wool is also yarn spun from the wool of animals which is used to knit, weave, and make such things as clothes, blankets, and carpets.

woollen woollens
ADJECTIVE 1 made from wool. ▶ NOUN 2 Woollens are clothes made of wool.

woolly woollier woolliest
ADJECTIVE 1 made of wool or looking like wool EG *a woolly hat.* 2 If you describe people or their thoughts as woolly, you mean that they seem confused and unclear.

woolshed woolsheds
NOUN In Australian and New Zealand English, a large building in which sheep are sheared.

woomera woomeras
NOUN a stick with a notch at one end used by Australian Aborigines to help fire a dart or spear.

word words wording worded
NOUN 1 a single unit of language in speech or writing which has a meaning. 2 A word can mean something brief said, such as a remark, statement, or conversation EG *a word of praise... Could I have a word?* 3 A word can also be a message EG *The word is that Sharon is exhausted.* 4 Your word is a promise EG *He gave me his word.* 5 The word can be a command EG *I gave the word to start.* ▶ PLURAL NOUN 6 The words of a play or song are the spoken or sung text. ▶ VERB 7 When you word something, you choose your words in order to express your ideas accurately or acceptably EG *the best way to word our invitations.*

wording
NOUN The wording of a piece of writing or a speech is the words

A
B
C
D
E
F
G
H
I
J
K
L
M
N
O
P
Q
R
S
T
U
V
W
X
Y
Z

used in it, especially when these words have been carefully chosen to have a certain effect.

word processor word processors
NOUN an electronic machine which has a keyboard and a visual display unit and which is used to produce, store, and organize printed material.

work works working worked
VERB **1** People who work have a job which they are paid to do EG *My husband works for a national newspaper*. **2** When you work, you do the tasks that your job involves. **3** To work the land is to cultivate it. **4** If someone works a machine, they control or operate it. **5** If a machine works, it operates properly and effectively EG *The radio doesn't work*. **6** If something such as an idea or a system works, it is successful EG *The housing benefit system is not working*. **7** If something works its way into a particular position, it gradually moves there EG *The cable had worked loose*. ▶ NOUN **8** People who have work or who are in work have a job which they are paid to do EG *She's trying to find work*. **9** Work is the tasks that have to be done. **10** something done or made EG *a work of art*. **11** In physics, work is transfer of energy. It is calculated by multiplying a force by the distance moved by the point to which the force has been applied. Work is measured in joules. ▶ PLURAL NOUN **12** A works is a place where something is made by an industrial process EG *the old steel works*. **13** Works are large scale building, digging, or general construction activities EG *building works*.
▤ (sense 4) control, handle, operate
▤ (sense 5) function, go, run
work out VERB **1** If you work out a solution to a problem, you find the solution. **2** If a situation works out in a particular way, it happens in that way.

work up VERB **1** If you work up to something, you gradually progress towards it. **2** If you work yourself up or work someone else up, you make yourself or the other person very upset or angry about something.
worked up ADJECTIVE

workable
ADJECTIVE Something workable can operate successfully or can be used for a particular purpose EG *a workable solution*.

workaholic workaholics
NOUN a person who finds it difficult to stop working and do other things.

worker workers
NOUN a person employed in a particular industry or business EG *a defence worker*.

workforce workforces
NOUN The workforce is the number of people who work in a particular place.

workhouse workhouses
NOUN In the past a workhouse was a building to which very poor people were sent and made to work in return for food and shelter.

working workings
ADJECTIVE **1** Working people have jobs which they are paid to do. **2** Working can mean related to, used for, or suitable for work EG *the working week… working conditions*. **3** Working can mean sufficient to be useful or to achieve what is required EG *a working knowledge of Hebrew*. ▶ PLURAL NOUN **4** The workings of a piece of equipment, an organization, or a system are the ways in which it operates EG *the workings of the European Union*.

working class working classes
NOUN The working class or working classes are the group of people in society who do not own much property and who do jobs which involve physical rather than intellectual skills.

workload workloads
NOUN the amount of work that a person or a machine has to do.

workman workmen
NOUN a man whose job involves using physical rather than intellectual skills.

workmanship
NOUN Workmanship is the skill with which something is made or a job is completed.

workmate workmates
NOUN Someone's workmate is the fellow worker with whom they do their job.

workout workouts
NOUN a session of physical exercise or training.

workshop workshops
NOUN **1** a room or building that contains tools or machinery used for making or repairing things EG *an engineering workshop*. **2** a period of discussion or practical work in which a group of people learn about a particular subject EG *a theatre workshop*.

world worlds
NOUN **1** The world is the earth, the planet we live on. **2** You can use 'world' to refer to people generally EG *The eyes of the world are upon me.* **3** Someone's world is the life they lead and the things they experience EG *We come from different worlds.* **4** A world is a division or section of the earth, its history, or its people, such as the Arab World, or the Ancient World. **5** A particular world is a field of activity and the people involved in it EG *the world of football.* ▶ ADJECTIVE **6** 'World' is used to describe someone or something that is one of the best or most important of its kind EG *a world leader.* ▶ PHRASE **7** If you **think the world** of someone, you like or admire them very much.
⌂ from Old English *weorold* from *wer* meaning 'man' and *ald* meaning 'age'

worldly worldlier worldliest
ADJECTIVE **1** relating to the ordinary activities of life rather than spiritual things EG *opportunities for worldly pleasures.* **2** experienced and knowledgeable about life.

world war world wars
NOUN a war that involves countries all over the world.

worldwide
ADJECTIVE throughout the world EG *a worldwide increase in skin cancers.*

World Wide Web
NOUN The World Wide Web is another name for the Internet, the worldwide communication system which people use through computers.

worm worms worming wormed
NOUN **1** a small thin animal without bones or legs, which lives in the soil or off other creatures. **2** an insect such as a beetle or moth at a very early stage in its life. ▶ VERB **3** If you worm an animal, you give it medicine in order to kill the worms that are living as parasites in its intestines.
worm out VERB If you worm information out of someone, you gradually persuade them to give you it.

worn
1 Worn is the past participle of **wear**. ▶ ADJECTIVE **2** damaged or thin because of long use. **3** looking old or exhausted EG *Her husband looks frail and worn.*

worn-out
ADJECTIVE **1** used until it is too thin or too damaged to be of further use EG *a worn-out cardigan.* **2** extremely tired EG *You must be worn-out after the drive.*

worried
ADJECTIVE unhappy and anxious about a problem or about something unpleasant that might happen.
▤ anxious, concerned, troubled

worry worries worrying worried

A B C D E F G H I J K L M N O P Q R S T U V W X Y Z

A
B
C
D
E
F
G
H
I
J
K
L
M
N
O
P
Q
R
S
T
U
V
W
X
Y
Z

VERB **1** If you worry, you feel anxious and fearful about a problem or about something unpleasant that might happen. **2** If something worries you, it causes you to feel uneasy or fearful EG *a puzzle which had worried her all her life*. **3** If you worry someone with a problem, you disturb or bother them by telling them about it EG *I didn't want to worry the boys with this*. **4** If a dog worries sheep or other animals, it frightens or harms them by chasing them or biting them. ▶ NOUN **5** Worry is a feeling of unhappiness and unease caused by a problem or by thinking of something unpleasant that might happen EG *the major source of worry*. **6** a person or thing that causes you to feel anxious or uneasy EG *Inflation is the least of our worries*.

worrying ADJECTIVE

📖 from Old English *wyrgan* meaning 'strangle'

▤ (sense 1) be anxious, fret
▤ (sense 2) bother, perturb, trouble
▤ (sense 5) anxiety, concern

worse

ADJECTIVE OR ADVERB **1** Worse is the comparative form of **bad** and **badly**. **2** If someone who is ill gets worse, they become more ill than before. ▶ PHRASE **3** If someone or something is **none the worse** for something, they have not been harmed by it EG *He appeared none the worse for the accident*.

worsen worsens worsening worsened

VERB If a situation worsens, it becomes more difficult or unpleasant EG *My relationship with my mother worsened*.

▤ decline, deteriorate, get worse

worse off

ADJECTIVE If you are worse off, you have less money or are in a more unpleasant situation than before EG *There are people much worse off than me*.

worship worships worshipping

worshipped

VERB **1** If you worship a god, you show your love and respect by praying or singing hymns. **2** If you worship someone or something, you love them or admire them very much. ▶ NOUN **3** Worship is the feeling of respect, love, or admiration you feel for something or someone.

worshipper NOUN

▤ (sense 2) adore, idolize, love
▤ (sense 3) adoration, devotion

worst

ADJECTIVE OR ADVERB Worst is the superlative of **bad** and **badly**.

worth

PREPOSITION **1** If something is worth a sum of money, it has that value EG *a house worth 85,000 dollars*. **2** If something is worth doing, it deserves to be done. ▶ NOUN **3** A particular amount of money's worth of something is the quantity of it that you can buy for that money EG *five pound's worth of petrol*. **4** Someone's worth is the value or usefulness they are considered to have.

worthless

ADJECTIVE having no real value or use EG *a worthless piece of junk*.

worthwhile

ADJECTIVE important enough to justify the time, money, or effort spent on it EG *a worthwhile career*.

worthy worthier worthiest

ADJECTIVE If someone or something is worthy of something, they deserve it EG *a worthy champion*.

would

VERB **1** You use 'would' to say what someone thought was going to happen EG *We were sure it would be a success*. **2** You use 'would' when you are referring to the result or effect of a possible situation EG *If readers can help I would be most grateful*. **3** You use 'would' when referring to someone's willingness to do something EG *I wouldn't change* *places with him if you paid me.* **4** You use 'would' in polite questions EG *Would you like some lunch?*

would-be
ADJECTIVE wanting to be or claiming to be EG *a would-be pop singer.*

wound wounds wounding wounded
NOUN **1** an injury to part of your body, especially a cut in your skin and flesh. ▶ VERB **2** If someone wounds you, they damage your body using a gun, knife, or other weapon. **3** If you are wounded by what someone says or does, your feelings are hurt.
wounded ADJECTIVE

wow
INTERJECTION Wow is an expression of admiration or surprise.

WPC WPCs
NOUN In Britain, a female member of the police force. WPC is an abbreviation for 'woman police constable'.

wrangle wrangles wrangling wrangled
VERB **1** If you wrangle with someone, you argue noisily or angrily, often about something unimportant. ▶ NOUN **2** an argument that is difficult to settle.
wrangling NOUN

wrap wraps wrapping wrapped
VERB **1** If you wrap something or wrap something up, you fold a piece of paper or cloth tightly around it to cover or enclose it. **2** If you wrap paper or cloth round something, you put or fold the paper round it. **3** If you wrap your arms, fingers, or legs round something, you coil them round it.
wrap up VERB If you wrap up, you put warm clothes on.

wrapped up
ADJECTIVE; AN INFORMAL USE If you are wrapped up in a person or thing, you give that person or thing all your attention.

wrapper wrappers
NOUN a piece of paper, plastic, or foil which covers and protects something that you buy EG *sweet wrappers.*

wrapping wrappings
NOUN Wrapping is the material used to cover and protect something.

wrath
Said "roth" NOUN; A LITERARY WORD Wrath is great anger EG *the wrath of his father.*

wreak wreaks wreaking wreaked
Said "reek" VERB To wreak havoc or damage is to cause it.

wreath wreaths
Said "reeth" NOUN an arrangement of flowers and leaves, often in the shape of a circle, which is put on a grave as a sign of remembrance for the dead person.

wreck wrecks wrecking wrecked
VERB **1** If someone wrecks something, they break it, destroy it, or spoil it completely. **2** If a ship is wrecked, it has been so badly damaged that it can no longer sail. ▶ NOUN **3** a vehicle which has been badly damaged in an accident. **4** If you say someone is a wreck, you mean that they are in a very poor physical or mental state of health and cannot cope with life.
wrecked ADJECTIVE

wreckage
NOUN Wreckage is what remains after something has been badly damaged or destroyed.

wren wrens
NOUN a very small brown songbird.

wrench wrenches wrenching wrenched
VERB **1** If you wrench something, you give it a sudden and violent twist or pull EG *Nick wrenched open the door.* **2** If you wrench a limb or a joint, you twist and injure it. ▶ NOUN **3** a metal tool with parts which can be adjusted to fit around nuts or bolts to loosen or tighten them. **4** a painful parting from someone or something.

A B C D E F G H I J K L M N O P Q R S T U V W X Y Z

845

A
B
C
D
E
F
G
H
I
J
K
L
M
N
O
P
Q
R
S
T
U
V
W
X
Y
Z

wrest wrests wresting wrested
Said "rest" VERB; A FORMAL WORD If you
wrest something from someone
else you take it from them
violently or with effort EG *to try and
wrest control of the island from the
Mafia.*

wrestle wrestles wrestling
wrestled
VERB **1** If you wrestle someone or
wrestle with them, you fight them
by holding or throwing them, but
not hitting them. **2** When you
wrestle with a problem, you try to
deal with it.
wrestler NOUN

wrestling
NOUN Wrestling is a sport in which
two people fight and try to win by
throwing or holding their
opponent on the ground.

wretch wretches
NOUN; AN OLD-FASHIONED WORD someone
who is thought to be wicked or
very unfortunate.
▥ from Old English *wrecca*
meaning 'exile' or 'despised person'

wretched
Said "ret-shid" ADJECTIVE **1** very
unhappy or unfortunate EG *a
wretched childhood.* **2** AN INFORMAL USE
You use wretched to describe
something or someone you feel
angry about or dislike EG *a wretched
bully.*

wriggle wriggles wriggling
wriggled
VERB **1** If someone wriggles, they
twist and turn their body or a part
of their body using quick
movements EG *He wriggled his arms
and legs.* **2** If you wriggle
somewhere, you move there by
twisting and turning EG *I wriggled
out of the van.*

wring wrings wringing wrung
VERB **1** When you wring a wet cloth
or wring it out, you squeeze the
water out of it by twisting it. **2** If
you wring your hands, you hold
them together and twist and turn

them, usually because you are
worried or upset. **3** If someone
wrings a bird's neck, they kill the
bird by twisting and breaking its
neck.

wrinkle wrinkles wrinkling
wrinkled
NOUN **1** Wrinkles are lines in
someone's skin, especially on the
face, which form as they grow old.
▶ VERB **2** If something wrinkles, folds
or lines develop on it EG *silk so rich it
doesn't wrinkle.* **3** When you wrinkle
your nose, forehead, or eyes, you
tighten the muscles in your face so
that the skin folds into lines.
wrinkled ADJECTIVE, **wrinkly** ADJECTIVE
▥ from Old English *wrinclian*
meaning 'to wind around'
▤ (sense 1) crease, fold

wrist wrists
NOUN the part of your body between
your hand and your arm which
bends when you move your hand.

writ writs
NOUN a legal document that orders a
person to do or not to do a
particular thing.

write writes writing wrote
written
VERB **1** When you write something,
you use a pen or pencil to form
letters, words, or numbers on a
surface. **2** If you write something
such as a poem, a book, or a piece
of music, you create it. **3** When you
write to someone or write them a
letter, you express your feelings in
a letter. **4** When someone writes
something such as a cheque, they
put the necessary information on it
and sign it.
write down VERB If you write
something down, you record it on
a piece of paper.
write up VERB If you write up
something, you write a full account
of it, often using notes that you
have made.

writer writers
NOUN **1** a person who writes books,

stories, or articles as a job. **2** The writer of something is the person who wrote it.

writhe writhes writhing writhed
Said "rieth" VERB If you writhe, you twist and turn your body, often because you are in pain.

writing writings
NOUN **1** Writing is something that has been written or printed EG *Apply in writing for the information.* **2** Your writing is the way you write with a pen or pencil. **3** Writing is also a piece of written work, especially the style of language used EG *witty writing.* **4** An author's writings are his or her written works.

written
1 Written is the past participle of **write.** ▶ ADJECTIVE **2** taken down in writing EG *a written agreement.*

wrong wrongs wronging wronged
ADJECTIVE **1** not working properly or unsatisfactory EG *There was something wrong with the car.* **2** not correct or truthful EG *the wrong answer.* **3** bad or immoral EG *It is wrong to kill people.* ▶ NOUN **4** an unjust action or situation EG *the wrongs of our society.* ▶ VERB **5** If someone wrongs you, they treat you in an unfair or unjust way.
wrongly ADVERB
■ (sense 2) erroneous, inaccurate, incorrect

wrongful
ADJECTIVE A wrongful act is regarded as illegal, unfair, or immoral EG *wrongful imprisonment.*

wrought iron
NOUN Wrought iron is a pure type of iron that is formed into decorative shapes.

wry
ADJECTIVE A wry expression shows that you find a situation slightly amusing because you know more about it than other people.
wryly ADVERB

A
B
C
D
E
F
G
H
I
J
K
L
M
N
O
P
Q
R
S
T
U
V
W
X
Y
Z

Xx Xx

X or x

1 'X' is used to represent the name of an unknown or secret person or place eg *The victim was referred to as Mr X throughout Tuesday's court proceedings*. **2** People sometimes write 'X' on a map to mark a precise position. **3** 'X' is used to represent a kiss at the bottom of a letter, a vote on a ballot paper, or the signature of someone who cannot write.

xenophobia

Said "zen-nof-**foe**-bee-a" NOUN Xenophobia is a fear or strong dislike of people from other countries.

xenophobic ADJECTIVE

📖 from Greek *xenos* meaning 'stranger' and *phobos* meaning 'fear'

Xerox Xeroxes

Said "**zeer**-roks" NOUN; A TRADEMARK **1** a machine that makes photographic copies of sheets of paper with writing or printing on them. **2** a copy made by a Xerox machine.

Xmas

NOUN; AN INFORMAL WORD Xmas means the same as Christmas.

X-ray X-rays X-raying X-rayed

NOUN **1** a stream of radiation of very short wavelength that can pass through some solid materials. X-rays are used by doctors to examine the bones or organs inside a person's body. **2** a picture made by sending X-rays through someone's body in order to examine the inside of it. ▶ VERB **3** If you are X-rayed, a picture is made of the inside of your body by passing X-rays through it.

xylem

Said "**zy**-lem" NOUN; A TECHNICAL WORD Xylem is a plant tissue that conducts water and mineral salts from the roots and carries them through the plant. It forms the wood in trees and shrubs.

xylophone xylophones

Said "**zy**-lo-fone" NOUN a musical instrument made of a row of wooden bars of different lengths. It is played by hitting the bars with special hammers.

yabby yabbies
NOUN a small edible Australian crayfish.

yacht yachts
Said "yot" NOUN a boat with sails or an engine, used for racing or for pleasure trips.

yachting
NOUN Yachting is the sport or activity of sailing a yacht.

yachtsman yachtsmen
NOUN a man who sails a yacht.
yachtswoman NOUN

yak yaks
NOUN a type of long-haired ox with long horns, found mainly in the mountains of Tibet.

yakka or **yacker**
NOUN; AN INFORMAL WORD In Australian and New Zealand English, yakka or yacker is work.

yam yams
NOUN a root vegetable which grows in tropical regions.

yank yanks yanking yanked
VERB 1 If you yank something, you pull or jerk it suddenly with a lot of force. ▶ NOUN 2 AN INFORMAL USE A Yank is an American.
☑ When *Yank* means 'an American' it starts with a capital letter.

Yankee Yankees
NOUN the same as a Yank.

yap yaps yapping yapped
VERB If a dog yaps, it barks with a high-pitched sound.

yard yards
NOUN 1 a unit of length equal to 36 inches or about 91.4 centimetres. 2 an enclosed area that is usually next to a building and is often used for a particular purpose EG *a ship repair yard*.

yardstick yardsticks
NOUN someone or something you use as a standard against which to judge other people or things EG *He had no yardstick by which to judge university*.

yarn yarns
NOUN 1 Yarn is thread used for knitting or making cloth. 2 AN INFORMAL USE a story that someone tells, often with invented details to make it more interesting or exciting.

yashmak yashmaks
NOUN a veil that some Muslim women wear over their faces when they are in public.

yawn yawns yawning yawned
VERB When you yawn, you open your mouth wide and take in more air than usual. You often yawn when you are tired or bored.

yawning
ADJECTIVE A yawning gap or opening is very wide.

ye
AN OLD WORD ▶ PRONOUN 1 Ye used to mean 'you'. ▶ ADJECTIVE 2 Ye also used to mean 'the'.

yeah
INTERJECTION; AN INFORMAL WORD Yeah means 'yes'.

year years
NOUN 1 a period of twelve months or 365 days (366 days in a leap year), which is the time taken for the earth to travel once around the sun. 2 a period of twelve consecutive months, not always January to December, on which administration or organization is based EG *the current financial year*. ▶ PHRASE 3 If something happens **year in, year out**, it happens every year EG *a tradition kept up year in, year out*.
yearly ADJECTIVE OR ADVERB

yearling yearlings
NOUN an animal between one and two years old.

yearn yearns yearning yearned

Rhymes with "learn" VERB If you yearn for something, you want it very much indeed EG *He yearned to sleep.*

yearning NOUN

yeast yeasts

NOUN Yeast is a kind of fungus which is used to make bread rise, and to make liquids ferment in order to produce alcohol.

yell yells yelling yelled

VERB 1 If you yell, you shout loudly, usually because you are angry, excited, or in pain. ▶ NOUN 2 a loud shout.

yellow yellower yellowest; yellows yellowing yellowed

NOUN OR ADJECTIVE 1 Yellow is the colour of buttercups, egg yolks, or lemons. ▶ VERB 2 When something yellows or is yellowed, it becomes yellow, often because it is old.
▶ ADJECTIVE 3 AN INFORMAL USE If you say someone is yellow, you mean they are cowardly.

yellowish ADJECTIVE

yellow box yellow boxes

NOUN a large spreading Australian tree which is a source of honey.

yellow fever

NOUN Yellow fever is a serious infectious disease that is found in tropical countries. It causes fever and jaundice.

yelp yelps yelping yelped

VERB 1 When people or animals yelp, they give a sudden, short cry. ▶ NOUN 2 a sudden, short cry.

yen

NOUN 1 The yen is the main unit of currency in Japan. 2 If you have a yen to do something, you have a strong desire to do it EG *Mike had a yen to try cycling.*

yes

INTERJECTION You use 'yes' to agree with someone, to say that something is true, or to accept something.

yesterday

NOUN OR ADVERB 1 Yesterday is the day before today. 2 You also use 'yesterday' to refer to the past EG *Leave yesterday's sadness behind you.*

yet

ADVERB 1 If something has not happened yet, it has not happened up to the present time EG *It isn't quite dark yet.* 2 If something should not be done yet, it should not be done now, but later EG *Don't switch off yet.* 3 'Yet' can mean there is still a possibility that something can happen EG *We'll make a soldier of you yet.* 4 You can use 'yet' when you want to say how much longer a situation will continue EG *The service doesn't start for an hour yet.* 5 'Yet' can be used for emphasis EG *She'd changed her mind yet again.*
▶ CONJUNCTION 6 You can use 'yet' to introduce a fact which is rather surprising EG *He isn't a smoker yet he always carries a lighter.*

yeti yetis

Said "yet-tee" NOUN A yeti, or abominable snowman, is a large hairy apelike animal which some people believe exists in the Himalayas.

yew yews

NOUN an evergreen tree with bright red berries.

Yiddish

NOUN Yiddish is a language derived mainly from German, which many Jewish people of European origin speak.
▤ from German *jüdisch* meaning 'Jewish'

yield yields yielding yielded

VERB 1 If you yield to someone or something, you stop resisting and give in to them EG *Russia recently yielded to US pressure.* 2 If you yield something that you have control of or responsibility for, you surrender it EG *They refused to yield control of their weapons.* 3 If something yields, it breaks or gives way EG *The handle* would yield to her grasp. **4** To yield something is to produce it EG *One season's produce yields food for the following year.* ▶ NOUN **5** A yield is an amount of food, money, or profit produced from a given area of land or from an investment.

yippee

INTERJECTION 'Yippee!' is an exclamation of happiness or excitement.

yob yobs

NOUN; AN INFORMAL WORD a noisy, badly behaved boy or young man.

yodel yodels yodelling yodelled

Said "yoe-dl" VERB When someone yodels, they sing normal notes with high quick notes in between. This style of singing is associated with the Swiss and Austrian Alps.

yoga

Said "yoe-ga" NOUN Yoga is a Hindu method of mental and physical exercise or discipline.
🔲 from Sanskrit *yoga* meaning 'union'

yogurt yogurts; also spelt yoghurt

Said "yog-gurt" NOUN Yogurt is a slightly sour thick liquid made from milk that has had bacteria added to it.

yoke yokes

NOUN **1** a wooden bar attached to two collars which is laid across the necks of animals such as oxen to hold them together, and to which a plough or other tool may be attached. **2** A LITERARY USE If people are under a yoke of some kind, they are being oppressed EG *two women who escape the yoke of insensitive men.*

yokel yokels

Said "yoe-kl" NOUN someone who lives in the country and is regarded as being rather stupid and old-fashioned.

yolk yolks

Rhymes with "joke" NOUN the yellow part in the middle of an egg.
🔲 from Old English *geoloca*, from *geolu* meaning 'yellow'

Yom Kippur

Said "yom kip-poor" NOUN Yom Kippur is an annual Jewish religious holiday, which is a day of fasting and prayers. It is also called the Day of Atonement.

yonder

ADVERB OR ADJECTIVE; AN OLD WORD over there EG *There's an island yonder.*

yore

AN OLD-FASHIONED PHRASE Of yore means existing a long time ago EG *nostalgia for the days of yore.*

Yorkshire pudding Yorkshire puddings

NOUN In Britain, Yorkshire pudding is a kind of baked batter made of flour, milk, and eggs, and usually eaten with roast beef.

you

PRONOUN **1** 'You' refers to the person or group of people that a person is speaking or writing to. **2** 'You' also refers to people in general EG *You can get a two-bedroom villa quite cheaply.*

young younger youngest

ADJECTIVE **1** A young person, animal, or plant has not lived very long and is not yet mature. ▶ NOUN **2** The young are young people in general. **3** The young of an animal are its babies.
🔳 (sense 1) immature, undeveloped
🔳 (sense 3) babies, offspring, progeny

youngster youngsters

NOUN a child or young person.

your

ADJECTIVE **1** 'Your' means belonging or relating to the person or group of people that someone is speaking to EG *I do like your name.* **2** 'Your' is used to show that something belongs or relates to people in general EG *Your driving ability is affected by just one or two drinks.*

yours

A B C D E F G H I J K L M N O P Q R S T U V W X Y Z

PRONOUN 'Yours' refers to something belonging or relating to the person or group of people that someone is speaking to EG *His hair is longer than yours*.

yourself yourselves

PRONOUN **1** 'Yourself' is used when the person being spoken to does the action and is affected by it EG *Why can't you do it yourself?*
2 'Yourself' is used to emphasize 'you' EG *Do you yourself want a divorce?*

youth youths

NOUN **1** Someone's youth is the period of their life before they are a fully mature adult. **2** Youth is the quality or condition of being young and often inexperienced. **3** a boy or young man. **4** The youth are young people thought of as a group EG *the youth of today*.
youthful ADJECTIVE

youth hostel youth hostels

NOUN a place where young people can stay cheaply when they are on holiday.

yo-yo yo-yos

NOUN a round wooden or plastic toy attached to a piece of string. You play by making the yo-yo rise and fall on the string.

Yugoslav Yugoslavs

Said "yoo-goe-slahv" ADJECTIVE
1 belonging or relating to the country that used to be known as Yugoslavia. ▶ NOUN **2** someone who came from the country that used be known as Yugoslavia.

Yule

NOUN; AN OLD WORD Yule means Christmas.
🔲 from Old English *geola* a pagan winter feast

yuppie yuppies

NOUN If you say people are yuppies, you think they are young, middle-class, and earn a lot of money which they spend on themselves.

Zz Zz

Zambian Zambians
*Said "**zam**-bee-an"* ADJECTIVE
1 belonging or relating to Zambia.
▶ NOUN **2** someone who comes from Zambia.

zany zanier zaniest
ADJECTIVE odd and ridiculous EG *zany humour.*
🏛 from Italian *zanni* meaning 'clown'

zap zaps zapping zapped
VERB; AN INFORMAL WORD **1** To zap someone is to kill them, usually by shooting. **2** To zap also is to move somewhere quickly EG *I zapped over to Paris.*

zeal
NOUN Zeal is very great enthusiasm.
zealous ADJECTIVE

zealot zealots
Said "zel-lot" NOUN a person who acts with very great enthusiasm, especially in following a political or religious cause.

zebra zebras
NOUN a type of African wild horse with black and white stripes over its body.

zebra crossing zebra crossings
NOUN a place where people can cross the road safely. The road is marked with black and white stripes.

Zen or Zen Buddhism
NOUN Zen is a form of Buddhism that concentrates on learning through meditation and intuition.

zenith
NOUN; A LITERARY USE The zenith of something is the time when it is at its most successful or powerful EG *the zenith of his military career.*

zero zeros or zeroes zeroing zeroed
1 Zero is the number 0. **2** Zero is freezing point, 0° Centigrade.
▶ ADJECTIVE **3** Zero means there is none at all of a particular thing EG

His chances are zero. ▶ VERB **4** To zero in on a target is to aim at or to move towards it EG *The headlines zeroed in on the major news stories.*
🏛 from Arabic *sifr* meaning 'cipher' or 'empty'

zest
NOUN **1** Zest is a feeling of pleasure and enthusiasm EG *zest for life.*
2 Zest is a quality which adds extra flavour or interest to something EG *brilliant ideas to add zest to your wedding list.* **3** The zest of an orange or lemon is the outside of the peel which is used to flavour food or drinks.

zigzag zigzags zigzagging zigzagged
NOUN **1** a line which has a series of sharp, angular turns to the right and left in it, like a continuous series of 'W's. ▶ VERB **2** To zigzag is to move forward by going at an angle first right and then left EG *He zigzagged his way across the racecourse.*

Zimbabwean Zimbabweans
*Said "zim-**bahb**-wee-an"* ADJECTIVE
1 belonging or relating to Zimbabwe. ▶ NOUN **2** someone who comes from Zimbabwe.

zinc
NOUN Zinc is a bluish-white metal used in alloys and to coat other metals to stop them rusting.

zing
NOUN; AN INFORMAL WORD Zing is a quality in something that makes it lively or interesting EG *There's a real zing around the studio.*

zip zips zipping zipped
NOUN **1** a long narrow fastener with two rows of teeth that are closed or opened by a small clip pulled between them. ▶ VERB **2** When you zip something or zip it up, you fasten it using a zip.

zipper zippers
NOUN the same as a zip.

A
B
C
D
E
F
G
H
I
J
K
L
M
N
O
P
Q
R
S
T
U
V
W
X
Y
Z

zodiac
Said "**zoe-dee-ak**" NOUN The zodiac is an imaginary strip in the sky which contains the planets and stars which astrologers think are important influences on people. It is divided into 12 sections, each with a special name and symbol.
▥ from Greek *zōidiakos kuklos* meaning 'circle of signs'

zombie zombies
NOUN **1** AN INFORMAL USE If you refer to someone as a zombie, you mean that they seem to be unaware of what is going on around them and to act without thinking about what they are doing. **2** In voodoo, a zombie is a dead person who has been brought back to life by witchcraft.
▥ from an African word *zumbi* meaning 'good-luck charm'

zone zones
NOUN an area that has particular features or properties EG *a war zone*.

zoo zoos
NOUN a place where live animals are kept so that people can look at them.

zoology
Said "**zoo-ol-loj-jee**" NOUN Zoology is the scientific study of animals.
zoological ADJECTIVE, **zoologist** NOUN

zoom zooms zooming zoomed
VERB **1** To zoom is to move very quickly EG *They zoomed to safety*. **2** If a camera zooms in on something, it gives a close-up picture of it.

zucchini
Said "**zoo-keen-nee**" PLURAL NOUN Zucchini are small vegetable marrows with dark green skin. They are also called **courgettes**.

Zulu Zulus
Said "**zoo-loo**" NOUN **1** The Zulus are a group of Black people who live in southern Africa. **2** Zulu is the language spoken by the Zulus.